ENVIRONMENTAL ETHICS

WHAT REALLY MATTERS
WHAT REALLY WORKS

THIRD EDITION

David Schmidtz

UNIVERSITY OF ARIZONA

Dan C. Shahar

UNIVERSITY OF NORTH CAROLINA AT CHAPEL HILL

NEW YORK   OXFORD
OXFORD UNIVERSITY PRESS

Oxford University Press is a department of the University of Oxford. It furthers the University's
objective of excellence in research, scholarship, and education by publishing worldwide.
Oxford is a registered trade mark of Oxford University Press in the UK and certain other countries.

Published in the United States of America by Oxford University Press
198 Madison Avenue, New York, NY 10016, United States of America.

For titles covered by Section 112 of the US Higher Education
Opportunity Act, please visit www.oup.com/us/he for the
latest information about pricing and alternate formats.

Library of Congress Cataloging-in-Publication Data

Names: Schmidtz, David, editor.
Title: Environmental ethics : what really matters, what really works /
   [edited by] David Schmidtz, University of Arizona, Dan C. Shahar,
   University of Arizona.
Description: Third Edition. | New York : Oxford University Press, 2018.
Identifiers: LCCN 2017038795 | ISBN 9780190259228 (pbk.)
Subjects: LCSH: Environmental ethics.
Classification: LCC GE42 .E585 2018 | DDC 179/.1—dc23
LC record available at https://lccn.loc.gov/2017038795

9 8 7 6 5 4 3 2
Printed by LSC Communications, Inc., United States of America

CONTENTS

PREFACE

Featuring accessible selections—from classic articles to today's most recent research—*Environmental Ethics: What Really Matters, What Really Works*, Third Edition, explores morality in theory and practice, from an environmental perspective. Asking what really matters, the book's first section focuses more on abstract ideas of human value and value in nature. The second section focuses more on what it takes to solve real problems, answering with empirically informed essays on applying environmental ethics to issues that matter right now.

One basic principle of ecology, informally stated, is that we are not in charge. Every action has more than one reaction. Every action ripples out into an ecological community in somewhat unpredictable and unintended ways. An ecosystem is a moving target. Also, an ecosystem is more like a neighborhood than a game of chess, in the sense that the other pieces on the board—our fellow humans and members of other species—are not pawns that we can move around at will. They each have a logic of their own, and some (our fellow humans at least) have hopes and dreams and plans of their own. If our plan requires that other people simply follow our orders, as if their own hopes and dreams were not relevant, then that will be where our plan falls apart. What matters and what works are different questions, and the connection is not automatic. If we aren't thinking hard about what works, then neither are we being serious about what matters.

Environmental ethics is a young field, though, full of intellectual energy, and a lot has happened. The first edition was compiled over three years. Elizabeth Willott and I finished in 2001, and the text was published in 2002. After that, we spent the best part of a fruitful decade compiling materials for the second. Tragically, Elizabeth passed away in 2015, at the age of fifty-nine. (She died of lung cancer complicated by cirrhosis of the liver. She was a nonsmoker and a nondrinker.)

Dan C. Shahar came to the project during our preparation of the second edition, and indeed contributed greatly to that volume. He now joins the project as coeditor of the third edition.

NEW TO THE THIRD EDITION

This third edition has thirty-four new articles in new or radically revised sections on the origins of environmental thought, humility, human excellence, suffering, wilderness, land management, food, citizenship, climate, and urban ecology. Many other sections have been streamlined in response to feedback from instructors on what was being used and what was not.

ACKNOWLEDGMENTS

This project is supported by a grant from the John Templeton Foundation. Opinions expressed here are those of the authors and editors and do not necessarily reflect views of the Templeton Foundation. Thanks especially to the Georgetown Institute for the Study of Markets and Ethics at Georgetown University's McDonough School of Business for hosting Schmidtz as a visiting scholar in the fall of 2016. Thanks also to the Department of Political Economy at King's College London for giving Schmidtz time to finish this project.

This new edition has benefited greatly from the input of reviewers Lauren Hartzell-Nichols (University of Washington), Lois Ann Lorentzen (University of San Francisco), Ben Minteer (Arizona State University), Darrel Moellendorf (San Diego State University), Judith Norman (Trinity University), Dan Perry (Texas Tech University), Mark Smillie (Carroll College), Gary Varner (Texas A&M), and Michael Weber (Bowling Green State University), plus two who are not named here.

Over the years, we have also been lucky to know and learn from (among many others) Nathan Ballantyne, Scott Boocher, Jason Brennan, Chris Brown, Michael Bukoski, Bill Dennis, Robert Ellickson, Chris Freiman, Robert Glennon, Nicole Hassoun, Kristen Hessler, Robert Hood, Cathleen Johnson, Avery Kolers, Mark LeBar, Andrew Light, Chris Maloney, Christina Mancuso, Robert Miller, Elissa Morris, Clare Palmer, Carol Rose, Dan Russell, Don Scherer, Jeremy Shearmur, Don Weidner, Clark Wolf, Sarah Wright, and Matt Zwolinski.

We have gotten helpful suggestions at several recent workshops in Tucson, Rocky Mountain National Park, and Oslo, Norway, for which we thank all the participants, including Jeremy Bendik-Keymer, David Boonin, Karol Boudreaux, Andrew Brennan, Philip Cafaro, Gary Comstock, Darren Domsky, Robert Elliot, Hans Eicholz, Espen Gamlund, Steve Gardiner, Hannes Gissurarson, Ben Hale, Ned Hettinger, Alan Holland, Dale Jamieson, Doug MacLean, Katie McShane, John O'Neill, Clare Palmer, Jim Petrik, Paul Pojman, Holmes Rolston III, Ronald Sandler, Lynn Scarlett, Clive Spash, Allen Thompson, Michael 't Sas-Rolfes, and Jenny Welchman.

INSTRUCTOR RESOURCES

Look up ppenetwork.org.

This network currently is maintained by Sagent Labs Inc. Our intention is that within this network site there will be an Environmental Ethics Store where you can access a library of supplemental readings, or add to that library by uploading any materials (consistent with the rules of fair use). You can establish a direct link to your course website so that your students can access the materials as well.

INTRODUCTION
Some Thoughts on Ethics

It is dawn. We have come to the mountains of eastern Arizona, seeking inspiration. We left our computer back at the trailhead, in the van, having no need for such fancy technology on our hike. We do need our state-of-the-art boots, though, for the hike up the west side of Mount Baldy is seven miles; the hike back down the east side is another twelve. We thank Mount Baldy for this glorious morning, but in fairness we also thank the van and all the other technological developments that enabled us to be here.

We inhabit a world of problems, but environmental ethics reminds us not only that these mountains need to be and can be saved but also that they're *worth* saving. Environmental ethics teaches us how to enjoy the world, not just how to fix it.

Not that we do not want to fix the world, of course, but fixing is a tricky, double-edged idea. On one hand, to "fix" is to repair or improve, and there is nothing wrong with wanting to fix things in principle. On the other, to "fix" is to stabilize or set in place so as to prevent further change, as when we describe a mortgage rate or a lecture schedule as fixed. Therein lies a problem, for in that second sense, ecologies are not fixed, and cannot be. It is of the essence of an ecosystem that it is not fixed. An ecosystem is essentially a thing in flux.

Of course, human nature being what it is, flux makes people nervous. Rightly or wrongly, we feel more secure when things are "fixed." So, we want to "fix" our ecosystem, but we cannot. Not without turning it into something other than the ongoing process it is. Ecosystems evolve. Human society evolves. Something decays and is lost in the process. Always. And we, like generations before us and generations to come, will lament its passing. There probably has never been a generation that did not view its world as going to hell in one way or another. We are only human. Still, we are here. We are now. Shouldn't we enjoy it?

Or perhaps "enjoy" is too mild a word to describe what it is like to be among wind-carved rocks, hearing the call of a crow, wondering for how many eons that call has echoed from that perch. Or stopping to count the growth rings in a fallen Ponderosa

Pine, one of the biggest we've ever seen, and giving up at 150, each of us silently aware that it was Aldo Leopold who inspired us to stop and look. Or stopping just short of Baldy's summit out of respect for the fact that the summit is marked as sacred ground by the Apache, wondering where the Apache were in 1492, wondering whether they already regarded this land as sacred when Columbus was still looking for a shorter route to India.

ENVIRONMENTAL ETHICS AS A BRANCH OF PHILOSOPHY

Throughout this book, we avoid jargon as much as we can. There are, however, some basic terms you need to know. The discipline of philosophy can be divided into fields. Typically it is divided into three. In the simplest terms: *metaphysics* is the study of the fundamental nature of reality; *epistemology* is the study of knowledge and how we acquire it; *ethics* is the study of goodness and rightness—what makes one outcome better than another, and (not the same question) what makes one outcome rather than another the one that is most worth striving for. To complicate matters in the real world, possible outcomes include not only what you *get*, but what you *become*. What kind of person you want to be is, on some views, the most important question you will ever ask.

The study of ethics generally is guided by certain presuppositions. Among the main presuppositions are these. First, we are more or less rational beings, capable of understanding the world. Second, we can act on the basis of what we understand. Third, our actions can serve a purpose—we can make a difference.

Ethics itself can be divided into subfields. *Normative ethics* is the study of rightness in action and goodness in states of affairs. *Descriptive ethics* is the study of opinions or beliefs about what is right and good. (Descriptive ethics often is considered to be the domain of anthropology, say, not philosophy. However, we insist on separating normative from descriptive ethics in order to emphasize that seeking the truth about ethics is not the same as cataloging opinions about ethics.) The third subfield, *metaethics,* studies the meanings and presuppositions of moral theories and moral language and asks what it would be like to justify a moral theory. In effect, then, where normative ethics is the enterprise of formulating theories about what is right and good, metaethics steps back to ask what we hope to accomplish by theorizing about it.

Within the subfield of normative ethics, we formulate theories of the *good*, sometimes called theories of value. We also formulate theories of the *right*. ("Good" and "right" often are interchangeable in ordinary use, but in philosophy we treat rightness as pertaining to what we should *do*, whereas goodness pertains to what we should *want*.)

When we try to apply the results of normative ethics to questions of practical policy and personal conduct such as those discussed in this volume, we move into the realm of applied ethics. The primary areas within applied ethics currently are medical ethics, business ethics, and environmental ethics.

Yet, lumping the three together is misleading. Business and medicine are professions, typically studied in separate professional schools rather than in colleges of art and science; thus business ethics and medical ethics currently are forms of professional ethics in large measure (although this may change). By contrast, the environment is not a profession, there are no environmental schools in the way there are professional schools in medicine and business, and environmental ethics is not the study of ethical issues specific to any particular occupation.

Environmental ethics is of course a way of applying normative ethics to a particular set of practical issues, but it also is a relatively new way of doing normative ethics in general. Environmental ethics asks what we owe to each other, and to ourselves, given our ecological context. It also asks what, if anything, we owe to nonhuman animals, to plants, to fragile geological wonders, to species, and even to ecosystems themselves. We ask what kind of life we should want to live, and what kind of world we should want to live in. We study the value of human life and the value of life in general. In short, part of the beauty of environmental ethics is that it not only *applies* but also *encompasses* normative ethics.

Much of the history of moral philosophy revolves around the project of articulating an adequate theory of morality. How do we construct a moral theory? We begin by asking a moral question, which is roughly to say, a question about what makes a particular kind of thing right or good, and that question defines the subject matter of our subsequent theorizing. For example, we might ask what makes an act right. We could have asked more specifically what makes an act permissible, or what makes an act obligatory. Or we could have asked about a different subject altogether, something other than acts. For example, we could ask about rules, laws, institutions, or character traits. Going even further, we could go way beyond what philosophers typically ask about, and ask what makes a particular specialization legitimate, or a particular jurisdiction, or a particular way of managing traffic. If it is wrong for a traffic cop to be presuming to pick people's destinations for them, why is it wrong? Is it wrong because it would be ridiculously inefficient to meddle in other people's lives that way, or is it wrong because it would be outrageously disrespectful?

If we ask what makes an action right, one plausible answer is that the right action is the one that does as much good as possible. Roughly speaking, this is the theory known as *utilitarianism.* The theory is most often associated with John Stuart Mill, and it is one of the simplest theories we have. An alternative theory: What makes an act right is not whether it *promotes* what is good so much as whether it *respects* what is good. Associated most often with Immanuel Kant, this theory is known as *deontology* and says, a bit more precisely, that an action is right if, but only if, it expresses respect for all persons as ends in themselves and therefore treats no person merely as a means to further ends.

Yet another alternative, *virtue theory,* is so different it might be best to see it not as an alternative answer to the same question but as responding to a different question altogether. Associated most often with Aristotle, virtue theory tells us that what is right is to be a certain kind of person, a person of virtue: courageous, modest, honest, evenhanded, industrious, wise. Moral life is less about doing the right thing and more about taking the best of our potential as persons and making it real.

We wish we could simply tell you which of these theories is right, then specify in simple terms what that correct theory tells you to do. For better or worse, though, moral life is more complicated than that. The three theories just described are the main theories we discuss in introductory classes in moral philosophy, but few philosophy professors believe that any of them expresses the whole truth about morality. Each contains a grain of truth. None can be treated as infallible.

We all need to understand, then, that the key to morality will not be found in a jingle, or even in a sophisticated professional code of ethics. Morality is complex. It calls for creativity and judgment in the same way that chess does. You may come to the game of chess hoping to learn a simple algorithm that picks out the winning play no matter what the situation. For human players, though, there is no algorithm. There is no substitute for creativity and good judgment, for the ability to think ahead and expect the unexpected. Even something as simple as a game of chess is full of surprises, yet the complexity involved in playing chess is nothing compared to the complexity involved in being moral.

Perhaps our first and most important practical task, then, is to understand what we should not be hoping for. What we naturally hope for is to be given a list of rules or a code of professional conduct. When moral philosophers try to do applied ethics, though, it becomes apparent that there is something artificial and unhelpful about trying to interpret morality as a set of rules. Rules function in our reasoning as trump cards. If we have a rule, and can believe with complete confidence that the rule ought to be followed, and if we ascertain that a certain course of action is forbidden by the rule, that settles it. The rule trumps all further reasoning, so no further reasoning is necessary.

How comforting it would be to have such rules. And of course, sometimes the situation actually is rule-governed. Not always, though. Often, there are reasons favoring an action, and reasons against, and neither trumps the other.

It may still be possible, though, to decide in a principled way. *Principles* are not like rules. Where rules function in our reasoning like trump cards, principles function like weights. If the applicable moral rule forbids X, then X is ruled out, so to speak. In contrast, principles can weigh against X without categorically ruling out X.

If you need to figure out what to do, don't look for rules. Look for principles.

Consider an analogy. Home builders might say, in describing their approach to building houses, "You have to minimize ductwork." Question: Is that a rule or a principle? The answer is that, interpreted as a rule, it would be silly. As a rule, it would say, no matter what weighs in favor of more extensive ductwork, minimize ductwork, period. In other words, zero ductwork?

In fact, "minimize ductwork" is a good principle rather than a bad rule. As a principle, it tells home builders to be mindful of energy wasted and living space consumed when heated or cooled air is piped to remote parts of the house. Other things equal, get the air to where it has to go by the shortest available route. This principle will seldom outweigh the principle that the ceiling should be a minimum of seven feet above the floor. That is to say, it is not a trump, but it does have weight. A good builder designs houses with that principle in mind, but does not treat the principle as if it were a rule.

When students sign up for courses in ethics, some of the most conscientious come hoping to learn the moral rules. It is a shock when we say we have been teaching ethics for thirty years, but for the most part, we don't know the moral rules, and we suspect there are too few to give comprehensive guidance regarding how we ought to live.

When making real-world practical decisions, the relevant considerations are more often principles than rules. So why, when we look to moral philosophy, do we hope to find rules rather than principles? What makes us want rules? The idea of following a rule is comforting, because it has the feel of relieving us of moral responsibility. If we follow the rules, it seems to guarantee our innocence. Unlike rules, principles offer no such escape. Rules are things we follow. Principles are things we apply. Principles leave us with no doubt as to who is responsible for weighing them, for making choices, and for bearing the consequences of those choices.

The upshot, and it is fundamental to understanding what being a moral agent is like in the real world: If you need to figure out what to do, don't look for rules; look for principles. Needless to say, this too is a principle, not a rule. It has exceptions. There are, after all, rules. Rules sometimes do trump all other considerations.

A few decades ago, Stanley Milgram ran now-infamous experiments on the phenomenon of obedience to authority. Volunteer subjects were told the experiment was designed to test whether we can enhance learning by using pain to motivate subjects to pay maximum attention to the learning task. A volunteer test giver watches as a test taker (actually an actor) is strapped down to a chair and wired to a machine that delivers the pain in the form of electric shock. The volunteer is asked by the experimenter to administer a multiple-choice word association test, and in the event of an incorrect answer, to hit a switch that sends the electric shock to the test taker. The test giver is also instructed to increase the voltage by fifteen volts after each incorrect answer, beginning at fifteen and eventually going beyond four hundred and fifty volts to settings marked XXX. After a few (scripted) mistakes the test taker howls with pain, complains of heart pain, then collapses into apparent unconsciousness.

The volunteers for the most part had no idea that it was an act. In films of the experiments, volunteer typically are extremely agitated, begging the experimenter to check the condition of the test taker to make sure he was all right, repeatedly begging the experimenter to discontinue the experiment. But when firmly told to continue with the experiment, volunteers most often did. Volunteers kept asking multiple-choice questions, to which the apparently dead or unconscious test taker did not respond. Having been instructed to treat nonanswers as incorrect answers, many of the volunteers kept sending ever more powerful electric shocks to that seemingly dead or unconscious body.[1]

Needless to say, there is a moral rule against strapping down innocent people and torturing them to death. It is safe to say none of the volunteer test givers were unaware of this rule. Yet, when told to break this rule, they did. Why? It seems that they broke the rule for no reason other than that they were told to do so. They did not wish to break the rule. Indeed, it was agonizing. Many were hysterical. However, they simply lacked whatever psychological resources a person needs in order to be able to disobey a direct order from someone perceived as an authority, even when they know that what they are being ordered to do is wrong.

Perhaps you feel sure that, if it had been you, you would not have obeyed. But no one thinks they would have obeyed. On the other hand, we just gave you this warning about the electric shock experiments, and we hope that will help you some day. But what if you were a Morton Thiokol engineer presenting your boss with reason to believe that seals on the space shuttle's booster rocket are not safe? What if your boss told you that the experiment requires you to continue? As it actually happened, the engineers bowed to authority and let it go. The Challenger space shuttle was launched. Seconds later, it exploded. The engineers' worst fears were confirmed.

Now, imagine yourself in their position, prior to the launch. Part of the problem is that if you refuse to back down and succeed in aborting the launch, there will always be an unanswered question. Perhaps the program will be halted until the seals are redesigned at great expense. The faulty seals would never be tested under full operation. You might be fired without anyone (including you!) ever knowing whether you were right or whether you were a troublemaking lunatic. You would be smart enough to see that.

When your turn comes, will you also be smart enough, and brave enough, to sound the alarm anyway? In the heat of the moment, will you remain calm enough to be able to call vividly to mind a picture of the kind of person you want to be?[2] In the heat of the moment, will you realize that while life has just raised the price of being that kind of person, it has not changed your reason for resolving to be that kind of person?

If we are looking for a moral code, the test of a code is not that it presents us with answers to all questions, but that it helps us to decide what questions to ask, when to ask them, and when not to settle for easy answers. Moral philosophy's value is not so much in the information it gives us regarding how to pass the test. Moral philosophy can indeed help us prepare for the test. But moral philosophy prepares us not so much by giving us the answers as by training us to recognize when the test has begun.

Moral philosophy prepares us not so much by giving us the answers as by training us to recognize when the test has begun.

We defined deontology as the theory that one ought never to treat persons merely as means but also as ends in themselves, not to be sacrificed to the ends of others. According to Immanuel Kant, another way to express the same idea is to say we ought to do only that which we could will to be a universal law. Whether this truly is the same idea is debatable, but in any case this new formulation contains a thought about the secret of being moral that has considerable value in practical terms. The thought is this: Act in such a way that you would be willing to let your action be presented to the whole world as an example of how a person ought to act. If you are doing that, then you are doing the right thing, or at least trying to the best of your ability.

Studying moral theory can make a person wiser, perhaps, but it is not obvious how the process works. Learning is somewhat mysterious. Especially when we are learning something that is more a skill than a list of facts, it can be hard to describe what we have learned or how. Thus, we know there is such a thing as learning how to ride a bicycle, yet we cannot teach a person to ride a bicycle simply by explaining how to do it. Being moral is like that. As teachers of moral philosophy, we try to explain how to be moral. But if our students are learning to be moral in our classrooms, it is not because they are memorizing information. Ethics is more skill than dogma. If students are learning to be moral, it is because they are getting a feel for what it is like to wrestle with hard choices. At least in their imaginations, they are practicing the art of acting with integrity in cases where integrity is not without cost.

NUMBERS DO NOT ALWAYS COUNT

Adam Smith was one of the greatest moral philosophers who ever lived. He also is credited with inventing economics as an academic discipline. Here is what he says about, in effect, playing God with other people's lives.

> The man of system . . . is apt to be very wise in his own conceit; and is often so enamoured with the supposed beauty of his own ideal plan of government, that he cannot suffer the smallest deviation from any part of it. He goes on to establish it completely and in all its parts, without any regard either to the great interests, or to the strong prejudices which may oppose it. He seems to imagine that he can arrange the different members of a great society with as much ease as the hand arranges the different pieces upon a chess-board. He does not consider that the pieces upon the chess-board have no other principle of motion besides that which the hand impresses upon them; but that, in the great chess-board of human society, every single piece has a principle of motion of its own, altogether different from that which the legislature might chuse to impress upon it.[3]

Smith's point is as relevant as ever. In moral philosophy, there has been much discussion of the following kind of case: Imagine that five patients lie on operating tables about to die for lack of suitable organ donors. A United Parcel Service delivery person walks into the hospital. She is a suitable organ donor for all five patients. If you kidnap her and harvest her organs, you will be saving five and killing one. Should you do it? Why or why not?

The answer is not simply a matter of numbers, of one versus five. The issue is more centrally a matter of trust. What gives society its utility for those who live in it? The answer is trust. Hospitals serve their purpose only when people can trust hospitals to treat patients and everyone else as rights bearers. Institutions have utility by creating conditions under which people can trust each other not to operate in a utilitarian way, as if other people were simply pawns to be moved around in such a way as to maximize the overall good.

Moral institutions work not so much by aiming at the best result as by imposing constraints on individual pursuits so as to bring individual pursuits into better harmony with each other. Institutions (e.g., hospitals) serve the common good by creating opportunities for mutual benefit, then trusting individuals to take advantage of them.

In effect, there are two sides to the sense in which institutional utility is based on trust. First, people have to be able to trust their society to treat them as rights bearers, not as mere pawns. Second, society has to trust people to make use of opportunities that people have as rights bearers within society. Even from a utilitarian perspective, then, numbers do not always count. There are times when simply treating values with respect is the best we can do to promote them.

So, the principle here is: Consider the consequences. However, when applying this principle, we must realize that, even when considering consequences, there are times when the numbers do not count. They paint a misleading picture of what is really at stake.

Here is one more illustration: a case that I used to present in my ethics courses.

TROLLEY: A trolley is rolling down a track on its way to killing five people. If you switch to another track on which there is only one person, you will save five and kill one.

When I presented the TROLLEY case, and asked audiences whether they would switch tracks, most would say, "There has to be another way!" On a trip to Kazakhstan, I presented the case to an audience of twenty-one professors from nine post-Soviet republics, and they said the same thing. I responded as I always did, saying, "Please, stay on topic. I'm trying to illustrate a point here. To see the point, you need to decide what to do when there is no other way." When I said this to my class of post-Soviet professors, though, they responded in a way no audience of mine ever had. They spoke briefly among themselves in Russian, then two of them quietly said (as others nodded, every one of them looking me straight in the eye), "Yes, we understand. We have heard this before. All our lives we were told the few must be sacrificed for the sake of many. We were told there is no other way. What we were told was a lie. There was always another way."

They were right. The real world does not dictate that there is no other way. Justice is about respecting the separateness of persons. We are not to sacrifice one person for the sake of another. If we find ourselves seemingly called on to sacrifice the few for the sake of the many, justice is about finding another way.

To summarize, being moral is not simply a matter of following rules. Nevertheless, there are such things as moral principles (many more than can be enumerated in a useful written code) that carry considerable weight and that fairly reliably lead us in the right direction. One example: Consider the consequences. However, do not treat people as if they were numbers, such that it appears permissible simply to sacrifice low numbers for the sake of high ones. Instead, treat all persons as ends in themselves.

One way to do philosophy is from the armchair, without facts. Would it be right to convert all the golf courses into marshland? To shut down all the factory farms? Is it wrong for Monsanto to develop and sell genetically engineered cotton seeds? Wrong for farmers to buy and plant genetically engineered seed, and eventually sell the harvest? Wrong for our colleagues in the agricultural sciences to advise cotton farmers as best they can on how to use the new seed while minimizing harmful environmental impacts? Wrong for you to support this whole system when you buy clothing made of genetically engineered cotton? Wrong not to shut down all fossil fuel consumption right now, even if only to atone for contributing to climate change?

We could try to answer these questions by consulting our abstract theories, backed by intuitions, fears, and uninformed assumptions. It is hard to avoid the thought, though, that doing environmental ethics without gathering pertinent facts is, in a word, unethical. Accordingly, while this book necessarily is about abstract theory, it also explores the efforts of various authors to learn how the world actually works. We hope you enjoy both parts, and we thank you for taking a look. In the following pages, we ask many questions. Indeed, we have more questions than answers. This is partly for pedagogical reasons, but also because some questions are too hard to settle here. We hope that you find our questions interesting, and that you enjoy the challenge of reaching your own conclusions.

NOTES

1. But for some doubts about the record-keeping, conduct, and results of this experiment (for example, how many subjects were fooled by the deception, and how many subjects actually obeyed) see Gina Perry, *Behind the Shock Machine* (New York: New Press, 2012).
2. A word of caution. Unwary readers could think of this idea as vaguely egoistic, without bothering to sort out what they mean by egoism. Suffice it to say, there is a world of difference between thinking that morality is centrally about getting as much good as you can get and thinking (a part of) morality is centrally about being as good a person as you can be. Only the former is egoistic in the normal pejorative sense of the word.
3. Adam Smith, *Theory of Moral Sentiments* (Indianapolis: Liberty Fund Press, 1976), Part VI ("Of the Character of Virtue").

1

HOW WE GOT HERE

RODERICK FRAZIER NASH

OLD WORLD ROOTS OF OPINION

The land is the Garden of Eden before them, and behind them a desolate wilderness.

—*Joel 2:3*

European discoverers and settlers of the New World were familiar with wilderness even before they crossed the Atlantic. Some of this acquaintance was first-hand, since in the late Middle Ages a considerable amount of wild country still existed on the Continent. Far more important, however, was the deep resonance of wilderness as a concept in Western thought. It was instinctively understood as something alien to man—an insecure and uncomfortable environment against which civilization had waged an unceasing struggle. The Europeans knew the uninhabited forest as an important part of their folklore and mythology. Its dark, mysterious qualities made it a setting in which the prescientific imagination could place a swarm of demons and spirits. In addition, wilderness as fact and symbol permeated the Judeo-Christian tradition. Anyone with a Bible had available an extended lesson in the meaning of wild land. Subsequent Christian history added new dimensions. As a result, the first

immigrants approached North America with a cluster of preconceived ideas about wilderness. This intellectual legacy of the Old World to the New not only helped determine initial responses but left a lasting imprint on American thought.

The value system of primitive man was structured in terms of survival. He appreciated what contributed to his well-being and feared what he did not control or understand. The "best" trees produced food or shelter while "good" land was flat, fertile, and well watered. Under the most desirable of all conditions the living was easy and secure because nature was ordered in the interests of man. Almost all early cultures had such a conception of an earthly paradise. No matter where they were thought to be or what they were called, all paradises had in common a bountiful and beneficent natural setting in accord with the original meaning of the word in Persian—luxurious garden. A mild climate constantly prevailed. Ripe fruit dropped from every bough, and there were no thorns to prick reaching hands. The animals in paradise lived in harmony with man. Fear as well as want disappeared in this ideal state of nature.[1]

Roderick Frazier Nash, *Wilderness and the American Mind*, 4th ed. (New Haven, Conn.: Yale University Press, [1967] 2001), pp. 8–22.

If paradise was early man's greatest good, wilderness, as its antipode, was his greatest evil. In one condition the environment, garden-like, ministered to his every desire. In the other it was at best indifferent, frequently dangerous, and always beyond control. And in fact, it was with this latter condition that primitive man had to contend. At a time when there was no alternative, existence in the wilderness was forbidding indeed. Safety, happiness, and progress all seemed dependent on rising out of a wilderness situation. It became essential to gain control over nature. Fire was one step; the domestication of some wild animals another. Gradually man learned how to control the land and raise crops. Clearings appeared in the forests. This reduction of the amount of wilderness defined man's achievement as he advanced toward civilization. But progress was slow. For centuries the wild predominated over the precarious defenses thrown up against its influence. Men dreamed of life without wilderness. Significantly, many traditions located paradise on an island or in some other enclosed area. In this way the wild hinterland normally surrounding and threatening the first communities was eliminated. Wilderness had no place in the paradise myth.

The wilds continued to be repugnant even in as relatively advanced civilizations as those of the Greeks and Romans. The celebrations of nature, which abound in classical literature, are restricted to the cultivated, pastoral variety. The beautiful in nature was closely related to the fruitful or otherwise useful.[2] The Roman poet of the first century B.C., Titus Lucretius Carus, spoke for his age in *De Rerum Natura* when he observed that it was a serious "defect" that so much of the earth "is greedily possessed by mountains and the forests of wild beasts." Apart from the areas man had civilized, it "is filled full of restless dread throughout her woods, her mighty mountains and deep forests." Yet Lucretius took hope because "these regions it is generally in our power to shun."

Turning to history, Lucretius drew a grim portrait of precivilized life in the wilderness. Men lived a nightmarish existence, hounded by dangers on every hand and surviving through the ancient code of eat or be eaten. With obvious satisfaction, Lucretius related how the race escaped this miserable condition through the invention of clothing, metals, and, eventually, "ships, agriculture, city walls, laws, arms, roads." These enabled man to control wild nature and achieve relative security. Cultural refinements and "all charms of life" followed the release from the wilderness.[3]

When Lucretius, Horace, Virgil and their contemporaries confessed their love of "nature" and expressed a desire to leave the towns for a "natural" way of life, they meant the pastoral or rural environment. Lucretius, for one, applauded the efforts of the first farmers whose labor "forced the forests more and more to climb the mountain-sides." This made room for the cultivated landscape that was so highly prized. It consisted of "fields, . . . crops, and joyous vineyards, and a gray-green strip of olives to run in between and mark divisions, . . . adorned and interspersed with pleasant fruits, and fenced by planting them all round with fruitful trees."[4] If this was the ideal, wilderness could only be forbidding and repulsive.

While the inability to control or use wilderness was the basic factor in man's hostility, the terror of the wild had other roots as well. One was the tendency of the folk traditions of many cultures to associate wilderness with the supernatural and monstrous. There was a quality of mystery about the wilderness, particularly at night, that triggered the imagination. To frightened eyes the limbs of trees became grotesque, leaping figures, and the wind sounded like a weird scream. The wild forest seemed animated. Fantastic creatures of every description were thought to lurk in its depths. Whether propitiated with sacrifices as deities or regarded as devils, these forest beings were feared.[5]

Classical mythology contained a whole menagerie of lesser gods and demons believed to inhabit wild places. Pan, the lord of the woods, was pictured as having the legs, ears, and tail of a goat and the body of a man. He combined gross sensuality with boundless, sportive energy. Greeks who had to pass through forests or mountains dreaded an encounter with Pan. Indeed, the word "panic" originated from the blinding fear that seized travelers upon hearing strange cries in the wilderness and assuming them to signify Pan's approach. Related to Pan were the tribe of satyrs— goat-men of a demoniacal character devoted to wine, dancing, and lust. They were thought to appear only at night and then solely in the darkest parts of the forest. According to Hellenic folklore, satyrs ravished women and carried off children who ventured into their wilderness lairs. Sileni and centaurs completed the Greek collection of forest spirits. These monsters had the torso and head of a man and the body and legs of a goat or horse. Usually, they were represented as carrying a club in the form of an uprooted tree which also served as a reminder of their favorite habitat. In Roman mythology satyr-like figures appeared as fauns and also lurked in thickly wooded regions.[6]

In early folk belief, the wildernesses of central and northern Europe also swarmed with supernatural beings. Some were worshipped, but generally with the fear characteristic of the attitude of the unsophisticated toward the incomprehensible. Others received classification as demons and cohorts of the devil. In the Scandinavian countries, for instance, it was thought that when Lucifer and his followers were expelled from heaven, some landed in the forests and became Wood-Sprites or Trolls. Many of the medieval European monsters were lineal descendants of the man-beasts of classical mythology. Russian, Czech, and Slovak folklore spoke of a creature living in forests and mountains with the face of a woman, body of a sow, and legs of a horse.[7] In Germany, when storms raged through the forests, it was widely believed that the ghostly Wild Huntsman was abroad with his pack of baying hounds, riding furiously and killing everything in his path. Man-eating ogres and the sinister werewolves were also identified with wild, remote regions. While in certain circumstances forest beings, like the elves, could be helpful to men, most were considered terrifying and added to the repulsiveness of wilderness.[8]

. . .

The Old Testament reveals that the ancient Hebrews regarded the wilderness as a cursed land and that they associated its forbidding character with a lack of water. Again, and again "the great and terrible wilderness" was described as a "thirsty ground where there was no water." When the Lord of the Old Testament desired to threaten or punish a sinful people, he found the wilderness condition to be his most powerful weapon: "I will lay waste the mountains and hills, and dry up all their herbage; I will turn the rivers into islands, and dry up the pools. . . . I will also command the clouds that they rain no rain upon it."[9]

Conversely, when the Lord wished to express his pleasure, the greatest blessing he could bestow was to transform wilderness into "a good land, a land of brooks of water, of fountains and springs." In the famous redemption passage in Isaiah, God promises that "The wilderness and the dry land shall be glad . . . for waters shall break forth in the wilderness and streams in the desert." To "give water in the wilderness" was a way God manifested his care.[10] It was a fitting image for a people so fearful of the desert.

The identification of the arid wasteland with God's curse led to the conviction that wilderness was the environment of evil, a kind of hell. There were several consequences. Like that of other cultures, the Hebraic folk imagination made the wilderness the abode of demons and devils. Among them were the howling dragon or *tan*, the winged female monster of the night called *Lilith*, and the familiar man-goat, *seirim*. Presiding over all was *Azazel*, the arch-devil of the wilderness. He was the key figure in an expiatory rite in which a live goat was brought before the chief priest of a community who symbolically laid upon it the sins of the group. The animal was then led to the edge of the cultivated land and "sent away into the wilderness of Azazel."[11] The ritual has significance not only as the origin of the conception of a "scapegoat" but as a demonstration of the Hebrews' opinion of wilderness.

This idea of the immorality of wild country is also evident in the Old Testament treatment of the paradise theme. From what little we are told about the Garden of Eden it appears to have been, in the tradition of other paradises, the antipode of wilderness. "Eden" was the Hebrew word for "delight," and Genesis represents it as a pleasant place, indeed. The Garden was well watered and filled with edible plants. Adam and Eve were relieved of the necessity of working in order to survive. Fear also was eliminated, since with one exception the creatures that shared paradise were peaceable and helpful. But the snake encouraged the first couple to eat the forbidden fruit and as a punishment they were driven out of the Garden. The world Adam and Eve now faced was a wilderness, a "cursed" land full of "thorns and thistles." Later in the Scripture, Eden and wilderness are juxtaposed in such a way as to leave no doubt about their original relationship. "The land is like the garden of Eden before them," wrote the author of Joel, "but after them a desolate wilderness." And Isaiah contains the promise that God will comfort Zion and "make her wilderness like Eden, her desert like the garden of the Lord."[12] The Story of the Garden and its loss embedded into Western thought the idea that wilderness and paradise were both physical and spiritual opposites.

The history of the Israelite nation added another dimension to the Judeo-Christian understanding of wilderness. After the Exodus from bondage in Egypt about 1225 B.C., the Jews under the leadership of Moses wandered in the wilderness of the Sinai Peninsula for an alleged forty years. The Old Testament account emphasizes the hardships encountered in this "howling waste of the wilderness";[13] yet the desert experience was immensely important to the tribes of Israel. During these years the God their fathers had worshipped revealed himself as Yahweh and promised to be their special protector. In the heart of the wilderness on Mount Sinai, Moses received the Ten Commandments which created a covenant between Yahweh and Israel. Thereafter the Lord demonstrated his protective power by the miraculous provision of water and food. He also promised that if the Israelites remained faithful to the covenant, he would allow them to escape the wilderness and enter Canaan, the promised land of milk and honey.[14]

The Israelites' experience during the forty-year wandering gave wilderness several meanings. It was understood, in the first place, as a sanctuary from a sinful and persecuting society. Secondly, wild country came to signify the environment in which to find and draw close to God. It also acquired meaning as a testing ground where a chosen people were purged, humbled, and made ready for the land of promise.[15] Wilderness never lost its harsh and forbidding character. Indeed, precisely *because* of them it was unoccupied and could be a refuge as well as a disciplinary force. Paradoxically, one sought the wilderness as a way of being purified and hence delivered from it into a promised land. There was no fondness in the Hebraic tradition for wilderness itself.

The Exodus experience established a tradition of going to the wilderness for freedom and the purification of faith. When a society became complacent and ungodly, religious leaders looked to the wilderness as a place for rededication and refuge. This is the meaning behind Jeremiah's plea: "Oh that I had in the desert a wayfarers' lodging place, that I might leave my people . . . for they are all adulterers, a company of treacherous men." When Elijah sought inspiration and guidance from God, he went into the wilderness a symbolic forty days and received it, like Moses, on a deserted mountain.[16] Sometimes an entire group left the settled parts of Israel for the wilderness with the intention of achieving a degree of purity and simplicity that would in fact prepare the way for the Messiah's coming. The most famous of these apocalyptic communities was that of the Essenes, who lived in caves near the Dead Sea in the second century before Christ. They hoped their sojourn, like the one of their ancestors in the Sinai desert, would lead to another and better promised land.

The importance of wilderness as a sanctuary was perpetuated in Christianity. John the Baptist was the New Testament counterpart to Moses, Elijah, and the Essenes. He sought the wild valley of the Jordan River to revitalize faith and make ready for the Messiah.[17] Each one of the Gospels connected John with the prophet mentioned in Isaiah whose voice could be heard crying "in the wilderness" to prepare God's way. When Jesus went to John in the Judean Desert for baptism the prophecy was fulfilled. Immediately thereafter Christ "was led up by the Spirit into the wilderness to be tempted by the devil."[18] This experience, complete with forty days of fasting, alluded to the testing of Israel during the Exodus. And wilderness retained its significance as the environment of evil and hardship where spiritual catharsis occurred. Jesus emerged from the wilderness prepared to speak for God.

In early and medieval Christianity, wilderness kept its significance as the earthly realm of the powers of evil that the Church had to overcome. This was literally the case in the missionary efforts to the tribes of northern Europe. Christians judged their work to be successful when they cleared away the wild forests and cut down the sacred groves where the pagans held their rites.[19] In a more figurative sense, wilderness represented the Christian conception of the situation man faced on earth. It was a compound of his natural inclination to sin, the temptation of the material world, and the forces of evil themselves. In this worldly chaos he wandered lost and forlorn, grasping at Christianity in the hope of delivery to the promised land that now was located in heaven.

Yet Christianity also retained the idea that wild country could be a place of refuge and religious purity. A succession of Christian hermits and monks (literally, one who lives alone) found the solitude of the wilderness conducive to meditation, spiritual insight, and moral perfection. Saint Anthony's lifelong retirement in the third century to the desert between the Nile and the Red Sea was the classic example. Subsequently monasticism flourished, and numerous zealots sought solitary retreats.[20] In the fourth century Saint Basil the Great established a monastery in the wilderness south of the Black Sea and proudly reported, "I am living . . . in the wilderness wherein, the Lord dwelt." Basil's description of the forested mountain on which he lived even suggested some recognition of beauty in wilderness,[21] but his virtual uniqueness in this respect dramatizes the general indifference in his time. On the whole the monks regarded wilderness as having value only for escaping corrupt society. It was the place in which they hoped to ignite the flame that would eventually transform all wilderness into a godly paradise.

The tradition of fleeing into uninhabited country to obtain freedom of worship persisted strongly into the Middle Ages. Late in the twelfth century, for instance, Peter Waldo, a merchant of Lyons, began advocating a form of Christian asceticism that included the surrender of all worldly wealth and pleasure. The established Church took a dim view of Waldo's implied criticism of its materialism. Excommunication followed in 1184, and Waldo and his followers were hounded as heretics. Refusing to surrender their beliefs and facing death at the hands of the Inquisition if they remained in society, several thousand Waldensians elected to flee into the Piedmontese Alps on the border between France and Italy. In the caves and secluded valleys of this wilderness they found escape from religious persecution as well as an environment conducive to their philosophy of self-abnegation.[22]

Among medieval Christians St. Francis of Assisi is the exception that proves the rule. He stood alone in a posture of humility and respect before the natural world. Assuming that birds, wolves, and other wild creatures had souls, St. Francis preached to them as equals. This challenge to the idea of man as above, rather than of, the natural world might have altered the prevailing conception of wilderness. But the Church stamped St. Francis' beliefs as heretical. Christianity had too much at stake in the notion that God set man apart from and gave him dominance over the rest of nature (Genesis 1:28) to surrender it easily.[23]

The belief that good Christians should maintain an aloofness from the pleasures of the world also helped determine attitude toward wilderness. The ideal focus for any Christian in the Middle Ages was the attainment of heavenly beatitudes, not enjoyment of his present situation. Such a point of view tended to check any appreciation of natural beauty. Thus, during the Renaissance, Christianity offered considerable resistance to the development of joy in perceiving wild landscapes. Petrarch's 1336 ascent of Mount Ventoux provides an example. He initially had no other purpose in wandering "free and alone, among the mountains, forests, and streams." After an all-day effort, Petrarch and his brother gained the summit. "The great sweep of view spread out before me," Petrarch wrote to a friend, and "I stood like one dazed." Clouds floated beneath his feet, and on the horizon, he could see the snow-covered Alps. Had he descended from the mountain at this point Petrarch might have retained an undiminished sense of enjoyment in the view, but it occurred to him to look at the copy of Saint Augustine's *Confessions* he was accustomed to carry. By chance he opened to the passage that admonished men not to take joy in mountains or scenery but rather to look after their salvation. Petrarch responded as a Christian: "I was abashed, and . . . I closed the book, angry with myself that I should still be admiring earthly things who might ago have learned . . . that nothing is wonderful but the soul." After this he hurriedly left the peak, "turned my inward eye upon myself," and returned to his inn, muttering imprecations at the way the world's beauty diverted men from their proper concerns.[24]

With the cases of St. Francis and Petrarch in mind, a comparison of early Western attitude toward wilderness with that of other cultures dramatizes the great influence of the Judeo-Christian tradition in arousing and nourishing antipathy. In the Far East, by way of contrast, the man–nature relationship was marked by respect, bordering on love, absent in the West. India's early religions, especially Jainism, Buddhism and Hinduism, emphasized compassion for all living things. Man was understood to be a part of nature.[25] And wilderness, in Eastern thought, did not have an unholy or evil connotation but was venerated as the symbol and even the very essence of the deity. As early as the fifth century B.C., Chinese Taoists postulated an infinite and benign force in the natural world. Wilderness was not excluded. Far from avoiding wild places, the ancient Chinese sought them out in the hope of sensing more clearly something of the unity and rhythm that they believed pervaded the universe.[26] In Japan the first religion, Shinto, was a form of nature worship that deified mountains, forests, storms, and torrents in preference to fruitful, pastoral scenes since the wild was thought to manifest the divine being more potently than the rural.[27] In linking God and the wilderness, instead of contrasting them as did the Western faiths, Shinto and Taoism fostered love of wilderness rather than hatred.

Largely as a result of their religious views but possibly also because their relatively advanced and populous civilizations had tamed most of their countries, Chinese and Japanese landscape painters celebrated wilderness over a thousand years before Western artists. By the sixth century, canvasses which hoped to capture the spiritual significance of nature were a major art form. Frequently the artist-philosopher made a pilgrimage into the wilderness and remained there many months to meditate, adore, and penetrate, if possible, to inner harmonies. Wild vistas dominated this genre, while human figures, if they appeared at all, took secondary importance to cliffs, trees, and rivers.[28]

Kuo Hsi, the eleventh-century Chinese master of landscapes, expressed his artistic philosophy with pen as well as brush. His *Essay on Landscape Painting* began by asking, rhetorically, "why does a virtuous man take delight in landscapes?" The answer was that away from civilization man "may nourish his nature." Expanding on this, Kuo Hsi continued: "the din of the dusty world and the locked-in-ness of human habitations are what human nature habitually abhors; while, on the contrary, haze, mist, and the haunting spirits of the mountains are what human nature seeks, and yet can rarely find." According to him the purpose of landscape painting was to make it possible for men to experience the delights and absorb the lessons of nature when they could not do so directly. That Kuo Hsi had wilderness in mind rather than the pastoral is evident from his lengthy opening section in the *Essay* where the emphasis was entirely on streams, rocks, pine trees, and, especially, mountains.[29]

Freed from the combined weight of Classicism, Judaism, and Christianity, Eastern cultures did not fear and abhor wilderness. Nor did they feel the conflict between religion and appreciation of natural beauty which caused Petrarch's anguish on Mount Ventoux. But Western thought generated a powerful bias against the wilderness, and the settlement of the New World offered abundant opportunity for the expression of this sentiment.

NOTES

1. Mircea Eliade, "The Yearning for Paradise in Primitive Tradition," *Daedalus*, 88 (1959), 255–67; Loren Baritz, "The Idea of the West," *American Historical Review*, 66 (1961), 618–40; Arthur O. Lovejoy and George Boas, *Primitivism and Related Ideas in Antiquity* (Baltimore, 1935), pp. 290–303; George Boas, *Essays on Primitivism and Related Ideas in the Middle Ages* (Baltimore, 1948), pp. 154–74.

2. Lovejoy and Boas, pp. 222–42; Henry Rushton Fairclough, *Love of Nature among the Greeks and Romans* (New York, 1930); Archibald Geikie, *The Love of Nature among the Romans during the Latter Decades of the Republic and the First Century of the Empire* (London, 1912); Charles Paul Segal, "Nature and the World of Man in Greek Literature," *Arion*, 2 (1963), 19–53.

3. *Titus Lucretius Carus on the Nature of Things*, trans. Thomas Jackson (Oxford, 1929), pp. 155, 160, 184ff., 201. Lovejoy and Boas, pp. 192–221, present other instances of "anti-primitivism" among Greek writers.

4. *Lucretius*, pp. 198–99.

5. Edward B. Taylor, *Primitive Culture* (2nd ed. 2 vols. London, 1873), 2, 214–29; Willhelm Mannhardt, *Wald- und feldkulte* (2 vols. Berlin, 1904–05); James Frazier, *The Golden Bough: A Study in Magic and Religion* (3rd rev. ed. 12 vols. New York, 1935), 2, 7–96; 9, 72–108; Alexander Porteus, *Forest Folklore, Mythology, and Romance* (New York, 1928), pp. 84–148.

6. Porteus, pp. 114–19; J.H. Philpot, *The Sacred Tree: The Tree in Religion and Myth* (London, 1897), pp. 55–58; Thomas Keightley, *The Mythology of Ancient Greece and Italy* (2nd ed. London, 1838), pp. 229–35, 316–18; Robert Graes et al., *Larousse Encyclopedia of Mythology* (New York, 1959), pp. 182–85.

7. Porteus, p. 84; Jan Machal, *Slavic Mythology: The Mythology of All Races*, ed. Louis Herbert Gray (13 vols. Boston, 1916), 3, 261–66.

8. The folk traditions of the Teutonic and Nordic peoples, which contain numerous references to

wilderness-dwelling spirits, are discussed extensively in Mannhardt; Jacob Grimm, *Teutonic Mythology*, trans. James Steven Stallybrass (4 vols. London, 1880); H.R. Ellis Davidson, *Gods and Myths of Northern Europe* (Baltimore, 1964); and Benjamin Thorpe, *Northern Mythology* (3 vols. London, 1851).

9. Deut. 8:15; Isaiah 42:15, 5:6. These and subsequent wordings are according to the *Holy Bible: Revised Standard Version* (New York, Thomas Nelson and Sons, 1952).

10. Deut. 8:7; Isaiah 35:1,6; Isaiah 43:20. See also Isaiah 41:18–19 and 32:15.

11. Deut. 16:10. On Hebrew folklore regarding the wilderness see Williams, p. 13; Frazier, 9, 109 ff.; and Angelo Rappoport, *The Folklore of the Jews* (London, 1937), pp. 39 ff.

12. Genesis 2:9, 3:17; Joel 2:3; Isaiah 51:3.

13. Deut. 32:10.

14. Martin Noth, *The History of Israel* (New York, 1958), pp. 107–37; W.O.E. Oesterley and Theodore H. Robinson, *A History of Israel* (2 vols. Oxford, 1932), 1, 67–111.

15. For amplification see Williams, pp. 15–19; Mauser, *Christ in the Wilderness*, pp. 20–36; and Robert T. Anderson, "The Role of the Desert in Israelite Thought," *Journal of the Bible and Religion, 27* (1959), 41–44.

16. Jeremiah 9:2; I Kings 19:4–18.

17. John H. Kraeling, *John the Baptist* (New York, 19510, pp. 1–32. The uses of wilderness in the New Testament are discussed in full in Mauser, pp. 62 ff.

18. Isaiah 40:3–5; Matthew 4:1.

19. Philpot, *Sacred Tree*, p. 18; Jacob Burckhardt, *The Civilization of the Renaissance in Italy* (New York, 1954), p. 218.

20. Walter Nigg, *Warriors of God: The Great Religious Orders and Their Founders*, ed. and trans. Mary Ilford (New York, 1959), pp. 19–49; Charles Kingsley, *The Hermits* (London, 1891), pp. 21–82; Helen Waddell, *The Desert Fathers* (London, 1936, pp. 41–53; Williams, pp. 28 ff.; Kenneth Scott Latourette, *A History of Christianity* (New York, 1953), pp. 221–35; Herbert B. Workman, *The Evolution of the Monastic Ideal* (London, 1913), pp. 29 ff.

21. *Saint Basil: The Letters*, trans. Roy J. Defarrari (4 vols. London, 1926), 1, 261; 107–11.

22. Emilio Comba, *History of the Waldenses of Italy* (London, 1889); Alexis Muston, *The Israel of the Alps: A Complete History of the Waldenses*, trans. John Montgomery (2 vols. London, 1875).

23. For this interpretation of St. Francis I am in debt to Lynn White, Jr.'s "The Historical Roots of our Ecologic Crisis," a paper read December 26, 1966 to the American Association for the Advancement of Science and scheduled for publication in a forthcoming issue of *Science* [155, no. 3767 (1967): 1203–1207]. The general problem of the conception of the man–land relationship in Western culture is considered in Clarence J. Glacken's monumental *Traces on the Rhodian Shore* which, at the author's kindness, I read in manuscript before its publication by the University of California Press.

24. James Harvey Robinson and Henry Winchester Rolfe, eds., *Petrarch: The First Modern Scholar and Man of Letters* (2nd rev. ed. New York, 1914), pp. 297, 313–14, 317–20. A relevant secondary discussion is Alfred Biese, *The Development of the Feeling for Nature in the Middle Ages and Modern Times* (London, 1905), pp. 109–20.

25. Albert Schweitzer, *Indian Thought and Its Development*, trans. Mrs. Charles E.B. Russell (New York, 1936), passim; A. L. Basham, *The Wonder That Was India* (New York, 1954), pp. 276 ff.

26. Joseph Needham, *Science and Civilization in China* (4 vols. Cambridge, 1962), 2, 33–164; Arthur Waley, *The Way and Its Power: A Study of Tao Te Ching and Its Place in Chinese Thought* (Boston, 1935), pp. 43 ff.; Maraharu Anesaki, *Art, Life, and Nature in Japan* (Boston, 1933), pp. 3–28.

27. G.B. Sansom, *Japan: A Short Cultural History* (rev. ed. New York, 1962), pp. 46–63; J.W.T. Mason, *The Meaning of Shinto* (New York, 1935).

28. Hugo Munsterberg, *The Landscape Painting of China and Japan* (Rutland, Vt., 1955), pp. 3 ff.; Michael Sullivan, *The Birth of Landscape Painting in China* (Berkeley, Cal., 1962); Arthur de Carle Sowerby, *Nature in Chinese Art* (New York, 1940), pp. 153–60; Otto Fischer, "Landscape as Symbol," *Landscape, 4* (1955), 24–33; Benjamin Roland, Jr., *Art in East and West* (Cambridge, Mass., 1954), pp. 65–68.

29. Kuo Hsi, *An Essay on Landscape Painting*, trans. Shio Sakanishi (London, 1935), p. 30.

MAN AND NATURE

The Roman Empire, at the period of its greatest expansion, comprised the regions of the earth most distinguished by a happy combination of physical advantages. The provinces bordering on the principal and the secondary basins of the Mediterranean enjoyed a healthfulness and an equability of climate, a fertility of soil, a variety of vegetable and mineral products, and natural facilities for the transportation and distribution of exchangeable commodities, which have not been possessed in an equal degree by any territory of like extent in the Old World or the New. The abundance of the land and of the waters adequately supplied every material want, ministered liberally to every sensuous enjoyment. Gold and silver, indeed, were not found in the profusion which has proved so baneful to the industry of lands richer in veins of the precious metals; but mines and river beds yielded them in the spare measure most favorable to stability of value in the medium of exchange, and, consequently, to the regularity of commercial transactions. The ornaments of the barbaric pride of the East, the pearl, the ruby, the sapphire, and the diamond—though not unknown to the luxury of a people whose conquests and whose wealth commanded whatever the habitable world could contribute to augment the material splendor of their social life—were scarcely native to the territory of the empire; but the comparative rarity of these gems in Europe, at somewhat earlier periods, was, perhaps, the very circumstance that led the cunning artists of classic antiquity to enrich softer stones with engravings, which invest the common onyx and carnelian with a worth surpassing, in cultivated eyes, the lustre of the most brilliant oriental jewels.

Of these manifold blessings the temperature of the air, the distribution of the rains, the relative disposition of land and water, the plenty of the sea, the composition of the soil, and the raw material of some of the arts, were wholly gratuitous gifts. Yet the spontaneous nature of Europe, of Western Asia, of Libya, neither fed nor clothed the civilized inhabitants of those provinces. Every loaf was eaten in the sweat of the brow. All must be earned by toil. But toil was nowhere else rewarded by so generous wages; for nowhere would a given amount of intelligent labor produce so abundant, and, at the same time, so varied returns of the good things of material existence. The luxuriant harvests of cereals that waved on every field from the shores of the Rhine to the banks of the Nile, the vines that festooned the hillsides of Syria, of Italy, and of Greece, the olives of Spain, the fruits of the gardens of the Hesperides, the domestic quadrupeds and fowls known in ancient rural husbandry—all these were original products of foreign climes, naturalized in new homes, and gradually ennobled by the art of man, while centuries of persevering labor were expelling the wild vegetation, and fitting the earth for the production of more generous growths.

Only for the sense of landscape beauty did unaided nature make provision. Indeed, the very commonness of this source of refined enjoyment seems to have deprived it of half its value; and it was only in the infancy of lands where all the earth was fair, that Greek and Roman humanity had sympathy enough with the inanimate world to be alive to the charms of rural and of mountain scenery. In later generations, when the glories of the landscape had been heightened by plantation,

George Perkins Marsh, Man and Nature: Or, Physical Geography as Modified by Human Action (Cambridge, Mass.: Harvard University Press, [1864] 1965), pp. 7–11, 18–19, 36–39, 42–46, 52.

and decorative architecture, and other forms of picturesque improvement, the poets of Greece and Rome were blinded by excess of light, and became, at last, almost insensible to beauties that now, even in their degraded state, enchant every eye, except, too often, those which a lifelong familiarity has dulled to their attractions.

PHYSICAL DECAY OF THE TERRITORY OF THE ROMAN EMPIRE, AND OF OTHER PARTS OF THE OLD WORLD

If we compare the present physical condition of the countries of which I am speaking, with the descriptions that ancient historians and geographers have given of their fertility and general capability of ministering to human uses, we shall find that more than one half of their whole extent—including the provinces most celebrated for the profusion and variety of their spontaneous and their cultivated products, and for the wealth and social advancement of their inhabitants—is either deserted by civilized man and surrendered to hopeless desolation, or at least greatly reduced in both productiveness and population. Vast forests have disappeared from mountain spurs and ridges; the vegetable earth accumulated beneath the trees by the decay of leaves and fallen trunks, the soil of the alpine pastures which skirted and indented the woods, and the mould of the upland fields, are washed away; meadows, once fertilized by irrigation, are waste and unproductive, because the cisterns and reservoirs that supplied the ancient canals are broken, or the springs that fed them dried up; rivers famous in history and song have shrunk to humble brooklets; the willows that ornamented and protected the banks of the lesser watercourses are gone, and the rivulets have ceased to exist as perennial currents, because the little water that finds its way into their old channels is evaporated by the droughts of summer, or absorbed by the parched earth, before it reaches the lowlands; the beds of the brooks have widened into broad expanses of pebbles and gravel, over which, though in the hot season passed dryshod, in winter sealike torrents thunder; the entrances of navigable streams are obstructed by sandbars, and harbors, once marts of an extensive commerce, are shoaled by the deposits of the rivers at whose mouths they lie; the elevation of the beds of estuaries, and the consequently diminished velocity of the streams which flow into them, have converted thousands of leagues of shallow sea and fertile lowland into unproductive and miasmatic morasses.

Besides the direct testimony of history to the ancient fertility of the regions to which I refer—Northern Africa, the greater Arabian Peninsula, Syria, Mesopotamia, Armenia, and many other provinces of Asia Minor, Greece, Sicily, and parts of even Italy and Spain—the multitude and extent of yet remaining architectural ruins, and of decayed works of internal improvement, show that at former epochs a dense population inhabited those now lonely districts. Such a population could have been sustained only by a productiveness of soil of which we at present discover but slender traces; and the abundance derived from that fertility serves to explain how large armies, like those of the ancient Persians, and of the Crusaders and the Tartars in later ages, could, without an organized commissariat, secure adequate supplies in long marches through territories which, in our times, would scarcely afford forage for a single regiment.

It appears, then, that the fairest and fruitfulest provinces of the Roman Empire, precisely that portion of terrestrial surface, in short, which, about the commencement of the Christian era, was endowed with the greatest superiority of soil, climate, and position, which had been carried to the highest pitch of physical improvement, and which thus combined the natural and artificial conditions best fitting it for the habitation and enjoyment of a dense and highly refined and cultivated population, is now completely exhausted of its fertility, or so diminished in productiveness, as, with the exception of a few favored oases that have escaped the general ruin, to be no longer capable of affording sustenance to civilized man. If to this realm of desolation we add the now wasted and solitary soils of Persia and the remoter East, that once fed their millions with milk and honey, we shall see that a territory larger than all Europe, the abundance of which sustained in bygone centuries a population scarcely inferior to that of the whole Christian world at the present day, has been entirely withdrawn from human use, or, at best, is thinly inhabited by tribes too few in numbers, too poor in superfluous products, and too little advanced in culture and the social arts, to contribute anything to the general moral and material interests of the great commonwealth of man.

CAUSES OF THIS DECAY

The decay of these once flourishing countries is partly due, no doubt, to that class of geological causes, whose action we can neither resist nor guide, and partly also to the direct violence of hostile human force; but it is, in a far greater proportion, either the result of man's ignorant disregard of the laws of nature, or an incidental consequence of war, and of civil and ecclesiastical tyranny and misrule.

. . .

GEOGRAPHICAL INFLUENCE OF MAN

. . . It is certain that man has done much to mould the form of the earth's surface, though we cannot always distinguish between the results of his action and the effects of purely geological causes; that the destruction of the forests, the drainage of lakes and marshes, and the operation of rural husbandry and industrial art have tended to produce great changes in the hygrometric, thermometric, electric, and chemical condition of the atmosphere, though we are not yet able to measure the force of the different elements of disturbance, or to say how far they have been compensated by each other, or by still obscurer influences; and, finally, that the myriad forms of animal and vegetable life, which covered the earth when man first entered upon the theatre of a nature whose harmonies he was destined to derange, have been, through his action, greatly changed in numerical proportion, sometimes much modified in form and product, and sometimes entirely extirpated.

The physical revolutions thus wrought by man have not all been destructive to human interests. Soils to which no nutritious vegetable was indigenous, countries which once brought forth but the fewest products suited for the sustenance and comfort of man—while the severity of their climates created and stimulated the greatest number and the most imperious urgency of physical wants—surfaces the most rugged and intractable, and least blessed with natural facilities of communication, have been

made in modern times to yield and distribute all that supplies the material necessities, all that contributes to the sensuous enjoyments and conveniences of civilized life. The Scythia, the Thule, the Britain, the Germany, and the Gaul which the Roman writers describe in such forbidding terms, have been brought almost to rival the native luxuriance and easily won plenty of Southern Italy; and, while the fountains of oil and wine that refreshed old Greece and Syria and Northern Africa have almost ceased to flow, and the soils of those fair lands are turned to thirsty and inhospitable deserts, the hyperborean regions of Europe have conquered, or rather compensated, the rigors of climate, and attained to a material wealth and variety of product that, with all their natural advantages, the granaries of the ancient world can hardly be said to have enjoyed.

These changes for evil and for good have not been caused by great natural revolutions of the globe, nor are they by any means attributable wholly to the moral and physical action or inaction of the peoples, or, in all cases, even of the races that now inhabit these respective regions. They are products of a complication of conflicting or coincident forces, acting through a long series of generations; here, improvidence, wastefulness, and wanton violence; there, foresight and wisely guided persevering industry.

. . .

DESTRUCTIVENESS OF MAN

Man has too long forgotten that the earth was given to him for usufruct alone, not for consumption, still less for profligate waste. Nature has provided against the absolute destruction of any of her elementary matter, the raw material of her works; the thunderbolt and the tornado, the most convulsive throes of even the volcano and the earthquake, being only phenomena of decomposition and recomposition. But she has left it within the power of man irreparably to derange the combinations of inorganic matter and of organic life, which through the night of æons she had been proportioning and balancing, to prepare the earth for his habitation, when, in the fullness of time, his Creator should call him forth to enter into its possession.

Apart from the hostile influence of man, the organic and the inorganic world are . . . bound together by such mutual relations and adaptations as secure, if not the absolute permanence and equilibrium of both, a long continuance of the established conditions of each at any given time and place, or at least, a very slow and gradual succession of changes in those conditions. But man is everywhere a disturbing agent. Wherever he plants his foot, the harmonies of nature are turned to discords. The proportions and accommodations which insured the stability of existing arrangements are overthrown. Indigenous vegetable and animal species are extirpated, and supplanted by others of foreign origin, spontaneous production is forbidden or restricted, and the face of the earth is either laid bare or covered with a new and reluctant growth of vegetable forms, and with alien tribes of animal life. These intentional changes and substitutions constitute, indeed, great revolutions; but vast as is their magnitude and importance, they are . . . insignificant in comparison with the contingent and unsought results which have flowed from them.

. . .

Man, the domestic animals that serve him, the field and garden plants the products of which supply him with food and clothing, cannot subsist and rise to the full development of their higher properties, unless brute and unconscious nature be effectually combated, and, in a great degree, vanquished by human art. Hence, a certain measure of transformation of terrestrial surface, of suppression of natural, and stimulation of artificially modified productivity becomes necessary. This measure man has unfortunately exceeded. He has felled the forests whose network of fibrous roots bound the mould to the rocky skeleton of the earth; but had he allowed here and there a belt of woodland to reproduce itself by spontaneous propagation, most of the mischiefs which his reckless destruction of the natural protection of the soil has occasioned would have been averted. He has broken up the mountain reservoirs, the percolation of whose waters through unseen channels supplied the fountains that refreshed his cattle and fertilized his fields; but he has neglected to maintain the cisterns and the canals of irrigation which a wise antiquity had constructed to neutralize the consequences of its own imprudence. While he has torn

the thin glebe which confined the light earth of extensive plains, and has destroyed the fringe of semi-aquatic plants which skirted the coast and checked the drifting of the sea sand, he has failed to prevent the spreading of the dunes by clothing them with artificially propagated vegetation. He has ruthlessly warred on all the tribes of animated nature whose spoils he could convert to his own uses, and he has not protected the birds which prey on the insects most destructive to his own harvests.

HUMAN AND BRUTE ACTION COMPARED

. . . The ravages committed by man subvert the relations and destroy the balance which nature had established between her organized and her inorganic creations; and she avenges herself upon the intruder, by letting loose upon her defaced provinces destructive energies hitherto kept in check by organic forces destined to be his best auxiliaries, but which he has unwisely dispersed and driven from the field of action. When the forest is gone, the great reservoir of moisture stored up in its vegetable mould is evaporated, and returns only in deluges of rain to wash away the parched dust into which that mould has been converted. The well-wooded and humid hills are turned to ridges of dry rock, which encumbers the low grounds and chokes the watercourses with its debris, and—except in countries favored with an equitable distribution of rain through the seasons, and a moderate and regular inclination of surface—the whole earth, unless rescued by human art from the physical degradation to which it tends, becomes an assemblage of bald mountains, of barren, turfless hills, and of swampy and malarious plains. There are parts of Asia Minor, of Northern Africa, of Greece, and even of Alpine Europe, where the operation of causes set in action by man has brought the face of the earth to a desolation almost as complete as that of the moon; and though, within that brief space of time which we call "the historical period," they are known to have been covered with luxuriant woods, verdant pastures, and fertile meadows, they are now too far deteriorated to be reclaimable by man, nor can they become again fitted for human use, except through great geological changes, or other mysterious influences or agencies of which we have no present knowledge, and over which we have no prospective control. The earth is fast becoming an unfit home for its noblest inhabitant, and another era of equal human crime and human improvidence, and of like duration with that through which traces of that crime and that improvidence extend, would reduce it to such a condition of impoverished productiveness, of shattered surface, of climatic excess, as to threaten the depravation, barbarism, and perhaps even extinction of the species.[1]

PHYSICAL IMPROVEMENT

True, there is a partial reverse to this picture. On narrow theatres, new forests have been planted; inundations of flowing streams restrained by heavy walls of masonry and other constructions; torrents compelled to aid, by depositing the slime with which they are charged, in filling up lowlands, and raising the level of morasses which their own overflows had created; ground submerged by the encroachments of the ocean, or exposed to be covered by its tides, has been rescued from its domain by diking,[2] swamps and even lakes have been drained, and their beds brought within the domain of agricultural industry; drifting coast dunes have been checked and made productive by plantation; seas and inland waters have been repeopled with fish, and even the sands of the Sahara have been fertilized by artesian fountains. These achievements are more glorious than the proudest triumphs of war, but, thus far, they give but faint hope that we shall yet make full atonement for our spendthrift waste of the bounties of nature.

It is, on the one hand, rash and unphilosophical to attempt to set limits to the ultimate power of man over inorganic nature, and it is unprofitable, on the other, to speculate on what may be accomplished by the discovery of now unknown and unimagined natural forces, or even by the invention of new arts and new processes. But since we have seen aerostation, the motive power of elastic vapors, the wonders of modern telegraphy, the destructive explosiveness of gunpowder, and even of a substance so harmless, unresisting, and inert as cotton, nothing in the way of mechanical achievement seems impossible, and it is hard to restrain the imagination from wandering forward a couple of generations to an epoch when our descendants shall have advanced as far beyond us in physical conquest, as we have marched beyond the trophies erected by our grandfathers.

I must therefore be understood to mean only, that no agencies now known to man and directed by him seem adequate to the reducing of great Alpine precipices to such slopes as would enable them to support a vegetable clothing, or to the covering of large extents of denuded rock with earth, and planting upon them a forest growth. But among the mysteries which science is yet to reveal, there may be still undiscovered methods of accomplishing even grander wonders than these. Mechanical philosophers have suggested the possibility of accumulating and treasuring up for human use some of the greater natural forces, which the action of the elements puts forth with such astonishing energy. Could we gather, and bind, and make subservient to our control, the power which a West Indian hurricane exerts through a small area in one continuous blast, or the momentum expended by the waves, in a tempestuous winter, upon the breakwater at Cherbourg,[3] or the lifting power of the tide, for a month, at the head of the Bay of Fundy, or the pressure of a square mile of sea water at the depth of five thousand fathoms, or a movement of the might of an earthquake or a volcano, our age—which moves no mountains and casts them into the sea by faith alone—might hope to scarp the rugged walls of the Alps and Pyrenees and Mount Taurus, robe them once more in a vegetation as rich as that of their pristine woods, and turn their wasting torrents into refreshing streams.[4]

Could this old world, which man has overthrown, be rebuilt, could human cunning rescue its wasted hillsides and its deserted plains from solitude or mere nomad occupation, from barrenness, from nakedness, and from insalubrity, and restore the ancient fertility and healthfulness of the Etruscan sea coast, the Campagna and the Pontine marshes, of Calabria, of Sicily, of the Peloponnesus and insular and continental Greece, of Asia Minor, of the slopes of Lebanon and Hermon, of Palestine, of the Syrian desert, of Mesopotamia and the delta of the Euphrates, of the Cyreniaica, of Africa proper, Numidia, and Mauritania, the thronging millions of Europe might still find room on the Eastern continent, and the main current of emigration be turned toward the rising instead of the setting sun.

But changes like these must await great political and moral revolutions in the governments and peoples by whom those regions are now possessed, a command of pecuniary and of mechanical means not at present enjoyed by those nations, and a more advanced and generally diffused knowledge of the processes by which the amelioration of soil and climate is possible, than now anywhere exists. Until such circumstances shall conspire to favor the work of geographical regeneration, the countries I have mentioned, with here and there a local exception, will continue to sink into yet deeper desolation, and in the mean time, the American continent, Southern Africa, Australia, and the smaller oceanic islands, will be almost the only theatres where man is engaged, on a great scale, in transforming the face of nature.

ARREST OF PHYSICAL DECAY OF NEW COUNTRIES

Comparatively short as is the period through which the colonization of foreign lands by European emigrants extends, great, and, it is to be feared, sometimes irreparable, injury has been already done in the various processes by which man seeks to subjugate the virgin earth; and many provinces, first trodden by the *homo sapiens Europæ* within the last two centuries, begin to show signs of that melancholy dilapidation which is now driving so many of the peasantry of Europe from their native hearths. It is evidently a matter of great moment, not only to the population of the states where these symptoms are manifesting themselves, but to the general interests of humanity, that this decay should be arrested, and that the future operations of rural husbandry and of forest industry, in districts yet remaining substantially in their native condition, should be so conducted as to prevent the widespread mischiefs which have been elsewhere produced by thoughtless or wanton destruction of the natural safeguards of the soil. This can be done only by the diffusion of knowledge on this subject among the classes that, in earlier days,

subdued and tilled the ground in which they had no vested rights, but who, in our time, own their woods, their pastures, and their ploughlands as a perpetual possession for them and theirs, and have, therefore, a strong interest in the protection of their domain against deterioration.

. . .

PHYSICAL DECAY OF NEW COUNTRIES

. . . The geological, hydrographical, and topographical surveys, which almost every general and even local government of the civilized world is carrying on, are making . . . important contributions to our stock of geographical and general physical knowledge, and, within a comparatively short space, there will be an accumulation of well-established constant and historical facts, from which we can safely reason upon all the relations of action and reaction between man and external nature.

But we are, even now, breaking up the floor and wainscoting and doors and window frames of our dwelling, for fuel to warm our bodies and seethe our pottage, and the world cannot afford to wait till the slow and sure progress of exact science has taught it a better economy. Many practical lessons have been learned by the common observation of unschooled men; and the teachings of simple experience, on topics where natural philosophy has scarcely yet spoken, are not to be despised.

NOTES

1. "And it may be remarked that, as the world has passed through these several stages of strife to produce a Christendom; so by relaxing in the enterprises it has learnt, does it tend downwards, through inverted steps, to wildness and the waste again. Let a people give up their contest with moral evil; disregard the injustice, the ignorance, the greediness, that may prevail among them, and part more and more with the *Christian* element of their civilization; and, in declining this battle with Sin, they will inevitably get embroiled with men. Threats of war and revolution punish their unfaithfulness; and if then, instead of retracing their steps, they yield again and are driven before

the storm—the very arts they had created, the structures they had raised, the usages they had established, are swept away; 'in that very day their thoughts perish.' The portion they had reclaimed from the young earth's ruggedness is lost; and failing to stand fast against man, they finally get embroiled with Nature, and are thrust down beneath her ever-living hand." (James M. Martineau, "The Good Soldier of Jesus Christ," *Endeavours after the Christian Life: Discourses, 2nd ser.*, new ed., Boston, 1858, pp. 419–420.)

2. The dependence of man upon the aid of spontaneous nature, in his most arduous material works, is curiously illustrated by the fact that one of the most serious difficulties to be encountered in executing the proposed gigantic scheme of draining the Zuiderzee in Holland, is that of procuring brushwood for the fascines to be employed in the embankments. See Bernard Pieter Gezienus van Diggelen, *Groote Werken in Nederland . . . Bedijking van de Zuiderzee* (Zwolle, 1855).

3. In heavy storms, the force of the waves as they strike against a sea wall is from one and a half to two tons to the square foot, and Stevenson, in one instance at Skerryvore, found this force equal to three tons per foot.

   The seaward front of the breakwater at Cherbourg exposes a surface of about 2,500,000 square feet. In rough weather the waves beat against this whole face, though at the depth of twenty-two yards, which is the height of the breakwater, they exert a very much less violent motive force than at and near the surface of the sea, because this force diminishes in geometrical, as the distance below the surface increases in arithmetic proportion. The shock of the waves is received several thousand times in the course of twenty-four hours, and hence the sum of impulse which the breakwater resists in one stormy day amounts to many thousands of millions of tons. The breakwater is entirely an artificial construction. If then man could accumulate and control the forces which he is able effectually to resist, he might be said to be, physically speaking, omnipotent.

4. Some well known experiments show that it is quite possible to accumulate the solar heat by a simple apparatus, and thus to obtain a temperature which might be economically important even in the climate of Switzerland. Saussure, by receiving the sun's rays in a nest of boxes blackened within and covered with glass, raised a thermometer enclosed in the inner box to the boiling point; and under the more powerful sun of the cape of Good Hope, Sir John Herschel cooked the materials for a family dinner by a similar process, using, however, but a single box, surrounded with dry sand and covered with two glasses. Why should not so easy a method of economizing fuel be restored to in Italy, and even in more northerly climates?

   The unfortunate John Davidson records in his journal that he saved fuel in Morocco by exposing his teakettle to the sun on the roof of his house, where the water rose to the temperature of one hundred and forty degrees, and, of course, needed little fire to bring it to boil. But this was the direct and simple, not the accumulated heat of the sun.

RALPH WALDO EMERSON

NATURE

To go into solitude, a man needs to retire as much from his chamber as from society. I am not solitary whilst I read and write, though nobody is with me. But if a man would be alone, let him look at the stars. . . . One might think the atmosphere was made transparent with this design, to give man, in the heavenly bodies, the perpetual presence of the sublime. Seen in the streets of cities, how great they are! If the stars should appear one night in a thousand years, how would men believe and adore; and preserve for many generations the remembrance of the city of God which had been shown! But every night come out these envoys of beauty, and light the universe with their admonishing smile.

The stars awaken a certain reverence, because though always present, they are inaccessible; but all natural objects make a kindred impression, when the mind is open to their influence. Nature never wears a mean appearance. Neither does the wisest man extort her secret, and lose his curiosity by finding out all her perfection. Nature never became a toy to a wise spirit. The flowers, the animals, the mountains, reflected the wisdom of his best hour, as much as they had delighted the simplicity of his childhood. When we speak of nature in this manner, we have a distinct but most poetical sense in the mind. We mean the integrity of impression made by manifold natural objects. It is this which distinguishes the stick of timber of the wood-cutter, from the tree of the poet. The charming landscape which I saw this morning, is indubitably made up of some twenty or thirty farms. Miller owns this field, Locke that, and Manning the woodland beyond. But none of them owns the landscape. There is a property in the horizon which no man has but he whose eye can integrate all the parts, that is, the poet. This is the best part of these men's farms, yet to this their warranty-deeds give no title. To speak truly, few adult persons can see nature. Most persons do not see the sun. At least they have a very superficial seeing. The sun illuminates only the eye of the man, but shines into the eye and the heart of the child. The lover of nature is he whose inward and outward senses are still truly adjusted to each other; who has retained the spirit of infancy even into the era of manhood. His intercourse with heaven and earth, becomes part of his daily food. In the presence of nature, a wild delight runs through the man, in spite of real sorrows. Nature says,—he is my creature, and maugre all his impertinent griefs, he shall be glad with me. Not the sun or the summer alone, but every hour and season yields its tribute of delight; for every hour and change corresponds to and authorizes a different state of the mind, from the breathless noon to the grimmest midnight. Nature is a setting that fits equally well in a comic or a mourning piece. In good health, the air is a cordial of incredible virtue. Crossing a bare common, in snow puddles, at twilight, under a clouded sky, without having in my thoughts any occurrence of special good fortune, I have enjoyed a perfect exhilaration. I am glad to the brink of fear. In the woods too, a man casts off his years, as the snake his slough, and at what period soever of life, is always a child. In the woods, is perpetual youth. Within these plantations of God, a decorum and sanctity reign, a perennial festival is dressed, and the guest sees not how he should tire of them in a thousand years. In the woods, we return to reason and faith. There I feel that nothing can befall me in life,—no disgrace, no calamity, (leaving me my

Emerson, Ralph Waldo, [1836] 1849, Nature, New Edition (Boston: James Munroe & Co.).

eyes,) which nature cannot repair. Standing on the bare ground,—my head bathed by the blithe air, and uplifted into infinite space,—all mean egotism vanishes. I become a transparent eye-ball; I am nothing; I see all; the currents of the Universal Being circulate through me; I am part or particle of God. The name of the nearest friend sounds then foreign and accidental: to be brothers, to be acquaintances,—master or servant, is then a trifle and a disturbance. I am the lover of uncontained and immortal beauty. In the wilderness, I find something more dear and connate than in streets or villages. In the tranquil landscape, and especially in the distant line of the horizon, man beholds somewhat as beautiful as his own nature.

The greatest delight which the fields and woods minister, is the suggestion of an occult relation between man and the vegetable. I am not alone and unacknowledged. They nod to me, and I to them. The waving of the boughs in the storm, is new to me and old. It takes me by surprise, and yet is not unknown. Its effect is like that of a higher thought or a better emotion coming over me, when I deemed I was thinking justly or doing right.

Yet it is certain that the power to produce this delight, does not reside in nature, but in man, or in a harmony of both. It is necessary to use these pleasures with great temperance. For, nature is not always tricked in holiday attire, but the same scene which yesterday breathed perfume and glittered as for the frolic of the nymphs, is overspread with melancholy today. Nature always wears the colors of the spirit. To a man laboring under calamity, the heat of his own fire hath sadness in it. Then, there is a kind of contempt of the landscape felt by him who has just lost by death a dear friend. The sky is less grand as it shuts down over less worth in the population.

COMMODITY

Whoever considers the final cause of the world, will discern a multitude of uses that result. . . . Under the general name of Commodity, I rank all those advantages which our senses owe to nature. This, of course, is a benefit which is temporary and mediate, not ultimate, like its service to the soul. Yet although low, it is perfect in its kind, and is the only use of nature

which all men apprehend. The misery of man appears like childish petulance, when we explore the steady and prodigal provision that has been made for his support and delight on this green ball which floats him through the heavens. What angels invented these splendid ornaments, these rich conveniences, this ocean of air above, this ocean of water beneath, this firmament of earth between? this zodiac of lights, this tent of dropping clouds, this striped coat of climates, this fourfold year? Beasts, fire, water, stones, and corn serve him. The field is at once his floor, his work-yard, his play-ground, his garden, and his bed.

"More servants wait on man
Than he'll take notice of."—

Nature, in its ministry to man, is not only the material, but is also the process and the result. All the parts incessantly work into each other's hands for the profit of man. The wind sows the seed; the sun evaporates the sea; the wind blows the vapor to the field; the ice, on the other side of the planet, condenses rain on this; the rain feeds the plant; the plant feeds the animal; and thus the endless circulations of the divine charity nourish man. The useful arts are reproductions or new combinations by the wit of man, of the same natural benefactors. He no longer waits for favoring gales, but by means of steam, he realizes the fable of Aeolus's bag, and carries the two and thirty winds in the boiler of his boat. To diminish friction, he paves the road with iron bars, and, mounting a coach with a ship-load of men, animals, and merchandise behind him, he darts through the country, from town to town, like an eagle or a swallow through the air. By the aggregate of these aids, how is the face of the world changed, from the era of Noah to that of Napoleon! The private poor man hath cities, ships, canals, bridges, built for him. He goes to the post-office, and the human race run on his errands; to the book-shop and the human race read and write of all that happens, for him; to the court-house, and nations repair his wrongs. He sets his house upon the road, and the human race go forth every morning, and shovel out the snow, and cut a path for him.

But there is no need of specifying particulars in this class of uses. The catalogue is endless, and the examples so obvious, that I shall leave them to the reader's reflection, with the general remark, that this mercenary benefit is one which has respect to a farther good. A man is fed, not that he may be fed, but that he may work.

BEAUTY

A nobler want of man is served by nature, namely, the love of Beauty.

The ancient Greeks called the world *kosmos*, beauty. Such is the constitution of all things, or such the plastic power of the human eye, that the primary forms, as the sky, the mountain, the tree, the animal, give us a delight *in and for themselves*; a pleasure arising from outline, color, motion, and grouping. This seems partly owing to the eye itself. The eye is the best of artists. By the mutual action of its structure and of the laws of light, perspective is produced, which integrates every mass of objects, of what character soever, into a well colored and shaded globe, so that where the particular objects are mean and unaffecting, the landscape which they compose, is round and symmetrical. And as the eye is the best composer, so light is the first of painters. There is no object so foul that intense light will not make beautiful. And the stimulus it affords to the sense, and a sort of infinitude which it hath, like space and time, make all matter gay. Even the corpse has its own beauty. But besides this general grace diffused over nature, almost all the individual forms are agreeable to the eye, as is proved by our endless imitations of some of them, as the acorn, the grape, the pine-cone, the wheat-ear, the egg, the wings and forms of most birds, the lion's claw, the serpent, the butterfly, seashells, flames, clouds, buds, leaves, and the forms of many trees, as the palm.

For better consideration, we may distribute the aspects of Beauty. . . .

1. First, the simple perception of natural forms is a delight. The influence of the forms and actions in nature, is so needful to man, that, in its lowest functions, it seems to lie on the confines of commodity and beauty. To the body and mind which have been cramped by noxious work or company, nature is medicinal and restores their tone. The tradesman, the attorney comes out of the din and craft of the street, and sees the sky and the woods,

and is a man again. In their eternal calm, he finds himself. The health of the eye seems to demand a horizon. We are never tired, so long as we can see far enough.

But in other hours, Nature satisfies by its loveliness, and without any mixture of corporeal benefit. I see the spectacle of morning from the hill-top over against my house, from day-break to sun-rise, with emotions which an angel might share. The long slender bars of cloud float like fishes in the sea of crimson light. From the earth, as a shore, I look out into that silent sea. I seem to partake its rapid transformations: the active enchantment reaches my dust, and I dilate and conspire with the morning wind. How does Nature deify us with a few and cheap elements! Give me health and a day, and I will make the pomp of emperors ridiculous. The dawn is my Assyria; the sun-set and moon-rise my Paphos, and unimaginable realms of faerie; broad noon shall be my England of the senses and the understanding; the night shall be my Germany of mystic philosophy and dreams.

. . .

But this beauty of Nature which is seen and felt as beauty, is the least part. The shows of day, the dewy morning, the rainbow, mountains, orchards in blossom, stars, moonlight, shadows in still water, and the like, if too eagerly hunted, become shows merely, and mock us with their unreality. Go out of the house to see the moon, and 't is mere tinsel; it will not please as when its light shines upon your necessary journey. The beauty that shimmers in the yellow afternoons of October, whoever could clutch it? Go forth and find it, and it is gone: 't is only a mirage as you look from the windows of diligence.

2. The presence of a higher, namely, of the spiritual element is essential to its perfection. The high and divine beauty which can be loved without effeminacy, is that which is found in combination with the human will. Beauty is the mark God sets upon virtue. Every natural action is graceful. Every heroic act is also decent, and causes the place and the bystanders to shine. We are taught by great actions that the universe is the property of every individual in it. Every rational creature has all nature for his dowry and estate. It is his, if he will. He may divest himself of it; he may creep into a corner, and abdicate his kingdom,

as most men do, but he is entitled to the world by his constitution. In proportion to the energy of his thought and will, he takes up the world into himself. "All those things for which men plough, build, or sail, obey virtue;" said Sallust. "The winds and waves," said Gibbon, "are always on the side of the ablest navigators. So are the sun and moon and all the stars of heaven. When a noble act is done,—perchance in a scene of great natural beauty; when Leonidas and his three hundred martyrs consume one day in dying, and the sun and moon come each and look at them once in the steep defile of Thermopylae; when Arnold Winkelried, in the high Alps, under the shadow of the avalanche, gathers in his side a sheaf of Austrian spears to break the line for his comrades; are not these heroes entitled to add the beauty of the scene to the beauty of the deed?

. . .

The world thus exists to the soul to satisfy the desire of beauty. This element I call an ultimate end. No reason can be asked or given why the soul seeks beauty. Beauty, in its largest and profoundest sense, is one expression for the universe. God is the all-fair. Truth, and goodness, and beauty, are but different faces of the same All. But beauty in nature is not ultimate. It is the herald of inward and eternal beauty, and is not alone a solid and satisfactory good. It must stand as a part, and not as yet the last or highest expression of the final cause of Nature.

GIFFORD PINCHOT

PRINCIPLES OF CONSERVATION

The principles which govern the conservation movement, like all great and effective things, are simple and easily understood. Yet it is often hard to make the simple, easy, and direct facts about a movement of this kind known to the people generally.

The first great fact about conservation is that it stands for development. There has been a fundamental misconception that conservation means nothing but the husbanding of resources for future generations. There could be no more serious mistake. Conservation does mean provision for the future, but it means also and first of all the recognition of the right of the present generation to the fullest necessary use of all the resources with which this country is so abundantly blessed. Conservation demands the welfare of this generation first, and afterward the welfare of the generations to follow.

The first principle of conservation is development, the use of the natural resources now existing on this continent for the benefit of the people who live here now. There may be just as much waste in neglecting the development and use of certain natural resources as there is in their destruction. We have a limited supply of coal, and only a limited supply. Whether it is to last for a hundred or a hundred and fifty or a thousand years, the coal is limited in amount, unless through geological changes which we shall not live to see, there will never be any more of it than there is now. But coal is in a sense the vital essence of our civilization. If it can be preserved, if

Gifford Pinchot, The Fight for Conservation (Seattle: University of Washington Press, 1910).

the life of the mines can be extended, if by preventing waste there can be more coal left in this country after we of this generation have made every needed use of this source of power, then we shall have deserved well of our descendants.

Conservation stands emphatically for the development and use of water-power now, without delay. It stands for the immediate construction of navigable waterways under a broad and comprehensive plan as assistants to the railroads. More coal and more iron are required to move a ton of freight by rail than by water, three to one. In every case and in every direction the conservation movement has development for its first principle, and at the very beginning of its work. The development of our natural resources and the fullest use of them for the present generation is the first duty of this generation. So much for development.

In the second place conservation stands for the prevention of waste. There has come gradually in this country an understanding that waste is not a good thing and that the attack on waste is an industrial necessity. I recall very well indeed how, in the early days of forest fires, they were considered simply and solely as acts of God, against which any opposition was hopeless and any attempt to control them not merely hopeless but childish. It was assumed that they came in the natural order of things, as inevitably as the seasons or the rising and setting of the sun. To-day we understand that forest fires are wholly within the control of men. So we are coming in like manner to understand that the prevention of waste in all other directions is a simple matter of good business. The first duty of the human race is to control the earth it lives upon.

We are in a position more and more completely to say how far the waste and destruction of natural resources are to be allowed to go on and where they are to stop. It is curious that the effort to stop waste, like the effort to stop forest fires, has often been considered as a matter controlled wholly by economic law. I think there could be no greater mistake. Forest fires were allowed to burn long after the people had means to stop them. The idea that men were helpless in the face of them held long after the time had passed when the means of control were fully within our reach. It was the old story that "as

a man thinketh, so is he"; we came to see that we could stop forest fires, and we found that the means had long been at hand. When at length we came to see that the control of logging in certain directions was profitable, we found it had long been possible. In all these matters of waste of natural resources, the education of the people to understand that they can stop the leakage comes before the actual stopping and after the means of stopping it have long been ready at our hands.

In addition to the principles of development and preservation of our resources there is a third principle. It is this: The natural resources must be developed and preserved for the benefit of the many, and not merely for the profit of a few. We are coming to understand in this country that public action for public benefit has a very much wider field to cover and a much larger part to play than was the case when there were resources enough for everyone, and before certain constitutional provisions had given so tremendously strong a position to vested rights and property in general.

A few years ago President Hadley, of Yale, wrote an article which has not attracted the attention it should. The point of it was that by reason of the XIVth amendment to the Constitution, property rights in the United States occupy a stronger position than in any other country in the civilized world. It becomes then a matter of multiplied importance, since property rights once granted are so strongly entrenched, to see that they shall be so granted that the people shall get their fair share of the benefit which comes from the development of the resources which belong to us all. The time to do that is now. By so doing we shall avoid the difficulties and conflicts which will surely arise if we allow vested rights to accrue outside the possibility of governmental and popular control.

The conservation idea covers a wider range than the field of natural resources alone. Conservation means the greatest good to the greatest number for the longest time. One of its great contributions is just this, that it has added to the worn and well-known phrase, "the greatest good to the greatest number," the additional words "for the longest time," thus recognizing that this nation of ours must be made to endure as the best possible home for all its people.

Conservation advocates the use of foresight, prudence, thrift, and intelligence in dealing with public matters, for the same reasons and in the same way that we each use foresight, prudence, thrift, and intelligence in dealing with our own private affairs. It proclaims the right and duty of the people to act for the benefit of the people. Conservation demands the application of common-sense to the common problems for the common good.

The principles of conservation thus described—development, preservation, the common good—have a general application which is growing rapidly wider. The development of resources and the prevention of waste and loss, the protection of the public interests, by foresight, prudence, and the ordinary business and home-making virtues, all these apply to other things as well as to the natural resources. There is, in fact, no interest of the people to which the principles of conservation do not apply.

The conservation point of view is valuable in the education of our people as well as in forestry; it applies to the body politic as well as to the earth and its minerals. A municipal franchise is as properly within its sphere as a franchise for water-power. The same point of view governs in both. It applies as much to the subject of good roads as to waterways, and the training of our people in citizenship is as germane to it as the productiveness of the earth. The application of common-sense to any problem for the Nation's good will lead directly to national efficiency wherever applied. In other words, and that is the burden of the message, we are coming to see the logical and inevitable outcome that these principles, which arose in forestry and have their bloom in the conservation of natural resources, will have their fruit in the increase and promotion of national efficiency along other lines of national life.

The outgrowth of conservation, the inevitable result, is national efficiency. In the great commercial struggle between nations which is eventually to determine the welfare of all, national efficiency will be the deciding factor. So from every point of view conservation is a good thing for the American people.

[handwritten marginalia: But what is "common sense"?]

JOHN MUIR

THE HETCH HETCHY VALLEY

It is impossible to overestimate the value of wild mountains and mountain temples as places for people to grow in, recreation grounds for soul and body. They are the greatest of our natural resources, God's best gifts, but none, however high and holy, is beyond reach of the spoiler. In these ravaging money-mad days monopolizing San Francisco capitalists are now doing their best to destroy the Yosemite Park, the most wonderful of all our great mountain national parks. Beginning on the Tuolumne side, they are trying with a lot of sinful ingenuity to get the Government's permission to dam and destroy the Hetch-Hetchy Valley for a reservoir, simply that comparatively private gain may be made out of universal public loss, while of course the Sierra Club is doing all it can to save the valley. The Honorable Secretary of the Interior has not yet announced his decision in the case, but in all that has come and gone nothing discouraging is yet in sight on our side of the fight.

. . .

John Muir, "Hetch Hetchy Valley," in The Yosemite (New York: The Century Company, 1912), pp. 249–262.

Hetch-Hetchy Valley, far from being a plain, common, rock-bound meadow, as many who have not seen it seem to suppose, is a grand landscape garden, one of Nature's rarest and most precious mountain mansions. As in Yosemite, the sublime rocks of its walls seem to the nature-lover to glow with life, whether leaning back in repose or standing erect in thoughtful attitudes, giving welcome to storms and calms alike. And how softly these mountain rocks are adorned, and how fine and reassuring the company they keep—their brows in the sky, their feet set in groves and gay emerald meadows, a thousand flowers leaning confidingly against their adamantine bosses, while birds, bees, and butterflies help the river and waterfalls to stir all the air into music—things frail and fleeting and types of permanence meeting here and blending, as if into this glorious mountain temple Nature had gathered here choices treasures, whether great or small, to draw her lovers into close confiding communion with her.

Strange to say, this is the mountain temple that is now in danger of being dammed and made into a reservoir to help supply San Francisco with water and light. This use of the valley, so destructive and foreign to its proper park use, has long been planned and prayed for, and is still being prayed for by the San Francisco board of supervisors, not because water as pure and abundant cannot be got from adjacent sources outside the park—for it can,—but seemingly only because of the comparative cheapness of the dam required.

Garden- and park-making goes on everywhere with civilization, for everybody needs beauty as well as bread, places to play in and pray in, where Nature may heal and cheer and give strength to body and soul. This natural beauty-hunger is displayed in poor folks' window-gardens made up of a few geranium slips in broken cups, as well as in the costly lily gardens of the rich, the thousands of spacious city parks and botanical gardens, and in our magnificent National parks—the Yellowstone, Yosemite, Sequoia, etc.—Nature's own wonderlands, the admiration and joy of the world. Nevertheless, like everything else worthwhile, however sacred and precious and well-guarded, they have always been subject to attack, mostly by despoiling gainseekers,—mischief-makers of every degree from Satan to supervisors, lumbermen, cattlemen, farmers, etc., eagerly trying to make everything dollarable, often thinly disguised in smiling philanthropy, calling pocket-filling plunder "Utilization of beneficent natural resources, that man and beast may be fed and the dear Nation grow great." Thus long ago a lot of enterprising merchants made part of the Jerusalem temple into a place of business instead of a place of prayer, changing money, buying and selling cattle and sheep and doves. And earlier still, the Lord's garden in Eden, and the first forest reservation, including only one tree, was spoiled. And so to some extent have all our reservations and parks. Ever since the establishment of the Yosemite National Park by act of Congress, October 8, 1890, constant strife has been going on around its borders and I suppose this will go on as part of the universal battle between right and wrong, however its boundaries may be shorn or its wild beauty destroyed. The first application to the Government by the San Francisco Supervisors for the use of Lake Eleanor and the Hetch Hetchy Valley was made in 1903, and denied December 22nd of that year by the Secretary of the Interior. In his report on this case he well says: "Presumably the Yosemite National Park was created such by law because of the natural objects, of varying degrees of scenic importance, located within its boundaries, inclusive alike of its beautiful small lakes, like Eleanor, and its majestic wonders, like Hetch-Hetchy and Yosemite Valley. It is the aggregation of such natural scenic features that makes the Yosemite Park a wonderland which the Congress of the United States sought by law to preserve for all coming time as nearly as practicable in the condition fashioned by the hand of the Creator—a worthy object of national pride and a source of healthful pleasure and rest for the thousands of people who may annually sojourn there during the heated months."

. . .

That anyone would try to destroy such a place seemed impossible; but sad experience shows that there are people good enough and bad enough for anything. The proponents of the dam scheme bring forward a lot of bad arguments to prove that the only righteous thing for Hetch-Hetchy is its destruction. These arguments are curiously like those of the devil devised for the destruction of the first garden—so much of the very best Eden fruit going to waste; so much of the best Tuolumne water. Very few of their statements are even partly true, and all are misleading. Thus, Hetch Hetchy, they say, is a "low-lying meadow."

On the contrary, it is a high-lying natural landscape garden.

"It is a common minor feature, like thousands of others."

On the contrary, it is a very uncommon feature; after Yosemite, the rarest and in many ways the most important in the park.

"Damming and submerging it 175 feet deep would enhance its beauty by forming a crystal-clear lake."

Landscape gardens, places of recreation and worship, are never made beautiful by destroying and burying them. The beautiful lake, forsooth, should be only an eyesore, a dismal blot on the landscape, like many others to be seen in the Sierra. For, instead of keeping it at the same level all the year, allowing Nature to make new shores, it would, of course, be full only a month or two in the spring, when the snow is melting fast; then it would be gradually drained, exposing the slimy sides of the basin and shallower parts of the bottom, with the gathered drift and waste, death and decay of the upper basins, caught here instead of being swept on to decent natural burial along the banks of the river or in the sea. Thus the Hetch Hetchy dam-lake would be only a rough imitation of a natural lake for a few of the spring months, an open mountain sepulcher for the others.

"Hetch Hetchy water is the purest, wholly unpolluted, and forever unpollutable."

On the contrary, excepting that of the Merced below Yosemite, it is less pure than that of most of the other Sierra streams, because of the sewerage of camp grounds draining into it, especially of the Big Tuolumne Meadows campgrounds, where hundreds of tourists and mountaineers, with their animals, are encamped for months every summer, soon to be followed by thousands of travelers from all the world.

These temple destroyers, devotees of ravaging commercialism, seem to have a perfect contempt for Nature, and, instead of lifting their eyes to the mountains, lift them to dams and town skyscrapers.

Dam Hetch-Hetchy! As well dam for water-tanks the people's cathedrals and churches, for no holier temple has ever been consecrated by the heart of man.

GIFFORD PINCHOT

THE HETCH HETCHY DAM SITE
Hearing before the House Committee on the Public Lands

Mr. Chairman and gentlemen of the committee, my testimony will be very short. I presume that you very seldom have the opportunity of passing upon any measure before the Committee on the Public Lands which has been so thoroughly thrashed out as this one. This question has been up now, I should say, more than 10 years, and the reasons for and against the proposition have not only been discussed over and

Hetch Hetchy Dam Site: Hearing Before the Committee on the Public Lands, House, 63rd Congress 1 (1913).

over again, but a great deal of the objections which could be composed have been composed. . . . [W]e come now face to face with the perfectly clean question of what is the best use to which this water that flows out of the Sierras can be put. As we all know, there is no use of water that is higher than the domestic use. Then, if there is, as the engineers tell us, no other source of supply that is anything like so reasonably available as this one; if this is the best, and, within reasonable limits of cost, the only means of supplying San Francisco with water, we come straight to the question of whether the advantage of leaving this valley in a state of nature is greater than the advantage of using it for the benefit of the city of San Francisco.

Now, the fundamental principle of the whole conservation policy is that of use, to take every part of the land and its resources and put it to that use in which it will best serve the most people, and I think there can be no question at all but that in this case we have an instance in which all weighty considerations demand the passage of the bill. There are, of course, a very large number of incidental changes that will arise after the passage of the bill. The construction of roads, trails, and telephone systems which will follow the passage of this bill will be a very important help in the park and forest reserves. The national forest telephone system and the roads and trails to which this bill will lead will form an important additional help in fighting fire in the forest reserves. As has already been set forth by the two Secretaries, the presence of these additional means of communication will mean that the national forest and the national park will be visited by very large numbers of people who cannot visit them now. I think that the men who assert that it is better to leave a piece of natural scenery in its natural condition have rather the better of the argument, and I believe if we had nothing else to consider than the delight of the few men and women who would yearly go into the Hetch Hetchy Valley, then it should be left in its natural condition. But the considerations on the other side of the question to my mind are simply overwhelming, and so much so that I have never been able to see that there was any reasonable argument against the use of this water supply by the city of San Francisco, provided the bill was a reasonable bill.

ALDO LEOPOLD

THE LAND ETHIC

When god-like Odysseus returned from the wars in Troy, he hanged all on one rope a dozen slave-girls of his household whom he suspected of misbehavior during his absence.

This hanging involved no question of propriety. The girls were property. The disposal of property was then, as now, a matter of expediency, not of right and wrong.

Concepts of right and wrong were not lacking from Odysseus' Greece: witness the fidelity of his wife through the long years before at last his black-prowed galleys clove the wine-dark seas for home. The ethical structure of that day covered wives, but it had not yet been extended to human chattels. During the three thousand years which have since elapsed, ethical criteria have been

A SAND COUNTY ALMANAC: AND SKETCHES HERE AND THERE by Leopold (1949) 3,512w from "Arizona and New Mexico" and "The Land Ethic" pp. 129–133, 201–205, 207–214, 223–226. © 1949, 1977 by Oxford University Press, Inc. By permission of Oxford University Press, USA.

extended to many fields of conduct, with corresponding shrinkages in those judged by expediency only.

THE ETHICAL SEQUENCE

This extension of ethics, so far studied only by philosophers, is actually a process in ecological evolution. Its sequences may be described in ecological as well as in philosophical terms. An ethic, ecologically, is a limitation on freedom of action in the struggle for existence. An ethic, philosophically, is a differentiation of social from anti-social conduct. These are two definitions of one thing. The thing has its origin in the tendency of interdependent individuals or groups to evolve modes of co-operation. The ecologist calls these symbioses. Politics and economics are advanced symbioses in which the original free-for-all competition has been replaced, in part, by co-operative mechanisms with an ethical content.

The complexity of co-operative mechanisms has increased with population density, and with the efficiency of tools. It was simpler, for example, to define the anti-social uses of sticks and stones in the days of the mastodons than of bullets and billboards in the age of motors.

The first ethics dealt with the relation between individuals; the Mosaic Decalogue is an example. Later accretions dealt with the relation between the individual and society. The Golden Rule tries to integrate the individual to society; democracy to integrate social organization to the individual.

There is as yet no ethic dealing with man's relation to land and to the animals and plants which grow upon it. Land, like Odysseus' slave girls, is still property. The land-relation is still strictly economic, entailing privileges but not obligations.

The extension of ethics to this third element in human environment is, if I read the evidence correctly, an evolutionary possibility and an ecological necessity. It is the third step in a sequence. The first two have already been taken. Individual thinkers since the days of Ezekiel and Isaiah have asserted that the despoliation of land is not only inexpedient but wrong. Society, however, has not yet affirmed their belief. I regard the present conservation movement as the embryo of such an affirmation.

An ethic may be regarded as a mode of guidance for meeting ecological situations so new or intricate, or involving such deferred reactions, that the path of social expediency is not discernible to the average individual. Animal instincts are modes of guidance for the individual in meeting such situations. Ethics are possibly a kind of community instinct in-the-making.

THE COMMUNITY CONCEPT

All ethics so far evolved rest upon a single premise that the individual is a member of a community of interdependent parts. His instincts prompt him to compete for his place in that community, but his ethics prompt him also to co-operate (perhaps in order that there may be a place to compete for).

The land ethic simply enlarges the boundaries of the community to include soils, waters, plants, and animals, or collectively: the land.

This sounds simple: do we not already sing our love for and obligation to the land of the free and the home of the brave? Yes, but just what and whom do we love? Certainly not the soil, which we are sending helter-skelter down river. Certainly not the waters, which we assume have no function except to turn turbines, float barges, and carry off sewage. Certainly not the plants, of which we exterminate whole communities without batting an eye. Certainly not the animals, of which we have already extirpated many of the largest and most beautiful species. A land ethic of course cannot prevent the alteration, management, and use of these "resources," but it does affirm their right to continued existence, and, at least in spots, their continued existence in a natural state.

In short, a land ethic changes the role of *Homo sapiens* from conqueror of the land-community to plain member and citizen of it. It implies respect for his fellow-members, and also respect for the community as such.

In human history, we have learned (I hope) that the conqueror role is eventually self-defeating. Why? Because it is implicit in such a role that the conqueror knows, *ex cathedra*, just what makes the community clock tick, and just what and who is valuable, and what and who is worthless, in community life. It always turns out that he knows neither, and this is why his conquests eventually defeat themselves.

In the biotic community, a parallel situation exists. Abraham knew exactly what the land was for: it was to drip milk and honey into Abraham's mouth. At the present moment, the assurance with which we regard this assumption is inverse to the degree of our education.

The ordinary citizen today assumes that science knows what makes the community clock tick; the scientist is equally sure that he does not. He knows that the biotic mechanism is so complex that its workings may never be fully understood.

. . .

THE ECOLOGICAL CONSCIENCE

Conservation is a state of harmony between man and land. Despite nearly a century of propaganda, conservation still proceeds at a snail's pace; progress still consists largely of letterhead pieties and convention oratory. On the back forty we still slip two steps backward for each forward stride.

The usual answer to this dilemma is "more conservation education." No one will debate this, but is it certain that only the *volume* of education needs stepping up? Is something lacking in the *content* as well?

It is difficult to give a fair summary of its content in brief form, but, as I understand it, the content is substantially this: obey the law, vote right, join some organizations, and practice what conservation is profitable on your own land; the government will do the rest.

Is not this formula too easy to accomplish anything worth-while? It defines no right or wrong, assigns no obligation, calls for no sacrifice, implies no change in the current philosophy of values. In respect of land use, it urges only enlightened self-interest. Just how far will such education take us? An example will perhaps yield a partial answer.

By 1930 it had become clear to all except the ecologically blind that southwestern Wisconsin's topsoil was slipping seaward. In 1933 the farmers were told that if they would adopt certain remedial practices for five years, the public would donate CCC labor to install them, plus the necessary machinery and materials. The offer was widely accepted, but the practices were widely forgotten when the five-year contract period was up. The farmers continued only those practices that yielded an immediate and visible economic gain for themselves.

This led to the idea that maybe farmers would learn more quickly if they themselves wrote the rules.

Accordingly the Wisconsin Legislature in 1937 passed the Soil Conservation District Law. This said to farmers, in effect: *We, the public, will furnish you free technical service and loan you specialized machines, if you will write your own rules for land-use. Each county may write its own rules, and these will have the force of law.* Nearly all the counties promptly organized to accept the proffered help, but after a decade of operation, *no county has yet written a single rule.* There has been visible progress in such practices as strip-cropping, pasture renovation, and soil liming, but none in fencing woodlots against grazing, and none in excluding plow and cow from steep slopes. The farmers, in short, have selected those remedial practices which were profitable anyhow, and ignored those which were profitable to the community, but not clearly profitable to themselves.

When asked why no rules have been written, one is told that the community is not yet ready to support them; education must precede rules. But the education actually in progress makes no mention of obligations to land over and above those dictated by self-interest. The net result is that we have more education but less soil, fewer healthy woods, and as many floods as in 1937.

The puzzling aspect of such situations is that the existence of obligations over and above self-interest is taken for granted in such rural community enterprises as the betterment of roads, schools, churches, and baseball teams. Their existence is not taken for granted, nor as yet seriously discussed, in bettering the behavior of the water that falls on the land, or in the preserving of the beauty or diversity of the farm landscape. Land use ethics are still governed wholly by economic self-interest, just as social ethics were a century ago.

To sum up: we asked the farmer to do what he conveniently could to save his soil, and he has done just that, and only that. The farmer who clears the woods off a 75 per cent slope, turns his cows into the clearing, and dumps its rainfall, rocks, and soil into the community creek, is still (if otherwise decent) a respected member of society. If he puts lime on his fields and plants his crops on contour, he is still entitled to all the privileges and emoluments of his Soil Conservation District. The District is a beautiful piece of social machinery, but it is coughing along on two cylinders because we have been too timid, and too anxious for quick success, to tell the farmer the true magnitude of his obligations. Obligations have no meaning without conscience, and the problem we face is the extension of the social conscience from people to land.

No important change in ethics was ever accomplished without an internal change in our intellectual emphasis, loyalties, affections, and convictions. The proof that conservation has not yet touched these foundations of conduct lies in the fact that philosophy and religion have not yet heard of it. In our attempt to make conservation easy, we have made it trivial.

SUBSTITUTES FOR A LAND ETHIC

When the logic of history hungers for bread and we hand out a stone, we are at pains to explain how much the stone resembles bread. I now describe some of the stones which serve in lieu of a land ethic.

One basic weakness in a conservation system based wholly on economic motives is that most members of the land community have no economic value. Wildflowers and songbirds are examples. Of the 22,000 higher plants and animals native to Wisconsin, it is doubtful whether more than 5 per cent can be sold, fed, eaten, or otherwise put to economic use. Yet these creatures are members of the biotic community, and if (as I believe) its stability depends on its integrity, they are entitled to continuance.

When one of these non-economic categories is threatened, and if we happen to love it, we invent subterfuges to give it economic importance. At the beginning of the century songbirds were supposed to be disappearing. Ornithologists jumped to the rescue with some distinctly shaky evidence to the effect that insects would eat us up if birds failed to control them. The evidence had to be economic in order to be valid.

It is painful to read these circumlocutions today. We have no land ethic yet, but we have at least drawn nearer the point of admitting that birds should continue as a matter of biotic right, regardless of the presence or absence of economic advantage to us.

A parallel situation exists in respect of predatory mammals, raptorial birds, and fish-eating birds. Time was when biologists somewhat overworked the evidence that these creatures preserve the health of game by killing weaklings, or that they control rodents for the farmer, or that they prey only on "worthless" species. Here again, the evidence had to be economic in order to be valid. It is only in recent years that we hear the more honest argument that predators are members of the community, and that no special interest has the right to exterminate them for the sake of a benefit, real or fancied, to itself. Unfortunately this enlightened view is still in the talk stage. In the field the extermination of predators goes merrily on: witness the impending erasure of the timber wolf by fiat of Congress, the Conservation Bureaus, and many state legislatures.

Some species of trees have been "read out of the party" by economics-minded foresters because they grow too slowly, or have too low a sale value to pay as timber crops: white cedar, tamarack, cypress, beech, and hemlock are examples. In Europe, where forestry is ecologically more advanced, the non-commercial tree species are recognized as members of the native forest community, to be preserved as such, within reason. Moreover some (like beech) have been found to have a valuable function in building up soil fertility. The interdependence of the forest and its constituent tree species, ground flora, and fauna is taken for granted.

Lack of economic value is sometimes a character not only of species or groups, but of entire biotic communities: marshes, bogs, dunes, and "deserts" are examples. Our formula in such cases is to relegate their conservation to governments as refuges, monuments, or parks. The difficulty is that these communities are usually interspersed with more valuable private lands; the government cannot possibly own or control such scattered parcels. The net effect is that we have relegated some of them to ultimate extinction over large areas. If the private owner were ecologically minded, he would be proud to be the custodian of a reasonable proportion of such areas, which add diversity and beauty to his farm and to his community.

In some instances, the assumed lack of profit in these "waste" areas has proved to be wrong, but only after most of them had been done away with. The present scramble to reflood muskrat marshes is a case in point.

There is a clear tendency in American conservation to relegate to government all necessary jobs that private landowners fail to perform. Government ownership, operation, subsidy, or regulation is now widely prevalent in forestry, range management, soil and watershed management, park and wilderness conservation, fisheries management, and migratory bird management, with more to come. Most of this growth in governmental conservation is proper and logical, some of it is inevitable. That I imply no disapproval of it is implicit in the fact that I have spent most of my life working for it. Nevertheless, the question arises: What is the ultimate magnitude of the enterprise? Will the tax base carry its eventual ramifications? At what point will governmental conservation, like the mastodon, become handicapped by its own dimensions? The answer, if there is any, seems to be in a land ethic, or some other force which assigns more obligation to the private landowner.

Industrial landowners and users, especially lumbermen and stockmen, are inclined to wail long and loudly about the extension of government ownership and regulation to land, but (with notable exceptions) they show little disposition to develop the only visible alternative: the voluntary practice of conservation on their lands.

When the private landowner is asked to perform some unprofitable act for the good of the community, he today assents only with outstretched palm. If the act costs him cash this is fair and proper, but when it costs only forethought, open-mindedness, or time, the issue is at least debatable. The overwhelming growth of land-use subsidies in recent years must be ascribed, in large part, to the government's own agencies for conservation education: the land bureaus, the agricultural colleges, and the extension services. As far as I can detect, no ethical obligation toward land is taught in these institutions.

To sum up: a system of conservation based solely on economic self-interest is hopelessly lopsided. It tends to ignore, and thus eventually to eliminate, many elements in the land community that lack commercial value, but that are (as far as we know) essential to its healthy functioning. It assumes, falsely, I think, that the economic parts of the biotic clock will function without the uneconomic parts. It tends to relegate to government many functions eventually too large, too complex, or too widely dispersed to be performed by government.

An ethical obligation on the part of the private owner is the only visible remedy for these situations.

. . .

THE OUTLOOK

It is inconceivable to me that an ethical relation to land can exist without love, respect, and admiration for land, and a high regard for its value. By value, of course, I mean something far broader than mere economic value; I mean value in the philosophical sense.

Perhaps the most serious obstacle impeding the evolution of a land ethic is the fact that our educational and economic system is headed away from, rather than toward, an intense consciousness of land. Your true modern is separated from the land by many middlemen, and by innumerable physical gadgets. He has no vital relation to it; to him it is the space between cities on which crops grow. Turn him loose for a day of the land, and if the spot does not happen to be a golf links of a "scenic" area, he is bored stiff. If crops could be raised by hydroponics instead of farming, it would suit him very well. Synthetic substitutes for wood, leather, wool, and other natural land products suit him better than the originals. In short, land is something he has "outgrown."

Almost equally serious as an obstacle to a land ethic is the attitude of the farmer for whom the land is still an adversary, or a taskmaster that keeps him in slavery. Theoretically, the mechanization of farming ought to cut the farmer's chains, but whether it really does is debatable. One of the requisites for an ecological comprehension of land is an understanding of ecology, and this is by no means co-extensive with "education"; in fact, much higher education seems deliberately to avoid ecological concepts. An understanding of ecology does not necessarily originate in courses bearing ecological labels; it is quite as likely to be labeled geography, botany, agronomy, history, or economics. This is as it should be, but whatever the label, ecological training is scarce.

The case for a land ethic would appear hopeless but for the minority which is in obvious revolt against these "modern" trends.

The "key-log" which must be moved to release the evolutionary process for an ethic is simply this: quit thinking about decent land-use as solely an economic problem. Examine each question in terms of what is ethically and esthetically right, as well as what is economically expedient. A thing is right when it tends to preserve the integrity, stability, and beauty of the biotic community. It is wrong when it tends otherwise.

It of course goes without saying that economic feasibility limits the tether of what can or cannot be done for land. It always has and it always will. The fallacy the economic determinists have tied around our collective neck, and which we now need to cast off, is the belief that economics determines *all* land use. This is simply not true. An innumerable host of actions and attitudes, comprising perhaps the bulk of all land relations, is determined by the land-users' tastes and predilections, rather than by his purse. The bulk of all land relations hinges on investments of time, forethought, skill, and faith rather than on investments of cash. As a land-user thinketh, so is he.

I have purposely presented the land ethic as a product of social evolution because nothing so important as an ethic is ever "written." Only the most superficial student of history supposes that Moses "wrote" the Decalogue: it evolved in the minds of a thinking community, and Moses wrote a tentative summary of it for a "seminar." I say tentative because evolution never stops.

The evolution of a land ethic is an intellectual as well as emotional process. Conservation is paved with good intentions which prove to be futile, or even dangerous, because they are devoid of critical understanding either of the land, or of economic land-use. I think it is a truism that as the ethical frontier advances from the individual to the community, its intellectual content increases.

The mechanism of operation is the same for any ethic: social approbation for right actions: social disapproval for wrong actions.

By and large, our present problem is one of attitudes and implements. We are remodeling the Alhambra with a steam-shovel, and we are proud of our yardage. We shall hardly relinquish the shovel, which after all has many good points, but we are in need of gentler and more objective criteria for its successful use.

WHAT REALLY MATTERS

Essays on Value in Nature

EDITORIAL

The Last Man and the Search for Objective Value

At a conference in 1973, Richard Sylvan (then known as Richard Routley) proposed a science fiction thought experiment that helped to launch environmental ethics as a branch of academic philosophy. (This is the only science fiction example you will find in this book. In environmental ethics, there is no need to make up strange cases, for the issues permeate everyday life.) Sylvan's thought experiment came to be known as the "Last Man" argument.

The thought experiment presents you with a situation like this: You are the last human being. When you are gone, the only life remaining will be plants, microbes, and invertebrates. For some reason, this thought runs through your head: Before I die, it sure would be fun to torch the last remaining Redwood.

Sylvan's audience was left to ponder. What, if anything, would be *wrong* with destroying that Redwood? Destroying it won't hurt anyone, so what's the problem? Environmental philosophers have been trying to answer that question ever since, and you will hear the question echoing through this book.

How would you answer it?

INSTRUMENTAL AND INTRINSIC VALUE

Perhaps the most fundamental question in environmental ethics is: What should be our attitude toward nature? No environmental ethicist says we should regard nature as merely a repository of natural resources, but we are divided over what *kind* of respect nature commands, or what kind of value we should regard nature as having. We will outline major divisions, but first, a word of caution about definitions. As in almost any field, writers use terms in different ways, so please do not assume every author you read will use these terms in exactly the same way. When we define a term, we aim to indicate, roughly speaking, how most people use the term. Also, we will keep the discussion as simple as we can, setting aside all but the most central issues. Be forewarned, though, that beneath the (relatively!) simple surface lies a nasty tangle of truly difficult philosophical problems that many smart people have spent lifetimes trying to untangle, with only partial success.

We can begin by noting that people value things like Redwoods in more than one way. Clearly, many objects are useful as means to further ends. We consider them valuable as tools or instruments rather than as intrinsically valuable in their own right. In environmental ethics, we refer to this sort of usefulness as an object's *instrumental* value.

By contrast, an object has *noninstrumental* value when it has a value apart from any use it may have as a means to further ends. If an object is good quite apart from what it is good for, it has noninstrumental value. The difference is like the difference between an excellent paintbrush and an excellent painting. Compared to the brush, the painting has a different kind of value, not just a different amount. Likewise, even if we have no interest in that last Redwood as a source of lumber, we might value it simply because it is the majestic living thing that it is. If we value the last Redwood in that way, then we are seeing it as having a kind of goodness that is independent of what it is good *for*. We are seeing it as more like the painting than like the paintbrush.

One of the main tasks in the field of environmental ethics is to be more precise about noninstrumental value, but achieving greater precision is not easy. People sometimes speak of an object's *intrinsic* value, and often they mean roughly what we have called noninstrumental value. For example, an art dealer might assess two paintings, and might say that while the first painting has a higher resale value under current market conditions, the second is actually the better painting when judged on its intrinsic merits. The painting has a kind of value simply because of its intrinsic beauty, independent of any usefulness it may have when used to raise money. In different words, we attach instrumental value to an object when we value what we can use it for, or exchange it for; we attach intrinsic value when we value what the object is, period.

Does that last Redwood have intrinsic value?

VALUED OBJECTS AND VALUING SUBJECTS

Saying an object is valued presupposes that some subject is doing the valuing. *Valuing* is a relation between valued object and valuing subject. Instrumental value is one kind of relation; intrinsic value is another. An object has instrumental value to me when it is useful to me. It has intrinsic value to me when I see it as valuable in its own right, independently of what it is good for. Both are values to me, although not in the same way.

One caution. We are tempted to think of "intrinsic" as a synonym for "really important." Likewise, we are tempted to see instrumental values as "merely" instrumental, as if instrumental values were necessarily small. Both assumptions are false. A souvenir postcard from the Grand Canyon can have a small intrinsic value; a kidney transplant can have a large instrumental value. The systematic difference between intrinsic and instrumental is not a matter of one being bigger. What separates the two kinds of value is the type of respect they command, not the amount.

After the last person is gone, there will be no valuing subjects left, therefore no one to whom the last Redwood can be useful, and therefore no possibility of the Redwood having *instrumental* value. Must we say the same about the Redwood's *intrinsic* value, since no one is left who can value the last Redwood for its own sake? When no one is left to value it, does that mean it will have no value?

IS VALUE SUBJECTIVE?

We will come back to these questions. First, a note about objectivity. To call valuing a relation between valuing subject and valued object is not to say value is subjective. For example, when I say vitamin C has instrumental value to me, my judgment can be correct or incorrect. It can be objectively true that vitamin C serves the purpose I think it serves, thus objectively true that vitamin C has that kind of value to me. I choose whether to care about my health, to some degree, but given that I do care, my valuing vitamin C is grounded in reality in a way it would not be if my beliefs about vitamin C were inaccurate.

The objectivity of intrinsic values is less obvious. On one hand, it is objectively true that Redwoods have the properties that inspire me to think of them as intrinsically valuable. They are alive; they truly are as old and as huge as I think they are, and so on. On the other hand, reasonable people can remain unconvinced that a Redwood's aesthetic (intrinsic) value is as objective as vitamin C's nutritional (instrumental) value.

We said valuing is a relation between valued object and valuing subject. Sometimes, when we value an object, we seem to be *creating* a relationship. (When I decide to start collecting stamps, stamps suddenly have a value to me that they did not have before my decision.) Other times, we seem to discover an existing relationship rather than create one. The existing relationship is this: given our nature and given the object's nature, we have reason to value the object even if we do not know it yet. Thus, ascorbic acid had value to us even before we discovered that ascorbic acid is an essential vitamin (i.e., vitamin C). Given what ascorbic acid is, and given what we are—we are beings who want to remain healthy and who need ascorbic acid to remain healthy—it is an objective fact that we have reason to value ascorbic acid.

What about the last Redwood? Is it like ascorbic acid? Is it an objective fact that we have reason to value Redwoods? Insofar as we have reason to value Redwoods, is our reason something we discover, or something we create?

DOES VALUE PRESUPPOSE A VALUER?

Now suppose, when the last person is gone, nothing will be left that needs ascorbic acid. Will it continue to be an objective fact that ascorbic acid has value? No. Ascorbic acid has value to us here and now, but in a world without animals that need it, there is nothing to whom ascorbic acid could have value.

Again, what about that last Redwood? Does it make sense to say the last Redwood would command respect? In a world devoid of sentient beings, whose respect would it command? Are Redwoods the sort of thing that have value to us here and now, but would not have value in a mindless world?

To this last question, some theorists would say yes, and add that we should not find this troubling. What matters is whether the last Redwood commands the last person's respect, which does not depend on whether the tree will have value after the last person is gone. Others will say this picture is missing something: the fact that Redwoods have value, period. They insist: the world would be a better place with that last Redwood in it, regardless of whether anyone is left to appreciate it. But why insist? Practically speaking, what difference does it make?

There is no easy way to settle this debate. The problem, in part, is that we use the word "value" in more than one way. Sometimes, we use the word as a verb. We say, "I value Redwoods." In that sense, value clearly presupposes a valuer; objects are valued only if valued by a valuing subject. Other times, we use the word as a noun, and then the relation between value and valuer is less clear. When I say, "Redwoods have value," that may be another way of saying, "I value Redwoods." Or, I may be saying something different, such as, "I have *reason* to value Redwoods." When I say Redwoods are intrinsically valuable, I seem to mean the latter. When I say the mindless planet would be a better place with that last Redwood in it, I am saying I would have reason (and so would you) to value the last Redwood. I cannot be saying the last Redwood would be valued by beings on *that* planet, because in the thought experiment valuing subjects no longer exist on that planet. For the same reason, I cannot mean anything on that planet has *reason* to value the last Redwood: the thought experiment stipulates that subjects capable of having reasons no longer exist. Presumably, what I mean is, valuers such as you and me, here and now, have reason to value Redwoods (even when Redwoods have no instrumental value), and therefore, in the world we are imagining, we *would* have reason to value the last Redwood.

Where does that leave us? We are in deep and treacherous philosophical waters here, but the upshot appears to be twofold. First, when I tell you the last Redwood has intrinsic value, I am not saying anyone actually is there to respect it. But second, I am saying that if we *were* there, it *would* be true that we ought to respect it. When everyone is gone, there will be no perspective in that world from which the last Redwood would have value, yet it remains true that the last Redwood would have value from my perspective, here and now. So if you ask me whether the last Redwood would have value, you are asking for my view here and now on the hypothetical Redwood's value, and that is what I am giving you when I answer, yes, it would have value.

Suppose the last person is a painter, and reasons as follows: My paintbrushes have value because they are useful. After I am gone, there will be no one to use them. Therefore, they will no longer be useful. Therefore, they will no longer have instrumental value. My paintings, though, are different. My paintings have value because they are beautiful. After I am gone, they will still be beautiful. (They are beautiful to me, and after I am gone, they will continue to be the kind of thing I *would* find beautiful if I were still around.) In that sense, won't they remain valu*able* even after I am gone? To answer yes is to see the paintings as having intrinsic value.

If this still seems too abstract, then here is something that people like you and me think about every day. Suppose I tell my insurance agent I want my children to be financially secure when I die, the agent does not say, "You're confused. The fact is, when you're dead, you're dead. You will no longer be a sentient valuing creature. Therefore, you won't care. So why not spend the money on something you care about?"

If my agent said that, I should reply, "Actually, you're the one who is confused. I am not saying that after I die, it will matter to me *then* what happens to my children. What I'm saying is, it matters to me now. I am imagining a world in which I no longer exist. Therefore, when I say I value my children's financial security in that world, I'm not saying I value it from a perspective that exists in *that* world. I'm saying I value it from my perspective right now. Here and now, I see my children's security as having a value that will survive my death. In other words, my attitude toward my children is that their value *does not depend on my attitude*. From my perspective, here and now, they are worthy of my love, and will continue to be worthy after I am gone."

That is what it is like to think the last Redwood would have value even after the last valuer is gone. It remains true that valuing does presuppose a valuer. *Intrinsic* valuing, though, presupposes a special *kind* of valuer, namely a kind of valuer who can see a valued object as having value, period—who can see an object as intrinsically worthy of respect.[1]

MORAL STANDING

The fundamental question is, as we said earlier: what should be our attitude toward nature? In particular, many theorists have pondered whether it is possible for nonhumans to have the sort of moral standing that humans have. As we understand the term, a being has *moral standing* just in case it has a right to be treated with respect. Things with moral standing are things to whom (or to which) we can have obligations. We can have obligations *regarding* a painting, but not *to* a painting. We ought to treat beautiful paintings with respect, but not because we have obligations to the paintings. We ought to respect them because they are beautiful (or because their owners have rights), not because they have rights.

What about plants, then? Does a Redwood command respect in the way an excellent painting commands respect? Or does it command respect in the way persons command respect? Is it enough for us to have obligations *regarding* Redwoods, or must we think of ourselves as having obligations *to* them as well?

What is your view? If we destroy that last Redwood, just for fun, is that like destroying a person for fun, or is it more like destroying a beautiful painting for fun?

Perhaps we should seek an intermediate position. Could we argue that moral standing comes in degrees? There are serious thinkers who view moral standing as a switch with only two settings. The switch is on or off. You either respect an entity or not. Other thinkers, equally serious, see moral standing as coming in degrees. Trees have some standing; people have more. Fish have some standing; dolphins have more. Mice have some; chimpanzees have more. Accordingly, if it seems preposterous that a mouse could have the same moral standing as a chimpanzee, it might be possible to argue that a mouse has a lesser, yet still real, moral standing.

WHAT KINDS OF THINGS HAVE MORAL STANDING?

Anything we can put to use is a potential bearer of instrumental value. Equally clearly, anything we can value simply because of what it is, independently of what it can be used for, is a potential bearer of intrinsic value. Paintings can have intrinsic value. Plants can have intrinsic value. Persons can have intrinsic value. But being a bearer of value (even intrinsic value) is a long way from having moral standing.

Almost everyone agrees that persons have moral standing, although theorists explain that obligation in different ways. Quickly put, some would say what separates plants from paintings is that plants have *lives*. What separates animals from plants is that animals have *perspectives*. What separates humans from other animals is that humans have *principles*. Humans have a unique or nearly unique capacity for self-conscious moral agency. (Do all humans have this capacity, though? Do all non-humans lack it?)

What is the connection between having the capacity for self-conscious moral agency and having moral standing? That capacity is the paradigmatic case of what most theorists consider sufficient for moral standing, but is it necessary?

Suppose we say that it is. Would that imply that only humans have moral standing? (Again, be forewarned: These are difficult issues on which consensus may never be achieved.) *Anthropocentrism* is the view that the answer is yes. *Nonanthropocentrism*, in contrast, is a view that at least some nonhuman life has moral standing, either because some nonhumans have a capacity for self-conscious moral agency, or because the capacity for self-conscious moral agency is not the only basis for moral standing. (*Weak* anthropocentrists stress that while only humans have a full-blown right to be treated with respect, various nonhumans ought to be treated with respect not because they have rights but because they have intrinsic value.)

Nonanthropocentrists say at least some nonhuman life has a full-blown right to be treated with respect, but they do not agree on which nonhuman life has such standing, or why. Animal liberationists like Peter Singer and Tom Regan (see their essays) depart from anthropocentrism in one direction. Rejecting the view that self-aware moral agency is the only proper basis for claiming moral rights, animal liberationists say sentience—the ability to feel pain and pleasure—would be a more properly inclusive basis. They say the realm of moral standing extends to all sentient animals. It is a further step to say that everything within that realm has equal standing, but some would defend that further step as well.

Other thinkers would extend moral standing literally to all living things. Where animal liberationists accuse anthropocentrists of being "speciesists," animal liberationists are in turn accused of speciesism or "sentientism" by *biocentrists*, who see sentience as an arbitrary cutoff and who endorse an even more radically inclusive view that simply being alive is the proper basis for moral standing. Among biocentrists, Paul Taylor (see his essay) says not only that the realm of moral standing extends to all living things but also that literally everything within that realm has equal standing. Gary Varner (see his essay) agrees that all living things have standing—they all command *some* respect—but denies that they all command *equal* respect. Thus, while Taylor and Varner are both biocentrists, only Taylor is a *species egalitarian*.

We distinguished different varieties of anthropocentrism and nonanthropocentrism. We also can distinguish between individualism and holism. *Individualism* is the view that only individual living things can have moral standing. Gary Varner thus calls himself a biocentric individualist. Opposed to individualism is *holism*, the view that individual living things are not the only kind of thing that can have moral standing. Can species have moral standing? How about fragile ecosystems? Biocentric holists such as Aldo Leopold and Holmes Rolston III (see their essays) say the most serious environmental issues concern not the suffering of individual animals, but the preservation of species and whole ecosystems: in a word, the environment. (See Sagoff's essay.) Clearly, holism and individualism are real options. Likewise, anthropocentrism and nonanthropocentrism are real options. You may be more attracted to one perspective rather than another, but each captures key insights in its own way.

When we commit to one view or the other, we risk losing sight of what is valuable in opposing views. We are tempted deliberately to distort opposing views, reducing them to cartoon caricatures. For example, we could have defined anthropocentrism as the view that only humans have intrinsic value and that anything nonhuman must have merely instrumental value at best. But that would be a caricature, not a serious theory. No one should deny that a vast array of objects, including Redwoods, are intrinsically valued. The genuine division between anthropocentrists, animal liberationists, and biocentrists, the issue that leaves us with serious thinkers on each side, is the question of whether (or which) nonhumans command respect in the same way (if not to the same degree) that self-aware moral agents do. If certain nonhumans do command respect, is it because certain nonhumans (dolphins, chimpanzees) *are* self-aware moral agents, or is it because self-aware moral agency is not necessary for moral standing?

We are human, of course, and therefore our values are human values. That is, our values necessarily are values of human subjects. But that does not make us anthropocentric, for anthropocentrism does not say merely that we are human. Instead, anthropocentrism is a theory about which *objects* have moral standing. In particular, it is the theory that nonhumans do not belong in that category. Should we be anthropocentric? Perhaps, but the bare fact that we are human does not make us anthropocentric. It does not commit us to thinking that only human beings have moral standing. We have a choice.

Whether we should be holists or individualists, and why, is an ongoing matter of hot debate. Whether we should be anthropocentric, or how far beyond humanity the realm of moral standing should extend, is likewise a matter of hot debate. However these debates are resolved, though, the fact remains that there is much to be gained from cultivating a more biocentric appreciation of nature. Simply appreciating nature—appreciating it for its own sake, treating it with respect—is how most of us begin to develop an environmental ethic. We learn that we live—and learn how to live—in a world of things worth appreciating.

WHAT REALLY WORKS

At the same time, we must also learn that we live, and how to live, in a world of never-ending disagreement about what we owe to each other and to our environment. For better or worse, we are, in many ways, free to choose how to live, and for the most part we choose as individuals. No person or government is in a position simply to decide how "We" are going to act. As individuals, we decide how to live in a world full of people trying to decide how to live, each coming to different conclusions. Therefore, when considering an issue such as climate change, there is this fact to consider: after we come to our own conclusions about what really matters, we still have a long way to go before we figure out what really works. Each of us needs to figure out how to live in peace—an environmentally friendly peace—with people who have come to different conclusions about what really matters.

NOTE

1. Tom Hill asks, what sort of person would destroy the natural environment? (See Hill's essays in Chapter 3.) What is Hill's answer? Do you agree? Why is that the question? Why does Hill not ask the seemingly simpler question, what is wrong with destroying the natural environment? How might Hill respond to Richard Sylvan's "Last Man" argument?

2

HUMILITY AND CONTROL

FOR DISCUSSION

Guilt

1. We grew up near a place called "Head-Smashed-In Buffalo Jump" in Southern Alberta. It is a Blackfoot name, translated into English. Before the Blackfoot acquired guns and horses from Europe, they hunted bison by stampeding whole herds over a cliff.[1] Dukeminier and Krier warn against forming

> an unduly romantic image of Native American culture prior to the arrival of "civiliza-
> tion." There is considerable evidence that some American Indian tribes, rather than
> being natural ecologists who lived in respectful harmony with the land, exploited the
> environment ruthlessly by overhunting and extensive burning of forests.[2]

What, then, should we think of Lynn White's thesis that the historical roots of our ecological crisis lie in Christianity? What crisis does White have in mind? Is White saying that if not for Christianity, there would be no environmental crises, or is his thesis something more subtle?

How should reflecting on our history affect our views about what we should do now? Does what we should do now depend on whether we are Christian?

2. Are things getting better or worse? How would we know? If things are getting worse, when exactly were they better? What facts would we have to know in order to have an educated opinion about this? Is the exhaust from today's cars more noxious than the "exhaust" from yesterday's horses?[3] Is there any general answer, or will it always be true that some things are getting better while other things get worse? What do you suppose the various authors in this section would say? Which trends (regarding pollution, resource depletion, etc.) are the most encouraging? Which are the most worrisome?

NOTES

1. Likewise, there were elephants in Spain 400,000 years ago. *Homo erectus* hunted them the same way the Blackfoot hunted bison here, stampeding them into swamps, according to Donald C. Johanson and Maitland A. Edey in *Lucy: The Beginnings of Humankind* (New York: Warner Books, 1981), pp. 73–74.
2. Jesse Dukeminier and James E. Krier. *Property*. 3rd ed. (Boston: Little, Brown, 1993), p. 62.
3. See Joel Tarr and Clay McShane, "The Centrality of the Horse to the Nineteenth-Century American City," in *The Making of Urban America*, ed. Raymond Mohl (New York: SR Publishers, 1997), pp. 105–130.

God said, "Let the waters abound with living creatures, and let birds fly above the earth in the open expanse of the sky." God created the large sea creatures and every living creature that moves with which the waters swarmed, after their kind, and every winged bird after its kind. God saw that it was good. God blessed them, saying, "Be fruitful, and multiply, and fill the waters in the seas, and let birds multiply on the earth." There was evening and there was morning, a fifth day.

God said, "Let the earth produce living creatures after their kind, livestock, creeping things, and animals of the earth after their kind"; and it was so. God made the animals of the earth after their kind, and the livestock after their kind, and everything that creeps on the ground after its kind. God saw that it was good.

God said, "Let's make man in our image, after our likeness. Let them have dominion over the fish of the sea, and over the birds of the sky, and over the livestock, and over all the earth, and over every creeping thing that creeps on the earth." God created man in his own image. In God's image he created him; male and female he created them. God blessed them. God said to them, "Be fruitful, multiply, fill the earth, and subdue it. Have dominion over the fish of the sea, over the birds of the sky, and over every living thing that moves on the earth." God said, "Behold, I have given you every herb yielding seed, which is on the surface of all the earth, and every tree, which bears fruit yielding seed. It will be your food. To every animal of the earth, and to every bird of the sky, and to everything that creeps on the earth, in which there is life, I have given every green herb for food"; and it was so.

God saw everything that he had made, and, behold, it was very good. There was evening and there was morning, a sixth day.

→ Humans are above animals. As he is "God's image

JOHN STUART MILL

ON NATURE

"Nature," "natural," and the group of words derived from them . . . have at all times filled a great place in the thoughts and taken a strong hold on the feelings of mankind. That they should have done so is not surprising when we consider what the words, in their primitive and most obvious signification, represent; but it is unfortunate that a set of terms which play so great a part in moral and metaphysical speculation should have acquired many meanings different from the primary one, yet sufficiently allied to it to admit of

Genesis 1:20-31 is excerpted from World English Bible, ed. Michael Paul Johnson (Rainbow Missions, 2000).
John Stuart Mill, "Nature," in Essays on Ethics, Religion and Society (Toronto: University of Toronto Press, [1874] 1985), pp. 373–375, 377–381, 385–386, 401–402.

confusion. The words have thus become entangled in so many foreign associations, mostly of a very powerful and tenacious character, that they have come to excite, and to be the symbols of, feelings which their original meaning will by no means justify, and which have made them one of the most copious sources of false taste, false philosophy, false morality, and even bad law.

. . .

The nature of any given thing is the aggregate of its powers and properties, [and] so Nature in the abstract is the aggregate of the powers and properties of all things. Nature means the sum of all phenomena, together with the causes which produce them; including not only all that happens, but all that is capable of happening. . . . All phenomena which have been sufficiently examined are found to take place with regularity, each having certain fixed conditions . . . on the occurrence of which it invariably happens . . . ; and the progress of science mainly consists in ascertaining those conditions. When discovered they can be expressed in general propositions, which are called the laws of the particular phenomenon, and also, more generally, Laws of Nature. Thus the truth, that all material objects tend toward one another with a force directly as their masses and inversely as the square of their distance, is a law of nature. The proposition, that air and food are necessary to animal life, if it be, as we have good reason to believe, true without exception, is also a law of nature, though the phenomenon of which it is the law is special, and not, like gravitation, universal.

Nature, then, in this, its simplest, acceptation, is a collective name for all facts, actual and possible; or (to speak more accurately) a name for the mode, partly known to us and partly unknown, in which all things take place. . . .

Such, then, is a correct definition of the word "nature." But this definition corresponds only to one of the senses of that ambiguous term. It is evidently inapplicable to some of the modes in which the word is familiarly employed. For example, it entirely conflicts with the common form of speech by which Nature is opposed to Art, and natural to artificial. For, in the sense of the word "nature" which has just been defined, and which is the true scientific sense, Art is as much Nature as anything else; and everything which is artificial is natural—Art has no independent power of its own: Art is

but the employment of the powers of Nature for an end. Phenomena produced by human agency, no less than those which as far as we are concerned are spontaneous, depend on the properties of the elementary forces, or of the elementary substances and their compounds. The united powers of the whole human race could not create a new property of matter in general, or of any one of its species. We can only take advantage for our purposes of the properties which we find. A ship floats by the same laws of specific gravity and equilibrium as a tree uprooted by the wind and blown into the water. The corn which men raise for food grows and produces its grain by the same laws of vegetation by which the wild rose and the mountain strawberry bring forth their flowers and fruit. A house stands and holds together by the natural properties, the weight and cohesion of the materials which compose it: a steam engine works by the natural expansive force of steam, exerting a pressure upon one part of a system of arrangements, which pressure, by the mechanical properties of the lever, is transferred from that to another part where it raises the weight or removes the obstacle brought into connection with it. In these and all other artificial operations the office of man is, as has often been remarked, a very limited one: it consists in moving things into certain places. We move objects, and, by doing this, bring some things into contact which were separate, or separate others which were in contact; and, by this simple change of place, natural forces previously dormant are called into action, and produce the desired effect. Even the volition which designs, the intelligence which contrives, and the muscular force which executes these movements, are themselves powers of Nature.

It thus appears that we must recognize at least two principal meanings in the word "nature." In one sense, it means all the powers existing in either the outer or the inner world and everything which takes place by means of those powers. In another sense, it means, not everything which happens, but only what takes place without the agency, or without the voluntary and intentional agency, of man. This distinction is far from exhausting the ambiguities of the word, but it is the key to most of those on which important consequences depend.

. . .

The employment of the word "nature" as a term of ethics seems to disclose a . . . meaning, in which

Nature does not stand for what is, but for what ought to be, or for the rule or standard of what ought to be. . . . Those who set up Nature as a standard of action . . . think they are giving some information as to what the standard of action really is. Those who say that we ought to act according to Nature . . . think that the word "nature" affords some external criterion of what we should do . . . .

The examination of this notion is the object of the present Essay. It is proposed to inquire into the truth of the doctrines which make Nature a test of right and wrong, good and evil, or which in any mode or degree attach merit or approval to following, imitating, or obeying Nature. . . .

When it is asserted, or implied, that Nature, or the laws of Nature, should be conformed to, is the Nature which is meant Nature in the first sense of the term, meaning all which is—the powers and properties of all things? But in this signification there is no need of a recommendation to act according to nature, since it is what nobody can possibly help doing, and equally whether he acts well or ill. There is no mode of acting which is not conformable to Nature in this sense of the term, and all modes of acting are so in exactly the same degree. Every action is the exertion of some natural power, and its effects of all sorts are so many phenomena of nature, produced by the powers and properties of some of the objects of nature, in exact obedience to some law or laws of nature. When I voluntarily use my organs to take in food, the act, and its consequences, take place according to the laws of nature: if instead of food I swallow poison, the case is exactly the same. To bid people to conform to the laws of nature when they have no power but what the laws of nature give them—when it is a physical impossibility for them to do the smallest thing otherwise than through some law of nature, is an absurdity. The thing they need to be told is what particular law of nature they should make use of in a particular case. When, for example, a person is crossing a river by a narrow bridge to which there is no parapet, he will do well to regulate his proceedings by the laws of equilibrium in moving bodies, instead of conforming only to the law of gravitation and falling into the river.

Yet, idle as it is to exhort people to do what they cannot avoid doing, and absurd as it is to prescribe as a rule of right conduct what agrees exactly as well with wrong, nevertheless a rational rule of conduct *may* be constructed out of the relation which it ought to bear to the laws of nature in this widest acceptation of the term. Man necessarily obeys the laws of nature, or in other words the properties of things; but he does not necessarily guide himself by them. Though all conduct is in conformity to the laws of nature, all conduct is not grounded on knowledge of them and intelligently directed to the attainment of purposes by means of them.

Though we cannot emancipate ourselves from the laws of nature as a whole, we can escape from any particular law of nature, if we are able to withdraw ourselves from the circumstances in which it acts. Though we can do nothing except through laws of nature, we can use one law to counteract another. According to Bacon's maxim, we can obey nature in such a manner as to command it. Every alteration of circumstances alters more or less the laws of nature under which we act; and by every choice which we make either of ends or of means we place ourselves to a greater or less extent under one set of laws of nature instead of another. If, therefore, the useless precept to follow nature were changed into a precept to study nature; to know and take heed of the properties of the things we have to deal with, so far as these properties are capable of forwarding or obstructing any given purpose; we should have arrived at the first principle of all intelligent action, or rather at the definition of intelligent action itself. And a confused notion of this true principle is, I doubt not, in the minds of many of those who set up the unmeaning doctrine which superficially resembles it. They perceive that the essential difference between wise and foolish conduct consists in attending, or not attending, to the particular laws of nature on which some important result depends. And they think that a person who attends to a law of nature in order to shape his conduct by it may be said to obey it, while a person who practically disregards it, and acts as if no such law existed, may be said to disobey it; the circumstance being overlooked, that what is thus called disobedience to a law of nature is obedience to some other, or perhaps to the very law itself. For example, a person who goes into a powder magazine either not knowing, or carelessly omitting to think of, the explosive force of gunpowder, is likely to do some act which will cause him to be blown to atoms in obedience to the very law which he has disregarded.

But, however much of its authority the "Naturam sequi" ["Follow nature"] doctrine may owe to its being confounded with the rational precept "Naturam observare" ["Observe nature"], its favourers and promoters unquestionably intend much more by it than that precept. To acquire knowledge of the properties of things, and make use of the knowledge for guidance, is a rule of prudence, for the adaptation of means to ends; for giving effect to our wishes and intentions whatever they may be. But the maxim of obedience to Nature, or conformity to Nature, is held up not as a simply prudential but as an ethical maxim; and by those who talk of *jus naturæ*, even as a law, fit to be administered by tribunals and enforced by sanctions. Right action, must mean something more and other than merely intelligent action: yet no precept beyond this last, can be connected with the word Nature in the wider and more philosophical of its acceptations. We must try it therefore in the other sense, that in which Nature stands distinguished from Art, and denotes, not the whole course of the phenomena which come under our observation, but only their spontaneous course.

Let us then consider whether we can attach any meaning to the supposed practical maxim of following Nature, in this second sense of the word, in which Nature stands for that which takes place without human intervention. In Nature as thus understood, is the spontaneous course of things when left to themselves, the rule to be followed in endeavouring to adapt things to our use? . . . [I]t is evident at once that the maxim, taken in this sense, is not merely, as it is in the other sense, superfluous and unmeaning, but palpably absurd and self-contradictory. For while human action cannot help conforming to Nature in the one meaning of the term, the very aim and object of action is to alter and improve Nature in the other meaning. If the natural course of things were perfectly right and satisfactory, to act at all would be a gratuitous meddling, which as it could not make things better, must make them worse. Or if action at all could be justified, it would only be when in direct obedience to instincts, since these might perhaps be accounted part of

the spontaneous order of Nature; but to do anything with forethought and purpose, would be a violation of that perfect order. If the artificial is not better than the natural, to what end are all the arts of life? To dig, to plough, to build, to wear clothes, are direct infringements of the injunction to follow nature.

Accordingly it would be said by every one, even of those most under the influence of the feelings which prompt the injunction, that to apply it to such cases as those just spoken of, would be to push it too far. Everybody professes to approve and admire many great triumphs of Art over Nature: the junction by bridges of shores which Nature had made separate, the draining of Nature's marshes, the excavation of her wells, the dragging to light of what she has buried at immense depths in the earth; the turning away of her thunderbolts by lightning rods, of her inundations by embankments, of her ocean by breakwaters. But to commend these and similar feats, is to acknowledge that the ways of Nature are to be conquered, not obeyed: that her powers are often towards man in the position of enemies, from whom he must wrest, by force and ingenuity, what little he can for his own use, and deserves to be applauded when that little is rather more than might be expected from his physical weakness in comparison to those gigantic powers. All praise of Civilization, or Art, or Contrivance, is so much dispraise of Nature; an admission of imperfection, which it is man's business, and merit, to be always endeavouring to correct or mitigate.

. . .

In sober truth, nearly all the things which men are hanged or imprisoned for doing to one another, are nature's every day performances. Killing, the most criminal act recognized by human laws, Nature does once to every being that lives; and in a large proportion of cases, after protracted tortures such as only the greatest monsters whom we read of ever purposely inflicted on their living fellow-creatures. If by an arbitrary reservation, we refuse to account anything murder but what abridges a certain term supposed to be allotted to human life, nature also does this to all but a small percentage of lives, and does it in all the modes, violent or insidious, in which the worst human beings take the lives of one another. Nature impales men, breaks them as if on the wheel, casts them to be devoured by wild beasts, burns them to death, crushes them with stones like the first christian martyr, starves them with hunger, freezes them with cold, poisons them by the quick or slow venom of her exhalations, and has hundreds of other hideous deaths in reserve, such as the ingenious cruelty of a Nabis or a Domitian never surpassed. All this, Nature does with the most supercilious disregard both of mercy and justice, emptying her shafts upon the best and noblest indifferently with the meanest and worst; upon those who are engaged in the highest and worthiest enterprises, and often as the direct consequence of the noblest acts; and it might almost be imagined as punishment for them. She mows down those on whose existence hangs the well-being of a whole people, perhaps the prospects of the human race for generations to come, with as little compunction as those whose death is a relief to themselves, or a blessing to those under their noxious influence. Such are Nature's dealings with life. Even when she does not intend to kill, she inflicts the same tortures in apparent wantonness. In the clumsy provision which she has made for that perpetual renewal of animal life, rendered necessary by the prompt termination she puts to it in every individual instance, no human being ever comes into the world but [when] another human being is literally stretched on the rack for hours or days, not unfrequently issuing in death. Next to taking life (equal to it according to a high authority) is taking the means by which we live; and Nature does this too on the largest scale and with the most callous indifference. A single hurricane destroys the hopes of a season; a flight of locusts, or an inundation, desolates a district; a trifling chemical change in an edible root starves a million of people. The waves of the sea, like banditti seize and appropriate the wealth of the rich and the little all of the poor with the same accompaniments of stripping, wounding, and killing as their human antitypes. Everything in short, which the worst men commit either against life or property is perpetrated on a larger scale by natural agents. Nature has Noyades more fatal than those of Carrier; her explosions of fire damp are as destructive as human artillery; her plague and cholera far surpass the poison cups of the Borgias. Even the love of "order" which is thought to be a following of the ways of Nature, is in fact a contradiction of them. All which people are accustomed to deprecate as "disorder" and its consequences, is precisely a counterpart of Nature's ways. Anarchy and the Reign of Terror are overmatched in injustice, ruin, and death, by a hurricane and a pestilence.

But, it is said, all these things are for wise and good ends. On this I must first remark that whether they are so or not, is altogether beside the point. Supposing it true that contrary to appearances these horrors when perpetrated by Nature, promote good ends, still as no one believes that good ends would be promoted by our following the example, the course of Nature cannot be a proper model for us to imitate. Either it is right that we should kill because nature kills; torture because nature tortures; ruin and devastate because nature does the like; or we ought not to consider at all what nature does, but what is good to do. . . .

It will be to sum up in a few words the leading conclusions of this Essay.

The word Nature has two principal meanings: it either denotes the entire system of things, with the aggregate of all their properties, or it denotes things as they would be, apart from human intervention.

In the first of these senses, the doctrine that man ought to follow nature is unmeaning; since man has no power to do anything else than follow nature; all his actions are done through, and in obedience to, some one or many of nature's physical or mental laws.

In the other sense of the term, the doctrine that man ought to follow nature, or in other words, ought to make the spontaneous course of things the model of his voluntary actions, is equally irrational and immoral.

Irrational, because all human action whatever, consists in altering, and all useful action in improving, the spontaneous course of nature:

Immoral, because the course of natural phenomena being replete with everything which when committed by human beings is most worthy of abhorrence, any one who endeavored in his actions to imitate the natural course of things would be universally seen and acknowledged to be the wickedest of men.

LYNN WHITE JR.

THE HISTORICAL ROOTS OF OUR ECOLOGICAL CRISIS

A conversation with Aldous Huxley not infrequently put one at the receiving end of an unforgettable monologue. About a year before his lamented death he was discoursing on a favorite topic: Man's unnatural treatment of nature and its sad results. To illustrate his point he told how, during the previous summer, he had returned to a little valley in England where he had spent many happy months as a child. Once it had been composed of delightful grassy glades; now it was becoming overgrown with unsightly brush because the rabbits that formerly kept such growth under control had largely succumbed to a disease, myxomatosis, that was deliberately introduced by the local farmers to reduce the rabbits' destruction of crops. Being something of a Philistine, I could be silent no longer, even in the interests of great rhetoric. I interrupted to point out that the rabbit itself had been brought as a domestic animal to England in 1176, presumably to improve the protein diet of the peasantry.

All forms of life modify their contexts. The most spectacular and benign instance is doubtless the coral polyp. By serving its own ends, it has created a vast undersea world favorable to thousands of other kinds of animals and plants. Ever since man became a numerous species he has affected his environment notably. The hypothesis that his fire-drive method of hunting created the world's great grasslands and helped to exterminate the monster mammals of the Pleistocene from much of the globe is plausible, if not proved. For 6 millennia at least, the banks of the lower Nile have been a human artifact rather than the swampy African jungle which nature, apart from man, would have made it. The Aswan Dam, flooding 5,000 square miles, is only the latest stage in a long process. In many regions terracing or irrigation, overgrazing, the cutting of forests by Romans to build ships to fight Carthaginians or by Crusaders to solve the logistics problems of their expeditions, have profoundly changed some ecologies. Observation that the French landscape falls into two basic types, the open fields of the north and the *bocage* of the south and west, inspired Marc Bloch to undertake his classic study of medieval agricultural methods. Quite unintentionally, changes in human ways often affect nonhuman nature. It has been noted, for example, that the advent of the automobile eliminated huge flocks of sparrows that once fed on the horse manure littering every street.

The history of ecologic change is still so rudimentary that we know little about what really happened, or what the results were. The extinction of the European aurochs as late as 1627 would seem to have been a simple case of overenthusiastic hunting. On more intricate matters it often is impossible to find solid information. For a thousand years or more the Frisians and Hollanders have been pushing back the North Sea, and the process is culminating in our own time in the reclamation of the Zuider Zee. What, if any, species of animals, birds, fish, shore life, or plants have died out in the process? In their epic combat with Neptune, have the Netherlanders overlooked ecological values in such a way that the quality of human life in the Netherlands has suffered? I cannot discover that the questions have ever been asked, much less answered.

People, then, have often been a dynamic element in their own environment, but in the present state of historical scholarship we usually do not know exactly when, where, or with what effects man-induced changes came. As we enter the last third of the 20th century, however, concern for the problem of ecologic backlash is mounting feverishly. Natural science, conceived as the effort to understand the nature of things, had flourished in several eras and among several peoples. Similarly there had been an age-old accumulation of technological skills, sometimes growing rapidly, sometimes slowly. But it was not until about four generations ago that Western Europe and North America arranged a marriage between science and technology, a union of the theoretical and the empirical approaches to our natural environment. The emergence in widespread practice of the Baconian creed that scientific knowledge means technological power over nature can scarcely be dated before about 1850, save in the chemical industries, where it is anticipated in the 18th century. Its acceptance as a normal pattern of action may mark the greatest event in human history since the invention of agriculture, and perhaps in nonhuman terrestrial history as well.

Almost at once the new situation forced the crystallization of the novel concept of ecology; indeed, the word *ecology* first appeared in the English language in 1873. Today, less than a century later, the impact of our race upon the environment has so increased in force that it has changed in essence. When the first cannons were fired, in the early 14th century, they affected ecology by sending workers scrambling to the forests and mountains for more potash, sulfur, iron ore, and charcoal, with some resulting erosion and deforestation. Hydrogen bombs are of a different order: a war fought with them might alter the genetics of all life on this planet. By 1285 London had a smog problem arising from the burning of soft coal, but our present combustion of fossil fuels threatens to change the chemistry of the globe's atmosphere as a whole, with consequences which we are only beginning to guess. With the population explosion, the carcinoma of planless urbanism, the now geological deposits of sewage and garbage, surely no creature other than man has ever managed to foul its nest in such short order.

There are many calls to action, but specific proposals, however worthy as individual items, seem too partial, palliative, negative: ban the bomb, tear down the billboards, give the Hindus contraceptives and tell them to eat their sacred cows. The simplest solution to any suspect change is, of course, to stop it, or, better

yet, to revert to a romanticized past: make those ugly gasoline stations look like Anne Hathaway's cottage or (in the Far West) like ghost-town saloons. The "wilderness area" mentality invariably advocates deep-freezing an ecology, whether San Gimignano or the High Sierra, as it was before the first Kleenex was dropped. But neither atavism nor prettification will cope with the ecologic crisis of our time.

What shall we do? No one yet knows. Unless we think about fundamentals, our specific measures may produce new backlashes more serious than those they are designed to remedy.

As a beginning we should try to clarify our thinking by looking, in some historical depth, at the presuppositions that underlie modern technology and science. Science was traditionally aristocratic, speculative, intellectual in intent; technology was lower-class, empirical, action-oriented. The quite sudden fusion of these two, towards the middle of the 19th century, is surely related to the slightly prior and contemporary democratic revolutions which, by reducing social barriers, tended to assert a functional unity of brain and hand. Our ecologic crisis is the product of an emerging, entirely novel, democratic culture. The issue is whether a democratized world can survive its own implications. Presumably we cannot unless we rethink our axioms.

THE WESTERN TRADITIONS OF TECHNOLOGY AND SCIENCE

One thing is so certain that it seems stupid to verbalize it: both modern technology and modern science are distinctively Occidental. Our technology has absorbed elements from all over the world, notably from China; yet everywhere today, whether in Japan or in Nigeria, successful technology is Western. Our science is the heir to all the sciences of the past, especially perhaps to the work of the great Islamic scientists of the Middle Ages, who so often outdid the ancient Greeks in skill and perspicacity: al-Razi in medicine, for example; or ibn-al-Haytham in optics; or Omar Khayyám in mathematics. Indeed, not a few works of such geniuses seem to have vanished in the original Arabic and to survive only in medieval Latin translations that helped to lay the foundations for later Western developments. Today, around the globe, all significant science is

Western in style and method, whatever the pigmentation or language of the scientists.

A second pair of facts is less well recognized because they result from quite recent historical scholarship. The leadership of the West, both in technology and in science, is far older than the so-called Scientific Revolution of the 17th century or the so-called Industrial Revolution of the 18th century. These terms are in fact outmoded and obscure the true nature of what they try to describe—significant stages in two long and separate developments. By A.D. 1000 at the latest—and perhaps, feebly, as much as 200 years earlier—the West began to apply water power to industrial processes other than milling grain. This was followed in the late 12th century by the harnessing of wind power. From simple beginnings but with remarkable consistency of style, the West rapidly expanded its skills in the development of power machinery, labor-saving devices, and automation. Those who doubt should contemplate that most monumental achievement in the history of automation: the weight-driven mechanical clock, which appeared in two forms in the early 14th century. Not in craftsmanship but in basic technological capacity, the Latin West of the later Middle Ages far outstripped its elaborate, sophisticated, and esthetically magnificent sister cultures, Byzantium and Islam. In 1444 a great Greek ecclesiastic, Bessarion, who had gone to Italy, wrote a letter to a prince in Greece. He is amazed by the superiority of Western ships, arms, textiles, glass. But above all he is astonished by the spectacle of waterwheels sawing timbers and pumping the bellows to blast furnaces. Clearly, he had seen nothing of the sort in the Near East.

By the end of the 15th century the technological superiority of Europe was such that its small, mutually hostile nations could spill out over all the rest of the world, conquering, looting, and colonizing. The symbol of this technological superiority is the fact that Portugal, one of the weakest states of the Occident, was able to become, and to remain for a century, mistress of the East Indies. And we must remember that the technology of Vasco da Gama and Albuquerque was built by pure empiricism, drawing remarkably little support or inspiration from science.

In the present-day vernacular of understanding, modern science is supposed to have begun in 1543, when both Copernicus and Vesalius published their great works. It is no derogation of their accomplishments, however, to point out that such structures as the *Fabrica* and the *De revolutionibus* do not appear overnight. The distinctive Western tradition of science, in fact, began in the late 11th century with a massive movement of translation of Arabic and Greek scientific works into Latin. A few notable books—Theophrastus, for example—escaped the West's avid new appetite for science, but within less than 200 years, effectively the entire corpus of Greek and Muslim science was available in Latin, and was being eagerly read and criticized in the new European universities. Out of criticism arose new observation, speculation, and increasing distrust of ancient authorities. By the late 13th century Europe had seized global scientific leadership from the faltering hands of Islam. It would be as absurd to deny the profound originality of Newton, Galileo, or Copernicus as to deny that of the 14th century scholastic scientists like Buridan or Oresme on whose work they built. Before the 11th century, science scarcely existed in the Latin West, even in Roman times. From the 11th century onward, the scientific sector of Occidental culture has increased in a steady crescendo.

Since both our technological and our scientific movements got their start, acquired their character, and achieved world dominance in the Middle Ages, it would seem that we cannot understand their nature or their present impact upon ecology without examining fundamental medieval assumptions and developments.

MEDIEVAL VIEW OF MAN AND NATURE

Until recently, agriculture has been the chief occupation even in "advanced" societies; hence, any change in methods of tillage has much importance. Early plows, drawn by two oxen, did not normally turn the sod but merely scratched it. Thus, cross-plowing was needed and fields tended to be squarish. In the fairly light soils and semi-arid climates of the Near East and Mediterranean, this worked well. But such a plow was inappropriate to the wet climate and often sticky soils of northern Europe. By the latter part of the 7th century after Christ, however, following obscure beginnings, certain northern peasants were using an entirely new kind of plow, equipped with a vertical knife to cut the line of the furrow, a horizontal share to slice under the sod, and a moldboard to turn it over. The friction of this plow with the soil was so great that it normally required not two but eight oxen. It attacked the land with such violence that cross-plowing was not needed, and fields tended to be shaped in long strips.

In the days of the scratch-plow, fields were distributed generally in units capable of supporting a single family. Subsistence farming was the presupposition. But no peasant owned eight oxen: to use the new and more efficient plow, peasants pooled their oxen to form large plow-teams, originally receiving (it would appear) plowed strips in proportion to their contribution. Thus, distribution of land was based no longer on the needs of a family but, rather, on the capacity of a power machine to till the earth. Man's relation to the soil was profoundly changed. Formerly man had been part of nature; now he was the exploiter of nature. Nowhere else in the world did farmers develop any analogous agricultural implement. Is it coincidence that modern technology, with its ruthlessness toward nature, has so largely been produced by descendants of these peasants of northern Europe?

This same exploitive attitude appears slightly before A.D. 830 in Western illustrated calendars. In older calendars the months were shown as passive personifications. The new Frankish calendars, which set the style for the Middle Ages, are very different: they show men coercing the world around them—plowing, harvesting, chopping trees, butchering pigs. Man and nature are two things, and man is master.

These novelties seem to be in harmony with larger intellectual patterns. What people do about their ecology depends on what they think about themselves in relation to things around them. Human ecology is deeply conditioned by beliefs about our nature and destiny—that is, by religion. To Western eyes this is very evident in, say, India or Ceylon. It is equally true of ourselves and of our medieval ancestors.

The victory of Christianity over paganism was the greatest psychic revolution in the history of our culture. It has become fashionable today to say that, for better or worse, we live in "the post-Christian age." Certainly the forms of our thinking and language have largely ceased to be Christian, but to my eye the substance often remains amazingly akin to that of the past. Our daily habits of action, for example, are dominated by an implicit faith in perpetual progress which was unknown either to Greco-Roman antiquity or to the Orient. It is rooted in, and is indefensible apart

from, Judeo-Christian teleology. The fact that Communists share it merely helps to show what can be demonstrated on many other grounds: that Marxism, like Islam, is a Judeo-Christian heresy. We continue today to live, as we have lived for about 1700 years, very largely in a context of Christian axioms.

What did Christianity tell people about their relations with the environment?

While many of the world's mythologies provide stories of creation, Greco-Roman mythology was singularly incoherent in this respect. Like Aristotle, the intellectuals of the ancient West denied that the visible world had had a beginning. Indeed, the idea of a beginning was impossible in the framework of their cyclical notion of time. In sharp contrast, Christianity inherited from Judaism not only a concept of time as nonrepetitive and linear but also a striking story of creation. By gradual stages a loving and all-powerful God had created light and darkness, the heavenly bodies, the earth and all its plants, animals, birds, and fishes. Finally, God had created Adam and, as an afterthought, Eve to keep man from being lonely. Man named all the animals, thus establishing his dominance over them. God planned all of this explicitly for man's benefit and rule: no item in the physical creation had any purpose save to serve man's purposes. And, although man's body is made of clay, he is not simply part of nature: he is made in God's image.

Especially in its Western form, Christianity is the most anthropocentric religion the world has seen. As early as the 2nd century both Tertullian and Saint Irenaeus of Lyons were insisting that when God shaped Adam he was foreshadowing the image of the incarnate Christ, the Second Adam. Man shares, in great measure, God's transcendence of nature. Christianity, in absolute contrast to ancient paganism and Asia's religions (except, perhaps, Zoroastrianism), not only established a dualism of man and nature but also insisted that it is God's will that man exploit nature for his proper ends.

At the level of the common people this worked out in an interesting way. In Antiquity every tree, every spring, every stream, every hill had its own *genius loci*, its guardian spirit. These spirits were accessible to men, but were very unlike men; centaurs, fauns, and mermaids show their ambivalence. Before one cut a tree, mined a mountain, or dammed a brook, it was important to placate the spirit in charge of that particular situation, and to keep it placated. By destroying pagan animism, Christianity made it possible to exploit nature in a mood of indifference to the feelings of natural objects.

It is often said that for animism the Church substituted the cult of saints. True; but the cult of saints is functionally quite different from animism. The saint is not *in* natural objects; he may have special shrines, but his citizenship is in heaven. Moreover, a saint is entirely a man; he can be approached in human terms. In addition to saints, Christianity of course also had angels and demons inherited from Judaism and perhaps, at one remove, from Zoroastrianism. But these were all as mobile as the saints themselves. The spirits *in* natural objects, which formerly had protected nature from man, evaporated. Man's effective monopoly on spirit in this world was confirmed, and the old inhibitions to the exploitation of nature crumbled.

When one speaks in such sweeping terms, a note of caution is in order. Christianity is a complex faith, and its consequences differ in differing contexts. What I have said may well apply to the medieval West, where in fact technology made spectacular advances. But the Greek East, a highly civilized realm of equal Christian devotion, seems to have produced no marked technological innovation after the late 7th century, when Greek fire was invented. The key to the contrast may perhaps be found in a difference in the tonality of piety and thought which students of comparative theology find between the Greek and the Latin Churches. The Greeks believed that sin was intellectual blindness, and that salvation was found in illumination, orthodoxy— that is, clear thinking. The Latins, on the other hand, felt that sin was moral evil, and that salvation was to be found in right conduct. Eastern theology has been intellectualist. Western theology has been voluntarist. The Greek saint contemplates; the Western saint acts. The implications of Christianity for the conquest of nature would emerge more easily in the Western atmosphere.

The Christian dogma of creation, which is found in the first clause of all the Creeds, has another meaning for our comprehension of today's ecologic crisis. By revelation, God had given man the Bible, the Book of Scripture. But since God had made nature, nature also must reveal the divine mentality. The religious study of nature for the better understanding of God was known as natural theology. In the early Church, and always in the Greek East, nature was conceived primarily as a symbolic system through which God speaks to men: the ant is a sermon to sluggards; rising flames are the symbol of the soul's aspiration. This view of nature was essentially artistic rather than scientific. While Byzantium preserved and copied great numbers of ancient Greek scientific texts, science as we conceive it could scarcely flourish in such an ambience.

However, in the Latin West by the early 13th century natural theology was following a very different bent. It was ceasing to be the decoding of the physical symbols of God's communication with man and was becoming the effort to understand God's mind by discovering how his creation operates. The rainbow was no longer simply a symbol of hope first sent to Noah after the Deluge: Robert Grosseteste, Friar Roger Bacon, and Theodoric of Freiberg produced startlingly sophisticated work on the optics of the rainbow, but they did it as a venture in religious understanding. From the 13th century onward, up to and including Leibniz and Newton, every major scientist, in effect, explained his motivations in religious terms. Indeed, if Galileo had not been so expert an amateur theologian he would have got into far less trouble: the professionals resented his intrusion. And Newton seems to have regarded himself more as a theologian than as a scientist. It was not until the late 18th century that the hypothesis of God became unnecessary to many scientists.

It is often hard for the historian to judge, when men explain why they are doing what they want to do, whether they are offering real reasons or merely culturally acceptable reasons. The consistency with which scientists during the long formative centuries of Western science said that the task and the reward of the scientist was "to think God's thoughts after him" leads one to believe that this was their real motivation. If so, then modern Western science was cast in a matrix of Christian theology. The dynamism of religious devotion, shaped by the Judeo-Christian dogma of creation, gave it impetus.

AN ALTERNATIVE CHRISTIAN VIEW

We would seem to be headed toward conclusions unpalatable to many Christians. Since both *science* and *technology* are blessed words in our contemporary vocabulary, some may be happy at the notions, first, that, viewed historically, modern science is an extrapolation of natural theology and, second, that modern technology is at least partly to be explained as an Occidental, voluntarist realization of the Christian dogma of man's transcendence of and rightful mastery over nature. But, as we now recognize, somewhat over a century ago science and technology—hitherto quite separate activities—joined to give mankind powers which, to judge by many of the ecologic effects, are out of control. If so, Christianity bears a huge burden of guilt.

I personally doubt that disastrous ecologic backlash can be avoided simply by applying to our problems more science and more technology. Our science and technology have grown out of Christian attitudes toward man's relation to nature which are almost universally held not only by Christians and neo-Christians but also by those who fondly regard themselves as post-Christians. Despite Copernicus, all the cosmos rotates around our little globe. Despite Darwin, we are *not*, in our hearts, part of the natural process. We are superior to nature, contemptuous of it, willing to use it for our slightest whim. The newly elected Governor of California, like myself a churchman but less troubled than I, spoke for the Christian tradition when he said (as is alleged), "when you've seen one redwood tree, you've seen them all." To a Christian a tree can be no more than a physical fact. The whole concept of the sacred grove is alien to Christianity and to the ethos of the West. For nearly 2 millennia Christian missionaries have been chopping down sacred groves, which are idolatrous because they assume spirit in nature.

What we do about ecology depends on our ideas of the man–nature relationship. More science and more technology are not going to get us out of the present ecologic crisis until we find a new religion, or rethink our old one. The beatniks, who are the basic revolutionaries of our time, show a sound instinct in their affinity for Zen Buddhism, which conceives of the man–nature relationship as very nearly the mirror image of the Christian view. Zen, however, is as deeply conditioned by Asian history as Christianity is by the experience of the West, and I am dubious of its viability among us.

Possibly we should ponder the greatest radical in Christian history since Christ: Saint Francis of Assisi. The prime miracle of Saint Francis is the fact that he did not end at the stake, as many of his left-wing followers did. He was so clearly heretical that a General of the Franciscan Order, Saint Bonaventura, a great and perceptive Christian, tried to suppress the early accounts of Franciscanism. The key to an understanding of Francis is his belief in the virtue of humility—not merely for the individual but for man as a species. Francis tried to depose man from his monarchy over creation and set up a democracy of all God's creatures. With him the ant is no longer simply a homily for the lazy, flames a sign of the thrust of the soul toward union with God; now they are Brother Ant and Sister Fire, praising the Creator in their own ways as Brother Man does in his.

Later commentators have said that Francis preached to the birds as a rebuke to men who would not listen. The records do not read so: he urged the little birds to praise God, and in spiritual ecstasy they flapped their wings and chirped rejoicing. Legends of saints, especially the Irish saints, had long told of their dealings with animals but always, I believe, to show their human dominance over creatures. With Francis it is different. The land around Gubbio in the Apennines was being ravaged by a fierce wolf. Saint Francis, says the legend, talked to the wolf and persuaded him of the error of his ways. The wolf repented, died in the odor of sanctity, and was buried in consecrated ground.

What Sir Steven Runciman calls "the Franciscan doctrine of the animal soul" was quickly stamped out. Quite possibly it was in part inspired, consciously or unconsciously, by the belief in reincarnation held by the Cathar heretics who at that time teemed in Italy and southern France, and who presumably had got it originally from India. It is significant that at just the same moment, about 1200, traces of metempsychosis are found also in western Judaism, in the Provençal *Cabbala*. But Francis held neither to transmigration of souls nor to pantheism. His view of nature and of man rested on a unique sort of pan-psychism of all things animate and inanimate, designed for the glorification of their transcendent Creator, who, in the ultimate gesture of cosmic humility, assumed flesh, lay helpless in a manger, and hung dying on a scaffold.

I am not suggesting that many contemporary Americans who are concerned about our ecologic crisis will be either able or willing to counsel with wolves or exhort birds. However, the present increasing disruption of the global environment is the product of a dynamic technology and science which were originating in the Western medieval world against which Saint Francis was rebelling in so original a way. Their growth cannot be understood historically apart from distinctive attitudes toward nature which are deeply grounded in Christian dogma. The fact that most people do not think of these attitudes as Christian is irrelevant. No new set of basic values has been accepted in our society to displace those of Christianity. Hence we shall continue to have a worsening ecologic crisis until we reject the Christian axiom that nature has no reason for existence save to serve man.

The greatest spiritual revolutionary in Western history, Saint Francis, proposed what he thought was an alternative Christian view of nature and man's relation to it: he tried to substitute the idea of the equality of all creatures, including man, for the idea of man's limitless rule of creation. He failed. Both our present science and our present technology are so tinctured with orthodox Christian arrogance toward nature that no solution for our ecologic crisis can be expected from them alone. Since the roots of our trouble are so largely religious, the remedy must also be essentially religious, whether we call it that or not. We must rethink and refeel our nature and destiny. The profoundly religious, but heretical, sense of the primitive Franciscans for the spiritual autonomy of all parts of nature may point a direction. I propose Francis as a patron saint for ecologists.

ALDO LEOPOLD

THINKING LIKE A MOUNTAIN

A deep chesty bawl echoes from rimrock to rimrock, rolls down the mountain, and fades into the far blackness of the night. It is an outburst of wild defiant sorrow, and of contempt for all the adversities of the world.

Every living thing (and perhaps many a dead one as well) pays heed to that call. To the deer it is a reminder of the way of all flesh, to the pine a forecast of midnight scuffles and of blood upon the snow, to the coyote a promise of gleanings to come, to the cowman a threat of red ink at the bank, to the hunter a challenge of fang against bullet. Yet behind these obvious and immediate hopes and fears there lies a deeper meaning, known only to the mountain itself. Only the mountain has lived long enough to listen objectively to the howl of a wolf.

Those unable to decipher the hidden meaning know nevertheless that it is there, for it is felt in all wolf country, and distinguishes that country from all other land.

It tingles in the spine of all who hear wolves by night, or who scan their tracks by day. Even without sight or sound of wolf, it is implicit in a hundred small events: the midnight whinny of a pack horse, the rattle of rolling rocks, the bound of a fleeing deer, the way shadows lie under the spruces. Only the ineducable tyro can fail to sense the presence or absence of wolves, or the fact that mountains have a secret opinion about them.

My own conviction on this score dates from the day I saw a wolf die. We were eating lunch on a high rimrock, at the foot of which a turbulent river elbowed its way. We saw what we thought was a doe fording the torrent, her breast awash in white water. When she climbed the bank toward us and shook out her tail, we realized our error: it was a wolf. A half-dozen others, evidently grown pups, sprang from the willows and all joined in a welcoming mêlée of wagging tails and playful maulings. What was literally a pile of wolves writhed and tumbled in the center of an open flat at the foot of our rimrock.

A SAND COUNTY ALMANAC: AND SKETCHES HERE AND THERE by Leopold (1949) 3,512w from "Arizona and New Mexico" and "The Land Ethic" pp. 129–133, 201–205, 207–214, 223–226. © 1949, 1977 by Oxford University Press, Inc. By permission of Oxford University Press, USA.

In those days we had never heard of passing up a chance to kill a wolf. In a second we were pumping lead into the pack, but with more excitement than accuracy: how to aim a steep downhill shot is always confusing. When our rifles were empty, the old wolf was down, and a pup was dragging a leg into impassable slide-rocks.

We reached the old wolf in time to watch a fierce green fire dying in her eyes. I realized then, and have known ever since, that there was something new to me in those eyes—something known only to her and to the mountain. I was young then, and full of trigger-itch; I thought that because fewer wolves meant more deer, that no wolves would mean hunters' paradise. But after seeing the green fire die, I sensed that neither the wolf nor the mountain agreed with such a view.

Since then I have lived to see state after state extirpate its wolves. I have watched the face of many a newly wolfless mountain, and seen the south-facing slopes wrinkle with a maze of new deer trails. I have seen every edible bush and seedling browsed, first to anaemic desuetude, and then to death. I have seen every edible tree defoliated to the height of a saddlehorn. Such a mountain looks as if someone had given God a new pruning shears, and forbidden Him all other exercise. In the end the starved bones of the hoped-for deer herd, dead of its own too-much, bleach with the bones of the dead sage, or molder under the high-lined junipers.

I now suspect that just as a deer herd lives in mortal fear of its wolves, so does a mountain live in mortal fear of its deer. And perhaps with better cause, for while a buck pulled down by wolves can be replaced in two or three years, a range pulled down by too many deer may fail of replacement in as many decades.

So also with cows. The cowman who cleans his range of wolves does not realize that he is taking over the wolf's job of trimming the herd to fit the range. He has not learned to think like a mountain. Hence we have dustbowls, and rivers washing the future into the sea.

We all strive for safety, prosperity, comfort, long life, and dullness. The deer strives with his supple legs, the cowman with trap and poison, the statesman with pen, the most of us with machines, votes, and dollars, but it all comes to the same thing: peace in our time. A measure of success in this is all well enough, and perhaps is a requisite to objective thinking, but too much safety seems to yield only danger in the long run. Perhaps this is behind Thoreau's dictum: In wildness is the salvation of the world. Perhaps this is the hidden meaning in the howl of the wolf, long known among mountains, but seldom perceived among men.

RACHEL CARSON

SILENT SPRING

THE OBLIGATION TO ENDURE

The history of life on earth has been a history of interaction between living things and their surroundings. To a large extent, the physical form and the habits of the earth's vegetation and its animal life have been molded by the environment. Considering the whole span of earthly time, the opposite effect, in which life actually modifies its surroundings, has been relatively slight. Only within the moment of time represented by the present century has one species—man—acquired significant power to alter the nature of his world.

During the past quarter century this power has not only increased to one of disturbing magnitude but it has changed in character. The most alarming of all man's assaults upon the environment is the contamination of air, earth, rivers, and sea with dangerous and even lethal materials. This pollution is for the most part irreversible; the chain of evil it initiates not only in the world that must support life but in living tissues is for the most part irreversible. In this now universal contamination of the environment, chemicals are the sinister and little-recognized partners of radiation in changing the very nature of the world—the very nature of its life. Strontium 90, released through nuclear explosions into the air, comes to earth in rain or drifts down as fallout, lodges in soil, enters into the grass or corn or wheat grown there, and in time takes up its abode in the bones of a human being, there to remain until his death. Similarly, chemicals sprayed on croplands or forests or gardens lie long in soil, entering into living organisms, passing from one to another in a chain of poisoning and death. Or they emerge and, through the alchemy of air and sunlight, combine into new forms that kill vegetation, sicken cattle, and work unknown harm on those who drink from once pure wells. As Albert Schweitzer has said, "Man can hardly even recognize the devils of his own creation."

It took hundreds of millions of years to produce the life that now inhabits the earth—eons of time in which that developing and evolving and diversifying life reached a state of adjustment and balance with its surroundings. The environment, rigorously shaping and directing the life it supported, contained elements that were hostile as well as supporting. Certain rocks gave out dangerous radiation; even within the light of the sun, from which all life draws its energy, there were short-wave radiations with power to injure. Given time—time not in years but in millennia—life adjusts, and a balance has been reached. For time is the essential ingredient; but in the modern world there is no time.

The rapidity of change and the speed with which new situations are created follow the impetuous and heedless pace of man rather than the deliberate pace of nature. Radiation is no longer merely the background radiation of rocks, the bombardment of cosmic rays, the ultraviolet of the sun that have existed before there was any life on earth; radiation is now the unnatural creation of man's tampering with the atom. The chemicals to which life is asked to make its adjustment are no longer merely the calcium and silica and copper and all the rest of the minerals washed out of the rocks and carried in rivers to the sea; they are the synthetic creations of man's inventive mind, brewed in his laboratories, and having no counterparts in nature.

To adjust to these chemicals would require time on the scale that is nature's; it would require not merely the years of a man's life but the life of generations. And even this, were it by some miracle possible, would be futile, for the new chemicals come from our laboratories in an endless stream; almost five hundred annually find their way into actual use in the United States alone. The figure is staggering and its implications are not easily grasped—500 new chemicals to which the bodies of men and animals are required somehow to adapt each year, chemicals totally outside the limits of biological experience.

Among them are many that are used in man's war against nature. Since the mid-1940's over 200 basic chemicals have been created for use in killing insects, weeds, rodents, and other organisms described in the modern vernacular as "pests"; and they are sold under several thousand different brand names.

These sprays, dusts, and aerosols are now applied almost universally to farms, gardens, forests, and homes—nonselective chemicals that have the power to kill every insect, the "good" and the "bad," to still the song of birds and the leaping of fish in the streams, to coat the leaves with a deadly film, and to linger on in soil—all this though the intended target may be only a few weeds or insects. Can anyone believe it is possible to lay down such a barrage of poisons on the surface of the earth without making it unfit for all life? They should not be called "insecticides," but "biocides."

The whole process of spraying seems caught up in an endless spiral. Since DDT was released for civilian use, a process of escalation has been going on in which ever more toxic materials must be found. This has happened because insects, in a triumphant vindication of Darwin's principle of the survival of the fittest, have evolved super races immune to the particular insecticide used, hence a deadlier one has always to be developed—and then a deadlier one than that. In has happened also because . . . destructive insects often undergo a "flareback," or resurgence, after spraying, in numbers greater than before. Thus the chemical war is never won, and all life is caught in its violent crossfire.

Along with the possibility of the extinction of mankind by nuclear war, the central problem of our age has therefore become the contamination of man's total environment with such substances of incredible potential for harm—substances that accumulate in the tissues of plants and animals and even penetrate the germ cells to shatter or alter the very material of heredity upon which the shape of the future depends.

Some would-be architects of our future look toward a time when it will be possible to alter the human germ plasm by design. But we may easily be doing so now by inadvertence, for many chemicals, like radiation, bring about gene mutations. It is ironic to think that man might determine his own future by something so seemingly trivial as the choice of an insect spray.

All this has been risked—for what? Future historians may well be amazed by our distorted sense of proportion. How could intelligent beings seek to control a few unwanted species by a method that contaminated the entire environment and brought the threat of disease and death even to their own kind? Yet this is precisely what we have done.

. . .

Have we fallen into a mesmerized state that makes us accept as inevitable that which is inferior or detrimental, as though having lost the will or the vision to demand that which is good? Such thinking, in the words of the ecologist Paul Shepard, "idealizes life with only its head out of water, inches above the limits of toleration of the corruption of its own environment. . . . Why should we tolerate a diet of weak poisons, a home in insipid surroundings, a circle of acquaintances who are not quite our enemies, the noise of motors with just enough relief to prevent insanity? Who would want to live in a world which is just not quite fatal?"

Yet such a world is pressed upon us. The crusade to create a chemically sterile, insect-free world seems to have engendered a fanatic zeal on the part of many specialists and most of the so-called control agencies. On every hand there is evidence that those engaged in spraying operations exercise a ruthless power. "The regulatory entomologists . . . function as prosecutor, judge and jury, tax assessor and collector and sheriff

to enforce their own orders," said Connecticut entomologist Neely Turner. The most flagrant abuses go unchecked in both state and federal agencies.

It is not my contention that chemical insecticides must never be used. I do contend that we have put poisonous and biologically potent chemicals indiscriminately into the hands of persons largely or wholly ignorant of their potentials for harm. We have subjected enormous numbers of people to contact with these poisons, without their consent and often without their knowledge. If the Bill of Rights contains no guarantee either by private individuals or by public officials, it is surely only because our forefathers, despite their considerable wisdom and foresight, could conceive of no such problem.

I contend, furthermore, that we have allowed these chemicals to be used with little or no advance investigation of their effect on soil, water, wildlife, and man himself. Future generations are unlikely to condone our lack of prudent concern for the integrity of the natural world that supports all life.

There is still very limited awareness of the nature of the threat. This is an era of specialists, each of whom sees his own problem and is unaware of or intolerant of the larger frame into which it fits. It is also an era dominated by industry, in which the right to make a dollar at whatever cost is seldom challenged. When the public protests, confronted with some obvious evidence of damaging results of pesticide applications, it is fed little tranquilizing pills of half truth. We urgently need an end to these false assurances, to the sugar coating of unpalatable facts. It is the public that is being asked to assume the risks that the insect controllers calculate. The public must decide whether it wishes to continue on the present road, and it can do so only when in full possession of the facts. In the words of Jean Rostand, "The obligation to endure gives us the right to know."

. . .

THE OTHER ROAD

We stand now where two roads diverge. But unlike the roads in Robert Frost's familiar poem, they are not equally fair. The road we have long been traveling is deceptively easy, a smooth superhighway on which we progress with great speed, but at its end lies disaster.

The other fork of the road—the one "less traveled by"—offers our last, our only chance to reach a destination that assures the preservation of our earth.

The choice, after all, is ours to make. If, having endured much, we have at last asserted our "right to know," and if, knowingly, we have concluded that we are being asked to take senseless and frightening risks, then we should no longer accept the counsel of those who tell us that we must fill our world with poisonous chemicals; we should look about and see what other course is open to us.

A truly extraordinary variety of alternatives to the chemical control of insects is available. Some are already in use and have achieved brilliant success. Others are in the stage of laboratory testing. Still others are little more than ideas in the minds of imaginative scientists, waiting for the opportunity to put them to the test. All have this in common: they are *biological* solutions, based on understanding of the living organisms they seek to control, and of the whole fabric of life to which these organisms belong. Specialists representing various areas of the vast field of biology are contributing—entomologists, pathologists, geneticists, physiologists, biochemists, ecologists—all pouring their knowledge and their creative inspirations into the formation of a new science of biotic controls.

. . .

Through all these new, imaginative, and creative approaches to the problem of sharing our earth with other creatures there runs a constant theme, the awareness that we are dealing with life—with living populations and all their pressures and counter-pressures, their surges and recessions. Only by taking account of such life forces and by cautiously seeking to guide them into channels favorable to ourselves can we hope to achieve a reasonable accommodation between the insect hordes and ourselves.

The current vogue for poisons has failed utterly to take into account these most fundamental considerations. As crude a weapon as the cave man's club, the chemical barrage has been hurled against the fabric of life—a fabric on the one hand delicate and destructible, on the other miraculously tough and resilient, and capable of striking back in unexpected ways. These extraordinary capacities of life have been ignored by the practitioners of chemical control who have brought to their task no "high-minded orientation," no humility before the vast forces with which they tamper.

The "control of nature" is a phrase conceived in arrogance, born of the Neanderthal age of biology and philosophy, when it was supposed that nature exists for the convenience of man. The concepts and practices of applied entomology for the most part date from that Stone Age of science. It is our alarming misfortune that so primitive a science has armed itself with the most modern and terrible weapons, and that in turning them against the insects it has also turned them against the earth.

HUMAN BEINGS

A. Human Suffering

PETER SINGER

FAMINE, AFFLUENCE, AND MORALITY

As I write this, in November 1971, people are dying in East Bengal from lack of food, shelter, and medical care. The suffering and death that are occurring there now are not inevitable, not unavoidable in any fatalistic sense of the term. Constant poverty, a cyclone, and a civil war have turned at least nine million people into destitute refugees; nevertheless, it is not beyond the capacity of the richer nations to give enough assistance to reduce any further suffering to very small proportions. The decisions and actions of human beings can prevent this kind of suffering. Unfortunately, human beings have not made the necessary decisions. At the individual level, people have, with very few exceptions, not responded to the situation in any significant way. Generally speaking, people have not given large sums to relief funds; they have not written to their parliamentary representatives demanding increased government assistance; they have not demonstrated in the streets, held symbolic fasts, or done anything else

directed toward providing the refugees with the means to satisfy their essential needs. At the government level, no government has given the sort of massive aid that would enable the refugees to survive for more than a few days. Britain, for instance, has given rather more than most countries. It has, to date, given £14,750,000. For comparative purposes, Britain's share of the non-recoverable development costs of the Anglo-French Concorde project is already in excess of £275,000,000, and on present estimates will reach £440,000,000. The implication is that the British government values a supersonic transport more than thirty times as highly as it values the lives of the nine million refugees. Australia is another country which, on a per capita basis, is well up in the "aid to Bengal" table. Australia's aid, however, amounts to less than one-twelfth of the cost of Sydney's new opera house. The total amount given, from all sources, now stands at about £65,000,000. The estimated cost of keeping the refugees alive for one year is

Singer, Peter. 1972. Famine, Affluence, and Morality. Philosophy & Public Affairs, 1:230–243. Copyright © 1972 by Princeton University Press. Reprinted with permission of the publisher.

£464,000,000. Most of the refugees have now been in the camps for more than six months. The World Bank has said that India needs a minimum of £300,000,000 in assistance from other countries before the end of the year. It seems obvious that assistance on this scale will not be forthcoming. India will be forced to choose between letting the refugees starve or diverting funds from her own development program, which will mean that more of her own people will starve in the future.[1]

These are the essential facts about the present situation in Bengal. So far as it concerns us here, there is nothing unique about this situation except its magnitude. The Bengal emergency is just the latest and most acute of a series of major emergencies in various parts of the world, arising both from natural and from man-made causes. There are also many parts of the world in which people die from malnutrition and lack of food independent of any special emergency. I take Bengal as my example only because it is the present concern, and because the size of the problem has ensured that it has been given adequate publicity. Neither individuals nor governments can claim to be unaware of what is happening there.

What are the moral implications of a situation like this? In what follows, I shall argue that the way people in relatively affluent countries react to a situation like that in Bengal cannot be justified; indeed, the whole way we look at moral issues—our moral conceptual scheme—needs to be altered, and with it, the way of life that has come to be taken for granted in our society.

In arguing for this conclusion I will not, of course, claim to be morally neutral. I shall, however, try to argue for the moral position that I take, so that anyone who accepts certain assumptions, to be made explicit, will, I hope, accept my conclusion.

I begin with the assumption that suffering and death from lack of food, shelter, and medical care are bad. I think most people will agree about this, although one may reach the same view by different routes. I shall not argue for this view. People can hold all sorts of eccentric positions, and perhaps from some of them it would not follow that death by starvation is in itself bad. It is difficult, perhaps impossible, to refute such positions, and so for brevity I will henceforth take this assumption as accepted. Those who disagree need read no further.

My next point is this: if it is in our power to prevent something bad from happening, without thereby sacrificing anything of comparable moral importance, we ought, morally, to do it. By "without sacrificing anything of comparable moral importance" I mean without causing anything else comparably bad to happen, or doing something that is wrong in itself, or failing to promote some moral good, comparable in significance to the bad thing that we can prevent. This principle seems almost as uncontroversial as the last one. It requires us only to prevent what is bad, and not to promote what is good, and it requires this of us only when we can do it without sacrificing anything that is, from the moral point of view, comparably important. I could even, as far as the application of my argument to the Bengal emergency is concerned, qualify the point so as to make it: if it is in our power to prevent something very bad from happening, without thereby sacrificing anything morally significant, we ought, morally, to do it. An application of this principle would be as follows: if I am walking past a shallow pond and see a child drowning in it, I ought to wade in and pull the child out. This will mean getting my clothes muddy, but this is insignificant, while the death of the child would presumably be a very bad thing.

The uncontroversial appearance of the principle just stated is deceptive. If it were acted upon, even in its qualified form, our lives, our society, and our world would be fundamentally changed. For the principle takes, firstly, no account of proximity or distance. It makes no moral difference whether the person I can help is a neighbor's child ten yards from me or a Bengali whose name I shall never know, ten thousand miles away. Secondly, the principle makes no distinction between cases in which I am the only person who could possibly do anything and cases in which I am just one among millions in the same position.

I do not think I need to say much in defense of the refusal to take proximity and distance into account. The fact that a person is physically near to us, so that we have personal contact with him, may make it more likely that we *shall* assist him, but this does not show that we *ought* to help him rather than another who happens to be further away. If we accept any principle of impartiality, universalizability, equality, or whatever, we cannot discriminate against someone merely because he is far away from us (or we are far away from him). Admittedly, it is possible that we are in a better position to judge what needs to be done to help a person near to us than one far away, and perhaps also to provide the assistance we judge to be necessary. If this were the case, it would be a reason for helping those near to us first. This may once have been a justification for being more concerned with the poor in one's own town than with famine victims in India. Unfortunately for those who like to keep their moral responsibilities limited, instant communication and swift transportation have changed the situation. From the moral point of view, the development of the world into a "global village" has made an important, though still unrecognized, difference to our moral situation. Expert observers and supervisors, sent out by famine relief organizations or permanently stationed in famine-prone areas, can direct our aid to a refugee in Bengal almost as effectively as we could get it to someone in our own block. There would seem, therefore, to be no possible justification for discriminating on geographical grounds.

There may be a greater need to defend the second implication of my principle—that the fact that there are millions of other people in the same position, in respect to the Bengali refugees, as I am, does not make the situation significantly different from a situation in which I am the only person who can prevent something very bad from occurring. Again, of course, I admit that there is a psychological difference between the cases; one feels less guilty about doing nothing if one can point to others, similarly placed, who have also done nothing. Yet this can make no real difference to our moral obligations. Should I consider that I am less obliged to pull the drowning child out of the pond if on looking around I see other people, no further away than I am, who have also noticed the child but are doing nothing? One has only to ask this question to see the absurdity of the view that numbers lessen obligation. It is a view that is an ideal excuse for inactivity; unfortunately most of the major evils—poverty, overpopulation, pollution—are problems in which everyone is almost equally involved.

The view that numbers do make a difference can be made plausible if stated in this way: if everyone in circumstances like mine gave £5 to the Bengal Relief Fund, there would be enough to provide food, shelter, and medical care for the refugees; there is no reason why I should give more than anyone else in the same circumstances as I am; therefore I have no obligation to give more than £5. Each premise in this argument is true, and the argument looks sound. It may convince us, unless we notice that it is based on a hypothetical premise, although the conclusion is not stated hypothetically. The argument would be sound if the conclusion were: if everyone in circumstances like mine were to give £5, I would have no obligation to give more than £5. If the conclusion were so stated, however, it would be obvious that the argument has no bearing on a situation in which it is not the case that everyone else gives £5. This, of course, is the actual situation. It is more or less certain that not everyone in circumstances like mine will give £5. So there will not be enough to provide the needed food, shelter, and medical care. Therefore by giving more than £5 I will prevent more suffering than I would if I gave just £5.

It might be thought that this argument has an absurd consequence. Since the situation appears to be that very few people are likely to give substantial amounts, it follows that I and everyone else in similar circumstances ought to give as much as possible, that is, at least up to the point at which by giving more one would begin to cause serious suffering for oneself and one's dependents—perhaps even beyond this point to the point of marginal utility, at which by giving more one would cause oneself and one's dependents as much suffering as one would prevent in Bengal. If everyone does this, however, there will be more than can be used for the benefit of the refugees, and some of the sacrifice will have been unnecessary. Thus, if everyone does what he ought to do, the result will not be as good as it would be if everyone did a little less than he ought to do, or if only some do all that they ought to do.

The paradox here arises only if we assume that the actions in question—sending money to the relief funds—are performed more or less simultaneously, and are also unexpected. For if it is to be expected that everyone is going to contribute something, then clearly each is not obliged to give as much as he would have been obliged to had others not been giving too. And if everyone is not acting more or less simultaneously, then those giving later will know how much more is needed, and will have no obligation to give more than

The motivation behind charitable action makes all the difference (is it within self or not) → shows if it is charitable.

is necessary to reach this amount. To say this is not to deny the principle that people in the same circumstances have the same obligations, but to point out that the fact that others have given, or may be expected to give, is a relevant circumstance: those giving after it has become known that many others are giving and those giving before are not in the same circumstances. So the seemingly absurd consequence of the principle I have put forward can occur only if people are in error about the actual circumstances—that is, if they think they are giving even when others are not, but in fact they are giving when others are. The result of everyone doing what he really ought to do cannot be worse than the result of everyone doing less than he ought to do, although the result of everyone doing what he reasonably believes he ought to do could be.

If my argument so far has been sound, neither our distance from a preventable evil nor the number of other people who, in respect to that evil, are in the same situation as we are, lessens our obligation to mitigate or prevent that evil. I shall therefore take as established the principle I asserted earlier. As I have already said, I need to assert it only in its qualified form: if it is in our power to prevent something very bad from happening, without thereby sacrificing anything else morally significant, we ought, morally, to do it.

The outcome of this argument is that our traditional moral categories are upset. The traditional distinction between duty and charity cannot be drawn, or at least, not in the place we normally draw it. Giving money to the Bengal Relief Fund is regarded as an act of charity in our society. The bodies which collect money are known as charities. These organizations see themselves in this way—if you send them a check, you will be thanked for your "generosity." Because giving money is regarded as an act of charity, it is not thought that there is anything wrong with not giving. The charitable man may be praised, but the man who is not charitable is not condemned. People do not feel in any way ashamed or guilty about spending money on new clothes or a new car instead of giving it to famine relief. (Indeed, the alternative does not occur to them.) This way of looking at the matter cannot be justified. When we buy new clothes not to keep ourselves warm but to look "well-dressed" we are not providing for any important need. We would not be sacrificing

anything significant if we were to continue to wear our old clothes, and give the money to famine relief. By doing so, we would be preventing another person from starving. It follows from what I have said earlier that we ought to give money away, rather than spend it on clothes which we do not need to keep us warm. To do so is not charitable, or generous. Nor is it the kind of act which philosophers and theologians have called "supererogatory"—an act which it would be good to do, but not wrong not to do. On the contrary, we ought to give money away, and it is wrong not to do so.

I am not maintaining that there are no acts which are charitable, or that there are no acts which it would be good to do but not wrong not to do. It may be possible to redraw the distinction between duty and charity in some other place. All I am arguing here is that the present way of drawing the distinction, which makes it an act of charity for a man living at the level of affluence which most people in the "developed nations" enjoy to give money to save someone else from starvation, cannot be supported. It is beyond the scope of my argument to consider whether the distinction should be redrawn or abolished altogether. There would be many other possible ways of drawing the distinction—for instance, one might decide that it is good to make other people as happy as possible, but not wrong not to do so.

Despite the limited nature of the revision in our moral conceptual scheme which I am proposing, the revision would, given the extent of both affluence and famine in the world today, have radical implications. These implications may lead to further objections, distinct from those I have already considered. I shall discuss two of these.

One objection to the position I have taken might be simply that it is too drastic a revision of our moral scheme. People do not ordinarily judge in the way I have suggested they should. Most people reserve their moral condemnation for those who violate some moral norm, such as the norm against taking another person's property. They do not condemn those who indulge in luxury instead of giving to famine relief. But given that I did not set out to present a morally neutral description of the way people make moral judgments, the way people do in fact judge has nothing to do with the validity of my conclusion. My conclusion follows from the principle which I advanced earlier, and unless that principle is rejected, or the arguments shown to be unsound, I think the conclusion must stand, however strange it appears.

It might, nevertheless, be interesting to consider why our society, and most other societies, do judge differently from the way I have suggested they should. In a well-known article, J. O. Urmson suggests that the imperatives of duty, which tell us what we must do, as distinct from what it would be good to do but not wrong not to do, function so as to prohibit behavior that is intolerable if men are to live together in society.[2] This may explain the origin and continued existence of the present division between acts of duty and acts of charity. Moral attitudes are shaped by the needs of society, and no doubt society needs people who will observe the rules that make social existence tolerable. From the point of view of a particular society, it is essential to prevent violations of norms against killing, stealing, and so on. It is quite inessential, however, to help people outside one's own society.

If this is an explanation of our common distinction between duty and super-erogation, however, it is not a justification of it. The moral point of view requires us to look beyond the interests of our own society. Previously, as I have already mentioned, this may hardly have been feasible, but it is quite feasible now. From the moral point of view, the prevention of the starvation of millions of people outside our society must be considered at least as pressing as the upholding of property norms within our society.

It has been argued by some writers, among them Sidgwick and Urmson, that we need to have a basic moral code which is not too far beyond the capacities of the ordinary man, for otherwise there will be a general breakdown of compliance with the moral code. Crudely stated, this argument suggests that if we tell people that they ought to refrain from murder and give everything they do not really need to famine relief, they will do neither, whereas if we tell them that they ought to refrain from murder and that it is good to give to famine relief but not wrong not to do so, they will at least refrain from murder. The issue here is: Where should we draw the line between conduct that is required and conduct that is good although not required, so as to get the best possible result? This would

seem to be an empirical question, although a very difficult one. One objection to the Sidgwick–Urmson line of argument is that it takes insufficient account of the effect that moral standards can have on the decisions we make. Given a society in which a wealthy man who gives five percent of his income to famine relief is regarded as most generous, it is not surprising that a proposal that we all ought to give away half our incomes will be thought to be absurdly unrealistic. In a society which held that no man should have more than enough while others have less than they need, such a proposal might seem narrow-minded. What it is possible for a man to do and what he is likely to do are both, I think, very greatly influenced by what people around him are doing and expecting him to do. In any case, the possibility that by spreading the idea that we ought to be doing very much more than we are to relieve famine we shall bring about a general breakdown of moral behavior seems remote. If the stakes are an end to widespread starvation, it is worth the risk. Finally, it should be emphasized that these considerations are relevant only to the issue of what we should require from others, and not to what we ourselves ought to do.

The second objection to my attack on the present distinction between duty and charity is one which has from time to time been made against utilitarianism. It follows from some forms of utilitarian theory that we all ought, morally, to be working full time to increase the balance of happiness over misery. The position I have taken here would not lead to this conclusion in all circumstances, for if there were no bad occurrences that we could prevent without sacrificing something of comparable moral importance, my argument would have no application. Given the present conditions in many parts of the world, however, it does follow from my argument that we ought, morally, to be working full time to relieve great suffering of the sort that occurs as a result of famine or other disasters. Of course, mitigating circumstances can be adduced—for instance, that if we wear ourselves out through overwork, we shall be less effective than we would otherwise have been. Nevertheless, when all considerations of this sort have been taken into account, the conclusion remains: we ought to be preventing as much suffering as we can without sacrificing something else of comparable moral importance. This conclusion is one which we may be reluctant to face. I cannot see, though, why it should be regarded as a criticism of the position for which I have argued, rather than a criticism of our ordinary standards of behavior. Since most people are self-interested to some degree, very few of us are likely to do everything that we ought to do. It would, however, hardly be honest to take this as evidence that it is not the case that we ought to do it.

It may still be thought that my conclusions are so wildly out of line with what everyone else thinks and has always thought that there must be something wrong with the argument somewhere. In order to show that my conclusions, while certainly contrary to contemporary Western moral standards, would not have seemed so extraordinary at other times and in other places, I would like to quote a passage from a writer not normally thought of as a way-out radical, Thomas Aquinas.

> Now, according to the natural order instituted by divine providence, material goods are provided for the satisfaction of human needs. Therefore the division and appropriation of property, which proceeds from human law, must not hinder the satisfaction of man's necessity from such goods. Equally, whatever a man has in superabundance is owed, of natural right, to the poor for their sustenance. So Ambrosius says, and it is also to be found in the *Decretum Gratiani*: "The bread which you withhold belongs to the hungry; the clothing you shut away, to the naked; and the money you bury in the earth is the redemption and freedom of the penniless."[3]

I now want to consider a number of points, more practical than philosophical, which are relevant to the application of the moral conclusion we have reached. These points challenge not the idea that we ought to be doing all we can to prevent starvation, but the idea that giving away a great deal of money is the best means to this end.

It is sometimes said that overseas aid should be a government responsibility, and that therefore one ought not to give to privately run charities. Giving privately, it is said, allows the government and the noncontributing members of society to escape their responsibilities.

This argument seems to assume that the more people there are who give to privately organized famine relief funds, the less likely it is that the government will take over full responsibility for such aid. This assumption is unsupported, and does not strike me as at all plausible. The opposite view—that if no one gives voluntarily, a government will assume that its citizens are uninterested in famine relief and would not wish to be forced into giving aid—seems more plausible. In any case, unless there were a definite probability that by refusing to give one would be helping to bring about massive government assistance, people who do refuse to make voluntary contributions are refusing to prevent a certain amount of suffering without being able to point to any tangible beneficial consequence of their refusal. So the onus of showing how their refusal will bring about government action is on those who refuse to give.

I do not, of course, want to dispute the contention that governments of affluent nations should be giving many times the amount of genuine, no-strings-attached aid that they are giving now. I agree, too, that giving privately is not enough, and that we ought to be campaigning actively for entirely new standards for both public and private contributions to famine relief. Indeed, I would sympathize with someone who thought that campaigning was more important than giving oneself, although I doubt whether preaching what one does not practice would be very effective. Unfortunately, for many people the idea that "it's the government's responsibility" is a reason for not giving which does not appear to entail any political action either. * WE MAKE EXCUSES.

Another, more serious reason for not giving to famine relief funds is that until there is effective population control, relieving famine merely postpones starvation. If we save the Bengal refugees now, others, perhaps the children of these refugees, will face starvation in a few years' time. In support of this, one may cite the now well-known facts about the population explosion and the relatively limited scope for expanded production.

This point, like the previous one, is an argument against relieving suffering that is happening now, because of a belief about what might happen in the future; it is unlike the previous point in that very good evidence can be adduced in support of this belief about the future. I will not go into the evidence here. I accept that the earth cannot support indefinitely a population rising at the present rate. This certainly poses a problem for anyone who thinks it important to prevent famine. Again, however, one could accept the argument without drawing the conclusion that it absolves one from any obligation to do anything to prevent famine. The conclusion that should be drawn is that the best means of preventing famine, in the long run, is population control. It would then follow from the position reached earlier that one ought to be doing all one can to promote population control (unless one held that all forms of population control were wrong in themselves, or would have significantly bad consequences). Since there are organizations working specifically for population control, one would then support them rather than more orthodox methods of preventing famine.

A third point raised by the conclusion reached earlier relates to the question of just how much we all ought to be giving away. One possibility, which has already been mentioned, is that we ought to give until we reach the level of marginal utility—that is, the level at which, by giving more, I would cause as much suffering to myself or my dependents as I would relieve by my gift. This would mean, of course, that one would reduce oneself to very near the material circumstances of a Bengali refugee. It will be recalled that earlier I put forward both a strong and a moderate version of the principle of preventing bad occurrences. The strong version, which required us to prevent bad things from happening unless in doing so we would be sacrificing something of comparable moral significance, does seem to require reducing ourselves to the level of marginal utility. I should also say that the strong version seems to me to be the correct one. I proposed the more moderate version—that we should prevent bad occurrences unless, to do so, we had to sacrifice something morally significant,—only in order to show that even on this surely undeniable principle a great change in our way of life is required. On the more moderate principle, it may not follow that we ought to reduce ourselves to the level of marginal utility, for one might hold that to reduce oneself and one's family to this level is to cause something significantly bad to happen. Whether this is so I shall not discuss, since, as I have said, I can see no good reason for holding the moderate version of the principle rather than the strong version. Even if we accepted the principle only

in its moderate form, however, it should be clear that we would have to give away enough to ensure that the consumer society, dependent as it is on people spending on trivia rather than giving to famine relief, would slow down and perhaps disappear entirely. There are several reasons why this would be desirable in itself. The value and necessity of economic growth are now being questioned not only by conservationists, but by economists as well.[4] There is no doubt, too, that the consumer society has had a distorting effect on the goals and purposes of its members. Yet looking at the matter purely from the point of view of overseas aid, there must be a limit to the extent to which we should deliberately slow down our economy; for it might be the case that if we gave away, say, forty percent of our Gross National Product, we would slow down the economy so much that in absolute terms we would be giving less than if we gave 25 percent of the much larger GNP that we would have if we limited our contribution to this smaller percentage.

I mention this only as an indication of the sort of factor that one would have to take into account in working out an ideal. Since Western societies generally consider one percent of the GNP an acceptable level for overseas aid, the matter is entirely academic. Nor does it affect the question of how much an individual should give in a society in which very few are giving substantial amounts.

It is sometimes said, though less often now than it used to be, that philosophers have no special role to play in public affairs, since most public issues depend primarily on an assessment of facts. On questions of fact, it is said, philosophers as such have no special expertise, and so it has been possible to engage in philosophy without committing oneself to any position on major public issues. No doubt there are some issues of social policy and foreign policy about which it can truly be said that a really expert assessment of the facts is required before taking sides or acting, but the issue of famine is surely not one of these. The facts about the existence of suffering are beyond dispute. Nor, I think, is it disputed that we can do something about it, either through orthodox methods of famine relief or through population control or both. This is therefore an issue on which philosophers are competent to take a position. The issue is one which faces everyone who has more money than he needs to support himself and his dependents, or who is in a position to take some sort of political action. These categories must include practically every teacher and student of philosophy in the universities of the Western world. If philosophy is to deal with matters that are relevant to both teachers and students, this is an issue that philosophers should discuss.

Discussion, though, is not enough. What is the point of relating philosophy to public (and personal) affairs if we do not take our conclusions seriously? In this instance, taking our conclusion seriously means acting upon it. The philosopher will not find it any easier than anyone else to alter his attitudes and way of life to the extent that, if I am right, is involved in doing everything that we ought to be doing. At the very least, though, one can make a start. The philosopher who does so will have to sacrifice some of the benefits of the consumer society, but he can find compensation in the satisfaction of a way of life in which theory and practice, if not yet in harmony, are at least coming together.

NOTES

1. There was also a third possibility: that India would go to war to enable the refugees to return to their lands. Since I wrote this paper, India has taken this way out. The situation is no longer that described above, but this does not affect my argument, as the next paragraph indicates.
2. J. O. Urmson, "Saints and Heroes," in *Essays in Moral Philosophy*, ed. A. I. Melden (Seattle: University of Washington Press, 1958), p. 214. For a related but significantly different view see also Henry Sidgwick, *The Methods of Ethics*, 7th ed. (London: Dover Press, 1907), pp. 220–21, 492–93.
3. *Summa Theologica*, II-II, Question 66, Article 7, in *Aquinas, Selected Political Writings*, ed. A. P. d'Entreves, trans. J. G. Dawson (Oxford: Basil Blackwell, 1948), p. 171.
4. See, for instance, John Kenneth Galbraith, *The New Industrial State* (Boston: Houghton Mifflin, 1967); and E. J. Mishan, *The Costs of Economic Growth* (New York: Praeger, 1967).

GARRET HARDIN

LIVING ON A LIFEBOAT

No generation has viewed the problem of the survival of the human species as seriously as we have. Inevitably, we have entered this world of concern through the door of metaphor. Environmentalists have emphasized the image of the earth as a spaceship—Spaceship Earth. Kenneth Boulding (1966) is the principal architect of this metaphor. It is time, he says, that we replace the wasteful "cowboy economy" of the past with the frugal "spaceship economy" required for continued survival in the limited world we now see ours to be. The metaphor is notably useful in justifying pollution control measures.

Unfortunately, the image of a spaceship is also used to promote measures that are suicidal. One of these is a generous immigration policy, which is only a particular instance of a class of policies that are in error because they lead to the tragedy of the commons (Hardin 1968). These suicidal policies are attractive

Garrett Hardin, author, BioScience, publisher.

because they mesh with what we unthinkably take to be the ideals of "the best people." What is missing in the idealistic view is an insistence that rights and responsibilities must go together. The "generous" attitude of all too many people results in asserting inalienable rights while ignoring or denying matching responsibilities.

For the metaphor of a spaceship to be correct the aggregate of people on board would have to be under unitary sovereign control (Ophuls 1974). A true ship always has a captain. It is conceivable that a ship could be run by a committee. But it could not possibly survive if its course were determined by bickering tribes that claimed rights without responsibilities.

What about Spaceship Earth? It certainly has no captain, and no executive committee. The United Nations is a toothless tiger, because the signatories of its charter wanted it that way. The spaceship metaphor is used only to justify spaceship demands on common resources without acknowledging corresponding spaceship responsibilities.

An understandable fear of decisive action leads people to embrace "incrementalism"—moving toward reform by tiny stages. As we shall see, this strategy is counterproductive in the area discussed here if it means accepting rights before responsibilities. Where human survival is at stake, the acceptance of responsibilities is a precondition to the acceptance of rights, if the two cannot be introduced simultaneously.

LIFEBOAT ETHICS

Before taking up certain substantive issues let us look at an alternative metaphor, that of a lifeboat. In developing some relevant examples the following numerical values are assumed. Approximately two-thirds of the world is desperately poor, and only one-third is comparatively rich. The people in poor countries have an average per capita GNP (Gross National Product) of about $200 per year; the rich, of about $3,000. (For the United States it is nearly $5,000 per year.) Metaphorically, each rich nation amounts to a lifeboat full of comparatively rich people. The poor of the world are in other, much more crowded lifeboats. Continuously, so to speak, the poor fall out of their lifeboats and swim for a while in the water outside, hoping to be admitted to a rich lifeboat, or in some other way to benefit from the "goodies" on board. What should the passengers on a rich lifeboat do? This is the central problem of "the ethics of a lifeboat."

First we must acknowledge that each lifeboat is effectively limited in capacity. The land of every nation has a limited carrying capacity. The exact limit is a matter for argument, but the energy crunch is convincing more people every day that we have already exceeded the carrying capacity of the land. We have been living on "capital"—stored petroleum and coal—and soon we must live on income alone.

Let us look at only one lifeboat—ours. The ethical problem is the same for all, and is as follows. Here we sit, say 50 people in a lifeboat. To be generous, let us assume our boat has a capacity of 10 more, making 60. (This, however, is to violate the engineering principle of the "safety factor." A new plant disease or a bad change in the weather may decimate our population if we don't preserve some excess capacity as a safety factor.)

The 50 of us in the lifeboat see 100 others swimming in the water outside, asking for admission to the boat, or for handouts. How shall we respond to their calls? There are several possibilities.

One. We may be tempted to try to live by the Christian ideal of being "our brother's keeper," or by the Marxian ideal (Marx 1875) of "from each according to his abilities, to each according to his needs." Since the needs of all are the same, we take all the needy into our boat, making a total of 150 in a boat with a capacity of 60. The boat is swamped, and everyone drowns. Complete justice, complete catastrophe.

Two. Since the boat has an unused excess capacity of 10, we admit just 10 more to it. This has the disadvantage of getting rid of the safety factor, for which action we will sooner or later pay dearly. Moreover, *which* 10 do we let in? "First come, first served?" The best 10? The neediest 10? How do we *discriminate*? And what do we say to the 90 who are excluded?

Three. Admit no more to the boat and preserve the small safety factor. Survival of the people in the lifeboat is then possible (though we shall have to be on our guard against boarding parties).

The last solution is abhorrent to many people. It is unjust, they say. Let us grant that it is.

"I feel guilty about my good luck," say some. The reply to this is simple: *Get out and yield your place to others.*

. . .

RUIN IN THE COMMONS

The fundamental error of the sharing ethic is that it leads to the tragedy of the commons. Under a system of private property the man (or group of men) who own property recognize their responsibility to care for it, for if they don't they will eventually suffer. A farmer, for instance, if he is intelligent, will allow no more cattle in a pasture than its carrying capacity justifies. If he overloads the pasture, weeds take over, erosion sets in, and the owner loses in the long run.

But if a pasture is run as a commons open to all, the right of each to use it is not matched by an operational responsibility to take care of it. It is no use asking independent herdsmen in a commons to act responsibly, for they dare not. The considerate herdsman who refrains from overloading the commons suffers more than a selfish one who says his needs are greater. (As Leo Durocher says, "Nice guys finish last.") Christian-Marxian idealism is counterproductive. That it *sounds* nice is no excuse. With distribution systems, as with individual morality, good intentions are no substitute for good performance.

A social system is stable only if it is insensitive to errors. To the Christian-Marxian idealist a selfish person is a sort of "error." Prosperity in the system of the commons cannot survive errors. If *everyone* would only restrain himself, all would be well; but it takes *only one less than everyone* to ruin a system of voluntary restraint. In a crowded world of less than perfect human beings—and we will never know any other—mutual ruin is inevitable in the commons. This is the core of the tragedy of the commons.

One of the major tasks of education today is to create such an awareness of the dangers of the commons that people will be able to recognize its many varieties, however disguised. There is pollution of the air and water because these media are treated as commons. Further growth of population and growth in the per capita conversion of natural resources into pollutants require that the system of the commons be modified or abandoned in the disposal of "externalities."

The fish populations of the oceans are exploited as commons, and ruin lies ahead. No technological invention can prevent this fate: in fact, all improvements in the art of fishing merely hasten the day of complete ruin. Only the replacement of the system of the commons with a responsible system can save oceanic fisheries.

The management of western range lands, though nominally rational, is in fact (under the steady pressure of cattle ranchers) often merely a government-sanctioned system of the commons, drifting toward ultimate ruin for both the range lands and the residual enterprisers.

WORLD FOOD BANKS

In the international arena we have recently heard a proposal to create a new commons, namely an international depository of food reserves to which nations will contribute according to their abilities, and from which nations may draw according to their needs. Nobel laureate Norman Borlaug has lent the prestige of his name to this proposal.

A world food bank appeals powerfully to our humanitarian impulses. We remember John Donne's celebrated line, "Any man's death diminishes me." But before we rush out to see for whom the bell tolls let us recognize where the greatest political push for international granaries comes from, lest we be disillusioned later. Our experience with Public Law 480 clearly reveals the answer. This was the law that moved billions of dollars worth of U.S. grain to food-short, population-long countries during the past two decades. When P.L. 480 first came into being, a headline in the business magazine *Forbes* (Paddock and Paddock 1970) revealed the power behind it: "Feeding the World's Hungry Millions: How it will mean billions for U.S. business."

And indeed it did. In the years 1960 to 1970 a total of $7.9 billion was spent on the "Food for Peace" program as P.L. 480 was called. During the years 1948 to 1970 an additional $49.9 billion were extracted from American taxpayers to pay for other economic aid programs, some of which went for food and food-producing machinery. (This figure does *not* include military aid.) That P.L. 480 was a give-away program was concealed. Recipient countries went through the motions of paying for P.L. 480 food—with IOU's. In December 1973 the charade was brought to an end as far as India was concerned when the United States "forgave" India's $3.2 billion debt (Anonymous 1974). Public announcement of the cancellation of the debt was delayed for two months: one wonders why.

"Famine–1975!" (Paddock and Paddock 1967) is one of the few publications that points out the commercial roots of this humanitarian attempt. Though all U.S. taxpayers lost by P.L. 480, special interest groups gained handsomely. Farmers benefited because they were not asked to contribute the grain—it was bought from them by the taxpayers. Besides the direct benefit there was the indirect effect of increasing demand and thus raising prices of farm products generally. The manufacturers of farm machinery, fertilizers, and pesticides benefited by the farmers' extra efforts to grow more food. Grain elevators profited from storing the grain for varying lengths of time. Railroads made money hauling it to port, and shipping lines by carrying it overseas. Moreover, once the machinery for P.L. 480 was established an immense bureaucracy had a vested interest in its continuance regardless of its merits.

Very little was ever heard of these selfish interests when P.L. 480 was defended in public. The emphasis was always on its humanitarian effects. The combination of multiple and relatively silent selfish interests with highly vocal humanitarian apologists constitutes a powerful lobby for extracting money from taxpayers. Foreign aid has become a habit that can apparently survive in the absence of any known justification. A news commentator in a weekly magazine (Lansner 1974), after exhaustively going over all the conventional arguments for foreign aid—self-interest, social justice, political advantage, and charity—and concluding that none of the known arguments really held water, concluded: "So the search continues for some logically compelling reasons for giving aid. . ." In other words, *Act now, Justify later*—if ever. (Apparently a quarter of a century is too short a time to find the justification for expending several billion dollars yearly.)

The search for a rational justification can be short-circuited by interjecting the word "emergency." Borlaug

uses this word. We need to look sharply at it. What is an "emergency?" It is surely something like an accident, which is correctly defined as *an event that is certain to happen, though with a low frequency* (Hardin 1972a). A well-run organization prepares for everything that is certain, including accidents and emergencies. It budgets for them. It saves for them. It expects them—and mature decision-makers do not waste time complaining about accidents when they occur.

What happens if some organizations budget for emergencies and others do not? If each organization is solely responsible for its own well-being, poorly managed ones will suffer. But they should be able to learn from experience. They have a chance to mend their ways and learn to budget for infrequent but certain emergencies. The weather, for instance, always varies and periodic crop failures are certain. A wise and competent government saves out of the production of the good years in anticipation of bad years that are sure to come. This is not a new idea. The Bible tells us that Joseph taught this policy to Pharaoh in Egypt more than 2,000 years ago. Yet it is literally true that the vast majority of the governments of the world today have no such policy. They lack either the wisdom or the competence, or both. Far more difficult than the transfer of wealth from one country to another is the transfer of wisdom between sovereign powers or between generations.

"But it isn't their fault! How can we blame the poor people who are caught in an emergency? Why must we punish them?" The concepts of blame and punishment are irrelevant. The question is, what are the operational consequences of establishing a world food bank? If it is open to every country every time a need develops, slovenly rulers will not be motivated to take Joseph's advice. Why should they? Others will bail them out whenever they are in trouble.

Some countries will make deposits in the world food bank and others will withdraw from it: there will be almost no overlap. Calling such a depository-transfer unit a "bank" is stretching the metaphor of *bank* beyond its elastic limits. The proposers, of course, never call attention to the metaphorical nature of the word they use.

. . .

An "international food bank" is really, then, not a true bank but a disguised one-way transfer device for moving wealth from rich countries to poor.

. . .

ECO-DESTRUCTION VIA THE GREEN REVOLUTION

The demoralizing effect of charity on the recipient has long been known. "Give a man a fish and he will eat for a day; teach him how to fish and he will eat for the rest of his days." So runs an ancient Chinese proverb. Acting on this advice the Rockefeller and Ford Foundations have financed a multipronged program for improving agriculture in the hungry nations. The result, known as the "Green Revolution," has been quite remarkable. "Miracle wheat" and "miracle rice" are splendid technological achievements in the realm of plant genetics.

Whether or not the Green Revolution can increase food production is doubtful (Harris 1972, Paddock 1970, Wilkes 1972), but in any event not particularly important. What is missing in this great and well-meaning humanitarian effort is a firm grasp of fundamentals. Considering the importance of the Rockefeller Foundation in this effort it is ironic that the late Alan Gregg, a much-respected vice president of the Foundation, strongly expressed his doubts of the wisdom of all attempts to increase food production some two decades ago. (This was before Borlaug's work—supported by Rockefeller—had resulted in the development of "miracle wheat.") Gregg (1955) likened the growth and spreading of humanity over the surface of the earth to the metastasis of cancer in the human body, wryly remarking that "Cancerous growths demand food; but, as far as I know, they have never been cured by getting it."

"Man does not live by bread alone"—the scriptural statement has a rich meaning even in the material realm. Every human being born constitutes a draft on all aspects of the environment—food, air, water, unspoiled scenery, occasional and optional solitude, beaches, contact with wild animals, fishing, hunting—the list is long and incompletely known. Food can, perhaps, be significantly increased: but what about clean beaches, unspoiled forests, and solitude? If we satisfy the need for food in a growing population we necessarily decrease the supply of other goods, and thereby increase the difficulty of equitably allocating scarce goods (Hardin 1969b, 1972b).

The present population of India is 600 million, and it is increasing by 15 million per year. The environmental load of this population is already great. The forests of India are only a small fraction of what they were three centuries ago. Soil erosion, floods, and the psychological costs of crowding are serious. Every one of the net 15 million lives added each year stresses the Indian environment more severely. *Every life saved this year in a poor country diminishes the quality of life for subsequent generations.*

Observant critics have shown how much harm we wealthy nations have already done to poor nations through our well-intentioned but misguided attempts to help them (Paddock and Paddock 1973). Particularly reprehensible is our failure to carry out post-audits of these attempts (Farvaar and Milton 1972). Thus we have shielded our tender consciences from knowledge of the harm we have done. Must we Americans continue to fail to monitor the consequences of our external "do-gooding"? If, for instance, we thoughtlessly make it possible for the present 600 million Indians to swell to 1,200 millions by the year 2001—as their present growth rate promises—will posterity in India thank *us* for facilitating an even greater destruction of *their* environment? Are good intentions ever a sufficient excuse for bad consequences?

IMMIGRATION CREATES A COMMONS

I come now to the final example of a commons in action, one for which the public is least prepared for rational discussion. The topic is at present enveloped by a great silence which reminds me of a comment made by Sherlock Holmes in A. Conan Doyle's story, "Silver Blaze." Inspector Gregory had asked, "Is there any point to which you would wish to draw my attention?" To this Holmes responded:

> "To the curious incident of the dog in the night-time."
> "The dog did nothing in the night-time," said the Inspector.
> "That was the curious incident," remarked Sherlock Holmes.

By asking himself what would repress the normal barking instinct of a watchdog Holmes realized that it must be the dog's recognition of his master as the criminal trespasser. In a similar way we should ask ourselves what repression keeps us from discussing something as important as immigration?

It cannot be that immigration is numerically of no consequence. Our government acknowledges a *net* flow of 400,000 a year. Hard data are understandably lacking on the extent of illegal entries, but a not implausible figure is 600,000 per year (Buchanan 1973). The natural increase of the resident population is now about 1.7 million per year. This means that the yearly gain from immigration is at least 19%, and may be 37%, of the total increase. It is quite conceivable that educational campaigns like that of Zero Population Growth, Inc., coupled with adverse social and economic factors—inflation, housing shortage, depression, and loss of confidence in national leaders—may lower the fertility of American women to a point at which all of the yearly increase in population would be accounted for by immigration. Should we not at least ask if that is what we want? How curious it is that we so seldom discuss immigration these days!

. . .

World food banks move food to the people, thus facilitating the exhaustion of the environment of the poor. By contrast, unrestricted immigration moves people to the food, thus speeding up the destruction of the environment in rich countries. Why poor people should want to make this transfer is no mystery, but why should rich hosts encourage it? This transfer, like the reverse one, is supported by both selfish interests and humanitarian impulses.

The principal selfish interest in unimpeded immigration is easy to identify: it is the interest of the employers of cheap labor, particularly that needed for degrading jobs. We have been deceived about the forces of history by the lines of Emma Lazarus inscribed on the Statue of Liberty:

> *Give me your tired, your poor*
> *Your huddled masses yearning to breathe free,*
> *The wretched refuse of your teeming shore,*
> *Send these, the homeless, tempest-tossed, to me:*
> *I lift my lamp beside the golden door.*

The image is one of an infinitely generous earth-mother, passively opening her arms to hordes of immigrants who come here on their own initiative. Such an image may have been adequate for the early days of colonization, but by the time these lines were written (1886) the force for immigration was largely manufactured inside our own borders by factory and mine owners who sought cheap labor not to be found among laborers already here. One group of foreigners after another was thus enticed into the United States to work at wretched jobs for wretched wages.

At present, it is largely the Mexicans who are being so exploited. It is particularly to the advantage of certain employers that there be many illegal immigrants. Illegal immigrant workers dare not complain about their working conditions for fear of being repatriated. Their presence reduces the bargaining power of all Mexican-American laborers. Cesar Chavez has repeatedly pleaded with congressional committees to close the doors to more Mexicans so that those here can negotiate effectively for higher wages and decent working conditions. Chavez understands the ethics of a lifeboat.

. . .

To be generous with one's own possessions is one thing; to be generous with posterity's is quite another. This, I think, is the point that must be gotten across to those who would, from a commendable love of distributive justice, institute a ruinous system of the commons, either in the form of a world food bank or that of unrestricted immigration. Since every speaker is a member of some ethnic group it is always possible to charge him with ethnocentrism. But even after purging an argument of ethnocentrism the rejection of the commons is still valid and necessary if we are to save at least some parts of the world from environmental ruin. Is it not desirable that at least some of the grandchildren of people now living should have a decent place in which to live?

THE ASYMMETRY OF DOOR-SHUTTING

We must now answer this telling point: "How can you justify slamming the door once you're inside? You say that immigrants should be kept out. But aren't we all immigrants, or the descendants of immigrants? Since we refuse to leave, must we not, as a matter of justice and symmetry, admit all others?"

. . .

We are all the descendants of thieves, and the world's resources are inequitably distributed, but we must begin the journey to tomorrow from the point where we are today. We cannot remake the past. We cannot, without violent disorder and suffering, give land and resources back to the "original" owners—who are dead anyway.

We cannot safely divide the wealth equitably among all present peoples, so long as people reproduce at different rates, because to do so would guarantee that our grandchildren—everyone's grandchildren—would have only a ruined world to inhabit.

. . .

Plainly many new problems will arise when we consciously face the immigration question and seek rational answers. No workable answers can be found if we ignore population problems. And—if the argument of this essay is correct—so long as there is no true world government to control reproduction everywhere it is impossible to survive in dignity if we are to be guided by Spaceship ethics. Without a world government that is sovereign in reproductive matters, mankind lives, in fact, on a number of sovereign lifeboats. For the foreseeable future survival demands that we govern our actions by the ethics of a lifeboat. Posterity will be ill served if we do not.

REFERENCES

Anonymous, *Wall Street Journal* February 19, 1974.

N. Borlaug, "Civilization's future: a call for international granaries." *Bull. At. Sci.* 29 (1973): 7–15.

K. Boulding, "The economics of the coming Spaceship earth." In H. Jarrett, ed. *Environmental Quality in a Growing Economy.* (Baltimore: Johns Hopkins Press, 1966)

W. Buchanan, "Immigration statistics." *Equilibrium* 1 (1973): no. 3: 16–19.

K. Davis, "Population." *Scientific American.* 209 (1963): no. 3, 62–71.

M. T. Farvar, and J. P. Milton, *The Careless Technology.* (Garden City, N.Y.: Natural History Press, 1972)

A. Gregg, "A medical aspect of the population problem." *Science* 121 (1955) 681–682.

G. Hardin, (1966) Chap. 9. in *Biology: Its Principles and Implications,* 2nd ed. Freeman, San Francisco.

G. Hardin (1968) "The tragedy of the commons." *Science* 162: 1243–1248.

G. Hardin (1969a) Page 18 in *Population, Evolution, and Birth Control,* 2nd ed. Freeman, San Francisco.

G. Hardin (1969b) "The economics of wilderness." *Nat Hist* 78(6): 20–27.

G. Hardin (1972a) Pages 81–82 in *Exploring New Ethics for Survival: The Voyage of the Spaceship Beagle.* Viking, N.Y.

G. Hardin (1972b) "Preserving quality on Spaceship Earth." *In* J. B. Trefethen, ed. *Translations of the Thirty-Seventh North American Wildlife and Natural Resources Conference* (Washington D.C.: Wildlife Management Institute, 1972) Washington D.C.

G. Hardin Chap. 23 in *Stalking the Wild Taboo.* (Los Altos, CA: Kaufmann, 1973)

M. Harris, "How green the revolution." *Nat Hist.* 81 (1972): no. 3, 28–30.

K. Lansner, "Should foreign aid begin at home?" *Newsweek,* February 11, 1974, p. 32.

K. Marx, (1875) "Critique of the Gotha program." Page 388 in R. C. Tucker, ed. *The Marx–Engels Reader.* (New York: Norton, 1972).

W. Ophuls, "The scarcity society." *Harpers* 248 (1974): no. 1487: 47–52.

W. C. Paddock, "How green is the green revolution?" *BioScience* 20 (1970): 897–902.

W. Paddock, and E. Paddock, *We Don't Know How.* (Ames, Iowa: Iowa State University Press, 1973)

W. Paddock, and E. Paddock, *Famine-1975!* (Boston: Little, Brown, 1967).

H. G. Wilkes, "The green revolution." *Environment* 14 (1972): no. 8, 32–39.

GITA SEN

WOMEN, POVERTY AND POPULATION
Issues for the Concerned Environmentalist

INTRODUCTION

Differences in perceptions regarding the linkages between population and environment became particularly acute during the preparatory build-up to the UN Conference on Environment and Development, variously known as the Earth Summit and Rio 92. Disagreement between Southern and Northern countries on the extent of attention to be given to population received considerable publicity. At the non-governmental level too, the issue of population has been, of late, a subject of considerable debate among environmentalists (especially those from the North), feminists and population lobbyists.

The basis of these differences often appears baffling; the apparent lack of willingness to compromise, or to acknowledge the obvious merits of opposing views seem to indicate a lack of analytical rigor. The debate appears, to some at least, to be based on passionately held but ultimately ephemeral differences. I wish to argue that, although the positions taken in the policy debate have been exaggerated at times, some of the oppositions have deeper roots. They arise from conceptual and possibly paradigmatic differences rather than from disagreements regarding the "truth-value" of particular scientific propositions. These shape the protagonists' perceptions of problems, the analytical methods used, and the weights assigned to different linkages and relationships. In particular, varying views regarding development strategies, the linkages between poverty and population growth, and the role of gender relations in shaping those links color the positions taken in the debate.

This chapter is an attempt to examine the different perspectives on these issues held by environmental scientists and environmental activists[1] on the one hand, and women's health researchers and feminist activists on the other. Its motivation is twofold: first, to identify the positions taken by these two broad groupings within the larger discourses on development and on population; secondly to propose a possible basis for greater mutual understanding.[2]

GENDER IN THE POPULATION FIELD

In the history of population policy, women have been viewed typically in one of three ways. The narrowest of these is the view of women as the principal "targets" of family planning programs; of women's bodies as the site of reproduction, and therefore as the necessary locus of contraceptive technology, and reproductive manipulation. The early history of population programs is replete with examples of such views; but even more recently, the "objectification" of women's bodies as fit objects for reproductive re-engineering, independent of a recognition of women as social subjects, continues apace. (Hubbard, 1990)

A second view of women which gained currency after the Bucharest Population Conference in 1983 was women as potential decision-makers whose capabilities in managing childcare, children's health in particular, could be enhanced through greater education. Women began to be viewed as social subjects in this case, but the attention given to women's education has not spun off (in the population policy literature) into a fuller consideration of the conditions under which the education of girls takes hold in a society, and therefore the extent to which education is embedded within a society, and therefore the extent to which education is

Sen, Gita. 1994. Women, Poverty, and Population: Issues for the Concerned Environmentalist. Feminist Perspectives on Sustainable Development. Edited by W. Harcourt. London: Zed. 216–25. Reprinted with permission of Society for International Development and the author.

embedded within larger social processes and structures. While this view represented a step away from objectification, women were still perceived as a means to a demographic end, with their own health and reproductive needs becoming thereby incidental to the process.

A third view which grew in the 1980s focused on maternal mortality as an important health justification for family planning. This view, which was at the core of the Safe Motherhood initiative, attempted to claim a health justification for family planning on the basis of rates of maternal mortality. In practice, the initiative has received relatively little funding or support.

CONCEPTUAL APPROACHES

Economic theories of fertility are closely associated with the "new" household economics. Premised on the belief that children are a source of both costs and benefits to their parents, such theories argue that parents determine their "optimum" number of children based on a balancing of costs and benefits at the margin. As a description of differences between societies where children are viewed as a source of both present and future streams of income vs. those where children are essentially a cost to parents (balanced by a measure of psychological satisfaction but not by a significant flow of money income), the theory has an appealing simplicity. It purports to explain why the former societies may be more pro-natalist than the latter. It also suggests that shifting children away from child labor (a source of parental income) towards schooling (a parental cost) might work to reduce fertility.

Such theories have been criticized on a number of grounds. The main criticism centers on the assumption that actual fertility is the result of choices made by a homogeneous household unit innocent of power and authority relations based on gender and age. Once such relations are acknowledged, and there is enough anthropological and historical evidence of their existence, the basis of decision-making within households has to be rethought in terms of differential short-term gains and losses for different members, as well as strategic choices by dominant members which will protect and ensure their continued dominance. For example, if the costs of child-raising increase, *ceteris paribus*, there may be little impact on fertility if the increased costs are largely borne by subordinate members of the household (such as younger women) who do not have much say in household decision-making.

Traditionally, in many societies the costs of high fertility in terms of women's health and work-burdens are rarely acknowledged as such, as long as the benefits in terms of access to a larger pool of subordinate children's labour or the social prestige inherent in being the father of many sons continue to accrue to men. Such authority relations are further cemented by ideologies which link woman's own personal status within the authoritarian household to her fertility. Newer game-theoretic models of household behavior (Sen, 1987) provide more interesting and complex theories that take better account of the differential distribution of types of assets as well as gains and losses within the household. These have not thus far, however, generated adequate explanations of fertility outcomes.[3]

AGAINST THE STREAM: GENDER RELATIONS AND REPRODUCTIVE RIGHTS

Many of the influential approaches to theory and policy within the population field have been less than able or equipped to deal with the complexity and pervasiveness of gender relations in households and the economies and societies within which they function. Both feminist researchers and activists within women's health movements have been attempting to change the terms of the debate and to expand its scope. An important part of this challenge is the critique of population policy and of family-planning programs as being biased (in gender, class and race terms) in their basic objectives and in the methods that they predominantly use.

The definition of a social objective of population limitation[4] which does not recognize that there may be costs to limiting family size that are differential across social classes and income groups, has long been criticized.[5] In particular, such costs are likely to be less than transparent in non-democratic politics or even within democratic states where the costs are disproportionately visited on groups that are marginal on ethnic racial bases and therefore do not have sufficient voice.[6]

Population policy has also been criticized by some as being a substitute for rather than complementary to economic development strategies that are broad-based in their allocation of both benefits and costs. For example, if impoverished peasants were persuaded or coerced to limit family size on the premise that their poverty is a result of high fertility, independent of the possible causal impact of skewed land-holding patterns, commercialization processes, or unequal access to development resources, then it is questionable whether smaller families would make them more or less poor.

The critique becomes more complicated once the gender dimension is introduced. Critics of population policy on class grounds have sometimes been as gender blind as the policy itself. Having many children may be an economic imperative for a poor family in certain circumstances, but the costs of bearing and rearing children are still borne disproportionately by the women of the household. Gender concerns cannot be subsumed under a notion of homogeneous national or global concerns. For feminist critics of population policy, development strategies that otherwise ignore or exploit poor women, while making them the main target of population programs, are highly questionable. But they do not believe that the interests of poor women in the area of reproduction are identical to those of poor men.

In general terms, the feminist critique agrees with many other critics that population control cannot be made a surrogate for directly addressing the crisis of economic survival that many poor women face. Reducing population growth is not a sufficient condition for raising livelihoods or meeting basic needs.[7] In particular, the critique qualifies the argument that reducing fertility reduces the health risks of poor women and therefore meets an important basic need. This would be true provided the means used to reduce fertility did not themselves increase the health hazards that women face, or were considerably and knowably less than the risks of childbearing. If family-planning programs are to do this, critics argue, they will have to function differently in the future than they have in the past.

The most trenchant criticism questions the objectives (population control rather than, and often at the expense of, women's health and dignity), the strategies (family planning gaining dominance over primary and preventive health care in the budgets and priorities of ministries and departments), the methods (use of individual incentives and disincentives for both "target" populations and program personnel, targets and quotas for field personnel, overt coercion, the prevalence of

"camps" and absence of medical care either before hand or afterwards, inadequate monitoring of side-effects), and the birth-control methods (a narrow range of birth prevention methods, technology that has not been adequately tested for safety, or which has not passed regulatory controls in Northern countries) advocated and supplied through population programs. A now extensive debate around the "quality of care" has focused particularly on the implications of alternative program methods and birth-control techniques for the quality of family program services. (Bruce, 1989) More broad-ranging evaluations of population policy objectives and strategies have found them guilty of biases of class, race/ethnicity and gender. (Hartmann, 1987)

Viewed as a development strategy, the critics see population policies as usually falling within a class of strategies that are "top-down" in orientation, and largely unconcerned with (and often violating) the basic human rights needs of target populations. Even the developmentalist concern with improving child health and women's education has received little real support from population programs despite the extensive research and policy debate it has generated.

The critical perspective argues that ignoring co-requisites, such as economic and social justice and women's reproductive health and rights, also makes the overt target of population policies (a change in birth rates) difficult to achieve. Where birth rates do fall (or rise as the case may be) despite this, the achievement is often predicated on highly coercive methods, and is antithetical to women's health and human dignity. The women's health advocates argue for a different approach to population policy—one that makes women's health and other basic needs more central to policy and program focus, and by doing so increases human welfare, transforms oppressive gender relations, and reduces population growth rates. (Germain and Ordway, 1989)

Around the world there is a growing emergence of positive statements about what human rights in the area of reproduction might encompass. (Petchesky and Weiner, 1990) Many of these statements are culturally and contextually specific, but they usually share a common critique of existing population programs, and a common understanding of alternative principles. Many of them prioritize the perspective of poor women, although they recognize that the reproductive rights of all women in most societies are less than satisfactory. Their attempt to recast population policies and programs is also, therefore, a struggle to redefine development itself to be more responsive to the needs of the majority.

ENTER THE ENVIRONMENTALISTS

Environmentalist concern with population growth pre-dates the public debate sparked by the UN Conference on Environment and Development (UNCED). Probably some of the most influential early documents were the Club of Rome's *Limits to Growth* and Ehrlich and Ehrlich's *The Population Bomb*. (Ehrlich, 1969) The interest in global and local carrying capacity, vis-à-vis growing human population sizes and densities, stimulated the production of considerable literature, both scientific and popular. Unfortunately, the popular and activist literature has tended to ignore some of the important anthropological debates about carrying capacity, as well as to disregard the inconclusiveness of empirical evidence linking environmental change to population growth.[8] It tends, furthermore, to treat the population–environment linkages as simple mathematical ones, linking numbers of people to their environments through technology.

But the argument of both developmentalists in the population field and women's health and rights advocates has been precisely that population is not just an issue of numbers, but of complex social relationships which govern birth, death and migration. People's interactions with their environments can be only partially captured by simple mathematical relationships which fail to take the distribution of resources, incomes and consumption into account; such mathematical relationships by themselves may therefore be inadequate as predictors of outcomes or as guides to policy.[9]

Furthermore, from a policy point of view, more precise modeling of population–environment interactions has not, thus far, provided much better guidance about appropriate population policy programs. Ignoring the wide disparities in the growth rates of consumption between rich and poor within developing countries and hence their relative environmental impacts, as well as the critiques of women's health advocates outlined in the previous sections,

leads to single-minded policy prescriptions directed once more simply to increasing family-planning funding and effort. The leap from over-aggregated population–environmental relations to policy prescriptions favoring increased family planning becomes an implicit choice of politics, of a particular approach to population policy, to environmental policy, and to development. Because it glosses over so many fundamental issues of power, gender and class relations, and of distribution, and because it ignores the historical experience of population programs, it has come to be viewed by many as a retrograde step in the population-development discourse.

POPULATION ACTORS

The preceding discussion suggests that important actors in the population field are as follows. First come those population specialists who traditionally have focused on the size and growth of populations, on age structures, migration and population composition. In general, they enter the development discourse primarily through their concern with what impact population growth might have on rates of economic growth. In addition, population projections are mapped onto planning needs in areas such as food production, energy, and other infrastructures, as well as health, education, and so on. These mappings can be said to belong to a class of simple mathematical planning models which usually ignore problems of distribution (based as they tend to be on per capita needs and availabilities), as well as the social and institutional aspects of making a plan actually work.

The second group are the developmentalists who focus less on the impact of demographic change, and more on the prerequisites of sustained decline in mortality and fertility rates. In particular they stress the importance of improving health and women's education. They thus represent a major revision of traditional population approaches, but all too often stop short of addressing the problem of sustainability or of livelihoods.

A third group, the fundamentalists, has become increasingly important in the population field during the 1980s, gaining political legitimacy through their links to mainstream political organizations. Their primary interest is not the size or growth of populations, but rather control over reproduction and a conservative concern to preserve traditional family structures and gender roles. The moral overtones of the US abortion debate notwithstanding, their interest in procreation appears to derive largely from an opposition to changing gender relations in society.

The fourth group are the Northern environmentalists. At the risk of oversimplification, one might argue that many of these individuals and groups focus mainly on the links between economic growth and ecological sustainability on the one hand, and the size and growth of population on the other.

The fifth important group of actors are the women's health groups which have evolved either out of the feminist movement or out of other social movements or population organizations. Their understanding of the population problem is distinctive in that they define it as primarily a question of reproductive rights and reproductive health, in the context of livelihoods, basic needs and political participation. They often acknowledge that economic growth and ecological sustainability are concerns, but believe these ought to be viewed in the context of reproductive rights and health. In particular, many of them give priority to the needs and priorities of poor women in defining issues, problems and strategies.

Each of these sets of population actors has a view of the population question that is consistent with a particular view of development; as such they tend to overlap with particular sets of development actors, and find a niche within a particular set of development ideas. For example, population specialists are attracted to problems of economic growth, developmentalists to basic needs issues, and women's health activists to the problems of livelihoods, basic needs and political empowerment. Many Northern environmentalists, on the other hand, tend to view population through the lens of ecological sustainability, and this accounts for a considerable amount of the dissonance between their views and those of grassroots groups in the South.

TOWARDS MORE SYNERGY BETWEEN ENVIRONMENTALISTS AND FEMINISTS

Despite the dissonance provoked by the population–environment debate, there is much in common between feminists and environmentalists in their visions of society and in the methods they use. Both groups (or at least their more progressive wings) have a healthy critical stance towards ecologically profligate and inequitable patterns of economic growth, and have been attempting to change mainstream perceptions in this regard. Both use methods that rely on grassroots mobilization and participation, and are therefore sensitive to the importance of political openness and involvement. As such, both believe in the power of widespread knowledge and in the rights of people to be informed and to participate in decisions affecting their lives and those of nations and the planet. Indeed, there are many feminists within environmental movements (North and South) and environmentalists within feminist movements.

Greater mutual understanding on the population question can result from a greater recognition that the core problem is that of development within which population is inextricably meshed. Privileging the perspective of poor women can help ground this recognition in the realities of the lives and livelihoods of many within the South.

Economic growth and ecological sustainability must be such as to secure livelihoods, basic needs, political participation and women's reproductive rights, not work against them. Thus, environmental sustainability must be conceptualized so as to support and sustain livelihoods and basic needs, and not in ways that automatically counterpose "nature" against the survival needs of the most vulnerable. Where trade-offs among these different goals exist or are inevitable, the costs and burdens must not fall on the poorest and most vulnerable, and all people must have a voice in negotiating resolutions through open and genuinely participatory political processes. Furthermore, environmental strategies that enhance livelihoods and fulfill needs can probably help lay the basis for reduced rates of mortality and fertility.

Population and family-planning programs should be framed in the context of health and livelihood agendas, should give serious consideration to women's health advocates, and be supportive of women's reproductive health and rights. This has to be more than lip-service; it requires reorienting international assistance and national policy, reshaping programs and rethinking research questions and methodologies.

Using the language of welfare, gender equity or health, while continuing advocacy for family planning as it is at present practiced will not meet the need.

Reproductive health strategies are likely to succeed in improving women's health and making it possible for them to make socially viable fertility decisions if they are set in the context of an overall support-ive health and development agenda. Where general health and social development are poorly funded or given low priority, as has happened in the develop-ment agendas of many major development agencies and countries during the last decade, reproductive rights and health are unlikely to get the funding or at-tention they need. Reproductive health programs are also likely to be more efficacious when general health and development are served. A poor female agricul-tural wage-laborer, ill-nourished and anemic, is likely to respond better to reproductive health care if her nutritional status and overall health improve at the same time.

The mainstream Northern environmental move-ment needs to focus more sharply on gender relations and women's needs in framing its own strategies, as well as on the issues raised by minority groups. These issues (such as those raised by native peoples and African Americans in the US) tend to link environmen-tal issues with livelihoods and basic needs concerns in much the same way as do the people's organizations in the South. Greater sensitivity to the one, therefore, might bring greater awareness of the other.

Wide discussion and acknowledgment of these principles could help to bridge some of the current gaps between feminists and environmentalists, and make it possible to build coalitions that can move both agendas forward.

NOTES

1. The dissonance addressed in this chapter is be-tween mainstream environmentalists from the North and women's health researchers and activ-ists from both North and South.
2. My own position is that of someone who has come to these debates from a background of working on issues of gender and development, and this chapter will perforce tilt heavily towards spelling out the positions taken from within the women's movements. I do not claim to be able to explicate how the mainstream of the environmen-tal movement (especially in the North) has come to the particular definitions it has of "the popula-tion problem."
3. A different theoretical approach that takes better ac-count of the shifts in patterns of inter-generational transfers, and therefore of age-based hierarchies, is contained in the work of Caldwell and Caldwell (1987).
4. Or, in the case of many parts of Europe, of popula-tion expansion through increased fertility.
5. For an influential early critique see Mamdani (1974).
6. See Scott (n.d.) for a look at Norplant use in the contemporary United States.
7. Even rapid fertility decline may sometimes be indic-ative of a strategy of desperation on the part of the poor who can no longer access the complementary resources needed to put children's labour to use.
8. Examples of the former are Little (1992), Blaikie (1985); of the latter, Shaw (1989) and UN (1992). The latter argues, for example, that "The failure to take fully into account the possible ef-fects of other factors that might contribute to environmental degradation characterizes many analyses of population–environmental interre-lationships at the national and global levels and thus limits their value in assessing the impact of demographic variables."
9. An example is the well known Ehrlich-Holden, identity, I = PAT, linking environmental impact (I) with population growth (P), growth in affluence/consumption per capita (A), and technological ef-ficiency (T).

REFERENCES

J. Bruce, "Fundamental Elements of the Quality of Care: A Simple Framework." The Population Council, Programmes Division Working Papers No. 1, May, 1989 New York.

J. Caldwell, and P. Caldwell, "The Cultural Context of High Fertility in Sub-Saharan Africa," in *Population and Development Review*, 13 (1987): 409–38.

P. Ehrlich, *The Population Bomb*. (New York: Ballantine Books, 1969)

A. Germain, and J. Ordway, *Population Control and Women's Health: Balancing the Scales*. (New York: International Women's Health Coalition, 1989)

B. Hartmann, *Reproductive Rights and Wrongs: The Global Politics of Population Control and Contraceptive Choice*. (New York: Harper and Row, 1987)

R. Hubbard, *The Politics of Women's Biology*. (New Brunswick: Rutgers Press, 1990)

P. Little, The Social Causes of Land Degradation in Dry Regions. (Binghamton: Institute of Development Anthropology, 1992): manuscript

M. Mamdani, *The Myth of Population Control*. (New York: Monthly Review Press, 1974)

R. Petchesky and J. Weiner, *Global Feminist Perspectives on Reproductive Rights and Reproductive Health*. Report on the Special Sessions at the Fourth International Interdisciplinary Congress on Women. (New York: Hunter College, 1990)

J. Scott, "Norplant: Its Impact on Poor Women and Women of Color." (Washington, D.C.: National Black Women's Health Project Public Policy/Education Office)

A. K. Sen, "Gender and Cooperative Conflicts." Discussion Paper No. 1342. (Cambridge: Harvard Institute of Economic Research, 1987)

R. P. Shaw, "Population Growth: Is It Ruining the Environment?" *Populi*, 16 (1989): 21–9.

HOLMES ROLSTON III

FEEDING PEOPLE VERSUS SAVING NATURE?

When we must choose between feeding the hungry and conserving nature, people ought to come first. A bumper sticker reads: Hungry loggers eat spotted owls. That pinpoints an ethical issue, pure and simple, and often one where the humanist protagonist, taking high moral ground, intends to put the environmentalist on the defensive. You wouldn't let the Ethiopians starve to save some butterfly, would you?

"Human beings are at the centre of concerns for sustainable development." So the *Rio Declaration* begins. Once this was to be an *Earth Charter*, but the developing nations were more interested in getting the needs of their poor met. The developed nations are wealthy enough to be concerned about saving nature. The developing nations want the anthropocentrism, loud and clear. These humans, they add, "are entitled to a healthy and productive life in harmony with nature," but there too they seem as concerned with their entitlements as with any care for nature.[1] Can we fault them for it?

We have to be circumspect. To isolate so simple a trade-off as hungry people versus nature is perhaps artificial. If too far abstracted from the complex circumstances of decision, we may not be facing any serious operational issue. When we have simplified the question, it may have become, minus its many qualifications, a different question. The gestalt configures the question, and the same question reconfigured can

So Humans are more Important?

Holmes Rolston III. Feeding People versus Saving Nature. World Hunger & Morality, 2nd ed. Edited by W. Aiken and H. LaFollette. Upper Saddle River, NJ: Prentice Hall. 248–267. Reprinted with permission of the author and Prentice-Hall.

be different. So we must analyze the general matrix, and then confront the more particular people-versus-nature issue.

Humans win? Nature loses? After analysis, sometimes it turns out that humans are not really winning, if they are sacrificing the nature that is their life support system. Humans win by conserving nature—and these winners include the poor and the hungry. "In order to achieve sustainable development, environmental protection shall constitute an integral part of the development process and cannot be considered in isolation from it."[2] After all, food has to be produced by growing it in some reasonably healthy natural system, and the clean water that the poor need is also good for fauna and flora. Extractive reserves give people an incentive to conserve. Tourism can often benefit both the local poor and the wildlife, as well as tourists. One ought to seek win–win solutions wherever one can. Pragmatically, these are often the only kind likely to succeed.

Yet there are times when nature is sacrificed for human development; most development is of this kind. By no means all is warranted, but that which gets people fed seems basic and urgent. Then nature should lose and people win. Or are there times when at least some humans should lose and some nature should win? We are here interested in these latter occasions. Can we ever say that we should save nature rather than feed people?

Do you RISK HURTING HUMANS or Do you RISK HURTING THE ENVIRONMENT?

ENDANGERED NATURAL VALUES

Natural values are endangered at every scale: global, regional, and local, at levels of ecosystems, species, organisms, populations, fauna and flora, terrestrial and marine, charismatic megafauna down to mollusks and beetles. This is true in both developed and developing nations, though we have under discussion here places where poverty threatens biodiversity.

Humans now control 40 percent of the planet's land-based primary net productivity, that is, the basic plant growth that captures the energy on which everything else depends.[3] If the human population doubles again, the capture will rise to 60 to 80 percent,

and little habitat will remain for natural forms of life that cannot be accommodated after we have put people first. Humans do not use the lands they have domesticated effectively. A World Bank study found that 35 percent of the Earth's land has now become degraded.[4] Daniel Hillel, in a soils study, concludes, "Present yields are extremely low in many of the developing countries, and as they can be boosted substantially and rapidly, there should be no need to reclaim new land and to encroach further upon natural habitats."[5]

Africa is a case in point, and Madagascar epitomizes Africa's future. Its fauna and flora evolved independently from the mainland continent; there are 30 primates, all lemurs; the reptiles and amphibians are 90 percent endemic, including two thirds of all the chameleons of the world; and plant species, of which 80 percent are endemic, including a thousand kinds of orchids. Humans came there about 1,500 years ago and lived with the fauna and flora more or less intact until this century. Now an escalating population of impoverished Malagasy people rely heavily on slash-and-burn agriculture, and the forest cover is one third of the original (27.6 million acres to 9.4 million acres), most of the loss occurring since 1950.[6] Madagascar is the most eroded nation on Earth, and little or none of the fauna and flora is safely conserved. Population is expanding at 3.2 percent a year; remaining forest is shrinking at 3 percent, almost all to provide for the expanding population. Are we to say that none ought to be conserved until after no person is hungry?

Tigers are sliding toward extinction. Populations have declined 95 percent in this century; the two main factors are loss of habitat and a ferocious black market in bones and other body parts used in traditional medicine and folklore in China, Taiwan, and Korea, uses that are given no medical credence. Ranthambhore National Park in Rajasthan, India, is a tiger sanctuary; there were 40 tigers during the late 1980s, reduced in a few years by human pressures—illicit cattle grazing and poaching—to 20 to 25 tigers today. There are 200,000 Indians within three miles of the core of the park—more than double the population when the park was launched, 21 years ago. Most depend on wood from the 150 square miles of park to cook their food. They graze in and around the park some 150,000 head of scrawny cattle, buffalo, goats, and camels. The cattle impoverish habitat and carry diseases to the ungulates that are the tiger's prey base. In May 1993, a young tigress gave birth to four cubs; that month 316 babies were born in the villages surrounding the park.[7]

The tigers may be doomed, but ought they to be? Consider, for instance, that there are minimal reforestation efforts, or that cattle dung can be used for fuel with much greater efficiency than is being done, or that, in an experimental herd of jersey and holstein cattle there, the yield of milk increased ten times that of the gaunt, freeranging local cattle, and that a small group of dairy producers has increased milk production 1,000 percent in just 3 years. In some moods we may insist that people are more important than tigers. But in other moods these majestic animals seem the casualties of human inabilities to manage themselves and their resources intelligently, a tragic story that leaves us wondering whether the tigers should always lose and the people win.

WHEN NATURE COMES FIRST

Ought we to save nature if this results in people going hungry? In people dying? Regrettably, sometimes, the answer is yes. In 20 years Africa's black rhinoceros population declined from 65,000 to 2,500, a loss of 97 percent; the species faces imminent extinction. Again, as with the tigers, there has been loss of habitat caused by human population growth, an important and indirect cause; but the primary direct cause is poaching, this time for horns. People cannot eat horns; but they can buy food with the money from selling them. Zimbabwe has a hard-line shoot-to-kill policy for poachers, and over 150 poachers have been killed.[8]

So Zimbabweans do not always put people first; they are willing to kill some, and to let others to go hungry rather than sacrifice the rhino. If we always put people first, there will be no rhinos at all. Always too, we must guard against inhumanity, and take care, so far as we can, that poachers have other alternatives for overcoming their poverty. Still, if it comes to this, the Zimbabwean policy is right. Given the fact that rhinos have been so precipitously reduced, given that the Zimbabwean population is escalating (the average

married woman there desires to have six children),[9] one ought to put the black rhino as a species first, even if this costs human lives.

But the poachers are doing something illegal. What about ordinary people, who are not breaking any laws? The sensitive moralist may object that, even when the multiple causal factors are known, and lamented, when it comes to dealing with individual persons caught up in these social forces, we should factor out overpopulation, overconsumption, and maldistribution, none of which are the fault of the particular persons who may wish to develop their lands. "I did not ask to be born; I am poor, not overconsuming; I am not the cause but rather the victim of the inequitable distribution of wealth." Surely there still remains for such an innocent person a right to use whatever natural resources one has available, as best one can, under the exigencies of one's particular life, set though this is in these unfortunate circumstances. "I only want enough to eat, is that not my right?"

Human rights must include, if anything at all, the right to subsistence. So even if particular persons are located at the wrong point on the global growth graph, even if they are willy-nilly part of a cancerous and consumptive society, even if there is some better social solution than the wrong one that is in fact happening, have they not a right that will override the conservation of natural value? Will it not just be a further wrong to them to deprive them of their right to what little they have? Can basic human rights ever be overridden by a society that wants to do better by conserving natural value?

This requires some weighing of the endangered natural values. Consider the tropical forests. There is more richness there than in other regions of the planet—half of all known species. In South America, for example, there are one fifth of the planet's species of terrestrial mammals (800 species); there are one third of the planet's flowering plants.[10] The peak of global plant diversity is in the three Andean countries of Columbia, Ecuador, and Peru, where over 40,000 species occur on just 2 percent of the world's land surface.[11] But population growth in South America has been as high as anywhere in the world,[12] and people are flowing into the forests, often crowded off other lands.

Again do we hurt humans/nature?

What about these hungry people? Consider first people who are not now there but might move there. This is not good agricultural soil, and such would-be settlers are likely to find only a short-term bargain, a long-term loss. Consider the people who already live there. If they are indigenous peoples, and wish to continue to live as they have already for hundreds and even thousands of years, there will be no threat to the forest. If they are cabaclos (of mixed European and native races), they can also continue the lifestyles known for hundreds of years, without serious destruction of the forests. Such peoples may continue the opportunities that they have long had. Nothing is taken away from them. They have been reasonably well fed, though often poor.

Can these peoples modernize? Can they multiply? Ought there to be a policy of feeding first all the children they bear, sacrificing nature as we must to accomplish this goal? Modern medicine and technology have enabled them to multiply, curing childhood diseases and providing better nutrition, even if these peoples often remain at thresholds of poverty. Do not such people have the right to develop? A first answer is that they do, but with the qualification that all rights are not absolute, some are weaker, some stronger, and the exercise of any right has to be balanced against values destroyed in the exercise of that right.

The qualification brings a second answer. If one concludes that the natural values at stake are quite high, and that the opportunities for development are low, because the envisioned development is inadvisable, then a possible answer is: No, there will be no development of these reserved areas, even if people there remain in the relative poverty of many centuries, or even if, with escalating populations, they become more poor. We are not always obligated to cover human mistakes with the sacrifice of natural values.

? WHAT DOES HE MEAN BY THIS?

NOTES

1. *Rio Declaration on Environment and Development*, Principle I, UNCED document A/CONF. 151/26, vol. 1, pp. 15–25.
2. *Rio Declaration*, Principle 4.
3. Peter M. Vitousek, Paul R. Ehrlich, Anne H. Ehrlich, and Pamela A. Matson, "Human Appropriation of the Products of Biosynthesis," *BioScience* 36(1986): 368–373.
4. Robert Goodland, "The Case That the World Has Reached Limits," pp. 3–22 in Robert Goodland, Herman E. Daly, and Salah El Serafy, eds., *Population, Technology, and Lifestyle* (Washington, DC: Island Press, 1992).
5. Daniel Hillel, *Out of the Earth* (New York: Free Press, Macmillan, 1991), p. 279.
6. E. O. Wilson, *The Diversity of Life* (Cambridge, MA: Harvard University Press, 1992), p. 267; Alison Jolly, *A World Like Our Own: Man and Nature in Madagascar* (New Haven: Yale University Press, 1980).
7. Geoffrey C. Ward, "The People and the Tiger," *Audubon* 96, no. 4 (1994): 62–69.
8. Joel Berger and Carol Cunningham, "Active Intervention and Conservation: Africa's Pachyderm Problem," *Science* 263(1994): 1241–1242.
9. John Bongaarts, "Population Policy Options in the Developing World," *Science* 263 (1994): 771–776.
10. Michael A. Mares, "Conservation in South America: Problems, Consequences, and Solutions," *Science* 233(1986): 734–739.
11. Wilson, *The Diversity of Life*, p. 197.
12. Ansley J. Coale, "Recent Trends in Fertility in the Less Developed Countries," *Science* 221(1983): 828–832.

B. Human Excellence

THOMAS E. HILL JR.

IDEALS OF HUMAN EXCELLENCE
AND PRESERVING NATURAL ENVIRONMENTS

The moral significance of preserving natural environments is not entirely an issue of rights and social utility, for a person's attitude toward nature may be importantly connected with virtues or human excellences. The question is, "What sort of person would destroy the natural environment—or even see its value solely in cost/benefit terms?" The answer I suggest is that willingness to do so may well reveal the absence of traits which are a natural basis for a proper humility, self-acceptance, gratitude, and appreciation of the good in others.

I

A wealthy eccentric bought a house in a neighborhood I know. The house was surrounded by a beautiful display of grass, plants, and flowers, and it was shaded by a huge old avocado tree. But the grass required cutting, the flowers needed tending, and the man wanted more sun. So he cut the whole lot down and covered the yard with asphalt. After all it was his property and he was not fond of plants.

It was a small operation, but it reminded me of the strip mining of large sections of the Appalachians. In both cases, of course, there were reasons for the destruction, and property rights could be cited as justification. But I could not help but wonder, "What sort of person would do a thing like that?"

Many Californians had a similar reaction when a recent governor defended the leveling of ancient redwood groves, reportedly saying, "If you have seen one redwood, you have seen them all."

Incidents like these arouse the indignation of ardent environmentalists and leave even apolitical observers with some degree of moral discomfort. The reasons for these reactions are mostly obvious. Uprooting the natural environment robs both present and future generations of much potential use and enjoyment. Animals too depend on the environment; and even if one does not value animals for their own sakes, their potential utility for us is incalculable. Plants are needed, of course, to replenish the atmosphere quite aside from their aesthetic value. These reasons for hesitating to destroy forests and gardens

Thomas E. Hill, Jr. 1983. Ideals of Human Excellence and Preserving Natural Environments. Environmental Ethics, 5: 211–24. Reprinted with permission of the author and the journal.

are not only the most obvious ones, but also the most persuasive for practical purposes. But, one wonders, is there nothing more behind our discomfort? Are we concerned solely about the potential use and enjoyment of the forests, etc., for ourselves, later generations, and perhaps animals? Is there not something else which disturbs us when we witness the destruction or even listen to those who would defend it in terms of cost/benefit analysis?

Imagine that in each of our examples those who would destroy the environment argue elaborately that, even considering future generations of human beings and animals, there are benefits in "replacing" the natural environment which outweigh the negative utilities which environmentalists cite.[1] No doubt we could press the argument on the facts, trying to show that the destruction is shortsighted and that its defenders have underestimated its potential harm or ignored some pertinent rights or interests. But is this all we could say? Suppose we grant, for a moment, that the utility of destroying the redwoods, forests, and gardens is equal to their potential for use and enjoyment by nature lovers and animals. Suppose, further, that we even grant that the pertinent human rights and animal rights, if any, are evenly divided for and against destruction. Imagine that we also concede, for argument's sake, that the forests contain no potentially useful endangered species of animals and plants. Must we then conclude that there is no further cause for moral concern? Should we then feel morally indifferent when we see the natural environment uprooted?

II

Suppose we feel that the answer to these questions should be negative. Suppose, in other words, we feel that our moral discomfort when we confront the destroyers of nature is not fully explained by our belief that they have miscalculated the best use of natural resources or violated rights in exploiting them. Suppose, in particular, we sense that part of the problem is that the natural environment is being viewed exclusively as a natural *resource*. What could be the ground of such a feeling? That is, what is there in our system of normative principles and values that could account for our remaining moral dissatisfaction?[2]

Some may be tempted to seek an explanation by appeal to the interests, or even the rights, of plants. After all, they may argue, we only gradually came to acknowledge the moral importance of all human beings, and it is even more recently that consciences have been aroused to give full weight to the welfare (and rights?) of animals. The next logical step, it may be argued, is to acknowledge a moral requirement to take into account the interests (and rights?) of plants. The problem with the strip miners, redwood cutters, and the like, on this view, is not just that they ignore the welfare and rights of people and animals; they also fail to give due weight to the survival and health of the plants themselves.

The temptation to make such a reply is understandable if one assumes that all moral questions are exclusively concerned with whether *acts* are right or wrong, and that this, in turn, is determined entirely by how the acts impinge on the rights and interests of those directly affected. On this assumption, if there is cause for moral concern, some right or interest has been neglected; <u>and if the rights and interests of human beings and animals have already been taken into account, then there must be some other pertinent interests, for example, those of plants.</u> A little reflection will show that the assumption is mistaken; but, in any case, the conclusion that plants have rights or morally relevant interests is surely untenable. We do speak of what is "good for" plants, and they can "thrive" and also be "killed." But this does not imply that they have "interests" in any morally relevant sense. Some people apparently believe that plants grow better if we talk to them, but the idea that the plants suffer and enjoy, desire and dislike, etc., is clearly outside the range of both common sense and scientific belief. The notion that the forests should be preserved to avoid *hurting* the trees or because they have a *right* to life is not part of a widely shared moral consciousness, and for good reason.[3]

Another way of trying to explain our moral discomfort is to appeal to certain religious beliefs. If one believes that all living things were created by a God who cares for them and entrusted us with the use of plants and animals only for limited purposes, then one has a reason to avoid careless destruction of the

PLANTS HAVE A SAY?

IF GOD GAVE US THE EARTH. WHY NOT PROTECT IT.

forests, etc., quite aside from their future utility. Again, if one believes that a divine force is immanent in all nature, then too one might have reason to care for more than sentient things. But such arguments require strong and controversial premises, and, I suspect, they will always have a restricted audience.

Early in this century, due largely to the influence of G. E. Moore, another point of view developed which some may find promising.[4] Moore introduced, or at least made popular, the idea that certain states of affairs are intrinsically valuable—not just valued, but valuable, and not necessarily because of their effects on sentient beings. Admittedly Moore came to believe that in fact the only intrinsically valuable things were conscious experiences of various sorts,[5] but this restriction was not inherent in the idea of intrinsic value. The intrinsic goodness of something, he thought, was an objective, nonrelational property of the thing, like its texture or color, but not a property perceivable by sense perception or detectable by scientific instruments. In theory at least, a single tree thriving alone in a universe without sentient beings, and even without God, could be intrinsically valuable. Since, according to Moore, our duty is to maximize intrinsic value, his theory could obviously be used to argue that we have reason not to destroy natural environments independently of how they affect human beings and animals. The survival of a forest might have worth beyond its worth *to* sentient beings.

This approach, like the religious one, may appeal to some but is infested with problems. There are, first, the familiar objections to intuitionism, on which the theory depends. Metaphysical and epistemological doubts about nonnatural, intuited properties are hard to suppress, and many have argued that the theory rests on a misunderstanding of the words *good, valuable*, and the like.[6] Second, even if we try to set aside these objections and think in Moore's terms, it is far from obvious that everyone would agree that the existence of forests, etc., is intrinsically valuable. The test, says Moore, is what we would say when we imagine a universe with just the thing in question, without any effects or accompaniments, and then we ask, "Would its existence be better than its nonexistence?" Be careful, Moore would remind us, not to construe this

question as, "Would you *prefer* the existence of that universe to its nonexistence?" The question is, "Would its existence have the objective, nonrelational property, intrinsic goodness?" *DON'T UNDERSTAND?*

Now even among those who have no worries about whether this really makes sense, we might well get a diversity of answers. Those prone to destroy natural environments will doubtless give one answer, and nature lovers will likely give another. When an issue is as controversial as the one at hand, intuition is a poor arbiter.

The problem, then, is this. We want to understand what underlies our moral uneasiness at the destruction of the redwoods, forests, etc., even apart from the loss of these as resources for human beings and animals. But I find no adequate answer by pursuing the questions, "Are rights or interests of plants neglected?" "What is God's will on the matter?" and "What is the intrinsic value of the existence of a tree or forest?" My suggestion, which is in fact the main point of this paper, is that we look at the problem from a different perspective. That is, let us turn for a while from the effort to find reasons why certain acts destructive of natural environments are morally wrong to the ancient task of articulating our ideals of human excellence. Rather than argue directly with destroyers of the environment who say, "Show me why what I am doing is *immoral*," I want to ask, "What sort of person would want to do what they propose?" The point is not to skirt the issue with an *ad hominem*, but to raise a different moral question, for even if there is no convincing way to show that the destructive acts are wrong (independently of human and animal use and enjoyment), we may find that the willingness to indulge in them reflects the absence of human traits that we admire and regard morally important.

This strategy of shifting questions may seem more promising if one reflects on certain analogous situations. Consider, for example, the Nazi who asks, in all seriousness, "Why is it wrong for me to make lampshades out of human skin—provided, of course, I did not myself kill the victims to get the skins?" We would react more with shock and disgust than with indignation, I suspect, because it is even more evident that the question reveals a defect in the questioner than that the proposed act is itself immoral. Sometimes we may not regard an act wrong at all though we see it as reflecting something objectionable about the person who does it. Imagine, for example, one who laughs spontaneously to himself when he reads a newspaper account of a plane crash that kills hundreds. Or, again, consider an obsequious grandson who, having waited for his grandmother's inheritance with mock devotion, then secretly spits on her grave when at last she dies. Spitting on the grave may have no adverse consequences and perhaps it violates no rights. The moral uneasiness which it arouses is explained more by our view of the agent than by any conviction that what he did was immoral. Had he hesitated and asked, "Why shouldn't I spit on her grave?" it seems more fitting to ask him to reflect on the sort of person he is than to try to offer reasons why he should refrain from spitting.

is the author trying to say basically we should think before we do??

III

What sort of person, then, would cover his garden with asphalt, strip mine a wooded mountain, or level an irreplaceable redwood grove? Two sorts of answers, though initially appealing, must be ruled out. The first is that persons who would destroy the environment in these ways are either shortsighted, underestimating the harm they do, or else are too little concerned for the well-being of other people. Perhaps too they have insufficient regard for animal life. But these considerations have been set aside in order to refine the controversy. Another tempting response might be that we count it a moral virtue, or at least a human ideal, to love nature. Those who value the environment only for its utility must not really love nature and so in this way fall short of an ideal. But such an answer is hardly satisfying in the present context, for what is at issue is *why* we feel moral discomfort at the activities of those who admittedly value nature only for its utility. That it is ideal to care for nonsentient nature beyond its possible use is really just another way of expressing the general point which is under controversy.

What is needed is some way of showing that this ideal is connected with other virtues, or human

excellences, not in question. To do so is difficult and my suggestions, accordingly, will be tentative and subject to qualification. The main idea is that, though indifference to nonsentient nature does not *necessarily* reflect the absence of virtues, it often signals the absence of certain traits which we want to encourage because they are, in most cases, a natural basis for the development of certain virtues. It is often thought, for example, that those who would destroy the natural environment must lack a proper appreciation of their place in the natural order, and so must either be ignorant or have too little humility. Though I would argue that this is not necessarily so, I suggest that, given certain plausible empirical assumptions, their attitude may well be rooted in ignorance, a narrow perspective, inability to see things as important apart from themselves and the limited groups they associate with, or reluctance to accept themselves as natural beings. Overcoming these deficiencies will not guarantee a proper moral humility, but for most of us it is probably an important psychological preliminary. Later I suggest, more briefly, that indifference to nonsentient nature typically reveals absence of either aesthetic sensibility or a disposition to cherish what has enriched one's life and that these, though not themselves moral virtues, are a natural basis for appreciation of the good in others and gratitude.[7]

Consider first the suggestion that destroyers of the environment lack an appreciation of their place in the universe.[8] Their attention, it seems, must be focused on parochial matters, on what is, relatively speaking, close in space and time. They seem not to understand that we are a speck on the cosmic scene, a brief stage in the evolutionary process, only one among millions of species on Earth, and an episode in the course of human history. Of course, they know that there are stars, fossils, insects, and ancient ruins; but do they have any idea of the complexity of the processes that led to the natural world as we find it? Are they aware how much the forces at work within their own bodies are like those which govern all living things and even how much they have in common with inanimate bodies? Admittedly scientific knowledge is limited and no one can master it all; but could one who had a broad and deep understanding of his place in nature really be indifferent to the destruction of the natural environment?

This first suggestion, however, may well provoke a protest from a sophisticated anti-environmentalist.[9] "Perhaps *some* may be indifferent to nature from ignorance," the critic may object, "but *I* have studied astronomy, geology, biology, and biochemistry, and I still unashamedly regard the nonsentient environment as simply a resource for our use. It should not be wasted, of course, but what should be preserved is decidable by weighing longterm costs and benefits." "Besides," our critic may continue, "as philosophers you should know the old Humean formula, 'You cannot derive an *ought* from an *is.*' All the facts of biology, biochemistry, etc., do not entail that I ought to love nature or want to preserve it. What one understands is one thing; what one values is something else. Just as nature lovers are not necessarily scientists, those indifferent to nature are not necessarily ignorant."

Although the environmentalist may concede the critic's logical point, he may well argue that, as a matter of fact, increased understanding of nature tends to heighten people's concern for its preservation. If so, despite the objection, the suspicion that the destroyers of the environment lack deep understanding of nature is not, in most cases, unwarranted, but the argument need not rest here.

The environmentalist might amplify his original idea as follows: "When I said that the destroyers of nature do not appreciate their place in the universe, I was not speaking of intellectual understanding alone, for, after all, a person can *know* a catalog of facts without ever putting them together and seeing vividly the whole picture which they form. To see oneself as just one part of nature is to look at oneself and the world from a certain perspective which is quite different from being able to recite detailed information from the natural sciences. What the destroyers of nature lack is this perspective, not particular information."

Again our critic may object, though only after making some concessions: "All right," he may say, "*some* who are indifferent to nature may lack the cosmic perspective of which you speak, but again there is no *necessary* connection between this failing, if it is one, and any particular evaluative attitude toward nature. In fact, different people respond

quite differently when they move to a wider perspective. When *I* try to picture myself vividly as a brief, transitory episode in the course of nature, I simply get depressed. Far from inspiring me with a love of nature, the exercise makes me sad and hostile. You romantics think only of poets like Wordsworth and artists like Turner, but you should consider how differently Omar Khayyam responded when he took your wider perspective. His reaction, when looking at his life from a cosmic viewpoint, was "Drink up, for tomorrow we die." Others respond in an almost opposite manner with a joyless Stoic resignation, exemplified by the poet who pictures the wise man, at the height of personal triumph, being served a magnificent banquet, and then consummating his marriage to his beloved, all the while reminding himself, "Even this shall pass away."[10] In sum, the critic may object, "Even if one should try to see oneself as one small transitory part of nature, doing so does not dictate any particular normative attitude. Some may come to love nature, but others are moved to live for the moment; some sink into sad resignation; others get depressed or angry. So indifference to nature is not necessarily a sign that a person fails to look at himself from the larger perspective."

The environmentalist might respond to this objection in several ways. He might, for example, argue that even though some people who see themselves as part of the natural order remain indifferent to nonsentient nature, this is not a common reaction. Typically, it may be argued, as we become more and more aware that we are parts of the larger whole we come to value the whole independently of its effect on ourselves. Thus, despite the possibilities the critic raises, indifference to nonsentient nature is still in most cases a sign that a person fails to see himself as part of the natural order.

If someone challenges the empirical assumption here, the environmentalist might develop the argument along a quite different line. The initial idea, he may remind us, was that those who would destroy the natural environment fail to *appreciate* their place in the natural order. "Appreciating one's place" is not simply an intellectual appreciation. It is also an attitude, reflecting what one values as well as what one knows. When we say, for example, that both the servile and the arrogant person fail to *appreciate* their place in a society of equals, we do not mean simply that they are ignorant of certain empirical facts, but rather that they have certain objectionable attitudes about their importance relative to other people. Similarly, to fail to appreciate one's place in nature is not merely to lack knowledge or breadth of perspective, but to take a certain attitude about what matters. A person who *understands* his place in nature but still views nonsentient nature merely as a resource takes the attitude that nothing is *important* but human beings and animals. Despite first appearances, he is not so much like the pre-Copernican astronomers who made the intellectual error of treating the Earth as the "center of the universe" when they made their calculations. He is more like the racist who, though well aware of other races, treats all races but his own as insignificant. *[handwritten: SO AUTHOR IS COMPARING NON-ENVIRONMENT PEOPLE TO RACIST]*

So construed, the argument appeals to the common idea that awareness of nature typically has, and should have, a humbling effect. The Alps, a storm at sea, the Grand Canyon, towering redwoods, and "the starry heavens above" move many a person to remark on the comparative insignificance of our daily concerns and even of our species, and this is generally taken to be a quite fitting response.[11] What seems to be missing, then, in those who understand nature but remain unmoved is a proper humility.[12] Absence of proper humility is not the same as selfishness or egoism, for one can be devoted to self-interest while still viewing one's own pleasures and projects as trivial and unimportant.[13] And one can have an exaggerated view of one's own importance while grandly sacrificing for those one views as inferior. Nor is the lack of humility identical with belief that one has power and influence, for a person can be quite puffed up about himself while believing that the foolish world will never acknowledge him. The humility we miss seems not so much a belief about one's relative effectiveness and recognition as an attitude which measures the importance of things independently of their relation to oneself or to some narrow group with which one identifies. A paradigm of a person who lacks humility is the self-important emperor who grants status to his family because it is *his*, to his subordinates because *he* appointed them,

and to his country because *he* chooses to glorify it. Less extreme but still lacking proper humility is the elitist who counts events significant solely in proportion to how they affect his class. The suspicion about those who would destroy the environment, then, is that what they count important is too narrowly confined insofar as it encompasses only what affects beings who, like us, are capable of feeling.

This idea that proper humility requires recognition of the importance of nonsentient nature is similar to the thought of those who charge meat eaters with "species-ism." In both cases it is felt that people too narrowly confine their concerns to the sorts of beings that are most like them. But, however intuitively appealing, the idea will surely arouse objections from our nonenvironmentalist critic. "Why," he will ask, "do you suppose that the sort of humility I *should* have requires me to acknowledge the importance of nonsentient nature aside from its utility? You cannot, by your own admission, argue that nonsentient nature *is* important, appealing to religious or intuitionist grounds. And simply to assert, without further argument, that an ideal humility requires us to view nonsentient nature as important for its own sake begs the question at issue. If proper humility is acknowledging the relative importance of things as one should, then to show that I must lack this you must first establish that one *should* acknowledge the importance of nonsentient nature."

Though some may wish to accept this challenge, there are other ways to pursue the connection between humility and response to nonsentient nature. For example, suppose we grant that proper humility requires only acknowledging a due status to sentient beings. We must admit, then, that it is logically possible for a person to be properly humble even though he viewed all nonsentient nature simply as a resource. But this logical possibility may be a psychological rarity. It may be that, given the sort of beings we are, we would never learn humility before persons without developing the general capacity to cherish, and regard important, many things for their own sakes. The major obstacle to humility before persons is self-importance, a tendency to measure the significance of everything by its relation to oneself and those with whom one identifies. The processes by which we overcome self-importance

[handwritten at bottom: GET OVER OURSELVES. NATURE IS ABOUT US. NOT FOR.]

are doubtless many and complex, but it seems unlikely that they are exclusively concerned with how we relate to other people and animals. Learning humility requires learning to feel that something matters besides what will affect oneself and one's circle of associates. What leads a child to care about what happens to a lost hamster or a stray dog he will not see again is likely also to generate concern for a lost toy or a favorite tree where he used to live.[14] Learning to value things for their own sake, and to count what affects them important aside from their utility, is not the same as judging them to have some intuited objective property, but it is necessary to the development of humility and it seems likely to take place in experiences with nonsentient nature as well as with people and animals. If a person views all nonsentient nature merely as a resource, then it seems unlikely that he has developed the capacity needed to overcome self-importance.

Building on the idea of ego, selfishness.

IV

This last argument, unfortunately, has its limits. It presupposes an empirical connection between experiencing nature and overcoming self-importance, and this may be challenged. Even if experiencing nature promotes humility before others, there may be other ways people can develop such humility in a world of concrete, glass, and plastic. If not, perhaps all that is needed is limited experience of nature in one's early, developing years; mature adults, having overcome youthful self-importance, may live well enough in artificial surroundings. More importantly, the argument does not fully capture the spirit of the intuition that an ideal person stands humbly before nature. That idea is not simply that experiencing nature tends to foster proper humility before other people; it is, in part, that natural surroundings encourage and are appropriate to an ideal sense of oneself as part of the natural world. Standing alone in the forest, after months in the city, is not merely good as a means of curbing one's arrogance before others; it reinforces and fittingly expresses one's acceptance of oneself as a natural being.

Previously we considered only one aspect of proper humility, namely, a sense of one's relative importance with respect to other human beings. Another aspect, I think, is a kind of *self-acceptance*. This involves

acknowledging, in more than a merely intellectual way, that we are the sort of creatures that we are. Whether one is self-accepting is not so much a matter of how one attributes *importance* comparatively to oneself, other people, animals, plants, and other things as it is a matter of understanding, facing squarely, and responding appropriately to who and what one is, e.g., one's powers and limits, one's affinities with other beings and differences from them, one's unalterable nature and one's freedom to change. Self-acceptance is not merely intellectual awareness, for one can be intellectually aware that one is growing old and will eventually die while nevertheless behaving in a thousand foolish ways that reflect a refusal to acknowledge these facts. On the other hand, self-acceptance is not passive resignation, for refusal to pursue what one truly wants within one's limits is a failure to accept the freedom and power one has. Particular behaviors, like dying one's gray hair and dressing like those twenty years younger, do not *necessarily* imply lack of self-acceptance, for there could be reasons for acting in these ways other than the wish to hide from oneself what one really is. One fails to accept oneself when the patterns of behavior and emotion are rooted in a desire to disown and deny features of oneself, to pretend to oneself that they are not there. This is not to say that a self-accepting person makes no value judgments about himself, that he likes all facts about himself, wants equally to develop and display them; he can, and should feel remorse for his past misdeeds and strive to change his current vices. The point is that he does not disown them, pretend that they do not exist or are facts about something other than himself. Such pretense is incompatible with proper humility because it is seeing oneself as better than one is.

Self-acceptance of this sort has long been considered a human excellence, under various names, but what has it to do with preserving nature? There is, I think, the following connection. As human beings we are part of nature, living, growing, declining, and dying by natural laws similar to those governing other living beings; despite our awesomely distinctive human powers, we share many of the needs, limits, and liabilities of animals and plants. These facts are neither good nor bad in themselves, aside from personal preference and varying conventional values. To say this is

→ We are similar to nature despite being apart from it.

to utter a truism which few will deny, but to accept these facts, as facts about oneself, is not so easy—or so common. Much of what naturalists deplore about our increasingly artificial world reflects, and encourages, a denial of these facts, an unwillingness to avow them with equanimity.

Like the Victorian lady who refuses to look at her own nude body, some would like to create a world of less transitory stuff, reminding us only of our intellectual and social nature, never calling to mind our affinities with "lower" living creatures. The "denial of death," to which psychiatrists call attention,[15] reveals an attitude incompatible with the sort of self-acceptance which philosophers, from the ancients to Spinoza and on, have admired as a human excellence. My suggestion is not merely that experiencing nature causally promotes such self-acceptance, but also that those who fully accept themselves as part of the natural world lack the common drive to disassociate themselves from nature by replacing natural environments with artificial ones. A storm in the wilds helps us to appreciate our animal vulnerability, but, equally important, the reluctance to experience it may *reflect* an unwillingness to accept this aspect of ourselves. The person who is too ready to destroy the ancient redwoods may lack humility, not so much in the sense that he exaggerates his importance relative to others, but rather in the sense that he tries to avoid seeing himself as one among many natural creatures.

V

My suggestion so far has been that, though indifference to nonsentient nature is not itself a moral vice, it is likely to reflect either ignorance, a self-importance, or a lack of self-acceptance which we must overcome to have proper humility. A similar idea might be developed connecting attitudes toward nonsentient nature with other human excellences. For example, one might argue that indifference to nature reveals a lack of either an aesthetic sense or some of the natural roots of gratitude.

When we see a hillside that has been gutted by strip miners or the garden replaced by asphalt, our first reaction is probably, "How ugly!" The scenes assault our aesthetic sensibilities. We suspect that no one with a keen sense of beauty could have left such a sight. Admittedly not everything in nature strikes us as

beautiful, or even aesthetically interesting, and sometimes a natural scene is replaced with a more impressive architectural masterpiece. But this is not usually the situation in the problem cases which environmentalists are most concerned about. More often beauty is replaced with ugliness.

At this point our critic may well object that, even if he does lack a sense of beauty, this is no moral vice. His cost/benefit calculations take into account the pleasure others may derive from seeing the forests, etc., and so why should he be faulted?

Some might reply that, despite contrary philosophical traditions, aesthetics and morality are not so distinct as commonly supposed. Appreciation of beauty, they may argue, is a human excellence which morally ideal persons should try to develop. But, setting aside this controversial position, there still may be cause for moral concern about those who have no aesthetic response to nature. Even if aesthetic sensibility is not itself a moral virtue, many of the capacities of mind and heart which it presupposes may be ones which are also needed for an appreciation of other people. Consider, for example, curiosity, a mind open to novelty, the ability to look at things from unfamiliar perspectives, empathetic imagination, interest in details, variety, and order, and emotional freedom from the immediate and the practical. All these, and more, seem necessary to aesthetic sensibility, but they are also traits which a person needs to be fully sensitive to people of all sorts. The point is not that a moral person must be able to distinguish beautiful from ugly people; the point is rather that unresponsiveness to what is beautiful, awesome, dainty, dumpy, and otherwise aesthetically interesting in nature probably reflects a lack of the openness of mind and spirit necessary to appreciate the best in human beings.

The anti-environmentalist, however, may refuse to accept the charge that he lacks aesthetic sensibility. If he claims to appreciate seventeenth-century miniature portraits, but to abhor natural wildernesses, he will hardly be convincing. Tastes vary, but aesthetic sense is not *that* selective. He may, instead, insist that he *does* appreciate natural beauty. He spends his vacations, let us suppose, hiking in the Sierras, photographing wildflowers, and so on. He might press his argument as follows: "I enjoy natural beauty as much as anyone, but I fail to see what this has to do with preserving the environment independently of human enjoyment and use. Nonsentient nature is a resource, but one of its best uses is to give us pleasure. I take this into account when I calculate the costs and benefits of preserving a park, planting a garden, and so on. But the problem you raised explicitly set aside the desire to preserve nature as a means to enjoyment. I say, let us enjoy nature fully while we can, but if all sentient beings were to die tomorrow, we might as well blow up all plant life as well. A redwood grove that no one can use or enjoy is utterly worthless."

The attitude expressed here, I suspect, is not a common one, but it represents a philosophical challenge. The beginnings of a reply may be found in the following. When a person takes joy in something, it is a common (and perhaps natural) response to come to cherish it. To cherish something is not simply to be happy with it at the moment, but to care for it for its own sake. This is not to say that one necessarily sees it as having feelings and so wants it to feel good; nor does it imply that one judges the thing to have Moore's intrinsic value. One simply wants the thing to survive and (when appropriate) to thrive, and not simply for its utility. We see this attitude repeatedly regarding mementos. They are not simply valued as a means to remind us of happy occasions; they come to be valued for their own sake. Thus, if someone really took joy in the natural environment, but was prepared to blow it up as soon as sentient life ended, he would lack this common human tendency to cherish what enriches our lives. While this response is not itself a moral virtue, it may be a natural basis of the virtue we call "gratitude." People who have no tendency to cherish things that give them pleasure may be poorly disposed to respond gratefully to persons who are good to them. Again the connection is not one of logical necessity, but it may nevertheless be important. A nonreligious person unable to "thank" anyone for the beauties of nature may nevertheless feel "grateful" in a sense; and I suspect that the person who feels no such "gratitude" toward nature is unlikely to show proper gratitude toward people.

Suppose these conjectures prove to be true. One may wonder what is the point of considering them. Is it to disparage all those who view nature merely as a resource? To do so, it seems, would be unfair, for, even if this attitude typically stems from deficiencies which affect one's attitudes toward sentient beings, there may be exceptions and we have not shown that their view of nonsentient nature is itself blameworthy. But when we set aside questions of blame and inquire what sorts of human traits we want to encourage, our reflections become relevant in a more positive way. The point is not to insinuate that all anti-environmentalists are defective, but to see that those who value such traits as humility, gratitude, and sensitivity to others have reason to promote the love of nature.

NOTES

1. When I use the expression "the natural environment," I have in mind the sort of examples with which I began. For some purposes it is important to distinguish cultivated gardens from forests, virgin forests from replenished ones, irreplaceable natural phenomena from the replaceable, and so on; but these distinctions, I think, do not affect my main points here. There is also a broad sense, as Hume and Mill noted, in which all that occurs, miracles aside, is "natural." In this sense, of course, strip mining is as natural as a beaver cutting trees for his dam, and, as parts of nature, we cannot destroy the "natural" environment but only alter it. As will be evident, I shall use *natural* in a narrower, more familiar sense.

2. This paper is intended as a preliminary discussion in *normative* ethical theory (as opposed to *metaethics*). The task, accordingly, is the limited, though still difficult, one of articulating the possible basis in our beliefs and values for certain particular moral judgments. Questions of ultimate justification are set aside. What makes the task difficult and challenging is not that conclusive proofs from the foundation of morality are attempted; it is rather that the particular judgments to be explained seem at first not to fall under the most familiar moral principles (e.g., utilitarianism, respect for rights).

3. I assume here that having a right presupposes having interests in a sense which in turn presupposes a capacity to desire, suffer, etc. Since my main concern lies in another direction, I do not argue the point,

but merely note that some regard it as debatable. See, for example, W. Murray Hunt, "Are *Mere Things* Morally Considerable?" *Environmental Ethics* 2 (1980): 59–65; Kenneth E. Goodpaster, "On Stopping at Everything," *Environmental Ethics* 2 (1980): 288–294; Joel Feinberg, "The Rights of Animals and Unborn Generations," in William Blackstone, ed., *Philosophy and Environmental Crisis* (Athens: University of Georgia Press, 1974), pp. 43–68; Tom Regan, "Feinberg on What Sorts of Beings Can Have Rights," *Southern Journal of Philosophy* (1976): 485–498; Robert Elliot, "Regan on the Sort of Beings That Can Have Rights," *Southern Journal of Philosophy* (1978): 701–705; Scott Lehmann, "Do Wildernesses Have Rights?" *Environmental Ethics* 2 (1981): 129–146.

4. G. E. Moore, *Principia Ethica* (Cambridge: Cambridge University Press, 1903); *Ethics* (London: H. Holt, 1912).

5. G. E. Moore, "Is Goodness a Quality?" *Philosophical Papers* (London: George Allen and Unwin, 1959), pp. 95–97.

6. See, for example, P. H. Nowell-Smith, *Ethics* (New York: Penguin, 1954).

7. The issues I raise here, though perhaps not the details of my remarks, are in line with Aristotle's view of moral philosophy, a view revitalized recently by Philippa Foot's *Virtue and Vice* (Berkeley: University of California Press, 1979), Alasdair McIntyre's *After Virtue* (Notre Dame: Notre Dame Press, 1981), and James Wallace's *Virtues and Vices* (Ithaca and London: Cornell University Press, 1978), and other works.

8. Though for simplicity I focus upon those who do strip mining, etc., the argument is also applicable to those whose utilitarian calculations lead them to preserve the redwoods, mountains, etc., but who care for only sentient nature for its own sake. Similarly the phrase "indifferent to nature" is meant to encompass those who are indifferent *except* when considering its benefits to people and animals.

9. For convenience I use the labels *environmentalist* and *anti-environmentalist* (or *critic*) for the opposing sides in the rather special controversy I have raised. Thus, for example, my "environmentalist" not only favors conserving the forests, etc., but finds something objectionable in wanting to destroy them even aside from the costs to human beings and animals. My "anti-environmentalist" is not simply one who wants to destroy the environment; he is a person who has no qualms about doing so independent of the adverse effects on human beings and animals.

10. "Even this shall pass away," by Theodore Tildon, in *The Best Loved Poems of the American People*, ed. Hazel Felleman (Garden City, N.Y.: Doubleday, 1936).

11. An exception, apparently, was Kant, who thought "the starry heavens" sublime and compared them with "the moral law within," but did not for all that see our species as comparatively insignificant.

12. By "*proper* humility" I mean that sort and degree of humility that is a morally admirable character trait. How precisely to define this is, of course, a controversial matter; but the point for present purposes is just to set aside obsequiousness, false modesty, underestimation of one's abilities, and the like.

13. I take this point from some of Philippa Foot's remarks.

14. The causal history of this concern may well depend upon the object (tree, toy) having given the child pleasure, but this does not mean that the object is then valued only for further pleasure it may bring.

15. See, for example, Ernest Becker, *The Denial of Death* (New York: Free Press, 1973).

PHILIP CAFARO

THOREAU, LEOPOLD, AND CARSON
Toward an Environmental Virtue Ethics

I. ENVIRONMENTAL VIRTUE ETHICS

Over the past twenty-five years, much scholarship in environmental ethics has focused on the intrinsic value or moral considerability of nonhuman nature. This valuable work has clearly formulated many environmentalists' intuitions that the destruction, overuse, or excessive appropriation of nature is morally wrong. It has given us plausible reasons for extending moral considerability beyond our own species, and limiting our conduct accordingly.

In contrast, little has been written in environmental ethics from a virtue ethics perspective which focuses on human excellence and flourishing. While individual authors such as Arne Naess and Erazim Kohak have discussed the joy and fulfillment to be found in a more environmentally conscious life, this theme has not been central within academic environmental ethics.[1] However, recent years have seen increased interest in developing an environmental virtue ethics, one which incorporates a respect for nature, conceives "human interests" broadly, and presents environmental protection as protection as being in our *enlightened* self-interest.[2] I believe that further development of such an environmental virtue ethics is timely and useful for two main reasons.

First, in the absence of an environmental virtue ethics, environmental ethics itself is incomplete and unbalanced. Recent virtue ethics proponents have made the (general) case forcefully.[3] An ethics which concentrates exclusively on rights and responsibilities, and judges our actions solely on whether they violate or uphold moral duty, ignores further, crucial ethical questions: what is the best life for a person and how can I go about living it? What is a good society and how can we move closer to achieving it? These questions are just as important within environmental ethics

as within ethics generally, because actions which affect the environment rebound and affect us, opening up or closing off possibilities. Our environmental decisions make us better or worse people and create better or worse societies: healthier or sicker, richer or poorer, more knowledgeable or more ignorant. Any complete valuation of our actions and lives must include a virtue ethics component, and any complete environmental ethics must include an environmental virtue ethics.

Second, there is a practical need to develop positive arguments for environmental protection. Often, the general public views environmentalists as killjoys, willing to countenance any trade-offs of human freedom or happiness in pursuit of their aims.[4] Partly this view is unavoidable. In defending wild nature and asserting its intrinsic value, environmentalists are necessarily proscriptive. Yet the writings of the great naturalists, and our own experiences, tell a story of joyful interrelation with nature. Just as classical virtue ethics provided strong self-interested reasons for treating others with respect—reasons based on a person's concern for his own virtue and flourishing—so an environmental virtue ethics can provide strong grounds for environmental protection. Above all, it can move us beyond our initial ethical response to environmental destruction—contrite self-abnegation—and toward a more positive, sustainable position of respectful dwelling in nature.[5]

II. THOREAU, LEOPOLD AND CARSON

While professional philosophers have largely neglected the subject, some of our greatest environmental writers can plausibly be seen as environmental virtue ethicists. In this section, I briefly discuss three: Henry David Thoreau, Aldo Leopold, and Rachel Carson.

"I went to the woods because I wished to live deliberately," Thoreau writes in a central passage in *Walden*:

Philip Cafaro. "Thoreau, Leopold, and Carson: Toward an Environmental Virtue Ethic," Environmental Ethics 23, no. 1 (2001): 3–17.

. . . to front only the essential facts of life, and see if I could not learn what it had to teach, and not, when I came to die, discover that I had not lived. . . . I wanted to live deep and suck all the marrow out of life . . . to know it by experience, and to be able to give a true account of it in my next excursion.[6]

Walden describes a life of personal development and enriched experience, centered on the pursuit of knowledge of self and nature. It advocates ethical, intellectual and creative striving. Thoreau alternately harangues his readers for their inertia and failure to demand more from life, and entices them onward with fair possibilities, noble ideals, and accounts of his own successes: Thoreau snug and secure in his well-built cabin, facing winter's blasts; Thoreau floating on the calm summer waters of Walden Pond, fishing pole in hand, a symbol of personal equilibrium and harmony with his surroundings. Interestingly, Thoreau uses the terms *flourishing*, *living well*, and *chief end* to describe his overall goal: words and phrases employed by recent scholars to translate and resurrect the proper ancient Greek understanding of *eudaimonia*, in place of our more subjective and trivial "happiness."[7]

Taking *Walden* as a whole, a clear picture of Thoreau's view of the good life emerges, which includes health, freedom, pleasure, friendship, a rich experience, knowledge (of self, nature, God), self-culture, and personal achievement.[8] He specifies his pursuit of these "goods" in detail, often in terms of his relationship to nature. Freedom, for Thoreau, includes not just the absence of physical coercion, but also having the time to explore his surroundings and the privilege to saunter through the local landscape without being arrested for trespassing. Perhaps some readers will define freedom similarly! He finds great physical pleasure and sensual stimulation in living and working in the woods, comparing his life favorably to the indoor lives of so many of his contemporaries; poor factory girls driven by necessity, but also wealthy Concord burghers who are free to live otherwise. Dwelling solitary and apart from people awakened him to possibilities for friendship and connection to the rest of nature, he reports. Thoreau makes it clear that he is not setting up rules that all must follow. But his experiment by the pond suggests possibilities for living well in nature, for those inclined to make the attempt.

It also suggests what we may give up in living a more urbanized existence.

Thoreau tries, in *Walden*, to recover the ancient sense of virtue as personal excellence, asserting that nowadays, "philanthropy is almost the only virtue which is sufficiently appreciated by mankind. Nay, it is greatly overrated."[9] His catalogue of virtues includes moral virtues such as sympathy, honesty, justice, and generosity, but also intellectual virtues such as curiosity, imagination, intelligence, and alertness, and even physical virtues such as health, beauty, and hardiness. Thoreauvian virtues crucial for the construction of an environmental virtue ethics include temperance, integrity, sensibility to beauty and, perhaps most important, simplicity.

Thoreau's "simplicity" is not simplicity of thought or experience, which he seeks to complicate and enrich. It is rather a limited use of external goods, combined with a focus on the task at hand. Simplicity, to borrow a concept from ecology, is a "keystone" virtue for Thoreau. It plays an important role in stabilizing and focusing our lives, and allows the development of a rich character manifesting diverse virtues. In a complicated world, such simplicity allows us to understand the effects of our actions and act with integrity.[10] Simplicity is also one key to freedom, for if we live simply, we need not trade most of our time to an employer, and can spend it as we wish.[11] Simplicity will be an important virtue for any environmental virtue ethics, for the obvious reason that living simply decreases our impact on other living things; but Thoreau, along with many environmentalists, also claims that living simply will improve our own lives.

Aldo Leopold can also be interpreted as an environmental virtue ethicist, as Bill Shaw recently argued . . . .[12] While Leopold's classic essay "The Land Ethic" makes a moving plea for moral extensionism and human self-restraint, he devotes much of *A Sand County Almanac* to showing the opportunities for knowledge and self-development made possible by a greater attentiveness to nature. "We abuse land because we regard it as a commodity belonging to us," he writes in the [foreword].

> When we see land as a community to which we belong, we may begin to use it with love and respect. There is no other way for land to survive the impact of mechanized man, *nor for us to reap from it the esthetic harvest it is capable, under science, of contributing to culture.*[13]

Along with classical extensionism, then, Leopold describes a parallel aesthetic and intellectual extensionism, in which "our ability to perceive quality in nature begins . . . with the pretty, [and] expands through the successive stages of the beautiful to ["higher"] values as yet uncaptured by language."[14] Capturing such values improves our lives. "To promote perception is the only truly creative part" of recreation management, he writes further on. "This fact is important, and its potential power for bettering "the good life' only dimly understood."[15] Here, and elsewhere, Leopold puts "the good life" in ironic quotation marks, suggesting that the *truly* good life is not defined solely or even mainly in material terms.

Leopold might appear to undermine this interpretation, when he writes of a "formula" for conservation which is "too easy to accomplish anything worthwhile," continuing:

> It defines no right or wrong, assigns no obligation, calls for no sacrifice, implies no change in the current philosophy of values. In respect of land-use, it urges only enlightened self-interest.[16]

Here Leopold accepts the modern dichotomy of altruistic moral action, as defined by moral philosophy, versus selfish, hedonistic action, as dealt with by the economists. This acceptance clarifies his moral extensionism but obscures his environmental virtue ethics. In fact, *A Sand County Almanac* explicitly and repeatedly asks us to recognize our "enlightened self-interest," contrasting it with a benighted, economistic and *mistaken* definition of self-interest.[17]

Wealthy Americans have reached the point, Leopold believes, where they cannot better their lives through increased wealth or possessions. Instead, building on a foundation of material sufficiency, they should strive to live lives that are rich in perception and knowledge of their surroundings. Along these lines Leopold makes a pioneering plea for a more environmentally informed understanding of human history. He praises and—more importantly—demonstrates an aesthetic appreciation of plants, animals, and places.[18] Reading the many dramas written in the animal tracks on his farm, or wading half a day in a marsh for a closer view of a family of grebes, he exhibits the peculiar virtues of the naturalist: patience, eagerness, physical endurance,

persistence, a keen perception, skill in making fine distinctions, precise description. Such activities make us happier and better people, he suggests.[19] They allow us to pursue knowledge and enrich our experience, without diminishing nature. Leopold asks us to conceive our own flourishing in ways which sustain—indeed, depend on—the flourishing of the natural communities of which we are part.

Reading *A Sand County Almanac*, it is striking how often Leopold praises the virtues of the nonhuman world: the "grace" of a plover, the "valor" of a chickadee, the "accumulated wisdom" of a stand of pine trees—a natural wisdom which silences the people who walk below—the "harmony" of a river ecosystem.[20] These expressions are more than metaphors. Human and nonhuman beings may share some virtues because we are in some respects similar. "How like fish we are," Leopold muses, in an interval between casts:

> . . . ready, nay eager, to seize upon whatever new thing some wind of circumstance shakes down upon the river of time! And how we rue our haste, finding the gilded morsel to contain a hook. Even so, I think, there is some virtue in eagerness, whether its object prove true or false. How utterly dull would be a wholly prudent man, or trout, or world![21]

Henry David Thoreau, fellow angler, concurs, adding that other species may exhibit virtues quite different from the human, which are no less genuine for all that:

> Away with the superficial and selfish phil-*anthropy* of men,—who knows what admirable virtue of fishes may be below low-water mark, bearing up against a hard destiny, not admired by that fellow creature who alone can appreciate it![22]

Environmental ethics here takes us back to philosophy's prehistory, beyond the reach of the army of philosophers who, from Aristotle onward, have patiently explained that only human beings have virtue—back to Homer, who could speak of the *arête* of a horse and have all Greece understand him.[23] This naturalizing of virtue is no mere literary conceit, but the very foundation of Leopold's land ethic. "A thing is right when it tends to preserve the integrity, stability, and beauty of the biotic community," he writes. "It is wrong when it tends otherwise."[24] Leopold identifies these three qualities as key virtues of natural and mixed human/natural communities; in a sense, they are "super-virtues," which promote the continuous generation of virtue in individual species and organisms, including us. Recognizing nature's excellence and ability to generate excellence gives us strong reasons to preserve it, for nature's sake and for our own.

Rachel Carson has been called the founder of the modern environmental movement, which some date, plausibly, to the publication of *Silent Spring* in 1962. *Silent Spring*'s case rests above all on numerous factual and scientific accounts of the use and abuse of agricultural and industrial chemicals. Ethically, its plea for restraint rests on the triple foundation of human health considerations, the moral considerability of nonhuman beings, and the value to humans of preserving wild nature.

Doubtless, more important for many readers were Carson's chapters on acute pesticide poisonings and these chemicals' potential to cause cancer and human birth defects. For these readers, Carson states the moral clearly: "Man, however much he may like to pretend the contrary, is part of nature. [He cannot] escape a pollution that is now so thoroughly distributed throughout the world."[25] Carson herself seems to have been equally if not more concerned with the destruction of wild nature and its resultant human loss. "I wrote [*Silent Spring*]," Carson told *Life* magazine, "because I think there is a great danger that the next generation will have no chance to know nature as we do."[26] As she finished *Silent Spring*, she was planning her next book, a guide to nature for parents and children, tentatively titled *Help Your Child to Wonder*.

Silent Spring clearly shows Rachel Carson's concern for all of life, human and nonhuman. Many of its arguments explicitly assert or implicitly rely on the moral considerability of nonhuman organisms:

> These creatures [birds, rabbits, domestic pets] are innocent of any harm to man. Indeed, by their very existence they and their fellows make his life more pleasant. Yet he rewards them with a death that is not only sudden but horrible.
>
> These insects [honeybees, wild bees and other pollinators], so essential to our agriculture and indeed to our landscape as we know it, *deserve something better from us* than the senseless destruction of their habitat.[27]

Silent Spring also expresses Carson's belief that preserving wild nature helps promote human happiness and flourishing. She approvingly quotes Paul Shepard and William O. Douglas on the aesthetic value and intellectual stimulation provided by wildlife and wild places, and adds her own arguments:

> To the bird watcher, the suburbanite who derives joy from birds in his garden, the hunter, the fisherman or the explorer of wild regions, anything that destroys the wildlife of an area for even a single year has deprived him of pleasure to which he has a legitimate right.
>
> Over increasingly large areas of the United States, spring now comes unheralded by the return of the birds, and the early mornings are strangely silent where once they were filled with the beauty of bird song . . . Can anyone imagine anything so cheerless and dreary as a springtime without a robin's song?
>
> Who has decided—who has the *right* to decide—for the countless legions of people who were not consulted that the supreme value is a world without insects, even though it be also a sterile world ungraced by the curving wing of a bird in flight. The decision is that of the authoritarian temporarily entrusted with power; he has made it during a moment of inattention by millions to whom beauty and the ordered world of nature still have a meaning that is deep and imperative.[28]

Before we can appreciate such ethical arguments, however, we must appreciate wild nature, and we cannot appreciate what we have not seen, experienced, or at least imagined. Carson's bestselling natural history writings—she once had two books on the *New York Times* best-seller list at the same time—took readers to places wilder and harder to imagine than any visited by Thoreau or Leopold: arctic tundra in the grip of winter; the weird, dark depths of the ocean; microscopic planktonic worlds. Just as surely, Carson uncovered the many details of nature close to hand: the fishing techniques of herons and skimmers; the fine structures and hidden beauties of jellyfish. Moreover, she was a great explainer of relationships and connections. "It is now clear that in the sea nothing lives to itself, she writes, and what holds true in the sea holds true throughout the biosphere.[29]

This oft-repeated message resounds somewhat ominously in *Silent Spring*, but even here Carson's clear message is that life's complexity and interconnections are cause for appreciation and celebration, if also for restraint. "One might easily suppose," she writes in an earlier book, "that nothing at all lived in or on or under these waters of the sea's edge," but by its end we know differently, and we come to the edge of the sea with new eyes, a better sense of "the spectacle of life in all its varied manifestations," and a desire to learn more.[30] Carson never doubted that increased knowledge was more precious than increased material wealth, or that a more widespread knowledge of nature would motivate people to protect it.[31] Knowledge, for her, was not simply learned, but lived and experienced, engaging and developing the senses and emotions as well as the mind, our imaginations as much as our analytic skills.

Carson saw humility as, perhaps, the cardinal environmental virtue. She concluded in *Silent Spring* that

> The "control of nature" is a phrase conceived in arrogance, born of the Neanderthal age of biology and philosophy, when it was supposed that nature exists for the convenience of man . . . [The] extraordinary capacities of life have been ignored by the practitioners of chemical control who have brought to their task . . . no humility before the vast forces with which they tamper.[32]

Speaking directly to millions of Americans on "CBS Reports" a few months before her death, she repeated the message: "We still talk in terms of conquest. . . . I think we're challenged, as mankind has never been challenged before, to prove our maturity and our mastery, not of nature but of ourselves."[33]

Carson's own genuine humility was not meek quiescence, however. She had a strong sense of her own abilities and responsibilities, shown in all areas of her life: personal, professional, and, when the need arose, political. No one else, she realized, had the combination of literary skill and scientific knowledge to write *Silent Spring*. Her determination to publish her book and defend its conclusions publicly, in the face of declining health and a well-financed, personal smear campaign by the chemical and agribusiness industries, is one of the heroic chapters in conservation history. In her final years as earlier, Carson epitomized the virtues that environmentalists will need in order to fight, and win, future battles: tenacity, intelligence, courage, and a passionate commitment to nature.

3. CONCLUSION

Thoreau, Leopold, and Carson provide inspiring accounts of human beings living well in nature. They suggest to me the rudiments of an environmental virtue ethics which is noble and challenging, and makes room for the rest of creation. To arguments for preserving nature in our own materialistic self-interest, and arguments for preserving nature for its intrinsic value, they add arguments for preserving nature in order to preserve human possibilities and help us become better people. That such arguments may convince and inspire is proven by these authors' enduring popularity and by their roles in shaping modern environmental consciousness.

There remains, of course, much to be said, and even more to be done, in furthering an environmental virtue ethics. Some of the challenges to the creation of an environmental virtue ethics are common to virtue ethics generally: is it possible to specify objective, unchanging standards of human excellence, or is excellence largely a matter of fitting in well to particular, historically contingent situations? Are the virtues unified or sometimes in conflict? Is a single, unitary and objective account of human virtue possible or desirable? Philosophers' faith in reason and our desire for theoretical simplicity lead us to choose the first options noted, but there might be limits to the possibility of finding such all-encompassing answers, and to their value if we did find them.

There are also issues more specific to an environmental virtue ethics. Perhaps the most important is the "artificial alternatives" argument: that when we have specified the good human life, we will find that it can be lived just as well in a largely artificial world: that we do not need wild nature. The answer here, I believe, must build on an appreciation of diversity and of the radical otherness of nonhuman nature; and on defending an account of the good life focusing on developing our higher capabilities, against accounts focused on status-seeking or increased consumption. For such an appreciation and defense, one need not argue the absolute superiority of the wild over the tame, but should rather try to specify an optimal mix of wildness and culture in individuals and landscapes. Given human dominance over so much of the biosphere, such considerations should strongly support the preservation of what wild nature remains, as well as extensive ecological restoration and "rewilding."

These and other complications exist; yet, the need for an environmental virtue ethics remains, for a strong case can be made that greater attention to our true happiness would do as much to protect the environment as the acceptance of the intrinsic value of wild nature for which so many environmental ethicists have argued. Both, if taken to heart, would result in less consumption and a more conscious production, and hence in less environmental damage.

Furthermore, issues of self-interest play an important part in environmental conflicts; if only for this reason, they compel our attention. When the dam builders and the river lovers argue before a town council or national parliament, they often clash over whether a free-flowing river and its wild inhabitants have an intrinsic value which must be respected. But they also clash over what sort of society is better: one with cheaper electricity and more factories, or one where it is still possible to walk along a natural river and see and study its wild inhabitants. Economists rightly point out that decisions concerning use or preservation always involve "opportunity costs." I believe a full *ethical* accounting must also tote up these "costs and benefits." It would be a mistake to dismiss such considerations and arguments as anthropocentric. They are important for the protagonists, and for coming to correct ethical judgments.

NOTES

1. This situation has partly been due to the commendable desire of most environmental ethicists to develop a nonanthropocentric ethical position. Arne Naess, *Ecology, Community and Lifestyle: Outline of an Ecosophy* (Cambridge: Cambridge University Press, 1989); Erazim Kohak, *The Embers and the Stars* (Chicago: University of Chicago Press, 1984).

2. See Bill Shaw, "A Virtue Ethics Approach to Aldo Leopold's Land Ethic," *Environmental Ethics* 19 (1997): 53–67; Thomas Hill Jr., "Ideals of Human Excellence and Preserving Natural Environments," *Environmental Ethics* 5 (1983): 211–24. Recently Louke Van Wensveen published the first book-length study of environmental virtue ethics, her excellent *Dirty Virtues: The Emergence of Ecological*

Virtue Ethics (Amherst, N.Y.: Prometheus Books, 2000).

3. See Alasdair MacIntyre, *After Virtue*, 2d ed. (Notre Dame: University of Notre Dame Press, 1984), pp. 118–19, and papers by Sarah Conly, R.Z. Friedman, and David Norton in Peter French et al., eds., *Ethical Theory: Character and Virtue* (Notre Dame: Notre Dame University Press, 1988).

4. "Without a change in consciousness, the ecological movement is experienced as a never-ending list of reminders: 'shame, you mustn't do that' and 'remember, you're not allowed to . . .'" With a change in mentality we can say 'think how wonderful it will be, if and when. . .,' 'look there! What a pity that we haven't enjoyed that before . . .' If we can clean up a little internally as well as externally, we can hope that *the ecological movement will be more of a renewing and joy-creating movement*" (Naess, *Ecology*, p. 91). I cannot follow Naess in his ultimate synthesis of deontological and eudaimonistic judgments, as self-interest is eclipsed by Self-interest (pp. 8–9). The important point remains that recognition of our enlightened self-interest gives us further incentive to respect wild nature's intrinsic value. This recognition can make doing our duty less onerous. Moreover, Naess is correct that it can help us lead better, more joyful lives.

5. See Kohak, *Embers*, pp. 90–91. This is not to say that self-interested arguments should supplant appeals or to the intrinsic value of wild nature. Rather, they should supplement them. As I see it, deontology and virtue ethics are the two necessary halves of a complete ethics.

6. Henry Thoreau, *Walden* (Princeton: Princeton University Press, 1989), pp. 90–91. For a discussion of Thoreau as a virtue ethicist, see Philip Cafaro, "Thoreau's Virtue Ethics in *Walden*," *The Concord Saunterer* 8 (2000): 23-47.

7. *Living Well*: Thoreau, *Walden*, p. 51, and J.L. Akrill, "Aristotle on Eudaimonia," in Amelie Rorty, ed., *Essays on Aristotle's Ethics* (Berkeley: University of California Press, 1980), p. 17. *Flourishing*: Thoreau, *Walden*, p. 79, and Martha Nussbaum, "Non-Relative Virtues: An Aristotelian Approach," in Martha Nussbaum and Amartya Sen, eds., *The Quality of Life* (Oxford: Oxford University Press,

1993), p. 243. *Chief end*: Thoreau, *Walden*, pp. 9, 90–91, and Julia Annas, *The Morality of Happiness* (Oxford: Oxford University Press, 1993), p. 46.

8. *Health* is often referred to as "hardiness." Thoreau several times speaks of his willingness to sacrifice health for higher goods (Thoreau, *Walden*, pp. 27, 60, 61). *Pleasure* is occasionally mentioned favorably in a fairly direct way, as on p. 240. More often it is assumed to be good, and more specific pleasures are noted. *Rich Experience*: pp. 42, 46, 51, 53, 61, 90. *Self-culture*: pp. 40, 77, 109–10, 328. *Freedom* is used interchangeably with *independence* and is one of Thoreau's most frequently mentioned goods (pp. 7, 8, 12, 15, 33, 37, 45, 56, 60, 63, 70, 84, etc.). *Friendship* receives its fullest discussion in Thoreau's earlier work, *A Week on the Concord and Merrimack Rivers* (Princeton: Princeton University Press, 1980), pp. 259–89. In *Walden* in the chapter entitled "Solitude" Thoreau asserts a certain independence from the need for human friendship, while in "Winter Visitors" he obliquely discusses his friendships with fellow transcendentalists Channing, Alcott and Emerson (Thoreau, *Walden*, pp. 129–39, 267–70). *Knowledge*: pp. 18, 20, 90, 95–97, 100, 321–22, 327, 330–31. *Achievement* in his chosen calling—writing—is referred to obliquely yet stirringly on pp. 16–21, 162.

9. Thoreau, *Walden*, p. 76.

10. Ibid., p. 91.

11. Ibid., pp. 15, 63.

12. Shaw, "A Virtue Ethics Approach to Aldo Leopold's Land Ethic."

13. Aldo Leopold, *A Sand County Almanac with Essays on Conservation from Round River* (New York: Ballantine Books, 1970), pp. xviii–xix (emphasis added).

14. Ibid., p. 102.

15. Ibid., p. 291.

16. Ibid., p. 244.

17. Ibid., pp. xvii, 50, 291.

18. For a detailed argument that aesthetic value can ground the preservation of nature, see Eugene Hargrove, *Foundations of Environmental Ethics* (Englewood Cliffs, N.J.: Prentice Hall, 1989).

19. Although superficially more modest than Thoreau's *Walden*, Leopold's *Almanac* also suggests that its author is a better person than most, due to his knowledge and finer appreciation of the world around him. Leopold whizzing across the former tall-grass prairie on the "Illinois Bus Rid" is the only passenger who knows its natural history or recognizes its remnants. This knowledge makes him better than them. The nice way to put such a point is to say that "you can improve your life through these activities," or, even more nicely, to simply suggest by example that such possibilities are open to the reader. Leopold does the latter. Thoreau takes the more direct route, saying that "a person is a better person if they do *x*, *y*, or *z*, rather than pile up useless possessions," or, even more obnoxiously, "*I* am better than *you*, because I know *x* or do *y*." Nevertheless, the authors imply the same ethical contrast by writing books in which they talk about themselves and their experiences to such a great extent. An environmental virtue ethics, like any virtue ethics, is essentially inegalitarian.

20. Leopold, *Almanac*, pp. 37, 94, 92, 158–59.

21. Ibid., p. 42.

22. Thoreau, *Week*, p. 37 (emphasis in the original). Note the fish puns.

23. Aristotle, *Nicomachean Ethics*, bk. 1, chap. 9. Similarly, perhaps, an environmental virtue ethics counters twenty-five centuries of privileging the mental by re-physicalizing the virtues. "If you have come quietly and humbly, as you should to any spot that can be beautiful only once," Leopold writes, if you "watch closely," "you may surprise a fox-red deer, standing knee-high in the garden of his delight" (Leopold, *Almanac*, pp. 55–56). Quietness and close watching are part of the virtue of humility here, not merely contingent aspects of the experience.

24. Leopold, *Almanac*, p. 262. Just as *nobility* is a key ethical term for Thoreau, so *beauty* is a key ethical term for Leopold. Here they clearly take us back to an ancient conception of ethics.

25. Rachel Carson, *Silent Spring* (New York: Fawcett World Library, 1962), p. 169.

26. Quoted in Linda Lear, *Rachel Carson: Witness for Nature* (New York: Henry Holt, 1997), p. 424.

27. Carson, *Silen Spring*, pp. 95, 73 (emphasis added).

28. Ibid., pp. 84, 97, 107, 118–19. Shepard and Douglas quoted on pp. 22 and 72.
29. Rachel Carson, *The Edge of the Sea* (Boston: Houghton Mifflin, 1955), p. 39.
30. Ibid., pp. 41–15.
31. Carson, *Silent Spring*, p. 118.
32. Ibid., p. 261.

33. Carson on "CBS Reports," 1962. Quoted in Lear, *Rachel Carson*, p. 450. Hill has also suggested that "a proper humility" is an important environmental virtue. Hill likewise broaches the possibility that "aesthetic sensibility" is a virtue, a position which Carson and our other naturalists would certainly endorse. See Hill, "Ideals of Human Excellence," pp. 216, 219, 223.

THOMAS E. HILL JR.

FINDING VALUE IN NATURE

BACKGROUND AND AIM

In an earlier paper, "Ideals of Human Excellence and Preserving Natural Environments," I argued against the assumption that the only factors morally relevant to environmental problems are human rights and welfare. This assumption seems less common now, but there is no general agreement on what the best alternative is. My concern was not only with environmental ethics. Some of the same narrowness of vision, I thought, affected philosophical ethics in general. In short, it is *not all about* human rights and welfare. A key question that opens the way to broader reflection is, "What sort of person would do that?' This calls for thinking about attitudes, understanding and sensibility more often discussed under the ethics of virtue than in theories of rights and costs and benefits. Apart from concerns about the natural environment, our attitudes and acts that express these attitudes are often objectionable even though they violate no one's rights and harm no one—or at least they are not objectionable solely because they violate rights or cause harm. Arguably what is objectionable in some cases is not that rights are violated or welfare is diminished. The ungrateful heir who spits on his grandmother's grave after the genuine mourners have left expresses an attitude that seems bad independently of rights, benefits and harms. Similarly, I argued, those who despoil the natural environment often express objectionable attitudes rooted in ignorance, self-importance and patterns of aesthetic insensitivity that, if not themselves vices, give evidence of deficiency in the natural bases of human excellences, such as proper humility, gratitude and aesthetic appreciation. *DOES EGO HAVE something?*

My argument appealed to common understandings of human virtues and vices that are often ignored in the rights and welfare literature, but it would not satisfy those who want an ethics and value theory that can support good environmental policies without relying on assumptions about human relations and attitudes. Insofar as it appealed to ideals of human excellence and attitudes, my main argument made no appeal to the intrinsic value of nature, or non-human animals,

Thomas E. Hill, Jr., "Finding Value in Nature," Environmental Values 15, no. 3 (2006): 331–341.

or eco-systems, at least as "intrinsic value" is often con-strued.[1] Although sceptical of uncritical talk of "intrinsic values," I also believe that the wrongness of most objectionable acts and attitudes is *over*-determined. It is usually a mistake to say that *the* reason that something is morally objectionable is such and such (just one thing). So whether there are other, less human-centred, reasons against the environmental practices I discussed is another issue—left open by my argument. My main point was that arguments from the intrinsic value of nature are *not necessary* to show the inadequacy of theories that appeal solely to human rights and welfare. Whether such arguments are tenable and provide additional support for the same conclusion is a further question.

Many familiar objections to an ethics exclusively focused on human rights and welfare appeal to the idea of animal rights or the intrinsic badness of pain in any sentient beings. Other arguments turn on the value of species or ecosystems. My earlier essay set these aside, not because they are unimportant but because I thought that, for my limited purposes, they were unnecessary. Even broadening the discussion to include "animal rights" arguably fails to capture the full range of values that are important to environmentalists and lovers of nature. My concern was to explore possible connections between attitudes towards the natural environment and familiar human virtues, such as humility, gratitude and aesthetic sensibility. The question raised, about strip-mining, logging old redwood groves and replacing gardens with asphalt, was not "Whose rights and interests were violated?' but "What sort of person would do that?" My suggestion in the end was that those who regard *only* human rights and welfare as reasons not to destroy the natural environment seem to lack the bases of the virtues of proper humility, gratitude and aesthetic appreciation.[2] My conclusion was limited, but implied that, barring special explanation, we can expect that virtuous persons will value nature for its own sake[3]—at least they will not regard the natural environment merely as a means to human welfare or as something whose treatment is constrained only by human rights, for example, property rights. My aim in that essay, frankly, was to capture some important environmental values without resorting to certain familiar ideas that I find unpromising, such as Native American animism, religious mysticism and metaphysical realism about values inherent in nature.

So much for background. Now I want to explore the idea that a proper valuing of natural environments is essential to (and not just a natural basis for) a broader human virtue that we might call "appreciation of the good." Those who are already committed to the value of nature, or various aspects of it, as a metaphysical fact should have no objection to this idea, but they are likely to insist that the "value of nature" is prior to and totally independent of human capacities for appreciation. In my view the relation is not so simple and one-directional. Values are not natural (or "non-natural") properties that we happen to "see" as pre-existing in a non-human world, but they are also not simply things we create or mere reflections of our subjective tastes. To understand all this is a major philosophical challenge, but, if successful, we would have gone beyond the aim and conclusion of my previous essay. That is, we would understand, without metaphysical obscurity or undue anthropocentrism, how and why it is good *to value* certain natural phenomena *for their own sakes* and to recognize and respond appropriately to *the value they have*, in a sense, independently of human rights and welfare.

THE COMMON EXPERIENCE OF FINDING VALUE IN NATURE AND ITS INTERPRETATION

Poets and novelists often express what many of us find difficult to put into words when we appreciate the beauty, variety, order, complexity and awesomeness of aspects of the natural world. But when thinking about the redwood groves, the Carlsbad caverns, and the interplay of living things in an unspoiled forest, most of us could say not only that we *want* to see them, but that we *value* them, value them *for their own sakes*, not just for their utility or as sources of aesthetic delight. Moreover, if challenged, we might add that we do not think this is just a matter of taste or fashion: they *are valuable*, and *would be* even if everyone were to become so crassly materialistic and self-absorbed that they cared about them only for profit, comfort and passing pleasures that they get from them. If human beings were to disappear from the earth tomorrow, many of us would still count it as a bad thing, a further misfortune or calamity, that the earth be reduced to a lifeless, smoldering rock. This is no doubt due largely (and for some entirely) to a concern for non-human animals, but it is not obvious that even sentient animal life is all that we care about apart from its utility.

Some philosophers want to explain this attitude as a commitment to a metaphysics of independently existing intrinsic values that I find obscure and unhelpful. As before, however, I want to explore alternatives. Following my previous strategy, I want to consider a certain human excellence, or virtue, that seems to have implications regarding our treatment of the environment. But this time the virtue in question itself requires us to consider the idea of intrinsic value, the very topic that earlier I tried to avoid. The virtue that I have in mind now, broadly speaking, is a *manifest readiness to appreciate the good* in all sorts of things, and not just as an instrument or resource for something else. Although this does not appear on every philosopher's list of moral virtues, arguably it is widely (and rightly) recognised as a human virtue or excellence, an admirable trait of character. The basic idea is simple enough. There seems something important missing in those who persistently ignore, cynically dismiss, or remain coldly indifferent to the vast range of things that are sources of joy, inspiration and value for others, and potentially for themselves. Obviously such people are more liable than most to behave in ways that mistreat, hurt and dampen the spirits of others, but, even apart from that, arguably their systematic lack of appreciation is a defect of character, at least a falling short of an ideal. We may hesitate to label this strictly a *moral vice*, comparable to cruelty, dishonesty and injustice, but we commonly treat the opposite trait as an aspect of an ideal person—that is, their openness to find and respond to value in a wide diversity of people, things and experiences.

Most readers would probably concede the general idea that it is an admirable trait *to appreciate what is good*, but . . . [w]hat is more controversial is whether the virtue of appreciating the good has any special application to our attitudes about the natural environment. It will be readily admitted, of course, that human life and pleasure are generally good things and so it matters that pretty scenes cause innocent pleasure and air pollution kills people. The deeper controversy is about whether values in nature are independent of such effects on human welfare and rights. Are there such values, and, if so, how are we to understand

them? Specifically, does the general virtue of appreciating the good . . . imply that we should value aspects of the non-human natural world independently of their utility and effects on our welfare? The answer seems to depend on whether we should think that those aspects of nature *are* good and valuable for their own sakes.[4] If so, a virtuous person should appreciate them; if not, appreciation would be optional, a matter of choice and not an issue of human excellence or virtue. For me the issue turns on whether we can plausibly affirm that aspects of nature are valuable in themselves, in an appropriate sense, without buying into a metaphysics that construes "intrinsic values" as independently existing natural (or "non-natural") properties of things.

VALUING AND APPRECIATING VALUE: IS A METAPHYSICS OF INTRINSIC VALUE NECESSARY?

Presumably we want to say not merely that many people do in fact *value* natural phenomena in themselves, but also that these phenomena *are valuable* in themselves. What is implied in this last claim? This is a large and difficult question, but a few things seem clear enough. When we say that something is valuable, and not merely valued by some, we imply that its being valued is not (or need not be) simply the result of mistakes of various kinds—for example, failure to understand it, confusion, bad reasoning, judgment skewed by irrelevant biases, and so on.[5] Moreover, we seem to imply that what is valuable has in itself features that make it worthy of being valued even when it is not. We readily acknowledge this with respect to unappreciated items of potential utility or delight to human beings—for example, a scientific discovery before its time, an unfashionable poem or painting, or a secret act of kindness. But the point could be extended. We may think that the aspects of nature that we value in themselves have features worthy of being valued in this non-instrumental way even if ignorance, greed and closed mindedness prevent all remaining generations of human beings from appreciating them. That is, we do not merely value them non-instrumentally, but also regard them *as valuable in themselves*, at least if this is understood in an ordinary sense. In my view, this is not a judgment that presupposes an untenable metaphysical value realism, but it does at least imply that, if these aspects of nature were to continue to be valued non-instrumentally, the attitude need not rest on mistakes (factual misunderstanding, bias, faulty inferences, etc.).

Moreover, as just noted, when we say that something is *valuable* in itself, not merely *valued* for its own sake, we imply that it is *worthy* of being valued for its own sake. We can perhaps imagine someone saying, "*I value* X for its own sake even though I admit X is not really worthy of this attitude," but could we understand someone who said, "X *is* intrinsically *valuable* but not worthy of being valued for its own sake"? Although we can only touch on the issue here, there are various ways that the further claim of worthiness could be interpreted without resorting to a metaphysics of intrinsic value as an independently existing property. For example, it seems, at least in part, to express the speaker's endorsement of valuing the object for its own sake, perhaps with an expectation that other reasonable, aware and informed persons would tend to share this attitude if appropriately situated. Any analysis of the meaning of these expressions is likely to remain controversial, but consideration of how we actually make and revise our judgments can be helpful. When we confirm that something has market value, it is sufficient to observe that very many people value it enough to exchange other things for it. If we learned that many, even most people, familiar with something valued it for its own sake, however, this would not by itself prove to us that the thing is intrinsically valuable. Their attitude, and not merely their beliefs about the object, might have been shaped by political indoctrination, cultural pressures, irrelevant associations and desires unrelated to the valued object. Discovery that the attitude was entirely due to such factors would undermine their claim that the object was intrinsically valuable. If, apart from such factors, the object itself has no stable disposition to lead anyone to value it for its own sake, then those who do value it for its own sake, do so not because it is worthy of such evaluation but for other reasons.

IS THIS ACCOUNT STILL TOO HUMAN CENTERED?

A persistent objection to accounts of the value of nature of the sort sketched here is that they still make the value too dependent on human nature. This is a kind of objection sometimes raised against any value theory that treats value judgments as involving a relation between facts, events and objects in the world and those who actually or potentially observe, experience, respond to them evaluatively.

. . .

Because "anthropocentrism" has become a term of abuse among some environmentalists, it may be helpful to raise again the question what this means and why it is a bad thing. "Anthropocentrism" can refer to significantly different ideas, and more or less radical ideas may be unfairly swept away with the same rhetorical brush. The following, for example, are prima facie significantly distinct claims: (i) Everything in nature except human beings exists solely for the material benefit of human beings; (ii) Everything in nature except human beings exists solely for the benefit of human beings; but this includes aesthetic and spiritual benefits as well as material benefits; (iii) All valid concerns about the natural environment derive ultimately from human rights and duties to respect human interests; (iv) It is good for us to value nonhuman animals, natural wildernesses and ecosystems noninstrumentally; that is, it is virtue of *human* beings, though not other creatures, to do this; (v) All moral obligations and duties, virtues and vices, blameworthiness and praiseworthiness are, strictly and literally, attributed only to human beings (or other "rational" beings); (vi) The ultimate justification for thinking that we should value nature noninstrumentally (and count it as "morally considerable") must appeal not only to the facts about the natural world and our place in it but also to the nature of moral justification—which is, in the end, a process dependent on human reason, sensibility, experience, dialogue and reflection; (vii) This process of moral justification, properly understood, is not a matter of either perceiving values that exist as facts in nature or of intuiting nonnatural "intrinsic values," and so, though we should *value* nonhuman nature and even *regard it as valuable* noninstrumentally, the ultimate justification cannot be "It simply exists with the non-relational property of intrinsic value" which we "see" or "intuit."

If being anthropocentric is to be objectionable, we should be careful to indicate which claims it encompasses. My own view is that the first three claims are the primary ones that environmentalists should protest. The fourth is environmentally friendly, for it endorses valuing nature noninstrumentally without denying other environmentalist themes. Controversies about the fifth—that only human beings, strictly, have moral virtues—will, I suspect, largely turn on whether we use "moral" in a sense that is narrow or broad, perhaps literal or metaphorical. The last two points, concerning ultimate justification, are subject to philosophical disagreement, but I see no practical or theoretical advantage for environmentalists to treat these claims as the enemy. To do so would require them to draw up battle lines against the major developments in moral theory this century, and much before, and quite *unnecessarily* as far as I can see. I suspect that confusing these claims, i.e., (vi) and (vii), with some of the others has been largely responsible for the idea that serious environmentalists must deny them.

NOTES *Can we value something w/out putting humans in the center?*

1. The term "intrinsic value" has been interpreted in different ways. As should become clear, my scepticism about its use applies primarily to interpretations, such as G.E. Moore's, that treat intrinsic value as a simple, non-natural metaphysical property. This is a special philosophical usage, not inherent in the common understanding of "good in itself" or "valuable for its own sake."

2. By "natural basis" for a virtue I mean a pervasive human disposition, not primarily the product of particular social and cultural influences, that is not itself a morally excellent or praiseworthy trait but is a background tendency necessary to (or usually important for) the development of a morally excellent or praiseworthy trait. For example, in "Human Excellence and Preserving Natural Environments" I conjectured that a natural basis for proper humility is a tendency to care about animals and things independently of their utility and a natural basis for gratitude is a disposition to cherish for their own sakes things that give us joy. Whether these conjectures are correct is, of course, an empirical question.

3. It is important to note here, and later, that "valuing something for its own sake" is not the same as "believing that something is intrinsically valuable." This is especially evident if the latter is interpreted as the belief that the thing in question has a metaphysical property ("intrinsic value") that exists independently of relations to anything else. "Valuing for its own sake" is an attitude about the thing in question, not a belief about its intrinsic properties or even its relation to other actual or potential valuers.

4. This is a point at which approaching environmental issues from a perspective on human virtues seems to require, rather than provide a way of avoiding, discussion of intrinsic value. My suggestion, however, is that practical judgments that aspects of nature are "intrinsically valuable," when understood in the ordinary sense relevant to real environmental debates, do not presuppose the metaphysical realist conception of intrinsic value that I have been trying to avoid. For present purposes I am not distinguishing "being intrinsically values," "having intrinsic value," and "being *valuable* for its own sake," though all of these, I assume, go beyond "being *valued* for its own sake."

5. The possibility of such mistakes about what is *valuable* is important to distinguish the concept from the weaker ideas that the thing *seems valuable* and *is valued*. It must make sense to say, "It seems valuable, it is valued (e.g. by many others), and I did value it, but really it is not valuable." The distinction, however, need not be explained as the difference between false and true attributions of a metaphysical property of the thing in question independent of its relation to those who do or might observe, experience, or otherwise respond to the thing. The difference has to do both with other possible errors and misjudgments as well as endorsement of something as *worthy* of being valued, a normative judgment that needs more discussion but does not necessarily invoke the kind of metaphysics of which I am sceptical.

4

ANIMAL SUFFERING

A. Traditional Perspectives

THOMAS AQUINAS — *ANIMALS ARE for HUMANS*

WHETHER IT IS UNLAWFUL TO KILL ANY LIVING THING

Objection 1. It seems that it is unlawful to kill any living thing. For the Apostle says (Romans 13:2): "They that resist the ordinance of God purchase to themselves damnation." Now Divine providence has ordained that all living things should be preserved, according to Psalm 146:8–9, "Who maketh grass to grow on the mountains . . . Who giveth to beasts their food." Therefore it seems unlawful to take the life of any living thing.

Objection 2. Further, murder is a sin because it deprives a man of life. Now life is common to all animals and plants. Hence for the same reason it is apparently a sin to slay dumb animals and plants.

Objection 3. Further, in the Divine law a special punishment is not appointed save for a sin.

Now a special punishment had to be inflicted, according to the Divine law, on one who killed another man's ox or sheep (Exodus 22:1). Therefore, the slaying of dumb animals is a sin.

On the contrary, Augustine says (De Civ. Dei i, 20): "When we hear it said, 'Thou shalt not kill,' we do not take it as referring to trees, for they have no sense, nor to irrational animals, because they have no fellowship with us. Hence it follows that the words, 'Thou shalt not kill' refer to the killing of a man."

I answer that, There is no sin in using a thing for the purpose for which it is. Now the order of things is such that the imperfect are for the perfect, even as in the process of generation nature proceeds from imperfection to perfection. Hence it is that just as in the generation

Thomas Aquinas, The Summa Theologica of St. Thomas Aquinas, Part II (Second Part), Second Number (QQ. XLVII–LXXIX) (New York: Benziger Brothers, [1485] 1918), pp. 195–197.

of a man there is first a living thing, then an animal, and lastly a man, so too things, like the plants, which merely have life, are all alike for animals, and all animals are for man. Wherefore it is not unlawful if man use plants for the good of animals, and animals for the good of man, as the Philosopher states (Polit. i, 3).

Now the most necessary use would seem to consist in the fact that animals use plants, and men use animals, for food, and this cannot be done unless these be deprived of life: wherefore it is lawful both to take life from plants for the use of animals, and from animals for the use of men. In fact this is keeping with the commandment of God Himself: for it is written (Genesis 1:29, 30): "Behold I have given you every herb . . . and all trees . . . to be your meat, and to all beasts of the earth": and again (Genesis 9:3): "Everything that moveth and liveth shall be meat to you."

Reply to Objection 1. According to the Divine ordinance the life of animals and plants is preserved not for themselves but for man. Hence, as Augustine says (De Civ. Dei i, 20), "by a most just ordinance of the Creator, both their life and their death are subject to our use."

Reply to Objection 2. Dumb animals and plants are devoid of the life of reason whereby to set themselves in motion; they are moved, as it were by another, by a kind of natural impulse, a sign of which is that they are naturally enslaved and accommodated to the uses of others.

Reply to Objection 3. He that kills another's ox, sins, not through killing the ox, but through injuring another man in his property. Wherefore this is not a species of the sin of murder but of the sin of theft or robbery.

IMMANUEL KANT — *ONLY HAVE MORAL DUTIES TO PERSON'S (COMPETENT ADULTS)*

DUTIES TOWARDS ANIMALS

So far as animals are concerned, we have no direct duties. Animals are not self-conscious and are there merely as a means to an end. That end is man. We can ask, "Why do animals exist?" But to ask, "Why does man exist?" is a meaningless question. Our duties towards animals are merely indirect duties towards humanity. Animal nature has analogies to human nature, and by doing our duties to animals in respect of manifestations which correspond to manifestations of human nature, we indirectly do our duty towards humanity. Thus, if a dog has served his master long and faithfully, his service, on the analogy of human service, deserves reward, and when the dog has grown too old to serve, his master ought to keep him until he dies. Such action helps to support us in our duties towards human beings, where they are bounden duties. If then any acts of animals are analogous to human acts and spring from the same principles, we have duties towards the animals because thus we cultivate the corresponding duties towards human *point* beings. If a man shoots his dog because the animal is no longer capable of service, he does not fail in his

Immanuel Kant, "Duties Towards Animals and Spirits," in Lectures on Ethics (New York: Harper & Row, 1963), pp. 239–241.

duty to the dog, for the dog cannot judge, but his act is inhuman and damages in himself that humanity which it is his duty to show towards mankind. If he is not to stifle his human feelings, he must practise kindness towards animals, for he who is cruel to animals becomes hard also in his dealings with men. We can judge the heart of a man by his treatment of animals. Hogarth[1] depicts this in his engravings. He shows how cruelty grows and develops. He shows the child's cruelty to animals, pinching the tail of a dog or a cat; he then depicts the grown man in his cart running over a child; and lastly, the culmination of cruelty in murder. He thus brings home to us in terrible fashion the rewards of cruelty, and this should be an impressive lesson to children. The more we come in contact with animals and observe their behavior, the more we love them, for we see how great is their care for their young. It is then difficult for us to be cruel in thought even to a wolf. Leibnitz used a tiny worm for purposes of observation, and then carefully replaced it with its leaf on the tree so that it should not come to harm through any act of his. He would have been sorry—a natural feeling for a humane man—to destroy such a creature for no reason. Tender feelings towards dumb animals develop humane feelings towards mankind. In England butchers and doctors do not sit on a jury because they are accustomed to the sight of death and hardened. Vivisectionists, who use living animals for their experiments, certainly act cruelly, although their aim is praiseworthy, and they can justify their cruelty, since animals must be regarded as man's instruments; but any such cruelty for sport cannot be justified. A master who turns out his ass or his dog because the animal can no longer earn its keep manifests a small mind. The Greeks' ideas in this respect were high-minded, as can be seen from the fable of the ass and the bell of ingratitude.[2] Our duties toward animals, then, are indirect duties towards mankind.

NOTES

1. Hogarth's four engravings, "The Stages of Cruelty," 1751.
2. Philipp Camerarius, *Operae horarum subcisivarum centuria prima*, 1644, cap. XXI.

JEREMY BENTHAM

CAN THEY SUFFER?

Ethics at large may be defined, the art of directing men's actions to the production of the greatest possible quantity of happiness, on the part of those whose interest is in view.

What then are the actions which it can be in a man's power to direct? They must be either his own actions, or those of other agents. Ethics, in as far as it is the art of directing a man's own actions, may be styled the *art of self-government*, or *private ethics*.

What other agents then are there, which, at the same time that they are under the influence of man's direction, are susceptible to happiness. They are of two sorts: 1. Other human beings who are styled persons. 2. Other animals, which, on account of their interests

Jeremy Bentham, An Introduction to the Principles of Morals and Legislation (Oxford: Clarendon Press, [1789] 1876), pp. 310–311, n. 1.

having been neglected by the insensibility of the ancient jurists, stand degraded into the class of *things*.

Under the Gentoo [Hindu] and Mahometan [Muslim] religions, the interests of the rest of the animal creation seem to have met with some attention. Why have they not universally, with as much as those of human creatures, allowance made for the difference in point of sensibility? Because the laws that are have been the work of mutual fear; a sentiment which the less rational animals have not had the same means as man has of turning to account. Why *ought* they not? No reason can be given. If the being eaten were all, there is very good reason why we should be suffered to eat such of them as we like to eat: we are the better for it, and they are never the worse. They have none of those long-protracted anticipations of future misery which we have. The death they suffer in our hands commonly is, and always may be, a speedier, and by that means a less painful one, than that which would await them in the inevitable course of nature. If the being killed were all, there is very good reason

why we should be suffered to kill such as molest us: we should be the worse for their living, and they are never the worse for being dead. But is there any reason why we should be suffered to torment them? Not that I can see. Are there any why we should *not* be suffered to torment them? Yes, several. . . . The French have already discovered that the blackness of the skin is no reason why a human being should be abandoned without redress to the caprice of a tormentor. (See Lewis XIV's Code Noir.) It may come one day to be recognized, that the number of the legs, the villosity of the skin, or the termination of the *os sacrum*, are reasons equally insufficient for abandoning a sensitive being to the same fate. What else is it that should trace the insuperable line? Is it the faculty of reason, or, perhaps, the faculty of discourse? But a full-grown horse or dog is beyond comparison a more rational, as well as a more conversable animal, than an infant of a day, or a week, or even a month, old. But suppose the case were otherwise, what would it avail? the question is not, Can they *reason*? nor, Can they *talk*? but, Can they *suffer*?

> *Does he then argue for rights of animal but not caring for the earth/nature in any different way since earth/nature cannot suffer?*

B. Contemporary Perspectives

FOR DISCUSSION: RESPECT FOR ANIMALS

1. I once attended a talk by Tom Regan in which he defended animal rights. When Tom concluded, the audience applauded, but the first question was an attack. "You say animals have rights," the questioner said, "but I can tell by looking at you that you are a hypocrite." That was all. The questioner sat down. The room was silent.

Finally, Tom said, "I never said I was perfect. I suppose when you say you can tell by looking that I'm a hypocrite, you're talking about my leather belt and my leather shoes and my woolen sports jacket." Tom continued. "I don't deny that I have blood on my hands. I could mention that the belt and shoes are actually vinyl, and the jacket is actually cotton. But how many animals were killed in the process of extracting the petroleum that went into making the vinyl? How many animals were killed in the process of growing and harvesting the cotton that went into the jacket? I have no idea. All I know is, I don't have clean hands. And all I can do from here is to avoid gratuitous killing as best I can."

So, Tom Regan has a problem. He has good intentions, but good intentions do not guarantee clean hands. How forgiving should Tom be of himself? How forgiving should Tom be of his fellow environmentalists, most of whom do not care nearly as much about animal suffering as does Tom?

What of holists whose top priority is the management of ecosystems, and who therefore would kill individual animals as a way of limiting herd size and thereby maintaining ecological balance? Is there any room for compromise?

2. Peter Singer may be today's most influential living philosopher. As Dale Jamieson observes, "While other philosophers have been more important in developing the discipline, none has changed more lives" (*Singer and His Critics*, p. 1). As Holmes Rolston III notes (in that same volume), "Few ethicists, indeed few persons responsible for the care and use of animals, are not more sensitive to animal welfare now than they were before the impact of Singer and his colleagues." In 1975, shampoos and cosmetics were tested by placing samples in rabbits' eyes. Today, the rabbit eye test is no longer legally required, and many manufacturers advertise "cruelty-free" products.

Was it wrong to use rabbits to test whether a new product is safe for humans? Why or why not? (If there were no alternative to using animals, if the only alternative to experimenting on animals would be, in effect, to experiment on human customers, would that make a difference?) If it was wrong to use animals, was it because animals have rights? Should we think of animals as having rights? Why or why not? If animals do not have rights, does that mean we can do whatever we want to them? Why or why not?

3. Although there is less cruelty to animals in laboratories today, other trends are more disturbing. In 1998, about 76,000 dogs and 25,000 cats were used in research. Is that a large number? To put it in perspective, between 2.4 million and 7.2 million unwanted cats and dogs were killed in American animal shelters in the same year, according to the Humane Society of America.[1] Yet, to judge from media coverage, we seem more concerned about animals killed in laboratories. Should we be? At the animal shelter, we simply kill the animal. At the laboratory, we first use the animal as a mere means to human ends. Is that an important difference? If so, which is worse? Why?

4. If and when we decide that animals (or plants) have rights, we will have some issues to work out regarding what is involved in respecting such rights in practice. For example, if we believe a deer has a right to life, is it enough simply to avoid killing deer ourselves, or are we also committed to protecting each deer against whatever threatens its life? Are we obligated to protect them from carnivores? Are we obligated to protect them from human hunters but not from "natural" predators? Are we obligated to feed them when they cannot feed themselves? Is our obligation to interfere with nature, on behalf of deer, or to avoid interfering?

NOTE

1. Lynne Lamberg, "Researchers urged to tell public how animal studies benefit human health" *Journal of the American Medical Association* (1999) 282 (7): 619–621.

PETER SINGER – *UTILITARIAN – Suffering Is Bad.* [handwritten]

ALL ANIMALS ARE EQUAL

In recent years a number of oppressed groups have campaigned vigorously for equality. The classic instance is the Black Liberation movement, which demands an end to the prejudice and discrimination that has made blacks second-class citizens. The immediate appeal of the black liberation movement and its initial, if limited, success made it a model for other oppressed groups to follow. We became familiar with liberation movements for Spanish-Americans, gay people, and a variety of other minorities. When a majority group—women—began their campaign, some thought we had come to the end of the road. Discrimination on the basis of sex, it has been said, is the last universally accepted form of discrimination, practiced without secrecy or pretense even in those liberal circles that have long prided themselves on their freedom from prejudice against racial minorities.

One should always be wary of talking of "the last remaining form of discrimination." If we have learnt anything from the liberation movements, we should have learnt how difficult it is to be aware of latent prejudice in our attitudes to particular groups until this prejudice is forcefully pointed out.

A liberation movement demands an expansion of our moral horizons and an extension or reinterpretation of the basic moral principle of equality. Practices that were previously regarded as natural and inevitable come to be seen as the result of an unjustifiable prejudice. Who can say with confidence that all his or her attitudes and practices are beyond criticism? If we wish to avoid being numbered amongst the oppressors, we must be prepared to re-think even our most fundamental attitudes. We need to consider them from the point of view of those most disadvantaged by our attitudes, and the practices that follow from these attitudes. If we can make this unaccustomed mental switch we may discover a pattern in our attitudes and practices that consistently operates so as to benefit one group—usually the one to which we ourselves belong—at the expense of another. In this way we may come to see that there is a case for a new liberation movement. My aim is to advocate that we make this mental switch in respect of our attitudes and practices towards a very large group of beings: members of species other than our own—or, as we popularly though misleadingly call them, animals. In other words, I am urging that we extend to other species the basic principle of equality that most of us recognize should be extended to all members of our own species.

All this may sound a little far-fetched, more like a parody of other liberation movements than a serious objective. In fact, in the past the idea of "The Rights of Animals" really has been used to parody the case for women's rights. When Mary Wollstonecraft, a forerunner of later feminists, published her *Vindication of the Rights of Women* in 1792, her ideas were widely regarded as absurd, and they were satirized in an anonymous publication entitled *A Vindication of the Rights of Brutes*. The author of this satire (actually Thomas Taylor, a distinguished Cambridge philosopher) tried to refute Wollstonecraft's reasonings by showing that they could be carried one stage further. If sound when applied to women, why should the arguments not be applied to dogs, cats, and horses? They seemed to hold equally well for these "brutes"; yet to hold that brutes had rights was manifestly absurd; therefore the reasoning by which this conclusion had been reached must be unsound, and if unsound when applied to brutes, it must also be unsound when applied to women, since the very same arguments had been used in each case.

Peter Singer. 1974. All Animals are Equal. Philosophical Exchange, 1: 103–116. Reprinted with permission of the author. © Peter Singer 1994.

One way in which we might reply to this argument is by saying that the case for equality between men and women cannot validly be extended to nonhuman animals. Women have a right to vote, for instance, because they are just as capable of making rational decisions as men are; dogs, on the other hand, are incapable of understanding the significance of voting, so they cannot have the right to vote. There are many other obvious ways in which men and women resemble each other closely, while humans and other animals differ greatly. So, it might be said, men and women are similar beings, and should have equal rights, while humans and nonhumans are different and should not have equal rights.

The thought behind this reply to Taylor's analogy is correct up to a point, but it does not go far enough. There *are* important differences between humans and other animals, and these differences must give rise to *some* differences in the rights that each have. Recognizing this obvious fact, however, is no barrier to the case for extending the basic principle of equality to nonhuman animals. The differences that exist between men and women are equally undeniable, and the supporters of Women's Liberation are aware that these differences may give rise to different rights. Many feminists hold that women have the right to an abortion on request. It does not follow that since these same people are campaigning for equality between men and women they must support the right of men to have abortions too. Since a man cannot have an abortion, it is meaningless to talk of his right to have one. Since a pig can't vote, it is meaningless to talk of its right to vote. There is no reason why either Women's Liberation or Animal Liberation should get involved in such nonsense. The extension of the basic principle of equality from one group to another does not imply that we must treat both groups in exactly the same way, or grant exactly the same rights to both groups. Whether we should do so will depend on the nature of the members of the two groups. The basic principle of equality, I shall argue, is equality of consideration; and equal consideration for different beings may lead to different treatment and different rights.

So there is a different way of replying to Taylor's attempt to parody Wollstonecraft's arguments, a way which does not deny the differences between humans and nonhumans, but goes more deeply into the question of equality, and concludes by finding nothing absurd in the idea that the basic principle of equality applies to so called "brutes." I believe that we reach this conclusion if we examine the basis on which our opposition to discrimination on grounds of race or sex ultimately rests. We will then see that we would be on shaky ground if we were to demand equality for blacks, women, and other groups of oppressed humans while denying equal consideration to nonhumans.

When we say that all human beings, whatever their race, creed or sex, are equal, what is it that we are asserting? Those who wish to defend a hierarchical, inegalitarian society have often pointed out that by whatever test we choose, it simply is not true that all humans are equal. Like it or not, we must face the fact that humans come in different shapes and sizes; they come with differing moral capacities, differing intellectual abilities, differing amounts of benevolent feeling and sensitivity to the needs of others, differing abilities to communicate effectively, and differing capacities to experience pleasure and pain. In short, if the demand for equality were based on the actual equality of all human beings, we would have to stop demanding equality. It would be an unjustifiable demand.

Still, one might cling to the view that the demand for equality among human beings is based on the actual equality of the different races and sexes. Although humans differ as individuals in various ways, there are no differences between the races and sexes *as such*. From the mere fact that a person is black, or a woman, we cannot infer anything else about that person. This, it may be said, is what is wrong with racism and sexism. The white racist claims that whites are superior to blacks, but this is false—although there are differences between individuals, some blacks are superior to some whites in all of the capacities and abilities that could conceivably be relevant. The opponent of sexism would say the same: a person's sex is no guide to his or her abilities, and this is why it is unjustifiable to discriminate on the basis of sex.

This is a possible line of objection to racial and sexual discrimination. It is not, however, the way that someone really concerned about equality would choose, because taking this line could, in some circumstances, force one to accept a most inegalitarian society. The fact that humans differ as individuals, rather than as races or sexes, is a valid reply to someone who defends a hierarchical society like, say, South Africa, in which all whites are superior in status to all blacks. The existence of individual variations that cut across the lines of race or sex, however, provides us with no defence at all against a more sophisticated opponent of equality, one who proposes that, say, the interests of those with I.Q. ratings above 100 be preferred to the interests of those with I.Q.s below 100. Would a hierarchical society of this sort really be so much better than one based on race or sex? I think not. But if we tie the moral principle of equality to the factual equality of the different races or sexes, taken as a whole, our opposition to racism and sexism does not provide us with any basis for objecting to this kind of inegalitarianism.

There is a second important reason why we ought not to base our opposition to racism and sexism on any kind of factual equality, even the limited kind which asserts that variations in capacities and abilities are spread evenly between the different races and sexes: we can have no absolute guarantee that these abilities and capacities really are distributed evenly, without regard to race or sex, among human beings. So far as actual abilities are concerned, there do seem to be certain measurable differences between both races and sexes. These differences do not, of course, appear in each case, but only when averages are taken. More important still, we do not yet know how much of these differences is really due to the different genetic endowments of the various races and sexes, and how much is due to environmental differences that are the result of past and continuing discrimination. Perhaps all of the important differences will eventually prove to be environmental rather than genetic. Anyone opposed to racism and sexism will certainly hope that this will be so, for it will make the task of ending discrimination a lot easier; nevertheless it would be dangerous to rest the case against racism and sexism on the belief that all significant differences are environmental in origin. The opponent of, say, racism who takes this line will be unable to avoid conceding that if differences in ability did after all prove to have some genetic connection with race, racism would in some way be defensible.

It would be folly for the opponent of racism to stake his whole case on a dogmatic commitment to one particular outcome of a difficult scientific issue which is still a long way from being settled. While attempts to prove that differences in certain selected abilities between races and sexes are primarily genetic in origin have certainly not been conclusive, the same must be said of attempts to prove that these differences are largely the result of environment. At this stage of the investigation we cannot be certain which view is correct, however much we may hope it is the latter.

Fortunately, there is no need to pin the case for equality to one particular outcome of this scientific investigation. The appropriate response to those who claim to have found evidence of genetically-based differences in ability between the races or sexes is not to stick to the belief that the genetic explanation must be wrong, whatever evidence to the contrary may turn up: instead we should make it quite clear that the claim to equality does not depend on intelligence, moral capacity, physical strength, or similar matters of fact. Equality is a moral ideal, not a simple assertion of fact. There is no logically compelling reason for assuming that a factual difference in ability between two people justifies any difference in the amount of consideration we give to satisfying their needs and interests. The principle of the equality of human beings is not a description of an alleged actual equality among humans: it is a prescription of how we should treat humans.

Jeremy Bentham incorporated the essential basis of moral equality into his utilitarian system of ethics in the formula: "Each to count for one and none for more than one." In other words, the interests of every being affected by an action are to be taken into account and given the same weight as the like interests of any other being. A later utilitarian, Henry Sidgwick, put the point in this way: "The good of any one individual is of no more importance, from the point of view (if I may say so) of the Universe, than the good of any other."[1] More recently, the leading figures in contemporary moral philosophy have shown a great deal of agreement in specifying as a fundamental presupposition of their moral theories some similar requirement which operates so as to give everyone's interests equal consideration—although they cannot agree on how this requirement is best formulated.[2]

It is an implication of this principle of equality that our concern for others ought not to depend on what they are like, or what abilities they possess—although precisely what this concern requires us to do may vary according to the characteristics of those affected by what we do. It is on this basis that the case against racism and the case against sexism must both ultimately rest; and it is in accordance with this principle that speciesism is also to be condemned. If possessing a higher degree of intelligence does not entitle one human to use another for his own ends, how can it entitle humans to exploit non-humans?

Many philosophers have proposed the principle of equal consideration of interests, in some form or other, as a basic moral principle; but, as we shall see in more detail shortly, not many of them have recognized that this principle applies to members of other species as well as to our own. Bentham was one of the few who did realize this. In a forward-looking passage, written at a time when black slaves in British dominions were still being treated much as we now treat non-human animals, Bentham wrote:

> The day *may* come when the rest of the animal creation may acquire those rights which never could have been witholden from them but by the hand of tyranny. The French have already discovered that the blackness of the skin is no reason why a human being should be abandoned without redress to the caprice of a tormentor. It may one day come to be recognized that the number of the legs, the villosity of the skin, or the termination of the *os sacrum*, are reasons equally insufficient for abandoning a sensitive being to the same fate. What else is it that should trace the insuperable line? Is it the faculty of reason, or perhaps the faculty of discourse? But a full grown horse or dog is beyond comparison a more rational, as well as a more conversable animal, than an infant of a day, or a week, or even a month, old. But suppose they were otherwise, what would it avail? The question is not, Can they reason? nor Can they *talk?* but, Can they suffer?[3]

In this passage Bentham points to the capacity for suffering as the vital characteristic that gives a being the right to equal consideration. The capacity for suffering—or more strictly, for suffering and/or enjoyment or happiness—is not just another characteristic like the capacity for language, or for higher mathematics. Bentham is not saying that those who try to mark "the insuperable line" that determines whether the interests of a being should be considered happen to have selected the wrong characteristic. The capacity for suffering and enjoying things is a pre-requisite for having interests at all, a condition that must be satisfied before we can speak of interests in any meaningful way. It would be nonsense to say that it was not in the interests of a stone to be kicked along the road by a schoolboy. A stone does not have interests because it cannot suffer. Nothing that we can do to it could possibly make any difference to its welfare. A mouse, on the other hand, does have an interest in not being tormented, because it will suffer if it is.

If a being suffers, there can be no moral justification for refusing to take that suffering into consideration. No matter what the nature of the being, the principle of equality requires that its suffering be counted equally with the like suffering—in so far as rough comparisons can be made—of any other being. If a being is not capable of suffering, or of experiencing enjoyment or happiness, there is nothing to be taken into account. This is why the limit of sentience (using the term as a convenient, if not strictly accurate, shorthand for the capacity to suffer or experience enjoyment or happiness) is the only defensible boundary of concern for the interests of others. To mark this boundary by some characteristic like intelligence or rationality would be to mark it in an arbitrary way. Why not choose some other characteristic, like skin color?

The racist violates the principle of equality by giving greater weight to the interests of members of his own race, when there is a clash between their interests and the interests of those of another race. Similarly the speciesist allows the interests of his own species to override the greater interests of members of other species.[4] The pattern is the same in each case. Most human beings are speciesists. I shall now very briefly describe some of the practices that show this.

For the great majority of human beings, especially in urban, industrialized societies, the most direct form of contact with members of other species is at mealtimes: we eat them. In doing so we treat them purely as means to our ends. We regard their life and well-being as subordinate to our taste for a particular kind of dish.

I say "taste" deliberately—this is purely a matter of pleasing our palate. There can be no defence of eating flesh in terms of satisfying nutritional needs, since it has been established beyond doubt that we could satisfy our need for protein and other essential nutrients far more efficiently with a diet that replaced animal flesh by soy beans, or products derived from soy beans, and other high-protein vegetable products.[5]

It is not merely the act of killing that indicates what we are ready to do to other species in order to gratify our tastes. The suffering we inflict on the animals while they are alive is perhaps an even clearer indication of our speciesism than the fact that we are prepared to kill them. In order to have meat on the table at a price that people can afford, our society tolerates methods of meat production that confine sentient animals in cramped, unsuitable conditions for the entire durations of their lives. Animals are treated like machines that convert fodder into flesh, and any innovation that results in a higher "conversion ratio" is liable to be adopted. As one authority on the subject has said, "cruelty is acknowledged only when profitability ceases."[6] So hens are crowded four or five to a cage with a floor area of twenty inches by eighteen inches, or around the size of a single page of the *New York Times*. The cages have wire floors, since this reduces cleaning costs, though wire is unsuitable for the hens' feet; the floors slope, since this makes the eggs roll down for easy collection, although this makes it difficult for the hens to rest comfortably. In these conditions all the birds' natural instincts are thwarted: they cannot stretch their wings fully, walk freely, dust-bathe, scratch the ground, or build a nest. Although they have never known other conditions, observers have noticed that the birds vainly try to perform these actions. Frustrated at their inability to do so, they often develop what farmers call "vices," and peck each other to death. To prevent this, the beaks of young birds are often cut off.

This kind of treatment is not limited to poultry. Pigs are now also being reared in cages inside sheds. These animals are comparable to dogs in intelligence, and need a varied, stimulating environment if they are not to suffer from stress and boredom. Anyone who kept a dog in the way in which pigs are frequently kept would be liable to prosecution, in England at least, but because our interest in exploiting pigs is greater than our interest in exploiting dogs, we object to cruelty to dogs while consuming the produce of cruelty to pigs. Of the other animals, the condition of veal calves is perhaps worst of all, since these animals are so closely confined that they cannot even turn around or get up and lie down freely. In this way they do not develop unpalatable muscle. They are also made anaemic and kept short of roughage, to keep their flesh pale, since white veal fetches a higher price; as a result they develop a craving for iron and roughage, and have been observed to gnaw wood off the sides of their stalls, and lick greedily at any rusty hinge that is within reach.

Since, as I have said, none of these practices cater for anything more than our pleasures of taste, our practice of rearing and killing other animals in order to eat them is a clear instance of the sacrifice of the most important interests of other beings in order to satisfy trivial interests of our own. To avoid speciesism we must stop this practice, and each of us has a moral obligation to cease supporting the practice. Our custom is all the support that the meat-industry needs. The decision to cease giving it that support may be difficult, but it is no more difficult than it would have been for a white Southerner to go against the traditions of his society and free his slaves: if we do not change our dietary habits, how can we censure those slaveholders who would not change their own way of living?

The same form of discrimination may be observed in the widespread practice of experimenting on other species in order to see if certain substances are safe for human beings, or to test some psychological theory about the effect of severe punishment on learning, or to try out various new compounds just in case something turns up. People sometimes think that all this experimentation is for vital medical purposes, and so will reduce suffering overall. This comfortable belief is very wide of the mark. Drug companies test new shampoos and cosmetics that they are intending to put on the market by dropping them into the eyes of rabbits, held open by metal clips, in order to observe what damage results. Food additives, like artificial colorings and preservatives, are tested by what is known as the "LD$_{50}$"—a test designed to find the level

Harmful Treatment is immoral. No reason for it.

of consumption at which 50% of a group of animals will die. In the process, nearly all of the animals are made very sick before some finally die, and others pull through. If the substance is relatively harmless, as it often is, huge doses have to be force-fed the animals, until in some cases sheer volume or concentration of the substance causes death.

Much of this pointless cruelty goes on in the universities. In many areas of science, non-human animals are regarded as an item of laboratory equipment, to be used and expended as desired. In psychology laboratories experimenters devise endless variations and repetitions of experiments that were of little value in the first place. To quote just one example, from the experimenter's own account in a psychology journal: at the University of Pennsylvania, Perrin S. Cohen hung six dogs in hammocks with electrodes taped to their hind feet. Electric shock of varying intensity was then administered through the electrodes. If the dog learnt to press its head against a panel on the left, the shock was turned off, but otherwise it remained on indefinitely. Three of the dogs, however, were required to wait periods varying from 2 to 7 seconds while being shocked before making the response that turned off the current. If they failed to wait, they received further shocks. Each dog was given from 26 to 46 "sessions" in the hammock, each session consisting of 80 "trials" or shocks, administered at intervals of one minute. The experimenter reported that the dogs, who were unable to move in the hammock, barked or bobbed their heads when the current was applied. The reported findings of the experiment were that there was a delay in the dogs' responses that increased proportionately to the time the dogs were required to endure the shock, but a gradual increase in the intensity of the shock had no systematic effect in the timing of the response. The experiment was funded by the National Institutes of Health, and the United States Public Health Service.[7] *HOW IS THIS ALLOWED???*

In this example, and countless cases like it, the possible benefits to mankind are either non-existent or fantastically remote; while the certain losses to members of other species are very real. This is, again, a clear indication of speciesism.

In the past, argument about vivisection has often missed this point, because it has been put in

absolutist terms: Would the abolitionist be prepared to let thousands die if they could be saved by experimenting on a single animal? The way to reply to this purely hypothetical question is to pose another: Would the experimenter be prepared to perform his experiment on an orphaned human infant, if that were the only way to save many lives? (I say "orphan" to avoid the complication of parental feelings, although in doing so I am being overfair to the experimenter, since the nonhuman subjects of experiments are not orphans.) If the experimenter is not prepared to use an orphaned human infant, then his readiness to use non-humans is simple discrimination, since adult apes, cats, mice and other mammals are more aware of what is happening to them, more self-directing and, so far as we can tell, at least as sensitive to pain, as any human infant. There seems to be no relevant characteristic that human infants possess that adult mammals do not have to the same or a higher degree. (Someone might try to argue that what makes it wrong to experiment on a human infant is that the infant will, in time and if left alone, develop into more than the nonhuman, but one would then, to be consistent, have to oppose abortion, since the fetus has the same potential as the infant—indeed, even contraception and abstinence might be wrong on this ground, since the egg and sperm, considered jointly, also have the same potential. In any case, this argument still gives us no reason for selecting a nonhuman, rather than a human with severe and irreversible brain damage, as the subject for our experiments.)

The experimenter, then, shows a bias in favor of his own species whenever he carries out an experiment on a nonhuman for a purpose that he would not think justified him in using a human being at an equal or lower level of sentience, awareness, ability to be self-directing, etc. No one familiar with the kind of results yielded by most experiments on animals can have the slightest doubt that if this bias were eliminated the number of experiments performed would be a minute fraction of the number performed today.

Experimenting on animals, and eating their flesh, are perhaps the two major forms of speciesism in our society. By comparison, the third and last form of speciesism is so minor as to be insignificant, but it is perhaps of some special interest to those for whom this article was written. I am referring to speciesism in contemporary philosophy.

Philosophy ought to question the basic assumptions of the age. Thinking through, critically and carefully, what most people take for granted is, I believe, the chief task of philosophy, and it is this task that makes philosophy a worthwhile activity. Regrettably, philosophy does not always live up to its historic role. Philosophers are human beings and they are subject to all the preconceptions of the society to which they belong. Sometimes they succeed in breaking free of the prevailing ideology: more often they become its most sophisticated defenders. So, in this case, philosophy as practiced in the universities today does not challenge anyone's preconceptions about our relations with other species. By their writings, those philosophers who tackle problems that touch upon the issue reveal that they make the same unquestioned assumptions as most other humans, and what they say tends to confirm the reader in his or her comfortable speciesist habits.

I could illustrate this claim by referring to the writings of philosophers in various fields—for instance, the attempts that have been made by those interested in rights to draw the boundary of the sphere of rights so that it runs parallel to the biological boundaries of the species *homo sapiens*, including infants and even mental defectives, but excluding those other beings of equal or greater capacity who are so useful to us at mealtimes and in our laboratories. I think it would be a more appropriate conclusion to this article, however, if I concentrated on the problem with which we have been centrally concerned, the problem of equality.

It is significant that the problem of equality, in moral and political philosophy, is invariably formulated in terms of human equality. The effect of this is that the question of the equality of other animals does not confront the philosopher, or student, as an issue itself—and this is already an indication of the failure of philosophy to challenge accepted beliefs. Still, philosophers have found it difficult to discuss the issue of human equality without raising, in a paragraph or two, the question of the status of other animals. The reason for this, which should be apparent from what I have said already, is that if humans are to be

regarded as equal to one another, we need some sense of "equal" that does not require any actual, descriptive equality of capacities, talents or other qualities. If equality is to be related to any actual characteristics of humans, these characteristics must be some lowest common denominator, pitched so low that no human lacks them—but then the philosopher comes up against the catch that any such set of characteristics which covers *all* humans will not be possessed *only by humans*. In other words, it turns out that in the only sense in which we can truly say, as an assertion of fact, that all humans are equal, at least some members of other species are also equal—equal, that is, to each other and to humans. If, on the other hand, we regard the statement "All humans are equal" in some nonfactual way, perhaps as a prescription, then, as I have already argued, it is even more difficult to exclude non-humans from the sphere of equality.

This result is not what the egalitarian philosopher originally intended to assert. Instead of accepting the radical outcome to which their own reasonings naturally point, however, most philosophers try to reconcile their beliefs in human equality and animal inequality by arguments that can only be described as devious.

As a first example, I take William Frankena's well-known article "The Concept of Social Justice."[8] Frankena opposes the idea of basing justice on merit, because he sees that this could lead to highly inegalitarian results. Instead he proposes the principle that:

> All men are to be treated as equals, not because they are equal, in any respect, but simply because they are human. They are human because they have emotions and desires, and are able to think, and hence are capable of enjoying a good life in a sense in which other animals are not.

But what is this capacity to enjoy the good life which all humans have, but no other animals? Other animals have emotions and desires, and appear to be capable of enjoying a good life. We may doubt that they can think—although the behavior of some apes, dolphins and even dogs suggests that some of them can—but what is the relevance of thinking? Frankena goes on to admit that by "the good life" he means "not so much the morally good life as the happy or satisfactory life," so thought would appear to be unnecessary for enjoying the good life; in fact to emphasize the need for thought would make difficulties for the egalitarian since only some people are capable of leading intellectually satisfying lives, or morally good lives. This makes it difficult to see what Frankena's principle of equality has to do with simply being *human*. Surely every sentient being is capable of leading a life that is happier or less miserable than some alternative life, and hence has a claim to be taken into account. In this respect the distinction between humans and non-humans is not a sharp division, but rather a continuum along which we move gradually, and with overlaps between the species, from simple capacities for enjoyment and satisfaction, or pain and suffering, to more complex ones.

Faced with a situation in which they see a need for some basis for the moral gulf that is commonly thought to separate humans and animals, but finding no concrete difference that will do the job without undermining the equality of humans, philosophers tend to waffle. They resort to high-sounding phrases like "the intrinsic dignity of the human individual";[9] they talk of the "intrinsic worth of all men" as if men (humans?) had some worth that other beings did not,[10] or they say that humans, and only humans, are "ends in themselves," while "everything other than a person can only have value for a person."[11]

This idea of a distinctive human dignity and worth has a long history; it can be traced back directly to the Renaissance humanists, for instance to Pico della Mirandola's *Oration on the Dignity of Man*. Pico and other humanists based their estimate of human dignity on the idea that man possessed the central, pivotal position in the "Great Chain of Being" that led from the lowliest forms of matter to God himself; this view of the universe, in turn, goes back to both classical and Judeo-Christian doctrines. Contemporary philosophers have cast off these metaphysical and religious shackles and freely invoke the dignity of mankind without needing to justify the idea at all. Why should we not attribute "intrinsic dignity" or "intrinsic worth" to ourselves? Fellow-humans are unlikely to reject the accolades we so generously bestow on them, and those to whom we deny the honor are unable to object. Indeed, when one thinks only of

humans, it can be very liberal, very progressive, to talk of the dignity of all human beings. In so doing, we implicitly condemn slavery, racism, and other violations of human rights. We admit that we ourselves are in some fundamental sense on a par with the poorest, most ignorant members of our own species. It is only when we think of humans as no more than a small sub-group of all the beings that inhabit our planet that we may realize that in elevating our own species we are at the same time lowering the relative status of all other species.

The truth is that the appeal to the intrinsic dignity of human beings appears to solve the egalitarian's problems only as long as it goes unchallenged. Once we ask *why* it should be that all humans—including infants, mental defectives, psychopaths, Hitler, Stalin and the rest—have some kind of dignity or worth that no elephant, pig, or chimpanzee can ever achieve, we see that this question is as difficult to answer as our original request for some relevant fact that justifies the inequality of humans and other animals. In fact, these two questions are really one: talk of intrinsic dignity or moral worth only takes the problem back one step, because any satisfactory defence of the claim that all and only humans have intrinsic dignity would need to refer to some relevant capacities or characteristics that all and only humans possess. Philosophers frequently introduce ideas of dignity, respect and worth at the point at which other reasons appear to be lacking, but this is hardly good enough. Fine phrases are the last resource of those who have run out of arguments.

In case there are those who still think it may be possible to find some relevant characteristic that distinguishes all humans from all members of other species, I shall refer again, before I conclude, to the existence of some humans who quite clearly are below the level of awareness, self-consciousness, intelligence, and sentience, of many nonhumans. I am thinking of humans with severe and irreparable brain damage, and also of infant humans. To avoid the complication of the relevance of a being's potential, however, I shall henceforth concentrate on permanently retarded humans.

Philosophers who set out to find a characteristic that will distinguish humans from other animals rarely take the course of abandoning these groups of humans by lumping them in with the other animals. It is easy to see why they do not. To take this line without re-thinking our attitudes to other animals would entail that we have the right to perform painful experiments on retarded humans for trivial reasons; similarly it would follow that we had the right to rear and kill these humans for food. To most philosophers these consequences are as unacceptable as the view that we should stop treating nonhumans in this way.

Of course, when discussing the problem of equality it is possible to ignore the problem of mental defectives, or brush it aside as if somehow insignificant.[12] This is the easiest way out. What else remains? My final example of speciesism in contemporary philosophy has been selected to show what happens when a writer is prepared to face the question of human equality and animal equality without ignoring the existence of mental defectives, and without resorting to obscurantist mumbo-jumbo. Stanley Benn's clear and honest article "Egalitarianism and Equal Consideration of Interests"[13] fits this description.

Benn, after noting the usual "evident human inequalities," argues, correctly I think, for equality of consideration as the only possible basis for egalitarianism. Yet Benn, like other writers, is thinking only of "equal consideration of human interests." Benn is quite open in his defence of this restriction of equal consideration:

> Not to possess human shape *is* a disqualifying condition. However faithful or intelligent a dog may be, it would be a monstrous sentimentality to attribute to him interests that could be weighed in an equal balance with those of human beings . . . if, for instance, one had to decide between feeding a hungry baby or a hungry dog, anyone who chose the dog would generally be reckoned morally defective, unable to recognize a fundamental inequality of claims.

This is what distinguishes our attitude to animals from our attitude to imbeciles. It would be odd to say that we ought to respect equally the dignity or personality of the imbecile and of the rational man . . . but there is nothing odd about saying that we should respect their interests equally, that is, that we should give to the interests of each the same serious consideration as claims to considerations necessary for some standard of well-being that we can recognize and endorse.

Benn's statement of the basis of the consideration we should have for imbeciles seems to me correct, but why should there be any fundamental inequality of claims between a dog and a human imbecile? Benn sees that if equal consideration depended on rationality, no reason could be given against using imbeciles for research purposes, as we now use dogs and guinea pigs. This will not do: "But of course we do distinguish imbeciles from animals in this regard," he says. That the common distinction is justifiable is something Benn does not question; his problem is how it is to be justified. The answer he gives is this:

> . . . we respect the interests of men and give them priority over dogs not *insofar* as they are rational, but because rationality is the human norm. We say it is *unfair* to exploit the deficiencies of the imbecile who falls short of the norm, just as it would be unfair, and not just ordinarily dishonest, to steal from a blind man. If we do not think in this way about dogs, it is because we do not see the irrationality of the dog as a deficiency or a handicap, but as normal for the species. The characteristics, therefore, that distinguish the normal man from the normal dog make it intelligible for us to talk of other men having interests and capacities, and therefore claims, of precisely the same kind as we make on our own behalf. But although these characteristics may provide the point of the distinction between men and other species, they are not in fact the qualifying conditions for membership, or the distinguishing criteria of the class of morally considerable persons; and this is precisely because a man does not become a member of a different species, with its own standards of normality, by reason of not possessing these characteristics.

The final sentence of this passage gives the argument away. An imbecile, Benn concedes, may have no characteristics superior to those of a dog; nevertheless this does not make the imbecile a member of "a different species" as the dog is. *Therefore* it would be "unfair" to use the imbecile for medical research as we use the dog. But why? That the imbecile is not rational is just the way things have worked out, and the same is true of the dog—neither is any more responsible for their mental level. If it is unfair to take advantage of an isolated defect, why is it fair to take advantage of a more general limitation? I find it hard to see anything in this argument except a defence of preferring the interests of members of our own species because they are members of our own species. To those who think there might be more to it, I suggest the following mental exercise. Assume that it has been proven that there is a difference in the average, or normal, intelligence quotient for two different races, say whites and blacks. Then substitute the term "white" for every occurrence of "men" and "black" for every occurrence of "dog" in the passage quoted; and substitute "high I.Q." for "rationality" and when Benn talks of "imbeciles" replace this term by "dumb whites"—that is, whites who fall well below the normal white I.Q. score. Finally, change "species" to "race." Now re-read the passage. It has become a defence of a rigid, no-exceptions division between whites and blacks, based on I.Q. scores, *not withstanding an admitted overlap* between whites and blacks in this respect. The revised passage is, of course, outrageous, and this is not only because we have made fictitious assumptions in our substitutions. The point is that in the original passage Benn was defending a rigid division in the amount of consideration due to members of different species, despite admitted cases of overlap. If the original did not, at first reading strike us as being as outrageous as the revised version does, this is largely because although we are not racists ourselves, most of us are speciesists. Like the other articles, Benn's stands as a warning of the ease with which the best minds can fall victim to a prevailing ideology.

NOTES

1. *The Methods of Ethics* (7th Ed.), p. 382.
2. For example, R. M. Hare, *Freedom and Reason* (Oxford, 1963) and J. Rawls, *A Theory of Justice* (Harvard, 1972); for a brief account of the essential agreement on this issue between these and other positions, see R. M. Hare, "Rules of War and Moral Reasoning," *Philosophy and Public Affairs*, 1:2 (1972).
3. *Introduction to the Principles of Morals and Legislation*, ch. XVII.
4. I owe the term "speciesism" to Dr. Richard Ryder.
5. In order to produce 1 lb. of protein in the form of beef or veal, we must feed 21 lbs. of protein to the animal. Other forms of livestock are slightly less inefficient, but the average ratio in the U.S. is still 1:8. It has been estimated that the amount of protein lost to humans in this way is equivalent to 90% of the annual world protein deficit. For a brief account, see Frances Moore Lappé, *Diet for a Small Planet* (New York: Friends of The Earth/Ballantine, 1971) pp. 4–11.
6. Ruth Harrison, *Animal Machines* (London: Stuart, 1964). For an account of farming conditions, see my *Animal Liberation* (New York Review Company, 1975).
7. *Journal of the Experimental Analysis of Behavior*, 13:1 (1970).
8. W. Frankena, "The Concept of Social Justice" in *Social Justice*, ed. R. Brandt, (Englewood Cliffs; Prentice Hall, 1962), p. 19.
9. Frankena, "The Concept of Social Justice," p. 23.
10. H. A. Bedau, "Egalitarianism and the Idea of Equality" in *Nomos IX: Equality*, ed. J. R. Pennock and J. W. Chapman (New York: Chapman, 1967)
11. G. Vlastos, "Justice and Equality" in Brandt, *Social Justice*, p. 48.
12. For example, Bernard Williams, "The Idea of Equality" in *Philosophy, Politics and Society* (second series), ed. P. Laslett and W. Runciman (Oxford: Blackwell, 1962), p. 118; J. Rawls, *A Theory of Justice*, pp. 509–10.
13. Bedau, *Nomos IX: Equality*. The passages quoted start on p. 62.

TOM REGAN

THE CASE FOR ANIMAL RIGHTS

— Subjects of Life Have Inherent Worth.

I regard myself as an advocate of animal rights—as a part of the animal rights movement. That movement, as I conceive of it, is committed to a number of goals, including:

- the total abolition of the use of animals in science;
- the total dissolution of commercial animal agriculture;
- the total elimination of commercial and sport hunting and trapping.

There are, I know, people who profess to believe in animal rights but do not avow these goals. Factory farming, they say, is wrong—it violates animals' rights—but traditional animal agriculture is all right. Toxicity tests of cosmetics on animals violates their rights, but important medical research—cancer research, for example—does not. The clubbing of baby seals is abhorrent, but not the harvesting of adult seals. I used to think I understood this reasoning. Not any more. You don't change unjust institutions by tidying them up.

What's wrong—fundamentally wrong—with the way animals are treated isn't the details that vary from case to case. It's the whole system. The forlornness of the veal calf is pathetic, heart wrenching; the pulsing pain of the chimp with electrodes planted deep in her brain is repulsive; the slow, tortuous death of the raccoon caught in the leg-hold trap is agonizing. But what is wrong isn't the pain, isn't the suffering, isn't the deprivation. These compound what's wrong. Sometimes—often—they make it much, much worse. But they are not the fundamental wrong.

The fundamental wrong is the system that allows us to view animals as *our resources*, here for *us*—to be eaten, or surgically manipulated, or exploited for sport or money. Once we accept this view of animals—as our resources—the rest is as predictable as it is regrettable. Why worry about their loneliness, their pain, their death? Since animals live for us, to benefit us in one way or another, what harms them really doesn't matter—or matters only if it starts to bother us, makes us feel a trifle uneasy when we eat our veal escalope, for example. So, yes, let us get veal calves out of solitary confinement, give them more space, a little straw, a few companions. But let us keep our veal escalope.

But a little straw, more space and a few companions won't eliminate—won't even touch—the basic wrong that attaches to our viewing and treating these animals as our resources. A veal calf killed to be eaten after living in close confinement is viewed and treated in this way: but so, too, is another who is raised (as they say) "more humanely." To right the wrong of our treatment of farm animals requires more than making rearing methods "more humane"; it requires the total dissolution of commercial animal agriculture.

How we do this, whether we do it or, as in the case of animals in science, whether and how we abolish their use—these are to a large extent political questions. People must change their beliefs before they change their habits. Enough people, especially those elected to public office, must believe in change—must want it—before we will have laws that protect the rights of animals. This process of change is very complicated, very demanding, very exhausting, calling for the efforts of many hands in education, publicity, political organization and activity, down to the licking of envelopes and stamps. As a trained and practising philosopher, the sort of contribution I can make is limited but, I like to think, important. The currency of philosophy is ideas—their meaning and rational foundation—not

Tom Regan, "The Case for Animal Rights," in Peter Singer (ed.), In Defense of Animals (New York: Basil Blackwell, 1985), pp. 13–26.

the nuts and bolts of the legislative process, say, or the mechanics of community organization. That's what I have been exploring over the past ten years or so in my essays and talks and, most recently, in my book, *The Case for Animal Rights*. I believe the major conclusions I reach in the book are true because they are supported by the weight of the best arguments. I believe the idea of animal rights has reason, not just emotion, on its side.

In the space I have at my disposal here I can only sketch, in the barest outline, some of the main features of the book. [Its] main themes—and we should not be surprised by this—involve asking and answering deep, foundational moral questions about what morality is, how it should be understood and what is the best moral theory, all considered. I hope I can convey something of the shape I think this theory takes. The attempt to do this will be (to use a word a friendly critic once used to describe my work) cerebral, perhaps too cerebral. But this is misleading. My feelings about how animals are sometimes treated run just as deep and just as strong as those of my more volatile compatriots. Philosophers do—to use the jargon of the day—have a right side to their brains. If it's the left side we contribute (or mainly should), that's because what talents we have reside there.

How to proceed? We begin by asking how the moral status of animals has been understood by thinkers who deny that animals have rights. Then we test the mettle of their ideas by seeing how well they stand up under the heat of fair criticism. If we start our thinking in this way, we soon find that some people believe that we have no duties directly to animals, that we owe nothing to them, that we can do nothing that wrongs them. Rather, we can do wrong acts that involve animals, and so we have duties regarding them, though none to them. Such views may be called indirect duty views. By way of illustration: suppose your neighbour kicks your dog. Then your neighbour has done something wrong. But not to your dog. The wrong that has been done is a wrong to you. After all, it is wrong to upset people, and your neighbour's kicking your dog upsets you. So you are the one who is wronged, not your dog. Or again: by kicking your dog your neighbour damages your property. And since it is wrong to damage another person's property, your neighbour has done something wrong—to you, of course, not to

your dog. Your neighbour no more wrongs your dog than your car would be wronged if the windshield were smashed. Your neighbour's duties involving your dog are indirect duties to you. More generally, all of our duties regarding animals are indirect duties to one another—to humanity.

How could someone try to justify such a view? Someone might say that your dog doesn't feel anything and so isn't hurt by your neighbour's kick, doesn't care about the pain since none is felt, is as unaware of anything as your windshield. Someone might say this, but no rational person will. . . . A second possibility is that though both humans and your dog are hurt when kicked, it is only human pain that matters. But, again, no rational person can believe this. Pain is pain wherever it occurs. If your neighbour's causing you pain is wrong because of the pain that is caused, we cannot rationally ignore or dismiss the moral relevance of the pain that your dog feels.

Philosophers who hold indirect duty views—and many still do—have come to understand that they must avoid the two defects just noted: that is, both the view that animals don't feel anything as well as the idea that only human pain can be morally relevant. Among such thinkers the sort of view now favored is one or other form of what is called contractarianism.

Here, very crudely, is the root idea: morality consists of a set of rules that individuals voluntarily agree to abide by, as we do when we sign a contract (hence the name contractarianism). Those who understand and accept the terms of the contract are covered directly; they have rights created and recognized by, and protected in, the contract. And these contractors can also have protection spelled out for others who, though they lack the ability to understand morality and so cannot sign the contract themselves, are loved or cherished by those who can. Thus young children, for example, are unable to sign contracts and lack rights. But they are protected by the contract none the less because of the sentimental interests of others, most notably their parents. So we have, then, duties involving these children, duties regarding them, but no duties to them. Our duties in their case are indirect duties to other human beings, usually their parents.

As for animals, since they cannot understand contracts, they obviously cannot sign; and since they cannot sign, they have no rights. Like children, however, some animals are the objects of the sentimental interest of others. You, for example, love your dog or cat. So those animals that enough people care about (companion animals, whales, baby seals, the American bald eagle), though they lack rights themselves, will be protected because of the sentimental interests of people. I have, then, according to contractarianism, no duty directly to your dog or any other animal, not even the duty not to cause them pain or suffering; my duty not to hurt them is a duty I have to those people who care about what happens to them. As for other animals, where no or little sentimental interest is present—in the case of farm animals, for example, or laboratory rats—what duties we have grow weaker and weaker, perhaps to vanishing point. The pain and death they endure, though real, are not wrong if no one cares about them.

When it comes to the moral status of animals' contractarianism could be a hard view to refute if it were an adequate theoretical approach to the moral status of human beings. It is not adequate in this latter respect, however, which makes the question of its adequacy in the former case, regarding animals, utterly moot. For consider: morality, according to the (crude) contractarian position before us, consists of rules that people agree to abide by. What people? Well, enough to make a difference—enough, that is, *collectively* to have the power to enforce the rules that are drawn up in the contract. That is very well and good for the signatories but not so good for anyone who is not asked to sign. And there is nothing in contractarianism of the sort we are discussing that guarantees or requires that everyone will have a chance to participate equally in framing the rules of morality. The result is that this approach to ethics could sanction the most blatant forms of social, economic, moral and political injustice, ranging from a repressive caste system to systematic racial or sexual discrimination. Might, according to this theory, does make right. Let those who are the victims of injustice suffer as they will. It matters not so long as no one else—no contractor, or too few of them—cares about it. Such a theory takes one's moral breath away . . . as if, for example, there would be nothing wrong with apartheid in South Africa if few white South Africans were upset by it. A theory with so

little to recommend it at the level of the ethics of our treatment of our fellow humans cannot have anything more to recommend it when it comes to the ethics of how we treat our fellow animals.

The version of contractarianism just examined is, as I have noted, a crude variety, and in fairness to those of a contractarian persuasion it must be noted that much more refined, subtle and ingenious varieties are possible. For example, John Rawls, in his *A Theory of Justice*, sets forth a version of contractarianism that forces contractors to ignore the accidental features of being a human being—for example, whether one is white or black, male or female, a genius or of modest intellect. Only by ignoring such features, Rawls believes, can we ensure that the principles of justice that contractors would agree upon are not based on bias or prejudice. Despite the improvement a view such as Rawls's represents over the cruder forms of contractarianism, it remains deficient: it systematically denies that we have direct duties to those human beings who do not have a sense of justice—young children, for instance, and many mentally retarded humans. And yet it seems reasonably certain that, were we to torture a young child or a retarded elder, we would be doing something that wronged him or her, not something that would be wrong if (and only if) other humans with a sense of justice were upset. And since this is true in the case of these humans, we cannot rationally deny the same in the case of animals.

Indirect duty views, then, including the best among them, fail to command our rational assent. Whatever ethical theory we should accept rationally, therefore, it must at least recognize that we have some duties directly to animals, just as we have some duties directly to each other. The next two theories I'll sketch attempt to meet this requirement.

The first I call the cruelty-kindness view. Simply stated, this says that we have a direct duty to be kind to animals and a direct duty not to be cruel to them. Despite the familiar, reassuring ring of these ideas, I do not believe that this view offers an adequate theory. To make this clearer, consider kindness. A kind person acts from a certain kind of motive—compassion or concern, for example. And that is a virtue. But there is no guarantee that a kind act is a right act. If I am a generous racist, for example, I will be inclined to act kindly towards members of my own race, favouring their interests above those of others. My kindness would be real and, so far as it goes, good. But I trust it is too obvious to require argument that my kind acts may not be above moral reproach—may, in fact, be positively wrong because rooted in injustice. So kindness, notwithstanding its status as a virtue to be encouraged, simply will not carry the weight of a theory of right action.

Cruelty fares no better. People or their acts are cruel if they display either a lack of sympathy for or, worse, the presence of enjoyment in another's suffering. Cruelty in all its guises is a bad thing, a tragic human failing. But just as a person's being motivated by kindness does not guarantee that he or she does what is right, so the absence of cruelty does not ensure that he or she avoids doing what is wrong. Many people who perform abortions, for example, are not cruel, sadistic people. But that fact alone does not settle the terribly difficult question of the morality of abortion. The case is no different when we examine the ethics of our treatment of animals. So, yes, let us be for kindness and against cruelty. But let us not suppose that being for one and against the other answers questions about moral right and wrong.

Some people think that the theory we are looking for is utilitarianism. A utilitarian accepts two moral principles. The first is that of equality: everyone's interests count, and similar interests must be counted as having similar weight or importance. White or black, American or Iranian, human or animal—everyone's pain or frustration matter, and matter just as much as the equivalent pain or frustration of anyone else. The second principle a utilitarian accepts is that of utility: do the act that will bring about the best balance between satisfaction and frustration for everyone affected by the outcome.

As a utilitarian, then, here is how I am to approach the task of deciding what I morally ought to do: I must ask who will be affected if I choose to do one thing rather than another, how much each individual will be affected, and where the best results are most likely to lie—which option, in other words, is most likely to bring about the best results, the best balance between satisfaction and frustration. That option, whatever it may be, is the one I ought to choose. That is where my moral duty lies.

The great appeal of utilitarianism rests with its uncompromising *egalitarianism:* everyone's interests count and count as much as the like interests of everyone else. The kind of odious discrimination that some forms of contractarianism can justify—discrimination based on race or sex, for example—seems disallowed in principle by utilitarianism, as is speciesism, systematic discrimination based on species membership.

The equality we find in utilitarianism, however, is not the sort an advocate of animal or human rights should have in mind. Utilitarianism has no room for the equal moral rights of different individuals because it has no room for their equal inherent value or worth. What has value for a utilitarian is the satisfaction of an individual's interests, not the individual whose interests they are. A universe in which you satisfy your desire for water, food and warmth is, other things being equal, better than a universe in which these desires are frustrated. And the same is true in the case of an animal with similar desires. But neither you nor the animal have any value in your own right. Only your feelings do.

Here is an analogy to help make the philosophical point clearer: a cup contains different liquids, sometimes sweet, sometimes bitter, sometimes a mix of the two. What has value are the liquids: the sweeter the better, the bitterer the worse. The cup, the container, has no value. It is what goes into it, not what they go into, that has value. For the utilitarian you and I are like the cup; we have no value as individuals and thus no equal value. What has value is what goes into us, what we serve as receptacles for; our feelings of satisfaction have positive value, our feelings of frustration have negative value.

Serious problems arise for utilitarianism when we remind ourselves that it enjoins us to bring about the best consequences. What does this mean? It doesn't mean the best consequences for me alone, or for my family or friends, or any other person taken individually. No, what we must do is, roughly, as follows: we must add up (somehow!) the separate satisfactions and frustrations of everyone likely to be affected by our choice, the satisfactions in one column, the frustrations in the other. We must total each column for each of the options before us. That is what it means to say the theory is aggregative. And then we must choose that option which is most likely to bring about the best balance of totaled satisfactions over totaled frustrations. Whatever act would lead to this outcome is the one we ought morally to perform—it is where our moral duty lies. And that act quite clearly might not be the same one that would bring about the best results for me personally, or for my family or friends, or for a lab animal. The best aggregated consequences for everyone concerned are not necessarily the best for each individual.

That utilitarianism is an aggregative theory—different individuals' satisfactions are added, or summed, or totaled—is the key objection to this theory. My Aunt Bea is old, inactive, a cranky, sour person, though not physically ill. She prefers to go on living. She is also rather rich. I could make a fortune if I could get my hands on her money, money she intends to give me in any event, after she dies, but which she refuses to give me now. In order to avoid a huge tax bite, I plan to donate a handsome sum of my profits to a local children's hospital. Many, many children will benefit from my generosity, and much joy will be brought to their parents, relatives and friends. If I don't get the money rather soon, all these ambitions will come to naught. The once-in-a-lifetime opportunity to make a real killing will be gone. Why, then, not kill my Aunt Bea? Oh, of course I *might* get caught. But I'm no fool and, besides, her doctor can be counted on to co-operate (he has an eye for the same investment and I happen to know a good deal about his shady past). The deed can be done . . . professionally, shall we say. There is *very* little chance of getting caught. And for my conscience being guilt-ridden, I am a resourceful sort of fellow and will take more than sufficient comfort—as I lie on the beach at Acapulco—in contemplating the joy and health I have brought to so many others.

Suppose Aunt Bea is killed and the rest of the story comes out as told. Would I have done anything wrong? Anything immoral? One would have thought that I had. Not according to utilitarianism. Since what I have done has brought about the best balance between totaled satisfaction and frustration for all those affected by the outcome, my action is not wrong. Indeed, in killing Aunt Bea the physician and I did what duty required.

This same kind of argument can be repeated in all sorts of cases, illustrating, time after time, how the utilitarian's position leads to results that impartial people find morally callous. It *is* wrong to kill my Aunt Bea in the name of bringing about the best results for others. A good end does not justify an evil means. Any adequate moral theory will have to explain why this is so. Utilitarianism fails in this respect and so cannot be the theory we seek.

What to do? Where to begin anew? The place to begin, I think, is with the utilitarian's view of the value of the individual—or, rather, lack of value. In its place, suppose we consider that you and I, for example, do have value as individuals—what we'll call *inherent value.* To say we have such value is to say that we are something more than, something different from, mere receptacles. Moreover, to ensure that we do not pave the way for such injustices as slavery or sexual discrimination, we must believe that all who have inherent value have it equally, regardless of their sex, race, religion, birthplace and so on. Similarly to be discarded as irrelevant are one's talents or skills, intelligence and wealth, personality or pathology, whether one is loved and admired or despised and loathed. The genius and the retarded child, the prince and the pauper, the brain surgeon and the fruit vender, Mother Teresa and the most unscrupulous used-car salesman—all have inherent value, all possess it equally, and all have an equal right to be treated with respect, to be treated in ways that do not reduce them to the status of things, as if they existed as resources for others. My value as an individual is independent of my usefulness to you. Yours is not dependent on your usefulness to me. For either of us to treat the other in ways that fail to show respect for the other's independent value is to act immorally, to violate the individual's rights.

Some of the rational virtues of this view—what I call the rights view—should be evident. Unlike (crude) contractarianism, for example, the rights view *in principle* denies the moral tolerability of any and all forms of racial, sexual or social discrimination; and unlike utilitarianism, this view *in principle* denies that we can justify good results by using evil means that violate an individual's rights—denies, for example, that it could be moral to kill my Aunt Bea to harvest beneficial consequences for others. That would be to sanction the disrespectful treatment of the individual in the name of the social good, something the rights view will not—categorically will not—ever allow.

The rights view, I believe, is rationally the most satisfactory moral theory. It surpasses all other theories in the degree to which it illuminates and explains the foundation of our duties to one another—the domain of human morality. On this score it has the best reasons, the best arguments, on its side. Of course, if it were possible to show that only human beings are included within its scope, then a person like myself, who believes in animal rights, would be obliged to look elsewhere.

But attempts to limit its scope to humans only can be shown to be rationally defective. Animals, it is true, lack many of the abilities humans possess. They can't read, do higher mathematics, build a bookcase or make *baba ghanoush*. Neither can many human beings, however, and yet we don't (and should) say that they (these humans) therefore have less inherent value, less of a right to be treated with respect, than do others. It is the *similarities* between those human beings who most clearly, most non-controversially have such value (the people reading this, for example), not our differences, that matter most. And the really crucial, the basic similarity is simply this: we are each of us the experiencing subject of a life, a conscious creature having an individual welfare that has importance to us whatever our usefulness to others. We want and prefer things, believe and feel things, recall and expect things. And all these dimensions of our life, including our pleasure and pain, our enjoyment and suffering, our satisfaction and frustration, our continued existence or our untimely death—all make a difference to the quality of our life as lived, as experienced, by us as individuals. As the same is true of those animals that concern us (the ones that are eaten and trapped, for example), they too must be viewed as the experiencing subjects of a life, with inherent value of their own.

Some there are who have resisted the idea, that animals have inherent value. "Only humans have such value," they profess. How might this narrow view be defended? Shall we say that only humans have the requisite intelligence, or autonomy, or reason? But there are many, many humans who fail to meet these standards and yet are reasonably viewed as having value

above and beyond their usefulness to others. Shall we claim that only humans belong to the right species, the species *Homo sapiens*? But this is blatant speciesism. Will it be said, then, that all—and only—humans have immortal souls? Then our opponents have their work cut out for them. I am myself not ill-disposed to the proposition that there are immortal souls. Personally, I profoundly hope I have one. But I would not want to rest my position on a controversial ethical issue on the even more controversial question about who or what has an immortal soul. That is to dig one's hole deeper, not to climb out. Rationally, it is better to resolve moral issues without making more controversial assumptions than are needed. The question of who has inherent value is such a question, one that is resolved more rationally without the introduction of the idea of immortal souls than by its use.

Well, perhaps some will say that animals have some inherent value, only less than we have. Once again, however, attempts to defend this view can be shown to lack rational justification. What could be the basis of our having more inherent value than animals? Their lack of reason, or autonomy, or intellect? Only if we are willing to make the same judgment in the case of humans who are similarly deficient. But it is not true that such humans—the retarded child, for example, or the mentally deranged—have less inherent value than you or I. Neither, then, can we rationally sustain the view that animals like them in being the experiencing subjects of a life have less inherent value. All who have inherent value have it *equally*, whether they be human animals or not.

Inherent value, then, belongs equally to those who are the experiencing subjects of a life. Whether it belongs to others—to rocks and rivers, trees and glaciers, for example—we do not know and may never know. But neither do we need to know, if we are to make the case for animal rights. We do not need to know, for example how many people are eligible to vote in the next presidential election before we can know whether I am. Similarly, we do not need to know how many individuals have inherent value before we can know that some do. When it comes to the case for animal rights, then, what we need to know is whether the animals that, in our culture, are routinely eaten, hunted, and used in our laboratories, for example, are like us in being subjects of a life. And we do know this. We do know that many—literally, billions and billions—of these animals are the subjects of a life in the sense explained and so have inherent value if we do. And since, in order to arrive at the best theory of our duties to one another, we must recognize our equal inherent value as individuals, reason—not sentiment, not emotion—reason compels us to recognize the equal inherent value of these animals and, with this, their equal right to be treated with respect.

That, *very* roughly, is the shape and feel of the case for animal rights. Most of the details of the supporting arguments are missing. They are to be found in the book to which I alluded earlier. Here, the details go begging, and I must, in closing, limit myself to four final points.

The first is how the theory that underlies the case for animal rights shows that the animal rights movement is a part of, not antagonistic to, the human rights movement. The theory that rationally grounds the rights of animals also grounds the rights of humans. Thus those involved in the animal rights movement are partners in the struggle to secure respect for human rights—the rights of women, for example, or minorities, or workers. The animal rights movement is cut from the same moral cloth as these.

Second, having set out the broad outlines of the rights view, I can now say why its implications for farming and science, among other fields, are both clear and uncompromising. In the case of the use of animals in science, the rights view is categorically abolitionist. Lab animals are not our tasters; we are not their kings. Because these animals are treated routinely, systematically as if their value were reducible to their usefulness to others, they are routinely, systematically treated with a lack of respect, and thus are their rights routinely, systematically violated. This is just as true when they are used in trivial, duplicative, unnecessary or unwise research as it is when they are used in studies that hold out real promise of human benefits. We can't justify harming or killing a human being (my Aunt Bea, for example) just for these sorts of reasons. Neither can we do so even in the case of so lowly a creature as a laboratory rat. It is not just refinement or reduction that is called for, not just larger, cleaner cages, not just more generous use of anaesthetic or the

elimination of multiple surgery, not just tidying up the system. It is complete replacement. The best we can do when it comes to using animals in science is—not to use them. That is where our duty lies, according to the rights view.

As for commercial animal agriculture, the rights view takes a similar abolitionist position. The fundamental moral wrong here is not that animals are kept in stressful close confinement or in isolation, or that their pain and suffering, their needs and preferences are ignored or discounted. All these *are* wrongs, of course, but they are not the fundamental wrong. They are symptoms and effects of the deeper, systematic wrong that allows these animals to be viewed and treated as lacking independent value, as resources for us—as, indeed, a renewable resource. Giving farm animals more space, more natural environments, more companions does not right the fundamental wrong, any more than giving lab animals more anaesthesia or bigger, cleaner cages would right the fundamental wrong in their case. Nothing less than the total dissolution of commercial animal agriculture will do this, just as, for similar reasons I won't develop at length here, morality requires nothing less than the total elimination of hunting and trapping for commercial and sporting ends. The rights view's implications, then, as I have said, are clear and uncompromising.

My last two points are about philosophy, my profession. It is, most obviously, no substitute for political action. The words I have written here and in other places by themselves don't change a thing. It is what we do with the thoughts that the words express—our acts, our deeds—that changes things. All that philosophy can do, and all I have attempted, is to offer a vision of what our deeds should aim at. And the why. But not the how.

Finally, I am reminded of my thoughtful critic, the one I mentioned earlier, who chastised me for being too cerebral. Well, cerebral I have been: indirect duty views, utilitarianism, contractarianism—hardly the stuff deep passions are made of. I am also reminded, however, of the image another friend once set before me—the image of the ballerina as expressive of disciplined passion. Long hours of sweat and toil, of loneliness and practice, of doubt and fatigue: those are the discipline of her craft. But the passion is there too, the fierce drive to excel, to speak through her body, to do it right, to pierce our minds. That is the image of philosophy I would leave with you, not "too cerebral" but *disciplined* passion. Of the discipline enough has been seen. As for the passion: there are times, and these not infrequent, when tears come to my eyes when I see, or read, or hear of the wretched plight of animals in the hands of humans. Their pain, their suffering, their loneliness, their innocence, their death. Anger. Rage. Pity. Sorrow. Disgust. The whole creation groans under the weigh of the evil we humans visit upon these mute, powerless creatures. It *is* our hearts, not just our heads, that call for an end to it all, that demands of us that we overcome, for them, the habits and forces behind their systematic oppression. All great movements, it is written, go through three stages: ridicule, discussion, adoption. It is the realization of this third stage, adoption, that requires both our passion and our discipline, our hearts and our heads. The fate of animals is in our hands. God grant we are equal to the task.

IT IS UP TO US TO CHANGE.

BONNIE STEINBOCK

SPECIESISM AND THE IDEA OF EQUALITY

Human Suffering is worse than Animal Suff[...]

Most of us believe that we are entitled to treat members of other species in ways which would be considered wrong if inflicted on members of our own species. We kill them for food, keep them confined, use them in painful experiments. The moral philosopher has to ask what relevant difference justifies this difference in treatment. A look at this question will lead us to re-examine the distinctions which we have assumed make a moral difference.

It has been suggested by Peter Singer[1] that our current attitudes are "speciesist," a word intended to make one think of "racist" or "sexist." The idea is that membership in a species is in itself not relevant to moral treatment, and that much of our behaviour and attitudes towards non-human animals is based simply on this irrelevant fact.

There is, however, an important difference between racism or sexism and "speciesism." We do not subject animals to different moral treatment simply because they have fur and feathers, but because they are in fact different from human beings in ways that could be morally relevant. It is false that women are incapable of being benefited by education, and therefore that claim cannot serve to justify preventing them from attending school. But this is not false of cows and dogs, even chimpanzees. Intelligence is thought to be a morally relevant capacity because of its relation to the capacity for moral responsibility.

What is Singer's response? He agrees that non-human animals lack certain capacities that human animals possess, and that this may justify different *treatment*. But it does not justify giving less consideration to their needs and interests. According to Singer, the moral mistake which the racist or sexist makes is not essentially the factual error of thinking that blacks or women are inferior to white men. For even if there were no factual error, even if it were true that blacks and women are less intelligent and responsible than whites and men, this would not justify giving less consideration to their needs and interests. It is important to note that the term "speciesism" is in one way like, and in another way unlike, the terms "racism" and

This reading is adapted from Bonnie Steinbock, "Speciesism and the Idea of Equality," *Philosophy* 53, no. 204 (1978): 247–256.

"sexism." What the term "speciesism" has in common with these terms is the reference to focusing on a characteristic which is, in itself, irrelevant to moral treatment. And it is worth reminding us of this. But Singer's real aim is to bring us to a new understanding of the idea of equality. The question is, on what do claims to equality rest? The demand for *human* equality is a demand that the interests of all human beings be considered equally, unless there is a moral justification for not doing so. But why should the interests of all human beings be considered equally? In order to answer this question, we have to give some sense to the phrase, "All men (human beings) are created equal." Human beings are manifestly *not* equal, differing greatly in intelligence, virtue and capacities. In virtue of what can the claim to equality be made?

It is Singer's contention that claims to equality do not rest on factual equality. Not only do human beings differ in their capacities, but it might even turn out that intelligence, the capacity for virtue, etc., are not distributed evenly among the races and sexes:

> The appropriate response to those who claim to have found evidence of genetically based differences in ability between the races or sexes is not to stick to the belief that the genetic explanation must be wrong, whatever evidence to the contrary may turn up; instead we should make it quite clear that the claim to equality does not depend on intelligence, moral capacity, physical strength, or similar matters of fact. There is no logically compelling reason for assuming that a factual difference in ability between two people justifies any difference in the amount of consideration we give to satisfying their needs and interests. The principle of equality of human beings is not a description of an alleged actual equality among humans: it is a prescription of how we should treat humans.[2]

In so far as the subject is human equality, Singer's view is supported by other philosophers. Bernard Williams, for example, is concerned to show that demands for equality cannot rest on factual equality among people, for no such equality exists.[3] The only respect in which all men are equal, according to Williams, is that they are all equally men. This seems to be a platitude, but Williams denies that it is trivial. Membership in the species *homo sapiens* in itself has no special moral significance, but rather the fact that all men are human serves as a *reminder* that being human involves the possession of characteristics that are morally relevant. But on what characteristics does Williams focus? Aside from the desire for self-respect (which I will discuss later), Williams is not concerned with uniquely human capacities. Rather, he focuses on the capacity to feel pain and the capacity to feel affection. It is in virtue of these capacities, it seems that the idea of equality is to be justified.

Apparently Richard Wasserstrom has the same idea as he sets out the racist's "logical and moral mistakes" in "Rights, Human Rights and Racial Discrimination."[4] The racist fails to acknowledge that the black person is as capable of suffering as the white person. According to Wasserstrom, the reason why a person is said to have a right not to be made to suffer acute physical pain is that we all do in fact value freedom from such pain. Therefore, if anyone has a right to be free from suffering acute physical pain, *everyone* has this right, for there is no possible basis of discrimination. Wasserstrom says, "For, if all persons do have equal capacities of these sorts and if the existence of these capacities is the reason for ascribing these rights to anyone, then all persons ought to have the right to claim equality of treatment in respect to the possession and exercise of these rights."[5] The basis of equality, for Wasserstrom as for Williams, lies not in some uniquely human capacity, but rather in the fact that all human beings are alike in their capacity to suffer. Writers on equality have focused on this capacity, I think, because it functions as some sort of lowest common denominator, so that whatever the other capacities of a human being, he is entitled to equal consideration because, like everyone else, he is capable of suffering.

If the capacity to suffer is the reason for ascribing a right to freedom from acute pain, or a right to well being, then it certainly looks as though these rights must be extended to animals as well. This is the conclusion Singer arrives at. The demand for human equality rests on the equal capacity of all human beings to suffer and to enjoy well being. But if this is the basis of the demand for equality, then this demand must also include all beings which have an equal capacity to suffer and enjoy well being. That is why Singer places at the basis of the demand for equality, not intelligence or reason, but sentience. And equality will mean, not equality of treatment, but "equal consideration of interests." The equal consideration of interests will often mean quite different treatment, depending on the nature of the entity being considered. (It would be as absurd to talk of a dog's right to vote, Singer says, as to talk of a man's right to have an abortion.)

. . .

I want to point out that the issue is not one of cruelty to animals. We all agree that cruelty is wrong, whether perpetrated on a moral or non-moral, rational or non-rational agent. Cruelty is defined as the infliction of unnecessary pain or suffering. What is to count as necessary or unnecessary is determined, in part, by the nature of the end pursued. Torturing an animal is cruel, because although the pain is logically necessary for the action to be torture, the end (deriving enjoyment from seeing the animal suffer) is monstrous. Allowing animals to suffer from neglect or for the sake of large profits may also be thought to be unnecessary and therefore cruel. But there may be some ends which are very good (such as the advancement of medical knowledge), which can be accomplished by subjecting animals to pain in experiments. Although most people would agree that the pain inflicted on animals used in medical research ought to be kept to a minimum, they would consider pain that could not be eliminated "necessary" and therefore not cruel. It would probably not be so regarded if the subjects were non-voluntary human beings. Necessity, then, is defined in terms of human benefit, but this is just what is being called into question. The topic of cruelty to animals, while important from a practical viewpoint, because much of our present treatment of animals involves the infliction of suffering for no good reason, is not very interesting philosophically. What is philosophically interesting is whether we are justified in having different standards of necessity for human suffering and for animal suffering.

Singer says, quite rightly I think, "If a being suffers, there can be no moral justification for refusing to take that suffering into consideration."[6] But he thinks that the principle of equality requires that, no matter what the nature of the being, its suffering be counted equally with the like suffering of any other being. In other words sentience does not simply provide us with reasons for acting; it is the *only* relevant consideration for equal consideration of interests. It is this view I wish to challenge.

I want to challenge it partly because it has such counter-intuitive results. It means, for example, that feeding starving children before feeding starving dogs is just like a Catholic charity's feeding hungry Catholics before feeding hungry non-Catholics. It is simply a matter of taking care of one's own, something which is usually morally permissible. But whereas we would admire the Catholic agency which did not discriminate, but fed all children, first come, first served, we would feel quite differently about someone who had this policy for dogs and children. Nor is this, it seems to me, simply a matter of a sentimental preference for our own species. I might feel much more love for my dog than for a strange child—and yet I might feel morally obliged to feed the child before I fed my dog. If I gave in to the feelings of love and fed my dog and let the child go hungry, I would probably feel guilty. This is not to say that we can simply rely on such feelings. Huck Finn felt guilty at helping Jim escape, which he viewed as stealing from a woman who had never done him any harm. But while the existence of such feelings does not settle the morality of an issue, it is not clear to me that they can be explained away. In any event, their existence can serve as a motivation for trying to find a rational justification for considering human interests above non-human ones.

However, it does seem to me that this *requires* a justification. Until now, common sense (and academic philosophy) have seen no such need. Benn says, "No one claims equal consideration for all mammals—human beings count, mice do not, though it would not be easy to say *why* not. . . . Although we hesitate to inflict unnecessary pain on sentient creatures, such as mice or dogs, we are quite sure that we do not need to show good reasons for putting human interests before theirs."[7]

I think we do have to justify counting our interests more heavily than those of animals. But how? Singer is right, I think, to point out that it will not do to refer vaguely to the greater value of human life, to human worth and dignity:

> Faced with a situation in which they see a need for some basis for the moral gulf that is commonly thought to separate humans and animals, but can

find no concrete difference that will do this without undermining the equality of humans, philosophers tend to waffle. They resort to high-sounding phrases like "the intrinsic dignity of the human individual." They talk of "the intrinsic worth of all men" as if men had some worth that other beings do not have or they say that human beings, and only human beings, are "ends in themselves," while "everything other than a person can only have value for a person." . . . Why should we not attribute "intrinsic dignity" or "intrinsic worth" to ourselves? Why should we not say that we are the only things in the universe that have intrinsic value? Our fellow human beings are unlikely to reject the accolades we so generously bestow upon them, and those to whom we deny the honour are unable to object.[8]

Singer is right to be sceptical of terms like "intrinsic dignity" and "intrinsic worth." These phrases are no substitute for a moral argument. But they may point to one. In trying to understand what is meant by these phrases, we may find a difference or differences between human beings and non-human animals that will justify different treatment while not undermining claims for human equality. While we are not compelled to discriminate among people because of different capacities, if we can find a difference in capacities between human and non-human animals, this could serve to justify regarding human interests as primary. It is not arbitrary or smug, I think, to maintain that human beings have a different moral status from members of other species because of certain capacities which are characteristic of being human. We may not all be equal in these capacities, but all human beings possess them to some measure, and non-human animals do not. For example, human beings are normally held to be responsible for what they do. In recognizing that someone is responsible for his or her actions, you accord that person a respect which is reserved for those possessed of moral autonomy, or capable of achieving such autonomy. Secondly, human beings can be expected to reciprocate in a way that non-human animals cannot. Non-human animals cannot be motivated by altruistic or moral reasons; they cannot treat you fairly or unfairly. This does not rule out the possibility of an animal being motivated by sympathy or pity. It does rule out altruistic motivation in the sense of motivation

due to the recognition that the needs and interests of others provide one with certain reasons for acting.[9] Human beings are capable of altruistic motivation in this sense. We are sometimes motivated simply by the recognition that someone else is in pain, and that pain is a bad thing, no matter who suffers it. It is this sort of reason that I claim cannot motivate an animal or any entity not possessed of fairly abstract concepts. (If some non-human animals do possess the requisite concepts—perhaps chimpanzees who have learned a language—they might well be capable of altruistic motivation.) This means that our moral dealings with animals are necessarily much more limited than our dealings with other human beings. If rats invade our houses, carrying disease and biting our children, we cannot reason with them, hoping to persuade them of the injustice they do us. We can only attempt to get rid of them. And it is this that makes it reasonable for us to accord them a separate and not equal moral status, even though their capacity to suffer provides us with some reason to kill them painlessly, if this can be done without too much sacrifice of human interests. Thirdly, as Williams points out, there is the "desire for self-respect": "a certain human desire to be identified with what one is doing, to be able to realize purposes of one's own, and not to be the instrument of another's will unless one has willingly accepted such a role."[10] Some animals may have some form of this desire, and to the extent that they do, we ought to consider their interest in freedom and self-determination. (Such considerations might affect our attitudes toward zoos and circuses.) But the desire for self-respect *per se* requires the intellectual capacities of human beings, and this desire provides us with special reasons not to treat human beings in certain ways. It is an affront to the dignity of a human being to be a slave (even if a well-treated one); this cannot be true for a horse or a cow. To point this out is of course only to say that the justification for the treatment of an entity will depend on the sort of entity in question. In our treatment of other entities, we must consider the desire for autonomy, dignity, and respect, but only where such a desire exists. Recognition of different desires and interests will often require different treatment, a point Singer himself makes.

But is the issue simply one of different desires and interests justifying and requiring different treatment?

I would like to make a stronger claim, namely, that certain capacities, which seem to be unique to human beings, entitle their possessors to a privileged position in the moral community. Both rats and human beings dislike pain, and so we have a *prima facie* reason not to inflict pain on either. But if we can free human beings from crippling diseases, pain and death through experimentation which involves making animals suffer, and if this is the only way to achieve such results, then I think that such experiment is justified because human lives are more valuable than animal lives. And this is because of certain capacities and abilities that normal human beings have which animals apparently do not, and which human beings cannot exercise if they are devastated by pain or disease.

My point is not that the lack of the sorts of capacities I have been discussing gives us a justification for treating animals just as we like, but rather that it is these differences between human beings and non-human animals which provide a rational basis for different moral treatment and consideration. Singer focuses on sentience alone as the basis of equality, but we can justify the belief that human beings have moral worth that non-human animals do not, in virtue of specific capacities, and without resorting to "high-sounding phrases."

Singer thinks that intelligence, the capacity for moral responsibility, for virtue, etc., are irrelevant to equality, because we would not accept a hierarchy based on intelligence any more than one based on race. We do not think that those with greater capacities ought to have their interests weighed more heavily than those with lesser capacities, and this, he thinks, shows that differences in such capacities are irrelevant to equality. But it does not show this at all. Kevin Donaghy argues (rightly, I think) that what entitles us human beings to a privileged position in the moral community is a certain minimal level of intelligence, which is a prerequisite for morally relevant capacities.[11] The fact that we would reject a hierarchical society based on degree of intelligence does not show that a minimal level of intelligence cannot be used as a cut-off point, justifying giving greater consideration to the interests of those entities which meet this standard.

Interestingly enough, Singer concedes the rationality of valuing the lives of normal human beings over the lives of non-human animals.[12] We are not required to value equally the life of a normal human being and the life of an animal, he thinks, but only their suffering. But I doubt that the value of an entity's life can be separated from the value of its suffering in this way. If we value the lives of human beings more than the lives of animals, this is because we value certain capacities that human beings have and animals do not. But freedom from suffering is, in general, a minimal condition for exercising these capacities, for living a fully human life. So, valuing human life more involves regarding human interests as counting for more. That is why we regard human suffering as more deplorable than comparable animal suffering.

But there is one point of Singer's which I have not yet met. Some human beings (if only a very few) are less intelligent than some non-human animals. Some have less capacity for moral choice and responsibility. What status in the moral community are these members of our species to occupy? Are their interests to be considered equally with ours? Is experimenting on them permissible where such experiments are painful or injurious, but somehow necessary for human well being? If it is certain of our capacities which entitle us to a privileged position, it looks as if those lacking those capacities are not entitled to a privileged position. To think it is justifiable to experiment on an adult chimpanzee but not on a severely mentally incapacitated human being seems to be focusing on membership in a species where that has no moral relevance. (It is being "speciesist" in a perfectly reasonable use of the word.) How are we to meet this challenge?

Donaghy is untroubled by this objection. He says that it is fully in accord with his intuitions, that he regards the killing of a normally intelligent human being as far more serious than the killing of a person so severely limited that he lacked the intellectual capacities of an adult pig. But this parry really misses the point. The question is whether Donaghy thinks that the killing of a human being so severely limited that he lacked the intellectual capacities of an adult pig would be less serious than the killing of that pig. If superior intelligence is what justifies privileged status in the moral community, then the pig who is smarter than a human being ought to have superior moral status. And I doubt that this is fully in accord with Donaghy's intuitions.

I doubt that anyone will be able to come up with a concrete and morally relevant difference that would justify, say, using a chimpanzee in an experiment rather than a human being with less capacity for reasoning, moral responsibility, etc. Should we then experiment on the severely retarded? Utilitarian considerations aside (the difficulty of comparing intelligence between species, for example), we feel a special obligation to care for the handicapped members of our own species, who cannot survive in this world without such care. Non-human animals manage very well, despite their "lower intelligence" and lesser capacities; most of them do not require special care from us. This does not, of course, justify experimenting on them. However, to subject to experimentation those people who depend on us seems even worse than subjecting members of other species to it. In addition, when we consider the severely retarded, we think, "That could be me." It makes sense to think that one might have been born retarded, but not to think that one might have been born a monkey. And so, although one can imagine oneself in the monkey's place, one feels a closer identification with the severely retarded human being. Here we are getting away from such things as "morally relevant differences" and are talking about something much more difficult to articulate, namely, the role of feeling and sentiment in moral thinking. We would be *horrified* by the use of the retarded in medical research. But what are we to make of this horror? Has it moral significance or is it "mere" sentiment, of no more import than the sentiment of whites against blacks? It is terribly difficult to know how to evaluate such feelings.[13] I am not going to say more about this, because I think that the treatment of severely incapacitated human beings does not pose an insurmountable objection to the privileged status principle. I am willing to admit that my horror at the thought of experiments being performed on severely mentally incapacitated human beings in cases in which I would find it justifiable and preferable to perform the same experiments on non-human animals (capable of similar suffering) may not be a moral emotion. But it is certainly not wrong of us to extend special care to members of our species, motivated by feelings of sympathy, protectiveness, etc. If this is speciesism, it is stripped of its tone of moral condemnation. It is not racist to provide special care to members of your own race; it is racist to fall below your moral obligation to a person because of his or her race. I have been arguing that we are morally obliged to consider the interests of all sentient creatures, but not to consider those interests equally with human interests. Nevertheless, even this recognition will mean some radical changes in our attitude toward and treatment of other species.[14]

NOTES

1. Peter Singer, *Animal Liberation* (A New York Review Book, 1975).
2. Singer, 5.
3. Bernard Williams, "The Idea of Equality," *Philosophy, Politics and Society* (Second Series), Laslett and Runciman (eds.) (Blackwell, 1962), 110–131, reprinted in *Moral Concepts*, Feinberg (ed.) (Oxford, 1970), 153–171.
4. Richard Wassertstrom, "Rights, Human Rights, and Racial Discrimination," *Journal of Philosophy* 61, No. 20 (1964), reprinted in *Human Rights*, A.I. Melden (ed.) (Wadsworth, 1970), 96–110.
5. Ibid., 106.
6. Singer, 9.
7. Benn, "Equality, Moral and Social," *The Encyclopedia of Philosophy* 3, 40.
8. Singer, 266–267.
9. This conception of altruistic motivation comes from Thomas Nagel's *The Possibility of Altruism* (Oxford, 1970).
10. Williams, op. cit., 157.
11. Kevin Donaghy, "Singer on Speciesism," *Philosophic Exchange* (Summer 1974).
12. Singer, 22.
13. We run into the same problem when discussing abortion. Of what significance are our feelings toward the unborn when discussing its status? Is it relevant or irrelevant that it looks like a human being?
14. I would like to acknowledge the help of, and offer thanks to, Professor Richard Arneson of the University of California, San Diego; Professor Sidney Gendin of Eastern Michigan University; and Professor Peter Singer of Monash University, all of whom read and commented on earlier drafts of this paper.

MARK SAGOFF

ANIMAL LIBERATION AND ENVIRONMENTAL ETHICS

Bad Marriage, Quick Divorce

— Environment as a moral community?

I.

"The land ethic," Aldo Leopold wrote in *A Sand County Almanac*, "simply enlarges the boundaries of the community to include soils, waters, plants, and animals, or collectively, the land."[1] What kind of community does Leopold refer to? He might mean a *moral* community, for example, a group of individuals who respect each other's right to treatment as equals or who regard one another's interests with equal respect and concern. He may also mean an *ecological* community, that is, a community tied together by biological relationships in interdependent webs or systems of life.[2]

Let us suppose, for a moment, that Leopold has a *moral* community in mind; he would expand our *moral* boundaries to include not only human beings, but also soils, waters, plants and animals. Leopold's view, then, might not differ in principle from that of Christopher Stone, who has suggested that animals and even trees be given legal standing, so that their interests may be represented in court.[3] Stone sees the expansion of our moral consciousness in this way as part of a historical progress by which societies have recognized the equality of groups of oppressed people, notably blacks, women and children.[4] Laurence Tribe eloquently makes the same point:

> What is crucial to recognize is that the human capacity for empathy and identification is not static; the very process of recognizing rights in those higher vertebrates with whom we can already empathize could well pave the way for still further extensions as we move upward along the spiral of moral evolution. It is not only the human liberation movements—involving

first blacks, then women, and now children—that advance in waves of increased consciousness.[5]

Peter Singer, perhaps more than any other writer, has emphasized the analogy between human liberation movements (for example, abolitionism and sufferagism) and "animal liberation" or the "expansion of our moral horizons" to include members of other species in the "basic principle of equality."[6] Singer differs from Stone and Tribe, however, in two respects. First, he argues that the capacity of animals to suffer pain or to enjoy pleasure or happiness places people under a moral obligation which does not need to be enhanced by a doctrine about rights. Second, while Stone is willing to speak of the interests of his lawn in being watered,[7] Singer argues that "only a being with subjective experiences, such as the experience of pleasure or the experience of pain, can have interests in the full sense of the term."[8] A tree, as Singer explains, may be said to have an "interest" in being watered, but all this means is that it needs water to grow properly as an automobile needs oil to function properly.[9] Thus, Singer would not include rocks, trees, lakes, rivers or mountains in the moral community or the community of morally equal beings.

Singer's thesis, then, is not necessarily that animals have rights which we are to respect. Instead, he argues that they have utilities that ought to be treated on an equal basis with those of human beings. Whether Tribe and Stone argue a weaker or a different thesis depends upon the rights they believe animals and other natural things to have. They may believe that all animals have a right to be treated as equals, in effect, they may agree with Singer that the interests of *all* animals should receive

Mark Sagoff. 1984. Animal Liberation and Environmental Ethics: Bad Marriage, Quick Divorce. Osgoode Hall Law Journal, 22: 297–307. Reprinted with permission of author.

equal respect and concern. On the other hand, Tribe, Stone or both may believe that animals have a right only to life or only to those very minimal and basic rights without which they could not conceivably enjoy any other right.[10] I will, for the moment, assume that Tribe and Stone agree that animals have basic rights, for example, a right to live or a right not to be killed for their meat. I will consider later the possibility that environmental law might protect the rights of animals without necessarily improving their welfare or protecting their lives.

Moral obligations to animals, to their well-being or to their rights, may arise in either of two ways. First, duties to non-human animals may be based on the principle that cruelty to animals is obnoxious, a principle nobody denies. Muckraking journalists (thank God for them) who depict the horrors which all too often occur in laboratories and on farms, appeal quite properly to the conviction and intuition that people should never inflict needless pain on animals and especially not for the sake of profit. When television documentaries or newspaper articles report the horrid ways in which domestic animals are often treated, the response is, as it should be, moral revulsion. This anger is directed at human responsibility for the callous, wanton and needless cruelty human beings inflict on domestic animals. It is not simply the pain but the way it is caused which justifies moral outrage.

Moral obligations, however, might rest instead on a stronger contention, which is that human beings are obliged to prevent and to relieve animal suffering however it is caused. Now, insofar as the animal equality or animal liberation movement makes a philosophically interesting claim, it insists on the stronger thesis, that there is an obligation to serve the interests, or at least to protect the lives, of *all* animals who suffer or are killed, whether on the farm or in the wild. Singer, for example, does not stop with the stultifying platitude that human beings ought not to be cruel to animals. No; he argues the controversial thesis that society has an obligation to prevent the killing of animals and even to relieve their suffering wherever, however, and as much as it is able, at a reasonable cost to itself.

II.

I began by supposing that Aldo Leopold viewed the community of nature as a *moral* community—one in which human beings, as members, have obligations to all other animals, presumably to minimize their pain. I suggested that Leopold, like Singer, may be committed to the idea that the natural environment should be preserved and protected only insofar as, and because, its protection satisfies the needs or promotes the welfare of individual animals and perhaps other living things. I believe, however, that this is plainly not Leopold's view. The principle of natural selection is not obviously a humanitarian principle; the predator–prey relation does not depend on moral empathy. Nature ruthlessly limits animal populations by doing violence to virtually every individual before it reaches maturity; these conditions respect animal equality only in the darkest sense. Yet these are precisely the ecological relationships which Leopold admires; they are the conditions which he would not interfere with, but protect. Apparently, Leopold does not think that an ecological system has to be an egalitarian moral system in order to deserve love and admiration. An ecological system has a beauty and an authenticity that demands respect—but plainly not on humanitarian grounds.

In a persuasive essay, J. Baird Callicott describes a number of differences between the ideas of Leopold and those of Singer—differences which suggest that Leopold's environmental ethic and Singer's humane utilitarianism lead in opposite directions. First, while Singer and other animal liberationists deplore the suffering of domestic animals, "Leopold manifests an attitude that can only be described as indifference."[11] Second, while Leopold expresses an urgent concern about the disappearance of species, Singer, consistently with his premises, is concerned with the welfare of individual animals, without special regard to their status as endangered species. Third, the preservation of wilderness, according to Leopold, provides "a means of perpetuating, in sport form, the more virile and primitive skills. . . ."[12] He had hunting in mind. Leopold recognized that since top predators are gone, hunters may serve an important ecological function. Leopold was himself an enthusiastic hunter and wrote unabashedly about his exploits pursuing game. The term "game" as applied to animals, Callicott wryly comments, "appears to be morally equivalent to referring to a sexually appealing young woman as a "piece" or to a strong, young black man as a "buck"—if animal rights, that is, are to be considered on par with women's rights and the rights of formerly enslaved races."[13]

Singer expresses disdain and chagrin at what he calls "environmentalist" organizations such as the Sierra Club and the Wildlife Fund, which actively support or refuse to oppose hunting. I can appreciate Singer's aversion to hunting, but why does he place the word "environmentalist" in shudder quotes when he refers to organizations like the Sierra Club? Environmentalist and conservationist organizations traditionally have been concerned with ecological, not humanitarian issues. They make no pretense of acting for the sake of individual animals; rather, they attempt to maintain the diversity, integrity, beauty and authenticity of the natural environment. These goals are ecological, not eleemosynary. Their goals are entirely consistent, then, with licensing hunters to shoot animals whose populations exceed the carrying capacity of their habitats. Perhaps hunting is immoral; if so, environmentalism is consistent with an immoral practice, but it is environmentalism without quotes nonetheless. The policies environmentalists recommend are informed by the concepts of population biology, not the concepts of animal equality. The S.P.C.A. does not set the agenda for the Sierra Club.

I do not in any way mean to support the practice of hunting; nor am I advocating environmentalism at this time. I merely want to point out that groups like the Sierra Club, the Wilderness Society and the World Wildlife Fund do not fail in their mission insofar as they devote themselves to causes other than the happiness or welfare of individual creatures; that never was their mission. These organizations, which promote a love and respect for the functioning of natural ecosystems, differ ideologically from organizations that make the suffering of animals their primary concern—groups like the Fund for Animals, the Animal Protection Institute, Friends of Animals, the American Humane Association, and various single issue groups such as Friends of the Sea Otter, Beaver Defenders, Friends of the Earthworm, and Worldwide Fair Play for Frogs.[14]

D. G. Ritchie, writing in 1916, posed a difficulty for those who argue that animals have rights or that we have obligations to them created simply by their capacity to suffer. If the suffering of animals creates a human obligation to mitigate it, is there not as much an obligation to prevent a cat from killing a mouse as to prevent a hunter from killing a deer? "Are we not to vindicate the rights of the persecuted prey of the stronger?"

Ritchie asks. "Or is our declaration of the rights of every creeping thing to remain a mere hypocritical formula to gratify pug-loving sentimentalists?"[15]

If the animal liberation or animal equality movement is not to deteriorate into "a hypocritical formula to gratify pug-loving sentimentalists," it must insist, as Singer does, that moral obligations to animals are justified, in the first place, by their distress, and, in the second place, by human ability to relieve that distress. The liberationist must morally require society to relieve animal suffering wherever it can and at a lesser cost to itself, whether in the chicken coop or in the wild. Otherwise, the animal liberationist thesis becomes interchangeable with the platitude one learns along with how to tie shoestrings: people ought not to be cruel to animals. I do not deny that human beings are cruel to animals, that they ought not to be, that this cruelty should be stopped and that sermons to this effect are entirely appropriate and necessary. I deny only that these sermons have anything to do with environmentalism or provide a basis for an environmental ethic.

III.

In discussing the rights of human beings, Henry Shue describes two that are basic in the sense that "the enjoyment of them is essential to the enjoyment of all other rights."[16] These are the right to physical security and the right to minimum subsistence. These are positive, not merely negative rights. In other words, these rights require governments to provide security and subsistence, not merely to refrain from invading security and denying subsistence. These basic rights require society, where possible, to rescue individuals from starvation; this is more than the merely negative obligation not to cause starvation. No; if people have basic rights—and I have no doubt they do—then society has a positive obligation to satisfy those rights. It is not enough for society simply to refrain from violating them.

This, surely, is true of the basic rights of animals as well, if we are to give the conception of "right" the same meaning for both people and animals. For example, to allow animals to be killed for food or to permit them to die of disease or starvation when it is within human power to prevent it, does not seem to balance fairly the interests of animals with those of human beings. To speak of the rights of animals, of treating them as equals, of liberating them, and at the same time to let nearly all of them perish unnecessarily in the most brutal and horrible ways is not to display humanity but hypocrisy in the extreme.

Where should society concentrate its efforts to provide for the basic welfare—the security and subsistence—of animals? Plainly, where animals most lack this security, when their basic rights, needs, or interests are most thwarted and where their suffering is most intense. Alas, this is in nature. Ever since Darwin, we have been aware that few organisms survive to reach sexual maturity; most are quickly annihilated in the struggle for existence. Consider as a rough but reasonable statement of the facts the following:

> All species reproduce in excess, way past the carrying capacity of their niche. In her lifetime a lioness might have 20 cubs; a pigeon, 150 chicks; a mouse, 1,000 kits; a trout, 20,000 fry, a tuna or cod, a million fry or more; an elm tree, several million seeds; and an oyster, perhaps a hundred million spat. If one assumes that the population of each of these species is, from generation to generation, roughly equal, then on the average only one offspring will survive to replace each parent. All the other thousands and millions will die, one way or another.[17]

The ways in which creatures in nature die are typically violent: predation, starvation, disease, parasitism, cold. The dying animal in the wild does not understand the vast ocean of misery into which it and billions of other animals are born only to drown. If the wild animal understood the conditions into which it is born, what would it think? It might reasonably prefer to be raised on a farm, where the chances of survival for a year or more would be good, and to escape from the wild, where they are negligible. Either way, the animal will be eaten: few die of old age. The path from birth to slaughter, however, is often longer and less painful in the barnyard than in the woods. Comparisons, sad as they are, must be made to recognize where a great opportunity lies to prevent or mitigate suffering. The misery of animals in nature—which humans can do much to relieve—makes every other form of suffering pale in comparison. Mother Nature is so cruel to her children she makes Frank Perdue look like a saint.

What is the practical course society should take once it climbs the spiral of moral evolution high enough to recognize its obligation to value the basic rights of animals equally with that of human beings? I do not know how animal liberationists, such as Singer, propose to relieve animal suffering in nature (where most of it occurs), but there are many ways to do so at little cost. Singer has suggested, with respect to pest control, that animals might be fed contraceptive chemicals rather than poisons.[18] It may not be beyond the reach of science to attempt a broad program of contraceptive care for animals in nature so that fewer will fall victim to an early and horrible death. The government is spending hundreds of millions of dollars to store millions of tons of grain. Why not lay out this food, laced with contraceptives, for wild creatures to feed upon? Farms which so overproduce for human needs might then satisfy the needs of animals. The day may come when entitlement programs which now extend only to human beings are offered to animals as well.

One may modestly propose the conversion of national wilderness areas, especially national parks, into farms in order to replace violent wild areas with more humane and managed environments. Starving deer in the woods might be adopted as pets. They might be fed in kennels; animals that once wandered the wilds in misery might get fat in feedlots instead. Birds that now kill earthworms may repair instead to birdhouses stocked with food, including textured soybean protein that looks and smells like worms. And to protect the brutes from cold, their dens could be heated, or shelters provided for the all too many who will otherwise freeze. The list of obligations is long, but for that reason it is more, not less, compelling. The welfare of all animals is in human hands. Society must attend not solely to the needs of domestic animals, for they are in a privileged class, but to the needs of all animals, especially those which without help, would die miserably in the wild. Now, whether you believe that this harangue is a *reductio* of Singer's position, and thus that it agrees in principle with Ritchie, or whether you think it should be taken seriously as an ideal is of no concern to me. I merely wish to point out that an environmentalist must take what I have said as a *reductio*, whereas an animal liberationist must regard it as stating a serious position, at least if the liberationist shares Singer's commitment to utilitarianism. Environmentalists cannot be animal liberationists. Animal liberationists cannot be environmentalists. The environmentalist would sacrifice the lives of individual creatures to preserve the authenticity, integrity and complexity of ecological systems. The liberationist—if the reduction of animal misery is taken seriously as a goal—must be willing, in principle, to sacrifice the authenticity, integrity and complexity of ecosystems to protect the rights, or guard the lives, of animals. *A DiffEREnCE BETWEEN ENVIRONMENTALIST AND LIBERATIONIST.*

IV.

A defender of the rights of animals may answer that my argument applies only to someone like Singer who is strongly committed to a utilitarian ethic. Those who emphasize the rights of animals, however, need not argue that society should enter the interests of animals equitably into the felicific calculus on which policy is based. For example, Laurence Tribe appeals to the rights of animals not to broaden the class of wants to be included in a Benthamite calculus but to "move beyond wants" and thus to affirm duties "ultimately independent of a desire-satisfying conception."[19] Tribe writes:

> To speak of "rights" rather than "wants," after all, is to acknowledge the possibility that want-maximizing or utility-maximizing actions will be ruled out in particular cases as inconsistent with a structure of agreed-upon obligations. It is Kant, not Bentham, whose thought suggests the first step toward making us "different persons from the manipulators and subjugators we are in danger of becoming."[20]

It is difficult to see how an appeal to rights helps society to "move beyond wants" or to affirm duties "ultimately independent of a desire-satisfying conception." Most writers in the Kantian tradition analyze rights as claims to something in which the claimant has an interest.[21] Thus, rights-theorists oppose utilitarianism not to go beyond wants but because they believe that some wants or interests are moral "trumps" over other wants and interests.[22] To say innocent people have a right not to be hanged for crimes they have not committed, even when hanging them would serve the general welfare, is to say that the interest of innocent people not to be hanged should outweigh the general interest in

deterring crime. To take rights seriously, then, is simply to take some interests, or the general interest, more seriously than other interests for moral reasons. The appeal to rights simply is a variation on utilitarianism, in that it accepts the general framework of interests, but presupposes that there are certain interests that should not be traded off against others.

A second problem with Tribe's reply is more damaging than the first. Only *individuals* may have rights, but environmentalists think in terms of protecting *collections, systems* and *communities.* Consider Aldo Leopold's oft-quoted remark: "A thing is right when it tends to preserve the integrity, stability, and beauty of the biotic community. It is wrong when it tends to do otherwise."[23] The obligation to preserve the "integrity, stability, and beauty of the biotic community," whatever those words mean, implies no duties whatever to individual animals in the community, except in the rare instance in which an individual is important to functioning of that community. For the most part, individual animals are completely expendable. An environmentalist is concerned only with maintaining a population. Accordingly, the moral obligation Leopold describes cannot be grounded in or derived from the rights of individuals. Therefore, it has no basis in rights at all.[24]

Consider another example: the protection of endangered species. An individual whale may be said to have rights, but the species cannot; a whale does not suddenly have rights when its kind becomes endangered.[25] No; the moral obligation to preserve species is not an obligation to individual creatures. It cannot, then, be an obligation that rests on rights. This is not to say that there is no moral obligation with regard to endangered species, animals or the environment. It is only to say that moral obligations to nature cannot be enlightened or explained—one cannot even take the first step—by appealing to the rights of animals and other natural things.

V.

Garrett Hardin, in his "Foreword" to *Should Trees Have Standing?*, suggests that Stone's essay answers Leopold's call for a "new ethic to protect land and other natural amenities. . . ."[26] But as one reviewer has pointed out,

> Stone himself never refers to Leopold, and with good reason; he comes from a different place, and his

proposal to grant rights to natural objects has emerged not from an ecological sensibility but as an extension of the philosophy of the humane movement.[27]

A humanitarian ethic—an appreciation not of nature, but of the welfare of animals—will not help us to understand or to justify an environmental ethic. It will not provide necessary or valid foundations for environmental law.

NOTES

1. Leopold, *A Sand County Almanac* (Oxford University Press, 1949) at 204.
2. For discussion, see Heffernan, "The Land Ethic: A Critical Appraisal," *Environmental Ethics* 4 (1982): 235. Heffernan notes that "when Leopold talks of preserving the 'integrity, stability and beauty of the biotic community' he is referring to preserving the characteristic structure of an ecosystem and its capacity to withstand change or stress." Leopold. *A Sand County Almanac* at 237.
3. Stone, *Should Trees Have Standing?* (Los Altos: Walter Kaufmann, 1974).
4. Stone, *Should Trees Have Standing?* at p. 44.
5. Tribe, "Ways Not to Think about Plastic Trees: New Foundations in Environmental Law," *Yale Law Journal* 83 (1973): 1315. See p. 1345.
6. Singer, "All Animals Are Equal" *Philosophic Exchange* 1 (1974): 103.
7. Stone, *Should Trees Have Standing?* at 24.
8. Singer, "Not For Humans Only: The Place of Nonhumans in Environmental Issues," in *Ethics and the Problems of the Twenty-first Century*, ed. Goodpaster and Sayre (1979), p. 194.
9. Singer, "Not For Humans Only," p. 195.
10. For a discussion of basic rights, see Shue, *Basic Rights* (1980).
11. Callicott, "Animal Liberation: A Triangular Affair" (1980), *Environmental Ethics* 2 (1980): 311. See p. 315.
12. Leopold, *A Sand County Almanac*, p. 269.
13. Callicott, "Animal Liberation," p. 314–15.
14. Singer, "Not For Humans Only," p. 201.
15. Ritchie, *Natural Rights* (3rd ed., 1916), p. 107. For an excellent discussion of this passage, see Clark, "The Rights of Wild Things," *Inquiry* 22 (1979): 171.
16. Shue, *Basic Rights*, p. 18–29.
17. Hapgood, *Why Males Exist* (1979). See p. 34.
18. Singer, "Not For Humans Only," p. 198.
19. Tribe, "From Environmental Foundations to Constitutional Structures: Learning From Nature's Future," *Yale Law Journal* 84 (1974): 545. See pp. 551–552.
20. Tribe, "From Environmental Foundations," p. 552.
21. For discussion, see Feinberg, "Duties, Rights, and Claims" (1966). *American Philosophical Quarterly* 3 (1966): 137.
22. See Dworkin, "Liberalism," in *Public and Private Morality* (1978), ed. Stuart Hampshire. Pages 113–143. Rights "function as trump cards held by individuals" (136).
23. Leopold, *A Sand County Almanac*, p. 262.
24. . . . Tom Regan discusses this issue in *The Case for Animal Liberation* (1983). See p. 362. Because paradigmatic rights-holders are individuals, and because the dominant thrust of contemporary environmental efforts (e.g., wilderness preservation) is to focus on the whole rather than on the part (i.e., the individual), there is an understandable reluctance on the part of environmentalists to "take rights seriously" or at least a reluctance to take them as seriously as the rights view contends we should. . . . A rights-based environmental ethic . . . ought not to be dismissed out of hand by environmentalists as being in principle antagonistic to the goals for which they work. It isn't. Were we to show proper respect for the rights of individuals who make up the biotic community, would not the *community* be preserved? I believe this is an empirical question, the answer to which is "no." The environmentalist is concerned about preserving evolutionary processes; whether these processes, e.g., natural selection, have deep enough respect for the rights of individuals to be preserved on those grounds, is a question that might best be addressed by an evolutionary biologist.
25. Feinberg, "The Rights of Animals and Unborn Generations," in *Philosophy and the Environmental Crisis*, ed. Blackstone, (1974), 43–end. See pp. 55–56.
26. Hardin, "Foreword," in Stone, *Should Trees Have Standing?* See p. xii.
27. Rodman, "The Liberation of Nature?" See p. 110.

5

LIFE

We think all humans are equal, in some way. What does that really mean? We do not believe all humans should be paid the same wage, but what exactly do we believe? We think all humans command equal respect in some sense, but not in every sense. In the human context, then, equality turns out to be a complex notion with uncertain implications. Similarly, if we say all species are equal, we need not be saying all animals (and all plants, for that matter) have equal rights. We need not be saying they should be treated as if they were human. But then, what *do* we mean?

Human beings have certain capacities that these other living things lack, but do these capacities make us superior? How do we even compare? We might claim that our distinctly human capacities are more *valuable* than those of the tree, but how do we know that they are not just more valuable from *our* point of view? How do we know our point of view is the relevant point of view for judging the value of a particular capacity? Or, we may say all living things have something in common, such as being alive, then claim *that* is what matters for deserving respect. Since all living things have it, they are all equally valuable. But is there any reason to think *that* aspect is what matters? What about all the other capacities that trees and chimpanzees and human beings have that distinguish them from each other? Do unique capacities give us reason to respect some things more than others? Do we have any good reason to decide one way rather than another?

What does it mean for all species to be worthy of equal respect? Why does Taylor think it matters? How might this work in practice? How should it affect the way we live?

GREGG EASTERBROOK

A MOMENT ON THE EARTH

If you would know the power of life over matter, know these things.

The sea turtle hatchling, born in the warm sands of a Florida beach, immediately stumbles to the ocean and throws itself in. Unknowing of the world, unaided by any parent, sought as prey by crabs and birds and perhaps facing its greatest danger from the featureless harshness of the cold waters, the hatchling begins floating among sargassum seaweeds, seeking to orient itself in the currents it will use to navigate as far as Ascension Island, thousands of miles distant. Answering some unknowable summons of antiquity the hatchling crosses the ocean alone, accomplishing without any physical technology a feat men and women in boats with radios and radars and turbo diesels and freeze-dried foods and ring-laser gyros have died attempting to accomplish.

Near the end of a life lived on the western shores of Africa the sea turtle answers a second summons, to return to the sands of its birth. This time it cannot float but must swim against the prevailing current. In some haunting way the turtle recalls exactly what it sensed as a hatchling—the precise successions of currents, wave patterns, salinity changes, and polarity from magnetic north. This is necessary because the goal is to return exactly to the patch of sand on which the turtle first knew the light of the temporal world. North America alone will not do; Florida alone will not do; it must be the same beach, the same feel and smell in every way.

Perhaps the sea turtle is a mere genetic automaton, driven by deterministic amino acid encodings toward a moot goal dropped into its DNA by some past random happenstance that signifies nothing. Or perhaps this journey has meaning.

Perhaps the turtle is willing to swim the breadth of the very ocean in order to experience once again the sweet tastes that accompanied it awakening to life—the early sensations of youth being the sweetest a living thing can ask to know. Perhaps this allows the sea turtle to end its days having not just existed and processed carbohydrates and excreted nitrogen and grown senescent but lived, taken a small yet noble role in an enterprise that may eventually fill the whole of the cosmos with meaning. Perhaps the turtle is driven not by mindless helixes but by longing—the longing of life over matter, the most insistent force in all the firmament.

One rare exception in a world of numbing pointlessness? Consider other examples of the profundity of life.

The spotted salamander lives underground almost the entire year. One day in spring when the temperature is at least 42 degrees Fahrenheit and it has rained hard the previous night, every spotted salamander emerges for a night of sporting and mating. When the night ends the salamanders return beneath the ground for another year. The timing of the emergence is always flawless.

Birds want berries for food. Plants want birds to distribute their gene lines by eating berries, flying somewhere, then relieving themselves of a portion of the berries designed to be indigestible: the seeds. Why do berries turn red? As a signal to birds that they are ripe and the time has come to eat them.

Each fall the yellow pine chipmunk collects and buries seeds of the yellow pine and the bitterbrush, a staple browsing food of deer. Some seeds the chipmunk returns to consume; some seeds the chipmunk forgets about. Forgotten seeds bloom in spring, perpetuating the yellow pine and the bitterbrush, which in turn feed the deer. The seeds have not only been dispersed by the chipmunk, they have been planted.

When a bear hibernates, in some unknown way its body recycles calcium to prevent osteoporosis and reabsorbs urea to prevent bladder failure. Bears can even carry a pregnancy through hibernation, continuing to make the necessary hormones; though in all nonhibernating mammals including people, fasting ends hormone production and causes miscarriage.

The sluggish caterpillar myrmecophilous, an attractive target for wasps, has two nectary glands that secrete a potion ants seem to consider champagne. If myrmecophilous thumps a branch in distress over the presence of a wasp, any nearby ants will rush to defend the caterpillar.

In the tree canopies of the tropical rainforest, star-shaped plants called bromeliads catch precipitation to form puddles. The puddles provide the plants with water, so they need not shoot roots to the ground: they also serve as little ponds for hundreds of other life forms.

Female guppies that live in streams where there are no predators prefer flashy males with bright markings and large fins. Female guppies that live in streams with many predators prefer plain males. Thus under safe conditions female guppies choose genes for attractiveness, to help their offspring get on socially. Under dangerous conditions female guppies choose genes for camouflage, to help their offspring survive by going unnoticed.

The opossum is believed to have existed for at least 60 million years. That is to say the opossum, a delicate thing easily harmed, is far older than the Rocky Mountains, a seemingly indestructible mass of dense minerals hewn from Earth's very continental plates. The whale is thought to have existed at least 12 million years, after somehow evolving from a land animal similar in appearance to a cow. That is to say the whale, a fragile living thing, is far older than the present alignment of ocean currents in which it swims. The sandhill crane seems to have existed for at least nine million years, perhaps making migratory stops along the area of the North Platte River of Nebraska, a favored present-day calling point, much of that time. The North Platte itself is somewhere around 15,000 years old. That is to say the sandhill crane, a fragile living thing today called endangered, is far, far older than the river at which it calls.

The monarch butterfly, a mere insect, migrates as much as 2,500 miles. Monarch brains no larger than a few grains of sand contain the topographical information necessary to navigate from the northern United States to Mexico. Several generations of the butterflies—born, metamorphosed, flying, mating, dying—are required to complete the passage of a family line from summering grounds to wintering area. Just try to guess what forces lead to the development of metamorphic creatures such as the butterfly, which essentially require two separate sets of genetic inheritances favored by two entirely separate circumstances of natural selection.

These are but a few of many, many examples of the wonder and complexity of life. I choose them because they may be less familiar than others. And I choose these two from genus Homo.

In the sediments of a lake near the Greek city of Nikopolis has been found a flint axe that is at least 200,000 and perhaps 500,000 years old. This tells us humans were not just quizzical primates, but tool users with minds already struggling to comprehend the world, an unimaginable length of time ago by our way of thinking.

In 1991 in the Qafzeh Cave near Haifa, Israel, archaeologists found the bones of a young human female delicately interned, arms wrapped around the bones of a neonate—suggesting mother and infant buried together after both died during childbirth. The bones are at least 100,000 years old. This tells us human beings had already begun to develop spiritual awareness—were already struggling with the meaning of life and the tragedy of its loss—an unimaginable length of time ago by our way of thinking.

PAUL W. TAYLOR

THE ETHICS OF RESPECT FOR NATURE

HUMAN-CENTERED AND LIFE-CENTERED SYSTEMS OF ENVIRONMENTAL ETHICS

In this paper I show how the taking of a certain ultimate moral attitude toward nature, which I call "respect for nature," has a central place in the foundations of a life-centered system of environmental ethics. I hold that a set of moral norms (both standards of character and rules of conduct) governing human treatment of the natural world is a rationally grounded set if and only if, first, commitment to those norms is a practical entailment of adopting the attitude of respect for nature as an ultimate moral attitude, and second, the adopting of that attitude on the part of all rational agents can itself be justified. When the basic characteristics of the attitude of respect for nature are made clear, it will be seen that a life-centered system of environmental ethics need not be holistic or organicist in its conception of the kinds of entities that are deemed the appropriate objects of moral concern and consideration. Nor does such a system require that the concepts of ecological homeostasis, equilibrium, and integrity provide us with normative principles from which could be derived (with the addition of factual knowledge) our obligations with regard to natural ecosystems. The "balance of nature" is not itself a moral norm, however important may be the role it plays in our general outlook on the natural world that underlies the attitude of respect for nature. I argue that finally it is the good (well-being, welfare) of individual organisms, considered as entities having inherent worth, that determines our moral relations with the Earth's wild communities of life.

In designating the theory to be set forth as life-centered, I intend to contrast it with all anthropocentric views. According to the latter, human actions affecting the natural environment and its nonhuman inhabitants are right (or wrong) by either of two criteria: they have consequences which are favorable (or unfavorable) to human well-being, or they are consistent (or inconsistent) with the system of norms that protect and implement human rights. From this human-centered standpoint it is to humans and only to humans that all duties are ultimately owed. We may have responsibilities *with regard to* the natural ecosystems and biotic communities of our planet, but these responsibilities are in every case based on the contingent fact that our treatment of those ecosystems and communities of life can further the realization of human values and/or human rights. We have no obligation to promote or protect the good of nonhuman living things, independently of this contingent fact.

A life-centered system of environmental ethics is opposed to human-centered ones precisely on this point. From the perspective of a life-centered theory, we have prima facie moral obligations that are owed to wild plants and animals themselves as members of the Earth's biotic community. We are morally bound (other things being equal) to protect or promote their good for *their* sake. Our duties to respect the integrity of natural ecosystems, to preserve endangered species, and to avoid environmental pollution stem from the fact that these are ways in which we can help make it possible for wild species populations to achieve and maintain a healthy existence in a natural state. Such obligations are due those living things out of recognition of their inherent worth. They are entirely additional to and independent of the obligations we owe to our fellow humans. Although many of the actions that fulfill one set of obligations will also fulfill the other, two different grounds of obligation are involved. Their

Paul Taylor. 1981. The Ethics of Respect for Nature. Environmental Ethics, 3: 197–218. Reprinted with permission of the author and the journal.

well-being, as well as human well-being, is something to be realized *as an end in itself*.

If we were to accept a life-centered theory of environmental ethics, a profound reordering of our moral universe would take place. We would begin to look at the whole of the Earth's biosphere in a new light. Our duties with respect to the "world" of nature would be seen as making prima facie claims upon us to be balanced against our duties with respect to the "world" of human civilization. We could no longer simply take the human point of view and consider the effects of our actions exclusively from the perspective of our own good.

THE GOOD OF A BEING AND THE CONCEPT OF INHERENT WORTH

What would justify acceptance of a life-centered system of ethical principles? In order to answer this it is first necessary to make clear the fundamental moral attitude that underlies and makes intelligible the commitment to live by such a system. It is then necessary to examine the considerations that would justify any rational agent's adopting that moral attitude.

Two concepts are essential to the taking of a moral attitude of the sort in question. A being which does not "have" these concepts, that is, which is unable to grasp their meaning and conditions of applicability, cannot be said to have the attitude as part of its moral outlook. These concepts are, first, that of the good (well-being, welfare) of a living thing, and second, the idea of an entity possessing inherent worth. I examine each concept in turn.

(1) Every organism, species population, and community of life has a good of its own which moral agents can intentionally further or damage by their actions. To say that an entity has a good of its own is simply to say that, without reference to any *other* entity, it can be benefited or harmed. One can act in its overall interest or contrary to its overall interest, and environmental conditions can be good for it (advantageous to it) or bad for it (disadvantageous to it). What is good for an entity is what "does it good" in the sense of enhancing or preserving its life and well-being. What is bad for an entity is something that is detrimental to its life and well-being.

We can think of the good of an individual nonhuman organism as consisting in the full development of its biological powers. Its good is realized to the extent that it is strong and healthy. It possesses whatever capacities it needs for successfully coping with its environment and so preserving its existence throughout the various stages of the normal life cycle of its species. The good of a population or community of such individuals consists in the population or community maintaining itself from generation to generation as a coherent system of genetically and ecologically related organisms whose average good is at an optimum level for the given environment. (Here *average good* means that the degree of realization of the good of *individual organisms* in the population or community is, on average, greater than it would be under any other ecologically functioning order of interrelations among those species populations in the given ecosystem.)

The idea of a being having a good of its own, as I understand it, does not entail that the being must have interests or take an interest in what affects its life for better or for worse. We can act in a being's interest or contrary to its interest without its being interested in what we are doing to it in the sense of wanting or not wanting us to do it. It may, indeed, be wholly unaware that favorable and unfavorable events are taking place in its life. I take it that trees, for example, have no knowledge or desires or feelings. Yet it is undoubtedly the case that trees can be harmed or benefited by our actions. We can crush their roots by running a bulldozer too close to them. We can see to it that they get adequate nourishment and moisture by fertilizing and watering the soil around them. Thus we can help or hinder them in the realization of their good. It is the good of trees themselves that is thereby affected. We can similarly act so as to further the good of an entire tree population of a certain species (say, all the redwood trees in a California valley) or the good of a whole community of plant life in a given wilderness area, just as we can do harm to such a population or community.

When construed in this way, the concept of a being's good is not coextensive with sentience or the capacity for feeling pain. William Frankena has argued for a general theory of environmental ethics in which the ground of a creature's being worthy of moral consideration is its sentience. I have offered some criticisms of this view elsewhere, but the full refutation of such a position, it seems to me, finally depends on the positive reasons for accepting a life-centered theory of the kind I am defending in this essay.[1]

It should be noted further that I am leaving open the question of whether machines—in particular, those which are not only goal directed, but also self-regulating—can properly be said to have a good of their own.[2] Since I am concerned only with human treatment of wild organisms, species populations, and communities of life as they occur in our planet's natural ecosystems, it is to those entities alone that the concept "having a good of its own" will here be applied. I am not denying that other living things, whose genetic origin and environmental conditions have been produced, controlled, and manipulated by humans for human ends, do have a good of their own in the same sense as do wild plants and animals. It is not my purpose in this essay, however, to set out or defend the principles that should guide our conduct with regard to their good. It is only insofar as their production and use by humans have good or ill effects upon natural ecosystems and their wild inhabitants that the ethics of respect for nature comes into play.

(2) The second concept essential to the moral attitude of respect for nature is the idea of inherent worth. We take that attitude toward wild living things (individuals, species populations, or whole biotic communities) when and only when we regard them as entities possessing inherent worth. Indeed, it is only because they are conceived in this way that moral agents can think of themselves as having validly binding duties, obligations, and responsibilities that are *owed* to them as their *due*. I am not at this juncture arguing why they *should* be so regarded; I consider it at length below. But so regarding them is a presupposition of our taking the attitude of respect toward them and accordingly understanding ourselves as bearing certain moral relations to them. This can be shown as follows:

What does it mean to regard an entity that has a good of its own as possessing inherent worth? Two general principles are involved: the principle of moral consideration and the principle of intrinsic value.

According to the principle of moral consideration, wild living things are deserving of the concern and consideration of all moral agents simply in virtue of their being members of the Earth's community of life. From the moral point of view their good must be taken into account whenever it is affected for better or worse by the conduct of rational agents. This holds no matter what species the creature belongs to. The good of each is to be accorded some value and so acknowledged as having some weight in the deliberations of all rational agents. Of course, it may be necessary for such agents to act in ways contrary to the good of this or that particular organism or group of organisms in order to further the good of others, including the good of humans. But the principle of moral consideration prescribes that, with respect to each being an entity having its own good, every individual is deserving of consideration.

The principle of intrinsic value states that, regardless of what kind of entity it is in other respects, if it is a member of the Earth's community of life, the realization of its good is something *intrinsically* valuable. This means that its good is prima facie worthy of being preserved or promoted as an end in itself and for the sake of the entity whose good it is. Insofar as we regard any organism, species population, or life community as an entity having inherent worth, we believe that it must never be treated as if it were a mere object or thing whose entire value lies in being instrumental to the good of some other entity. The well-being of each is judged to have value in and of itself.

Combining these two principles, we can now define what it means for a living thing or group of living things to possess inherent worth. To say that it possesses inherent worth is to say that its good is deserving of the concern and consideration of all moral agents, and that the realization of its good has intrinsic value, to be pursued as an end in itself and for the sake of the entity whose good it is.

The duties owed to wild organisms, species populations, and communities of life in the Earth's natural ecosystems are grounded on their inherent worth. When rational, autonomous agents regard such entities as possessing inherent worth, they place intrinsic value on the realization of their good and so hold themselves responsible for performing actions that will have this effect and for refraining from actions having the contrary effect.

. . .

THE JUSTIFIABILITY OF THE ATTITUDE OF RESPECT FOR NATURE

The attitude we take toward living things in the natural world depends on the way we look at them, on what kind of beings we conceive them to be, and on how we understand the relations we bear to them. Underlying and supporting our attitude is a certain belief system that constitutes a particular world view or outlook on nature and the place of human life in it. To give good reasons for adopting the attitude of respect for nature, then, we must first articulate the *belief system* which underlies and supports that attitude. If it appears that the belief system is internally coherent and well-ordered, and if, as far as we can now tell, it is consistent with all known scientific truths relevant to our knowledge of the object of the attitude (which in this case includes the whole set of the Earth's natural ecosystems and their communities of life), then there remains the task of indicating why scientifically informed and rational thinkers with a developed capacity of reality awareness can find it acceptable as a way of conceiving of the natural world and our place in it. To the extent we can do this we provide at least a reasonable argument for accepting the belief system and the ultimate moral attitude it supports.

I do not hold that such a belief system can be *proven* to be true, either inductively or deductively. As we shall see, not all of its components can be stated in the form of empirically verifiable propositions. Nor is its internal order governed by purely logical relationships. But the system as a whole, I contend, constitutes a coherent, unified, and rationally acceptable "picture" or "map" of a total world. By examining each of its main components and seeing how they fit together, we obtain a scientifically informed and well-ordered conception of nature and the place of humans in it.

This belief system underlying the attitude of respect for nature I call (for want of a better name) "the biocentric outlook on nature." Since it is not wholly analyzable into empirically confirmable assertions, it should not be thought of as simply a compendium of the biological sciences concerning our planet's ecosystems. It might best be described as a philosophical world view, to distinguish it from a scientific theory or explanatory system. However, one of its major tenets is the great lesson we have learned from the science of ecology: the interdependence of all living things in an organically unified order whose balance and stability are necessary conditions for the realization of the good of its constituent biotic communities.

. . .

THE BIOCENTRIC OUTLOOK ON NATURE

The biocentric outlook on nature has four main components. (1) Humans are thought of as members of the Earth's community of life, holding that membership on the same terms as apply to all the nonhuman members. (2) The Earth's natural ecosystems as a totality are seen as a complex web of interconnected elements, with the sound biological functioning of each being dependent on the sound biological functioning of the others. (This is the component referred to above as the great lesson that the science of ecology has taught us.) (3) Each individual organism is conceived of as a teleological center of life, pursuing its own good in its own way. (4) Whether we are concerned with standards of merit or with the concept of inherent worth, the claim that humans by their very nature are superior to other species is a groundless claim and, in the light of elements (1), (2), and (3) above, must be rejected as nothing more than an irrational bias in our own favor.

The conjunction of these four ideas constitutes the biocentric outlook on nature. In the remainder of this paper I give a brief account of the first three components, followed by a more detailed analysis of the fourth. I then conclude by indicating how this outlook provides a way of justifying the attitude of respect for nature.

HUMANS AS MEMBERS OF THE EARTH'S COMMUNITY OF LIFE

We share with other species a common relationship to the Earth. In accepting the biocentric outlook we take the fact of our being an animal species to be a fundamental feature of our existence. We consider it an essential aspect of "the human condition." We do not deny the differences between ourselves and other species, but we keep in the forefront of our consciousness the fact that in relation to our planet's natural ecosystems we are but one species population among many. Thus, we acknowledge our origin in the very same evolutionary process that gave rise to all other species and we recognize ourselves to be confronted with similar environmental challenges to those that confront them. The laws of genetics, of natural selection, and of adaptation apply equally to all of us as biological creatures. In this light we consider ourselves as one with them, not set apart from them. We, as well as they, must face certain basic conditions of existence that impose requirements on us for our survival and well-being. Each animal and plant is like us in having a good of its own. Although our human good (what is of true value in human life, including the exercise of individual autonomy in choosing our own particular value systems) is not like the good of a nonhuman animal or plant, it can no more be realized than their good can without the biological necessities for survival and physical health.

When we look at ourselves from the evolutionary point of view we see that not only are we very recent arrivals on Earth, but that our emergence as a new species on the planet was originally an event of no particular importance to the entire scheme of things. The Earth was teeming with life long before we appeared. Putting the point metaphorically, we are relative newcomers, entering a home that has been the residence of others for hundreds of millions of years, a home that must now be shared by all of us together.

The comparative brevity of human life on Earth may be vividly depicted by imagining the geological time scale in spatial terms. Suppose we start with algae, which have been around for at least 600 million years. (The earliest protozoa actually predated this by several *billion* years.) If the time that algae have been here were represented by the length of a football field (300 feet), then the period during which sharks have been swimming in the world's oceans and spiders have been spinning their webs would occupy three quarters of the length of the field; reptiles would show up at about the center of the field; mammals would cover the last third of the field; hominids (mammals of the family *Hominidae*) the last two feet; and the species *Homo sapiens* the last six inches.

Whether this newcomer is able to survive as long as other species remains to be seen. But there is surely something presumptuous about the way humans look down on the "lower" animals, especially those that have become extinct. We consider the dinosaurs, for example, to be biological failures, though they existed on our planet for 65 million years. One writer has made the point with beautiful simplicity:

> We sometimes speak of the dinosaurs as failures; there will be time enough for that judgment when we have lasted even for one tenth as long. . . .[3]

The possibility of the extinction of the human species, a possibility which starkly confronts us in the contemporary world, makes us aware of another respect in which we should not consider ourselves privileged beings in relation to other species. This is the fact that the well-being of humans is dependent upon the ecological soundness and health of many plant and animal communities, while their soundness and health does not in the least depend upon human well-being. Indeed, from their standpoint the very existence of humans is quite unnecessary. Every last man, woman, and child could disappear from the face of the Earth without any significant detrimental consequence for the good of wild animals and plants. On the contrary, many of them would be greatly benefited. The destruction of their habitats by human "developments" would cease. The poisoning and polluting of their environment would come to an end. The Earth's land, air, and water would no longer be subject to the degradation they are now undergoing as the result of large-scale technology and uncontrolled population growth. Life communities in natural ecosystems would gradually return to their former healthy state. Tropical forests for example, would again be able to make their full contribution to a life-sustaining atmosphere for the whole planet. The rivers, lakes, and oceans of the world would (perhaps) eventually become clean again. Spilled oil, plastic trash, and even radioactive waste might finally, after many centuries, cease doing their terrible work. Ecosystems would return to their proper balance, suffering only the disruptions of natural events such as volcanic eruptions and glaciation. From these the community of life could recover, as it has so often done in the past. But the ecological disasters now perpetrated on it by humans—disasters from which it might never recover—these it would no longer have to endure.

If, then, the total, final, absolute extermination of our species (by our own hands?) should take place and if we should not carry all the others with us into oblivion, not only would the Earth's community of life continue to exist, but in all probability its well-being would be enhanced. Our presence, in short, is not needed. If we were to take the standpoint of the community and give voice to its true interest, the ending of our six-inch epoch would most likely be greeted with a hearty "Good riddance!"

THE NATURAL WORLD AS AN ORGANIC SYSTEM

To accept the biocentric outlook and regard ourselves and our place in the world from its perspective is to see the whole natural order of the Earth's biosphere as a complex but unified web of interconnected organisms, objects, and events. The ecological relationships between any community of living things and their environment form an organic whole of functionally interdependent parts. Each ecosystem is a small universe itself in which the interactions of its various species populations comprise an intricately woven network of cause–effect relations. Such dynamic but at the same time relatively stable structures as food chains, predator–prey relations, and plant succession in a forest are self-regulating, energy-recycling mechanisms that preserve the equilibrium of the whole.

As far as the well-being of wild animals and plants is concerned, this ecological equilibrium must not be destroyed. The same holds true of the well-being of humans. When one views the realm of nature from the perspective of the biocentric outlook, one never forgets that in the long run the integrity of the entire biosphere of our planet is essential to the realization of the good of its constituent communities of life, both human and nonhuman.

Although the importance of this idea cannot be overemphasized, it is by now so familiar and so widely acknowledged that I shall not further elaborate on it here. However, I do wish to point out that this "holistic" view of the Earth's ecological systems does not itself constitute a moral norm. It is a factual aspect of biological reality, to be understood as a set of causal connections in ordinary empirical terms. Its significance for humans is the same as its significance for nonhumans, namely, in setting basic conditions for

the realization of the good of living things. Its ethical implications for our treatment of the natural environment lie entirely in the fact that our *knowledge* of these causal connections is an essential *means* to fulfilling the aims we set for ourselves in adopting the attitude of respect for nature. In addition, its theoretical implications for the ethics of respect for nature lie in the fact that it (along with the other elements of the biocentric outlook) makes the adopting of that attitude a rational and intelligible thing to do.

INDIVIDUAL ORGANISMS AS TELEOLOGICAL CENTERS OF LIFE

As our knowledge of living things increases, as we come to a deeper understanding of their life cycles, their interactions with other organisms, and the manifold ways in which they adjust to the environment, we become more fully aware of how each of them is carrying out its biological functions according to the laws of its species-specific nature. But besides this, our increasing knowledge and understanding also develop in us a sharpened awareness of the uniqueness of each individual organism. Scientists who have made careful studies of particular plants and animals, whether in the field or in laboratories, have often acquired a knowledge of their subjects as identifiable individuals. Close observation over extended periods of time has led them to an appreciation of the unique "personalities" of their subjects. Sometimes a scientist may come to take a special interest in a particular animal or plant, all the while remaining strictly objective in the gathering and recording of data. Nonscientists may likewise experience this development of interest when, as amateur naturalists, they make accurate observations over sustained periods of close acquaintance with an individual organism. As one becomes more and more familiar with the organism and its behavior, one becomes fully sensitive to the particular way it is living out its life cycle. One may become fascinated by it and even experience some involvement with its good and bad fortunes (that is, with the occurrence of environmental conditions favorable or unfavorable to the realization of its good). The organism comes to mean something to one as a unique, irreplaceable individual. The final culmination of this process is the achievement of a genuine understanding of its point of view and, with that understanding, an ability to "take" that point of view. *Conceiving of it as a center of life, one is able to look at the world from its perspective.*

This development from objective knowledge to the recognition of individuality, and from the recognition of individuality to full awareness of an organism's standpoint, is a process of heightening our consciousness of what it means to be an individual living thing. We grasp the particularity of the organism as a teleological center of life, striving to preserve itself and to realize its own good in its own unique way.

It is to be noted that we need not be falsely anthropomorphizing when we conceive of individual plants and animals in this manner. Understanding them as teleological centers of life does not necessitate "reading into" them human characteristics. We need not, for example, consider them to have consciousness. Some of them may be aware of the world around them and others may not. Nor need we deny that different kinds and levels of awareness are exemplified when consciousness in some form is present. But conscious or not, all are equally teleological centers of life in the sense that each is a unified system of goal-oriented activities directed toward their preservation and well-being.

When considered from an ethical point of view, a teleological center of life is an entity whose "world" can be viewed from the perspective of *its* life. In looking at the world from that perspective we recognize objects and events occurring in its life as being beneficent, maleficent, or indifferent. The first are occurrences which increase its powers to preserve its existence and realize its good. The second decrease or destroy those powers. The third have neither of these effects on the entity. With regard to our human role as moral agents, we can conceive of a teleological center of life as a being whose standpoint we can take in making judgments about what events in the world are good or evil, desirable or undesirable. In making those judgments it is what promotes or protects the being's own good, not what benefits moral agents themselves, that sets the standard of evaluation. Such judgments can be made about anything that happens to the entity which is favorable or unfavorable in relation to its good. As was pointed out earlier, the entity itself need not have any

(conscious) *interest* in what is happening to it for such judgments to be meaningful and true.

It is precisely judgments of this sort that we are disposed to make when we take the attitude of respect for nature. In adopting that attitude those judgments are given weight as reasons for action in our practical deliberation. They become morally relevant facts in the guidance of our conduct.

THE DENIAL OF HUMAN SUPERIORITY

This fourth component of the biocentric outlook on nature is the single most important idea in establishing the justifiability of the attitude of respect for nature. Its central role is due to the special relationship it bears to the first three components of the outlook. This relationship will be brought out after the concept of human superiority is examined and analyzed.[4]

In what sense are humans alleged to be superior to other animals? We are different from them in having certain capacities that they lack. But why should these capacities be a mark of superiority? From what point of view are they judged to be signs of superiority and what sense of superiority is meant? After all, various nonhuman species have capacities that humans lack. There is the speed of a cheetah, the vision of an eagle, the agility of a monkey. Why should not these be taken as signs of *their* superiority over humans?

One answer that comes immediately to mind is that these capacities are not as *valuable* as the human capacities that are claimed to make us superior. Such uniquely human characteristics as rational thought, aesthetic creativity, autonomy and self-determination, and moral freedom, it might be held, have a higher value than the capacities found in other species. Yet we must ask: valuable to whom, and on what grounds?

The human characteristics mentioned are all valuable to humans. They are essential to the preservation and enrichment of our civilization and culture. Clearly it is from the human standpoint that they are being judged to be desirable and good. It is not difficult here to recognize a begging of the question. Humans are claiming human superiority from a strictly human point of view, that is, from a point of view in which the good of humans is taken as the standard of judgment. All we need to do is to look at the capacities of nonhuman animals (or plants, for that matter) from the standpoint of *their* good to find a contrary judgment of superiority. The speed of the cheetah, for example, is a sign of its superiority to humans when considered from the standpoint of the good of its species. If it were as slow a runner as a human, it would not be able to survive. And so for all the other abilities of nonhumans which further their good but which are lacking in humans. In each case the claim to human superiority would be rejected from a nonhuman standpoint.

When superiority assertions are interpreted in this way, they are based on judgments of *merit*. To judge the merits of a person or an organism one must apply grading or ranking standards to it. (As I show below, this distinguishes judgments of merit from judgments of inherent worth.) Empirical investigation then determines whether it has the "good-making properties" (merits) in virtue of which it fulfills the standards being applied. In the case of humans, merits may be either moral or nonmoral. We can judge one person to be better than (superior to) another from the moral point of view by applying certain standards to their character and conduct. Similarly, we can appeal to nonmoral criteria in judging someone to be an excellent piano player, a fair cook, a poor tennis player, and so on. Different social purposes and roles are implicit in the making of such judgments, providing the frame of reference for the choice of standards by which the nonmoral merits of people are determined. Ultimately such purposes and roles stem from a society's way of life as a whole. Now a society's way of life may be thought of as the cultural form given to the realization of human values. Whether moral or nonmoral standards are being applied, then, all judgments of people's merits finally depend on human values. All are made from an exclusively human standpoint.

The question that naturally arises at this juncture is: why should standards that are based on human values be assumed to be the only valid criteria of merit and hence the only true signs of superiority? This question is especially pressing when humans are being judged superior in merit to nonhumans. It is true that a human being may be a better mathematician than a monkey, but the monkey may be a better tree climber than a human being. If we humans value mathematics more than tree climbing, that is because

our conception of civilized life makes the development of mathematical ability more desirable than the ability to climb trees. But is it not unreasonable to judge nonhumans by the values of human civilization, rather than by values connected with what it is for a member of *that* species to live a good life? If all living things have a good of their own, it at least makes sense to judge the merits of nonhumans by standards derived from *their* good. To use only standards based on human values is already to commit oneself to holding that humans are superior to nonhumans, which is the point in question.

A further logical flaw arises in connection with the widely held conviction that humans are *morally* superior beings because they possess, while others lack, the capacities of a moral agent (free will, accountability, deliberation, judgment, practical reason). This view rests on a conceptual confusion. As far as moral standards are concerned, only beings that have the capacities of a moral agent can properly be judged to be *either* moral (morally good) *or* immoral (morally deficient). Moral standards are simply not applicable to beings that lack such capacities. Animals and plants cannot therefore be said to be morally inferior in merit to humans. Since the only beings that can have moral merits *or be deficient in such merits* are moral agents, it is conceptually incoherent to judge humans as superior to nonhumans on the ground that humans have moral capacities while nonhumans don't.

Up to this point I have been interpreting the claim that humans are superior to other living things as a grading or ranking judgment regarding their comparative merits. There is, however, another way of understanding the idea of human superiority. According to this interpretation, humans are superior to nonhumans not as regards their merits but as regards their inherent worth. Thus, the claim of human superiority is to be understood as asserting that all humans, simply in virtue of their humanity, have *a greater inherent worth* than other living things.

The inherent worth of an entity does not depend on its merits.[5] To consider something as possessing inherent worth, we have seen, is to place intrinsic value on the realization of its good. This is done regardless of whatever particular merits it might have or might lack, as judged by a set of grading or ranking standards.

In human affairs, we are all familiar with the principle that one's worth as a person does not vary with one's merits or lack of merits. The same can hold true of animals and plants. To regard such entities as possessing inherent worth entails disregarding their merits and deficiencies, whether they are being judged from a human standpoint or from the standpoint of their own species.

The idea of one entity having more merit than another, and so being superior to it in merit, makes perfectly good sense. Merit is a grading or ranking concept, and judgments of comparative merit are based on the different degrees to which things satisfy a given standard. But what can it mean to talk about one thing being superior to another in inherent worth? In order to get at what is being asserted in such a claim it is helpful first to look at the social origin of the concept of degrees of inherent worth.

The idea that humans can possess different degrees of inherent worth originated in societies having rigid class structures. Before the rise of modern democracies with their egalitarian outlook, one's membership in a hereditary class determined one's social status. People in the upper classes were looked up to, while those in the lower classes were looked down upon. In such a society one's social superiors and social inferiors were clearly defined and easily recognized.

Two aspects of these class-structured societies are especially relevant to the idea of degrees of inherent worth. First, those born into the upper classes were deemed more worthy of respect than those born into the lower orders. Second, the superior worth of upper class people had nothing to do with their merits nor did the inferior worth of those in the lower classes rest on their lack of merits. One's superiority or inferiority entirely derived from a social position one was born into. The modern concept of a meritocracy simply did not apply. One could not advance into a higher class by any sort of moral or nonmoral achievement. Similarly, an aristocrat held his title and all the privileges that went with it just because he was the eldest son of a titled nobleman. Unlike the bestowing of knighthood in contemporary Great Britain, one did not earn membership in the nobility by meritorious conduct.

We who live in modern democracies no longer believe in such hereditary social distinctions. Indeed, we would wholeheartedly condemn them on moral grounds as being fundamentally unjust. We have come to think of class systems as a paradigm of social injustice, it being a central principle of the democratic way of life that among humans there are no superiors and no inferiors. Thus we have rejected the whole conceptual framework in which people are judged to have different degrees of inherent worth. That idea is incompatible with our notion of human equality based on the doctrine that all humans, simply in virtue of their humanity, have the same inherent worth. (The belief in universal human rights is one form that this egalitarianism takes.)

The vast majority of people in modern democracies, however, do not maintain an egalitarian outlook when it comes to comparing human beings with other living things. Most people consider our own species to be superior to all other species and this superiority is understood to be a matter of inherent worth, not merit. There may exist thoroughly vicious and depraved humans who lack all merit. Yet because they are human they are thought to belong to a higher class of entities than any plant or animal. That one is born into the species *Homo sapiens* entitles one to have lordship over those who are one's inferiors, namely, those born into other species. The parallel with hereditary social classes is very close. Implicit in this view is a hierarchical conception of nature according to which an organism has a position of superiority or inferiority in the Earth's community of life simply on the basis of its genetic background. The "lower" orders of life are looked down upon and it is considered perfectly proper that they serve the interests of those belonging to the highest order, namely humans. The intrinsic value we place on the well-being of our fellow humans reflects our recognition of their rightful position as our equals. No such intrinsic value is to be placed on the good of other animals, unless we choose to do so out of fondness or affection for them. But their well-being imposes no moral requirement on us. In this respect there is an absolute difference in moral status between ourselves and them.

This is the structure of concepts and beliefs that people are committed to insofar as they regard humans to be superior in inherent worth to all other species. I now wish to argue that this structure of concepts and beliefs is completely groundless. If we accept the first three components of the biocentric outlook and from that perspective look at the major philosophical traditions which have supported that structure, we find it to be at bottom nothing more than the expression of an irrational bias in our own favor. The philosophical traditions themselves rest on very questionable assumptions or else simply beg the question. I briefly consider three of the main traditions to substantiate the point. These are classical Greek humanism, Cartesian dualism, and the Judeo-Christian concept of the Great Chain of Being.

The inherent superiority of humans over other species was implicit in the Greek definition of man as a rational animal. Our animal nature was identified with "brute" desires that need the order and restraint of reason to rule them (just as reason is the special virtue of those who rule in the ideal state). Rationality was then seen to be the key to our superiority over animals. It enables us to live on a higher plane and endows us with a nobility and worth that other creatures lack. This familiar way of comparing humans with other species is deeply ingrained in our Western philosophical outlook. The point to consider here is that this view does not actually provide an argument *for* human superiority but rather makes explicit the framework of thought that is implicitly used by those who think of humans as inherently superior to nonhumans. The Greeks who held that humans, in virtue of their rational capacities, have a kind of worth greater than that of any nonrational being, never looked at rationality as but one capacity of living things among many others. But when we consider rationality from the standpoint of the first three elements of the ecological outlook, we see that its value lies in its importance for *human* life. Other creatures achieve their species-specific good without the need of rationality, although they often make use of capacities that human lack. So the humanistic outlook of classical Greek thought does not give us a neutral (nonquestion-begging) ground on which to construct a scale of degrees of inherent worth possessed by different species of living things.

The second tradition, centering on the Cartesian dualism of soul and body, also fails to justify the claim to human superiority. That superiority is supposed to derive from the fact that we have souls while animals do not. Animals are mere automata and lack the divine element that makes us spiritual beings. I won't go into the now familiar criticisms of this two-substance view. I only add the point that, even if humans are composed of an immaterial, unextended soul and a material, extended body, this in itself is not a reason to deem them of greater worth than entities that are only bodies. Why is a soul substance a thing that adds value to its possessor? Unless some theological reasoning is offered here (which many, including myself, would find unacceptable on epistemological grounds), no logical connection is evident. An immaterial something which thinks is better than a material something which does not think only if thinking itself has value, either intrinsically or instrumentally. Now it is intrinsically valuable to humans alone, who value it as an end in itself, and it is instrumentally valuable to those who benefit from it, namely humans.

For animals that neither enjoy thinking for its own sake nor need it for living the kind of life for which they are best adapted, it has no value. Even if "thinking" is broadened to include all forms of consciousness, there are still many living things that can do without it and yet live what is for their species a good life. The anthropocentricity underlying the claim to human superiority runs throughout Cartesian dualism.

A third major source of the idea of human superiority is the Judeo-Christian concept of the Great Chain of Being. Humans are superior to animals and plants because their Creator has given them a higher place on the chain. It begins with God at the top, and then moves to the angels, who are lower than God but higher than humans, then to humans, positioned between the angels and the beasts (partaking of the nature of both), and then on down to the lower levels occupied by nonhuman animals, plants, and finally inanimate objects. Humans, being "made in God's image," are inherently superior to animals and plants by virtue of their being closer (in their essential nature) to God.

The metaphysical and epistemological difficulties with this conception of a hierarchy of entities are, in my mind, insuperable. Without entering into this matter here, I only point out that if we are unwilling to accept the metaphysics of traditional Judaism and Christianity, we are again left without good reasons for holding to the claim of inherent human superiority.

The foregoing considerations (and others like them) leave us with but one ground for the assertion that a human being, regardless of merit, is a higher kind of entity than any other living thing. This is the mere fact of the genetic makeup of the species *Homo sapiens*. But this is surely irrational and arbitrary. Why should the arrangement of genes of a certain type be a mark of superior value, especially when this fact about an organism is, taken by itself, unrelated to any other aspect of its life? We might just as well refer to any other genetic makeup as a ground of superior value. Clearly we are confronted here with a wholly arbitrary claim that can only be explained as an irrational bias in our own favor.

That the claim is nothing more than a deep-seated prejudice is brought home to us when we look at our relation to other species in the light of the first three elements of the biocentric outlook. Those elements taken conjointly give us a certain overall view of the natural world and of the place of humans in it. When we take this view we come to understand other living things, their environmental conditions, and their ecological relationships in such a way as to awake in us a deep sense of our kinship with them as fellow members of the Earth's community of life. Humans and nonhumans alike are viewed together as integral parts of one unified whole in which all living things are functionally interrelated. Finally, when our awareness focuses on the individual lives of plants and animals, each is seen to share with us the characteristic of being a teleological center of life striving to realize its own good in its own unique way.

As this entire belief system becomes part of the conceptual framework through which we understand and perceive the world, we come to see ourselves as bearing a certain moral relation to nonhuman forms of life. Our ethical role in nature takes on a new significance. We begin to look at other species as we look at ourselves, seeing them as beings which have a good they are striving to realize just as we have a good we are striving to realize. We accordingly develop the disposition to view the world from the standpoint of their good as well as from the standpoint of our own good. Now if the groundlessness of the claim that humans are inherently superior to other species were brought

clearly before our minds, we would not remain intellectually neutral toward that claim but would reject it as being fundamentally at variance with our total world outlook. In the absence of any good reasons for holding it, the assertion of human superiority would then appear simply as the expression of an irrational and self-serving prejudice that favors one particular species over several million others.

Rejecting the notion of human superiority entails its positive counterpart: the doctrine of species impartiality. One who accepts that doctrine regards all living things as possessing inherent worth—the *same* inherent worth, since no one species has been shown to be either "higher" or "lower" than any other. Now we saw earlier that, insofar as one thinks of a living thing as possessing inherent worth, one considers it to be the appropriate object of the attitude of respect and believes that attitude to be the only fitting or suitable one for all moral agents to take toward it.

Here, then, is the key to understanding how the attitude of respect is rooted in the biocentric outlook of nature. The basic connection is made through the denial of human superiority. Once we reject the claim that humans are superior either in merit or in worth to other living things, we are ready to adopt the attitude of respect. The denial of human superiority is itself the result of taking the perspective on nature built into the first three elements of the biocentric outlook.

Now the first three elements of the biocentric outlook, it seems clear, would be found acceptable to any rational and scientifically informed thinker who is fully "open" to the reality of the lives of nonhuman organisms. Without denying our distinctively human characteristics, such a thinker can acknowledge the fundamental respects in which we are members of the Earth's community of life and in which the biological conditions necessary for the realization of our human values are inextricably linked with the whole system of nature. In addition, the conception of individual living things as teleological centers of life simply articulates how a scientifically informed thinker comes to understand them as the result of increasingly careful and detailed observations. Thus, the biocentric outlook recommends itself as an acceptable system of concepts and beliefs to anyone who is clear-minded, unbiased, and factually enlightened, and who has a developed capacity of reality awareness with regard to the lives of individual organisms. This, I submit, is as good a reason for making the moral commitment involved in adopting the attitude of respect for nature as any theory of environmental ethics could possibly have.

MORAL RIGHTS AND THE MATTER OF COMPETING CLAIMS

I have not asserted anywhere in the foregoing account that animals or plants have moral rights. This omission was deliberate. I do not think that the reference class of the concept, bearer of moral rights, should be extended to include nonhuman living things. My reasons for taking this position, however, go beyond the scope of this paper.[6] I believe I have been able to accomplish many of the same ends which those who ascribe rights to animals or plants wish to accomplish. There is no reason, moreover, why plants and animals, including whole species populations and life communities, cannot be accorded *legal* rights under my theory. To grant them legal protection could be interpreted as giving them legal entitlement to be protected, and this, in fact, would be a means by which a society that subscribed to the ethics of respect for nature could give public recognition to their inherent worth.

There remains the problem of competing claims, even when wild plants and animals are not thought of as bearers of moral rights. If we accept the biocentric outlook and accordingly adopt the attitude of respect for nature as our ultimate moral attitude, how do we resolve conflicts that arise from our respect for persons in the domain of human ethics and our respect for nature in the domain of environmental ethics? This is a question that cannot adequately be dealt with here. My main purpose in this paper has been to try to establish a base point from which we can start working toward a solution to the problem. I have shown why we cannot just begin with an initial presumption in favor of the interests of our own species. It is after all within our power as moral beings to place limits on human population and technology with the deliberate intention of sharing the Earth's bounty with other species. That such sharing is an ideal difficult to realize even in an approximate way does not take away its claim to our deepest moral commitment.

NOTES

1. W.K. Frankena, "Ethics and the Environment," in *Ethics and Problems of the 21st Century*, ed. K.E. Goodpaster and K.M. Sayre, (South Bend: University of Notre Dame Press, 1979), pp. 3–20. I critically examine Frankena's views in "Frankena on Environmental Ethics," *Monist*, 64 (July 1981), no. 3: 313–324.

2. In the light of considerations set forth in Daniel Dennett's *Brainstorms: Philosophical Essays on Mind and Psychology* (Montgomery, Vermont: Bradford Books, 1978), it is advisable to leave this question unsettled at this time. When machines are developed that function in the way our brains do, we may well come to deem them proper subjects of moral consideration.

3. Stephen R. L. Clark, *The Moral Status of Animals* (Oxford: Clarendon Press, 1977), p. 112.

4. My criticisms of the dogma of human superiority gain independent support from a carefully reasoned essay by R. and V. Routley showing the many logical weaknesses in arguments for human-centered theories of environmental ethics. R. and V. Routley, "Against the Inevitability of Human Chauvinism," in *Ethics and Problems of the 21st Century*, ed. K. E. Goodpaster & K. M. Sayre, (South Bend: University of Notre Dame Press, 1979), pp. 36–59.

5. For this way of distinguishing between merit and inherent worth, I am indebted to Gregory Vlastos, "Justice and Equality," in *Social Justice*, ed. R. Brandt (Englewood Cliffs, N.J.: Prentice-Hall, 1962), pp. 31–72.

6. Editor's Note: For further discussion, see Paul Taylor, *Respect for Nature* (Princeton: Princeton University Press, 1986), pp. 245ff.

GARY VARNER

BIOCENTRIC INDIVIDUALISM

CREATE AS MUCH VALUE AS POSSIBLE IN THE WORLD

INTRODUCTION

As a boy, I often wandered in the woods near my home in central Ohio. One August day, I dug up a maple seedling from the woods and planted it in one of my mother's flowerbeds beside the house. Within hours, the seedling was terribly wilted. Convinced that I had mortally wounded the plant, I felt a wave of guilt and, wishing to hasten what I believed to be its inevitable and imminent demise, I pulled it up, broke its small stalk repeatedly, and stuffed it in the trash. When my mother later explained that the plant was only in temporary shock from being transplanted into full sun, I felt an even larger wave of guilt for having dispatched it unnecessarily.

Was I just a soft-headed lad? Even then, I did not think that the plant was conscious, and since childhood, I have not again tried to "euthanize" a doomed plant. I feel no guilt about weeding the garden, mowing the lawn, or driving over the plants which inevitably crowd the four wheel drive paths I gravitate towards while camping. Nevertheless, I now let "weeds" grow indiscriminately in my wooded backyard, I mow around the odd wildflower that pops up amid the Bermuda grass out front, and I sometimes swerve to avoid a plant when tracking solitude in my truck. I believe that insects are not conscious, that they are in the same category, morally speaking, as plants, yet I often carry cockroaches and wasps outside rather than kill them. I'll even pause while mowing to let a grasshopper jump to safety. My relative diffidence regarding insects could just be erring on the side of caution. I believe that insects *probably* are not conscious, whereas I am *cock-sure* that plants are not; so when I do dispatch an insect, I make a point of crushing it quite thoroughly, including its head. Similarly, my current plant-regarding decisions are doubtless inspired in part by aesthetic judgments rather than concern for

their non-conscious well-being. The wildflowers in my front yard are just more interesting to look at than a continuous stretch of Bermuda grass, and my unkempt backyard buffers me from my neighbors. Still, I believe it is better—*morally* better—that plants thrive rather than die, even if they do not benefit humans or other, conscious creatures. So if I was just soft-headed to feel bad about that maple seedling, then my grey matter hasn't quite firmed up yet.

But *am* I just soft-headed, or is there a rational case to be made for plants and other presumably non-conscious organisms? A few philosophers have thought so. The famous doctor and theologian, Albert Schweitzer, wrote:

> A man is truly ethical only when he obeys the compulsion to help all life which he is able to assist, and shrinks from injuring anything that lives. He does not ask how far this or that life deserves one's sympathy as being valuable, nor, beyond that, whether and to what degree it is capable of feeling. Life as such is sacred to him. He tears no leaf from a tree, plucks no flower, and takes care to crush no insect. If in summer he is working by lamplight, he prefers to keep the window shut and breathe a stuffy atmosphere rather than see one insect after another fall with singed wings upon his table.
>
> If he walks on the road after a shower and sees an earthworm which has strayed on it, . . . he lifts if from the deadly stone surface, and puts it on the grass. If he comes across an insect which has fallen into a puddle, he stops a moment in order to hold out a leaf or a stalk on which it can save itself. (1955, p. 310)

And in the contemporary literature of environmental ethics, Paul Taylor's 1986 book, *Respect For Nature: A Theory of Environmental Ethics*, is a must-read for any serious student of the field. In it (and in a 1981 essay which is reproduced in this volume) Taylor argues that extending a Kantian ethic of respect to non-conscious individuals is plausible once one understands that organisms, "conscious or not, all are equally teleological centers of life in the sense that each is a unified system of goal-oriented activities directed toward their preservation and well-being," that each has a good of its own which is "prima facie worthy of being preserved or promoted as an end in itself and for the sake of the entity whose good it is" (1981, pp. 210, 201 reprinted in this volume).

I call views like Schweitzer's and Taylor's *biocentric individualism*, because they attribute moral standing to all living things while denying that holistic entities like species or ecosystems have moral standing. Hence they are *bio*-centric—rather than, say anthropocentric or sentientist—but they are still *individualist* views—rather than versions of holism.

Schweitzer's and Taylor's views differ in important ways. Perhaps most significantly, Schweitzer talks as if we incur guilt every time we harm a living thing, even when we do so to preserve human life. He writes:

> Whenever I in any way sacrifice or injure life, I am not within the sphere of the ethical, but I become guilty, whether it be egoistically guilty for the sake of maintaining my own existence or welfare, or unegoistically guilty for the sake of maintaining a greater number of other existences or their welfare. (1955, p. 325).

In the 40s and 50s, Schweitzer was celebrated in the popular media for bringing modern hospital services to the heart of Africa. Yet he appears to have thought that he incurred guilt when he saved human lives by killing disease microbes, not to mention when he killed things to eat. By contrast, in his book, Taylor makes it clear that he believes we are justified in violating plants' (and some animals') most basic interests in a range of cases: certainly for the sake of surviving, but also for the sake of furthering non-basic, but culturally important, interests of humans. He does impose on this a requirement of "minimum wrong," that is, harming as few living things as possible in the process (1986, p. 289), but Taylor, unlike Schweitzer, believes that we can prioritize interests in a way that justifies us in preserving our own lives and pursuing certain non-basic interests at the expense of plants' (and some animals') most basic interests.

I will return to this question of which interests take precedence in various cases of conflict later. That is certainly an important question for any biocentric individualist. After all, if you think that even disease microbes and radishes have moral standing, then you need an explanation of how your interests can override those of millions of plants and microbes which must be doomed in the course of living a full human life. Otherwise, you are left with Schweitzer's perpetual guilt. But if I wasn't just being a soft headed lad when I regretted killing that maple seedling—if there is a rational case to be made for plants (and other non-conscious organisms) having moral standing—then the first question is: Why think this?

WHY THINK THAT PLANTS HAVE MORAL STANDING?

I have two basic arguments for the conclusion that they do. Before discussing these arguments, however, it is important to be more clear about what, specifically, is being asked.

As I use the terms, to say that an entity has moral standing is to say that it has interests, and to say that it has interests is to say that it has needs and/or desires, and that the satisfaction of those needs and/or desires creates intrinsic value. When I say that their satisfaction creates intrinsic value, I mean that it makes the world a better place, independent of the entity's relations to other things. As the introduction to this volume emphasizes, the term "intrinsic value" is a key one in environmental ethics, but it is also a very nuanced one. There certainly is a distinction to be drawn between valuing something because it is useful, and valuing it apart from its usefulness. One way of expressing the biocentric individualist stance, then, would be to describe it as the view that moral agents ought to value plants' lives intrinsically rather than merely instrumentally. However, putting it this way suggests that plants' flourishing might not be a good thing if there were no conscious valuers around to consider it, and one of my arguments for biocentric individualism purports to show that plants' flourishing is a good thing independently of there being any conscious valuers around at all. So I define biocentric individualism in terms of plants having interests, the satisfaction of which creates intrinsic value as defined above, whether or not there are any conscious valuers around.

A second thing to be clear about is what I mean by "plants." For simplicity's sake, I will speak simply of "plants," but unless stated otherwise, what I mean by this is *all non-conscious organisms*. Later I will take up the question of which non-human animals lack consciousness. For now, suffice it to say that even after the taxonomic revisions of the 1970s, the animal kingdom includes a number of organisms that are poor candidates for consciousness, e.g., barnacles and sponges. Besides plants, the new taxonomy includes three whole kingdoms, the members of which are equally poor candidates. The fungi are just heterotrophic plants. Organisms in the new kingdoms monera and protista—single celled organisms like bacteria and amoebas (respectively)—were previously classified as animals. But in this essay, "plants" is a shorthand for all of these non-conscious organisms.

In summary, I assume the following definitions of these key terms:

Moral standing: An entity has moral standing if and only if it has interests.

Interests: An entity has interests if and only if the fulfillment of its needs and/or desires creates intrinsic value.

Intrinsic value: Intrinsic value is the value something has independently of its relationships to other things. If a thing has intrinsic value, then its existence (flourishing, etc.) makes the world a better place, independently of its value to anything else or any other entity's awareness of it.

Plants: Unless stated otherwise, "plants" refers to all non-conscious organisms, including (presumably) all members of the plant kingdom, but also all members of the kingdoms fungi, monera, and protista, as well as some members of the animal kingdom (to be specified later).

So the question is: Why think that all those "plants" have interests, the satisfaction of which creates intrinsic value, independently of any conscious organism's interest in them?

My first argument for this conclusion is developed in detail in my book, *In Nature's Interests?* (Varner 1998, chapter three). There I argue against the dominant, mental state theory of individual welfare (for short, the mental state theory). The dominant account of individual welfare in recent Western moral philosophy has identified what is in an individual's interests with what the individual actually desires, plus what the individual would desire if he or she were both adequately informed and impartial across phases of his or her life. This dominant account then identifies what is in an individual's *best* interests with the latter, with what he or she would desire under those idealized conditions. Formally:

The mental state theory of individual welfare: Something, X, is in an individual A's interests just in case:

1. A actually desires X, or
2. A would desire X if A were sufficiently informed and impartial across phases of his or her life; and
3. what is in A's *best* interests is defined in terms of clause (2).

Something like this theory is accepted by most contemporary moral and political philosophers.

My first argument for the moral standing of plants begins by pointing to an inadequacy of the mental state theory.

Argument #1: The mental state theory seems to provide an inadequate account of the interests of conscious individuals. If that is so, and if the way to fix it involves acknowledging that intrinsic value is created by the satisfaction of non-conscious, biologically-based needs of such individuals, then it makes sense to attribute interests to plants. For although plants are incapable of having desires, they have biologically-based needs just as do conscious individuals.

Here is an example that brings out the problem I see in the mental state theory:

Example 1 (the nineteenth century mariners): By the nineteenth century, British mariners were carrying citrus fruit on long sea voyages to prevent the debilitating disease of scurvy. It was not until this century that scientists discovered that we need about 10 milligrams of ascorbic acid a day, and that citrus fruits prevent scurvy because they contain large amounts of it.

To see how this raises a problem, consider what is meant by being "adequately informed" in the second clause of the mental state theory. Some authors limit "adequate information" to the best scientific knowledge of the day. But then it would be false that those mariners had any interest in getting 10 milligrams of ascorbic acid a day. This is because they did not in fact desire it (they did not even know it exists), and even having the best scientific knowledge of the day would not have led them to desire it (because no one then knew about it). The problem is that it certainly seems wrong to say that getting 10 milligrams of ascorbic acid a day was not in their interests.

This problem is easily avoided by adding a clause about biologically-based needs to our theory of individual welfare. Renamed appropriately, the theory would now be something like this:

The psycho-biological theory of individual welfare: Something, X, is in an individual A's interests just in case:

1. A actually desires X,
2. A would desire X if A were sufficiently informed and impartial across phases of his or her life, or
3. X serves some biologically-based need of A.

In my book (Varner 1998, pp. 64–71) I give a detailed analysis of the complex notion of a biologically-based need, arguing that these can be determined by examining the evolutionary history of an organism. Here, I think it unnecessary to revisit that analysis. Pretty clearly, ascorbic acid served a biologically-based need of sailors before modern scientists discovered it. So, on this psycho-biological theory, it was in those sailors' interest to get enough of it, even though no one knew anything about ascorbic acid at the time.

Note that this new theory says nothing about what is in one's *best* interests. I replaced clause (3) in the mental state theory rather than adding another clause, because identifying what is in one's best interests with what one would desire under ideal motivational and information conditions—clause (2)—faces similar problems. Other things being equal, it seems that getting enough ascorbic acid was in those mariners' best interests, even though they would still not have desired it even under the best motivational and information conditions. So even after adding a clause about biologically-based needs, it would still be a mistake to identify what is in one's best interests with clause (2).

One limitation of the nineteenth century mariners example is that being "sufficiently informed" can be analyzed other than in terms of having "the best scientific knowledge of the day." We could, for instance, analyze it in terms of having all the scientific knowledge that humans will ever or could ever accumulate. I believe there are other problems with this analysis (see Varner 1998, pp. 58–60), but it would solve the problem raised by the above example. However, here is another example, which brings out the same kind of problem with the mental state theory, and where the alternative analysis of "sufficiently informed" doesn't help:

Example 2 (Nanci's desire to go outside): Like many cat owners, I grapple with the question of whether and when to allow my cat, Nanci, to go outside. Cats find the outdoors endlessly fascinating, but they also encounter health risks outside, including exposure to feline leukemia virus (FeLV) and fleas (which Nanci happens to be allergic to).

I frankly do not know whether or not keeping Nanci indoors is in her best interests, all things considered. Nonetheless, it does seem clear that keeping her inside would serve some interests of hers, in at least some ways. For instance, it would prevent exposure to FeLV and fleas. Yet the mental state theory does not support this intuition, because it is not clear that it even makes sense to talk about what an animal like Nanci would desire if she were "sufficiently informed and impartial across phases of her life." I assume that Nanci is congenitally incapable of understanding the relevant information about FeLV and fleas. So on the mental state theory, what are we to say about her going outside? It looks like we have to conclude that, whenever she in fact wants to go out, she has no interest whatsoever in staying inside, because clause (2) is irrelevant in her case. It just doesn't make sense, in the case of animals like Nanci, to talk about what they would desire were they "sufficiently informed" (let alone "impartial across phases of their lives"). Thus, in the case of animals like Nanci, what is in their interests is whatever they happen to desire at any moment in time. This is another counter-intuitive implication of the mental state theory, and one which the psycho-biological theory avoids. Although the psycho-biological theory as formulated above is silent on the issue of what is in an individual's best interests, it at least supports the intuition that Nanci has some interest in staying inside (because doing so would serve her biologically-based needs by preventing exposure to FeLV and fleas), even if she now desires to go outside and no sense can be made of what an animal like her would desire under ideal epistemological and motivational conditions.

The examples of Nanci and the nineteenth century mariners together illustrate a general problem for the mental state theory. The theory ties all of our interests to what we desire, either actually or under ideal epistemological and motivational conditions, but not all of our interests are tied in this way to our conscious desires and beliefs. Most (maybe even all) of our desires are tied to our beliefs about the world, because as our beliefs change, our desires change. For instance, suppose that I desire to marry Melody, primarily because I believe that she is a fine fiddler. When I find out that my belief about her is false, my desire to marry her will presumably be extinguished. Similarly, if I do not desire to marry Melinda only because I believe that she is a lousy fiddler, when I find out that she is actually a virtuoso, I will presumably form a desire to marry her. My interest in marrying each woman comes and goes with my beliefs about her. However, nothing I could possibly believe about the world, whether true or false, could change the fact that I need about 10 milligrams a day of ascorbic acid to stay healthy, and no matter how strongly I might desire it, I will never be able to make it true that going without ascorbic acid is in my interest. My interest in ascorbic acid is determined by a biological need that exists wholly independent of my beliefs and desires. This is a central advantage of the psycho-biological theory over the mental state theory. Some things are only in our interests if we happen to desire them or have certain beliefs about the world, but other things are in our interests no matter what we desire or believe, or what we would desire and believe under ideal conditions. We can refer to the former as preference interests and to the latter as biological interests. The mental state theory errs by identifying all of our interests with our preference interests. The psycho-biological theory acknowledges these, but also accounts for biological interests which are wholly independent of our preference interests.

That being said, my first argument for the moral standing of plants is now complete. The above examples are intended to illustrate how the dominant, mental state theory of individual welfare is flawed, because it ties all of individuals' interests to their actual or hypothetical desires. An obvious way to fix this problem is to hold that individuals also have biological interests in the fulfillment of their various biologically-based needs, whether they (like the nineteenth century mariners) could only become aware of these needs under special circumstances, or they (like Nanci the cat) are congenitally incapable of desiring that those needs be fulfilled. But then, since plants too have biologically-based needs, they too have interests, even though they are congenitally incapable of desiring anything at all.

I did not include my second argument for the view that plants have moral standing in my 1998 book, because, frankly, I doubted that it would be persuasive to anyone not already essentially convinced. Nevertheless, I think that this second argument expresses very clearly the most basic value assumption of the biocentric individualist. It also ties in to famous thought experiments in ethical theory and environmental ethics, and so I include it here.

The argument is driven by a variant of a famous thought experiment which British philosopher G. E. Moore used to cast doubt on sentientism (the view that only sentient—that is conscious—organisms have moral standing). Moore discussed the classical utilitarians (Jeremy Bentham, John Stuart Mill, and Henry Sidgwick—who were all sentientists) at length and in particular responded to Sidgwick's claim that "No one would consider it rational to aim at the production of beauty in external nature, apart from any possible contemplation of it by human beings." Moore responded:

> Well, I may say at once, that I, for one, do consider this rational; and let us see if I cannot get any one to agree with me. Consider what this admission really means. It entitles us to put the following case. Let us imagine one world exceedingly beautiful. Imagine it as beautiful as you can; put into it whatever on this earth you most admire—mountains, rivers, the sea; trees, and sunsets, stars and moon. Imagine these all combined

in the most exquisite proportions, so that no one thing jars against another, but each contributes to increase the beauty of the whole. And then imagine the ugliest world you can possibly conceive. Imagine it simply one heap of filth, containing everything that is most disgusting to us, for whatever reason, and the whole, as far as may be, without one redeeming feature. Such a pair of worlds we are entitled to compare: they fall within Prof. Sidgwick's meaning, and the comparison is highly relevant to it. The only thing we are not entitled to imagine is that any human being ever has or ever, by any possibility, *can*, live in either, can ever see and enjoy the beauty of the one or hate the foulness of the other. Well, even so, supposing them quite apart from any possible contemplation by human beings; still, is it irrational to hold that it is better that the beautiful world should exist, than the one which is ugly? Would it not be well, in any case, to do what we could to produce it rather than the other?

Moore thought we would agree with him in answering yes. But then, he continued:

If it be once admitted that the beautiful world *in itself* is better than the ugly, then it follows, that however many beings may enjoy it, and however much better their enjoyment may be than it is itself, yet its mere existence adds *something* to the goodness of the whole . . . (pp. 83–85; emphases in original)

That is, Moore concluded, the mere existence of beauty adds intrinsic value to the world.

I have always been unsure what to think about Moore's thought experiment, so apparently I am of two minds when it comes to saying that the mere existence of beauty adds intrinsic value to the world. However, I have always felt certain about my answer to an analogous question. Suppose that instead of choosing between creating a beautiful world and an ugly world, the choice were between creating a world devoid of life and a world brimming with living things, neither of which would ever evolve conscious life or even be visited or known about by any conscious organisms. If, like me, you believe that it matters which world is produced and that it would be better to produce the world chock-full of non-conscious life, then you seem to be committed to biocentric individualism. For you appear to believe that life—even non-conscious life—has intrinsic value. To paraphrase Moore:

Argument 2: If we admit that a world of non-conscious living things is *in itself* better than a world devoid of all life, then it follows that however much better it is to be both conscious and alive, the mere existence of non-conscious life adds *something* to the goodness of the world.

Note that this contrasts with the "last man" thought experiment, as characterized in the introduction to this volume (where the last person on earth destroys a tree "Just for fun"), in two important ways. First, in my variant of Moore's thought experiment, it is stipulated that there is no person on the scene at all. This is important because an anthropocentrist might try to explain the problem with the last man in terms of his action's effects on his own character. Second, and more importantly, in the "last man" case, the tree is said to be "the last remaining Redwood," but in my variant of Moore's thought experiment, nothing is said about the plants in question being rare. If we agree that it matters which of my worlds is produced, and that it would be better to produce the plant-filled world, then we seem to agree that the lives of even the most mundane plants add intrinsic value to the world.

JUST WHAT ARE PLANTS' INTERESTS WORTH?

The next question has to be: Just *how valuable* are the interests of plants, in relation to those of humans and other animals? Moral hierarchies are unpopular in many quarters. In particular, feminist philosophers often condemn hierarchical views of beings' relative moral significance for being instruments of patriarchal oppression (see, for instance, Karen Warren's contribution to this volume). But as a biocentric individualist, I feel forced to endorse one. Otherwise, how could I live with myself? I gleefully tear radishes from the garden for a snack, swatting mosquitoes all the while. I take antibiotics for a persistent sinus infection, and (at least when I'm not on antibiotics) I send countless intestinal bacteria on a deadly joyride into the city sewer system every morning. Unless I can give good reasons for thinking that my interests somehow trump those of microbes and plants (if not also animals), I am left with Albert Schweitzer's view, quoted above, that we "become guilty" whenever we "in any way sacrifice or injure life," even when fighting off disease organisms, eating, and defecating. In my book (Varner 1998, chapter four), I argue that a plausible assumption about what I call "hierarchically structured interests" does the trick, when coupled with empirical observations about certain broad categories of interests.

Here is what I mean by hierarchically structured interests:

> **Hierarchically structured interests:** Two interests are hierarchically structured when the satisfaction of one requires the satisfaction of the other, but not vice-versa.

Certain types of interests clearly stand in this relationship to other types of interests. For example, satisfying my desire to succeed professionally requires the satisfaction of innumerable more particular desires across decades, but not vice-versa. It takes years to succeed professionally, and therefore I have to satisfy innumerable day-to-day desires to eat this or that in the course of completing that long-term project. But each particular desire to eat can be satisfied without satisfying my long-term desire to succeed professionally. So my desires to eat and to succeed professionally are hierarchically structured in the above sense.

Generally, what the contemporary American philosopher Bernard Williams calls "ground projects" and "categorical desires" stand in this relationship to day-to-day desires for particular things. Here is how Williams defines these terms:

> **"Ground projects" and "categorical desires":** A ground project is "a nexus of projects . . . which are closely related to [one's] existence and which to a significant degree give a meaning to [one's] life," and a categorical desire is one that answers the question "Why is life worth living?" (Williams 1981, pp. 13, 12; 1973, pp. 85–86)

A person's ground project normally is a nexus of categorical desires, and generally, a ground project requires decades to complete. There are, of course, exceptions. It is conceivable that a person might have literally only one categorical desire, a desire which she could satisfy in one fell swoop. Perhaps a young gymnast aiming at a gold medal in the Olympics is a realistic approximation of this, but notice that even in the case of the gymnast: (1) satisfying the desire for a gold medal

requires years of training, and (2) we would probably think it unhealthy and abnormal if the gymnast had no other ground project, if there were no other, longer-term desires that made her life worth living beyond the Olympics. So a ground project normally involves a host of very long-term desires which bear the above kind of hierarchical relationship with the individual's day-to-day desires for this or that specific thing.

Here is a plausible assumption about interests that are clearly hierarchically structured:

> **Assumption:** Generally speaking, ensuring the satisfaction of interests from similar levels in similar hierarchies of different individuals creates similar amounts of value, and the dooming of interests from similar levels in similar hierarchies of different individuals creates similar levels of disvalue.

In stating the assumption in this way, I do not mean to imply that we can make very fine-tuned judgements about which interests are more valuable than others.[1] All I claim is that interests from certain very broad categories *generally* bear this relationship to interests from other very broad categories. In particular, I argue that the following two principles are reasonable in light of the assumption:

> **Principle P1 (the priority of desires principle):** Generally speaking, the death of an entity that has desires is a worse thing than the death of an entity that does not.

> **Principle P2′ (the priority of ground projects principle):** Generally speaking, the satisfaction of ground projects is more important than the satisfaction of non-categorical desires.

Since I introduced the above assumption by discussing human ground projects, let me begin with principle P2′.

I call it P2′, rather than just P2, because in my book I first introduce, and dismiss, this principle:

> **Principle P2 (the priority of *human* desires principle):** The satisfaction of the desires of humans is more important than the satisfaction of the desires of animals.

Principle P2 would solve the problem under discussion in this section, but it is transparently speciesist.

It says that humans' desires are more important than any other organisms' simply because they are desires of *humans*. Principle P2′ compares ground projects to non-categorical desires without asserting that humans' desires are more important than any other organisms'. If it turns out that some non-human animals have ground projects, then Principle P2′ applies equally to theirs. Which animals, if any, have ground projects is an empirical question, as is the question of whether all human beings do. Surely some human beings do not. For instance, anencephalic babies and the permanently comatose clearly do not, and perhaps others, like the most profoundly retarded, or those who have lost the will to live, do not. Regarding animals, my hunch is that very few if any non-human animals have ground projects, but maybe some do (perhaps some great apes or cetaceans). The crucial thing to note is that principle P2′ is not speciesist. It does not say that humans' interests are more important *because they are humans' interests*. Principle P2′ only says that ground projects, wherever they occur, generally have more value than non-categorical desires. P2′ leaves the question of which beings have ground projects open for empirical investigation; it does not stipulate that only humans have this especially valuable kind of interest.

So why think that ground projects are more valuable than non-categorical desires? The reason is that, as we saw above, ground projects normally stand in a hierarchical relationship to day-to-day desires for particular things; satisfying a ground project requires the satisfaction of innumerable day-to-day desires for particular things, but not vice-versa. So under the above assumption (that various interests within each type generally have similar amounts of value), satisfying a ground project generally creates more value than satisfying any such day-to-day desire.

I will discuss the implications of P2′ in the next section, along with those of P1. First, however, let me discuss the justification of P1. Notice that P1 does not assert that just any desire trumps any biological need or set thereof. Some day-to-day desires for particular things are incredibly trivial and it would be implausible to say that these trivial desires trump seemingly important biological interests like one's biological interest in good cardiovascular health. But all that principle P1 states is that "Generally speaking, the death

of an entity that has desires is a worse thing than the death of an entity that does not." This is plausible under the assumption stated above, given the following general fact: maintenance of the capacity to form and satisfy desires requires the on-going satisfaction of the lion's share of one's biological needs. Certainly not every biological need of a conscious organism must be fulfilled for it to go on forming desires. In particular, the account I give in my book implies that the continued functioning of my vasa deferentia is in my biological interest (Varner 1998, p. 97), but obviously I would go on desiring sex (among other things) after a vasectomy. One of the deep challenges to my position (as Vermont philosopher Bill Throop has driven home to me in conversation) is deciding how to individuate interests. Do I have just one biological interest in the continued functioning of my whole cardiovascular system? One interest in the functioning of my heart and another in the functioning of my vascular system? Or do I have myriad interests, in the functioning of my various ventricles, veins, arteries, and so on? This is a difficult issue, but however it gets sorted out, it seems plausible to say that just as satisfying a ground project requires the satisfaction of innumerable day-to-day desires for particular things, maintaining the general capacity to form and satisfy desires requires the on-going satisfaction of the lion's share of one's biological needs. As a conscious process, maintenance of the capacity to form and satisfy desires presumably requires maintenance of myriad biological organs and subsystems, including, at the very least, the respiratory and cardio-vascular systems, and most of the central nervous system. The argument for principle P1, then, is this: The only interests plants have in common with conscious organisms are biological interests. The ability to form and satisfy desires stands in a hierarchical relationship to such biological interests. But if interests of these two types generally have similar value, then conscious animals' lives have more value than plants' lives, because animals satisfy both types of interests in the course of their lives, whereas plants satisfy only one type.

The question posed in this section has not been answered precisely. My argument has not shown precisely how much the interests of plants are worth, relative to the interests of humans or other animals. For reasons given in my book (Varner 1998, pp. 80–88), I think it is impossible to give such a precise answer to this question. However, if principle P1 is indeed justified by the principle of inclusiveness (coupled with the assumption articulated above), then it is plausible to conclude that the *lives* of plants are, generally, less valuable than the *lives* of desiring creatures, including yours and mine. And that goes a long way towards showing that biocentric individualism is a practicable view, although most environmental philosophers have doubted that it is.

IS BIOCENTRIC INDIVIDUALISM PRACTICABLE?

One reason for doubt would be that before Paul Taylor, the only well-known biocentric individualist was Albert Schweitzer and, as we have seen, he said flatly that we are guilty for merely keeping ourselves alive by eating and fighting disease. However, as the foregoing section shows, a biocentric individualist can reasonably endorse a hierarchy of interests and related principles showing why it is better that we do this than let ourselves perish. We can at least say that my view implies this rough hierarchy of value:

> ground projects
>
> non-categorical desires
>
> biological interests

Principle P2' states that the satisfaction of a ground project is better than (creates more value than) the satisfaction of any interest of the other two kinds. Thus killing an individual with a ground project robs the world of a special kind of value. According to principle P1, the lives of many non-human animals have more value than the lives of plants, because these conscious organisms have both biological interests and non-categorical desires, whereas plants have only biological interests. Thus killing an animal robs the world of more value than does killing a plant.

The second part of this value hierarchy focuses attention on questions about consciousness that were alluded to earlier: which animals are conscious, which ones have desires? These questions are related, but not equivalent. I assume that all "genuine" desires are conscious, or at least potentially conscious, just as pain is. However, the evidence for desires in non-human animals may not overlap the evidence for pain, because I also assume that desires require relatively sophisticated cognitive capacities, whereas the bare consciousness of pain may not. A detailed treatment of this issue is beyond the scope of this essay, but here is a summary of the conclusions I reach from the more detailed treatment in my book (Varner 1998, pp. 26–30). All normal, mature mammals and birds very probably *do* have desires, and there is a somewhat weaker case for saying that "herps" (reptiles and amphibians) do too. The case for saying that fish have desires is decisively weaker. However, the available evidence makes it very likely that all vertebrates, including fish, can feel pain. This is a curious result—it sounds odd to say that fish could feel pain without desiring an end to it—and so I suspect that as more kinds of scientific studies are available than I considered in my book, the evidence for pain and for desire in the animal kingdom will converge. However, for the sake of discussion here, I assume that although mammals and birds have desires, fish and invertebrates do not.[2]

We can now spell out more specifically the implications of the principles defended in the preceding section. Principle P1 tells us that it is better to kill desireless organisms than desiring ones. This addresses Schweitzer's hyperbolic guilt, because it shows that it would be worse for a human being to kill herself than it would be for her to kill any plant or microbe for the sake of good nutrition or fighting off disease. However, in light of the above discussion of consciousness, this does not imply that vegetarian diets are better, since most invertebrates apparently lack consciousness, and even fish may lack desires. Also, since it is possible to obtain animal byproducts like eggs and dairy foods from animals without killing them, a lacto-ovo diet might be perfectly respectful of animals' intrinsic value. (There are other ethical considerations, of course, as well as complicated issues in human nutrition. For an overview, see the essays in Comstock 1994.)

I also suspect that Principle P2' can be used to make a case for the humane killing of animals who clearly have (non-categorical) desires. My reasoning is as follows. To the extent that hunting and slaughter-based animal agriculture play an important role in sustainable human communities, the value of protecting the background conditions for satisfying humans' ground projects would seem to support the necessary killing, at least if the animals live good lives and are killed humanely. Obviously, various animals, including mammals and birds, played a very large role in both paleolithic hunting-gathering societies and in the emergence of agriculture. Domesticated mammals continue to have a crucial role in sustainable agricultural systems in so-called "developing" nations, where they provide not only food but draft power and fertilizer. But at present it is still unclear to me just how much killing of animals might be necessary in utopian sustainable communities of the future.

In light of these implications of Principles P1 and P2', the biocentric individualist stance hardly looks unlivable in the way Schweitzer's talk of perpetual guilt would suggest. There is a deeper reason that many environmental philosophers dismiss the biocentric individualist stance, however. They fear that it somehow devalues nature and thus, even if it is not literally an unlivable ethic, it is "inadequate" as an *environmental* ethic. This charge of "inadequacy" takes at least two distinct forms, and the biocentric individualist response to each must be different.

First, it is often claimed that individualist theories in general (that is, anthropocentrism and sentientism in addition to biocentric individualism) have implications that do not comport with the environmentalist agenda, which includes things like endangered species programs, the elimination of exotic species from natural areas, and the whole emphasis on preserving remaining natural areas. The heart of this claim is that because they focus on individuals, such theories get the wrong answers in a range of cases. For instance, environmentalists are keenly interested in preserving remaining natural areas, but, so this objection goes, biocentric individualism cannot justify this emphasis. For if we compare a woods and a cultivated field, or an old growth forest and a managed timber lot, they may look equally valuable from a biocentric individualist stance. Simply put, if only biological interests are at stake, then a cultivated area supporting thousands of thriving plants creates just as much value as a wild area that supports the same number of plants. Similarly, the biological interests of common plants seem no more valuable than the biological interests of rare plants.

This first version of the "inadequacy" charge misfires precisely because there *is* more at stake than the biological interests of the plants involved. Environmentalists commonly claim that in order to preserve the ecological context in which humans can live healthy, productive, and innovative lives into the indefinite future, we must stop the current trend of species extinctions and preserve most remaining wild areas. Characterizing the environmentalists' claim as a general need to safeguard background biological diversity in our environment, my response to the first version of the inadequacy charge is this. Principle P2' attaches preeminent importance to safeguarding humans' ability to satisfy their ground projects. But if safeguarding this ability requires safeguarding background biological diversity in our environment, then doing so is of preeminent importance, at least instrumentally, on my view. That is, to the extent that environmentalists are correct that their practical agenda safeguards long-term human interests, any version of biocentric individualism which, like mine, attributes preeminent importance to certain interests of humans can probably endorse their agenda.

At this point it is important to note that two senses of the term "anthropocentric" are sometimes conflated in discussions of environmental ethics. In one sense of the term, a view is anthropocentric just in case it denies that non-human nature has any intrinsic value whatsoever. Obviously, biocentric individualism is not anthropocentric in this sense. But in another sense, a view is called anthropocentric if it gives pride of place to certain interests which only humans have. Schweitzer's version of biocentric individualism is not anthropocentric in this second sense, but because I doubt that any non-human animals have ground projects, mine is. For clarity's sake, I use the labels "valuational anthropocentrism" and "axiological anthropocentrism" to refer, respectively, to views that deny all intrinsic value to non-humans and to views that acknowledge the intrinsic value of some non-human beings but insist that only humans have certain preeminently important interests (1998, p. 121).

The other form of the "inadequacy" charge focuses on the fact that for the biocentric individualist, even if holistic entities like species and ecosystems have enormous value, this value is still only instrumental. Environmentalists, it is claimed, tend to think that such entities have intrinsic value rather than merely instrumental value, and thus environmentalists tend to think more like holists.

I think this version of the "inadequacy" charge misconstrues one of the central questions of environmental ethics. As environmental philosophers, we should not think of ourselves as focusing on the question: What do environmentalists *in fact* think has intrinsic value? Rather, we should be asking: What *should* we think has intrinsic value? Or: What do we *have good reasons* to think has intrinsic value? Defining an "adequate" environmental ethic as one that matches the pre-theoretic intuitions of self-professed environmentalists turns the discipline of environmental ethics into a kind of moral anthropology rather than a reasoned search for truth. In this essay, I have not developed a case against environmental holism, but the arguments of this section do show that biocentric individualism cannot be summarily dismissed as impracticable, either generally or in regard to environmental policy specifically.

CONCLUSION

My larger goal in this essay has been to show that one need not be soft-headed to think that it matters, morally speaking, how we treat plants. It would, in my judgment, be unreasonable to obsess on the microbes one's immune system is killing every day or on how one's dinner vegetables were dealt their death-blows, but it is not irrational to think that it is good to save the life of plants and non-conscious animals when one can. Good arguments can be given for thinking this, and someone who thinks this can consistently live a good human life.

And, of course, if it is reasonable to think that plants' lives have intrinsic value, then it was not irrational for me to feel at least a little bit guilty about killing that maple seedling unnecessarily.

SOURCES CITED

Gary Comstock, "Might Morality Require Veganism?" Special issue of *Journal of Agricultural and Environmental Ethics* 7 (1994) no. 1.

G. E. Moore, *Principia Ethica*. (London: Cambridge University Press, 1903).

Albert Schweitzer, *The Philosophy of Civilization*. (New York: Macmillan, 1955).

Paul Taylor, "The Ethics of Respect for Nature." *Environmental Ethics* 3 (1981) 197–218.

Paul Taylor, *Respect for Nature: A Theory of Environmental Ethics*. (Princeton: Princeton University Press, 1986).

Gary E. Varner, *In Nature's Interests? Interests, Animal Rights, and Environmental Ethics*. (New York: Oxford University Press, 1998).

Bernard Williams, *Problems of the Self*. (Cambridge: Cambridge University Press, 1973).

Bernard Williams, *Moral Luck*. (Cambridge: Cambridge University Press, 1981).

NOTES

1. Strictly speaking, my view is that the *satisfaction* of interests creates intrinsic value, but in this essay I speak interchangeably of "the value of various interests," "the value of various interests' satisfaction," and "the value created by the satisfaction of various interests."

2. The issue is further complicated by the phenomenon of convergent evolution—some invertebrates could have evolved coping strategies which most other invertebrates have not. In particular, cephalopods (octopus, squid, and cuttlefish) may have evolved consciousness of pain and cognitive capacities which other invertebrates lack but most or all vertebrates have.

DAVID SCHMIDTZ

ARE ALL SPECIES EQUAL?

Species egalitarianism is the view that all living things have equal moral standing. To have moral standing is, at a minimum, to command respect, to be more than a mere thing. Is there reason to believe that all living things have moral standing in even this most minimal sense? If so—that is, if all living things command respect—is there reason to believe they all command *equal* respect?[1]

I explain why members of other species command our respect but also why they do not command equal respect. The intuition that we should respect nature is one motive for embracing species egalitarianism, but we need not be species egalitarians to have respect for nature. I question whether species egalitarianism is even compatible with respect for nature.

I. RESPECT FOR NATURE

According to Paul Taylor, anthropocentrism "gives either exclusive or primary consideration to human interests above the good of other species."[2] The alternative to anthropocentrism is biocentrism, and it is biocentrism that, in Taylor's view, grounds species egalitarianism.

Four beliefs form the core of Taylor's biocentrism:

(a) Humans are members of the Earth's community of life in the same sense and on the same terms in which other living things are members of that community.

(b) All species, including humans, are integral parts of a system of interdependence.

(c) All organisms are teleological centers of life. Each is a unique individual pursuing its own good in its own way.

(d) Humans are not inherently superior to other living beings.[3]

Taylor concludes, "Rejecting the notion of human superiority entails its positive counterpart: the doctrine of species impartiality. One who accepts that doctrine regards all living things as possessing inherent worth—the *same* inherent worth, since no one species has been shown to be either higher or lower than any other."[4] Taylor does not call this a valid argument (he acknowledges that it is not), but he thinks that if we concede (a), (b), and (c), it would be unreasonable not to move to (d), and then to his egalitarian conclusion. Is he right? For those who accept Taylor's three premises, and who thus interpret those premises in terms innocuous enough to render them acceptable, there are two responses. First, we may go on to accept (d), following Taylor, yet deny that there is any warrant for moving from there to Taylor's egalitarian conclusion. Having accepted that our form of life is not superior, we might instead regard it as inferior. More plausibly, we might view our form of life as noncomparable. The question of how we compare to nonhumans has a simple answer: we don't. We are not equal. We are not superior. We are not inferior. We are simply different.

Alternatively, we may reject (d) and say humans are inherently superior, but then go on to say that our superiority is a moot point. Whether we are inherently superior—that is, superior as a form of life—does not matter much. Even if we are superior, within the web of ecological interdependence mentioned in premises (a) and (b), it would be a mistake to ignore the needs and the telos of any species referred to in premise (c). Thus, there are two ways of rejecting Taylor's argument for species egalitarianism. Neither alternative is committed to species equality, yet each, on its face, is compatible with the respect for nature that motivates Taylor's egalitarianism in the first place.

Previously published in Journal of Applied Philosophy, 15 (1998): 57–67. Reprinted by permission of the author and the Society for Applied Philosophy.

These are preliminary worries about Taylor's argument. Taylor's critics have been harsh, perhaps overly harsh. After building on some of their criticisms and rejecting others, I explore some of our reasons to have respect for nature and ask whether they translate into reasons to be species egalitarians. I conclude that Taylor's biocentrism has a point, but that biocentrism does not require any commitment to species equality.

II. IS SPECIES EGALITARIANISM HYPOCRITICAL?

Taylor is among the most intransigent of species egalitarians, yet he allows that human needs override the needs of nonhumans. In response, Peter French argues that species egalitarians cannot have it both ways. French perceives a contradiction between the egalitarian principles that Taylor officially endorses and the unofficial principles he offers as the real principles by which we should live. Having proclaimed that we are all equal, French asks, what licenses Taylor to say that, in cases of conflict, nonhuman interests can legitimately be sacrificed to vital human interests?[5]

Good question. Yet, somehow Taylor's alleged inconsistency is too obvious. Perhaps his position is not as blatantly inconsistent as it appears. Let me suggest how Taylor could respond: Suppose I find myself in a situation of mortal combat with an enemy soldier. If I kill my enemy to save my life, that does not entail that I regard my enemy as an inferior form of life. Likewise, if I kill a bear to save my life, that does not entail that I regard the bear as inherently inferior. Therefore, Taylor can, without hypocrisy, deny that species egalitarianism requires a radically self-effacing pacifism.

What, then, does species egalitarianism require? It requires us to avoid mortal combat whenever we can, not only with other humans but with living things in general. On this view, we ought to regret finding ourselves in kill-or-be-killed situations that we could have avoided. There is no point in regretting the fact that we must kill in order to eat, though, for there is no avoiding that. Species egalitarianism is compatible with our having a limited license to kill.

Many, including vegetarians, will say that it matters *what* we kill. Most vegetarians think it is worse to kill a cow than to kill a carrot. Are they wrong? Yes they are, according to species egalitarianism. Therein

lies egalitarianism's failure to respect nature. I agree with Taylor that we have reason to respect nature, but if we treat a chimpanzee no better than we would treat a carrot, that is a failure of respect, not a token of it. Failing to respect what makes living things different is not a way of respecting them. It is instead a way of being indiscriminate.

III. IS SPECIES EGALITARIANISM ARBITRARY?

According to premise (c) of Taylor's argument for the biocentric outlook, as discussed in section I, a being has intrinsic worth if it has a good of its own. He notes that even plants have a good of their own in the relevant sense. They seek their own good in their own way. Taylor defines anthropocentrism as giving exclusive or primary consideration to human interests above the good of other species. So, if we acknowledge that the ability to think is a valuable capacity and if we further acknowledge that some but not all living things possess this capacity, are we giving exclusive or primary consideration to human interests? Not at all. All we are doing is acknowledging that living things, including humans, can be valuable in various ways, and that some living things may be *more* valuable than humans along some dimensions. We acknowledge that not all living things are equal along all dimensions. Some are faster, some are smarter, and so on. We consider the possibility that all values are commensurable. (If they are not commensurable, then neither can they be equal.) We note that *if* all values are commensurable, then in principle we can add up the values of all living things along all dimensions. If we do this, it might turn out that all living things have equal value. But that would be quite a fluke.

It will not do to defend species egalitarianism by singling out a property that all living things possess, arguing that this property is important, then concluding that all living things are therefore of equal moral importance. Why not? Because where one property such as simply being alive provides a basis for moral standing, there might be others. Other properties such as sentience might be possessed by some but not all living things, and might provide bases for different kinds or degrees of moral standing.

Taylor realizes that not all living things can think, and never denies that the capacity for thought is valuable. What he would say is that it begs the question to rank the ability to think as *more* valuable than the characteristic traits of plants and other animals. Taylor assumes that human rationality is on a par with, for example, a cheetah's foot-speed: no less valuable, but no more valuable either.[6] In this case, though, Taylor is missing the point.[7] Let us concede to Taylor that the good associated with the ability to think is not superior (not even by our unavoidably human standards) to the good associated with a tree's ability to grow and reproduce. The point is, it doesn't matter. Suppose we let *a* be the good of being able to grow and reproduce, let *b* be the good of sentience, and let *c* be the good of being rational. Contra Taylor, anthropocentrists need not assume that *c* has a higher value than *a*. All they need assume is that the value of *a* + *c* is higher than the value of *a* by itself. The point is independent of any standard by which we might evaluate *a* or *c*. No matter how much we value the ability to grow and reproduce, the fact would remain that chimpanzees have what trees have, plus more.

One valid response: it is a little odd to treat properties of living things as if some property called "able to grow and reproduce" were manifested by all living things identically, or as if a property called "able to run" were manifested in an identical way by all animals that run, and so on. In truth, not all *a*'s are equal. Acknowledging this does not help the case for species equality, but it does complicate things. Perhaps a tree's vegetative good is greater than a chimpanzee's vegetative good, so that the additional animal good of chimpanzees just suffices to balance the vegetative superiority of trees.

Although this response is interesting in its own right, I think it is unavailable to biocentric egalitarians such as Taylor. Taylor says that all living things are equal in the sense that they all have lives of their own.[8] As soon as Taylor acknowledges that there are other dimensions of value, he has to choose. On the one hand, he can arbitrarily assign different values to each living thing's *a* so as to preserve an overall equality:

$$a_{tree} = a_{animal} + b = a_{human} + b + c$$

Alternatively, and more plausibly, Taylor can concede that equality is not the real issue. It never was. There is a real issue here, and there always was, but the issue is this: Wouldn't the world would be a better place if we stopped thinking of ourselves as superior, and acknowledged that we live in a world of value extending far beyond the human realm? The plea implicit in this question is the common sense intuition that motivates biocentrism—nothing more, nothing less. This intuition is best grounded not in some tortured argument that everything is equal, but rather in the simple and plausible thought that the goods of trees and chimpanzees (and humans) are not comparable. They each have goods of their own, and their goods are incomparable. Period.

Although both trees and chimpanzees are teleological centers of life, and although we can agree that this status is valuable and that trees and chimpanzees share equally in this particular value, we cannot infer that trees and chimpanzees have equal value. We are entitled to conclude only that they are of equal value so far as being a teleological center of life is concerned. From that, we may infer that *one* alleged ground of our moral standing (that we grow and reproduce) is shared by all living things. Beyond that, nothing about equality even suggests itself. It is okay to admit (and morality does not require us to pretend not to notice) that there are grounds for moral standing that humans do not share with all living things.

IV. SPECIESISM AND SOCIAL POLICY

Peter Singer and others talk as if speciesism—the idea that some species are superior to others—is necessarily a kind of bias in favor of humans and against nonhuman animals. (Singer has no problem with being "biased" against plants.) Not so. If we have more respect for chimpanzees than for mice, then we are speciesists, no matter what status we accord to human beings. A speciesist is taking no stance with regard to humanity when she says to an egalitarian, we *should* respect chimpanzees more than we respect mice, shouldn't we? Or if not, shouldn't we at least respect chimpanzees more than carrots?

Suppose we take an interest in how the moral standing of chimpanzees compares to that of mice and wonder what we would do in an emergency where we could save a drowning chimpanzee or a drowning mouse but not both. More realistically, suppose we conclude that we must do experiments involving animals, because it's the only way to cure an otherwise catastrophic disease, and now we have to choose which animals. Whichever we use, the animals we use will die. We decide to use mice. Then a species egalitarian says, "Why not use chimpanzees? They're all the same anyway, morally speaking, and you'll get more reliable data." Would that sort of egalitarianism be monstrous? I think so. But if we believe all living things are equal, then *why not* use the chimpanzee instead of the mouse?

If chimpanzees are, morally speaking, the wrong *kind* of animal to experiment on when researchers could use mice, then speciesism is to that extent closer to the moral truth than is species egalitarianism. Although in philosophy we tend to use science fiction examples, the situation just described is an everyday problem in the scientific community. Suppose researchers had to choose between harvesting the organs of a chimpanzee or a severely brain-damaged human baby. Peter Singer says we cannot have it both ways. Singer argues that if the ability to think is what makes the difference, then the brain-damaged infant commands no more respect than a chimpanzee, and should indeed command less. Singer concludes that if we need to use one or the other in a painful or lethal medical experiment, and if it does not matter which one we use so far as the experiment is concerned, then we ought to use the infant, not the chimpanzee.[9]

I am not trying to have it both ways when I note that, if we claimed that the rightness of eating beef has to be settled individual cow by individual cow, because some cows are brain damaged, Singer would agree in principle, then go on to insist that cows are the wrong *kind* of thing for us to be eating. He would say that we need a policy governing our exploitation of cows as a species, and that it should not be up to individual consumers to decide case by case whether the cow they want to eat is sentient or brain-dead, or whether the benefits of eating this particular cow exceed the costs. Singer would allow that the benefits sometimes do exceed the costs, but would insist that we need laws—laws governing how we treat cows in general.

Again, Singer would insist that researchers cannot be trusted to decide on a case by case basis whether to use mice or chimpanzees or defective people in their experiments, when turnips would do just as well. Likewise, Singer wants to insist that individual consumers should not decide on a case by case basis whether to eat cows or turnips—rather, they ought to quit eating cows, period. In the medical research policy area, we rightly ignore Singer's point that some animals are smarter than some people. Singer would want us to ignore his point in that context (and in this sense he wants it both ways). We instead formulate policy on the basis of characteristic features of species. Brain-dead infants are not representative of humanity as a species, any more than brain-dead cows represent cows as a species. In either case, unrepresentative individuals are not relevant as a basis for policy decisions that will apply to humans or cows in general.

Think about it this way: suppose we say Canadians should have a right to free speech. Suppose Singer responds by calling us Canadianists, and says being a Canadianist is like being a racist. When we ask Singer where we went wrong, imagine Singer telling us some Canadians are brain-damaged ("Just look at their arguments," he says); therefore, he says, it is mere chauvinism to assert that Canadians as a general class should have so special a right.

In that case, we should reply to Singer that what matters is that it is compellingly good policy for every Canadian to have that kind of legal protection as a default presumption. Whether every Canadian has what it takes to exercise that right is not even relevant. Singer would, and does, endorse some applications of this form of argument. For example, he would insist that it is compellingly good policy for every cow to have certain kinds of legal protection, regardless of whether each and every cow has what it takes to benefit from it.

None of this is a criticism of Singer. I aim only to interpret his writings in a charitable way. Some of Singer's arguments seem to commit him to an extreme egalitarianism, but Singer does, when pressed, decline to bite that bullet. He says that many species are broadly equal to humans in terms of their characteristic capacities to feel pleasure and pain, but at the same time acknowledges that the characteristic cognitive capacities of normal humans are such that they tend to have more at stake than would other animals otherwise similarly situated. That's why he would feed starving humans before feeding starving animals.[10]

V. EQUALITY AND TRANSCENDENCE

Even if speciesists are right to see a nonarbitrary distinction between humans and cows as types, the fact remains that claims of superiority do not easily translate into justifications of domination.[11] We can have reasons to treat nonhuman species with respect, regardless of whether we consider them to be on a moral par with *Homo sapiens*.

Why respect members of other species? We might respect chimpanzees or mice on the grounds that they are sentient. Even mice have a rudimentary point of view and rudimentary hopes and dreams, and we might well respect them for that. But what about plants? Plants, unlike mice and chimpanzees, do not care what happens to them. They could not care less. So, why should we care? Is it even possible for us to have any good reason to care what happens to plants beyond caring instrumentally about how plants can benefit us?

I say yes. Here is why. When we are alone in a forest and wondering whether it would be fine to chop down a tree for fun, our perspective on what happens to the tree is, so far as we know, the only perspective there is. The tree does not have its own. Thus, explaining our reason to care about trees requires us to explain caring from our point of view, since that (we are supposing) is all there is. We do not have to satisfy *trees* that we are treating them properly; rather, we have to satisfy ourselves. Again, can we have reasons for caring about trees separate from their instrumental value as lumber and such?

One reason to care (not the only one) is that gratuitous destruction is a failure of self-respect. It is a repudiation of the kind of self-awareness and self-respect that we can achieve by repudiating wanton vandalism. So far as I know, no one finds anything puzzling in the idea that we have reason to treat our lawns or living rooms with respect. Lawns and living rooms have instrumental value, but there is more to it than that. Most of us have the sense that taking reasonable care of our lawns and living rooms is somehow a matter of self-respect, not merely a matter of preserving their instrumental value. Do we have similar reasons to treat forests with respect? I think we do. There is an aesthetic involved, the repudiation of which would be a failure of self-respect. Obviously, not everyone feels the same

way about forests. Not everyone feels the same way about lawns and living rooms, either. However, our objective here is to make sense of respect for nature, not to argue that respect for nature is in fact universal or that failing to respect nature is irrational. If and when we identify with a Redwood, in the sense of being inspired by it, having respect for its size and age and so on, then as a psychological fact, we face questions about how we ought to treat it. When we come to see a Redwood in that light, subsequently turning our backs on it becomes a kind of self-effacement, because the values we thereby fail to take seriously are *our* values, not the tree's.

So, the attitude we take toward gazelles, for example, raises issues of self-respect insofar as we see ourselves as relevantly like gazelles. Here is a different and complementary way of looking at the issue. Consider that lions owe nothing to gazelles. Therefore, if we owe it to gazelles not to hunt them, it must be because we are *unlike* lions, not—or not only—because we are *like* gazelles. Unlike lions, we have a choice about whether to hunt gazelles, and we are capable of deliberating about that choice in a reflective way. We are capable of caring about the gazelle's pain, the gazelle's beauty, the gazelle's hopes and dreams, such as they are. So, on the one hand, if we do care, then in a more or less literal way, something is wrong with us—we are less than fully, magnificently, human—if we cannot adjust our behavior in light of what we care about. On the other hand, if we do not care, then we are missing something. For a human being, to lack a broad respect for living things and beautiful things and well-functioning things is to be stunted in a way.

Taylor could agree with this argument. He says that all living things are equal because they all have lives of their own, but then concedes that we can systematically privilege animals over plants because animals are sentient, and sentience gives animals, in effect, a superior kind of life. Where does this leave us? What Taylor is rightly conceding here is that when it is time actually to live our lives, we give up on saying all living things are *equal*, and we acknowledge that the moral point is to treat all living things with *respect*. Taylor, moreover, sees a basic connection between self-respect and respect for the world in which one lives.[12]

Our coming to see members of other species as commanding respect is a way of transcending our animal natures. It is ennobling. It is part of our natures unthinkingly to see ourselves as superior and to try to dominate accordingly; as noted, our capacity to see ourselves as equal is part of what makes humans unique. It may be part of what makes us superior. Aldo Leopold expressed a related thought. When the Cincinnati Zoo erected a monument to the passenger pigeon, Leopold wrote, "We have erected a monument to commemorate the funeral of a species. . . . For one species to mourn the death of another is a new thing under the sun. . . . In this fact . . . lies objective evidence of our superiority over the beasts."[13] Trying to see all living things as equal may not be the best way of transcending our animal natures, but it is one way.

Another way of transcending our animal natures and expressing due respect for nature is simply to not bother with keeping score. This way is more respectful of our own reflective natures. It does not dwell on rankings. It does not insist on seeing equality where a more reflective being simply would see what is there to be seen and would not shy away from respecting what is unique as well as what is common. Someone might say we need to rank animals as our equals to be fair, but that appears to be false: I can be fair to my friends without ranking them. For most purposes, it is better to let them simply remain the unique and priceless friends that they are. Sometimes, respect is simply respect. It need not be based on a pecking order.

Children rank their friends. It is one of the things children do before they are old enough to understand friendship. Sometimes, the idea of ranking things, even as equals, is a child's game. It is beneath us.

VI. RESPECT FOR EVERYTHING

Therefore, a broad respect for living or beautiful or well-functioning things need not translate into *equal* respect. It need not translate into *universal* respect, either. Part of our responsibility as moral agents is to be somewhat choosy about what we respect and how we respect it. I can see why people shy away from openly accepting that responsibility, but they still have it. We might suppose speciesism is as arbitrary as racism unless we can show that the differences are morally relevant. This is a popular sentiment among animal liberationists such as Peter Singer and Tom Regan. However, are we really like racists when we think it is worse to kill a dolphin than to kill a tuna? The person who asserts that there is a relevant similarity between speciesism and racism has the burden of proof: identify the similarity.

Burden of proof, crucial to many philosophical arguments, is a slippery notion. Do we need good reason to exclude plants and animals from the realm of things we regard as commanding respect? Or do we need reason to *in*clude them? The latter seems more natural to me, so I am left supposing the burden of proof lies with those who claim we should have respect for all living things. I could be wrong.[14] But suppose Alf says oatmeal commands respect. Betty asks why. Alf responds by saying, "I don't need an argument. It's up to you to prove that oatmeal *doesn't* command respect." Something has gone wrong. Alf has mislocated the burden of proof. He fails to see that he implied that he has reason to believe that oatmeal commands respect. Taking the obvious implication of Alf's statement at face value, Betty asked Alf to state his reason, and Alf's response suggests that he does not have one. The way to rebut someone who says oatmeal doesn't command respect is to explain why it does. After the positive side of a debate says there is a reason for believing X and the negative side says, "I doubt it," it's always up to the positive side to go ahead and state the reason.

But I do not mean to suggest that the positive side's burden in the case at hand is unbearable. One reason to have regard for other living things has to do with self-respect. As I said earlier, when we mistreat a tree that we admire, the values we fail to respect are our values, not the tree's. A second reason has to do with self-realization. As I said, exercising our capacity for moral regard is a form of self-realization. Finally, some species share with human beings, to varying degrees, precisely those moral and intellectual characteristics that lead us to see human life as especially worthy of esteem. For example, Lawrence Johnson describes experiments in which rhesus monkeys show extreme reluctance to obtain food by means that would subject monkeys in neighboring cages to electric shock. He describes the case of Washoe, a chimpanzee who learned sign language.[15] Anyone who has tried to learn a foreign language ought to appreciate how astonishing an intellectual feat it is that an essentially nonlinguistic creature could learn a language—a language that is not merely foreign but the language of another species.[16]

Although he believes Washoe has moral standing, Johnson does not believe that the moral standing of chimpanzees, and indeed of all living creatures, implies that we must resolve never to kill. Johnson, an Australian, supports killing introduced animal species such as feral dogs, rabbits, and so forth to protect Australia's native species, including native plant species.[17] Is Johnson advocating a speciesist version of the Holocaust? Has he shown himself to be no better than a racist? I think not. Johnson is right to want to take drastic measures to protect Australia's natural flora, and the idea of respecting trees is intelligible. One thing I feel in the presence of California Redwoods or Australia's incredible eucalyptus forests is a feeling of respect. However, I doubt that what underlies Johnson's willingness to kill feral dogs is mere respect for Australia's native plants. I suspect that his approval of such killings turns to some extent on needs and aesthetic sensibilities of human beings, not just interests of plants. For example, if the endangered species were a malaria-carrying mosquito, and if we thought that introducing an exotic species of amphibian would finish the job of wiping them out, I would not blame Johnson for being wary of a plan to introduce yet another exotic species. Johnson has seen Australia go down that road before. But I doubt Johnson would advocate wiping out an exotic species of amphibian simply to protect native mosquitoes.

Aldo Leopold urged us to see ourselves as plain citizens of, rather than conquerors of, the biotic community,[18] but there are species with whom we can never be fellow citizens. Rabbits that once ate flowers in my back yard in Ohio and cardinals now eating my cherry tomatoes in Arizona are neighbors, and I cherish their company, minor frictions notwithstanding. However, I feel no sense of community with mosquitoes and not merely because they are not warm and fuzzy. Some mosquito species are so adapted to making human beings miserable that mortal combat is not accidental; rather, combat is a natural state. It is how such creatures live. It is fair to say that human beings are not equipped to respond to malaria-carrying mosquitoes in a caring manner. At the very least, most of us would think less of a person who did respond to them in a caring manner. We would regard the person's caring as a parody of respect for nature.

The conclusion that *all* living things have moral standing is unmotivated. There is no evidence for it, and believing it would serve no purpose. By contrast, for human beings, viewing apes as having moral standing is motivated, for the reasons just described. One further conjecture: Like redwoods and dolphins, apes capture our imagination. We identify with some animals, perhaps even some plants. We feel gripped by their stories. Now, this is a flimsy thing to say, in a way. If we were talking about reasons to see charismatic species as rights-bearers rather than talking about reasons simply to cherish them, it would be too flimsy. I offer this remark in a tentative way. It is not the kind of consideration that moral philosophers are taught to take seriously, yet it may be closer to our real reasons for valuing charismatic species than are abstract philosophical arguments. Our finding a species inspiring, or our identifying with beings of a given kind, implies that if we fail to care about how their stories turn out, the failure is a failure of self-respect, a failure to care about *our* values.

Viewing viruses as having moral standing is not the same thing. It is good to have a sense of how amazing living things are, but being able to marvel at living things is not the same as thinking that all living things have moral standing. Life as such commands respect only in the limited but important sense that for self-aware and reflective creatures who want to act in ways that make sense, deliberately killing something is an act that does not make sense unless we have good reason to do it. Destroying something for no good reason is, at best, the moral equivalent of vandalism.

VII. THE HISTORY OF THE DEBATE

There is an odd project in the history of philosophy that equates what seem to be three distinct projects:

1. determining the essence of human beings;
2. specifying how humans are different from all other species;
3. specifying what makes humans morally important.

Equating these three projects has important ramifications. Suppose for the sake of argument that what makes humans morally important is that we can suffer.

If what makes us morally important is necessarily the same property that constitutes our essence, then our essence is that we can suffer. And if our essence necessarily is what makes us different from all other species, then we can straightforwardly deduce that dogs cannot suffer. (I wish this were merely a tasteless joke.)

Likewise with rationality. If rationality is our essence, then it is what makes us morally important and also what makes us unique. Therefore, we can deduce that chimpanzees are not rational. Alternatively, if some other animal becomes rational, does that mean our essence will change? Perhaps this sort of reasoning accounts for why some people find Washoe, the talking chimpanzee, threatening.

The three projects should not be conflated in the way philosophy historically has conflated them, but we can reject species equality without conflation. As noted earlier, we can select a property with respect to which all living things are the same, such as being teleological centers of life, but we need not ignore the possibility that there are other morally important properties, such as sentience, with respect to which not all living things are equal.

There is room to wonder whether species egalitarianism is even compatible with respect for nature. Is the moral standing of dolphins truly no higher than that of tuna? Is the standing of chimpanzees truly no higher than that of mice? Undoubtedly some people embrace species egalitarianism on the assumption that endorsing species egalitarianism is a way of giving dolphins and chimpanzees the respect they deserve. It is not. Species egalitarianism not only takes humans down a notch. It takes down dolphins, chimpanzees, and redwoods, too. It takes down any species we regard as special. But we have reason to regard some species as special—especially intelligent, especially beautiful, especially long-lived, especially beneficial to humans, especially complex, or even especially fast on its feet. There is no denying that it demeans us to destroy living things we find beautiful or otherwise beneficial. What about living things in which we find neither beauty nor benefit? It is, upon reflection, obviously in our interest to enrich our lives by discovering in them something beautiful or beneficial, if we can. By and large, we must agree with Leopold that it is too late for conquering the biotic community. Our task now is to find ways of fitting in. Species egalitarianism is one way of trying to understand how we fit in, but all things considered it is not an acceptable way. Respecting nature and being a species egalitarian are different things.[19]

NOTES

1. Paul Taylor, "In Defense of Biocentrism," *Environmental Ethics* 5 (1983): 237–43, at 240.
2. Paul Taylor, *Respect for Nature* (Princeton: Princeton University Press, 1986): 99ff. See also Paul W. Taylor, "The Ethics of Respect for Nature," *Environmental Ethics* 5 (1981): 197–218, at 217.
3. Taylor, "The Ethics of Respect," 217.
4. William C. French, "Against Biospherical Egalitarianism," *Environmental Ethics* 17 (1995): 39–57, esp. 44ff. See also James C. Anderson, "Species Equality and the Foundations of Moral Theory," *Environmental Values* 2 (1993): 347–65, at 350.
5. Taylor, "The Ethics of Respect," 211.
6. In passing, let me be clear that Paul Taylor (1923–2015) did not miss much. The adult interpretation of my criticism here is that there was something missing in Taylor's argument as Taylor wrote it down at a particular time in his life. When I pointed out what his argument was missing, Taylor simply said, that's roughly what he had in mind and he wished he had said it my way. I told him Jim Anderson's article (cited above and below) had inspired my thinking on this topic. Taylor said, "me too." He was too generous, too grown-up, and had seen too much in his life to ever feel threatened by a philosophical argument.
7. For a similar critique of Taylor from an Aristotelian perspective, see Anderson, "Species Equality," 348. See also Louis G. Lombardi, "Inherent Worth, Respect, and Rights," *Environmental Ethics* 5 (1993): 257–70.
8. Peter Singer, *Animal Liberation*, 2nd ed. (New York: Random House, 1990): 1–23. See also Lawrence Johnson, *A Morally Deep World* (New York: Cambridge Press, 1991), 52.
9. See Peter Singer, "Reply to Schmidtz," *Singer under Fire*, ed. Schaler (NY: Open Court, 2009), 455–62, at 461.
10. This is effectively argued by Anderson, "Species Equality," 362.

11. Taylor, *Respect*, 42–43. Note: I have not discussed rights in this essay, but on Taylor's theory it is impossible for nonhumans to have rights. To have rights, on Taylor's view, a being has to be capable of self-conscious self-respect. Interestingly, although Taylor denies that nonhumans can have moral rights, he grants that there can be reason to treat trees and animals as having legal rights (Taylor, *Respect*, 246). It is not exactly called for on metaphysical grounds, but it would be a way of treating them with respect. I thank Dan Shahar for educating me on this point.

12. Aldo Leopold, *A Sand County Almanac* (New York: Oxford University Press, 1966; 1st published in 1949), 116–17.

13. For a discussion of what it takes to deserve respect, see Part II of David Schmidtz, *Elements of Justice* (New York: Cambridge University Press, 2006).

14. Johnson, *Morally Deep World*, 64n.

15. This is what I wrote in the original version of this article. I since have heard that in the wild, families of lowland gorillas have their own fairly complicated language of hand signals, so I would no longer describe chimpanzees as *essentially* nonlinguistic, except insofar as they lack the vocal cords and the descended larynx that enabled homo sapiens to articulate the elements of spoken language.

16. Johnson (1991), 174.

17. Leopold (1966), 240.

18. For further reading, see Jason Brennan, "Dominating Nature," *Environmental Values* 16 (2007): 513–28; Christopher Brown, "Kantianism and Mere Means," *Environmental Ethics* 32 (2010): 265–83; Christopher Freiman, "Goodwill Toward Nature," *Environmental Values* 18 (2009): 343–59.

6

WILDERNESS

HOLMES ROLSTON III

VALUE IN NATURE AND THE NATURE OF VALUE

VALUABLE SPECIES

On our travels we may see endangered species. If so, we will value them. But are we seeing, and valuing, species? Or just that trumpeter swan, this grizzly bear, that we are lucky enough to see? That is partly a scientific and partly a philosophical problem. I have seen, and valued, swans and bears in Yellowstone over four decades. But not the same individuals, rather bear replaced by bear replaced by bear, swan-swan-swan. . . .

We must ask whether singular somatic identity conserved is the only process that is valuable. A species is another level of biological identity reasserted genetically over time. Identity need not attach solely to the centred or modular organism; it can persist as a discrete pattern over time.

The life that the organismic individual has is something passing through the individual as much as something it intrinsically possesses. The genetic set, in which is coded the *telos*, is as evidently the property of the species as of the individual through which it passes. Value is something dynamic to the specific form of life. The species *is* a bigger event than the individual with its interests or sentience. Events can be good for the well-being of the species, considered collectively, although they are harmful if considered as distributed to individuals. When a wolf is tearing up an elk, the individual elk is in distress, but *Cervus Canadensis* is in no distress. The species is being improved, shown by the fact that wolves will subsequently find elk harder to catch. If the predators are removed, and the carrying capacity is exceeded, wildlife managers may have to benefit a species by culling its member individuals.

Even the individuals that escape external demise die of old age; and their deaths, always to the disadvantage of individuals, are a necessity for the species. A finite life span makes room for those replacements

This reading is adapted from Holmes Rolston III, "Value in Nature and the Nature of Value," Royal Institute of Philosophy Supplement 36 (1994): 13–30, pp. 19–30.

that enable development, allowing the population to improve in fitness or to adapt to a shifting environment. The surplus of young, with most born to perish prematurely, is disadvantageous to such individuals, but advantageous to the species. Without the "flawed" reproduction that incorporates mutation and permits variation, without selection of the more fit few, and death of the less fit, which harms most individuals, the species would soon be extinct in a changing environment. The individual is a receptacle of the form, and the receptacles are broken while the form survives, but the form cannot otherwise survive.

Reproduction is typically assumed to be a need of individuals, but since any particular individual may flourish somatically without reproducing at all, indeed may be put through duress and risk or spend much energy reproducing, by another logic we can interpret reproduction as the species staying in place by its replacement. In this sense a female grizzly does not bear cubs to be healthy herself. Rather, her cubs are *Ursus arctos*, threatened by nonbeing, recreating itself by continuous performance. A female animal does not have mammary glands nor a male testicles because the function of these is to preserve its own life; these organs are defending the line of life bigger than the somatic individual. The locus of the value that is defended over generations is as much in the form of life, since the individuals are genetically impelled to sacrifice themselves in the interests of reproducing their kind.

An insistent individualist can claim that species-level phenomena (vitality in a population, danger to a species, reproduction of a life form, tracking a changing environment) are only epiphenomena, byproducts of aggregated individuals in their interrelationships. But our more comprehensive account, interpreting the species itself as a kind of individual, historical lineage over time, is just as plausible. Biologists have often and understandably focused on individual organism, and some recent trends interpret biological processes from the perspective of genes. But a consideration of species reminds us that many events can be interpreted at this level too. Properly understood, the story at the microscopic genetic level reflects the story at the ecosystemic specific level, with the individual

a macroscopic mid-level between. The genome is a kind of map coding the species; the individual is an instance incarnating it.

. . . The single, organismic-directed course is part of a bigger picture in which a species . . . runs a telic course through the environment, using individuals resourcefully to maintain its course over much longer periods of time. The species line is the *vital* living system, the whole, of which individual organisms are the essential parts. The species defends a particular form of life, pursuing a pathway through the world, resisting death (extinction), by regeneration maintaining a normative identity over time. It is as logical to say that the individual is the species' way of propagating itself as to say that the embryo or egg is the individual's way of propagating itself. The value resides in the dynamic form; the individual inherits this, exemplifies it, and passes it on. If so, what prevents value existing at that level? The appropriate survival unit is the appropriate location of valuing.

Even a species is a kind of valuer. Species as historical lines have a defended biological identity, though they do not have any subjective experience. Species are quite real; that there really is a bear-bear-bear sequence is about as certain as anything we believe about the empirical world. Species are lively and full of life, they are processes, they are wholes, they have a kind of unity and integrity. The species line too is value-able, able to conserve a biological identity. Indeed it is more real, more value-able than the individual, necessary though individuals are for the continuance of this lineage.

We said earlier that natural selection picks out whatever traits an organism has that are valuable to it, relative to its survival. But if we ask what is the essence of this value, it is not the somatic survival of the organismic individual; this value ability is the ability to reproduce. That locates value-ability innate or intrinsic within the organism, but it just as much locates the value-ability as the capacity to re-produce a next generation, and a next generation positioned to produce a next generation after that. Any biocentrism that focuses on individuals has got to argue away the fact that natural selection is rather careless with individuals; the test to which it puts them is whether they can pass on the historical lineage.

VALUABLE ECOSYSTEMS

Exploring, we will see different ecosystems: an oak-hickory forest, a tall grass prairie. At least we see trees and grasses. But do we see ecosystems? Maybe we immerse ourselves in them, for an ecosystem is not so much an object in the focus of vision as an enveloping community, a place in space, a process in time, a set of vital relationships. This can mean that philosophers have difficulty seeing, and valuing, ecosystems. Yet, really, the ecosystem is the fundamental unit of development and survival.

Humans can value whatever they wish in nature. This can include ecosystems. "A thing is right," concluded Aldo Leopold, "when it tends to preserve the integrity, stability, and beauty of the biotic community. It is wrong when it tends otherwise."[1] Leopold wanted a "land ethic." So humans can value ecosystem communities intrinsically—for what they are in themselves—as well as instrumentally. But can ecosystems be valuable all by themselves?

Actually, there is a deeper worry again, partly scientific and partly philosophical. Perhaps ecosystems do not exist—or exist in too loose a way to be valuers. They are nothing but aggregations of their more real members, like a forest is (some say) nothing more than a collection of trees. Even a human will have trouble valuing what does not really exist. We can value collections, as of stamps, but this is just the aggregated value of individual stamps. Still, an ecosystem, if it exists, is rather different. Nothing in the stamp collection is alive; the collection is neither self-generating nor self-maintaining. Neither stamp nor collection is valuable on its own. But perhaps ecosystems are both valuable to humans and, if they exist, value-able as systems in themselves.

We need ecology to discover what biotic community means as an organizational mode. Then we can reflect philosophically to discover the values there. Ecosystems can seem little more than stochastic processes. A sea-shore, a tundra, is a loose collection of externally related parts. Much of the environment is not organic at all (rain, groundwater, rocks, nonbiotic soil particles, air). Some is dead and decaying debris (fallen trees, scat, humus). These things have no organized needs; the collection of them is a jumble. The fortuitous interplay between organisms is simply a matter of distribution and abundance of organisms, how they get dispersed, birth rates and death rates, population densities, moisture regimes, parasitism and predation, checks and balances. There is really not enough centred process to call community.

An ecosystem has no brain, no genome, no skin, no self-identification, no *telos*, no unified program. It does not defend itself against injury or death. It is not irritable. The parts (foxes, sedges) are more complex than the wholes (forests, grasslands). So it can begin to seem as if an ecosystem is too low a level of organization to be the direct focus of concern. Ecosystems do not and cannot care; they have no interests about which they or we can care.

But this is to misunderstand ecosystems, to make a category mistake. To fault *communities* as though they ought to be organismic *individuals* is to look at one level for what is appropriate at another. One should look for a matrix of interconnections between centres, for creative stimulus and open-ended potential. Everything will be connected to many other things, sometimes by obligative associations, more often by partial and pliable dependencies; and, among other components, there will be no significant interactions. There will be shunts and criss-crossing pathways, cybernetic subsystems and feedback loops. One looks for selection pressures and adaptive fit, not for irritability or repair of injury, for speciation and life support, not for resisting death. We must think more systemically, and less organismically.

An ecosystem generates a spontaneous order that envelops and produces the richness, beauty, integrity, and dynamic stability of the component parts. Though these organized interdependencies are loose in comparison with the tight connections within an organism, all these metabolisms are as vitally linked as are liver and heart. The equilibrating ecosystem is not merely push–pull forces. It is an equilibrating of values.

We do not want in an undiscriminating way to extrapolate criteria of value from organism to biotic community, any more than from person to animal or from animal to plant. Rather, we want to discriminate the criteria appropriate to this level. The selective forces in ecosystems at once transcend and produce the lives of individual plants and animals. Evolutionary ecosystems over ecological time have increased the numbers of species on Earth from zero to five million or more. R.H. Whittaker found that on continental scales and for most groups "increase of species diversity . . . is a self-augmenting evolutionary process without any evident limit." There is a tendency toward what he called "species packing."[2]

Superimposed on this, the quality of individual lives in the upper trophic rungs of ecological pyramids has risen. One-celled organisms evolved into many-celled, highly integrated organisms. Photosynthesis evolved and came to support locomotion—swimming, walking, running, flight. Stimulus–response mechanisms became complex instructive acts. Warm-blooded animals followed cold-blooded ones. Neural complexity, conditioned behaviour, and learning emerged. Sentience appeared—sight, smell, hearing, taste, pleasure, pain. Brains evolved, coupled with hands. Consciousness and self-consciousness arose. Persons appeared with intense concentrated unity. The products are valuable, able to be valued by these humans; but why not say that the process is really what is value-able, able to produce these values?

Ecosystems are selective systems, as surely as organisms are selective systems. The system selects over the long ranges for individuality, for diversity, for adapted fitness, for quantity and quality of life. Organisms defend only their own selves or kinds, but the system spins a bigger story. Organisms defend their continuing survival; ecosystems promote new arrivals. Species increase their kinds, but ecosystems increase kinds, and increase the integration of kinds. The system is a kind of field with characteristics as vital for life as any property contained within particular organisms. The ecosystem is the depth source of individual and species alike.

In the current debate among biologists about the levels at which selection takes place—individual organisms, populations, species, genes—the recent tendency to move selective pressures down to the genetic level forgets that a gene is always emplaced in an organism that is emplaced in an ecosystem. The molecular configurations of DNA are what they are because they record the story of a particular form of life in the macroscopic, historical ecosystem. What is generated arises from molecular mutations, but what

survives is selected for adaptive fit in an ecosystem. We cannot make sense of biomolecular life without understanding ecosystemic life, the one level as vital as the other.

Philosophers, sometimes encouraged by biologists, may think ecosystems are just epiphenomenal aggregations. This is a confusion. Any level is real if there is significant downward causation. Thus the atom is real because the pattern shapes the behaviour of electrons; the cell because that pattern shapes the behaviour of amino acids; the organism because that pattern co-ordinates the behaviour of hearts and lungs; the community because the niche reshapes the morphology and behaviour of the foxes within it. Being real requires an organisation that shapes the existence and the behaviour of members or parts.

. . .

VALUABLE EARTH

Viewing Earthrise, Edgar Mitchell, was entranced: "Suddenly from behind the rim of the moon, in long–slow motion moments of immense majesty, there emerges a sparkling blue and white jewel, a light, delicate sky-blue sphere laced with slowly swirling veils of white, rising gradually like a small pearl in a thick sea of black mystery. It takes more than a moment to fully realize this is earth . . . home."[3] Michael Collins was Earthstruck: "When I travelled to the moon, it wasn't my proximity to that battered rockpile I remember so vividly, but rather what I saw when I looked back at my fragile home—a glistening, inviting beacon, delicate blue and white, a tiny outpost suspended in the black infinity. Earth is to be treasured and nurtured, something precious that *must* endure."[4]

Pearls are, a philosopher might object, valuable only when humans come around. But this mysterious Earth-pearl, a biologist will reply, is a home long before we humans come. This is the only biosphere, the only planet with an ecology. Earth may not be the only planet where anything is valuable—able to be valued by humans intrinsically or instrumentally—but it is the only place able to produce vitality before humans come. The view from space symbolizes all this.

. . .

Environmental valuing is not over until we have risen to the planetary level. Earth is really the relevant survival unit. But valuing the whole Earth is unfamiliar and needs philosophical analysis. We may seem to be going to extremes. Earth is, after all, just earth. The belief that dirt could have intrinsic value is sometimes taken as a *reductio ad absurdum* in environmental philosophy. Dirt is not the sort of thing that has value by itself. Put like that, we agree. An isolated clod defends no intrinsic value and it is difficult to say that it has much value in itself. But that is not the end of the matter, because a clod of dirt is integrated into an ecosystem; earth is a part, Earth the whole. Dirt is product and process in a systemic nature. We should try to get the global picture, and switch from a lump of dirt to the Earth system in which it has been created.

Earth is, some will insist, a big rockpile like the moon, only one on which rocks are watered and illuminated in such way that they support life. So maybe it is really the life we value and not the Earth, except as instrumental to life. We do not have duties to rocks, air, ocean, dirt, or Earth; we have duties to people, or living things. We must not confuse duties to the home with duties to the inhabitants. We do not praise so much the dirt as what is in the dirt, not earth so much as what is on Earth. But this is not a systemic view of what is going on. We need some systematic account of the valuable Earth we now behold, before we beheld it, not just some value that is generated in the eye of the beholder. Finding that value will generate a global sense of obligation.

The evolution of rocks into dirt into fauna and flora is one of the great surprises of natural history, one of the rarest events in the astronomical universe. Earth is all dirt, we humans too arise up from the humus, and we find revealed what dirt can do when it is self-organizing under suitable conditions. This is pretty spectacular dirt. Really, the story is little short of a series of "miracles," wondrous, fortuitous events, unfolding of potential; and when Earth's most complex product, *Homo sapiens*, becomes intelligent enough to reflect over this cosmic wonderland, everyone is left stuttering about the mixtures of accident and necessity out of which we have evolved. For some the black mystery will be numinous and signal transcendence; for some the mystery may be impenetrable. Perhaps we do not have to have all the cosmological answers. Nobody has much doubt that this is a precious place, a pearl in a sea of black mystery.

The elemental chemicals of life—carbon, oxygen, hydrogen, nitrogen—are common enough throughout the universe. They are made in the stars. But life, rare elsewhere, is common on Earth, and the explanation lies in the ordinary elements in an extraordinary setting, the super-special circumstances in which these common chemicals find themselves arranged on Earth, that is, in the self-organizing system. On an everyday scale, earth, dirt, seems to be passive, inert, an unsuitable object of moral concern. But on a global scale?

The scale changes nothing, a critic may protest, the changes are only quantitative. Earth is no doubt precious as life support, but it is not precious in itself. There is nobody there in a planet. There is not even the vitality of an organism, or the genetic transmission of a species line. Earth is not even an ecosystem, strictly speaking; it is a loose collection of myriads of ecosystems. So we must be talking loosely, perhaps poetically or romantically, of valuing Earth. Earth is a mere thing, a big thing, a special thing for those who happen to live on it, but still a thing, and not appropriate as an object of intrinsic or systemic valuation. We can, if we insist on being anthropocentrists, say that it is all valueless except as our human resource.

But we will not be valuing Earth objectively until we appreciate this marvelous natural history. This really is a superb planet, the most valuable entity of all, because it is the entity able to produce all the Earthbound values. At this scale of vision, if we ask what is principally to be valued, the value of life arising as a creative process on Earth seems a better description and a more comprehensive category.

Perhaps you think that species are unreal. Perhaps you still insist that ecosystems are unreal, only aggregations, but how about Earth? Will you say that Earth too, being a higher level entity, is unreal? Only an aggregation, and not a systemic whole? There is no such thing as a biosphere? Surely, Earth has some rather clear boundaries, does it not? Will you say that this is a planet where nothing matters? Nothing matters to Earth, perhaps, but everything matters on Earth, for Earth.

Do humans sometimes value Earth's life-supporting systems because they are valuable, and not always the other way round? Is this value just a matter of late-coming human interests? Or is Earth not historically a remarkable, valuable place, a place able to produce value prior to the human arrival, and even now valuable antecedently to the human uses of it? It seems parochial to say that our part alone in the drama establishes all its worth. The production of value over the millenia [sic] of natural history is not something subjective that goes on in the human mind. In that sense, a valuable Earth is not the *reductio ad absurdum* of valuing dirt. It is not even locating the most valuable thing in the world; it is locating the ultimate value of the world itself. The creativity within the natural system we inherit, and the values this generates, are the ground of our being, not just the ground under our feet. Earth could be the ultimate object of duty, short of God, if God exists.

VALUABLE NATURE

William James, toward the beginning of our century, starkly portrayed the utterly valueless world, transfigured as a gift of the human coming:

> Conceive yourself, if possible, suddenly stripped of all the emotion with which your world now inspires you, and try to imagine it *as it exists*, purely by itself, without your favorable or unfavorable, hopeful or apprehensive comment. It will be almost impossible for you to realize such a condition of negativity and deadness. No one portion of the universe would then have importance beyond another; and the whole collection of its things and series of its events would be without significance, character, expression, or perspective. Whatever of value, interests, or meaning our respective worlds may appear endued with are thus pure gifts of the spectator's mind.[5]

At the end of this century, this is not what the astronauts think at all. They do not see Earth as negativity and deadness, nor do they think that this portion of the universe has no significance beyond any other part, except by gift of our spectating minds. They did not say that the world was valuable only because they took along an indubitable self into space and projected value onto Earth. They rather see that human life arises in a spectacular place, in a nature of whose creative patterns they are part.

. . .

It is true that humans are the only evaluators who can reflect about what is going on at this global scale, who can deliberate about what they ought to do conserving it. When humans do this, they must set up the scales; and humans are the measurers of things. Animals, organisms, species, ecosystems, Earth, cannot teach us how to do this evaluating. But they can display what it is that is to be valued. The axiological scales we construct do not constitute the value, any more than the scientific scales we erect create what we thereby measure.

Humans are not so much lighting up value in a merely potentially valuable world, as they are psychologically joining ongoing natural history in which there is value wherever there is positive creativity. While such creativity can be present in subjects with their interests and preferences, it can also be present objectively in living organisms with their lives defended, and in species that defend an identity over time, and in systems that are self-organizing and the project storied achievements. The valuing subject in an otherwise valueless world is an insufficient premise for the experienced conclusions of those who value natural history.

NOTES

1. Aldo, Leopold, *A Sand County Almanac: and Sketches Here and There* (New York: Oxford University Press, 1966): 240

2. R. H. Whittaker, "Evolution and Measurement of Species Diversity," *Taxon* 21 (1972): 213–5, at 214.

3. Kevin W. Kelley, *The Home Planet* (Boston: Da Capo Press, 1988) at photographs 42–45.

4. Roy A. Gallant, *Our Universe* (Colchester: The Book Service, 1980), at p. 6.

5. William James, *Pragmatism* (New York; Longman's, 1925) at p. 150.

J. BAIRD CALLICOTT

HOLISTIC ENVIRONMENTAL ETHICS AND THE PROBLEM OF ECOFASCISM

THE HOLISM OF THE LAND ETHIC

According to Leopold, "a land ethic implies respect for . . . fellow-members *and also for the community as such*" (emphasis added).[1] The land ethic, in other words, has a holistic dimension to it that is completely foreign to the mainstream Modern moral theories.

. . .

In the Leopold land ethic, . . . the holistic aspect eventually eclipses the individualistic aspect. Toward the beginning of "The Land Ethic," Leopold, as noted, declares that a land ethic "implies respect for fellow-members" of the biotic community, as well as "for the community as such." Toward the middle of "The Land Ethic," Leopold speaks of a "biotic right" to "continue" but such a right accrues, as the context indicates, to species, not to specimens.[2] Toward the end of the essay, Leopold writes a summary moral maxim, a golden rule, for the land ethic: "A thing is right when it tends to preserve the integrity, stability, and beauty of the biotic community. It is wrong when it tends otherwise."[3] In it there is no reference at all to "fellow members." They have gradually dropped out of account as "The Land Ethic" proceeds to its climax.

Why? One reason . . . is that conservationists, among whom Leopold counted himself, are professionally concerned about biological and ecological wholes—populations, species, communities, ecosystems—not their individual constituents. And the land ethic is tailored to suit conservation concerns, which are often confounded by concerns for individual specimens. For example, the conservation of endangered plant species is often most directly and efficiently effected by the deliberate eradication of the feral animals that threaten them. Preserving the integrity of a biotic community often requires reducing the populations of some component species, be they native or non-native, wild or feral. Certainly animal liberation and animal rights—advocated by Peter Singer and Tom Regan, respectively—would prohibit such convenient but draconian solutions to conservation problems. So would a more inclusive individualistic environmental ethic, such as that proffered by Paul Taylor.[4] Another reason is that ecology is about metaorganismic entities—biotic communities and ecosystems—not individuals, and the land ethic is expressly informed by ecology and reflects an ecological worldview. Its holism is precisely what makes the land ethic the environmental ethic of choice among conservationists and ecologists. In short, its holism is the land ethic's principal asset.

Whether by the end of the essay he forgets it or not, Leopold does say in "The Land Ethic" that fellow-members" of the "land community" deserve "respect." How can we pretend to respect them if, in the interest of integrity, stability, and beauty, we chop some down, gun others down, set fire to still others, and so on? Such brutalities are often involved in what conservationists call "wildlife" management. . . . [T]o resolve this conundrum, we may consult Darwin, who indicates that ethics originate among Homo sapiens in the first place to serve the welfare of the community. Certainly, among the things that threaten to dissolve a human community are "murder, robbery, treachery, &c.[5]" However, as ethics evolve correlatively to social evolution, not only do they widen their scope, they change in content, such that what is wrong correlative to one stage of social development, may not be wrong correlative to the next. In a tribal society, as Darwin observes, exogamy is a cardinal precept. It is not in a republic. Nevertheless, in all human communities—from the savage clan to the family of man—the "infamy" of murder, robbery, treachery, etc. remains "everlasting." But the multi-species *biotic* community is so different from all our human communities that we cannot assume that what is wrong for one human being to do to another, even at every level of *social* organization, is wrong for one fellow member of the *biotic* community to do to another.

The currency of the economy of nature, we must remember, is energy. And it passes from one member to another, not from hand to hand like money in the human economy, but from stomach to stomach. As Leopold observes of the biotic community, "The only truth is that its members must suck hard, live fast, and die often."[6] In the biotic community there are producers and consumers; predators and prey. One might say that the integrity and stability of the biotic community depends upon death as well as life; indeed, one might say further, that the life of one member is premised squarely on the death of another. So one could hardly argue that our killing of fellow members of the biotic community is, prima facie, land ethically wrong. It depends on who is killed, for what reasons, under what circumstances, and how. The filling of these blanks would provide, in each case, an answer to the question about respect. Models of respectful, but often violent and lethal, use of fellow members of the biotic community are provided by traditional American Indian peoples.[7]

THE PROBLEM OF ECOFASCISM

Its holism is the land ethic's principle strength, but also its principal liability. Remember that according to Leopold, evolutionary and ecological biology reveal that "land [is] a community to which we belong" not "a commodity belonging to us" and that from the point of view of the land ethic, we are but "plain members and citizens of the biotic community." Then it would seem that the summary moral maxim of the land ethic applies to Homo sapiens no

less than to other members and citizens of the biotic community, plain or otherwise. A human population of more than six billion individuals is a dire threat to the integrity, stability, and beauty of the biotic community. Thus the existence of such a large human population is land ethically wrong. To right that wrong should we not do what we do when a population of white-tailed deer or some other species irrupts and threatens the integrity, stability, and beauty of the biotic community? We immediately and summarily reduce it, by whatever means necessary, usually by randomly and indiscriminately shooting the members of such a population to death—respectfully, of course—until its numbers are optimized. It did not take the land ethic's critics long to draw out the vitiating—but, as I shall go on to argue directly, only apparent—implication of the land ethic. According to William Aiken, from the point of view of the land ethic, "massive human diebacks would be good. It is our duty to cause them. It is our species' duty, relative to the whole, to eliminate 90 percent of our numbers."[8] Its requirement that individual organisms, apparently also including *human* organisms, be sacrificed for the good of the whole, makes the land ethic, according to Tom Regan, a kind of "environmental fascism."[9] Frederick Ferré echoes and amplifies Aiken's and Regan's indictment of the land ethic: 'Anything we could do to exterminate excess people . . . would be morally 'right'! To refrain from such extermination would be 'wrong'! . . . Taken as a guide for human culture, the land ethic—despite the best intentions of its supporters—would lead toward classical fascism, the submergence of the individual person in the glorification of the collectivity, race, tribe, or nation."[10] Finally, Kristin Shrader-Frechette adds her voice to those expressing moral outrage at the land "ethic": "In subordinating the welfare of all creatures to the integrity, stability, and beauty of the biotic community, then one subordinates individual human welfare, in all cases, to the welfare of the biotic community."[11]

Michael Zimmerman had defended the land ethic against the charge of ecofascism, pointing out that in addition to subordinating the welfare of the individual to that of the community, fascism involves other characterizing features, salient among them nationalism and militarism. And there is no hint of nationalism and militarism in the land ethic.[12] But however one labels it, if the land ethic implies what Aiken, Regan, Ferré, and Shrader-Frechette allege that it does, it must be rejected as monstrous. Happily, it does not. To think that it does, one must assume that Leopold proffered the land ethic as a substitute for, not an addition to, our venerable and familiar human ethics. But he did not. Leopold refers to the various stages of ethical development—from tribal mores to universal human rights and, finally, to the land ethic—as "accretions." Accretion means an "increase by external addition or accumulation." The land ethic is an accretion—that is, an addition—to our several accumulated social ethics, not something that is supposed to replace them. . . . [W]ith the advent of each new stage in the accreting development of ethics, the old stages are not erased or replaced, but added to. I, for example, am a citizen of a republic, but I also remain a member of an extended family, and a resident of a municipality. And it is quite evident to us all, from our own moral experience, that the duties attendant on citizenship in a republic (to pay taxes, to serve in the armed forces or in the Peace Corps, for example) do not cancel or replace the duties attendant on membership in a family (to honor parents, to love and educate children, for example) or residence in a municipality (to support public schools, to attend town meetings). Similarly, it is equally evident— at least to Leopold and his exponents, if not to his critics—that the duties attendant upon citizenship in the biotic community (to preserve its integrity, stability, and beauty) do not cancel or replace the duties attendant on membership in the human global village (to respect human rights).

individual is sacrificed for the good of the whole.

PRIORITIZING THE DUTIES GENERATED BY MEMBERSHIP IN MULTIPLE COMMUNITIES

This consideration has led Varner to argue that any proponent of the land ethic, Leopold presumably included, must be a moral pluralist.[13] True enough, if by moral pluralist one means only that one tries simultaneously to adhere to multiple moral maxims (Honor thy Father and thy Mother; Love thy Country; Respect the Rights of All Human Beings Irrespective of Race

Creed, Color, or National Origin; Preserve the Integrity, Stability, and Beauty of the Biotic Community, for example). But if being a moral pluralist means espousing multiple moral philosophies and associated ethical theories, as it does in Christopher Stone's celebrated and influential *The Case for Moral Pluralism*,[14] then proponents of the land ethic are not necessarily committed to pluralism. On the contrary, the univocal theoretical foundations of the land ethic naturally generate multiple sets of moral duties—and correlative maxims, principles, and precepts—each related to a particular social scale (family, republic, global village, biotic community, for parallel example) all within a single moral philosophy.

. . .

The land ethic involves a limited pluralism (multiple moral maxims, multiple sets of duties, or multiple principles and precepts) not a thoroughgoing pluralism of moral philosophies *sensu* Stone[15]—Aristotelian ethics for this quandary, Kantian ethics for that, utilitarianism here, social-contract theory there. . . Thus, as Shrader-Frechette points out, the land ethic must provide "second-order ethical principles and a priority ranking system that specifies the respective conditions under which [first-order] holistic and individualistic ethical principles ought to be recognized."[16] Leopold provides no such second-order principles for prioritizing among first-order principles, but they can easily be derived from the communitarian foundations of the land ethic. By combining two second-order principles we can achieve a priority ranking among first-order principles, when, in a given quandary, they conflict. The first second-order principle (SOP-1) is that obligations generated by membership in more venerable and intimate communities take precedence over those generated in more recently-emerged and impersonal communities. I think that most of us, for example, feel that our family duties (to care for aged parents, say, to educate minor children) take precedence over our civic duties (to contribute to United Way charities, say, to vote for higher municipal taxes to better support more indigent persons on the dole), when, because of limited means, we are unable to perform both family and civic duties. The second second-order principle (SOP-2) is that stronger interests (for lack of a better word) generate duties that take precedence over duties generated by weaker interests. For example, while duties to one's own children, all things being equal, properly take precedence over duties toward unrelated children in one's municipality, one would be ethically remiss to shower one's own children with luxuries while unrelated children in one's municipality lacked the basic necessities (food, shelter, clothing, education) for a decent life. Having the bare necessities for a decent life is a stronger interest than is the enjoyment of luxuries, and our duties to help supply proximate unrelated children with the former take precedence over our duties to supply our own children with the latter.

. . .

THE PRIORITY PRINCIPLES APPLIED TO THE OLD-GROWTH FOREST QUANDARY

Let me consider now those kinds of quandaries in which our duties to human beings conflict with our duties to *biotic* communities as such. Varner supplies a case in point:

> Suppose that an environmentalist enamored with the Leopoldian land ethic is considering how to vote on a national referendum to preserve the spotted owl by restricting logging in Northwest forests. . . . He or she would be required to vote, not according to the land ethic, but according to whatever ethic governs closer ties to a human family and/or larger human community. Therefore, if a relative is one of 10,000 loggers who will lose jobs if the referendum passes, the environmentalist is obligated to vote against it. Even if none of the loggers is a family member, the voter is still obligated to vote against the referendum.[17]

The flaw in Varner's reasoning is that he applies only SOP-1—that obligations generated by membership in more venerable and intimate communities take precedence over those generated in more recently emerged and impersonal communities. If that were the only second-order communitarian principle then he would be right. But SOP-2—that stronger interests generate duties that take precedence over duties generated by weaker interests—reverses the priority determined by applying SOP-1 in this case. The spotted owl is threatened with preventable anthropogenic

extinction—threatened with biocide, in a word—and the old-growth forest biotic communities of the Pacific North-west are threatened with destruction. These threats are the environmental–ethical equivalent of genocide and holocaust. The loggers, on the other hand, are threatened with economic losses, for which they can be compensated dollar for dollar. More important to the loggers, I am told, their lifestyle is threatened. But livelihood and lifestyle, for both of which adequate substitutes can be found, is a lesser interest than life itself. If we faced the choice of cutting down millions of four-hundred-year-old trees or cutting down thousands of forty-year-old loggers, our duties to the loggers would take precedence by SOP-1, nor would SOP-1 be countermanded by SOP-2. But that is not the choice we face. The choice is between cutting down four-hundred-year-old trees, rendering the spotted [owl] extinct, and destroying the old growth forest biotic community, on the one hand, and displacing forest workers in an economy that is already displacing them through automation and raw-log exports to Japan and other foreign markets. And the old-growth logging lifestyle is doomed, in any case, for it will come to an end with the "final solution" to the old-growth forest question, if the jack-booted timber barons (who disingenuously blame the spotted owl for the economic insecurity of loggers and other workers in the timber industry) continue to have their way. With SOP-2 supplementing SOP-1, the indication of the land ethic is crystal clear in the exemplary quandary posed by Varner, and is opposite to the one Varner, applying only SOP-1, claims it indicates.

CONCLUSION

The holistic Leopoldian land ethic is not a case of ecofascism. The land ethic is intended to supplement, not replace, the more venerable community-based social ethics, in relation to which it is an accretion or addition. Neither is the land ethic a "paper tiger," an environmental ethic with no teeth. Choice among which community-related principle should govern a moral agent's conduct in a given moral quandary may be determined by the application of two second-order principles. The first, SOP-1, requires an agent to give priority to the first-order principles generated by the more venerable and more intimate community memberships. Thus, when holistic environment-oriented duties are in direct conflict with individualistic human-oriented duties, the human-oriented duties take priority. The land ethic is, therefore, not a case of ecofascism. However, the second second-order principle, SOP-2, requires an agent to give priority to the stronger interests at issue. When the indication determined by the application of SOP-1 is reinforced by the application of SOP-2, an agent's choice is clear. When the indication determined by the application of SOP-1 is contradicted by the application of SOP-2, an agent's choice is equally clear: SOP-2 countermands SOP-1. Thus, when holistic environment-oriented duties are in direct conflict with individualistic human-oriented duties, and the holistic environmental interests at stake are significantly stronger than the individualistic human interests at issue, the former take priority.

BIBLIOGRAPHY

Aiken, W. 1984. "Ethical Issues in Agriculture." In *Earthbound: New Introductory Essays in Environmental Ethics*, edited by T. Regan, 247–288. New York: Random House.

Callicott, J.B., and T. W. Overholt. 1993. "American Indian Attitudes Toward Nature." In *Philosophy from Africa to Zen: An Invitation to World Philosophy*, edited by R.C. Solomon and K.M. Higgins, 55–80. Lanham, Md.: Rowman and Littlefield.

Darwin, C.R. [1871] 1987. *The Descent of Man & Selection in Relation to Sex*. London: J. Murray.

Ferré, F. 1996. "Persons in Nature: Toward an Applicable and Unified Environmental Ethics." *Ethics and the Environment* 1: 15–25.

Leopold, A. 1949. *A Sand County Almanac and Sketches from Here and There*. New York: Oxford University Press.

Nelson, M. 1996. "Holism and Fascists and Paper Tigers . . . Oh My!" *Ethics and the Environment* 2: 103–107.

Regan, T. 1983. *The Case for Animal Rights*. Berkeley: University of California Press.

Shrader-Frechette, K.S. 1996. "Individualism, Holism, and Environmental Ethics." *Ethics and the Environment* 1: 55–69.

Stone, C.D. 1987. *Earth & Other Ethics*. New York: Harper & Row.

Taylor, P. 1986. *Respect for Nature: A Theory of Environmental Ethics*. Princeton: Princeton University Press.

Varner, G.E. 1991. "No Holism without Pluralism." *Environmental Ethics* 19: 175–179.

Zimmerman, M.E. 1995. "The Threat of Ecofascism." *Social Theory and Practice* 21: 207–238.

NOTES

1. Leopold 1949, 204.
2. Ibid., 210.
3. Ibid., 224–225.
4. Taylor 1986.
5. Darwin [1871] 1987, 93.
6. Leopold 1949, 107.
7. Callicott and Overholt 1993.
8. Aiken 1984, 269.
9. Regan 1983, 262.
10. Ferré 1996, 18.
11. Shrader-Frechette 1996, 63.
12. Zimmerman 1995.
13. Varner 1991.
14. Stone 1987.
15. Ibid.
16. Shrader-Frechette 1996, 63.
17. Varner 1991, 176.

NED HETTINGER AND BILL THROOP

REFOCUSING ECOCENTRISM
De-emphasizing Stability and Defending Wildness

At the beginning of the century, the howl of wolves still haunted Yellowstone National Park. But wolves were considered "varmints" and were poisoned, trapped, and shot as part of an official government policy of predator extermination that succeeded in eradicating wolves from Yellowstone by 1940. Today, most environmentalists believe that the extermination of the wolf was wrong and that its recent restoration was right.

Several widely held rationales for these judgments are rooted in ecocentric ethics. An ecocentric ethic treats natural systems as intrinsically valuable and/ or morally considerable. This ethic is holistic in that it bases moral concern primarily on features of natural systems rather than on the individuals in them. Traditionally, ecocentric ethics has relied heavily on "holistic" ecological theory to provide its empirical foundation. It has evaluated human impacts on the environment primarily in terms of their effect on the integrity, stability, and balance of ecosystems.

Many have argued, for example, that without wolves the Yellowstone ecosystem was incomplete. Wolves were in Yellowstone long before modern settlement of the area, and they are integral to the identity of that ecosystem. Holmes Rolston, III says that Yellowstone is the "largest nearly intact ecosystem in the temperate zone of earth"[1] and suggests that the wolf was one of the few missing components. Wolf biologist David Mech supports wolf reintroduction by arguing that "one of the mandates of the national parks is to preserve complete natural systems. Somehow Yellowstone was shorted. For more than sixty years it has preserved an incomplete system."[2] On this view, returning the wolf helps restore Yellowstone's integrity by making it whole again.

Many also support returning the wolves in order to restore the balance and stability of the Yellowstone ecosystem.[3] Wolf predation helps to control ungulate populations. Absent a major predator with which they coevolved, the elk population in Yellowstone increased dramatically. Vast herds of elk confined year round in this hunting sanctuary have eaten so much of the aspen and willow that these species are not regenerating. The decline in aspens and willows led to the decline of the beaver, a keystone species in maintaining riparian areas and park hydrology. On these grounds, Alston Chase, among others, argues that the balance of the Yellowstone ecosystem was upset by the restriction of the range of the ungulate population, by fire suppression, and by human eradication of wolves and other predators. Restoring the wolf is perceived to be an important step in allowing the Yellowstone equilibrium to return.

The idea that integrity and stability fundamentally characterize natural systems is far from uncontroversial. According to numerous ecologists, disturbance, disequilibria, and chaotic dynamics characterize many natural systems at a variety of scales.[4] Ecosystems are frequently interpreted by these ecologists as historically contingent, transient associations, rather than as persisting, integrated communities. Although many ecologists continue to find stable dimensions of some ecosystems, the presence of instability is trouble for traditional ecocentric ethics. It is risky to advocate preserving the integrity of natural systems when such integrity may not exist, and it is questionable to criticize humans for causing instability in what may already be unstable natural systems.

In this article, we assess the implications of instability models in ecological theory for ecocentric ethics.

Ned Hettinger and Bill Throop, "Refocusing Ecocentrism: De-emphasizing Stability and Defending Wildness," Environmental Ethics 21, no. 1 (1999): 3–21.

We use the elimination and restoration of wolves in Yellowstone to illustrate troubles for traditional eco-centric ethics caused by ecological models emphasizing instability in natural systems. We identify several other problems for a stability-integrity based ecocentrism as well. We show how an ecocentric ethic can avoid these difficulties by emphasizing the value of wildness in natural systems. . . . We do not attempt a full-fledged justification of ecocentrism; in particular, we do not defend ecocentrism against individualistic or anthropocentric environmental ethics.

THE ECOLOGY OF STABILITY

The ecological theories on which traditional ecocentric ethics are based, theories we call collectively the "ecology of stability," were developed by Frederic Clements and Eugene Odum, among others. They tended to view natural systems as integrated, stable wholes that are either at, or moving toward, mature equilibrium states. The terms *equilibrium*, *balance*, *stability*, and *integrity* often go unexplained in traditional ecocentric ethics. Kristin Shrader-Frechette and Earl McCoy have identified over twenty different uses of *stability* and *equilibrium* in ecology.[5] Central among these are the following uses.

A system is in equilibrium if the various forces acting on it are sufficiently balanced that the system is constant and orderly with respect to those features under consideration; thus *balance* and *equilibrium* are closely related. A balance or equilibrium can be either static or dynamic: equilibrium is displayed both by a constancy in tree species in a mature forest ecosystem and by a regular oscillation in a predator–prey system. A system is stable (1) if it is relatively constant over time, (2) if it resists alteration (i.e., it is not fragile), (3) if upon being disturbed it has a strong tendency to return to its pre-disturbance state (i.e., it is resilient), or (4) if it moves toward some end point ("matures"), despite differences in starting points ("trajectory stability").[6] Whether a system is in equilibrium and/or stable depends on the features under consideration and the scale at which the system is described. Vernal pools that exist for perhaps a dozen weeks each year and then dry up are ephemeral on a time scale of months but constant if the scale is years.

Integrity is also used in a variety of senses. The general idea is that the elements of the ecosystem are blended into a unified whole. This idea is commonly associated with the view that ecosystems come in fixed packages of species whose coordinated function creates a unified community. A system which has integrity is characterized by a high degree of integration of its parts. Complex patterns of interdependency weave the parts into a well-integrated unit.

In the ecology of stability, natural systems do undergo some changes, such as fluctuations in the populations of predators and prey, but usually such changes are regular and predictable (as in the cycling of predator and prey according to the Lotka–Volterra equations). Disturbances are considered atypical, and when they occur, ecosystems resist upset. When a natural system is disturbed, it typically returns to its pre-disturbance state or trajectory. Successional ecosystems will move through a predictable series of stages to their mature climax states. In these end states, biotic and abiotic elements of the ecosystem are in balance and the system has "as large and diverse an organic structure" as is possible given available energy and environmental limitations.[7] According to this paradigm, the loss of a species, such as the wolf, upsets the balance and often results in a decline in ecosystem stability, for species diversity in an ecosystem is thought to be proportional to its stability. Thus, ecosystem integrity, stability, and diversity are seen to be closely interrelated phenomena.

This conception of natural systems provides a powerful and seemingly objective basis for determining when ecosystems have been damaged or their value diminished.[8] Integrity, stability, and balance are properties that have widespread and powerful normative appeal. In an ecocentric ethic that emphasizes these properties, our duties to natural systems seem to arise from the nature of ecosystems themselves, rather than from human preferences concerning natural systems. An ecosystem missing a top predator is not simply one that environmentalists do not like; it is a damaged ecosystem. Ignoring this damage betrays ecological ignorance. Ecological science thus appears to underwrite environmental ethics and environmentalist policies. Further, because nature tends towards these states absent human intervention, the ethic based on this normative ecological paradigm warrants preserving ecosystems intact, limiting human impacts, and restoring nature after human degradation.

Advocates of ecocentric ethics frequently appeal to the basic notions of the ecology of stability. Aldo Leopold's often quoted summary maxim—"A thing is right when it tends to preserve the integrity, stability, and beauty of the biotic community; it is wrong when it tends otherwise"—relies on these ideas.[9] Many, such as J. Baird Callicott, have taken Leopold's views as the basis for their environmental ethic.[10] In articulating his ecocentrism, Holmes Rolston puts considerable evaluative weight on the integrity and stability of biotic communities: "A biotic community is a dynamic web of interacting parts in which lives are supported and defended, where there is integrity (integration of the members) and health (niches and resources for the flourishing of species), stability and historical development (dependable regeneration, resilience, and evolution) . . ."[11] Although Rolston's ecocentrism relies on a number of values that systematically make nature valuable (such as diversity, complexity, creativity, and a tendency to produce increasingly valuable "ecological achievements"), ecosystem integrity and stability are central among them.[12]

THE ECOLOGY OF INSTABILITY

An ethic based on the integrity, stability, and balance of natural systems ill accords with some trends in ecology.[13] The more radical proponents of what we call the "ecology of instability" argue that disturbance is the norm for many ecosystems and that natural systems typically do not tend toward mature, stable, integrated states.[14] On a broad scale, climatic changes show little pattern, and they ensure that over the long term, natural systems remain in flux. On a smaller scale, fires, storms, droughts, shifts in the chemical compositions of soils, chance invasions of new species, and a wealth of other factors continually alter the structures of natural systems in ways that do not create repeating patterns of return to the same equilibrium states.[15]

Many empirical studies show that populations fluctuate irregularly.[16] Simple predator/prey models in which numbers of predators and prey oscillate predictably over time ignore the myriad of factors that affect population size. Major population explosions and declines are inherent features of numerous natural systems. Some ecologists suggest that many interacting

populations are chaotic systems, in the mathematical sense of *chaos*.[17] Although these systems are fully deterministic, accurate predictions about them are impossible because tiny (and thus hard to measure) differences in initial conditions can produce drastically different results. Furthermore, ecologists no longer assume a tight correlation between stability and diversity. There is evidence that an intermediate level of disturbance can increase diversity.[18] Also, some stable ecosystems are not very diverse, such as east coast U.S. salt marsh grass ecosystems where *Spartina alterniflora* grows in vast stands that are simple in species composition but quite stable.

With flux taken to be the norm on a variety of levels, it becomes more difficult to interpret natural systems as well-integrated, persisting wholes, much like organisms. Ecosystem integrity becomes problematic when species relationships are opportunistic. Noting that co-occurrence of species is determined by abiotic factors as much as by species interactions and that typical interactions between species involve competition, predation, parasitism, and disease, one well-known conservation biologist claims that "the idea that species live in integrated communities is a myth."[19] Evidence suggests that species groupings are historically contingent and are not fixed packages that come and go as units.[20] Insofar as species associations are transient, individualistic, biotic assemblages, we must begin to question the ideas that ecosystems are supposed to have certain species, that without all of its species an ecosystem is "incomplete," and that exotic species do not belong.

Indeed, the very notion of an ecosystem has become suspect in some quarters. A number of ecologists now investigate the dynamics of "patches" of land, giving up on the idea of homogenous ecosystems. Others retain the notion of an ecosystem, but drop the organismic assumptions often associated. We follow the latter course, recognizing that without these assumptions, what counts as an ecosystem depends on our purposes as well as on the empirical facts.

. . .

We want to stress that there are important ways in which many natural systems display significant degrees of integrity and stability in various respects. Ecosystems are certainly not mere jumbles of self-sufficient individuals. No one denies the existence of causal connections between individuals in ecosystems or dependencies between species. Species adapt to each other, to disturbances, and to changing environments. Sometimes these adaptations can make ecosystems more resistant (and persistent), as when a keystone tree species on hurricane-prone barrier islands evolves a thicker trunk and begins to hug the ground. Selective pressures also put a brake on species self-aggrandizement, for example, by working against predator species that drive their prey to extinction and parasites that destroy their hosts. Many dimensions of natural systems clearly persist on human time scales.

The ecology of instability is far from achieving the status of a dominant paradigm. There continues to be ongoing fruitful work on stability at larger scales and in systems where the disturbance interval is long relative to recovery time.[21] Some recent experimental research supports the claim that increases in diversity produce increases in stability.[22] Additionally, ongoing research in group selection (i.e., natural selection operating on higher levels of organization than the individual), including selection at the community level, may provide support for ecosystem stability and integrity of certain sorts.[23]

Some respected ecologists even suggest that the emphasis on disturbance, instability, and chaos is as much a function of sociological factors, such as the novelty of research on disequilibrium, as it is of new data in ecology.[24] Ecologists are exploring a variety of fruitful metaphors drawn from other sciences and society at large. The success of population biology and of chaos theory outside ecology, as well as our culture's increasing individualism, provide resources for plausible sociological explanations of the popularity of the metaphors and models informing contemporary ecology. Nonetheless, these models have also proved to be empirically fruitful.

Although it would be unreasonable to reject wholesale the ecology of stability, the dangers of basing an environmental ethic on that ecology are significant. An ecocentrism that emphasizes preserving the stability and integrity in ecosystems would seem to leave those ecosystems which lack significant stability or integrity largely unprotected. If an ecocentric ethic is based on valuing stability, would it not follow, implausibly, that less stable and integrated ecosystems

were less valuable and thus less worthy of protection? Michael Soulé thinks it positively dangerous to emphasize the equilibrial, self-regulating, stability producing tendencies of ecosystems.[25] If nature is so stable, it ought to be able to handle human disturbance. If it can, it seems we ought to be protecting the more fragile ecosystems rather than the more stable ones. Moreover, what about the different kinds of stability? Would ecosystems that lacked resilience, but had constancy, such as tundra ecosystems, be subject to more or less protection than those that are resilient, but less constant, such as fire-prone chaparral? Would more tightly integrated biotic communities (e.g., ecosystems with keystone species) take precedence over looser species assemblages? Such questions indicate how developments in ecology muddy the waters for an ecocentrism that emphasizes stability and integrity and leave it with a range of unpalatable implications. Leopold's dictum that what is right is what "preserves the integrity, stability and beauty of the biotic community" seems all too vulnerable to the charge that we may be obligating ourselves to preserve something that frequently does not exist.

In particular, consider the implications of viewing the case of the Yellowstone wolves through the lens of the ecology of instability. It is no longer clear that ecocentrists can justify the claims that elimination of wolves from Yellowstone damaged the ecosystem and that their restoration is desirable. Perhaps those who hunted and poisoned the wolves did not disrupt any significant stability and integrity of the system. They might have merely changed the system, much like other phenomena might change it (e.g., an ice age, disease, etc.); now it is governed by a different set of dynamics.

Of course, it may be that characteristics of the Yellowstone ecosystem relevant to wolves can be most fruitfully explained by stability models. But what if, in relevant respects, Yellowstone is better interpreted using instability models? Suppose that elk populations would fluctuate dramatically and irregularly with or without wolves and that such fluctuations had a variety of unpredictable impacts on animals dependent on elk forage. Do we want our obligations to Yellowstone to depend on how stable or unstable, integrated or loosely organized it is? We think not. We may, of course, decide that we should restore wolves to Yellowstone for other reasons, perhaps because we enjoy seeing wolves and want our children to be able to experience them. But then we have abandoned an ecocentric ethic, and this, we believe, is premature.

WILDNESS AND ECOCENTRISM

We think that advocates of ecocentric ethics should shift the emphasis away from integrity and stability toward other intrinsically valuable features of natural systems, such as diversity, complexity, creativity, beauty, fecundity, and wildness. For reasons we outline below, we think that the value of wildness plays a central role in this nexus of values. Emphasizing wildness provides the most promising general strategy for defending ecocentric ethics. Others have suggested that the wildness of some natural systems gives us a strong reason for valuing them intrinsically.[26] We support this claim by showing how wildness value is in reflective equilibrium with many considered judgments, [and] by showing how a focus on wildness avoids a number of problems with traditional ecocentrism. . . .

The term *wild* has a variety of meanings, many of which are not relevant to our defense of ecocentrism. For example, by *wild* we do not mean "chaotic," "fierce," or "uncontrollable." As we use the term, something is wild in a certain respect to the extent that it is *not humanized* in that respect. An entity is humanized in the degree to which it is influenced, altered, or controlled by humans. While one person walking through the woods does little to diminish its wildness, leaving garbage, culling deer, or clear cutting do diminish wildness, although in different degrees. Do we tend to value wildness so defined?

Numerous examples from ordinary life suggest that people do value wildness in a variety of contexts. For instance, admiration of a person's attractive features is likely to diminish when it is learned that they were produced by elective plastic surgery. People prefer the birth of a child without the use of drugs or a Caesarean section, and they do so not just because the former may be more conducive to health. Picking raspberries discovered in a local ravine is preferable to procuring the store-bought commercial variety (and not just because of the beauty of the setting). Our appreciation of catching cut-throat trout in an isolated and rugged

mountain valley is reduced by reports that the Department of Fish and Game stocked the stream the previous week. Imagine how visitors to Yellowstone would feel about Old Faithful if they thought that the National Park Service put soap into the geyser to regulate and enhance its eruptions. In each example, people value more highly what is less subject to human alterations or control than a more humanized variant of the same phenomenon. The value differential may result from several features of these cases, but central among them is the difference in wildness. Notice that if we focus on different aspects of these situations, the judgment of wildness changes: the mountain stream may be wild in many respects, even if its fish are not. Although we value wildness in many things, an ecocentric ethic will focus on the value of the wildness of natural systems.

In addition to such specific judgments, there are powerful and widespread general intuitions that support the value of the nonhumanized. People rightfully value the existence of a realm not significantly under human control—the weather, the seasons, the mountains, and the seas. This is one reason why the idea of humans as planetary managers is so objectionable to many.[27] Consider a world in which human beings determine when it rains, when spring comes, how the tides run, and where mountains rise. The surprise and awe we feel at the workings of spontaneous nature would be replaced by appraisal of the decisions of these managers. Our wonder at the mystery of these phenomena would not survive such management. People value being a part of a world not of their own making. Valuing the wild acknowledges that limits to human mastery and domination of the world are imperative.

Humans also need to be able to confront, honor, and celebrate the "other."[28] In an increasingly secular society, "Nature" takes on the role of the other. Humans need to be able to feel small in comparison with something nonhuman which is of great value. Confronting the other helps humans to cultivate a proper sense of humility. Many people find the other powerfully in parts of nature that do not bend to our will and where the nonhuman carries on in relative autonomy, unfolding on its own.

With dramatic humanization of the planet, wildness becomes especially significant. In general, when something of value becomes rare, that value increases.

Today, the spontaneous workings of nature are becoming increasingly rare. Reportedly, humans appropriate between twenty and forty percent of the photosynthetic energy produced by terrestrial plants.[29] Humans now rival the major geologic forces in our propensity to move around soil and rock.[30] Human population, now approaching six billion, is projected to increase by fifty percent by the middle of the next century. Leaving out Antarctica, there are now 100 humans for every square mile of the land surface of the Earth.[31] Almost everyone knows a special natural area that has been "developed" and is now gone. The increasing importance of biotechnology further manifests our domestication, artificialization, and humanization of nature. Wildness is threatened on a variety of fronts, and the passions that fuel many environmental disputes can often be explained by this rapid loss of the wild and the consequent increase in the value of what remains.

By positing wildness as a significant value-enhancing property, we account for a wide range of intuitions. Of course, the nature that we value in virtue of its wildness is also valuable because it is complex, creative, fecund, diverse, beautiful, and so on. Why focus on wildness, rather than on biodiversity, as is currently fashionable (or on some other characteristic)? We believe that the emphasis on wildness is justified by the transformative and intensifying roles it plays in this nexus of values. These roles suggest that wildness is a kind of "root" value, that is, a significant source of these other values.

Wildness is transformative in that it can combine with a property that has neutral or even negative value and turn the whole into a positive value. For example, wildness helps to transform biodiversity into the powerful value it is in today's environmental debates. Biodiversity is not by itself valuable. If it were, we could add value to ecosystems by integrating large numbers of genetically engineered organisms into them. But doing so seems unacceptable. It is *wild* biodiversity that people wish to protect. Wildness transforms biodiversity into a significant value-bearing property. The presence or absence of wildness frequently transforms our evaluation of things; a beautiful sunset is diminished in value when it is caused by pollution. Wildness also intensifies the value of properties that are already valuable.[32] For example, wildness often significantly enhances the value of beauty. As Eugene Hargrove argues,

"our aesthetic admiration and appreciation for natural beauty is an appreciation of the achievement of complex form that is entirely unplanned. It is in fact because it is unplanned and independent of human involvement that the achievement is so amazing, wonderful, and delightful."[33]

An ecocentrism that emphasizes wildness value also puts a brake on alleged human improvements of nature through anthropogenic production of the properties in virtue of which we value nature. A stability and integrity based ecocentrism would have to judge human activity that enhanced ecosystem stability or integrity as value increasing. A highly humanized ecosystem could be more stable, integrated, and diverse than a natural ecosystem that it replaced. For example, an engineered beach with breakwaters and keystone exotics that held the sand might be more stable, integrated, and diverse than the naturally eroding beach it replaced. Only an ecocentrism that puts its central focus on wildness value can prevent the unpalatable conclusion that such human manipulation of nature would, if successful, increase intrinsic value.

. . .

RESTORATION, WOLVES, AND THE WILD

Appealing to the value of wildness provides strong reasons to believe that it was wrong to extirpate wolves from Yellowstone. Eliminating wolves involved significant human alteration of the processes that characterized that system. In the context of the twentieth century, this loss of wildness in Yellowstone carried with it significant loss of value. Nonetheless, we cannot directly infer from the loss of wild value in Yellowstone that wildness counts in favor of restoration of wolves, for reintroducing wolves involves significant additional human alteration and management of Yellowstone, and it is hard to see how such a reintroduction can be sanctioned by the value of wildness. Indeed, intuitions about the positive value of restoration result in [an] objection to wildness value. As Robin Attfield puts the point, "How can anything be restored by human agency the essence of which is to be independent of human agency?"[34] Restoration is a contentious environmental issue. Some philosophers disparage restorations as fakes or artifacts.[35] Other philosophers stress our obligations to restore nature and suggest that certain types of restoration can increase value significantly.[36] We believe that an ecocentric ethic that emphasizes the value of wildness has the virtue of maintaining and explaining this ambivalent attitude. Although restoration typically fails to increase wildness in the short run, it can speed recovery of wildness by helping humanization wash out of natural systems.

Notice that a stability-integrity ecocentrism must be quite sanguine about restoration (at least in theory). If an ecosystem's stability or integrity is restored, no loss has occurred. In contrast, restoration designed to enhance wildness value wears its limitations on its sleeve. Not only will the additional human activity involved in restoration tend to detract from wildness value, but restoring the original system's wildness will not be possible in one respect: human activity will forever remain part of the causal chain leading to that ecosystem. Nevertheless, wildness value can count in favor of restoration projects. By returning the system to what it would have been had humans not altered it, restoration can help diminish human influence.

A number of factors affect the speed and extent of "washout." In general, the greater the human influence on a system, the longer it will take for the humanization to wash out. For example, previous levels of wildness will return more quickly to a selectively-cut forest than to a clear-cut forest. Temporal distance from the humanization also affects washout. The mere fact that it has been at least six hundred years since humans removed the trees from Dartmoor makes that landscape significantly wilder than it would be had the deforestation occurred fifty years ago. Complete washout of human influence can occur rapidly. A volcanic eruption that destroys a humanized landscape and covers it with a thick layer of lava would seem to return the full wildness of the landscape almost instantaneously. The land becomes very much like what it would have been whether or not it had been humanized. Such transformations suggest that washout is also a function of the extent to which a system instantiates a pattern it would have displayed absent some relatively recent humanization. A fourth factor affecting washout is the extent to which natural processes rework a humanized area, whether or not the result instantiates what it would have been absent humanization. For example, Dartmoor has

recovered more of its lost wildness than have the cliffs of Mount Rushmore because natural processes have been more successful in changing the humanized state.

We think that restoring wolves to Yellowstone is a case in which additional human activity can help humanization washout of a natural system. The human involvement in the restoration does initially subtract from wildness in important respects: humans transporting wolves from Canada into the park, attaching radio collars to the animals, and then tracking their movements involves additional and significant human activity in natural systems and it alters natural systems as they are currently constituted. Yellowstone would become wilder sooner if wolves returned without human assistance. Still, we believe this additional human activity will eventually decrease the degree to which Yellowstone is a humanized environment. By putting wolves back, we diminish the overall impact of humans on Yellowstone, much the way picking up litter in a forest diminishes the human impact on the forest or removing a dam reduces the human impact on a river—despite involving additional human activity. Contrast wolf restoration with introducing snow leopards into Yellowstone. Wildness value counts significantly in favor of wolf restoration rather than snow leopard introduction because wolves and not snow leopards would have been in Yellowstone today. An ecocentrism based on stability would have no reason to support putting back the native species rather than a functionally equivalent exotic.

CONCLUSION

We have argued that an ecocentric ethic that emphasizes the value of wildness of natural systems has a number of virtues in comparison with traditional ecocentrism. Most importantly, it avoids the ecologically and philosophically troubling assumptions that natural systems worthy of protections are integrated and stable. Moreover, by focusing on wildness, ecocentrism can avoid the counterintuitive result that humans can improve ecosystems' value by increasing their integrity, stability, biodiversity, and so on. An ecocentrism that emphasizes wildness allows for a more ambivalent assessment of restoration than the overly sanguine approach resulting from traditional ecocentrism.

. . .

It seems unwise to ground ecocentrism in general theories, such as the ecology of stability or the ecology of instability, when nature displays so much variation and complexity. Powerful intuitions about the value of wildness that are accepted by many people can provide that grounding. Other values can also play important roles in a fully developed ecocentric ethic, though, if we are right, their roles will usually depend on wildness.

NOTES

1. Holmes Rolston, III, "Biology and Philosophy in Yellowstone," *Biology & Philosophy* 5 (1990): 242.
2. David Mech, "Returning the Wolf to Yellowstone," in Robert Keiter and Mark Boyce, eds., *The Greater Yellowstone Ecosystem* (New Haven: Yale University Press, 1991), p. 309.
3. The following account comes from Alston Chase, *Playing God in Yellowstone* (San Diego: Harcourt Brace Jovanovich, 1987), pp. 19–30, 382.
4. For an overview of this emphasis in ecology, see Donald Worster, "The Ecology of Order and Chaos," *Environmental History Review* 14 (1990): 1–18.
5. K.S. Shrader-Frechette and E.D. McCoy, *Method in Ecology* (New York: Cambridge University Press, 1993), pp. 65–67.
6. Compare Gordon Orians, "Diversity, Stability and Maturity in Natural Ecosystems," W.H. van Dobben and R.H. Lowe-McConnell, eds., *Unifying Concepts in Ecology* (The Hague: Dr. W. Junk B. V. Publishers, 1975), pp. 139–50.
7. See Worster, "The Ecology of Order," p. 41, quoting Odum.
8. A number of U.S. environmental laws use concepts like balance and stability to define the goals they set for public policy. See Mark Sagoff, "Fact and Value in Ecological Science," *Environmental Ethics* 7 (1985): 101.
9. Aldo Leopold, *A Sand County Almanac* (New York: Oxford University Press, 1949), p. 240.
10. J. Baird Callicott, *In Defense of the Land Ethic* (Albany: SUNY Press, 1989).
11. Holmes Rolston, III, *Conserving Natural Value* (New York: Columbia Press, 1994), p. 78.

12. In arguing that the most important natural value is the "systemic value" of ecosystems, that is, their ability to create value, Rolston says: "the stability, integrity, and beauty of biotic communities is what is most fundamentally to be conserved" (ibid., p. 177). Rolston is well aware of ecologists' ambivalence toward ecosystem stability and integrity. He ties his discussion of ecosystem stability to a discussion of historical change. At one point, he calls the notion that ecosystems tend toward equilibrium "a half-truth."
13. For one development of this argument, see Kristin Shrader-Frechette, "Ecological Theories and Ethical Imperatives," in William Shea and Beat Sitter, eds., *Scientists and Their Responsibility* (Canton, Mass.: Watson Publishing International, 1989).
14. See Daniel Botkin, *Discordant Harmonies* (New York: Oxford University Press, 1990). In "Nonequilibrium Determinants of Biological Community Structure," *American Scientist* 82 (1994): 427, Seth Reice contends that "equilibrium is an unusual state for natural ecosystems. . . . the normal state of communities and ecosystems is to be recovering from the last disturbance. Natural systems are so frequently disturbed that equilibrium is rarely achieved.
15. See the articles in S.T.A. Pickett and P.S. White, eds., *The Ecology of Natural Disturbance and Patch Dynamics* (Orlando: Academic Press, 1985), for examples of research in this area.
16. Botkin, *Discordant Harmonies*, chap. 3.
17. Ibid. For research documenting the chaotic behavior of populations independent of perturbations, see Alan Hastings and Kevin Higgins, "Persistence of Transients in Spatially Structured Ecological Models," *Science* 263 (1994): 1133–36.
18. See Reice, "Nonequilibrium Determinants," p. 428.
19. Michael Soulé, "The Social Siege of Nature," in Michael Soulé and Gary Lease, eds., *Reinventing Nature?* (Washington, D.C.: Island Press, 1995), p. 143.
20. Looking at the fossil record of the last 50,000 years, David Jablonski says, "The most important message . . . is that ecological communities do not respond as units to environmental change. . . . Species are highly individualistic in their behavior,

so that few, if any, modern terrestrial communities existed in their present form 10,000 years ago." See Jablonski's "Extinction: A Paleontological Perspective," *Science* 253 (1991): 756. In a similar vein, Michael Soulé suggests that historical "studies are undermining typological concepts of community composition, structure, dynamics, and organization by showing that existing species once constituted quite different groupings or 'communities.'" See Soulé's, "The Onslaught of Alien Species, and Other Challenges in the Coming Decades," *Conservation Biology* 4 (1990): 234.

21. See Stuart Pimm, *The Balance of Nature?* (Chicago: University of Chicago Press, 1991) and Monica G. Turner et al., "A Revised Concept of Landscape Equilibrium: Disturbance and Stability on Scaled Landscapes," *Landscape Ecology* 8 (1993): 213–27. Frank Golley's informative *A History of the Ecosystem Concept in Ecology* (New Haven: Yale University Press, 1994) traces the development of ecosystem ecology and responds to some of the important challenges to it.

22. See Elizabeth Culotta, "Exploring Biodiversity's Benefits," *Science* 273 (1996): 1045–46.

23. Charles Goodnight, "Experimental Studies of Community Evolution I: The Response at the Community Level," *Evolution* 44 (1990): 1614–24.

24. David Ehrenfeld calls this emphasis a "fad." See "Ecosystem Health and Ecological Theories," in Robert Costanza, Bryan Norton, and Benjamin Haskell, eds., *Ecosystem Health* (Washington, D.C.: Island Press, 1992), p. 140. For another suggestion that the focus on instability is due to sociological factors, see P. Koetsier et al., "Rejecting Equilibrium Theory—A Cautionary Note," *Bulletin of the Ecology Society of America* 71 (1990): 229–30.

25. See Soulé, "The Social Siege of Nature," p. 160.

26. Although a number of philosophers have appealed to wildness and the related notion of naturalness, there is no uniform agreement on its meaning or justification. See Robert Elliot, "Extinction, Restoration, Naturalness," *Environmental Ethics* 16 (1994): 135–44, and "Faking Nature," *Inquiry* 25 (1982): 81–93; Eric Katz, "The Big Lie: The Human Restoration of Nature," *Research in Philosophy and Technology* 12 (1992: 231–41, and "The Call of the Wild," *Environmental Ethics* 14 (1992): 265–73.

27. For a powerful treatment of this topic, see Rolston, *Conserving Natural Value*, pp. 223–28.

28. Tom Birch discusses wildness as "otherness" in "The Incarceration of Wildness: Wilderness Areas as Prisons," *Environmental Ethics* 12 (1990): 3–26.

29. See Edward O. Wilson, *The Diversity of Life* (Cambridge: The Belknap Press of Harvard University Press, 1992), p. 272.

30. Richard Monastersky, "Earthmovers: Humans Take Their Place alongside Wind, Water, and Ice," *Science News* 146 (1994): 432.

31. Donald Worster, "The Nature We Have Lost," in *The Wealth of Nature* (New York: Oxford University Press, 1993), p. 6.

32. According to Robert Elliot, "Extinction, Restoration, Naturalness," p. 138, "intensification of value occurs when the co-instantiation of value-adding properties yields more value than the sum of the values of the properties would have if they were instantiated singly."

33. Eugene Hargrove, "The Paradox of Humanity: Two Views of Biodiversity and Landscapes," in Ke Chung Kim and Robert D. Weaver, eds., *Biodiversity and Landscapes* (Cambridge: Cambridge University Press, 1994), p. 183.

34. Robin Attfield, "Rehabilitating Nature and Making Nature Habitable," in Robin Attfield and Andrew Belsey, eds., *Philosophy and the Natural Environment* (New York: Cambridge University Press, 1994), p. 45.

35. See Elliot's "Faking Nature" and Katz's "The Big Lie."

36. See, for example, Richard Sylvan's "Mucking with Nature," in Sylvan, *Against the Main Stream*, Discussion Papers in Environmental Philosophy, no. 21 (Canberra: Research School of Social Sciences, Australia National University, 1994).

7

NATURE

FOR DISCUSSION: HOW WILD DOES NATURE HAVE TO BE?

1. Years ago (Schmidtz reports) my sister visited me in Tucson. She lives in Canada; the desert was completely new to her. I took her to the Sonoran Desert Museum just outside Tucson. At the museum is a cave, which I took her to see. As we descended into the cave, my sister marveled at how beautiful it was. After a few minutes, though, her eyes became accustomed to the dark. She took a closer look, and reached out to touch the wall. "It isn't real. It's concrete," she said softly, embarrassed by her earlier wonderment.

Why was she disappointed? What difference does it make whether the cave is natural or artificial? What do you suppose Martin Krieger would say?

2. If you go to zoos, you have probably witnessed little kids ignoring the tigers and zebras and squealing with excitement about a ground squirrel running down the path beside them. The kids know: in some way, the ground squirrel is real in a way zoo animals are not. Somehow, there is more meaning in the wild, in encounters with nature that have not been scripted for us by someone else. But what exactly is missing? What are the kids seeing in the squirrel that they do not see in caged tigers? What do you suppose Martin Kreiger would say?

3. Today, in the temperate climates of Europe and North America, mosquitoes are primarily an irritant. In the tropics of Africa, Asia, and South America, mosquitoes are among the most dangerous animals you could ever have the misfortune to meet, for they transmit diseases that kill millions of human beings every year.

DDT is an inexpensive insecticide still used to control malaria-transmitting mosquitoes in many parts of the world. In the United States, we could afford to ban the use of DDT, and did so in 1972. We had alternatives. We put screens on our windows. We drained wetlands and eradicated mosquito habitat. In many countries, such measures are unaffordable. Do people in developing countries have the right to use DDT to save themselves from mosquito-transmitted diseases? If or when they have an obligation *not* to use DDT, to whom or to what do they have this obligation? To consumers of their agricultural products? To the birds and fish that might be put at risk? To the mosquitoes themselves? To the malaria parasite?

MARTIN KRIEGER

WHAT'S WRONG WITH PLASTIC TREES?

A tree's a tree. How many more [redwoods] do you need to look at? If you've seen one, you've seen them all.

—Attributed to Ronald Reagan, then candidate
for governor of California.

A tree is a tree, and when you've seen one redwood, given your general knowledge about trees, you have a pretty good idea of the characteristics of a redwood. Yet most people believe that when you've seen one, you haven't seen them all. Why is this so? What implications does this have for public policy in a world where resources are not scarce, but do have to be manufactured; where choice is always present; and where the competition for resources is becoming clearer and keener? In this article, I attempt to explore some of these issues, while trying to understand the reasons that are given, or might be given, for preserving certain natural environments.

THE ECOLOGY MOVEMENT

In the past few years, a movement concerned with the preservation and careful use of the natural environment in this country has grown substantially. This ecology movement, as I shall call it, is beginning to have genuine power in governmental decision-making and is becoming a link between certain government agencies and the publics to which they are responsible. The ecology movement should be distinguished from related movements concerned with the conservation and wise use of natural resources. The latter, ascendant in the United States during the first half of this century, were mostly concerned with making sure that natural resources and environments were used in a fashion that reflected their true worth to man. This resulted in a utilitarian conception of environments and in the adoption of means to partially preserve them—for example, cost–benefit analysis and policies of multiple use on federal lands.

The ecology movement is not necessarily committed to such policies. Noting the spoliation of the environment under the policies of the conservation movement, the ecology movement demands much greater concern about what is done to the environment, independently of how much it may cost. The ecology movement seeks to have man's environment valued in and of itself and thereby prevent its being traded off for the other benefits it offers to man.

It seems likely that the ecology movement will have to become more programmatic and responsive to compromise as it moves into more responsible and bureaucratic positions vis-à-vis governments and administrative agencies. As they now stand, the policies of the ecology movement may work against resource-conserving strategies designed to lead to the movement's desired ends in 20 or 30 years. Meier has said:[1]

> The best hope, it seems now, is that the newly evolved ideologies will progress as social movements. A number of the major tenets of the belief system may then be expected to lose their centrality and move to the periphery of collective attention. Believers may thereupon only "satisfice" with respect to these principles; they are ready to consider compromises.

What is needed is an approach midway between the preservationist and conservationist-utilitarian policies. It is necessary to find ways of preserving the opportunity for experiences in natural environments, while having, at the same time, some flexibility in the alternatives that the ecology movement could advocate.

Martin H. Krieger. 1973. What's Wrong with Plastic Trees? Science, 179: 446–455. Reprinted with permission of the American Association for the Advancement of Science.

A new approach is needed because of the success of economic arguments in the past. We are now more concerned about social equity and about finding arguments from economics for preserving "untouched" environments. Such environments have not been manipulated very much by mankind in the recent past (hundreds or thousands of years). Traditional resource economics has been concerned not as much with preservation as with deciding which intertemporal (the choice of alternative times at which one intervenes) use of natural resources over a period of years yields a maximum return to man, essentially independent of considerations of equity. If one believes that untouched environments are unlikely to have substitutes, then this economics is not very useful. In fact, a different orientation toward preservation has developed and is beginning to be applied in ways that will provide powerful arguments for preservation. At the same time, some ideas about how man experiences the environment are becoming better understood, and they suggest that the new economic approach will be in need of some modification, even if most of its assumptions are sound.

I first examine what is usually meant by natural environments and rarity; I will then examine some of the rationales for preservation. It is important to understand the character and the weak points of the usual arguments. I also suggest how our knowledge and sophistication about environments and our differential access to them are likely to lead to levers for policy changes that will effectively preserve the possibility of experiencing nature, yet offer alternatives in the management of natural resources.

One limitation of my analysis should be made clear. I have restricted my discussion to the nation-state, particularly to the United States. If it were possible to take a global view, then environmental questions would be best phrased in terms of the world's resources. If we want undisturbed natural areas, it might be best to develop some of them in other countries. But we do not live in a politically united world, and such a proposal is imperialistic at worst and unrealistic at best. Global questions about the environment need to be considered, but they must be considered in terms of controls that can exist. If we are concerned about preserving natural environments, it seems clear that, for the moment, we will most likely have to preserve them in our own country.

THE AMERICAN FALLS: KEEPING IT NATURAL

For the last few thousand years, Niagara Falls has been receding. Water going over the Falls insinuates itself into crevices of the rock, freezes and expands in winter, and thereby causes cracks in the formation. The formation itself is a problem in that the hard rock on the surface covers a softer substratum. This weakness results not only in small amounts of erosion or small rockfalls, but also in very substantial ones when the substratum gives way. About 350,000 cubic yards (1 cubic yard equals 0.77 cubic meter) of talus lie at the base of the American Falls.

The various hydroelectric projects that have been constructed during the years have also affected the amount of water that flows over the Falls. It is now possible to alter the flow of water over the American Falls by a factor of 2 and, consequently, to diminish that of the Horseshoe (Canadian) Falls by about 10%. As a result of these forces, the quality of the Falls—its grandeur, its height, its smoothness of flow—changes over the millennia and the months.

There is nothing pernicious about the changes wrought by nature; the problem is that Americans' image of the Falls does not change. Our ideal of a waterfall, an ideal formed by experiences with small, local waterfalls that seem perfect and by images created by artists and photographers, is not about to change without some effort.

When one visits the Falls today, he sees rocks and debris at the base, too much or too little water going over the edge, and imperfections in the flow of water. These sights are not likely to make anyone feel that he is seeing or experiencing the genuine Niagara Falls. The consequent effects on tourism, a multimillion-dollar-per year industry, could be substantial.

At the instigation of local forces, the American Falls International Board has been formed under the auspices of the International Joint Commission of the United States and Canada. Some $5 to $6 million are being spent to investigate, by means of "dewatering" the Falls and building scale models, policies for intervention. That such efforts are commissioned suggests that we, as a nation, believe that it is proper and possible to do something about the future evolution of the Falls. A "Fallscape" committee, which is especially concerned with the visual quality of the Falls, has been formed. It suggests that three strategies, varying in degree of intervention, be considered.

1. The Falls can be converted into a monument. By means of strengthening the structure of the Falls, it is possible to prevent rockfalls. Also, excess rock from the base can be removed. Such a strategy might cost tens of millions of dollars, a large part of this cost being for the removal of talus.
2. The Falls could become an event. Some of the rocks at the base could be removed for convenience and esthetics, but the rockfalls themselves would not be hindered. Instead, instruments for predicting rockfalls could be installed. People might then come to the Falls at certain times, knowing that they would see an interesting and grand event, part of the cycle of nature, such as Old Faithful.
3. The Falls might be treated as a show. The "director" could control the amount of water flowing over the Falls, the size of the pool below, and the amount of debris, thereby producing a variety of spectacles. Not only could there be *son et lumière*, but it could take place on an orchestrated physical mass.

Which of these is the most nearly natural environment? Current practice, exemplified by the National Park Service's administration of natural areas, might suggest that the second procedure be followed and that the Falls not be "perfected." But would that be the famous Niagara Falls, the place where Marilyn Monroe met her fate in the movie *Niagara*? The answer to this question lies in the ways in which efforts at preservation are presented to the public. If the public is seeking a symbolic Falls, then the Falls has to be returned to its former state. If the public wants to see a natural phenomenon at work, then the Falls should be allowed to fall.

Paradoxically, the phenomena that the public thinks of as "natural" often require great artifice in their creation. The natural phenomenon of the Falls today has been created to a great extent by hydroelectric projects over the years. Esthetic appreciation of the Falls has been conditioned by the rather mundane considerations of routes of tourist excursions and views from hotel windows, as well as the efforts of artists.

I think that we can provide a smooth flow of water over the Falls and at the same time not be completely insensitive to natural processes if we adopt a procedure like that described in the third proposal. Niagara Falls is not a virgin territory, the skyscrapers and motels will not disappear. Therefore, an aggressive attitude toward the Falls seems appropriate. This does not imply heavy-handedness in intervention (the first proposal), but a willingness to touch the "sacred" for esthetic as well as utilitarian purposes.

The effort to analyze this fairly straightforward policy question is not trivial. Other questions concerning preservation have fuzzier boundaries, less clear costs (direct and indirect), and much more complicated political considerations. For these reasons it seems worthwhile to examine some of the concepts I use in this discussion.

NATURAL ENVIRONMENTS

What is considered a natural environment depends on the particular culture and society defining it. It might be possible to create for our culture and society a single definition that is usable (that is, the definition would mean the same thing to many people), but this, of course, says nothing about the applicability of such a definition to other cultures. However, I restrict my discussion to the development of the American idea of a natural environment.

The history of the idea of the wilderness is a good example of the development of one concept of natural environment. I follow Nash's discussion in the following.

A wilderness may be viewed as a state of mind, as an attitude toward a collection of trees, other plants, animals, and the land on which they all exist. The idea that a wilderness exists as a product of an intellectual movement is important. A wilderness is not discovered in the sense that some man from a civilization looked upon a piece of territory for the first time. It is the meanings that we attach to such a piece of territory that convert it to a wilderness.

The Romantic appreciation of nature, with its associated enthusiasm for the "strange, remote, solitary and mysterious," converted territory that was a threatening wildland into a desirable area capable of producing an invigorating spirit of wilderness. The appreciation of the wilderness in this form began in cities, for whose residents the wildland was a novelty. Because of the massive destruction of this territory for resources (primarily timber), city dwellers, whose livelihood did not depend on these resources and who were not familiar with the territory, called for the preservation of wildlands. At first, they did not try to keep the most easily accessible, and therefore most economically useful, lands from being exploited, but noted that Yellowstone and the Adirondacks were rare wonders and had no other utility. They did not think of these areas as wilderness, but as untouched lands. Eventually, a battle developed between conservationists and preservationists. The conservationists (Pinchot, for example) were concerned with the wise use of lands, with science and civilization and forestry; the preservationists (Muir, for example) based their argument on art and wilderness. This latter concept of wilderness is the significant one. The preservationists converted wildland into wilderness— a good that is indivisible and valuable in itself.

This capsule history suggests that the wilderness, as we think of it now, is the product of a political effort to give a special meaning to a biological system organized in a specific way. I suspect that this history is the appropriate model for the manner in which biological systems come to be designated as special.

But it might be said that natural environments can be defined in the way ecosystems are—in terms of complexity, energy and entropy flows, and so on. This is true, but only because of all the spadework that has gone into developing in the public a consensual picture of natural environments. What a society takes to be a natural environment is one.

Natural environments are likely to be named when there are unnatural environments and are likely to be noted only when they are outnumbered by these unnatural environments. The wildlands of the past, which were frightening, were plentiful and were not valued. The new wilderness, which is a source of revitalization, is rare and so valued that it needs to be preserved.

WHEN IS SOMETHING RARE?

Something is considered to be rare when there do not exist very many objects or events that are similar to it. It is clear that one object must be distinguishable from another in order to be declared rare, but the basis for this distinction is not clear.

One may take a realist's or an idealist's view of rarity. For the realist, an object is unique within a purview: given a certain boundary, there exists no other object like it. Certainly the Grand Canyon is unique within the United States. Perhaps Niagara Falls is also unique. But there are many other waterfalls throughout the world that are equally impressive, if not of identical dimensions.

For the idealist, a rare object is one that is archetypal: it is the most nearly typical of all the objects it represents, having the most nearly perfect form. We frequently preserve archetypal specimens in museums and botanical gardens. Natural areas often have these qualities.

A given object is not always rare. Rather, it is designated as rare at one time and may, at some other time, be considered common. How does this happen? Objects become rare when a large number of people change their attitudes toward them. This may come about in a number of ways, but it is necessary that the object in question be noticed and singled out. Perhaps one individual discovers it, or perhaps it is common to everyone's experience. Someone must convince the public that the object is something special. The publicist must develop in others the ability to differentiate one object from among a large number of others, as well as to value the characteristic that makes the particular object different. If he convinces a group of people influential in the society, people who are able to affect a much larger group's beliefs, then he will have succeeded in his task. Thus it may be important that some form of snob appeal be created for the special object.

In order to create the differentiations and the differential valuations of characteristics, information and knowledge are crucial. A physical object can be transformed into an instrument of beauty, pleasure, or pride, thereby developing sufficient characteristics to be called rare, only by means of changing the knowledge we have of it and of its relation to the rest of the world. In this sense, knowledge serves an important function in the creation of rare environments, very much as knowledge in society serves an important function in designating what should be considered natural resources.

Advertising is one means of changing states of knowledge—nor does such advertising have to be wholly sponsored by commercial interests. . . . As a *result* of the social process of creating a rare object, the usual indicators of rarity become important. Economically, prices rise; physically, the locations of the rare objects become central, or at least highly significant spatially; and socially, rare objects and their possessors are associated with statuses that are valued and activities that are considered to be good.

ENVIRONMENTS CAN BE AND ARE CREATED

To recapitulate, objects are rare because men decide that they are and, through social action, convince others that they are. The rarity of an object is created through four mechanisms: designating the object as rare; differentiating it from other objects of the same species; establishing its significance; and determining its position in the context of society. The last two mechanisms are especially important, for the meaning that an environment has and its relation to other things in the society are crucial to its being considered rare. That a rare environment be irreproducible or of unchanging character is usually a necessary preliminary to our desire to preserve it. Technologies, which may involve physical processes or social organization and processes, determine how reproducible an object is, for we may make a copy of the original or we may transfer to another object the significance attached to the original. (Copying natural environments may be easier than copying artistic objects because the qualities of replicas and forgeries are not as well characterized in the case of the natural environment.) Insofar as we are incapable of doing either of these, we may desire to preserve the original environment.

In considering the clientele of rare environments, one finds that accessibility by means of transportation and communication is important. If there is no means of transportation to a rare environment then it is not likely that the public will care about that environment. An alternative to transportation is some form of communication, either verbal or pictorial, that simulates a feeling of being in the environment.

I am concerned here with the history of environments that, at first, are not considered unique.

However, a similar argument could be applied to environments regarded as unique (for example, the Grand Canyon), provided they were classed with those environments most like them. . . . For example, suppose that a particular kind of environment is plentiful and that, over a period of time, frequent use causes it to become polluted. (Note that pollution need not refer just to our conventional concepts of dirtying the environment, but to a wide variety of uncleanliness and stigma as well.) Because there is a substantial amount of that environment available, man's use of it will, at first, have little effect on his perception of its rarity. As time goes on, however, someone will notice that there used to be a great deal more of that particular environment available. Suddenly, the once vast quantities of that environment begin to look less plentiful. The environment seems more special as it becomes distinguishable from the polluted environments around it. At that point, it is likely that there will be a movement to designate some fraction of the remaining environment as rare and in need of protection. There will also be a movement to restore those parts of the environment that have already been polluted. People will intervene to convert the polluted environment to a simulation of the original one.

REASONS FOR PRESERVATION

That something is rare does not imply that it must be preserved. The characteristics that distinguish it as rare must also be valued. Arguments in favor of preserving an object can be based on the fact that the object is a luxury, a necessity, or a merit.

We build temples or other monuments to our society (often by means of preservation) and believe that they represent important investments in social unity and coherence. If a forest symbolizes the frontier for a society and if that frontier is meaningful in the society's history, then there may be good reasons for preserving it. An object may also be preserved in order that it may be used in the future. Another reason, not often given but still true, for preserving things is that there is nothing else worth doing with them. For example, it may cost very little to preserve something that no one seems to have any particular reason for despoiling; therefore, we expend some small effort in trying to keep it untouched.

Natural environments are preserved for reasons of necessity also. Environments may provide ecological samples that will be useful to future generations. Recently, the long-lived bristlecone pine has helped to check radiocarbon dating and has thereby revised our knowledge of early Europe. It may be that the preservation of an environment is necessary for the preservation of an ecosystem and that our destruction of it will also destroy, as a product of a series of interactions, some highly valued aspects of our lives. Finally, it may be necessary to preserve environments in order that the economic development of the adjacent areas can proceed in a desired fashion.

Other reasons for preservation are based on merit: it may be felt by the society that it is good to preserve natural environments. It is good for people to be exposed to nature. Natural beauty is worth having, and the amenity resulting from preservation is important.

RARITY, UNIQUENESS, AND FORGERY: AN ARTISTIC INTERLUDE

The problems encountered in describing the qualities that make for "real" artistic experiences and genuine works of art are similar to those encountered in describing rare natural objects. The ideas of replica and forgery will serve to make the point.

Kubler[2] observes that, if one examines objects in a time sequence, he may decide that some are prime objects and the rest are replicas. Why should this be so? One may look at the properties of earlier objects and note that some of them serve as a source of later objects; however, since the future always has its sources in the present, any given object is a source. Therefore, one must distinguish important characteristics, perhaps arbitrarily, and say that they are seminal. Prime objects are the first to clearly and decisively exhibit important characteristics.

Why are there so few prime objects? By definition, prime objects exhibit characteristics in a clear and decisive way, and this must eliminate many other objects from the category; but why do artists not constantly create new objects, each so original that it would be prime? Not all artists are geniuses, it might be said.

But this is just a restatement of the argument that most objects do not exhibit important characteristics in a clear, decisive manner. It might also be said that, if there are no followers, there will be no leaders, but this does not explain why some eras are filled with prime works and others are not.

Kubler suggests that invention, especially if too frequent, leads to chaos, which is frightening. Replication is calmer and leads only to dullness. Therefore, man would rather repair, replicate what he has done, than innovate and discard the past. We are, perhaps justifiably, afraid of what the prime objects of the future will be. We prefer natural environments to synthesized ones because we are familiar with techniques of managing the natural ones and know what the effects of such management are. Plastic trees are frightening.

What about those replicas of prime objects that are called forgeries? Something is a forgery if its provenance has been faked. Why should this bother us? If the forgery provides us with the same kind of experience we might have had with the original, except that we know it is a forgery, then we are snobbish to demand the original. But we do not like to be called snobs. Rather, we say that our opinion of the work, or the quality of our experience of it, depends on its context. History, social position, and ideology affect the way in which we experience the object. It may be concluded that our appreciation of something is only partly a product of the thing itself.

Art replicas and forgeries exist in an historical framework. So do the prime and genuine objects. And so do natural environments.

CRITERIA FOR PRESERVATION

Whatever argument one uses for preservation, there must be some criteria for deciding what to preserve. Given that something is rare and is believed to be worth preserving, rarity itself, as well as economic, ecological, or socio-historical reasons, can be used to justify preservation. I consider each of these here.

There are many economic reasons for planned intervention to achieve preservation, and I discuss two of them: one concerns the application of cost–benefit analysis to preservation; the other concerns the argument that present value should be determined by future benefits.

The work of Krutilla[3] is an ingenious application of economics; it rescues environments from current use by arguing for their future utility. The crux of the argument follows.

Nature is irreproducible compared to the materials it provides. There have been enough substitutions of natural materials to obviate the idea of a shortage of nature resources. It also seems likely that the value of nature and of experiences in nature will increase in the future, while the supply of natural environments will remain constant. Because it is comparatively easy to produce substitutes for the materials we get from natural environments, the cost of not exploiting an environment is small, compared to the cost of producing that environment. Finally, there is an option demand for environments: that is, there will be a demand, at a certain price, for that environment in the future. If a substantial fraction of the supply of the environment is destroyed now, it will be impossible to fill the demand in the future at a reasonable price. Therefore, we are willing to pay to preserve that option. The problem is not the intertemporal use of natural environments (as it is for natural resources), but the preservation of our options to use environments in the future, or at least the reduction of uncertainty about the availability of environments in the future.

Fisher[4] has applied optimal investment theory, including a possibility of restoring environments to a quasi-natural state, to the problem of preservation as formulated by Krutilla. Krutilla *et al.* have applied an analysis similar to Fisher's to the preservation of Hell's Canyon.[5]

Robinson[6] has criticized Krutilla's argument from the following perspectives: he suggests that the amenity valued so highly by Krutilla is not necessarily that valuable; that the experiences of nature are reproducible; that refraining from current use may be costly; and that the arguments for public intervention into such environments depend on the collective consumption aspects of these environments. That is, these environments benefit everyone, and, since people cannot be differentially charged for using them, the public must pay for these environments collectively, through government. It is well known that the users of

rare environments tend to be that small fraction of the population who are better off socially and economically than the majority. However, a greater difficulty than any of these may be discerned.

It seems to me that the limitations of Krutilla's argument lie in his assumptions about how quickly spoiled environments can be restored (rate of reversion) and how great the supply of environments is. Krutilla *et al.* are sensitive to the possibility that the rate of reversion may well be amenable to technological intervention:

> Perhaps more significant, however, is the need to investigate more fully the presumption of asymmetric implications of technological progress for the value of attributes of the natural environment when used as intermediate goods, compared with their retention as assets supplying final consumption services. Irreproducibility, it might be argued, is not synonymous with irreplaceability. If reasonably good substitutes can be found, by reliance on product development, the argument for the presumption of differential effects of technological progress is weakened; or if not weakened, the value which is selected [for the reversion rate] . . . would not remain unaffected.[7]

The supply of natural environments is affected by technology in that it can manipulate both biological processes and information and significance. The advertising that created rare environments can also create plentiful substitutes. The supply of special environments can be increased dramatically by highlighting (in ways not uncommon to those of differentiating among groups of equivalent toothpastes) significant and rare parts of what are commonly thought to be uninteresting environments.

The accessibility of certain environments to population centers can be altered to create new rare environments. Also, environments that are especially rare, or are created to be especially rare, could be very far away, since people would be willing to pay more to see them. Thus it may be possible to satisfy a large variety of customers for rare environments. The following kind of situation might result.

1) Those individuals who demand "truly" natural environments could be encouraged to fly to some isolated location where a national park with such

an environment is maintained; a substantial sum of money would be required of those who use such parks.

2) For those who find a rare environment in state parks or perhaps in small national parks, such parks could be made more accessible and could be developed more. In this way, a greater number of people could use them and the fee for using them would be less than the fee for using isolated areas.

3) Finally, for those who wish to have an environment that is just some trees, some woods, and some grass, there might be a very small park. Access would be very easy, and the rareness of such environments might well be enhanced beyond what is commonly thought possible by means of sophisticated methods of landscape gardening.

It seems to me that, as Krutilla suggests, the demand for rare environments is a learned one. It also seems likely that conscious public choice can manipulate this learning so that the environments which people learn to use and want reflect environments that are likely to be available at low cost. There is no lack of merit in natural environments, but this merit is not canonical.

THE VALUATION OF THE FUTURE

In any cost–benefit analysis that attempts to include future values, the rate at which the future is discounted is crucial to the analysis. (That is, a sum of money received today is worth more to us now than the same sum received in the future. To allow for this, one discounts, by a certain percent each year, these future payments.) Changes in discount rates can alter the feasibility of a given project. If different clientele's preferences for projects correspond to different discount rates at which these projects are feasible, then the choice of a particular discount rate would place the preferences of one group over another. Preservation yields benefits that come in the future. The rich have a low rate of discount compared to the poor (say, 5 percent as opposed to 10 or 20 percent) and would impute much higher present value to these future benefits than the poor would. Baumol suggests (though it is only a hunch) that:

> by and large, the future can be left to take care of itself. There is no need to lower artificially the social rate of

discount in order to increase further the prospective wealth of future generations. . . . However, this does not mean that the future should in every respect be left at the mercy of the free market. . . . Investment in the preservation of such items then seems perfectly proper, but for this purpose the appropriate instrument would appear to be a set of selective subsidies rather than a low general discount rate that encourages indiscriminately all sorts of investment programs whether or not they are relevant [8]

Baumol is saying that the process of preserving environments may not always be fruitfully analyzed in terms of cost–benefit analyses; we are preserving things in very special cases, and each choice is not a utilitarian choice in any simple sense, but represents a balancing of all other costs to the society of having *no* preserved environments. Preservation often entails a gross change in policy, and utilitarian analyses cannot easily compare choices in which values may be drastically altered.

OTHER CRITERIA

We may decide to preserve things just because they are rare. In that case, we need to know which things are rarer than others. Leopold has tried to do this for a set of natural environments.[9] He listed a large number of attributes for each environment and then weighted each attribute as follows. For any single attribute, determine how many environments share that attribute and assign each of them a value of $1/N$ units, where N is the number of environments that share an attribute. Then add all the weights for the environments; the environment with the largest weight is the rarest. It is clear that, if an environment has attributes which are unique, it will get one unit of weight for each attribute and thus its total weight will just equal the number of attributes. If all of the environments are about the same, then each of them will have roughly the same weight, which will equal the number of attributes divided by the number of environments. The procedure is sensitive to how differentiated we wish to make our attributes and to the attributes we choose. It is straightforward and usable, as Leopold has shown.

It seems to me that there are two major difficulties in this approach. The first, and more important, is that the accessibility of environments to their clientele, which Leopold treats as one of his 34 attributes, needs to be further emphasized in deciding what to preserve. An environment that is quite rare but essentially inaccessible may not be as worthy of preservation as one that is fairly common but quite accessible. The other difficulty is that probably the quantity that should be used is the amount of information possessed by each environment—rather than taking $1/N$, one should take a function of its logarithm to the base 2.

An ecological argument is that environments which contribute to our stability and survival as an ecosystem should be preserved. It is quite difficult to define what survival means, however. If it means the continued existence of man in an environment quite similar to the one he lives in now, then survival is likely to become very difficult as we use part of our environment for the maintenance of life and as new technologies come to the fore. If survival means the maintenance of a healthy and rich culture, then ecology can only partially guide us in the choices, since technology has substantially changed the risk from catastrophe in the natural world. Our complex political and social organizations may serve to develop means for survival and stability sufficient to save man from the catastrophic tricks of his own technology.

If a taxonomy of environments were established, a few environments might stand out from all the rest. But what would be the criteria involved in such a taxonomy?

Another possibility is to search for relics of cultural, historical, and social significance to the nation. Such physical artifacts are preserved because the experiences they represent affect the nature of the present society. In this sense, forests are preserved to recall a frontier, and historic homes are preserved to recall the individuals who inhabited them. Of course the problem here is that there is no simple way of ordering the importance of relics and their referents. Perhaps a survey of a large number of people might enable one to assign priorities to these relics.

Finally, it might be suggested that preservation should only be used, or could sometimes be used, to serve the interests of social justice. Rather than preserving things for what they are or for the experiences they provide, we preserve them as monuments to people who deserve commemoration or as a means

of redistributing wealth (when an environment is designated as rare, local values are affected). Rather than buy forests and preserve them, perhaps we should preserve slums and suitably reward their inhabitants.

All of these criteria are problematic. Whichever ones are chosen, priorities for intervention must still be developed.

PRIORITIES FOR PRESERVING THE ENVIRONMENT

Not every problem in environmental quality is urgent, nor does every undesirable condition that exists need to be improved. We need to classify environmental problems in order that we can choose from among the possible improvements.

1) There are conditions about which we must do something soon or we will lose a special thing. These conditions pertain especially to rare environments, environments we wish to preserve for their special beauty or their uniqueness. We might allocate a fixed amount of money every year to such urgent problems. Niagara Falls might be one of these, and it might cost a fraction of a dollar per family to keep it in good repair. Wilderness and monument maintenance have direct costs of a few dollars per family per year.

2) There are situations in which conditions are poor, but fairly stable. In such situations, it might be possible to handle the problem in 10 years without too much loss. However, the losses to society resulting from the delayed improvement of these facilities need to be carefully computed. For example, the eutrophied Lake Erie might be such a project. There, society loses fishing and recreational facilities. It might cost $100 per family, locally, to clean up the lake. Perhaps our environmental dollar should be spent elsewhere.

3) There are also situations in which conditions are rapidly deteriorating and in which a small injection of environmental improvement and amelioration would cause dramatic changes in a trend. Smog control devices have probably raised the cost of driving by 2 or 3 percent, yet their contribution to the relative improvement of the environment in certain areas (for example, Los Angeles) has been

substantial. Fifty dollars per car per year is the estimated current cost to the car owner.

4) There may be situations in which large infusions of money are needed to stop a change. These problems are especially irksome. Perhaps the best response to them would be to change the system of production sufficiently that we can avoid such costs in the future. The costs of such change, one-time costs we hope, may be much smaller than the long-term costs of the problems themselves, although this need not be the case. The development of cleaner industrial processes is a case in point.

This is not an all-inclusive or especially inventive classification of problems, but I have devised it to suggest that many of the "urgent" problems are not so urgent.

Rare environments pose special problems and may require an approach different from that required by other environments. A poor nation is unlikely to destroy very much of its special environments. It lacks the technical and economic power to do so. It may certainly perform minor miracles of destruction through a series of small decisions or in single, major projects. These latter are often done with the aid of rich countries.

The industrialized, but not wealthy, nations have wreaked havoc with their environments in their efforts to gain some degree of wealth. It is interesting that they are willing to caution the poor nations against such a course, even though it may be a very rapid way of developing. At the U.N. Conference on the Environment this year, the poor nations indicated their awareness of these problems and their desire to develop without such havoc.

The rich nations can afford to have environments that are rare and consciously preserved. These environments are comparable to the temples of old, in that these environments will be relics of *our* time, yet this is no criterion for deciding how much should be spent on "temple building." The amount of money needed is only a small proportion of a rich country's wealth (as opposed to the cost of churches in medieval times).

Politically, the situation is complicated. There are many small groups in this country for whom certain environments are highly significant. The problem for each group is to somehow get its piece of turf, preferably uncut, unrenewed, or untouched. It seems likely that the ultimate determinant of which environments are preserved will be a process of political trade-off, in which some environments are preserved for some groups and other environments for others. Natural environments are likely to be viewed in a continuum with a large number of other environments that are especially valued by some subgroup of the society. In this sense, environmental issues will become continuous with a number of other special interests and will no longer be seen as a part of a "whole earth" movement. The power of the intellectuals, in the media, and even in union bureaucracies, with their upper middle class preferences for nature, suggests that special interest groups who are advocates for the poor and working classes will have to be wary of their own staffs.

Projects might be ranked in importance on the basis of the net benefits they provide a particular group. Marglin has suggested a means by which income redistribution could be explicitly included in cost–benefit calculations for environmental programs.[10] If one wishes to take efficiency into account, costs minus benefits could be minimized with a constraint relating to income redistribution. This is not a simple task, however, because pricing some commodities at zero dollars, seemingly the best way of attempting a redistribution of income, may not be politically desirable or feasible. As Clawson and Knetsch have pointed out, we have to be sure that in making some prices low we do not make others prohibitively high and thereby deny the persons who are to benefit access to the low-priced goods.[11] In any case, Marglin shows that the degree to which income is redistributed will depend on how the same amount of money might have been spent in alternative activities (marginal opportunity cost). This parallels Kneese and Bower's view that the level of pollution we tolerate, or is "optimal," is that at which the marginal benefits of increasing pollution are balanced by the marginal costs of abatement measures.[12]

In doing these cost–benefit calculations, one must consider the value of 10 years of clean lake (if we can clean up the lake now) versus 10 years of uneducated man (if we wait 10 years for a manpower training program). According to Freeman:

> equity characteristics of projects *within* broad classifications ... will be roughly similar. If this surmise is correct, then the ranking of projects within these

classes is not likely to be significantly affected by equity considerations. On the other hand, we would expect more marked differences in distribution patterns among classes of projects, e.g., rural recreation vs. urban air quality.[13]

He goes on to point out that it is unlikely that such seemingly incommensurable kinds of projects will be compared with respect to equity. I suspect that it is still possible to affect specific groups in the design of a given project; furthermore, equity can be taken into consideration more concretely at this level. Careful disaggregation, in measuring effects and benefits, will be needed to ensure that minorities are properly represented.

AN ETHICAL QUESTION

I still feel quite uncomfortable with what I have said here. I have tried to show that the utilitarian and manipulative rationality inherited from the conservationist movement and currently embodied in economic analyses and modes of argument can be helpful in deciding questions of preservation and rarity. By manipulating attitudes, we have levers for intervening into what is ordinarily considered fixed and uncontrollable. But to what end?

Our ability to manipulate preferences and values tends to lead to systems that make no sense. For example, an electrical utility encourages its customers to use more electricity, and the customers proceed to do so. As a result, there are power shortages. Similarly, if we allocate resources now in order to preserve environments for future generations, their preferences for environments may be altered by this action, and there may be larger shortages.

I also fear that my own proposals might get out of hand. My purpose in proposing interventions is not to preserve man's opportunity to experience nature, although this is important, but to promote social justice. I believe that this concern should guide our attempts to manipulate, trade off, and control environments. A summum bonum of preserving trees has no place in an ethic of social justice. If I took this ethic seriously, I could not argue the relative merits of schemes to manipulate environments. I would argue that the ecology movement is wrong and would not answer its question about what we are going to do about the earth—I would be worried about what we are going to do about men.

CONCLUSION

With some ingenuity, a transformation of our attitudes toward preservation of the environment will take place fairly soon. We will recognize the symbolic and social meanings of environments, not just their economic utility; we will emphasize their historical significance as well as the future generations that will use them.

At the same time, we must realize that there are things we may not want to trade at all, except in the sense of letting someone else have his share of the environment also. As environments become more differentiated, smaller areas will probably be given greater significance, and it may be possible for more groups to have a share.

It is likely that we shall want to apply our technology to the creation of artificial environments. It may be possible to create environments that are evocative of other environments in other times and places. It is possible that, by manipulating memory through the rewriting of history, environments will come to have new meaning. Finally, we may want to create proxy environments by means of substitution and simulation. In order to create substitutes, we must endow new objects with significance by means of advertising and by social practice. Sophistication about differentiation will become very important for appreciating the substitute environments. We may simulate the environment by means of photographs, recordings, models, and perhaps even manipulations in the brain. What we experience in natural environments may actually be more controllable than we imagine. Artificial prairies and wildernesses have been created, and there is no reason to believe that these artificial environments need be unsatisfactory for those who experience them.

Rare environments are relative, can be created, are dependent on our knowledge, and are a function of policy, not only tradition. It seems likely that economic arguments will not be sufficient to preserve environments or to suggest how we can create new ones. Rather, conscious choice about what matters, and then a financial and social investment in an effort to create significant experiences and environments will become a policy alternative available to us.

What's wrong with plastic trees? My guess is that there is very little wrong with them. Much more can be done with plastic trees and the like to give most people the feeling that they are experiencing nature. We will have to realize that the way in which we experience nature is conditioned by our society—which more and more is seen to be receptive to responsible interventions.

NOTES

1. R. Meier, *J. Amer. Inst. Plann.* **37**, 211, 1971.
2. G. Kubler, *The Shape of Time* (New Haven: Yale Univ. Press, 1962).
3. J. Krutilla, *Amer. Econ. Rev.* **57**, 777, 1967.
4. A. Fisher, "The optimum uses of natural areas." (Xeroxed, Brown Univ., Providence, R.I.)
5. J. V. Krutilla, C. M. Clechetti, A. M. Freeman III, C. S. Russell, in *Environmental Quality Analysis*, A. V. Kneese and B. T. Bowers, Eds, (Baltimore: Johns Hopkins Press, 1972). See pp. 69–112.
6. W. Robinson, *Land Econ.* **45**, 453, 1969.
7. Krutilla *et al.*, *Environmental Quality Analysis*, pp. 69–112.
8. W. Baumol, *Amer. Econ. Rev.* **58**, 788, 1968.
9. L. Leopold, *Nat. Hist.* **78**, (4), p. 36 October 1969; L. Leopold and M. O. Marchand, *Water Resour. Res.* **4**, 709, 1968.
10. S. A. Marglin, in *Design of Water-Resource Systems*, A. Maass, M. M. Hufschmidt, R. Dorfman, H. A. Thomas, Jr., S. A. Marglin, G. M. Fair, Eds. Harvard Univ. Press, Cambridge, Mass., 1962 pp. 159–225; *Public Investment Criteria* M.I.T. Press, Cambridge, Mass., 1967.
11. M. Clawson and J. Knetsch, *Economics of Outdoor Recreation*. Johns Hopkins Press, Baltimore, 1966.
12. A. Kneese & B. Bower, *Managing Water Quality: Economics, Technology & Institutions*. John Hopkins, Baltimore, 1968.
13. A. Freeman III, in *Environmental Quality Analysis*. Johns Hopkins Press, Baltimore, 972, pp. 243–278.

ERIC KATZ

THE CALL OF THE WILD
The Struggle against Domination and the Technological Fix of Nature

In this essay, I use encounters with the white-tailed deer of Fire Island to explore the "call of the wild"— the *attraction to value* that exists in a natural world outside of human control. Value exists in nature to the extent that it avoids modification by human technology. Technology "fixes" the natural world by improving it for human use or by restoring degraded ecosystems. Technology creates a "new world," an artifactual reality that is far removed from the "wildness" of nature. The technological "fix" of nature thus raises a moral issue: how is an artifact morally different from a natural and wild entity? Artifacts are human instruments; their value lies in their ability to meet human needs. Natural entities have no intrinsic functions; they were not created for any instrumental purpose. To attempt to manage natural entities is to deny

Katz, Eric. 1992. The Call of the Wild. Environmental Ethics, 14: 265–273. Reprinted with permission of the author and the journal.

their inherent autonomy: a form of domination. The moral claim of the wilderness is thus a claim against human technological domination. We have an obligation to struggle against this domination by preserving as much of the natural world as possible.

I.

During the summer I live with my family on Fire Island, a barrier beach off the coast of Long Island. Most mornings, if I wake up early, I can look out my window and watch white-tailed deer munching their breakfast of flowers and leaves from the trees surrounding my house. The deer are rather tame; they have become accustomed to the transient human population that invades the island each summer. A few years ago, if they had heard me walking onto the deck, they would have jumped and run off into the thicker underbrush. Now, if they hear me, they might look up to see if I have a carrot; more likely still, they will simply ignore me and continue foraging. My experiences with these deer are the closest encounters I have with what I like to call the "wild."

Using the adjective *wild* to describe these deer is obviously a distortion of terminology. These are animals that live in and around a fairly dense human community; they consume, much to the dismay of many residents, the cultivated gardens of flowers and vegetables; they seek handouts from passing humans—my daughters often feed them breadsticks and pretzels. Yet, seeing them is different than my experience with any other animal, surely different than seeing white-tailed deer in the zoo, on a petting farm, or in a nature documentary film on television. The mornings when I find them in my yard are something special. If I walk close to one, unaware, at night, my heart beats faster. These animals are my connection to "wild nature." Despite their acceptance of the human presence, they embody something untouched and beyond humanity. They are a deep and forceful *symbol* of the wild "other." The world—my world—would be a poorer place if they were not there.

In this essay, I explore this "call of the wild"—our *attraction to value* that exists in a natural world outside of human control. To understand this value, we must understand the relationship between technology and the natural world, the ways in which humanity attempts to "fix" and mold nature to suit human purposes. Thomas

Birch has described this project as the "control of otherness,"[1] a form of domination that includes the control of nature and all such outsiders of human society. Here I bring together several ideas about the philosophy of technology and the nature of artifacts, and combine them with themes raised by Birch. I argue that value exists in nature to the extent it avoids the domination of human technological practice. Technology can satisfy human wants by creating the artifactual products we desire, but it cannot supply, replace, or restore the "wild."

II.

One promise of the technological enterprise is the creation of "new worlds." This optimistic view of the ability of technology to improve the human condition is based on the belief that humanity has the power to alter the physical structure of the world. Consider the words of Emmanuel Mesthene:

> We . . . have enough . . . power actually at hand to create new possibilities almost at will. By massive physical changes deliberately induced, we can literally pry new alternatives out of nature. The ancient tyranny of matter has been broken, and we know it. . . . We can change it and shape it to suit our purposes.[2]

No longer limited by the physical necessities of the "given" natural world, our technological power enables us to create a new world of our dreams and desires. Nature can be controlled; its limitations overcome; humanity can achieve its highest potential. For Mesthene, "our technical prowess literally bursts with the promise of new freedom, enhanced human dignity, and unfettered aspiration."[3]

I admit to being mesmerized by the resonances of meaning in the concept of the "new world." The technological promise of a new dignity and freedom, a limitless opportunity, an unchained power, sounds suspiciously like the promise envisioned in the new political and social conditions of the New World of the European discovery, our homeland, the Americas. But the "new world" of the European discovery was not, in fact, a *new* world; indeed, it was a very *old* world, the world of a wild untamed nature, with a minimal human presence that was itself quite old. The freedom, dignity, and benefits of the new human population were achieved, to some degree, at the expense of the older natural world. For the new world to be useful to humanity, it had to be developed and cultivated.[4] The New World had to cease being wild.[5]

The comparison between the taming of the American wilderness and the technological control of brute physical matter is disturbing. I do not believe that the technological control of nature is a desirable end of human activity. The control of nature is a dream, an illusion, a hallucination. It involves the replacement of the wild natural environment with a human artifactual environment. It creates a fundamental change in the value of the world. This change in value, in turn, forces a reexamination of the ethical relationship between humanity and the natural environment.

III.

It is a commonplace to refer to the improvements of technology as a "technological fix." It is supposed that the advanced technology of the contemporary world can "fix" nature. The term *fix* is used here in two complementary ways: it implies either that something is broken or that it can be improved. Thus, the technological fix of nature means that natural processes can be "improved" to maximize human satisfaction and good; alternatively, damage to the environment can be repaired by the technological reconstruction of degraded ecological systems. Humans use nature to create benefits for humanity, and we can restore natural environments after they have been damaged by use. The only new aspect of this technological activity is its increased scope and power. The practical control of natural processes has increased to such an extent that we no longer acknowledge the impossibility of doing anything; nature can be improved and restored to any extent that we wish.

Both processes—the improvement-use and the restoration of nature—lead to serious questions about value and moral obligation. The idea that nature ought to be used (and improved, if necessary) for human benefit is the fundamental assumption of "resource environmentalism"—arguably the mainstream of the American conservation movement. Under this doctrine, environmental policies are designed to maximize human satisfactions or minimize human harms. The pollution of the atmosphere is a problem because of the health hazards to human beings. The extinction of a species is a problem because the extinct species

may be useful to humans, or the resulting instability in the ecosystem may be harmful. The greenhouse effect is a problem because the changes in climate may have dramatic impacts on agriculture and coastal geography. With all environmental problems, the effects on humanity are the primary concern.[6]

These "human interest" resource arguments for environmental protection have been criticized by thinkers in several disciplines concerned with environmental philosophy and environmental ethics. A full inventory of the arguments against so-called "anthropocentric" environmental ethics is clearly beyond the scope of this discussion.[7] Here I focus on one particular implication of the anthropocentric resource view, i.e., the creation of an artificial world that more adequately meets the demands of human welfare. As Martin Krieger has written:

> Artificial prairies and wildernesses have been created, and there is no reason to believe that these artificial environments need be unsatisfactory for those who experience them. . . . What's wrong with plastic trees? My guess is that there is very little wrong with them. Much more can be done with plastic trees and the like to give most people the feeling that they are experiencing nature.[8]

Krieger thus argues for "responsible interventions" to manage, manipulate, and control natural environments for the promotion of human good. "A summum bonum of preserving trees has no place in an ethic of social justice."[9] Because human social justice, the production and distribution of human goods, is the primary policy goal, the manipulation of natural processes and the creation of artificial environments is an acceptable (and probably required) human activity.

Krieger's vision of a "user-friendly" plasticized human environment is chilling; it is not a world view that has many advocates. Nevertheless, the point of his argument is that a primary concern for the human uses of the natural environment leads inevitably to a policy of human intervention and manipulation in nature, and the subsequent creation of artificial environments. If humanity is planning to "fix" the natural environment, to use it and improve it to meet human needs, wants, and interests, the conclusion of the process is a technologically created "new" world of our own design. "Wild" nature will no longer exist, merely the controlled nature that offers pleasant experiences.

The restoration of nature, the policy of repairing damaged ecosystems and habitats, leads to similar results. The central issue is the *value* of the restored environments. If a restored environment is an adequate replacement for the previously existing natural environment, then humans can use, degrade, destroy, and replace natural entities and habitats with no moral consequences whatsoever. The value in the original natural entity does not require preservation.

The value of the restored environment, however, is questionable. Robert Elliot has argued that even a technologically perfect reproduction of a natural area is not equivalent to the original.[10] Elliot uses the analogy of an art forgery, in which even a perfect copy loses the value of the original artwork. What is missing in the forgery is the causal history of the original, the fact that a particular human artist created a specific work in a specific historical period. Although the copy may be as superficially pleasing as the original, the knowledge that it is not the work created by the artist distorts and disvalues our experience. Similarly, we value a natural area because of its "special kind of continuity with the past." This history, Eugene Hargrove argues, provides the authenticity of nature. He writes: "Nature is not simply a collection of natural objects; it is a process that progressively transforms those objects. . . . When we admire nature, we also admire that history."[11] Thus, a restored nature is a fake nature; it is an artificial human creation, not the product of a historical natural process.

The technological "fix" of repairing a damaged and degraded nature is an illusion and a falsehood; elsewhere, I have called it "the big lie."[12] As with all technology, the product of nature restoration is a human artifact, not the end result of a historically based natural process. Artifacts, of course, can have positive or negative value. However, what makes the value in the artifactually restored natural environment questionable is its ostensible claim to be the original.

Both forms of technological intervention in the natural world thus lead to the same result: the establishment of an artifactual world rather than a natural one. When our policy is to use nature to our best advantage, we end up with a series of so-called "responsible interventions" that manipulate natural processes to create the most pleasant human experiences possible. When our policy is to restore and repair a degraded natural environment, we end up with an unauthentic copy of the original. The technological "fix" of nature merely produces artifacts for the satisfaction of human interests.

IV.

The issue of *value* now has a sharper focus. We can ask, "What is the value of artifacts and what are the moral obligations that derive from that value?" More precisely, "How is the value of the artifacts, and the derivative moral obligations, different from the value and moral obligations concerning 'wild' nature?" Framed in this manner, the answer to the problem is clear: artifacts differ from natural entities in their anthropocentric and instrumental origins. Artifacts are products of the larger human project of the domination of the natural world.

The concepts of function and purpose are central to an understanding of artifacts.[13] Artifacts, unlike natural objects, are created for a specific purpose. They are essentially anthropocentric instruments, tools or objects, that serve a function in human life. The existence of artifacts is centered on human life. It is impossible to imagine an artifact that is not designed to meet a human purpose, for without a foreseen use the object would not have been created.

The anthropocentric instrumentality of artifacts is completely different from the essential characteristics of natural entities, species, and ecosystems. Living natural entities and systems of entities evolve to fill ecological niches in the biosphere; they are not designed to meet human needs or interests. Andrew Brennan thus argues that natural entities have no "intrinsic functions": they are not created for a particular purpose; they have no set manner of use. We may speak as if natural individuals (e.g., predators) have roles to play in ecosystemic wellbeing (the maintenance of optimum population levels), but this talk is either metaphorical or fallacious. No one created or designed the mountain lion as a regulator of the deer population.[14]

From a moral point of view, the difference between purposely designed artifacts and evolving natural entities is not generally problematic. The anthropocentric instrumentality of artifacts is not a serious moral concern, for most artifacts are designed for use in human social and cultural contexts. Nevertheless, the human intervention into "wild" nature is a different process entirely. Hargrove notes how human intervention alters the aesthetic evaluation of nature: "To attempt to manipulate nature, even for aesthetic reasons, alters nature adversely from an aesthetic standpoint. Historically, manipulation of nature, even to improve it, has been considered subjugation or domination."[15] This domination resulting from human intervention can be generalized beyond aesthetic valuations; it leads to more than just a loss of beauty. The management of nature results in the imposition of our anthropocentric purposes on areas that exist outside human society. We intervene in nature to create so-called natural objects and environments based on models of human desires, interests, and satisfactions. In doing so, we engage in the project of the human domination of nature: the reconstruction of the natural world in our own image, to suit our purposes.

Need we ask why domination is a moral issue? In the context of human social and political thought, domination is the evil that restricts, denies, or distorts individual (and social) freedom and autonomy. In the context of environmental philosophy, domination is the anthropocentric alteration of natural processes. The entities and systems that comprise nature are not permitted to be free, to pursue their own independent and unplanned course of development. Even Hargrove, who emphasizes the aesthetic value of nature, judges this loss of freedom the crucial evil of domination: it "reduces [nature's] ability to be creative."[16] Wherever it exists, in nature or in human culture, the process of domination attacks the preeminent value of self-realization.

Is the analysis of domination appropriate here? Does it make sense to say that we can deny the autonomy, the self-realization, of natural nonhuman entities? The central assumption of this analysis is that natural entities and systems have a value in their own right, a value that transcends the instrumentality of human concerns, projects, and interests. Nature is not merely the physical matter that is the *object* of technological practice and alteration; it is also a *subject*, with its own process and history of development independent of human intervention and activity. Nature thus has a value that can be subverted and destroyed by the process of human domination. In this way, human domination, alteration, and management are issues of moral concern.

V.

But does the "wild" have a moral claim on humanity? The answer to this question determines the moral status of the human domination of nature. Does the wilderness, the world of nature untouched by the technological alteration of humanity, possess a moral value worth preserving? Is the creation of a technological "new world" morally harmful? Does it destroy the value of the original New World of the European discovery of American, the untamed and "wild" wilderness? How do we discern a method for answering these questions?

It is at this point that my thoughts return to my encounters with the white-tailed deer on Fire Island. They are not truly wild, for they are no longer afraid of the human presence on the island. They seem to realize that the summer residents are not hunters. These humans come with pretzels, not rifles. Nevertheless, there are some human residents who are deeply disturbed by the existence of the deer. The deer carry ticks that are part of the life cycle of Lyme disease. They eat the flowers and vegetables of well-tended gardens. They are unpredictable, and they can knock a person down. A considerable portion of the human community thus wants the deer hunted and removed from the island.

Just the thought of losing these deer disturbs me—and until recently I did not understand why. In my lucid rational moments, I realize that they are not "wild," that they have prospered on Fire Island due to an unnatural absence of predators; their population could be decreased with no appreciable harm to the herd or the remaining natural ecosystem of the barrier beach. Nevertheless, they are the vestiges of a truly wild natural community; they are reminders that the forces of domination and subjugation do not always succeed.

Birch describes the process of wilderness preservation as "incarceration" by "the technological imperium"— i.e., by the primary social–political force of the contemporary world.[17] The entire process of creating and maintaining wilderness reservations by human law is contradictory, for the wildness is destroyed by the power of the human–technological system:

> Wilderness reservations are not meant to be voids in the fabric of domination where "anarchy" is permitted, where nature is actually liberated. Not at all. The rule of law is presupposed as supreme. Just as

wilderness reservations are created by law, so too they can be abolished by law. The threat of annihilation is always maintained.[18]

The domination of natural wildness is just one example of the system of power. "The whole point, purpose, and meaning of imperial power, and its most basic legitimation, is to give humans control over otherness."[19]

It is here that Birch sees the contradiction in the imperial technological domination of wild nature. "The wildness is still there, and it is still wild," and it maintains its own integrity.[20] The wildness, the otherness of nature, remains, I suggest, because the forces of the imperial power require its existence. If there is no "other" recognized as the victim of domination, then the power of the imperium is empty. There would be nothing upon which to exercise power. But maintaining the existence of the wild other, even in the diminished capacity of wilderness reservations managed by the government, lays the seeds for the subversion of the imperial domination of technology.

Birch thus recommends that we view wilderness, wherever it can be found, as a "sacred space" acting as "an implacable counterforce to the momentum of totalizing power." Wilderness appears anywhere: "old roadbeds, wild plots in suburban yards, flower boxes in urban windows, cracks in the pavement. . . ."[21] And it appears, in my life, in the presence of the white-tailed deer of Fire Island. My commitment to the preservation of the deer in my community is part of my resistance to the total domination of the technological world.

This resistance is based on yet a deeper moral commitment: the deer themselves are members of my moral and natural community. The deer and I are partners in the continuous struggle for the preservation of autonomy, freedom, and integrity. This shared partnership creates obligations on the part of humanity for the preservation and protection of the natural world. This is the *call of the wild*—the moral claim of the natural world.

We are all impressed by the power and breadth of human technological achievements. Why is it not possible to extend this power further, until we control and dominate the entire natural universe? This insidious dream of domination can only end by respecting freedom and self-determination, wherever it exists, and by recognizing the true extent of the moral community in the natural world.

NOTES

1. Thomas H. Birch, "The Incarceration of Wildness: Wilderness Areas as Prisons," *Environmental Ethics* 12 (1990): 18.
2. Emmanuel G. Mesthene, "Technology and Wisdom," *Philosophy and Technology: Readings in the Philosophical Problems of Technology*, ed. Carl Mitcham and Robert Mackey (New York: Free Press, 1983), p. 110.
3. Mesthenem, "Technology and Wisdom," p. 111.
4. One of the best examples of this attitude from a historical source contemporaneous with the period of European expansion is the discussion of property by John Locke, *Second Treatise on Government*, chap. 5, especially, secs. 40–43. Locke specifically mentions the lack of value in American land because of the absence of labor and cultivation.
5. For my purposes, it is irrelevant to raise the question, whether North America ever really was wild. It existed then, and now, as a *symbol* of nature uncontrolled by human civilization. Of course, it may have been altered and modified through fire and hunting by Native American populations. Such practices, however, do not change its *significance* as wild and untamed. . . .
6. There are sound political and motivational reasons for arguments that outline the threat to human interests caused by environmental degradation. These arguments have been the rallying cry of popular conservationists from Rachel Carson, *Silent Spring* (New York: Houghton Mifflin, 1962), to Barry Commoner, *The Closing Circle: Nature, Man, and Technology* (New York: Knopf, 1971), to Bill McKibben, *The End of Nature* (New York: Random House, 1989). My philosophical criticisms of these views do not diminish my respect for the positive social and political changes these works have inspired.
7. A complete listing of the relevant literature is impossible. One of the best early works is David Ehrenfeld, *The Arrogance of Humanism* (New York: Oxford University Press, 1978). Other major representative works of nonanthropocentric strands in environmental ethics are Holmes Rolston, III,

Environmental Ethics: Duties to and Values in the Natural World (Philadelphia: Temple University Press, 1988), J. Baird Callicott, *In Defense of the Land Ethic* (Albany: SUNY Press, 1989), Paul Taylor, *Respect for Nature: A Theory of Environmental Ethics* (Princeton: Princeton University Press, 1986), Arne Naess, *Ecology, Community and Lifestyle*, trans. and ed. David Rothenberg (Cambridge: Cambridge University Press, 1989). For a discussion of enlightened anthropocentric views, see Bryan G. Norton, *Why Preserve Natural Variety?* (Princeton: Princeton University Press, 1987), Eugene C. Hargrove, *The Foundations of Environmental Ethics* (Englewood Cliffs: Prentice Hall, 1989), and Mark Sagoff, *The Economy of the Earth: Philosophy, Law, and the Environment* (Cambridge: Cambridge University Press, 1988).

8. Martin H. Krieger, "What's Wrong with Plastic Trees?" *Science* 179 (1973): 453.

9. Krieger, "What's Wrong with Plastic Trees?" p. 453.

10. Robert Elliot, "Faking Nature," *Inquiry* 25 (1982): 81–93, specifically, p. 86.

11. Hargrove, *The Foundations of Environmental Ethics*, p. 195.

12. Eric Katz, "The Big Lie: Human Restoration of Nature," *Research in Philosophy and Technology*, 12 (1992): 231–41.

13. The argument of this section is based on Katz, "The Big Lie." See also Michael Losonsky, "The Nature of Artifacts," *Philosophy* 65 (1990): 81–88.

14. Andrew Brennan, "The Moral Standing of Natural Objects," *Environmental Ethics* 6 (1984): 41–44.

15. Hargrove, *The Foundations of Environmental Ethics*, p. 195.

16. Hargrove, *The Foundations*.

17. Birch, "The Incarceration of Wildness," p. 10.

18. Birch, "The Incarceration of Wildness," p. 10.

19. Birch, "The Incarceration of Wildness," p. 18.

20. Birch, "The Incarceration of Wildness," pp. 21–22.

21. Birch, "The Incarceration of Wildness," pp. 24–25.

DAVID PITCHER AND JENNIFER WELCHMAN

CAN AN ENVIRONMENTAL PARADISE BE REGAINED?
The Hetch Hetchy Valley Question

Dam Hetch Hetchy! As well dam for water-tanks the people's cathedrals and churches, for no holier temple has ever been consecrated by the heart of man.

—John Muir, 1912

With support from a dedicated public, imagination and a willingness on the part of officials to work together, perhaps an American paradise can be regained.

—*Environmental Defense, 2004*[1]

With the passage of the 1913 Raker Act, John Muir and the Sierra Club lost their seven-year battle with the city and county of San Francisco over the fate of Hetch Hetchy Valley, a three-mile long, glacier carved valley on the Tuolumne River in Yosemite National Park. The Raker Act gave San Francisco permission to turn the valley into a reservoir.[2] Construction of the dam began in 1914. Muir died the same year, "his death hastened by his grief at this unbelievable calamity,"[3] the drowning of a valley Muir once described as "one of Nature's rarest and most precious mountain temples."[4]

Hetch Hetchy Valley had been occupied by Native American groups long before its discovery by Europeans in the mid-nineteenth century.[5] The earliest known non-native people to enter the valley were Joseph and Nathan Screech, two of the many "49ers" who had come to California to prospect for gold.[6] The Screech brothers explored the valley in 1850, naming it "Hetch Hetchy Valley" after *hatchatchie*, a Native American word for an edible grass they found growing there. Word of the valley's open meadows spread. By 1860s, the native inhabitants had largely been displaced by sheep herders seeking summer grazing for their flocks. John Muir first visited the valley in 1871 and was struck by its beauty. He wrote ecstatically about "this wonderful valley" with its "rocks and waterfalls, meadows and groves, of Yosemite size and kind, and grouped in Yosemite style."[7] "How perfectly would the pure soul of Thoreau have mingled with those glorious trees," he continued, assuring his readers that "it certainly is worth while riding a few miles out of a direct course to assure one's self that the world is so rich as to possess at least two Yosemites instead of one."[8] To protect Hetch Hetchy from further development, Muir campaigned successfully for inclusion of the valley within the boundaries of the new Yosemite National Park, established in 1890. Not long afterwards, however, the city of San Francisco asked the federal government for permission to use Hetch Hetchy as a reservoir. Muir and colleagues in the recently founded Sierra Club were initially able to persuade the federal government to reject the request. But after a 1906 earthquake triggered a devastating fire that leveled the city, San Francisco's appeals to be allowed to build a reservoir in Hetch Hetchy garnered new sympathy. Muir and other preservationists continued their opposition but only succeeded in delaying the drowning of the valley. After construction on the O'Shaughnessy dam was completed in 1923, the dam began supplying water and hydroelectric power to San Francisco. Hetch Hetchy's fate seemed to have been settled.

However, dams like the O'Shaughnessy require frequent and expensive maintenance. By the 1980s, the projected costs of maintenance and repair to keep the dam functioning into the next century were growing so high as to raise questions about whether the returns on such an investment would recover the costs. It appeared that the dam was becoming obsolete. Other dams and reservoirs built in the intervening years, if expanded, might replace the bulk of the water stored in the Hetch Hetchy reservoir. Were new water conservation measures adopted to make up the shortfall, it seemed possible that the dam might be decommissioned without substantial cost to the city's water supply. Moreover, the dam's contributions to the city's and state's hydroelectric supplies were of minimal and decreasing significance. Some estimates put the reservoir's overall contribution to the California's total electrical supply at no more than 0.2%.[9] In 1987, the Secretary of the Interior Department, Donald Hodel, proposed study of deconstruction of the dam and the draining of Hetch Hetchy valley.[10] A 1988 National Park Service report concluded that if drained, reclamation of the valley as a wilderness recreation area was feasible.[11]

Hodel's proposal was greeted enthusiastically by environmental groups such as the Sierra club, the Environmental Defense Fund, and a new organization, Restore Hetch Hetchy, which began lobbying the state to undertake a comprehensive feasibility study of removing the dam and restoring the valley. In 2006, the State of California Resources Agency released a preliminary review which affirmed that "[i]t does appear technically feasible to restore the Hetch Hetchy Valley," but concluded that it was not yet possible to "to evaluate its financial feasibility."[12] This was because:

> There are major gaps in vital information. For example, objectives for replacing the water supply for the Bay Area, dam removal methods and impacts, and considerations of the public use and benefit of a restored Valley remain largely undefined. Another critical, missing element is a formal public involvement process to engage agencies, Native American tribes, stakeholders and other interested parties in this issue.[13]

Among the gaps in the information vital for comprehensive cost–benefit accounting identified by the report was public agreement on just what the objective of the project should be. In other words, the report threw the ball back into the public's court. Precisely what objective was the state to try to achieve on behalf of its citizens? Should the state's objective be reclamation of Hetch Hetchy as public land for recreation, restoration of the valley to the "pristine" wilderness condition in which Screech brothers found it in 1850, or a "rewilded" valley in which natural forces would once again determine the valley's natural features.

North American policy documents and regulations typically understand *reclamation* of a disturbed landscape as "repurposing" its development in such a way as to ensure that its value after reclamation is equivalent to its value prior to disturbance. For example, reclamation of lands disturbed by mining or industrial development is often directed to recovery of its value for earlier uses, such as agriculture, housing, or recreation. However, the ultimate goal in reclamation is simply to achieve equivalent use value, not to restore the entities or processes that constituted the landscape prior to its disturbance. Prior to being dammed, Hetch Hetchy Valley's flora and fauna were harvested by Native Americans; its meadows later provided grazing for domesticated sheep, and later still the valley became an aesthetic and recreational resource for nature lovers, artists, and wilderness tourists. If we chose to focus upon the most recent of these prior uses, reclamation would mean repurposing the valley as a wilderness park with recreational and related use values equivalent to, but not necessarily identical with, those the valley possessed prior to 1914. But committing ourselves to reclaiming Hetch Hetchy would not constrain us to choosing this objective. Redeveloping the valley for sheep grazing or for subsistence hunting and harvesting by the Native groups who formerly inhabited the region would be equally legitimate objectives for reclamation.

Among proponents of draining the valley, the most popular objective appears to be reclamation of the valley as a wilderness park primarily for recreation, with the expansion of open land capable of supporting locally endangered species an important secondary objective. Doing so would entail adopting a loose interpretation of the 1964 Wilderness Act's definition of wilderness as areas "where the earth and its community of life are untrammeled by

man, where man himself is a visitor who does not remain."[14] A number of different Native Americans groups have historically made use of Hetch Hetchy valley for a variety of purposes—even after it was incorporated into Yosemite National Park. So "untrammeled by man" would have to be interpreted as meaning untrammeled by *non-native* human beings. The use values the valley had for non-native groups cannot be left out of consideration.

With this proviso, however, reclaiming the valley as wilderness park land would seem technically feasible. Once the dam was removed and the valley drained, one could simply surrender the valley to re-colonization by local plant and animal species. Since achieving equivalent value would be the sole objective, it would not matter precisely which native species were to re-colonize the area, whether invasive non-native species gained a foothold, or whether the valley floor had the same contours as it had prior to 1914. Nor would it matter if improved campgrounds and hiking trails were established that had not previously been present. Progress in reaching equivalent use value by this means would be slow, so more direct intervention in the form of replanting and restocking might be preferred.

However, any method that eventually results in establishing equivalent use values might be adopted. Even building a Disney-style theme park in the newly drained valley could count as reclamation if overall equivalent use value was achieved. A theme park could provide employment for local people, stimulate tourism in the valley and its neighboring parks, and offer many forms of recreation for families. Various rides and attractions could be built on the meadow and along the river, without obstructing views of Hetch Hetchy's distinctive canyon walls or waterfalls. Some areas of the valley could be revegetated to allow for electric tram rides through artistically created "wilderness" scenes. And heritage values could be promoted by inclusion of a museum and interpretive center. In fact, legal obstacles probably make this sort of repurposing of Hetch Hetchy impossible. Because the Raker Act's authorization of the development of Hetch Hetchy was restricted to the uses San Francisco originally proposed (which did not include a theme park), reclamation plans would presumably be constrained by the regulations governing operations in the surrounding Yosemite Park. These would seem to favor reclamation of Hetch Hetchy along the lines of Yosemite Valley. Nevertheless, building a Disney-style theme park could in principle be a perfectly legitimate form of reclamation for Hetch Hetchy.

To *restore* disturbed land is to return it to its "original" condition, prior to damage or disturbance by human beings. Just as the aim of art restoration is to return a damaged or decaying painting or sculpture to its pristine original condition, the aim of environmental restoration of Hetch Hetchy would be to return the environment of the valley to its pristine original condition, i.e. to replace the valley's original flora and fauna and to reinstate the dynamic processes (patterns of drainage, predation, etc.) that formerly held sway. If restoration is the objective, extensive human intervention would be required to ensure that the restored valley would closely resemble its original condition. It would be necessary to reseed and restock all and only those species known to have inhabited the valley prior to its inundation and bar incursions by non-native species. It would also be necessary to recontour the valley floor (scarred by the removal of rock for dam construction) and to re-establish the river's original course. As traditional forms of hunting and harvesting by Native Americans were among the dynamic processes that shaped the valley's ecosystems prior to inundation, restoration would not be complete unless these were restored as well. Though it would be tempting to try to recover some of the costs involved, as one might under reclamation strategies, by locating revenue-generating campgrounds or other amenities in the valley, these would not seem consistent with a restoration objective.

Clearly restoration poses more significant and probably more costly practical challenges than mere reclamation. But, in addition to these, restoration poses special theoretical challenges. Assuming that all the practical challenges could be met, would it be correct to think of the end product as a "restored" Hetch Hetchy? Given the discontinuity of the processes of restoration from the natural processes responsible for the valley's original condition, mightn't it seem more accurate to call the end product a "replica" rather than a restoration? Or worse yet, a "forgery"? Robert Elliot

has argued that restoration of natural environments amounts to little more than the "faking" of nature. Elliot notes

> John Muir's remarks about Hetch Hetchy Valley are a case in point. Muir regarded the valley as a place where he could have direct contact with primeval nature; he valued it, not just because it was a place of great beauty, but because it was also a part of the world that had not been shaped by human hand. Muir's valuation was conditional upon certain facts about the valley's genesis.[15]

Because a "restored" Hetch Hetchy would be product of human rather than natural production, perhaps it would be simply a "carefully contrived elaborate ecological artifact."[16] If so, the distinctive values Hetch Hetchy possessed in virtue of its natural origins could never literally be restored.[17]

Another theoretical challenge can be raised to the very notion of a landscape having an "original" condition to which it can be restored, as if natural environments existed in a sort of static condition prior to "disturbance" by human activity. The geological features that defined Hetch Hetchy in the 19th century were not permanent features of the landscape, but were instead only the most recent results of dynamic geological processes that had been continually reshaping the region for millions of years. So one might ask on what grounds we could justify treating the landscape's condition in the mid-nineteenth century as its "original" condition as opposed to other yet earlier periods, including those occurring before the valley had even begun to form? What is true of the geological features of the valley is equally true of its flora and fauna. All have changed drastically over the eons it has taken the valley to form. Which communities of life should we regard as "original" to the valley and why?

Even if we overlook such theoretical issues, the practical challenges of restoring Hetch Hetchy to its condition prior to inundation are daunting and possibly insurmountable. The appearance of the valley prior to 1914 is well-documented with respect to cartography, native presence, and representation of large predator and prey species. However, the 1988 National Park Service report noted that "the identity of all plant taxa inhabiting Hetch Hetchy before inundation is unknown" consequently efforts to restore the original flora "would be based on speculation."[18] Some of the documented predator and prey species have been extirpated over the years, making restocking difficult or impossible. Moreover, extensive ongoing human management would be required to prevent invasive non-native species colonizing the valley as they have colonized so many others in the Sierras.

Nevertheless, the benefits might seem to outweigh the costs involved. A restored valley would be an important heritage site insofar as it would be an example of a 19th century ecosystem. There would also be important aesthetic values in allowing future generations to behold the beauty and sublimity of the valley as it was perceived and extolled by Muir and the Sierra Club. Equally important, restoring access to the valley to Native American groups would be an act of restorative justice, helping to rectify the past wrongs done during non-native settlement of the region. However, given the theoretical and practical challenges involved in restoring Hetch Hetchy, restoration might not seem a viable alternative to reclamation.

Rewilding is a relatively new concept for which there is as yet no single common definition. But while definitions differ, they agree on certain key respects: to *rewild* disturbed land is to alter or remove human intrusions into a landscape that inhibit the operation of dynamic natural processes that would otherwise shape the natural environment.[19] With rewilding, the objective is not to recreate lost wilderness but rather to create conditions conducive to the evolution of new wild lands in formerly developed areas. Rewilding projects often look to the past for ideas about how to remediate disturbed areas, but not necessarily to eras prior to human occupation and development. In Europe, where restoration to pre-human conditions is wholly impractical, rewilding projects have offered a viable alternative to restoration and reclamation schemes.

One striking early example is the Dutch nature reserve, Oostvaardersplassen, established on a "polder" (i.e., drained land), that had originally been submerged under the Zuiderzee. The polder had been created in the 1960s for industrial use.[20] When an economic down-turn delayed development, migratory

waterfowl began to use portions of property which were then set aside as a bird sanctuary. However to support a wide range of migratory birds, it was necessary to create and maintain open grass lands near the water's edge. Rather that resort to intensive human management (mowing, herbicides, etc.) to hold back the trees, the Dutch opted to "rewild" the area by reintroducing the sorts of wild-roaming herbivores that controlled tree invasions into grass lands as late as the middle ages, including aurochs (wild cattle), tarpans (wild horses), wisent (European bison,) elk, wild boar, and deer. In the 1980s, managers began introducing "proxies" for extinct cattle and horses (modern Heck Cattle and konik horses) and then moved on to the reintroduction of locally extirpated species of deer. The experiment has been an enormous success in creating and maintaining suitable habitat for a wide range of species. Further introductions of large animals into Oostvaardersplassen are being considered (wisent, wild boar, and possibly wolves.) Although Oostvaardersplassen would not count as "wilderness" under the 1964 Wilderness Act because human management continues, it is now home to communities of wild flora and fauna evolving in response to predominantly natural environmental processes. And as a sanctuary for migratory wild species, it plays an important role in protecting wilderness areas in other countries whose character would be irrevocably changed were those migratory species to be lost.

With a rewilding project like Oostvaardersplassen, it is important to remember that the past is a resource to draw upon and not an original to be reinstated. Returning Oostvaardersplassen to its original condition would mean sinking it below a restored Zuiderzee, to the loss of the many communities of life, human and non-human, that currently benefit from it. The object of rewilding is simply to redevelop disturbed areas so that wild natural processes again play a key role in shaping its ecological systems. But at the same time, adopting a rewilding strategy does not preclude one's choosing to closely model some specific period in an area's earlier history, provided that the outcome meets the overall objectives of rewilding. In the United States, proponents of rewilding have argued for projects of this type, especially what has come to be known as "Pleistocene rewilding," e.g., the development of nature reserves modeled on the natural condition of the North America prior to the arrival of the first human beings approximately 13000 years ago.[21] Before human hunters and gatherers arrived, North America was inhabited by many different large species of herbivores and carnivores now extinct, similar to modern cheetahs, camels, and elephants. Proponents of Pleistocene rewilding have proposed the creation of new nature reserves modeled on the Pleistocene era, using modern proxies for extinct North American species. As many relevantly similar modern species, such as the African cheetahs, are endangered in their homelands, it is argued Pleistocene parklands could help preserve global biodiversity. A related but less radical suggestion, proposed by an American organization, The Rewilding Institute, is the rewilding of "corridors" between existing wilderness reserves to support the reintroduction of large carnivores and their prey species into reserves currently too small to support them.

What might rewilding mean for Hetch Hetchy? That would depend on the form of rewilding chosen. If the goal is simply to permit natural processes to predominate in the evolution of the landscape, simply surrendering the drained valley to recolonization by surrounding native species might be sufficient, but with greater limits on human interventions (such as the inclusion of improved campgrounds) of the sort that straightforward reclamation schemes would permit. If the goal was to establish ecosystems like the ones that existed prior to 1914, then proxy species might be deliberately introduced to replace extinct species and locally extirpated species reintroduced. If, however, the goal was Pleistocene rewilding, a variety of proxy species might have to be imported from other countries. To prevent their spread into the neighboring mountains and valleys of Yosemite National Park, Hetch Hetchy would have to be fenced in, isolating its ecosystems from those around it. For safety reasons, access by Native American groups and tourists would need to be tightly controlled. Thus recreational, aesthetic, and justice values might be curtailed, depending upon the type of rewilding scheme adopted. On the other hand, some types of rewilding would offer special opportunities for promoting bio-diversity, protecting endangered wildlife,

and facilitating scientific understanding through observation of the interactions of flora and fauna in a rewilded valley.

Given the wide disparity of the goals that might be adopted for a drained Hetch Hetchy Valley, the position taken in the 2006 California Resources Agency report was reasonable. No conclusions can possibly be drawn about the overall feasibility of proceeding until some decision is made about what the overall objective is to be—reclamation, restoration, or rewilding. Each alternative would offer advantages that the other alternatives could not match. Each would present unique practical, legal, and ethical problems to be solved. Public consultation to ensure fairness to all viewpoints would be essential. But significant as the hurdles may be to identifying a mutually acceptable goal for Hetch Hetchy Valley, this should not discourage all those involved from tackling them. Removal of a dam of the size of the O'Shaunessey would be a historic first, one that could mark an important turning point in human interactions with nature on the North American continent. As Larry Fahn, a past president of the Sierra Club, has observed, "*a fitting tribute to John Muir would be for us to find the wisdom and the will to restore the grandeur of Hetch Hetchy Valley, in the early 21st century, for our families and all future generations.*"[22]

NOTES

1. Environmental Defense, *Paradise Regained: Solutions for Restoring Yosemite's Hetch Hetchy Valley,* (2004) Web Site (accessed 30 Dec 2009) http://www.environmentaldefense.org/.
2. Raker Act, United States 38 Stat. 242 (1913).
3. Robert U. Johnson, "John Muir as I knew Him," *John Muir Exhibit,* Sierra Club Bulletin, vol. 10, no. 1 (1916) Web page (accessed 30 Dec 2009) http://www.sierraclub.org/john_muir_exhibit/ January 7, 2010.
4. John Muir, "Hetch Hetchy Valley," in *The Yosemite* (New York: Anchor Books, 1962) 192–202, 197.
5. The presence of Native Americans in the valley prior to its discovery by non-native explorers is supported by oral traditions and archeological evidence. On the latter, see S. Montague and W. J. Mundy, *The 1991 Hetch Hetchy Reservoir*

Archeological Survey, Yosemite Research Center Technical Report, No. 1. National Park Service Yosemite National Park, California (1995).

6. On the history of the damming of Hetch Hetchy, see Holway Jones, *John Muir and the Sierra Club: The Battle for Yosemite*, Sierra Club (1965), and Robert W Righter, *The Battle Over Hetch Hetchy—America's Most Controversial Dam and the Birth of Modern Environmentalism*, New York: Oxford University Press (2005).

7. John Muir, "The Hetch Hetchy Valley," *Boston Weekly Transcript*, (March 25, 1873) Web page (accessed 30 Dec 2009) http://www.yosemite.ca.us/john_muir_writings/muir_hetch_hetchy_boston_25mar1873.html/.

8. Ibid.

9. Gerald H. Meral. "Beyond and Beneath O'Shaughnessy Dam: Options to Restore Hetch Hetchy Valley and Replace Water and Energy Supplies," *Golden Gate University Environmental Law Journal*, 2 (2008): 22–68, 24.

10. California Resources Agency, *Hetch Hetchy Restoration Study*, Department of Water Resources, Department of Parks and Recreation (2006), 20.

11. United States Bureau of Reclamation, *Hetch Hetchy: Water and Power Replacement Concepts*, Sacramento (1988) Web (accessed 30 Dec 2009) http://www.hetchhetchy.org/pdf/reclamation_water_replacement_body.pdf/.

12. California Resources Agency, 50.

13. California Resources Agency, 5.

14. California Resources Agency, 18.

15. Robert, Elliot, "Faking Nature," Inquiry 25 (1982): 81–94, 86.

16. Elliot, 86.

17. Specialists in the field of environmental restoration acknowledge that historically accurate restoration is often impossible. See, e.g., Society for Ecological Restoration International Science & Policy Working Group, *The SER International Primer on Ecological Restoration*, Tucson: Society for Ecological Restoration International, 2004.

18. Richard Riegelhuth, Steve Botti, Jeff Keay, *Alternatives for Restoration of Hetch Hetchy Valley Following Removal of the Dam and Reservoir*, Yosemite National Park (1988), 3.

19. The definition given here is wider than some popular in North America, for example the definitions offered in a current Wikipedia article (*http://en.wikipedia.org/wiki/Rewilding*, accessed December 30, 2009) and the definition currently offered by the Rewilding Institute, which reflect the interests of North American environmentalists (see the discussion of Pleistocene rewilding below) and thus exclude older understandings of rewilding common in Great Britain and in Europe. It should also be noted that the Wikipedia article is incorrect in suggesting that the term "rewilding" was coined as recently as 2003, as there are many instances of its use prior to that date. (See, e.g., Martin Soulé & Reed Noss., "Rewilding and Biodiversity: Complementary Goals for Continental Conservation," *Wild Earth*, vol. 7 no. 3 (1998) 19–28.)

20. On Oostvaardersplassen see, Frans M.W. Vera, "Large-scale Nature Development—the Oostvaardersplassen," *British Wildlife* (June 2009) 28–36, and Hein-Anton Van Der Heijden, "Ecological Restoration, Environmentalism and the Dutch Politics of 'New Nature,'" *Environmental Values* **14** (2005): 427–46. Wicken Fen is a notable British example of rewilding, see "Wicken Fen Vision", The Nation Trust, online at www.wicken.org.uk/vision/WFVstrategy2009.pdf (accessed December 30, 2009.) For information on other rewilding schemes, see Emma Marris, "Reflecting the Past," *Nature* 462 (November 2009): 30–32.

21. See, e.g., Josh Donlan, "Re-wilding North America," *Nature* 436 (August 2005): 913–914, and Soulé & Noss.

22. Fahn, Larry, December 1, 2004, Quoted on the Sierra Club's Hetch Hetchy main page, Web (accessed 03 Dec 2009) http://www.sierraclub.org/ca/hetchhetchy/.

ELIZABETH WILLOTT

RESTORING NATURE, WITHOUT MOSQUITOES?

The benefits of wetlands are now widely appreciated. Less widely known is that historically many wetlands were drained to help eliminate malaria and other deadly problems. This essay's general theme is that there are pros and cons to restoration or creation of wetlands. The specific theme is that mosquitoes pose practical and theoretical problems. In particular, abundant mosquitoes should not be regarded as an after-the-fact surprising *side* effect. Rather, abundant mosquitoes are a primary and foreseeable effect of providing habitat suitable for them. Yet our funding mechanisms and educational institutions often fail to suitably address the reality that restoring or creating wetlands has a downside.

INTRODUCTION

Attempts to restore, rehabilitate, or create riparian and wetland habitats are funded and otherwise supported by private citizens, corporations, non-profit groups and all levels of government. The result has been the creation of wonderful places to enjoy nature. In addition to the aesthetic benefit, wetland and restored riparian areas aid in flood control. They purify water and provide habitat for many species. However, do we want to increase populations of pathogen-transmitting mosquitoes when we build or restore wetlands and riparian habitats? If we don't want that, what can we do?

Wetlands and mosquitoes have always tended to go together; so have mosquitoes and devastating diseases (For an introduction to mosquitoes, see Gillett 1972; Spielman & D'Antonio 2001). People have recognized the association between disease and wetlands a long time. Warshaw (1949: 39) writes, "Even in the days when disease was attributed to evil spirits, the relationship between malaria and swamps was so

apparent that the particular evil spirits responsible for malaria were said to reside in the depths of marshes."

Draining swamps and marshes to control malaria has a long history, dating back at least to the early Romans. Cato considered land in a marshy region to be unhealthy and impossible to live upon in summer; he advised the removal of surface water to promote drying of swamps (Celli 1933, p.23). Vitruvius, Augustus Caesar's military engineer, gave instructions on choosing sites for towns and how to drain cities built in marshy areas, so that pestilence could be avoided (Celli 33). Several Roman Catholic popes were involved in drainage schemes: Pope John XV (985–96) enhanced drainage around Lake Porto to improve human health; by the time of Pope John XVIII (1003–9) fevers were so common that the Pope is said to have referred to the lake as a "cursed little stagnant water"; Pope John XIX (1024–32) cleared the drains and the situation improved so much that he called the lake "Blessed" for its beauty and usefulness (Russell 1955, p.128). More recently, but still many years before the scientific proof that mosquitoes transmitted the malaria parasite, an 1812 municipal regulation for Freetown, Sierra Leone, urged drainage of water which bred mosquitoes and fever (Carlson 1984, p.33). Malaria most likely arrived in Oregon's Willamette Valley approximately 1830, killing a great number of Indians, and making many of the settlers and soldiers ill (Boyd 1975; Boyd 1986). In 1928, a Dr. C. J. Smith interviewed the ten oldest physicians in the state. They all claimed that malaria had been present, but that they had not seen cases since 1900. The decline around St. Helens was attributed to draining: "(T)wo little spots that were lakes in the winter and swamps in summer, swarming with mosquitoes, were drained, since which time ague is not a problem here" (Smith 1928; cited in Boyd 1975).

Willott, Elizabeth. 2004. Restoring Nature, Without Mosquitoes? Restoration Ecology, 147–153. Reprinted with permission of the journal.

Draining wetter areas not only reduced disease but also typically exposed good agricultural land, so it is often impossible to separate drainage for health reasons and drainage to provide agricultural land. Hence, malaria "gradually disappeared from England as the marshy parts were drained" (Jones 1977, p.83). Smillie writes that the decline in malaria in the United States during the latter part of the 1800s was due not to quinine or the knowledge that mosquitoes transmitted the malaria parasite, but to a transition to "improved cultivation of the land [read this in part as drainage of crop land], better rural housing, more cattle, more drainage of the bottom land [i.e., swamps], rapid transportation, replacement of the village mill and its mill pond by centralized milling, and all the other components of an advancing civilization"(Smillie 1952, p.71).

In the U.S. in 1860, the average life expectancy was 40 years; in 2002 it was 77 years (Population Resource Center 2003). The increase in life-span is due to many factors, but dramatic decreases in infant, child, and early adult mortality are attributable, in part, to securing reliable clean water and the decrease in diseases such as malaria, cholera, typhoid, and diphtheria (Doull 1952). In 1850, of deaths due to disease, malaria killed more than any other diseases except tuberculosis, cholera, and dysentery/diarrhea (Smillie 1952, p.70). In general, weakness due to chronic malaria would make people more susceptible to other diseases, so mortality figures may underestimate the impact of malaria.

Even the northern states faced major problems due to malaria. The swampy area south of Toledo, Ohio was considered almost uninhabitable due to disease, presumably malaria, until most of the swamp was drained between 1870 and 1920 (American Society of Mechanical Engineers 1988; Kinney 1999). The last major epidemic struck central Illinois in 1872. One physician wrote: "This endemic lasted from the last days of July till the coming of a killing frost and within the bounds of my practice I think almost no one escaped an attack" (Johnson 1926: 131). People in the Missouri and Arkansas valleys also suffered. Malaria was so common that one author wrote:

> The valley of the Arkansas, with very little exception, is sickley (sic). Remittents and intermittents are so common, that when a person has no more than

simple fever and ague, he is hardly allowed to claim the immunities of sickness, and it is remarked that he has only the ague. The autumn that I was there, it appeared to me that more than half the inhabitants, not excepting the Creoles, had the ague (Flint 1826: 256).

In the early to mid 1900s, U.S. malaria-control literature consistently advocated draining wetter areas for mosquito control (for examples, see Herms 1913, especially p.53; Tennessee Valley Authority 1941). The Prudential Life Insurance Company published a report in 1933 that studied the decline in malaria in Virginia, North Carolina and South Carolina. The author concluded: "Drainage operations on a vast scale have made large areas of fertile land available for cultivation, reaffirming the conclusion that nothing is more effective in malaria reduction than progressive agriculture and the draining of lands to make them suitable for crops" (Hoffman 1933, p.10–11). Mortality from malaria was 32.2/100,000 for North Carolina in 1910 (earliest figure given); by 1932 the rate was reduced to 1.6/100,000 (Hoffman 1933, p.30). Draining swamps worked in multiple ways to reduce disease: it decreased the mosquito populations and it often created rich agricultural land that thereby permitted people to increase their standard of living. The result was that houses were better built, people had better diets, and they could isolate the sick.

Even the desert Southwest was not exempt: several U.S. Army camps, including Fort Wallen and Camp Goodwin, both in what is now southern Arizona, were closed due to malaria (Fink 1998). That the U.S. has a west at all is perhaps largely due to an abundance of mosquitoes, making Louisiana too difficult for the French to defend (Gillett 1972, see p.249). In 1802, Napoleon sent 33,000 men to conquer Haiti and the Mississippi; 29,000 died of yellow fever. Unable to sustain that kind of loss, France sold Louisiana to the United States in 1803, thereby facilitating the U.S.'s western expansion.

Now, two hundred years later, we recreate and restore swamps and wetlands. I am not claiming that malaria or yellow fever would return with the same force as they did in the early days of this country. Houses are better built, most Americans can afford window screens, and people sick with malaria or yellow fever would have access to appropriate treatment. It is therefore unlikely that these illnesses could prevail as they did historically. However, reviewing history should remind us that we should acknowledge that nature can be a threat.

WHAT WE FACE

I painted a grim history of malaria and yellow fever, but ended by saying these particular diseases do not appear to pose major threats to those of us in the U.S. now or in the foreseeable future. (Elsewhere in the world, malaria remains a major factor.) Western and Eastern equine encephalitis, St. Louis encephalitis, and LaCrosse encephalitis are endemic over much of the U.S. and regularly sicken and kill people. West Nile virus, introduced into the U.S. in New York in the late 1990s, is spreading across the United States.[1] The virus causes either a mild illness or much more serious meningitis or encephalitis. Between 6–10% of people diagnosed with the encephalitis or meningitis die. In 2002, 284 people died; in 2003, 222 deaths have been reported according to the Centers for Disease Control website, http://www.cdc.gov/ncidod/dvbid/westnile/ (January 24, 2004). Mosquito-transmitted viruses present in other parts of the world could cause problems if introduced to the U.S. (see Russell 1999 for a discussion of some viruses currently a concern for Australians). The introduction of either an exotic species of mosquito or an exotic virus can have serious consequences, since an endemic virus in an exotic mosquito host or an exotic virus in an endemic host may result in greater disease transmission.

When we restore or create riparian and wetland habitat, we typically create excellent mosquito habitat, including habitat for mosquitoes that transmit viruses responsible for diseases. Surely this is important. Sometimes the increase in mosquitoes is dramatic. For Sweetwater Wetlands in Tucson Arizona, a surface-flow, waste-water treatment constructed wetland, mosquitoes increased 100-fold after starting operation in 1998 (Karpiscak et al. 2004). Weekly monitoring and a variety of abatement methods, including removal of vegetation and weekly applications of larvicide, along with judicious use of adulticides when necessary, have resulted in significant control of the mosquitoes in recent years; and it has served as an instructive example for others building wetlands.

WHAT WE WANT FROM RESTORATION

"Restoration" to most lay persons suggests returning something to a prior state. However, given that we lack adequate information about any current complex ecosystem, much less those of 150, 1500, or 15,000 years ago, it is not possible to restore a habitat in the sense of putting all the original components back in place. Nor is it desirable to return to conditions in which humans suffered as they did. In some cases, we are not capable of removing and excluding all introduced exotics that have come to this country and invaded particular habitats. For example, starlings, house sparrows, and dandelions are almost ubiquitous. The mosquitoes *Culex quinquefasciatus* and *Aedes aegypti* were probably introduced to the U.S. via European ships (Spielman & D'Antonio 2001, p.79). In the mid-1980s, the mosquito *Aedes albopictus* arrived in the U.S., most likely in used tires shipped into Texas from southeast Asia (Craven et al. 1988). *A. albopictus* now has spread throughout much of the eastern U.S. often via transport of desiccation-resistant eggs in used tires but sometimes in graveyard floral arrangements, as shown in Florida (O'Meara et al. 1992). Shipments of living bamboo and banana plants provide excellent opportunities for *A. albopictus* to spread to more of the country as people readily order them on-line or purchase them in stores stocked via trucks moving all around the country. Another mosquito species, *Ochlerotatus japonicus*, has also arrived recently (Peyton et al. 1999). Any of these mosquito species may facilitate the spread of already established or newly introduced viruses and pathogens. Or, they may allow exotic viruses to establish and spread in North America. For example, preliminary work indicated that Japanese encephalitis virus can be transmitted by *O. japonicus* (Takashima & Rosen 1989; cited in Peyton et al. 1999); the introduction of Japanese encephalitis virus is possibly more a threat now that *O. japonicus* is here. These introduced mosquito species, along with starlings, house sparrows, and dandelions, are likely permanently here.

Hence, we cannot completely "restore" sites containing these irremovable exotics. In other cases, we are faced with a local species going extinct or being so rare that it cannot serve its function in the ecosystem. Under such circumstances, perhaps it is better to introduce a different species that can occupy the same, or very similar niche. This introduces a danger, but the danger created by the vacancy of a species may sometimes outweigh the danger of the introduced species. Aldo Leopold's classic example can serve: if wolves are exterminated from an area and they cannot be reintroduced (for whatever reason), then humans may need to control deer and elk populations (Leopold 1966). Sometimes, therefore, management and continued intervention are essential parts of a project.

What we want is captured not by recreating a prior state but by a different interpretation of "restoration," one that makes more sense when applied to ecosystems and can accommodate situations involving non-removable exotics or too rare species.

By "restoration" we aim to *restore underlying capacities* that permit elements of the ecosystem to interact in a way that promotes flourishing of species suitable (more on that later) for the region. The common word "rehabilitating," meaning "making capable again," captures this sense. The concept of restoration as "making capable again" grounds many restoration projects and underlies much of conservation biology as both a theoretical and practical subject. The idea is to restore function, not to make the ecosystem resemble that of some earlier time. (The opening two paragraphs of the Society for Restoration Ecology's Primer (SER 2002), which gives an extended definition of "ecological restoration," seems to accord with this view.) The interest in restoring function is to restore a kind and level of function suitable not only for wildlife but also for the humans who form part of the ecosystem as they use, maintain, and otherwise co-exist with that ecosystem. This interest in function constrains what can or cannot be considered suitable species; a "suitable" species at least does not interfere with the ecosystem functioning as an ecosystem.

In a letter paying tribute to H. T. Odum, Marsha Gilliland comments that Odum had the gift of "asking the key question, at the key moment, and at the key scale that most of us don't think about" (Gilliland 1994). Out in the marshes of Cedar Key, the mosquitoes were, in Gilliland's words, "really, really bad." Someone commented on the mosquitoes and Odum answered "the real issue is to ask and understand what the mosquitoes are doing for the system." In her letter,

Gilliland concluded by asking the question: "What are we doing for the system?"

It is easier to think about deer and elk, wolf and bear, than mosquitoes and humans. The interactions of macrofauna present themselves more readily to our senses than do mosquitoes; their interactions lack the complexity of human interactions. Hindsight allows us to see that sometimes, depending on context, we are right to interfere with the macrofauna: if wolves have been extirpated, we may need to cull deer and elk. Or, if elk or bear become too habituated to humans, they may need to be translocated (to protect themselves and humans) or killed (to protect the humans). What ought to be our parallel response to microfauna that threaten us? In particular for this paper's topic, what is our appropriate response to mosquitoes that threaten us—or threaten other elements of the ecosystem? Like with deer and elk, management and intervention are relevant.

Historically, one role of mosquitoes has been to help keep human populations in check. However, as Holmes Rolston has observed (personal communication): "In a medically skilled culture, suffering from malaria is pointless." There are better ways to control human population than for people to be cursed with malaria (or other vector-borne diseases); the malaria parasite need no longer fulfill the function of human population control. Our improved health and well-being now allow us to focus more on improving the health and wellbeing of our ecosystems. More of us now can *want* wetlands for our children.

Humans can—and do—value biodiversity, habitat loss, and much more, even when there is no apparent benefit for humans. Our values are not narrowly anthropocentric; we can act on values beyond the narrowly anthropocentric. Some writers refer to these beyond-anthropocentric interests as "aesthetic" interests, others refer to the "intrinsic worth" of nature. In different ways, the authors are discussing interests that are not solely human-centered. (For a longer discussion, see chapter 14 of a commonly used Conservation Biology text (Meffe & Carroll 1994 p.409–438).

When we say we desire to experience nature (even as restored environments), what most of us mean is that we desire to experience selected aspects of nature. We generally would prefer *not* to experience dangers posed by nature. We prefer to have safe drinking water come from our taps and not be concerned about dangers in the water—either non-human generated (excess arsenic naturally present) or human-generated (disease-causing agents such as hepatitis virus or cholera-causing bacteria). More generally, while recognizing the importance of predators in an ecosystem, we prefer that our families are not the prey.

Generally we prefer not to have mosquitoes bite us only if the means of preventing their bites jeopardizes us less than their presence. Some people go further and desire that risks to wildlife, possibly even "nature" in general, also serve as a constraint. We often draw a distinction between risks we accept at home and those acceptable when we journey to a national park to experience "nature." Even within "nature" we draw distinctions. Some parts of nature are best left isolated from humans. There, abundant mosquitoes and black flies can serve the very useful function of keeping most humans away; they thereby allow the ecosystem to flourish with minimal human influence (I thank Philip Cafaro for succinctly pointing out this "keeping out the riff-raff effect"). We also make distinctions regarding endangered species: we may be comfortable with thousands of crows dying from West Nile, yet want to intervene—if we can—to protect condors.

Some people make a distinction between human-inhabited space (culture) and wild-space (nature). However, in some respects this is more a conceptual boundary than an ecological one: mosquitoes fail to respect it. For example, in southern Arizona, the mosquito *C. quinquefasciatus* breeds readily in either wetland areas or in human-made containers such as empty watering jugs or discarded cups or jars. (It is a possible vector for West Nile virus according to Goddard et al. 2002.)

Our preference does not lead us to zero-risk tolerance (see Callicott & Mumford 1997 for a discussion of what constraints we may need to consider as appropriate for different habitats). This is consistent with our preferences in other areas of our lives: we find *some* risk, even deadly risk, tolerable. For example, we prefer that our children not be killed in traffic, but that preference does not lead us to refuse to have roads near schools. Instead, it leads us to restricted speed limits, and we accept that some children will die in traffic. Something similar operates with our preference for avoiding hazards in nature. We can accept that some people will die from encephalitis arising from mosquito-transmitted viruses, but as with children dying in traffic we want the number to be small.

WHAT CONSTITUTES ADEQUATELY ADDRESSING MOSQUITOES IN OUR BODY OF LITERATURE?

Given that mosquitoes and water go together so well, that virtually everyone has experienced the irritation caused by mosquitoes, and hence has some personal experience with some of nature's disvalue, and given the role of mosquitoes in human history and U.S. history within the last two hundred years, one might expect mosquito and water issues to be addressed in general biology and ecology texts and in books and papers on restoration or wetland construction or ecology. Yet, at present, mosquito issues are rarely or only cursorily addressed in books on conservation biology, in restoration proposals, or in research papers in journals for water management personnel. This does not mean no one works in the area. People work on mosquito-related issues. However, the primary texts in conservation biology and the majority of research papers addressing restoration and wetland construction generally do not acknowledge that mosquitoes create practical implementation problems and also problems for the theoretical basis for restoration as it is currently presented in much of the literature.

To discover texts currently used in courses on Conservation Biology, I searched the web for syllabi for Conservation Biology courses. The most common textbooks were Meffe and Carroll, 1994, 1997 and Primack, 2000. These texts either do not, or barely, mention mosquitoes or the negative consequences to humans—or wildlife—of restoring or developing wetlands. In talking of the restoration of wetlands, Meffe and Carroll write:

> Wetlands throughout the world have declined extensively in the last few centuries. In the coterminous United States, some 53% of the estimated original extent of wetlands has been lost in the last two centuries. Swamps, floodplains, bogs, sloughs, marshes, springs, and other wetlands that serve vital

ecosystemic functions and are centers of biological diversity have been drained, pumped, and diked. The *obvious* restoration action in such cases is to reinstate former hydrological conditions by reestablishing historical water flows. Ditches may be closed, pumping stopped, dikes removed, and so forth. (Meffe & Carroll 1994, p.433, emphasis added)

To those who know the history of vector-borne disease in this country, there is nothing "obvious" about this. The truly obvious result—increase in mosquitoes, and hence in potential spread of vector-borne disease—is not discussed. If students are not taught the history—that many swamps were drained at least in part for health reasons—they are being misled.

Elsewhere in the text, Meffe and Carroll write of the dangers of introducing the fish *Gambusia affinis* and *G. holbrooki. Gambusia* can cause reductions, even local extinctions, of some fish species, including some endangered fish (Meffe & Carroll 1994, see p.223–224). They never mention that *Gambusia*, often called mosquitofish, are frequently used in constructed wetlands and water rehabilitation projects to control mosquitoes.

Another key conservation biology text, Primack's *A Primer of Conservation Biology*, has no entry for either "mosquito" or "insects" in the index. Primack writes, "Wetlands are often filled in or damaged, because their importance in flood control, maintenance of water quality, and preservation of biological communities is either not known or not appreciated" (2002, 232). Although this may explain why wetlands are currently being filled in or damaged, and certainly in the early settling of this country people would have been unaware of some of the ecological functions, a more complete explanation for filling in wetlands should acknowledge that at least some of those who filled or drained wetlands knew and appreciated something that Primack perhaps does not, namely the importance—at least historically—of wetlands in spreading disease.

To test whether professionals working and publishing scholarly articles in the field of water treatment addressed mosquitoes, I searched in Kadlec and Knight's book for professionals, *Treatment Wetlands* and in three key journals (*Journal of the American Water Resources Association; Wetlands;* and *Ecological Engineering*).

According to several colleagues active in the field, the key reference book on wetland construction is Kadlec and Knight's, *Treatment Wetlands.* "Mosquitoes" is not in the index but with guidance or thorough searching one can discover that mosquitoes are discussed on two of the 893 pages (Kadlec & Knight 1996a). The authors' conclusion: Mosquitoes are not usually much of a problem because mosquito population levels are often no higher than in surrounding wetland areas unless organic loadings are excessive, or bulrush or cattail concentrations get too high, or there is debris (like floating dead cattails) on the surface. At the end of the two pages, they recommend: "Mosquito larvae and mosquitofish populations in wetland treatment systems should be monitored regularly to determine the need for restocking or other operational controls" (Kadlec & Knight 1996b, p. 710).

Despite this overt caution, the chapter's Summary of Treatment Wetland Operational Guidelines fails even to mention routine monitoring for mosquitoes and concludes:

Few operational controls are available in most natural wetland treatment systems. Typically, the only system controls available are variation of inflow loading rates through changes in pretreatment or through storage or diversion of flows, system rotation between alternate discharge locations or wetlands, and some control over water levels within the wetland. Vegetation management might include planting tree species, selective clearing, and the controlled use of fire. Through conservative design and preventive maintenance, natural wetland systems can operate almost care free for many years." (p.713)

In practice, if the wetland is close to residential or recreational areas with significant human contact, it may need to be monitored for mosquitoes at least every two weeks during mosquito season and aggressive intervention is likely necessary several times throughout the year. Vegetation grows, debris accumulates, mosquitofish die. Kadlec and Knight cite thirteen references on mosquitoes and constructed wetlands. One reference they cite concludes:

Good preventive design coupled with water management and vegetation control will normally be enough to minimize mosquito problems. *Continued surveillance is necessary*, though, because problems at treatment plants or unusually hot weather can easily kill off resident mosquito fish populations, resulting in emergence of very large numbers of mosquitoes in a short period of time. Mosquito control must be a basic element of the preproject planning as well as in operation and management documents for all treated-effluent systems. (Dill 1989, emphasis added)

In California, between 1974 and 1988, at least *five of nine* pilot water treatment plants using aquatic macrophytes went out of duty because of mosquito problems (Martin & Eldridge 1989, p.396). (For a more detailed discussion of the problem see Eldridge & Martin 1987.)

These references—and others—suggest that mosquitoes can be a significant problem unless planned for in advance and continuously managed.

For the *Journal of the American Water Resources Association*, "mosquito" is not a searchable word. "Insects" yielded two articles, neither of which addressed mosquitoes. Nor were mosquitoes mentioned in the seven articles (published since 1995) retrieved by searching "constructed wetland." For six of the articles this makes sense since they specifically addressed other aspects of wetlands, but one (Sauter & Leonard 1997) discussed wetland design methods for residential water treatment. In the introduction, the authors list several advantages, but no disadvantages, of using wetlands for treating wastewater:

In response to the need for practical alternatives for on-site treatment, constructed wetlands are garnering much interest. A natural wetland has many positive environmental advantages including flood abatement, reducing erosion, providing habitat for fish and wildlife, and naturally improving water quality. Similarly, a well designed constructed (or artificial) wetland will imitate a natural wetland and result in a highly efficient natural water treatment system (Sauter & Leonard 1997, p.155).

The authors are aware that mosquitoes may be a problem, since they write:

Because constructed wetlands are an above-ground treatment method, their aesthetic impact, both positive and negative, cannot be overlooked. For example, education of the community, or bordering neighbors,

may be appropriate and advisable to help address concerns over odor or *perceived* vector problems prior to ground-breaking. (Sauter & Leonard 1997, p.162, emphasis added).

We may wish mosquitoes were only a "perceived" problem, curable by "education." Sometimes, though, educating neighbors will not be enough to prevent vector problems from becoming a reality.

In *Wetlands*, of about 254 research articles since 2000, 15 contained the term "mosquito." One thanks mosquito control personnel for assistance when studying ducks and aquatic invertebrate ecology (but does not mention mosquitoes in the text) (Szalay et al. 2003); one mentions a dike built in the 1930's for mosquito control (Raposa & Roman 2001); another mentions that extensive ditching was done in the mid 1900's for mosquito control (Ehrenfeld et al. 2003); another notes that new stands of *Phragmites australis* often established along mosquito ditches (Bart & Hartman 2002); two discuss plankton ecology in a national park in Spain and mosquitofish are discussed (Ortega-Mayagoitia et al. 2000; Ortega-Mayagoitia et al. 2002); one discusses bird ecology and mentions mosquitofish breeding rates (Frederick & Ogden 2001); another mentions that "mosquito-control spraying of pools, drainage, and development of continuous upland habitat also threaten vernal pool wildlife" (Tiner 2003).

Three articles talk of people's perceptions of wetlands and mosquitoes. One, in the introduction has the sentence: "Initially perceived as wastelands that produced mosquitoes and as impediments to agricultural production, federal policies targeted wetlands for conversion to cropland and other land uses" (Euliss Jr et al. 2001, p.223). Another, on zooplankton in restored depressional wetlands in Wisconsin, states:

The biological function of wetlands, while obvious in general context to most wildlife biologists or ecologists, is often questioned by developers, engineers, and the public. This is especially true when those wetlands are small, transient or temporary, hinder human attempts to farm, build roads, or construct other structures, or where the wetlands simply appear to serve as breeding areas for hoards of nuisance mosquitoes. (Dodson & Lillie 2001, p.293)

The third paper discusses a survey that indicated people in Halifax, Nova Scotia did not ascribe the term "mosquito" to their urban wetlands (Manuel 2003).

Three papers describe the use of hemi-marsh design. Although not primarily addressing mosquitoes, they are relevant: One paper mentions the advantage of the hemi-marsh configuration:

> The design of wastewater treatment wetlands for wildlife habitat may not necessarily preclude use for treatment functions. Sartoris and Thullen (1998) suggested that interspersion of emergent vegetation and open water habitats would create alternating aerobic and anoxic environments and allow for nitrogen treatment and degradation of dissolved organic matter, along with providing a mosaic of habitat types for wildlife use. Our studies suggest that some combination of oxygen-producing open water and detritus-producing emergent plant zones maximizes invertebrate biodiversity. This sort of habitat mosaic may also result in benefits to human health because of the increased numbers of predatory macroinvertebrates that decrease populations of mosquitoes (Walton and Workman, 1998). (Nelson et al. 2000, p.413).

Originally constructed in 1994, a wetland in San Jacinto, California was reconfigured in 1998/99 to a hemi-marsh to "improve its ammonia nitrogen removal function, reduce nuisance mosquito populations (Walton & Workman 1998), and maintain or perhaps improve avian habitat diversity" (Andersen et al. 2003, p. 425). Studies on mosquito dispersal from the site suggested that for a region of 23 km^2, the "wetland would be the primary source of western encephalitis mosquitoes" (Walton 2002). The wetland reached maturity relatively quickly which Smith et al. (2000) note is not unprecedented in the Southwest, where Sweetwater Wetlands in Tucson, Arizona needed to clear vegetation "after approximately three years of operation, in order to maintain flow and reduce mosquito breeding habitat" (quote is from Smith et al. 2000, p. 694, referencing Prior 2000). Bruce Prior notes that although Sweetwater has all the features mentioned in Nelson, 2000, including abundant predatory aquatic macroinvertebrates, it still requires significant investment in mosquito control (personal communication, on file with author).

These two papers, by citing other papers, thereby do allow entry into the literature. Of the three relevant papers they cite, only one is in the primary literature and that is not in a wetlands journal but rather is in the *Journal of the American Mosquito Control Association*.

The remaining paper, the only one emphasizing mosquitoes, addresses the history of wetlands in Willamette Valley, Oregon, noting that several lines of evidence support a belief that wetlands were extensive, mosquitoes abundant, and that malaria killed many of the Indians soon after the Europeans arrived (Taft & Haig 2003).

A search of *Ecological Engineering* of the approximately 560 papers since 1993 revealed that 22 supposedly contained the term "mosquito" (or its variations). Eleven of these referred to mosquitofish (not in the context of mosquito control), to mosquito fern, to a place with Mosquito as part of the name, or did not contain the term (*Ecological Engineering* admits to a problem with their indexing). Eight papers mentioned mosquito in a single sentence or two to indicate the following: that mosquitofish were added to control mosquitoes (Costa-Pierce 1998, p.344); that in Morocco, constructed wetlands using water hyacinths had a "proliferation of mosquitoes" (Kivaisi 2001, p.553); that reed beds are normally kept with all water subsurface to "minimise the risk of mosquito breeding and unpleasant odors" (Mars et al. 1999, p.58); that vertical flow with its lack of exposed water thereby excludes mosquitoes (Lantzke et al. 1999, p.103); that historically a lake, now being restored, had been created to eliminate "stagnant mosquito-breeding areas" and to establish a recreational area (Ruley & Rusch 2002, p.266); that impoundments of salt marshes to control mosquitoes began in the 1940s and extended into the late 1980s (Weinstein & Weishar 2002, p.188); or that restoration projects sometimes include in their goals controlling mosquitoes (Thom 2000, p.368). Although the three remaining papers primarily address mosquitoes and wetlands, only one is about U.S. wetlands.

One studied mosquitoes in a macrophyte-based wastewater treatment system in the Cameroon. The overall system was a good breeding ground for some species of mosquitoes, although some treatment ponds were less attractive than others (Kengne et al. 2003).

Another paper is a well-cited paper giving an Australian perspective on constructed wetlands and mosquitoes, pointing out health risks pertinent to Australia (Russell 1999). This paper includes many important citations to the literature of wetland design that incorporates measures for managing mosquitoes. The author concludes: "(M)osquito management must be an integral objective of modern wetland design and maintenance in order to minimise health hazards" (Russell 1999, p.107). The third paper looked at how vegetation management strategies affected mosquito production and water quality at the Sacramento Constructed Wetlands Demonstration Project in California (Thullen et al. 2002). This paper concluded that a combination of open water and vegetation (i.e., the hemi-marsh design) gave better water purification and lower mosquito production than the alternatives tested.

Perhaps others will have a different opinion, however, I think only one research paper devoted to managing mosquitoes in current U.S. wetlands seems to be on the low side.

MANAGING MOSQUITOES

Managing mosquitoes in restoration sites or at water treatment sites is not new. In a short search of the Web using "mosquito" and "restoration" I discovered several sites addressing the issue of managing mosquitoes in constructed wetlands. Several conferences and workshops have been held which were sufficiently interdisciplinary that mosquito concerns have been addressed and relevant papers published (see, for example, Dill 1989; Martin & Eldridge 1989; Pries 2002) although some proceedings papers and books are not easily accessed.

We have resources available now that were not available before. Our choices are not limited to only two: have no wetlands, or, have wetlands with all their hazards, known and unknown, acknowledged and unacknowledged. We can inform ourselves about relevant history and teach it so our students have greater awareness of the past. We can stay informed about potential problems for the future. As indicated by some of the papers cited above, we can develop better management strategies and technologies to protect humans and non-humans.

Controlling mosquitoes is not simply a narrow, anthropocentric concern. On the contrary, mosquito-transmitted viruses also threaten non-human species. West Nile virus primarily affects birds. Humans and horses are sometimes called "dead-end hosts" because they do not support an epidemic. The "real" target of West Nile virus is birds (for more information see the Centers for Disease Control webpages, http://www.cdc.gov/ncidod/dvbid/westnile/). In North America, birds of over 100 species can be killed by West Nile, and for some species the death toll is substantial. In certain situations, to protect a particular bird species, it may be beneficial for us to manage mosquito populations. We may find ourselves in the following dilemma:

1. Mosquitoes transmitting virus may threaten bird populations that are also desirable inhabitants of that ecosystem (Consider, for example, the ferruginous pygmy owl, peregrine falcon, American condor, or whooping crane).

2. Adding fish such as *Gambusia* that eat mosquito larvae might help control the mosquitoes and hence reduce the risk to the birds, but the *Gambusia* may threaten directly some other species of fish and other aquatic organisms that are desirable inhabitants of an ecosystem.

What do we do? That biodiversity and ecological stability are important is not enough to tell us whether a proposed intervention will be beneficial. Sometimes intervening may be good, sometimes not—it will depend on the local context. We need to address how we can control mosquito populations when diseases spread by mosquitoes *unduly* threaten us *or desired local species*. People will differ in what they define as "unduly" but we can make better decisions if we know as much as reasonably possible about our options and the consequences of our actions.

Sometimes, if we communicate interests, rather than digging in to opposing positions, better solutions can emerge. We want to preserve native species *and* we want to reduce the risk of spread of vector-borne diseases that threaten humans (and, arguably, sometimes non-human animals). One attractive possibility is to use endangered native species of fish to control mosquitoes in wetlands and private ponds. Some wetland managers hesitate to introduce endangered fish because then the wetland project would be subject to significantly more regulation. In Arizona, private citizens have been unable to acquire some native species of fish because it has been illegal for pet stores to sell them. These problems are being addressed by various governments. Native species such as the Gila topminnow and desert pupfish may get more of a chance soon in Arizona (Weedman 2003).

CONCLUSION

Do we want to restore mosquito populations? Likely not. If possible, presumably we prefer to experience nature with few mosquitoes (or at least with few pathogen-transmitting mosquitoes). However, nature without mosquitoes is not an option. Minimizing mosquito populations, while restoring wetlands, requires planning and frequent intervention. Incorporating that insight into the design of a restoration or rehabilitation project is better than addressing the problem later when financial and ecological costs will likely be higher and the benefits of the project may be lost during renovations.

Several obstacles block people from frankly discussing mosquito problems. Financing for restoration projects is often short-term. Grants lasting three years are considered long-term in some circles; it can be three years before vegetation grows, debris accumulates, and mosquito problems get serious. People reason: "Why mention it as a problem in the initial grant application since the funding isn't going to last that long. And no agency is going to fund rehabilitation of a restoration project that is only three years old. We need to focus on the success we can achieve in the period of funding."

Even if the funding duration might be adequate, some people believe that talking about the negative aspects of a project increases the likelihood the project will not receive funding since it gives the funding agency a reason to reject the proposal. Perhaps in some cases this is true. However, when I have spoken with representatives of funding agencies, virtually all say that discussing obvious negatives *and addressing the concerns reasonably well* is one of the strongest approaches a proposal can take. There are measures that can be taken to minimize mosquito problems and

thereby increase safety for humans and other animals. These can be incorporated into proposed projects, thereby strengthening the proposals.

Restoring mosquito habitat has both advantages and disadvantages; we want wetlands, but we don't want the disease and death that historically accompanied wetlands; nor do we want to increase any risk that currently exists to humans or non-humans. As a society, we do a reasonable, if imperfect, job managing risks posed by things like cars traveling near schools. We can manage, also imperfectly, risks associated with wetlands or other restoration projects.

One of the prices of restoring wetlands will be continuous monitoring. By integrating mosquito awareness and control into an entire project, it seems not unreasonable that just as people volunteer to monitor bird species and numbers, some volunteers could be found for monitoring mosquito species and numbers. There is evidence that people can be supportive: Since getting mosquitoes under control at Rumney Marsh, Park Avenue Restorations Project in Massachusetts, the superintendent of the project wrote: "Public interest and support for preserving and protecting this marsh with mosquito control as a major component has increased" (Montgomery 1998).

I want to close by moving from ecological to social considerations. When we create or restore wetlands, we not only restore or create wildlife habitat for humans to enjoy; we also create human social environments. What type of human social environments are we fostering if we write, fund, encourage, or implement proposals or books that ignore or minimize known problems?[2]

NOTES

1. Since 2004 West Nile virus has spread throughout the United States and Canada, affecting people each mosquito season. It is expected to persist at low levels each mosquito season, perhaps with larger outbreaks every few years in some areas as susceptible bird pools increase in response to particular weather patterns or other ecological conditions.

2. I thank the University of Arizona–based Institute for the Study of Planet Earth and the Udall Center for Study of Public Policy for a fellowship in the fall of 2002 that permitted me to start this paper,

for the chance to present a draft at a fellow's luncheon, and for their continued support. I thank David Soren for suggestions for accessing the historical literature. Many people at the 2002 Ecological Society of America/Society for Restoration Ecology meeting in Tucson, at various granting agency forums, at the Udall Center, in graduate ecology seminars at the University of North Carolina–Chapel Hill and at Ohio University shared their personal experiences and ideas. Phil Cafaro, Ken Kingsley, Cynthia Lindquist, Frank Ramberg, Robert Varady, Margaret Zinser, three reviewers for Restoration Ecology, and especially David Schmidtz offered encouragement and criticism for which I am grateful.

REFERENCES

Ackerknecht, E. H. 1945. Malaria in the upper Mississippi Valley 1760–1900. Supplements to the Bulletin of the History of Medicine, Vol. 4. The Johns Hopkins Press, Baltimore, Maryland.

American Society of Mechanical Engineers. 1988. International historic mechanical engineering landmark: Buckeye steam traction ditcher. Findlay, Ohio. Hancock Historical Museum Association. http://www.asme.org/history/brochures/h133.pdf

Andersen, D. C., J. J. Sartoris, J. S. Thullen, and P. G. Reusch. 2003. The effects of bird use on nutrient removal in a constructed wastewater-treatment wetland. Wetlands 23: 423–435.

Bart, D., and J. M. Hartman. 2002. Environmental constraints on early establishment of *Phragmites australis* in salt marshes. Wetlands 22: 201–213.

Boyd, R. 1986. Strategies of Indian burning in the Willamette Valley. Canadian Journal of Anthropology 5: 65–86.

Boyd, R. T. 1975. Another look at the "Fever and Ague" of Western Oregon. Ethnohistory 22: 135–54.

Callicott, J. B., and K. Mumford. 1997. Ecological sustainability as a conservation concept. Conservation Biology 11: 32–40.

Carlson, D. G. 1984. African fever: a study of British science, technology, and politics in West Africa, 1787–1864. Science History Publications. Watson Publishing, Massachusetts.

Celli, A. 1933. The history of malaria in the Roman Compagna. John Bale, Sons & Danielsson, reprinted 1977, translation of *Storia della malaria*, London.

Costa-Pierce, B. A. 1998. Preliminary investigation of an integrated aquaculture-wetland ecosystem using tertiary-treated municipal wastewater in Los Angeles County, California. Ecological Engineering 10: 341–354.

Craven, R. B., D. A. Eliason, D. B. Francy, P. Reiter, E. G. Campos, W. L. Jakob, G. C. Smith, C. J. Bozzi, C. G. Moore, G. O. Maupin, and T. P. Monath. 1988. Importation of *Aedes albopictus* and other exotic mosquito species into the United States in used tires from Asia. Journal of the American Mosquito Control Association 4: 138–142.

Dill, C. H. 1989. Wastewater wetlands: user friendly mosquito habits. 664–667 in D. A. Hammer, ed. Constructed wetlands for wastewater treatment: municipal, industrial, and agricultural. Lewis Publishers, Chelsea, MI.

Dodson, S. I., and R. A. Lillie. 2001. Zooplankton communities of restored depressional wetlands in Wisconsin, USA. Wetlands 21: 292–300.

Doull, J. A. 1952. The bacteriological era (1876–1920). 74–113 in F. H. Top, ed. The History of American epidemiology. The C. V. Mosby Company, St. Louis.

Ehrenfeld, J., H. Bowman Cutway, R. Hamilton IV, and E. Stander. 2003. Hydrologic description of forested wetlands in northeastern New Jersey, USA—an urban/suburban region. Wetlands 23: 685–700.

Eldridge, B. F., and C. V. Martin. 1987. Mosquito problems in sewage treatment plants using aquatic macrophytes in California. Proceedings and Papers of the 55th Annual Conference of the California Mosquito and Vector Control Association, Inc,

Euliss Jr, N. H., D. M. Mushet, and D. H. Johnson. 2001. Use of macroinvertebrates to identify cultivated wetlands in the prairie pothole region. Wetlands 21: 223–231.

Fink, T. M. 1998. John Spring's account of "malarial fever" at Camp Wallen, A.T., 1866–1869. Journal of Arizona History 39: 67–84.

Flint, T. 1826. Recollections. (cited in Ackerknecht), Boston.

Frederick, P. C., and J. C. Ogden. 2001. Pulsed breeding of long-legged wading birds and the importance of infrequent severe drought conditions in the Florida Everglades. Wetlands 21: 484–491.

Gillett, J. D. 1972. The Mosquito: its life, activities, and impact on human affairs. Doubleday & Company, Garden City, New York.

Gilliland, M. 1994. *Letter to the editor.* Ecological Engineering 3: 89.

Goddard, L. B., A. E. Roth, W. K. Reisen, and T. W. Scott. 2002. Vector competence of California mosquitoes for West Nile virus. Emerging Infectious Diseases 8: 02-2536.htm.

Herms, W. B. 1913. Malaria: cause and control. MacMillan, New York.

Hoffman, F. L. 1933. Malaria in Virginia, North Carolina and South Carolina. The Prudential Life Insurance Company of America, Newark NJ.

Johnson, C. B. 1926. Sixty years in medical harness. (cited in Ackerknecht), New York.

Jones, W. H. S. 1977. Malaria and Greek history. Manchester University Press, reprint of 1909, Manchester.

Kadlec, R. H., and R. L. Knight. 1996a. Treatment wetland operation and maintenance. 701–713 in Treatment wetlands. CRC Lewis Publishers, Boca Raton.

Kadlec, R. H., and R. L. Knight. 1996b. Treatment wetlands. Lewis Publishers, Gainesville, Florida.

Karpiscak, M. M., K. J. Kingsley, R. D. Wass, F. A. Amalfi, J. Friel, A. M. Stewart, J. Tabor, and J. Zauderer. 2004. Constructed wetland technology and mosquito populations in Arizona. Journal of Arid Environments 56: 681–707.

Kengne, I. M., F. Brissaud, A. Akoa, R. A. Eteme, J. Nya, A. Ndikefor, and T. Fonkou. 2003. Mosquito development in a macrophyte-based wastewater treatment plant in Cameroon (Central Africa). Ecological Engineering 21: 53–61.

Kinney, K. 1999. Black Swamp once ruled the land and people. Sentinel Tribune. Bowling Green, Ohio. June 10, 1999. http://www.nwoet.org/swamp/PDF/black_swamp_people.PDF

Kivaisi, A. K. 2001. The potential for constructed wetlands for wastewater treatment and reuse in developing countries: a review. Ecological Engineering 16: 545–560.

Lantzke, I. R., D. S. Mitchell, A. D. Heritage, and K. P. Sharma. 1999. A model of factors controlling orthophosphate removal in planted vertical flow wetlands. Ecological Engineering 12: 93–105.

Leopold, A. 1966. Thinking like a mountain. 137–141 in *A Sand County Almanac* with essays on conservation from Round River. Oxford University Press, Oxford.

Manuel, P. M. 2003. Cultural perceptions of small urban wetlands: cases from the Halifax regional municipality, Nova Scotia, Canada. Wetlands 23: 921–940.

Mars, R., K. Mathew, and G. Ho. 1999. The role of the submergent macrophyte *Triglochin huegelii* in domestic greywater treatment. *Ecological Engineering* 12: 57–66.

Martin, C. V., and B. F. Eldridge. 1989. California's experience with mosquitoes in aquatic wastewater treatment systems. 393–398 in D. A. Hammer, ed. Constructed wetlands for wastewater treatment: municipal, industrial, and agricultural. Lewis Publishers, Chelsea, MI.

Meffe, G. K., and C. R. Carroll. 1994. Principles of conservation biology. Sinauer Associates, Sunderland, Massachusetts.

Montgomery, W. G. 1998. Rumney Marsh, Park Avenue Restorations Project. 44th Annual Meeting of the Northeastern Mosquito Control Association, Dec 7–9, 1998, Lincoln, New Hampshire, NMCA. http://www.nmca.org/conten98.htm

Nelson, M. S., R. A. Roline, J. S. Thullen, J. Sartoris, and J. Boutwell. 2000. Invertebrate assemblages and trace element bioaccumulation associated with constructed wetlands. Wetlands 20: 406–415.

O'Meara, G. F., A. D. Gettman, L. F. Evans Jr, and F. D. Scheel. 1992. Invasion of cemeteries in Florida by *Aedes albopictus.* Journal of the American Mosquito Control Association 8: 1–10.

Ortega-Mayagoitia, E., X. Armengol, and C. Rojo. 2000. Structure and dynamics of zooplankton in a semi-arid wetland, the National Park las Tablas de Daimiel (Spain). Wetlands 20: 629–638.

Ortega-Mayagoitia, E., M. A. Rodrigo, C. Rojo, and M. Álvarez-Cobelas. 2002. Picoplankton dynamics in a hypertrophic semiarid wetland. Wetlands 22: 575–587.

Peyton, E., S. R. Campbell, T. M. Candeletti, M. Romanowski, and W. J. Crans. 1999. *Aedes (Finlaya) japonicus japonicus* (Theobald), a new introduction into the United States. Journal of the American Mosquito Control Association 15: 238–241.

Population Resource Center. 2003. Providing the Demographic Dimensions of Public Policy: Executive Summary: Population Glossary. http://www.prcdc.org/summaries/popglossary/popglossary.html

Pries, J., ed. 2002. Treatment wetlands for water quality improvement. CH2MHILL, Waterloo.

Primack, R. B. 2000. A primer of conservation biology. 2nd ed. Sinauer Associates, Sunderland, MA.

Prior, B. M. 2000. Sweetwater Wetlands mosquito control update. Mosquito Connection (published by the City of Tucson Water Department; phone 520-791-5080, ext. 1403) 5: 4–5.

Raposa, K. B., and C. T. Roman. 2001. Seasonal habitat-use patterns of nekton in a tide-restricted and unrestricted New England salt marsh. Wetlands 21: 451–461.

Rolston, H. 1992. Disvalues in nature. The Monist 75: 250–278.

Ruley, J. E., and K. A. Rusch. 2002. An assessment of long-term post-restoration water quality trends in a shallow, subtropical, urban hypereutrophic lake. Ecological Engineering 19: 265–280.

Russell, P. F. 1955. Man's mastery of malaria. Oxford University Press, London.

Russell, R. C. 1999. Constructed wetlands and mosquitoes: health hazards and management options—an Australian perspective. Ecological Engineering 12: 107–124.

Sartoris, J. J., and J. S. Thullen. 1998. Developing a habitat-driven approach to CWWT (constructed wetlands for wastewater treatment) design. Engineering Approaches to Ecosystem Restoration: Proceedings of the 1998 Wetlands Engineering and River Restoration Conference, Denver CO, American Society of Civil Engineers (ASCE), Reston VA. CD ISBN 0-7844-0382-1.

Sauter, G., and K. Leonard. 1997. Wetland design methods for residential wastewater treatment. Journal of the American Water Resources Association 33: 155–162.

Society for Ecological Restoration Science & Policy Working Group. 2002. The SER Primer on Ecological Restoration. Society for Ecological Restoration. www.ser.org

Smillie, W. G. 1952. The period of great epidemics in the United States (1800–1875). 52–73 in F. H. Top, ed. The history of American epidemiology. C.V. Mosby, St. Louis.

Smith, C. J. 1928. Malaria (Typewritten manuscript, University of Oregon Health Sciences Center Library; cited in Boyd, 1975).

Smith, L. K., J. J. Sartoris, J. S. Thullen, and D. C. Andersen. 2000. Investigation of denitrification rates in an ammonia-dominated constructed wastewater-treatment wetland. Wetlands 20: 684–696.

Spielman, A., and M. D'Antonio. 2001. Mosquito: the story of man's deadliest foe. Hyperion, NY.

Szalay, F. A. d., L. C. Carroll, J. A. Beam, and V. H. Resh. 2003. Temporal overlap of nesting duck and aquatic invertebrate abundances in the Grasslands Ecological Area, California, USA. Wetlands 23: 739–749.

Taft, O. W., and S. M. Haig. 2003. Historical wetlands in Oregon's Willamette Valley: implications for restoration of winter waterbird habitat. Wetlands 23: 51–64.

Takashima, I., and L. Rosen. 1989. Horizontal and vertical transmission of Japanese encephalitis virus by *Aedes japonicus* (Diptera: Culicidae). Journal of Medical Entomology 26: 454–458.

Tennessee Valley Authority. Health and Safety Department. 1941. Malaria control: I. How the community can help. II. An educational project for the use of community leaders. Chattanooga, Tennessee. Tennessee Valley Authority.

Thom, R. M. 2000. Adaptive management of coastal ecosystem restoration projects. *Ecological Engineering* 15: 365–372.

Thullen, J. S., J. J. Sartoris, W. E. Walton. 2002. Effects of vegetation management in constructed wetland treatment cells on water quality and mosquito production. *Ecological Engineering* 18: 441–57.

Tiner, R. W. 2003. Geographically isolated wetlands of the United States. *Wetlands* 23: 494–516.

Tobin, M. 2003. Pact could put four endangered species in ponds. *Arizona Daily Star*. Tucson.

Walton, W. E. 2002. Multipurpose constructed treatment wetlands in the arid southwestern United States: are the benefits worth the risks? 115–123 in J. Pries, ed. Treatment Wetlands for Water Quality Improvement: Quebec 2000 Conference, August 6–12, 2000.

Walton, W. E., and P. D. Workman. 1998. Effect of marsh design on the abundance of mosquitoes in experimental constructed wetlands in southern California. *Journal of the American Mosquito Control Association* 14: 95–107.

Warshaw, L. J. 1949. Malaria: the biography of a killer. Rinehart & Co., New York.

Weedman, D. 2003. Natives effective at mosquito control. Gila topminnow vs. western mosquitofish: an update. *Mosquito Connection* 9: 4–5 (published by the City of Tucson Water Department; phone 520-791-5080, ext. 1465).

Weinstein, M. P., and L. L. Weishar. 2002. Beneficial use of dredged material to enhance the restoration trajectories of formerly diked lands. *Ecological Engineering* 19: 187–201.

VAL PLUMWOOD

BEING PREY

A CROCODILE ATTACK CAN REVEAL THE TRUTH ABOUT NATURE IN AN INSTANT

In the early wet season, Kakadu's paperbark wetlands are especially stunning, as the water lilies weave white, pink, and blue patterns of dreamlike beauty over the shining thunderclouds reflected in their still waters. Yesterday, the water lilies and the wonderful bird life had enticed me into a joyous afternoon's idyll as I ventured onto the East Alligator Lagoon for the first time in a canoe lent by the park service. "You can play about on the backwaters," the ranger had said, "but don't go onto the main river channel. The current's too swift, and if you get into trouble, there are the crocodiles. Lots of them along the river!" I followed his advice and glutted myself on the magical beauty and bird life of the lily lagoons, untroubled by crocodiles. Today, I wanted to repeat that experience despite the drizzle beginning to fall as I neared the canoe launch site. I set off on a day trip in search of

an Aboriginal rock art site across the lagoon and up a side channel. The drizzle turned to a warm rain within a few hours, and the magic was lost. The birds were invisible, the water lilies were sparser, and the lagoon seemed even a little menacing. I noticed now how low the 14-foot canoe sat in the water, just a few inches of fiberglass between me and the great saurians, close relatives of the ancient dinosaurs. Not long ago, saltwater crocodiles were considered endangered, as virtually all mature animals in Australia's north were shot by commercial hunters. But after a decade and more of protection, they are now the most plentiful of the large animals of Kakadu National Park. I was actively involved in preserving such places, and for me, the crocodile was a symbol of the power and integrity of this place and the incredible richness of its aquatic habitats.

After hours of searching the maze of shallow channels in the swamp, I had not found the clear channel

Permission to reprint this article kindly granted by Val Plumwood's Literary Executors and Terra Nova.

leading to the rock art site, as shown on the ranger's sketch map. When I pulled my canoe over in driving rain to a rock outcrop for a hasty, sodden lunch, I experienced the unfamiliar sensation of being watched. Having never been one for timidity, in philosophy or in life, I decided, rather than return defeated to my sticky trailer, to explore a clear, deep channel closer to the river I had travelled along the previous day.

The rain and wind grew more severe, and several times I pulled over to tip water from the canoe. The channel soon developed steep mud banks and snags. Farther on, the channel opened up and was eventually blocked by a large sandy bar. I pushed the canoe toward the bank, looking around carefully before getting out in the shallows and pulling the canoe up. I would be safe from crocodiles in the canoe I had been told but swimming and standing or wading at the water's edge were dangerous. Edges are one of the crocodile's favourite food-capturing places. I saw nothing, but the feeling of unease that had been with me all day intensified.

The rain eased temporarily, and I crossed a sandbar to see more of this puzzling place. As I crested a gentle dune, I was shocked to glimpse the muddy waters of the East Alligator River gliding silently only 100 yards away. The channel had led me back to the main river. Nothing stirred along the riverbank, but a great tumble of escarpment cliffs up on the other side caught my attention. One especially striking rock formation a single large rock balanced precariously on a much smaller one held my gaze. As I looked, my whispering sense of unease turned into a shout of danger. The strange formation put me sharply in mind of two things: of the indigenous Gagadgu owners of Kakadu, whose advice about coming here I had not sought, and of the precariousness of my own life, of human lives. As a solitary specimen of a major prey species of the saltwater crocodile, I was standing in one of the most dangerous places on earth.

I turned back with a feeling of relief. I had not found the rock paintings, I rationalized, but it was too late to look for them. The strange rock formation presented itself instead as a telos of the day, and now I could go, home to trailer comfort.

As I pulled the canoe out into the main current, the rain and wind started up again. I had not gone more than five or ten minutes down the channel when, rounding a bend, I saw in midstream what looked like a floating stick one I did not recall passing on my way up. As the current moved me toward it, the stick developed eyes. A crocodile! It did not look like a large one. I was close to it now but was not especially afraid; an encounter would add interest to the day.

Although I was paddling to miss the crocodile, our paths were strangely convergent. I knew it would be close, but I was totally unprepared for the great blow when it struck the canoe. Again it struck, again and again, now from behind, shuddering the flimsy craft. As I paddled furiously, the blows continued. The unheard of was happening; the canoe was under attack! For the first time, it came to me fully that I was prey. I realized I had to get out of the canoe or risk being capsized.

The bank now presented a high, steep face of slippery mud. The only obvious avenue of escape was a paperbark tree near the muddy bank wall. I made the split-second decision to leap into its lower branches and climb to safety. I steered to the tree and stood up to jump. At the same instant, the crocodile rushed up alongside the canoe, and its beautiful, flecked golden eyes looked straight into mine. Perhaps I could bluff it, drive it away, as I had read of British tiger hunters doing. I waved my arms and shouted, "Go away!" (We're British here.) The golden eyes glinted with interest. I tensed for the jump and leapt. Before my foot even tripped the first branch, I had a blurred, incredulous vision of great toothed jaws bursting from the water. Then I was seized between the legs in a red-hot pincer grip and whirled into the suffocating wet darkness.

Our final thoughts during near-death experiences can tell us much about our frameworks of subjectivity. A framework capable of sustaining action and purpose must, I think, view the world "from the inside," structured to sustain the concept of a continuing, narrative self; we remake the world in that way as our own, investing it with meaning, reconceiving it as sane, survivable, amenable to hope and resolution. The lack of fit between this subject-centered version and reality comes into play in extreme moments. In its final, frantic attempts to protect itself from the knowledge that threatens the narrative framework, the mind can instantaneously fabricate terminal doubt of extravagant proportions: This is not really happening. This is a nightmare from which I will soon awake. This desperate delusion split apart as I hit the water. In that flash, I glimpsed the world for the first time "from the outside," as a world no longer my own, an unrecognizable bleak landscape composed of raw necessity, indifferent to my life or death.

Few of those who have experienced the crocodile's death roll have lived to describe it. It is, essentially, an experience beyond words of total terror. The crocodile's breathing and heart metabolism are not suited to prolonged struggle, so the roll is an intense burst of power designed to overcome the victim's resistance quickly. The crocodile then holds the feebly struggling prey underwater until it drowns. The roll was a centrifuge of boiling blackness that lasted for an eternity, beyond endurance, but when I seemed all but finished, the rolling suddenly stopped. My feet touched bottom, my head broke the surface, and, coughing, I sucked at air, amazed to be alive. The crocodile still had me in its pincer grip between the legs. I had just begun to weep for the prospects of my mangled body when the crocodile pitched me suddenly into a second death roll.

When the whirling terror stopped again I surfaced again, still in the crocodile's grip next to a stout branch of a large sandpaper fig growing in the water. I grabbed the branch, vowing to let the crocodile tear me apart rather than throw me again into that spinning, suffocating hell. For the first time I realized that the crocodile was growling, as if angry. I braced myself for another roll, but then its jaws simply relaxed; I was free. I gripped the branch and pulled away, dodging around the back of the fig tree to avoid the forbidding mud bank, and tried once more to climb into the paperbark tree.

As in the repetition of a nightmare, the horror of my first escape attempt was repeated. As I leapt into the same branch, the crocodile seized me again, this time around the upper left thigh, and pulled me under. Like the others, the third death roll stopped, and we came up next to the sandpaper fig branch again. I was growing weaker, but I could see the crocodile taking a long time to kill me this way. I prayed for a quick finish and decided to provoke it by attacking it with my hands. Feeling back behind me along the head, I encountered two lumps. Thinking I had the eye sockets, I jabbed

my thumbs into them with all my might. They slid into warm, unresisting holes (which may have been the ears, or perhaps the nostrils), and the crocodile did not so much as flinch. In despair, I grabbed the branch again. And once again, after a time, I felt the crocodile jaws relax, and I pulled free.

I knew I had to break the pattern; up the slippery mud bank was the only way. I scrabbled for a grip, then slid back toward the waiting jaws. The second time I almost made it before again sliding back, braking my slide by grabbing a tuft of grass. I hung there, exhausted. I can't make it, I thought. It'll just have to come and get me. The grass tuft began to give way. Flailing to keep from sliding farther, I jammed my fingers into the mud. This was the clue I needed to survive. I used this method and the last of my strength to climb up the bank and reach the top. I was alive! Escaping the crocodile was not the end of my struggle to survive. I was alone, severely injured, and many miles from help. During the attack, the pain from the injuries had not fully registered. As I took my first urgent steps, I knew something was wrong with my leg. I did not wait to inspect the damage but took off away from the crocodile toward the ranger station.

After putting more distance between me and the crocodile, I stopped and realized for the first time how serious my wounds were. I did not remove my clothing to see the damage to the groin area inflicted by the first hold. What I could see was bad enough. The left thigh hung open, with bits of fat, tendon, and muscle showing, and a sick, numb feeling suffused my entire body. I tore up some clothing to bind the wounds and made a tourniquet for my bleeding thigh, then staggered on, still elated from my escape. I went some distance before realizing with a sinking heart that I had crossed the swamp above the ranger station in the canoe and could not get back without it.

I would have to hope for a search party, but I could maximize my chances by moving downstream toward the swamp edge, almost two miles away. I struggled on, through driving rain, shouting for mercy from the sky, apologizing to the angry crocodile, repenting to this place for my intrusion. I came to a flooded tributary and made a long upstream detour looking for a safe place to cross.

My considerable bush experience served me well, keeping me on course (navigating was second nature). After several hours, I began to black out and had to crawl the final distance to the swamp's edge. I lay there in the gathering dusk to await what would come. I did not expect a search party until the following day, and I doubted I could last the night.

The rain and wind stopped with the onset of darkness, and it grew perfectly still. Dingoes howled, and clouds of mosquitoes whined around my body. I hoped to pass out soon, but consciousness persisted. There were loud swirling noises in the water, and I knew I was easy meat for another crocodile. After what seemed like a long time, I heard the distant sound of a motor and saw a light moving on the swamp's far side. Thinking it was a boat, I rose up on my elbow and called for help. I thought I heard a faint reply, but then the motor grew fainter and the lights went away. I was as devastated as any castaway who signals desperately to a passing ship and is not seen.

The lights had not come from a boat. Passing my trailer, the ranger noticed there was no light inside it. He had driven to the canoe launch site on a motorized trike and realized I had not returned. He had heard my faint call for help, and after some time, a rescue craft appeared. As I began my 13-hour journey to Darwin Hospital, my rescuers discussed going upriver the next day to shoot a crocodile. I spoke strongly against this plan: I was the intruder, and no good purpose could be served by random revenge. The water around the spot where I had been lying was full of crocodiles. That spot was under six feet of water the next morning, flooded by the rains signaling the start of the wet season.

In the end I was found in time and survived against many odds. A similar combination of good fortune and human care enabled me to overcome a leg infection that threatened amputation or worse. I probably have Paddy Pallin's incredibly tough walking shorts to thank for the fact that the groin injuries were not as severe as the leg injuries. I am very lucky that I can still walk well and have lost few of my previous capacities. The wonder of being alive after being held quite literally in the jaws of death has never entirely left me. For the first year, the experience of existence as an unexpected blessing cast a golden glow over my life, despite the injuries and the pain. The glow has slowly faded, but some of that new gratitude for life endures, even if I remain unsure whom I should thank. The gift of gratitude came from the searing flash of near-death knowledge, a glimpse "from the outside" of the alien, incomprehensible world in which the narrative of self has ended.

I had survived the crocodile attack, but not the cultural drive to represent it in terms of the masculinist monster myth: the master narrative. The encounter did not immediately present itself to me as a mythic struggle. I recall thinking with relief, as I struggled from the attack site, that I now had a good excuse for being late with an overdue article and a foolish but unusual story to tell a few friends. Crocodile attacks in North Queensland have often led to massive crocodile slaughters, and I feared that my experience might have put the creatures at risk again. That's why I tried to minimize publicity and save the story for my friends alone.

This proved to be extremely difficult. The media machine headlined a garbled version anyway, and I came under great pressure, especially from the hospital authorities, whose phone lines had been jammed for days, to give a press interview. We all want to pass on our story, of course, and I was no exception. During those incredible split seconds when the crocodile dragged me a second time from tree to water, I had a powerful vision of friends discussing my death with grief and puzzlement. The focus of my own regret was that they might think I had been taken while risking a swim. So important is the story and so deep the connection to others, carried through the narrative self, that it haunts even our final desperate moments.

By the same token, the narrative self is threatened when its story is taken over by others and given an alien meaning. This is what the mass media do in stereotyping and sensationalizing stories like mine and when they digest and repackage the stories of indigenous peoples and other subordinated groups. As a story that evoked the monster myth, mine was especially subject to masculinist appropriation. The imposition of the master narrative occurred in several ways: in the exaggeration of the crocodile's size, in portraying the encounter as a heroic wrestling match, and especially in its sexualization. The events seemed to provide irresistible material for the pornographic imagination, which encouraged male identification with the crocodile and interpretation of the attack as sadistic rape.

Although I had survived in part because of my active struggle and bush experience, one of the major meanings imposed on my story was that the bush was no place for a woman. Much of the Australian media had trouble accepting that women could be competent in the bush, but the most advanced expression of this masculinist mind-set was Crocodile Dundee, which was filmed in Kakadu not long after my encounter. Two recent escape accounts had both involved active women, one of whom had actually saved a man. The film's story line, however, split the experience along conventional gender lines, appropriating the active struggle and escape parts for the male hero and representing the passive "victim" parts in the character of an irrational and helpless woman who has to be rescued from the crocodile-sadist (the rival male) by the bushman hero.

I had to wait nearly a decade before I could repossess my story and write about it in my own terms. For our narrative selves, passing on our stories is crucial, a way to participate in and be empowered by culture. Retelling the story of a traumatic event can have tremendous healing power. During my recovery, it seemed as if each telling took part of the pain and distress of the memory away. Passing on the story can help us transcend not only social harm, but also our own biological death. Cultures differ in how well they provide for passing on their stories. Because of its highly privatized sense of the individual, contemporary Western culture is, I think, relatively impoverished in this respect. In contrast, many Australian Aboriginal cultures offer rich opportunities for passing on stories. What's more, Aboriginal thinking about death sees animals, plants, and humans sharing a common life force. Their cultural stories often express continuity and fluidity between humans and other life that enables a degree of transcendence of the individual's death.

In Western thinking, in contrast, the human is set apart from nature as radically other. Religions like Christianity must then seek narrative continuity for the individual in the idea of an authentic self that belongs to an imperishable realm above the lower sphere of nature and animal life. The eternal soul is the real, enduring, and identifying part of the human self, while the body is animal and corrupting. But transcending death this way exacts a great price; it treats the earth as a lower, fallen realm, true human identity as outside nature, and

it provides narrative continuity for the individual only in isolation from the cultural and ecological community and in opposition to a person's perishable body.

It seems to me that in the human supremacist culture of the West there is a strong effort to deny that we humans are also animals positioned in the food chain. This denial that we ourselves are food for others is reflected in many aspects of our death and burial practices the strong coffin, conventionally buried well below the level of soil fauna activity, and the slab over the grave to prevent any other thing from digging us up, keeps the Western human body from becoming food for other species. Horror movies and stories also reflect this deep-seated dread of becoming food for other forms of life: Horror is the wormy corpse, vampires sucking blood, and alien monsters eating humans. Horror and outrage usually greet stories of other species eating humans. Even being nibbled by leeches, sandflies, and mosquitoes can stir various levels of hysteria.

This concept of human identity positions humans outside and above the food chain, not as part of the feast in a chain of reciprocity but as external manipulators and masters of it: Animals can be our food, but we can never be their food. The outrage we experience at the idea of a human being eaten is certainly not what we experience at the idea of animals as food. The idea of human prey threatens the dualistic vision of human mastery in which we humans manipulate nature from outside, as predators but never prey. We may daily consume other animals by the billions, but we ourselves cannot be food for worms and certainly not meat for crocodiles. This is one reason why we now treat so inhumanely the animals we make our food, for we cannot imagine ourselves similarly positioned as food. We act as if we live in a separate realm of culture in which we are never food, while other animals inhabit a different world of nature in which they are no more than food, and their lives can be utterly distorted in the service of this end.

Before the encounter, it was as if I saw the whole universe as framed by my own narrative, as though the two were joined perfectly and seamlessly together. As my own narrative and the larger story were ripped apart, I glimpsed a shockingly indifferent world in which I had no more significance than any other edible being. The thought, "This can't be happening to me, I'm a human being. I am more than just food!"

was one component of my terminal incredulity. It was a shocking reduction, from a complex human being to a mere piece of meat. Reflection has persuaded me that not just humans but any creature can make the same claim to be more than just food. We are edible, but we are also much more than edible. Respectful, ecological eating must recognize both of these things. I was a vegetarian at the time of my encounter with the crocodile, and remain one today. This is not because I think predation itself is demonic and impure, but because I object to the reduction of animal lives in factory farming systems that treat them as living meat. Large predators like lions and crocodiles present an important test for us. An ecosystem's ability to support large predators is a mark of its ecological integrity. Crocodiles and other creatures that can take human life also present a test of our acceptance of our ecological identity. When they're allowed to live freely, these creatures indicate our preparedness to coexist with the otherness of the earth, and to recognize ourselves in mutual, ecological terms, as part of the food chain, eaten as well as eater.

Thus the story of the crocodile encounter now has, for me, a significance quite the opposite of that conveyed in the master/monster narrative. It is a humbling and cautionary tale about our relationship with the earth, about the need to acknowledge our own animality and ecological vulnerability. I learned many lessons from the event, one of which is to know better when to turn back and to be more open to the sorts of warnings I had ignored that day. As on the day itself, so even more to me now, the telos of these events lies in the strange rock formation, which symbolized so well the lessons about the vulnerability of humankind I had to learn, lessons largely lost to the technological culture that now dominates the earth. In my work as a philosopher, I see more and more reason to stress our failure to perceive this vulnerability, to realize how misguided we are to view ourselves as masters of a tamed and malleable nature. The balanced rock suggests a link between my personal insensitivity and that of my culture. Let us hope that it does not take a similar near-death experience to instruct us all in the wisdom of the balanced rock.

ARNE NAESS

THE SHALLOW AND THE DEEP, LONG-RANGE ECOLOGY MOVEMENT
A Summary

Ecologically responsible policies are concerned only in part with pollution and resource depletion. There are deeper concerns which touch upon principles of diversity, complexity, autonomy, decentralization, symbiosis, egalitarianism, and classlessness.

The emergence of ecologists from their former relative obscurity marks a turning point in our scientific communities. But their message is twisted and misused. A shallow, but presently rather powerful movement, and a deep, but less influential movement,

Naess, Arne. The Shallow and the Deep, Long-Range Ecology Movement: A Summary. Inquiry, 16 (1973), 95–100. Reprinted with permission of the journal.

compete for our attention. I shall make an effort to characterize the two.

1. *The Shallow Ecology movement:* Fight against pollution and resource depletion. Central objective: the health and affluence of people in the developed countries.

2. *The Deep Ecology movement:*

(1) Rejection of the man-in-environment image in favor of *the relational, total-field image.* Organisms as knots in the biospherical net or field of intrinsic relations. An intrinsic relation between two things *A* and *B* is such that the relation belongs to the definitions or basic constitutions of *A* and *B*, so that without the relation, *A* and *B* are no longer the same things. The total-field model dissolves not only the man-in-environment concept, but *every* compact thing-in-milieu concept—except when talking at a superficial or preliminary level of communication.

(2) *Biospherical egalitarianism*—in principle. The "in principle" clause is inserted because any realistic praxis necessitates some killing, exploitation, and suppression. The ecological field-worker acquires a deep-seated respect, or even veneration, for ways and forms of life. He reaches an understanding from within, a kind of understanding that others reserve for fellow men and for a narrow section of ways and forms of life. To the ecological field-worker, *the equal right to live and blossom* is an intuitively clear and obvious value axiom. Its restriction to humans is an anthropocentrism with detrimental effects upon the life quality of humans themselves. This quality depends in part upon the deep pleasure and satisfaction we receive from close partnership with other forms of life. The attempt to ignore our dependence and to establish a master–slave role has contributed to the alienation of man from himself.

Ecological egalitarianism implies the reinterpretation of the future- research variable, "level of crowding," so that *general* mammalian crowding and loss of life-equality is taken seriously, not only human crowding. (Research on the high requirements of free space of certain mammals has, incidentally, suggested that theorists of human urbanism have largely underestimated human life-space requirements. Behavioral crowding symptoms (neuroses, aggressiveness, loss of traditions) are largely the same among mammals.)

(3) *Principles of diversity and of symbiosis.* Diversity enhances the potentialities of survival, the chances of new modes of life, the richness of forms. And the so-called struggle of life, and survival of the fittest, should be interpreted in the sense of ability to coexist and cooperate in complex relationships, rather than ability to kill, exploit, and suppress. "Live and let live" is a more powerful ecological principle than "Either you or me."

The latter tends to reduce the multiplicity of kinds of forms of life, and also to create destruction within the communities of the same species. Ecologically inspired attitudes therefore favor diversity of human ways of life, of cultures, of occupations, of economies. They support the fight against economic and cultural, as much as military, invasion and domination, and they are opposed to the annihilation of seals and whales as much as to that of human tribes or cultures.

(4) *Anti-class posture.* Diversity of human ways of life is in part due to (intended or unintended) exploitation and suppression on the part of certain groups. The exploiter lives differently from the exploited, but both are adversely affected in their potentialities of self-realization. The principle of diversity does not cover differences due merely to certain attitudes or behaviors forcibly blocked or restrained. The principles of ecological egalitarianism and of symbiosis support the same anti-class posture. The ecological attitude favors the extension of all three principles to any group conflicts, including those of today between developing and developed nations. The three principles also favor extreme caution towards any over-all plans for the future, except those consistent with wide and widening classless diversity.

(5) Fight against *pollution and resource depletion.* In this fight ecologists have found powerful supporters, but sometimes to the detriment of their total stand. This happens when attention is focused on pollution and resource depletion rather than on the other points, or when projects are implemented which reduce pollution but increase evils of the other kinds. Thus, if prices of life necessities increase because of the installation of anti-pollution devices, class differences increase too. An ethics of responsibility implies that ecologists do not serve the shallow, but the deep

ecological movement. That is, not only point (5), but all seven points must be considered together.

Ecologists are irreplaceable informants in any society, whatever their political color. If well organized, they have the power to reject jobs in which they submit themselves to institutions or to planners with limited ecological perspectives. As it is now, ecologists sometimes serve masters who deliberately ignore the wider perspectives.

(6) *Complexity, not complication.* The theory of ecosystems contains an important distinction between what is complicated without any Gestalt or unifying principles—we may think of finding our way through a chaotic city—and what is complex. A multiplicity of more or less lawful, interacting factors may operate together to form a unity, a system. We make a shoe or use a map or integrate a variety of activities into a workaday pattern. Organisms, ways of life, and interactions in the biosphere in general, exhibit complexity of such an astoundingly high level as to color the general outlook of ecologists. Such complexity makes thinking in terms of vast systems inevitable. It also makes for a keen, steady perception of the profound *human ignorance* of biospherical relationships and therefore of the effect of disturbances.

Applied to humans, the complexity-not-complication principle favors division of labor, *not fragmentation of labor.* It favors integrated actions in which the whole person is active, not mere reactions. It favors complex economies, an integrated variety of means of living. (Combinations of industrial and agricultural activity, of intellectual and manual work, of specialized and non-specialized occupations, of urban and non-urban activity, of work in city and recreation in nature with recreation in city and work in nature.)

It favors soft technique and "soft future-research," less prognosis, more clarification of possibilities. More sensitivity towards continuity and live traditions, and—most importantly—towards our state of ignorance.

The implementation of ecologically responsible policies requires in this century an exponential growth of technical skill and invention—but in new directions, directions which today are not consistently and liberally supported by the research policy organs of our nation-states.

(7) *Local autonomy and decentralization.* The vulnerability of a form of life is roughly proportional to the weight of influences from afar, from outside the local region in which that form has obtained an ecological equilibrium. This lends support to our efforts to strengthen local self-government and material and mental self-sufficiency. But these efforts presuppose an impetus towards decentralization. Pollution problems, including those of thermal pollution and recirculation of materials, also lead us in this direction, because increased local autonomy, if we are able to keep other factors constant, reduces energy consumption. (Compare an approximately self-sufficient locality with one requiring the importation of foodstuff, materials for house construction, fuel and skilled labor from other continents. The former may use only five per cent of the energy used by the latter.) Local autonomy is strengthened by a reduction in the number of links in the hierarchical chains of decision. (For example a chain consisting of local board, municipal council, highest sub-national decision-maker, a state-wide institution in a state federation, a federal national government institution, a coalition of nations, and of institutions, e.g. E.E.C. top levels, and a global institution, can be reduced to one made up of local board, nation-wide institution, and global institution.) Even if a decision follows majority rules at each step, many local interests may be dropped along the line, if it is too long.

Summing up, then, it should, first of all, be borne in mind that the norms and tendencies of the Deep Ecology movement are not derived from ecology by logic or induction. Ecological knowledge and the life-style of the ecological field-worker have *suggested, inspired, and fortified* the perspectives of the Deep Ecology movement. Many of the formulations in the above seven-point survey are rather vague generalizations, only tenable if made more precise in certain directions.

But all over the world the inspiration from ecology has shown remarkable convergencies. The survey does not pretend to be more than one of the possible condensed codifications of these convergencies.

Secondly, it should be fully appreciated that the significant tenets of the Deep Ecology movement are clearly and forcefully *normative.* They express a value priority system only in part based on results (or lack of results, cf. point [6]) of scientific research. Today, ecologists try to influence policy-making bodies largely through threats, through predictions concerning pollutants and resource depletion, knowing that policy-makers accept at least certain minimum *norms* concerning health and just distribution. But it is clear that there is a vast number of people in all countries, and even a considerable number of people in power, who accept as valid the wider norms and values characteristic of the Deep Ecology movement. There are political potentials in this movement which should not be overlooked and which have little to do with pollution and resource depletion. In plotting possible futures, the norms should be freely used and elaborated.

Thirdly, in so far as ecology movements deserve our attention, they are *ecophilosophical* rather than ecological. Ecology is a *limited* science which makes *use* of scientific methods. Philosophy is the most general forum of debate on fundamentals, descriptive as well as prescriptive, and political philosophy is one of its subsections. By an *ecosophy* I mean a philosophy of ecological harmony or equilibrium. A philosophy as a kind of *sofia* wisdom, is openly normative, it contains *both* norms, rules, postulates, value priority announcements *and* hypotheses concerning the state of affairs in our universe. Wisdom is policy wisdom, prescription, not only scientific description and prediction.

. . .

BILL DEVALL AND GEORGE SESSIONS

DEEP ECOLOGY

The term *deep ecology* was coined by Arne Naess in his 1973 article, "The Shallow and the Deep, Long-Range Ecology Movement."[1] Naess was attempting to describe the deeper, more spiritual approach to Nature exemplified in the writings of Aldo Leopold and Rachel Carson. He thought that this deeper approach resulted from a more sensitive openness to ourselves and non-human life around us. The essence of deep ecology is to keep asking more searching questions about human life, society, and Nature as in the Western philosophical tradition of Socrates. As examples of this deep questioning, Naess points out "that we ask why and how, where others do not. For instance, ecology as a science does not ask what kind of a society would be the best for maintaining a particular ecosystem—that is considered a question for value theory, for politics, for ethics." Thus deep ecology goes beyond the so-called factual scientific level to the level of self and Earth wisdom.

Deep ecology goes beyond a limited piecemeal shallow approach to environmental problems and attempts to articulate a comprehensive religious and philosophical worldview. The foundations of deep ecology are the basic intuitions and experiencing of ourselves and Nature which comprise ecological consciousness. Certain outlooks on politics and public policy flow naturally from this consciousness. And in the context of this book, we discuss the minority

Bill Devall and George Sessions. 1985. Deep Ecology: Living as if Nature Mattered. Salt Lake City, UT: Peregrine Smith. Pages 65–77. Reprinted with permission of the publisher, Gibbs Smith.

tradition as the type of community most conducive both to cultivating ecological consciousness and to asking the basic questions of values and ethics addressed in these pages.

Many of these questions are perennial philosophical and religious questions faced by humans in all cultures over the ages. What does it mean to be a unique human individual? How can the individual self maintain and increase its uniqueness while also being an inseparable aspect of the whole system wherein there are no sharp breaks between self and the *other*? An ecological perspective, in this deeper sense, results in what Theodore Roszak calls "an awakening of wholes greater than the sum of their parts. In spirit, the discipline is contemplative and therapeutic."[2]

Ecological consciousness and deep ecology are in sharp contrast with the dominant worldview of technocratic-industrial societies which regards humans as isolated and fundamentally separate from the rest of Nature, as superior to, and in charge of, the rest of creation. But the view of humans as separate and superior to the rest of Nature is only part of larger cultural patterns. For thousands of years, Western culture has become increasingly obsessed with the idea of dominance: with dominance of humans over nonhuman Nature, masculine over the feminine, wealthy and powerful over the poor, with the dominance of the West over non-Western cultures. Deep ecological consciousness allows us to see through these erroneous and dangerous illusions.

For deep ecology, the study of our place in the Earth household includes the study of ourselves as part of the organic whole. Going beyond a narrowly materialist scientific understanding of reality, the spiritual and the material aspects of reality fuse together. While the leading intellectuals of the dominant worldview have tended to view religion as "just superstition," and have looked upon ancient spiritual practice and enlightenment, such as found in Zen Buddhism, as essentially subjective, the search for deep ecological consciousness is the search for a more objective consciousness and state of being through an active deep questioning and meditative process and way of life.

Many people have asked these deeper questions and cultivated ecological consciousness within the context of different spiritual traditions—Christianity,

Taoism, Buddhism, and Native American rituals, for example. While differing greatly in other regards, many in these traditions agree with the basic principles of deep ecology.

Warwick Fox, an Australian philosopher, has succinctly expressed the central intuition of deep ecology: "It is the idea that we can make no firm ontological divide in the field of existence: That there is no bifurcation in reality between the human and the non-human realms . . . to the extent that we perceive boundaries, we fall short of deep ecological consciousness."[3]

From this most basic insight or characteristic of deep ecological consciousness, Arne Naess has developed two *ultimate norms* or intuitions which are themselves not derivable from other principles or intuitions. They are arrived at by the deep questioning process and reveal the importance of moving to the philosophical and religious level of wisdom. They cannot be validated, of course, by the methodology of modern science based on its usual mechanistic assumptions and its very narrow definition of data. These ultimate norms are *self-realization* and *biocentric equality*.

SELF-REALIZATION

In keeping with the spiritual traditions of many of the world's religions, the deep ecology norm of self-realization goes beyond the modern Western *self* which is defined as an isolated ego striving primarily for hedonistic gratification or for a narrow sense of individual salvation in this life or the next. This socially programmed sense of the narrow self or social self dislocates us, and leaves us prey to whatever fad or fashion is prevalent in our society or social reference group. We are thus robbed of beginning the search for our unique spiritual/biological personhood. Spiritual growth, or unfolding, begins when we cease to understand or see ourselves as isolated and narrow competing egos and begin to identify with other humans from our family and friends to, eventually, our species. But the deep ecology sense of self requires a further maturity and growth, an identification which goes beyond humanity to include the nonhuman world. We must see beyond our narrow contemporary cultural assumptions and values, and the conventional wisdom of our time and place, and this is best achieved by the meditative deep questioning process. Only in this way can we hope to attain full mature personhood and uniqueness.

A nurturing nondominating society can help in the "real work" of becoming a whole person. The "real work" can be summarized symbolically as the realization of "self-in-Self" where "Self" stands for organic wholeness. This process of the full unfolding of the self can also be summarized by the phrase, "No one is saved until we are all saved," where the phrase "one" includes not only me, an individual human, but all humans, whales, grizzly bears, whole rain forest ecosystems, mountains and rivers, the tiniest microbes in the soil, and so on.

BIOCENTRIC EQUALITY

The intuition of biocentric equality is that all things in the biosphere have an equal right to live and blossom and to reach their own individual forms of unfolding and self-realization within the larger Self-realization. This basic intuition is that all organisms and entities in the ecosphere, as parts of the interrelated whole, are equal in intrinsic worth. Naess suggests that biocentric equality as an intuition is true in principle, although in the process of living, all species use each other as food, shelter, etc. Mutual predation is a biological fact of life, and many of the world's religions have struggled with the spiritual implications of this. Some animal liberationists who attempt to side-step this problem by advocating vegetarianism are forced to say that the entire plant kingdom including rain forests have no right to their own existence. This evasion flies in the face of the basic intuition of equality.[4] Aldo Leopold expressed this intuition when he said humans are "plain citizens" of the biotic community, not lord and master over all other species.

Biocentric equality is intimately related to the all-inclusive Self-realization in the sense that if we harm the rest of Nature then we are harming ourselves. There are no boundaries and everything is interrelated. But insofar as we perceive things as individual organisms or entities, the insight draws us to respect all human and nonhuman individuals in their own right as parts of the whole without feeling the need to set up hierarchies of species with humans at the top.

The practical implications of this intuition or norm suggest that we should live with minimum rather than maximum impact on other species and on the Earth in general. Thus we see another as our guiding principle: "simple in means, rich in ends."

. . .

A fuller discussion of the biocentric norm as it unfolds itself in practice begins with the realization that we, as individual humans, and as communities of humans, have vital needs which go beyond such basics as food, water, and shelter to include love, play, creative expression, intimate relationships with a particular landscape (or Nature taken in its entirety) as well as intimate relationships with other humans, and the vital need for spiritual growth, for becoming a mature human being.

Our vital material needs are probably more simple than many realize. In technocratic-industrial societies there is overwhelming propaganda and advertising which encourages false needs and destructive desires designed to foster increased production and consumption of goods. Most of this actually diverts us from facing reality in an objective way and from beginning the "real work" of spiritual growth and maturity.

Many people who do not see themselves as supporters of deep ecology nevertheless recognize an overriding vital human need for a healthy and high-quality natural environment for humans, if not for all life, with minimum intrusion of toxic waste, nuclear radiation from human enterprises, minimum acid rain and smog, and enough free flowing wilderness so humans can get in touch with their sources, the natural rhythms and the flow of time and place.

Drawing from the minority tradition and from the wisdom of many who have offered the insight of interconnectedness, we recognize that deep ecologists can offer suggestions for gaining maturity and encouraging the processes of harmony with Nature, but that there is no grand solution which is guaranteed to save us from ourselves.

The ultimate norms of deep ecology suggest a view of the nature of reality and our place as an individual (many in the one) in the larger scheme of things. They cannot be fully grasped intellectually but are ultimately experiential.

. . .

BASIC PRINCIPLES OF DEEP ECOLOGY

In April 1984, during the advent of spring and John Muir's birthday, George Sessions and Arne Naess summarized fifteen years of thinking on the principles of deep ecology while camping in Death Valley, California. In this great and special place, they articulated these principles in a literal, somewhat neutral way, hoping that they would be understood and accepted by persons coming from different philosophical and religious positions.

Readers are encouraged to elaborate their own versions of deep ecology, clarify key concepts and think through the consequences of acting from these principles.

Basic Principles

1. The well-being and flourishing of human and nonhuman Life on Earth have value in themselves (synonyms: intrinsic value, inherent value). These values are independent of the usefulness of the nonhuman world for human purposes.
2. Richness and diversity of life forms contribute to the realization of these values and are also values in themselves.
3. Humans have no right to reduce this richness and diversity except to satisfy *vital* needs.
4. The flourishing of human life and cultures is compatible with a substantial decrease of the human population. The flourishing of nonhuman life requires such a decrease.
5. Present human interference with the nonhuman world is excessive, and the situation is rapidly worsening.
6. Policies must therefore be changed. These policies affect basic economic, technological, and ideological structures. The resulting state of affairs will be deeply different from the present.
7. The ideological change is mainly that of appreciating *life quality* (dwelling in situations of inherent value) rather than adhering to an increasingly higher standard of living. There will be a profound awareness of the difference between big and great.
8. Those who subscribe to the foregoing points have an obligation directly or indirectly to try to implement the necessary changes.

NAESS AND SESSIONS PROVIDE COMMENTS ON THE BASIC PRINCIPLES:

RE (1). This formulation refers to the biosphere, or more accurately, to the ecosphere as a whole. This includes individuals, species, populations, habitat, as well as human and nonhuman cultures. From our current knowledge of all-pervasive intimate relationships, this implies a fundamental deep concern and respect. Ecological processes of the planet should, on the whole, remain intact. "The world environment should remain 'natural'" (Gary Snyder).

The term "life" is used here in a more comprehensive nontechnical way to refer also to what biologists classify as "nonliving"; rivers (watersheds), landscapes, ecosystems. For supporters of deep ecology, slogans such as "Let the river live" illustrate this broader usage so common in most cultures.

Inherent value as used in (1) is common in deep ecology literature ("The presence of inherent value in a natural object is independent of any awareness, interest, or appreciation of it by a conscious being.")[5]

RE (2). More technically, this is a formulation concerning diversity and complexity. From an ecological standpoint, complexity and symbiosis are conditions for maximizing diversity. So-called simple, lower, or primitive species of plants and animals contribute essentially to the richness and diversity of life. They have value in themselves and are not merely steps toward the so-called higher or rational life forms. The second principle presupposes that life itself, as a process over evolutionary time, implies an increase of diversity and richness. The refusal to acknowledge that some life forms have greater or lesser intrinsic value than others (see points 1 and 2) runs counter to the formulations of some ecological philosophers and New Age writers.

Complexity, as referred to here, is different from complication. Urban life may be more complicated than life in a natural setting without being more complex in the sense of multifaceted quality.

RE (3). The term "vital need" is left deliberately vague to allow for considerable latitude in judgment. Differences in climate and related factors, together with differences in the structures of societies as they now exist, need to be considered (for some Eskimos, snowmobiles are necessary today to satisfy vital needs).

People in the materially richest countries cannot be expected to reduce their excessive interference with the nonhuman world to a moderate level overnight. The stabilization and reduction of the human population will take time. Interim strategies need to be developed. But this in no way excuses the present complacency—the extreme seriousness of our current situation must first be realized. But the longer we wait the more drastic will be the measures needed. Until deep changes are made substantial decreases in richness and diversity are liable to occur: the rate of extinction of species will be ten to one hundred times greater than any other period of earth history.

RE (4). The United Nations Fund for Population Activities in their State of World Population Report (1984) said that high human population growth rates (over 2.0 percent annum) in many developing countries "were diminishing the quality of life for many millions of people." During the decade 1974–1984, the world population grew by nearly 800 million—more than the size of India. "And we will be adding about one Bangladesh (population 93 million) per annum between now and the year 2000."

The report noted that "The growth rate of the human population has declined for the first time in human history. But at the same time, the number of people being added to the human population is bigger than at any time in history because the population base is larger."

Most of the nations in the developing world (including India and China) have as their official government policy the goal of reducing the rate of human population increase, but there are debates over the types of measures to take (contraception, abortion, etc.) consistent with human rights and feasibility.

The report concludes that if all governments set specific population targets as public policy to help alleviate poverty and advance the quality of life, the current situation could be improved.

As many ecologists have pointed out, it is also absolutely crucial to curb population growth in the so-called developed (i.e., overdeveloped) industrial societies. Given the tremendous rate of consumption and waste production of individuals in these societies, they represent a much greater threat and impact on the biosphere per capita than individuals in Second and Third World countries.

RE (5). This formulation is mild. For a realistic assessment of the situation, see the unabbreviated version of the I.U.C.N.'s *World Conservation Strategy*. There are other works to be highly recommended, such as Gerald Barney's *Global 2000 Report to the President of the United States*.

The slogan of "noninterference" does not imply that humans should not modify some ecosystems as do other species. Humans have modified the earth and will probably continue to do so. At issue is the nature and extent of such interference.

The fight to preserve and extend areas of wilderness or near wilderness should continue and should focus on the general ecological functions of these areas (one such function: large wilderness areas are required in the biosphere to allow for continued evolutionary speciation of animals and plants). Most present designated wilderness areas and game preserves are not large enough to allow for such speciation.

RE (6). Economic growth as conceived and implemented today by the industrial states is incompatible with (1)–(5). There is only a faint resemblance between ideal sustainable forms of economic growth and present policies of the industrial societies. And "sustainable" still means "sustainable in relation to humans."

Present ideology tends to value things because they are scarce and because they have a commodity value. There is prestige in vast consumption and waste (to mention only several relevant factors).

Whereas "self-determination," "local community," and "think globally, act locally," will remain key terms in the ecology of human societies, nevertheless the implementation of deep changes requires increasingly global action—action across borders.

Governments in Third World countries (with the exception of Costa Rica and a few others) are uninterested in deep ecological issues. When the governments of industrial societies try to promote ecological measures through Third World governments, practically nothing is accomplished (e.g., with problems of desertification). Given this situation, support for global action through non-governmental international organizations becomes increasingly important. Many of these organizations are able to act globally "from grassroots to grassroots," thus avoiding negative governmental interference.

Cultural diversity today requires advanced technology, that is, techniques that advance the basic goals of each culture. So-called soft, intermediate, and alternative technologies are steps in this direction.

RE (7). Some economists criticize the term "quality of life" because it is supposed to be vague. But on closer inspection, what they consider to be vague is actually the nonquantitative nature of the term. One cannot quantify adequately what is important for the quality of life as discussed here, and there is no need to do so.

RE (8). There is ample room for different opinions about priorities: what should be done first, what next? What is most urgent? What is clearly necessary as opposed to what is highly desirable but not absolutely pressing?

NOTES

1. Arne Naess, "The Shallow and the Deep, Long-Range Ecology Movements: A Summary," *Inquiry* 16 (Oslo, 1973), pp. 95–100.
2. Theodore Roszak, *Where the Wasteland Ends* (New York: Anchor, 1972).
3. Warwick Fox, "The Intuition of Deep Ecology" (Paper presented at the Ecology and Philosophy Conference, Australian National University, September, 1983). To appear in *The Ecologist* (England, Fall 1984).
4. Tom Regan, *The Case for Animal Rights* (New York: Random House, 1983). For excellent critiques of the animal rights movement, see John Rodman, "The Liberation of Nature?" *Inquiry* 20 (Oslo, 1977). J. Baird Callicott, "Animal Liberation," *Environmental Ethics* 2, 4, (1980).
5. Tom Regan, "The Nature and Possibility of an Environmental Ethic," *Environmental Ethics* 3 (1981): 19–34.

MURRAY BOOKCHIN

SOCIAL ECOLOGY VERSUS DEEP ECOLOGY

The environmental movement has traveled a long way beyond those annual "Earth Day" festivals when millions of school kids were ritualistically mobilized to clean up streets and their parents were scolded by Arthur Godfrey, Barry Commoner, and Paul Ehrlich. The movement has gone beyond a naive belief that patchwork reforms and solemn vows by EPA bureaucrats will seriously arrest the insane pace at which we are tearing down the planet.

This shopworn "Earth Day" approach toward "engineering" nature so that we can ravage the Earth with minimal effects on ourselves—an approach that I called "environmentalism"—has shown signs of giving way to a more searching and radical mentality. Today, the new word in vogue is "ecology"—be it "deep ecology," "human ecology," "biocentric ecology," "anti-humanist ecology," or, to use a term uniquely rich in meaning, "*social* ecology."

Murray Bookchin. 1988. Social Ecology versus Deep Ecology. Socialist Review, 88: 11–29. Reprinted with permission of the journal.

Happily, the new relevance of the word "ecology" reveals a growing dissatisfaction with attempts to use our vast ecological problems for cheaply spectacular and politically manipulative ends. Our forests disappear due to mindless cutting and increasing acid rain; the ozone layer thins out from widespread use of fluorocarbons; toxic dumps multiply all over the planet; highly dangerous, often radioactive pollutants enter into our air, water, and food chains. These innumerable hazards threaten the integrity of life itself, raising far more basic issues than can be resolved by "Earth Day" cleanups and faint-hearted changes in environmental laws.

For good reason, more and more people are trying to go beyond the vapid "environmentalism" of the early 1970s and toward an *ecological* approach: one that is rooted in an ecological philosophy, ethics, sensibility, image of nature, and, ultimately, an ecological movement that will transform our domineering market society into a nonhierarchical cooperative one that will live in harmony with nature, because its members live in harmony with each other. They are beginning to sense that there is a tie-in between the way people deal with each other as social beings—men with women, old with young, rich with poor, white with people of color, first world with third, elites with "masses"—and the way they deal with nature.

The questions that now face us are: what do we really mean by an *ecological* approach? What is a *coherent* ecological philosophy, ethics, and movement? How can the answers to these questions and many others *fit together* so that they form a meaningful and creative whole? If we are not to repeat all the mistakes of the early seventies with their hoopla about "population control," their latent anti-feminism, elitism, arrogance, and ugly authoritarian tendencies, so we must honestly and seriously appraise the new tendencies that today go under the name of one or another form of "ecology."

TWO CONFLICTING TENDENCIES

Let us agree from the outset that the word "ecology" is no magic term that unlocks the real secret of our abuse of nature. It is a word that can be as easily abused, distorted, and tainted as words like "democracy" and "freedom." Nor does the word "ecology" put us all—whoever

"we" may be—in the same boat against environmentalists who are simply trying to make a rotten society work by dressing it in green leaves and colorful flowers, while ignoring the deep-seated *roots* of our ecological problems.

It is time to face the fact that there are differences within the so-called "ecology movement" of the present time that are as serious as those between the "environmentalism" and "ecologism" of the early seventies. There are barely disguised racists, survivalists, macho Daniel Boones, and outright social reactionaries who use the word "ecology" to express their views, just as there are deeply concerned naturalists, communitarians, social radicals, and feminists who use the word "ecology" to express theirs.

The differences between these two tendencies in the so-called "ecology movement" consist not only in quarrels over theory, sensibility, and ethics. They have far reaching *practical* and *political* consequences on the way we view nature, "humanity," and ecology. Most significantly, they concern how we propose to *change* society and by what *means*.

The greatest differences that are emerging within the so-called "ecology movement" of our day are between a vague, formless, often self-contradictory ideology called "deep ecology" and a socially oriented body of ideas best termed "social ecology." Deep ecology has parachuted into our midst quite recently from the Sunbelt's bizarre mix of Hollywood and Disneyland, spiced with homilies from Taoism, Buddhism, spiritualism, reborn Christianity, and, in some cases, ecofascism. Social ecology, on the other hand, draws its inspiration from such radical decentralist thinkers as Peter Kropotkin, William Morris, and Paul Goodman, among many others who have challenged society's vast hierarchical, sexist, classruled, statist, and militaristic apparatus.

Bluntly speaking, deep ecology, despite all its social rhetoric, has no real sense that our ecological problems have their roots in society and in social problems. It preaches a gospel of a kind of "original sin" that accuses a vague species called "humanity"—as though people of color were equatable with whites, women with men, the third world with the first, the poor with the rich, and the exploited with their exploiters. This vague, undifferentiated humanity is seen as an ugly "anthropocentric" thing—presumably a malignant product of natural evolution—that is "over-populating" the planet, "devouring" its resources, destroying its wildlife and the biosphere. It assumes that some vague domain called "nature" stands opposed to a constellation of non-natural things called "human beings," with their "technology," "minds," " society," and so on. Formulated largely by privileged white male academics, deep ecology has brought sincere naturalists like Paul Shepard into the same company with patently anti-humanist and macho mountain-men like David Foreman, who writes in *Earth First!*—a Tucson-based journal that styles itself as the voice of a wilderness-oriented movement of the same name—that "humanity" is a cancer in the world of life.

It is easy to forget that this same kind of crude eco-brutalism led Hitler to fashion theories of blood and soil that led to the transport of millions of people to murder camps like Auschwitz. The same eco-brutalism now reappears a half-century later among self-professed deep ecologists who believe that famines are nature's "population control" and immigration into the US should be restricted in order to preserve "our" ecological resources.

Simply Living, an Australian periodical, published this sort of eco-brutalism as part of a laudatory interview of David Foreman by Professor Bill Devall, co-author of *Deep Ecology*, the manifesto of the deep ecology movement. Foreman, who exuberantly expressed his commitment to deep ecology, frankly informs Devall that

> When I tell people how the worst thing we could do in Ethiopia is to give aid—the best thing would be to just let nature seek its own balance, to let the people there just starve—they think this is monstrous. . . . Likewise, letting the USA be an overflow valve for problems in Latin America is not solving a thing. It's just putting more pressure on the resources we have in the USA.

One could reasonably ask what it means for "nature to seek its own balance" in a part of the world where agribusiness, colonialism, and exploitation have ravaged a once culturally and ecologically stable area like East Africa. And who is this all-American "our" that owns the "resources we have in the USA"? Is it the

ordinary people who are driven by sheer need to cut timber, mine ores, operate nuclear power plants? Or are they the giant corporations that are not only wrecking the good old USA, but have produced the main problems in Latin America that are sending Indian folk across the Rio Grande? As an ex-Washington lobbyist and political huckster, David Foreman need not be expected to answer these subtle questions in a radical way. But what is truly surprising is the reaction—more precisely, the *lack* of any reaction—which marked Professor Devall's behavior. Indeed, the interview was notable for his almost reverential introduction and description of Foreman.

WHAT IS "DEEP ECOLOGY"?

Deep ecology is enough of a "black hole" of half-digested and ill-formed ideas that a man like Foreman can easily express utterly vicious notions and still sound like a fiery pro-ecology radical. The very words "deep ecology" clue us into the fact that we are not dealing with a body of clear ideas, but with an ideological toxic dump. Does it make sense, for example, to counterpose "deep ecology" with "superficial ecology" as though the word "ecology" were applicable to *everything* that involves environmental issues? Does it not completely degrade the rich meaning of the word "ecology" to append words like "shallow" and "deep" to it? Arne Naess, the pontiff of deep ecology—who, together with George Sessions and Bill Devall, inflicted this vocabulary upon us—have taken a pregnant word—ecology—and stripped it of any inner meaning and integrity by designating the most pedestrian environmentalists as "ecologists," albeit "shallow" ones, in contrast to their notion of "deep."

This is not an example of mere wordplay. It tells us something about the mindset that exists among these "deep" thinkers. To parody the word "shallow" and "deep ecology" is to show not only the absurdity of this terminology but to reveal the superficiality of its inventors. In fact, this kind of absurdity tells us more than we realize about the confusion Naess–Sessions–Devall, not to mention eco-brutalists like Foreman, have introduced into the current ecology movement. Indeed, this trio relies very heavily on the ease with which people forget the history of the ecology movement, the way in which the wheel is re-invented every few years by newly arrived individuals who, well-meaning as they may be, often accept a crude version of highly developed ideas that appeared earlier in a richer context and tradition of ideas. At worst, they shatter such contexts and traditions, picking out tasty pieces that become utterly distorted in a new, utterly alien framework. No regard is paid by such "deep thinkers" to the fact that *the new context in which an idea is placed may utterly change the meaning of the idea itself.* German "National Socialism " was militantly "anti-capitalist." But its "anti-capitalism" was placed in a strongly racist, imperialist, and seemingly "naturalist" context which extolled wilderness, a crude biologism, and anti-rationalism—features one finds in latent or explicit form in Sessions' and Devall's *Deep Ecology*.[1]

Neither Naess, Sessions, nor Devall have written a single line about decentralization, a nonhierarchical society, democracy, small-scale communities, local autonomy, mutual aid, communalism, and tolerance that was not already conceived in painstaking detail and brilliant contextualization by Peter Kropotkin a century ago. But what the boys from Ecotopia do is to totally recontextualize the framework of these ideas, bringing in personalities and notions that basically change their radical libertarian thrust. *Deep Ecology* mingles Woody Guthrie, a Communist Party centralist who no more believed in decentralization than Stalin, with Paul Goodman, an anarchist who would have been mortified to be placed in the same tradition with Guthrie. In philosophy, the book also intermingles Spinoza, a Jew in spirit if not in religious commitment, with Heidegger, a former member of the Nazi party in spirit as well as ideological affiliation—all in the name of a vague word called "process philosophy." Almost opportunistic in their use of catch-words and what Orwell called "double-speak," "process philosophy" makes it possible for Sessions–Devall to add Alfred North Whitehead to their list of ideological ancestors because he called his ideas "processual."

One could go on indefinitely describing this sloppy admixture of "ancestors," philosophical traditions, social pedigrees, and religions that often have nothing in common with each other and, properly conceived, are commonly in sharp opposition with each other. Thus, a reactionary like Thomas Malthus

and the tradition he spawned is celebrated with the same enthusiasm in *Deep Ecology* as Henry Thoreau, a radical libertarian who fostered a highly humanistic tradition. Eclecticism would be too mild a word for this kind of hodge-podge, one that seems shrewdly calculated to embrace everyone under the rubric of deep ecology who is prepared to reduce ecology to a religion rather than a systematic and critical body of ideas. This kind of "ecological" thinking surfaces in an appendix to the Devall–Sessions book, called *Ecosophy T* by Arne Naess, who regales us with flow diagrams and corporate-type tables of organization that have more in common with logical positivist forms of exposition (Naess, in fact, was an acolyte of this school of thought for years) than anything that could be truly called organic philosophy.

If we look beyond the spiritual eco-babble and examine the *context* in which demands like decentralization, small-scale communities, local autonomy, mutual aid, communalism, and tolerance are placed, the blurred images that Sessions and Devall create come into clearer focus. These demands are not intrinsically ecological or emancipatory. Few societies were more decentralized than European feudalism, which was structured around small-scale communities, mutual aid, and the communal use of land. Local autonomy was highly prized, and autarchy formed the economic key to feudal communities. Yet few societies were more hierarchical. The manorial economy of the Middle Ages placed a high premium on autarchy or "self-sufficiency" and spirituality. Yet oppression was often intolerable and the great mass of people who belonged to that society lived in utter subjugation by their "betters" and the nobility.

If "nature worship," with its bouquet of wood sprites, animistic fetishes, fertility rites and other such ceremonies, paves the way to an ecological sensibility and society, then it would be hard to understand how ancient Egypt, with its animal deities and all-presiding goddesses, managed to become one of the most hierarchical and oppressive societies in the ancient world. The Nile River, which provided the "life-giving" waters of the valley, was used in a highly ecological manner. Yet the entire society was structured around the oppression of millions of serfs by opulent nobles, such that one wonders how notions of spirituality can be given priority over the need for a critical evaluation of social structures.

Even if one grants the need for a new sensibility and outlook—a point that has been made repeatedly in the literature of social ecology—one can look behind even this limited context of deep ecology to a still broader context. The love affair of deep ecology with Malthusian doctrines, a spirituality that emphasizes self-effacement, a flirtation with a *super*naturalism that stands in flat contradiction to the refreshing naturalism that ecology has introduced into social theory, a crude positivism in the spirit of Naess—all work against a truly organic dialectic so needed to understand *development*. We shall see that all the bumper-sticker demands like decentralization, small-scale communities, local autonomy, mutual aid, communalism, tolerance, and even an avowed opposition to hierarchy, go awry when we place them in the larger context of anti-humanism and "biocentrism" that mark the authentic ideological infrastructure of deep ecology.

THE ART OF EVADING SOCIETY

The seeming ideological "tolerance" and pluralism which deep ecology celebrates has a sinister function of its own. It not only reduces richly nuanced ideas and conflicting traditions to their lowest common denominator; it legitimates extremely primitivistic and reactionary notions in the company of authentically radical contexts and traditions.

Deep ecology reduces people from social beings to a simple species—to zoological entities that are interchangeable with bears, bison, deer, or, for that matter, fruit flies and microbes. The fact that people can consciously change themselves and society, indeed enhance that natural world in a free ecological society, is dismissed as "humanism." Deep ecology essentially ignores the social nature of humanity and the social origins of the ecological crises.

This "zoologization" of human beings and of society yields sinister results. The role of capitalism with its competitive "grow or die" market economy—an economy that would devour the biosphere whether there were 10 billion people on the planet or 10 million—is simply vaporized into a vapid spiritualism. Taoist and Buddhist pieties replace the need for social and economic analysis, and self-indulgent encounter groups replace the need for political organization and action. Above all, deep ecologists explain the destruction of human beings in terms of the same "natural laws" that are said to govern the population vicissitudes of lemmings. The fact that major reductions of populations would not diminish levels of production and the destruction of the biosphere in a capitalist economy totally eludes Devall, Sessions, and their followers.

In failing to emphasize the unique characteristics of human societies and to give full due to the self-reflective role of human consciousness, deep ecologists essentially evade the *social* roots of the ecological crisis. Deep ecology contains no history of the emergence of society out of nature, a crucial development that brings social theory into organic contact with ecological theory. It presents no explanation of—indeed, it reveals no interest in—the emergence of hierarchy out of society, of classes out of hierarchy, of the state out of classes—in short, the highly graded social as well as ideological developments which are at the roots of the ecological problem.

Instead, we not only lose sight of the social differences that fragment "humanity" into a host of human beings—men and women, ethnic groups, oppressors and oppressed—we lose sight of the individual self in an unending flow of eco-babble that preaches the "realization of self-in-Self where the 'Self' stands for organic wholeness." More of the same cosmic eco-babble appears when we are informed that the "phrase 'one' includes not only men, an individual human, but all humans, grizzly bears, whole rain forest ecosystems, mountains and rivers, the tiniest microbes in the soil, and so on."

ON SELFHOOD AND VIRUSES

Such flippant abstractions of human individuality are extremely dangerous. Historically, a "Self" that absorbs all real existential selves has been used from time immemorial to absorb individual uniqueness and freedom into a supreme "Individual" who heads the state, churches of various sorts, adoring congregations, and spellbound constituencies. The purpose is the same, no matter how much such a "Self" is dressed up in ecological, naturalistic, and "biocentric" attributes. The Paleolithic shaman, in reindeer skins and horns, is the predecessor of the Pharaoh, the Buddha, and, in more recent times, of Hitler, Stalin, and Mussolini.

That the egotistical, greedy, and soloist bourgeois "self" has always been a repellent being goes without saying, and deep ecology as put forth by Devall and Sessions makes the most of it. But is there not a free, independently minded, ecologically concerned, idealistic self with a unique personality that can think of itself as different from "whales, grizzly bears, whole rain forest ecosystems (no less!), mountains and rivers, the tiniest microbes in the soil, and so on"? Is it not indispensable, in fact, for the individual self to disengage itself from a Pharonic "Self," discover its own capacities and uniqueness, and acquire a sense of personality, of self-control and self-direction—all traits indispensable for the achievement of *freedom*? Here, one can imagine Heidegger grimacing with satisfaction at the sight of this self-effacing and passive personality so yielding that it can easily be shaped, distorted, and manipulated by a new "ecological" state machinery with a supreme "Self" at its head. And this all in the name of a "biocentric equality" that is slowly reworked as it has been so often in history, into a social hierarchy. From Shaman to Monarch, from Priest or Priestess to Dictator, our warped social development has been marked by "nature worshippers" and their ritual Supreme Ones who produced unfinished individuals at best or deindividuated the "self-in-Self" at worst, often in the name of the "Great Connected Whole" (to use exactly the language of the Chinese ruling classes who kept their peasantry in abject servitude, as Leon E. Stover points out in his *The Cultural Ecology of Chinese Civilization*).

What makes this eco-babble especially dangerous today is that we are already living in a period of massive de-individuation. This is not because deep ecology or Taoism is making any serious in-roads into our own cultural ecology, but because the mass media, the commodity culture, and a market society are "reconnecting" us into an increasingly depersonalized "whole" whose essence is passivity and a chronic vulnerability to economic and political manipulation. It is not an excess of "selfhood" from which we are suffering, but rather the surrender of personality to the security and control of corporations, centralized government, and

the military. If "selfhood" is identified with a grasping, "anthropocentric," and devouring personality, these traits are to be found not so much among ordinary people, who basically sense they have no control over their destinies, but among the giant corporations and state leaders who are not only plundering the planet, but also robbing from women, people of color, and the underprivileged. It is not deindividuation that the oppressed of the world require, but *re*individuation that will transform them into active agents in the task of remaking society and arresting the growing totalitarianism that threatens to homogenize us all into a Western version of the "Great Connected Whole."

We are also confronted with the delicious "and so on" that follows the "tiniest microbes in the soil" with which our deep ecologists identify the "Self." Taking their argument to its logical extreme, one might ask: why stop with the "tiniest microbes in the soil" and ignore the leprosy microbe, the viruses that give us smallpox, polio, and, more recently, AIDS? Are they, too, not part of "all organisms and entities in the ecosphere . . . of the interrelated whole . . . equal in intrinsic worth . . . ," as Devall and Sessions remind us in their effluvium of eco-babble? Naess, Devall, and Sessions rescue themselves by introducing a number of highly debatable qualifiers:

> The slogan of "noninterference" does not imply that humans should not modify some ecosystems as do other species. Humans have modified the Earth and will probably continue to do so. At issue is the nature and extent of such interference.

One does not leave the muck of deep ecology without having mud all over one's feet. Exactly *who* is to decide the "nature" of human "interference" in nature and the "extent" to which it can be done? What are "some" of the ecosystems we can modify and which ones are not subject to human "interference"? Here, again, we encounter the key problem that deep ecology poses for serious, ecologically concerned people: the *social* bases of our ecological problems and the role of the human species in the evolutionary scheme of things.

Implicit in deep ecology is the notion that a "Humanity" exists that accurses the natural world; that individual selfhood must be transformed into a cosmic

"Selfhood" that essentially transcends the person and his or her uniqueness. Even nature is not spared from a kind of static, prepositional logic that is cultivated by the logical positivists. "Nature," in deep ecology and David Foreman's interpretation of it, becomes a kind of scenic view, a spectacle to be admired around the campfire. It is not viewed as an *evolutionary* development that is cumulative and *includes* the human species.

The problems deep ecology and biocentricity raise have not gone unnoticed in the more thoughtful press in England. During a discussion of "biocentric ethics" in *The New Scientist* 69 (1976), for example, Bernard Dixon observed that no "logical line can be drawn" between the conservation of whales, gentians, and flamingoes on the one hand and the extinction of pathogenic microbes like the smallpox virus. At which point David Ehrenfeld, in his *Arrogance of Humanism*,[2] work that is so selective and tendentious in its use of quotations that it should validly be renamed "The Arrogance of Ignorance"—cutely observes that the smallpox virus is "an endangered species." One wonders what to do about the AIDS virus if a vaccine or therapy should threaten its "survival"? Further, given the passion for perpetuating the "ecosystem" of every species, one wonders how smallpox and AIDS viruses should be preserved? In test tubes? Laboratory cultures? Or, to be truly "ecological" in their "native habitat," the human body? In which case, idealistic acolytes of deep ecology should be invited to offer their own bloodstreams in the interests of "biocentric equality." Certainly, "if nature should be permitted to take its course"—as Foreman advises for Ethiopians and Indian peasants—plagues, famines, suffering, wars, and perhaps even lethal asteroids of the kind that exterminated the great reptiles of the Mesozoic should not be kept from defacing the purity of "first nature" by the intervention of human ingenuity and—yes!—*technology*. With so much absurdity to unscramble, one can indeed get heady, almost dizzy, with a sense of polemical intoxication.

At root, the eclecticism which turns deep ecology into a goulash of notions and moods is insufferably reformist and surprisingly environmentalist—all its condemnations of "superficial ecology" aside. Are you, perhaps, a mild-mannered liberal? Then do not fear: Devall and Sessions give a patronizing nod to "reform legislation,"

"coalitions," "protests," the "women's movement" (this earns all of ten lines in their "Minority Tradition and Direct Action" essay), "working in the Christian tradition," "questioning technology" (a hammering remark, if there ever was one), "working in Green politics" (which faction, the "fundies" or the "realos"?). In short, everything can be expected in so "cosmic" a philosophy. Anything seems to pass through deep ecology's donut hole: anarchism at one extreme and eco-fascism at the other. Like the fast food emporiums that make up our culture, deep ecology is the fast food of quasi-radical environmentalists.

Despite its pretense of "radicality," deep ecology is more "New Age" and "Aquarian" than the environmentalist movements it denounces under those names. Indeed, the extent to which deep ecology accommodates itself to some of the worst features of the "dominant view" it professes to reject is seen with extraordinary clarity in one of its most fundamental and repeatedly asserted demands—namely, that the world's population must be drastically reduced, according to one of its devotees, to 500 million. If deep ecologists have even the faintest knowledge of the "population theorists" Devall and Sessions invoke with admiration—notably, Thomas Malthus, William Vogt, and Paul Ehrlich—then they would be obliged to add: by measures that are virtually eco-fascist. This specter clearly looms before us in Devall's and Sessions' sinister remark: ". . . the longer we wait [for population control], the more drastic will be the measures needed."

THE "DEEP" MALTHUSIANS

Devall and Sessions often write with smug assurance on issues they know virtually nothing about. This is most notably the case in the so-called "population debate," a debate that has raged for over two hundred years and more and involves explosive political and social issues that have pitted the most reactionary elements in English and American society against authentic radicals. In fact, the eco-babble which Devall and Sessions dump on us in only two paragraphs would require a full-sized volume of careful analysis to unravel.

Devall and Sessions hail Thomas Malthus (1766–1854) as a prophet whose warning "that human population growth would exponentially outstrip food production . . . was ignored by the rising tide of industrial/technological optimism." First of all, Thomas Malthus was not a prophet; he was an apologist for the misery that the Industrial Revolution was inflicting on the English peasantry and working classes. His utterly fallacious argument that population increases exponentially while food supplies increase arithmetically was not ignored by England's ruling classes; it was taken to heart and even incorporated into social Darwinism as an explanation of why oppression was a necessary feature of society and why the rich, the white imperialists, and the privileged were the "fittest" who were equipped to "survive"—needless to say, at the expense of the impoverished many. Written and directed in great part as an attack upon the liberatory vision of William Godwin, Malthus' mean-spirited *Essay on the Principle of Population* tried to demonstrate that hunger, poverty, disease, and premature death are *inevitable* precisely because population and food supply increase at different rates. Hence war, famines, and plagues (Malthus later added "moral restraint") were necessary to keep population down—needless to say, among the "lower orders of society," whom he singles out as the chief offenders of his inexorable population "laws."[3] Malthus, in effect, became the ideologue par excellence for the land-grabbing English nobility in its effort to dispossess the peasantry of their traditional common lands and for the English capitalists to work children, women, and men to death in the newly emergent "industrial/technological" factory system.

Malthusianism contributed in great part to that meanness of spirit that Charles Dickens captured in his famous novels, *Oliver Twist* and *Hard Times*. The doctrine, its author, and its overstuffed wealthy beneficiaries were bitterly fought by the great English anarchist, William Godwin, the pioneering socialist, Robert Owen, and the emerging Chartist movement of English workers in the early 19th century. However, Malthusianism was naively picked up by Charles Darwin to explain his theory of "natural selection." It then became the bedrock theory for the new *social* Darwinism, so very much in vogue in the late nineteenth and early twentieth centuries, which saw society as a "jungle" in which only the "fit" (usually, the rich and white) could "survive" at the expense of the "unfit" (usually, the poor and people of color). Malthus, in

effect, had provided an ideology that justified class domination, racism, the degradation of women, and, ultimately, British imperialism.

Malthusianism was not only revived in Hitler's Third Reich; it also reemerged in the late 1940s, following the discoveries of antibiotics to control infectious diseases. Riding on the tide of the new Pax Americana after World War II, William F. Vogt and a whole bouquet of neo-Malthusians were to challenge the use of the new antibiotic discoveries to control disease and prevent death—as usual, mainly in Asia, Africa, and Latin America. Again, a new "population debate" erupted, with the Rockefeller interests and large corporate sharks aligning themselves with the neo-Malthusians, and caring people of every sort aligning themselves with third world theorists like Josua de Castro, who wrote damning, highly informed critiques of this new version of misanthropy.

Zero Population Growth fanatics in the early seventies literally polluted the environmental movement with demands for a government bureau to "control" population, advancing the infamous "triage" ethic, according to which various "underdeveloped" countries would be granted or refused aid on the basis of their compliance to population control measures. In *Food First*, Francis Moore Lappé and Joseph Collins have done a superb job in showing how hunger has its origins not in "natural" shortages of food or population growth, but in social and cultural dislocations. (It is notable that Devall and Sessions do *not* list this excellent book in their bibliography.) The book has to be read to understand the reactionary implications of deep ecology's demographic positions.

Demography is a highly ambiguous and ideologically charged social discipline that cannot be reduced to a mere numbers game in biological reproduction. Human beings are not fruit flies (the species which the neo-Malthusians love to cite). Their reproductive behavior is profoundly conditioned by cultural values, standards of living, social traditions, gender relations, religious beliefs, socio-political conflicts, and various sociopolitical expectations. Smash up a stable, precapitalist culture and throw its people off the land into city slums, and, due to demoralization, population may soar rather than decline. As Gandhi told the British, imperialism left India's wretched poor and homeless with little more in life than the immediate gratification provided by sex and an understandably numbed sense of personal, much less social, responsibility. Reduce women to mere reproductive factories and population rates will explode.

Conversely, provide people with decent lives, education, a sense of creative meaning in life, and, above all, expand the role of women in society—and population growth begins to stabilize and population rates even reverse their direction. Nothing more clearly reveals deep ecology's crude, often reactionary, and certainly superficial ideological framework—all its decentralist, antihierarchical, and "radical" rhetoric aside—than its suffocating "biological" treatment of the population issue and its inclusion of Malthus, Vogt, and Ehrlich in its firmament of prophets.

Not surprisingly, the *Earth First!* newsletter, whose editor professes to be an enthusiastic deep ecologist, carried an article titled "Population and AIDS" which advanced the obscene argument that AIDS is desirable as a means of population control. This was no spoof. It was earnestly argued and carefully reasoned in a Paleolithic sort of way. Not only will AIDS claim large numbers of lives, asserts the author (who hides under the pseudonym of "Miss Ann Thropy," a form of black humor that could also pass as an example of machomale arrogance), but it "may cause a breakdown in technology (read: human food supply) and its export which could also decrease human population." These people feed on human disasters, suffering, and misery, preferably in third world countries where AIDS is by far a more monstrous problem than elsewhere.

We have little reason to doubt that this mentality is perfectly consistent with the "more drastic . . . measures" Devall and Sessions believe we will have to explore. Nor is it inconsistent with Malthus and Vogt that we should make no effort to find a cure for this disease which may do so much to depopulate the world. "Biocentric democracy," I assume, should call for nothing less than a "hands-off" policy on the AIDS virus and perhaps equally lethal pathogens that appear in the human species.

WHAT IS SOCIAL ECOLOGY?

Social ecology is neither "deep," "tall," "fat," nor "thick." It is *social*. It does not fall back on incantations, sutras, flow diagrams or spiritual vagaries. It is avowedly *rational*.

It does not try to regale metaphorical forms of spiritual mechanism and crude biologism with Taoist, Buddhist, Christian, or shamanistic ecobabble. It is a coherent form of *naturalism* that looks to *evolution* and the *biosphere*, not to deities in the sky or under the earth for quasi-religious and supernaturalistic explanations of natural and social phenomena.

Philosophically, social ecology stems from a solid organismic tradition in Western philosophy, beginning with Heraclitus, the near-evolutionary dialectic of Aristotle and Hegel, and the critical approach of the famous Frankfurt School—particularly its devastating critique of logical positivism (which surfaces in Naess repeatedly) and the primitivistic mysticism of Heidegger (which pops up all over the place in deep ecology's literature).

Socially, it is revolutionary, not merely "radical." It critically unmasks the entire evolution of hierarchy in all its forms, including neo-Malthusian elitism, the ecobrutalism of David Foreman, the anti-humanism of David Ehrenfeld and "Miss Ann Thropy," and the latent racism, first-world arrogance, and Yuppie nihilism of postmodernistic spiritualism. It is noted in the profound eco-anarchistic analyses of Peter Kropotkin, the radical economic insights of Karl Marx, the emancipatory promise of the revolutionary Enlightenment as articulated by the great encyclopedist, Denis Diderot, the *Enragés* of the French Revolution, the revolutionary feminist ideals of Louise Michel and Emma Goldman, the communitarian visions of Paul Goodman and E. A. Gutkind, and the various eco-revolutionary manifestoes of the early 1960s.

Politically, it is *green*—radically green. It takes its stand with the left-wing tendencies in the German Greens and extra-parliamentary street movements of European cities; with the American radical ecofeminist movement; with the demands for a new politics based on citizens' initiatives, neighborhood assemblies, and New England's tradition of town-meetings; with nonaligned anti-imperialist movements at home and abroad; with the struggle by people of color for complete freedom from the domination of privileged whites and from the superpowers.

Morally, it is *humanistic* in the high Renaissance meaning of the term, not the degraded meaning of "humanism" that has been imparted to the world by

David Foreman, David Ehrenfeld, and a salad of academic deep ecologists. Humanism from its inception has meant a shift in vision from the skies to the earth, from superstition to reason, from deities to people—who are no less products of natural evolution than grizzly bears and whales. Social ecology accepts neither a "biocentricity" that essentially denies or degrades the uniqueness of human beings, human subjectivity, rationality, aesthetic sensibility, and the ethical potentiality of humanity, nor an "anthropocentricity" that confers on the privileged few the right to plunder the world of life, including human life. Indeed, it opposes "centricity" of *any* kind as a new word for hierarchy and domination—be it that of nature by a mystical "Man" or the domination of people by an equally mystical "Nature." It firmly denies that nature is a static, scenic view which Mountain Men like a Foreman survey from a peak in Nevada or a picture window that spoiled yuppies view from their ticky-tacky country homes. To social ecology, nature *is* natural *evolution*, not a cosmic arrangement of beings frozen in a moment of eternity to be abjectly revered, adored, and worshipped like Gods and Goddesses in a realm of "*super*-nature." Natural evolution is nature in the very real sense that it is composed of atoms, molecules that have evolved into amino acids, proteins, unicellular organisms, genetic codes, invertebrates and vertebrates, amphibia, reptiles, mammals, primates, and human beings—all, in a cumulative thrust toward ever-greater complexity, ever-greater subjectivity, and finally, an ever greater capacity for conceptual thought, symbolic communication, and self-consciousness.

This marvel we call "Nature" has produced a marvel we call *Homo sapiens*—"thinking man"—and, more significantly for the development of society, "thinking woman," whose primeval domestic domain provided the arena for the origins of a caring society, human empathy, love, and idealistic commitment. The human species, in effect, is no less a product of natural evolution and differentiation than blue–green algae. To degrade the human species in the name of "anti-humanism," to deny people their uniqueness as thinking beings with an unprecedented gift for conceptual thought, is to deny the rich fecundity of natural evolution itself. To separate human beings and society from nature is to dualize and truncate nature itself, to

diminish the meaning and thrust of natural evolution in the name of a "biocentricity" that spends more time disporting itself with mantras, deities, and supernature than with the realities of the biosphere and the role of society in ecological problems.

Accordingly, social ecology does not try to hide its critical and reconstructive thrust in metaphors. It calls "technological/industrial" society *capitalism*—a word which places the onus for our ecological problems on the *living* sources and *social* relationships that produce them, not on a cutesy "Third Wave" abstraction which buries these sources in technics, a technical "mentality," or perhaps the technicians who work on machines. It sees the domination of women not simply as a "spiritual" problem that can be resolved by rituals, incantations, and shamannesses, important as ritual may be in solidarizing women into a unique community of people, but in the long, highly graded, and subtly nuanced development of hierarchy, which long preceded the development of classes. Nor does it ignore class, ethnic differences, imperialism, and oppression by creating a grab-bag called "Humanity" that is placed in opposition to a mystified "Nature," divested of all development.

All of which brings us as social ecologists to an issue that seems to be totally alien to the crude concerns of deep ecology: natural evolution has conferred on human beings the capacity to form a "second" or cultural nature out of "first" or primeval nature. Natural evolution has not only provided humans with the *ability*, but also the *necessity* to be purposive interveners into "first nature," to consciously *change* "first nature" by means of a highly institutionalized form of community we call "society." It is not alien to natural evolution that a species called human beings have emerged over the billions of years who are capable of thinking in a sophisticated way. Nor is it alien for human beings to develop a highly sophisticated form of symbolic communication which a new kind of community—institutionalized, guided by thought rather than by instinct alone, and ever-changing—has emerged called "society."

Taken together, all of these human traits—intellectual, communicative, and social—have not only emerged from natural evolution and are inherently human; they can also be placed at the *service* of natural evolution to consciously increase biotic diversity, diminish suffering, foster the further evolution of new and ecologically valuable life-forms, reduce the impact of disastrous accidents or the harsh effects of mere change.

Whether this species, gifted by the creativity of natural evolution, can play the role of a nature rendered self-conscious or cut against the grain of natural evolution by simplifying the biosphere, polluting it, and undermining the cumulative results of organic evolution is above all a *social* problem. The primary question ecology faces today is whether an ecologically oriented society can be created out of the present anti-ecological one.

Unless there is a resolute attempt to fully anchor ecological dislocations in social dislocations; to challenge the vested corporate and political interests we should properly call *capitalism*; to analyze, explore, and attack hierarchy as a *reality*, not only as a sensibility; to recognize the material needs of the poor and of third world people; to function politically, and not simply as a religious cult; to give the human species and mind their due in natural evolution, rather than regard them as "cancers" in the biosphere; to examine economies as well as "souls," and freedom instead of scholastic arguments about the "rights" of pathogenic viruses—unless, in short, North American Greens and the ecology movement shift their focus toward a *social ecology* and let deep ecology sink into the pit it has created for us, the ecology movement will become another ugly wart on the skin of society.

What we must do, today, is return to *nature*, conceived in all its fecundity, richness of potentialities, and subjectivity—not to *super*nature with its shamans, priests, priestesses, and fanciful deities that are merely anthropomorphic extensions and distortions of the "Human" as all-embracing divinities. And what we must "enchant" is not only an abstract image of "Nature" *that often reflects our own systems of power, hierarchy, and domination*—but rather human beings, the human mind, the human spirit.

NOTES

1. Unless otherwise indicated, all future references and quotes come from Bill Devall and George Sessions, *Deep Ecology* (Layton, Utah: Gibbs M. Smith, 1985), a book which has essentially become the bible of the "movement" that bears its name.

2. David Ehrenfeld, *The Arrogance of Humanism* (New York: Modern Library, 1978), pp. 207–211.

3. Chapter five of his *Essay*, which, for all its "concern" over the misery of the "lower classes," inveighs against the poor laws and argues that the "pressures of distress on this part of the community is an evil so deeply seated that no human ingenuity can reach it." Thomas Malthus, *On Population* (New York: The Modern Library), p. 34.

II

WHAT REALLY WORKS

Essays on Human Ecology

EDITORIAL
Reflections on What Works

1. MANAGING WILDLIFE

Kobus Krüger worked for eighteen years as a ranger in Kruger National Park, located along South Africa's eastern border with Mozambique. He often rescued orphaned animals. He once hand-reared an orphaned lion at his own expense. More than once, he tranquilized elephants so as to treat wounds they had suffered, occasionally tracking them long enough to do follow-up treatments. He spent days and sometimes weeks in the bush, on his own, without supplies or fire or radio, risking his life to track and stop poachers.

Kobus took us (that is, David Schmidtz and Elizabeth Willott) on a tour of the Park. He was visibly upset one day when we hit a rabbit that darted in front of our car. He stopped the car and moved the rabbit off the road so that animals stopping to feed on the carcass would not suffer the same fate. He was visibly delighted when we encountered sizable herds of healthy elephant and Cape buffalo. We have never met a person who loves animals more than he does.

However, although Kruger Park is huge, it is not a self-sustaining ecosystem. To keep herds within the Park's carrying capacity, the Park Service at one time culled a variety of large mammals. The current view is that natural predators, starvation, and disease naturally suffice to control most animal populations. The one exception is the elephant. In Africa, humans are not an introduced species. Human hunters are Africa's keystone natural predator, and the only predator that preys on elephants.

Kobus was the last ranger in Kruger Park to be assigned the task of culling elephants. Kobus shot them from a helicopter with an automatic rifle, killing as many as a dozen at a time in the same number of seconds with the same number of shots through the brain. At his elbow sat monitors from organizations such as Society for Prevention of Cruelty to Animals.

The SPCA did not stop the culling, but in 1995, public pressure did. There were 7,200 elephants at the time. As of 2001, there were 9,600, according to Kruger National Park's senior scientist in charge of elephant management, Ian Whyte (see his article in chapter 8). As of 2009, William Mabasa reports (private communication) that there are 13,500. It is visibly apparent that the park is not producing enough food to sustain them indefinitely. Section Ranger Aari Schreiber (chief ranger for an area covering about a quarter of the park), told us in 1999 that if elephants were to disappear today, it would take twenty years for the land to recover from the damage the elephants have done since 1995.

The Park Service moved 1,100 elephants to Mozambique over four years between 2001 and 2005. There were roughly 10,300 elephants left in Kruger National Park when the relocation process was complete (with no plan for protecting relocated elephants from poachers). Barring a resumption of culling, the Park Service has been trying to concentrate the elephants in an area constituting about half the park. While the elephants strip their half of the park, the Park Service is preserving biodiversity as best it can in the remainder. Is there a better alternative?

One way or another, thousands upon thousands of elephants have to go, and for most of them there is nowhere to go. We talked to a number of rangers. They all said it is only a matter of time before the culling begins again. So, Kobus is waiting for the phone to ring—waiting for someone to say it has started again and they need Kobus's help. The prospect horrifies him. What should he do?

In 2008, the South African government lifted its moratorium on elephant culling, according to the *Washington Post* (February 26, 2008). Ian Whyte, chief scientist in charge of large herbivore management at Kruger National Park (now retired), interviewed for that article, said of the resumption of culling, "I believe it is necessary. I am relieved that I do not have to be involved." Despite the lifting of the ban, the culling has not actually resumed.

It was Kobus Krüger who introduced us to Ian Whyte, whose essay appears in chapter 8. For more on Kobus Krüger, see his wife's memoir on the precarious and sometimes hilarious adventure of raising three daughters and assorted animals in Kruger Park's most remote wilderness. Kobie Krüger, *The Wilderness Family* (New York: Ballantine, 2001.) For more on Ian Whyte, see John F. Walker, *Ivory's Ghosts* (New York: Atlantic Monthly Press, 2009).

2. MANAGING THE LOGIC OF THE COMMONS

Sustainability is a central concept of environmental economics. Originally applied to renewable resources such as forests and fish, the idea was to calculate a maximum rate of harvesting the resource that would not deplete the stock. Following the landmark study, *Our Common Future*, people have begun to treat sustainability as the more vague but more inclusive idea of meeting today's needs without compromising people's ability to meet needs in the future.

Here, in essence, is the problem. Suppose there is a plot of land. The land has a *carrying capacity*, which is the number of animals the land can sustain more or less indefinitely. Suppose the parcel's carrying capacity is 100 animals. The land is jointly owned by ten shepherds, each of whom owns ten animals for a total flock of 100 animals. The land is thus at its carrying capacity. As things stand, each animal is worth (let's say) one dollar to its owner, so that, at carrying capacity, 100 animals are worth $100. Crucially, although the ten shepherds treat their individual flocks as private property, they jointly treat the land as one large pasture, with no internal fences, so that each of their animals grazes freely.

> 10 shepherds × 10 animals each = 100 animals.
> Individual flock's value = 10 animals × $1 = $10
> Total flock's value = 100 animals × $1 = $100

Now suppose one shepherd adds an eleventh animal. We now have 101 animals altogether, and thus exceed the land's carrying capacity. There is not quite enough food per animal now; therefore they are a bit leaner, and the value per animal drops to 95 cents per head. At that rate, the total stock of 101 animals is now worth $95.95, which is $4.95 less than the total stock was worth before, when it was kept within the land's carrying capacity.

> Total flock's value = 101 animals × 0.95 = $95.95

So, why would a shepherd add the extra animal, when it so clearly is a losing proposition? Here is why. At the original carrying capacity, the individual flocks of ten were worth $10. Having added one more sheep, the shepherd now has eleven and each is worth 95 cents. That works out to $10.45, which means that the individual shepherd actually made a profit of forty-five cents by adding the extra animal, even though the value of the total stock went from $100 to $95.95.

> Individual flock's value = 11 animals × 0.95 = $10.45

It appears that the same decision, whether to add another sheep, represents both a net loss of $4.05 and a net gain of $0.45. Is this possible? Was one of our calculations fallacious?

What happened is this: Although the total cost to the group of adding the extra animal exceeded the total benefit, the individual shepherd receives 100 percent of the benefit while paying only 10 percent of the cost. The remaining 90 percent is paid by the other nine shepherds: because they own 90 percent of the animals, they suffer 90 percent of the loss involved in the falling price per head. Individual shepherds, though, see only individual costs and benefits, and act accordingly. The logic of the commons has begun its seemingly inevitable grind toward its tragic fate.

What can the shepherds do? See Hardin's essay in chapter 10.

3. MANAGING OVERPOPULATION

UTILITARIANISM: A THEORY ABOUT HOW TO THEORIZE ABOUT WHAT WORKS

Peter Singer is contemporary philosophy's foremost expositor and defender of the moral theory known as *utilitarianism*. The utilitarianism of the 1700s was a theory about what works; thus, philosophers David Hume and Adam Smith studied tariffs, trade, contract law, and property law. Where do such things have a history of helping citizens to know what to expect from each other, and how to be of service to each other, or simply how to avoid being in each other's way?

Today's utilitarianism would be unrecognizable to Hume and Smith. Today's utilitarianism concerns a different question, not just a different answer. Contemporary utilitarianism asks not what has a record of working but instead asks what you, personally, ought to do. Today's utilitarianism answers the new question by saying, your moral duty is to do the best you can right now. One possible implication of this seemingly common sense idea is that you should look through your pockets right now, then figure out how to get that money to someone who needs it more than you do. If you can save a life with money you otherwise would spend on a movie ticket, then save the life. See Singer (chapter 3).[1]

STUDYING WHAT WORKS VERSUS PROVING YOUR HEART IS IN THE RIGHT PLACE

Or should you? What if saving a life would contribute to overpopulation? Are you trying to do as much good as you can, or to convince Peter Singer that you have a good heart? If you want to do as much good as you can, then you want to get your facts right.

The usual way of thinking about overpopulation is inspired by (or haunted by) Paul Ehrlich. Ehrlich started his book, *The Population Bomb*, with the words, "The battle to feed all of humanity is over. In the 1970's the world will undergo famines—hundreds of millions of people are going to starve to death in spite of any crash programs embarked upon now. At this late date nothing can prevent a substantial increase in the world death rate."[2] Ehrlich convinced a generation that we were descending into a hell of overpopulation.

Ehrlich, like many others, believed extreme measure "The birth rate must be brought into balance with the death rate or mankind will breed itself into oblivion. We can no longer afford merely to treat the symptoms of the cancer of population growth; the cancer itself must be cut out. Population control is the only answer." By population control, he did not mean handing out free condoms. In keeping with the cancer metaphor, he later wrote, "The operation will demand many apparently brutal and heartless decisions. The pain may be intense. But the disease is so far advanced that only with radical surgery does the patient have a chance of survival."[3]

Did humanity "breed itself into oblivion" in the 1970s? Did Ehrlich get his facts right? Was he even close? If birth rates were falling sharply and falling death rates—rising life expectancy—continues to be the main reason why population is rising, how afraid should we be of life expectancy continuing to rise in the future? Suggestion: do a search right now. Search for the terms "world population trend" or "world fertility trend." Check World Bank interactive charts on fertility rates: http://data.worldbank.org/indicator/SP.DYN.TFRT.IN. Check figures for population growth: http://data.worldbank

.org/indicator/SP.POP.GROW. Or check http://worldhunger.org, which in 2017 says, "The vast majority of hungry people live in developing regions, which saw a 42 percent reduction in the prevalence of undernourished people between 1990–92 and 2012–14."

These figures change; that's why you need to check for yourself. People are starving, and in horrific numbers, yet the trend is going in the opposite direction from what Ehrlich predicted, and probably also in the opposite direction from what you've been told, and will continue to be told. What do you suppose McKibben (chapter 15) would say?

4. MANAGING FOREIGN AID

As I walked across the border from Zimbabwe into Zambia in July 1999, I saw a large sign warning that bringing second-hand clothing into Zimbabwe from Zambia is strictly prohibited. I wondered whether authorities were concerned that second-hand clothing might carry some form of plague.

Once across the border, I met Phillip Roberts, a construction worker who owned a Jeep, had some experience as a tour guide, was not otherwise working that day, and was willing to show me some of the country. We drove off. After a half hour of delightfully animated conversation, I asked Phillip about the sign. The smile left his face and he said, "I can't tell you," After a silent minute in which he seemed to be struggling with something, he said, "I can show you, though." He said that if I wanted to understand the sign, we needed to make a stop in the town of Livingstone, Zambia. We reached the town, and I heard its story.

A few years previously, there had been a drought. Relief agencies wanted to help. Sending money was a problem, though, because money often is used to buy guns, as in Somalia. Sending food was a problem. Food sent to India, improperly stored, had become a breeding ground for plague-carrying rats. When plague broke out, people who had flooded in from the countryside seeking food fled back to their villages, taking plague with them. So the agencies wanted to lend aid in a form that at least would do no harm. They decided that what Zambia could use, which would at least do no harm, was planeloads of second-hand clothing.

Until then, Livingstone had been the hub of Zambia's textile industry. Cotton was grown, processed, and woven into cloth there. As was the case in North America as recently as a generation ago, consumers bought the cloth and did the sewing themselves. Livingstone cloth could not compete with factory-made clothing, though, especially free factory-made clothing. Livingstone's unemployment rate had hovered around 90 percent ever since. Finally, I understood: the plague was the clothing itself, carried by a swarm of well-meaning but ignorant foreigners like me.[4]

The problem was not faulty execution by particular agencies, but something more fundamental: failing to appreciate that solutions to problems of developing countries ultimately lie in their own local economies. To be effective in the long term, foreign aid must assist local producers, not put them out of business.

In chapter 3, Holmes Rolston III claimed that G-7 nations consume, and also produce, about 80 percent of the world's food while containing less than 20 percent of the world's population. What would happen if G-7 nations consumed, and produced, less? Would we be better off? Would Zambia? Under what circumstances?

If we consumed less, would people in developing countries be better off? How so? Does our reason for consuming less stand or fall with whether importing less from developing countries would somehow improve their standard of living? Or is the main reason for living a simpler life closer to home, namely that a simpler life is a better life? What would Sagoff, or Gambrel and Cafaro (chapter 15) say?

5. MANAGING CONFLICT

Many people would argue that it is morally wrong for the crew of Paul Watson's *Sea Shepherd* (chapter 16) to be destroying fishing boats. Others would disagree. Can such disagreements be settled? If not, where does that leave us? What should be done?

Are the Japanese fishermen in Watson's story as innocent as the little girl in Norton's story? How do you suppose the fishermen felt about having their boats destroyed? How would you feel if the *Sea Shepherd* crew singled you out, making an example of you by destroying your car to stop you from using it to pollute the atmosphere?

Can you recall episodes in your own life in which you have faced a dilemma like Bryan Norton's, where the "aggregationist" approach would prove too little, while the moral approach would prove too much? See chapter 13.

Norton's tale of sand dollar "strip mining" is a case in which the story's villain is an innocent little girl. But innocent though she may be, environmentalist rhetoric will not impress her. She is not ready to listen. How often is that the case? How often are polluters and overconsumers simply innocent people who mean no harm? Does that affect how (or whether) we ought to confront them? What would Andrew Light (chapter 16) say?

6. MANAGING CITIES

According to Jane Jacobs, cities are almost as old as the human race itself, and are considerably older than the institution that we now call agriculture. There had to be marketplaces where people could exchange their agricultural surplus before there could be any point in having farms large enough to produce a surplus. There also had to be marketplaces before farmers could acquire tools with which to go beyond being the most primitive kind of hunter-gatherers. That means that the problems that go with cities have been with us for eons.

Yet, cities remain an underexplored frontier in environmental ethics. Urban ecosystems are where most of us spend most of our lives. So, for most of us, the good life, and the sustainable life, has to be a life lived mainly in a city. We need not lament this. Indeed, the idea of "making the best of it" seems unduly glum. Life in the city can be joyful. Life in the city can be sustainable too, to a far greater degree than it has been under previously available technologies. At very least, we can have fun trying.

Cities have acquired a bad reputation, ecologically speaking. Cities are where the pollution is, the reasoning seems to go, so if we get rid of the cities, won't we be getting rid of the pollution at the same time?

Do we know how the environmental footprint of a city dweller compares to that of someone who lives in the countryside? Do we even know which generally is larger? Feeling nostalgia for the simple life we never had, we want to extol the virtues of living off the land in a low-tech, "natural" way, ignoring the fact that it takes a *lot* of land for a family to support itself that way, even at a bare subsistence level. As described by Nordhaus and Schellenberger in chapter 8, Brazilian cities have been sending people back to the land—that is, the Amazon rainforest—and the migration back to the forest has been among the world's most infamous ecological disasters. In fact, given the size of the world's human population, what forests need is high-tech, space-saving, energy-saving, high-rise cities. Above all, what the forests do not need is people going back to the land and using trees for firewood. Ironically, the focus on decentralization, small-scale development, and self-sufficiency ignores the fact that "urbanization can ease land pressures in the countryside, thus reducing rates of deforestation and desertification."[5]

What, then, are the real alternatives to the status quo in which most of us live in familiar urban and suburban neighborhoods? Which alternatives would be worse, and which would be better, environmentally speaking? Further, what can you do, and what should you do, as individuals and as communities, to reduce your consumption of natural resources, to reduce your production of pollutants, and more generally to reduce your environmental impact?

What happens when we price water or electricity as if such things were not scarce? Do consumers consume more or less when there is no charge for consuming more? Does our current regime of artificially low prices teach people to consume thoughtlessly? What would have happened to the whales if, in the nineteenth century, we had heavily subsidized whale-oil consumption? Imagine selling food by charging each household a flat monthly fee, then simply turning people loose on the supermarkets. Would we run out of food? Would more food be wasted? What forms of urban ecology does our world need?

From an environmental perspective, we want consumers to economize, to moderate their demand. But to make consumers stop to think before consuming that extra unit, the extra unit needs to have a price. We live in a complex world in which there are many relevant considerations, but as a rule, if you want to save whales, do not subsidize the consumption of whale oil. Do not give cash prizes to people for doing things you do not want them to do. So, under what conditions should we subsidize the consumption of scarce resources? When do we have moral reason to prevent markets from teaching consumers to economize?

We would not normally think of the preservation of whales as a question of urban ecology, but that could be a mistake. If we build cities in a way that makes their population dependent on a particular energy source, then any discussion we had about conserving that particular energy source will not be serious unless we pay heed to the pressure we put on the resource when we build cities like that. See the two essays by Adriana Zuniga-Teran (chapter 15) for a preview of some of those most central topics in urban ecology that environmental ethics will need to engage in years to come.

7. MANAGING YOUR LIFESTYLE

Perhaps the most important lesson a student of environmental ethics could learn is how good the life of an environmentalist can be. People can get the wrong idea about being "green": that an environmentalist is constantly on the lookout for things to feel guilty about, or for things to try to make other people feel guilty about: in short, I'm not okay, you're not okay.

In *The Global Living Handbook*, though, Jim Merkel says, "We realize that we are not martyrs and we are not victims. If we ride our bikes to prove a point we will feel bitter. If we ride because we love getting exercise, hearing the birds, and watching the moon scribe the sky, then our life enters the realm of poetics. Let's face it: the corporations may be trying to dominate the planet, but they are not *making* us buy their cars and gas. We have a choice."[6]

How do you suppose your life would change if you were to be more environmentally conscious? In what ways would a more environmentally sound lifestyle represent a sacrifice on your part? What would you truly miss? Are there ways in which life might be *more* satisfying? If so, then why not start gently phasing them into your life? Why not today?

Freya Mathews (chapter 15) imagines how to live in a city without getting caught up in its frantic modern pace. What sort of relationship does she see between living a simple life and living an ecologically sustainable life? Does the "desire to make things better" lead us to waste our time fighting for something, when there are better things to do with our time than fight? Mathews seems to say there is a sense in which environmental ethics is not "natural." That is, environmental activists often fail to live "within the framework of the given." What does Mathews mean? Does she have a point? If she is right, does that change how we ought to think about environmental ethics?

Mathews also writes that we should stop "nursing the desire to make things better." That urge is the "motor of modern civilization" and the cause of environmental crises. Do you agree? Are modern civilizations the first civilizations to run into environmental problems? If not, what were the motors of environmental crisis in the past?

8. MANAGING THE CLIMATE

Climate change looks like the ultimate commons tragedy. Yet, in a fairly obvious way, there is a personal dimension to questions about how to live a good life as a city dweller, and those questions come up when we ask about living ethically in a world whose climate is changing. Do questions of climate change have personal implications? How would we know?

There are still people who are skeptical about whether the climate is changing. Others think the climate is changing, but doubt that the change is anthropocentric (caused by human activity). Does it matter? Does anything depend on whether climate change happens naturally, has happened before, and will happen again?

If or when these discussions run their course, a new layer of questions emerge. Those who agree that climate change is a crisis do not necessarily agree on what to do about it. Suffice it to say, if climate change really matters, then sooner or later we had better ask what really works.

What are our policy options? What are the costs and benefits of our options? Do we have any good information? Does the current state of our meteorological science give us a basis for estimating how much we need to reduce anthropogenic greenhouse emissions in order to make a real difference to atmospheric greenhouse gas levels within the next century? Perhaps that is not the right question, but if not, why not?

We hope this will change soon, but as we write this, in 2017, it appears that if you try to track down research on how to prevent climate change, almost everything you find will consist of lists of things you can do to prove your heart is in the right place. You can live close enough to work to cycle. You can recycle. You can vote for your government to require 50 percent cuts in carbon emissions. Do we have evidence that, if everyone did that, it would help? What do our best models predict? *When* would it make a difference? Do you know? Does anyone? If we have no such evidence, why would we even be talking about such things? For that matter, even if we did have evidence about what would happen if everyone did *x*, how is that supposed to be a reason for you to do *x*? (Recall our discussion of the moral theory known as deontology at the beginning of this book.)

Environmental ethicists and environmental activists often proceed as if what really matters is agreeing that there is a problem and that we should feel guilty. But what if our ecological challenges are as serious as we have been led to expect? In that case, what can we do, without devastating cost to future generations, that would actually help? If solving the problem is no longer possible, then what can we do to give future generations the cultural and technological tools they will need to cope with the problem we anticipate leaving them?[7] For the sake of coming generations, we need to get our science right. (See chapter 14.)

NOTES

1. See also David Schmidtz, "After Solipsism," *Oxford Studies in Normative Ethics* 6 (2016) 145–65.
2. Paul Ehrlich, *The Population Bomb* (Cutchogue, NY: Buccaneer Books, 1968) p. xi.
3. Ehrlich, *Population Bomb*, p. 166–67.
4. As it turned out, the Zambians did not know the exact point of the sign back at the Zimbabwe border. Zimbabwe may have been trying to nurture its own domestic textile

industry, or trying to force Zimbabweans to go back to buying Zambian cloth, thereby helping to revive Livingstone's industry.

5. Martin Lewis, "Third World Development and Population," *Survey of Ecological Economics,* ed. R. Krishnan, J. Harris, & N. Goodwin (Washington: Island Press, 1995), 314–17, at 316.

6. Jim Merkel was once an electrical engineer. He made his living selling military technology. He gave it up, and for ten years lived on five thousand dollars per year. For more on the Global Living Project, contact Jim Merkel (http://radicalsimplicity.org/).

7. See https://www.ipcc.ch/publications_and_data/ar4/wg1/en/spmsspm-projections-of.html

8

TOWARD A HUMANE ENVIRONMENTALISM

A. Ecology and Imperialism

RAMACHANDRA GUHA

RADICAL AMERICAN ENVIRONMENTALISM AND WILDERNESS PRESERVATION

A Third World Critique

I present a Third World critique of the trend in American environmentalism known as deep ecology, analyzing each of deep ecology's central tenets: the distinction between anthropocentrism and biocentrism, the focus on wilderness preservation, the invocation of Eastern traditions, and the belief that it represents the most radical trend within environmentalism.

I argue that the anthropocentrism/biocentrism distinction is of little use in understanding the dynamics of environmental degradation, that the implementation of the wilderness agenda is causing serious deprivation in the Third World, that the deep ecologist's interpretation of Eastern tradition is highly selective, and that in other cultural contexts (e.g., West Germany and India) radical environmentalism manifests itself quite differently, with a far greater emphasis on equity and the integration of ecological concerns with livelihood and work. I conclude that despite its claims to universality, deep ecology is firmly rooted in American environmental and cultural history and is inappropriate when applied to the Third World.

> Even God dare not appear to the poor man except in the form of bread.
>
> —*Mahatma Gandhi*

INTRODUCTION

The respected radical journalist Kirkpatrick Sale recently celebrated "the passion of a new and growing movement that has become disenchanted with the environmental establishment and has in recent years mounted a serious and sweeping attack on it—style,

Ramachandra Guha, "Radical American Environmentalism and Wilderness Preservation: A Third World Critique," Environmental Ethics 11 (1989). Reprinted with permission.

substance, systems, sensibilities and all."[1] The vision of those whom Sale calls the "New Ecologists"—and what I refer to in this article as deep ecology—is a compelling one. Decrying the narrowly economic goals of mainstream environmentalism, this new movement aims at nothing less than a philosophical and cultural revolution in human attitudes toward nature. In contrast to the conventional lobbying efforts of environmental professionals based in Washington, it proposes a militant defense of "Mother Earth," an unflinching opposition to human attacks on undisturbed wilderness. With their goals ranging from the spiritual to the political, the adherents of deep ecology span a wide spectrum of the American environmental movement. As Sale correctly notes, this emerging strand has in a matter of a few years made its presence felt in a number of fields: from academic philosophy (as in the journal *Environmental Ethics*) to popular environmentalism (for example, the group Earth First!).

In this article I develop a critique of deep ecology from the perspective of a sympathetic outsider. I critique deep ecology not as a general (or even a foot soldier) in the continuing struggle between the ghosts of Gifford Pinchot and John Muir over control of the U.S. environmental movement, but as an outsider to these battles. I speak admittedly as a partisan, but of the environmental movement in India, a country with an ecological diversity comparable to the U.S., but with a radically dissimilar cultural and social history.

My treatment of deep ecology is primarily historical and sociological, rather than philosophical, in nature. Specifically, I examine the cultural rootedness of a philosophy that likes to present itself in universalistic terms. I make two main arguments: first, that deep ecology is uniquely American, and despite superficial similarities in rhetorical style, the social and political goals of radical environmentalism in other cultural contexts (e.g., West Germany and India) are quite different; second, that the social consequences of putting deep ecology into practice on a worldwide basis (what its practitioners are aiming for) are very grave indeed.

THE TENETS OF DEEP ECOLOGY

While I am aware that the term deep ecology was coined by the Norwegian philosopher Arne Naess, this article refers specifically to the American variant.

Adherents of the deep ecological perspective in this country, while arguing intensely among themselves over its political and philosophical implications, share some fundamental premises about human–nature interactions. As I see it, the defining characteristics of deep ecology are fourfold:

First, deep ecology argues that the environmental movement must shift from an "anthropocentric" to a "biocentric" perspective. In many respects, an acceptance of the primacy of this distinction constitutes the litmus test of deep ecology. A considerable effort is expended by deep ecologists in showing that the dominant motif in Western philosophy has been anthropocentric—i.e., the belief that man and his works are the center of the universe—and conversely, in identifying those lonely thinkers (Leopold, Thoreau, Muir, Aldous Huxley, Santayana, etc.) who, in assigning man a more humble place in the natural order, anticipated deep ecological thinking. In the political realm, meanwhile, establishment environmentalism (shallow ecology) is chided for casting its arguments in human-centered terms. Preserving nature, the deep ecologists say, has an intrinsic worth quite apart from any benefits preservation may convey to future human generations. The anthropocentric–biocentric distinction is accepted as axiomatic by deep ecologists, it structures their discourse, and much of the present discussion remains mired within it.

The second characteristic of deep ecology is its focus on the preservation of unspoilt wilderness—and the restoration of degraded areas to a more pristine condition—to the relative (and sometimes absolute) neglect of other issues on the environmental agenda. I later identify the cultural roots and portentous consequences of this obsession with wilderness. For the moment, let me indicate three distinct sources from which it springs. Historically, it represents a playing out of the preservationist (read radical) and utilitarian (read reformist) dichotomy that has plagued American environmentalism since the turn of the century. Morally, it is an imperative that follows from the biocentric perspective; other species of plants and animals, and nature itself, have an intrinsic right to exist. And finally, the preservation of wilderness also turns on a scientific argument—viz., the value of biological diversity in stabilizing ecological regimes and in retaining a gene pool for future generations. Truly radical policy proposals have been put forward by deep ecologists on the basis of these arguments. The influential poet Gary Snyder, for example, would like to see a 90 percent reduction in human populations to allow a restoration of pristine environments, while others have argued forcefully that a large portion of the globe must be immediately cordoned off from human beings.[2]

Third, there is a widespread invocation of Eastern spiritual traditions as forerunners of deep ecology. Deep ecology, it is suggested, was practiced both by major religious traditions and at a more popular level by "primal" peoples in non-Western settings. This complements the search for an authentic lineage in Western thought. At one level, the task is to recover those dissenting voices within the Judeo-Christian tradition; at another, to suggest that religious traditions in other cultures are, in contrast, dominantly if not exclusively "biocentric" in their orientation. This coupling of (ancient) Eastern and (modern) ecological wisdom seemingly helps consolidate the claim that deep ecology is a philosophy of universal significance.

Fourth, deep ecologists, whatever their internal differences, share the belief that they are the "leading edge" of the environmental movement. As the polarity of the shallow/deep and anthropocentric/biocentric distinctions makes clear, they see themselves as the spiritual, philosophical, and political vanguard of American and world environmentalism.

TOWARD A CRITIQUE

Although I analyze each of these tenets independently, it is important to recognize, as deep ecologists are fond of remarking in reference to nature, the interconnectedness and unity of these individual themes.

(1) Insofar as it has begun to act as a check on man's arrogance and ecological hubris, the transition from an anthropocentric (human-centered) to a biocentric (humans as only one element in the ecosystem) view in both religious and scientific traditions is only to be welcomed.[3] What is unacceptable are the radical conclusions drawn by deep ecology, in particular, that intervention in nature should be guided primarily by the need to preserve biotic integrity rather than by the needs of humans. The latter for deep ecologists is anthropocentric, the former biocentric. This dichotomy is, however, of very little use in understanding the dynamics of environmental degradation.

The two fundamental ecological problems facing the globe are (i) overconsumption by the industrialized world and by urban elites in the Third World and (ii) growing militarization, both in a short-term sense (i.e., ongoing regional wars) and in a long-term sense (i.e., the arms race and the prospect of nuclear annihilation). Neither of these problems has any tangible connection to the anthropocentric–biocentric distinction. Indeed, the agents of these processes would barely comprehend this philosophical dichotomy. The proximate causes of the ecologically wasteful characteristics of industrial society and of militarization are far more mundane: at an aggregate level, the dialectic of economic and political structures, and at a microlevel, the life style choices of individuals. These causes cannot be reduced, whatever the level of analysis, to a deeper anthropocentric attitude toward nature; on the contrary, by constituting a grave threat to human survival, the ecological degradation they cause does not even serve the best interests of human beings! If my identification of the major dangers to the integrity of the natural world is correct, invoking the bogy of anthropocentrism is at best irrelevant and at worst a dangerous obfuscation.

(2) If the above dichotomy is irrelevant, the emphasis on wilderness is positively harmful when applied to the Third World. If in the U.S. the preservationist/utilitarian division is seen as mirroring the conflict between "people" and "interests," in countries such as India the situation is very nearly the reverse. Because India is a long settled and densely populated country in which agrarian populations have a finely balanced relationship with nature, the setting aside of wilderness areas has resulted in a direct transfer of resources from the poor to the rich. Thus, Project Tiger, a network of parks hailed by the international conservation community as an outstanding success, sharply posits the interests of the tiger against those of poor peasants living in and around the reserve. The designation of tiger reserves was made possible only by the physical displacement of existing villages and their inhabitants; their management requires the continuing exclusion of peasants and livestock. The initial impetus for setting up parks for the tiger and other large mammals such as the rhinoceros and elephant came from two social groups, first, a class of ex-hunters turned conservationists belonging mostly to the declining Indian feudal elite and second,

representatives of international agencies, such as the World Wildlife Fund (WWF) and the International Union for the Conservation of Nature and Natural Resources (IUCN), seeking to transplant the American system of national parks onto Indian soil. In no case have the needs of the local population been taken into account, and as in many parts of Africa, the designated wildlands are managed primarily for the benefit of rich tourists. Until very recently, wildlands preservation has been identified with environmentalism by the state and the conservation elite; in consequence, environmental problems that impinge far more directly on the lives of the poor—e.g., fuel, fodder, water shortages, soil erosion, and air and water pollution—have not been adequately addressed. Deep ecology provides, perhaps unwittingly, a justification for the continuation of such narrow and inequitable conservation practices under a newly acquired radical guise. Increasingly, the international conservation elite is using the philosophical, moral, and scientific arguments used by deep ecologists in advancing their wilderness crusade. A striking but by no means atypical example is the recent plea by a prominent American biologist for the takeover of large portions of the globe by the author and his scientific colleagues. Writing in a prestigious scientific forum, the *Annual Review of Ecology and Systematics*, Daniel Janzen argues that only biologists have the competence to decide how the tropical landscape should be used. As "the representatives of the natural world," biologists are "in charge of the future of tropical ecology," and only they have the expertise and mandate to "determine whether the tropical agroscape is to be populated only by humans, their mutualists, commensals, and parasites, or whether it will also contain some islands of the greater nature—the nature that spawned humans, yet has been vanquished by them." Janzen exhorts his colleagues to advance their territorial claims on the tropical world more forcefully, warning that the very existence of these areas is at stake: "if biologists want a tropics in which to biologize, they are going to have to buy it with care, energy, effort, strategy, tactics, time, and cash."[4]

This frankly imperialist manifesto highlights the multiple dangers of the preoccupation with wilderness preservation that is characteristic of deep ecology. As I have suggested, it seriously compounds the neglect by

the American movement of far more pressing environmental problems within the Third World. But perhaps more importantly, and in a more insidious fashion, it also provides an impetus to the imperialist yearning of Western biologists and their financial sponsors, organizations such as the WWF and the IUCN. The wholesale transfer of a movement culturally rooted in American conservation history can only result in the social uprooting of human populations in other parts of the globe.

(3) I come now to the persistent invocation of Eastern philosophies as antecedent in point of time but convergent in their structure with deep ecology. Complex and internally differentiated religious traditions—Hinduism, Buddhism, and Taoism—are lumped together as holding a view of nature believed to be quintessentially biocentric. Individual philosophers such as the Taoist Lao Tzu are identified as being forerunners of deep ecology. Even an intensely political, pragmatic, and Christian influenced thinker such as Gandhi has been accorded a wholly undeserved place in the deep ecological pantheon. Thus the Zen teacher Robert Aitken Roshi makes the strange claim that Gandhi's thought was not human-centered and that he practiced an embryonic form of deep ecology which is "traditionally Eastern and is found with differing emphasis in Hinduism, Taoism and in Theravada and Mahayana Buddhism."[5] Moving away from the realm of high philosophy and scriptural religion, deep ecologists make the further claim that at the level of material and spiritual practice "primal" peoples subordinated themselves to the integrity of the biotic universe they inhabited.

I have indicated that this appropriation of Eastern traditions is in part dictated by the need to construct an authentic lineage and in part a desire to present deep ecology as a universalistic philosophy. Indeed, in his substantial and quixotic biography of John Muir, Michael Cohen goes so far as to suggest that Muir was the "Taoist of the [American] West."[6] This reading of Eastern traditions is selective and does not bother to differentiate between alternate (and changing) religious and cultural traditions; as it stands, it does considerable violence to the historical record. Throughout most recorded history the characteristic form of human activity in the "East" has been a finely tuned but nonetheless conscious and dynamic manipulation of nature. Although mystics such as Lao Tzu did reflect on the spiritual essence of human relations with nature, it must be recognized that such ascetics and their reflections were supported by a society of cultivators whose relationship with nature was a far more active one. Many agricultural communities do have a sophisticated knowledge of the natural environment that may equal (and sometimes surpass) codified "scientific" knowledge; yet, the elaboration of such traditional ecological knowledge (in both material and spiritual contexts) can hardly be said to rest on a mystical affinity with nature of a deep ecological kind. Nor is such knowledge infallible; as the archaeological record powerfully suggests, modern Western man has no monopoly on ecological disasters.

In a brilliant article, the Chicago historian Ronald Inden points out that this romantic and essentially positive view of the East is a mirror image of the scientific and essentially pejorative view normally upheld by Western scholars of the Orient. In either case, the East constitutes the Other, a body wholly separate and alien from the West; it is defied by a uniquely spiritual and nonrational "essence," even if this essence is valorized quite differently by the two schools. Eastern man exhibits a spiritual dependence with respect to nature—on the one hand, this is symptomatic of his prescientific and backward self, on the other, of his ecological wisdom and deep ecological consciousness. Both views are monolithic, simplistic, and have the characteristic effect—intended in one case, perhaps unintended in the other—of denying agency and reason to the East and making it the privileged orbit of Western thinkers.

The two apparently opposed perspectives have then a common underlying structure of discourse in which the East merely serves as a vehicle for Western projections. Varying images of the East are raw material for political and cultural battles being played out in the West; they tell us far more about the Western commentator and his desires than about the "East." Inden's remarks apply not merely to Western scholarship on India, but to Orientalist constructions of China and Japan as well:

> . . . The adherents of the romantic view, best exemplified academically in the discourses of Christian liberalism and analytic psychology, concede the realm of the public and impersonal to the positivist. Taking

their succour not from governments and big business, but from a plethora of religious foundations and self-help institutes, and from allies in the "consciousness industry," not to mention the important industry of tourism, the romantics insist that India embodies a private realm of the imagination and the religious which modern, western man lacks but needs. They, therefore, like the positivists, but for just the opposite reason, have a vested interest in seeing that the Orientalist view of India as "spiritual," "mysterious," and "exotic" is perpetuated.[7]

(4) How radical, finally, are the deep ecologists? Notwithstanding their self-image and strident rhetoric (in which the label "shallow ecology" has an opprobrium similar to that reserved for "social democratic" by Marxist-Leninists), even within the American context their radicalism is limited and it manifests itself quite differently elsewhere. To my mind deep ecology is best viewed as a radical trend within the wilderness preservation movement. Although advancing philosophical rather than aesthetic arguments and encouraging political militancy rather than negotiation, its practical emphasis—viz., preservation of unspoilt nature—is virtually identical. For the mainstream movement, the function of wilderness is to provide a temporary antidote to modern civilization. As a special institution within an industrialized society, the national park "provides an opportunity for respite, contrast, contemplation, and affirmation of values for those who live most of their lives in the workaday world."[8] Indeed, the rapid increase in visitations to the national parks in postwar America is a direct consequence of economic expansion. The emergence of a popular interest in wilderness sites, the historian Samuel Hayes points out, was "not a throwback to the primitive, but an integral part of the modern standard of living as people sought to add new 'amenity' and 'aesthetic' goals and desires to their earlier preoccupation with necessities and conveniences."[9]

Here, the enjoyment of nature is an integral part of the consumer society. The private automobile (and the life style it has spawned) is in many respects the ultimate ecological villain, and an untouched wilderness the prototype of ecological harmony; yet, for most Americans it is perfectly consistent to drive a thousand miles to spend a holiday in a national park. They possess a vast, beautiful, and sparsely populated continent and are also able to draw upon the natural resources of large portions of the globe by virtue of their economic and political dominance. In consequence, America can simultaneously enjoy the Material benefits of an expanding economy and the aesthetic benefits of unspoilt nature. The two poles of "wilderness" and "civilization" mutually coexist in an internally coherent whole, and philosophers of both poles are assigned a prominent place in this culture. Paradoxically as it may seem, it is no accident that Star Wars technology and deep ecology both find their fullest expression in that leading sector of Western civilization, California.

Deep ecology runs parallel to the consumer society without seriously questioning its ecological and sociopolitical basis. In its celebration of American wilderness, it also displays an uncomfortable convergence with the prevailing climate of nationalism in the American wilderness movement. For spokesmen such as the historian Roderick Nash, the national park system is America's distinctive cultural contribution to the world, reflective not merely of its economic but of its philosophical and ecological maturity as well. In what Walter Lippman called the American century, the "American invention of national parks" must be exported worldwide. Betraying an economic determinism that would make even a Marxist shudder, Nash believes that environmental preservation is a "full stomach" phenomenon that is confined to the rich, urban, and sophisticated. Nonetheless, he hopes that "the less developed nations may eventually evolve economically and intellectually to the point where nature preservation is more than a business."[10]

The error which Nash makes (and which deep ecology in some respects encourages) is to equate environmental protection with the protection of the wilderness. This is a distinctively American notion, borne out of a unique social and environmental history. The archetypal concerns of radical environmentalists in other cultural contexts are in fact quite different. The German Greens, for example, have elaborated a devastating critique of industrial society which turns on the acceptance of environmental limits to growth. Pointing to the intimate links between industrialization, militarization, and conquest, the Greens argue that economic growth in the West has historically rested on the economic and ecological exploitation of the Third World. Rudolf Bahro is characteristically blunt:

> The working class here [in the West] is the richest lower class in the world. And if I look at the problem from the point of view of the whole of humanity, not just from that of Europe, then I must say that the metropolitan working class is the worst exploiting class in history. . . . What made poverty bearable in eighteenth or nineteenth-century Europe was the prospect of escaping it through exploitation of the periphery. But this is no longer a possibility, and continued industrialism in the Third World will mean poverty for whole generations and hunger for millions.[11]

Here the roots of global ecological problems lie in the disproportionate share of resources consumed by the industrialized countries as a whole and the urban elite within the Third World. Since it is impossible to reproduce an industrial monoculture worldwide, the ecological movement in the West must begin by cleaning up its own act. The Greens advocate the creation of a "no growth" economy, to be achieved by scaling down current (and clearly unsustainable) consumption levels. This radical shift in consumption and production patterns requires the creation of alternate economic and political structures—smaller in scale and more amenable to social participation—but it rests equally on a shift in cultural values. The expansionist character of modern Western man will have to give way to an ethic of renunciation and self-limitation, in which spiritual and communal values play an increasing role in sustaining social life. This revolution in cultural values, however, has as its point of departure an understanding of environmental processes quite different from deep ecology.

Many elements of the Green program find a strong resonance in countries such as India, where a history of Western colonialism and industrial development has benefited only a tiny elite while exacting tremendous social and environmental costs. The ecological battles presently being fought in India have as their epicenter the conflict over nature between the subsistence and largely rural sector and the vastly more powerful commercial–industrial sector. Perhaps the most celebrated of these battles concerns the Chipko (Hug the Tree) movement, a peasant movement against deforestation in the Himalayan foothills. Chipko is only one of several movements that have sharply questioned the nonsustainable demand being placed on the land and vegetative base by urban centers and industry. These include opposition to large dams by displaced peasants, the conflict between small artisan fishing and large-scale trawler fishing for export, the countrywide movements against commercial forest operations, and opposition to industrial pollution among downstream agricultural and fishing communities.

Two features distinguish these environmental movements from their Western counterparts. First, for the sections of society most critically affected by environmental degradation—poor and landless peasants, women, and tribals—it is a question of sheer survival, not of enhancing the quality of life. Second, and as a consequence, the environmental solutions they articulate deeply involve questions of equity as well as economic and political redistribution. Highlighting these differences, a leading Indian environmentalist stresses that "environmental protection per se is of least concern to most of these groups. Their main concern is about the use of the environment and who should benefit from it."[12] They seek to wrest control of nature away from the state and the industrial sector and place it in the hands of rural communities who live within that environment but are increasingly denied access to it. These communities have far more basic needs, their demands on the environment are far less intense, and they can draw upon a reservoir of cooperative social institutions and local ecological knowledge in managing the "commons"—forest, grasslands, and the waters—on a sustainable basis. If colonial and capitalist expansion has both accentuated social inequalities and signaled a precipitous fall in ecological wisdom, an alternate ecology must rest on an alternate society and polity as well.

This brief overview of German and Indian environmentalism has some major implications for deep ecology. Both German and Indian environmental traditions allow for a greater integration of ecological concerns with livelihood and work. They also place a greater emphasis on equity and social justice (both within individual countries and on a global scale) on the grounds that in the absence of social regeneration environmental regeneration has very little chance of succeeding. Finally, and perhaps most significantly,

they have escaped the preoccupation with wilderness preservation so characteristic of American cultural and environmental history.

A HOMILY

In 1958, the economist J. K. Galbraith referred to overconsumption as the unasked question of the American conservation movement. There is a marked selectivity, he wrote, "in the conservationist's approach to materials consumption. If we are concerned about our great appetite for materials, it is plausible to seek to increase the supply, to decrease waste, to make better use of the stocks available, and to develop substitutes. But what of the appetite itself? Surely this is the ultimate source of the problem. If it continues its geometric course, will it not one day have to be restrained? Yet in the literature of the resource problem this is the forbidden question. Over it hangs a nearly total silence."[13]

The consumer economy and society have expanded tremendously in the three decades since Galbraith penned these words; yet his criticisms are nearly as valid today. I have said "nearly," for there are some hopeful signs. Within the environmental movement several dispersed groups are working to develop ecologically benign technologies and to encourage less wasteful life styles. Moreover, outside the self-defined boundaries of American environmentalism, opposition to the permanent war economy is being carried on by a peace movement that has a distinguished history and impeccable moral and political credentials. It is precisely these (to my mind, most hopeful) components of the American social scene that are missing from deep ecology. In their widely noticed book, Bill Devall and George Sessions make no mention of militarization or the movements for peace, while activists whose practical focus is on developing ecologically responsible life styles (e.g., Wendell Berry) are derided as "falling short of deep ecological awareness."[14] A truly radical ecology in the American context ought to work toward a synthesis of the appropriate technology, alternate life style, and peace movements. By making the (largely spurious) anthropocentric–biocentric distinction central to the debate, deep ecologists may have appropriated the moral high ground, but they are at the same time doing a serious disservice to American and global environmentalism.

DEEP Ecology is a DISTRACTION.

NOTES

1. Kirkpatrick Sale, "The Forest for the Trees: Can Today's Environmentalists Tell the Difference," *Mother Jones* 11 (November 1986): 26.
2. Gary Snyder, quoted in Sale, "The Forest for the Trees," p. 32.
3. Donald Worster, *Nature's Economy: The Roots of Ecology* (San Francisco: Sierra Club, 1977).
4. D. Janzen, "The Future of Tropical Ecology," *Annual Rev. Ecology & Systematics* 17 (1986): 305–6.
5. Robert Aitken Roshi, "Gandhi, Dogen, and Deep Ecology," reprinted as appendix C in Devall and Sessions, *Deep Ecology: Living as if Nature Mattered* (Salt Lake: Peregrine Smith, 1985).
6. Michael Cohen, *The Pathless Way* (Madison: University of Wisconsin Press, 1984), p. 120.
7. Ronald Inden, "Orientalist Constructions of India," *Modern Asian Studies* 20 (1986): 401–46, at 442.
8. Joseph Sax, *Mountains Without Handrails: Reflections on the National Parks* (Ann Arbor: University of Michigan Press, 1980), p. 42.
9. Samuel Hayes, "From Conservation to Environment: Environmental Politics in the United States since World War Two," *Environmental Review* 6 (1982): 21.
10. Roderick Nash, *Wilderness and the American Mind* (New Haven: Yale University Press, 1982).
11. Rudolf Bahro, *From Red to Green* (London: Verso Books, 1984).
12. Anil Agarwal, "Human–Nature Interactions in a Third World Country," *The Environmentalist* 6 (1986): 165–83, at 167. [Note: This journal is now called *Environment Systems and Decisions*.]
13. John Kenneth Galbraith, "How Much Should a Country Consume?" in *Perspectives on Conservation*, ed. Henry Jarrett (Baltimore: Johns Hopkins Press, 1958), pp. 91–92.
14. Devall and Sessions, *Deep Ecology*, p. 122.

DAVID SCHMIDTZ

WHEN PRESERVATIONISM DOESN'T PRESERVE

Is it okay to shoot an elephant so that you can carve the tusks into fancy ivory chess pieces? Is it okay to chop down a Redwood so that you can take a picture of people dancing on the stump? Probably not. What exactly is wrong with such things, though? That is a tougher question, and there is a controversy in environmental ethics over how to answer it.

One approach is what we call conservationism. The idea is that elephants and Redwoods are a precious resource, too precious to waste on trifles. Scarce and precious resources should be conserved. They should be used wisely, taking into account costs and benefits for future generations as well as our own. Chopping down a Redwood so you can take pictures of people dancing on the stump is a waste: a waste of lumber or of a tourist attraction.

What if it is not a waste, though? What if the lumber is used efficiently and the tree stump dance floor itself becomes a major tourist attraction—a source of human happiness for generations to come? Wouldn't it still be wrong? Don't Redwoods somehow deserve more *respect* than that? Among people who do environmental ethics, conservationism has to some degree been supplanted by a second approach, which we call

David Schmidtz. 1997. When Preservationism Doesn't Preserve. Environmental Values, 6: 327–339. Reprinted here with permission of White Horse Press, Cambridge, U.K. Revised.

preservationism. Although we cannot avoid exploiting the natural world to some extent, preservationism's core idea is that nature has a moral status independent of its utility for humankind. Some ecosystems should simply be left alone to evolve according to their own lights, free of human use and human interference. The conservationist slogan is "wise use." The preservationist slogan is "let it be." According to preservation ethics, we should not think of wilderness as a mere resource. Wilderness commands reverence in a way mere resources do not.

One concern a preservationist might have about conservation ethics, then, is that it fails to make room for reverence. There are other, more contingent concerns as well. First, we ought to be skeptical about wise use policies regarding resources whose range of potential uses is largely unknown. "Wise use" of rain forests, for example, might not be very wise in the long term because there might be goods we do not know about yet that we unwittingly are squandering. Second, there might be other goods, like atmospheric oxygen, that rain forests would go on producing for us if we just left them alone. In that case, *using* a resource interferes with *benefiting* from it. Third, "wise use" of rain forests might be exposing us to diseases that otherwise would have stayed in the rain forests. There are species of mosquitoes that live only in the rain forest canopy. They feed only on monkeys that live in the canopy and they transmit diseases only to those monkeys. When you chop down the trees, though, those mosquitoes are suddenly on the forest floor where they have never been before. They and the organisms they carry suddenly are exposed to a population of six billion human beings. It would not be like them to let that much food go to waste.

So, there are reasons why people plausibly could say the wisest use of rain forests is virtually no use at all, at least for now. And when wise use is tantamount to no use at all, we have a situation where preservationism has won out on conservationism's own grounds. It is no surprise, then, that many (perhaps most) environmental ethicists today see conservationism as an ethic whose time has passed. My sympathies, too, lie mainly (although not exclusively) with preservationism.

However, after reading Raymond Bonner's book on wildlife conservation in Africa, and after travelling to South Africa, Zimbabwe, Botswana, and Zambia to see as much as I could for myself, I have had to rethink the wisdom of preservationism, at least in the African context.[1] Bonner was in Africa on other business when he stumbled into an ugly debate over the legitimacy of the ivory trade. Was it a good idea to ban international trade in ivory products? I do not know. This paper's purpose is not to take sides in that debate but rather to do something more philosophical: to reflect on what Bonner's experience, and mine, reveals about the practical limitations of preservationist philosophy.

If you were writing a Hollywood movie script, you would have the bad guys being in favor of shooting elephants for ivory (at "sustainable levels" of course). The good guys would say elephants are a sacred world heritage and it is a moral crime to be hacking their faces off and turning their tusks into trinkets. That is how you would be expected to write the script and that is just what Bonner expected to find. What he actually found was quite different.

VIGILANTE PRESERVATIONISM

Guy Grant bought his ranch in Kenya in 1963. He had twenty-five zebra at the time. Today he has over a thousand. He once sold hunting rights to zebra, elephant, buffalo, and warthogs, which provided a third of his income. In any case, he needs to keep the zebra population down to have room to graze cattle. Sport hunting, however, was banned in 1977. He could not sell hunting licenses anymore, so he had to hunt zebra himself. He still made money selling meat and hides, but trade in wildlife products was banned in 1978, so he lost that income too. Now, because of the ban, he has to graze more cattle to make ends meet. And he still has to keep the zebra population down. Otherwise it will bankrupt him. The only change is that he cannot make money from the zebra. Think about what that means. Without income from zebra, Grant had to graze more cattle to make the same money, which means he had less room for zebra, which means he had to shoot more zebra than otherwise would have been necessary *because of the ban on hunting them for sport*. The ban transformed zebra: not from crops into sacred objects but from crops into weeds.

The situation on Guy Grant's ranch is far from unique. For better or worse, Kenya had become one of

Africa's most enlightened countries, at least in terms of paying lip service to preservationist ideals. Wildlife in general was protected by law. Even outside the national parks, hunting was tightly regulated. In particular, poaching elephants in Kenya was as illegal as dealing cocaine in Brooklyn. With similar results.

What do you do when your laws are treated with contempt? Naturally, you get tough on crime. That is what voters want. That is what lobbyists want. And that is what they got. In 1988, Kenya's president ordered that poachers be shot on sight. Forty-one suspected poachers were killed in the next eight months. No park rangers were killed. In Zimbabwe, with the same shoot-to-kill policy, one hundred and forty-five suspected poachers were killed between 1984 and 1991. Four rangers were killed in the same time frame.

The trouble is, when the score in favor of the game wardens is forty-one to zero in one country and one hundred and forty-five to four in another, it begins to seem absurd to think the alleged poachers are well-armed, war-hardened mercenaries. In fact, it was average rural peasants who were being shot. According to Richard Leakey, director of Kenya's wildlife department at the time, there were no more than a hundred hardcore poachers in Kenya and for the most part, their identities were known (p. 18).[2] Many were wildlife rangers. By some accounts, over a third of the rhinos poached in the 1970s, when the population crashed from twenty thousand to under one thousand, were taken by members of the wildlife department itself (p. 134).[3] Perhaps the darkest spin on this is that, if you are a game warden and some hard-luck farmer chasing a stray goat accidentally catches you sawing tusks off an elephant, it is awfully convenient to have a license to kill. You have the carcass right there as proof that he was poaching. (You can even keep the tusks. Just claim that the poacher had a confederate who escaped.) However we explain the statistics, though, the fact remains that shoot-to-kill did not work. Farmers were getting shot. Poaching was escalating.

What else could you do? One suggestion: regulate trade in ivory. The Convention on International Trade in Endangered Species determined in 1977 that elephants were not yet an endangered species but would become so if the ivory trade were not brought under control. The Convention proposed that each exporting country establish self-imposed quotas on ivory exports, based on sustainable off-take—a level that would maintain existing populations.

What happened? To give one example, in 1986, Somalia voluntarily limited its export quota to seventeen thousand tusks per year. The odd thing is that Somalia had only six thousand elephants to begin with. Where were all those tusks coming from? Probably Kenya, its neighbor to the southwest.

If *regulating* commerce in ivory does not work, how about *banning* it? The case against a ban is this: Elephant populations in many countries were not decreasing, and were in fact near carrying capacity. Ivory was an important source of revenue for conservation programs. In theory, at least, legal exports from countries like South Africa dampen demand for poached ivory from countries like Kenya where elephants are threatened. For better or worse, these considerations failed to carry the day. The World Wide Fund for Nature and the African Wildlife Foundation originally opposed a ban for the reasons just mentioned, then changed their minds. Bonner suspects that they could not afford to pass up the millions of dollars they stood to gain through highly publicized campaigns to ban ivory.[4]

Here is a different issue. Even if the ivory ban eliminated poaching entirely, the wildlife would still be disappearing (p. 212). In Theodore Roosevelt's time, Africa's human population was 100 million. Now it is 450 million. As Bonner puts it, "People were once an island in a sea of wildlife. Now wildlife survives in parks that are islands in an ocean of people" (p. 8). Competition for water, disruption of migration routes, and farmers defending crops (and their families) against marauding wildlife will decimate wildlife with or without poaching. Clearly, the poaching has to stop, but in the long run, that will not be enough to save the elephants. Whether we like it or not, the elephants will not survive except by sharing the land with people, which means their long-term survival depends on whether the people of Africa can afford to share.

THE LARGER PROBLEM

As Laura Westra tells us, "An Arab proverb says, Before the palm tree can be beautiful, our bellies must be full of dates. It is a truism, as indeed survival comes before aesthetic enjoyment. Unfortunately environmental concern is seen as aesthetic preference rather than ur-gently needed for survival."[5] Westra has a point when she calls it a mistake to see environmental issues as a luxury. At the same time, it also would be a mistake to ignore the fact that environmental concern falls by the wayside in a personal crunch. Being able to think in terms of long-term survival is itself a luxury of a kind, and not one that everyone can afford. From an indi-vidual perspective, the survival of one's family comes first. Compared to that, environmental concern is indeed a luxury, and Westra's real take-home message is that the rest of us do not have the luxury of ignoring that point.

Presumably, there are exceptions to this general rule. For example, Ramachandra Guha cringes at de-picting environmental concern as a "full stomach" phenomenon and makes note of peasant movements against deforestation and industrial pollution in India.[6] Guha's point is well-taken, but it bears adding that, as Guha himself stresses, "environmental protec-tion is of least concern to most of these groups. Their main concern is about the use of the environment and who should benefit from it."[7] Thus, even if our own attitude is one of deep and unconditional reverence for wilderness, we have to be aware that other people may have, in their own eyes, more pressing things to think about. If we really care about wilderness, we cannot just look at it through our own eyes. Part of our job is to help create the kind of society in which, for other people, from their perspectives, respecting wil-derness is worth the cost. We can say preservation is morally right; therefore the Maasai tribes are morally obligated to preserve; therefore we should not have to bribe them to do what they are obligated to do. They should just do it. If we say that, though, we are kidding ourselves. Under such circumstances, David Western (director of the Kenyan Wildlife Service) observes, "the African farmer's enmity toward elephants is as visceral as western mawkishness is passionate."[8]

Like us, the people of Africa care for their natural heritage when they can afford to do so, when rewards for doing so go to them and not just to others, and when they know how to do so. Some of them have been practicing wise use for a long time, killing wild-life when it threatens their families, hunting it for food, and for sport as well. When we try to impose our preservationist ideals on local villagers who have to live with wildlife, we risk starting a war between locals and wildlife, a war that both sides lose. The problem is that preservation ethics does not allow the local people to profit from wildlife, and not allowing people to profit from wildlife effectively pits people against wildlife, which is bad for wildlife as well as the local people. Kreuter and Simmons say that, because elephants "compete directly with humans for use of fertile land, we believe elephants will continue to be eliminated unless they provide . . . direct personal benefits to the people who incur the cost of co-existing with them. If the western preservationists do not respect the need for Africans to benefit from their resources, they will one day stand justly accused of promoting rather than abating the demise of Africa's elephants."[9] Our own ex-periences and our conversations with a dozen people from five African countries suggests that Kreuter and Simmons are right, and that the hard choice in south-ern Africa is not so much between people and wildlife as between a pragmatic humanism that benefits both and an uninformed environmentalism that benefits neither. When it comes to African wildlife, preserva-tion ethics runs into a problem. In a nutshell, preser-vationism does not preserve. It fails by its own lights. We need alternatives.

WISE USE ALTERNATIVES

Namibia's Auxiliary Guard: In several countries, elephant numbers are increasing. Is it because of the ivory ban? That seems reasonable, but it does not explain why the numbers in some countries were increasing even before the ban. Nor does it explain why the numbers have in-creased only in some countries, not others. One variable that separates countries is their success in controlling poaching. (And successful countries seem to be those that see poaching as a symptom of more fundamental problems.) In contrast to Kenya, Namibia's Kaokoveld region, for example, is doing fairly well. In 1982, a con-servation officer named Garth Owen-Smith diagnosed Namibia's problem as follows. Local villagers once had customs that effectively limited their own hunt-ing activities to sustainable levels. Then foreign hunters started showing up in large numbers. It was a classic tragedy of the commons. Self-restraint seemed point-less, and villagers did not restrain themselves. They were helping to destroy wildlife and were destroying their own future in the process, and it was partly their fault. Somehow, the villagers had to reverse the deterioration of their own social norms, and they had to do something about trespassing poachers from outside. To western environmentalists, one obvious solution was to shoot the villagers (after all, they were poaching), but that had been tried. Instead of shooting the villagers, Owen-Smith asked them for help.

He asked village headmen to assemble troops of auxiliary guards to act as neighborhood watch organizations. These watchdog organizations radically reduced poaching by outsiders, and also provided an institutional framework that made it easier to reassert community standards and re-establish norms of self-restraint. It was a simple idea, but it worked. Five years later, Owen-Smith went further. By then elephants, lions, and other animals were returning to the Kaokoveld, and with them came the tourists. The plan was to sell crafts to visitors coming through to see wildlife and also to tax visitors for overnight stays within their territory. Both sources of income ultimately are tied to wildlife, so incentives to preserve are put in place (p. 33).

Does the program demean the animals? Perhaps, but we should keep in mind that we are not talking here about locking them up in zoos. Elephants have their value to the local people to the extent that they are wild and free and living in a natural setting. That is what the tourists (and hunters) are paying to see.

Revenue Sharing: To Westerners, the commercial value of tourism is a panacea (p. 218). Tourism could indeed help, but it depends on how the money is distributed. In Kenya, Richard Leakey announced in 1990 that twenty-five percent of entrance fees would go to local Maasai tribes (p. 222). Involving the Maasai is crucial, since eighty percent of Kenya's wildlife lives outside of its parks, and much of it is migratory. Thus, it is imperative that local farmers and herdsmen tolerate big animals coming and going, circulating among seasonal food and water supplies. And they were tolerant, after they started to get some of the money. In fact, the Maasai now use some of their share to hire their own wardens to track and protect animals outside the park—a remarkable change of attitude.

In Zambia, businesses that cater to the tourist industry take a percentage of their annual gross revenues and distribute it in equal shares amongst their entire staff. Accordingly, everyone you meet who is involved in the tourism industry, from janitors and dishwashers to maids and managers, directly profits from every dollar you spend, and thus is personally committed to making their business as attractive as possible to tourists. And since unspoiled land and especially wildlife is what draws the tourists, they have a personal interest in conservation as well.[10]

In Botswana, the Moremi Game Reserve was created in 1964—the first wildlife area to be set aside by tribal chiefs rather than by colonial powers. Licenses for doing business in the Reserve are allocated according to competitive bids. Winning bids receive a five year lease, renewable up to two times for a total of fifteen years maximum. From a European or North American perspective, it makes no sense at first, since it undercuts incentives to make long term investments in durable infrastructure. In Botswana, though, it may prove a brilliant solution to a vexing problem. Botswana needs foreign investment, but at the same time it does not want to find itself owned by white foreigners. So, under the current leasing arrangement, foreigners are investing and building infrastructure, but their buildings are flimsy shacks (with wooden rather than concrete foundations, for example). The roads are dirt trails built for Jeeps. In other words, investors are planning not to leave much behind when they leave, and as a result seem to be building in a way that minimizes their environmental impact. Meanwhile, native Botswanan students (now about twenty years old) are being sent abroad to study tourism, management, ecology, and so on, returning home during the tourist season to work in the national parks as tour guides, assistant managers, and so on. Non-native entrepreneurs will help get Botswana's tourist industry going, and the hope is that, after they make a quick profit and a graceful exit, a generation of internationally trained and locally experienced Botswanans (who by that time will be about thirty-five years old) will be ready to take over.[11] We will see.

Tanzania's Bounty Hunters: In the Maswa Preserve, near Serengeti, Robin Hurt once led hunting safaris. Tanzania banned hunting in 1973, so Hurt went elsewhere. Tanzania legalized hunting again in 1984. Robin Hurt came back in 1985. During that twelve year moratorium on hunting, the wildlife virtually disappeared. Why? Because of poachers. Without licensed hunters to keep poachers in line, poachers ran amok.

But what is the difference between a poacher and a hunter? A hunter is just a poacher by another name, no? In fact, the difference is enormous. Hunters hunt with rifles. In Tanzania, poachers hunt with *snares*, and snares are a disaster for the wildlife (p. 236). The people of Makao, for example, were laying snares around water holes, or along timeworn paths to water holes, or they would cut new paths in the bushes and lay snares along those. Robin Hurt found twenty lion skulls in one snare line. He found snare lines that ran for two miles. More often than not, the animal caught is not what the poacher wants. Even if it is, vultures or hyenas often get to the animal before the poacher does. Snare-hunting is catastrophically wasteful from an ecological perspective, but from a poacher's perspective it is a lot easier than hunting with bow and arrow. The Makao switched to snares.[12]

When Hurt resumed operations in 1985, he began a casual anti-poaching effort, picking up snares as he went, in his spare time. Gradually realizing the magnitude of the problem, he concluded that the Makao had to be enlisted. How? Well, why not just pay them to turn in snares and poachers? Here, too, I would have worried about incentive problems. (If Hurt pays too much for the snares, won't people respond by making more snares?) Still, it was an idea worth trying. Hurt raised enough money to try it. It worked (p. 249).

Zimbabwe's Local Autonomy: There have been problems in Zimbabwe, as in other countries, with wildlife molesting villagers, to the point where villagers came to feel that government wildlife protection was persecuting people for the sake of the animals. And they were basically right. One major effect of the bans on commerce in wildlife was to prevent locals from making significant money. "It was clear that to the local people, the wildlife was simply a nuisance. Elephants and other large herbivores raided their meager crops and sometimes even trampled their huts, while lions and other large carnivores occasionally preyed on their domestic stock. The wild animals often moved into the communal lands from national parks and other protected areas, but because the locals saw no direct benefit from these areas, they saw no reason

to protect this errant game."[13] Wildlife groups had failed to ask: What could make it *rational* for villagers to choose wildlife over cattle?

Consider this example. Shortly after Zimbabwe gained political independence in 1980, its Department of National Parks and Wildlife Management concluded that conventional agricultural practices were ecologically and economically unsound throughout much of Zimbabwe. (The soil is not right, and there is not enough water.) The best use of the land was as a reservoir for wildlife. The Department also realized that the problem would be solved only if it were handed over to the local people. Over a period of years, the Department created the CAMPFIRE program. They surveyed community areas, assessed wildlife populations, and came to conclusions about what sort of numbers could be considered surplus game. They then gave local communities a nearly free hand in deciding what to do with the surplus.

Local communities were granted authority to cull herds, sell hunting permits, or set up tourist ventures, and since 1992 they have been allowed to keep eighty percent of the money. (The rest goes to wildlife management and rural district administration.) They put some of that money in a fund for compensating farmers when lions take their goats or elephants trample their crops, which defuses much of the resentment of wildlife. In some districts, rangers periodically hunt impala and sell meat to local villagers at a price that covers cost of the hunt, making villagers less dependent on cattle as a source of protein. The issue is not just money, but self-sufficiency. Decisions are made in the village square. In that setting, people have more knowledge, more understanding, more voice. There is less room for corruption. Decision-making is more efficient and more equitable.

A note of caution: there are programs in southern Africa that call themselves community-based but merely gesture at sharing revenue and at granting communities authority to set local policy. Such programs do not work.[14] Political corruption in Africa is deep and pervasive, and there is no magic cure for it. CAMPFIRE, however, seems to have worked. "The foundation of community empowerment lies in devolution of management decisions to the local level. Just giving the communities economic resources from wildlife is not CAMPFIRE. In CAMPFIRE, the concept of community empowerment means actually giving the community the power to decide on the allocation of these resources."[15]A pamphlet published by the CAMPFIRE Association says,

> Today, the total land mass devoted to wildlife conservation is more than 33% whereas only 13% is officially designated as such in the form of Protected Areas. . . . In the immediate period before the introduction of CAMPFIRE, Protected Areas were in danger of becoming ecological islands, threatening the maintenance of genetic and species diversity. CAMPFIRE has re-opened traditional migration routes of animals within the community, thus making a contribution to the preservation of biodiversity and the natural environment.[16]

In the village of Masoka, in 1993, only a few years after launching their own local CAMPFIRE program, thirty-five percent of Masoka's household heads reported their primary employment to be a direct result of the program, mainly through safari camps.[17] Enough money came in from hunting that villagers turned their land over to wildlife rather than grazing cattle. This is crucial because the bigger threat to wildlife tends to be cattle, not hunting. Cattle crowds out wildlife. (Actually, pastoral herds are one problem; farms and ranches are another. Nomadic Maasai herdsmen compete with wildlife for space and water, but at least they do not cut off migration routes by erecting fences or otherwise defending their turf.[18])

Villages (directly or through tour guides) sell elephant hunting licenses. Hunters currently pay as much as $30,000 for the privilege. It is a lot of money in a country where the per capita annual income is around $2000. As of 1999, when I was in Zimbabwe, there were thirty-seven such districts, occupying well over half of the country (and containing 56 percent of the country's population), and much of the land in those districts was reserved for wildlife.

There is a sad end to this encouraging tale, though. Within a year of my visit, Zimbabwe became one of the world's most brutal dictatorships, its economy shattered. So-called war veterans were authorized first to resettle the lands of evicted white farmers. Having eaten everything they could find on once-productive farms, these people are now rumored to be settling in the national parks, presumably poaching the wildlife. Little news escapes, and it remains to be seen whether or to what extent CAMPFIRE has survived the carnage.[19]

What about the morality of sport hunting? Is it something a sane person would do? Winston Churchill once shot a rhinoceros, but failed to kill it. The wounded rhino charged. The hunting party opened fire. The rhino kept coming into a hail of bullets, swerving aside at the last moment before more bullets finally brought it down. Churchill later wrote that, even in the midst of the charge, "There is time to reflect with some detachment that, after all, we it is who have forced the conflict by an unprovoked assault with murderous intent upon a peaceful herbivore; that if there is such a thing as right and wrong between man and beast—and who shall say there is not?—right is plainly on his side."[20]

I grew up on a farm, in a family of hunters, but I never joined in. I loved to shoot at targets, but I was never able to make sense of killing sentient beings for fun. Perhaps you feel the same way. And yet, we should hesitate before concluding that regular tourism is benign whereas hunting is destructive. Actually, tourism may do more damage than hunting relative to the money it brings in. Why? Mainly because, dollar for dollar, hunting does not need as much infrastructure as tourism does. Hunters in jeeps do not use precious water the way tourist hotels do, and do not demand wilderness-fragmenting highways the way tourist hotels do.

ANIMAL RIGHTS

I have been talking about selling hunting licenses as an alternative to grazing cattle that compete with wildlife for space. As things stand, though, it sometimes is necessary to cull elephant herds for straightforwardly ecological reasons—to preserve habitat, other animal species, and even the elephants themselves. In the Volcans National Park in Rwanda, a choice had to be made between elephants and gorillas. As the elephants deplete food sources in the park, they normally migrate, coming back only when the park has replenished itself. As human populations increase and human settlements surround the parks, though, elephants are forced to turn back into the parks, destroying habitat for everything else in the park as well as for themselves. To prevent that, Rwanda's two remaining elephant herds, about seventy animals each, were wiped out in 1973.[21]

Uganda also culled elephant herds for ecological reasons. Not Kenya. The elephant population in Kenya's Tsavo Park had reached forty thousand in the 1960s. "Some conservationists and wildlife officials wanted to cull three thousand elephants. Others argued that man should do nothing, that nature should be allowed to take its course" (p. 104). Preservationists prevailed, but during a subsequent drought, six to nine thousand elephants died of starvation, and they took several hundred rhinos with them.[22]

Today, the same thing is happening again, as we saw with our own eyes—especially in the Chobe and Moremi Game Reserves in Botswana and in Kruger National Park in South Africa. In many places, there are far too many elephants, and they are ruining the woodland. They are leaving both themselves and all the other wildlife without viable habitat. Mopalo Setswantsho has been taking people on hiking and canoe trips into the Okavango Delta in the interior of Botswana since 1983 and has lived in the area all his life. I asked whether there were fewer animals now. He answered that, on the contrary, there are more animals now, but the trees are disappearing.

Do we have the right to put a stop to it? Animal rights organizations say no. Their approach is individualistic rather than holistic. They focus on saving animals rather than on saving populations or habitat. Their view is particularly salient in the case of elephants. When rangers cull elephants, they take out whole families in order to avoid leaving behind orphans and other remnants of shattered families. The horrible thing is that, under favorable conditions, elephants can hear the sound of a culling operation up to thirty kilometers away, and elephants are smart—smart enough to understand and share the terror of the ones being shot. Cynthia Moss, who has written fascinating and convincing books about what it is like to be an elephant, says elephants deserve something better than to be exterminated like rodents. She has a point.[23]

Lawrence Johnson, though, argues that there are times when "the interests of species are not adequately protected by a concern for individuals."[24] The individualistic animal rights position is powerful, given the nature of elephants, but it leaves us in a horrible quandary, for the price of absolute rights may be extinction. Nonetheless, elephants are not like zebra. They are not the kind of creature that we have a right to treat as mere means. Cynthia Moss (p. 226) said she would rather see elephants go extinct than see individual animals murdered for the sake of population control, and she is not alone. If elephants had a voice in the matter, perhaps they would thank Moss for her stand. Perhaps not.

PERSONAL AND INTERPERSONAL MORALITY

I asked what makes it wrong to cut down a Redwood in order to use the stump as a dance floor, or to shoot an elephant in order to use the tusks for ivory. Do we have an answer? We may have more than one. I say that partly because, in my view, morality is more than one thing. One part of morality ranges over the subject of personal aspiration—which goals we should spend our lives trying to achieve. Another part of morality ranges over the subject of interpersonal constraint—especially which socially or institutionally embedded constraints we ought to respect as we pursue our goals in a social setting.[25] In those terms, then, I still believe in preservationism as part of a morality of personal aspiration. Committing ourselves to preservationist ideals—to reverence for nature and to a policy of "no use at all" at least in some contexts—is one way of giving ourselves something to live for.

I also believe a preservationist "no use at all" policy can work among people who share a commitment to preservationist ideals. What I mean by this is that when people accept the ideals behind a set of institutional constraints, and individually and collectively commit themselves to living within those constraints on behalf of those ideals, the institution has a decent chance of functioning in such a way as actually to further those ideals.

However, I have come to realize that preservationism often and predictably does not work in the context of a social arrangement in which the cost of upholding preservationist ideals has to be born by people who do not embrace those ideals. Even given that preservationism is acceptable as a personal ideal, it remains a bad idea to create institutions that depend upon people who do not share that ideal to take responsibility for realizing it. Ramachandra Guha [see the preceding essay in this volume] goes so far as to say our foisting preservationist ideals on third world countries is a form of imperialism.

Some of our most beloved environmental heroes, such as Aldo Leopold, were unrepentant hunters. They saw hunting as part of an environmentally benign overall pattern. Even if they were wrong, and even if their philosophy has no place within an enlightened morality of personal aspiration, it would be neither personally enlightened nor environmentally benign to interfere with hunting by other people when such hunting is a community's way of allowing people and wildlife to live together in some semblance of harmony.

NOTES

1. Raymond Bonner, *At the Hand of Man*, New York: Vintage (1993). Unless otherwise noted, page references in the text are to this book. Bonner's sources include interviews, memos, minutes of committee meetings, and newsletters. His reporting is consistent with my own experience and with other sources I have been able to check, except where otherwise noted.

2. Bonner's source is a publicly circulated 1989 report by Leakey to the U.S. State Department.

3. If it seems astonishing both that this could be true and that Leakey would publicly admit it, consider that, first, there was pervasive corruption at the highest levels of government, enabling well-connected poachers to operate with impunity. Second, many rangers were paid less than a living wage. Thus, Leakey sometimes had to put up with poaching within his own ranks.

4. Yet, in hindsight, it now seems clearer that the ivory ban did reduce poaching and did depress prices. Why? My speculation is that the ban choked off American demand for ivory, not because border officials have any power to stop the influx of contraband but because ivory's main value in America is as a status symbol. Ivory today is politically incorrect as well as illegal, which ruins it as a status symbol. Since sales of ivory have resumed (twenty tons each to Japan from Botswana, Zimbabwe, and

Namibia), though, there seems to have been an uptick in black market prices. Why? I do not know. However, sixty tons is not very much; perhaps the gesture at legalization is doing more to increase demand than to increase supply.

5. Laura Westra, "The Principle of Integrity and *The Economy of the Earth*," in W. Michael Hoffman, Robert Frederick, & Edward S. Petry, editors, *The Corporation, Ethics, and the Environment*, New York: Quorum Books (1990): 227–40, at 232.

6. Ramachandra Guha, "Radical American Environmentalism and Wilderness Preservation: A Third-World Critique," in this volume.

7. Guha here is quoting Anil Agarwal, "Human–Nature Interactions In a Third World Country," *The Environmentalist*, 6 (1986) 165–83, at 167.

8. David Western, "The Balance of Nature," *Wildlife Conservation* 96 (March/April, 1993) p. 52.

9. Urs P. Kreuter & Randy Simmons, "Who Owns the Elephants?" *Wildlife in the Marketplace*, ed. T. Anderson & P. J. Hill, Lanham: Rowman and Littlefield (1995): 147–65, at 161.

10. Source: Conversation (Livingstone, Zambia, July 28, 1999) with Phillip Roberts, a native of Zambia and proprietor of Wilderness Wheels Africa, a company that specializes in wildlife tours for customers in wheelchairs.

11. Source: Conversation (Moremi Game Reserve, Botswana, July 24 and 26, 1999) with Isrea Batlanang, a native of Botswana, assistant manager of Oddballs' Lodge in Moremi Game Reserve. Batlanang also studied for a degree in Tourism at Semmering University in Austria.

12. Even on private reserves, snare-poaching can be a problem. Khame Game Reserve in Zimbabwe spans about ten thousand acres, and employs five full-time rangers, which makes it reasonably well-policed compared to most national parks. Even so, when we visited the manager, Brianna Carne, she said they had caught a trespassing snare poacher the previous week. Rangers had so far picked up ten snares, fearing they might yet find another two hundred.

13. David Holt-Biddle, "CAMPFIRE: An African Solution To An African Problem," *Africa Environment and Wildlife*, 2 (1994) 33–35, here p. 33.

14. Alexander N. Songorwa, "Community-Based Wildlife Management in Tanzania: Are the Communities Interested?" *World Development*, 27 (1999) 2061–79.

15. Gordon Matzke and Nontokozo Nabane, "Outcomes of a Community Controlled Wildlife Utilization Program in a Zambezi Valley Community," *Human Ecology* 24 (1996) 65–85, at p. 73.

16. See http://www.campfirezimbabwe.org or write campfir@id.co.zw for further information.

17. Matzke and Nabane, p. 80.

18. See Cynthia Moss, *Elephant Memories*, New York: William Morrow (1988) p. 209, 301.

19. However, in November, 2017, as we make final revisions to this edition of the text, Robert Mugabe has been arrested and deposed. Perhaps there is hope.

20. Winston S. Churchill, *My African Journey*, London: Hodder and Stoughton (1908) p. 17.

21. J.C. Haigh, I.S.C. Parker, D.A. Parkinson, and A.L. Archer, "An Elephant Extermination," *Environmental Conservation*, 6 (1979) 305–10.

22. Bonner's figure is nine thousand. Daniel Botkin says six thousand in *Discordant Harmonies: A New Ecology For the 21st Century*, New York: Oxford University Press (1990) p. 18.

23. Moss, p. 317.

24. L. Johnson, *A Morally Deep World*, New York: Cambridge University Press (1991) p. 173.

25. See David Schmidtz, *Rational Choice and Moral Agency*, Princeton University Press (1995).

IAN JOHN WHYTE

THE ELEPHANT MANAGEMENT DILEMMA

The dilemmas of managing elephants in reserves are generally poorly understood. The different attitudes to basic management philosophies have led to many acrimonious debates and deep rifts have developed between some of the respective proponents. While those from the anti-culling lobby have condemned the killing of elephants, the non-interference policies are not without their own ethical dilemmas. It is not the purpose of this article to try to favour either one of these two elemental points of view, but to try to set the situation in Kruger National Park (South Africa) against the background of other national parks in Africa. The intention is to get to the heart of the elephant dilemma so that readers themselves may understand the issues and have some empathy with elephant managers and the decisions with which they are faced.

There are many viewpoints emanating from a diverse variety of sources on the subject. These come from scientists from academic institutions involved in elephant research, animal rights and animal welfare groups, "absentee or ex-situ conservationists," ex-patriot conservationists and other interested and affected parties. It is the purpose of this paper to examine the problems specifically from the viewpoint of managers tasked with elephant management. These are the people who ultimately are accountable for the outcomes of any management actions undertaken. The people and groups who work on the fringes seldom fall into this category, and they are not accountable for their sometimes radical proposals and solutions. They can walk away from any resulting adverse ecological outcomes without the serious personal consequences faced by managers. They are therefore likely to view the issues in an entirely different light to those faced with the hard realities.

Before the advent of firearms, the elephants of Africa were probably not greatly influenced by Man, though there is a view held by an increasing number of prominent conservationists that indigenous Africans were well capable of influencing the dynamics of African elephant populations well before the advent of firearms. There is also archaeological evidence of proboscidean "overkills" elsewhere in the world. Be this as it may, the ability to easily kill large elephants increased as firearms began to proliferate, and the populations started to decline. Initially this was due to the demand for ivory in Europe and Asia and there was no control over the off-take. This situation possibly persisted for two hundred years or more, and in spite of the establishment of reserves and national parks throughout Africa, many (if not most) elephants roamed outside of these parks and remained vulnerable. The numbers of elephants on the African continent in earlier times are not known, but by 1979 they had been reduced to an estimated 1.3 million. By this time the range states (countries which have elephant populations) north of Zimbabwe and Namibia were in the grip of a poaching epidemic which reduced the continental population to 609,000 by 1989.

Concern over this dramatic trend resulted in the banning by CITES (Convention on the International Trade in Endangered Species) of international trade in elephant products in 1989. Although one study four years later concluded that in most countries the ban had not halted the illegal off-take, it is widely believed that the ban had achieved much in reducing the poaching. The worst of the poaching was experienced in the countries to the north of the Zambezi and Cunene rivers. South of this, although increased poaching was experienced, this was not at a scale which significantly reduced elephant numbers. In Kruger the first case of elephant poaching was recorded in 1975. Since then the incidence has been sporadic except during the years 1981–1985 when a sharp increase in the incidence was experienced. During this time, 193 were known to have been shot. Active anti-poaching measures solved the problem to a large degree and elephant poaching has occurred only sporadically since. Populations in

the southern range states have continued to grow and by 2007 were estimated at a definite total of 298,000, with the possibility that there could be as many as 358,500. The disparity between these two geographical zones has had the result that northern range states generally favour the ban while southern countries do not. Southern wildlife departments maintain that they could benefit enormously from the financial returns that the sale of elephant products could bring, particularly as elephant management in these countries is now impeded by financial constraints. So while the northern African range states welcome the ban as perceived protection for their populations, most southern African range states are seeking ways of limiting their elephant numbers. But why would you want to limit elephant numbers? Why manage elephants at all? Why not just let them be?

THE PROBLEM

In many African countries today, elephant populations are confined to national parks and reserves. This is also true of most other wildlife species, both plant and animal. In South Africa nature reserves and national parks are conservation "islands" whose boundaries are hard-edged up against the activities of people. In these conservation islands, it is usually the wildlife manager's job to try to protect all of these species as part of biodiversity maintenance programs, but there are some reserves that have been proclaimed specifically for the protection of particularly endangered species and biodiversity may be considered of lesser importance. But there are some countries such as Kenya who can still claim that as much as 70% of their wildlife exists outside of national parks. Wildlife managers in these countries have their own set of problems, usually concerned with interactions between man and wild animals, and the dilemmas of conserving elephants in closed systems have not yet really become part of their conservation priorities. Large parts of east Africa, particularly in Kenya and Tanzania, is Maasai country. Maasai were semi-nomadic pastoralists who traditionally had little interest in wildlife. They saw wild animals as "God's cattle" and their whole lives were centred around their own herds of cattle and goats. As agriculture was not practised at all, competition with wildlife was confined to incidents where people or their livestock were killed or injured by animals, but by and large they could co-exist in relative harmony. But this situation is changing slowly for two main reasons. Dramatic human population increases and hunger for land no longer affords people a nomadic life style, or their herds free access to rangeland, and many are switching from pastoralism to agriculture. Agriculture is rarely compatible with wild animals as crops planted by people are a highly attractive to the larger herbivores. In the early 1990's the African Elephant Specialist Group considered human/elephant conflict to be the greatest current problem facing elephant conservation. These clashes will gradually force wild animals more and more into sanctuaries set aside for them. Secondly, college education of the Maasai youth means that they have tasted the offerings of civilisation and are no longer satisfied with the pastoralist's simple life style. They want jobs, houses, and access to electricity and running water, and to the trappings of the modern world, none of which are compatible with pastoralism.

These two forces will probably ensure that the wildlife in these countries will also eventually occur only in reserves, and the problems of maintaining biodiversity in these "conservation islands" will be brought into sharper focus.

As a general rule of thumb, the smaller the conservation island, the greater the degree of management it will require as some of the essential ecological processes will be missing. An example of this is that many small parks can not accommodate the larger predators, and in the absence of the population checks which these predators impose on prey populations, man has to take over this role. But if the "island" is large enough (and the Kruger National Park is considered to be one of these) the vast majority of its component species and ecosystem processes will require little or no management at all. Throughout time, these species and processes have co-evolved to form a complex matrix of competition, inter-dependence and above all, survival. This is the way it should be and it is accepted that managers should interfere with these processes only when it is considered unavoidable.

In nature, nothing is static. Rainfall and temperature are the engines of ecological processes, and these are never constant. There are years when rainfall is abundant and others of drought. In most of Africa these conditions are cyclic and there are periods of a few years of above average rainfall followed by periods below average. In Kruger, records show that rainfall cycles average about 20 years in duration—ten dry years followed by ten wet ones, though it is usual to experience one or more dry years during the wet part of the cycle and vice-versa, and the length of a wet or dry cycle may also vary considerably.

Different species respond differently to the prevailing conditions, some increasing during the wetter years, but some also favour the dry conditions and their populations flourish during the drier parts of the cycle. In Kruger wildebeest and zebra favour the drier years when the grass has been grazed short and trampled to create more open conditions. These animals rely on their good eyesight to avoid predators, so when the grass becomes long and rank during the wetter years, lions have enough cover to get up close and make their kills more easily.

But most species prefer the wetter times and have developed ways of reducing the threat of predators in long grass. When food is abundant, buffalo congregate in large herds and the adults are aggressive to predators and protective of the younger animals and calves. But when droughts come, each individual buffalo is forced to compete with the others for the meagre grass reserves that are available. Food shortages force them to split off in smaller groups to allow more effective foraging. Being in a weakened physical condition, these small groups are much more vulnerable to lions. A single large herd of buffalo will find itself in only one lion pride's territory at any one time, but when a herd splits, more prides have access to the herd and individuals are in poorer physical condition, rendering them less able to defend themselves against these predators. Furthermore, water is in short supply and buffalo have to drink. Lions wait at the water and in their more vulnerable condition, buffalo can be killed almost at will. Many cases have been recorded of lions making multiple buffalo kills during these times. It is a predator's instinct to kill, and each time the buffalo herd approaches the water, the lions kill another. During the severe droughts of 1992/3, Kruger's buffalo population declined by more than 50% from nearly 30 000 to less than 15 000.

Kudu have other strategies for avoiding lions in long grass. They have excellent eyesight, smell and hearing and live in small groups who forage silently. During droughts they lose condition and are forced to forage in habitats they would normally avoid. As with buffalo, they are forced also to drink at the few remaining waterholes, which is where the lions are waiting. In most cases these population fluctuations are driven by the short-term (± 20 year) climatic cycles.

But elephants do not conform to this pattern. In today's imperfect world, Africa is no longer what it was before the advent of technological man, and the continent-wide ecological processes which used to operate, can now no longer do so. The functioning of most of these processes is lost in the mists of time and can now only be speculated upon. The population cycles of elephants is one of these. Elephants had few natural enemies in those times, and the questions of how their populations were regulated are unanswered. It is sure of course, that no population can continue to grow forever, as eventually they will exceed the resources upon which they are dependant. There must come a time when conditions are less favourable and the population will enter a phase of decline. Did elephant populations build up over centuries in local "events" to the point that food became limiting and then die out to a much lower level? Or did they move away when food became scarce? If so, where did they go? And what would have happened to the elephants already occupying the area to which they moved? Did disease play a role? Was pre-technological Man really capable of limiting elephant numbers? These are all questions which nobody can answer with surety, and maybe nobody ever will.

What is known is that elephants have the intellect and constitution to exploit a wider range of food resources than any other animal (except Man). When grass and browse are not available, they can eat twigs and branches or use their tusks to prise bark off trees, and can even push trees over to reach the leaves in the canopy or to expose the roots. The latter two activities will almost invariably result in the death of the tree. Elephants are selective feeders, and it is the favoured food species that are initially affected. But as these are depleted they are forced to switch their feeding activities to other less palatable plant species. These in turn will also be depleted as the elephant population grows.

Natural limitation of elephant numbers will only begin to occur once even these resources have been depleted and the elephants become nutritionally stressed, but by this time the environment will have been subjected to severe impacts. In this process, the question is what would have happened to the other species—both plant and animal—occupying these habitats? Some may have even been extirpated (local extinction).

In the old Africa, this would not necessarily have resulted in the extinction of species as other populations would likely have occurred elsewhere and recolonisation by both plants and animals could have taken place naturally, even though it may have taken hundreds of years. In evolutionary time, time scales like this are irrelevant. Some species that were unable to adapt or recolonise may have been pushed to extinction, but this is nature's way—adapt or die!

But the old Africa has now gone forever. No longer can species range far and wide, and no longer can most terrestrial life forms naturally recolonise areas where they have been extirpated. And so elephants, with their ability to drastically modify habitats, are a threat to many species within these confined reserves. A reserve like Kruger, which is large enough to allow for minimum management of most species, is still considered to be too small to accommodate elephant population fluctuations without environmental damage. And thus, if the objective of a national park is the long-term conservation of all the indigenous biota occurring there, then something will ultimately have to be done to limit elephant numbers.

A theory proposed recently is that if an elephant population is left long enough without artificial limitation of its numbers, it will eventually attain a state where it will stabilise numerically. At this point the population would have achieved what is known as a "stable age structure" and a decline of the population growth rate to zero. Put simply, in a growing population the most numerous age class will be the youngest, i.e. there will be more individuals under one year than there are one year olds, more one year olds than two year olds and so on through all the age classes. For a population's growth rate to decline to zero (no increase in the number of individuals in the population), the number of deaths (mortality) must equal the number of births (natality). For this to happen, either the number of births must decline, or else a significant number of younger animals must die. In this case the age structure would show much reduced proportions of calves and juveniles. Over time, this structure would remain largely unaltered, giving rise to the concept of a "stable age structure." There are no epidemic diseases known to affect elephants and predation is negligible. Lowered fecundity rates and increased mortality of juveniles therefore implies that the individuals in the population would have to be severely stressed nutritionally. Elephants are extremely successful and efficient foragers capable of exploiting nearly all parts of both grass and woody plants, and for them to reach a state where they are not in condition to breed or to where they may die from food deprivation, the habitat would be in a severely degraded state.

There is as yet no evidence to suggest that an elephant population will attain such a stable age structure, or evidence which may indicate the environmental conditions which would give rise to such an age structure. The question for the Manager is whether he can risk allowing the elephant population to increase until a possible stable age structure and zero growth rate in the population was achieved? What would have been lost in the process from the habitats in his charge?

HISTORY OF THE KRUGER NATIONAL PARK ELEPHANT POPULATION

Elephant populations throughout Africa were decimated by the early hunters whose writings were more concerned with the thrill of the hunt than of natural history. In the Lowveld areas of South Africa where Kruger is situated, all the elephants had been shot out before the park was proclaimed in 1898. Nobody knows how abundant elephants were in this area, or how they utilised their range, but there is evidence from some sources which suggests that elephant numbers were never high in the Kruger area before the advent of the white man and his guns.

The San (Bushmen), whose characteristic rock paintings are still visible in rock shelters in both the south-western and northern areas of the KNP, were associated with the latter part of the Late Stone Age between 7000 B.C. and 300 A.D. Elephants must have occurred in the KNP area during this time as one of the paintings in a shelter along the Nwatindlopfu River shows a group of five of these animals. Of the 109 shelters containing rock art so far discovered in the KNP area, this is the only one featuring elephants. One other shelter with elephant paintings has been found in the area, some 30 kms to the west of the KNP.

It would be expected that a large, dramatic and dangerous animal like the elephant would feature prominently in Bushman folk lore. Elephants were a popular theme for paintings elsewhere in southern Africa as they provided a lot of meat and were associated with water and rain which the Bushmen artists were keen to influence. Bushmen were capable of hunting elephants by "ham-stringing" (as was shown in a painting near Molteno in the eastern Cape) or through the use of poisoned arrows—particularly on the younger animals. San art is believed to have been of considerable spiritual significance to the artists, depicting the spiritual experiences of shamans during states of altered consciousness induced by ritual dances. San art was not narrative of their lifestyles nor "menus" representative of their diet, and that the incidence of different species in their art may not be reflective of their relative abundance. But elephants have been shown to be of "special symbolic importance" to San peoples elsewhere in South Africa. Human figures with trunks and even with heads of elephants have been painted. Given then that elephants were of considerable cultural significance to the San people, their relative scarcity in the rock art of the KNP and surrounding area may indicate that these animals were relatively rare during the San era.

There is also a lack of evidence of old elephant utilisation of baobab trees. Elephants strip off the bark of these trees for food and scars persist for hundreds of years. One baobab in Kruger, carries the inscription "BRISCOE 1890" carved in its bark. This carving, now 110 years old, is still as clearly visible as if it was carved only a year or two ago, and will probably persist for another 100 years or more. If elephants were utilising baobabs 100 or even 200 years or more ago, it could be expected that the scars would still be clearly visible. Yet more than 50% of trees in the far north of the park show no sign of utilisation by elephants. Baobabs outside the Park show no signs of old elephant damage, but clearly show the impacts of earlier people who cut "panels" of bark from the trees for domestic use.

A third clue comes from the writings of early travellers to the area who made little mention of these animals. Francois de Cuiper and his party were the first to visit the area in 1752. His mission from Delagoa Bay (now Maputo in Mozambique) was to establish trade with the interior in gold, ivory and copper. They saw few elephants and were informed by the indigenous people that if they wanted ivory and gold, they would have to go far to the north to the area now known as Zimbabwe. Copper could be obtained from the area now known as Phalaborwa. This last information has proved to be correct for gold and copper, so the information on ivory was probably also correct. Louis Trichardt on his trek through Kruger in 1838 also made no mention of elephants in his diaries, though he mentioned an elephant hunt once they arrived in Delagoa Bay. Joâo Albasini was the first white settler in the Kruger area. He arrived in Delagoa Bay in 1831 and established himself as a hunter and trader in Mozambique and the eastern Transvaal. He formed a company in Lorenco Marques whose objective was to hunt elephants and increase the trade in ivory. This lasted only six months and he then established himself as a hunter and trader in the Phabeni area in the southern part of Kruger. After two years there he abandoned the store and moved to Ohrigstad. Though no records exist, the outcome of these ventures hint at an elephant population at too low a density to sustain viable hunting and trade.

Of the later hunters who left any written record, it is perhaps significant that none who hunted elephants (e.g. Selous, Finaughty) did so in the KNP area while those that did hunt there (Vaughn Kirby, Glynn) did not hunt elephants.

A final speculative clue may come from the floral and faunal diversity which still exists in the Kruger today. Over two thousand plant species have been recorded, some of which are known to be vulnerable to elephant. If there had been successive episodes of high densities of elephants over time, this complex diversity may have been much reduced.

Why elephant densities may have been low is not known, but one theory speculates that perhaps numbers could have been held in check by early man. If densities were low, and man had the means to kill elephant calves, say using poisoned arrows, they would not have to kill many to impose limits on their population growth. But however many elephants that there

may have been, they were shot out by hunters, and by 1903 James Stevenson-Hamilton, the park's first warden, reported that there were no elephants to be found. They responded quickly to the new sanctuary, and by 1905 his staff had found evidence of their occurrence near the confluence of the Letaba and Olifants rivers which is located roughly midway between the Park's northern and southern boundaries. From there they gradually recolonised the whole Park. Diaries of the earlier Rangers recorded the first sightings of elephants in new localities. The recolonisation process to the northern and southern extremities of the Park occurred at about the same rate. Northward to the Luvuvhu River took until 1945 (40 years to cover 290 kms) while the spread southward to the confluence of the Crocodile and Sigaas rivers, was slightly slower, taking until 1958 (53 years to cover 280 kms).

Numbers increased steadily during this time and concern over the evident impact they were having was shown as early as 1942. In that year an early park ranger by the name of Steyn made the following tongue in cheek comment in his annual report: "With regard to the question of the control (culling) of elephants in certain areas where it may become necessary, the following idea has come to mind, i.e. to use a 10 or 12 ton armoured car to remove them from any region. This will naturally only be possible after the present war and I leave the details to the imagination of the reader."

Early estimates of population size were made by Park rangers based on their observations, but without the modern aids like helicopters, these estimates were clearly severe underestimates. The concerns intensified until 1967 when the first comprehensive aerial census was conducted and the population estimate of 6,586 proved to be nearly 3 times larger than the 1964 estimate of 2,374. The decision was then taken to limit the population to around 7,000 and culling was initiated.

This figure concurred with those of biologists working elsewhere in Africa at around that time. The elephant population density in Murchison Falls National Park in Uganda was 5 elephants per square mile and it was felt that this considerably exceeded the carrying capacity. In Tsavo National Park, Kenya, the early recommendation was that one per square mile was the right number (this recommendation was never implemented). The 7,000 for Kruger, which has an area of 20,000 square kilometres (8,000 square miles), was just below this. This number gave an average area of 2.7 square kilometres per elephant. As this policy was implemented to prevent the loss of biodiversity from the Kruger's ecosystems, it was undoubtedly successful as no species are known to have been lost from the Park.

So how was the Kruger elephant population managed to maintain it at the prescribed level of around 7,000? A unique technique was developed for the censusing of Kruger's elephant population, which is the most intensive and accurate census of elephant conducted anywhere in the world, though recent intensive fixed wing census techniques in Tsavo using multiple teams and GPS (Global Positioning System) technology probably give comparable results. The Kruger census is conducted annually during August and September to capitalise on the late dry season conditions. At this time of year the animals tend to congregate in the vicinity of watercourses and waterholes, and visibility is at its best due to the trees having shed their leaves. A helicopter is preferred as it can fly at extremely low speeds and can hover as well. In large, loose aggregations of elephants, the pilot can manoeuvre the aircraft systematically from group to group at low level until all have been exactly counted. In contrast, fixed-wing aircraft are forced to maintain forward speed which necessitates circling of the groups which is confusing to observers. Because of the helicopter's manoeuvrability, a flight pattern which follows the watercourses is flown. Kruger is particularly suitable for this as its undulating savanna terrain is drained by a well spaced network of watercourses which are clearly visible from the air. The pilot begins by flying along one bank of a major watercourse, keeping close enough to it to allow careful scanning of this denser vegetation but yet far enough from it to allow adequate scanning of the ground as far as the watershed. He then turns up each tributary and sub-tributary, following it up one bank to its source and back down the other bank. In this way each drainage system is systematically covered before moving on to the next. The watercourses give the pilot visual cues as to where to fly and systematic ground coverage thereafter is almost automatic. The census is conducted at an altitude of about 200 m above ground depending on the terrain

and visibility. The whole census is completed in 18 days and about 130 hours of flying time. Research has shown that census totals have never exceeded 7% of the expected result. Once the census result was known, a committee (known as the Standing Committee for Wildlife Management) made up of the senior nature conservation staff of the Kruger met to decide on an appropriate culling quota to conform with the elephant management policy. This quota was then achieved either through capture and translocation to other conservation areas where they could be accommodated, or through culling.

But whereas the Kruger managers decided to limit elephant population growth, a *laissez faire* (non-interference) policy was adopted in east Africa. This policy's roots almost certainly originated from compassion for the elephants themselves. To sit quietly in the close proximity of a herd of elephants who are going quietly about their business is an emotional experience that can not easily be described to anyone unfamiliar with these animals. Their sheer size alone induces a feeling of awe, and you will not have to sit for long before their intelligence, playfulness, compassion and tolerance become evident. All of these attributes of elephants combine to instil in those lucky enough to have experienced them, a feeling of empathy which intensifies the longer that exposure to elephants lasts. These emotions are not comfortable bedfellows with the concepts of killing these wonderful animals.

Elephants are also considered to be a "keystone species"—one upon which other species are dependant for their own survival. Elephants open up areas of thick woodland affording habitats to species favouring those of a more open character. They also pass seeds through the gut to be deposited in seedbeds of fertile dung assisting germination. Trees pushed over give refuge and food to many lesser vertebrates and invertebrates. These refuges are essential to their survival and without these, populations of these species would be severely compromised. Elephants also excavate holes in sandy riverbeds to gain access to the water below. These water holes give other species access to water which would otherwise be unavailable allowing them to survive in arid environments out of the rainy season.

But to stand under the canopy of a massive old baobab tree (*Adansonia digitata*) and to ponder a little on the size and age of such old giants, is an emotional experience of a different kind, but one which in its own way is no less soul stirring than that which may be gained from elephants. It is perhaps also their size which makes the initial impression, but the aura of age is tangible. The age that these trees may attain is not known as the pithy wood shows none of the rings which allow the determination of age in other tree species. The "Briscoe" baobab is not a particularly large tree suggesting that it is not one of the older ones, yet it was more than a hundred years ago since the carving was carried out. The tree can have changed little in the intervening 120 years, so some of the older ones must be many hundreds if not thousands of years old!

Baobabs are also a keystone species and a little examination of some of these trees will reveal their significance in the environment. The convolutions in the trunks of these benevolent old giants form cracks and holes which provide shelter to many small animals and birds and offer ideal sites to rear their young. To some species, the presence of baobabs is critical—in Kruger the only known nesting sites of both the Böhm's Spinetail *(Neafrapus boehmi)* and the Mottled Spinetail *(Telecanthura ussheri)* are in hollow baobabs. Thus without these trees, these birds would simply not occur in the area. Mosque Swallows *(Hirundo senegalensis)* and Grey-headed Parrots *(Poicephalus fuscicollis)* also favour these trees for breeding and any decline in the number of baobabs would also have its effects on the populations of these birds also. Barn owls *(Tyto alba)* would occur at much lower densities if the nesting holes offered by baobabs were not available, and White-headed Vultures *(Aegypius occipitalis)* favour baobabs for building their nests as well.

So, quite apart from their aesthetic appeal, both elephants and baobabs play important but different ecological roles—the elephant in its capacity to accelerate nutrient cycling and alter their environments, and the baobab because of its importance to many species of animals as a source of food and shelter. But elephants also feed on baobabs, stripping the bark off and even chipping away the pithy wood with their tusks. In extreme cases the trees may become so weakened that they eventually topple and die. Most tree species die when ring-barked, but baobabs have a remarkable capacity to regenerate bark. They are therefore resistant

to utilisation by elephants up to a point, but one of the major causes of mortality in baobabs is drought, particularly once they have had excessive amounts of bark removed by elephants which probably accelerates moisture loss. Anyone visiting the northern parts of Kruger will not fail to notice that most baobabs have suffered considerable bark removal. During aerial censuses of the Kruger elephant population, dead baobabs are also recorded and this has showed that over the past few years, more than 200 have died due to the combined effects of drought and elephant utilisation.

But baobabs are not the only plants which are vulnerable to utilisation by elephants. The knobthorn *(Acacia nigrescens)* is another keystone species as it is favoured by a wide number of raptors and other birds for nesting. Wahlberg's *(Aquila wahlbergi)* and Tawny *(A. rapax)* eagles, White-backed vultures *(Gyps africanus)* and some of the small goshawks *(Accipiter spp.)* also favour the mature knobthorns, while quelea finches *(Quelea quelea)* and Wattled starlings *(Creatophora cinerea)* are communal breeders favouring stands of the stunted forms of this species. They breed in thousands (even millions) in these stands and are a staple food of migrant Steppe and Lesser Spotted eagles. Luckily the knobthorn is a very common species but few mature knobthorns in Kruger are free of some form of elephant utilisation and many have been ring-barked resulting in the death of the tree. Absence of mature knobthorns would have severe consequences for many of these species. Marula trees *(Sclerocarya birrea)* are often debarked or pushed over and even the branches up to the thickness of a man's forearm are eaten. Numbers of marulas have also declined over the years. Other plant species at risk are fever trees *(Acacia xanthophloea)*, kiaat *(Pterocarpus angolensis)* and star chestnut *(Sterculia rogersii)*. These are just a few of the species favoured by elephants but where elephant densities increase to the point where food availability becomes limiting on the elephant population, nearly all plant species are at some degree of risk. In some parks elsewhere in Africa, this has meant loss of species from systems with unlimited elephant populations.

In Amboseli National Park (Kenya) for example, an extremely high density of elephants has led to a decline in the woodland in the park resulting in the extirpation (local extinction) of both lesser kudu

(Tragelaphus imberbis) and bushbuck *(Tragelaphus scriptus)*. Other species favouring woodland such as gerenuk *(Litocranius walleri)*, giraffe *(Giraffa camelopardalis)*, baboons *(Papio* species) and monkeys *(Cercopithicus* species) have also declined inside the Park. In Tsavo National Park (Kenya), dense woodland was changed into open savanna and baobabs are now very rare where they were once common.

The Tsavo story is an interesting one. The huge elephant herds that modified Tsavo's landscapes this way are now severely depleted—by poachers, not managers! Apart from being one of Africa's most famous national parks, it gained initial fame through the book, "The man-eaters of Tsavo" which tells the story of two lions which killed at least 28 labourers and even held up the construction of the railway in 1898. J. H. Patterson, the author of this book was a keen observer and he described the nature of the bush as "interminable nyika . . . the whole country covered in low stunted trees . . . the only clearing being the narrow track of the railway." Elephants are hardly mentioned in the book. In 1903, the writer/traveller Mienertzhagen found "very few" elephants in the thick Tsavo bush, but by 1970, this had changed and human developments outside had compressed the population into the park—an area roughly the same size as Kruger. Aerial surveys in that year estimated the population to stand at 45,000. These elephants had a huge impact and by 1974, severe droughts had reduced the population to 36,000. Nine thousand elephants had died and at the same time, 4,000 black rhino also died of starvation. The carcasses of these animals offered an opportunity to local people and corrupt staff to establish an illegal trade in the horns and tusks. Having become established, this trade turned to the poaching of live elephants and rhinos and by 1989, the Tsavo elephant population had been reduced to just 6,000. Thirty thousand elephants had been poached and black rhinos had been all but extirpated. Tsavo today is an open savanna which has favoured the grassland species, and the removal of the trees has had some other interesting consequences. Fountains have appeared where they were not known to occur before—the moisture which once was sucked up by the trees and transpired into the atmosphere, now seeps into the drainage lines. These changes are perceived by some as benefits to the Tsavo ecosystem induced by high densities of elephants, and their role in this transformation has often been lauded. But an unanswered question remains—what would Tsavo look like today had the 30,000 elephants not been removed from the system by the poachers?

The poaching has now been contained and the most recent census of Tsavo's elephants in 2007 yielded a total of close to 9,000.

ELEPHANT MANAGEMENT OPTIONS

Given this background, the obvious basic question about elephant management in any confined reserve is whether or not to limit elephant numbers. If the management authority decides that the maintenance of biodiversity is the objective, what options are available? In order to limit the population growth of **any** species (and cynically, this applies even to humans), there are only three possible options. These are translocation, contraception and culling or a combination of these. Others such as hunting are just variations of one or more of these options. In western society, non-lethal means of population limitation would clearly be preferable to the killing of elephants, but there is a strong body of opinion in Africa which supports the sustainable use of wild animals (even elephants) to provide benefits to local people and communities. Who is right? Westerners who live far removed from the problems or local people who often suffer terrible depredations from living close to elephants and see the killing of the animals as a desirable solution? For them, if the problem animals are removed, the meat becomes available and revenues can even be generated. In some areas such as in Zimbabwe, problem or excess animals are hunted by professional hunters in schemes known as CAMPFIRE (Communal Areas Management Programme For Indigenous Resources). These hunters pay for the privilege and the money is given back to the people for community development projects.

If non-lethal means are to be employed, there are three options available—range expansion, translocation and contraception. Range expansion would usually be the first choice if it were available, but of course, very little land is now still available to allow for this. Perhaps one of the last large remaining patches of land that could still be zoned for conservation was recently proclaimed on Kruger's eastern boundary in Mozambique. Known now as the Limpopo National Park (LNP), it is half the size of Kruger. Even here there are still many people (an estimated 22,000) still living on the land, and there are many problems associated with this that still need to be overcome. In the modern era people can no longer simply be relocated. There were very few elephants in this area when it was proclaimed and it was initially seen as a considerable opportunity for Kruger to dispose of its excess elephants.

RANGE EXPANSION

There was a common perception that once the game proof fence between Kruger and the proposed park had been removed, elephants would immediately move off into Mozambique, alleviating the need to limit the population in Kruger. But studies of elephant movement in Kruger have revealed that they show a remarkable degree of fidelity to their home ranges. These home ranges have an average size of about 1,200 square kilometres. Factors which may be expected to stimulate movements, such as rainfall in nearby areas and culling, have little effect on their movements except within their respective home ranges. They may be induced to move to other parts of their home range, but they do not leave these well defined areas. This is certainly because these ranges are the areas where they are most comfortable. The old matriarchs know the area well—they know where water will be found in the dry season, where food availability may be best—information and experience that they have built up over their long life times. They also have the ability to extract sufficient nutrition from the available vegetation even during severe droughts, so they have no real necessity to move.

After the proclamation, 25 elephants (three family units of seven each and four adult bulls) were translocated into the new park. All of these animals returned to Kruger and made their way back to their original home ranges. This illustrated that translocation over a relatively short distance will not be successful unless the elephants are prevented from returning to their original home ranges by very robust, intact and well maintained fences.

However, more recently, three sections of the eastern boundary fence between the Limpopo and

Olifants rivers were removed to allow for natural re-colonisation of game in this new trans-frontier conservation area. At certain river crossings (Shingwedzi and Nshawu rivers) wash-aways had also occurred creating more gaps in the fence. A problem with simply creating gaps in a fence is that only the animals whose home ranges border on the fence will even be aware that a gap has been created. The vast majority of Kruger's elephants will not even know that there is a fence there, or that that there is now an opportunity to expand their home ranges to the east. There can therefore be no sudden spill of elephants into the new area. The resident elephants will start the process by exploring the opened up area and will gradually expand this deeper and deeper into Mozambique. This may relieve population pressure in the immediate area of the gaps, but not in the vast remaining area of the Kruger.

In October 2006 an aerial survey of the Shingwedzi River basin area of the LNP was conducted, and a total of 630 elephants were recorded at widespread localities in the survey area. This census result showed that the natural recolonisation process had begun, but censuses within the Kruger showed that no decline had occurred. Population growth within Kruger was negating any emigration to Mozambique.

An aspect of the concept of range expansion is a new idea of corridors connecting conservation areas to enable the establishment of what are called "metapopulations." A metapopulation is a group of spatially separated populations of the same species which interact through dispersal. In this instance, dispersal is supposed to occur through the established corridors. The promoters of this theory suggest that such an arrangement could allow for stabilisation of population numbers through a model known as a source-sink.

This is a model used to describe how variation in habitat quality may affect population growth. Source patches are high quality habitat in which a population will increase while in the sinks, low quality habitat can not support a population and survival is reduced. The theory holds that excess individuals from the source will move to the sink. The supposition in the case of elephants is that in the sinks mortality rates would be higher than birth rates and higher than in the source population. Those advocating this idea suggest that by emigration from source to sink elephant numbers could be prevented from increasing to levels that are deemed undesirable. They acknowledge that sink population numbers must be limited, and while they advocate natural control, they concede that there may be a need for people to reduce numbers in sinks. This they see as "natural" given that human predation is considered a major historical source of impact on elephant numbers. To manage sinks effectively, local communities could be allowed to hunt elephants in a controlled and authorised manner. They argue that this must be seen in the context of sustainable resource use and must provide tangible benefits (for instance in the form of meat or revenue from sports hunting) to these communities.

While there would be a few benefits emanating from the implementation of this model (benefits to local communities, genetic exchange within the metapopulation, there also seem to be a number of potential problems. These are:

- Mortality rates in sinks must exceed birth rates in the source population and in the overall metapopulation. Normal increase in an elephant population is between 5% and 7%. In a large population this means a considerable mortality must take place (675–945 deaths). If the habitat was that poor as to induce mortality of this scale, why would elephants want to go there? Similarly if local communities were allowed to hunt elephants, it would need to be conducted at a similar scale. Elephants are not stupid and with the harassment of hunting, they will be unlikely to remain in the sink and will quickly move back to the source.
- It is not clear how hunting in the sinks differs from culling at source. If the objective is to obviate culling, why is hunting acceptable? Sports hunters may be interested in hunting adult bulls, but what about the family groups? Hunting or culling of individuals from family groups is seen as inhumane due to the special social bonds which exist between family members and the trauma involved in killing individuals. This form of elephant management is banned by legislation in the National Norms and Standards for the Management of Elephants in South Africa. It would therefore not be acceptable for local communities to be allowed to hunt elephants for meat or revenue in these sinks.

- Corridors. The same problem exists for corridors connecting metapopulations as for range expansion—very little land is now still available to allow for this. Can they be established in areas where people are already established? What about human–elephant conflict issues in the corridors? Can elephants be induced to use the corridors if people are present?
- Very few elephants will be in a position to utilise the corridors. As is the case with fence gaps, only the elephants whose home ranges border on the corridor opening will even be aware that a corridor has been created. The vast majority of the rest of the elephant population will be unaffected by its creation. It is unlikely that sufficient elephants will use the corridor to affect the population size within the source.

TRANSLOCATION

Translocation is the second option and is one that most will find ethically acceptable. Whole families can now be moved together so splitting of families does not occur, and it has the additional advantage of establishing other elephant populations elsewhere. In southern Africa today however, saturation point has almost been reached. Most conservation areas already now have elephants and their managers understand the consequences of too many elephants and do not wish to increase their populations any further. Translocations are very expensive and ultimately the areas acquiring excess elephants from one conservation area will one day be faced with exactly the same dilemmas—the problems are merely transferred. Translocations are therefore still not the ideal solution. They provide temporary respite, but in a population as large as Kruger's translocations can not be conducted at a rate fast enough to reduce numbers, and there are currently no reserves requiring elephants.

CONTRACEPTION

Contraception is the third non-lethal option. Two methods have received attention so far, the first being through hormonal control using oestrogens. A project researching this method was terminated in Kruger on humane grounds as there was strong evidence that the hormones were drastically affecting behaviour of the vaccinated cows and attendant bulls. Females were induced into a state of "false oestrus," and bulls were attempting to mate with them while they were not receptive. This led to harassment of the cows by the bulls to the point that they got separated from their families, and even from their small calves. Three of the calves died during the research period, either through starvation or predation.

The other approach achieves contraception through Porcine Zona Pellucida (pZP) vaccination of adult elephant females. This vaccine is made from the ovaries of pigs obtained from commercial slaughterhouses. The vaccine stimulates the animal's immune system to produce antibodies which bind to the outer membrane (zona pellucida) of the elephant cow's egg cells (oocytes) and prevents penetration of sperm. This method has no hormonal or behavioural consequences. But in an area the size of Kruger with a population of 13,500 elephants, even this method is unlikely to provide a solution for logistical reasons. Computer modelling has shown that to stabilise an elephant population, approximately 70% of all breeding females have to be under treatment at any one time. In Kruger this means about 5,500 females. Currently the technology will give a contraceptive effect for up to about 2.5 years. The expense would almost certainly be prohibitive. In a smaller reserve however, contraception programs using pZP vaccines have been implemented with great success.

A problem with the use of contraception is that it can not reduce a population over the short term. Contraception prevents additions to the population and thus stabilises the population, but to achieve a decline in numbers, you have to await natural mortality. Elephants are long lived (± 60 years) and many years will have to pass before a significant decline will have occurred.

An unexplored possible negative consequence of limiting an elephant population through contraception would be a decline in the sizes of matriarchal (family) units. Young cows stay with their mothers for as long as the mother remains alive. The normal elephant family is thus a large extended one consisting of the old matriarch, her surviving daughters, and all of their respective offspring. A cow may have as many as eight or ten calves in her life of which half could be expected to be female. A family could thus be comprised of five or six adult females with calves of varying

ages in a group size of around 15 or more. This is an important social structure among savanna elephants in which young animals learn essential lessons in life, particularly with regard to birth, death, mating behaviour and rearing of young. If the objective of a contraception program was aimed at stabilizing numbers in the population, each cow would theoretically only be allowed to have two offspring, one of which could be expected to be a male. The outcome of this would be that the average group would thus consist of only the old female, a single daughter and possibly one or two calves. Given the social importance of the family, would this enforced change in elephant society be ethically acceptable?

CULLING

Culling is currently the only remaining long-term alternative, and here there are also a few options. Anaesthetic drugs would be ideal but they can not be used for such purposes as the meat may subsequently not be used for human consumption. The leaving of such contaminated carcasses in the field for scavengers is therefore also questionable. The only drug that has been approved which allows for later human consumption of the meat is succinylcholine chloride (scoline) whose component compounds occur naturally in mammalian bodies. Scoline is a neuro/muscular blocking agent which paralyses the animal by preventing the brain's impulses from reaching the muscles. This was used in Kruger to cull elephants in the past as it had the clear advantage of obviating wounding and provided a far greater safety margin for staff and scientists attending such culls. However, research conducted in Kruger showed that the use of this drug on elephants was inhumane as the heart muscle remained largely unaffected by the scoline. The locomotory muscles were the first to be affected followed by those controlling breathing (the diaphragm). This meant that the animal was fully conscious but paralysed and unable to breathe, and therefore died of suffocation if it could not be brain-shot immediately after becoming recumbent. The use of scoline was then discontinued and the only method now considered humane is by a sharpshooter using a rifle and live ammunition from a helicopter at close range. Only whole family units or single bulls would be culled to prevent trauma to surviving family members.

Culling is the only option which can generate revenues adequate for covering the costs involved. Translocations and contraception are expensive as are land acquisitions for range expansion and corridors.

PREVIOUS AND CURRENT POLICIES

The policy of limiting the Kruger elephant population to a level around 7,000 was maintained until 1994 when it was challenged by an animal rights group. A decision was then taken to place a moratorium on culling until the policy had been reviewed. This review compiled a new policy by 1999 which was never implemented due to sensitivities surrounding elephant culling. The policy has now once again been reviewed in 2008, but has also still to be implemented. In the mean time, the population has increased to an estimated 13,500 at the last (2009) census.

The text below has been extracted from the new policy and gives a brief summary. This policy can be viewed in full at: *http://www.sanparks.org/parks/kruger/conservation/scientific/key_issues/plans/elephant/*. In essence this new policy focuses less on numbers of elephants than on the impacts that they are having. The park has been divided into various areas constituting designated areas of high elephant impact and low elephant impact. The impact zoning approach considered several aspects including various biodiversity values, incidences of and risks from damage-causing animals, tourism expectations, landscape linkages and trans-frontier opportunities. Five key elephant management objectives have been developed for Kruger:

Objective 1 seeks SANParks to manage elephant impact and human interactions through inducing spatial and temporal variation in elephant use of landscapes through "High" and "Low" elephant impact zones. This should be achieved through:

1. Minimizing the number of additional water points and dams;
2. Mimicking the effect of natural water distribution;
3. Expanding land through contracts and agreements; and
4. Removing restrictions such as fences. This objective deals with direct influences that elephants have on the landscape and the associated suite of values.

Objective 2 focuses on reactive responses and associated actions to ensure that management accommodates both the consequences of historic biodiversity, elephant and tourism-related management philosophies and the current expectations as articulated in the broad Kruger park management objectives. This objective thus strives to ensure that the consequences of historic management actions are minimized by proposing short- to medium-term actions, evaluating risks to other objectives, and implementing actions that do not compromise SANParks' strategic objectives and primary mandate of biodiversity conservation.

Objective 3 focuses on the effects that elephants have on stakeholders through aligning SANParks' Elephant Management Plan with co-management and contractual agreements and, where appropriate, revisiting and establishing agreements with stakeholders and affected parties. These actions focus on assessing concerns and issues of various stakeholders, acting on these, informing stakeholders and evaluating how SANParks' actions affect stakeholders.

Objective 4 strives to align SANParks and Trans Frontier Conservation Area (TFCA) Elephant Management Policies through appropriate bilateral approaches.

Objective 5 is directed at expanding understanding through focused research, namely to evaluate, inform and revise elephant management through collaborative research agreements. This provides for the critical evaluation both internally and externally of SANParks' achievements against the intentions articulated in this Kruger Elephant Management Plan. The actions provide explicitly for the opportunity to generate information as well as to inform, review and accommodate variance in management actions on annual, bi-annual, five-yearly and ten-yearly intervals.

Through the implementation of this policy, much information should be gained on the dynamics of elephant population cycles, and the consequences of large elephant populations on biodiversity and ecosystem functioning.

SUMMING UP—THE DILEMMA

This brings us finally to the headaches and heartaches that are experienced by *all* managers of elephants. A decision has to be made before elephant damage occurs as to whether the area for which they are responsible will be managed as an elephant reserve or whether the maintenance of biodiversity will be the priority. The two approaches are mutually exclusive. The decision to manage as an elephant sanctuary is a valid one which is usually taken out of respect for the elephants themselves. Elephants are wonderful animals with which most people easily empathise, and there should be areas where they can live out their lives free from the stresses of the various management options. Amboseli is probably a good case in point. The wonderful research that has been conducted there by Cynthia Moss and her colleagues has taught us most of what we know about the complexities of elephant society and behaviour. There is still much to learn about long-term elephant cycles and Amboseli, with its huge data base and intimate knowledge of the elephants and their ecosystem, may be the best place to study these. The Addo Elephant National Park in South Africa is another. This park was created as a sanctuary for the last remaining elephants in the Cape region. Recent expansions to the park have perhaps shifted the focus towards a biodiversity approach, but elephants will probably always remain the conservation priority.

But a decision to allow unlimited growth of an elephant population needs to be taken consciously by the management authority, in the full awareness of the consequences—they must be aware that ultimately, other species *will* begin to disappear from the system due to over-utilisation or habitat changes induced by elephants. In some cases this will mean extirpation and perhaps even extinction. Ultimately also, when times of drought come (as they inevitably will in Africa), they must be prepared for the die-offs of elephants which will occur. These will be controversial, disturbing and emotional times.

But if the maintenance of biodiversity is the priority, something will have to be done (usually culling) to limit the numbers and densities of elephants before biodiversity is affected. This is also not an easy decision—the killing of elephants is never one that can or should be taken lightly. But here there lies yet another moral dilemma. At what level should

the population be held? To maintain a population at any particular level requires the removal from the population of a number of animals equal to the population's annual increase. The average increase in Kruger's elephant population has been calculated at a rate of 6.2% per year. To maintain a population at a low level would require the annual removal of a relatively few individuals. Maintaining it at a higher level requires the annual removal of proportionately more animals. As we have seen, when such numbers are involved, the only option for the removal of most of them would be through culling. If you agonize over the morality and ethics of culling elephants, then the issue will be greatly compounded by having to cull a much larger number. Is it not better to keep a population low at the level where few animals need to be culled or better still, at a level where most excess animals could be translocated rather than culled?

There is no middle of the road on the issue of elephant management—in large national parks with large elephant populations a choice has to be made for either one of these options: to cull or not to cull? If the choice is for the latter of these options (which is a valid one depending on the conservation priority for the designated area), there is no going back once extensive damage has occurred. When plant and/or animals species have been lost, it may (through the management of the elephant population) be able to maintain the remaining biodiversity, but the restoration of the system to its former richer state of biodiversity and function will scarcely be possible, particularly while elephants are still present in the system. The dilemma is in weighing up the sacrifice of individual elephants against the sacrifice of species. Either way, the decision taken will always trouble the consciences of those involved in the process. You should not have cold feet if you enter the elephant management arena, and be prepared to be castigated for your opinions and decisions whichever side of the debate they may lie.

So, if the decision were yours, what would you do?

B. Conflicting Values, Conflicting Priorities

RAMACHANDRA GUHA

DEEP ECOLOGY REVISITED

I.

"Radical Environmentalism and Wilderness Preservation: A Third World Critique" was written at the end of an extended period of residence in the United States, which followed directly upon several years of research on the origins of Indian environmentalism. That background might explain the puzzlement and anger which, in hindsight, appear to mark the essay. To my surprise, the article evoked a variety of responses, both pro and con. The veteran Vermont radical, Murray Bookchin, himself engaged in a polemic with American deep ecologists, offered a short (three-line) letter of congratulation. A longer (thirty-page) response came from the Norwegian philosopher Arne Naess, the originator of the term "deep ecology." Naess felt bound to assume responsibility for the ideas I had challenged, even though I had distinguished between his emphases and those of his American interpreters. Other correspondents, lesser known but no less engaged, wrote in to praise and to condemn.

. . .

The essay has acquired a life of its own. This postscript allows me to look at the issues anew, to expand and strengthen my case with the aid of a few freshly arrived examples.

II.

Woodrow Wilson once remarked that the United States was the only idealistic nation in the world. It is indeed this idealism which explains the zest, the zeal, the almost unstoppable force with which Americans have sought to impose their vision of the good life on the rest of the world. American economists urge on other nations their brand of energy-intensive, capital-intensive, market-oriented development. American spiritualists, saving souls, guide pagans to one or another of their eccentrically fanatical cults, from Southern Baptism to Moral Rearmament. American advertisers export the ethic of disposable containers—of all sizes, from coffee cups to automobiles—and Santa Barbara.

Adapted from Ramachandra Guha, "Deep Ecology Revisited," in J. Baird Callicott and Michael P. Nelson (eds.), The Great New Wilderness Debate (Athens, Ga.: University of Georgia Press, 1998).

Of course, other people have had to pay for the fruits of this idealism. The consequences of the forward march of American missionaries include the undermining of political independence, the erosion of cultures, and the growth of an ethic of sheer greed. In a dozen parts of the world, those fighting for political, economic, or cultural autonomy have collectively raised the question whether the American way of life is not, in fact, the Indian (or Brazilian, or Somalian) way of death.

One kind of U.S. missionary, however, has attracted virtually no critical attention. This is the man who is worried that the rest of the world thinks his country has a dollar sign for a heart. The dress he wears is also colored green, but it is the green of the virgin forest. A deeply committed lover of the wild, in his country he has helped put in place a magnificent system of national parks. But he also has money, and will travel. He now wishes to convert other cultures to his gospel, to export the American invention of national parks worldwide.

The essay to which these paragraphs are a coda was one of the first attacks on an imperialism previously reckoned to be largely benign. After all, we are not talking here of the Marines, with their awesome firepower, or even of the World Bank, with its money power and the ability to manipulate developing country governments. These are men (and more rarely, women) who come preaching the equality of all species, who worship all that is good and beautiful in Nature. What could be wrong with them?

I had suggested in my essay that the noble, apparently disinterested motives of conservation biologists and deep ecologists fueled a territorial ambition—the physical control of wilderness in parts of the world other than their own—that led inevitably to the displacement and harsh treatment of the human communities who dwelt in these forests. Consider in this context a recent assessment of global conservation by Michael Soulé, which complains that the language of policy documents has "become more humanistic in values and more economic in substance, and correspondingly less naturalistic and ecocentric." Soulé seems worried that in theory (though certainly not in practice!) some national governments and international conservation organizations (or ICOs) now pay more attention to the rights of human communities. Proof of this shift is the fact that "the top and middle management of most ICOs are economists, lawyers, and development specialists, not biologists." This is a sectarian plaint, a trade union approach to the problem spurred by an alleged takeover of the international conservation movement by social scientists, particularly economists.[1]

Soulé's essay, with its talk of conspiracies and takeover bids, manifests the paranoia of a community of scientists which has a *huge* influence on conservation policy yet wants to be the sole dictator of it. A scholar acclaimed by his peers as the "dean of tropical ecologists" has expressed this ambition more nakedly than most. Daniel Janzen, in a paper in the *Annual Review of Ecology and Systematics*, urges upon his fellow biologists the cultivation of the ability to raise cash so as to buy space and species to study. Let me now quote from a report he wrote on a new national park in Costa Rica, whose tone and thrust perfectly complement the other, ostensibly "scientific" essay. "We have the seed and the biological expertise: we lack control of the terrain," wrote Janzen in 1986. This situation he was able to remedy for himself by raising enough money to purchase the forest area needed to create Guanacaste National Park. One can only marvel at Janzen's conviction that he and his fellow biologists know all, and that the inhabitants of the forest know nothing. He justifies the taking over of the forest and the dispossession of the forest farmer by claiming that "today virtually all of the present-day occupants of the western Mesoamerican pastures, fields and degraded forests are deaf, blind, and mute to the fragments of the rich biological and cultural heritage that still occupies the shelves of the unused and underappreciated library in which they reside."[2]

This is an ecologically updated version of the White Man's Burden, where the biologist (rather than the civil servant or military official) knows that it is in the native's true interest to abandon his home and hearth and leave the field and forest clear for the new rulers of his domain. In Costa Rica we only have Janzen's word for it, but elsewhere we are better placed to challenge the conservationist's point of view. A remarkable recent book on African conservation has laid bare the imperialism, unconscious and explicit, of Western wilderness lovers and biologists working on that luckless continent. I cannot here summarize the massive documentation of Raymond Bonner's *At the Hand of Man*, so let me simply quote some of his conclusions:

> Above all, Africans [have been] ignored, overwhelmed, manipulated and outmaneuvered by a conservation crusade led, orchestrated and dominated by white Westerners.
>
> Livingstone, Stanley and other explorers and missionaries had come to Africa in the nineteenth century to promote the three C's—Christianity, commerce, and civilization. Now a fourth was added: conservation. These modern secular missionaries were convinced that without the white man's guidance, the Africans would go astray.
>
> [The criticisms] of egocentricity and neocolonialism . . . could be leveled fairly at most conservation organizations working in the Third World.
>
> As many Africans see it, white people are making rules to protect animals that white people want to see in parks that white people visit. Why should Africans support these programs? . . . The World Wildlife Fund professed to care about what the Africans wanted, but then tried to manipulate them into doing what the Westerners wanted: and those Africans who couldn't be brought into line were ignored.
>
> Africans do not use the parks and they do not receive any significant benefits from them. Yet they are paying the costs. There are indirect economic costs—government revenues that go to parks instead of schools. And there are direct personal costs [i.e., of the ban on hunting and fuel collecting, or of displacement].[3]

Bonner's book focuses on the elephant, one of the half-a-dozen or so animals that have come to acquire "totemic" status among Western wilderness lovers. Animal totems existed in most pre-modern societies, but as the Norwegian scholar Arne Kalland points out, in the past the injunction not to kill the totemic species applied only to members of the group. Hindus do not ask others to worship the cow, but those who love and cherish the elephant, seal, whale, or tiger try and impose a worldwide prohibition on its killing. No

one, they say, anywhere, anytime, shall be allowed to touch the animal they hold as sacred even if (as with the elephant and several species of whale) scientific evidence has established that small-scale hunting will not endanger its viable populations and will, in fact, save human lives put at risk by the expansion, after total protection, of the *lebensraum* of the totemic animal. The new totemists also insist that their species is the "true, rightful inhabitant" of the ocean or forest, and ask that human beings who have lived in the same terrain (and with the animals) for millennia be taken out and sent elsewhere.[4]

I turn, last of all, to an ongoing controversy in my own bailiwick. The Nagarhole National Park in southern Karnataka has an estimated forty tigers, the species toward whose protection enormous amounts of Indian and foreign money and attention have been directed. Now Nagarhole is also home to about 6,000 tribals, who have been in the area longer than anyone can remember, perhaps as long as the tigers themselves. The state Forest Department wants the tribals out, claiming they destroy the forest and kill wild game. The tribals answer that their demands are modest, consisting in the main of fuel wood, fruit, honey, and the odd quail or partridge. They do not own guns, although coffee planters living on the edge of the forest do. Maybe it is the planters who poach big game? In any case, they ask the officials, if the forest is only for tigers, why have you invited India's biggest hotel chain to build a hotel inside it while you plan to throw us out?

Into this controversy jumps a green missionary, passing through Karnataka. Dr. John G. Robinson works for the Wildlife Conservation Society in New York, for whom he oversees 160 projects in 44 countries. He conducts a whistle-stop tour of Nagarhole, and before he flies off to the next project on his list, hurriedly calls a press conference in the state capital, Bangalore. Throwing the tribals out of the park, he says, is the only means to save the wilderness. This is not a one-off case but a sacred principle, for in Robinson's opinion "relocating tribal or traditional people who live in these protected areas is the single most important step toward conservation." Tribals, he explains, "compulsively hunt for food," and compete with tigers for prey. Deprived of food, tigers cannot survive, and "their extinction means that the balance of the ecosystem is upset and this has a snowballing effect."[5]

One does not know how many tribals Robinsons met (none, is the likely answer). Yet the Nagarhole case is hardly atypical. All over India, the management of parks has sharply pitted the interests of poor tribals who have traditionally lived in them against those of wilderness lovers and urban pleasure seekers who wish to keep parks "free of human interference"—that is, free of other humans. These conflicts are being played out in the Rajaji sanctuary in Uttar Pradesh, in Simlipal in Orissa, in Kanha in Madhya Pradesh, and in Melghat in Maharashtra.[6] Everywhere, Indian wildlifers have ganged up behind the Forest Service to evict the tribals and relocate them far outside the forests. In this they have drawn sustenance from American biologists and conservation organizations, who have thrown the prestige of science and the power of the dollar behind the crusade to kick the original owners of the forest out of their home.

Specious nonsense about the equal rights of all species cannot hide the plain fact that green imperialists are possibly as dangerous and certainly more hypocritical than their economic or religious counterparts. For the American advertiser and banker hopes for a world in which everyone, regardless of color, will be in an economic sense an American—driving a car, drinking a Pepsi, owning a fridge and a washing machine. The missionary, having discovered Jesus Christ, wants pagans also to share in the discovery. The conservationist wants to "protect the tiger (or whale) for posterity," yet expects *other* people to make the sacrifice.

Moreover, the processes unleashed by green imperialism are well-nigh irreversible. For the consumer titillated into eating Kentucky Fried Chicken can always say, "once is enough." The Hindu converted to Christianity can decide later to revert to his original faith. But the poor tribal, thrown out of his home by the propaganda of the conservationist, is condemned to the life of an ecological refugee in a slum, a fate, for these forest people, which is next only to death.

III.

The illustrations offered above throw serious doubts on Arne Naess's claim that the deep ecology movement is "from the point of view of many people all over the world, the most precious gift from the North American continent in our time."[7] For deep ecology's signal contribution has been to privilege, above all other varieties and concerns of environmentalism, the protection of wild species and wild habitats, and to provide high-sounding, self-congratulatory but nonetheless dubious moral claims for doing so. Treating "biocentric equality" as a moral absolute, tigers, elephants, whales, and so on will need more space to grow, flourish and reproduce, while humans—poor humans—will be expected to make way for them.

By no means do I wish to see the world completely dominated by "human beings, their mutualists, commensals and parasites." I have time for the tiger and the rainforest, and wish also to try and protect those islands of nature not yet fully conquered by us. My plea rather is to put wilderness protection (and its radical edge, deep ecology) in its place, to recognize it as a distinctively North American brand of environmentalism, whose export and expansion must be done with caution, care, and above all, with humility. For in the poor and heavily populated countries of the South, protected areas cannot be managed with guns and guards but must, rather, be managed with full cognizance of the rights of the people who lived in (and oftentimes cared for) the forest before it became a national park or a world heritage site.

Putting deep ecology in its place is to recognize that trends it derides as "shallow" ecology might in fact be varieties of environmentalism that are more apposite, more representative, and more popular in the countries of the South. When Arne Naess says that "conservation biology is the spearhead of scientifically based environmentalism"[8] one wonders why "agro-ecology," "pollution abatement technology" or "renewable energy studies" cannot become the "spearhead of scientifically based environmentalism." For the Costa Rican peasant, the Ecuadorian fisherman, the Indonesian tribal, or the slum dweller in Bombay, wilderness preservation can hardly be more "deep" than pollution control, energy conservation, ecological urban planning, or sustainable agriculture.

NOTES

1. Michael Soulé, *The Tigress and the Little Girl* (unpublished manuscript), Chapter 6, "International Conservation Politics and Programs."
2. Daniel H. Janzen, *Guanacaste National Park: Tropical Ecological and Cultural Restoration* (San José, Costa Rica, Editorial Universidad Estatal a Distancia, 1986).
3. Raymond Bonner, *At the Hand of Man: Peril and Hope for Africa's Wildlife* (New York: Alfred A. Knopf, 1993), pp. 36, 65, 70, 85, 221. [For more on Bonner, see Schmidtz, "When Preservationism Doesn't Preserve," in this volume.]
4. Arne Kalland, "Seals, Whales and Elephants: Totem Animals and Anti-Use Campaigns," in *Proceedings of the Conference on Responsible Wildlife Management* (Brussels: European Bureau for Conservation and Development, 1994). Also, Arne Kalland, "Management by Totemization: Whale Symbolism and the Anti-Whaling Campaign," *Arctic* 46 (1993).
5. Quoted in *The Deccan Herald*, Bangalore, 5 November 1995.
6. A useful countrywide overview is provided in Ashish Kothari, Saloni Suri, and Neena Singh, "Conservation in India: A New Direction," *Economic and Political Weekly*, 28 October 1995.
7. Arne Naess, "Comments on the Article 'Radical American Environmentalism and Wilderness Preservation: A Third World Critique' by Ramachandra Guha," typescript (1989), p. 23.
8. Arne Naess, *Ecology, Community, and Lifestyle*, translated by David Rothenberg (Cambridge: Cambridge University Press, 1990), p. 45.

DAVID SCHMIDTZ

NATURAL ENEMIES
An Anatomy of Environmental Conflict

For many who live in modern cities, nature is a haven, a refuge from an urban jungle. The frustrations of the city make it easy to feel nostalgia for a simple life that never was: days spent hiking in the Grand Canyon, nights spent curled up by the fireplace after a hot shower and something nice from the refrigerator.

But nature is not a national park, as people who make their living in its midst are aware. My ancestors emigrated from Germany to North America in the 1850's, settling in Minnesota and Saskatchewan. Like most settlers, they had mixed feelings about nature.[1]

Beautiful it may have been, but it was not the innocuous beauty that city dwellers find in art galleries. Nature was wild, literally. It could be kind. It could be indifferent. Or it could be an appalling enemy, a promise of hard life and sudden death. My mother lost a brother to diphtheria. A mile down the road, her uncle watched his whole family, a wife and three children, die of diphtheria in the space of three days. She grew up on a farm that got virtually no rain for a stretch of ten years.[2] She once told me, "You'd see black clouds boiling on the horizon. If you didn't know better you'd think the rain was finally coming. But it wasn't rain.

Ted Nerdhaus, Michael Shellenberger, Break Through: Why We Can't Leave Saving the Planet to Environmentalists, 2009, Houghton Mifflin Harcourt.

When you got up in the morning everything would be covered by a carpet of dust. Or grasshoppers." For many of the world's people today, nature remains as it was for my ancestors—red in tooth and claw. It comes in the night to kill their children.[3] No hot shower. No refrigerator.

Western civilization has given me the luxury of being an environmentalist. I am insulated against nature, and this insulation gives me the luxury of no longer needing to see nature as a threat. Unfortunately, not everyone is so insulated, and thus not everyone is in a position to join me in treating wilderness preservation as an urgent priority. Therein lies a source of conflict, a kind of conflict that is bad for the environment and that we cannot resolve unless we understand that it is not like other kinds of conflict.

This essay describes three kinds of environmental conflict, concentrating on a subtle but crucial contrast between conflicting values and conflicting priorities.[4] I discuss what it takes to avoid, manage, and resolve these kinds of environmental conflict. I discuss the contingent connection between environmental conflict resolution and environmental justice. Finally, I argue that economics can help us understand how to resolve environmental conflict. While we need not (and should not) attempt to reduce all values to economic values, we do need to understand that there is a certain logic to the working of economic systems. To ignore the logic of human economy is to ignore the logic of human ecology and thus to ignore the logic of any ecology in which humans play a role. Anyone who truly cares about the environment would not do that.

THREE KINDS OF ENVIRONMENTAL CONFLICT

I will treat as basic a kind of conflict in which people simply find themselves in each other's way. I will refer to this as *conflict in use*. Conflict in use manifests itself in traffic jams, figuratively or literally. A pattern of overall use results in congestion, such that people trying to use a resource end up interfering with each other.[5] Conflict in use is resolved by institutions that literally or figuratively direct traffic, such as a system of property rights that lets people know who has the right of way when their intentions put them on a collision course. Such institutions help people avoid, manage, and resolve conflict when they facilitate orderly use

of a common resource, when they facilitate orderly removal of resources from the commons, and when they help people cope with *externalities*, including new externalities that emerge as property regimes evolve.[6] Property regimes can be a kind of public good if and when they solve commons problems and induce overall patterns of sustainable use.

Some environmental conflicts, though, cannot be addressed merely by settling on a system of property rights. In particular, some of our most serious conflicts concern what should be property in the first place. Thus, there is a second kind of conflict that ultimately is a matter of conflicting *values*. Should Maasai tribes be allowed to own and sell elephants as if elephants were pieces of property? One thing to be said on behalf of conferring such rights is that it would give the Maasai reason to protect elephants against poachers.[7] However, some would say turning elephants into a commodity is another way of destroying them. Even when it does not literally destroy the elephants, it still destroys what elephants stand for in the minds of those who cherish the idea of nature wild and free. This is not a conflict we can resolve by deciding who owns the resource. The parties disagree on whether anyone has the right to regard elephants as a resource in the first place.

Environmentalists sometimes distinguish between anthropocentric (i.e., human-centered) and biocentric (i.e., nature-centered) orientations toward nature. *Conservationists* care about nature in an anthropocentric way, saying nature should be used wisely. *Preservationists* care about nature in a biocentric way, saying that, although we (like any living creature) cannot avoid using nature, nature nevertheless has moral standing independent of its utility for humans.[8] A preservationist will say some ecosystems or species should be left to evolve according to their own lights, as free as possible from human interference. We should not think of wilderness as a mere resource. Wilderness commands reverence; mere resources do not. We may call this clash a case of contested commodification. It exemplifies the second kind of conflict: conflict in values.

There is a third kind of environmental conflict: conflicting *priorities*. We misunderstand this kind of conflict if we see it simply as another case of conflicting values. The difference is that people's immediate goals can be incompatible even when their values are relevantly similar. International conservation groups raise money by pledging to fight for preservationist "no use at all" policies. Sometimes, though, farmers do not join in pursuing cosmopolitan environmentalist goals because they cannot *afford* to.

This kind of conflict could occur even among people who all feel precisely the same way about where elephants should rank in our hierarchy of values. To give a crude illustration, suppose we all agree that our children outrank elephants but elephants outrank chess sets carved out of ivory. Even so, we could come into conflict when North Americans denounce hunting elephants to acquire ivory for carving chess sets, while Africans defend the practice because ivory revenues are feeding their children. Although both sides have the same values, they do not face the same cost. For one person, no elephant hunting means no ivory chess sets; for another person, no elephant hunting means no children.

Subsistence farmers for whom getting enough food is a day-by-day proposition can have priorities unlike ours not because their values are different but precisely because their values are the same. Thus, there is a kind of conflict that originates not so much from a difference of values as from a difference in which values people can afford to pursue under their differing circumstances.

Moreover, there is an additional problem, a feature of real-world conflict that some preservationists fail to appreciate. In parts of Africa, the dilemma for subsistence farmers is this: if they cannot commodify elephants (by selling ivory, hunting licenses, or photo safaris), then they will have to push elephants out of the way to make room for livestock or crops. In the abstract, exploiting elephants seems obviously wrong, but it stops being obvious after one spends time in rural Africa, and sees that when rural people cannot exploit elephants in some fashion, their only alternative is to convert elephant habitat into farmland.

Whether we like it or not, elephants will not survive except by sharing the land with people, which means their long-term survival depends on whether people can afford to share. Realistically, at least in parts of Africa where this kind of conflict is extreme, threatened species will have to contribute to the local

economy if they are to have any hope of survival. Thus, according to Brian Child, "wildlife will survive in Africa only where it can compete financially for space. The real threat to wildlife is poverty, not poaching."[9] With equal bluntness, Norman Myers says, "In emergent Africa, you either use wildlife or lose it. If it pays its own way, some of it will survive."[10]

And please understand: coexisting with elephants is costly. We are not talking about animals one looks at through a pair of binoculars, at a safe distance, while on vacation at a national park. Elephants are an integral part, and a dangerous part, of everyday life. Although I knew this at an intellectual level, such knowledge left me unprepared when the time came to learn it from experience. In July of 1999, my wife and I arrived at Oddballs' Camp in Botswana's Okavanga Delta in an airplane just big enough for three passengers. (The wings of the plane were reinforced with duct tape.) The airstrip was dirt. As we landed, baboons and warthogs scattered before us. The person who was to meet us was late because, while walking to the airstrip from the camp, he had to detour around a herd of Cape Buffalo, reputedly among the most dangerous animals in the world. After a fifteen-minute walk through the marsh, we arrived at the campground.

That night, we slept with the sound of baboons howling in the foreground and lions roaring in the background. Around four in the morning, we woke up to what sounded like trees being shaken by a gale-force wind. I got up and found myself standing in the open air, right next to a twelve-foot elephant. The elephant had been pressing its forehead against a lala palm, whipping the tree back and forth (thereby making sound that woke us up) in order to shake down the fruit higher up. Tiring of that, the elephant had torn the whole tree out of the ground and was taking an experimental munch at the roots. (The elephant knew I was there. Perhaps it deliberately avoided letting the tree fall on us. Some elephants are considerate in that way. Some aren't.)

Elephants rarely sleep and spend about eighty percent of their lives eating, and there usually were a few roaming the campground. It is important to grasp that these elephants were not pets. The camp did not adopt them. There was nothing domestic about them. There was nothing cute about them. They were magnificent by day and literally breathtaking by night. They were there because despite everyone's efforts to keep elephants out of camp, the bottom line is that if an elephant takes an interest in something inside camp, it is coming in and nothing is going to stop it. Our experience makes for a great story and an unforgettable visit, but imagine spending your whole life that way, going to bed not knowing what will be left of your crop or garden or house or children when you get up in the morning. Would you love wildlife?

Again, even people who embrace environmentalist values will act contrary to those values when they cannot afford to act in accordance with them. There are times when conflict is a matter of conflicting priorities.[11]

IDEALS, COMPROMISE, AND STEWARDSHIP

To some extent a philosopher's job is to say how the world ought to be in the grand scheme of things. It is an honorable job. But where environmental ethics is a study of ideals, environmental conflict resolution is the art of compromise in a world that is not a blank canvas. Conflict mediation typically involves trying to help negotiate win–win solutions.

Sometimes the negotiation is between people who would not both win in a more perfect world. Often, though, conflicts are not clashes between good and evil. When we try to stop people from burning the rain forest, the situation may be a conflict of *values* between us and evil condominium developers burning forests for the sheer thrill of raping the planet. However, it is as likely to be a conflict of *priorities* between us and displaced farmers who just want to feed their children. If we understood each other, we might have no quarrel whatsoever with each other's values, and might well have taken each other's side if circumstances had been different. We often have no reason at all to be trying to win by making our adversary lose.

In choosing our priorities, we sometimes need to be sensitive not only to our own values but to other people's as well, sometimes even when we *do not care* about other people's values. Why? Because we cannot *decide* that people will act according to our view of what is best for Gaia. People decide for themselves. We have to ask what their values are, what their priorities are, and what could lead people with such values and priorities to act in environmentally benign ways.

The most basic principle of conflict resolution is that mediators should try to get people to focus on their *interests*, not their *positions*.[12] In other words, it is better if negotiation does not turn into a contest of wills (drawing lines in the sand, as they say) but instead revolves around the actual problem, as defined by actual benefits that might be realized if negotiation leads to agreement.

Consider what this implies for the familiar idea that we are not owners of the land so much as stewards of it. If we see ourselves as stewards, then we see ourselves as obliged to care for the land on behalf of future generations. But if we are to take our stewardship role seriously, we need to understand that honest stewardship is a commitment to environmental interests, not environmentalist positions.[13] Commitment to interests sometimes mandates compromise on positions. It sometimes requires negotiation. Sometimes, what people call values are dressed-up positions that have little to do with any real interests. We make a huge mistake if we equate what is bad for our enemies (corporations, economists, ranchers, Western patriarchy, whatever) with what is good for the environment.

Mark Sagoff says government regulations have expressive and symbolic value. I agree that "regulation expresses what we believe, what we are, what we stand for as a nation."[14] Nevertheless, we need to be careful not to endorse a regulation merely because of what it symbolizes. If we want to make sure a law does not undermine a value in the course of symbolizing it, we must stop to ask what sort of behavior the law will induce when put in place.[15] Otherwise, when we glorify a regulation's symbolic value, we glorify the taking of environmentalist positions at the expense of environmental interests. We will be doing exactly what experience in the theory and practice of conflict resolution tells us to avoid.

My father was a farmer. When I was eight years old, a pair of red foxes built a den and raised a litter in our wheat field. I can remember watching Dad on his tractor in the late afternoon, giving the foxes a wide berth, and leaving that part of our field uncultivated that year. He protected the den because he could afford to (and even then, I admired him for it). If there had been a law prohibiting farming on land inhabited by foxes, analogous to laws that prohibit logging in forests inhabited by spotted owls, then Dad would have had to make sure his land was not inhabited by foxes. Which is to say, Dad probably would have killed them. Although he loved them, he would not have been able to afford to let them live.[16]

A LESSON FOR ENVIRONMENTAL ETHICS

Environmental philosophers often talk about environmental justice, but almost never talk about environmental conflict resolution. This is unfortunate. From a mediator's perspective, progress requires negotiation and compromise. Moreover, achieving acceptable and stable compromise can be more important from an environmental perspective than getting it right in some idealized sense that abstracts from political realities. Where the world can go from here is constrained by the histories of stakeholders and by a plurality of values. Mediators deal with the situation as it is.

The practical relevance of environmental ethics depends on our ability to do likewise. We need to think about conflict, not merely about how the world ought to be in the grand scheme of things. If humanity were a decision-making entity, and if its component parts had no interests of their own, this entity might rationally decide to prune itself back, amputating overgrown parts for the sake of the whole, thereby leaving more room for wildlife. In Africa, though, and in the developing world more generally, if people manage to protect their land and wildlife, it will be because doing so is in their interest, not because doing so is in the interest of "the whole." If we fail to treat them as players with interests of their own, we will be our own worst enemies.

In formal terms, philosophy of law distinguishes between procedural and substantive justice. *Substantive* justice is, roughly, a property of outcomes. It is about people (or any entities with moral standing) receiving what they are due. *Procedural* justice is about following fair procedures: procedures intended to be impartial. When philosophers discuss environmental justice, they usually have one or another notion of substantive justice in mind. In large measure, though, conflict mediation tends to involve seeking justice in a procedural sense.

Perhaps mediators should and do seek to ground negotiations in principles of substantive justice as well. I am not a mediator and have no direct practical experience with institutions of conflict mediation, so it is hard for me to say. What I can say with confidence is that philosophers need to do their part to complete the circle. What I have in mind is that while mediators are trying to ground their practice in a sound theory, we could do our part by trying to ground our theories in the requirements of sound practice. If we say our philosophical principles ought to be put into practice, then we implicitly if not explicitly are warranting those principles as compatible with sound practice. However, if we make no effort to ground our theories in requirements of sound practice, then it would be fraudulent to recommend our theory to practitioners. In that case, if and when practitioners respond by ignoring us, they will be doing the right thing.[17]

ECONOMICS AS ECOLOGY

Conflict in priorities often is not only an environmental conflict. Often, perhaps typically, it is an economic conflict, too—a conflict rooted in differing economic circumstances—and it will not be resolved as an environmental conflict unless it also is resolved as an economic conflict.

Unfortunately, people who embrace ecological reasoning often reject that very reasoning as applied to human ecology. Environmentalists tend to be pretty far left of center, and they tend to think of economics as a tool of their enemies. It is not only ecofeminists and deep ecologists who tend to reject economics out of hand; even more mainstream philosophers such as Eugene Hargrove sometimes flatly reject what they call "the economic approach to nature preservation."[18] This attitude may sometimes be apt. I am an economist as well as a philosopher, but I too reject the economic approach insofar as "economic approach" refers to trying to reduce all values to economic values.[19]

However, rejecting economic value-reductionism and ignoring the real-world logic of economic systems are two different things. In cases of conflicting priorities, ignoring the economic approach to understanding the logic of human interaction is bad for the environment.[20] If in that sense we are not taking an economic approach, then we are not taking a genuinely ecological approach either. We need to pay attention to the logic of human ecology lest we stand rightly accused of not truly caring about ecology at all. Murray Bookchin offers "social" ecology as an alternative to "deep" ecology.[21] My point in Bookchin's terms is that to seriously promote deep ecology's values, we have to seriously respect social ecology's logic.

Like economic reasoning, ecological reasoning is reasoning about equilibria and perturbations that keep systems from converging on equilibria. Like economic reasoning, ecological reasoning is reasoning about competition, scarcity, unintended consequences, and the internal logic of systems, a logic that dictates how a system responds to attempts to manipulate it. Environmental activism and regulation do not automatically improve the environment. It is a truism in ecology, as in economics, that well-intentioned interventions need not translate into good results. Ecology (human and nonhuman) is complicated, our knowledge is limited, and environmentalists are themselves only human.

Intervention that works with a system's logic rather than against it can have good consequences. Even in a centrally planned economy, the shape taken by the economy mainly is a function not of the central plan but of how people respond to it, and people respond to central plans in ways that best serve their purposes, not the central planner's. Thus, even a dictator is in no position simply to decide how things are going to go. Ecologists understand that the same point applies in their own discipline. They understand that an ecology's internal logic limits the directions in which would-be ecological engineers can take it.

Within environmental philosophy, most of us have come around to something like Aldo Leopold's view of humans as plain citizens of the biotic community.[22] As Bryan Norton notes, the contrast between anthropocentrism and biocentrism obscures the fact that we increasingly need to be nature-centered to be properly human-centered; we need to focus on "saving the ecological systems that are the context of human cultural and economic activities."[23] If we do not tend to what is good for nature, we will not be tending to what is good for people either. As Gary Varner once put it, on purely anthropocentric grounds we have reason to think biocentrically.[24]

I completely agree. My point is that the converse is also true: on purely biocentric grounds, we have reason to think anthropocentrically. We need to be human-centered to be properly nature-centered; unless we tend to what is good for people, we will not be tending to what is good for nature either. From a biocentric perspective, preservationists sometimes are not anthropocentric enough. They sometimes advocate policies and regulations with no concern for values and priorities that differ from their own. Even from a biocentric perspective, such slights are illegitimate. Policy makers who ignore human values and priorities other than their own will, in effect, be committed to mismanaging the ecology of which those ignored values and priorities are an integral part.

Africans seem to understand this, and in some cases they have been able to structure their policies in ways that do not slight the priorities of rural people who pay the price of co-existing with the wildlife. They understand that rural people must also benefit from co-existing with wildlife if wildlife is to survive.[25]

CONCLUSION

Those who embrace economic values and those who embrace preservationist values are not natural enemies. If we want other people's actions (or our own, for that matter) to be environmentally benign, then we will have to understand and work with human ecology. Environmentalists need to avoid thinking of economics as the enemy, because that antipathy interferes with understanding what it takes to resolve conflicting priorities in environmentally benign ways.

In cases of conflicting priorities, we need to think about people first, if we care about people, or even if we do not. If we care about wildlife, we need to accept that wildlife will survive to the extent that people who have to live with it are better off taking care of it. It is roughly that simple. Requiring subsistence farmers to cooperate in putting the interests of wildlife before (or even on a par with) their own is not a winning strategy for helping the wildlife. We need their cooperation, and the terms of cooperation will have to address not only our interest in preserving wildlife but also their interest in being able to live with it.

Wildlife will survive only if people can afford to share the land. If they cannot share, then they will not share, and the wildlife will die.

NOTES

1. I thank Don Scherer for his thoughts on how attitudes toward nature have changed over the centuries. See also Eugene C. Hargrove, "The Historical Foundations of American Environmental Attitudes," *Environmental Ethics* 1 (1979): 209–40.

2. I was the fifth of six children, and the first to be born into a house with running water and an indoor toilet. Before then, families like ours got through the summer on melted snow.

3. Malaria, for example, is transmitted by mosquitoes. In the 1850's, malaria was widespread as far north as the Great Lakes. See Erwin H. Ackerknecht, *Malaria in the Upper Mississippi Valley, 1760–1900* (Baltimore: Johns Hopkins Press, 1945). Malaria remains endemic in many regions. When I was in Zambia, a young woman told me that like everyone else in her village, she contracts malaria two or three times per year.

4. I use the term "environmental conflict" to refer to conflict in which at least one party is voicing concerns about the environmental impact of another party's projects.

5. A *commons tragedy* occurs if and when individually rational use of a common resource culminates in a pattern of collective overuse that exceeds the resource's capacity for self-renewal.

6. A resource use has an *external* cost when some of the activity's costs are born by people other than the user, without their consent. Air and water pollution are the standard examples. One lesson of Ronald Coase's seminal essay "The Problem of Social Cost" is that it takes two to make an externality. Someone has to be literally or figuratively downstream, in position to be affected by an activity. That raises questions about who should do what in order to contain that cost. It might for example be far less costly to avoid being downstream than to avoid being a polluter.

7. Such schemes seem to have had that effect in places where they have been tried. For a number of cases studies describing the successes and failures of attempts to turn wildlife to the advantage of local economies in developing countries, thereby turning local economies to the advantage of wildlife, see *Natural Connections: Perspectives in Community-Based Conservation*, ed. David Western, R. Michael Wright, and Shirley C. Strum, Washington: Island Press (1994).

8. Some people equate preservationism with environmentalism. This paper uses "environmentalist" to refer equally to conservationists and preservationists. I agree with Bryan Norton that it is easy to exaggerate the distinction's practical importance. See Bryan Norton, *Toward Unity Among Environmentalists* (New York: Oxford University Press, 1991) pp. 12–13.

9. Brian Child, "The Elephant as a Natural Resource," *Wildlife Conservation* (March, 1993) p. 60.

10. Norman Myers, "A Farewell to Africa," *International Wildlife* 11 (1981) p. 36.

11. Of course, the different kinds of conflict are not mutually exclusive. They can occur together.

12. Roger Fisher and William Ury, *Getting To Yes* (New York: Penguin Books, 2nd ed., 1991).

13. On the issue of climate change and environmental conflict, see Jason Scott Johnston, "Global Warming and the End of Environmental Law," University of Virginia working paper, 2012.

14. Mark Sagoff, *The Economy of the Earth* (Cambridge: Cambridge University Press, 1988), p. 16.

15. In passing, we also need to accept that what we stand for as a nation differs from what we *want* to stand for as a nation. The things for which nations stand are a product of ongoing piecemeal compromise. We do well not to glorify the expressive value of such compromised ideals.

16. A "No Surprises" regulation was incorporated into the Endangered Species Act in 1998, offering some protection from possibilities to landowners who enter into a long-term agreement on a Habitat Conservation Plan. The regulation is controversial and survived a serious legal challenge in 2007. I thank Lynn Scarlett, former Deputy Secretary of the Interior, for helpful conversation.

17. It would be far beyond the scope of this paper to defend a particular conception of substantive justice, but let me suggest what sort of conception could count as completing the circle. Consider the principle that people ought to take responsibility

for environmental consequences of their own actions: not just legally relevant consequences as determined by some regulatory agency, but the real consequences, to the honest best of people's ability to ascertain them. In short, people ought to take responsibility for internalizing externalities. I believe such a principle is intuitively just. I also believe that promulgating this principle as a principle of justice could help mediators resolve real world conflicts in a principled way. (As far as I know, the connection between internalizing externalities and being substantively just has not been explored in the literature.)

18. Eugene Hargrove, *Foundations of Environmental Ethics* (Englewood Cliffs: Prentice-Hall, 1989): 210.
19. See Mark Sagoff, "At the Shrine of Our Lady of Fatima, or Why Political Questions Are Not All Economic," *Arizona Law Review* 23 (1981): 1283–98.
20. Of course, it can be bad for people too. Ramachandra Guha rails against those who assume that so long as they are "cutting edge radicals" they are ipso facto champions of the world's oppressed poor and thus are relieved of any responsibility for gathering real information concerning the effect their policy proposals would have on the world's oppressed poor. See "Radical American Environmentalism and Wilderness Preservation: A Third-World Critique," in this volume.
21. Murray Bookchin, "Social Ecology versus Deep Ecology," in this volume. Roughly, Bookchin's terms refer to our social environment as understood by social scientists versus our natural environment as understood by preservationist environmentalists.
22. Aldo Leopold, *Sand County Almanac* (New York: Oxford Press, 1966, 1st pub. 1949) p. 240.
23. Bryan Norton, *Toward Unity*, p. 252. See the selections from Norton together with Katie McShane's response in Chapter 13, this volume.
24. Gary Varner, *In Nature's Interests?* (New York: Oxford University Press, 1998) p. 129.
25. For some examples, see my "When Preservationism Doesn't Preserve," in this volume.

TED NORDHAUS AND MICHAEL SHELLENBERGER

THE FOREST FOR THE TREES

On July 24, 1993, millions of people worldwide awoke to newspaper photographs of dead children wearing little more than rags lying in copious amounts of blood in the shadow of Nossa Senhora da Candelária, one of Rio de Janeiro's most cherished cathedrals.

The children, some of whom had been on the streets since they were three years old, dozed each night in front of the cathedral located in the heart of downtown Rio. Whether for lack of food or fear of violence, they could no longer sleep at home. Huddled together for warmth on flattened cardboard boxes and soiled newspapers, the children thought they were safe under the protective arches of the church.

For Officer Marcos Emmanuel and seven other off-duty cops, the children who took refuge each night at the Candelária were nothing more than filthy street vermin. It was obvious to him and everyone else that they were behind the street crime in the area—the indecorous begging, the stealing from merchants, the

Ted Nordhaus and Michael Shellenberger, *Break Through* (Boston: Houghton Mifflin, 2007), chapter 2, pp. 41–65.

stickups of tourists. When word got out that a pack of them had pummeled a local patrol car with rocks, trying to shatter the windows and the resolve of the men inside, Emmanuel and the other officers decided to take dramatic action.

The children were asleep when the cops pulled up. Emmanuel and another officer grabbed three of the older kids who they suspected were the gang's ringleaders, shoved them into the car, and shot each of them in the head three times. They dumped the bodies on a lawn across from the Museum of Modern Art a short distance away and sped back to the Candelária. On their return they found that the other officers had nearly finished shooting forty children. By the end of the evening, eight of the children were dead.

The next day's news coverage felt, for most Brazilians, like a stiff brush over an infected wound. The occasional extrajudicial killing of delinquents was one thing: doing it under the protective gaze of Nossa Senhora was quite another. Even those Brazilians who had been ranting at the nearby street-corner soda counters about the annoying *molecas* couldn't look at the newspaper photos and not feel disgusted by the whole thing: the kids, the cops, the country. There was no shortage of Brazilians who called radio stations the next day to say that they thought it was about time somebody cleaned up the street filth. But for most, the spectacle summed up what Brazilians hate most about their country.[1]

Thanks to the audacity and symbolic setting of the crime, and the fact that July 23, 1993, was a slow news day internationally, demands that the government do something poured in from abroad. Brazil's social movement of street children and their allies held demonstrations throughout the country. Politicians promised to root out the evildoers, send them to prison, and reform the system. Strongly worded editorials were written. International conferences were held. A few low-level officers went to prison. A few midlevel officers were let go or transferred. In short, nothing of consequence was done.[2] Around five children continue to be murdered every day in Brazil. Their deaths are for the most part quiet. Of the sixty-two children who survived the Candelária massacre, thirty-nine are now dead—likely more, by the time you read this—from drugs, guns, or police.[3] What was unusual about Candelária was that it got any attention whatsoever.[4]

When a record thirty civilians were randomly gunned down on March 31, 2005, by off-duty cops seeking blanket revenge for fallen comrades, hardly anybody outside of Brazil heard about it. Two days later, massacre-fatigued Brazilians had the death of Pope John Paul II to grieve.[5]

The colossus of the south today continues to offer up sensational killings that occasionally attract international attention, and the street children's movement is a firmly established and respectable interest group. But more often than not, everyday acts of terrorism, from the murder of small children to the police shootings of bystanders are, like the burning of the Amazon, little more than background noise in our cacophonous modern world.[6]

1. The killing of street children is but one manifestation of the violence that keeps half of all Brazilians living in poverty. Most street children are not orphans. They have parents and even homes. They just can't, for lack of food or the certainty of abuse, live in them.

The everyday violence in Rio de Janeiro is a mirror of the destruction in the Amazon. Both are manifestations of extreme poverty and inequality. Brazil has the world's highest death toll from guns—about 36,000 per year.[7] Many Brazilians carry guns for self-defense because the government cannot guarantee personal safety. And recently, drug gangs operating from within Brazil's prisons have started unleashing terrorist attacks against civilian targets, including churches, in order to win better conditions from the government. More than 180 people were left dead from attacks in May 2006. Because the gangs have better weaponry than the police—such as grenades and mortars—the federal government had to send ten thousand army troops into São Paulo.[8]

Seeking protection as much from the police as from criminals, many of the poorest people in Brazil reluctantly welcomed heavily armed drug traffickers into their communities in the 1990s. "Drug trafficking has a good and a bad side to it," one Rio *favela* (slum) resident told a group of documentary filmmakers in 2000.

Before there were dealers, when the police entered the *favela* they would break down doors. So, when these guns entered the community from the drugs, they forced the police to behave more cautiously. Now, the negative side, the cruelty of the guns, is that when they come to collect debts from people in the community, they don't care if that person is a minor or not. They will kill and cut up and quarter that person to display as an example for everyone to see.[9]

And yet Brazil is a fantastically wealthy country. Larger in size than the continental United States, it boasts sophisticated manufacturing, mining, biotechnology, and agricultural industries. It is a major exporter of coffee, soybeans, iron ore, orange juice, steel, and even high-tech airplanes, which it manufactures for companies like the U.S. airline JetBlue.

Few are more articulate about the nexus of lawlessness, corruption, and violence than Brazil's cops. The former chief of police of Rio de Janeiro explained the situation this way:

> The police are corrupt. The institution was designed to be violent and corrupt. Why do I say this? Because it was created to protect the state and the elite. I practice law enforcement to protect the *status quo*. There's no beating around the bush about this. It keeps the *favelas* under control. How do you keep two million underprivileged people [in Rio] who make 112 *reais* [less than $50] per month under control? With repression, of course.[10]

Brazil's richest 10 percent of the population has an annual income nineteen times higher than that of the poorest 40 percent. For poverty to be managed in a society as wealthy as Brazil, what's required is, in the words of the police chief, an institution "designed to be violent and corrupt."[11] It is through this prism of violence, poverty, and inequality that the destruction of the Amazon must be understood.

2. Land in Brazil is like oil in Nigeria: as much a curse as a blessing. Its control by the few denies prosperity to the many. The most affluent 1 percent of Brazilian landlords own 45 percent of the land, some of it inherited, some of it bought, and much of it stolen. Today, roughly 4.5 million peasants are without land; many millions more have left the countryside to live in the 100,000-plus-person slums, or *favelas*, of the country's largest cities.[12]

Since its founding by the Portuguese crown, Brazil has long hoped to colonize its seemingly limitless interior. The country's 1891 constitution stipulated the construction of a new capital in the center of the country that was meant to replace Rio de Janeiro. The idea was that the new city would be a launching pad for development northward into the Amazon forest, an area eleven times the size of France. By 1893 a site was selected, and in 1955 President Juscelino Kubitschek announced plans to create a new capital in the parched, empty center of Brazil, calling for "fifty years' progress in five."[13] Kubitschek wanted Brasília, the new capital, to catapult Brazil into the modern world.

But Brasília and the expansion into the Amazon came at a terrible price. Because Brazil had little money to pay for the new capital, Kubitschek simply printed more money. This triggered Brazil's long struggle with inflation, which rose from 9 percent in 1950 to 58 percent in 1965 to 235 percent in 1985 to an astonishing 1,783 percent in 1989.

In 1964, taking advantage of the country's economic and political chaos, Brazil's generals staged a coup d'état with the support of the U.S. government.[14] Upon seizing power, they were quickly confronted with the same confounding thicket of impossible demands, intractable conflicts, and irremediable problems that every Brazilian leader, militarily imposed or democratically elected, has faced since. Rampant inflation and crushing debt forced Brazil's leaders to choose between satisfying the demands of foreign investors—and thus cutting public investments in education, health care, and emergent industries—or making the public investments and risk being cut off from the foreign capital and markets they needed.

Looking for a way out of the nation's many conflicts and contradictions, Brazil's generals, like generations of Brazilian leaders before and after, placed their faith in the one seemingly inexhaustible resource that has been an endless source of fascination and fantasy for five hundred years: the Amazon forest.

From a strictly economic point of view, Brazil would have been better off if it had left the Amazon alone and focused its agricultural and economic development elsewhere. But massively unequal land ownership—a residue of the colonial land system set up by the Portuguese crown—concentrated national wealth in impractically large, idle estates, some the size of small European countries, resulting in almost ritualized conflicts between peasants and Brazil's powerful landlords. Government leaders who attempted meaningful land reform faced the wrath of landowners, who, through corruption and other forms of political influence, had long been a part of the state itself.

Development of the Amazon seemed to offer an alternative to the impossible conflicts facing the nation, and Brazil's generals jumped at the prospect, believing that in doing so they would entice foreign investment, earn foreign capital, grow the economy, and obviate the need for land reform all at the same time.

In 1966, Brazil's dictator president, General Castello Branco, announced that "Amazonian occupation will proceed as though we are waging a strategically conducted war," branding the colonization effort as a national project of unification—a march toward *orden e progresso*.[15] The effort included massive tax breaks for investors, huge development projects such as the paving of the Belém to Brasília highway and the construction of massive new dams, and an Amazonian version of the Homestead Act to encourage the colonization of the Amazon by settlers. Aping the old Israeli slogan, Brazil's generals declared the Amazon to be "a land without people for a people without land."

The result was a disaster by everyone's estimation, including the generals'. Brazil's elite sensed a land rush and began buying up land in the region. Hopeful homesteaders arrived in the Amazon only to discover that people had already made claims to their land, often fraudulently. Because the easiest and in some cases the only way of proving ownership was to demonstrate use, the first thing farmers, large and small alike, did was log and burn the rain forest. Given the utter lack of law enforcement in the area, landlords blithely tortured and killed peasants who got in their way. Brazilian peasants who cleared land for cattle and farming discovered after a few years that slash-and-burn agriculture couldn't sustain them, and so millions fled to the overcrowded *favelas* of nearby cities.[16]

3. Brazil's inflation, its debt, and its inequitable land distribution would become the macrodrivers of hunger, misery, and deforestation for a half century to come. In response to the widely publicized failures of colonization, Brazil's military rulers shifted their emphasis to massive infrastructure development—roads, dams, and industrial agriculture—financed with loans from private lenders, the World Bank, and the Inter-American Development Bank.

After the first OPEC oil shock, in 1973, the military took the nation's debt to a new level when the dictatorship borrowed billions from foreign lenders at low but also *variable* interest rates in order to cover the abrupt increase in fuel costs. The generals' borrowing accelerated after the second oil shock, in 1979, when oil accounted for 43 percent of Brazil's imports.[17]

The moment of reckoning arrived in 1981, when the U.S. Federal Reserve raised the prime rate. By 1982, having exhausted nearly all of its hard currency for foreign exchange, Brazil defaulted on its loan payments to its private creditors.[18] The consequences were harsh, both for the Brazilian people and their national treasure, the Amazon forest. From 1982 on, Brazil spent much of its foreign exchange reserves servicing the foreign debt. Brazil repeatedly rolled over its debt, accepting the burden of paying more interest in the future to make smaller payments in the present.[19]

As of 2007, Brazil was one of the world's largest debtors, owing an astonishing $511 billion[20]—an amount it has paid off several times over even as the principal has increased.[21] One disastrous result of Brazil's debt is a skyrocketing rate of deforestation. By 1990, the year that Brazil discontinued direct subsidies for cattle ranching, roughly 587,000 square kilometers (317,000 square miles) of rain forest had been destroyed.[22] And the number of non-Indian Brazilians living in the Amazon increased from ten million in 1970 to twenty-one million in 2000.[23]

The Amazon remains the top destination of poor Brazilian migrants seeking a better life. Many come from the impoverished northeastern states of Maranhão and Piauí, often escaping the violence of landlords in already colonized states. One of Brazil's leading Amazon reporters, *Veja* magazine's Leonardo Coutinho, told us, "Impoverished and punished by violence, they come to the Amazon to serve as semi-enslaved workers clearing the forest. In some cases they become hired guns themselves."[24]

The criminal mafias who oversee illegal logging and deforestation—and the murders of peasant leaders—often also traffic in drugs and guns. Even when Brazil's financially strapped and corrupt environmental enforcement agencies crack down on illegal deforestation, they find themselves badly outmatched by land speculators and cattle ranchers, who use sophisticated satellite equipment and deforest in stages in order to evade law enforcement.[25] "Even when the government is able to spot illegal deforestation using satellite images," Coutinho points out, "it usually takes a week for agents to arrive in the field. By that point, the loggers have taken what they wanted and moved on. The state simply doesn't function out here. The law of the Amazon is made by the bullet."[26]

One of Brazil's most frustrating paradoxes is that it has some of the most progressive environmental and human rights laws on the books but is mostly unable to enforce them. It is illegal to export hardwoods from the Amazon, and yet every year Brazil sells nearly $400 million worth of them to foreign buyers.[27] Slavery was officially banned in 1888, but today somewhere between twenty-five and fifty thousand souls toil away as slaves in gruesome conditions, logging mahogany and other hardwoods for sale on global markets.[28] For the most part, this is a consequence of Brazil's economic reality: when pushed to choose between servicing its foreign debt and investing in law enforcement, it chooses to service its debt.

The Brazilian government simply doesn't have the resources to eliminate slavery or govern the *favelas* in Rio patrolled by drug traffickers, much less properly enforce land and environmental laws in the Amazon. Reassured by the virtual absence of state power in the Amazon, Brazil's powerful agricultural, logging, mining, and other interests hardly bother opposing environmental laws and regulations in Brasília.[29]

Everyone acknowledges that there are macroeconomic drivers of deforestation, from the government's infrastructure projects to cattle and soy exports. And yet Brazil's debt is the elephant in the room that few environmentalists discuss—much less prioritize—even as the global movement to "make poverty history" through debt relief gains momentum.

It has long been obvious that what drives the murder of street children is what drives the murder of peasant leaders—and that what drives the growth of *favelas* in Rio is what drives the decimation of the Amazon. Why then do Brazilian and non-Brazilian environmentalists alike make the violence and poverty in the Amazon part of their politics but not the poverty and violence that afflict the rest of Brazil?

. . .

6. . . . Thanks to the efforts of people like rock star Bono, Harvard economist Jeffrey Sachs, and the Jubilee Coalition for debt relief, the last few years would have been an excellent time for environmentalists in Brazil, the United States, and Europe to champion a global solution to Brazil's dictatorship debt. But because environmentalists believe conservation and economic development are separate issues, that thought apparently never crossed their minds.

7. A cynic might suggest that the lack of enthusiasm for global debt relief among North American conservationists could have something to do with the fact that they have long advanced their own proposal for debt relief—one predicated on the idea that the developed world should swap Brazilian debt for Amazon forest. And therein lies an important difference. Whereas Bono, Sachs, and the debt relief movement point out that the debts owed by developing nations like Brazil were incurred by dictatorships, and should thus be considered immoral, the environmental movement treats Brazil's debt as a bargaining chip to be used to secure the Amazon forest without regard for Brazil's economic aspirations. In doing so, environmentalists have done more to define environmentalism as an alien concern than anyone else.

The failure to pursue an approach that protects both the Amazon and Brazil's national interests has stoked concerns that conservation masks a conspiracy to enrich the developed world at Brazil's expense. Today, 75 percent of Brazilians say they fear a foreign country could invade Brazil to take advantage of its natural resources.[30]

The debt-for-nature idea was first proposed in 1984 by the biologist Dr. Thomas Lovejoy, then with the World Wildlife Fund. Lovejoy wrote an opinion piece for the *New York Times* proposing that conservationists and governments purchase developing world debt and trade it for conservation.[31] At first the Brazilian government opposed debt-for-nature swaps as a threat to their national sovereignty. Although the government reversed its official opposition in 1991, debt-for-nature never took off in Brazil, encountering opposition from both the right, which feared encroachments on sovereignty, and the left, which argued that the military-incurred debt should be forgiven outright. To this day, the concept triggers the ire of Brazilians.

The concern about debt-for-nature continues to annoy Lovejoy, now the president of the Heinz Center for Science, Economics and the Environment in Washington, D.C. "It's an irrational response," he told us.

> If you're going to have a sovereignty issue, it should apply equally to debt for equity, where somebody buys discounted debt and uses it to buy an industry in Brazil. Nobody has ever done a debt-for-nature swap when a country didn't want it. Brazil has always had this paranoia and it's odd, but it's endemic.[32]

8. . . . Lovejoy's argument to us—that because Brazil's sovereignty concerns aren't triggered when foreign investors use foreign debt to purchase national companies, they shouldn't be triggered when foreign environmentalists use Brazil's debt to conserve the forest—ignores the powerful symbolic, romantic, and geopolitical importance the Amazon has had for Brazilians since the sixteenth century. And given the history of U.S. intervention in Latin America—its support for Brazil's military coup and its help propping up dictators in Argentina, Uruguay, Paraguay, and Chile—not to mention its outright invasion of Iraq in 2003, what's surprising is not that Brazilians have sovereignty concerns but rather that American environmentalists are so dismissive of them.

Lovejoy is an accomplished biologist whose contributions to understanding the Amazon are significant. That Lovejoy has spent years living and working with Brazilians makes it all the more disappointing that he can dismiss their genuine concerns.

Brazilians rightly see their country as a colossus—a regional superpower with the military, economic, and political potential to become a global one. As a country of great artists, architects, diplomats, designers, and engineers, and as a people who speak Portuguese in a region where Spanish dominates, Brazilians justifiably see themselves as special and unique. At the same time, many Brazilians are ashamed of the persistence of widespread poverty, violence, and lawlessness. For many years Brazilians played on a slogan from the Kubitschek era that "Brazil is the country of the future!"

by slyly adding, "And always will be!" But is a joke used to mask their feelings of indignation and resentment.

This stew of national pride and shame results in Brazil's love–hate relationship with the United States. Environmentalists' efforts to reassure Brazilians that their attempts to save the Amazon are in Brazil's best interests not only fail to assuage Brazilian concerns, they trigger Brazil's fear of being patronized, which in part explains why Brazilians get more irritated with do-gooder efforts to save the Amazon than commercial ventures to buy Brazilian corporations.

Brazilians continue to see environmental proposals—such as working with foreigners to conduct a comprehensive inventory of the Amazon's biological assets—as suspicious. Do these foreigners actually care about us? Brazilians ask themselves. Or is this a plot by the CIA or the pharmaceutical companies to rob us of our wealth? Are environmental efforts to win Brazil greenhouse gas credits that can be bought or sold as part of an international treaty on global warming really in Brazil's best interests? Or are they a conspiracy to prevent the country from developing economically? (A question, incidentally, that is being asked by developing countries around the world, from India to China.)

American and European environmentalists have certainly learned to pay lip service to questions of economic development and poverty. "There are many more people living [in the Amazon today than forty years ago], so a reasonable solution is a reasonable quality of life that protects the forest," Lovejoy conceded. "But if you wait around for [the Brazilians] to fix their economic problems it will be too late."

Little surprise, then, that in their relationships with foreign conservationists, Brazilians, no matter their political orientation, often wonder, "Do you care about us or just our forest?"

9. The most explicit and influential case for the internationalization of the Amazon was made by renowned conservation biologist John Terborgh, who heads the prestigious Center for Tropical Conservation at Duke University in North Carolina. Terborgh spends much of his 1999 book *Requiem for Nature* arguing that ecological hot spots such as the Amazon should be controlled and patrolled by the United Nations. "In my opinion, the best—perhaps the only—hope lies

in the internationalization of nature protection," he writes. "Biodiversity transcends national boundaries and belongs to no one."[33]

Terborgh's opinions are hardly unique. Terborgh is one of the best-known conservation biologists in the world and is influential among American conservation groups. His book was glowingly blurbed by then-president of the World Wildlife Fund Katherine Fuller; *Collapse* author Jared Diamond; and the famous biologist Edward O. Wilson. *Requiem* had a major influence on American conservation organizations and their funders.[34]

On the one hand, Terborgh stresses that conservation and economics are separate issues, arguing in his book, "Ultimately, nature and biodiversity must be conserved for their own sakes, not because they have present utilitarian value . . . Instead, the fundamental arguments for conserving nature must be spiritual and aesthetic, motivated by feelings that well up from our deepest beings."[35] When we interviewed him he told us, "Poverty alleviation is not what conservation is all about. It's a different enterprise. It's a separate issue."[36] On the other hand, Terborgh repeatedly praises Peru's former dictator Alberto Fujimori for his "enlightened macroeconomic policies."[37]

When we asked Terborgh about the contradiction between his praise for Fujimori's economic program and his insistence that poverty alleviation and conservation should not be linked, Terborgh became more effusive in his praise for Fujimori. "I think he's the best thing that ever happened to Peru," he told us. "Corruption was very low. What he did was thrilling." Terborgh offered these views to us even though Peru's prosecutors had recently charged Fujimori with stealing $162 million, bribing the media, and murdering his critics.[38]

One gets a sense of how Terborgh would like to see conservation happen in his praise for the way Fujimori—who declared himself dictator in 1992 and dissolved the country's congress and supreme court—ruled Peru. "Active protection of parks requires a top-down approach," he wrote in *Requiem*, "because enforcement is invariably in the hands of police and other armed forces that respond only to orders from their commanders."[39]

Exhibit A in Terborgh's case for internationalizing the Amazon is Manú Park in Peru, where he has worked for three decades. His concern: the handful of indigenous and mixed-race people who he believes shouldn't live in the park. In a chapter ominously titled "The Danger Within," Terborgh laments that the "settlements swarm with children, most of whom survive to adulthood because they have access to public health services provided by the government. Where there are now ten families, in another eighteen years there will be twenty—that is, if nothing else changes, which is unlikely."[40]

Terborgh refers to the situation as a case of overpopulation—a curious description, given that there are only twenty people per square kilometer in Peru, compared to twenty-nine people per square kilometer in the United States, a country that uses per capita far more of the world's resources.[41] What Terborgh is referring to when he speaks of overpopulation is the fact that so many poor and landless peasants are seeking to meet their most basic needs in the forest.

"Is there a solution?" Terborgh asks. "There is." Terborgh proceeds to argue that the government should use cash and other incentives to lure the younger generation of Indians away from the park. "What I propose is a carefully constructed and voluntary relocation program built on the manifest desire of contacted indigenous groups to acquire goods and an education for their children and to participate in the money economy."[42]

Terborgh laments that his plan might be opposed because "in the present political environment of Perú, indigenous rights are being championed by many groups including the government. . . . In this political climate, proposing the relocation of an indigenous population would be analogous to advocating racial segregation in the United States."[43]

Terborgh spends much of his book attacking "Integrated Conservation and Development Programs" because, in his words, they are "tantamount to social engineering" (in contrast, apparently, to paying Manú Park's Indians to abandon their homes and way of life).[44] "Am I a misanthrope?" Terborgh asks in his book. "I don't think so."[45]

And maybe he isn't. But after reading page after page of Terborgh raging against the encroachments into a piece of nonhuman nature by "squatters," it becomes increasingly clear how one of the world's most influential and prominent conservation biologists would answer the Brazilians' question "Do you care about us or just our forest?"[46]

10. The way Brazil thinks about the Amazon hasn't changed all that much since 1988, when Brazil's foreign minister declared that "Brazil does not want to transform itself into an ecological reserve for humanity. Our greatest duty is with economic development." Nor has it changed much since 1972, when the interior minister said, "A country that has not achieved a minimal standard of living is not in a position to spend its valuable resources protecting the environment."[47]

In early 2007, in response to another intergovernmental report on global warming, Brazil's president Lula da Silva said, "The wealthy countries are very smart, approving protocols, holding big speeches on the need to avoid deforestation, but they already deforested everything."[48]

And President Lula da Silva was, of course, right: every one of the world's wealthiest countries long ago destroyed their ancient forests in order to develop. Had Brazil developed like the United States—and had the United States developed like Brazil—then today there would exist large organizations of upper-middle-class Brazilians funded by Brazilian philanthropists referring to America's forests as the "lungs of the world." Given all of this, the most educated and prosperous inhabitants of the world's wealthiest countries are not in a particularly strong position to pressure Brazil to do more to save the Amazon.

None of this is to deny the ecological reality. The burning of forests, the loss of their role as net absorbers and storage banks of carbon, and the reality of global warming make the increasingly rapid destruction of the Amazon even more alarming than it was back in the mid-1980s, when the Amazon first became appreciated for its biodiversity. Even if we reduced greenhouse gases by 70 percent worldwide overnight, the continued destruction of the Amazon would still leave the global climate system in jeopardy.

The political problem remains that the destruction of the Amazon is, to the vast majority of Brazilians, far less alarming than the fear of losing their jobs, their life savings, or their lives on the mean streets of Rio de Janeiro. The same is doubly true for the people who eke out a living in the Amazon.

For too long, environmentalists have believed their cause—protecting nature—to be so transparently right that they have thought little about their failure to appeal to deeply held national aspirations. It has thus been inconceivable to environmentalists that they might do more to protect the Amazon by addressing, for example, Brazil's desire to be an agricultural superpower, a UN Security Council member, or an industrial leader in biotechnology.

Until the world's wealthiest countries seriously support Brazil's goals for itself, the colossus of the south will have neither the means nor the motives to save the Amazon. In a country where one out of five people goes to bed hungry every night, where drug traffickers control 100,000-person *favelas* in Rio, and where middle-class professionals fear for their financial security and their personal safety, saving the Amazon simply will never become a top concern. Protecting the Amazon and ensuring future rainfall is in long-term economic interests, to be sure, but as long as its short-term and long-term interests collide, the forest will continue to burn.

If our answer to the Brazilians' question "Do you care about us or just our forest?" is indeed "We care about you," then we must do something for Brazil before we can do anything for the Amazon.

NOTES

1. Michael S. Serrill and Ian McClusky, "Unholy Confession," *Time*, May 13, 1996; Mac Margolis, "Nightmare for Brazil," *Los Angeles Times*, September 4, 1993.

2. This despite the fact that additional pressure came in the form of a new massacre one month later, when forty off-duty cops shrouded in black hoods machine-gunned down twenty-one random passersby in Vigario Geral, a poor neighborhood in Rio. The cops were seeking revenge for four comrades who had been gunned down the day before by drug traffickers. Tracking down the killers would have been difficult and dangerous, so the police took their rage out on ordinary innocents—retirees, porters, mechanics, a fifteen-year-old girl—who had made the fatal mistake of walking through their neighborhood when justice needed to be served. Sebastian Rotella, "Brazil Tries to Rein In Its Police," *Los Angeles Times*, August 27, 1996.

3. Tony Smith, "Child Poverty Still Plagues Latin America," Associated Press, September 16, 2001.

4. Sometimes the traumatized come back for revenge. On June 12, 2000, Sandro do Nascimento, a survivor of Candelária, held up midday traffic in Rio de Janeiro by hijacking a bus and threatening to kill everyone on board. The incident inspired an extraordinary 2002 documentary—Bus 174—winning international awards and critical accolades.

5. A Nexis database search revealed a single AP story about the massacre, aptly entitled, "Brutal Massacre in Rio Slum Gets Little Attention Due to Rich–Poor Divide and Pope's Death," written a week later. Michael Astor, Associated Press, April 8, 2005.

6. The violence against children is just the tip of the iceberg: according to a UN study, 500,000 Brazilians were killed by guns between 1979 and 2003—four times as many as have died in the Arab Israeli conflict in the last fifty years. Steve Kingstone, "UN Highlights Brazil Gun Crisis," *BBC News*, June 27, 2005.

7. Juliana Resende, "Gunshot Wounds 'Endemic' in Rio de Janeiro," *San Francisco Chronicle*, June 27, 2005.

8. Larry Rohter, "New Attacks by a Heavily Armed Gang Rattle Brazil and Set Off Political Wrangling," *New York Times*, August 13, 2006.

9. *Notes from a Personal War*, documentary film, on DVD of *City of God*, 2001.

10. Ibid.

11. Harry Vanden, "Brazil's Landless Hold Their Ground," *NACLA Report on the Americas*, March 1, 2005.

12. Ibid.

13. Thomas Skidmore, *Brazil: Five Centuries of Change* (New York: Oxford University Press, 1999), 147.

14. See Physllis Parker, *Brazil and the Quiet Intervention* (Austin: University of Texas Press, 1964, 1979), and Jan Knippers Brack, *United States Penetration of Brazil* (Philadelphia: University of Pennsylvania Press, 1977).

15. Quoted in Susanna Hecht and Alexander Cockburn, *The Fate of the Forest: Developers, Destroyers and Defenders of the Amazon* (New York: Harper Perennial, 1990), 104.

16. For discussions of the history of Amazon colonization, see Skidmore, *Brazil*; Hecht and Cockburn, *Fate of the Forest*; Marianne Schmink and Charles H. Wood, *Contested Frontiers in Amazonia* (New York: Columbia University Press, 1992); Bertha K. Becker, "Amazônia: Desenvolvimento, Governabilidade e Soberania, Documento para o IPEA [Instituto de Pesquisa Econômica Aplicada]: O Estado de Nação," in *Brasil: o estado de uma nação*, ed. Fernando Rezende and Paulo Tafner (São Paulo: Instituto de Pesquisa Econômica Aplicada, 2005).

17. Skidmore, *Brazil*, 147–49, 178. Inflation figures are from Werner Baer, *The Brazilian Economy*, 4th ed. (Westport, CT: Praeger Publishers, 1995), 392–93.

18. Skidmore, *Brazil*, 180–81.

19. Ibid.

20. Fabio Alves and Adriana Brasileiro, "Brazil Fixed-Rate Debt to Exceed Floating in 2007," *Bloomberg News*, January 17, 2007.

21. Latin America as a whole has also paid off the equivalent of its debt in interest payments, more than $730 billion between 1982 and 1996, but it still has not reduced its debt inventory. Alicia Asper, "Latin American Debt Relief: There is Less Than Meets the Eye," Council on Hemispheric Affairs Analysis, August 2, 2005.

22. Daniel C. Nepstad, Claudia M. Stickler, and Oriana T. Almeida, "Globalization of the Amazon Soy and Beef Industries: Opportunities for Conservation," in *Conservation Biology* 20, no. 6 (December 2006): 1595.

23. Censos Demogáficos, IBGE, cited in Becker, "Amazônia."

24. Leonardo Coutinho, e-mail correspondence, November 3, 2005.

25. In his reporting, Coutinho notes that only 25 percent of the budget pledged for environmental law was ever released—enough to last until August 2005, precisely the time that the burning season began. If the Amazon was divided equally among the 695 officers assigned to enforce environmental laws in the region, each officer would be responsible for an area five times larger than the megalopolis of São Paulo. And 80 percent of the fines levied by the environmental agency are never

paid. Leonardo Coutinho, "As 7 Pragas da Amazônia," *Veja*, October 12, 2005, 111–12.

26. Leonardo Countinho, telephone interview with Mark Shellenberger, June 6, 2005.

27. Numbers are from the Brazilian government. Kevin G. Hall, "Slavery Exists Out of Sight in Brazil," Knight-Ridder Newspapers, September 5, 2004.

28. Ibid.

29. For discussion of law enforcement failure in the Amazon, see Leonardo Coutinho, "Fiscal, espécie rara," *Veja*, January 28, 2004. "With about 54 million hectares protected by law in 250 federal reserves, the law enforcement branch of the Environment Ministry relies on 1,483 agents. With each one responsible for monitoring an area of 36,400 hectares, the size of Belo Horizonte, But in a region of forests, mountains, and gorges." The same is true for the rest of the world. According to the International Tropical Timber Organization, . . . 95 percent of the world's remaining tropical forests exist without actual physical protection, even though two-thirds are under some sort of legal protection. Lisa Adams, "Tropical Forests Still Unprotected, Report Concludes," Associated Press, May 25, 2006. For original report, see www .itto.or.jp/live/PageDisplayHandler?pageID=27 &id=1262.

30. Alex Bugge, "Brazilians Fear Riches May Spark Invasion," Reuters, June 5, 2005. The poll was conducted among two thousand Brazilians, April 8–13, 2005, by the polling firm IBOPE for the animal welfare group Renctas.

31. T.E. Lovejoy, "Aid Debtor Nations' Ecology," *New York Times*, October 4, 1984.

32. Thomas Lovejoy, telephone interview with M.S., August 23, 2005.

33. John Terborgh, *Requiem for Nature* (Washington, DC: Island Press, 1999), 198. "The notion that biodiversity is a global commons, belonging only to the planet earth, is not new. To date, however, governments and international bodies have failed to take this idea seriously," he adds.

34. E.O. Wilson calls Terborgh "a distinguished biologist" and claims that *Requiem* was written with "compelling documentation." Jared Diamond calls the book a "must read" and refers to Terborgh as "one of the world's greatest field biologists."

35. "What is absolute, enduring, and irreplaceable is the primordial nourishment of our psyches afforded by a quiet walk in an ancient forest or the spectacle of a thousand snow geese against a blue sky on a crisp winter day," Terborgh adds. *Requiem*, 19.

36. John Terborgh, telephone interview with M.S., April 20, 2005.

37. Terborgh, *Requiem*, 38.

38. Tyler Bridges, "Fugitive Fujimori Plans Run for Peru Presidency," *Miami Herald*, August 19, 2005. Bridges writes, "'In all, 42 people have been convicted of crimes involving the Fujimori government,' said special anti-corruption prosecutor Antonio Maldonado. He said the Toledo government has collected $162 million illegally stashed abroad." When we pressed Professor Terborgh on his unabashed Fujimori boosterism, he said, "Fujimori changed the country in many, many ways that are almost all to the good, but got tangled up with [intelligence chief] Montesinos." But Peruvian prosecutors pointed to strong evidence that Fujimori knew full well about Montesinos's death-squad activities. Javier Ciurlizza, special legal adviser to the Foreign Ministry, told the *New York Times*, "Fujimori is not just another Latin American president who is in trouble. We are in front of a mafia, the leader of a mafia." As of October 25, 2005, Fujimori faced eighteen corruption and four human rights charges in Peru.

39. Terborgh, *Requiem*, 170.

40. Ibid., 53.

41. This information per the World Resources Institute can be found at http://earthtrends.wri.org/ pdf_library/country_profiles/pop_cou_604.pdf and http://earthtrends.wri.org/pdf_library/country_profiles/pop_cou_840.pdf.

42. Terborgh, *Requiem*, 56.

43. Ibid., 57.

44. Terborgh thus decries in no uncertain terms efforts to help the poor. "In the United States, government-sponsored experiments in social engineering have expended hundreds of billions of dollars in funds and yet have achieved only modest

progress toward the goal of reducing poverty. The social problems of the big cities remain stubbornly intractable. Attempting to carry out social engineering in a foreign culture that is undergoing rapid social and economic change within the period of a five-year assistance project can, in my view, be likened to pouring water into the Sahara Desert." Ibid., 203.

45. Ibid., 188.

46. Terborgh calls these peaceful occupations "*invasions*"—the word used by Latin America's landlords and ruling elite—and labels them "unlawful." In fact, many Latin American governments, including Brazil's, allow for the peaceful occupation of idle land, which often leads to its purchase or expropriation so that it can be used for growing food. There's little question where Terborgh's sympathies lie: "Landless migrants to the city gather together, target a vacant plot, and, on an appointed night, rush in to erect makeshift shanties of cardboard and sheet metal before dawn. The next morning, the land-owner is faced with a *fait accompli*." Ibid., 167.

47. Kim MacQueen, "Roads to Ruin," *FSU Research in Review*, Summer 1994.

48. *New York Times*, "Brazil's Leader Speaks Out," February 7, 2007.

HENRY SHUE

GLOBAL ENVIRONMENT AND INTERNATIONAL INEQUALITY

My aim is to establish that three commonsense principles of fairness, none of them dependent upon controversial philosophical theories of justice, give rise to the same conclusion about the allocation of the costs of protecting the environment.

Poor states and rich states have long dealt with each other primarily upon unequal terms. The imposition of unequal terms has been relatively easy for the rich states because they have rarely needed to ask for the voluntary cooperation of the less powerful poor states. Now the rich countries have realized that their own industrial activity has been destroying the ozone in the earth's atmosphere and has been making far and away the greatest contribution to global warming. They would like the poor states to avoid adopting the same form of industrialization by which they themselves became rich. It is increasingly clear that if poor states pursue their own economic development with the same disregard for the natural environment and the economic welfare of other states that rich states displayed in the past during their development, everyone will continue to suffer the effects of environmental destruction. Consequently, it is at least conceivable that rich states might now be willing to consider dealing cooperatively on equitable terms with poor states in a manner that gives due weight to both the economic development of poor states and the preservation of the natural environment.

If we are to have any hope of pursuing equitable cooperation, we must try to arrive at a consensus about what equity means. And we need to define equity, not as a vague abstraction, but concretely and specifically in the context of both development of the economy in poor states and preservation of the environment everywhere.

. . .

GREATER CONTRIBUTION TO THE PROBLEM

All over the world parents teach their children to clean up their own mess. This simple rule makes good sense from the point of view of incentive: if one learns that one will not be allowed to get away with simply walking away from whatever messes one creates, one is given a strong negative incentive against making messes in the first place. Whoever makes the mess presumably does so in the process of pursuing some benefit—for a child, the benefit may simply be the pleasure of playing with the objects that constitute the mess. If one learns that whoever reaps the benefit of making the mess must also be the one who pays the cost of cleaning up the mess, one learns at the very least not to make messes with costs that are greater than their benefits.

Economists have glorified this simple rule as the "internalization of externalities." If the basis for the price of a product does not incorporate the costs of cleaning up the mess made in the process of producing the product, the costs are being externalized, that is, dumped upon other parties. Incorporating into the basis of the price of the product the costs that had been coercively socialized is called internalizing an externality.

At least as important as the consideration of incentives, however, is the consideration of fairness or equity. If whoever makes a mess receives the benefits and does not pay the costs, not only does he have no incentive to avoid making as many messes as he likes, but he is also unfair to whoever does pay the costs. He is inflicting costs upon other people, contrary to their interests and, presumably, without their consent. By making himself better off in ways that make others worse off, he is creating an expanding inequality.

Once such an inequality has been created unilaterally by someone's imposing costs upon other people, we are justified in reversing the inequality by imposing extra burdens upon the producer of the inequality. There are two separate points here. First, we are justified in assigning additional burdens to the party who has been inflicting costs upon us. Second, the minimum extent of the compensatory burden we are justified in assigning is enough to correct the inequality previously unilaterally imposed. The purpose of the extra burden is to restore an equality that was disrupted unilaterally and arbitrarily (or to reduce an inequality that was enlarged unilaterally and arbitrarily). In order to accomplish that purpose, the extra burden assigned must be at least equal to the unfair advantage previously taken. This yields us our first principle of equity:

> When a party has in the past taken an unfair advantage of others by imposing costs upon them without their consent, those who have been unilaterally put at a disadvantage are entitled to demand that in the future the offending party shoulder burdens that are unequal at least to the extent of the unfair advantage previously taken, in order to restore equality.

In the area of development and the environment, the clearest cases that fall under this first principle of equity are the partial destruction of the ozone layer and the initiation of global warming by the process of industrialization that has enriched the North but not the South. Unilateral initiatives by the so-called developed countries (DCs) have made them rich, while leaving the less developed countries (LDCs) poor. In the process the industrial activities and accompanying lifestyles of the DCs have inflicted major global damage upon the earth's atmosphere. Both kinds of damage are harmful to those who did not benefit from Northern industrialization as well as to those who did. Those societies whose activities have damaged the atmosphere ought, according to the first principle of equity, to bear sufficiently unequal burdens henceforth to correct the inequality that they have imposed. In this case, everyone is bearing costs—because the damage was universal—but the benefits have been overwhelmingly skewed towards those who have become rich in the process.

GREATER ABILITY TO PAY

The second principle of equity is widely accepted as a requirement of simple fairness. It states:

> Among a number of parties, all of whom are bound to contribute to some common endeavour, the parties who have the most resources normally should contribute the most to the endeavour.

This principle of paying in accordance with ability to pay, if stated strictly, would specify what is often called a progressive rate of payment: insofar as a party's assets are greater, the rate at which the party should contribute to the enterprise in question also becomes greater. The progressivity can be strictly proportional—those with double the base amount of assets contribute at twice the rate at which those with the base amount contribute, those with triple the base amount of assets contribute at three times the rate at which those with the base amount contribute, and so on. More typically, the progressivity is not strictly proportional—the more a party has, the higher the rate at which it is expected to contribute, but the rate does not increase in strict proportion to increases in assets.

The general principle itself is sufficiently fundamental that it is not necessary, and perhaps not possible, to justify it by deriving it from considerations that are more fundamental still. Nevertheless, it is possible to explain its appeal to some extent more fully. The basic appeal of payment in accordance with ability to pay as a principle of fairness is easiest to see by contrast with a flat rate of contribution, that is, the same rate of contribution by every party irrespective of different parties' differing assets. At first thought, the same rate for everyone seems obviously the fairest imaginable arrangement. What could possibly be fairer, one is initially inclined to think, than absolutely equal treatment for everyone? Surely, it seems, if everyone pays an equal rate, everyone is treated the same and therefore fairly? This, however, is an exceedingly abstract approach, which pays no attention at all to the actual concrete circumstances of the contributing parties. In addition, it focuses exclusively upon the contribution process and ignores the position in which, as a result of the process, the parties end up. Contribution according to ability to pay is much more sensitive both to concrete circumstance and to final outcome.

Suppose that Party A has 90 units of something, Party B has 30 units, and Party C has 9 units. In order to accomplish their missions, it is proposed that everyone should contribute at a flat rate of one-third. This may seem fair in that everyone is treated equally: the same rate is applied to everyone, regardless of circumstances. When it is considered that A's contribution will be 30 and B's will be 10, while C's will be only 3,

the flat rate may appear more than fair to C who contributes only one-tenth as much as A does. However, suppose that these units represent $100 per year in income and that where C lives it is possible to survive on $750 per year but on no less. If C must contribute 3 units—$300—he will fall below the minimum for survival. While the flat rate of one-third would require A to contribute far more ($3,000) than C, and B to contribute considerably more ($1,000) than C, both A (with $6,000 left) and B (with $2,000 left) would remain safely above subsistence level. A and B can afford to contribute at the rate of one-third because they are left with more than enough while C is unable to contribute at that rate and survive.

While flat rates appear misleadingly fair in the abstract, they do so largely because they look at only the first part of the story and ignore how things turn out in the end. The great strength of progressive rates, by contrast, is that they tend to accommodate final outcomes and take account of whether the contributors can in fact afford their respective contributions.

A single objection is usually raised against progressive rates of contribution: disincentive effects. If those who have more are going to lose what they have at a greater rate than those who have less, the incentive to come to have more in the first place will, it is said, be much less than it would have been with a flat rate of contribution. Why should I take more risks, display more imagination, or expend more effort in order to gain more resources if the result will only be that, whenever something must be paid for, I will have to contribute not merely a larger absolute amount (which would happen even with a flat rate) but a larger percentage? I might as well not be productive if much of anything extra I produce will be taken away from me, leaving me little better off than those who produced far less.

Three points need to be noticed regarding this objection. First, of course, being fair and providing incentives are two different matters, and there is certainly no guarantee in the abstract that whatever arrangement would provide the greatest incentives would also be fair. Second, concerns about incentives often arise when it is assumed that maximum production and limitless growth are the best goal. It is increasingly clear that many current forms of production and growth are unsustainable and that the last thing we should do is to give people self-interested reasons to consume as many resources as they can, even where the resources are consumed productively. These issues cannot be settled in the abstract either, but it is certainly an open question—and one that should be asked very seriously—whether in a particular situation it is desirable to stimulate people by means of incentives to maximum production. Sometimes it is desirable, and sometimes it is not. This is an issue about ends. Third, there is a question about means. Assuming that it had been demonstrated that the best goal to have in a specific set of circumstances involved stimulating more production of something, one would then have to ask: how much incentive is needed to stimulate that much production? Those who are preoccupied with incentives often speculate groundlessly that unlimited incentives are virtually always required. Certainly it is true that it is generally necessary to provide some additional incentive in order to stimulate additional production. Some people are altruistic and are therefore sometimes willing to contribute more to the welfare of others even if they do not thereby improve their own welfare. It would be completely unrealistic, however, to try to operate an economy on the assumption that people generally would produce more irrespective of whether doing so was in their own interest—they need instead to be provided with some incentive. However, some incentive does not mean unlimited incentive.

It is certainly not necessary to offer unlimited incentives in order to stimulate (limited) additional production by some people (and not others). Whether people respond or not depends upon individual personalities and individual circumstances. It is a factual matter, not something to be decreed in the abstract, how much incentive is enough: for these people in these circumstances to produce this much more, how much incentive is enough? What is clearly mistaken is the frequent assumption that nothing less than the maximum incentive is ever enough.

In conclusion, insofar as the objection based on disincentive effects is intended to be a decisive refutation of the second principle of equity, the objection fails. It is not always a mistake to offer less than the maximum possible incentive, even when the goal of thereby increasing production has itself been justified.

There is no evidence that anything less than the maximum is even generally a mistake. Psychological effects must be determined case by case.

On the other hand, the objection based on disincentive effects may be intended—much more modestly—simply as a warning that one of the possible costs of restraining inequalities by means of progressive rates of contribution, in the effort of being fair, may (or may not) be a reduction in incentive effects. As a caution rather than a (failed) refutation, the objection points to one sensible consideration that needs to be taken into account when specifying which variation upon the general second principle of equity is the best version to adopt in a specific case. One would have to consider how much greater the incentive effect would be if the rate of contribution were less progressive, in light of how unfair the results of a less progressive rate would be.

This conclusion that disincentive effects deserve to be considered, although they are not always decisive, partly explains why the second principle of equity is stated, not as an absolute, but as a general principle. It says: "... the parties who have the most resources *normally* should contribute the most ..."—not always, but normally. One reason why the rate of contribution might not be progressive, or might not be as progressive as possible, is the potential disincentive effects of more progressive rates. It would need to be shown case by case that an important goal was served by having some incentive and that the goal in question would not be served by the weaker incentive compatible with a more progressive rate of contribution.

...

GUARANTEED MINIMUM

We noted earlier that issues of equity or fairness can arise only if there is something that must be divided among different parties. The existence of the following circumstances can be taken as grounds for thinking that certain parties have a legitimate claim to some of the available resources: (a) the aggregate total of resources is sufficient for all parties to have more than enough; (b) some parties do in fact have more than enough, some of them much more than enough; and (c) other parties have less than enough. American philosopher Thomas Nagel has called such circum-stances radical inequality.[1] Such an inequality is radi-cal in part because the total of available resources is so great that there is no need to reduce the best-off people to anywhere near the minimum level in order to bring the worst-off people up to the minimum: the existing degree of inequality is utterly unnecessary and easily reduced, in light of the total resources already at hand. In other words, one could preserve consid-erable inequality—in order, for instance, to provide incentives, if incentives were needed for some impor-tant purpose—while arranging for those with less than enough to have at least enough.

Enough for what? The answer could of course be given in considerable detail, and some of the details would be controversial (and some, although not all, would vary across societies). The basic idea, however, is of enough for a decent chance for a reasonably healthy and active life of more or less normal length, barring tragic accidents and interventions. "Enough" means the essentials for at least a bit more than mere physical survival—for at least a distinctively human, if modest, life. For example, having enough means owning not merely clothing adequate for substantial protection against the elements but clothing adequate in ap-pearance to avoid embarrassment, by local standards, when being seen in public, as Adam Smith noted.

In a situation of radical inequality—a situation with the three features outlined above—fairness de-mands that those people with less than enough for a decent human life be provided with enough. This yields the third principle of equity, which states:

When some people have less than enough for a decent human life, other people have far more than enough, and the total resources available are so great that everyone could have at least enough without pre-venting some people from still retaining considerably more than others have, it is unfair not to guarantee everyone at least an adequate minimum.

Clearly, provisions to guarantee an adequate minimum can be of many different kinds, and, concerning many of the choices, equity has little or nothing to say. The arrangements to provide the minimum can be local, regional, national, international or, more likely, some complex mixture of all, with secondary arrangements

at one level providing a backstop for primary arrange-ments at another level.[2]

. . .

Children, it is worth emphasizing, are the main beneficiaries of this principle of equity. When a family drops below the minimum required to maintain all its members, the children are the most vulnerable. Even if the adults choose to allocate their own share of an insufficient supply to the children, it is still quite likely that the children will have less resistance to disease and less resilience in general. And of course not all adults will sacrifice their own share to their children. Or, in quite a few cultures, adults will sacrifice on behalf of male children but not on behalf of female children. All in all, when essentials are scarce, the proportion of children dying is far greater than their proportion in the population, which in poorer countries is already high—in quite a few poor countries, more than half the population is under the age of 15.

One of the most common objections to this third principle of equity flows precisely from this point about the survival of children. It is what might be called the over-population objection. I consider this objection to be ethically outrageous and factually groundless, as explained elsewhere.[3]

The other most common objection is that while it may be only fair for each society to have a guaranteed minimum for its own members, it is not fair to expect members of one society to help to maintain a guaran-tee of a minimum for members of another society.[4] This objection sometimes rests on the assumption that state borders—national political boundaries—have so much moral significance that citizens of one state cannot be morally required, even by consider-ations of elemental fairness, to concern themselves with the welfare of citizens of a different political jurisdiction. A variation on this theme is the conten-tion that across state political boundaries moral man-dates can only be negative requirements not to harm and cannot be positive requirements to help. I am unconvinced that, in general, state political borders and national citizenship are markers of such extraor-dinary and over-riding moral significance. Whatever may be the case in general, this second objection is especially unpersuasive if raised on behalf of citizens of the industrialized wealthy states in the context of international cooperation to deal with environmental problems primarily caused by their own states and of greatest concern in the medium term to those states. To help to maintain a guarantee of a minimum could mean either of two things: a weaker requirement (a) not to interfere with others' ability to maintain a minimum for themselves; or a stronger requirement (b) to provide assistance to others in maintaining a minimum for themselves. If everyone has a general obligation, even towards strangers in other states and societies, not to inflict harm on other persons, the weaker requirement would follow, provided only that interfering with people's ability to maintain a minimum for themselves counted as a serious harm, as it certainly would seem to. Accordingly, persons with no other bonds to each other would still be obliged not to hinder the others' efforts to provide a minimum for themselves.

One could not, for example, demand as one of the terms of an agreement that someone make sacrifices that would leave the person without necessities. This means that any agreement to cooperate made between people having more than enough and people not having enough cannot justifiably require those who start out without enough to make any sacrifices. Those who lack essentials will still have to agree to act cooperatively, if there is in fact to be cooperation, but they should not bear the costs of even their own cooperation. Because a demand that those lacking essentials should make a sacrifice would harm them, making such a demand is unfair.

That (a), the weaker requirement, holds, seems perfectly clear. When, if ever, would (b), the stronger requirement to provide assistance to others in maintaining a minimum for themselves, hold? Consider the case at hand. Wealthy states, which are wealthy in large part because they are operating industrial processes, ask the poor states, which are poor in large part because they have not industrialized, to cooperate in controlling the bad effects of these same industrial processes, like the destruction of atmospheric ozone and the creation of global warming. Assume that the citizens of the wealthy states have no general obligation, which holds prior to and independently of any agreement to work together on environmental problems, to contribute to the provision of a guaranteed minimum for the citizens of the poor states. The citizens of the poor states certainly have no general obligation, which holds prior to and independently of any agreement, to assist the wealthy states in dealing with the environmental problems that the wealthy states' own industrial processes are producing. It may ultimately be in the interest of the poor states to see ozone depletion and global warming stopped, but in the medium term the citizens of the poor states have far more urgent and serious problems—like lack of food, lack of clean water and lack of jobs to provide minimal support for themselves and their families. If the wealthy states say to the poor states, in effect, "our most urgent request of you is that you act in ways that will avoid worsening the ozone depletion and global warming that we have started," the poor states could reasonably respond, "our most urgent request of you is assistance in guaranteeing the fulfillment of the essential needs of our citizens."

In other words, if the wealthy have no general obligation to help the poor, the poor certainly have no general obligation to help the wealthy. If this assumed absence of general obligations means that matters are to be determined by national interest rather than international obligation, then surely the poor states are as fully at liberty to specify their own top priority as the wealthy states are. The poor states are under no general prior obligation to be helpful to the wealthy states in dealing with whatever happens to be the top priority of the wealthy states. This is all the more so as long as the wealthy states remain content to watch hundreds of thousands of children die each year in the poor states for lack of material necessities, which the total resources in the world could remedy many times over. If the wealthy states are content to allow radical inequalities to persist and worsen, it is difficult to see why the poor states should divert their attention from their own worst problems in order to help out with problems that for them are far less immediate and deadly. It is as if I am starving to death, and you want me to agree to stop searching for food and instead to help repair a leak in the roof of your house without your promising me any food. Why should I turn my attention away from my own more severe problem to your less severe one, when I have no guarantee that if

I help you with your problem you will help me with mine? If any arrangement would ever be unfair, that one would.

Radical human inequalities cannot be tolerated and ought to be eliminated, irrespective of whether their elimination involves the movement of resources across national political boundaries: resources move across national boundaries all the time for all sorts of reasons. I have not argued here for this judgment about radical inequality, however.[5]

NOTES

1. See Thomas Nagel, "Poverty and food: why charity is not enough," in Peter G. Brown and Henry Shue, eds, *Food policy: the responsibility of the United States in the life and death choices* (New York: Free Press, 1977), pp. 54–62.

2. On the importance of backstop arrangements, or the allocation of default duties, see "Afterword" in Henry Shue, *Basic rights: subsistence, affluence, and US foreign policy*, 2nd ed (Princeton, NJ: Princeton University Press, 1996).

3. *Basic rights*, ch. 4.

4. This objection has recently been provided with a powerful and sophisticated Kantian formulation that deserves much more attention than space here allows—see Richard W. Miller, "Cosmopolitan respect and patriotic concern." *Philosophy & Public Affairs* 27 (1998): 202–24.

5. And for the argument to the contrary see Miller, "Cosmopolitan respect and patriotic concern."

9

FEMINIST ECOLOGICAL ETHICS

DANIEL SILVERMINT

THREE MODELS OF OPPRESSION

Although we all share a world, developing ecological realities impact us in different ways. Ecofeminists explore how intersectional identity categories like gender, race, and class mediate our risk and shape our opportunities. Many ecofeminists also make a stronger claim: the systematic mistreatment and exploitation of the natural world parallels the oppression of women, because both kinds of harm stem from the same assumptions and values and entitled attitudes, and both are routinely dismissed as entirely "natural"—as just the way things are. Feminism can thus teach us something about the underlying causes of environmental injustice, and understanding the scope of that injustice can reveal just how ingrained and structural the problem really is. But we can't appreciate the implications of this framework without pausing on the notion of oppression at the heart of its comparison. What does it mean *to oppress*, or to *be oppressed*?

There's more than one way to model oppression, its harms, and the responsibility individuals bear for those harms. And different models lead to unique interpretations of ecofeminism. I think there are three basic models of oppression: the *action model*, the *group relationship model*, and the *effects model*. What does ecofeminism look like under each of these?

According to the action model, some behaviors, practices, and abuses of power are straightforwardly oppressive. Banning women from attending school is oppressive. So too are various attempts to limit the role of women in political and economic life, or to control women's sexuality, or to punish women who deviate from expected gender roles. Even a sexist joke or catcall can oppress—especially when it's the fifth one you've heard that morning, aggregating into a hostile climate for someone who's just trying to go about her day. Some harms are so bad or so brazenly unfair that we can't describe them any other way. The advantage of the action model is that it singles out such mistreatment, and gives us clear guidance on the appropriate way to interact with each other.

What does ecofeminism look like under the action model? If the goal is to act in a just manner, then which environmental practices rise to the level of oppression? What ways of treating the natural world are wrong? It obviously won't be the same list of offenses that harm women, or strive to keep women "in their place," because those offenses are ways of mistreating women *because* they're women. What wrongs a person doesn't wrong an ecosystem, and vice versa. So which actions should go on the list? And how would we decide that, without falling into anthropomorphism or falling back on question-begging assumptions about the kinds of environmental actors we ought to be? Where is the line between making use of a resource and abusing that resource? And what if we determine that an economic practice or industry does count as oppressive, but it proves incredibly advantageous for humankind? Does the importance of ending environmental oppression immediately trump all other concerns, as it does (or should) for social oppression? Or might it be appropriate to try and justify the practice anyway? In other words, does the label "oppressive" have the same force in environmental contexts?

Instead of locating oppression in particular acts, many feminists point to structural hierarchies to explain the wrongs that women suffer. The group relationship model understands oppression in terms of domination and subordination, of institutions arranged to benefit some at the direct expense of the rest. And because those in a dominant social position are allowed or even encouraged to privilege their interests above the interests of others, the vulnerability, exploitation, and marginalization of those others only grows. The sexual division of labor is an example of how structurally unequal relationships result in oppression: many men not only gain from the uncompensated domestic and emotional labor of women but also see that labor as natural and expected, and experience social change as a direct attempt to disadvantage *them*.

It's easy to see the same self-serving, hierarchical attitudes in how some people relate to the natural world. But in the environmental case, is it obvious that such attitudes are wrong? Gendered domination and exploitation are oppressive because women and men have equal moral worth and because their interests command equal moral attention. Is the same true for

humans and animals, or humans and natural objects, or human societies and ecosystems? What would it mean for the environment to have interests or claims on us, and how should we weigh them if it does? Even if people have the same moral worth as the world we inhabit, does that understanding rule out the extraction of resources or the cultivation of land for individual use, or explain what it would mean for the world to have equal authority over us? What arrangements would we have to abandon or adopt to manifest such equality? And does it even make sense to think in terms of our relationship to the world and its ecosystems, as if we stand apart from them instead of being part of them?

The final approach is the effects model. Here oppression refers to ongoing victimizing effects, or to the kinds of experiences that make a person a victim of oppression. The oppressed face institutional and interpersonal barriers that wrongfully burden their life prospects, limit their opportunities, interfere with the exercise of their autonomy or the pursuit of their projects, erode their sense of security, undermine their self-respect and social worth, deny them valuable external goods, and so much more. We identify cases of oppression when we see people living the kinds of lives they shouldn't have to live, and confronting the kinds of burdens that we simply can't excuse.

But once again, the comparison to gendered burdens isn't perfect. What does it mean for nature to *experience* oppression? Even when some occupants of the natural world suffer burdened life prospects or constrained options as the result of human activity, do they experience it the same way we do? Do they feel wearied, or stumble under the emotional weight of longstanding discrimination? Does that matter? Do they have autonomy, or conceptions of the good, or self-respect in the rich moral sense? Even if some of them do, can we generalize these experiences to species, or ecosystems, or natural objects? The effects model of oppression is explicitly grounded in assumptions about human well-being, in claims about what makes lives like ours go well and go wrong. And it's not clear that we properly respect constituents of the natural world—or ourselves, for that matter—when we act as if these intimate differences don't shape what we deserve, or speak in broadly metaphorical terms about the very real harms that women face. Instead, perhaps there's a set of oppressive effects that apply uniquely to the natural world, given the kind of thing *it* is. That's a promising approach, but if so, we once again face the question of what to include on the list and how we should decide that.

Each model of oppression requires us to think about how we see ourselves, and the natural world, and our relationship to that world. It may turn out that the best model for understanding the oppression of women isn't the best way to think about environmental harms, or our unexamined attitudes about those harms. Or maybe the same system really does underlie it all, requiring that we make environmental concerns part of the fight for gender equality and considerations of gender part of the fight for environmental justice. Either way, getting clear about what we mean by oppression can only help.

V. RUKMINI RAO

WOMEN FARMERS OF INDIA'S DECCAN PLATEAU
Ecofeminists Challenge World Elites

This article describes the collective efforts of several thousand rural women and the staff of the Deccan Development Society. It is the story of economically and socially deprived, poor women farmers living on the Deccan Plateau in Andhra Pradesh, a state in the south of India. The Deccan Plateau is one of the most ecologically sensitive regions in the country. It is a semi-arid desert with erratic rainfall and mostly poor quality soil. Government policies over the years have led to the deterioration of natural resources. Pricing policy, which favored rice and wheat production in the country, led to the near collapse of coarse grain production in the region such as sorghum and pearl millet. The increasing costs of modern agricultural inputs also made it difficult for small and marginal farmers to continue production. As a result, large tracts of land now remain fallow in the drought-prone areas. The government has also encouraged the production of sugar cane by providing loans to dig bore-wells and setting up a sugar factory to process the cane. This has resulted in wealthy farmers overusing ground water at the cost of poor farmers whose shallow wells go dry. While 99 percent of the women farmers do not own their own land, through a number of initiatives they have established more control over agriculture, in the process conserving and enriching the soils.

SOCIOECONOMIC CONDITIONS OF DALIT WOMEN

Dalit[1] women and men belong to a number of sub-castes, which divides them.[2] Elite castes and classes in the village consider them "untouchable," which in effect means apartheid. Dalit women are not allowed to collect water from village hand pumps and they cannot sit together with other communities. In public places they stand at a distance from upper castes because they are considered to be "polluting." They suffer from discrimination in the worst forms.

At the same time the dalit communities do all the agricultural hard labor such as ploughing, sowing, planting, weeding, and harvesting. They are exploited on a daily basis: they are paid extremely low wages, have little or no job security, and have no maternity or child care benefits.[3] In addition, women are at risk of sexual exploitation because they are poor and typically economically dependent on male landowners.[4] Dalit male farmers in the region own small plots of agricultural land on which they try to grow food for home consumption. Due to soil erosion, and lack of access to irrigation and credit, their lands are kept fallow, resulting in poverty. Most men and women are in the grip of moneylenders who charge 60 to 120 percent annual interest on loans, often cheating farmers of their lands. Drought years leave the dalit community further in debt. While the government enacted legislation, which outlaws practices of untouchability, the practice of untouchability continues due to prevailing social customs imposed by upper castes and classes on the poor. Though the government has promoted affirmative action for the community with special quotas in educational institutions and jobs, the overall conditions remain grim. Literacy rates among dalit women are well below 10 percent, and 98 percent of the women work as daily wage workers without job security.

THE SUPPORT ORGANIZATION

The Deccan Development Society (DDS) was set up in 1983 by a group of professional men to help poor communities develop themselves. A few professional women have been in and out of senior management positions. The DDS works with approximately two hundred part-time and full-time staff, and 95 percent of the staff are local men and women. The DDS recognizes that the livelihoods of the rural poor can improve only when the environment in which they live is regenerated. Deprived people need organizational and financial support because they have been exploited for many generations. A number of European donors support the DDS. Also, the government of India funds some of the DDS programs. The Deccan Development Society believes that people have a right to a decent livelihood and government resources must be accessed to help them.

Initially, the DDS attempted to organize men to take up development activities, believing that since farmers owned some land, they could benefit if irrigation wells were provided along with electrical pumps to ensure irrigation. As a result of frequent voltage fluctuations, however, the pumps were damaged, increasing a farmer's costs rather than improving his economy. In some cases farmers excavated wells and found there was too little ground water to be used. The wells went dry.

A second effort was to improve livestock. This also did not work for a number of reasons. The male groups were encouraged to start saving regularly to take up additional income-generating activities. The groups asked for large sums of matching grants to start small businesses. Usually women's groups of fifteen to twenty women who start saving may be given financial support of INR Rs.15,000 in addition to their own savings to start very small businesses. The men expect to be given individual loans of Rs.5,000 to Rs.10,000 each and a group of fifteen men would expect Rs.150,000 (US $1 is approximately 43 Indian rupees). The financial investment demanded by the men was much higher than the support DDS could provide.

Men's groups quickly fall apart for a number of reasons. Men have strong political identities, so groups break up during election periods when members canvass for and support rival candidates. In most villages men are sharply divided along political lines owing allegiance to local leaders in the different political parties. Leaders help their own supporters to access development projects and show undue favor regularly. Conflicts among groups are common. Also, men quarrel for leadership positions much more bitterly than women do. Dissatisfied men leave a group taking a small following with them, ultimately leading to the collapse of the whole group.

While the men's groups failed, women came forward to set up local groups called Sangams. The DDS now works only with women, because it recognizes that dalit women suffer from the triple burden of caste, class, and gender. Over the years, the organization has come to understand the situation of the rural poor and developed a strategy to work toward self-reliance. It works mainly with dalit women who are poor. Poor women from other castes are also included in the Sangam if they accept norms of equality and respect for each other, irrespective of caste. The groups are self-selected and members belong to Christian, Hindu, and Islamic communities.

Women in the thrift groups quarrel over a number of issues. If there are mistakes in bookkeeping and accounting the women quarrel, but usually such mistakes are easily sorted out. If the group fails in any collective task, individuals tend to blame each other but after some loud quarreling spread over two to three meetings everyone calms down and life returns to normal. In spite of differences, women are very keen to stay and work together because they can see clear benefits from working together. While some women also struggle to establish leadership they are much more willing to accommodate each other. This may be partly due to the fact that women are overburdened by work outside and inside the home and are willing to allow others to take the burden of group management.

Over the past fifteen years more than five thousand women have been organized into self-help groups that are on the path to sustainable development. The village of Edakulapalli illustrates the developments of the region.

THE STRUGGLE OF DALIT WOMEN IN EDAKULAPALLI VILLAGE

FINANCIAL SELF-HELP

A group of dalit women approached DDS in 1992, asking for assistance in starting a women's group. Forty-seven women from different subcastes came together and started a savings program. Though the women were very poor and indebted, regular saving of a small amount of money helps the women to create basic resources. Collectively, the fund creates space for action to improve consumption and take new economic initiatives. The individual members saved Rs.5 every week (approximately US $0.12).

A year after coming together, the group fell apart. The women developed strong differences among themselves. Male family members also created trouble for the group. To compound the problem, a DDS staff member who left the organization also created divisions. This is a common experience when the poor

organize themselves. Upper-caste and -class men, men from the dalit community, male political leaders who feel threatened, and insensitive activists often cause the collapse of groups. However, two women leaders who had tasted the initial benefits of organization were determined to restart. They regrouped and started over with thirty-six members.

The group savings were strengthened by adding matching grants from donor funds. Over a seven-year period the group now holds Rs.124,915 (US $2,905) as a revolving fund. This revolving fund was initially used to take loans for consumption of food grains, to buy clothes for women at Christmas, and for emergency relief in case of serious health problems. Since rural healthcare is practically inaccessible to most of the poor, immediate support to rush the sick to hospital is very important. Consumption loans to overcome the seasonal shortages of food at a low interest rate of 12 percent per annum instead of 60 to 120 percent help the women and their families maintain essential nutritional levels and prevent illnesses that can ruin a family's economic stability and earning capacity. The core thrift and credit activities work as a safety net to members of the Sangam. In addition, the women have accessed government funds to take up income generating activities. A group of twelve hundred women who started organizing themselves at the same time now manage a revolving fund of Rs 3,500,000 (US $81,395).

ENVIRONMENT REGENERATION

A major impact of the poor conditions of agriculture lands and small family holdings is that they are left fallow. Big landlords also cultivate only part of their holdings to grow sugar cane and other irrigated crops while leaving the rest fallow. This leads to (1) lack of employment; (2) lack of basic food, since farm laborers are paid in kind when they harvest crops; (3) high rates of soil erosion; and eventually (4) forced migration of landless, small, and marginal farmers. The vulnerability of the poor leads to inhuman practices such as annual bondage of young boys (for a very small wage),[5] preventing them from going to school. Girls belonging to poor families are experienced as burdens and are considered fair game for sexual harassment, and so are married at the age of ten to twelve years.[6] To overcome this deteriorating negative cycle, DDS has over the years worked out a program in collaboration with the women's groups. In Edakulapalli it took the following forms:

1. Create Summer Employment and Improve the Quality of Land: Each summer, the women's groups identify agricultural land for development. Small plots of poor quality land are usually owned by men in their families. The women pick stones from fields, improve drainage, and build contour bunds to prevent soil erosion. These activities help to improve the productivity of the land and increase yields. Because the owners do not have the financial resources to take up the necessary activities, DDS provides a 50 percent subsidy to individual woman farmers. The whole group benefits because employment is created during the summer when no other employment is available to women. For example, in each village during the summer, DDS provides ten women a loan of US $23 each to improve their lands. A total of US $230 is spent in the village to improve farmland. This creates four hundred days of employment at existing wage rates. Each individual returns 50 percent of the loan during the following year to the thrift fund. The four hundred days of employment created in the village is shared among the twenty members of the group. Each member gets twenty days of wage employment over a period of one or two months. With support to buy farm implements and bullocks for ploughing, small farmers who had never cultivated land turn into farmers who are able to grow food and to make an income.

2. Lease the Land: Since land is the most productive resource in the region, the women form small groups and lease land. This provides employment and food and also improves land quality because the farmers are encouraged to undertake organic agriculture. Group farming has given women access to this productive resource. As individuals they could not afford to farm and provide necessary inputs, but as a collective the women have gained recognition as farm managers and are not seen only as unskilled workers.

3. Control the Seed: Since seeds are the most critical input into agriculture, the women have collected a variety of seeds, which they lend to each other and

other poor farmers. The traditional system of returning double the amount of borrowed seed has led to women creating their own seed banks.

COMMUNITY SEED BANKS

In India, as in most third world countries, a battle to control seeds rages between all farmers and multinational companies such as Monsanto and Novartis. The control over new seed varieties, including genetically modified seeds, coupled with intellectual property rights and the patent regime spells doom for small farmers. If they become dependent on seeds, fertilizers, and pesticides bought in the market, they will be pushed out of agriculture because they cannot afford the escalating costs.

Traditionally, people have survived drought and hardships in the region because of the rich biodiversity of food crops cultivated in the area. Elderly farmers (women and men) have identified more than eighty varieties of food crops that were grown locally. The DDS is working toward regaining the vast biodiversity of the region. Twenty-four women farmers in the village have taken the responsibility to identify different food crops grown in the area and replant them on their own lands. A community seed bank has been set up in the village. Throughout the region, women's groups have set up their own seed banks and reduced dependence on the market for seeds.

PROTECTING AND REGENERATING PRODUCTIVE RESOURCES

Because of rapid industrialization, poor farmers are tempted to sell their lands when prices escalate. Once they sell their lands, they are forced to migrate to nearby towns and live a life of destitution. Women in the Sangam prevented their men folk from selling away their barren land. Women in the Sangam do not have any legal rights to stop the men (their husbands) from selling their lands. However as a group they have social power to influence men in the community. More importantly, women used their economic power to access loans to demonstrate to the men that barren lands could be made productive. The men were tempted to sell the land because it was barren and would fetch a high price if sold to an industry. The women are more conscious of the need to safeguard land, the main productive asset they own, and they work hard to make it productive. While wives cannot individually influence major decisions of their spouses, collectively they can strategize and influence community decisions. The women's Sangam has provided leadership: they negotiated a loan and subsidies from DDS to improve and develop ninety-five acres of their own land. With soil and moisture conservation efforts, barren land has been made productive. More than twenty varieties of cereals, pulses, oil seeds, spices, and vegetables have been grown on this land. The men have worked in the fields and supported the women.

ADDITIONAL INCOME-GENERATING ACTIVITIES

Since most farmers own only small plots of land and the climate conditions are harsh, the women need to secure their incomes through additional activities. Milk production and raising goats for meat production are lucrative. Women have also started selling vegetables and setting up village tea shops, which are managed by men in the family. The women use their revolving thrift fund to buy assets, create an income, and repay loans. Over a period of six to seven years, women's incomes have increased gradually. When the Sangam started functioning, a survey of the economic conditions of the members showed that all were indebted to moneylenders. Many had pawned their lands for small amounts to raise money during emergencies such as ill health or consumption during drought years. Today only one member is still indebted, and the group is planning a strategy to redeem her assets.

BASIC NEEDS VERSUS STRATEGIC NEEDS

One school of development thinking has emphasized the need to ensure women's basic needs are met. Another group insists that this is not enough. They emphasize the need to address issues of power relationships within society. If society is not gender balanced in terms of power, then economic gains made to meet basic needs can easily be lost.

In the efforts described previously, it is clear that both basic needs and power relationships have to be addressed. For example, leasing of land by the women's group meets their basic need of ensuring incomes and food. At the same time, leasing of land has broken down class and caste barriers in the Indian village society. It is usually the large landowners who have land to lease out. Once the women's groups have the funds and the skills to take up collective farming, upper-caste male landowners are coming to women and offering them leases. They come to the settlements where the dalits live, drink tea with the dalit women, request the women politely to lease the lands. This is a complete role reversal. Earlier, the landless dalit women would go begging the landlord for work. She was usually kept standing outside the house, and when employed as a daily wage worker, was told to come back a week later to collect her wages.

THE ETHIC OF CARE

In neighboring villages where wastelands were available, the women's groups have developed community forestry and woodlots. In some villages the women's group is growing traditional medicinal plants. Where extensive fallow land was available, the women have developed community grain banks. In their collective efforts, the women demonstrate a caring ethic. For example, paid employment is provided to elderly women and childcare facilities are set up to support young mothers. Intergenerational care is established as a norm. The women also show the same caring attitude to livestock. They regard livestock as more than mere production machines, and consider the overall welfare of the animal. This consideration runs throughout their decision-making. When asked why they prefer traditional varieties of sorghum, even though it has lower grain yield, their answer is: "What about our animals—the new dwarf variety means our animals will have little food. We need to feed our animals too!"

The dalit women are building on their traditional knowledge and wisdom to improve their environment. They combine traditional wisdom with modern practices such as participatory rural appraisals (PRAs) to plan for medicinal plantations, watershed development, and crop planning. They also use PRA techniques to reduce conflicts. For example, wealth-ranking exercises, done publicly and collectively by the group, identify the most needy women as top priorities for receiving aid. They are assisted by staff from the organization to plan their activities.

The women have rejected use of chemical fertilizers and pesticides as harmful to the earth. They are experimenting with nonchemical approaches to pest management. To ensure long-term sustainability, they are working to establish regional federations and cooperatives which will produce and market traditional organic food.

FEMINISM IN PRACTICE

With success in improving their environment, women now have the confidence to tackle social problems. They intervene in domestic disputes and are able to influence local police and traditional leaders, leading to more gender-just decisions. Because the women's group supported the victim, for the first time in the area a rapist was punished in court.

Urban middle-class feminists worked closely with women's groups to create awareness of the contribution women make to family incomes. During workshops the women could discuss among themselves the long hours of housework they contribute to ensure family well-being. When the housework was assigned an economic value the women clearly understood that though they brought home lower cash income, they contribute more than men to the family. For example, collecting fuelwood, washing clothes, cooking, and so forth, all had economic value. Caste bias also increased women's workload. While upper-caste women collect drinking water from a well in the center of the village, dalit women may have to walk a longer distance if untouchability is practiced. Discussing such issues allowed women to work out some strategies for change. The most important understanding that emerged was the need for women to work collectively.

Through sharing experiences the women realize both their individual worth and the potential of collective functioning to overcome gender discrimination. In collaboration with urban feminists, mainstream institutional norms for giving credit have been challenged and changed. The women as part of collectives are now able to access resources from institutions such as government development departments and banks. The working models set up by the women's groups have been adopted by government agencies.

QUESTIONS FOR THE FUTURE

Government policies in India, such as pricing policies that promote rice, wheat, and sugar cane production have led to deterioration of natural resources. Often this deterioration has most harshly struck the poor, who are either landless or own marginal land. With globalization of agricultural marketing, many farmers have become dependent on relatively costly inputs like commercial seed, fertilizers, and pesticides. This has put or kept many poorer farmers in continual debt. The widespread cultural practice of discriminating against people on the basis of caste, class, and gender continues, despite official government legislation outlawing the practice. Again this has a greater effect on the poor. Yet the poor have discovered local resources to work against these difficulties. With a little outside financial and organizational help, poor women have formed groups dedicated to norms of equality and respect for each other, irrespective of caste. They have established local seed banks, brought fallow land back into production, and promoted sustainable, organic agriculture. In accomplishing these things, they have begun to incrementally acquire the power needed to change cultural norms that have held them down in society.

Women leaders in the area are very sensitive to issues of oppression and alert about their rights. Yet due to traditional gender values, most women still prefer sons and want them to inherit family property. At the same time a growing number of women question prevailing patriarchal ideology. Through years of hard work, the women have demonstrated an alternative to technoindustrial agriculture[7] and the potential for development without destroying nature. With the support of DDS the women have set up a local radio station and a media group of women videographers to propagate alternate values. Under what circumstances they succeed remains to be seen.

NOTES

1. "Dalit" is a self-proclaimed name for a group of people who are considered untouchable. They belong to fifty-five subcastes in Andhra Pradesh. The word literally means "oppressed broken people."

2. Indian society is stratified into caste groups. Traditionally the pure caste groups were the Brahmins,

Kshatriyas, Viashyas, and Shudras. They represented the four basic occupations: priests, warriors, businessmen, and workers. Today, Indian caste society is complex, with many subcastes. An individual is born into the caste of his parents and remains in that caste for life. The lowest castes are usually the poorest, and some are designated untouchable. The lowest caste groups live in separate parts of the village and are not allowed to use the common drinking water source. (In contrast, the word "class" is used to describe differences in wealth and access to productive resources and employment. Usually upper-class people also belong to higher castes, but with rapid changes in the economy this is not always true. You can find very poor Brahmins and some rich dalit families in the cities.)

3. The main exploitation is the extremely low pay. In the Deccan area, the government has fixed a minimum wage of Rs.32 per day (US $0.77) for eight hours of work for male and female unskilled workers. In spite of this, women are usually paid only half the minimum wage and well below the wages of men. Though the official wage rate is revised regularly, real wages continue to be low. Women also work more than eight hours per day. There are no maternity benefits or childcare facilities.

4. When women go to work on farms, some farmers pressure or seduce women into sexual relationships. These are not based on mutuality, since women are economically dependent on the farmers for their daily wages and livelihoods. The same farmers may be the main money lenders in the village, thus increasing the dependence of women, leading them to accept unwanted sexual advances.

5. When families are extremely poor and need loans to meet basic food needs or to deal with an emergency health problem, they pledge their sons to work with a landlord for a period of one year.

A boy aged eight to twelve years may be forced to work for one year to pay off a loan of U.S. $35 to $46. The boy will clean cowsheds, take the landlord's livestock out for grazing during the day, and is expected to do any housework assigned to him such as sweeping the house. Some boys are expected to irrigate the farmer's fields during the day or night, while some are allowed to go home at the end of the day. There are no fixed hours of employment. Some boys are given food by the landlord during the day. Others eat only a morning meal before leaving for work and then again upon returning home at night. Boys living in bondage are usually underweight and have no opportunity for schooling. Children may be bonded for four to five years with the same landlord or with different ones. Adult men may also enter bondage when the family faces desperate poverty. They are paid half the minimum wage for the year.

6. Although some harassment consists "only" of making obscene remarks when girls or women are going by, or trying to touch the women physically, the situation can be much worse. Rape is a serious problem. Even when violence is not used, there is an element of coercion in most premarital sexual relationships involving dalit teenage girls because it is upper-caste men who have premarital sexual relations with lower-caste women. Since the women work as laborers in the fields of the upper-caste families they are vulnerable to economic pressure. Upper-caste families stand together when facing a problem, often ostracizing the poorer, lower-caste families and refusing them wage employment if they file complaints with the police.

7. Technoindustrial agriculture is characterized by excessive use of chemicals, dangerous pesticides, biotechnology and overproduction, which destroys natural resources, pollutes water, and degrades soil quality.

KRISTEN HESSLER AND ELIZABETH WILLOTT

FEMINISM AND ECOFEMINISM

In 1848, in Seneca Falls, New York, at a convention on women's rights, women's rights activist Elizabeth Cady Stanton proposed the radical idea that women should be given the right to vote. In her "Declaration of Sentiments" (modeled on the Declaration of Independence), Stanton declared: "Now, in view of this entire disenfranchisement of one-half the people of this country . . . and because women do feel themselves aggrieved, oppressed, and fraudulently deprived of their most sacred rights, we insist that they have immediate admission to all the rights and privileges which belong to them as citizens of the United States."[1] This convention is generally viewed as the official beginning of the women's rights movement in the United States. In 1920, after more than seventy years of feminist activism and lobbying against severe resistance from both men and women, women finally received the right to vote.

Liberal feminists believe the best way to combat women's oppression is to continue to seek equal rights for women, just as early American feminists sought the right to vote. This variant of feminism is based on the ideals of liberalism, the political ideology that emphasizes individual freedom—usually understood as individual rights—and the political equality of all citizens. Liberal feminism is a moderate doctrine in the sense that, at least in liberal democracies, it does not advocate a social revolution for the sake of women's liberation. Instead, liberal feminists believe women's liberation consists in gaining equal status and rights for women within a liberal society.

Radical feminists, by contrast, see the domination of women by men as so basic that merely reforming the existing political or social structure will not eliminate women's oppression. Therefore, they advocate revolutionary social change for the sake of women's liberation. Many radical feminists argue that fundamental changes in our basic values are necessary for the liberation of women. They point out that women's lives traditionally have been private—concerned with the home and the family. In contrast, men have occupied the public realm, including most professions and government. Some radical feminists believe that, instead of seeking equality for women in the public realm, feminists should work to change our values so we ascribe positive value to the traditional roles of women.

Gains in women's status have not come easily. Women in the United States had to fight for the right to own property on the same terms as men. They had to fight to change laws that, as recently as the 1980s, made it impossible for a man to be charged with raping his wife.[2] Feminists are still working to improve representation of women in their governments, to end discrimination and sexual harassment in the workplace, to combat rape and domestic abuse, and to create arrangements for raising families so that women who choose to raise children are not disadvantaged in work.

Much progress has been made, not only in Western democracies, but much work still needs to be done. Asian women no longer have their feet mutilated. On the other hand, thousands of Asian women and girls each year are kidnapped or sold into forced prostitution or domestic slavery, often with the tacit permission of police.[3] In most countries, female genital mutilation[4] has been made illegal. On the other hand, it still occurs. In some countries, women are at risk of being killed by their families if even suspected of impermissible sexual conduct. In some cases, the best protection the legal system can offer is to put a woman in jail, where her family cannot get to her. Some women have been in jail for years.[5]

In some countries, women have lost ground. In the mid-1990s, women in Afghanistan lost their right to work outside the home, attend university, and even to leave their houses without a male relative. They must wear clothing that covers them from head to foot; an ankle or wrist exposed can lead to a vicious public beating by members of the Department for the Propagation of Virtue and the Suppression of Vice. Prior to these decrees, women made up 40 percent of the physicians in the capital city Kabul; in September 1997, not only were women forbidden to work as physicians in the hospitals but also they were banned as patients from receiving medical care at them. Instead, a single, poorly equipped, clinic was to serve all 500,000 women who lived in the city. Because of international outcry, that has been rescinded—by May 1998, women are officially granted limited access to healthcare in all but military hospitals and some female healthcare providers were permitted to return to work.[6]

Feminist theory asks why and how women are oppressed. *Feminist activism* tries to do something about it: educating people about women's subordination and its causes and teaching them how to resist in a constructive way. In feminism, as in other social movements, theory and activism usually work together: activism often is informed by theory, and theory often is a product of the systematic thinking of concerned and engaged activists.

Ecofeminism is short for "ecological feminism." Whether radical or liberal, ecofeminists share a belief that the oppression of women is importantly linked to the domination of nature. Ecofeminist theorists are still working on accounts of how these oppressions are linked. Some ecofeminists think men's psychology drives men to oppress both women and nature. Others argue that Western society has traditionally identified women with nature and has devalued both compared to men and culture.

Ecofeminism has prompted examination of several issues: Are attitudes toward women importantly similar to attitudes toward nature? Can nature be oppressed in the same ways that people, specifically women, can be oppressed? What should we make of the fact that women have contributed to the disappearance of wilderness and other environmental damage? Are strategies designed to liberate women, but that ignore environmental degradation, bound to fail in the long term? Are strategies designed to preserve the environment, but that ignore the domination of women, destined—or at least more likely—to fail? Do we need to care about both the oppression of women and the environment, simultaneously, to achieve optimal results for either? Ecofeminist theorists continue to work on answers to such questions. Meanwhile, ecofeminist activists are working to protect our environment, as well as to combat the oppression of women.

NOTES

1. Elizabeth Cady Stanton, "Declaration of Sentiments," *Women's Rights Conventions: Seneca Falls and Rochester 1848* (New York: Arno and *New York Times*, 1969), p. 7.

2. Diana H. Russell, *Rape in Marriage*, expanded and revised edition (Bloomington: Indiana University Press, 1990) p. 21.

3. *Human Rights Watch Global Report on Women's Human Rights* (New York: Human Rights Watch, 1995), chap. 4. Indeed, the police are sometimes customers at brothels where women are forced to work, or they capture women who escape and return them to the brothels.

4. Female genital mutilation refers to surgical removal of the clitoris. However, the "surgery" is sometimes performed without anesthetic and under highly unsterile conditions.

5. Douglas Jehl, "Arab Honor's Price: A Woman's Blood," *New York Times*, Sunday, June 20, 1999. p. 1.

6. Zohra Rasekh, Heidi M. Bauer, M. Michele Manos, and Vincent Iacopino, "Women's Health and Human Rights in Afghanistan," *Journal of the American Medical Association* 280 (2000): 449–455. The situation for men is also horrific: men can be beaten if their beards are not long enough and for other spurious reasons. Also see US Department of State, Bureau of Democracy, Human Rights, and Labor, *Country Reports on Human Rights Practices for 1999—Afghanistan* (US Dept. of State, February 2000) http://www.usis.usemb.se/human/human1999/afghanis.html.

KAREN J. WARREN

THE POWER AND THE PROMISE
OF ECOLOGICAL FEMINISM

Ecological feminism is the position that there are important connections—historical, symbolic, theoretical between the domination of women and the domination of nonhuman nature. I argue that because the conceptual connections between the dual dominations of women and nature are located in an oppressive patriarchal conceptual framework characterized by a logic of domination, (1) the logic of traditional feminism requires the expansion of feminism to include ecological feminism, and (2) ecological feminism provides a framework for developing a distinct feminist environmental ethic. I conclude that any feminist theory and any environmental ethic which fails to take seriously the interconnected domination of women and nature is simply inadequate.

INTRODUCTION

Ecological feminism (ecofeminism) has begun to receive a fair amount of attention lately as an alternative feminism and environmental ethic. Since Francoise d'Eaubonne introduced the term *ecofeminisme* in 1974 to bring attention to women's potential for bringing about an ecological revolution,[1] the term has been used in a variety of ways. As I use the term in this paper, ecological feminism is the position that there are important connections—historical, experiential, symbolic, theoretical—between the domination of women and the domination of nature, an understanding of which is crucial to both feminism and environmental ethics. I argue that the promise and power of ecological feminism is that *it provides a distinctive framework both for reconceiving feminism and for developing an environmental ethic which takes seriously connections between the domination of women*

and the domination of nature. I do so by discussing the nature of a feminist ethic and the ways in which ecofeminism provides a feminist and environmental ethic. I conclude that any feminist theory *and* any environmental ethic which fails to take seriously the twin and interconnected dominations of women and nature is at best incomplete and at worst simply inadequate.

FEMINISM, ECOLOGICAL FEMINISM, AND CONCEPTUAL FRAMEWORKS

Whatever else it is, feminism is at least the movement to end sexist oppression. It involves the elimination of any and all factors that contribute to the continued and systematic domination or subordination of women. While feminists disagree about the nature of and solutions to the subordination of women, all feminists agree that sexist oppression exists, is wrong, and must be abolished.

A "feminist issue" is any issue that contributes in some way to understanding the oppression of women. Equal rights, comparable pay for comparable work, and food production are feminist issues wherever and whenever an understanding of them contributes to an understanding of the continued exploitation or subjugation of women. Carrying water and searching for firewood are feminist issues wherever and whenever women's primary responsibility for these tasks contributes to their lack of full participation in decision making, income producing, or high status positions engaged in by men. What counts as a feminist issue, then, depends largely on context, particularly the historical and material conditions of women's lives.

Environmental degradation and exploitation are feminist issues because an understanding of them

Karen J. Warren. 1990. The Power and the Promise of Ecological Feminism. Environmental Ethics, 12: 125–146. Reprinted with permission of the author and the journal.

contributes to an understanding of the oppression of women. In India, for example, both deforestation and reforestation through the introduction of a monoculture species tree (e.g., eucalyptus) intended for commercial production are feminist issues because the loss of indigenous forests and multiple species of trees has drastically affected rural Indian women's ability to maintain a subsistence household. Indigenous forests provide a variety of trees for food, fuel, fodder, household utensils, dyes, medicines, and income-generating uses, while monoculture-species forests do not.[2] Although I do not argue for this claim here, a look at the global impact of environmental degradation on women's lives suggests important respects in which environmental degradation is a feminist issue.

Feminist philosophers claim that some of the most important feminist issues are *conceptual* ones: these issues concern how one conceptualizes such mainstay philosophical notions as reason and rationality, ethics, and what it is to be human. Ecofeminists extend this feminist philosophical concern to nature. They argue that, ultimately, some of the most important connections between the domination of women and the domination of nature are conceptual. To see this, consider the nature of conceptual frameworks.

A *conceptual framework* is a set of *basic* beliefs, values, attitudes, and assumptions which shape and reflect how one views oneself and one's world. It is a socially constructed lens through which we perceive ourselves and others. It is affected by such factors as gender, race, class, age, affectional orientation, nationality, and religious background.

Some conceptual frameworks are oppressive. An *oppressive conceptual framework* is one that explains, justifies, and maintains relationships of domination and subordination. When an oppressive conceptual framework is *patriarchal*, it explains, justifies, and maintains the subordination of women by men.

I have argued elsewhere that there are three significant features of oppressive conceptual frameworks: (1) value-hierarchical thinking, i.e., "up–down" thinking which places higher value, status, or prestige on what is "up" rather than on what is "down"; (2) value dualisms, i.e., disjunctive pairs in which the disjuncts are seen as oppositional (rather than as complementary)

and exclusive (rather than as inclusive), and which place higher value (status, prestige) on one disjunct rather than the other (e.g., dualisms which give higher value or status to that which has historically been identified as "mind," "reason," and "male" than to that which has historically been identified as "body," "emotion," and "female"); and (3) logic of domination, i.e., a structure of argumentation which leads to a justification of subordination.

The third feature of oppressive conceptual frameworks is the most significant. A logic of domination is not just a logical structure. It also involves a substantive value system, since an ethical premise is needed to permit or sanction the "just" subordination of that which is subordinate. This justification typically is given on grounds of some alleged characteristic (e.g., rationality) which the dominant (e.g., men) have and the subordinate (e.g., women) lack.

Contrary to what many feminists and ecofeminists have said or suggested, there maybe nothing inherently problematic about "hierarchical thinking" or even "value-hierarchical thinking" in contexts other than contexts of oppression. Hierarchical thinking is important in daily living for classifying data, comparing information, and organizing material. Taxonomies (e.g., plant taxonomies) and biological nomenclature seem to require some form of "hierarchical thinking." Even "value-hierarchical thinking" may be quite acceptable in certain contexts. (The same may be said of "value dualisms" in non-oppressive contexts). For example, suppose it is true that what is unique about humans is our conscious capacity to radically reshape our social environments (or "societies"), as Murray Bookchin suggests.[3] Then one could truthfully say that humans are better equipped to radically reshape their environments than are rocks or plants—a "value-hierarchical" way of speaking.

The problem is not simply that value-hierarchical thinking and value dualisms are used, but the way in which each has been used in oppressive conceptual frameworks to establish inferiority and to justify subordination.[4] It is the logic of domination, coupled with value-hierarchical thinking and value dualisms, which "justifies" subordination. What is explanatorily basic, then, about the nature of oppressive conceptual frameworks is the logic of domination.

For ecofeminism, that a logic of domination is explanatorily basic is important for at least three reasons. First, without a logic of domination, a description of similarities and differences would be just that—a description of similarities and differences. Consider the claim, "Humans are different from plants and rocks in that humans can (and plants and rocks cannot) consciously and radically reshape the communities in which they live, humans are similar to plants and rocks in that they are both members of an ecological community." Even if humans are "better" than plants and rocks with respect to the conscious ability of humans to radically transform communities, one does not thereby get any morally relevant distinction between humans and nonhumans, or an argument for the domination of plants and rocks by humans. To get those conclusions one needs to add at least two powerful assumptions, viz., (A2) and (A4) in argument A below:

(Al) Humans do, and plants and rocks do not, have the capacity to consciously and radically change the community in which they live.

(A2) Whatever has the capacity to consciously and radically change the community in which it lives is morally superior to whatever lacks this capacity.

(A3) Thus, humans are morally superior to plants and rocks.

(A4) For any X and Y, if X is morally superior to Y, then X is morally justified in subordinating Y.

(A5) Thus, humans are morally justified in subordinating plants and rocks.

Without the two assumptions that humans are morally superior to (at least some) nonhumans, (A2), and that superiority justifies subordination, (A4), all one has is some difference between humans and some nonhumans. This is true even if that difference is given in terms of superiority. Thus, it is the logic of domination, (A4), which is the bottom line in ecofeminist discussions of oppression.

Second, ecofeminists argue that, at least in Western societies, the oppressive conceptual framework which sanctions the twin dominations of women and nature is a patriarchal one characterized by all three features of an oppressive conceptual framework. Many ecofeminists claim that, historically, within at least the dominant Western culture, a patriarchal conceptual framework has sanctioned the following argument B:

(B1) Women are identified with nature and the realm of the physical; men are identified with the "human" and the realm of the mental.

(B2) Whatever is identified with nature and the realm of the physical is inferior to ("below") whatever is identified with the "human" and the realm of the mental; or, conversely, the latter is superior to ("above") the former.

(B3) Thus, women are inferior to ("below") men; or, conversely, men are superior to ("above") women.

(B4) For any X and Y, if X is superior to Y, then X is justified in subordinating Y.

(B5) Thus, men are justified in subordinating women.

If sound, argument B establishes patriarchy, i.e., the conclusion given at (B5) that the systematic domination of women by men is justified. But according to ecofeminists, (B5) is justified by just those three features of an oppressive conceptual framework identified earlier: value-hierarchical thinking, the assumption at (B2); value dualisms, the assumed dualism of the mental and the physical at (B1) and the assumed inferiority of the physical vis-à-vis the mental at (B2); and a logic of domination, the assumption at (B4), the same as the previous premise (A4). Hence, according to ecofeminists, insofar as an oppressive patriarchal conceptual framework has functioned historically (within at least dominant Western culture) to sanction the twin dominations of women and nature (argument B), both argument B and the patriarchal conceptual framework, from whence it comes, ought to be rejected.

Of course, the preceding does not identify which premises of B are false. What is the status of premises (Bl) and (B2)? Most, if not all, feminists claim that (Bl), and many ecofeminists claim that (B2), have been assumed or asserted within the dominant

Western philosophical and intellectual tradition. As such, these feminists assert, as a matter of historical fact, that the dominant Western philosophical tradition has assumed the truth of (Bl) and (B2). Ecofeminists, however, either deny (B2) or do not affirm (B2). Furthermore, because some ecofeminists are anxious to deny any ahistorical identification of women with nature, some ecofeminists deny (Bl) when (B1) is used to support anything other than a strictly historical claim about what has been asserted or assumed to be true within patriarchal culture—e.g., when (Bl) is used to assert that women properly are identified with the realm of nature and the physical. Thus, from an ecofeminist perspective, (Bl) and (B2) are properly viewed as problematic though historically sanctioned claims: they are problematic precisely because of the way they have functioned historically in a patriarchal conceptual framework and culture to sanction the dominations of women and nature.

What all ecofeminists agree about, then, is the way in which the logic of domination has functioned historically within patriarchy to sustain and justify the twin dominations of women and nature.[5] Since all feminists (and not just ecofeminists) oppose patriarchy, the conclusion given at (B5), all feminists (including ecofeminists) must oppose at least the logic of domination, premise (B4), on which argument B rests—whatever the truth-value status of (Bl) and (B2) outside of a patriarchal context.

That *all* feminists must oppose the logic of domination shows the breadth and depth of the ecofeminist critique of B: it is a critique not only of the three assumptions on which this argument for the domination of women and nature rests, viz., the assumptions at (Bl), (B2), and (B4); it is also a critique of patriarchal conceptual frameworks generally, i.e., of those oppressive conceptual frameworks which put men "up" and women "down," allege some way in which women are morally inferior to men, and use that alleged difference to justify the subordination of women by men. Therefore, ecofeminism is necessary to any feminist critique of patriarchy, and, hence, necessary to feminism (a point I discuss again later).

Third, ecofeminism clarifies why the logic of domination, and any conceptual framework which gives rise to it, must be abolished in order both to make possible a meaningful notion of difference which does not breed domination and to prevent feminism from becoming a "support" movement based primarily on shared experiences. In contemporary society, there is no one "woman's voice," no woman (or human) *simpliciter*: every woman (or human) is a woman (or human) of some race, class, age, affectional orientation, marital status, regional or national background, and so forth. Because there are no "monolithic experiences" that all women share, feminism must be a "solidarity movement" based on shared beliefs and interests rather than a "unity in sameness" movement based on shared experiences and shared victimization.[6] In the words of Maria Lugones, "Unity—not to be confused with solidarity—is understood as conceptually tied to domination."[7]

Ecofeminists insist that the sort of logic of domination used to justify the domination of humans by gender, racial or ethnic, or class status is also used to justify the domination of nature. Because eliminating a logic of domination is part of a feminist critique—whether a critique of patriarchy, white supremacist culture, or imperialism—ecofeminists insist that *naturism* is properly viewed as an integral part of any feminist solidarity movement to end sexist oppression and the logic of domination which conceptually grounds it.

ECOFEMINISM RECONCEIVES FEMINISM

The discussion so far has focused on some of the oppressive conceptual features of patriarchy. As I use the phrase, the "logic of traditional feminism" refers to the location of the conceptual roots of sexist oppression, at least in Western societies, in an oppressive patriarchal conceptual framework characterized by a logic of domination. Insofar as other systems of oppression (e.g., racism, classism, ageism, heterosexism) are also conceptually maintained by a logic of domination, appeal to the logic of traditional feminism ultimately locates the basic conceptual interconnections among all systems of oppression in the logic of domination. It thereby explains at a conceptual level why the eradication of sexist oppression requires the eradication of the other forms of oppression. It is by clarifying this conceptual connection between systems of oppression that a movement to end sexist oppression—traditionally the special turf of feminist theory and practice—leads to a reconceiving of feminism as a movement to end all forms of oppression.

Suppose one agrees that the logic of traditional feminism requires the expansion of feminism to include other social systems of domination (e.g., racism and classism). What warrants the inclusion of nature in these "social systems of domination"? Why must the logic of traditional feminism include the abolition of "naturism" (i.e., the domination or oppression of nonhuman nature) among the "isms" feminism must confront? The conceptual justification for expanding feminism to include ecofeminism is twofold. One basis has already been suggested: by showing that the conceptual connections between the dual dominations of women and nature are located in an oppressive and, at least in Western societies, patriarchal conceptual framework characterized by a logic of domination, ecofeminism explains how and why feminism, conceived as a movement to end sexist oppression, must be expanded and reconceived as also a movement to end naturism. This is made explicit by the following argument C:

(C1) Feminism is a movement to end sexism.

(C2) But Sexism is conceptually linked with naturism (through an oppressive conceptual framework characterized by a logic of domination).

(C3) Thus, Feminism is (also) a movement to end naturism.

Because, ultimately, these connections between sexism and naturism are conceptual—embedded in an oppressive conceptual framework—the logic of traditional feminism leads to the embracement of ecological feminism.

The other justification for reconceiving feminism to include ecofeminism has to do with the concepts of gender and nature. Just as conceptions of gender are socially constructed, so are conceptions of nature. Of course, the claim that women and nature are social constructions does not require anyone to deny that there are actual humans and actual trees, rivers, and plants. It simply implies that how women and nature are conceived is a matter of historical and social reality. These conceptions vary cross-culturally and by historical time

period. As a result, any discussion of the "oppression or domination of nature" involves reference to historically specific forms of social domination of nonhuman nature by humans, just as discussion of the "domination of women" refers to historically specific forms of social domination of women by men. Although I do not argue for it here, an ecofeminist defense of the historical connections between the dominations of women and of nature, claims (B1) and (B2) in argument B, involves showing that within patriarchy the feminization of nature and the naturalization of women have been crucial to the historically successful subordinations of both.[8]

If ecofeminism promises to reconceive traditional feminism in ways which include naturism as a legitimate feminist issue, does ecofeminism also promise to reconceive environmental ethics in ways which are feminist? I think so. This is the subject of the remainder of the paper.

CLIMBING FROM ECOFEMINISM TO ENVIRONMENTAL ETHICS

Many feminists and some environmental ethicists have begun to explore the use of first-person narrative as a way of raising philosophically germane issues in ethics often lost or underplayed in mainstream philosophical ethics. Why is this so? What is it about narrative which makes it a significant resource for theory and practice in feminism and environmental ethics? Even if appeal to first-person narrative is a helpful literary device for describing ineffable experience or a legitimate social science methodology for documenting personal and social history, how is first-person narrative a valuable vehicle of argumentation for ethical decision making and theory building? One fruitful way to begin answering these questions is to ask them of a particular first-person narrative.

Consider the following first-person narrative about rock climbing:

> For my very first rock climbing experience, I chose a somewhat private spot, away from other climbers and on-lookers. After studying "the chimney," I focused all my energy on making it to the top. I climbed with intense determination, using whatever strength and skills

I had to accomplish this challenging feat. By midway I was exhausted and anxious. I couldn't see what to do next—where to put my hands or feet. Growing increasingly more weary as I clung somewhat desperately to the rock, I made a move. It didn't work. I fell. There I was, dangling midair above the rocky ground below, frightened but terribly relieved that the belay rope had held me. I knew I was safe. I took a look up at the climb that remained. I was determined to make it to the top. With renewed confidence and concentration, I finished the climb to the top.

On my second day of climbing, I rappelled down about 200 feet from the top of the Palisades at Lake Superior to just a few feet above the water level. I could see no one—not my belayer, not the other climbers, no one. I unhooked slowly from the rappel rope and took a deep cleansing breath. I looked all around me—really looked—and listened. I heard a cacophony of voices—birds, trickles of water on the rock before me, waves lapping against the rocks below. I closed my eyes and began to feel the rock with my hands—the cracks and crannies, the raised lichen and mosses, the almost imperceptible nubs that might provide a resting place for my fingers and toes when I began to climb. At that moment I was bathed in serenity. I began to talk to the rock in an almost inaudible, child-like way, as if the rock were my friend. I felt an overwhelming sense of gratitude for what it offered me—a chance to know myself and the rock differently, to appreciate unforeseen miracles like the tiny flowers growing in the even tinier cracks in the rock's surface, and to come to know a sense of being in relationship with the natural environment. It felt as if the rock and I were silent conversational partners in a longstanding friendship. I realized then that I had come to care about this cliff which was so different from me, so unmovable and invincible, independent and seemingly indifferent to my presence. I wanted to be with the rock as I climbed. Gone was the determination to conquer the rock, to forcefully impose my will on it; I wanted simply to work respectfully with the rock as I climbed. And as I climbed, that is what I felt. I felt myself *caring* for this rock and feeling thankful that climbing provided the opportunity for me to know it and myself in this new way.

There are at least four reasons why use of such a first-person narrative is important to feminism and environmental ethics. First, such a narrative gives voice to a felt sensitivity often lacking in traditional analytical ethical discourse, viz., a sensitivity to conceiving of oneself as fundamentally "in relationship with" others, including the nonhuman environment. It is a modality which takes relationships themselves seriously. It thereby stands in contrast to a strictly reductionist modality that takes relationships seriously only or primarily because of the nature of the relators or parties to those relationships (e.g., relators conceived as moral agents, right holders, interest carriers, or sentient beings). In the rock-climbing narrative above, it is the climber's relationship with the rock she climbs which takes on special significance—which is itself a locus of value—in addition to whatever moral status or moral considerability she or the rock or any other parties to the relationship may also have.

Second, such a first-person narrative gives expression to a variety of ethical attitudes and behaviors often overlooked or underplayed in mainstream Western ethics, e.g., the difference in attitudes and behaviors toward a rock when one is "making it to the top" and when one thinks of oneself as "friends with" or "caring about" the rock one climbs.[9] These different attitudes and behaviors suggest an ethically germane contrast between two different types of relationship humans or climbers may have toward a rock: an imposed conqueror-type relationship, and an emergent caring-type relationship. This contrast grows out of, and is faithful to, felt, lived experience.

The difference between conquering and caring attitudes and behaviors in relation to the natural environment provides a third reason why the use of first-person narrative is important to feminism and environmental ethics: it provides a way of conceiving of ethics and ethical meaning as emerging out of particular situations moral agents find themselves in, rather than as being imposed on those situations (e.g., as a derivation or instantiation of some predetermined abstract principle or rule). This emergent feature of narrative centralizes the importance of *voice*. When a multiplicity of cross-cultural voices are centralized, narrative is able to give expression to a range of attitudes, values, beliefs, and behaviors which may be overlooked or silenced by imposed ethical meaning and theory. As a reflection of and on felt, lived experiences, the use of narrative in ethics provides a stance from which ethical discourse can be held accountable to the historical, material, and social realities in which moral subjects find themselves.

Lastly, and for our purposes perhaps most importantly, the use of narrative has argumentative significance. Jim Cheney calls attention to this feature of narrative when he claims, "To contextualize ethical deliberation is, in some sense, to provide a narrative or story, from which the solution to the ethical dilemma emerges as the fitting conclusion."[10] Narrative has argumentative force by suggesting what counts as an appropriate conclusion to an ethical situation. One ethical conclusion suggested by the climbing narrative is that what counts as a proper ethical attitude toward mountains and rocks is an attitude of respect and care (whatever that turns out to be or involve), not one of domination and conquest.

In an essay entitled "In and Out of Harm's Way: Arrogance and Love," feminist philosopher Marilyn Frye distinguishes between "arrogant" and "loving" perception as one way of getting at this difference in the ethical attitudes of care and conquest.[11] Frye writes:

> The loving eye is a contrary of the arrogant eye.
>
> The loving eye knows the independence of the other. It is the eye of a seer who knows that nature is indifferent. It is the eye of one who knows that to know the seen, one must consult something other than one's own will and interests and fears and imagination. One must look at the thing. One must look and listen and check and question.
>
> The loving eye is one that pays a certain sort of attention. This attention can require a discipline but *not* a self-denial. The discipline is one of self-knowledge, knowledge of the scope and boundary of the self. . . . In particular, it is a matter of being able to tell one's own interests from those of others and of knowing where one self leaves off and another begins. . . .
>
> The loving eye does not make the object of perception into something edible, does not try to assimilate it, does not reduce it to the size of the seer's desire, fear and imagination, and hence does not have to simplify. It knows the complexity of the other as something which will forever present new things to be known. The science of the loving eye would favor The Complexity Theory of Truth [in contrast to The Simplicity Theory of Truth] and presuppose The Endless Interestingness of the Universe.[12]

According to Frye, the loving eye is not an invasive, coercive eye which annexes others to itself, but one which "knows the complexity of the other as something which will forever present new things to be known."

When one climbs a rock as a conqueror, one climbs with an arrogant eye. When one climbs with a loving eye, one constantly "must look and listen and check and question." One recognizes the rock as something very different, something perhaps totally indifferent to one's own presence, and finds in that difference joyous occasion for celebration. One knows "the boundary of the self," where the self—the "I," the climber—leaves off and the rock begins. There is no fusion of two into one, but a complement of two entities acknowledged as separate, different, independent, yet in relationship; they are in relationship if only because the loving eye is perceiving it, responding to it, noticing it, attending to it.

An ecofeminist perspective about both women and nature involves this shift in attitude from "arrogant perception" to "loving perception" of the nonhuman world. Arrogant perception of nonhumans by humans presupposes and maintains sameness in such a way that it expands the moral community to those beings who are thought to resemble (be like, similar to, or the same as) humans in some morally significant way. Any environmental movement or ethic based on arrogant perception builds a moral hierarchy of beings and assumes some common denominator of moral considerability in virtue of which like beings deserve similar treatment or moral consideration and unlike beings do not. Such environmental ethics are or generate a "unity in sameness." In contrast, "loving perception" presupposes and maintains difference—a distinction between the self and other, between human and at least some nonhumans—in such a way that perception of the other as other is an expression of love for one who/which is recognized at the outset as independent, dissimilar, different. As Maria Lugones says, in loving perception, "Love is seen not as fusion and erasure of difference but as incompatible with them."[13] "Unity in sameness" alone is an erasure of difference.

"Loving perception" of the nonhuman natural world is an attempt to understand what it means for humans to care about the nonhuman world, a world acknowledged as being independent, different, perhaps even indifferent to humans. Humans are different from rocks in important ways, even if they are also both members of some ecological community. A moral community based on loving perception of oneself in relationship with a rock, or with the natural environment as a whole, is one which acknowledges and respects difference, whatever "sameness" also exists.[14] The limits of loving perception are determined only by the limits of one's (e.g., a person's, a community's) ability to respond lovingly (or with appropriate care, trust, or friendship)—whether it is to other humans or to the nonhuman world and elements of it.[15]

If what I have said so far is correct, then there are very different ways to climb a mountain and how one climbs it and how one narrates the experience of climbing it matter ethically. If one climbs with "arrogant perception," with an attitude of "conquer and control," one keeps intact the very sorts of thinking that characterize a logic of domination and an oppressive conceptual framework. Since the oppressive conceptual framework which sanctions the domination of nature is a patriarchal one, one also thereby keeps intact, even if unwittingly, a patriarchal conceptual framework. Because the dismantling of patriarchal conceptual frameworks is a feminist issue, how one climbs a mountain and how one narrates—or tells the story—about the experience of climbing also are feminist issues. In this way, ecofeminism makes visible why, at a conceptual level, environmental ethics is a feminist issue. I turn now to a consideration of ecofeminism as a distinctively feminist and environmental ethic.

ECOFEMINISM AS A FEMINIST AND ENVIRONMENTAL ETHIC

A feminist ethic involves a twofold commitment to critique male bias in ethics wherever it occurs, and to develop ethics which are not male-biased. Sometimes this involves articulation of values (e.g., values of care, appropriate trust, kinship, friendship) often lost or underplayed in mainstream ethics.[16] Sometimes it involves engaging in theory building by pioneering in new directions or by revamping old theories in gender sensitive ways. What makes the critiques of old theories or conceptualizations of new ones "feminist" is that they emerge out of sex–gender analyses and reflect whatever those analyses reveal about gendered experience and gendered social reality.

As I conceive feminist ethics in the pre-feminist present, it rejects attempts to conceive of ethical theory in terms of necessary and sufficient conditions, because it assumes that there is no essence (in the sense of some transhistorical, universal, absolute abstraction) of feminist ethics. While attempts to formulate joint necessary and sufficient conditions of a feminist ethic are unfruitful, nonetheless, there are some necessary conditions, what I prefer to call "boundary conditions," of a feminist ethic. These boundary conditions clarify some of the minimal conditions of a feminist ethic without suggesting that feminist ethics has some ahistorical essence. They are like the boundaries of a quilt or collage. They delimit the territory of the piece without dictating what the interior, the design, the actual pattern of the piece looks like. Because the actual design of the quilt emerges from the multiplicity of voices of women in a cross-cultural context, the design will change over time. It is not something static.

What are some of the boundary conditions of a feminist ethic? First, nothing can become part of a feminist ethic—can be part of the quilt—that promotes sexism, racism, classism, or any other "isms" of social domination. Of course, people may disagree about what counts as a sexist act, racist attitude, classist behavior. What counts as sexism, racism, or classism may vary cross-culturally. Still, because a feminist ethic aims at eliminating sexism and sexist bias, and (as I have already shown) sexism is intimately connected in conceptualization and in practice to racism, classism, and naturism, a feminist ethic must be anti-sexist, anti-racist, anti-classist, anti-naturist and opposed to any "ism" which presupposes or advances a logic of domination.

Second, a feminist ethic is a *contextualist* ethic. A contextualist ethic is one which sees ethical discourse and practice as emerging from the voices of people located in different historical circumstances. A contextualist ethic is properly viewed as a collage or mosaic, a tapestry of voices that emerges out of felt experiences. Like any collage or mosaic, the point is not to have one picture based on a unity of voices, but a pattern which emerges out of the very different voices of people located in different circumstances. When a contextualist ethic is feminist, it gives central place to the voices of women.

Third, since a feminist ethic gives central significance to the diversity of women's voices, a feminist ethic must be structurally pluralistic rather than unitary or reductionistic. It rejects the assumption that there is "one voice" in terms of which ethical values, beliefs, attitudes, and conduct can be assessed.

Fourth, a feminist ethic reconceives ethical theory as theory in process which will change over time. Like all theory, a feminist ethic is based on some generalizations.[17] Nevertheless, the generalizations associated with it are themselves a pattern of voices within which the different voices emerging out of concrete and alternative descriptions of ethical situations have meaning. The coherence of a feminist theory so conceived is given within a historical and conceptual context, i.e., within a set of historical, socioeconomic circumstances (including circumstances of race, class, age, and affectional orientation) and within a set of basic beliefs, values, attitudes, and assumptions about the world.

Fifth, because a feminist ethic is contextualist, structurally pluralistic, and "in-process," one way to evaluate the claims of a feminist ethic is in terms of their inclusiveness: those claims (voices, patterns of voices) are morally and epistemologically favored (preferred, better, less partial, less biased) which are more inclusive of the felt experiences and perspectives of oppressed persons. The condition of inclusiveness requires and ensures that the diverse voices of women (as oppressed persons) will be given legitimacy in ethical theory building. It thereby helps to minimize empirical bias, e.g., bias rising from faulty or false generalizations based on stereotyping, too small a sample size, or a skewed sample. It does so by ensuring that any generalizations which are made about ethics and ethical decision making include—indeed cohere with—the patterned voices of women.[18]

Sixth, a feminist ethic makes no attempt to provide an "objective" point of view, since it assumes that in contemporary culture there really is no such point of view. As such, it does not claim to be "unbiased" in the sense of "value-neutral" or "objective." However, it does assume that whatever bias it has as an ethic centralizing the voices of oppressed persons is a better bias—"better" because it is more inclusive and therefore less partial—than those which exclude those voices.[19]

Seventh, a feminist ethic provides a central place for values typically unnoticed, underplayed, or misrepresented in traditional ethics, e.g., values of care, love, friendship, and appropriate trust.[20] Again, it need not do this at the exclusion of considerations of rights, rules, or utility. There may be many contexts in which talk of rights or of utility is useful or appropriate. For instance, in contracts or property relationships, talk of rights may be useful and appropriate. In deciding what is cost effective or advantageous to the most people, talk of utility may be useful and appropriate. In a feminist *qua* contextualist ethic, whether or not such talk is useful or appropriate depends on the context; other values (e.g., values of care, trust, friendship) are not viewed as reducible to or captured solely in terms of such talk.

Eighth, a feminist ethic also involves a reconception of what it is to be human and what it is for humans to engage in ethical decision making, since it rejects as either meaningless or currently untenable any gender-free or gender-neutral description of humans, ethics, and ethical decision making. It thereby rejects what Alison Jaggar calls "abstract individualism," i.e., the position that it is possible to identify a human essence or human nature that exists independently of any particular historical context.[21] Humans and human moral conduct are properly understood essentially (and not merely accidentally) in terms of networks or webs of historical and concrete relationships.

All the props are now in place for seeing how ecofeminism provides the framework for a distinctively feminist and environmental ethic. It is a feminism that critiques male bias wherever it occurs in ethics (including environmental ethics) and aims at providing an ethic (including an environmental ethic) which is not male biased—and it does so in a way that satisfies the preliminary boundary conditions of a feminist ethic.

First, ecofeminism is quintessentially anti-naturist. Its anti-naturism consists in the rejection of any way of thinking about or acting toward nonhuman nature that reflects a logic, values, or attitude of domination. Its anti-naturist, anti-sexist, anti-racist, anti-classist (and so forth, for all other "isms" of social domination) stance forms the outer boundary of the quilt: nothing gets on the quilt which is naturist, sexist, racist, classist, and so forth.

Second, ecofeminism is a contextualist ethic. It involves a shift *from* a conception of ethics as primarily a matter of rights, rules, or principles predetermined and applied in specific cases to entities viewed as competitors in the contest of moral standing, *to* a conception of ethics as growing out of what Jim Cheney calls "defining relationships," i.e., relationships conceived in some sense as defining who one is. As a contextualist ethic, it is not that rights, or rules, or principles are not relevant or important. Clearly they are in certain contexts and for certain purposes. It is just that what makes them relevant or important is that those to whom they apply are entities in relationship with others.

Ecofeminism also involves an ethical shift from granting moral consideration to nonhumans exclusively on the grounds of some similarity they share with humans (e.g., rationality, interests, moral agency, sentiency, rightholder status) to "a highly contextual account to see clearly what a human being is and what the nonhuman world might be, morally speaking, for human beings."[22] For an ecofeminist, how a moral agent is in relationship to another becomes of central significance, not simply that a moral agent is a moral agent or is bound by rights, duties, virtue, or utility to act in a certain way.

Third, ecofeminism is structurally pluralistic in that it presupposes and maintains difference—difference among humans as well as between humans and at least some elements of nonhuman nature. Thus, while ecofeminism denies the "nature/culture" split, it affirms that humans are both members of an ecological community (in some respects) and different from it (in other respects). Ecofeminism's attention to relationships and community is not, therefore, an erasure of difference but a respectful acknowledgment of it.

Fourth, ecofeminism reconceives theory as theory in process. It focuses on patterns of meaning which emerge, for instance, from the storytelling and first-person narratives of women (and others) who deplore the twin dominations of women and nature. The use of narrative is one way to ensure that the content of the ethic—the pattern of the quilt—may/will change over time, as the historical and material realities of women's lives change and as more is learned about women–nature connections and the destruction of the nonhuman world.

Fifth, ecofeminism is inclusivist. It emerges from the voices of women who experience the harmful domination of nature and the way that domination is tied to their domination as women. It emerges from listening to the voices of indigenous peoples such as Native Americans who have been dislocated from their land and have witnessed the attendant undermining of such values as appropriate reciprocity, sharing, and kinship that characterize traditional Indian culture. It emerges from listening to voices of those who, like Nathan Hare, critique traditional approaches to environmental ethics as white and bourgeois, and as failing to address issues of "black ecology" and the "ecology" of the inner city and urban spaces.[23] It also emerges out of the voices of Chipko women who see the destruction of "earth, soil, and water" as intimately connected with their own inability to survive economically.[24] With its emphasis on inclusivity and difference, ecofeminism provides a framework for recognizing that what counts as ecology and what counts as appropriate conduct toward both human and non-human environments is largely a matter of context.

Sixth, as a feminism, ecofeminism makes no attempt to provide an "objective" point of view. It is a social ecology. It recognizes the twin dominations of women and nature as social problems rooted both in very concrete, historical, socioeconomic circumstances and in oppressive patriarchal conceptual frameworks which maintain and sanction these circumstances.

Seventh, ecofeminism makes a central place for values of care, love, friendship, trust, and appropriate reciprocity—values that presuppose that our relationships to others are central to our understanding of who we are.[25] It thereby gives voice to the sensitivity that in climbing a mountain, one is doing something in relationship with an "other," an "other" whom one can come to care about and treat respectfully.

Lastly, an ecofeminist ethic involves a reconception of what it means to be human, and in what human ethical behavior consists. Ecofeminism denies abstract individualism. Humans are who we are in large part by virtue of the historical and social contexts and the relationships we are in, including our relationships with nonhuman nature. Relationships are not something extrinsic to who we are, not an "add on" feature of human nature; they play an essential role in shaping what it is to be human. Relationships of humans to the nonhuman environment are, in part, constitutive of what it is to be a human.

By making visible the interconnections among the dominations of women and nature, ecofeminism shows that both are feminist issues and that explicit acknowledgment of both is vital to any responsible environmental ethic. Feminism must embrace ecological feminism if it is to end the domination of women because the domination of women is tied conceptually and historically to the domination of nature.

A responsible environmental ethic also must embrace feminism. Otherwise, even the seemingly most revolutionary, liberational, and holistic ecological ethic will fail to take seriously the interconnected dominations of nature and women that are so much a part of the historical legacy and conceptual framework that sanctions the exploitation of nonhuman nature. Failure to make visible these interconnected, twin dominations results in an inaccurate account of how it is that nature has been and continues to be dominated and exploited and produces an environmental ethic that lacks the depth necessary to be truly inclusive of the realities of persons who at least in dominant Western culture have been intimately tied with that exploitation, viz., women. Whatever else can be said in favor of such holistic ethics, a failure to make visible ecofeminist insights into the common denominators of the twin oppressions of women and nature is to perpetuate, rather than overcome, the source of that oppression.

This last point deserves further attention. It may be objected that as long as the end result is "the same"— the development of an environmental ethic which does not emerge out of or reinforce an oppressive conceptual framework—it does not matter whether that ethic (or the ethic endorsed in getting there) is feminist or not. Hence, it simply is not the case that any adequate environmental ethic must be feminist. My argument, in contrast, has been that it does matter, and for three important reasons. First, there is the scholarly issue of accurately representing historical reality, and that, ecofeminists claim, requires acknowledging the historical feminization of nature and naturalization of women as part of the exploitation of nature. Second, I have shown that the conceptual connections between the domination of women and the domination of nature are located in an oppressive and, at least in Western societies, patriarchal conceptual framework characterized by a logic of domination. Thus, I have shown that failure to notice the nature of this connection leaves at best an incomplete, inaccurate, and partial account of what is required of a conceptually adequate environmental ethic. An ethic which does not acknowledge this is simply not the same as one that does, whatever else the similarities between them. Third, the claim that, in contemporary culture, one can have an adequate environmental ethic which is not feminist assumes that, in contemporary culture, the label feminist does not add anything crucial to the nature or description of environmental ethics. I have shown that at least in contemporary culture this is false, for the word feminist currently helps to clarify just how the domination of nature is conceptually linked to patriarchy and, hence, how the liberation of nature, is conceptually linked to the termination of patriarchy. Thus, because it has critical bite in contemporary culture, it serves as an important reminder that in contemporary sex-gendered, raced, classed, and naturist culture, an unlabeled position functions as a privileged and "unmarked" position. That is, without the addition of the word *feminist*, one presents environmental ethics as if it has no bias, including male-gender bias, which is just what ecofeminists deny: failure to notice the connections between the twin oppressions of women and nature *is* male-gender bias.

One of the goals of feminism is the eradication of all oppressive sex–gender (and related race, class, age, affectional preference) categories and the creation of a world in which *difference does not breed domination*— say, the world of 4001. If in 4001 an "adequate environmental ethic" is a "feminist environmental ethic," the word *feminist* may then be redundant and unnecessary.

However, this is not 4001, and in terms of the current historical and conceptual reality the dominations of nature and of women are intimately connected. Failure to notice or make visible that connection in 1990 perpetuates the mistaken (and privileged) view that "environmental ethics" is not a feminist issue, and that *feminist* adds nothing to environmental ethics.

CONCLUSION

I have argued in this paper that ecofeminism provides a framework for a distinctively feminist and environmental ethic. Ecofeminism grows out of the felt and theorized about connections between the domination of women and the domination of nature. As a contextualist ethic, ecofeminism refocuses environmental ethics on what nature might mean, morally speaking, for humans, and on how the relational attitudes of humans to others—humans as well as nonhumans—sculpt both what it is to be human and the nature and ground of human responsibilities to the nonhuman environment. Part of what this refocusing does is to take seriously the voices of women and other oppressed persons in the construction of that ethic.

A Sioux elder once told me a story about his son. He sent his seven-year-old son to live with the child's grandparents on a Sioux reservation so that he could "learn the Indian ways." Part of what the grandparents taught the son was how to hunt and kill the four leggeds of the forest. As I heard the story, the boy was taught, "to shoot your four-legged brother in his hind area, slowing it down but not killing it. Then, take the four legged's head in your hands, and look into his eyes. The eyes are where all the suffering is. Look into your brother's eyes and feel his pain. Then, take your knife and cut the four-legged under his chin, here, on his neck, so that he dies quickly. And as you do, ask your brother, the four-legged, for forgiveness for what you do. Offer also a prayer of thanks to your four-legged kin for offering his body to you just now, when you need food to eat and clothing to wear. And promise the four-legged that you will put yourself back into the earth when you die, to become nourishment for the earth, and for the sister flowers, and for the brother deer. It is appropriate that you should offer this blessing for the four-legged and, in due time,

reciprocate in turn with your body in this way, as the four-legged gives life to you for your survival." As I reflect upon that story, I am struck by the power of the environmental ethic that grows out of and takes seriously narrative, context, and such values and relational attitudes as care, loving perception, and appropriate reciprocity, and doing what is appropriate in a given situation—however that notion of appropriateness eventually gets filled out. I am also struck by what one is able to see, once one begins to explore some of the historical and conceptual connections between the dominations of women and of nature. A re-conceiving and re-visioning of both feminism and environmental ethics, is, I think, the power and promise of ecofeminism.

NOTES

1. Francoise d'Eaubonne, *Le Feminisme ou la Mort* (Paris: Pierre Horay, 1974).

2. I discuss this in my paper, "Toward an Ecofeminist Ethic."

3. Murray Bookchin, "Social Ecology versus 'Deep Ecology'", in *Green Perspectives: Newsletter of the Green Program Project*, no. 4–5 (Summer 1987): 9.

4. It may be that in contemporary Western society, which is so thoroughly structured by categories of gender, race, class, age, and affectional orientation, that there simply is no meaningful notion of "value-hierarchical thinking" which does not function in an oppressive context. For purposes of this paper, I leave that question open.

5. I make no attempt here to defend the historically sanctioned truth of these premises.

6. See, e.g., Bell Hooks, *Feminist Theory: From Margin to Center* (Boston: South End Press, 1984), pp. 51–52.

7. Maria Lugones, "Playfulness, 'World-Travelling,' and Loving Perception," *Hypatia* 2 (Summer 1987): 3.

8. See, e.g., Gray, *Green Paradise Lost*; Griffin, *Women and Nature*; Merchant, *The Death of Nature*; and Ruether, *New Woman/New Earth*.

9. It is interesting to note that the image of being friends with the Earth is one which cytogeneticist Barbara McClintock uses when she describes the importance of having "a feeling for the organism," "listening to the material [in this case the corn

plant]," in one's work as a scientist. See Evelyn Fox Keller, "Women, Science, and Popular Mythology," in *Machina Ex Dea: Feminist Perspectives on Technology*, ed. Joan Rothschild (New York: Pergamon Press, 1983), and Evelyn Fox Keller, *A Feeling For the Organism: The Life and Work of Barbara McClintock* (San Francisco: W. H. Freeman, 1983).

10. Cheney, "Eco-Feminism and Deep Ecology," 144.

11. Marilyn Frye, "In and Out of Harm's Way: Arrogance and Love," *The Politics of Reality* (Trumansburg, New York: The Crossing Press, 1983), pp. 66–72.

12. Ibid., pp. 75–76.

13. Maria Lugones, "Playfulness," p. 3.

14. Cheney makes a similar point in "Eco-Feminism and Deep Ecology," p. 140.

15. Ibid., p. 138.

16. This account of a feminist ethic draws on my "Toward an Ecofeminist Ethic."

17. Marilyn Frye makes this point in her illuminating paper, "The Possibility of Feminist Theory," read at the American Philosophical Association Central Division in Chicago, 1986. My discussion of feminist theory is inspired largely by that paper and by Kathryn Addelson's paper "Moral Revolution," in *Women and Values: Reading in Recent Feminist Philosophy*, ed. Marilyn Pearsall (Belmont: Wadsworth, 1986) pp. 291–309.

18. Notice that the standard of inclusiveness does not exclude the voices of men. It is just that those voices must cohere with the voices of women.

19. For a more in-depth discussion of the notions of impartiality and bias, see my paper, "Critical Thinking and Feminism," *Informal Logic* 10, no. 1 (Winter 1988): 31–44.

20. The burgeoning literature on these values is noteworthy. See, e.g., Carol Gilligan, *In a Different Voice: Psychological Theories and Women's Development* (Cambridge: Harvard University Press, 1982); *Mapping the Moral Domain: A Contribution of Women's Thinking to Psychological Theory and Education*, ed. Carol Gilligan, Janie Victoria Ward, and Jill McLean Taylor, with Betty Bardige (Cambridge: Harvard University Press, 1988); Nel Noddings, *Caring: A Feminine Approach to Ethics and Moral Education* (Berkeley: University of California Press, 1984); Maria Lugones and Elizabeth V. Spelman, "Have We Got a Theory for You! Feminist Theory, Cultural Imperialism, and the Women's Voice," *Women's Studies International Forum* 6 (1983): 573–81; Maria Lugones, "Playfulness"; Annette C. Baier, "What Do Women Want in a Moral Theory?" *Nous* 19 (1985): 53–63.

21. Alison Jaggar, *Feminist Politics and Human Nature* (Totowa: Rowman and Allanheld, 1980): pp. 42–44.

22. Cheney, "Eco-Feminism and Deep Ecology," p. 144.

23. Nathan Hare, "Black Ecology," in *Environmental Ethics*, ed. K. S. Shrader-Frechette (Pacific Grove, Calif.: Boxwood Press, 1981), pp. 229–36.

24. For an ecofeminist discussion of the Chipko movement, see my "Toward an Ecofeminist Ethic," and Shiva's *Staying Alive*.

25. See Cheney, "Eco-Feminism and Deep Ecology," p. 122.

1 0

LAND

GARRETT HARDIN

THE TRAGEDY OF THE COMMONS

In economic affairs, *The Wealth of Nations* popularized the "invisible hand," the idea that an individual who "intends only his own gain," is, as it were, "led by an invisible hand to promote . . . the public interest."[1] Adam Smith did not assert that this was invariably true, and perhaps neither did any of his followers. But he contributed to a dominant tendency of thought that has ever since interfered with positive action based on rational analysis, namely, the tendency to assume that decisions reached individually will, in fact, be the best decisions for an entire society. If this assumption . . . is not correct, we need to reexamine our individual freedoms to see which ones are defensible.

TRAGEDY OF FREEDOM IN A COMMONS

The rebuttal to the invisible hand in population control is to be found in a scenario first sketched in a little-known pamphlet[2] in 1833 by a mathematical amateur named William Forster Lloyd (1794–1852). We may well call it "the tragedy of the commons," using the word "tragedy" as the philosopher Whitehead used it:[3] "The essence of dramatic tragedy is not unhappiness. It resides in the solemnity of the remorseless working of things." He then goes on to say, "This inevitableness of destiny can only be illustrated in terms of human life by incidents which in fact involve unhappiness. For it is only by them that the futility of escape can be made evident in the drama."

The tragedy of the commons develops in this way. Picture a pasture open to all. It is to be expected that each herdsman will try to keep as many cattle as possible on the commons. Such an arrangement may work reasonably satisfactorily for centuries because tribal wars, poaching, and disease keep the numbers of both man and beast well below the carrying capacity of the land. Finally, however, comes the day of reckoning,

This reading is adapted from Garrett Hardin, "The Tragedy of the Commons," Science 162, no. 3859 (1968): 1243–1248.

that is, the day when the long-desired goal of social stability becomes a reality. At this point, the inherent logic of the commons remorselessly generates tragedy.

As a rational being, each herdsman seeks to maximize his gain. Explicitly or implicitly, more or less consciously, he asks, "What is the utility *to me* of adding one more animal to my herd?" This utility has one negative and one positive component.

1. The positive component is a function of the increment of one animal. Since the herdsman receives all the proceeds from the sale of the additional animal, the positive utility is nearly +1.
2. The negative component is a function of the additional overgrazing created by one more animal. Since, however, the effects of overgrazing are shared by all the herdsmen, the negative utility for any particular decision-making herdsman is only a fraction of –1.

Adding together the component partial utilities, the rational herdsman concludes that the only sensible course for him to pursue is to add another animal to his herd. And another; and another.... But this is the conclusion reached by each and every rational herdsman sharing a commons. Therein is the tragedy. Each man is locked into a system that compels him to increase his herd without limit—in a world that is limited. Ruin is the destination toward which all men rush, each pursuing his own best interest in a society that believes in the freedom of the commons. Freedom in a commons brings ruin to all.

Some would say that this is a platitude. Would that it were! In a sense, it was learned thousands of years ago, but natural selection favors the forces of psychological denial.[4] The individual benefits as an individual from his ability to deny the truth even though society as a whole, of which he is a part, suffers.

Education can counteract the natural tendency to do the wrong thing, but the inexorable succession of generations requires that the basis for this knowledge be constantly refreshed.

A simple incident that occurred a few years ago in Leominster, Massachusetts, shows how perishable the knowledge is. During the Christmas shopping season the parking meters downtown were covered with plastic bags that bore tags reading: "Do not open until

after Christmas. Free parking courtesy of the mayor and city council." In other words, facing the prospect of an increased demand for already scarce space, the city fathers reinstituted the system of the commons. (Cynically, we suspect that they gained more votes than they lost by this retrogressive act.)

In an approximate way, the logic of the commons has been understood for a long time, perhaps since the discovery of agriculture or the invention of private property in real estate. But it is understood mostly only in special cases which are not sufficiently generalized. Even at this late date, cattlemen leasing national land on the western ranges demonstrate no more than an ambivalent understanding, in constantly pressuring federal authorities to increase the head count to the point where overgrazing produces erosion and weed-dominance. Likewise, the oceans of the world continue to suffer from the survival of the philosophy of the commons. Maritime nations still respond automatically to the shibboleth of the "freedom of the seas." Professing to believe in the "inexhaustible resources of the oceans," they bring species after species of fish and whales closer to extinction.[5]

The National Parks present another instance of the working out of the tragedy of the commons. At present, they are open to all, without limit. The parks themselves are limited in extent—there is only one Yosemite Valley—whereas population seems to grow without limit. The values that visitors seek in the parks are steadily eroded. Plainly, we must soon cease to treat the parks as commons or they will be of no value to anyone.

What shall we do? We have several options. We might sell them off as private property. We might keep them as public property, but allocate the right to enter them. The allocation might be on the basis of wealth, by the use of an auction system. It might be on the basis of merit, as defined by some agreed-upon standards. It might be by lottery. Or it might be on a first-come, first-served basis, administered to long queues. These, I think, are all the reasonable possibilities. They are all objectionable. But we must choose—or acquiesce in the destruction of the commons that we call our National Parks.

POLLUTION

In a reverse way, the tragedy of the commons reappears in problems of pollution. Here it is not a question of taking something out of the commons, but of putting something in—sewage, or chemical, radioactive, and heat wastes into water; noxious and dangerous fumes into the air, and distracting and unpleasant advertising signs into the line of sight. The calculations of utility are much the same as before. The rational man finds that his share of the cost of the wastes he discharges into the commons is less than the cost of purifying his wastes before releasing them. Since this is true for everyone, we are locked into a system of "fouling our own nest," so long as we behave only as independent, rational, free-enterprisers.

The tragedy of the commons as a food basket is averted by private property, or something formally like it. But the air and waters surrounding us cannot readily be fenced, and so the tragedy of the commons as a cesspool must be prevented by different means, by coercive laws or taxing devices that make it cheaper for the polluter to treat his pollutants than to discharge them untreated. We have not progressed as far with the solution of this problem as we have with the first. Indeed, our particular concept of private property, which deters us from exhausting the positive resources of the earth, favors pollution. The owner of a factory on the bank of a stream—whose property extends to the middle of the stream, often has difficulty seeing why it is not his natural right to muddy the waters flowing past his door. The law, always behind the times, requires elaborate stitching and fitting to adapt it to this newly perceived aspect of the commons.

The pollution problem is a consequence of population. It did not much matter how a lonely American frontiersman disposed of his waste. "Flowing water purifies itself every 10 miles," my grandfather used to say, and the myth was near enough to the truth when he was a boy, for there were not too many people. But as population became denser, the natural chemical and biological recycling processes became overloaded, calling for a redefinition of property rights.

HOW TO LEGISLATE TEMPERANCE?

Analysis of the pollution problem as a function of population density uncovers a not generally recognized principle of morality, namely: *the morality of an act is a function of the state of the system at the time it is performed.*[6] Using the commons as a cesspool does not harm the general public under frontier conditions, because there is no public; the same behavior in a metropolis is unbearable. A hundred and fifty years ago a plainsman could kill an American bison, cut out only the tongue for his dinner, and discard the rest of the animal. He was not in any important sense being wasteful. Today, with only a few thousand bison left, we would be appalled at such behavior.

In passing, it is worth noting that the morality of an act cannot be determined from a photograph. One does not know whether a man killing an elephant or setting fire to the grassland is harming others until one knows the total system in which his act appears. "One picture is worth a thousand words," said an ancient Chinese; but it may take 10,000 words to validate it. It is as tempting to ecologists as it is to reformers in general to try to persuade others by way of the photographic shortcut. But the essence of an argument cannot be photographed: it must be presented rationally—in words.

That morality is system-sensitive escaped the attention of most codifiers of ethics in the past. "Thou shalt not . . ." is the form of traditional ethical directives which make no allowance for particular circumstances. The laws of our society follow the pattern of ancient ethics, and therefore are poorly suited to governing a complex, crowded, changeable world. Our epicyclic solution is to augment statutory law with administrative law. Since it is practically impossible to spell out all the conditions under which it is safe to burn trash in the back yard or to run an automobile without smog-control, by law we delegate the details to bureaus. The result is administrative law, which is rightly feared for an ancient reason—*Quis custodiet ipsos custodes?*—"Who shall watch the watchers themselves?" John Adams said that we must have "a government of laws and not men." Bureau administrators, trying to evaluate the morality of acts in the total system, are singularly liable to corruption, producing a government by men, not laws.

Prohibition is easy to legislate (though not necessarily to enforce); but how do we legislate temperance? Experience indicates that it can be accomplished best through the mediation of administrative law. We limit possibilities unnecessarily if we suppose that the sentiment of *Quis custodiet* denies us the use of administrative law. We should rather retain the phrase as a perpetual reminder of fearful dangers we cannot avoid. The great challenge facing us now is to invent the corrective feedbacks that are needed to keep custodians honest. We must find ways to legitimate the needed authority of both the custodians and the corrective feedbacks.

. . .

PATHOGENIC EFFECTS OF CONSCIENCE

If we ask a man who is exploiting a commons to desist "in the name of conscience," what are we saying to him? What does he hear?—not only at the moment but also in the wee small hours of the night when, half asleep, he remembers not merely the words we used but also the nonverbal communication cues we gave him unawares? Sooner or later, consciously or subconsciously, he senses that he has received two communications, and that they are contradictory: (i) (intended communication) "If you don't do as we ask, we will openly condemn you for not acting like a responsible citizen"; (ii) (the unintended communication) "If you do behave as we ask, we will secretly condemn you for a simpleton who can be shamed into standing aside while the rest of us exploit the commons."

. . .

When we use the word responsibility in the absence of substantial sanctions are we not trying to browbeat a free man in a commons into acting against his own interest? Responsibility is a verbal counterfeit for a substantial *quid pro quo*. It is an attempt to get something for nothing.

If the word responsibility is to be used at all, I suggest that it be in the sense Charles Frankel uses it.[7] "Responsibility," says this philosopher, "is the product of definite social arrangements." Notice that Frankel calls for social arrangements—not propaganda.

MUTUAL COERCION MUTUALLY AGREED UPON

The social arrangements that produce responsibility are arrangements that create coercion, of some sort. Consider bank-robbing. The man who takes money from a bank acts as if the bank were a commons. How do we prevent such action? Certainly not by trying to control his behavior solely by a verbal appeal to his sense of responsibility. Rather than rely on propaganda we follow Frankel's lead and insist that a bank is not a commons; we seek the definite social arrangements that will keep it from becoming a commons. That we thereby infringe on the freedom of would-be robbers we neither deny nor regret.

The morality of bank-robbing is particularly easy to understand because we accept complete prohibition of this activity. We are willing to say "Thou shalt not rob banks," without providing for exceptions. But temperance also can be created by coercion. Taxing is a good coercive device. To keep downtown shoppers temperate in their use of parking space we introduce parking meters for short periods, and traffic fines for longer ones. We need not actually forbid a citizen to park as long as he wants to; we need merely make it increasingly expensive for him to do so. Not prohibition, but carefully biased options are what we offer him. A Madison Avenue man might call this persuasion; I prefer the greater candor of the word coercion.

Coercion is a dirty word to most liberals now, but it need not forever be so. As with the four-letter words, its dirtiness can be cleansed away by exposure to the light, by saying it over and over without apology or embarrassment. To many, the word coercion implies arbitrary decisions of distant and irresponsible bureaucrats; but this is not a necessary part of its meaning. The only kind of coercion I recommend is mutual coercion, mutually agreed upon by the majority of the people affected.

To say that we mutually agree to coercion is not to say that we are required to enjoy it, or even to pretend we enjoy it. Who enjoys taxes? We all grumble about them. But we accept compulsory taxes because we recognize that voluntary taxes would favor the conscienceless. We institute and (grumblingly) support taxes and other coercive devices to escape the horror of the commons.

An alternative to the commons need not be perfectly just to be preferable. With real estate and other material goods, the alternative we have chosen is the institution of private property coupled with legal inheritance. Is this system perfectly just? As a genetically trained biologist I deny that it is. It seems to me that, if there are to be differences in individual inheritance, legal possession should be perfectly correlated with biological inheritance—that those who are biologically more fit to be the custodians of property and power should legally inherit more. But genetic recombination continually makes a mockery of the doctrine of "like father, like son" implicit in our laws of legal inheritance. An idiot can inherit millions, and a trust fund can keep his estate intact. We must admit that our legal system of private property plus inheritance is unjust— but we put up with it because we are not convinced, at the moment, that anyone has invented a better system. The alternative of the commons is too horrifying to contemplate. Injustice is preferable to total ruin.

It is one of the peculiarities of the warfare between reform and the status quo that it is thoughtlessly governed by a double standard. Whenever a reform measure is proposed it is often defeated when its opponents triumphantly discover a flaw in it. As Kingsley Davis has pointed out,[8] worshippers of the status quo sometimes imply that no reform is possible without unanimous agreement, an implication contrary to historical fact. As nearly as I can make out, automatic rejection of proposed reforms is based on one of two unconscious assumptions: (i) that the status quo is perfect; or (ii) that the choice we face is between reform and no action; if the proposed reform is imperfect, we presumably should take no action at all, while we wait for a perfect proposal.

But we can never do nothing. That which we have done for thousands of years is also action. It also produces evils. Once we are aware that the status quo is action, we can then compare its discoverable advantages and disadvantages with the predicted advantages and disadvantages of the proposed reform, discounting as best we can for our lack of experience. On the basis of such a comparison, we can make a rational decision which will not involve the unworkable assumption that only perfect systems are tolerable.

RECOGNITION OF NECESSITY

Perhaps the simplest summary of this analysis of man's population problems is this: the commons, if justifiable at all, is justifiable only under conditions of low-population density. As the human population has increased, the commons has had to be abandoned in one aspect after another.

First we abandoned the commons in food gathering, enclosing farm land and restricting pastures and hunting and fishing areas. These restrictions are still not complete throughout the world.

Somewhat later we saw that the commons as a place for waste disposal would also have to be abandoned. Restrictions on the disposal of domestic sewage are widely accepted in the Western world; we are still struggling to close the commons to pollution by automobiles, factories, insecticide sprayers, fertilizing operations, and atomic energy installations.

In a still more embryonic state is our recognition of the evils of the commons in matters of pleasure. There is almost no restriction on the propagation of sound waves in the public medium. The shopping public is assaulted with mindless music, without its consent. Our government is paying out billions of dollars to create supersonic transport which will disturb 50,000 people for every one person who is whisked from coast to coast 3 hours faster. Advertisers muddy the airwaves of radio and television and pollute the view of travelers. We are a long way from outlawing the commons in matters of pleasure. Is this because our Puritan inheritance makes us view pleasure as something of a sin, and pain (that is, the pollution of advertising) as the sign of virtue?

Every new enclosure of the commons involves the infringement of somebody's personal liberty. Infringements made in the distant past are accepted because no contemporary complains of a loss. It is the newly proposed infringements that we vigorously oppose; cries of "rights" and "freedom" fill the air. But what does "freedom" mean? When men mutually agreed to pass laws against robbing, mankind became more free, not less so. Individuals locked into the logic of the commons are free only to bring on universal ruin; once they see the necessity of mutual coercion, they become free to pursue other goals. I believe it was Hegel who said, "Freedom is the recognition of necessity."

NOTES

1. Smith, A., *The Wealth of Nations* 423 (1937).
2. W. F. Lloyd, *Two Lectures on the Checks to Population*, excerpt, in G. Hardin, ed. *Population, Evolution, and Birth Control* (Freeman, San Francisco, 1964), p. 37.

3. A. N. Whitehead, *Science and the Modern World* 17 (1948).

4. G. Hardin, *Population, Evolution, and Birth Control* (Freeman, San Francisco, 1964) p. 54.

5. S. McVay, *Scientific American* **216** (No. 8) 13 (1966).

6. J. Fletcher, *Situation Ethics* (Westminster, Philadelphia, 1966).

7. C. Frankel, *The Case for Modern Man* (Harper, New York, 1955), p. 203.

8. J. D. Roslansky, *Genetics and the Future of Man* 177 (Appleton–Century–Crofts, New York, 1966).

THE INSTITUTION OF PROPERTY

The evolution of property law is driven by an ongoing search for ways to internalize what economists call externalities: positive externalities associated with productive effort and negative externalities associated with misuse of commonly held resources.[1] If all goes well, property law enables would-be producers to enjoy the benefits of productive effort. It also enables people to insulate themselves from external costs associated with activities around the neighborhood. Property law is not perfect. To further reduce external costs that neighbors might otherwise impose on each other, people resort to nuisance and zoning laws, regulatory agencies, and so on, all with a view to supplementing and perfecting the critical role that property law plays in minimizing external costs.

Philosophers speak of the ideal of society as a cooperative venture for mutual advantage. To be a cooperative venture for mutual advantage, though, society must first be a setting in which mutually advantageous interaction is possible. In other words, borrowing a term from game theory, society must be a positive sum game. What determines the extent to which society is a positive sum game? This essay explains how property institutions convert negative-sum games to positive-sum games, setting the stage for society's flourishing as a cooperative venture.

The term "property rights" is used to refer to a bundle of rights that could include rights to sell, lend, bequeath, and so on. In what follows, I use the phrase to refer primarily to the right of owners to exclude nonowners.[2] Private owners have the right to exclude nonowners, but the right to exclude is a feature of property rights in general rather than the defining feature of private ownership in particular.[3] The National Park Service claims a right to exclude. Communes claim a right to exclude nonmembers. This essay does not settle which kind or which mix of public and private property institutions is best. Instead, it asks how we could justify *any* institution that recognizes a right to exclude.

I. ORIGINAL APPROPRIATION: THE PROBLEM

The right to exclude presents a philosophical problem. Consider how full-blooded rights differ from mere liberties. My being at liberty to plant a garden means my planting a garden is permitted. That leaves open the possibility of you being at liberty to interfere with my gardening as you see fit. Thus, mere liberties are not full-blooded rights. When I stake a claim to a piece of land, though, I claim to be changing other people's liberties—canceling them somehow—so that other people no longer are at liberty to use the land without my permission. To say I have a right to the land is to say I have a right to exclude.

From where could such rights come? There must have been a time when no one had a right to exclude. Everyone had liberties regarding the land, but not rights. (Perhaps this does not seem obvious, but if no one owns the land, no one has a right to exclude. If no one has a right to exclude, everyone has liberties.) How, then, did we get from each person having a liberty to someone having an exclusive right to the land? What justifies original appropriation, that is, staking a claim to previously unowned resources?

To justify a claim to unowned land, people need not make as strong a case as would be needed to justify confiscating land already owned by someone else. Specifically, since there is no prior owner in original appropriation cases, there is no one from whom one can or needs to get consent. What, then, must a person do? Locke's idea was that any residual (perhaps need-based) communal claim to the land could be met if a person could appropriate it without prejudice to other people, in other words, if a person could leave "enough and as good" for others.[4] This so-called Lockean Proviso can be interpreted in many ways, but an adequate interpretation will note that this is its point: to license claims that can be made without making other people worse off.

We also should consider whether the "others" who are to be left with enough and as good include not just people currently on the scene but latecomers as well, including people not yet born. John Sanders asks, "What possible argument could at the same time require that the present generation have scruples about leaving enough and as good for one another, while shrugging off such concern for future generations?"[5] Most theorists accept the more demanding interpretation. It fits better with Locke's idea that the preservation of humankind (which includes future generations) is the ultimate criterion by which any use of resources is assessed. Aside from that, we have a more compelling defense of an appropriation (especially in environmental terms) when we can argue that there was enough left over not just for contemporaries but also for generations to come.

Of course, when we justify original appropriation, we do not in the process justify expropriation. Some say institutions that license expropriation make

people better off; I think our histories of violent expropriation are ongoing tragedies for us all. Capitalist regimes have tainted histories. Communist regimes have tainted histories. Indigenous peoples have tainted histories. Europeans took land from Algonquin tribes, and before that, Algonquin tribes took the same land from Iroquois tribes. We may regard those expropriations as the history of markets or governments or Christianity or tribalism or simply as the history of the human race. It makes little difference. This essay discusses the history of property institutions, not because their history can justify them, but rather because their history shows how some of them enable people to make themselves and the people around them better off without destroying their environment. Among such institutions are those that license original appropriation (and not expropriation).

II. ORIGINAL APPROPRIATION: A SOLUTION

Private property's philosophical critics often have claimed that justifying original appropriation is the key to justifying private property, frequently offering a version of Locke's Proviso as the standard of justification. Part of the Proviso's attraction for such critics was that it seemingly could not be met. Many critics conclude that the Proviso is, at least in the case of land appropriation, logically impossible to satisfy, and thus that (private) property in land cannot possibly be justified along Lockean lines.

The way Judith Thomson puts it, if "the first labor-mixer must literally leave as much and as good for others who come along later, then no one can come to own anything, for there are only finitely many things in the world so that every taking leaves less for others."[6] To say the least, Thomson is not alone:

> "We leave enough and as good for others only when what we take is not scarce."[7]
>
> "The Lockean Proviso, in the contemporary world of overpopulation and scarce resources, can almost never be met."[8]
>
> "Every acquisition worsens the lot of others—and worsens their lot in relevant ways."[9]
>
> "The condition that there be enough and as good left for others could not of course be literally satisfied by any system of private property rights."[10]
>
> "If the 'enough and as good' clause were a necessary condition on appropriation, it would follow that, in

these circumstances, the only legitimate course for the inhabitants would be death by starvation . . . since *no* appropriation would leave enough and as good in common for others."[11]

And so on. If we take something out of the cookie jar, we *must* be leaving less for others. This appears self-evident. It has to be right.

But it isn't right, for two reasons.

1. APPROPRIATION IS NOT A ZERO-SUM GAME

First, it is hardly impossible—certainly not logically impossible—for a taking to leave as much for others. We can at least imagine a logically possible world of magic cookie jars in which, every time you take out one cookie, more and better cookies take its place.

Second, the logically possible world I just imagined is the sort of world we actually live in. Philosophers writing about original appropriation tend to speak as if people who arrive first are luckier than those who come later. The truth is, first appropriators begin the process of resource creation; latecomers get most of the benefits. Consider America's first permanent English settlement, the Jamestown colony of 1607. (Or, if you prefer, imagine the lifestyles of people crossing the Bering Strait from Asia twelve thousand years ago.) Was their situation better than ours? How so? They were never caught in rush-hour traffic jams, of course. For that matter, they never worried about being overcharged for car repairs. They never awoke in the middle of the night to the sound of noisy refrigerators, leaky faucets, or even flushing toilets. They never wasted a minute at airports waiting for delayed flights. They never had to change a light bulb. They never agonized over the choice among cellular telephone companies. They never faced the prospect of a dentist's drill; after their teeth fell out, in their thirties, they could subsist for a while on liquids. Life was simple.

Philosophers are taught to say, in effect, that original appropriators got the good stuff for free. We have to pay for crumbs. But in truth, original appropriation benefits latecomers far more than it benefits original appropriators. Original appropriation is a cornucopia of wealth, but mainly for latecomers. The people who got here first literally could not even have imagined what we latecomers take for granted. Our life expectancies exceed theirs by several *decades*.

Original appropriation diminishes the stock of what can be originally appropriated, at least in the case of land, but that is not the same thing as diminishing the stock of what can be owned.[12] On the contrary, in taking control of resources and thereby removing those particular resources from the stock of goods that can be acquired by original appropriation, people typically generate massive increases in the stock of goods that can be acquired by trade. The lesson is that appropriation typically is not a zero-sum but a positive-sum game. As Locke himself stressed, it creates the possibility of mutual benefit on a massive scale. It creates the possibility of society as a cooperative venture.

The point is not merely that enough is produced in appropriation's aftermath to compensate latecomers who lost out in the race to appropriate. The point is that being an original appropriator is not the prize. The prize is prosperity, and latecomers win big, courtesy of those who arrived first. If anyone had a right to be compensated, it would be the first appropriators.

2. THE COMMONS BEFORE APPROPRIATION IS NOT ZERO-SUM EITHER

The next point is that the commons before appropriation is not a zero-sum game either. Typically it is a negative sum game. Let me tell two stories. The first comes from the coral reefs of the Philippine and Tongan Islands.[13] People once fished those reefs with lures and traps, but then began bleach-fishing, which involves dumping bleach into the reefs. Fish cannot breath sodium hypochlorite. Suffocated, they float to the surface where they are easy to collect.[14]

The problem is, the coral itself is composed of living animals. The coral suffocates along with the fish, and the dead reef is no longer a viable habitat. (Another technique, blast-fishing, involves dynamiting the reefs. The concussion produces an easy harvest of stunned fish and dead coral.) Perhaps your first reaction is to say people ought to be more responsible. They ought to preserve the reefs for their children.

But that would miss the point, which is that individual fishermen lack the option of saving the coral for their children. Individual fishermen obviously have the option of not destroying it themselves, but what happens if they elect not to destroy it? What they want is for the reef to be left for their children; what is actually happening is that the reef is left for the next blast-fisher down the line. If a fisherman wants to have anything at all to give his children, he must act quickly, destroying the reef and grabbing the fish himself. It does no good to tell fishermen to take responsibility. They are taking responsibility—for their children. Existing institutional arrangements do not empower them to take responsibility in a way that would save the reef.

Under the circumstances, they are at liberty to not destroy the reef themselves, but they are not at liberty to do what is necessary to save the reef for their children. To save the reef for their children, fishermen must have the power to restrict access to the reef. They must claim a right to exclude blast-fishers. Whether they stake that claim as individuals or as a group is secondary, so long as they actually succeed in restricting access. One way or another, they must have, and must effectively exercise, a right to restrict access.

The second story comes from the Cayman Islands.[15] The Atlantic Green Turtle has long been prized as a source of meat and eggs. The turtles were a commonly held resource and were being harvested in an unsustainable way. In 1968, when by some estimates there were as few as three to five thousand left in the wild, a group of entrepreneurs and concerned scientists created Mariculture Ltd. (sold in 1976 and renamed Cayman Turtle Farm) and began raising and selling captive-bred sea turtles. In the wild, as few as one tenth of one percent of wild hatchlings survive to adulthood. Most are seized by predators before they can crawl from nest to sea. Cayman Farm, though, boosted the survival rate of captive-bred animals to fifty percent or more. At the peak of operations, they were rearing over a hundred thousand turtles. They were releasing one percent of their hatchlings into the wild at the age of ten months, an age at which hatchlings have a decent chance of surviving to maturity.

In 1973, commerce in Atlantic Green Turtles was restricted by CITES (the Convention on International Trade in Endangered Species) and, in the United States, by the Fish and Wildlife Service, the Department of Commerce, and the Department of the Interior. Under the newly created Endangered Species Act, the U.S. classified the Atlantic Green Turtle as an endangered species, but Cayman Farm's business was unaffected, at first, because regulations pertaining to commerce in Atlantic Green Turtles covered only wild turtles, implicitly exempting commerce in captive-bred animals. In 1978, however, the regulations were published in their final form, and although exemptions were granted for trade in captive-bred animals of other species, no exemption was made for turtles. The company could no longer do business in the U.S. Even worse, the company no longer could ship its products through American ports, so it no longer had access via Miami to world markets. The Farm exists today only to serve the population of the Cayman Islands themselves.[16]

What do these stories tell us? The first tells us we do not need to justify failing to preserve the commons in its pristine, original, unappropriated form, because preserving a pristine commons is not an option. Leaving our environment in the commons is not like putting our environment in a time capsule as a legacy for future generations. There are ways to take what we find in the commons and preserve it—to put it in a time capsule—but before we can put something in a time capsule, we have to appropriate it.[17]

3. JUSTIFYING THE GAME

Note a difference between justifying *institutions* that regulate appropriation and justifying particular *acts* of appropriation. Think of original appropriation as a game and of particular acts of appropriation as moves within the game. Even if the game is justified, a given move within the game may have nothing to recommend it. Indeed, we could say (for argument's sake) that any act of appropriation will seem arbitrary when viewed in isolation, and some will seem unconscionable. Even so, there can be compelling reasons for an institutional framework to recognize property claims on the basis of moves that would carry no moral weight in an institutional vacuum. Common law implicitly acknowledges morally weighty reasons for not requiring original appropriators to supply morally weighty reasons for their appropriations. Carol Rose argues that a rule of first possession, when the world is notified in an unambiguous way, induces discovery (and future productive activity) and minimizes disputes over discovered objects.[18] Particular acts of appropriation are justified not because they carry moral weight but because they are permitted moves within a game that carries moral weight.

Needless to say, the cornucopia of wealth generated by the appropriation and subsequent mobilization of resources is not an unambiguous benefit. Commerce made possible by original appropriation creates pollution, and other negative externalities as well. Further, there may be people who attach no value to the increases in life expectancy and other benefits that accompany the appropriation of resources for productive use. Some people may prefer a steady-state system that indefinitely supports their lifestyles as hunter-gatherers, untainted by the shoes, tents, fishing rods, and safety matches of Western culture. If original appropriation forces such people to participate in a culture they want no part of, then from their viewpoint, the game does more harm than good.

Here are two things to keep in mind, though. First, as I said, the commons is not a time capsule. It does not preserve the status quo. For all kinds of reasons, quality of life could drop after appropriation. However, pressures that drive waves of people to appropriate are a lot more likely to compromise quality of life when those waves wash over an unregulated commons. In an unregulated commons, those who conserve pay the costs but do not get the benefits of conservation, while overusers get the benefits but do not pay the costs of overuse. An unregulated commons is thus a prescription for overuse, not for conservation.

Second, the option of living the life of a hunter-gatherer has not entirely disappeared. It is not a comfortable life. It never was. But it remains an option. There are places in northern Canada and elsewhere where people still live that way. As a bonus, those who opt to live as hunter-gatherers retain the option of participating in western culture on a drop-in basis during medical emergencies, to trade for supplies, and so on. Obviously, someone might respond, "Even if the hunter-gatherer life is an option now, that option is disappearing as expanding populations equipped with advancing technologies claim the land for other purposes." Well, probably so. What does that prove? It proves that, in the world as it is, if hunter-gatherers want their children to have the option of living as hunter-gatherers, then they need to stake a claim to the territory on which they intend to preserve that option.

They need to argue that they, as rightful owners, have a right to regulate access to it. If they want a steady-state civilization, they need to be aware that they will not find it in an unregulated commons. They need to exclude oil companies, for example, which would love to treat northern Canada as an unregulated commons.

When someone says appropriation does not leave enough and as good for others, the reply should be "compared to what?" Compared to the commons as it was? As it is? As it will be? Often, in fact, leaving resources *in the commons* does not leave enough and as good for others. The Lockean Proviso, far from forbidding appropriation of resources from the commons, actually requires appropriation under conditions of scarcity.

Removing goods from the commons stimulates increases in the stock of what can be owned and limits losses that occur in tragic commons. Appropriation replaces a negative sum with a positive sum game. Therein lies a justification for social structures enshrining a right to remove resources from the unregulated commons: when resources become scarce, we need to remove them if we want them to be there for our children. Or anyone else's.

III. WHAT KIND OF PROPERTY INSTITUTION IS IMPLIED?

I have defended appropriation of, and subsequent regulation of access to, scarce resources as a way of preserving (and creating) resources for the future. When resources are abundant, the Lockean Proviso permits appropriation; when resources are scarce, the Proviso requires appropriation. It is possible to appropriate without prejudice to future generations. Indeed, when the burden of common use begins to exceed a resource's ability to renew itself, leaving the resource in the commons is what would be prejudicial to future generations.

Private property enables people (and gives them an incentive) to take responsibility for conserving scarce resources. It preserves resources under a wide variety of circumstances. It is the preeminent vehicle for turning negative sum commons into positive sum property regimes. However, it is not the only way. Evidently, it is not always the best way, either. Public property is ubiquitous, and it is not only rapacious governments and mad ideologues who create it. It has a history of evolving spontaneously in response to real problems, enabling people to remove a resource from an unregulated commons and collectively take responsibility for its management. The following sections discuss research by Martin Bailey, Harold Demsetz, Robert Ellickson, and Carol Rose, showing how various property institutions help to ensure that enough and as good is left for future generations.

1. THE UNREGULATED COMMONS

An unregulated commons need not be a disaster. An unregulated commons will work well enough so long as the level of use remains within the land's carrying capacity. However, as use nears carrying capacity, there will be pressure to shift to a more exclusive regime. For a real-world example of an unregulated commons evolving into a regime of private parcels as increasing traffic began to exceed carrying capacity, consider economist Harold Demsetz's classic account of how property institutions evolved among indigenous tribes of the Labrador Peninsula. As Demsetz tells the story, the region's people had, for generations, treated the land as an open-access commons. The human population was small. There was plenty to eat. Thus, the pattern of exploitation was within the land's carrying capacity.[19] The resource maintained itself. In that situation, the Proviso, as interpreted above, was satisfied. Original appropriation would have been permissible, other things equal, but it was not required.

With the advent of the fur trade, though, the scale of hunting and trapping activity increased sharply. The population of game animals began to dwindle. The unregulated commons had worked for a while, but now the tribes were facing a classic "tragedy of the commons."[20] The tragedy of the commons is one version of a more general problem of externalities. In this case, the benefits of exploiting the resource were internalized but the costs were not, and the arrangement was no longer viable. In response, tribal members began to mark out family plots. The game animals in question were small animals like beaver and otter that tend not to migrate from one plot to another. Thus, marking out plots of land effectively privatized small game as well as the land itself. In sum, the tribes converted the commons in nonmigratory fur-bearing game to family parcels when the fur trade began to spur a rising demand that exceeded the land's carrying capacity. When demand began to exceed carrying capacity, that was when the Proviso came not only to permit but to require original appropriation.

One other nuance of the privatization of fur-bearing game: although the fur was privatized, the meat was not. There was still plenty of meat, so tribal law allowed people to hunt for meat on each other's land. Unannounced visitors could kill a beaver and take the meat, but had to leave the pelt, prominently displayed to signal that they had eaten and had respected the owner's right to the pelt. The new customs went to the heart of the matter, privatizing what had to be privatized, leaving intact liberties that people had always enjoyed with respect to other resources where unrestricted access had not yet become a problem.

2. THE COMMUNAL ALTERNATIVE[21]

We can contrast the unregulated or open-access commons with communes. A commune is a restricted-access commons. In a commune, property is owned by the group rather than by individual members. People as a group claim and exercise a right to exclude. Typically, communes draw a sharp distinction between members and nonmembers, and regulate access accordingly. Public property tends to restrict access by time of day or year. Some activities are permitted; others are prohibited.

Ellickson believes a broad campaign to abolish either private property or public and communal property would be ludicrous. Each kind of property serves social welfare in its own way. Likewise, every ownership regime has its own externality problems. Communal management leads to overconsumption and to shirking on maintenance and improvements, because people receive only a fraction of the value of their labor, and pay only a fraction of the costs of their consumption. To minimize these disincentives, a commune must monitor production and consumption activities.

In practice, communal regimes can lead to indiscriminate dumping of wastes, ranging from piles of unwashed dishes to ecological disasters that threaten whole continents. Privately managed parcels also can lead to indiscriminate dumping of wastes and to various other uses that ignore spillover effects on neighbors.[22] One advantage of private property is that owners can buy each other out and reshuffle their holdings in such a way as to minimize the extent to which their activities bother each other. But it does not always work out so nicely, and the reshuffling itself can be a waste. There are transaction costs. Thus, one plausible social goal would be to have a system that combines private and public property in a way that reduces the sum of transaction costs and the cost of externalities.

IV. LOCAL VERSUS REMOTE EXTERNALITIES

Is it generally better to convert an unregulated commons to smaller private parcels or to manage it as a commune with power to exclude nonmembers? It depends on what kind of problem the property regime needs to solve. Not all problems are of equal scale; some are more local than others. As a problem's scale changes, there will be corresponding changes in which responses are feasible and effective. An individual sheep eating grass in the pasture is what Ellickson and Demsetz would call a *small* event, affecting only a small area relative to the prevailing parcel size. If the commons is being ruined by small events, there is an easy solution: cut the land into parcels. We see this solution everywhere. If we can divide the land into parcels of a certain size, such that the cost of grazing an extra sheep is borne entirely by the individual owner who decides whether to graze the extra sheep, then we have internalized externalities and solved the problem. If we divide the pasture into private parcels, then what a particular sheep eats on a particular owner's pasture is no one else's concern. The grass is no longer a common pool.

For better or worse, events come in more than one size. For the sake of example, suppose six parcels are situated over a pool of oil in such a way that, via oil wells, each of the six owners has access to the common pool. The more wells individual owners sink, the more oil they can extract, up to a point. As the number of wellheads rises, oil pressure per wellhead declines. Not only is the reserve of oil ultimately fixed but the practically extractable reserve eventually begins to decline with the number of wells sunk. Past a point, we no longer have a situation where what individual owners do on their property is of no concern to other owners. Instead, the six owners become part of a *medium* event, a kind of problem that neighbors cannot solve

simply by putting up fences. This kind of problem occurs when an event is too large to be contained on a single parcel, or does not have a precise and confined location, or migrates from one location to another. For one reason or another, the event is large enough that its effects spill over onto neighboring parcels.

In an unfenced commons, there is in effect only one parcel, so "small," "medium" and "large" would refer simply to the radius over which the effects of an event are felt, that is, small, medium or large parts of the whole parcel. In a regime that has been cut into smaller parcels, the more interesting distinction is between a small event that affects a single owner, a medium event that affects immediate neighbors, and a large event that affects remote parts of the community. When land is divided into parcels, whether an event is small, medium, or large will depend on the size of the parcels. Whether a regime succeeds in internalizing externalities will depend on whether it succeeds in carving out parcel sizes big enough to contain those events whose effects it is most crucial to internalize. In effect, if an individual owner's parcel size could be increased without limit, any event could be made "small."

Ellickson says private regimes are clearly superior as methods for minimizing the costs of small and medium events. Regarding small events, the first point is that the external effects of small events are by definition vanishingly small. Neighbors do not care when we pick tomatoes on our own land; they do care when we pick tomatoes on their communal plot. In the former case, we are minding our own business; in the latter, we are minding theirs. (In effect, there are no small events on communal land. Everything we do affects our neighbors. Even doing nothing at all affects our neighbors, given that we could instead have been helping to tend the communal gardens.) The second point regarding small events concerns the cost of monitoring. To internalize externalities, whatever the property regime, owners must be able to monitor other would-be users. On a private regime, though, it is only boundary crossings that need monitoring; guard dogs and motion sensors can handle that. By contrast, the monitoring needed within a communal regime involves evaluating whether workers are just going through the motions, whether they are taking more than their share, and so on. In sum, "detecting the presence of a trespasser is much less demanding than evaluating the conduct of a person who is privileged to be where he is."[23] Thus, the external cost of small events is lower on private parcels. Monitoring, while still required, is relatively cheap and relatively nonintrusive in a parcelized regime.

The effects of medium events tend to spill over onto one's neighbors, and thus can be a source of friction. Nevertheless, privatization has the advantage of limiting how many people need to be consulted about how to handle the externality, which cuts transaction costs. Instead of consulting the entire community of communal owners, each at liberty with respect to the affected area, one consults a handful of people who own parcels in the immediate area of the medium event. A further virtue of privatization is that disputes arising from medium events tend to be left in the hands of people in the immediate vicinity, who tend to better understand local conditions and thus are in a better position to devise resolutions without harmful unintended consequences. They are in a better position to foresee the costs and benefits of a medium event.[24]

When it comes to large events, though, there is no easy way to say which mix of private and public property is best. Large events involve far-flung externalities among people who do not have face-to-face relationships. The difficulties in detecting such externalities, tracing them to their source, and holding people accountable for them are difficulties for any kind of property regime. It is no easy task to devise institutions that encourage pulp mills to take responsibility for their actions while simultaneously encouraging people downstream to take responsibility for their welfare, and thus to avoid being harmed by large-scale negative externalities. Ellickson says there is no general answer to the question of which regime best deals with them.

Large events fall into one of two categories. Releasing toxic wastes into the atmosphere, for example, may violate existing legal rights or community norms. Or, such laws or norms may not yet be in place. Most of the problems arise when existing customs or laws fail to settle who (in effect) has the right of way. That is not a problem with parceling land per se but rather with the fact that key resources like air and waterways remain in a largely unregulated commons.

So, privatization exists in different degrees and takes different forms. Different forms have different incentive properties. Simply parceling out land or sea is not always enough to stabilize possession of resources that make land or sea valuable in the first place. Suppose that fish are known to migrate from one parcel to another. In that case, owners have an incentive to grab as many fish as they can whenever the school passes through their own territory. Thus, simply dividing fishing grounds into parcels may not be enough to put fishermen in a position to avoid collectively exceeding sustainable yields. It depends on the extent to which sought-after fish migrate from one parcel to another, and on continuously evolving conventions that help neighbors deal with the inadequacy of their fences (or other ways of marking off territory). Clearly, then, not all forms of privatization are equally good at internalizing externalities. Privatization per se is not a panacea, and not all forms of privatization are equal.

There are obvious difficulties with how private property regimes handle large events. The nature and extent of the difficulties depends on details. So, for purposes of comparison, Ellickson looked at how communal regimes handle large events.

V. JAMESTOWN AND OTHER COMMUNES

The Jamestown Colony is North America's first permanent English settlement. It begins in 1607 as a commune, sponsored by London-based Virginia Company. Land is held and managed collectively. The colony's charter guarantees to each settler an equal share of the collective product regardless of the amount of work personally contributed. Of the original group of one hundred and four settlers, two thirds die of starvation and disease before their first winter. New shiploads replenish the colony; the winter of 1609 cuts the population from five hundred to sixty. Colonist William Simmons writes, "It were too vile to say (and scarce to be believed) what we endured, but the occasion was only our own for want of providence, industry, and government, and not the barrenness and defect of the country, as is generally supposed."[25] In 1611, career soldier Thomas Dale (appointed by Governor Thomas Gates to administer martial law) arrives to find living skeletons[26] bowling in the streets, waiting for someone else to plant the crops.[27] Their main food source consists of wild animals such as turtles and raccoons, which settlers hunt and eat by dark of night before neighbors arrive to demand equal shares.[28]

Colonist George Percy writes that bad water accounted for many deaths, but most deaths were from "meere famine."[29] Archeologist Ivor Hume reacts with wonder: "The James Fort colonists' unwillingness or inability to work toward their own salvation remains one of American history's great mysteries."[30] Newly arriving ship's crew members, fishing the Chesapeake, caught seven-foot sturgeon and oysters the size of dinner plates, and left fishing gear with the colonists. How could colonists starve? Moreover, "Percy's recognition that bad water was the cause of many deaths leaves one asking why, then, nothing was done to combat its dangers. That foul water was bad for you had been known for centuries . . ."[31]

In 1614, (by now Governor) Thomas Dale has seen enough. He assigns three-acre plots to individual settlers, which reportedly increases productivity at least seven-fold. (I found no verification of this, but colonist Captain John Smith observes that, "When our people were fed out of the common store, and laboured jointly together, glad was he could slip from his labour, or slumber over his taske he care not how, nay, the most honest among them would hardly take so much true paines in a weeke, as now for themselves they will doe in a day")[32] The colony converts the rest of its land holdings to private parcels in 1619.[33]

Why go communal in the first place? Are there advantages to communal regimes? One advantage is obvious. Communal regimes can help people spread risks under conditions where risks are substantial and where alternative risk-spreading mechanisms, like insurance, are unavailable. The Company was sending settlers to a frontier where, without help, something as simple as a sprained ankle could be fatal. The only form of insurance available was, in effect, mutual insurance among the settlers, backed up by their ability to work overtime for less fortunate neighbors. But as communities build up capital reserves to the point where they can offer insurance, they tend to privatize, for insurance lets them secure a measure of risk-spreading without having to endure the externalities that tend to afflict communal regimes.

A communal regime might also be an effective response to economies of scale in large public works

that are crucial in getting a community started. To build a fort, man its walls, dig wells, and so on, a communal economy is an obvious choice as a way of mobilizing the teams of workers needed to execute these urgent tasks. But again, as these tasks are completed and community welfare increasingly comes to depend on small events, the communal regime gives way to private parcels. At Jamestown, Plymouth, the Amana colonies, and Salt Lake, formerly communal settlers "understandably would switch to private land tenure, the system that most cheaply induces individuals to undertake small and medium events that are socially useful."[34] (The legend of Salt Lake says the sudden improvement in the fortunes of once-starving Mormons occurred in 1848 when God sent sea gulls to save them from plagues of locusts, at the same time as they coincidentally were switching to private plots. Similarly, the Jamestown tragedy sometimes is attributed to harsh natural conditions, as if those conditions suddenly changed in 1614, multiplying productivity seven-fold while Governor Dale coincidentally was cutting the land into parcels.)

Of course, the tendency toward decentralized and individualized forms of management is only a strong tendency and, in any case, there are tradeoffs. For example, what would be a small event on a larger parcel becomes a medium event under more crowded conditions. Loud music is an innocuous small event on a ranch but an irritating medium event in an apartment complex. Changes in technology or population density affect the scope or incidence of externalities. The trend, though, is that as people become aware of and concerned about a medium or large event, they seek ways of reducing the extent to which the event's cost is externalized. Social evolution is partly a process of perceiving new externalities and devising institutions to internalize them.

Historically, the benefits of communal management have not been enough to keep communes together indefinitely. Perhaps the most enduring and successful communes in human memory are the agricultural settlements of the Hutterites, dating back to sixteenth century Austria. They migrated to the Dakotas in the 1870s, then to Canada (to avoid compulsory military service during World War I). North American Hutterite communities now contain around forty thousand people (mostly on the Canadian prairies). Hutterites believe in a fairly strict sharing of assets. They forbid radio and television, to give one example of how strictly they control contact with the outside world.

Ellickson says Hutterite communities have three special things going for them: 1. A population cap: when a settlement reaches a population of one hundred and twenty, a portion of the community must leave to start a new community. The cap helps them retain a close-knit society; 2. Communal dining and worship: people congregate several times a day, which facilitates a rapid and intense monitoring of individual behavior and a ready avenue for supplying feedback to those whose behavior deviates from expectations; 3. A ban on birth control: the average woman bears ten children (the highest documented fertility rate of any human population) which more than offsets the trickle of emigration.[35] We might add that Hutterite culture and education leave people ill-prepared to live in anything other than Hutterite society, which accounts for the low emigration rate.

Ellickson discusses other examples of communal property regimes. But the most pervasive example of communal ownership in America, Ellickson says, is the family household. American suburbia consists of family communes nested within a network of open-access roadways. Family homes tacitly recognize limits to how far we can go in converting common holdings to individual parcels. Consider your living room. You could fully privatize, having one household member own it while others pay user fees. The fees could be used to pay family members or outside help to keep it clean. In some respects, it would be better that way. The average communal living room today, for example, is notably subject to overgrazing and shirking on maintenance. Yet we put up with it. No one charges user fees to household members. Seeing the living room degraded by communal use may be irritating, but it is better than treating it as one person's private domain.

Some institutions succeed while embodying a form of ownership that is essentially collective. History indicates, though, that members of successful communes internalize the rewards that come with that collective responsibility. In particular, they reserve the right to exclude nonmembers. A successful commune is not run as an open-access commons.

VI. GOVERNANCE BY CUSTOM

Many commons (such as our living rooms) are regulated by custom rather than government, so saying there is a role for common property and saying there is a role for government management of common property are two different things. As Ellickson notes, "Group ownership does not necessarily imply government ownership, of course. The sorry environmental records of federal land agencies and Communist regimes are a sharp reminder that governments are often particularly inept managers of large tracts."[36] Carol Rose tells of how, in the nineteenth century, public property was thought to be owned by society at large. The idea of public property often was taken to imply no particular role for government beyond whatever enforcement role is implied by private property. Society's right to such property was held to precede and supersede any claim by government. Rose says, "Implicit in these older doctrines is the notion that, even if a property should be open to the public, it does not follow that public rights should necessarily vest in an active governmental manager."[37] Sometimes, rights were held by an "unorganized" rather than a "governmentally organized" public.[38]

Along the same lines, open-field agricultural practices of medieval times gave peasants exclusive cropping rights to scattered thin strips of arable land in each of the village fields. The strips were private only during the growing season, after which the land reverted to the commons for the duration of the grazing season.[39] Thus, ownership of parcels was usufructuary in the sense that once the harvest was in, ownership reverted to the common herdsmen without negotiation or formal transfer.[40] A farmer had an exclusive claim to the land only so long as he was using it to bring in a harvest. The scattering of strips was a means of diversification, reducing the risk of being ruined by small or medium events: small fires, pest infestations, etc.. The post-harvest commons in grazing land exploited economies of scale in fencing and tending a herd. Scattering the strips also made it harder for a communal herdsman to position livestock exclusively over his own property, thus promoting more equitable distribution of manure (i.e., fertilizer).[41]

According to Martin Bailey, the pattern observed by Rose and Ellickson also was common among aboriginal tribes. That is, tribes that practiced agriculture treated the land as private during the growing season, and often treated it as a commons after the crops were in. Hunter-gatherer societies did not practice agriculture, but they too tended to leave the land in the commons during the summer when game was plentiful. It was during the winter, when food was most scarce, that they privatized. The rule among hunter-gatherers is that where group hunting's advantages are considerable, that factor dominates. But in the winter, small game is relatively more abundant, less migratory, and evenly spread. There was no "feast or famine" pattern of the sort one expects to see with big-game hunting. Rather, families tended to gather enough during the course of the day to get themselves through the day, day after day, with little to spare.[42]

Although this pattern corroborates my general thesis, I admit to being surprised. I might have predicted that it would be during the hardest times that families would band together and throw everything into the common pot in order to pull through. Not so. It was when the land was nearest its carrying capacity that they recognized the imperative to privatize.

Customary use of medieval commons was hedged with restrictions limiting depletion of resources. Custom prohibited activities inconsistent with the land's ability to recover.[43] In particular, the custom of "stinting" allowed the villagers to own livestock only in proportion to the relative size of their (growing season) land holdings. Governance by custom enabled people to avoid commons tragedies.[44]

Custom is a form of management unlike exclusive ownership by individuals or governments. Custom is a self-managing system for according property rights.[45] For example, custom governs rights-claims you establish by taking a place in line at a supermarket checkout counter. Rose believes common concerns often are best handled by decentralized, piecemeal, self-managing customs that tend to arise as needed at the local level. So, to the previous section's conclusion that a successful commune does not operate as an open-access commons, we can add that a successful commune does not entrust its governance to a distant bureaucracy.

VII. THE HUTTERITE SECRET

I argued that the original appropriation of (and subsequent regulation of access to) scarce resources is

justifiable as a mechanism for preserving opportunities for future generations. There are various means of exclusive control, though. Some internalize externalities better than others, and how well they do so depends on the context. There is no single form of exclusive control that uniquely serves this purpose. Which form is best depends on what kind of activities are most prevalent in a community at any given time. It also depends on the extent to which public ownership implies control by a distant bureaucracy rather than by local custom.

As mentioned earlier, I have heard people say Jamestown failed because it faced harsh natural conditions. But communal (and noncommunal) settlements typically face harsh natural conditions. Jamestown had to deal with summer in Virginia. Hutterites dealt with winter on the Canadian prairie. It is revealing, not misleading, to compare Jamestown to settlements that faced harsher conditions more successfully. It also is fair to compare the two Jamestowns: the one before and the one following Governor Dale's mandated privatization. What distinguished the first Jamestown from the second was not the harshness of the former's natural setting but the thoroughness with which it stopped people from internalizing externalities.

Michael Hechter considers group solidarity to be a function of (a) the extent to which members depend on the group and (b) the extent to which the group can monitor and enforce compliance with expectations that members will contribute to the group rather than free ride upon it.[46] On Hechter's analysis, it is unsurprising that Hutterite communal society has been successful. Members are extremely dependent, for their upbringing leaves them unprepared to live in a non-Hutterite culture. Monitoring is intense. Feedback is immediate. But if that is the Hutterite secret, why did Jamestown fail? They too were extremely dependent on each other. They too had nowhere else to go. Monitoring was equally straightforward. Everyone knew who was planting crops (no one) and who was bowling (everyone). What was the problem?

The problem lay in the guarantee embedded in Jamestown's charter. The charter entitled people to an equal share regardless of personal contribution, which is to say it ensured that individual workers would be maximally alienated from the fruits of their labors—that they would think of their work as disappearing into an open-access commons.

Robert Goodin says, "Working within the constraints set by natural scarcity, the greatest practical obstacle to achieving as much justice as resources permit is, and always has been, the supposition that each of us should cultivate his own garden."[47] However, Jamestown's charter did not suppose each of us should cultivate his own garden. It supposed the opposite. Colonists abided by the charter, and starved. Only a few years later, with a new charter, colonists were tending their own gardens, and thriving.

We should applaud institutions that encourage people to care for each other. But telling people they are required to tend someone else's garden rather than their own does not encourage people to care for each other. It does the opposite. It encourages spite. The people of Jamestown reached the point where they would rather die, bowling in the street, than tend the gardens of their free-riding neighbors, and die they did.

REFERENCES

Bailey, Martin J. 1992. Approximate Optimality of Aboriginal Property Rights. *Journal of Law and Economics.* 35: 183–98.

Bogart, J. H. 1985. Lockean Provisos and State of Nature Theories. *Ethics* 95: 828–36.

Chesher, R. 1985. Practical Problems in Coral Reef Utilization and Management: a Tongan Case Study. *Proceedings of the Fifth International Coral Reef Congress* 4: 213–24.

Davis, Frederick R. *The Man Who Saved Sea Turtles: Archie Carr and the Origins of Conservation Biology.* New York: Oxford University Press (2007).

Demsetz, Harold. 1967. Toward a Theory of Property Rights. *American Economic Review* (Papers & Proceedings) 57: 347–59.

Dukeminier, Jesse, and James E. Krier. 1993. *Property.* 3rd edn. Boston: Little, Brown.

Ellickson, Robert C. 1993. Property in Land. *Yale Law Journal* 102: 1315–1400.

Fosdick, Peggy, and Sam Fosdick. 1994. *Last Chance Lost?* York, PA: Irvin S. Naylor Publishing.

Fried, Barbara. 1995. Wilt Chamberlain Revisited: Nozick's "Justice in Transfer" and the Problem of Market-Based Distribution. *Philosophy and Public Affairs* 24: 226–45.

Gomez, E, A. Alcala, and A. San Diego. 1981. Status of Philippine Coral Reefs—1981. *Proceedings of the Fourth International Coral Reef Symposium* 1: 275–85.

Goodin, Robert E. 1985. *Protecting the Vulnerable: Toward a Reanalysis of Our Social Responsibilities.* Chicago: University of Chicago Press.

Haile, Edward W. Editor. *Jamestown Narratives: Eye Witness Accounts of the Virginia Colony, The First Decade, 1607–1617.* Champlain, Virginia: Roundhouse, 1998.

Hardin, Garrett. "The Tragedy of the Commons," *Science* 162 (1968): 1243–48.

Hardin, Garrett. 1977. The Ethical Implications of Carrying Capacity. In G. Hardin and J. Baden, eds., *Managing the Commons.* San Francisco: W. H. Freeman.

Hechter, Michael. 1983. A Theory of Group Solidarity. In Hechter, ed., *Microfoundations of Macrosociology.* Philadelphia: Temple University Press. 16–57.

Held, Virginia. 1980. Introduction. In Held, ed., *Property, Profits, & Economic Justice.* Belmont: Wadsworth.

Hohfeld, Wesley. 1919. *Fundamental Legal Conceptions.* New Haven: Yale University Press.

Hume, Ivor N. 1994. *The Virginia Adventure.* Charlottesville: University of Virginia Press.

Locke, John. 1690. *Second Treatise of Government.* Ed. P. Laslett. Cambridge: Cambridge University Press (reprinted 1960).

Merrill, Thomas W. 1998. Property and the Right to Exclude. *Nebraska Law Review.* 77: 730–55.

Mydans, Seth. 1989. "Hmong Refugees Import a Near Record Birthrate," *New York Times* (August 27).

Lewis, John. (1888), *Law of Eminent Domain* (Chicago: Callaghan and Co.).

Nash, J. Madeleine. 1996. Wrecking the Reefs. *Time* (September 30): 60–2.

Rose, Carol. 1985. Possession as the Origin of Property. *University of Chicago Law Review.* 52: 73–88.

Rose, Carol. 1986. The Comedy of the Commons: Custom, Commerce, and Inherently Public Property. *University of Chicago Law Review* 53: 711–87.

Sanders, John T. 1987. Justice and the Initial Acquisition of Private Property. *Harvard Journal of Law and Public Policy* 10: 367–99.

Sartorius, Rolf. 1984. Persons and Property. In Ray Frey, ed., *Utility and Rights*. Minneapolis: University of Minnesota Press.

Schmidtz, David, and Robert E. Goodin. 1998. *Social Welfare and Individual Responsibility*. Cambridge: Harvard University Press.

Schmidtz, David, and Elizabeth Willott. "The Tragedy of the Commons." In R.G. Frey & Christopher Wellman, eds., *Blackwell Companion to Applied Ethics*. Oxford: Blackwell, 2003. 662–73.

Thomson, Judith Jarvis. 1990. *The Realm of Rights*. Cambridge: Harvard University Press.

Waldron, Jeremy. 1976. Enough and as Good Left for Others. *Philosophical Quarterly* 29: 319–28.

NOTES

1. A negative externality or external cost is a cost (of a decision or transaction) paid by bystanders who were not consulted and whose interests were not taken into account. A transaction may also, analogously, create positive externalities, that is, have external benefits.

2. Since John Lewis (1888) described property as a "bundle of sticks" we have treated property rights as bundles that could include rights to sell, lend, bequeath, use as collateral, or even destroy. Yet, the right to exclude is not merely one stick in a bundle of rights but is instead more like the trunk of a tree, where all the other sticks (the right to use, lend, bequeath, use as collateral, and so on) are branches. Not everyone sees it the same way, but there is precedent in the common law for calling the right to exclude "one of the most essential sticks in the bundle of rights that are commonly characterized as property." *Kaiser Aetna* v. *United States, 444 U.S. 164*, 176 (1979). When the right of property owners to exclude is combined with the right of citizens not to be excluded from the community's day to day business, the uneasy but productive compromise became the foundation of the 19th century philosophy known as liberalism.

3. Merrill (1998).

4. See Locke (1969/1690, Chap. 5). Locke sometimes uses other locutions, such as "as much and as good."

5. Sanders (1987) 377.

6. Thomson (1990) 330.

7. Fried (1995) 230n.

8. Held (1980) 6.

9. Bogart (1985) 834.

10. Sartorius (1984) 210.

11. Waldron (1976) 325.

12. Is it fair for latecomers to be excluded from acquiring property by rules allowing original appropriation? Sanders (1987, 385) notes that latecomers "are *not* excluded from acquiring property by these rules. They are, instead, excluded from being the first to own what has not been owned previously. Is *that* unfair?"

13. Chesher (1985). See also Gomez, Alcala, and San Diego (1981).

14. Nash (1996) says fishermen currently pump 330,000 pounds of cyanide per year into Philippine reefs.

15. I thank Peggy Fosdick at the National Aquarium in Baltimore for correspondence and documents. See also Fosdick and Fosdick (1994).

16. As later sections stress, privatization may be a key to avoiding commons tragedies, but it is not a panacea. In this case, there was concern that the farming of turtles would spur demand, and that rising demand would lead to rising prices, which would mean an increased poaching pressure on wild populations. This is unlikely. As a rule, the prices of scarce wild animals do not rise when people begin bringing to market large quantities of farm-bred alternatives. One real danger, though, is that large-scale farms (salmon farms, cattle farms, etc.) breed disease and put wild as well as domestic populations at risk. As with any other new industry, there are always unanticipated problems and newly emerging externalities that need to be contained. See Davis (2007).

17. A private non-profit organization, The Nature Conservancy, is pursuing such a strategy. Although not itself an original appropriator, it has acquired over a billion dollars' worth of land in an effort to preserve natural ecosystems. Note that this includes habitat for endangered species that have no market value.

18. Rose (1985).

19. This was not true everywhere. I have seen places where tribes hunted bison by stampeding whole herds over the edge of a cliff. (The Blackfoot name for one such place translates as "head-smashed-in buffalo jump.") So I accept Dukeminier and Krier's warning against forming "an unduly romantic

image of Native American culture prior to the arrival of 'civilization.' There is considerable evidence that some American Indian tribes, rather than being natural ecologists who lived in respectful harmony with the land, exploited the environment ruthlessly by overhunting and extensive burning of forests" (1993, 62).

20. Hardin (1968) 1243. The cases described in previous sections are examples of the "tragedy of the commons," where unregulated access to a resource results in overuse by a population of users who lack the effective right to exclude other users and thus whose only rational alternative is to jump in and overuse while they can. See also Schmidtz & Willott (2003).

21. This essay discusses Ellickson's article in some detail. While I take little credit for the ideas in the next few sections, any errors are presumably mine.

22. Alchian and Demsetz represent the general nature of the tradeoff in this way. As we move toward a more communal arrangement, "the immediate problem is replaced by another: the problem of providing incentives to work. Thus, if we suppose that the communal right to hunt is supplemented by the stipulation that killed animals belong to the community, in which all citizens can share according to custom, and do not belong exclusively to the hunter, then the incentive to hunt will be diminished. This may cure the over-hunting problem by creating an under-hunting problem in which the able-bodied wait for others to do the hunting, the results of which will be shared by all. In order to reduce the severity of the shirking problem that is thereby created, it is necessary for societies which fail to establish private rights to move ever closer to a social organization in which the behavior of individuals is directly regulated by the state or indirectly influenced by cultural indoctrination. The option to hunt or not to hunt cannot be left with the individual who, unable to claim the fruit of his effort, will tend to shirk. Instead, the state will find it increasingly necessary to *order* the hunt, to insist on participation in it, and to regulate more closely the sharing of the kill." Armen Alchian and Harold Demsetz, "The Tasks of Economic History," *Journal of Economic History* 33 (1973):16–27, at 23.

23. Ellickson (1993) 1327.

24. Ellickson (1993) 1331.

25. Haile (1998) 340.

26. The word chosen by eyewitness George Percy was "anatomies" (Haile, 1998, 507).

27. Eyewitness Ralph Hamor refers to Thomas Dale arriving at Jamestown where "the most company were, and their daily and usuall workes, bowling in the streetes." Dale declared martial law, conscripting people to repair their buildings, plant corn, etc. (Hume, 1994, 298).

28. As reported by CNN, September 13, 1996, on the occasion of the original fort's excavation.

29. Hume (1994) 159.

30. Hume (1994) 160.

31. Hume (1994) 160. Hume adds, "Although considering the geology of Jamestown Island, it would have been fruitless to try to reach sustained freshwater by digging wells, they were not to know that—but nobody even tried!" (161). While visiting the Jamestown excavation in 2007, I saw new diggings indicating that colonists had indeed tried to dig a well, but Hume's point still holds. When the well project failed, colonists seemed to give up. Just as inexplicably, they seem to have torn down sections of the fort to use as firewood, even though eyewitnesses described the forest edge as "within a stone's throw." Apart from the need for firewood, the forest should have been cut back for the sake of securing the fort's perimeter.

32. Quoted by Ellickson (1993) 1337. After visiting Jamestown in 2007, talking to four history buffs who work there, and reading scholarly work published since the first version of this essay (including Haile's extraordinary collection of eyewitness accounts), I now suspect that several factors exacerbated the communal charter's corrosive incentive effects. First, the Virginia Company intended to make a profit, so eventually skimming the produce of the colony was precisely the point. Colonists resented having been misled about how hard life would be, and the idea of working harder than required for their own subsistence, largely to profit the lying fat cats who put them in their plight to begin with, was intolerable. Second, the colonists wanted to go home, and had the idea that they could win a deadly game of Chicken. The idea, as reported by a

horrified Thomas Dale, was, "We will weary out the Company at home in sending us provisions, and then, when they grow weary and see that we do not prosper here, they will send for us home. Therefore let us weary them out" (Haile, 1998, 779).

33. Under the new "Headright" system, settlers are given 50-acre plots, plus an additional 50 acres for each servant in their employ. So, they plant tobacco, harvest a crop, and use the money to return to England to recruit new servant/settlers. The recruiter collects the new settler's 50-acre grant. The new settler gets transport to Virginia and some portion of the fifty acres in return for working the recruiter's land for a few seasons while learning the essential skills. Recruiters thus begin to cobble together large plantations, new recruits in turn become recruiters themselves, and Virginia's tobacco economy begins to gallop.

34. Ellickson (1993) 1342.

35. Mydans (1989).

36. Ellickson (1993) 1335.

37. Rose (1986) 720.

38. Rose (1986) 736.

39. Ellickson (1993) 1390.

40. For an excellent discussion of the issue of adverse possession, see Rose (1985). A "usufructuary" right is an entitlement that persists only so long as the owner is using an item for its customary purpose. For example, you establish a usufructuary right to a park bench by sitting on it, but you abandon that right when you leave.

41. Ellickson (1993) 1390.

42. Bailey (1992).

43. Rose (1986) 743.

44. Of course, no one thinks governance by custom automatically solves commons problems. Custom works when local users can restrict outsider access and monitor insider behavior, but those conditions are not always met, and tragedies like those discussed earlier continue to occur.

45. Rose (1986) 742.

46. Hechter (1983) 21.

47. Goodin (1985, 1). Goodin and I debate the issue at length in Schmidtz & Goodin (1998).

CAROL M. ROSE

LIBERTY, PROPERTY, AND ENVIRONMENTALISM

In the conventional wisdom, environment and property are opposites. "The environment" consists of a kind of supposedly natural background of resources that are not subject to individual property rights, usually because they are so large or diffuse or distant. The atmosphere, the oceans, groundwater aquifers, remote forests and the wildlife that inhabits them—all these resources often carry the label "environmental." But this label also signifies that they are not owned by any individual, except perhaps metaphorically by "the sovereign,"[1] which in the United States would presumably mean "the people."

Moreover, another aspect of the conventional wisdom is that the absence of ownership is a great source of trouble for environmental resources: since no one owns them, no one invests in them or protects them from overuse. If any of their attributes become valuable, they have no defenders against the archetypical tragedy of the commons.[2] The issue is not lack of value. Quite the contrary, environmental resources are

Carol M. Rose, "Liberty, Property, Environmentalism," Social Philosophy & Policy 26 (2009): 1–25. Republished with permissions of the author and the journal.

of enormous value, even or perhaps especially in their large and diffuse undivided form. The issue is rather that no one can claim exclusive rights—that is to say, property rights—over these resources in their undivided form. The tragedy ensues because individuals slice away claimable bite-sized portions as individual property, until the whole is ruined. Millions of bison kills drove the once fabulously multitudinous herds to collapse. Millions of exhaust pipes can turn the air into an opaque and unbreathable brew. With respect to environmental resources, the usual utilitarian virtues of property—encouragement of effort, planning, investment, and trade—seem to be totally missing, turning environmental resources into scenes of waste, profligacy, and immiseration.

Given this conventional opposition between property and environment, perhaps it is not surprising that much early environmentalism relied very little on ordinary property rights. Instead, most efforts went into governmental measures like the purchase or retention of park areas, and somewhat later into command-and-control legislation specifying required measures for the use of a large array of environmental resources, ranging from catalytic converters on automobiles to double liners on hazardous waste sites to turtle exclusion devices on shrimp trawlers.[3]

All the more interesting, then, is the turn to property-rights approaches in the current effort to stave off climate change—reputedly the most gigantic environmental problem yet faced by human beings. Cap-and-trade programs are popping up throughout the international discussions of climate-change controls—that is, programs that cap the total allowable output of particular greenhouse gases, divide the allowable total into smaller individual allowances, and then allow the recipients to treat their allowances as tradable property rights. The Europeans have gone as far as anyone down the road to constraints on greenhouse gas emissions, and while they previously rejected cap-and-trade programs of all kinds as immoral trafficking in bad things, they have now developed their own active (if sometimes problematic) trading programs for greenhouse emissions. In the United States, a laggard with respect to greenhouse emission control, virtually all the legislative proposals of late 2007 and early 2008 embraced some version of market-based approaches to controlling greenhouse gases, generally cap-and-trade.[4]

Meanwhile, another form of property-rights approach to environmental protection has grown rapidly both in the United States and in the wider world, namely, conservation easements in private parcels, and conservation reserves orchestrated through nongovernmental environmental groups. The latter in particular may ultimately connect with climate-change initiatives, insofar as forestry protection becomes a larger part of the effort to sequester carbon emissions.[5]

All this property-related activity on the climate-change front raises intriguing questions about the relationship of property rights to environmental protection. Contrary to the conventional view of environmental resources as unowned or even unownable, the new initiatives hope to deploy property rights as a central means by which to conserve these seemingly unmanageable, vulnerable, and valuable resources.

Can property rights help to solve environmental problems after all, especially the one problem that currently looms largest in the world's consciousness, climate change? The answer I put forward in this essay is that property-rights approaches are important and feasible, but that there are many pitfalls that will need to be avoided. Those pitfalls can be observed from our experience with property-rights regimes for much less ambitious subjects—subjects like land, minerals, wild animals, and terrestrial water sources.

I. EVOLUTIONARY STORIES

The "tragedy of the commons" is a pessimistic story, named by the biologist Garrett Hardin in his 1968 essay of that name, but well known to resource economists considerably earlier.[6] The basic idea is that resources subject to open access—like a grazing field, a fishery, or the atmosphere—present potential users with a miniature cost–benefit calculation. Use of these resources (for grazing, fishing, or pollution storage, respectively) brings the full benefit of the taken portion to the user, while costing that user only a fraction of any damage inflicted on the larger resource, since the cost of the damage is spread out among all the other users. Conversely, investing in the larger resource's maintenance or regeneration imposes the entire investment cost on the user while bringing her only a fraction of the benefit, since she shares the benefits with all the other users. These scenarios give powerful incentives to exploit the resource and to refrain from investing. This is particularly true because the user suspects that all or most other users are making the same calculations. Essentially, the tragedy of the commons is a failure of coordination among players who could do best collectively by cooperating and deploying a modicum of self-restraint, but whose individual motivations are all to consume without restraint. Hardin suggested, and his disciple William Ophuls strongly argued, that the solution to this problem was necessarily either a turn to property rights or to the state, Leviathan.[7] More manageable and more easily divisible resources like land might be turned into property, but because large and diffuse environmental resources are so resistant to propertization, the upshot seems to be that only Leviathan can manage them. The problem is that property regimes on a smaller scale, and Leviathan on a larger one, do not simply emerge spontaneously; both institutions require coordination, and coordination raises the same "tragic" collective-action issues that appear in the original commons problem.[8]

In the opposite corner from the tragedy of the commons, however, is another widely told and much more optimistic story about property, one that does not go deeply into the coordination or collective-action problem but that nevertheless argues that property rights do emerge as the need for them unfolds. An early teller of this optimistic story was the eighteenth century legal scholar William Blackstone, who described the supposed origin and evolution of property before laying out the details of English property law in his *Commentaries*.[9] A much more recent narrator is the economist Harold Demsetz, whose story about the emergence of property rights in the eighteenth-century Canadian fur trade appeared in a now classic essay.[10]

A particularly clear exposition of the optimistic story, together with several interesting examples, can be found in an essay by two other modern economists, Terry Anderson and P. J. Hill. They begin with the premise that property rights are not costless, and hence property is unlikely to develop when it is not worth it to anyone, notably when a given resource is plentiful by comparison to the demand for it. But if a resource becomes more valuable (or the cost drops for defining and maintaining property rights), then the relevant parties will expend the necessary effort to subject the resource to property rights, and indeed to

ever more refined versions of property rights. Hence, on the account offered by Anderson and Hill, shortly after the middle of the nineteenth century cattlemen began to run their stock on the open range without many signals of ownership. But as the number of stock (and potential thieves) multiplied, cattlemen began to use roundups and branding as rudimentary methods of signaling and enforcing property rights, and finally turned to fenced-in range, particularly after the invention of barbed wire. All these moves, Anderson and Hill argue, occurred in tandem with the increased value of beef and, thanks to barbed wire, the lower cost of defending property rights.[11]

Here as in other versions of this much-told optimistic tale, property regimes emerged to meet increasing needs for resource management. It takes very little to project this story onto new-fangled conservation easements, or onto the almost ethereal property rights created for greenhouse gas allotments. Both can be envisioned as simply another ratcheting up of the level of inventiveness and sophistication, as people meet increasingly intense resource challenges with new kinds of property rights and regimes.

II. WHAT CAN GO WRONG?

Tragedy or comedy? Will property stories tend toward a woeful demise or a happy and fruitful ending, for environmental resources as well as others? The pure tragedy story is obviously overly lugubrious. As institutional economists, political scientists, and historians have pointed out repeatedly, people somehow do overcome their collective-action problems to deal with some resource issues—perhaps most dramatically, to manage the very "tragic" example that Hardin used as a metaphor, the medieval agricultural commons, whose common-field governance regimes in fact enjoyed a longevity of almost a thousand years.[12] And the medieval common fields are not the only example. Certain kinds of groups—especially those whose members know one another well and who can observe and interact with one another—often manage to establish effective property regimes, especially when they are working with certain kinds of resources. Robert Ellickson calls these groups "close-knit"; they are likely to be linked together by ties of family, geography, and perhaps religion. All over the world, people in groups like these have organized property regimes to manage common-pool resources, typically in agriculture, grazing, irrigation, fishing, and more modernly, scientific information.[13]

Nonetheless, the comedy or happy-ending story is clearly not always correct either. If it were, we would be unlikely to have evidence of so many decimations of valuable fish and wildlife, desertified former forests and grasslands, polluted waterbodies, or murderously filthy air.[14] No effective property regimes emerged in time to manage these valuable resources when they came under pressure.

In assessing the chances for managing environmental resources—and particularly climate change—through property-rights approaches, it is important to consider what can go wrong with the evolution of property rights to meet resource needs. In the following five subsections, I offer a compilation of some of the major things that can go wrong, though the list is certainly not exhaustive. I use examples from property regimes in resources that are simpler and more easily subjected to property rights than greenhouse gases ever will be, on the theory that if things can go wrong with these resources that are more readily and cheaply brought under a property regime, we should be on the lookout for related problems all the more with respect to climate change.

Here is the list:

A. POTENTIAL PARTICIPANTS MAY FAIL TO AGREE ON A PROPERTY REGIME

There are, of course, a great number of reasons why people never come to agreement at all on a new or revised system of property rights to give order to their use of resources.

The most obvious reason is that while property rights may be private, a modern property *regime* is a public good, either a formal public good like national defense, or an informal one like the cattle roundups that Anderson and Hill describe. A property regime serves an entire collectivity of people who hold and observe property rights. Nothing is lost to the regime by any individual's participation, a feature that much reduces any motivations to exclude others from the regime.[15] By the same token, however, no one has any particular motivation to create the regime in the first place. A property regime requires investment to get underway—often investment in the form of discussions, committee meetings, and cajoling others—but any such investment is little more than a gift to the others who can participate in the regime without bothering to go to the initial meetings. Under those circumstances, unless some Solon steps up, a property regime may never get off the ground, or if it does, it does so for almost accidental reasons. Anthropologist Bonnie McCay, a student of informal property regimes among fishing communities, has made the very useful observation that these informal property regimes often spring up simply as a means for managing and avoiding disputes,[16] an observation to which I will return. But in the absence of some lasting agreement to solve disputes through a system of mutually recognized entitlements, the relevant parties may simply continue to fight and grab, with the accompanying waste of resources and human efforts.

Similarly, even if people do manage to establish a property regime, they may be unable to change the regime to conform to new situations. Fishermen may agree, for example, on some variation of a first-possession rule favoring the first one to capture an individual fish, or they may develop some other kind of allocation rules for larger and more dangerous marine animals, whose capture requires group efforts. But they may never come up with property rules to manage the stock as a whole. This was a problem for nineteenth-century whalers; the whalers' on-the-spot rules for possessory rights added to the efficiency of the hunt, reducing conflict and encouraging cooperative efforts within small groups, but if anything their localized cooperation exacerbated the never-addressed global problem of declining whale stocks.[17] The global problem involved whaling communities from all over the world, and until very recently, none ever even considered creating the global public good of an overarching property regime to maintain worldwide stocks.

A second reason why people often cannot agree on a property regime (whether initially or at a revision stage) is that they get snarled in the distributional conflicts that a property regime raises. Property rights make obvious the issue of who gets what, and this can cause problems. From a purely utilitarian point of view, the initial distribution of entitlements in a valuable resource is a distinctly secondary issue if the entitlements can be traded, since trade will enhance the movement of goods and services to those who value them most, no matter who received them in the first instance. Besides, much wealth is created simply through trade, which encourages specialization in the areas of each trading partner's comparative advantage. On this utilitarian perspective, the important thing is simply to get a new or revised property regime under way for valuable resources, no matter who gets what at the outset.[18]

But distributional issues matter a great deal to the parties involved, both from a perspective of self-interest and from a perspective of fairness and desert.[19] Natural resources are replete with instances in which parties fail to reach value-maximizing agreements over entitlements because they cannot agree on distribution, leading to situations that would be ludicrous if they were not so wasteful. A nineteenth-century case in the early Pennsylvania oilfields gives an example. In *Hague v. Wheeler* (1893), a natural gas developer sued a neighboring landowner to stop him from flaring off the natural gas that underlay both their properties; this was evidently a kind of extortionate effort on the part of the neighboring landowner, aimed at inducing the gas entrepreneur to run a pipeline to his property. The trial court held that flaring off natural gas was an unreasonable use of their common-pool property, but the Supreme Court of Pennsylvania reversed the lower court's decision, holding that the landowner was entitled to do as he pleased—which included wasting the commonly-held resource.[20]

Even in cases like this, when courts step in to allocate entitlements, bad blood may still keep the neighbors from ever coming to terms over a trade.[21] Cap-and-trade systems are now working their way into American fish stock management, but it has taken the biological collapse of many important fisheries to induce fishermen to try these property-rights schemes. A major stumbling block has been the choice of a basis for allocating newly-limited rights: Should the basis be each fisherman's past catch levels? Boat ownership? Boat capacity? Time spent as a crew member? All these possibilities yield different distributions, and the parties involved are acutely aware of the differences.[22] Gary Libecap, an economist who studies such common-pool problems, argues that distributional

issues routinely disrupt the process of what he calls "contracting for property rights," and the larger and more heterogeneous the group that must agree, the slimmer the chances and the longer the delay before they arrive (if ever) at property arrangements that can staunch the common pool hemorrhage.[23]

A third reason why people often fail to come to terms on a property-rights regime is that falling back on Leviathan offers an escape from the knotty problems that property rights present. That is to say, people may settle on a command-and-control regime to manage resources, because command-and-control on the surface appears to require the same performance of all participants, thus evading the difficult distributional issues. Efforts to manage fish stocks often take a command-and-control turn long before turning to property approaches. For example, early-stage regulatory efforts are often prohibitions of certain kinds of gear or permission to fish only in certain time periods, precisely because command-and-control regulations like these avoid difficult confrontations over the distribution of entitlements. The disadvantage of these regulations, however, is that they can be very wasteful, with examples that would again be ludicrous if they were not so sad—like the tightly limited fishing seasons that fishermen turn into "derbies," taking on so many fish that their boats sometimes sink under the weight.[24] And indeed, even the appearance of egalitarianism is deceptive in command-and-control regulation. We learned early on from command-and-control air pollution measures that seemingly equal requirements have great cost differences in different locations and under different circumstances.[25] Failure to agree is thus an important and multifaceted reason why property regimes never come into place or fail to assimilate to new pressures on resources. But there are other reasons as well for the failure of property regimes.

B. A PROPERTY REGIME MAY BE INEFFECTIVE OR INCONSISTENT

There are a number of reasons why property regimes may be ineffective, many leading back to governmental incapacity. In the simplest case, a government may lack the financial resources and administrative capacity to project the basic elements of a modern property regime throughout its territory. Record systems, impartial enforcement, and dispute resolution are elements of a property regime that may not function in a weak government. Corruption can corrode the effectiveness of property systems even further, as when technical objections block land registration until the landowner pays under the table, or when supposedly neutral enforcement agents wink at violations by favored persons or firms.

Of course, formal property regimes are not the only option. Even in the absence of modern forms of property rights, people use informal systems to manage resources that are important to them. These regimes are not perfect, however, either from the perspective of economic development or of libertarian independence. For one thing, informal regimes are generally limited to resources that are relatively easily monitored, usually involving extractive activities of one sort or another, like grazing or water use. Indeed, an important criterion for the success of informal property rights is that individual entitlements can be ordered in such a way that they can be monitored by members of the group, and particularly by the most affected members of the group. As an example, Elinor Ostrom cites the community-based irrigation systems in which each farmer along the channel can observe the time and rough quantity of water that is diverted by the neighboring farmer who precedes him in turn.[26] But informal regimes do relatively little to address issues of pollution, which are much harder to monitor, and in any event, community members may be indifferent to pollution that affects outsiders rather than the community members themselves. In addition, long-lasting informal rights regimes depend for enforcement on the community and its implicit or explicit hierarchies. Customary practices are likely to favor certain groups over others (notably men over women); and they are generally not welcoming to outsiders, since outsiders could disrupt the social relations that hold the community together. Moreover, customary informal property regimes tend to be very complex; these complexities serve a purpose by cementing ties among the community members, but they further limit the ability of outsiders to participate through trade. Hence informal regimes are constrained in a variety of significant ways: for example, in their ability to raise capital or to make room for new ideas.[27]

Modern property regimes depend on governmental intervention. With their formal rights, relatively easy trading conditions, and openness to the participation of strangers, these rights regimes are aimed at overcoming the limitations of informal regimes. Perhaps the worst-case scenario for resource management, however, occurs when a nominally rational and modern central government attempts to impose a modernist system of formal property rights on a customary regime, and succeeds only partially. Under those circumstances, citizens live in a paralyzing situation of what Daniel Fitzpatrick calls "legal pluralism," a condition of conflicting regimes of entitlement that leaves all participants insecure in their claims, and that encourages all to take while the taking is possible. Among his many examples of this problem, Fitzpatrick cites several areas in Africa, where earlier colonial efforts to modernize property rights served chiefly to undermine long-standing customary regimes without providing citizens with effective modernist property institutions.[28] In the absence of a unified and effective system of property protections, natural resources are much at risk.

A variant on the theme of legal pluralism may occur within a national government itself, a situation that is illustrated strikingly in a study of the modern Brazilian Amazon region by economists Lee Alston, Gary Libecap, and Bernardo Mueller. As they argue, the Brazilian legal system provides strong property protection in the civil code, yet not only does that protection go unenforced in remote areas, but it is contradicted by an opposing constitutional policy that allows settlers to claim "unproductive" lands for themselves. These contradictory legal elements result in great uncertainty about property rights, and they fuel the violent confrontations that occur between land-hungry settlers and their proponents on the one hand, and determined owners of outsized land grants, the old *latifundia*, on the other. Caught in the middle is the Brazilian rainforest, subject to burns and clearing as both sides use self-help to staunch their claims with proof of "productive" use.[29]

C. EVEN AN EFFECTIVE PROPERTY REGIME MAY REVOLVE AROUND PURPOSES INCOMPATIBLE WITH ENVIRONMENTAL PROTECTION

Another major category of things that can go wrong is that people may develop strong and efficacious property regimes, but these regimes may focus on goals that treat environmental resources with indifference or hostility.

The mining camp rules of the mid-nineteenth-century California gold rush are often used as an example of the spontaneous generation of property regimes not only within a close-knit group, but among complete strangers. Newly arrived prospectors quickly hit upon rules for the size of individual claims, for the events that would count as abandonment, and for the mechanisms to be used in resolving disputes, as well as other rules about the priority of claims to use the waters in nearby streams for mining purposes. Historians have discussed the degree to which the mining camp rules were original to the gold rush participants. But original or not, these rule systems were certainly a remarkable achievement for men who were pouring in from all over the world and who were strangers to one another—a motley collection of men who from all appearances should have turned gold mining into a total free-for-all.[30]

From an environmental perspective, however, one of the notable features of the mining camp rules was that—as anthropologist Bonnie McCay has observed of many informal regimes—they focused entirely on assisting miners to avoid disputes and to invest more or less rationally in their quest for gold. These rules completely ignored the enormous impact that mining had on the surrounding environment. Gold rush miners ripped the hills apart with hydraulic water jets, and they trashed salmon runs with sediments and debris (meanwhile casually murdering complaining indigenous salmon fishers).[31] The detritus left by gold rush miners is still visible to this day in the California hill country. If anything, quite like the whalers' rules, the gold miners' rules increased the environmental depredations simply because they reduced conflicts among miners themselves. Over the longer run, the gold rush mining camp rules about water set the stage for the creation of the appropriative water rights regimes of the western states, regimes that have been used to provide water for western agriculture as well as mining and a number of other uses. Appropriative systems follow rules of priority, whereby the first to divert water from a stream and use it for a "beneficial" purpose may continue to claim the amount of water diverted in subsequent seasons. The second diverter comes second in

priority, and so it goes until the stream water is entirely claimed or, in many cases, over-claimed. It is often said that agriculture would have been impossible in the dry west without this striking deviation from the humid eastern states' "riparian" rules, which linked water usage to adjacent landownership and which generally attempted to keep water in the stream for subsequent streamside users.[32]

There are many critiques of western water law, but for many years the system has served agricultural, mining, and other commercial and municipal activities in the western states. What it has not served well is the set of environmental resources that depend on water that remains in the stream—notably fish and other wildlife, as well as wetlands and their numerous ecological services, not to speak of recreational river rafting. There is a version of "path dependency" in western water law that keeps this body of law from easy transformation toward more conservationist ends —that is, a difficulty in adapting because of prior institutional choices. The central method for claiming appropriative rights is diversion of water from the stream, but this is obviously an activity that is difficult to square with claiming rights for instream uses. This problem of rights-definition can be addressed, as it has been in some states, but it involves a major shift in people's thinking about the ways that water rights can be claimed.[33] Another kind of path dependency occurs simply because people have acquired rights with one purpose in mind and only later realize that another purpose might have been more valuable; by that time, it may be costly to change course. Resource economist Dean Lueck, for example, writes that farmers generally attempt to make the most valuable uses of their land *net of transaction costs*. Those uses could theoretically include wildlife conservation (e.g., for a birding preserve or hunting club).[34] But the transaction costs are the rub: if farmland has already been divided among a number of farmers, they may find that the high cost of bargaining among themselves impedes them from consolidating their holdings into a single unit that is large enough to be useful for wildlife purposes. Much the same occurs with oil and gas discoveries. As economists Gary Libecap and Steven Wiggins have illustrated, after a number of landowners divide up the surface property that overlays an oil or gas reservoir, they may never succeed in negotiating a voluntary unitization agreement for the most efficient exploitation of a later-discovered underlying resource.[35]

In all these instances, property rights have been defined with certain purposes in mind, while ignoring other possible goals—notably, environmental ones—and in fact they may make the vindication of other goals either difficult or impossible.

D. METHODS FOR DEFINING PROPERTY MAY NOT WORK WELL FOR ENVIRONMENTAL RESOURCES

Because property rights must command the respect of nonowners, it is important that property rights give off signals that are recognizable to the relevant universe of nonowners.[36] One very important reason why environmental resources are often not included in property-rights regimes is that it is difficult to find recognizable markers for environmental resources. Land rights can be signaled relatively easily by fences or cultivation. But water, air, and wildlife stocks are much more difficult to mark in any tangible way. Moreover, the tangible methods of marking out rights often entail the destruction of environmental resources. Diversion from streams under western water law was mentioned above. Diversion is a tangible way to claim a right to a certain amount of water, since nonowners can observe the diversion itself, but diversion necessarily removes the water from the stream. Similarly, a person can claim the right to particular animals or fish in a wildlife stock by killing or capturing them, but this method of rights-marking necessarily removes the animals from the larger stock. Even land rights are often signaled by environmentally destructive methods. Cutting trees or planting crops are common methods of signaling ownership of land, but an uncultivated or un-logged forest lot may appear to be unclaimed or abandoned, even though the owner has purposefully kept the area wild. In general, passive uses are at a disadvantage in property regimes. Nonphysical claim-marking methods like recording or registration systems can ease many of these difficulties, but these systems are apt to be at their weakest in the remote areas in which environmental resources may be most valuable.[37]

Another feature of property rights also undercuts their effectiveness for environmental uses. A very important aspect of modern property rights is that they may be traded widely, because, as I mentioned earlier, trade encourages specialization and allows resources to gravitate to those who most wish to have them. But if property rights are to be tradable to the world at large, they must also be maintained in relatively simple and standardized form; otherwise, potential buyers will be uncertain what they are getting, and they may be frightened out of transactions where they have to be on guard for idiosyncratic forms of property.[38] Idiosyncratic and complex property regimes can work reasonably well in small and close-knit groups, where the members are familiar with local complexities, but they will not serve a larger market well. But it is larger marketability that adds to the value of entitlements.

The problem for environmental resources is that these resources themselves are often complex, and they are not easily shaped into fungible, standardized rights that can be traded back and forth over a wide range. For example, if a wetland is to provide such ecosystem services as flood control or fish spawning, its location matters, as does the consistency of its plant and animal life. Tradable environmental property regimes within the United States have functioned reasonably well for sulfur dioxide emissions, the major precursor gases to acid rain, although even here there are important nonfungibilities of location; trades from downwind to upwind are considerably more damaging than trades in the opposite direction. Trades have been far more problematic for wetlands or habitat. These more complex resources cannot be traded against one another without significant alterations in the very features that make them valuable: location makes a difference, for example, to a wetland's ability to tame floodwaters or provide fish spawning grounds. One may take other measures to assure against losing the distinctive ecosystem values of wildlife habitat, old growth forests, or wetlands (for example, by allowing trades only within restricted specifications), but such specifications necessarily limit the pool of potential trading possibilities.[39]

Considerable thought has gone into the ways that various aspects of environmental resources might be broken down and classified in trade—for example, creating elaborate point systems for the different ecosystem services performed by wetlands, which are the subjects of trade under some legislation.[40] If a real estate developer of, say, a beach hotel cannot avoid destroying legally protected wetlands, the ecosystem damage can be added up and the developer can purchase an offsetting quantity in a "wetlands bank" established elsewhere by an environmental entrepreneur. Flood protection would receive a certain number of points, aquifer recharge a certain amount more, bird habitat still more, and so on. Property rights regimes of this sort are certainly conceivable, but they are likely to be complex and expensive. Indeed, wetlands banks exist now for purposes of real estate development trades, but with a few exceptions, these banks use only very simple comparative-value calculations, resulting in trades that may in fact forfeit substantial wetlands values.[41]

Efforts to turn complex environmental resources into property rights thus face serious obstacles, and these can only be overcome in ways that are all at least somewhat unattractive. First, one can ignore the differences among various environmental resources and allow trading in gross rights, despite potential losses. Second, one can account for the differences through constraints and hedges on trading. And third, one can pay the costs of property definitions that take into account the distinctive features of particular environmental resources. The first option is one that the United States has taken with the cap-and-trade program in sulfur dioxide; the second with wetlands trades; the third is still under development, no doubt because of the expense.

E. MODERN PROPERTY REGIMES TEND TO CREATE RESOURCE MONOCULTURES, AND THESE MAY UNDERMINE ENVIRONMENTAL RESOURCES

Private property and freedom of contract are the basic building blocks of capitalism. The relative simplicity of modern property rights makes them tradable to a worldwide pool of bidders, and this feature in turn means that goods and services can circulate all over the globe. Moreover, the possibility of trade encourages individuals as well as regions to specialize in the activities in which they have a comparative advantage.

By the same token, however, trade and specialization also reduce local diversity in production. By contrast, small-scale economies are by necessity diversified

and more or less self-sufficient on a local scale, because people in such economies must produce on the spot most or all of what they consume. But wider trade seriously modifies local diversification. Why buy the local leather goods if imported goods are cheaper and better? Indeed, this question raises one of the chief complaints against globalized trade: that products from elsewhere outcompete the array of locally grown or locally manufactured products, and this competition ultimately forces the locality to die off or to find a specialization of its own. The complaint is not a new one; a growing international trade in woolens encouraged the enclosure movement in sixteenth-century England, when landowners disrupted diversified common-field agricultural communities and enclosed the fields for the sole purpose of raising sheep.[42] Just as trade allowed those landowners to produce wool for distant markets, trade obviated their need for locally diversified goods. Then as now, local diversification is unnecessary where trade allows consumers to satisfy their needs from better if more distant sources.

The pattern described above is typical of an expanding capitalism: it tends toward localized monocultures. Another example is the relationship between the city of Chicago and its hinterlands during the nineteenth century, admirably described in William Cronon's 1991 book *Nature's Metropolis*. In order to feed the city's enormous appetites, both in its own right and as a trading depot for other parts of the United States, midwestern farmers turned the diverse tallgrass prairie into monocultures of wheat and corn; Michigan and Wisconsin loggers stripped bare the old growth forests; while ranchers in the west turned the public lands into a vast feeding ground for beef cattle.[43]

Needless to say, these particular specializations had serious consequences for native plants and animals. But more generally, insofar as environmental resources (e.g., wildlife stocks) require diversified ecosystems, they are likely to suffer under an expanding capitalist resource regime that tends toward specialization and regional monocultures. This is not to say that modern property rights and freedom of contract, the essential elements of capitalism, are the bane of environmentalism. They are not, or at least not necessarily. Capitalism makes societies wealthier, and wealthier societies tend to lavish much more concern on environmental issues than poor ones do.[44] It is simply to note that one important aspect of capitalism—specialization—can run contrary to the well-being of environmental goods that require a diversified resource base.

III. CLIMATE CHANGE AND WHAT MAY GO WRONG WITH PROPERTY REGIMES

With this incomplete listing of potential problems that property-rights regimes may pose for the environment, let us turn to climate change, and to the efforts to use property-rights regimes to combat global warming. Are these efforts likely to encounter similar issues? Clearly they are. Very briefly, the following subsections illustrate how climate change control efforts map onto the environmental problem areas for property regimes more generally.

A. THE FIRST PROBLEM: POTENTIAL PARTICIPANTS MAY FAIL TO AGREE ON A PROPERTY REGIME

Climate change is a worldwide issue, and there could scarcely be a more daunting task than garnering worldwide agreement on any property regime, about any subject. Since the Rio Conference on climate change in 1992, a mix of national governments and nongovernmental organizations (NGOs) has been at work on crafting some kind of property regime to govern the emissions of the chief greenhouse gases (GHGs). But major disagreements still split the international community on what must be the most basic issue of all: Shall there be a worldwide cap on greenhouse gas production, to which all are committed? The United States has insisted on such a universal cap, to which less-developed countries (LDCs) must also commit, whereas the LDCs themselves adamantly refuse, taking the view that the major responsibility for emission control lies with already developed economies.[45] A partial accord was reached in the 1997 Kyoto Protocol; this agreement binds the developed countries to reduce GHGs by an average of just over 5 percent by 2012, but it has placed no binding obligations on LDCs.[46] The United States refused to ratify the protocol. As a result, as of the writing of this essay in 2008, neither the United States nor major LDC producers of greenhouse gases, notably China and India, had

committed to curb emissions to a particular capped level. This lag may well prove to be only temporary, but it suggests some of the difficulties of coming to agreement on the most basic property-rights issues for environmental protection.

Negotiations over a cap-and-trade property regime for greenhouse gases have also illustrated how wrangles can develop over much subtler issues, many of them, quite predictably, involving distributional questions. For example, if GHG caps are to be determined on the basis of a rollback of existing emissions—the most prevalent method for setting caps—then the choice of a rollback date matters a great deal, since any given target date affects different countries quite differently. The chosen rollback date of 1990 favored the European signatories while disfavoring the nonratifying United States; during the 1990s, the Europeans had made a number of moves toward non-carbon-based energy for other reasons, and thus fortuitously had already met more of their obligations.[47] Further disagreements have occurred over what counts or does not count as a suitable offset for GHG emissions—that is, what can be traded for what under the Kyoto Protocol. Credits for forests (as so-called carbon sinks, removing carbon dioxide from the air) have been particularly contentious, again pitting Europe, with its few forests, against the much more forested United States.[48] With these numerous serious disagreements, it is remarkable that any movement at all has occurred with respect to property-rights-oriented greenhouse gas controls.

B. THE SECOND PROBLEM: A PROPERTY REGIME MAY BE INEFFECTIVE OR INCONSISTENT

The great advantage of cap-and-trade programs is that they allow for substitute performance. A GHG emitter has the option of reducing emissions or buying emission permits from some other source, but purchased permits necessarily come from other sources which have reduced or otherwise sequestered GHGs. Here as in all trading regimes, the great advantage of substitute performance is that it allows all parties to take advantage of the lowest-cost options for pollution reduction, and it encourages multiple parties to experiment in developing those low-cost options.[49]

The credibility of the entire system, however, depends on reliable monitoring and enforcement at the business end—that is to say, where the emission reduction or sequestration is supposed to take place. It is at that point that ineffective or weak property rights could be most damaging. Greenhouse gas emitters in developed countries could well find numerous opportunities to purchase emission rights by contracting for reduced emissions in less-developed countries (LDCs); among other things, it is likely to be cheaper to install controls on new plants in LDCs than to retrofit older ones in more-developed countries. But LDC leaders may well have conflicting motives about such trades, given their sense of urgency about enhancing economic growth; meanwhile, on-the-scene local actors may well disdain what they regard as do-gooder meddlers from far away. Those patterns could well lead to widespread surreptitious flouting of the terms of GHG trades, coupled with lax enforcement on domestic industries that are purportedly decreasing emissions.[50] LDCs are not the only offenders, of course. In all parts of the world, unverified promises to offset GHGs by reduced emissions are already a feature of trading regimes, and much hucksterism may be expected in the future.[51]

C. THE THIRD PROBLEM: EVEN AN EFFECTIVE PROPERTY REGIME MAY REVOLVE AROUND PURPOSES INCOMPATIBLE WITH ENVIRONMENTAL PROTECTION

With respect to questions of climate change, this third problem is nowhere near as serious as the first two, i.e., garnering agreement and securing consistent and effective enforcement. Cap-and-trade programs for GHGs are obviously aimed directly at a serious environmental problem, and quasi-property rights under these programs will be a central element of any climate-change regime that includes the world's major industrial powers.[52] Nevertheless, we have learned from other environmental endeavors that efforts to solve one kind of environmental issue can create other environmental problems. In a well-known example, technology to reduce sulfur dioxide from factory emissions has created large quantities of toxic sludge, resulting in a kind of trade-off between air cleanup and land disposal.[53] Experience with the Kyoto Protocol has already hinted at another such displacement problem

that affects cap-and-trade: the sidelining and potential disturbance of old-growth forests. The protocol allows GHG emitters in developed countries to meet their emission reduction requirements by "offsetting" their own emissions with certain kinds of approved carbon sequestrations elsewhere, both within the developed countries and in LDCs. These offsetting sequestrations include newly planted vegetation, which absorbs and fixes carbon dioxide from the air, but the offset plantings must be an addition to what might have been planted in the ordinary course of what is called "business as usual."

Since the preservation of old-growth forests is not an "additional" form of carbon sequestration, however, parties to Kyoto have been unable to use old-growth forestry conservation activities as offsets, eliminating an important potential source of funds for LDC forest conservation. Newly planted trees, in contrast, do count as additional offsetting measures under Kyoto, so that it is certainly conceivable that old-growth forests could be clearcut or burned to make way for newly planted tree monocultures, losing the benefits of old-growth biodiversity while possibly causing a net increase in atmospheric GHGs. Such results cause dismay among rainforest conservation experts, who point out that the burnoffs of old-growth forests are already contributing heavily to worldwide carbon dioxide formation. They cause dismay as well among the leaders of some less developed countries, who fear that their old-growth forests are doomed without the infusion of resources that eligibility for offset credits might provide. The Kyoto signatories are aware of this forestry problem and have begun to address it since the followup Bali conference in 2007, but solutions may be difficult or incomplete, for reasons to be addressed next.[54]

D. THE FOURTH PROBLEM: METHODS FOR DEFINING PROPERTY RIGHTS MAY NOT WORK WELL FOR ENVIRONMENTAL RESOURCES

This fourth problem, like the third, amounts to a vexing set of peripheral problems in climate-change programs rather than the kind of deal-breaking difficulties presented by agreement and enforcement. Nevertheless, the vexation is a durable one: as with other environmental resources, it can be difficult to find good property-rights markers for contributions to climate change. The United States' widely acclaimed cap-and-trade program for acid rain control has shown a comparable feature. The real problem of acid rain is the acidification of soils and water bodies, but we are unable to measure and mark those damages directly, so we instead control acid rain by measuring and permitting trades of tons of emissions. So too with climate change. The main object of course is to avoid damage, but damage, in the form of contribution to climate change, is far too difficult to measure, so that cap-and-trade programs use tons of GHGs as a proxy for damage.[55] But the use of these proxies raises other problems. For example, carbon is relatively easy to measure, but methane is not. Hence carbon trades against other carbon sources are relatively straightforward, but carbon emissions offset by methane necessarily involve a metric that is at best approximate.[56] An even more troublesome situation faces the prospect of using forestry sequestration to offset GHGs. Forests differ greatly in their capacities to absorb GHGs, depending among other things on location, composition, and the age of the trees involved.[57] Indeed, some believe that while forests in the earth's cold regions do sequester GHGs, they may actually make global warming worse by substituting dark green ground-cover for reflective white snow.[58] If forests are to be incorporated into GHG cap-and-trade programs as offsets, some unit or units of measurement must be found. A simple measure like acreage is highly advantageous for purposes of creating thick market trading, but highly disadvantageous for purposes of precision in offsets. All these issues add up to a problem that one might call "proxy slippage": the things we can measure for purposes of defining property rights have only an inexact relationship to the objects for which we create the property regime in the first place. This will be true in GHG cap-and-trade programs as it is in other property regimes.

E. THE FIFTH PROBLEM: MODERN PROPERTY REGIMES TEND TO CREATE RESOURCE MONOCULTURES, AND THESE MAY UNDERMINE ENVIRONMENTAL RESOURCES

A generic pattern in property regimes is that modern tradable rights promote regional specialization, and specialization tends toward monoculture. One environmental version of this pattern is the "hotspot" problem. This can occur, for example, if pollutants are treated as tradable rights and then traded toward one direction, leading some particular area to "specialize" in toxicity. Hotspots have been a particular focus for environmental justice concerns, since the pollutants in question may well gravitate toward locations occupied by the poor, where the concentration of pollutants may make them more hazardous than they would have been if still dispersed. However, this hotspot pattern is much less serious for climate change cap-and-trade programs than it can be for other kinds of property or quasi-property regimes. Carbon dioxide, the main GHG, is immune from the hotspot problem, because carbon dioxide mixes into a uniform mass in the atmosphere, no matter where it comes from or where it goes. Moreover, certain kinds of trading-induced regional specialization can actually be of benefit to biodiversity. It is widely thought, for example, that even though there are many problems about wetlands trades, nevertheless wetlands trades can result in larger, concentrated wetland areas that have more benefits to wildlife than do smaller and isolated wetland fragments. Insofar as GHG offset trading does come to include old-growth forestry, specialization could be a particular benefit for biodiversity. GHG emissions in any part of the globe could be traded for the preservation of large tracts of intact old-growth forest.

In sum, then, property-rights approaches to climate change can be expected to face many of the same environmental issues as do property-rights regimes in other resource domains. These issues vary in seriousness, however, from extreme to much less serious. Taken together, they suggest that property-rights regimes can be very important contributors in confronting climate change, but that they cannot be adopted without overcoming significant obstacles, and that they will never be perfect once adopted.

IV. CONCLUSION

I conclude this essay with two sets of observations. The first set concerns the place of ordinary property and environmental property regimes in a more general libertarian project. The second set concerns the scale on which property rights—and environmental property regimes—are most meaningful.

First, the libertarian project: Property rights loom large in libertarian thinking because property preserves a zone of freedom for the owner. But from the same libertarian perspective, property rights pale to almost nothing by comparison to open access. In a regime of open access, anyone can do anything. The philosopher J. E. Penner is a great advocate of property, but his work suggests strongly that property rights for the most part define not rights in the owner, but duties in the nonowner. He gives the very prosaic example of an amble through a parking lot where the person on foot knows nothing about the vehicles or their owners except one thing: the vehicles do not belong to him, and he had better keep his hands off.[59] Game theorists make much the same point in rather different language. They define property rights as a hawk/dove "game" in which the owner gets to play hawk, while all nonowners play dove.[60] In a functioning property regime, one plays dove vastly more frequently than one plays hawk. How much more liberating, then, is the grand free-for-all of open access, where one can hunt and fish and roam about at will! To be sure, open access has its inconveniences, all those aggravating interlopers and that damned tragedy of the commons. From a certain perspective, however, property regimes are a distinct retreat from the freedom of open access, a concession to reality that, yes, rewards effort and investment, but that still preserves only a little zone of freedom. By comparison to open access, that zone can only be considered, in the vernacular, dinky. By the same token, the grand environmental dream is the vast wilderness, untamed, unowned, and unsullied. Environmental management regimes of any sort are a distinct wet blanket on such romantic dreams of the wild, a kind of stern reminder that, like it or not, it is all a zoo out there—no part of the globe is safe from the baleful impact of human activity. Efforts to mitigate the damage of climate change are only the latest and the largest of such wet-blanket reminders. Under the circumstances we face, though, property-based regimes like cap-and-trade offer the same kind of limited consolation that ordinary property offers after the retreat from open access: at least a bit of freedom, a small opportunity to decide for oneself how to allocate one's allotment, and how to augment that allotment by striking up agreements with others. And as

with ordinary property, planning and trading can open up vast new arenas of activity and opportunity. Putting to one side all the practical difficulties that environmental property regimes may present—the main subject of this essay—a system of free choice in tradable environmental rights may uncover whole new realms of now unexpected and even unimagined conservationist innovation, if only a vanishingly faint glimmer of the romance of the wild.

A second set of observations concerns the parallels between property rights and environmental concerns with respect to scale. While property rights may be generated spontaneously in nongovernmental groups and communities, the property that counts, both for wealth creation and for liberty, is not bottom-up but top-down, that is to say, state-sponsored. There are small-scale community-based property regimes the world over, but they define rights that are excruciatingly detailed, that are policed by nosy neighbors and local bosses, and that cannot be traded or even understood by outsiders. By and large, the rights that count for amassing commercial wealth are modernist: these property rights are relatively simple; they are capable of being recorded and registered; they can be traded anywhere and to anyone; and they depend on science, technology, and literacy for monitoring, and on agencies and courts for enforcement.

By the same token, small communities may have only a light impact on the environment, and they may coexist for long periods amid abundant environmental resources. But the environmental friendliness of small-scale communities is easily overwhelmed by shifts in market demand or changes in technology. Such communities often lack the knowledge, power, or desire to protect environmental resources in the face of market or technological alterations, leading some to conclude that community based environmentalism exists only because of isolation and technological limitations.[61]

These observations coalesce in environmental property rights regimes like cap-and-trade. These regimes offer great promise for innovation and cost-saving, and in some cases they can even be deployed to reenergize community-based environmentalism, as in community-based fishing quotas.[62] The rights they put in play are tremendously sophisticated, however, and they depend critically on modernist property instruments of definition, recordkeeping, and enforcement. We may dream of perfect liberty and a natural equilibrium in an undisturbed commons. But that is not the stuff of modern environmental protection, including environmental protection based on property rights. For modern environmental property rights to function, the central object of concern must be accountable, clean, willing, capable, and energetic government.

NOTES

1. See William Blackstone, *Commentaries on the Laws of England* (1766; Chicago and London: University of Chicago Press, 1979), 2:14–15 (attributing otherwise unowned things to the ownership of the "sovereign").
2. Garrett Hardin, "The Tragedy of the Commons," *Science* 162, no. 3859 (1968): 1243–48.
3. The first national park was Yellowstone, reserved in 1872. For a brief history of federal park reservations and related wilderness protection in the United States, see George Cameron Coggins, Charles F. Wilkinson, John D. Leshy, and Robert L. Fischman, *Federal Public Land and Resources Law*, 6th ed. (New York: Foundation Press, 2007), 1009–13. For the general pattern of command-and-control legislation in the generation after 1970 and the more recent move to market-oriented regulation, see Carol M. Rose, "Environmental Law Grows Up (More or Less), and What Science Can Do to Help," *Lewis and Clark Law Journal* 9 (2005): 273–94. For the specifics of turtle exclusion devices (TEDs), for which the United States' requirements have encountered international opposition on free-trade grounds, see George Cavros, "The Hidden Cost of Free Trade: The Impact of United States World Trade Organization Obligations on United States Environmental Sovereignty," *ILSA Journal of International and Comparative Law* 9 (2003): 563, 564–65.
4. For a summary and analysis of congressional legislative proposals as of late 2007 and some comparisons with European efforts, see Victor B. Flatt, "Taking the Legislative Temperature: Which Federal Climate Change Proposal is 'Best'?" *Northwestern University Law Review Colloquy* 102 (2007): 123–50.

5. See Mashiro Amano and Roger A. Sedjo, "Forest Sequestration: Performance in Selected Countries in the Kyoto Period and the Potential Role of Sequestration in Post-Kyoto Agreements" (2006), http://www.rff. org/Documents/RFF-Rpt-ForestSequestrationKyoto. pdf. See also Carol M. Rose, "Big Roads, Big Rights: Varieties of Public Infrastructure and Their Impact on Environmental Resources," *Arizona Law Review* 50, no. 2 (2008): 409–43.
6. See Hardin, "Tragedy of the Commons." For an earlier and more precise treatment by a resource economist, see H. Scott Gordon, "The Economic Theory of a Common Property Resource: The Fishery," *Journal of Political Economy* 62, no. 2 (1954): 124–42.
7. William Ophuls, *Ecology and the Politics of Scarcity* (San Francisco: W. H. Freeman, 1977), 147–56.
8. James E. Krier, "The Tragedy of the Commons, Part II," *Harvard Journal of Law and Public Policy* 15 (1992): 325, 336–38.
9. Blackstone, *Commentaries*, 2:2–11.
10. Harold Demsetz, "Toward a Theory of Property Rights," *American Economic Review Papers and Proceedings* 57, no. 2 (1967): 347–58.
11. Terry L. Anderson and P. J. Hill, "The Evolution of Property Rights: A Study of the American West," *Journal of Law and Economics* 18, no. 1 (1975): 163–79.
12. See Susan Jane Buck Cox, "No Tragedy of the Commons," *Environmental Ethics* 7 (Spring 1985): 49–61 (illustrating the absence of "tragedy" on the medieval common fields). See also Henry E. Smith, "Semicommon Property Rights and Scattering in the Open Fields," *Journal of Legal Studies* 29, no. 1 (2000): 131–69 (describing and offering an economic analysis of the elaborate medieval village systems for scattering individual fields and rotating them in and out of common grazing usage). Smith reports that there is some evidence that particular commons originated with individual farmers who agreed to "common" their holdings.
13. Robert C. Ellickson, *Order without Law: How Neighbors Settle Disputes* (Cambridge, MA: Harvard University Press, 1991), 177–83. For a variety of examples, see Elinor Ostrom, *Governing the Commons: The Evolution of Institutions for Collective*

Action (Cambridge: Cambridge University Press, 1990). For specific examples, see Robert McC. Netting, *Balancing on an Alp: Ecological Change and Continuity in a Swiss Mountain Community* (Cambridge and New York: Cambridge University Press, 1981) (community grazing); Paul B. Trawick, *The Struggle for Water in Peru: Comedy and Tragedy in the Andean Commons* (Stanford, CA: Stanford University Press, 2003) (community irrigation); James M. Acheson, *The Lobster Gangs of Maine* (Hanover, NH: University Press of New England, 1988) (fishing community); and Robert P. Merges, "Property Rights Theory and the Commons: The Case of Scientific Research," *Social Philosophy and Policy* 13, no. 2 (1996): 145–67.

14. See, e.g., Warren Dean, *With Broadax and Firebrands* (Berkeley, Los Angeles, and London: University of California Press, 1995) (describing the long decimation of the Brazilian Atlantic Forest); Joshua Hamer, "A Prayer for the Ganges: Across India, Environmentalists Battle a Tide of Troubles to Clean Up a River Revered as the Source of Life," *Smithsonian* 38, no. 8 (November 1, 2007): 74 (describing the extreme pollution of the Ganges); and William Wise, *Killer Smog: The World's Worst Air Pollution Disaster* (Chicago: Rand McNally, 1968) (recounting London's smog attack in the 1930s).

15. This is not to say that property regimes do not sometimes exclude particular persons from taking ownership roles. Notable historical examples in U.S. society are slaves and married women, neither of which group was allowed to own property in the past. In other societies, there have been classes of the non-elite for whom some resources were *tabu* or *kapu*, as in Hawai'i until some years into the nineteenth century. Absence of ownership rights keeps these persons in dependent or subordinate roles. Nevertheless, even dependent persons are part of the property regime's system of *obligations*—they are not to disrupt the property of others. For property regimes as a source of obligations on all participants, see J. E. Penner, *The Idea of Property in Law* (Oxford and New York: Oxford University Press, 1997), 25–27.

16. Bonnie J. McCay, "Emergence of Institutions for the Commons: Contexts, Situations, and Events,"

in Elinor Ostrom et al., eds., *The Drama of the Commons* (Washington, DC: National Academy Press, 2002), 361, 370–71.

17. At the local point of the kill, whalers adopted different rules for ownership of speared whales. Sometimes the right to the carcass was allocated to the whalers who successfully killed the animal and tagged it with a waif-pole; but for more dangerous whale species, where the first approach was particularly perilous, property in the carcass was allocated to the first whalers to cast a spear that the whale could not throw off, even if the kill were completed by others. Other participants in the hunt received various forms of compensation for their contributions. All these local rules aided any particular hunt, but did not address and may have exacerbated the larger issue of overhunting by all whalers. See Ellickson, *Order without Law*, 196–206.

18. For the locus classicus of this argument, see Ronald H. Coase, "The Problem of Social Cost," *Journal of Law and Economics* 3, no. 1 (1960): 1–44.

19. For an exploration of distributional conflicts that may delay new or revised property regimes, see Gary Libecap, *Contracting for Property Rights* (Cambridge: Cambridge University Press, 1989); see also Robert Cooter, "The Cost of Coase," *Journal of Legal Studies* 11 (1982): 1–33. The question of fairness and desert, for example, undoubtedly affected popular attitudes toward Russia's newly wealthy "oligarchs" and cleared the way for President Vladimir Putin's prosecution of these entrepreneurs. See Carol M. Rose, "Privatization—The Road to Democracy?" *Saint Louis University Law Journal* 50, no. 3 (2006): 691, 707.

20. *Hague v. Wheeler*, 27 A. 714 (Pa. 1893).

21. Ward Farnsworth, "Do Parties in Nuisance Cases Bargain after Judgment? A Glimpse Inside the Cathedral," *University of Chicago Law Review* 69 (1999): 373–436 (describing the dearth of bargaining after nuisance suits are settled in favor of one party or the other).

22. See Katrina Wyman, "From Fur to Fish: Reconsidering the Evolution of Private Property," *New York University Law Review* 80, no. 1 (2005): 117, 193–97 (describing some of the conflicts over allocation of

fishing rights); see also Tom Tietenberg, "The Tradable Rights Approach to Protecting the Commons: What Have We Learned?" in Ostrom et al., eds., *The Drama of the Commons,* 197, 208–9.

23. Libecap, *Contracting for Property Rights,* 21–23.

24. Shi-ling Hsu, "Fairness vs. Efficiency in Environmental Law," *Ecology Law Quarterly* 31 (2004): 303, 375–76, notes that uniform restrictions on technology predate market-based regulations because they seem more fair and raise fewer objections. For "derby" or "olympic" fishing practices, see Carrie A. Tipton, "Protecting Tomorrow's Harvest: Developing a National System of Individual Transferable Quotas to Conserve Ocean Resources," *Virginia Environmental Law Journal* 14 (1995): 381, 391–95.

25. Hsu, "Fairness vs. Efficiency," 370, notes with respect to air pollution control that a coal-burning plant in one location might more cheaply burn low-sulfur coal, whereas another plant elsewhere would install exhaust pipe scrubbers; a uniform technology requirement to install scrubbers favors the latter over the former. Similarly, it is more difficult to meet uniform air quality standards in a heavily populated inversion area like Los Angeles than in a windswept and lightly populated area like the western plains. On this issue, see James E. Krier, "The Irrational National Air Quality Standards: Macro and Micro-Mistakes," *UCLA Law Review* 22, no. 1 (1974): 323–42.

26. Ostrom, *Governing the Commons,* 73–74.

27. For these and other pros and cons of community-based management regimes, see Carol M. Rose, "Common Property, Regulatory Property, and Environmental Protection: Comparing Community-Based Management to Tradable Environmental Allowances," in Ostrom et al., eds., *The Drama of the Commons,* 233–57.

28. Daniel Fitzpatrick, "Evolution and Chaos in Property Rights Systems: The Third World Tragedy of Contested Access," *Yale Law Journal* 115 (2006): 996–1048; for African examples, see pp. 1041–42.

29. Lee J. Alston, Gary D. Libecap, and Bernardo Mueller, *Titles, Conflict, and Land Use: The Development of Property Rights and Land Reform on the Brazilian Amazon Frontier* (Ann Arbor: University of Michigan Press, 1999), 17, 22–25, 176–77, 202.

30. For a very modest sampling of the literature on the generation of legalistic rules among gold rush miners, see John Umbeck, "The California Gold Rush: A Study of Emerging Property Rights," *Explorations in Economic History* 14, no. 3 (1977): 197–226; Richard O. Zerbe and C. Leigh Anderson, "Culture and Fairness in the Development of Institutions in the California Gold Fields," *Journal of Economic History* 61, no. 1 (2001): 114–43; and Andrea McDowell, "Real Property, Spontaneous Order, and Norms in the Gold Mines," *Law and Social Inquiry* 29, no. 4 (2004): 771–818.

31. Arthur F. McEvoy, *The Fisherman's Problem: Ecology and Law in the California Fisheries* (Cambridge: Cambridge University Press, 1986), 44, 47–48.

32. See, e.g., David B. Schorr, "Appropriation as Agrarianism: Distributive Justice in the Creation of Property Rights," *Ecology Law Quarterly* 32, no. 3 (2005).

33. For rights-definition issues in water and their impact on instream flows, see Carol M. Rose, "From H2O to CO2: Lessons of Water Rights for Carbon Trading," *Arizona Law Review* 50 (2008): 91–110; for some of the practical issues, see Janet Neuman, "The Good, the Bad, and the Ugly: The First Ten Years of the Oregon Water Trust," *Nebraska Law Review* 83 (2004): 432–84.

34. Dean Lueck, "Property Rights and the Economic Logic of Wildlife Institutions," *Natural Resources Journal* 35 (Summer 1995): 625–28, 635–44.

35. Gary D. Libecap and Steven N. Wiggins, "Contractual Responses to the Common Pool: Prorationing of Crude Oil Production," *American Economic Review* 74, no. 1 (1984): 87–98.

36. Henry Smith, "The Language of Property: Form, Context, and Audience," *Stanford Law Review* 55 (April 2003): 1105–91. See also Carol M. Rose, "Property and Language," *Yale Journal of Law and the Humanities* 18, no. 1 (2006): 1–28.

37. See Rose, "Big Roads, Big Rights."

38. Thomas W. Merrill and Henry E. Smith, "Optimal Standardization in the Law of Property: The *Numerus Clausus* Principle," *Yale Law Journal* 110, no. 1 (2000): 1–70.

39. James Salzman and J. B. Ruhl, "Currencies and the Commodification of Environmental Law," *Stanford Law Review* 53 (2000): 607, 637.

40. Lisa Wainger, Dennis King, James Salzman, and James Boyd, "Wetland Value Indicators for Scoring Mitigation Trades," *Stanford Environmental Law Journal* 20 (2001): 413–78. For a more general discussion of the issues of valuation, see James Salzman, "Valuing Ecosystem Services: Notes from the Field," *New York University Law Review* 80 (2005): 870–961. The chief U.S. legislation allowing trades is the Clean Water Act (Federal Water Pollution Control Act, 1972), sec. 404, which protects wetlands but under certain circumstances permits unavoidable damage to wetlands, so long as the damage is offset by wetlands created elsewhere. See Salzman, "Valuing Ecosystem Services," 908–9.

41. Salzman, "Valuing Ecosystem Services," 909–10.

42. Carl J. Dahlman, *The Open Field System and Beyond: A Property Rights Analysis of an Economic Institution* (Cambridge and New York: Cambridge University Press, 1980), 153–70.

43. William Cronon, *Nature's Metropolis: Chicago and the Great West* (New York: W. W. Norton, 1991), 97–102, 151–55, 200–204, 213–25.

44. See Daniel C. Esty, "Bridging the Trade–Environment Gap," *Journal of Economic Perspectives* 15 (2001): 113, 115, 119 (describing the "Kuznets curve" of worsening followed by improving environmental protection over the course of new economic development).

45. Paul G. Harris, "Common but Differentiated Responsibilities: The Kyoto Protocol and United States Policy," *New York University Environmental Law Journal* 7 (1999): 27–48.

46. For background about the Kyoto Protocol as well as extensive up-to-date information on this and other efforts to deal with climate change, see the Pew Center on Global Climate Change Web site, www.pewclimate.org. The chief features of the Kyoto Protocol are that during the period 2008–2012, it requires developed countries to reduce greenhouse gas emissions by an average of 5.12 percent below 1990 levels, with further reductions to be negotiated in later rounds; it permits compliance via emission trades; it also permits emitters in developed countries to offset their own emissions by undertaking projects in LDCs that reduce GHGs there below the emission levels that would have otherwise occurred (the "additionality" requirement).

47. Bruce Yandle and Stuart Buck, "Bootleggers, Baptists, and the Global Warming Battle," *Harvard Environmental Law Review* 26, no. 1 (2006): 177, 217–19.

48. Ibid., 221–23.

49. Bruce A. Ackerman and Richard B. Stewart, "Reforming Environmental Law," *Stanford Law Review* 37 (1955): 1333, 1341–42.

50. Flatt, "Taking the Legislative Temperature," 143. Keith Bradsher, "Outsize Profits, and Questions, in Effort to Cut Warming Gases," *New York Times*, December 21, 2006, A1, describes a notorious example in which payments were made to dismantle a Chinese air-conditioning chemical production plant, but were then applied to the expansion of the manufacturing operation.

51. For example, Jeffrey Ball, "The Carbon-Neutral Vacation," *Wall Street Journal*, July 28, 2007, P1, P5–6, describes resorts that offer varying strategies for carbon-neutrality, including investment in "offsets" in vaguely defined carbon sequestration projects.

52. Flatt, "Taking the Legislative Temperature," 135–38.

53. Lakshman Guruswamy, "Integrating Thoughtways: Reopening of the Environmental Mind?" *Wisconsin Law Review* (1989): 463, 490–92, notes some early cases in which the cross-boundary pollution issue, including scrubber sludge disposal, was raised but dismissed.

54. Amano and Sedjo, "Forest Sequestration," 8–9, 31–32 (describing narrow forestry credits actually allowed for trade credit under Kyoto Clean Development Mechanism). On new verification technology, as well as increased concern to permit credits for existing forests, see Tom Wright, "New Tool May Help in Fight to Curb CO_2: Radar Enables Better Monitoring of Commitments to Preserve Forests," *Wall Street Journal*, January 3, 2008, B3.

55. Rose, "From H_2O to CO_2: Lessons of Water Rights for Carbon Trading," 91, 104.

56. Salzman and Ruhl, "Currencies and the Commodification of Environmental Law," 627–30.

57. Brandon Scarborough, "Trading Forest Carbon: A Panacea or Pipe Dream to Address Climate Change?" *PERC Policy Series* PS-40 (July 2007): 7–10, 20.

58 Ken Caldeira, "When Being Green Raises the Heat," *New York Times*, January 16, 2007, A21.

59. Penner, *The Idea of Property in Law*, 75.

60. Zerbe and Anderson, "Culture and Fairness," 133–35. Zerbe and Anderson call the game a "chicken/hawk" game rather than a "dove/hawk" game, but the game is the same.

61. Two contributions in *The Question of the Commons: The Culture and Ecology of Communal Resources*, ed. Bonnie J. McCay and James M. Acheson (Tucson: University of Arizona Press, 1988) sharply question the idea that community-based resource regimes are conservation oriented in any systematic way: Raymond Hames, "Game Conservation or Efficient Hunting?" 92–107; and James G. Carrier, "Marine Tenure and Conservation in Papua New Guinea," 142–67. Rose, "Common Property,

Regulatory Property, and Environmental Protection," 233, 248–50, describes some of the weaknesses of traditional community-based regimes with respect to commerce—including communities with some conservationist practices.

62. Alison Rieser, "Property Rights and Ecosystem Management in U.S. Fisheries: Contracting for the Commons?" *Environmental Law Quarterly* 24 (1997): 813, 830–32, approvingly describes the allocation of fishing quotas to some Alaskan native communities. See also John Tierney, "A Tale of Two Fisheries," *New York Times Magazine*, August 27, 2000, 38. Among other things, the latter describes the way in which holders of individual tradable fishing quotas in Australia have come together to form a new common-property regime for managing the tuna fishery.

MARK PENNINGTON

LIBERTY, MARKETS, AND ENVIRONMENTAL VALUES

FREE-MARKET ENVIRONMENTALISM VERSUS GREEN COMMUNITARIANISM

Environmental problems for much of the postwar period were treated as classical examples of "market failure," a treatment inspired by developments in neoclassical welfare economics. In this perspective, market processes result in socially suboptimal environmental decisions because private decision makers are not held properly to account for the consequences of their actions owing to the prevalence of collective goods and externality problems. Seen in this light, the task of environmental policy is to devise ways of correcting imbalances in the market system via the judicious use of taxes,

subsidies, and regulatory controls in order to ensure the appropriate provision of environmental goods.

The emergence of free-market environmentalism represents a significant advance in how environmental problems are conceived. Building on the work of Ronald Coase,[1] Harold Demsetz,[2] and developments in public-choice theory, free-market environmentalism suggests that the mere identification of market failures is *not* a sufficient justification for widespread government intervention. Insofar as markets are prone to "fail" in the environmental sphere, they do so mainly because of the high costs of establishing private-property rights. These obstacles to market exchange

"Liberty, Markets, and Environmental Values: A Hayekian Defense of Free-Market Environmentalism," Author: Mark Pennington. This article has been reprinted with permission from the publisher of The Independent Review: A Journal of Political Economy (Summer 2005, Volume 10, no. 1, pp. 39–57), Copyright 2005, Independent Institute, 100 Swan Way, Oakland, CA 94621-1428 USA; info@independent.org; www.independent.org.

prevent the successful internalization of spillover effects. Transaction costs are not the sole preserve of the market system, however, and we commit the "nirvana fallacy" if we suggest that the alternative to an imperfect market is a government immune from the same sort of problems. Public-choice theory, in particular, suggests that the interaction of voters, interest groups, politicians, and bureaucrats is characterized by a distinctive set of transaction costs that may result in chronic examples of government failure. What we need, therefore, is a comparative framework for examining the extent to which institutional provisions in the private and public sectors encourage or inhibit the internalization of all costs.

In this framework, free-market environmentalism has made a strong case for much greater use of private-property rights and "imperfect" market processes as an alternative to the regulatory state. Authors such as Terry Anderson and Donald Leal have documented numerous examples of environmental goods that can be and are supplied successfully in private markets, and empirical researchers examining state-centered models of environmental management have highlighted numerous cases of government failure.[3] For land-based environmental assets such as forests and minerals, for example, evidence suggests that private-property solutions are highly successful in generating the necessary incentives that encourage resource conservation and help to overcome the problems of "free-riding" associated with open-access conditions.[4] Thus, the record of forest management in Sweden under a predominantly private regime has been noticeably more impressive than the record of forest management under government ownership in the United States, Canada, and Great Britain. Similarly, the private ownership of wildlife in countries such as Botswana has had markedly more success in protecting stocks than government-sponsored trade bans on ivory products that have been put in place over much of Africa.[5]

Although proponents of free-market environmentalism recognize that environmental markets have limits owing to the prevalence of transaction costs, they contend that these problems are more likely to be overcome within an institutional framework supportive of private contractual arrangements. In this perspective, *all* environmental externalities represent potential profit opportunities for entrepreneurs who can devise ways of defining private-property rights and arranging contracts (via technological innovations, for example) so that those currently free riding on collective goods or imposing negative external effects (for example, water pollution) on their neighbors are required to bear the full costs of their actions. A land owner, for example, may introduce fences and install entrance points to the grounds of a park in order to exclude nonpayers from the park's aesthetic benefits. Likewise, if technologies develop in the future that enable the "fencing" of the atmosphere, then entrepreneurs will have incentives to define property rights to the air and to charge those who are currently polluting without compensating those injured by their action. In the market economy, therefore, if people are imposing costs on others or are benefiting from the provision of certain goods without payment, entrepreneurs have incentives to find ways of eliminating such involuntary transfers *over time*.

The political process, by contrast, tends in its very nature to *externalize* costs through the coercive mechanisms of collective decision. The all-or-nothing nature of political decision making means that once a majority coalition has been assembled, costs can be imposed on those outside the ruling group. As a consequence, politicians *always* have an incentive to find ways of externalizing costs—providing benefits to some groups at the direct expense of others. In light of these incentives, advocates of free-market environmentalism suggest that we should rely on government action only in those situations where it is inconceivable that a market solution might be forthcoming. At present, for example, transboundary air-quality management seems to fall in this category. As yet, technological developments have not allowed the effective "fencing" of atmospheric resources, so government action may be warranted as a last resort.

Recognizing the limits of property-rights solutions in this regard, free-market environmentalists argue nonetheless that "market-like" incentives, such as those established by a tradable-permit scheme, be built into whatever policy interventions are required, eschewing the adoption of a command-and-control approach. In this perspective, command-and-control policies, such as fixed-emission quotas, do not provide sufficient incentives to deliver improvements in environmental quality *beyond* those specified by government mandates. Market-like approaches, such as tradable permits, by contrast, give externalities a price tag that producers can reduce in a process of substitution. Thus, in the case of tradable pollution permits, if a firm reduces its emissions below its allocated quota, it can sell the unneeded share of its quota to other firms that are less efficient in producing emissions reductions. In turn, because firms, whatever their efficiency, have a positive incentive to continue reducing pollution, the state has less need to employ armies of inspectors to ensure compliance with the law.

Despite the substantial body of evidence to support the case for free-market environmentalism, the approach has made little headway either in policy-making or with regard to developments in green political theory. Although some green theorists are now willing to concede that certain environmental goods *can* be supplied in private markets, they reject the view that these goods *should* be provided in that way.

Similarly, although many greens are willing to concede the "efficiency" case for tradable permits and other market-like instruments, they continue to favor reliance on command-and-control policy tools. Their objections rest on the contention that the rational-choice model of decision making is entirely inappropriate to the nature of the matters at issue. In making these claims, green political theorists draw heavily on the communitarian critique of market liberalism that has come to the fore over the past twenty years.[6]

At the core of communitarian objections to the use of environmental markets is a belief that support for market processes presupposes that the purpose of social institutions is to facilitate the efficient satisfaction of individual preferences. From a communitarian perspective, such an approach is neglectful of the moral context in which individual preferences are shaped and eschews any sense of the "common good." Alisdair MacIntyre, for example, argues that liberalism reduces ethical questions to matters of personal preference in such a way that morality becomes an entirely relativistic concept.[7] Insofar as liberals have a conception of the common good, it is seen to reflect the aggregate sum of individual preferences. As MacIntyre points out, however, without some overarching sense of morality that *transcends* the individual actor, liberalism is a potentially self-destructive ideology because principles such as respect for private-property rights become matters of purely personal preference.

In response to such perceived deficiencies, communitarians argue that the individual should be conceived as a thoroughly social being whose preferences are derived from a relationship to a shared or intersubjective conception of the good reflective of the community *as a whole*. The common good, therefore, should provide a standard by which the virtue of individual preferences can properly be judged. According to this view, the "selfishness" of market-driven consumerism must be kept in its place because the exit mechanisms that pervade markets allow people to "disconnect" from their communities and render them unable to relate their choices to a shared conception of the good.[8] In contrast, democratic deliberation and collective choice in the "public realm," it is argued, enable individuals to educate their values through a dialogue in which the virtue of preferences can be judged by the community according to the articulation of the "best reasons."

Applying such arguments in the environmental sphere, green political theorists contend that environmental problems are quintessential collective-good problems that can be dealt with only by institutions that transcend a concern for individual preference. This line of thought has several dimensions.

First, it is argued that environmental problems are "systematic" and therefore cannot be dealt with effectively by using approaches that treat individual issues in isolation from others.[9] Ecological systems are complex interrelated wholes in which decisions that affect one particular dimension (such as land management) inevitably ripple outward to affect other aspects of the human/ecological interface (such as water management). Because green thinkers tend to apply to ecological processes the notion that "the whole is greater than the sum of its parts," they regard it as imperative that environmental decisions be based on holistic decision practices, whereby concerned citizens collectively analyze how their choices affect and impinge on the environment and the lives of other human beings. A focus on market freedom, they argue, "atomizes" individual decisions and discourages people from thinking about how their behavior affects the health of the community as a whole.

A second and related objection to free-market environmentalism derives from its focus on incentives. Seen in this light, property-rights approaches emphasize concrete personal gains to be realized from environmental protection rather than encourage people to reflect on the abstract moral virtue of ecologically sensitive behavior. The focus on individual incentives in cases where the market *can* supply environmental goods, therefore, is likely to intensify prisoners' dilemma–type problems in cases where markets *cannot* deliver such goods owing to the culture of "selfishness" that these institutions perpetuate.[10] Command-and-control models of regulation it is suggested, are by contrast more likely to inculcate other-regarding behavior by enforcing a communal conception of morally appropriate resource use.

A third and final set of objections to free-market environmentalism maintains that individual willingness to pay is simply not a valid criterion for a large . . . number of goods deemed to reflect fundamental moral and ethical values, which cannot be bought or sold. According to this view, free-market environmentalism takes individual preferences as fixed and predetermined, thus neglecting the possibility that people can be educated to an appreciation of alternative lifestyles given a context that encourages debate and argument rather than a consumerist gratification of individual wants.[11]

Moreover, in the perspective of green communitarianism, the use of a common denominator such as money to aggregate individual preferences into an "efficient" social welfare function is entirely inappropriate where incommensurable moral ends are involved and the aggregation of conflicting values is therefore impossible. Moral conflicts over resource use should not be considered according to the utilitarian criterion of willingness to pay, but should instead be dealt with by means of democratic debate and compromise.[12] The analogy invoked here is the approach to scientific theories; it is considered inappropriate to decide the merits of competing theories according to the intensity of individual preference. Likewise, for communitarian greens, the value of environmental public goods should be resolved by collective judgment in accordance with the "power of the better argument," not by a willingness to pay.

The overall essence of the green communitarian case is captured in the distinction that Mark Sagoff draws between "consumer" and "citizen" preferences.[13]

When asking a group of students if they would visit a new ski resort proposed for construction in a national park, Sagoff noted that the majority of respondents indicated that they would gladly visit the resort to benefit from the recreational opportunities. When he asked this same group of individuals whether they would in fact *support* the construction of the relevant resort, however, many replied in the negative. For Sagoff, the difference between these responses reflects the distinction between consumer and citizen preferences. As participants in a market for amoral consumer goods, individuals welcomed the opportunity for new skiing facilities to satisfy their individual recreational wants. In their capacity as critical moral citizens, however, the same individuals were morally opposed to the destruction of valued wilderness, which they considered of value to their community *as a whole*. If we do not want to live in a degraded environment, therefore, we should choose collective citizen deliberation over individual consumer choice more often than not.

F.A. HAYEK: "THE LIBERAL AS COMMUNITARIAN"

It is evident from the previous sketch that much of the objection to free-market environmentalism stems not from concerns about the practicality of market solutions to environmental issues, but rather from a rejection of the ontological framework from which these solutions derive.[14] Green political theorists are unlikely to accept proposals grounded in the assumptions of rational-choice theory. As a consequence, much of the debate between free-market environmentalists and communitarian greens resembles a dialogue between people who cannot hear or understand one another. Such a resemblance is notably apparent in some recent exchanges between Mark Sagoff, on one side, and Terry Anderson and Donald Leal, on the other. According to Sagoff, free-market environmentalism relies on an aggregate conception of allocative efficiency, scarcely distinguishable from neoclassical welfare economics, and it thus fails to recognize that environmentalists are concerned not with efficiency, but with the *moral* status of conserving the natural world.[15] On the other side, Anderson and Leal accuse Sagoff of providing little more than a sophisticated apology for a disguised form of rent seeking by environmental campaigners.[16]

I do not intend to debate here the virtues of the rational-choice model or to engage deeply in the debate between classical liberals and communitarians that has raged in recent years. Having adopted a liberal rational-choice perspective,[17] I simply note that many of the objections to this account of human behavior are weak and can be dealt with from inside the rational-choice framework itself.[18] Rather, my purpose here is to demonstrate that even if one accepts all the communitarian arguments against rational-choice liberalism, *none* of these arguments provides an effective case against market institutions and environmental markets in particular. On the contrary, a Hayekian perspective shares many of the ontological assumptions of communitarian thought and yet provides a radical endorsement of the case for private markets. In this section, I sketch the similarities and differences between Hayek's liberalism and modern theories of communitarianism. In the subsequent section, I apply these Hayekian concepts to mount a defense of free-market environmentalism against the communitarian greens' claims.[19]

The most immediate similarity between Hayekian liberalism and communitarian thinking is evident in the notion of "true" individualism. True individualism acknowledges that individuals are *inherently* social creatures (or *situated selves*, to use communitarian terminology), who acquire many of their preferences, values, and practices in a process of emulation and imitation. For Hayek, true individualism is distinct from the "false" individualism that conceives of society as the rational creation of individuals seeking to design optimal social institutions: "This fact should by itself be sufficient to refute the silliest of misunderstandings: the belief that individualism postulates (or bases its arguments on the assumption of) the existence of isolated or self-contained individuals, instead of starting from men whose whole nature and character is determined by their existence in society."[20]

To recognize that people are a product of their society is not, however, to imply that society is itself the result of deliberate human action. On the contrary, the social and cultural environment is in large part the unintended by-product of many individual acts, whose effects are beyond the purview of any one actor or group. For Hayek, the defining feature of individuals as social beings is their incapacity, owing to the constitutional limits of the human mind, to comprehend more than a tiny portion of the society of which they are a part. Individuals and organizations are situated within much larger "spontaneous ordering" processes, the results of which are far greater than and hence beyond the comprehension of their constituent parts. Language, for example, though developing out of the human capacity for communication, emerges as the unintended by-product of multiple communicative acts. As new words and combinations spread by a process of imitation and adaptation, their initiators are *not* consciously aware of how others will use and adapt such practices. Similarly, the users of language are typically unaware of the multiple individual nodes that have initiated the words and phrases in common usage and the "reasons" why such symbols have been adopted. In the latter sense, complex social wholes such as language are greater than the sum of their parts.

. . .

A HAYEKIAN DEFENSE OF FREE-MARKET ENVIRONMENTALISM

Hayek's version of liberalism clearly is not susceptible to many of the charges that communitarians level at more orthodox forms of liberal theory. With its socialized conception of the individual and of rationality, "true individualism" is not guilty of the atomistic fallacy. Similarly, with its concept of spontaneous order or catallaxy, this approach cannot be accused of seeing society in narrowly aggregate terms. More important, the Hayekian defense of the market makes *no* assumptions about individual motivations. The problem is *not* that individuals are insufficiently altruistic and lack the necessary incentives under socialism, but that in the absence of the signaling function of market prices, they can never possess the appropriate *knowledge* to adjust their behavior in a manner consistent with others' interests.

THE LIMITS OF SOCIAL CONSCIOUSNESS

The latter point is central to Hayekian objections against communitarian proposals that environmental decisions be made collectively by citizens who *consciously* analyze how their actions affect others' lives.

In a Hayekian perspective, although the self is socially situated, the notion of a socially conscious citizen is an epistemological impossibility. Given the cognitive limits of the mind, individuals and groups *cannot* be aware of all the different ramifications of their actions, either for themselves or for society at large. This is not to suggest that other-regarding behavior is itself impossible, but that such action may occur only within a small cognitive sphere, confined perhaps to family, friends, and colleagues. Consumer choices, therefore, are not necessarily selfish—a consumer may be seeking out the best value in the market on the behalf of friends, colleagues, or a charity. Given the cognitive limits of the mind, however, the ends about which people know will always be a tiny fraction of the needs of dispersed and multitudinous others. *The cen*tral problem of social coordination, therefore, is to enable people to adjust to circumstances and interests of which they are not directly aware. For Hayek, this enablement is precisely the role performed by market-generated spontaneous order.

In this light, the normative relevance of the communitarian distinction between altruistic citizenship and selfish consumerism collapses. Consider the earlier example provided by Sagoff, in which it was argued that consumer action to satisfy recreational wants would favor the construction of a ski resort in a national park, whereas citizen action would oppose the destruction of unspoiled wilderness of value to the community as a whole. At first sight, this example seems to illustrate the merits of the communitarian case, but on closer inspection it fails to justify Sagoff's conclusion.

Sagoff concedes that most environmental decisions are *not*, after all, akin to matters of scientific truth, which can be judged right or wrong on the basis of reasoned argument.[21] Rather, such decisions involve trade-offs and marginal adjustments between competing values. Even for communitarians, therefore, it would seem that economic factors such as the intensity of preferences and the availability of substitutes must be taken into account. Thus, "We must acknowledge, however idealistic we may be, that clean air, workplace safety and the like have a price and at some point the additional amount of cleanliness or safety may be grossly disproportionate to the goods and services that we must forego in order to pay for

it . . . . But how to determine what is appropriate from an ethical point of view?"[22] With specific regard to the ski resort example, therefore, it is not so much that people have a community-centered objection to ski resorts per se, but that they are opposed to the construction of such a venture in a particular wilderness area. The underlying problem is to discover a mechanism that will help us to decide where new resorts should be developed as well as how many there should be. For Sagoff, such decisions should be made through a deliberative democratic process based on debate and compromise. Precisely at this juncture, however, democratic deliberation faces the epistemological problems highlighted by Hayek. Democratic representatives can never have access to or process the multitude of factors needed to adjust the demand for ski resorts rationally. Information pertaining to ethics, local conditions, pressures on land use, and so forth does not exist as a coherent integrated whole. The dispersed bits of information may be communicated, however, by market prices, which transmit context-specific factors in coded form across the overlapping perspectives of many different actors—shifting demand for ski resorts away from more environmentally valued and hence relatively more expensive sites, for example. *Regardless* of whether the participants are acting as consumers or citizens, therefore, they are unlikely to bring about the desired process of mutual adjustment without market-derived relative prices.

The latter point does not deny the existence of alternative forms of mutual adjustment that can occur in other networked structures such as linguistic communication or even pluralist politics. It does suggest, however, that there is no effective equivalent to market prices when the adjustments required are fine-grained responses to shifting patterns of relative scarcity. Absent the common denominator provided by money prices, citizens and politicians lack the capacity to make rational marginal adjustments. How, for example, are politicians to judge whether to weight the receipt of a phone call from a citizen more or less than the receipt of another citizen's letter or the sight of a third citizen's participation in a demonstration? Even processes of single-issue direct democracy (the preferred method of many communitarian greens) provide no means equivalent to prices for adjusting to the *intensity* of individual valuations. In such processes, the vote of someone who values a particular good very highly counts for no more than that of someone else who places the same good much farther down his scale of values.[23]

To take the analysis further, it is useful to compare Hayekian arguments for a property-rights approach to the problem of open-access environmental resources with those arguments associated with rational-choice versions of economic liberalism. According to the latter, establishing private-property rights over resources such as water or fish is crucial in helping to change the incentives that self-interested actors face, in internalizing costs, and hence in overcoming the free-rider problem.[24] The Hayekian argument for property rights and markets, however, is by no means dependent on the assumption of individual self-interest and the significance of incentives. Suppose that an individual is altruistically motivated as a concerned citizen to reduce his water consumption to a "socially responsible amount." In the absence of property rights and market prices for water, the individual has no way to ascertain how much to adjust his consumption to take the interests of others properly into account. As Steele points out, even the most altruistically inclined person faced with this situation is likely to consume as much water as he personally requires *because at least he knows what that amount is*, whereas the "socially responsible" amount of consumption is shrouded in a fog of ignorance.[25] Such problems will be multiplied many times over, of course, when the choice is between the vast array of production and consumption possibilities that make up an advanced economy and the complex environmental consequences of these possibilities. In short, without the information provided by market-generated relative prices, citizens will find it impossible to communicate their values to one another and to adjust their behavior accordingly.

PREFERENCE ELEVATION AND THE MARKET ECONOMY

In a Hayekian perspective, people simply cannot know in some collective or deliberative sense how to act in the public good; therefore, the claim that other-regarding behavior is more likely to be generated by collective choice looks extremely dubious. Equally significant, however, is that many of the educative advantages usually attributed to communitarian politics may be more likely to arise in the private market. If individual preferences are shaped by the social environment, then for communitarians it follows that the resultant values should be subject to a process of democratic criticism and debate in which the community as a whole can examine the virtue of these values. Seen through a Hayekian lens, this argument rests on a complete non sequitur.

Predetermined or innate preferences in human beings are probably confined to a few basic desires for food, shelter, and sex. As Hayek notes, "It would scarcely be an exaggeration to say that contemporary man, in all fields where he has not yet formed firm habits, tends to find out what he wants by looking at what his neighbors do and at various displays of goods (physical or in catalogues or advertisements) and then choosing what he likes best."[26] The vast majority of the goods that people desire, therefore, are things that they learn to desire because they see other people enjoying them. The desire for literature, for example, is probably not innate, but is largely an acquired taste derived from the cultural environment.[27] Can anyone suggest seriously that the production and consumption of literature, therefore, ought to be subject to state control and that the *only* literary values exercised in society be those arrived at by majority approval? The "citizen versus consumer" dichotomy central to communitarian thought does not appear to provide clear grounds for deciding whether such decisions should be subject to social-democratic procedures. It might be argued, of course, that because environmental goods are collective goods, democratic-choice mechanisms are the most appropriate. This claim, however, reduces the argument for citizenship to a purely technical question of defining the boundaries of a collective good. If it turns out that environmental goods can be supplied privately, then no necessary merit resides in making a decision between citizen action and consumer choice.

For Hayek, market institutions are evolutionary discovery processes that expose people to a wide variety of competing ideas and enable them to discover previously unforeseen production and consumption values. Market processes allow contradictory ideas to be tested *simultaneously* against one another without the need for majority approval. Employing the exit option enables individuals who dissent from the majority to follow their own ideas without impinging on the ability of those who support the majority opinion to follow theirs. Market processes, therefore, allow a greater range of production and consumption decisions to be tried and tested, and hence they bring more knowledge into the public realm than would ever be the case under a strictly majoritarian system. As Wohlgemuth observes, the most that majoritarian procedures can do is to conduct consecutive experiments in which only one option or a small set of options is being tried out at any time.[28] Similarly, the most that politicians and interest groups that do not form part of the majority can do is to offer verbal critiques of current policies. They cannot actively supply alternative packages of goods. The range of plans that may actually be implemented, therefore, will necessarily be less than the range generated in a context of private exchange.

Paradoxical as it may seem, the learning advantages of markets arise because they do not rely heavily on the transmission of knowledge by explicit articulation. This aspect is, of course, one of the primary objects of the complaints that communitarians raise against markets. In a Hayekian perspective, however, although discussion is an important way to impart knowledge, and although democracy is or should be government by discussion, this explicit articulation of argument is not the most important way by which people can actually decide what is best.[29] On the contrary, a large body of tacit knowledge can be communicated only by multiple examples of private action. A crucial distinction separates the sort of social learning that takes place when people enter into verbal conversation or read a written text and that which occurs when they observe and emulate the behavior of others.[30] The latter exemplifies learning by results—imitating successful courses of action and avoiding unsuccessful ones even when the reasons behind such successes and failures cannot be articulated explicitly. The emphasis on explicit reasoning in a communitarian democracy is therefore likely to stultify the dissemination of new values by choking off those forms of tacit knowledge that cannot be communicated by the articulate persuasion of majorities. Moreover, procedures that rely exclusively on the statement of explicit reasons are likely to exclude systematically those individuals who are less able to engage in articulate persuasion of majorities, but who may still possess valuable knowledge embodied in the exercise of entrepreneurship or a practical skill. Unlike the relatively easy comparisons of value and the knowledge transmission that markets facilitate, which both the rich and the poor, the articulate and the inarticulate, can make, deliberative institutions give special advantage to those skilled in the use of articulate persuasion alone.[31] The latter point reflects Hayek's contention in *The Fatal Conceit: The Errors of Socialism* that intellectuals who tend to be the most vociferous advocates of deliberative democracy overvalue the power of explicit reason in the communication of knowledge.[32]

The communitarian claim that the elevation of individual values is more likely to occur in a context of collective citizen deliberation is therefore without foundation. As Michael Polanyi has shown, the spread of knowledge in markets, the arts, and academia does not proceed by collective deliberation, but rather advances best when individuals and groups have a private sphere that secures the freedom to experiment with projects that do not conform to majority opinions.[33] Then, as a result, the prevailing wisdom changes incrementally over time. With regard to "green" consumption, for example, it is doubtful whether the massive growth in the organic food market that has occurred in recent years would ever have developed if production decisions in the agricultural sector had been subject to collectivist procedures. For years, organic food was viewed as the concern of hapless eccentrics. Precisely because private property affords minorities the space to try out experimental ideas (the merits of which may be indiscernible) rather than simply talking about them, more and more people are now able to emulate such role models as the benefits become more visible.[34]

This argument does not suggest that the market process necessarily will generate ideas that are good for the environment, but that a process that allows for a greater degree of experimental adaptation is more likely to do so than a collectivist regime bound by majority decisions. Open-ended discovery processes, such as the market, necessarily allow mistakes and are characterized by an element of disequilibrium. Bad decisions cannot be eliminated from evolution and are essential to a process characterized by trial-and-error learning. As research conducted since the early 1980s suggests, ecosystems are themselves far from static entities.[35] Ecological systems are subject to constant change, both natural and human induced, some of which may be beneficial, some harmful. A process of experimental adaptation akin to that of the market may therefore be more appropriate than steering a sustainable-development path, the approach favored by communitarian greens.[36] Indeed, the notion of steering may be totally inappropriate in the context of a dynamic, open-ended system. The essentially unpredictable nature of such systems implies that collectives simply cannot know where they are supposed to be going. Experience suggests that governments are not in the best position to pick industrial winners, so we have little reason to believe that they can select an appropriate development path, sustainable or otherwise.

Deliberative democracy therefore is unlikely to generate the necessary process of evolutionary adaptation appropriate to dynamic human/environmental conditions. Indeed, it is not clear that communitarian greens are especially committed to evolutionary learning per se. For all the claims made in favor of communication and debate, theorists of this persuasion tend to have decidedly strong views about appropriate locations for chemicals, how much people should be allowed to travel, and what is to constitute sustainable development. Barry, for example, argues that international trade is inherently unsustainable,[37] and Daly and Cobb espouse a "massive program of education" to reorient citizens to a preference for rural as opposed to urban ways of life.[38] With certainties of this order, the parameters for open-ended debate seem extremely limited.

THE CASH NEXUS AND MORAL VALUES

The remaining objection to environmental markets is that willingness to pay is simply not a valid criterion for a large number of goods deemed to reflect moral and ethical values. Again, Sagoff's example about the preservation of wilderness or the development of ski resorts falls clearly into this category. From a Hayekian perspective, however, this tack is an especially weak one. The fundamental reason for instituting property rights over environmental assets is precisely that they allow property owners to say no to inappropriate

offers, whether on ethical grounds or for some other reason important to them—rather than having bureaucrats make such judgments. Just as one may refuse to sell the family home to the highest bidder because of personal history or identity, so a property right to a forest or waterway would allow individuals and groups not to sell extraction rights if the compensation offered were inappropriate to the moral attachments concerned. Monetary payment does not necessarily mean a decrease in moral attachments. There is no evidence to suggest, for example, that in societies in which monetary payment for sexual services is legal, a greater proportion of the population considers prostitution to be a valid career option. Moreover, as Richard Epstein has argued, to outlaw the offer of monetary payments where moral issues are involved is to devalue actively the ethical fortitude of individuals who resist monetary inducements.[39] If cash payments are utterly inappropriate, then an important social signaling function that indicates different actors' character and values is lost by prohibiting such payments from being made.[40]

Communitarian greens complain that the use of a common denominator such as money is inappropriate where incommensurable moral ends are involved and where the aggregation of conflicting values is therefore impossible. As already argued, however, the Hayekian case for market prices is not that they facilitate the aggregation of values into a yardstick of social welfare, but that they allow people with conflicting ends to engage in an impersonal process of mutual adjustment. For Hayek, it is precisely because people have conflicting values that money prices are required to facilitate adjustments among their diverse interests. Critics of money prices appear to have no such qualms about the use of a common denominator when it comes to their own deliberative designs, all of which resort to some form of majority voting.[41] For the reasons outlined earlier, however, such processes are far less likely to facilitate mutual adjustment than a set of market-generated relative prices. In addition, the all-or-nothing nature of the political process entails that once a majority coalition has been formed, the interests of minorities can easily be ignored as they are effectively forced to consume (and pay for) policies that they did not actually demand. It is therefore an error to suggest that moral values cannot be reflected by the cash nexus because every decision not to buy or sell, for moral or other reasons, will be reflected in the relevant markets.[42] Moreover, a case surely can be made that it is precisely for the ends people value most highly that they should be required to make a personal sacrifice, including perhaps a material sacrifice. It is ironic that communitarian greens urge that people should sacrifice the material benefits of growth for a better quality of life, while refusing to countenance the possibility that people should be faced directly with the material opportunity costs of such decisions.

CONCLUSION

In the preceding discussion, I have defended a case for a property-rights approach to issues of environmental protection against the green communitarian . . . challenge to the liberal market. Unlike existing defenses of free-market environmentalism, however, the defense I have set out adopts a critique that deals with the concerns of the communitarian greens *on their own terms*. A Hayekian approach is well suited to perform this task and suggests that a focus on the situated self, the systemic nature of environmental problems, and a non-aggregate account of social decisions offers greater support for liberal markets than for a communitarian citizen democracy. Insofar as the extension of private-property arrangements has genuine limits, those limits should be identified by assessing the logistical obstacles to environmental markets and not by making the spurious distinction between the virtues of citizenship and the supposed evils of market-driven consumer choice.

REFERENCES

Alchian, A., and H. Demsetz. 1973. The Property Rights Paradigm. *Journal of Economic History* 3: 16–27.

Anderson, T., and D. Leal. 2001. *Free Market Environmentalism*. 2d ed. New York: Palgrave.

Baden, J., and R. Stroup. 1979. Property Rights and Natural Resource Management. *Literature of Liberty* 2: 5–44.

Barber, B. 1984. *Strong Democracy*. Berkeley: University of California Press.

Barry, J. 1999. *Rethinking Green Politics*. London: Sage.

Botkin, D. 1990. *Discordant Harmonies*. New York: Oxford University Press.

Chase, A. 1995. *The Fight over Forests and the Tyranny of Ecology*. Boston: Houghton Mifflin.

Coase, R. 1960. The Problem of Social Cost. *Journal of Law and Economics* 3: 1–44.

Daly, H., and J. Cobb. 1989. *For the Common Good*. London: Greenprint.

De Alessi, L. 2003. Gains from Private Property: The Empirical Evidence. In *Property Rights: Cooperation, Conflict, and Law*, edited by T. Anderson and F. McChesney, 90–112. Princeton, N.J.: Princeton University Press.

Demsetz, H. 1969. Information and Efficiency: Another Viewpoint. *Journal of Law & Economics* 12: 1–22.

Dryzek, J. 1987. *Rational Ecology: Environment and Political Economy*. Oxford: Blackwell.

Epstein, R. 2003. *Skepticism and Freedom*. Chicago: University of Chicago Press.

Hayek, F.A. 1948a. Economics and Knowledge. In *Individualism and Economic Order*, 33–56. Chicago: University of Chicago Press.

Hayek, F.A. 1948b. Individualism: True and False. In *Individualism and Economic Order*, 1–32. Chicago: University of Chicago Press.

Hayek, F.A. 1948c. The Use of Knowledge in Society. In *Individualism and Economic Order*, 77–91. Chicago: University of Chicago Press.

Hayek, F.A. 1960. *The Constitution of Liberty*. London: Routledge.

Hayek, F.A. 1967. The Non Sequitur of the Dependence Effect. In *Studies in Philosophy, Politics, and Economics*, 313–17. London: Routledge.

Hayek, F.A. 1973. *Rules and Order*. Chicago: Chicago University Press.

Hayek, F.A. 1978. Competition as a Discovery Procedure. In *New Studies in Politics, Economics, and the History of Ideas*, 179–90. London: Routledge.

Hayek, F.A. 1988. *The Fatal Conceit: The Errors of Socialism*. London: Routledge.

Horwitz, S. 1992. Monetary Exchange as an Extra-linguistic Communications Medium. *Review of Social Economy* 50, no. 2: 193–214.

Jacobs, M. 1997. Environmental Valuation, Deliberative Democracy, and Public Decision-Making Institutions. In *Valuing Nature*, edited by J. Foster, 211–31. London: Routledge.

Lewin, P. 1998. The Firm, Money, and Economic Calculation: Considering the Institutional Nexus of

Market Production. *American Journal of Economics and Sociology* 57 (October): 499–512.

MacIntyre, A. 1984. *After Virtue*. South Bend: University of Indiana Press.

McCann, C.R. 2002. F.A. Hayek: The Liberal as Communitarian. *Review of Austrian Economics* 15: 5–34.

McCoy, E.D., and K.S. Shrader-Frechette. 1994. The Concept of Community in Community Ecology. *Perspectives on Science* 2: 445–75.

Mill, J.S. 1848. *The Principles of Political Economy*. Oxford: Oxford University Press.

Ostrom, E. 1990. *Governing the Commons*. Cambridge: Cambridge University Press.

Pennington, M. 2000. *Planning and the Political Market: Public Choice and the Politics of Government Failure*. London: Athlone Press, Continuum International.

Pennington, M. 2001. Environmental Markets versus Environmental Deliberation: A Hayekian Critique of Green Political Economy. *New Political Economy* 6, no. 2: 171–190.

Pennington, M. 2003. Hayekian Political Economy and the Limits of Deliberative Democracy. *Political Studies* 51, no. 4: 722–39.

Polanyi, M. 1951. *The Logic of Liberty*. Chicago: University of Chicago Press.

Polanyi, M. 1957. *Personal Knowledge*. Chicago: University of Chicago Press.

Sagoff, M. 1988. *The Economy of the Earth*. Cambridge: Cambridge University Press.

Sagoff, M. 1994. Environmentalism vs. Value Subjectivism: Rejoinder to Anderson and Leal. *Critical Review* 8: 467–73.

Smith, G. 2003. *Deliberative Democracy and the Environment*. London: Routledge.

Steele, D. 1992. *From Marx to Mises*. La Salle, Ill.: Open Court.

Sugg, I., and R. Kreuter. 1994. *Elephants and Ivory*. London: Institute of Economic Affairs.

Sunstein, C. 1991. Preferences and Politics. *Philosophy and Public Affairs* 20: 3–24.

Wohlgemuth, M. 1995. Economic and Political Competition in Neo-classical and Evolutionary Perspective. *Constitutional Political Economy* 6: 71–96.

Wohlgemuth, M. 1999. Entry Barriers in Politics, or: Why Politics, Like Natural Monopoly, Is Not Organized as an On-Going Market Process. *Review of Austrian Economics* 12: 175–200.

NOTES

1. Coase 1960.
2. Demsetz 1969.
3. Anderson and Leal 2001.
4. De Alessi 2003.
5. Sugg and Kreuter 1994.
6. In using this term, I do not intend to imply that *all* people who describe themselves as *green* are communitarians. Nonetheless, the term does capture a range of arguments that constitutes a majority of green opinion, covering the so-called "social ecology" school, the "deep ecology" school, and a large body of green opinion influenced by the Frankfurt school of critical theory. For a critique of the latter from a Hayekian perspective, see Pennington 2001.
7. MacIntyre 1984.
8. See, for example, Barber 1984, Sunstein 1991.
9. See, for example, Dryzek 1987; Barry 1999; Smith 2003.
10. Jacobs 1997.
11. See, for example, Barry 1999.
12. See, for example, Smith 2003.
13. Sagoff 1988.
14. I borrow the phrase "the liberal as communitarian" from the title of an excellent review article (McCann 2002) that compares and contrasts Hayekian liberalism with the main elements of communitarian thought.
15. Sagoff 1994.
16. Anderson and Leal 2001, 24.
17. See, for example, Pennington 2000.
18. See, for example, Epstein 2003.
19. It should be recognized that Anderson and Leal make excellent use of Hayek's work at various points in their book *Free Market Environmentalism* (2001). They fail, however, to set these arguments in a broader philosophical/epistemological context and as a consequence do not address Sagoff's and other communitarian greens' arguments *on their own terms*.
20. Hayek 1948b, 6.
21. Sagoff 1988, 80.
22. Ibid.
23. Steele 1992, 316–17.
24. See, for example, Baden and Stroup 1979.
25. Ibid., 205. One way of overcoming this problem is to rely on traditional communal rules

to regulate resource exploitation, as is the case with the common-property regimes examined in depth by Ostrom (1990). Such approaches are more likely to be effective in small-scale, isolated economies where resource demands are relatively predictable. They are, however, much less suitable in a more complex, interdependent economy, in which pressures on resource use are subject to considerable fluctuation and where resource demands may vary considerably among actors. In these circumstances, a flexible set of relative resource prices brought about by trading in private markets is more likely to facilitate the necessary mutual adjustment (Alchian & Demsetz 1973).

26. Hayek 1967, 315.
27. Hayek 1967.
28. Wohlgemuth 1995, 1999.
29. Hayek 1960, 110.
30. Horwitz 1992; Pennington 2003.
31. Pennington 2003, 734.
32. Hayek 1988.
33. Polanyi 1951, 1957.
34. This process might have progressed more speedily were it not for the communitarian justifications so frequently advanced in support of the European Union Common Agricultural Policy.
35. See, for example, Botkin 1990; McCoy and Shrader-Frechette 1994; Chase 1995.
36. See, for example, Jacobs 1997.
37. Barry 1999, 165.
38. Daly and Cobb 1989, 277.
39. Epstein 2003.
40. Ibid., 157.
41. See, for example, Smith 2003.
42. That cultural and moral factors affect relative prices has long been recognized in liberal political economy; see, for example, Mill 1848, book 2, chap. 5.

11

AT WHAT COST?

J. H. DALES

SIMPLE PROBLEMS, SIMPLE SOLUTIONS

Economists have found that it is usually very helpful to attack complex problems like pollution by assuming away all their complexities and then solving the artificially simplified problems that remain. The value of the technique lies *not* in the answer to the artificial problem (ask an artificial question and you'll get an artificial answer) but in the making of the assumptions that allow us to solve it, for these assumptions help us to identify exactly what features of the original problem make it complex and difficult. And it is only when we know exactly what the difficulties are that we can begin to zero in on them. Let us, then, begin our study of the economics of pollution with a very simple problem, taking great care to note exactly *why* it is so simple.

THE FIRST PROBLEM

Imagine a city of 100,000 voters located on the shore of a small lake. There is only one pollutant that enters the lake, human wastes from the city's population. Pollution of the lake has been gradually increasing through the years because the inflow of wastes exceeds the capacity of the lake to degrade or dilute them sufficiently to prevent the quality of the water from deteriorating; until very recently, however, this fact has been unknown, no one having taken the trouble to keep track of what was going on in the lake. At the time our analysis begins the lake water has just been declared dangerous for drinking purposes, and the citizens find themselves face-to-face with a pollution problem.

J. H. Dales, Pollution, Property & Prices: An Essay in Policy-Making and Economics (Toronto: University of Toronto Press, 1968), pp. 27–38. Reproduced with permission of the Licensor through PLSclear.

Now for the assumptions that will allow us to solve the problem:

1. There is only one pollutant.
2. There is only one group of polluters; and each member of the group pollutes to exactly the same extent as every other member.
3. Each member of the group takes exactly the same view of the medical warning as every other member.
4. Each member would be willing to pay up to $10 a year, but no more, in order to avoid the risk involved in drinking water that might be harmful to his health.
5. The risk can be avoided in two, and only two, ways: each family can boil its own drinking water at a cost of $6 per year, or $600,000 for the entire population; a city water treatment plant can be provided at a cost of $250,000 per year, or $2.50 per voter.
6. Everyone expects that within the next ten years the lake will be declared unfit for swimming. Each would be willing to pay a dollar per year from now on to avoid that eventuality. They discover, though, that the cheapest way of avoiding it would be to pay for sewage treatment, which would cost each of them $3.00 a year. (The sewage treatment plant would not solve the drinking water problem: see assumption 5.)
7. No one expects further damage, except to swimming, from continued pollution of the lake.

The answer is easy, isn't it? The citizens vote to build a water treatment plant, and that's that! (The swimming problem, of course, is still hanging over their heads, but it is not worth doing anything about it right now, so they forget it.) Even though the answer is self-evident, it will be well to construct a simple table—which we shall call a benefit–cost table—to make sure we know *how* we got the answer. Looking at Row 4 of the table we see that the policy of building the water treatment plant is indeed the best solution to our problem because the net benefit of this policy is greater than that of any other (including doing nothing about the problem). Row 6 gives us a further check on our reasoning because it shows that our society's total waste disposal costs are minimized by building the water treatment plant. We have therefore found the proper balance between the various components of waste disposal cost. (We could get rid of the welfare damage of $1 by building a sewage plant, thereby raising our total waste disposal costs from $3.50 to $5.50; but it does not make sense to raise costs by $2 in order to get rid of damage valued at $1.)

We must now ask *why* the answer to our problem was so easy. The first reason is the so-called people we have invented. They are certainly a dull lot, because they are all exactly the same (assumptions 2, 3, 4, 6, and 7). It is almost as if we were dealing with one individual instead of a society of individuals because the social problem is simply 100,000 times any individual's problem; and the solution to the social problem is simply 100,000 times any individual's solution to his own problem. There really wouldn't be any *social* problem if we all thought alike—and the essence of the pollution problem in the real world is that most

BENEFIT–COST TABLE I

1	POLICY	water treatment plant	boil water	water and sewage plants	do nothing
2	GROSS BENEFIT value of damage avoided	(health) $10.00	(health) $10.00	(health and swimming) $11.00	$0.00
3	COST OF AVOIDING DAMAGE	$2.50	$6.00	$5.50	$0.00
4	NET BENEFIT (item 2 – 3)	$7.50	$4.00	$5.50	$0.00
5	WELFARE DAMAGE REMAINING	(swimming) $1.00	(swimming) $1.00	$0.00	(health and swimming) $11.00
6	WASTE DISPOSAL COSTS (item 3 + 5)	$3.50	$7.00	$5.50	$11.00

people don't seem to take it as seriously as we do! Our "people" are also pretty ignorant (assumption 7), since damage to other uses of the lake will certainly become manifest if pollution continues unabated. Some of us may be willing to say, moreover, that they are a pretty insensitive lot because they know they are going to ruin the lake for swimming and really ought to be willing to pay for that sewage treatment plant; but then *we* don't all think alike, especially when it comes to opinions about what people ought to do.

The second reason why the answer is so easy is that everything about the problem is so cut-and-dried; all the benefits (that is, all the damages avoided) and all the costs of every possible line of action are known, are measurable in dollars, and have in fact been measured and presented to the citizens in dollar amounts. Choice is simple when everything is cut-and-dried, and everything is cut-and-dried when all aspects of a problem can be exactly measured in some common unit, such as dollars. There are two reasons why our artificial problem can be expressed in exact dollar terms; we shall label them reasons 2A and 2B. Reason 2A is that everyone knows exactly what his welfare damage would be if he did nothing about his pollution problem (assumptions 4 and 6). Reason 2B is that the only possible solutions are "all-or-nothing" solutions (assumptions 5 and 6); we shall look at a problem in a moment where it is possible to buy different degrees of protection from risk for different prices.

The third reason why the answer to our initial problem is so easy is that the technical problem is very simple, mainly because there is only one pollutant (assumption 1). If there were ten pollutants it would not always be possible to calculate the damage done by each, and then add them up to get the total damage. As we have seen, pollutants often interact, sometimes to escalate their individual damages, sometimes to reduce them; pollutant damages are not always additive, as the mathematicians would say. When two pollutants, X and Y, escalate, and you pay to get rid of one of them, say X, you get a bonus because Y is much less damaging by itself than it was with X. (In the early days of chemical insecticides, DDT was used to kill coddling moths in apple orchards; it did not, however, kill mites, whose numbers had formerly been kept in check by coddling moths, who ate them; the result was

that after the moths were killed the mites had a field day, and orchardists suffered more mite damage than they would have believed possible.) In this [chapter], however, I am going to ignore the non-additive aspects of pollution problems. They only complicate the calculation of the damage figures that the economic analysis of pollution uses; they do not affect the analysis itself.

Finally, a fourth artificiality must be mentioned, a fourth reason why our first problem is so easy to solve. We considered only one city, one area (assumption 2), so we didn't have to worry about how pollution in one area by one group might affect the well-being of other groups in other areas. . . . When we remove the "one-area" artificiality from our analysis, complications come flooding in.

In summary, we have *made* our problem easy—even ridiculously easy—by imposing on it a number of simplifications. Two of these are unimportant because they only simply technical aspects of the problem: we shall not discuss further the assumption of only one pollutant (reason 3) because in the real world engineers could in most cases provide good data on the effects of more than one pollutant; and we shall show in a moment how we can dispense with the reason 2B simplification of "all-or-nothing" solutions. But all of our other carefully contrived constraints on our simplified "pollution" problem touch on essentials; they not only simplify actual pollution problems—they also distort them.

. . .

THE SECOND PROBLEM

The 2B simplification made pollution problems "all-or-nothing" propositions—they were either solved or not solved. Sometimes, perhaps, that is the way things are; but usually we have to choose among different "degrees of solution" to pollution problems. (The question is not whether I will keep my car clean or dirty, but how clean—or dirty—I will keep it.) Let us therefore change the character of our first problem so that "partial solutions" as well as "all-or-nothing" solutions become possible, and see whether we can find an answer to this more complicated problem.

The voters are now told by the City Engineer that he can provide them with a treatment plant that will remove all of the noxious wastes from drinking water for a cost of $5 per voter per year; or one that will remove 75 per cent of the wastes at a cost of $3.50, or one that will remove half the wastes (and thus prevent half the damage) for $2 per voter per year. Each voter now asks himself how much he would pay to avoid all the damage, three-quarters of the damage, and half the damage that he expects to suffer if nothing is done about the condition of the city drinking water. Since all the voters are exactly the same, we might as well stick with the City Engineer, who is of course a voter. He says to himself: "If nothing is done I expect to be sick one day a year, and I'll pay $10 to avoid a day's sickness; thus a treatment plant that was 100 per cent effective would be worth $10 to me. If only half the wastes are removed I expect I would be sick only about three days in ten years; I think the harm done by the wastes goes up faster than the amount of wastes I imbibe, so that as the dosage doubles the harm more than doubles; so if I halve the dosage I'll cut down my sickness by more

BENEFIT–COST TABLE II
TWO MEASURES WITH VARYING DEGREES OF TREATMENT

1	DEGREE OF TREATMENT	100%	75%	50%	0%
2	GROSS BENEFIT value of sickness avoided	$10.00	$9.00	$7.00	$0.00
3	COST OF AVOIDING DAMAGE				
	boiling	$6.00	$4.50	$3.00	$0.00
	city plant	$5.00	$3.50	$2.00	$0.00
4	NET BENEFIT (item 2 – 3)				
	boiling	$4.00	$4.50	$4.00	$0.00
	city plant	$5.00	$5.50	$5.00	$0.00
5	WELFARE DAMAGE REMAINING*				
	boiling	$0.00	$1.00	$3.00	$0.00
	city plant	$0.00	$1.00	$3.00	$0.00
6	WASTE DISPOSAL COSTS (item 3 + 5)				
	boiling	$6.00	$5.50	$6.00	$0.00
	city plant	$5.00	$4.50	$5.00	$0.00

* Value of sickness not avoided, i.e., $10 minus item 2

than 50 per cent, by more than half a day a year; three tenths of a day a year sounds about right, so a treatment plant that would cut my losses from $10 to $3 a year would be worth $7 a year to me. Similarly, if a plant that is 75 per cent effective cut my sickness to one day in ten years, it would save me $9 a year in sickness costs; that's what the plant would be worth to me."

The Engineer then recalls that it would cost him $6 a year to boil his drinking water, and with the help of his slide rule he quickly calculates that if he boiled half his water (or all of his water half the time) the cost would be $3, and that to boil it 75 per cent of the time would cost $4.50. The Engineer then thinks a moment and decides that he will refer to "the value of sickness avoided" as the "gross benefit" of each scheme, and that he will describe the costs of boiling water or paying for a water treatment plant as "damage avoidance costs." The "net benefit" of any given scheme he defines as gross benefit less damage avoidance costs.

This is all the information the Engineer needs to solve his problem, but, being an engineer, he wants to check his reasoning by working out the problem another way. To do so, he defines two more magnitudes. Some of the schemes he is considering do not avoid all the pollution damage, and the "psychic" cost to him of the risk of sickness that he does *not* avoid by adopting any particular scheme he decides to call "welfare damage." The total cost to him of dealing with the pollution problem is therefore the sum of his damage avoidance costs (paid in money) plus the value of the welfare damage (which he simply grins and bears); this sum he labels "waste disposal costs." He is now ready to put all his findings into a table.

The effort of preparing the table has obviously been worthwhile, because the solution now leaps to the eye. We choose the scheme with the *highest* net benefit, which turns out to be the 75 per cent effective city treatment plant. By looking at Row 6 we see that this plan results in the lowest total cost of disposing of the wastes—which is, of course, as it should be. By adopting the 75 per cent treatment plant, total waste disposal costs have been reduced from $10 to $4.50; a profit or net benefit of $5.50 has been made on the deal. (On either the 100 per cent treatment plant or the 50 per cent treatment plant the profit would only be $5.00.)

It is obvious, of course, that the answer we get depends entirely on the numbers we have assumed. If, for example, the cost of providing a 100 per cent treatment plant had been $4 instead of $5, and all the other numbers had remained the same, the net benefit of this policy would been $6, waste disposal costs would have been reduced to $4, and our best choice would have been the 100 per cent treatment plant. Or if the costs of all treatment plants were $2 higher than the figures we have chosen, the best solution would turn out to be to boil all drinking water. You can play around with the figures all you like, and rig them in such a way as to get seven different answers—one for each active policy and one for a policy of doing nothing. (If the costs of avoiding damage by all of the six "positive" policies is greater than $10, then the best policy is to do nothing.)

You can imagine that tables of the type illustrated above could become very complicated if there were, say, half a dozen different types of damage to be considered and seven or eight different ways of either avoiding it (damage avoidance schemes) or preventing the pollution that occasions it (pollution control schemes), each of which would probably help to control different proportions of different types of damage. Benefit–cost calculations, as they are called, of actual pollution problems might easily become so complex, especially if we were to include the Reason-3 difficulties occasioned by interacting pollutants, that we might very well want to buy a little bit of high-speed computer time in order to work them all out and arrive at the net benefit figures.

What is important, though, is that they always *can* be worked out—provided, of course, that we remain within our very artificial world where Reason-1 assumptions protect us from real people and let us deal with very dull "creatures," all of whom are exactly alike; where 2A assumptions ensure that we have all the information we need to solve the problem; and where the Reason-4 artificiality means that we are dealing with a one-community world.

A CONCLUDING CAVEAT

A major purpose of this chapter has been to illustrate a certain way of thinking about pollution problems.

The technique has been to balance the benefits against the costs of different policies (including a policy of doing nothing) in order to find the most profitable policy. This "cost–benefit–profit" apparatus is simply a formal description of the process of making a choice. Every day everyone makes choices, i.e., decides to do this rather than that. In order to get the benefit of doing "this" one must incur a cost, even if the cost consists only of giving up the pleasure (or profit) associated with doing "that." Every line of action (including "zero-action" or inaction) involves both costs and benefits, and sensible behavior consists of nothing more than adopting that line of action that yields the greatest profit, i.e., the greatest excess of benefit over costs.

In the present chapter the benefit–cost apparatus has provided us with an orderly way of thinking about our simplified problems; and it will serve the same function in the discussion of *any* problem of choice, no matter how complicated. A guide to straight thinking is not, of course, a dramatic break-through in the pollution field, but it does constitute an essential base for any rational attack on the problem. If you look carefully at many proposed "solutions" to pollution problems you will be astonished to find how often authors forget that every benefit has its cost and how often, in their enthusiasm, they argue as if the great benefits of their pet anti-pollution schemes could be obtained at no cost.

In the simplified problems dealt with in the present chapter, benefit–cost analysis has perhaps seemed to be much more than a guide to straight thinking; it may have seemed, indeed, to be a magic machine that actually solved problems for us. But do not be deceived! The problems were *not* solved by the benefit–cost machine; they were solved because we took great pains to adopt assumptions that *made* them solvable. A brief discussion of some of the complications involved in choices about real-world pollution problems will serve to suggest why the actual making of decisions about such problems cannot be reduced to a mechanical, numerical procedure.

We all know that a personal decision about a major matter—say the choice of a career—is apt to have an important effect on other aspects of our lives: where we live, our opportunities for travel and recreation, our income level, and perhaps even on our choice of mate. Everyone faced with a major personal decision is aware of such interrelations and in trying to make a wise choice from among the different possibilities open to him no doubt makes a sort of mental cost–benefit analysis; but no one, surely, would maintain that he could actually draw up a numerical benefit–cost table that would show him how to live happily forever afterwards! The main reason why we would have little faith in numerical "measurements" of benefits and costs that relate to major decisions is, I think, the realization that what we decide today may well affect our lives so much that ten years from now we will probably look on things very differently from how we look on them today. The result is that we will probably never know whether we have made the "best" choice available to us. Twenty years ago I could have decided to be an architect instead of an economist; I have no way of knowing now whether I chose wisely or not. Indeed the very concept of choice becomes tenuous when we deal with areas of life in which there are normally very few second chances (so that we have little opportunity to learn by a trial-and-error process) and where what we do today has a strong effect not only on what we are likely to be doing tomorrow, but also on what sort of person we are likely to *be* tomorrow. It is notable, though, that despite the uncertain outcome of such choices—or, somewhat perversely, because of the uncertainty—we always make special efforts to come to "wise" decisions about them. In the choice of career, for example, we seek to assess our own strong points and weak points in an attempt to make as fruitful a combination as possible between our capabilities, our desires, and the apparent demands and rewards of different career lines. And despite the fact that very few of us would pretend to be able to make (or to have made) a scientific decision about choice of career, most of us probably make a reasonably sensible choice, though we can never be sure that we couldn't have done better.

Major social decisions, such as the choice of a pollution policy, are analogous to major individual decisions. We know that what we do about pollution (or don't do about it) is going to affect many other aspects of our lives—the cost of living, where we live, where we work, what we do for recreation, and so on, and on.

Society is bound to adjust in scores of ways to whatever policy about pollution is adopted, and in order to list all the benefits and costs of a given policy we must try to imagine what the new situation would be like—just as, in deciding on a career, we have to try to imagine what it would be like to be a doctor, or a farmer, or an economist. To some extent the social decision may be more amenable than the individual decision to objective calculation; social scientists, at least, believe that it is easier to forecast the average reaction of a large number of interacting individuals to a change in circumstance than it is to forecast the reaction of any particular individual. We may therefore have some basis for "imagining" the changes in society that would result from the adoption of any given rule about pollution. As a practical matter, of course, it is much easier to predict the direction of a change than its magnitude, so that social science predictions in numerical form are usually very inaccurate. Moreover, when we make decisions that will in all likelihood affect the well-being of people twenty years hence—including those yet unborn—we cannot assume that "people then" (including those of us who survive) will have the same attitudes about pollution as those held by "people now." It then becomes impossible in principle, as well as in practice, to choose the best pollution policy for all concerned—unless someone is willing to gaze into his crystal ball and forecast what people's attitudes will be twenty years from now. But again, as in the corresponding individual decision, gross uncertainty about the outcome of a decision should serve as a challenge to make it carefully and in the light of as much knowledge as possible, not as an excuse for pretending that questions that cannot be answered scientifically are not worth worrying about.

Pollution problems are *social* problems; and decisions about them must result from some process of "social choice." I have so far avoided the problem of whether there actually exists a unique, best solution to any "social choice," and for the most part I shall go right on avoiding it because it is probably insoluble. The problem is simply that if ten people have to make a joint decision about something—say a pollution question—there will be at least ten views about what decision should be made. How, then, can individual preferences be combined to produce a "social preference"? What is really at issue here is a set of age-old questions: What is a society? How should it be governed? How can it make decisions that reflect the general will? The long search for utopia has not so far yielded completely logical answers to these questions; actual governments are only more or less workable institutions, not fully logical creations. If we could find some benefit–cost analysis that would always produce the best answer to social questions we would, in fact, have found utopia.

Which is unlikely. We should be content that benefit–cost analysis provides us with an orderly way of thinking about pollution problems, and not try to make it into an all-purpose decision machine. Indeed to most problems in social choice, as to the most important of all social questions—how shall we govern ourselves?—there is probably no one best solution. Social decisions lead to social change. But who knows the way to utopia?

THEME ???

STEVEN KELMAN

COST–BENEFIT ANALYSIS
An Ethical Critique

A t the broadest and vaguest level, cost benefit analysis may be regarded simply as systematic thinking about decision making. Who can oppose, economists sometimes ask, efforts to think in a systematic way about the consequences of different courses of action? The alternative, it would appear, is unexamined decision making. But defining cost benefit analysis so simply leaves it with few implications for actual regulatory decision making. Presumably, therefore, those who urge regulators to make greater use of the technique have a more extensive prescription in mind. I assume here that their prescription includes the following views:

1. There exists a strong presumption that an act should not be undertaken unless its benefits outweigh its costs.

2. In order to determine whether benefits outweigh costs, it is desirable to attempt to express all benefits and costs in a common scale or denominator, so that they can be compared with each other, even when

some benefits and costs are not traded on markets and hence have no established dollar values.

3. Getting decision makers to make more use of cost–benefit techniques is important enough to warrant both the expense required to gather the data for improved cost–benefit estimation and the political efforts needed to give the activity higher priority compared to other activities, also valuable in and of themselves.

My focus is on cost–benefit analysis as applied to environmental, safety, and health regulation. In that context, I examine each of the above propositions from the perspective of formal ethical theory, that is, the study of what actions it is morally right to undertake. My conclusions are:

1. In areas of environmental, safety, and health regulation, there may be many instances where a certain decision might be right even though its benefits do not outweigh its costs.

Reprinted with the permission of The American Enterprise Institute for Public Policy Research, Washington, D.C.

2. There are good reasons to oppose efforts to put dollar values on non-marketed benefits and costs.

3. Given the relative frequency of occasions in the areas of environmental, safety, and health regulation where one would not wish to use a benefits-outweigh-costs test as a decision rule, and given the reasons to oppose the monetizing of non-marketed benefits or costs that is a prerequisite for cost–benefit analysis, it is not justifiable to devote major resources to the generation of data for cost–benefit calculations or to undertake efforts to "spread the gospel" of cost–benefit analysis further.

How do we decide whether a given action is morally right or wrong and hence, assuming the desire to act morally, why it should be undertaken or refrained from? Like the Molière character who spoke prose without knowing it, economists who advocate use of cost–benefit analysis for public decisions are philosophers without knowing it: the answer given by cost benefit analysis, that actions should be undertaken so as to maximize net benefits, represents one of the classic answers given by moral philosophers—that given by utilitarians. To determine whether an action is right or wrong, utilitarians tote up all the positive consequences of the action in terms of human satisfaction. The act that maximizes attainment of satisfaction under the circumstances is the right act. That the economists' answer is also the answer of one school of philosophers should not be surprising. Early on, economics was a branch of moral philosophy, and only later did it become an independent discipline.

Before proceeding further, the subtlety of the utilitarian position should be noted. The positive and negative consequences of an act for satisfaction may go beyond the act's immediate consequences. A facile version of utilitarianism would give moral sanction to a lie, for instance, if the satisfaction of an individual attained by telling the lie was greater than the suffering imposed on the lie's victim. Few utilitarians would agree. Most of them would add to the list of negative consequences the effect of the one lie on the tendency of the person who lies to tell other lies, even in instances when the lying produced less satisfaction for him than dissatisfaction for others. They would also add the negative effects of the lie on the general level of social regard for truth-telling, which has many consequences for future utility. A further consequence may be added as well. It is sometimes said that we should include in a utilitarian calculation the feeling of dissatisfaction produced in the liar (and perhaps in others) because, by telling a lie, one has "done the wrong thing." Correspondingly, in this view, among the positive consequences to be weighed into a utilitarian calculation of truth-telling is satisfaction arising from "doing the right thing." This view rests on an error, however, because it *assumes* what it is the purpose of the calculation to *determine*—that telling the truth in the instance in question is indeed the right thing to do. Economists are likely to object to this point, arguing that no feeling ought "arbitrarily" to be excluded from a complete cost–benefit calculation, including a feeling of dissatisfaction at doing the wrong thing. Indeed, the economists' cost–benefit calculations would, at least ideally, include such feelings. Note the difference between the economist's and the philosopher's cost–benefit calculations, however. The economist may choose to include feelings of dissatisfaction in his cost–benefit calculation, but what happens if somebody asks the economist, "Why is it right to evaluate an action on the basis of a cost–benefit test?" If an answer is to be given to that question (which does not normally preoccupy economists but which does concern both philosophers and the rest of us who need to be persuaded that cost–benefit analysis is right), then the circularity problem reemerges. And there is also another difficulty with counting feelings of dissatisfaction at doing the wrong thing in a cost–benefit calculation. It leads to the perverse result that under certain circumstances a lie, for example, might be morally right if the individual contemplating the lie felt no compunction about lying and morally wrong only if the individual felt such a compunction!

This error is revealing, however, because it begins to suggest a critique of utilitarianism. Utilitarianism is an important and powerful moral doctrine. But it is probably a minority position among contemporary moral philosophers. It is amazing that economists can proceed in unanimous endorsement of cost–benefit analysis as if unaware that their conceptual framework is highly controversial in the discipline from which it arose—moral philosophy.

Let us explore the critique of utilitarianism. The logical error discussed before appears to suggest that we have a notion of certain things being right or wrong that *predates* our calculation of costs and benefits. Imagine the case of an old man in Nazi Germany who is hostile to the regime. He is wondering whether he should speak out against Hitler. If he speaks out, he will lose his pension. And his action will have done nothing to increase the chances that the Nazi regime will be overthrown: he is regarded as somewhat eccentric by those around him, and nobody has ever consulted his views on political questions. Recall that one cannot add to the benefits of speaking out any satisfaction from doing "the right thing," because the purpose of the exercise is to determine whether speaking out *is* the right thing. How would the utilitarian calculation go? The benefits of the old man's speaking out would, as the example is presented, be nil, while the costs would be his loss of his pension. So the costs of the action would outweigh the benefits. By the utilitarians' cost–benefit calculation, it would be *morally wrong* for the man to speak out.

Another example: two very close friends are on an Arctic expedition together. One of them falls very sick in the snow and bitter cold, and sinks quickly before anything can be done to help him. As he is dying, he asks his friend one thing, "Please, make me a solemn promise that ten years from today you will come back to this spot and place a lighted candle here to remember me." The friend solemnly promises to do so, but does not tell a soul. Now, ten years later, the friend must decide whether to keep his promise. It would be inconvenient for him to make the long trip. Since he told nobody, his failure to go will not affect the general social faith in promise-keeping. And the incident was unique enough so that it is safe to assume that his failure to go will not encourage him to break other promises. Again, the costs of the act outweigh the benefits. A utilitarian would need to believe that it would be *morally wrong* to travel to the Arctic to light the candle.

A third example: a wave of thefts has hit a city and the police are having trouble finding any of the thieves. But they believe, correctly, that punishing someone for theft will have some deterrent effect and will decrease the number of crimes. Unable to arrest any actual perpetrator, the police chief and the prosecutor arrest a person whom they know to be innocent and, in cahoots with each other, fabricate a convincing case against him. The police chief and the prosecutor are about to retire, so the act has no effect on any future actions of theirs. The fabrication is perfectly executed, so nobody finds out about it. Is the *only* question involved in judging the act of framing the innocent man that of whether his suffering from conviction and imprisonment will be greater than the suffering avoided among potential crime victims when some crimes are deterred? A utilitarian would need to believe that it is *morally right to punish the innocent man* as long as it can be demonstrated that the suffering prevented outweighs his suffering.

And a final example: imagine two worlds, each containing the same sum total of happiness. In the first world, this total of happiness came about from a series of acts that included a number of lies and injustices (that is, the total consisted of the immediate gross sum of happiness created by certain acts, minus any long-term unhappiness occasioned by the lies and injustices). In the second world the same amount of happiness was produced by a different series of acts, none of which involved lies or injustices. Do we have any reason to prefer the one world to the other? A utilitarian would need to believe that the choice between the two worlds is a *matter of indifference.*

To those who believe that it would not be morally wrong for the old man to speak out in Nazi Germany or for the explorer to return to the Arctic to light a candle for his deceased friend, that it would not be morally right to convict the innocent man, or that the choice between the two worlds is not a matter of indifference—to those of us who believe these things, utilitarianism is insufficient as a moral view. We believe that some acts whose costs are greater than their benefits may be morally right and, contrariwise, some acts whose benefits are greater than their costs may be morally wrong.

This does not mean that the question whether benefits are greater than costs is morally irrelevant. Few would claim such. Indeed, for a broad range of individual and social decisions, whether an act's benefits outweigh its costs is a sufficient question to ask. But not for all such decisions. These may involve situations where certain duties—duties not to lie, break promises, or kill, for example—make an act wrong, even if it would result in an excess of benefits over costs. Or they may involve instances where people's rights are at stake. We would not permit rape even if it could be demonstrated that the rapist derived enormous happiness from his act, while the victim experienced only minor displeasure. We do not do cost–benefit analyses of freedom of speech or trial by jury. The Bill of Rights was not RARGed.[1] As the United Steelworkers noted in a comment on the Occupational Safety and Health Administration's economic analysis of its proposed rule to reduce worker exposure to carcinogenic coke-oven emissions, the Emancipation Proclamation was not subjected to an inflationary impact statement. The notion of human rights involves the idea that people may make certain claims to be allowed to act in certain ways or to be treated in certain ways, even if the sum of benefits achieved thereby does not outweigh the sum of costs. It is this view that underlies the statement that "workers have a right to a safe and healthy work place" and the expectation that OSHA's decisions will reflect that judgment.

In the most convincing versions of nonutilitarian ethics, various duties or rights are not absolute. But each has a prima facie moral validity so that, if duties or rights do not conflict, the morally right act is the act that reflects a duty or respects a right. If duties or rights do conflict, a moral judgment, based on conscious deliberation, must be made. Since one of the duties non-utilitarian philosophers enumerate is the duty of beneficence (the duty to maximize happiness), which in effect incorporates all of utilitarianism by reference, a nonutilitarian who is faced with conflicts between the results of cost–benefit analysis and nonutility-based considerations will need to undertake such deliberation. But in that deliberation, additional elements, which cannot be reduced to a question of whether benefits outweigh costs, have been introduced. Indeed, depending on the moral importance we attach to the right or duty involved, cost–benefit questions may, within wide ranges, become irrelevant to the outcome of the moral judgment.

In addition to questions involving duties and rights, there is a final sort of question where, in my view, the issue of whether benefits outweigh costs should not govern moral judgment. I noted earlier that, for the common run of questions facing individuals and societies, it is possible to begin and end our judgment simply by finding out if the benefits of the contemplated act outweigh the costs. This very fact means that one way to show the great importance, or value, attached to an area is to say that decisions involving the area should not be determined by cost–benefit calculations. This applies, I think, to the view many environmentalists have of decisions involving our natural environment. When officials are deciding what level of pollution will harm certain vulnerable people—such as asthmatics or the elderly—while not harming others, one issue involved may be the right of those people not to be sacrificed on the altar of somewhat higher living standards for the rest of us. But more broadly than this, many environmentalists fear that subjecting decisions about clean air or water to the cost–benefit tests that determine the general run of decisions removes those matters from the realm of specially valued things.

In order for cost–benefit calculations to be performed the way they are supposed to be, all costs and benefits must be expressed in a common measure, typically dollars, including things not normally bought and sold on markets, and to which dollar prices are therefore not attached. The most dramatic example of such things is human life itself; but many of the other benefits achieved or preserved by environmental policy—such as peace and quiet, fresh-smelling air, swimmable rivers, spectacular vistas—are not traded on markets either.

Economists who do cost–benefit analysis regard the quest after dollar values for nonmarket things as a difficult challenge—but one to be met with relish. They have tried to develop methods for imputing a person's "willingness to pay" for such things, their approach generally involving a search for bundled goods that *are* traded on markets and that vary as to whether they include a feature that is, *by itself*, not marketed. Thus, fresh air is not marketed, but houses in different parts of Los Angeles that are similar except for the degree of smog are. Peace and quiet is not marketed, but similar houses inside and outside airport flight paths are. The risk of death is not marketed, but similar jobs that have different levels of risk are. Economists have produced many often ingenious efforts to impute dollar prices to non-marketed things by observing the premiums accorded homes in clean air areas over similar homes in dirty areas or the premiums paid for risky jobs over similar non-risky jobs.

These ingenious efforts are subject to criticism on a number of technical grounds. It may be difficult to control for all the dimensions of quality other than the presence or absence of the non-marketed thing. More important, in a world where people have different preferences and are subject to different constraints as they make their choices, the dollar value imputed to the non-market things that most people would wish to avoid will be lower than otherwise, because people with unusually weak aversion to those things or unusually strong constraints on their choices will be willing to take the bundled good in question at less of a discount than the average person. Thus, to use the property value discount of homes near airports as a measure of people's willingness to pay for quiet means to accept as a proxy for the rest of us the behavior of those least sensitive to noise, of airport employees (who value the convenience of a near-airport location) or of others who are susceptible to an agent's assurances that "it's not so bad." To use the wage premiums accorded hazardous work as a measure of the value of life means to accept as proxies for the rest of us the choices of people who do not have many choices or who are exceptional risk seekers.

A second problem is that the attempts of economists to measure people's willingness to pay for non-marketed things assume that there is no difference between the price a person would require for *giving up* something to which he has a preexisting right and the price he would pay to *gain* something to which he enjoys no right. Thus, the analysis assumes no difference between how much a homeowner would need to be paid in order to give up an unobstructed mountain view that he already enjoys and how much he would be willing to pay to get an obstruction moved once it is already in place. Available evidence suggests that most people would insist on being paid far more to assent to a worsening of their situation than they would be willing to pay to improve their situation. The difference arises from such factors as being accustomed to and psychologically attached to that which one believes one enjoys by right. But this creates a circularity

problem for any attempt to use cost–benefit analysis to determine *whether* to assign to, say, the homeowner the right to an unobstructed mountain view. For willingness to pay will be different depending on whether the right is assigned initially or not. The value judgment about whether to assign the right must thus be made first. (In order to set an upper bound on the value of the benefit, one might hypothetically assign the right to the person and determine how much he would need to be paid to give it up.)

Third, the efforts of economists to impute willingness to pay invariably involve bundled goods exchanged in *private* transactions. Those who use figures garnered from such analysis to provide guidance for *public* decisions assume no difference between how people value certain things in private individual transactions and how they would wish those same things to be valued in public collective decisions. In making such assumptions, economists insidiously slip into their analysis an important and controversial value judgment, growing naturally out of the highly individualistic microeconomic tradition—namely, the view that there should be no difference between private behavior and the behavior we display in public social life. An alternative view—one that enjoys, I would suggest, wide resonance among citizens— would be that public, social decisions provide an opportunity to give certain things a higher valuation than we choose, for one reason or another, to give them in our private activities.

Thus, opponents of stricter regulation of health risks often argue that we show by our daily risk-taking behavior that we do not value life infinitely, and therefore our public decisions should not reflect the high value of life that proponents of strict regulation propose. However, an alternative view is equally plausible. Precisely because we fail, for whatever reasons, to give life-saving the value in everyday personal decisions that we in some general terms believe we should give it, we may wish our social decisions to provide us the occasion to display the reverence for life that we espouse but do not always show. By this view, people do not have fixed unambiguous "preferences" to which they give expression through private activities and which therefore should be given expression in public decisions. Rather, they may have what they themselves regard as "higher" and "lower" preferences. The latter may come to the fore in private decisions, but people may want the former to come to the fore in public decisions. They may sometimes display racial prejudice, but support antidiscrimination laws. They may buy a certain product after seeing a seductive ad, but be skeptical enough of advertising to want the government to keep a close eye on it. In such cases, the use of private behavior to impute the values that should be entered for public decisions, as is done by using willingness to pay in private transactions, commits grievous offense against a view of the behavior of the citizen that is deeply engrained in our democratic tradition. It is a view that denudes politics of any independent role in society, reducing it to a mechanistic, mimicking recalculation based on private behavior.

Finally, one may oppose the effort to place prices on a non-market thing and hence in effect incorporate it into the market system out of a fear that the very act of doing so will reduce the thing's perceived value. To place a price on the benefit may, in other words, reduce the value of that benefit. Cost–benefit analysis thus may be like the thermometer that, when placed in a liquid to be measured, itself changes the liquid's temperature.

Examples of the perceived cheapening of a thing's value by the very act of buying and selling it abound in everyday life and language. The disgust that accompanies the idea of buying and selling human beings is based on the sense that this would dramatically diminish human worth. Epithets such as "he prostituted himself," applied as linguistic analogies to people who have sold something, reflect the view that certain things should not be sold because doing so diminishes their value. Praise that is bought is worth little, even to the person buying it. A true anecdote is told of an economist who retired to another university community and complained that he was having difficulty making friends. The laconic response of a critical colleague—"If you want a friend why don't you buy yourself one"—illustrates in a pithy way the intuition that, for some things, the very act of placing a price on them reduces their perceived value.

The first reason that pricing something decreases its perceived value is that, in many circumstances, non-market exchange is associated with the production of certain values not associated with market exchange. These may include spontaneity and various other feelings that come from personal relationships. If a good becomes less associated with the production of positively valued feelings because of market exchange, the perceived value of the good declines to the extent that those feelings are valued. This can be seen clearly in instances where a thing may be transferred both by market and by non-market mechanisms. The willingness to pay for sex bought from a prostitute is less than the perceived value of the sex consummating love. (Imagine the reaction if a practitioner of cost–benefit analysis computed the benefits of sex based on the price of prostitute services.)

Furthermore, if one values in a general sense the existence of a non-market sector because of its connection with the production of certain valued feelings, then one ascribes added value to any non-marketed good simply as a repository of values represented by the nonmarket sector one wishes to preserve. This seems certainly to be the case for things in nature, such as pristine streams or undisturbed forests: for many people who value them, part of their value comes from their position as repositories of values the non-market sector represents.

The second way in which placing a market price on a thing decreases its perceived value is by removing the possibility of proclaiming that the thing is "not for sale," since things on the market by definition are for sale. The very statement that something is not for sale affirms, enhances, and protects a thing's value in a number of ways. To begin with, the statement is a way of showing that a thing is valued for its own sake. Furthermore, to say that something cannot be transferred in that way places it in the exceptional category— which requires the person interested in obtaining that thing to be able to offer something else that is exceptional, rather than allowing him the easier alternative of obtaining the thing for money that could have been obtained in an infinity of ways. This enhances its value. If I am willing to say "You're a really kind person" to whoever pays me to do so, my praise loses the value that attaches to it from being exchangeable only for an act of kindness.

In addition, if we have already decided we value something highly, one way of stamping it with a cachet affirming its high value is to announce that it is "not for sale." Such an announcement does more, however, than just reflect a preexisting high valuation. It signals a thing's distinctive value to others and helps us persuade them to value the thing more highly than they otherwise might. It also expresses our resolution to safeguard that distinctive value. To state that something is not for sale is thus also a source of value for that thing, since if a thing's value is easy to affirm or protect, it will be worth more than an otherwise similar thing without such attributes.

If we proclaim that something is not for sale, we make a once-and-for-all judgment of its special value. When something is priced, the issue of its perceived value is constantly coming up, as a standing invitation to reconsider that original judgment. Were people constantly faced with questions such as "how much money could get you to give up your freedom of speech?" or "how much would you sell your vote for if you could?", the perceived value of the freedom to speak or the right to vote would soon become devastated as, in moments of weakness, people started saying "maybe it's not worth *so much* after all." Better not to be faced with the constant questioning in the first place. Something similar did in fact occur when the slogan "better red than dead" was launched by some pacifists during the Cold War. Critics pointed out that the very posing of this stark choice—in effect, "would you *really* be willing to give up your life in exchange for not living under communism?"—reduced the value people attached to freedom and thus diminished resistance to attacks on freedom.

Finally, of some things valued very highly it is stated that they are "priceless" or that they have "infinite value." Such expressions are reserved for a subset of things not for sale, such as life or health. Economists tend to scoff at talk of pricelessness. For them, saying that something is priceless is to state a willingness to trade off an infinite quantity of all other goods for one unit of the priceless good, a situation that empirically appears highly unlikely. For most people, however, the word priceless is pregnant with meaning. Its value-affirming and value-protecting functions cannot be bestowed on expressions that merely denote a determinate, albeit high, valuation. John Kennedy in his inaugural address proclaimed that the nation was ready to "pay any price [and] bear any burden . . . to assure the survival and the success of liberty." Had he said instead that we were willing to "pay a high price" or "bear a large burden" for liberty, the statement would have rung hollow.

An objection that advocates of cost–benefit analysis might well make to the preceding argument should be considered. I noted earlier that, in cases where various non-utility-based duties or rights conflict with the maximization of utility, it is necessary to make a deliberative judgment about what act is finally right. I also argued earlier that the search for commensurability might not always be a desirable one, that the attempt to go beyond expressing benefits in terms of (say) lives saved and costs in terms of dollars is not something devoutly to be wished.

In situations involving things that are not expressed in a common measure, advocates of cost–benefit analysis argue that people making judgments "in effect" perform cost–benefit calculations anyway. If government regulators promulgate a regulation that saves 100 lives at a cost of $1 billion, they are "in effect" valuing a life at (a minimum of) $10 million, whether or not they say that they are willing to place a dollar value on a human life. Since, in this view, cost–benefit analysis "in effect" is inevitable, it might as well be made specific.

This argument misconstrues the real difference in the reasoning processes involved. In cost–benefit analysis, equivalencies are established *in advance* as one of the raw materials for the calculation. One determines costs and benefits, one determines equivalencies (to be able to put various costs and benefits into a common measure), and then one sets to toting things up—waiting, as it were, with bated breath for the results of the calculation to come out. The outcome is determined by the arithmetic; if the outcome is a close call or if one is not good at long division, one does not know how it will turn out until the calculation is finished. In the kind of deliberative judgment that is performed without a common measure, no establishment of equivalencies occurs in advance. Equivalencies are not aids to the decision process. In fact, the decision maker might not even be aware of what the "in effect" equivalencies were, at least before they are revealed to him afterwards by someone pointing out what he had "in effect" done. The decision maker would see himself as simply having made a deliberative judgment; the "in effect" equivalency number did not play a causal role in the decision but at most merely reflects it. Given this, the argument against making the process explicit is the one discussed earlier in the discussion of problems with putting specific quantified values on things that are not normally quantified—that the very act of doing so may serve to reduce the value of those things.

My own judgment is that modest efforts to assess levels of benefits and costs are justified, although I do not believe that government agencies ought to sponsor efforts to put dollar prices on non-market things. I also do not believe that the cry for more cost–benefit analysis in regulation is, on the whole, justified. If regulatory officials were so insensitive about regulatory costs that they did not provide acceptable raw material for deliberative judgments (even if not of a strictly cost–benefit nature), my conclusion might be different. But a good deal of research into costs and benefits already occurs—actually, far more in the U.S. regulatory process than in that of any other industrial society. The danger now would seem to come more from the other side.

NOTE

1. Editor's note: RARG stands for "Regulatory Analysis Review Group," a group set up during the Ford Administration to do cost–benefit analyses of regulatory proposals. In Washington circles at the time, it was common to speak of a proposal as having been "RARGed."

KRISTIN SHRADER-FRECHETTE

ENVIRONMENTAL JUSTICE

World War III has already begun, according to environmental activist Dave Foreman. In this struggle of humans against the earth, he says "there are no sidelines, there are no civilians."[1] Founder of Earth First!, Foreman and his followers have been fighting this world war by performing acts of "monkey-wrenching," or "ecotage" (ecological sabotage, the destruction of machines or property that are used to destroy the natural world). Monkey-wrenching includes acts such as pulling up survey stakes, destroying tap lines, putting sand in the crankcases of bulldozers, cutting down billboards, and spiking trees so they cannot be logged. Foreman claims such acts of ecological sabotage are part of a proud American tradition of civil disobedience, like helping slaves escape through the Underground Railroad or dumping English tea into Boston Harbor. Rather than slaves or colonists, monkeywrenchers say they are not protecting humans, but earth itself.

As Foreman's remarks suggest, environmentalists have tended to focus on protecting the earth rather than the humans who inhabit it. This book argues not only for protection of the planet but also for public-interest advocacy on behalf of people victimized by environmental injustice. Environmental injustice occurs whenever some individual or group bears

Kristin Shrader-Frechette, Environmental Justice: Creating Equality, Reclaiming Democracy (New York: Oxford University Press, 2002), pp. 3–18. Republished with permission of the author and the publisher.

disproportionate environmental risks, like those of hazardous waste dumps, or has unequal access to environmental goods, like clean air, or has less opportunity to participate in environmental decision-making. In every nation of the world, poor people and minorities face greater environmental risks, have less access to environmental goods, and have less ability to control the environmental insults imposed on them.

This chapter focuses on six key questions: (1) Why have so many environmentalists called for protection of the environment, even as they remained misanthropic and ignored the plight of humans? (2) How did environmentalists come to recognize problems of environmental justice (EJ)? (3) What are the characteristics of environmental injustice? (4) What are some key examples of environmental injustice, both in developed and in developing nations? (5) Why do some people deny EJ problems, and how defensible are their denials? (6) Why do critics of the EJ movement tend to reject various solutions to EJ problems, and are their rejections reasonable?

. . .

ENVIRONMENTALISM AND BIOCENTRISM

To understand why people have ignored environmental injustices for so long, it might be helpful to examine the attitudes and priorities of various environmentalists, like Dave Foreman. Foreman's priorities were called into question several years ago after an accident at the Louisiana-Pacific sawmill in Cloverdale, California. On May 8, 1987, a band saw struck an 11-inch, spike embedded in a redwood log. The saw shattered, and pieces of blade flew across the room. A large section hit workman George Alexander. It broke his jaw and knocked out several teeth. Foreman called the California accident "tragic"; nonetheless, the attitudes and writings of many environmentalists seem to encourage disrespect for humans even as they call for a greater respect for nature and the earth. Such writings often are exclusively nature centered (biocentric) rather than also human centered (anthropocentric).[2]

In "Animal Liberation: A Triangular Affair," J. Baird Callicott claims that "the extent of misanthropy in modern environmentalism . . . may be taken as a measure of the degree to which it is biocentric." And most environmentalists have heard Edward Abbey's famous remark that he would rather shoot a human than a snake. Garrett Hardin even went so far as to recommend that people injured in wilderness areas not be rescued; he worried that rescue attempts would damage pristine wildlife. Even Paul Taylor, in *Respect for Nature*, writes that "in the contemporary world the extinction of the species Homo sapiens would be beneficial to the Earth's Community of Life as a whole." In *Eco-Warriors*, Rik Scarce advocates extermination of humanity as "an environmental cure-all."[3]

Gene Hargrove believes that several factors explain the misanthropy of many environmentalists. One reason is that the early U.S. environmentalists, like Teddy Roosevelt, were the most educated and powerful people in the country. Their environmentalism frequently consisted of bird-watching or expensive ecotourism, not addressing areas of greatest pollution where poor people live. Another reason is that there was no significant conflict between environmentalists and the government until the 1950s, when the Sierra Club had a falling out with the U.S. Forest Service over logging policy.[4] Prior to that, environmentalists were aligned with powerful commercial and government interests, not with poor people. A third reason for traditional environmentalists' emphasis on protection for nature, rather than humans, is that many environmental ethicists have claimed that problems of planetary degradation can be blamed on anthropocentrism, or human-centered values. Callicott's remark, just quoted, is a good example. Rejecting anthropocentric ethics, many environmental philosophers have called for biocentric norms. They have argued for evaluating human actions on the basis of how well they promote ecological, not human, welfare.

Often this biocentrism or ecocentrism is coupled with an appeal to holism, to valuing nature as a whole, rather than valuing its individual species or parts, like humans. Because biocentrists focus on the good of the whole (ecosystems, habitats, and so on), philosophers like Tom Regan have charged them with "environmental fascism." Regan and others believe an ethics of maximizing biotic or ecological welfare could lead to violating human rights in order to serve environmental welfare. Indeed, the misanthropic words of Callicott, Hardin, and Taylor, already quoted, give some credence to the charge of environmental fascism.[5]

Contrary to environmental fascists and misanthropic biocentrists, . . . protection for people and the planet go hand in hand. . . . Poor and minorities are the most frequent victims of all societal risks, including environmental degradation.[6]

. . .

FROM ENVIRONMENTALISM TO ENVIRONMENTAL JUSTICE

Early in the twentieth century many environmentalists were aligned with governmental and industrial interests. The environmental movement of that era conjured up images of backpackers and bird-watchers, Boy Scouts and nature lovers. The images were of white upper- or middle-class people concerned with conserving a pristine wilderness or an important sanctuary. The environmental movement often focused on action to protect threatened forests, rivers, and non-human species, not humans. Even in the academic community, environmental scholarship and particularly, environmental ethics traditionally have focused on esoteric topics such as whether to give "rights" to trees and rocks and whether nature has intrinsic or inherent value.[7] Have they been playing the violin while Rome burned?

Two decades ago, while wealthy environmentalists focused on leisure activities and environmental scholars wrote about ivory-tower topics, the grassroots environmental movement began to notice society's most vulnerable groups. They recognized that poor and minorities have been especially damaged by societal threats such as environmental pollution, runaway development, and resource depletion. This grassroots movement saw farm-worker communities victimized by pesticides, Native American tribes devastated by radioactive waste, African-American ghettos beset with urban pollutants, Latino settlements plagued by hazardous waste incinerators, and Appalachian towns controlled by absentee-owned coal companies.[8] They saw minority communities forced to trade unemployment for environmental pollution, to exchange a shrinking local tax base for toxic dumps, to trade no bread for a

bloody half loaf. Such trade-offs arose in communities more worried about starvation, unemployment, and violent crime than about health threats from industrial pollution. As Professor Bob Bullard, U.S. sociologist and EJ advocate, notes, this situation has changed. Most minority communities are no longer willing to make such no-win exchanges. They realize they constitute the path of least resistance for polluters and developers, and they have begun to take action. In fact, Bullard says that 80 percent of minority-community resistance groups began as environmental organizations. The tactics of such groups have been demonstrations, marches, hearings, public workshops, research, and lawsuits.[9]

Many people believe that traditional environmental activists, as opposed to EJ advocates, have different goals and backgrounds because often they come from different worlds. This book suggests, however, that the two movements are merely different sides of the same coin. What affects the welfare of the planet affects us all. And once polluters and developers learn that their costs of doing business must be borne by everyone and not shifted to the poor and the powerless, "greening" the ghetto may be the first step in "greening" the entire society.

UNDERSTANDING ENVIRONMENTAL INJUSTICE

The grassroots, minority-led movement for political equality, self-determination, and EJ has sprung up mainly in the urban centers of America. Led largely by women of color, this movement combines many of the philosophies and goals of civil rights and environmental activism. But what is the environmental justice movement? It is the attempt to equalize the burdens of pollution, noxious development, and resource depletion. Environmental justice requires both a more equitable distribution of environmental goods and bads and greater public participation in evaluating and apportioning these goods and bads. Evidence indicates that minorities (e.g., African Americans, Appalachians, Pacific Islanders, Hispanics, and Native Americans) who are disadvantaged in terms of education, income, and occupation not only bear a disproportionate share of environmental risk and death but also have less power to protect themselves.[10] Even children represent a minority victimized by environmental injustice. They are more sensitive to all forms of environmental pollution, and frequently schools have been built atop closed hazardous waste sites.[11] Studies consistently show that socio-economically deprived groups are more likely than affluent whites to live near polluting facilities, eat contaminated fish, and be employed at risky occupations. Research also confirms that they are less able to prevent and to remedy such inequities.[12] Because minorities are statistically more likely to be economically disadvantaged, some scholars assert that "environmental racism" or "environmental injustice" is the central cause of these disparities. Other social scientists have found that race is an independent factor, not reducible to socioeconomic status, in predicting the distribution of air pollution, contaminated fish consumption, municipal landfills and incinerators, toxic waste dumps, and lead poisoning in children.[13] Members of communities facing such threats typically are too poor to "vote with their feet" and move elsewhere.

Often the sources of environmental injustice are the corporations and governments who site questionable facilities among those least able to be informed about, or to stop, them. Zoning boards, influenced by politically and economically powerful developers and their friends, also have helped create much environmental injustice. If [I am] correct, however, we the people ultimately are responsible for environmental injustice. We have allowed corporate and government abuses to disenfranchise the weakest among us.

To understand environmental injustice, consider a typical situation that began several decades ago in Texarkana, Texas. Patsy Ruth Oliver, a former resident of Carver Terrace, a polluted African-American suburb of Texarkana, began to notice dark patches of "gunk" seeping up through withered lawns, around puddles, and into the cracked centers of streets. The suburb also had an unusual cluster of medical problems. Their cause finally emerged in 1979, one year after residents of Love Canal, New York, discovered leaking barrels of dioxin beneath their homes. When Congress ordered the largest chemical firms in the United States to identify their hazardous waste sites, the Koppers

Company of Pittsburgh identified Carver Terrace as one of its problem areas. For over 50 years, Koppers had used creosote (a known carcinogen) to coat railroad ties. In 1961, when it closed its Carver Terrace operation, it bulldozed over most of its facilities, including the creosote tanks. Not realizing the dangers left by Koppers, poor families eagerly bought plots in the new Carver Terrace. When Koppers finally admitted the risks at the site, the Environmental Protection Agency (EPA) brought in scientists in full protective gear. They declared the Carver Terrace soil contaminated, but the scientists–did not bother to interview the residents. Instead they claimed that the area posed "no immediate health threat" to citizens. Oliver and her neighbors were enraged. They formed the Carver Terrace Community Action Group and soon discovered that the EPA had failed to notify them of two other EPA studies that concluded the site posed immediate health hazards. Oliver argued that the government should "buy out" her community, just as it did for Love Canal. She also concluded that racism was the only reason her neighborhood was treated differently from Love Canal. "I have a master's degree in Jim Crow," she said. Eventually Oliver forced the government to purchase the homes in Carver Terrace, although the buyout destroyed the African-American community there. In 1984, Texas officials asked the U.S. EPA to place Carver Terrace on the Superfund list, the $1.3 billion trust that Congress established in 1980 to clean up toxic waste dumps.[14] Bob Bullard says that the Patsy Olivers of the world are typical of the EJ movement. Struggling to protect their families and homes, they are not traditional activists. They are just trying to survive. On December 17, 1993, the day demolition of homes began in Carver Terrace, Patsy Oliver died of a heart attack.

ENVIRONMENTAL INJUSTICE AT HOME AND ABROAD

Inspired by the example of Patsy Oliver, many EJ activists also trace their beginnings to 1982 when North Carolina decided to build a polychlorinated biphenyl (PCB) disposal site in Shocco Township in Warren County. The township is 75 percent African American, and the average per capita income of the county is 97th (of 100 counties) in North Carolina. The U.S. EPA allowed state officials to place the waste only 7 feet above the water table instead of the normal 50 feet required for PCBs. Outraged by this discrimination, 16,000 residents (mostly African Americans and Native Americans) organized marches and protests. Officials arrested more than 500 local residents. They lost their battle, the state opened the dump, and PCBs have been leaching into the soil. Their actions, however, helped begin the EJ movement.[15]

As in the North Carolina PCB case, African-American communities have been among those hardest hit by environmental injustice. Often the government is the culprit, as in West Dallas, Texas, where, in 1954, the Dallas Housing Authority built a large public housing project—3,500 units—immediately adjacent to a lead smelter. During its peak operations in the 1960s, each year the smelter released 269 tons of lead into the air. West Dallas, children had blood lead levels that were 36 percent higher than those in children in control areas. Such exposures are significant because even small amounts of lead can impair learning, interfere with red blood cell production, and damage the liver and brain. Despite repeated studies showing that the public-housing children were in danger from the smelter, officials did nothing. For 20 years local and federal officials ignored citizens of West Dallas who asked merely that the city and state enforce existing lead-emission standards. Finally, in 1983 the city and state sued the smelter for violations of city, state, and federal lead-emissions standards. Within two years, the smelter agreed to clean up lead-contaminated soil, to screen children and pregnant women for lead poisoning, and to provide $45 million in compensation to several generations, including hundreds of children exposed to the lead.[16]

Perhaps the most notorious example of environmental injustice against African Americans has occurred in the "Cancer Alley" region of Louisiana. An 85-mile stretch of the Mississippi River between Baton Rouge and New Orleans, Cancer Alley produces one-quarter of the nation's petrochemicals. More than 125 companies there produce fertilizers, paints, plastics, and gasoline. Each year more than a billion pounds of toxic chemicals are emitted in the alley. An advisory committee to the U.S. Civil Rights Commission concluded that African-American communities have been disproportionately impacted by Cancer Alley for at least two reasons. One is that the system of state and local permitting for Louisiana hazardous facilities is unfair. The other reason is that citizens living in Cancer Alley have low socioeconomic status and limited political influence.[17]

Besides African Americans, indigenous peoples repeatedly have been victims of environmental injustice. Among Native Americans, some of the most serious abuses have occurred in connection with uranium mining in the West. Churchrock, New Mexico, in Navajo Nation, the territory of the largest Native American tribe, is a case in point. Churchrock is the site of the longest continuous uranium mining in Navajo Nation, from 1954 until 1986. Navajo tribal governments leased mining rights to companies such as Kerr–McGee, but they did not obtain either the consent of Navajo families or any information as to the consequences of company activities. Because rainfall at Churchrock is about only 7 inches per year, mining companies withdrew as much as 5,000 gallons of water per minute from the Morrison aquifer to support construction and operation of the mines. Once this groundwater was contaminated with uranium, the companies released it into the Rio Puerco, the main water source for the Navajos. As a result, companies like Kerr–McGee not only significantly reduced the groundwater from which many families drew well water but also contaminated the only main surface water supply. For years, the two main companies, Kerr–McGee and United Nuclear Corporation, argued that the Federal Water Pollution Control Act did not apply to them. They said their activities took place on Native-American land that is not subject to any environmental protections. It was not until 1980 that the courts forced the companies to comply with U.S. clean water regulations.[18] Among Latinos, one of the most common forms of environmental injustice is that faced by farmworkers exposed to pesticides. In 1972, the United States banned many chlorinated hydrocarbon pesticides such as DDT, aldrin, dieldrin, and chlordane, in part because they were so long-lived and remained on fruits and vegetables when they were consumed by the public. Instead farmers began using the much shorter-lived but much more toxic pesticides known as "organophosphates." The pesticides pose less threat to consumers because they are less persistent, but they are a greater threat to farm-workers. A large proportion of farm-workers are Mexican Americans, often illegal aliens who work for less-than-minimum wage and typically under difficult or illegal working conditions. Given such circumstances, the workers are in no position to complain about pesticide exposure. Moreover, what pesticide laws exist typically are not enforced, so farm-workers have little protection.[19]

People in developing nations usually face similar or worse environmental threats. In the case of pesticides, for example, after the United States banned many chlorinated hydrocarbons, U.S. and multinational chemical companies merely began shipping them abroad. Currently about one-third of the pesticides manufactured in the United States are not allowed to be used in the United States and are exported, mostly to developing nations. According to the World Health Organization, the chemicals contribute to approximately 40,000 pesticide-related deaths annually in the developing world. The case of Gammalin 20 is fairly typical. A highly toxic relative of DDT known as "lindane," Gammalin 20 has been banned in the United States for about 30 years. After it was imported into Ghana for use as a pesticide, the local fishermen along the shores of Lake Volta found it had another use as well. When they dumped it into the water, many dead fish floated to the top of the water, and the fishermen could easily collect them, sell them, and feed them to their families. Soon the fish population began dropping off at the rate of about 10 percent per year, and the Ghana villagers began experiencing the classic symptoms of nausea, vomiting, convulsions, circulatory disorders, and liver damage. The people did not connect their ailments to the chemical they dumped into the lake, and their problems continued until a Ghanaian nongovernmental organization explained what had happened.[20]

The 1984 chemical spill in Bhopal, India, also illustrated that people in developing nations receive far less protection from environmental threats than do citizens in the developed world. When a toxic gas, MIC, leaked from Union Carbide pesticide plant in Bhopal, the accident killed nearly 4,000 people and permanently disabled another 50,000. The company later settled with survivors and the disabled, for only several thousand dollars per person. After Bhopal, the predominantly African-American community of Institute, West Virginia, became the center of a violent conflict. West Virginia's Kanawha Valley, "the chemical capital of the world," is the site of the only Union Carbide facility in the United States that manufactures MIC. On the one side, Union Carbide workers fought for their jobs. On the other side, local residents said they fought for their lives. Both the company and the EPA stonewalled citizens' demands for investigation of their health complaints and the chemical odors that saturated the valley's air. Citizens claimed at the EPA attempted to show there was no public health threat by continually revising its risk-assessment methods[21] so as to obtain the answers Union Carbide wanted. Apart from the lax standards that U.S. and multinational corporations employ in their plants in poor areas, including developing nations like India, groups in the industrialized world also often intentionally dump toxic wastes in the Third World. Each year companies and local governments offer nations in the Caribbean and in West Africa hundreds of dollars for every 55-gallon barrel of toxic waste that can be dumped legally. For example, in 1988, the city of Philadelphia hired a Norwegian company, Bulkhandlung, to transport 15,000 tons of toxic incinerator ash to the African nation of Guinea. After plant and animal life died at the waste site, the African government ordered Bulkhandlung to remove the ash and return it to Philadelphia. The Africans appealed to the 1989 Basel Convention on the Control of Transboundary Movements of Hazardous Wastes and Their Disposal, ratified by more than one hundred nations, including the United States. According to the convention, companies wishing to ship hazardous waste must notify the receiving country. In fact, exporters must receive written permission from the importing nation. Because the Basel Convention allows any country to refuse permission, it has helped address waste-related EJ problems. Nevertheless, corruption and lack of information often keep the citizens of waste receiving countries from knowing what their leaders have accepted in exchange for payment. Thus it is questionable whether people in many developing nations actually give free informed consent to imports of hazardous waste that may threaten them.[22]

A chief economist from the World Bank recently created a massive controversy when he wrote an internal memo explaining the economic rationale for such waste transfers. The memo was leaked to the press in 1991. It said: "just between you and me, shouldn't the World Bank be encouraging MORE migration of the dirty industries to the LDCs [less-developed countries]?" The memo further enraged ethicists and environmentalists by offering three reasons that developing nations were a good place to dump toxics: their citizens already had a lower life expectancy; such countries were relatively "under-polluted"; and impairing the health of the people with the lowest wages made the "greatest economic sense." [23]

Over the last two decades, many studies have documented the fact that polluters, both at home and abroad, appear to be following the advice of the World Bank economist. In 1983, Bob Bullard showed that, from the later 1920s to the late 1970s, Houston placed all its city-owned landfills in largely African-American neighborhoods. Although they comprised 28 percent of the city's population, African-American communities received 15 of 17 landfills and 6 of 8 incinerators. Bullard pointed out that such dumping has magnified the myriad social ills—crime, unemployment, poverty, drugs—that already plague inner-city areas.[24] Journalists also have shown that the dirtiest zip code in California, a one-square-mile section of Los Angeles County, is filled with waste dumps, smokestacks, and wastewater pipes from polluting industries. In one zip code, where 18 companies discharge five times as much pollution as they emit in the next-worst zip code, the population is 59 percent African-American and 38 percent Latino.[25]

In 1984, Cerell Associates, a private consulting firm hired by the California Waste Management Board, issued a report titled "Political Difficulties Facing Waste-to-Energy Conversion Plant Siting." The report concluded that all socioeconomic groups resist the siting of hazardous facilities in their neighborhoods and adopt positions of NIMBY ("Not in My Back Yard"). Nevertheless, the study showed that because lower-income groups have fewer resources to fight corporate and government siting decisions, they usually lose.[26] Further "confirming the Cerell findings, in 1986 the Center for Third World Organizing in Oakland, California, issued the report, "Toxics and Minority Communities." It showed that 2 million tons of radioactive uranium tailings, left from uranium mining, had been dumped on Native-American lands. As a result, the study argued, cancers of the reproductive organs among Navajo teenagers had climbed to 17 times the national average. Later, in April 1987 the United Church of Christ Commission for Racial Justice released a widely quoted report that documented environmental racism throughout the United States.[27] Ben Chavis, the executive director of the National Association for the Advancement of Colored People (NAACP), organized a study that later showed that 60 percent of African Americans live in communities endangered by hazardous waste landfills. The report revealed that the largest U.S. hazardous waste landfill, which receives toxics from 45 states, is in Emelle, Alabama; Emelle is 79 percent African American. The study also demonstrated that the greatest concentration of hazardous waste sites in the United States is in the predominately minority South Side of Chicago. Typically minority communities have agreed to take the sites in exchange for jobs and other benefits that have never become a reality. A more recent report, published in 1992 in the *National Law Journal*, concluded that government agencies do not guarantee equal political power and equal participation to all groups victimized by environmental injustice. In fact, the study showed that government agencies treat polluters based in minority areas less severely than those in largely white communities. The same report showed that toxic cleanup programs, under the federal Superfund law, take longer and are less thorough in minority neighborhoods.[28]

A 1992 EPA report likewise found significant evidence that low-income, nonwhite communities are disproportionately exposed to lead, air pollution, hazardous waste facilities, contaminated fish, and pesticides. When the report recommended greater attention to environmental injustice,[29] the EPA established the Office of Environmental Equity (OEE). Also in 1992 the General Accounting Office (GAO) began an ongoing study to examine the EPA's activities related to EJ.

The Clinton administration likewise emphasized environmental justice when it selected a prominent leader of the EJ movement, Bob Bullard, to serve on the Clinton–Gore transition team. On February 11, 1994, Clinton signed an executive order that directed each federal agency to develop an EJ strategy for "identifying and addressing ... disproportionately high and adverse human health or environmental effects of its programs, policies, and activities on minority and low income populations." [30]

Bullard says that Clinton's actions are not enough. He claims the United States and other nations need an EJ equivalent of the 1964 Civil Rights Act and the 1968 Fair Housing Act. Every year since 1994, Congress has been debating bills designed to guarantee environmental justice. Because none has ever passed, current efforts to promote EJ rest on three bases: Clinton's executive order, the environmental justice division of the EPA, and the 1969 National Environmental Policy Act (NEPA). [31] Before leaving office in January 2001, President Clinton set the budget of the EJ branch of EPA at roughly the same amounts for 2001 and for 2002 as it was for the year 2000. President Bush is expected to cut both the overall EPA budget and the environmental justice program of the EPA.

Why have local, national, and international media not helped more to promote EJ? One reason is that small-town leaders like Patsy Oliver are typically unknown women. Both sexism and racism combine to silence them in the press. Another reason is that the Patsy Olivers of the world typically do not want media attention and public glory. They want results: health and safety for their families and communities. A third reason is that even the EPA has been slow to acknowledge environmental justice. Only in 1990, in its report "Environmental Equity: Reducing Risks for All Communities," did it finally admit that minority communities have borne more than their "fair share" of environmental-pollution. [32] Policymakers bear some of the blame for the failure to confront environmental racism. They typically use quantitative risk assessment and benefit–cost analysis in ways that are not sensitive to justice issues. Both methods incorporate aggregation methods that often hide inequitable impacts. Those using both methods also usually try to trace the causes of specific problems to particular

hazardous substances. [33] However, EJ proponents say that scientists should assess the total risks that a given community faces because many health threats are a combination of several factors. They also argue that often no one addresses the cumulative and synergistic public health and environmental burdens that minority communities often bear.

Apart from deficiencies in media attention, science, and law, another reason that society has been slow to confront issues of environmental injustice is the backwardness of environmental organizations. Groups like the Sierra Club sometimes mirror the biases of the larger society. Organizing at a time when discrimination was the norm, early Sierra Club leaders did not link social justice to the conservation cause. In fact, in 1959 the Sierra Club vetoed an explicit antidiscrimination policy and said membership already was open to everyone. And in 1971 members voted against addressing conservation issues related to the poor and minorities. Even today, many environmentalists view alliances with the disenfranchised as "too political." Nevertheless, in Los Angeles, Virginia, and Florida, many Sierra Club groups have taken up EJ issues on behalf of Latinos, Native Americans, and African Americans. [34]

DENIAL OF ENVIRONMENTAL INJUSTICE CHARGES

In response to repeated calls for EJ, critics typically make two responses, one based on denying environmental injustice and another based on excusing it. The "denial" retort is that although EJ is desirable, because flaws in existing research make it almost impossible to identify particular instances of environmental injustice, most supposed cases can be challenged. The "excuse" response is to admit that there are instances of environmental injustice but to claim that the benefits of avoiding them do not outweigh the costs of correcting them. Proponents of the first, or "denial," argument often say that although poor and minority communities appear to be victimized, much of the evidence for their discrimination is "largely anecdotal." Attacking Bob Bullard's daily study of environmental racism in Houston, they note that the lawsuit based on it, *Bean v. Southwestern Waste Management Corp.*, was unsuccessful. They also claim that authors often assume rather than prove that actual risks near hazardous facilities are higher than elsewhere.[35]

While it is wrong to assume that risks always are higher near dangerous facilities, critics of EJ research ignore the fact that, all things being equal, public health risks probably are higher near noxious facilities, and research is needed to determine their level. Proponents of the denial argument also ignore the fact that such sites lower nearby property values.

Many proponents of the "denial" argument specifically attack a widely discussed General Accounting Office (GAO) analysis that alleges environmental racism. This 1983 report examined community demographics near commercial waste treatment, storage, and disposal facilities. After assessing data from four noxious facilities in EPA Region IV (the Southeast), the GAO researchers found that the populations in three of the four areas surrounding the problematic sites were predominantly African American, even though they were only a minority in the state's population. Objecting to the GAO study, critics argue that it is ambiguous with respect to how one ought to characterize a community as minority. Christopher Boerner and Thomas Lambert, for example, claim that defining a minority community as one in which the percentage of minority residents exceeds the percentage in the entire population may be problematic. According to this definition, they note that Staten Island, New York, home of the nation's largest landfill, is a minority community even though more than 60 percent of its residents are white.[36]

One problem with the preceding Boerner–Lambert criticism, however, is that it confuses the neighborhood near the landfill with all of Staten Island. Just because Staten Island is only 20 percent nonwhite does not mean that the area immediately around the landfill is only 20 percent nonwhite. Because most residents within several miles of the landfill are African American, Boerner's and Lambert's attempted criticism is questionable.

Critics of EJ research use the "denial" argument to make other allegations. They claim many EJ studies err in ignoring population density when they characterize a community as "minority." They say the real issue is the total number of people affected by some noxious facility, not just the percentage of nonwhites

around it.[37] While the total number of people affected is important, this criticism begs the question of the importance of distributive justice. It arguably is worse for some people to be discriminated against than for everyone to be treated the same and exposed to similar threats. Such discrimination is worse because it entails threats both to life and to equal treatment, whereas the same treatment of different groups may jeopardize only rights to life and not also rights to equal treatment.

Critics of the EJ movement also employ the "denial" argument to challenge the 1987 report of the Commission for Racial Justice (CRJ) of the United Church of Christ. Correlating percentages of nonwhites, within zip codes, with numbers of waste plants, the CRJ analysis showed that the percentage of nonwhites in zip codes with one facility was twice that in zip codes having no such plant. For zip codes with more than one waste facility, the percentage of nonwhites was three times that in zip codes with no such plant. The CRJ also revealed that race was statistically more significant than either mean household income or mean value of owner-occupied housing as a determinant of where noxious facilities were located.[38]

In response to the CRJ findings, proponents of the "denial" argument allege that environmental injustice often disappears once one stops aggregating data from large areas such as zip codes. They say that how one defines the relevant geographic area determines whether or not there is environmental injustice. Such criticisms, of course, are reasonable. One often can gerrymander geographic regions so as to exhibit or to cover up some spatially related effect. Nevertheless, the criticism is beside the point. If the area closest to a noxious facility tends to have a population of nonwhites rather than whites, then regardless of what zip codes (or any other systems of aggregation) reflect, there is likely to be environmental racism. Moreover, if even large aggregates appear to reveal evidence of environmental injustice, the appropriate response is to determine whether the apparent disparate impact is real. The appropriate response is not to say that there are ways of aggregating the data so that the injustice "disappears," because the real question is the defensibility of such methods of aggregation. And this question should be analyzed on a case-by-case basis. It would be surprising if there were never any real environmental injustice, and if poor or powerless people never were subject to more noxious facilities than wealthier ones.[39]

UTILITARIAN EXCUSES
FOR ENVIRONMENTAL INJUSTICE

Using the "excuse" response, critics of the EJ movement do not deny environmental injustice. Instead they give two arguments to put the alleged injustice into perspective. They argue that (1) on balance, victims of alleged environmental insults may benefit from living near noxious facilities. They say victims might suffer worse from higher unemployment and housing costs if they did not live near dangerous sites. Likewise they charge that (2) the mere correlation of hazardous sites and the presence of poor or minority communities does not prove that racism or injustice actually caused the siting there. They say that African Americans, for example, may have moved to risky or undesirable areas because housing was cheaper or because of some other factor.[40] Both of these "excuse" arguments are questionable. Complaint (1) ignores the fact that, apart from the ultimate balance of costs and benefits (such as more employment) near a risky facility, the evidence of what residents want is clear. Poor people and minorities usually do not want most of the dangerous or undesirable sites to be located near them. And nearby residents have the right to control the risks that others impose on them. Critics of the EJ movement who use this "excuse" response seem to forget principles of equal human rights and instead to use utilitarian grounds to attempt to defend injustice. Such a defense is obviously flawed because all people, especially innocent potential victims, have rights to exercise their preferences regarding what threatens their welfare—particularly when others profit from the threats.

"Excuse" argument (2), that the correlation between race and risky facilities does not prove discrimination, is correct. Nevertheless, it is misleading. The issue is not whether people, corporations, or governments deliberately discriminate against poor people or minorities in siting decisions and therefore cause them to live in polluted areas. Even if minorities moved to an area after it was polluted, the issue is whether some citizens ought to have less than equal

opportunity to breathe clean air, drink clean water, and be protected from environmental toxins, if they do have less than equal opportunity, even though no one may have deliberately discriminated against them, the situation may need to be remedied, at least in part because people have rights to equal treatment. Moreover, racism or injustice need not be deliberate. Many people believe in racist or sexist ways even when they have no idea of their prejudices. Their ignorance of their own faults may limit their guilt, but it provides no evidence of the absence of those faults. Absence of evidence for deliberate discrimination is not the same as evidence of the absence of deliberate discrimination. Admittedly, in the landmark case of *Washington, May of Washington D.C., et al. v. Davis et al.*, the court set a stringent standard of proof for damage awards in cases of environmental harm.[41] The standard is stringent because the court ruled that a plaintiff seeking damages must prove that harmful actions taken by an individual or group were intended to cause the plaintiff harm and not merely that the harm occurred as an unexpected by-product of the action. Just because such a standard of proof is required before a defendant must pay legal damages, however, does not mean that environmental injustice occurs only when the same standard of proof is met. Rather, the legal standard is stricter (1) because defendants must be presumed innocent until proved guilty, (2) because courts must be conservative in meting out punishment, and (3) because courts must be cautious in making damage awards. Although the "discriminatory intent" ruling in the *Washington* case damages some civil rights and environmental justice cases, because it is almost impossible to prove the subjective motivations of a decision maker, it applies only to legal rulings. The limits of truth or moral responsibility are not the same as the limits of what can be proved in a court of law as a basis for a damage award. Lack of legal proof for deliberate discrimination does not entail the absence of environmental injustice. Besides, . . . even if citizens, corporations, and governments do not deliberately discriminate, they nevertheless may be responsible for the institutional structures that indirectly cause disparate impacts on poor or minority groups.

. . .

Many critics of the EJ movement use the "excuse" argument in a third way. They claim that alleged solutions to environmental injustice are even worse than the original injustice. They tend to focus on three such solutions: (1) eliminating all social costs (like pollution) of industrial processes; (2) locating these costs evenly throughout the population; or (3) compensating the individuals who bear more of these costs. With respect to the first solution to environmental injustice, critics of the EJ movement say that it would cause greater harm to society than does environmental injustice, and they probably are right, insofar as it is impossible to eliminate all pollution. In the case of pesticides, for example, critics claim (correctly) that because some pollution is inevitable, the "costs to society" of completely eliminating these chemicals are far higher than those of environmental injustice.[42]

Nevertheless, proponents of the "excuse" argument beg a crucial question. Costs to whom? Costs to poor and minority communities might not be greater if society reduced or eliminated pollution near them. Moreover, in the specific case of pesticides, experts have argued that most of these chemicals are not essential to society and agriculture but instead are used to make foods look more appetizing. The same experts argue that biological forms of pest control are safer alternatives than chemicals.[43] The most basic problem, however, with this first solution to environmental injustice—eliminating all pollution—is that it is not realistic. It is a straw-man solution, one easy to reject because it is so extreme. A more realistic solution would be to reduce pollution to levels as low as practical. But critics of EJ do not consider this less extreme option.

What about a second solution to EJ problems, distributing pollution equally? Critics of the EJ movement also reject this alternative on the grounds that not siting noxious facilities in poor neighborhoods would have undesirable consequences, such as reducing the tax base and employment in areas needing them most.[44] This criticism, however, ignores the fact . . . that residents of poor neighborhoods typically do not feel deprived of economic benefits when someone protects them from dangerous facilities. And if not, then rejecting this second solution to EJ problems errs because it ignores the authentic consent and

the well-confirmed opinions of those who have been most victimized by environmental injustice. To argue that communities desire health threats in exchange for economic benefits presupposes that the communities have given free informed consent to the noxious facilities. But proponents of the "excuse" argument typically have not established this presupposition. The argument also assumes that there is no right to a livable environment. Probably EJ advocates would argue that all people do have such rights and that they ought not be traded for money, especially if what is traded is the health and safety of innocent victims such as children.

Critics of the EJ movement also reject a third solution to EJ problems, compensating individuals who are disproportionately impacted by pollution from which society benefits. They reject this compensation solution on the grounds that paying the poor to take health risks amounts to bribery or coercion. To avoid bribery or coercion, they claim that society should compensate only nonpoor or nonminorities, those who can freely consent to the risks. But if only they are paid, proponents of the "excuse" argument say the payment schemes ultimately would raise the level of unemployment and poverty. Are they correct? No; this third objection is flawed in that it ignores the fact that if compensation is owed, then some is better than none. It also begs the question of whether compensation, as such, would increase poverty and unemployment. After all, there are ways to increase employment and reduce poverty, independent of compensating people for accepting noxious facilities. The criticism likewise errs because it presupposes that society has no responsibility to help correct unemployment and poverty, independent of its solutions to EJ problems. Moreover, it is desirable to consider the option of compensation in part because it forces society to ask whether the pollution costs associated with a proposed facility may be so high as to make it undesirable in any location. It forces society to ask whether polluters genuinely are able to pay the full market costs of their actions. A key benefit of compensation schemes thus is that they force polluters to internalize the social costs of pollution and not to try to save money by dumping their burdens on the unwilling, the vulnerable, and the poor. In this regard, one model of compensating host communities for noxious facilities may be the 1982 Wisconsin program for landfill negotiation/arbitration.[45] One compensation model that appears not to have worked is the one created by the U.S. Department of Energy (DOE) for the proposed Yucca Mountain radioactive waste facility. This model failed, in part, because the DOE did not secure free informed consent from potential victims, did not disclose the complete risks to them, and severely limited all liability for the site. The conclusion to draw from cases like Yucca Mountain is not that compensation for environmental injustice is unworkable but that not all compensation schemes are just and reasonable.[46]

NOTES

1. Dave Foreman, *Confessions of an Eco-Warrior* (New York: Harmony Books, 1991), pp. viii–ix, hereafter cited as: Foreman, CEW.

2. Foreman, CEW, pp. ix, 118–119, 149, 165, See also Dave Foreman, "Ecotage Updated," *Mother Jones* 15, 7 (November–December 1990): 49, 76, 80–81.

3. Callicott, Scarce, and others are quoted in Gene Hargrove, foreword to *Faces of Environmental Racism*, edited by Laura Westra and Peter Wenz (Lanham, MD: Rowman and Littlefield, 1995), pp. ix–xiii; hereafter cited as: Hargrove, Foreword, in Westra and Wenz, FER. See also David E. Newton, *Environmental Justice* (Oxford, England: ABC-CLIO, IS96); hereafter cited as Newton, EJ.

4. Hargrove, Foreword, pp. ix–xi.

5. Hargrove, Foreword, in Westra and Wenz, FER, pp. x–xiii.

6. See Wendell Berry, *A Continuous Harmony* (New York: Harcourt, Brace, Jovanovich, 3972), p. 79; see also Avner De-Shalit, *The Environment in Theory and in Practice* (Oxford: Oxford University Press, 2000).

7. J. Baird Callicott, *In Defense of the Land Ethic* (Albany: State University Press of New York, 1989); Holmes Rolston, *Environmental Ethics* (Philadelphia: Temple University Press, 1988); Laura Westra, *Our Environmental Proposal for Ethics* (Lanham, MD: Rowman and Littlefield, 1994); Byron G. Norton, "Environmental Ethics and the Rights of Non-humans," *Environmental Ethics* 4 (1982): 17–35.

8. Kristin Shrader-Frechette & L. K. Caldwell, *Policy for Land* (Savage: Rowman & Littlefield, 1993).

9. Robert Bullard, *Confronting Environmental Racism; Voices from the Grassroots* (Boston: South End Press, 1996); hereafter cited as: Racism. See P. Cotton, "Pollution and Poverty Overlap Becomes Issue, Administration Promises Action," *Journal of the American Medical Association* 271, 13 (April 6, 1994); 967–969; Mary E. Northridge and Peggy M. Shepard, "Environmental Racism and Public Health" *American Journal of Public Health* 87 (May 1997); 730–732.

10. R. Bullard, *Dumping in Dixie: Race, Class, and Environmental Quality* (Boulder: Westview, 1990).

11. Stacy A. Telcher, "Schools atop Dumps: Environmental Racism?" *Christian Science Monitor* 91 (1999): 3.

12. J. Gould, *Quality of Life in American Neighborhoods: Levels of Affluence, Toxic Waste and Cancer Mortality in Residential Zip Codes Areas* (Boulder: Westview, 1988).

13. R. D. Bullard, "Environmental Racism in America?" *Environmental Protection* 206 (1991): 25–26; Bullard, "Anatomy of Environmental Racism and the Environmental Justice Movement," in Bullard, *Racism*, p. 21.

14. Quoted by Ruth Rosen, "Who Gets Polluted? The Movement for Environmental Justice," in *Toting Sides: Clashing Views on Controversial Environmental Issues*, ed. Theodore Goldfarb (Guilford, CT: Dushkin/McGraw-Hill, 1977), pp. 67–68; hereafter cited as; Rosen, "Who Gets Polluted?"

15. Newton, EJ, pp. 1–2.

16. Ibid., pp. 6–7.

17. Ibid., pp. 9–11.

18. Ibid., pp. 7–9.

19. Ibid., pp. 11–12.

20. Newton, EJ, pp. 13–14.

21. Rosen, "Who Gets Polluted?" pp. 64–65.

22. H. Shue, "Exporting Hazards," In *Boundaries*, edited by P. Brown and H. Shue (Totowa, NJ: Rowman and Littlefield, 1981), p. 107. For the Burkhandlug case, see Newton, EJ, pp. 47–48; for the text of the Basel Convention, see Newton, EJ, pp. 131–134.

23. Rosen, "Who Gets Polluted?" p. 66; see Meena Singh, "Environmental Security," *Social Justice* 23 (winter 1996): 125–134.

24. Bullard, *Dumping.*
25. Rosen, "Who Gets Polluted?" pp. 65–66; see Raquel Pinderhughes, "The Impact of Race on Environmental Quality," *Sociological Perspectives* 39 (summer 1996): 231–249; hereafter cited as: Pinderhughes, "Impact."
26. Rosen, "Who Gets Polluted?" p. 66.
27. UCC, Toxic Wastes.
28. *National Law Journal* 15, no. 3, special issue, "Unequal Protection; The Racial Divide in Environmental Law" (September 21, 1992); Rosen, "Who Gets Polluted?" p. 66.
29. EPA, Equity.
30. Executive Order #12698, Sec. 1–101. For the full text of the order, see *Environment* 36 (May 1994): 16–19.
31. Thomas M. Parris, "Spinning the Web of Environmental Justice," *Environment* 39 (May 1097): 44–46; Rosen, "Who Gets Polluted?" pp. 69–70. The 1967 NEPA requires assessors to take account of distributive inequities in environmental impacts. For the text of NEPA, see Newton, EJ, pp. 92–97.
32. Pinderhughes, "Impact," pp. 231–249.
33. See Kristin Shrader-Frechette, *Risk and Rationality* (Berkeley: University of California Press, 1991); Kristin Shrader-Frechette, *Risk Analysis and Scientific Method* (Boston: Kluwer, 1985).
34. Baxter, "Environmental Justice."
35. Christopher Boomer and Thomas Lambert, "Environmental Injustice: Industrial and Waste Facilities Must Consider the Human Factor," in Goldfarb, *Taking Sides,* pp. 73–75; hereafter cited as: Boerner and Lambert, " Environmental Injustice."
36. Bosrner and Lambert, "Environmental Injustice," 74; see also Ralph M. Perhac, Jr., "Environmental Justice: The Issue of Disproportionality," *Environmental Ethics* 21 (1999): 81–92.
37. Boerner and Lambert, "Environmental Injustice," p. 75
38. Boerner and Lambert, "Environmental Injustice," p. 75.
39. See Pinderhughes, "Impact," pp. 231–249.
40. Deb Starkey, "Environmental Justice," *State Legislature* 20 (March 1994): 27–31; Boerner and Lambert, "Environmental Injustice," p. 75. Payne, "Environmental Injustice," also makes this objection, as do Been, "Locally Undesirable" (note 38), and John S. Baker, "Dissent," in Louisiana Advisory Committee to the US Commission on Civil Rights, The Battle for Environmental Justice in Louisiana (Kansas City: US Commission on Civil Rights, 1993).
41. For discussion of the Washington case, see Newton, EJ, pp. 44–45, 142–144.
42. Boerner and Lambert, "Environmental Injustice," pp. 76–77.
43. Kristin Shrader-Frechette, *Environmental Ethics* (Pacific Grove, CA: Boxwood Press, 1991), pp. 270–324; David Pimentel et al., "Assessment of Environmental and Economic Impacts of Pesticide Use," in *Technology and Values,* ed. Kristin Shrader-Frechette and L. Westra (New York: Rowman & Littlefield, 1997), pp. 375–414.
44. See Starkey, "Environmental Justice," pp. 27–31.
45. Ibid., pp. 81–82.
46. Kristin Shrader-Frechette, *Burying Uncertainty* (Berkeley, CA: University of California Press, 1893), pp. 15–23, 96–98, 204–207.

DAVID SCHMIDTZ

A PLACE FOR COST–BENEFIT ANALYSIS

From time to time, we need to decide. When unsure, we tend to weigh pros and cons. Occasionally, we make the weighing explicit, listing pros and cons and assigning numbers. What could go wrong? In fact, things can go terribly wrong. This paper reflects on the nature and limits of cost–benefit analysis: what it can do, and what it cannot.

I. WHAT IS CBA, AND WHAT IS IT FOR?

Many critics of cost–benefit analysis (henceforth CBA) seem driven by a gut feeling that CBA is heartless. They think, in denouncing CBA, they are taking a stand against heartlessness. This is unfortunate. In truth, weighing a proposal's costs and benefits does not make you a bad person. What makes you a bad person is *ignoring* costs—costs you impose on others.

Problems arise not when decision makers take costs and benefits into account, but rather when they *neglect* to do so. The problem in general terms is a problem of *external* cost. External costs are costs that decision makers ignore, leaving them to be paid by someone else.

We naturally are prone to ignoring external costs. Every time you drive a car, you are risking other people's lives, and you probably never feel guilty about it. (And just like you, industrial polluters defend themselves by saying, "But everybody does it!") It is only human.

No ethicist would defend forms of CBA that explicitly set aside external cost. What is controversial is whether there exists any defensible other form of CBA. Those with expertise in accounting draw fine-grained distinctions among variations on the basic theme of CBA. Full Cost Accounting, for example, refers to an attempt to carry out CBA in such a way as to take *all* known costs, external as well as internal, into account. From here on, except where otherwise noted, when I speak of CBA, I will be referring to cost–benefit analysis with Full Cost Accounting. (The technical terms here are not quite standardized. What I call Full Cost Accounting is sometimes called Multiple Accounts Analysis or Life Cycle Analysis. Whatever term we use, I have in mind CBA that does not deliberately ignore any cost whatever.)

Under what circumstances, then, should we want policy makers to employ CBA? Two answers come to mind: first, when one group pays the cost of a regulation while another group gets the benefit; second, and more generally, whenever regulators have an incentive not to take full costs into account. When benefits of political decisions are concentrated while costs are dispersed, we see special interest groups pushing through policies even when costs to the larger population outweigh benefits. To contain the proliferation of unconscionable policies, we may require that policies be justified by the lights of a proper CBA. Making a CBA available for public scrutiny is one way of trying to teach regulators to take environmental costs into account. We want social, cultural, and legal arrangements that encourage people to be aware of the full cost of what they do.

If a business pollutes, would it be wrong to insist that the business should pay the cost? No. The fundamental argument for CBA is that a proper CBA is not merely an accounting method. It is a commitment to being accountable for the consequences of one's actions. As a mechanism for holding regulators publicly accountable for external costs, CBA can identify projects as not worthwhile when external costs are taken into account, thereby making CBA potentially a friend of the environment.

Current environmentalist opinion generally is anti-CBA, but CBA per se is merely an analytical tool, no more, no less. Consider this argument. Everything we care about is either a cost or a benefit. So to say we should do CBA is simply to say we should take what we care about into account. There is a grain of truth this argument, but also two problems.

First, we can say that everything we care about is a cost or a benefit, but saying it does not make it so. When we add up costs and benefits, we add up weights. Yet, not everything is a weight. Insofar as moral rights in particular are trumps rather than weights, treating rights as weights fails to respect the fact that rights have a gravity that goes beyond mere *weight*. For example, we can agree that it is better for a doctor to save five patients than to save one, while also thinking that this does not even begin to show that doctors have a right to *kill* one patient to save five, despite the weight of what is stake being the same in both cases: five lives versus one.

A second problem with being too cavalier about costs and benefits is this: We are only human, and humans are wired to seek evidence confirming what they want to believe. When we deal with weights, we aren't built to be impartial. We exaggerate weights in favor of what we want to believe, and discount anything weighing against what we want to believe. Critics and defenders of CBA alike do this, just like anyone else. With that caveat, the following sections consider reasons (some cogent, some not) for distrusting CBA.

II. IS CBA ANTHROPOCENTRIC?

Is it only human interests that CBA can take into account? Is CBA essentially anthropocentric? No. CBA as construed here is partly an accounting procedure, and partly a way of organizing public debate. In no way is it a substitute for philosophical debate. Animal liberationists who think full costs must include pain suffered by animals must argue for that point in philosophical debate with those who think otherwise. If CBA presupposed one or the other position, thereby falsely implying that there is no room for philosophical debate, that would be a real flaw.

III. DOES CBA PRESUPPOSE UTILITARIAN MORAL THEORY?

Current utilitarian moral theory holds that X is right if and only if X maximizes utility, where maximizing utility is a matter of producing the best balance of benefits over costs. Does CBA presuppose utilitarianism? No. CBA is a way of organizing a public forum expressing respect for persons: not only persons present at the meeting but other persons as well, on whose behalf those present can speak (citizens of faraway countries, future generations, etc.). For that matter, those present at the forum will speak on behalf of whatever they care about: not only people but animals, trees, canyons, historic sites, etc. The forum is defensible on utilitarian grounds, but does not presuppose utilitarianism. Neither deontologists nor utilitarians would endorse a CBA that ignores external cost, but CBA with Full Cost Accounting could be endorsed by either.

IV. DOES CBA TELL US TO SACRIFICE THE ONE FOR THE SAKE OF THE MANY?

We can imagine advocates of CBA assuming that actions are justified *whenever* benefits exceed costs. That would be a mistake.

Suppose a doctor, contemplating killing one patient to save five, performs CBA and concludes that, well, five is more than one. Does that mean killing one patient is permitted? Required? No. It would be only human if we tried to get the answer that we *want* by fiddling with the calculation, but if we did that, we would miss what is fundamental. Namely, CBA offers relevant guidance when our mandate is to promote the best balance of costs and benefits, but not all situations are mandates to maximize net benefit. Promoting value is not always the best way of respecting it. There are times when morality calls on us not to maximize value but simply to respect it.

I argued that CBA does not presume the truth of utilitarianism. Now I may appear to be arguing that CBA presumes utilitarianism is false! Not so. Even from a broadly utilitarian perspective, it would be a terrible idea to give doctors or anyone else a license to kill whenever they think they can do a lot of good in the process. Some institutions have utility precisely by taking utilitarian calculation out of the hands of citizens. Hospitals, for example, cannot serve their purpose unless people can trust hospitals to treat people as rights-bearers. Respecting people's rights is part of what helps make it safe to visit hospitals. And making it safe to visit hospitals is a prerequisite of hospitals functioning properly. Therefore, even a utilitarian should not try to justify killing one patient to save five simply by saying five is more than one. Sometimes, even a utilitarian should see that numbers do not count. Sometimes, refusing to count—acknowledging that one has no right to count—is good policy.

Consider the case of *Peeveyhouse vs. Garland Coal* (Morris, 2000, 144). Having completed a strip-mining operation on Peeveyhouse property, Garland Coal refused to honor its contractual promise to restore the land to its original condition. The restored land would have been worth only $300 and would have cost $29,000 to restore. Still, Peeveyhouse wanted the land restored and Garland Coal had promised to do it.

Incredibly, the Oklahoma court awarded Peeveyhouse only the $300, judging that Garland Coal could not be held liable for a restoration when such restoration would not be cost-effective. The Court's verdict generally is regarded as utterly mistaken. One way of understanding the mistake is to see it as failing to understand the limits of CBA's legitimate scope. We live in a society where Garland Coal normally honors contracts. Thus, we know where we stand. We need not be perpetually preparing to prove before a tribunal that strip-mining our land or killing us to save other patients is *inefficient*. Instead, we have a simple right to say no, and that simple right to say no empowers us to live with dignity in a community. In giving us moral space that we govern by right, our laws limit how much energy we need to waste: trying to influence regulators, fighting to keep what belongs to us, fighting to *take* what belongs to others.

Crucially, our being able to say no teaches regulators and other people to search for ways to get what they want in such a way as to benefit everyone. CBA in its crudest form allows sacrificing the few for the sake of the many. However, the proper purpose of CBA is not to give us a license to sacrifice the few. If we see CBA as indicating when takings are permissible, we will have a problem: breaking contracts, or taking things from people (especially their lives!) whenever benefit exceeds cost is not a way of respecting people. However, if we instead treat CBA as a *constraint* on takings, ruling out inefficient takings without licensing efficient takings, then it is not disrespectful. So, when one ascertains that winners are gaining more than losers are losing, the properly circumspect conclusion is not that we thereby have a license to take but only that the taking has passed one crucial test.

CBA so construed becomes a way of stopping people from treating each other as mere means. Requiring people to offer an accounting of the true costs and benefits of their operations is a way of holding them publicly accountable for failing to treat fellow citizens as ends in themselves. CBA will *not* filter out every proposal that ought to be filtered out, but it will help to filter out many of the most flagrantly disrespectful proposals, and that is its proper purpose.

V. MUST CBA TREAT ALL VALUES AS MERE COMMODITIES?

As Mark Sagoff notes, there are people who believe that "neither worker safety nor environmental quality should be treated as a commodity to be traded at the margin for other commodities, but rather each should be valued for its own sake" (Sagoff, 1981, 1288–89). Sagoff may be correct, but note that CBA is perfectly compatible with the idea that worker safety and environmental quality should be valued for their own sake. Suppose a recycling process improves environmental quality, but inevitably poses some risk to workers. Workers risk getting their hands caught in the machines, and so on. Notice: if we treat both environmental quality and worker safety as ends in themselves, we still have to weigh the operation's costs and benefits. Is the increment of environmental quality worth the risk? We would be ignoring the question if we said "environmental quality is valued for its own sake."

CBA would be needed even if environmental quality were the *sole* value at stake. Suppose recycling saves paper (therefore trees), but only at the cost of all the water and electricity used in the process. Trucks use gasoline collecting paper from recycling bins. Therefore, recycling has environmental costs as well as environmental benefits. I suggest that we need to know these costs and benefits just in case environmental quality *matters*. "Recycling" is a politically correct word, but does that mean we support any operation using the word in its title, even if the operation is environmentally catastrophic? Or should we instead stop to think about costs and benefits? Those concerned only to maintain politically correct environmentalist appearances do not worry about such things, but stopping to think can be a way of showing respect.

In a nutshell, we sometimes find ourselves in situations of conflicting values. Critics of CBA sometimes seem to say, when values are important, that is when we should *not* think hard about costs and benefits of resolving conflicts in one way rather than another. That seems backwards.

Sagoff asserts that CBA "treats all value judgments other than those made on its behalf as nothing but statements of preference, attitude, or emotion" (Sagoff, 1981, 1290–91). Many things are going on in this passage; I will mention only two. First, Sagoff considers it a mistake to see all values as reducible to costs and benefits. I agree. On one hand, an economist's job is to go as far as possible in treating values as preferences; within economics narrowly construed, this reductionist bias serves a purpose. On the other hand, when we switch to philosophical analysis, we cannot treat values as mere preferences, as if valuing honesty were on a par with valuing chocolate. We cannot jump from economic to philosophical discussion without acknowledging that what we take for granted in one discussion cannot be taken for granted in the other.

Second, Sagoff is saying is that CBA characteristically treats all values as mere preferences. Perhaps, if Sagoff means to say CBA *typically* does so. But saying CBA *necessarily* does so would be incorrect. CBA is about weighing costs and benefits. It does not presume everything is either a cost or a benefit. We have to decide what to treat as mere preferences, costs, or benefits, and what to treat separately, as falling outside the scope of CBA. CBA itself does not decide for us.

To be clear, it is true by definition that to care about X is to have a preference regarding X. However, we can care about X without thinking X *itself* is merely a preference. CBA assumes nothing about the nature of values, other than that values sometimes conflict. Further, CBA does not assume choice is unproblematic; it assumes only that we sometimes do, after all, need to choose.

CAN CBA HANDLE QUALITATIVE VALUES?

Steven Kelman says CBA presupposes the desirability of being able to express all values as dollar values. However, as Kelman correctly notes, converting values to dollars can distort the nature of the values at stake. On the other hand, it would be incorrect to think CBA *requires* us to represent all value as dollar values. If we care about elephants and do a CBA of alternative ways of protecting them, nothing in that process even suggests we have reduced the value of elephants to dollars.

More generally, we sometimes put a dollar value on X despite knowing perfectly well that X's value to us is essentially different from the value of dollars. Note also: an object's having intrinsic value does not imply that the object is priceless. There is such a thing as limited intrinsic value. A painting can have an intrinsic value that is real without being infinite, or even particularly large. The value I would get from selling it is its instrumental value to me. The value it has to me in and of itself, simply because it is a beautiful painting, is its intrinsic value to me. Both values are real, but one is instrumental and the other is intrinsic. Neither is necessarily huge. Suppose I sell a painting. Kelman says, "selling a thing for money demonstrates that it was valued only instrumentally" (Kelman, 1981, 39). Not so fast. The money I receive from the sale is the painting's instrumental value to me, but does my deciding to sell imply that the painting had no intrinsic value? No. Suppose I love the painting, but I desperately need to quickly raise a large sum of money, so I sell. The implication is not that the painting lacks intrinsic value but rather that the instrumental value of selling it can outweigh the intrinsic value of keeping it, at least in desperate circumstances.

Incommensurability of values is not an insurmountable obstacle to CBA. When competing values cannot be reduced to a common measure without distortion, that makes it harder to know the bottom line. Indeed, there may not be a unitary bottom line to be known. Sometimes the bottom line is simply that one precious and irreplaceable thing is gained while another precious and irreplaceable thing is lost. Even so, that does not mean there is a problem with the very idea of taking costs and benefits into account. It just means we should not assume too much about what kind of bottom line we can expect to see.

Crucially, there often is no point in trying to convert a qualitative balancing into something that *looks* like a precise quantitative calculation and thus *looks* scientific but in fact remains the same qualitative balancing, only now its qualitative nature is disguised by the attaching of made-up numbers.

SOME THINGS ARE PRICELESS. SO WHAT?

Critics of CBA think they capture the moral high ground when they say some things are beyond price. They miss the point. Choosing to regard elephants as priceless does not settle what is to be done about them. We still need to look at costs and benefits of protecting them in one way rather than another. First, we want our protection to be an effective way of spending whatever dollars we have available to spend on protection. Second, we need to know whether we are saving them at a cost of sacrificing something equally priceless.

If baby Jessica has fallen into an abandoned well in Midland, Texas and it will cost nine million dollars to rescue her, is it worth the cost? It seems wrong even to ask; after all, it is only money. But it is not wrong. If it would cost nine million to save Jessica's life, what would the nine million otherwise have purchased? Could it have been sent to Africa where it might have saved nine thousand lives? Consider an even more expensive case. If a public utility company in Pennsylvania (in the wake of a frivolous lawsuit blaming high-voltage power lines for a child's leukemia) calculates that burying its power lines underground will cost two billion dollars, in the process maybe preventing one or two deaths from leukemia, is it only money? If the two billion could have been sent to Africa where

it might have saved two million lives, is it obvious a decent person would not even *think* about it?

Critics like to say not all values are economic values. Yes. In fact, no values are purely economic values. Even money itself is never only money. In a small town in Texas in 1987, a lot of money was spent to save a baby's life—money that took several lifetimes to produce. It was not only money. It did after all save a baby's life. It also gave a community a chance to show the world what it stands for. These are not trivial things. Neither are many other things that on which nine million could have been spent.

There are things so valuable to us that we view them as beyond price. What does this plain fact imply? Not much. When we must make tradeoffs, should we ignore items we consider priceless, or take them into account? The hard fact is, priceless values sometimes conflict. When that happens, and we try rationally to weigh our options, we in effect put a price on what is priceless. In that case, CBA is not the problem. It is a response to the problem. The world has handed us a painful choice, and trying rationally to weigh our options is our way of trying to cope (but see Holland's [2002] warning against viewing all choices as tradeoffs).

Although critics often speak of incommensurable values, incommensurability is not strictly the issue. Consider the central dilemma of the novel, *Sophie's Choice* (1979). Sophie's two children are about to be executed by a concentration camp commander. The commander says he will kill both unless Sophie picks one to be killed, in which case the commander will spare the other. Now, to Sophie, both children are beyond price. She does not value one more than the other. In some way, she values each more than anything. Nevertheless, she does in the end pick one for execution, thereby saving the other. The point: although her values were incommensurate, she was still able to pick in a situation where the cost of failing to pick would have meant losing both. The values were incommensur*ate*, but not incommensur*able*. To Sophie, both children were beyond price, but when forced to put a price on them, she could.

Of course, as the sadistic commander foresaw, forcing Sophie to rank those particular values would destroy her. At some level, commensuration is *always* possible, but there are times when something (our innocence, perhaps) is lost in the process of commen-surating. That may explain why some critics want to reject CBA; they see in CBA a mechanism for ranking values that should not be ranked.

Elizabeth Anderson voices this concern when she says life and environmental quality are not "mere commodities. By regarding them only as commodity values, cost–benefit analysis fails to consider the proper roles they occupy in public life" (Anderson 1995, 190). But if we *blame Sophie* for treating her children as commodities subject to tradeoffs, we blame the victim. Sophie's treating her children this way is unquestionably a catastrophic failure to honor their value. But when Sophie does CBA, her calculation is not *causing* the catastrophe so much as acknowledging and coping with it. Reducing values to mere commodities can indeed be a terrible thing, but sometimes the world forces tradeoffs on us that in a better world we would have been lucky enough to avoid. Although we can hope people like Sophie will never need to rank their children and can instead go on thinking of each child as having infinite value, and although we can wish we never had to choose between worker safety and environmental quality, or between different aspects of environmental quality, the fact remains that we live in a world that sometimes requires tradeoffs.

VI. DOES CBA WORK?

When agencies engage in CBA, they typically ask how much they should be willing to pay. That is an obvious and legitimate question because agencies are, after all, constrained by their budget. Sometimes, though, what legislators ponder is how much they are willing to make *other* people pay. That is a problem. In that case, paying is an external cost, and it is no surprise if legislators seem cavalier about it. I said that failing CBA—finding that losers will lose more than winners will gain—should pretty much end the conversation. Unfortunately, in the real world, the conversation does not always stop there. When benefits are concentrated within influential constituencies, legislators conceal how costly the program is to taxpayers at large. Again, it is not because they are evil. They are only human. Situations where we are not fully accountable—where we have the option of not paying the price of our decisions—tend not to bring

out the best in us. CBA with Full Cost Accounting is one way of making corporations and governments rethink what they owe to the environment.

But we need to concede that there is much corruption in the world and nothing like CBA will ever put an end to it. As with any other accounting method, the quality of the output typically will be only as good as the quality of the inputs. Biased inputs generate biased outputs. CBA is potentially a smokescreen for the real action that takes place before numbers get added.

Can anything guarantee that CBA will not be subject to the same political piracy that CBA was supposed to limit? Probably not. I mentioned that the verdict in *Peeveyhouse* generally is regarded as mistaken. What I did not mention is that, as Andrew Morriss notes, "Shortly after the *Peeveyhouse* decision, a corruption investigation uncovered more than thirty years of routine bribery of several of the court's members" (Morriss, 2000, 144). CBA per se does not correct for corrupted inputs. Neither does CBA stop people from applying CBA to cases where CBA has no legitimate role. However, if the process is public, with affected parties having a chance to protest when their interests are ignored, public scrutiny will have some tendency to correct for biased inputs. It also will encourage planners to supply inputs that can survive scrutiny in the first place. If the process is public, people can step forward to scrutinize not only valuations, but also the list of options, suggesting possibilities that planners have concealed or overlooked.

Even if we know the costs and benefits of any particular factor, that does not guarantee that we have considered everything. In the real world, we must acknowledge that for any actual calculation we perform, it very often turns out that we overlooked some cost or benefit or risk. How can we avoid overlooking what in retrospect will become painfully obvious? Although it is no guarantee, the best thing I can think of is to open the process to public scrutiny.

Kelman says CBA presumes we should spare no cost in enabling policy makers to make decisions in accordance with CBA. Kelman is right to mock such a presumption, for CBA is itself an activity with costs and benefits. Analyzing costs and benefits can be a waste of time. It is not always warranted on cost–benefit grounds, and therefore proper CBA on its own grounds recognizes limits to CBA's legitimate scope.

VII. MUST CBA MEASURE VALUATIONS IN TERMS OF WILLINGNESS TO PAY?

CBA often is depicted as requiring us to measure a good's value by asking what people would pay for it. One problem: willingness to pay is a function not only of perceived values but also of resources available for bidding on those values. Poorer people show up as less willing to pay even if, in some other sense, they care about the good just as much.

Another problem is that surveys designed to measure willingness to pay often fail to take willingness to pay seriously. They ask subjects to declare not willingness to pay but *hypothetical* willingness to pay. Such surveys spuriously justify building waste treatment plants in poorer neighborhoods because we *judge* that poorer people would not pay as much as richer people would pay to have the plant built elsewhere. Critics call this environmental racism (because minorities tend to live in poorer neighborhoods). Whatever we call it, we should concede that it does indeed look preposterous.

Is there an alternative that would be more respectful of neighborhoods that provide the most likely building sites? Suppose we initially choose sites by random lottery. Suppose that by random luck, Beverly Hills is selected as the site of a new waste treatment plant. We then ask Beverly Hills's rich residents what they are willing to pay to site the plant elsewhere. Suppose they say they jointly would pay ten billion dollars to locate the plant elsewhere. Suppose we then announce that the people of Beverly Hills are actually, not just hypothetically, offering ten billion to any neighborhood willing to serve as the alternate host of that waste treatment facility. Suppose a poor neighborhood accepts the bid. Would that be respectful?

Or instead, suppose no one accepts the Beverly Hills offer, so the plant is built in Beverly Hills. Is anything wrong with richer residents leaving, selling their houses to poorer people happy to live near a waste treatment plant if that means being able to own far nicer houses than they otherwise could afford? If siting a waste treatment plant drives down property values so that poorer people can afford to live in Beverly Hills, while rich people take their money elsewhere, is that so bad?

Note that even a random lottery inevitably will produce nonrandom results. Regardless of where waste treatment facilities are built, home buyers who opt to move in, accepting the nuisance in order to have a nicer house at a lower price, will tend to be poorer than buyers who opt to pay higher prices to live farther from the nuisance. One thing will never change: waste treatment facilities will be found in poorer neighborhoods. *Not even putting them all in Beverly Hills* could ever change that.

Oddly, activists in effect agitate for plants to be sited as far as possible from people who work in them, since siting waste treatment facilities within walking distance of the homes of people who might want the kind of jobs that waste treatment plants provide is classified as environmental racism. Perhaps questions about how far poor people are commuting to work is not important; normally, though, environmentalists urge us to pay more attention to such issues. In any case, if waste treatment plants need to be near populations that produce the waste being treated, neighbors will be affected. Someone will have to pay, and no accounting tool is to blame for that.

Critics presume the process of siting waste treatment facilities will *not* be conducted in a respectful manner. They presume politicians will site waste treatment facilities in response to calculations about what will minimize adverse effects on campaign contributions and ultimately on reelection bids. The critics may be right. Kristin Shrader-Frechette (in this volume) makes a strong case, and I would bet that she is right about the particular cases she mentions. Under those circumstances, the point of subjecting a CBA to public scrutiny is to lead (quite possibly racist) politicians not to recalculate answers so much as to start asking the right questions.

Just to be clear, however, I would suggest that at least some of the right questions are questions about the future and about long-term trends. Are life expectancies and infant-mortality rates improving for all groups? If so, that is a massively different situation from the situation where indices for some groups are improving while indices for minorities are crashing. The latter manifestly would be cause for alarm, perhaps even outrage. However, if what provokes our outrage is nothing more than the fact that people with more money can afford more than people with less money can, then whether we have a serious complaint is very much in doubt.

VIII. MUST FUTURE GENERATIONS BE DISCOUNTED?

In financial markets, a dollar acquired today is worth more than a dollar to be acquired in a year. Dollars acquired today can be put to work immediately. At worst, dollars put in the bank can collect interest. Therefore, if you ask me how much I would pay today to be given a dollar a year from now, I certainly would not pay as much as a dollar. I might pay a few percent less. Properly valued, then, future dollars sell at a discount. Therefore, borrowing to get a profitable project off the ground can be rational, even when the cost of borrowing a thousand dollars now will be more than a thousand later.

Here is the catch. There is nothing wrong with taking out a loan, so long as we *pay it back*. But there is something wrong with taking out a loan we have no intention of repaying. Discounting is one thing when the cost of raising capital is internal, and something else when we borrow against *someone else's* future rather than our own. Let me stress: the problem here is not discounting; it is the same problem of external cost with which this essay began. We have no right to discount the price that *others* will have to pay for our projects.

In any case, if we undertake a CBA to evaluate the merits of borrowing against our futures, we decide how or whether to discount. CBA will not decide for us.

CONCLUSIONS

I talked about CBA with Full Cost Accounting, but no mechanical procedure can be guaranteed to take all costs into account. For any mechanical procedure we devise, there will be cases where the people who carry out that procedure overlook something important. This is reason not to reject the very idea of CBA, though, but rather to be wary of the desire to make decisions in a mechanical way. We cannot wait for someone to devise a perfect procedure, guaranteed to give everything its proper weight. Whatever procedures we devise for making decisions as individuals or as a community, we need to exercise judgment. At some point we draw the line, make a decision, and get on with our lives, realizing that any real-world decision procedure inevitably will be of limited value. It will not be perfect. It never will be beyond question.

CBA is an important response to a real problem. However, it is not magic. There is a limit to what it can do. CBA is a way of organizing information. It can be a forum for eliciting further information. It can be a forum for correcting biased information. It can be a forum for giving affected parties a voice in community decision making, thereby leading to better understanding of, and greater acceptance of, the tradeoffs involved in running a community. CBA can be all of these good things, but it is not necessarily so. CBA can constrain a system's tendency to invite abuse, but CBA is prone to the same abuse that infects the system as a whole. It is no panacea. It is an antidote to abuse that is itself subject to abuse.

CBA is not inherently biased, but if inputs are biased, then so will be the outputs, generally speaking. However, although the method does not inherently correct for biased inputs, if the process is conducted publicly, so that people can publicly challenge suppliers of biased inputs, there can be some tendency for the process to correct for biased inputs as well. We can hope those with minority viewpoints will have a forum for challenging mainstream biases, but we cannot guarantee it. The most we can say is that CBA done in public view helps to give democracies a fighting chance to operate as democracies are supposed to operate.

REFERENCES

Anderson, Elizabeth. *Value in Ethics and Economics* (Harvard University Press, 1995).

Kelman, Steven. "Cost–Benefit Analysis: An Ethical Critique." *Regulation* 5 (1981): 33–40.

Morriss, Andrew. "Lessons for Environmental Law from the American Codification Debate," *The Common Law & the Environment*, ed. Roger Meiners & A. Morriss (Lanham: Rowman & Littlefield, 2000) 130–57.

Sagoff, Mark. "At the Shrine of Our Lady of Fatima, or Why Political Questions Are Not All Economic," *Arizona Law Review* 23 (1981): 1283–98.

1 2

FOOD

GARY L. FRANCIONE AND ANNA E. CHARLTON

ANIMAL RIGHTS: THE ABOLITIONIST APPROACH

ANIMALS: OUR MORAL SCHIZOPHRENIA

We claim to take animals seriously. We all agree that it is morally wrong to inflict "unnecessary" suffering or death on animals. But what do we mean by this? Whatever else it means, it must mean that it is wrong to inflict suffering or death on animals merely because we derive pleasure or amusement from doing so, or because it is convenient to do so, or because it is just plain habit. But the overwhelming portion of our animal use—just about all of it—cannot be justified by anything other than pleasure, amusement, convenience, or habit.

Most animals are killed for food. According to the Food and Agricultural Organization (FAO) of the United Nations, humans kill approximately 53 billion animals—that's 53,000,000,000—for food per year not including fish and other sea animals. And this number is rising and will double in the second part of this century.

HOW CAN WE JUSTIFY THIS SLAUGHTER?

We cannot justify it on the ground that we need to eat animal products for reasons of health. We clearly do not need to do so. In fact, the evidence increasingly shows that animal products are detrimental to human health.

We cannot justify it on the ground that it is "natural" because humans have been eating animals for thousands of years. The fact that we have been doing something for a long time does not make it morally right. Humans have been racist and sexist for centuries and we now recognize that racism and sexism are morally wrong.

Gary L. Francione and Anna E. Charlton, Animal Rights: The Abolitionist Approach (2008), available online at http://www.abolitionistapproach.com/wp-content/uploads/2015/09/20150902-ARAA_Pamphlet_English_USLetter.pdf.

We cannot justify it as necessary for the global ecology. There is a growing consensus that animal agriculture is an environmental disaster.

- According to the FAO, animal agriculture generates more greenhouse gas emissions than does the use of gasoline in cars, trucks, and other vehicles used for transport.
- Livestock use 30% of the earth's entire land surface, including 33% of the global arable land used for producing feed for livestock.
- Animal agriculture is resulting in deforestation as forests are cleared to make way for new pastures and in serious widespread degradation of land through overgrazing, compaction, and erosion.
- Animal agriculture is a major threat to the world's increasingly scarce water resources. Large quantities of water are needed to produce feed for livestock; widespread overgrazing disturbs water cycles; and animal agriculture is a serious source of water pollution.
- Animals consume more protein than they produce. For every kilogram (2.2 pounds) of animal protein produced, animals consume an average of almost 6 kilograms, or more than 13 pounds, of plant protein from grains and forage.
- It takes more than 100,000 liters of water to produce one kilogram of beef, and approximately 900 liters to produce one kilogram of wheat.

Because animals consume much more protein than they produce, grains that should be consumed by humans are consumed by animals instead. Thus, along with other factors, animal agriculture condemns many human beings to starvation.

The *only* justification we have for inflicting suffering and death on 53 billion animals per year is that we get pleasure from eating them; that it is convenient for us to eat them; that it is a habit. In other words, we have no good justification at all.

Our thinking about nonhuman animals is very confused. Many of us live, or have lived, with companion animals, such as dogs, cats, rabbits, etc. We love these animals. They are important members of our families. We grieve when they die. But we stick forks into other animals no different from the ones we love. That makes no sense.

OUR TREATMENT OF ANIMALS

We not only use animals for all sorts of purposes that cannot be considered as "necessary," but we treat them in ways that would be considered as torture if humans were involved. There are animal welfare laws that require us to treat animals "humanely," but these laws are largely meaningless because animals are property; they are economic commodities that have no value other than what we accord them. As far as the law is concerned, nonhuman animals are no different from cars, furniture, or any other property that we own. Because animals are property, we generally allow people to use animals for whatever purpose they want and to inflict horrible suffering on them in the process.

WHY NOT GET BETTER LAWS AND INDUSTRY STANDARDS?

Most animal protection organizations in the United States and Europe maintain that the solution to the problem of animal exploitation is to improve animal welfare laws or to pressure industry to improve standards of treatment. These organizations campaign for more "humane" methods of slaughter, more "humane" systems of confinement, such as larger cages, etc. Some of these organizations maintain that by improving treatment, animal use will one day be ended altogether or will at least be reduced significantly.

But is this the solution? No, it is not.

The economic realities are such that welfare reforms provide little, if any, improvements. A "cage-free" egg involves as much suffering as a conventional egg. The characterization of animal exploitation as becoming more "humane" encourages the public to become more comfortable about animal use and this encourages continued consumption of animal products and may even *increase* net suffering and death.

Moreover, there is absolutely no proof whatsoever that animal welfare reforms will lead to the end of animal use or significantly reduced animal use. We have had animal welfare standards and laws for more than 200 years now and we are exploiting more animals in more horrible ways than at any time in human history. And, most importantly, reforming exploitation ignores the fundamental question: how can we justify using animals at all as our resources—however "humanely" we treat them?

WHAT IS THE SOLUTION?

The solution is to abolish the exploitation of animals, not to regulate it. The solution is to recognize that just as we recognize that every human, irrespective of her particular characteristics, has the fundamental right not to be treated as the property of another, we must recognize that every sentient (perceptually aware) nonhuman has that right as well.

WHAT DOES THAT MEAN AS A PRACTICAL MATTER?

You are probably asking how you can do anything to abolish animal exploitation. There is something that you can do. You can go vegan. Now.

Veganism means that you no longer eat or otherwise consume animal products. Veganism is not merely a matter of diet; it is a moral and political commitment to abolition on the individual level and extends not only to matters of food, but to clothing, other products, and personal actions and choices.

Veganism is the one thing that we can all do today—right now—to help animals. It does not require an expensive campaign, the involvement of a large organization, legislation, or anything other than our recognition that if "animal rights" means anything, it means that we cannot justify killing and eating animals. Veganism reduces animal suffering and death by decreasing demand. It represents a rejection of the commodity status of nonhumans and our recognition of their inherent value.

Veganism is also a commitment to nonviolence. The animal rights movement should be a movement of peace and should reject violence against all animals—human and nonhuman.

Veganism is the most important form of political activism that we can undertake on behalf of animals. And once you go vegan, start to educate your family, friends, and others in your community to go vegan. If we want to abolish animal exploitation, a vegan movement is a necessary prerequisite. And that movement begins with the decision of the individual.

BUT WHAT'S WRONG WITH EATING ANIMAL PRODUCTS OTHER THAN MEAT?

There is no meaningful distinction between eating flesh and eating dairy or other animal products. Animals exploited for dairy, eggs, or other products are treated as badly if not worse than "meat" animals, and they end up in the same slaughterhouse after which we consume their flesh anyway. There is every bit as much suffering and death in a glass of milk, ice cream cone, or an egg as there is in a steak.

To maintain that there is a moral distinction between eating flesh and eating dairy, eggs, or other animal products is as silly as maintaining that there is a moral difference between eating large cows and eating small cows. As long as more than 99% of people think that it is acceptable to consume animal products, nothing will ever really change for animals.

SO . . .

The decision is yours. No one can make it for you. But if you believe that the lives of nonhumans have moral value, then stop participating in the killing of animals, however "humanely" they are treated. Join the vegan movement. Go vegan. Today. It is easy to go vegan. And it's the right thing to do.

MARK BRYANT BUDOLFSON

IS IT WRONG TO EAT MEAT FROM FACTORY FARMS? IF SO, WHY?

According to [Peter] Singer, purchasing and eating meat from factory farms is wrong because it has unacceptable consequences on balance for welfare. For example, if I purchase and eat a factory-farmed steak, Singer would claim that my gustatory pleasure is greatly outweighed by the suffering that the cow experiences in order to bring me that pleasure; as a result, Singer would claim that the welfare effects of my eating that steak are unacceptably negative on balance, even if I really enjoy it—and Singer believes that this shows that it is generally impermissible to consume animal products from factory farms.[1]

Although Singer's argument is powerful and initially appealing, there is an important objection . . . —the inefficacy objection—that claims it is too quick. The inefficacy objection is that even if we agree (as we should) with Singer's premises about the magnitude of animal suffering and the comparative unimportance of gustatory and other human pleasures, his conclusion about the welfare effects of consumption by individuals does not follow, and, upon careful reflection, turns out to be false. That is because an individual's decision to consume animal products cannot really be expected to have any effect on the number of animals that suffer or the extent of that suffering, given the actual nature of the supply chain that stands in between individual consumption decisions and production decisions; at the same time, an individual's decision to consume animal products does have a positive effect on that individual's own welfare. As a result, Singer's premises about animal suffering and human pleasures, together with the actual empirical facts about the workings of the marketplace, entail that an individual should expect the effect of his or her decision to consume animal products to be *positive* on balance, in contrast to what Singer assumes. If this inefficacy objection is correct, it undermines the idea that individuals have welfare-based reasons not to consume ethically objectionable products, and shows that Singer's utilitarian principles actually imply that individuals who would do better by consuming such products are *required* to do so, which is the opposite of what philosophers like Singer want us to believe.[2]

To make the inefficacy objection a little more vivid, note that everyone can agree that there is a dramatic ethical difference between the following two ways of consuming a T-bone steak: in the first case, a dumpster diver snags a T-bone steak from the garbage and eats it; in the second case, a diner enjoys a T-bone steak at Jimmy's You-Hack-It-Yourself Steakhouse, where customers brutally cut their steaks from the bodies of live cows, which are kept alive throughout the excruciating butchering process. (Once a cow bleeds to death, customers shift their efforts to a new live cow.)[3]

Everyone can agree that enjoying a steak at Jimmy's You-Hack-It-Yourself is objectionable, whereas enjoying a steak acquired through dumpster diving is far less objectionable, because the welfare effects of eating a steak at Jimmy's are substantially negative on balance, whereas a dumpster diver's consumption has no negative effect on welfare. According to welfarists like Singer, that is the only relevant difference between these two ways of consuming a T-bone steak.

But now consider this question: if you purchase animal products at a supermarket or restaurant, are the welfare effects more like those of buying a steak at Jimmy's or more like those of acquiring a steak through dumpster diving? Conventional wisdom among consequentialist moral philosophers says that the effects are more like eating at Jimmy's; however,

Mark Bryant Budolfson, "Is It Wrong to Eat Meat from Factory Farms? If So, Why?" in Ben Bramble and Bob Fischer (eds.), The Moral Complexities of Eating Meat (New York: Oxford University Press, 2015), pp. 80–98, pp. 83–90, pp. 93–98.

the empirical facts suggest that they may be more like dumpster diving, because it is virtually impossible for an individual's consumption of animal products at supermarkets and restaurants to have any effect on the number of animals that suffer and the extent of that suffering, just as it is virtually impossible for an individual's consumption of products acquired through dumpster diving to have any effect on animal welfare. If this claim about the inefficacy of a single individual's consumption decisions is correct, then the upshot is that consuming animal products from factory farms is not objectionable for welfare-based reasons, because there is then no important difference in (expected) welfare effects between an individual consuming factory-farmed products from a store versus a dumpster—and there is nothing wrong with consuming factory-farmed products from a dumpster, as even Peter Singer would agree.[4] (Singer endorses the permissibility of eating meat acquired through dumpster diving on the grounds that such a strategy is "impeccably consequentialist.")

The key empirical claims here relevant to the ethics of consumption are that many products we consume are delivered by a massive and complex supply chain in which there is waste, inefficiency, and other forms of *slack* at each link. Arguably, that slack serves as a *buffer* to absorb any would-be effects from the links before. Furthermore, production decisions are arguably insensitive to the informational signal generated by a single consumer because the sort of slack just described together with other kinds of noise in the extended transmission chain from consumers to producers ensures that significant-enough threshold effects are not likely enough to arise from an individual's consumption decisions to justify equating the effect of an individual's decision with anything approaching the average effect of such decisions. As a result, for many products in modern society, it may seem empirically implausible that even a lifetime of consumption decisions by a single individual would make any difference to quantity produced and thus the harm that lies behind those products.

For a particularly clear illustration of this, consider the supply chain for American beef. When ranchers who own their own grazing land decide how many cattle to raise, their decisions are sensitive to their own financial situation, the number of cattle their land can

support, the expected price of any additional feed that will be needed, bull semen and other "raw materials" that go into cattle production, and the expected price that the cattle will fetch when they are ultimately sold to feedlots. Of these, small changes in the last item—the price that cattle will fetch at the feedlot—are of the least importance, because insofar as ranchers judge that capital should be invested in raising cattle rather than other investments, they will tend to raise as many cattle as they can afford to breed and feed within that budget, letting the ultimate extent of their profits fall where it may at the feedlot. Many ranchers also use the nutritional well-being of their herd as a buffer to absorb adverse changes in market conditions, feeding their cattle less and less to whatever point maximizes the new expectation of profits as adverse conditions develop, or even sending the entire herd to premature slaughter if, say, feed prices rise to levels that are unacceptably high. This serves to shift the ranchers' emphasis in decision-making relevant to herd size even further away from the price of beef. As a result, even if an individual's consumption decisions managed to have a $0.01 effect on the price of cattle at feedlots, the effect on the number of cattle produced would be much smaller than it would have to be in order for the possibility of such a threshold effect to justify equating the expected marginal effect of an individual's consumption of beef with the average effect of such consumption decisions. These facts, together with those that follow, seem to show that there is good empirical reason to think that the actual effect (and expectation) of a single individual's consumption decisions on production is nearly zero and is not to be equated with the average effect of similar consumption decisions across society, contrary to what philosophers such as Peter Singer, Alastair Norcross, and Shelly Kagan have claimed in defending utilitarian arguments against the inefficacy objection.

Furthermore, in the absence of a large shock to the expected price of beef, ranchers who lease grazing land from the government will collectively tend to purchase all of the scarce and independently determined number of grazing permits and raise the maximum number of cattle that are allowed by those permits, because it tends only to make economic sense to hold such permits (rather than sell them to another rancher) if one grazes the maximum number of cattle allowed on the relevant parcels of land. As a result, the number of animals that are raised on land leased from the government appears insensitive to tiny changes in the price of cattle at feedlots.

More importantly, because animal production is so many links in the supply chain away from grocery stores and restaurants, and because each of the intervening links involves waste, inefficiency, and other forms of slack that serve as a buffer to absorb any effect that your personal consumption might otherwise have, it is arguably unrealistic to think that your personal consumption could really have any effect on decisions made at the production end of the supply chain, even when your consumption is considered over the course of an entire lifetime, as noted above. That is because the actual mechanisms by which information is conveyed and decisions are made throughout the supply chain do not seem to give rise to the sort of threshold effects that philosophers tend to imagine as driving the expected marginal effect of an act of consumption toward the average effect of such consumption; instead, waste, inefficiency, and other forms of slack may seem to ensure that the real expected marginal effect of an individual's consumption is essentially zero, because the change in the signal received at the production end of the supply based on a change in a single individual's consumption decisions is almost certainly zero. It does not have a significant chance of giving rise to any tangible expected effects.

Here it may help to focus on the way that decisions are actually made and prices are actually determined at each link in the supply chain, focusing especially on the fact that many of these decisions and price determinations are the result of intuitive human judgment, strategic considerations, and preexisting contracts rather than the result of a frictionless optimization procedure—which means that in practice such determinations are even less sensitive to the noise generated by a single consumer's decisions than they might initially appear. For example, consider the actual human participants at cattle auctions: wearing cowboy boots, standing around in dirt and manure, smoking cigarettes, often distracted and occasionally irrational, and sometimes aiming only to express machismo by means of their bids in the auction. Similarly, consider the actual human participants in production decisions:

wearing suits, sitting around in board rooms, drinking coffee, smoking big cigars, often distracted and occasionally irrational, and sometimes doing what is best for themselves rather than promoting the interest of their firms.

As these considerations help make vivid, the actual price and quantity produced are the result of decision processes that have many inputs, and those inputs are arguably insensitive to a change in a single individual's consumption decisions, especially given the actual mechanisms that tend to absorb the signal from a single individual at each stage in the signal transmission chain that lies behind those inputs.

. . .

Another important consideration is that even if you would convince many others to be a vegetarian by becoming one yourself, that does not translate into strong welfare-based reasons to become a vegetarian, because even if your vegetarian lifestyle ultimately caused, say, one hundred others to become vegetarians who would not otherwise have done so, their collective consumption decisions might still not have any appreciable effect on the number of animals that are raised and mistreated, because the actual mechanisms in the marketplace may be insensitive to the distributed effects of even one hundred consumers. Of course, this reasoning does not hold true when applied to an influential person like Peter Singer who really does influence enough people to make a difference, but it does hold true when applied to almost everyone else, which means that utilitarianism does not require most individuals to become vegetarians, even if it requires a few influential people like Peter Singer to be vegetarians. For example, just as morality does not require us to act as if we had the talents, influence, and resources that Warren Buffett has, so too morality does not require us to act as if we had the talents, influence, and resources that Peter Singer has.

A related observation is that individual vegetarian acts often have negative unintended consequences that must also be properly accounted for. For example, if I am a vegetarian, I might easily alienate others with my vegetarian acts if they are interpreted as self-righteous, and thus cause others to adopt a policy of never reducing their consumption of meat and never taking vegetarian arguments seriously—and if vegetarians are generally interpreted as self-righteous, that might lead to a consensus among most members of society that vegetarians are radical, self-righteous jerks who should not be taken seriously and who should be scoffed at by others—which then raises the cost of making vegetarian choices for everyone, and is counterproductive in other ways.[5]

So, the inefficacy problem raises an important objection for arguments like Peter Singer's against consuming ethically objectionable products and seems to have a sound basis in the empirical workings of the marketplace.

. . .

How then can we explain the ethically relevant differences between consuming products that are produced in an ethically objectionable way and those that are not? After all, most people would agree that even if what you consume as a single individual really makes no difference, there are still some *particularly objectionable ways* of being connected to evil that are impermissible. This, then, leads to the philosophical question of how exactly to distinguish the particularly objectionable ways of being connected to evil from the relatively innocuous ways of being connected to evil.

. . .

One intuitively appealing way of making the distinction between permissible and impermissible connection to evil is to invoke the notion of *the degree of essentiality of harm to an act*, claiming that, for example, consumption of a product is particularly objectionable the more essential it is to that product that harm or the violation of rights lies behind it. To illustrate this basic idea, consider a can of vegetables sold at a supermarket that is produced in a normal way. Although the production of those vegetables might depend on petroleum products and thus involve a surprisingly high footprint[6] of harm and connection to evil, it is nonetheless *highly inessential* to that product that such evils occur in the background, because there is nothing in the nature, actual production, actual consumption, and so on of that product that necessitates harm or the violation of significant rights. This provides a principled reason for explaining why you do not have

strong reasons not to consume a can of vegetables even though you know that they have a surprisingly high footprint of harm. . . . As a result, invoking this idea allows for a principled distinction between connections to evil that seem innocuous and connections that are not, and avoids overgeneralizing and implying that it is impermissible to consume everything, even a can of corn. . . .

Setting aside for a moment the precise details of this notion of *degree of essentiality*, for current purposes it is worth noting that it is embedded in moral common sense, and as a result it seems essential to an intuitive explanation of the relevant cases, especially in light of the failure of more familiar ethical notions to adequately explain those cases. For an example of its use in moral common sense, consider the ethical view that is probably endorsed by most actual vegetarians, which is suggested by one interpretation of this quote from Michael Pollan:

> Like any self-respecting vegetarian (and we are nothing if not self-respecting) I will now burden you with my obligatory compromises and ethical distinctions. I'm not a vegan (I will eat eggs and dairy), because eggs and milk can be coaxed from animals without hurting or killing them.[7]

There are two ways of understanding the underlying ethical principle here. On one interpretation, the idea is that consuming animal products is permissible only if those products do not *actually* have any footprint of harm or killing. However, that cannot be the interpretation of this principle that is endorsed by most actual vegetarians, because most actual vegetarians are ovo-lacto vegetarians who believe it is permissible to consume factory-farmed dairy products—even though those products have a very high footprint of harm.[8] This suggests that most actual vegetarians interpret this principle in a way that leans heavily on the idea that even factory-farmed dairy products *can* be coaxed from animals without hurting or killing them. Presumably, the idea here is that even if factory-farmed eggs or cheese have a disturbingly high footprint of harm, nonetheless it is highly *inessential* to those products that such harm lies behind them, and as a result consuming them does not connect one to harm in a way that is impermissible. So on this second interpretation, the crucial ethical issue is whether a particular animal product *can* be produced without harm—and taken at face value, this is subtly different than the issue of whether a particular product *actually is* produced without harm. And as we've just seen, this second interpretation and its invocation of the degree of essentiality of harm seem deeply rooted in the moral thinking of most actual vegetarians.

As further confirmation of this, note that alternative interpretations of most vegetarians' underlying ethical principle would imply, contrary to their view, that eating eggs and dairy is generally *more* objectionable than eating beef, because the actual suffering of laying hens and dairy cows on factory farms is far more extreme than the actual suffering of cattle raised for slaughter, given that most cattle raised for slaughter tend to be raised in good conditions on ranches, and only encounter factory-farming operations when transported to feedlots and then to slaughterhouses— and even then, significant suffering tends to be visited probabilistically on only some of the cows. This is in contrast to the laying hens and dairy cows that are used to produce factory-farmed eggs and dairy products, which experience the worst treatment of any animals in contemporary agribusiness. As a result, the harm footprint associated with each calorie of energy from factory-farmed eggs or dairy is generally higher than the harm footprint associated with beef, and similar remarks apply to other measures of ethical objectionability that would be relevant to other familiar ethical theories; nonetheless, most ovo-lacto-vegetarians believe that eating meat is wrong, but that consuming factory-farmed eggs and dairy is permissible, which is why familiar ethical theories do not provide a charitable interpretation of their view. Instead, the most charitable interpretation of their view is that what matters is whether it is *highly essential* to an animal product that harm or killing lies behind it. The idea of ovo-lacto-vegetarians is, presumably, that it is not essential to eggs and dairy that harm or killing lies behind them, whereas it is quite essential—given actual facts about cause and effect and facts about technological possibility and feasibility in the actual world—that killing lies behind eating meat; therefore, eating meat is impermissible, whereas consuming eggs and dairy is permissible, even if the harm footprint of the latter is greater than the harm footprint of the former.

Setting aside the views of actual vegetarians, further confirmation of the explanatory power of this notion of degree of essentiality is provided by consideration of other cases. For example, suppose you learn that a computer you are interested in purchasing is made from metals and other inputs that are themselves produced in a way that is objectionable. Although that harm might be serious, it might also be true that there is no practical way that the computer manufacturer can do anything about it, and it is in no way central to the design or functioning of those computers that such harm lies behind them. In such a case, buying the computer need not be impermissible even if some action that lies far behind them is impermissible. This is in contrast to a different case involving the same harm footprint in which it is *fairly essential* to the computer that such harm lies behind it, perhaps because of some engineering decision that requires it to be produced in a way or from materials that involve such harm.[9]

Why would morality make such a distinction between ways of being connected to evil? If there were no good answer to this question, then we should doubt whether a principle that invoked the degree of essentiality of harm was a genuine moral principle, even if it seemed to correctly capture our initial intuitive judgments about cases. However, on further reflection it is not that surprising that morality would make such a distinction, as it seems to be a consequence of the more general compelling idea that morality distinguishes between what is within a single individual's control and what is not. If it is highly inessential to an action open to you that harm lies behind it, but at the same time background actions by others that you cannot change and that are far removed from any direct connection to any action of yours would give that option a high harm footprint, the current proposal is that morality does not assign that as much negative weight as if a similarly high degree of harm would be directly caused by your choosing an option, or if it is relatively essential to an option that a similarly high degree of harm lies behind it. This is merely one way that morality distinguishes between relevant facts that are within a single individual's control and facts that are not.

In sum, the discussion above suggests that the best explanation of what consumers are required to do when products are produced in morally objectionable ways is more subtle than it initially appears. Among other things, it suggests that typical appeals are too quick to the welfare effects of consumption or connection to evil practices that lie behind our products, and do not invoke principles that are ultimately defensible. At the same time, appealing to the *degree of essentiality of harm* seems to allow a better explanation of the cases that we care about and remains consistent with the compelling idea that, for example, the most decisive fact relevant to the ethics of eating meat is that a person's gustatory pleasure is of little ethical significance compared to the suffering that animals must experience in the service of that pleasure. And arguably, this view implies that there is something that is genuinely more objectionable about eating meat from factory farms than eating humanely raised meat. The general philosophical point is that facts about the pleasure that we get from products and facts about the harm that lies behind those products do not lead to conclusions in the simple way that utilitarian reasoning might initially suggest, but must instead be marshaled into more subtle arguments. As these subtleties are clarified, many of our prior judgments will be vindicated—but a few may also have to be revised.[10]

NOTES

1. Singer, "Utilitarianism and Vegetarianism," and Singer, *Animal Liberation*.

2. I examine the inefficacy objection in much more detail in other papers (including "The Inefficacy Objection to Consequentialism" and "The Inefficacy Objection to Deontology"). Among other things, I argue at greater length that an important response due to Peter Singer (and later endorsed by Alastair Norcross and Shelly Kagan) does not succeed. The inefficacy objection has been noted by many authors, although not in connection with the range of related issues discussed here.

3. If this example seems callous at first glance, it may help to note that its purpose is to make salient by analogy some of the horrors of factory farming—for example, some cows are dismembered while fully conscious because of mistakes made in the stunning process at slaughterhouses. Although some such mistakes are inevitable, the actual number of such mistakes is arguably inexcusable, on the grounds that most mistakes could be eliminated by slowing the processing line speed at slaughterhouses to a reasonable level—which would also save countless workers from disabling injuries each year. For a moving discussion of this last issue, see "The Most Dangerous Job" in Eric Schlosser, *Fast Food Nation*.

4. Peter Singer and Jim Mason, *The Ethics of What We Eat* (US paperback edition) p. 268, and more generally pp. 260–269.

5. Here it may be useful to note that many undergraduate students respond to vegetarian arguments by pledging to eat more meat to "cancel out" the effects of vegetarians.

6. The *footprint* of an act of a particular type is simply the *average effect* of all actual acts of that type for some particular kind of effect. I discuss the relevance of footprints to ethics and public policy in my paper "Collective Action, Climate Change, and the Ethical Significance of Futility," where I argue that they are overemphasized and sometimes mistaken guides to what should be done, and that ethical reasoning that depends on footprints generally commits what I call *The Average Effects Fallacy*, which is the fallacy of equating the ethically relevant effects of a particular act with the average effects of all of the actual acts of that type. I suspect that consequentialists who quickly dismiss the inefficacy objection are often tacitly committing a version of this fallacy.

7. Michael Pollan, *The Omnivore's Dilemma*, p. 313.

8. Note that such a principle is implausible because (as explained above) it overgeneralizes and implies that it is impermissible to consume almost everything in contemporary society, since almost every product has a surprisingly high footprint of harm or killing.

9. As another example, consider that the law makes a similar appeal to the degree of essentiality of harm. For example, in *New York v. Ferber* and in *Ashcroft v. Free Speech Coalition* the US Supreme Court held that a compelling state interest exists to prohibit the promotion and consumption of child pornography insofar as that pornography is "intrinsically related to the sexual abuse of children." This appeal to the notion of the degree of essentiality

of harm that lies behind sexually explicit materials involving children provides an important part of the court's basis for distinguishing between, on the one hand, objectionable child pornography that may be constitutionally prohibited by legislation (e.g., actual videos of child sex acts, where it is *highly essential* to the pornography that harm lies behind it), and on the other hand, constitutionally protected and arguably unobjectionable depictions of children engaging in sexual acts (for

example, drawings in textbooks, or depictions by actors in fictional films).

10. For further discussion of the ethics of collective action and some prior judgments that may need to be revised, see my paper "Collective Action, Climate Change, and the Ethical Significance of Futility." The current chapter is intended for a general audience. I discuss other possible responses to the inefficacy objection and related issues in much greater detail in other papers, as referenced in several notes above.

CORA DIAMOND

EATING MEAT AND EATING PEOPLE

This paper is a response to a certain kind of argument defending the rights of animals. Part I is a brief explanation of the background and of the sort of argument I want to reject; Part II is an attempt to characterize those arguments: they contain fundamental confusions about moral relations between people and people *and* between people and animals. And Part III is an indication of what I think can still be said on—as it were—the animals' side.

I

The background to the paper is the recent discussions of animals' rights by Peter Singer and Tom Regan and a number of other philosophers.[1] The basic type of argument in many of these discussions is encapsulated in the word "speciesism." The word I think is originally Richard Ryder's, but Peter Singer is responsible for making it popular in connection with an obvious sort of argument: that in our attitude to members of other species we have prejudices which are completely analogous to the prejudices people may have with regard

to members of other races, and these prejudices will be connected with the ways we are blind to our own exploitation and oppression of the other group. We are blind to the fact that what we do to them deprives them of their rights; we do not want to see this because we profit from it, and so we make use of what are really morally irrelevant differences between them and ourselves to justify the difference in treatment.

Putting it fairly crudely: if we say "You cannot live here because you are black," this would be supposed to be parallel to saying "You can be used for our experiments, because you are only an animal and cannot talk." If the first is unjustifiable prejudice, so equally is the second. In fact, both Singer and Regan argue, if we, as a justification for differential treatment, point to things like the incapacity of animals to use speech, we should be committed to treating in the same way as animals those members of our own species who (let us say) have brain damage sufficient to prevent the development of speech—committed to allowing them to be used as laboratory animals or as food or whatever. If we say, "These *animals* are not rational, so we have

This reading is adapted from Cora Diamond, "Eating Meat and Eating People," Philosophy 53, no. 206 (1978): 465–479.

a right to kill them for food," but we do not say the same of *people* whose rationality cannot develop or whose capacities have been destroyed, we are plainly not treating like cases alike.

The fundamental principle here is one we could put this way (the formulation is based on Peter Singer's statements): We must give equal consideration to the interests of any being which is capable of having interests; and the capacity to have interests is essentially dependent only on the capacity for suffering and enjoyment. This we evidently share with animals.

. . .

It is on the basis of this sort of claim, that the rights of all animals should be given equal consideration, that Singer and Regan and Ryder and others have argued that we must give up killing animals for food, and must drastically cut back—at least—the use of animals in scientific research. And so on.

That argument seems to me to be confused. I do not dispute that there are analogies between the case of our relations to animals and the case of a dominant group's relation to some other group of human beings which it exploits or treats unjustly in other ways. But the analogies are not simple and straightforward, and it is not clear how far they go. The Singer-Regan approach makes it hard to see what is important *either* in our relationship with other human beings *or* in our relationship with animals. And that is what I shall try to explain in Part II. My discussion will be limited to eating animals, but much of what I say is intended to apply to other uses of animals as well.

II

Discussions of vegetarianism and animals' rights often start with discussion of human rights. We may then be asked what is it that grounds the claims that people have such rights, and whether similar grounds may not after all be found in the case of animals.

All such discussions are beside the point. For they ask why we do not kill people (very irrational ones, let us say) for food, or why we do not treat people in ways which would cause them distress or anxiety and so on, when for the sake of meat we are willing enough to kill *animals* or treat them in ways which cause them

distress. This is a totally wrong way of beginning the discussion, because it ignores certain quite central facts—facts which, if attended to, would make it clear that *rights* are not what is crucial. *We do not eat our dead,* even when they have died in automobile accidents or been struck by lightning, and their flesh might be first class. We do not eat them; or if we do, it is a matter of extreme need, or of some special ritual—and even in cases of obvious extreme need, there is very great reluctance. We also do not eat our amputated limbs. (Or if we did, it would be in the same kinds of special circumstances in which we eat our dead.)

Now the fact that we do not eat our dead is not a consequence—not a direct one in any event—of our unwillingness to kill people for food or other purposes. It is not a direct consequence of our unwillingness to cause distress to people. Of course it *would* cause distress to people to think that they might be eaten when they were dead, but it causes distress because of what it is to eat a dead person. Hence we cannot elucidate what (if anything) is wrong—if that is the word—with eating people by appeal to the distress it would cause, in the way we can point to the distress caused by stamping on someone's toe as a reason why we regard it as a wrong to kill him.

Now if we do not eat people who are already dead and also do not kill people for food, it is at least prima facie plausible that our reasons in the two cases might be related, and hence must be looked into by anyone who wants to claim that we have no good reasons for not eating people which are not also good reasons for not eating animals. Anyone who, in discussing this issue, focuses on our reasons for not killing people or our reasons for not causing them suffering quite evidently runs a risk of leaving altogether out of his discussion those fundamental features of our relationship to other human beings which are involved in our not eating them.

It is in fact part of the way this point is usually missed that arguments are given for not eating animals, for respecting their rights to life and not making them suffer, which imply that there is absolutely nothing queer, nothing at all odd, in the vegetarian eating the cow that has obligingly been struck by lightning. That is to say, there is nothing in the discussion which suggests that a cow is *not* something to eat; it is only that one must not help the process along: one must not, that is, interfere with those rights that we should usually have to interfere with if we are to eat animals at all conveniently. But if the point of the Singer–Regan vegetarian's argument is to show that the eating of meat is, morally, in the same position as the eating of human flesh, he is not consistent unless he says that it is just squeamishness, or something like that, which stops us eating our dead. If he admitted that what underlies our attitude to dining on ourselves is the view that *a person is not something to eat,* he could not focus on the cow's right not to be killed or maltreated, as if that were the heart of it.

I write this as a vegetarian, but one distressed by the obtuseness of the normal arguments, in particular, I should say, the arguments of Singer and Regan. For if vegetarians give arguments which do not begin to get near the considerations which are involved in our not eating people, those to whom their arguments are addressed may not be certain how to reply, but they will not be convinced either, and really are quite right. They themselves may not be able to make explicit what it is they object to in the way the vegetarian presents our attitude to not eating people, but they will be left feeling that beyond all the natter about "speciesism" and equality and the rest, there is a difference between human beings and animals which is being ignored.

This is not just connected with the difference between what it is to eat one and what it is to eat the other. It is connected with the difference between giving people a funeral and giving a dog one, with the difference between miscegenation and *chacun à son goût* with consenting adult gorillas. (Singer and Regan give arguments which certainly appear to imply that a distaste for the latter is merely that, and would no more stand up to scrutiny than a taboo on miscegenation.) And so on.

It is a mark of the shallowness of these discussions of vegetarianism that the only tool used in them to explain what differences in treatment are justified is the appeal to the capacities of the beings in question. That is to say, such-and-such a being—a dog, say—might be said to have, like us, a right to have its interests taken into account; but its interests will be different because its capacities are. Such an appeal may then be used by the vegetarian to explain why he need not in consistency demand votes for dogs (though even there it is not really adequate), but as an explanation of the appropriateness of a funeral for a child two days old and not for a puppy

it will not do; and the vegetarian is forced to explain that—if he tries at all—in terms of what it is *to us,* a form of explanation which for him is evidently dangerous.

. . .

I do not think it an accident that the arguments of vegetarians have a nagging moralistic tone. They are an attempt to show something to be morally wrong, on the assumption that *we all agree* that it is morally wrong to raise people for meat, and so on.

Now the objection to saying that *that* is morally wrong is not, or not merely, that it is too weak. What we should be going against in adopting Swift's "Modest Proposal" is something we should be going against in salvaging the dead more generally: useful organs for transplantation, and the rest for supper or the compost heap. And "morally wrong" is not too weak for that, but in the wrong dimension.

One could say that it would be impious to treat the dead so, but the word "impious" does not make for clarity, it only asks for explanation. We can most naturally speak of a kind of action as morally wrong when we have some firm grasp of what *kind* of beings are involved. But there are some actions, like giving people names, that are part of the way we come to understand and indicate our recognition of *what* kind it is with which we are concerned. And "morally wrong" will often not fit our refusals to act in such a way, or our acting in an opposed sort of way, as when Gradgrind calls a child "Girl number twenty." Doing her out of a name is not like doing her out of an inheritance to which she has a right and in which she has an interest. Rather, Gradgrind lives in a world, or would like to, in which it makes no difference whether she has a name, a number being more efficient, and in which a human being is not *something to be named, not numbered.*

Again, it is not "morally wrong" to eat our pets; people who ate their pets would not have pets in the same sense of that term. (If we call an animal that we are fattening for the table a pet, we are making a crude joke of a familiar sort.) A pet is not something to eat, it is given a name, is let into our houses and may be spoken to in ways in which we do not normally speak to cows or squirrels. That is to say, it is given some part of the character of a person. (This may be more or less sentimental; it need not be sentimental at all.)

Treating pets in these ways is not at all a matter of recognizing some *interest* which pets have in being so treated. There is not a class of beings, pets, whose nature, whose capacities, are such that we owe it to them to treat them in these ways. Similarly, it is not out of respect for the interests of beings of the class to which we belong that we give names to each other, or that we treat human sexuality or birth or death as we do, marking them—in their various ways—as significant or serious. And again, it is not respect for our interests which is involved in our not eating each other. These are all things that go to determine what sort of concept "human being" is.

Similarly with having duties to human beings. This is not a consequence of what human beings are, it is not justified by what human beings are: it is itself one of the things which go to build our notion of human beings. And so too—very much so—the idea of the difference between human beings and animals. We learn what a human being is in—among other ways—sitting at a table where WE eat THEM. We are around the table and they are on it. The difference between human beings and animals is not to be discovered by studies of Washoe or the activities of dolphins. It is not that sort of study or ethology or evolutionary theory that is going to tell us the difference between us and animals: the difference is, as I have suggested, a central concept for human life and is more an object of contemplation than observation (though that might be misunderstood; I am not suggesting it is a matter of intuition).

One source of confusion here is that we fail to distinguish between "the difference between animals and people" and "the differences between animals and people"; the same sort of confusion occurs in discussions of the relationships of men and women. In both cases people appeal to scientific evidence to show that "the difference" is not as deep as we think; but all that such evidence can show, or show directly, is that the differences are less sharp than we think. In the case of the difference between animals and people, it is clear that we form the idea of this difference, create the concept of the difference, knowing perfectly well the overwhelmingly obvious similarities.

. . .

III

What then is involved in trying to show someone that he ought not eat meat? I have drawn attention to one curious feature of the Peter Singer sort of argument, which is that your Peter Singer vegetarian should be perfectly happy to eat the unfortunate lamb that has just been hit by a car. I want to connect this with a more general characteristic of the utilitarian vegetarians' approach. They are not, they say, especially fond of, or interested in, animals. They may point [out that] they do not "love them." They do not want to anthropomorphize them, and are concerned to put their position as distinct from one which they see as sentimental anthropomorphizing. Just as you do not have to prove that underneath his black skin the black man has a white man inside in order to recognize his rights, you do not have to see animals in terms of your emotional responses to people to recognize their rights. So the direction of their argument is: *we* are only one kind of *animal*; if what is fair for us is concern for our interests, that depends only on our being living animals *with* interests—and if that *is* fair, it is fair for *any* animal. They do not, that is, want to move from concern for people to concern for four-legged people or feathered people—to beings who deserve that concern only because we think of them as having a little person inside.

To make a contrast, I want to take a piece of vegetarian propaganda of a very different sort.

Learning to be a Dutiful Carnivore[2]
Dogs and cats and goats and cows,
Ducks and chickens, sheep and sows,
Woven into tales for tots,
Pictured on their walls and pots.
Time for dinner! Come and eat
All your lovely, juicy meat.
One day ham from Percy Porker
(In the comics he's a corker),
Then the breast from Mrs. Cluck
Or the wing from Donald Duck.
Liver next from Clara Cow
(No, it doesn't hurt her now).
Yes, that's leg from Peter Rabbit
Chew it well; make that a habbit.
Eat the creatures killed for sale,
But never pull the pussy's tail.

Eat the flesh from "filthy hogs"
But never be unkind to dogs.
Grow up into double-think—
Kiss the hamster; skin the mink.
Never think of slaughter, dear,
That's why animals are here.
They only come on earth to die,
So eat your meat, and don't ask why.
Jane Legge

What that is trying to bring out is a kind of inconsistency, or confusion mixed with hypocrisy—what it sees as that—in our ordinary ways of thinking about animals, confusions that come out, not only but strikingly, in what children are taught about them. That is to say, the poem does not ask you to feel in this or the other way about animals. Rather, it takes a certain range of feelings for granted. There *are* certain ways of feeling reflected in our telling children classical animal stories, in our feeding birds and squirrels in the winter, say—in our interfering with what children do to animals as we interfere when they maltreat smaller children: "Never pull the pussy's tail." The poem does not try to get us to behave like that, or to get us to feel a "transport of cordiality" towards animals. Rather, it is addressed to people whose response to animals already includes a variety of such kinds of behavior, and taking that for granted it suggests that other features of our relationship to animals show confusion or hypocrisy.

It is very important, I think, that it does not attempt any justification for this range of responses against the background of which certain other kinds of behavior are supposed to look hypocritical. There is a real question whether justification would be in place for these background responses. I want to bring this out by another poem, not a bit of vegetarian or any other propaganda. This is a poem of Walter de la Mare's.

Titmouse
If you would happy company win,
Dangle a palm-nut from a tree,
Idly in green to sway and spin,
Its snow-pulped kernel for bait; and see
A nimble titmouse enter in.
Out of earth's vast unknown of air,
Out of all summer, from wave to wave,
He'll perch, and prank his feathers fair,

Jangle a glass-clear wildering stave,
And take his commons there—
This tiny son of life; this spright,
By momentary Human sought,
Plume will his wing in the dappling light,
Clash timbrel shrill and gay—
And into Time's enormous Nought,
Sweet-fed will flit away

What interests me here is the phrase "This tiny son of life." It is important that this is connected in the poem with the bird's appearing out of earth's vast unknown of air, and flitting off into Time's enormous Nought. He is shown as fellow creature, with this very striking phrase "son of life." I want to say some things about the idea of a fellow creature.

First, that it indicates a direction of thought very unlike that of the Singer argument. There we start supposedly from the biological fact that we and dogs and rats and titmice and monkeys are all species of animal, differentiated indeed in terms of this or the other capacity, but what is appropriate treatment for members of our species would be appropriate to members of any whose capacities gave them similar interests. We are all equally animals, though, for a start—with, therefore, an equal right to have whatever our interests are taken into account. The starting point for our thought is what is general and in common and biologically given.

Implicitly in the Jane Legge poem, and explicitly in the de la Mare, we have a different notion, that of a living creature, or fellow creature—which is *not* a biological concept. It does not mean, biologically an animal, something with *biological life*—it means a being in a certain boat, as it were, of whom it makes sense to say, among other things, that it goes off into Time's enormous Nought, and which may be sought as *company*.

The response to animals as our fellows in mortality, in life on this earth (think here of Burns's description of himself to the mouse as "thy poor earthborn companion, / An' fellow mortal"), depends upon a conception of *human* life. It is an extension of a non-biological notion of what human life is. You can call it anthropomorphic, but only if you want to create confusion. The confusion, though, is created only because we do not have a clear notion of what the phenomena the word "anthropomorphic" might cover, and tend to use it for cases which are sentimental in certain characteristic ways, which the de la Mare poem avoids, however narrowly.

The extension to animals of modes of thinking characteristic of our responses to human beings is extremely complex, and includes a great variety of things. The idea of an animal as company is a striking kind of case; it brings out that the notion of a fellow creature does not involve just the extension of moral concepts like charity or justice. Those are, indeed, among the most familiar of such extensions; thus the idea of a fellow creature may go with feeding birds in winter, though of as something akin to charity, or again with giving a hunted animal a sporting chance, where that is thought of as something akin to justice or fairness.

. . .

Independence is another of the important extended concepts, or rather, the idea of an independent life, subject, as any is, to contingencies; and this is closely connected with the idea of something like *respect* for the animal's independent life. We see such a notion in, for example, many people's objections to the performance of circus tricks by animals, as an *indignity*. The conception of a hunted animal as a "respected enemy" is also closely related. *Pity* is another central concept here, as expressed, for example, in Burns' "To a Mouse"; and I should note that the connection between pity and sparing someone's life is wholly excluded from vegetarian arguments of the sort attacked in Part I—it has no place in the rhetoric of a "liberation" movement.

It does normally, or very often, go with the idea of a fellow creature, that we do eat them. But it then characteristically goes with the idea that they must be hunted fairly or raised without bad usage. The treatment of an animal as simply a stage (the self-moving stage) in the production of a meat product is not part of this mode of thinking; and I should suggest also that the concept of "vermin" is at least sometimes used in excluding an animal from the class of fellow creatures. However, it makes an importantly different kind of contrast with "fellow creature" from the contrast you have when animals are taken as stages in the production of a meat product, or as "very delicate pieces of machinery" (as in a recent BBC programme on the use of animals in research).

I shall have more to say about these contrasts later; the point I wish to make now is that it is not a *fact* that a titmouse *has a life*; if one speaks that way it expresses a particular relation within a broadly specifiable range to titmice. It is no more biological than it would be a biological point should you call another person a "traveller between life and death": that is not a biological point dressed up in poetical language.

The fellow-creature response sits in us alongside others. This is brought out by another poem of de la Mare's, "Dry August Burned," which begins with a child weeping her heart out on seeing a dead hare lying limp on the kitchen table. But hearing a team of field artillery going by to manoeuvres, she runs out and watches it all in the bright sun. After they have passed, she turns and runs back into the house, but the hare has vanished—"Mother," she asks, "please may I go and see it skinned?"

In a classic study of intellectual growth in children, Susan Isaacs describes at some length what she calls the extraordinarily confused and conflicting ways in which we adults actually behave towards animals in the sight of children, and in connection with which children have to try to understand our horror at the cruelty they may display towards animals, our insistence that they be "kind" to them.[3] She mentions the enormously varied ways in which animal death and the killing of animals are a matter-of-course feature of the life children see and are told about. They quite early grasp the relation between meat and the killing of animals, see insect pests killed, or spiders or snakes merely because they are distasteful; they hear about the killing of dangerous animals or of superfluous puppies and kittens, and are encouraged early to fish or collect butterflies—and so on.

I am not concerned here to ask whether we should or should not do these things to animals, but rather to bring out what is meant by doing something *to an animal*, what is meant by something's being an animal, is shaped by such things as Mrs. Isaacs describes. Animals—these objects we are acting upon—are not given for our thought independently of such a mass of ways of thinking about and responding to them.

. . .

This mass of responses, and more, Mrs. Isaacs called confused and contradictory. But there are significant patterns in it; it is no more just a lot of confused and contradictory modes of response than is the mass which enables us to think of our fellow human beings as such. For example, the notion of vermin makes sense against the background of the idea of animals in general as not mere things. Certain groups of animals are then singled out as *not* to be treated fully as the rest are, where the idea might be that the rest are to be hunted only fairly and not meanly poisoned. Again, the killing of dangerous animals in self-defense forms part of a pattern in which circumstances of immediate danger make a difference, assuming as background the independent life of the lion (say), perceived in terms not limited to the way it might serve our ends.

What I am suggesting here is that certain modes of response may be seen as withdrawals from *some* animals ("vermin"), or from animals in *some* circumstances (danger), of what would otherwise belong to recognizing them as animals, just as the notion of an enemy or of a slave may involve the withdrawing from the person involved of some of what would belong to recognition of him as a human being. Thus for example in the case of slaves, there may be no formal social institution of the slave's name in the same full sense as there is for others, or there may be a denial of socially significant ancestry, and so on. Or a man who is outlawed may be killed like an animal. Here then the idea would be that the notion of a slave or an enemy or an outlaw assumes a background of response to persons, and recognition that what happens in *these* cases is that we have something which we are *not* treating as what it—in a way—is.

Of course, even in these cases, a great deal of the response to "human being" may remain intact, as for example what may be done with the dead body. Or again, if the enemyhood is so deep as to remove even these restraints, and men dance on the corpses of their enemies, as for example recently in Lebanon, the point of this can only be understood in terms of the violation of what is taken to be how you treat the corpse of a human being. It is because you know it *is* that, that you are treating it with some point as that is *not* to be treated. And no one who does it could have the slightest difficulty—whatever contempt he might feel—in

understanding why someone had gone off and been sick instead.

Now suppose I am a practical-minded hardheaded slaveholder whose neighbour has, on his deathbed, freed his slaves. I might regard such a man as foolish, but not as batty, not batty in the way I should think of someone if he had, let us say, freed his cows on his deathbed. Compare the case Orwell describes, from his experience in the Spanish Civil War, of being unable to shoot at a half-dressed man who was running along the top of a trench parapet, holding up his trousers with both hands as he ran. "I had come here to shoot at 'Fascists,' but a man who is holding up his trousers is not a 'Fascist,' he is visibly a fellow-creature, similar to yourself, and you do not feel like shooting at him."[4] The notion of enemy ("Fascist") and fellow creature are there in a kind of tension, and even a man who could shoot at a man running holding his trousers up might recognize perfectly well why Orwell could not. The tension there is in such cases (between "slave" or "enemy" and "fellow human being") may be reflected not merely in recognition of the point of someone else's actions, but also in defensiveness of various sorts, as when you ask someone where he is from and the answer is "South Africa and you do not treat them very well here either." And that is like telling someone I am a vegetarian and getting the response "And what are your shoes made of?"

What you have then with an image or a sight like that of the man running holding his trousers up is something which may check or alter one's actions, but something which is not compelling, or not compelling for everyone who can understand its force, and the possibility, even where it is not compelling for someone, of making for discomfort or of bringing discomfort to awareness. I should suggest that the Jane Legge poem is an attempt to bring a similar sort of discomfort closer to the surface—but that images of fellow creatures are naturally much less compelling ones than images of "fellow human beings" can be.

I introduced the notion of a fellow creature in answer to the question: How might I go about showing someone that he had reason not to eat animals? I do not think I have answered that so much as shown a direction in which I should look for an answer. And clearly the approach I have suggested is not usable with someone in whom there is no fellow-creature response, nothing at all in that range.

I am not therefore in a weaker position than those who would defend animals' rights on the basis of an abstract principle of equality. For although they purport to be providing reasons which are reasons for anyone, Martian or human being or whatnot, to respect the rights of animals, Martians and whatnot, in fact what they are providing, I should say, is images of a vastly more uncompelling sort.

. . .

If we appeal to people to prevent suffering, and we, in our appeal, try to obliterate the distinction between human beings and animals and just get people to speak or think of "different species of animals," there is no footing left from which to tell us what we ought to do, because it is not members of one among species of animals that have moral obligations to do anything. The moral expectations of other human beings demand something of me as other than an animal; and we do something like imaginatively read into

animals something like such expectations when we think of vegetarianism as enabling us to meet a cow's eyes. There is nothing wrong with that; there *is* something wrong with trying to keep that response and destroy its foundation. . . .

NOTES

1. See especially Peter Singer, *Animal Liberation* (New York: New York Review, 1975), Tom Regan and Peter Singer, eds, *Animal Rights and Human Obligations* (Englewood Cliffs: Prentice Hall, 1976), Stanley and Roslind Godlovitch and John Harris, eds, *Animals, Men and Morals* (New York: Grove, 1972), and Richard Ryder, "Speciesism: The Ethics of Vivisection" (Edinburgh: Scottish Society for the Prevention of Vivisection, 1974).
2. *The British Vegetarian*, Jan/Feb 1969, p. 59.
3. *Intellectual Growth in Young Children* (London: Routledge, 1930), pp. 160–162.
4. *Collected Essays, Journalism and Letters* (London: Secker and Warburg, 1968), Vol. II, p. 254.

MICHAEL POLLAN

THE (AGRI)CULTURAL CONTRADICTIONS OF OBESITY

Sometimes even complicated social problems turn out to be simpler than they look. Take America's "obesity epidemic," arguably the most serious public-health problem facing the country. Three of every five Americans are now overweight, and some researchers predict that today's children will be the first generation of Americans whose life expectancy will actually be shorter than that of their parents. The culprit, they say, is the health problems associated with obesity. You hear several explanations. Big food companies are pushing supersize portions of unhealthful foods on us and our children. We have devolved into a torpid nation of couch potatoes. The family dinner has succumbed to the fast-food outlet. All these explanations are true, as far as they go. But it pays to go a little further, to look for the cause behind the causes. Which, very simply, is this: when food is abundant and cheap, people will eat more of it and get fat. Since 1977, an American's average daily intake of calories has jumped by more than 10 percent. Those 200 or so extra calories have to go somewhere. But the interesting question is: Where, exactly, did all those extra calories come from in the first place? And the answer takes us back to the source of all calories: the farm.

It turns out that we have been here before, sort of, though the last great American binge involved not food, but alcohol. It came during the first decades of the 19th century, when Americans suddenly began drinking more than they ever had before or have since, going on a collective bender that confronted the young republic with its first major public-health crisis—the obesity epidemic of its day. Corn whiskey, suddenly superabundant and cheap, was the drink of choice, and in the 1820's the typical American man was putting away half a pint of the stuff every day. That works out to more than five gallons of spirits a year for every American. The figure today is less than a gallon. As W.J. Rorabaugh tells the story in "The Alcoholic Republic," we drank the hard stuff at breakfast, lunch and dinner, before work and after and very often during. Employers were expected to supply spirits over the course of the workday; in fact, the modern coffee break began as a late-morning whiskey break called "the elevenses." (Just to pronounce it makes you sound tipsy.) Except for a brief respite Sunday mornings in church, Americans simply did not gather—whether for a barn raising or quilting bee, corn husking or political campaign— without passing the jug. Visitors from Europe—hardly models of sobriety themselves—marveled at the free flow of American spirits. "Come on then, if you love toping," the journalist William Cobbett wrote his fellow Englishmen in a dispatch from America. "For here you may drink yourself blind at the price of sixpence."

The results of all this toping were entirely predictable: a rising tide of public drunkenness, violence and family abandonment and a spike in alcohol-related diseases. Several of the founding fathers—including George Washington, Thomas Jefferson and John Adams—denounced the excesses of the "alcoholic republic," inaugurating the American quarrel over drinking that would culminate a century later in Prohibition. But the outcome of our national drinking binge is not nearly as relevant to our present predicament as its underlying cause. Which, put simply, was this: American farmers were producing way too much corn, especially in the newly settled areas west of the Appalachians, where fertile soil yielded one bumper crop after another. Much as it has today, the astounding productivity of American farmers proved to be their own worst enemy, as well as a threat to the public health. For when yields rise, the market is flooded with grain, and its price collapses. As a result, there is a surfeit of cheap calories that clever marketers sooner or later will figure out a way to induce us to consume.

In those days, the easiest thing to do with all that grain was to distill it. The Appalachian range made it difficult and expensive to transport surplus corn from the lightly settled Ohio River Valley to the more populous markets of the East, so farmers turned their corn into whiskey—a more compact and portable "value-added commodity." In time, the price of whiskey plummeted, to the point that people could afford to drink it by the pint, which is precisely what they did. Nowadays, for somewhat different reasons, corn (along with most other agricultural commodities) is again abundant and cheap, and once again the easiest thing to do with the surplus is to turn it into more compact and portable value-added commodities: corn sweeteners, cornfed meat and chicken and highly processed foods of every description. The Alcoholic Republic has given way to the Republic of Fat, but in both cases, before the clever marketing, before the change in lifestyle, stands a veritable mountain of cheap grain. Until we somehow deal with this surfeit of calories coming off the farm, it is unlikely that even the most well-intentioned food companies or public-health campaigns will have much success changing the way we eat.

The underlying problem is agricultural overproduction, and that problem (while it understandably never receives quite as much attention as underproduction) is almost as old as agriculture itself. Even in the Old Testament, there's talk about how to deal not only with the lean times but also with the fat: the Bible advises creation of a grain reserve to smooth out the swings of the market in food. The nature of farming has always made it difficult to synchronize supply and demand. For one thing, there are the vagaries of nature: farmers may decide how many acres they will plant, but precisely how much food they produce in any year is beyond their control.

The rules of classical economics just don't seem to operate very well on the farm. When prices fall, for example, it would make sense for farmers to cut back on production, shrinking the supply of food to drive up its price. But in reality, farmers do precisely the opposite, planting and harvesting more food to keep their total income from falling, a practice that of course depresses prices even further. What's rational for the individual farmer is disastrous for farmers as a group. Add to this logic the constant stream of improvements in agricultural technology (mechanization, hybrid seed, agrochemicals and now genetically modified crops—innovations all eagerly seized on by farmers hoping to stay one step ahead of falling prices by boosting yield), and you have a sure-fire recipe for overproduction—another word for way too much food.

All this would be bad enough if the government weren't doing its best to make matters even worse, by recklessly encouraging farmers to produce even more unneeded food. Absurdly, while one hand of the federal government is campaigning against the epidemic of obesity, the other hand is actually subsidizing it, by writing farmers a check for every bushel of corn they can grow. We have been hearing a lot lately about how our agricultural policy is undermining our foreign-policy goals, forcing third-world farmers to compete against a flood tide of cheap American grain. Well, those same policies are also undermining our public-health goals by loosing a tide of cheap calories at home. While it is true that our farm policies are making a bad situation worse, adding mightily to the great mountain of grain, this hasn't always been the case with government support of farmers, and needn't be the case even now. For not all support programs are created equal, a fact that has been conveniently overlooked in the new free-market campaign to eliminate them.

In fact, farm programs in America were originally created as a way to shrink the great mountain of grain, and for many years they helped to do just that. The Roosevelt administration established the nation's first program of farm support during the Depression, though not, as many people seem to think, to feed a hungry nation. Then, as now, the problem was too much food,

not too little; New Deal farm policy was designed to help farmers reeling from a farm depression caused by what usually causes a farm depression: collapsing prices due to overproduction. In Churdan, Iowa, recently, a corn farmer named George Naylor told me about the winter day in 1933 his father brought a load of corn to the grain elevator, where "the price had been 10 cents a bushel the day before," and was told that suddenly, "the elevator wasn't buying at any price." The price of corn had fallen to zero. New Deal farm policy, quite unlike our own, set out to solve the problem of overproduction. It established a system of price supports, backed by a grain reserve, that worked to keep surplus grain off the market, thereby breaking the vicious cycle in which farmers have to produce more every year to stay even. It is worth recalling how this system worked, since it suggests one possible path out of the current subsidy morass.

Basically, the federal government set and supported a target price (based on the actual cost of production) for storable commodities like corn. When the market price dropped below the target, a farmer was given an option: rather than sell his harvest at the low price, he could take out what was called a "nonrecourse loan," using his corn as collateral, for the full value of his crop. The farmer then stored his corn until the market improved, at which point he sold it and used the proceeds to repay the loan. If the market failed to improve that year, the farmer could discharge his debt simply by handing his corn over to the government, which would add it to something called, rather quaintly, the "ever-normal granary." This was a grain reserve managed by the U.S.D.A., which would sell from it whenever prices spiked (during a bad harvest, say), thereby smoothing out the vicissitudes of the market and keeping the cost of food more or less steady—or "ever normal."

This wasn't a perfect system by any means, but it did keep cheap grain from flooding the market and by doing so supported the prices farmers received. And it did this at a remarkably small cost to the government, since most of the loans were repaid. Even when they weren't, and the government was left holding the bag (i.e., all those bushels of collateral grain), the U.S.D.A. was eventually able to unload it, and often did so at a profit. The program actually made money in good years. Compare that with the current subsidy regime, which costs American taxpayers about $19 billion a year and does virtually nothing to control production.

So why did we ever abandon this comparatively sane sort of farm policy? Politics, in a word. The shift from an agricultural-support system designed to discourage overproduction to one that encourages it dates to the early 1970's—to the last time food prices in America climbed high enough to generate significant political heat. That happened after news of Nixon's 1972 grain deal with the Soviet Union broke, a disclosure that coincided with a spell of bad weather in the farm belt. Commodity prices soared, and before long so did supermarket prices for meat, milk, bread and other staple foods tied to the cost of grain. Angry consumers took to the streets to protest food prices and staged a nationwide meat boycott to protest the high cost of hamburger, that American birthright. Recognizing the political peril, Nixon ordered his secretary of agriculture, Earl (Rusty) Butz, to do whatever was necessary to drive down the price of food.

Butz implored America's farmers to plant their fields "fence row to fence row" and set about dismantling 40 years of farm policy designed to prevent overproduction. He shuttered the ever-normal granary, dropped the target price for grain and inaugurated a new subsidy system, which eventually replaced nonrecourse loans with direct payments to farmers. The distinction may sound technical, but in effect it was revolutionary. For instead of lending farmers money so they could keep their grain off the market, the government offered to simply cut them a check, freeing them to dump their harvests on the market no matter what the price.

The new system achieved exactly what it was intended to: the price of food hasn't been a political problem for the government since the Nixon era. Commodity prices have steadily declined, and in the perverse logic of agricultural economics, production has increased, as farmers struggle to stay solvent. As you can imagine, the shift from supporting agricultural prices to subsidizing much lower prices has been a boon to agribusiness companies because it slashes the cost of their raw materials. That's why Big Food, working with the farm-state Congressional delegations it lavishly supports, consistently lobbies to maintain a farm policy geared to high production and cheap grain. (It doesn't hurt that those lightly populated farm states exert a disproportionate influence in Washington, since it takes far fewer votes to elect a senator in Kansas than in California. That means agribusiness can presumably "buy" a senator from one of these under-populated states for a fraction of what a big-state senator costs.)

But as we're beginning to recognize, our cheap-food farm policy comes at a high price: first there's the $19 billion a year the government pays to keep the whole system afloat; then there's the economic misery that the dumping of cheap American grain inflicts on farmers in the developing world; and finally there's the obesity epidemic at home—which most researchers date to the mid-70's, just when we switched to a farm policy consecrated to the overproduction of grain. Since that time, farmers in the United States have managed to produce 500 additional calories per person every day; each of us is, heroically, managing to pack away about 200 of those extra calories per day. Presumably the other 300—most of them in the form of surplus corn—get dumped on overseas markets or turned into ethanol.

Cheap corn, the dubious legacy of Earl Butz, is truly the building block of the "fast-food nation." Cheap corn, transformed into high-fructose corn syrup, is what allowed Coca-Cola to move from the svelte 8-ounce bottle of soda ubiquitous in the 70's to the chubby 20-ounce bottle of today. Cheap corn, transformed into cheap beef, is what allowed McDonald's to supersize its burgers and still sell many of them for no more than a dollar. Cheap corn gave us a whole raft of new highly processed foods, including the world-beating chicken nugget, which, if you study its ingredients, you discover is really a most ingenious transubstantiation of corn, from the corn-fed chicken it contains to the bulking and binding agents that hold it together.

You would have thought that lower commodity prices would represent a boon to consumers, but it doesn't work out that way, not unless you believe a 32-ounce Big Gulp is a great deal. When the raw materials for food become so abundant and cheap, the clever strategy for a food company is not necessarily to lower prices—to do that would only lower its revenues. It makes much more sense to compete for the consumer's dollar by increasing portion sizes—and as Greg Critser points out in his recent book "Fat Land," the bigger the portion, the more food people will eat.

So McDonald's tempts us by taking a 600-calorie meal and jacking it up to 1,550 calories. Compared with that of the marketing, packaging and labor, the cost of the added ingredients is trivial.

Such cheap raw materials also argue for devising more and more highly processed food, because the real money will never be in selling cheap corn (or soybeans or rice) but in "adding value" to that commodity. Which is one reason that in the years since the nation moved to a cheap-food farm policy, the number and variety of new snack foods in the supermarket have ballooned. The game is in figuring out how to transform a penny's worth of corn and additives into a $3 bag of ginkgo biloba–fortified brain-function-enhancing puffs, or a dime's worth of milk and sweeteners into Swerve, a sugary new "milk based" soft drink to be sold in schools. It's no coincidence that Big Food has suddenly "discovered" how to turn milk into junk food: the government recently made deep cuts in the dairy-farm program, and as a result milk is nearly as cheap a raw material as water.

As public concern over obesity mounts, the focus of political pressure has settled on the food industry and its marketing strategies—supersizing portions, selling junk food to children, lacing products with transfats and sugars. Certainly Big Food bears some measure of responsibility for our national eating disorder—a reality that a growing number of food companies have publicly accepted. In recent months, Kraft, McDonald's and Coca-Cola have vowed to change marketing strategies and even recipes in an effort to help combat obesity and, no doubt, ward off the coming tide of litigation.

There is an understandable reluctance to let Big Food off the hook. Yet by devising ever more ingenious ways to induce us to consume the surplus calories our farmers are producing, the food industry is only playing by a set of rules written by our government. (And maintained, it is true, with the industry's political muscle.) The political challenge now is to rewrite those rules, to develop a new set of agricultural policies that don't subsidize overproduction—and overeating. For unless we somehow deal with the mountain of cheap grain that makes the Happy Meal and the Double Stuff Oreo such "bargains," the calories are guaranteed to keep coming.

PAUL SCHWENNESEN

ON THE ETHICS OF RANCHING

"I always feel there's no real balance of gain in my work on the land, and yet one does it. . . . It's a sort of duty one feels to the land."

—*Konstantin Levin, Anna Karenina*

"Local," so the saying goes, "never goes out of season." People holding this view typically emblazon it on the back of expensive hybrids and consume above average quantities of whole grains. And they have a point. The counterpoint, meanwhile, is subtly delivered in weekly specials of "89 cents a pound!" and is made by corpulent grocers driving SUVs. They also have a point.

Like all catchphrases they happily ignore some important truths. At Double Check Ranch, we're caught between the two as we fervently try to discover the proper balance between sustainable stewardship, pragmatic economics, and our own personal pursuit of happiness.

BACKGROUND:

As an individual response to the often fickle, steadily worsening cattle market, our family began direct marketing grassfed beef 15 years ago. My mother and father patiently pioneered Tucson's earliest farmers' markets, diligently explaining the benefits of grassfed beef to people who assumed that all cows ate grass all the time. Now, a decade and a half later, my wife and I are trying to meet the increasing demand for local grassfed beef. In the process we're hopefully demonstrating a new model for family-scale ranching, one that can preserve the inherently stable, decentralized nature of an agrarian land ethic.

Our operation is unique in that we own the entire beef cycle. From "pasture to palate," we control every aspect of the product our customers eat. We raise cattle on eleven thousand acres of Arizona/New Mexico range, finishing them on irrigated pasture along the San Pedro River north of Tucson. After finishing, we slaughter and butcher right on the ranch in our own state-inspected packinghouse which enables us to control the final, critical stages of beef production.

Owning the whole process more than doubles the per head return of a standard cow–calf ranching operation (with only four times the work!), enabling us to contemplate stewardship projects that might otherwise go undone and to focus on the things that make us happy. It's too early to call our model lucrative, but it certainly appears to be financially and emotionally sustainable.

MANAGEMENT:

Not long ago, someone asked, "How do you manage it, way out there in the sticks?" It probably didn't answer the question, but we replied, "Intensively . . . ."

Indeed, we intensively manage our primary physical tool (cattle), grazing and rotating them in patterns reminiscent of the herd effect of large wild ungulate grazers like bison. This is an intense activity which pushes plant matter and manure back into the soil, increases rainfall absorption and leads to a vibrant energy, water, and mineral cycle that positively feeds upon itself, generating plenty where once there was little. We do not kill coyotes, mountain lions, rattlesnakes or other predators unless they are clearly deviant. We don't use pesticides or herbicides on our land or antibiotics or steroids in our animals. And, partly as a consequence of our approach, our pastures and riparian areas are home to one of North America's greatest concentrations of mammal and avian species[1], and it is not uncommon to find tourists from as far away as Europe coming to see the variety of life that makes its home here.

EXPLOITING ECOLOGY (AS GOD INTENDED)

We maintain a cautiously opportunistic approach to Nature out here. Rather than "conquering" her, we have opted for a kind of Jujitsu approach, attempting to turn existing conditions to our favor rather than trying to counter them head on. For instance, mesquite (a leguminous, shrubby tree) is considered a nuisance and often chained or poisoned out of most farmland. A hardy survivor, it can indeed choke out other growth and create a tangled, thorny thicket that is practically unusable. However, we have found that judicious pruning (as opposed to outright cutting) can garner tremendous benefits. In addition to valuable shade, the pruned trees provide significant nitrogen fixing, leaf litter, and at 20% crude protein, excellent livestock feed. Moreover, the brush pile trimmings from these trees makes excellent bird habitat, attracting a variety of life forms (including birdwatchers . . .)

WASTE NOT, WANT NOT . . .

Operating a meat-processing plant presents a number of disposal challenges that are usually environmental liabilities. As entrepreneurs, however, we view "waste" as simply an underutilized asset and have therefore turned two horrible, disgusting problems into two rather neat solutions. Beef tallow, which we normally have to pay to have removed, is rendered and catalyzed into biodiesel that runs our tractors and trucks, reducing one of our largest overhead expenses. Slaughterhouse offal (rumen, blood, bone, etc.) is mixed with local wood chips to make excellent high-octane compost. Each year, we spread 50,000 pounds of this compost on our pastures and have seen a marked increase in the organic response to this input. The grass, not surprisingly, really *is* greener when you feed it. . . .

A RIVER RUNS THROUGH IT (WELL, MOST OF THE TIME . . .)

We manage two hundred acres of San Pedro River bottomland that floods frequently. Rather than damming or building gabions to protect our pastureland banks from erosion (a neighbor to the north "protected" his banks with dozens of enormous mine-truck tires which promptly washed away in the first major flood), we have chosen to use pulsed and specifically timed grazing in the bottoms to promote cottonwood and willow seedling establishment along the banks.

If allowed to graze continuously year-round, cattle will eat the young seedlings and tree establishment can take decades. We time our bottomland grazing in such a way that peak seedling season is off limits to grazing; young trees thrive and the forest corridor thrives as a consequence. Additionally, we have established perennial native grass species along the upper banks to provide a permanent root mat to hold back topsoil and keep our groomed pastures from washing away. Coupled with shameless exploitation of all-volunteer labor, we have smoothed the bank from a vertical cut to a more natural angle of repose.

While these activities may seem terribly eco-conscious, it is not in jest that I say we "exploit" our local ecology. In this, we are not alone. It is our firm conviction that humans exist as an element of the natural order and as such we behave according to the same ecological rules as, say, wombats (of which we have seen very few I'm afraid to say). *Every* species exploits its environment, it is precisely this unmanaged resource race which leads to the blossoming of life. What one species excretes is another's welcome treat. The relatively oxygen-rich atmosphere we enjoy today is the poisonous result of cyanobacterial "off-gassing" (flatulence hadn't been coined yet) from the Archaen.[2]

Granted, our ability to alter our environment is remarkably fast-paced, but there is nothing unnatural in this. Our roles (and responsibilities, I hasten to add) are not fully understood, but our importance *to* Nature is increasingly clear.[3]

"SUSTAINABLE" STEWARDSHIP

This is one of those wince-inducing phrases that means almost all things to all people. For us, it means profitably harvesting a wholesome food source with practically no external inputs beyond sunlight, water, and our own creative energy; an activity that can reasonably be expected to continue unchanged for generations to come.

Our stewardship begins by countering the common misunderstanding that livestock are inevitably destructive toward landscapes, and that their impacts should be limited or mitigated by enforcement agencies with the wisdom and resources to control them. Viewing livestock as an inherently damaging force to be minimized entirely ignores the well-established relationship between herbivory and grassland ecology. Grasslands, and to some extent riparian and forest systems, have co-evolved for eons with grazing ungulates and generally respond positively to periodic tissue removal. To be sure, livestock impacts *can* be detrimental (so can buffalo or grasshoppers). But the overgrazing effects that can lead to landscape denuding, erosion, and biodiversity loss are not a factor of livestock activity or numbers per se, but result entirely from the mismanagement of that livestock impact's *timing*. Landscape ecological health is dependent on rest/recovery as well as grazing, and it is vitally important that livestock impacts be concentrated, pulsed, *and removed* after the impact. These traditional concepts are not new (as many an old-timer rancher will tell you) and were clearly articulated in the resource management literature by Allan Savory[4] and others over forty years ago. Proper livestock management has had remarkable applied success around the globe, turning barren landscapes into vibrant grasslands, improving watershed rainfall effectiveness, and restoring biodiversity.

In short, managed grazing which capitalizes on a natural structure of concentrated grazing followed by established rest periods can turn livestock into an ecological asset rather than a liability.

ARE WE "GREEN?"

People who emotionally relate to our way of life commend us for our "greenness" all the time. Calling someone "green" used to lead to gunfights out here, but now it means we attract attention from the vegetarian set. While I fully commend consumers for their concerns (and share many of them!) I doubt if we're as green as they think. People get terribly excited about the notion of "food-miles," the premise being that the fewer miles food travels to reach one's mouth, the better. This may resonate in some quaint corner of our minds, but I doubt that the carbon footprint a pound of my beef creates in traveling to Tucson towed by a diesel pickup (biodiesel notwithstanding) is significantly lower than a pound of Uruguayan beef traveling by shipping container. "Big" is the new "Bad," in today's vernacular, but economies of scale do often create efficiency and it would be foolish for us to assume that small is always best.

If being green means that we produce our beef without relying on taxpayer funded, artificially cheap corn feeds,[5] without externalizing our costs into local aquifers and impinging on our neighbor's property with obnoxious noise, dust, and pollutants, then I guess we're "green." But if being "green" means that we are following the ecological trend du jour, then we humbly beg off. We care deeply about the landscape that supports us because our good management benefits *us*, not some vague notion of the "planet's well-being." I know it's not politically correct, but brazen self-interest (within an appropriate "rule of law" framework) is the only way to make the world a better place. . . .

A BEEF WITH "BIODIVERSITY"

"Biodiversity," while a socially exciting and politically potent term, is nevertheless a complex and poorly understood one. Despite this, it is touted as an unmitigated *good*, at least when it exists in the proper places. Biodiversity is usually frowned upon when found in our bathrooms, for instance. Often the term is co-opted by advocacy groups who use it to justify intentions of maintaining status quo or of a return to an ill-defined "pristine" state. Misanthropy seems to be the common theme in most discussions over biodiversity.

We take a more pragmatic view. At its most basic, biodiversity refers to the degree of genetic variation found within a particular biome or ecosystem. In this sense, our ranching decisions are tuned toward managing for biodiversity for we find that creating optimal conditions for diversity creates inherent stability. Monocultures, we've learned, teeter toward collapse.

The fact that we, as agricultural producers, would voluntarily engage in conservation-friendly activities often comes as a surprise to those familiar with large-scale agriculture modeled on industrial production systems. But it really should not be such a surprise; family-scale agriculture has had a long tradition of carefully preserving and enhancing local environments and increasing biodiversity since long before the term had been coined.

Of the 11–14 million distinct species estimated to exist on the globe, fewer than 13% have actually been discovered.[6] This dramatic shortfall in baseline data should give us pause when touting policies that "favor" biodiversity or when declaiming activities that "reduce" it. That said, the concept of "ecological stability" and its relationship to variety (a kind of biological corollary to political democratization) is a compelling one that informs our particular approach.

Management is an awful word (particularly if you happen to be the one being "managed"), but is nevertheless crucial in an ethical understanding of the pressures affecting our environment. Even choosing *not* to manage is a management decision. The ability, nay *imperative*, to manage our surroundings is perhaps a uniquely human characteristic that we ignore at our own peril.

ECONOMICS:

THE POLITICS OF "LOCAL"

"Ah," the flinty-eyed economist in you says, "but isn't this grassfed, boutique-scale of production terribly inefficient, supported only by the bubble-heads infatuated with local food?" And he would be right, we're the first to admit that this particular method of converting solar energy into cashflow is subject to the whims of a health/eco-conscious clientele. But frankly, we'll take our chances with the whims of a clientele we can see and know over an impersonal industrial system that insists on ninety-nine cent Whoppers for two decades in a row. For years now, corporate cattle buyers have been offering lower prices to producers even as they grow feedlot production and processing systems beyond any resemblance to the picture-perfect farms they display on their packaging. In 1970, a pound of beef cost nearly five adjusted dollars. Now it costs two. In 1970, a rancher could buy a new pickup (the standard "Square State" asset index) with fifteen steers. Now it takes forty-four. For the economist, this tells you practically everything you need to know about the beef industry, and it isn't pretty.

BIG MEAT

Indeed, the dramatic decline in the commodity price of beef has gotten many in the ranching industry wondering if something is "going on" in the meat industry. In fact, the perception that large corporate meat packers are manipulating markets even prompted the U.S. Attorney General (Eric Holder) and USDA Secretary (Tom Vilsack) to recently host a public forum on "Competition Issues Facing Farmers in Today's Agricultural Marketplaces" —and to consider a potential anti-trust probe. Despite the grandiose title, the topic of the day was really about the growing concerns over consolidation in the meat-packing industry leading to lower prices for calves in the auction market. By the way, if you're wondering why the beef industry ought to concern you or your environment, consider that nearly a billion acres are classified as "rangeland"; anything that influences the commodities raised on these rangelands affects 36% of the land area of the country.[7] That's an awful lot of environment. . . .

While the majority attending this forum had hats, it seemed that an awful lot of them were in hands, not on heads. Appealing for help to the "suits," the audience was unashamedly suggesting that government rescue the small family rancher. Now, don't get me wrong; I share the common concern over the demise of a way of life. I, too, am disturbed at how far cattle prices have fallen over the years. It disturbs me that 80% of the meat-packing industry is in the hands of four conglomerates. But asking government to break the back of "Big Meat" is like asking the schoolyard bully to make your friend share his lunch money. So many unintended possibilities . . . !

For the record, I would be the first to rally if substantiated findings showed that Cargill, Tyson, National, or JBS were engaged in price-fixing or fraud (after all, it is one of the limited functions of government, according to Jefferson, to "prevent men from injuring one another"). But after six hours of public testimony at the forum hosted by Holder and Vilsack, no inkling of such manipulation emerged. What emerged was that some producers in the industry would rather see higher prices for their cattle (no kidding?!), that ranchers ought to get a "fair shake" (whatever that means: I think it's shorthand for "more for me"), and that the big guys should open the books to their private transactions to let the rest of us see what's "going on."

The difficulty with these proposals is that they ignore the underlying economics, replacing them with emotional subterfuge. In my mind, the consolidation of the meat industry is a predictable economic response to consumer demand for cheap food, aided and abetted by misguided (or purposefully twisted) policy. In fact, the *primary* reason for megalithic consolidation is unrelated to corporate meat processors. "Big Meat" is simply the result of two seemingly "good" government programs: 1) agricultural subsidies, and 2) stringent regulation of food processing.[8]

SUBSIDIES

Upwards of $30 billion taxpayer dollars a year are funneled into cash subsides to farmers and owners of farmland each year. Seventy-two percent of it goes to the ten largest subsidized farms,[9] effectively (though not surprisingly) countering the original New Deal intention of supporting small family farmers. The ironclad law of unintended consequences hits hardest when programs are large and centrally managed. The Cato Institute neatly summarizes the problems associated with an entrenched subsidy program:

> The extensive federal welfare system for farm businesses is costly to taxpayers and it creates distortions in the economy. Subsidies induce farmers to overproduce, which pushes down prices and creates political demands for further subsidies. Subsidies inflate land prices in rural America. And the flow of subsidies from Washington hinders farmers from innovating, cutting costs, diversifying their land use, and taking the actions needed to prosper in a competitive global economy.[10]

In the meat industry artificially subsidized feeder grain has clearly altered the cow–calf business, allowing cheap grain to generally depress calf prices by as much as

60 cents per head with greater impacts on those unable or unwilling to participate in the skewed market.[11] Cheap feed grain, moreover, facilitates concentrated feedlot systems and these systems naturally tend to conglomerate as the efficiencies scale up beyond imagination (500,000 head of cattle in one feed yard is not unheard of today). It is this tremendous efficiency and scale that leads to lower calf prices at the sale yard.

Accusing feedlots and packers of "collusion" and "price-fixing" in the marketplace is probably stretching a point since they are simply doing what everyone else is doing: buying as low as they can and selling as high as possible. That they've offered lower and lower calf prices over the years is not their fault, they're not charities after all. And while I don't claim that they have spotless records, I'm awfully suspicious of centralized solutions to guarantee ranchers "fair" prices for their calves.

Perhaps our national farm subsidy program ought to be addressed as it was in New Zealand in 1984. New Zealand's farmers and ranchers are significantly better off today than in the heyday of government "assistance." The number of farmers in active production has remained steady (at 11.4%, compared to less than 2% in the U.S.), the number of farmed acres has decreased (increasing wildlife habitat) while production has increased (at 5.9% per year compared with 1% during the subsidized regime.)[12] Eliminating corrosive subsidy programs has done wonders for the Kiwi agrarian.

OVER-REGULATION

If you think subsidies are bad, over-regulation of food-processing has done more to hurt ranching families than they even know. Heavy regulation makes it extremely difficult to enter the slaughter and processing sector since the financial risks are high and the regulatory hurdles are immense. It's easier to build a centralized feedlot/packing house if you are a Cargill with huge capital reserves and an army of technicians than it is to build a certified mom-and-pop local packing facility. Reams of paperwork, tests, constantly updated inspection requirements and complicated procedures create an almost insurmountable barrier-to-entry.

The inability to process animals locally has guaranteed that cow–calf producers are locked in to the local auction yards and the attendant cattle-buyers. Alternative marketing opportunities such as direct-marketing

finished product are hugely more difficult if the processing facilities don't exist.

As an owner of a tiny packinghouse myself, I can attest to the forbidding array of regulatory restrictions that hamper my creativity and production. For instance, we thought that grassfed hotdogs would be a popular item to sell. It turns out that the facilities capable of making them will not accept our state-inspected meat (even though they would be happy to accept non-USDA inspected meat from abroad). Or take jerky: while all-natural grassfed jerky would probably be an excellent and desirable product, inspectors have dismissed the notion out of hand ("Have you seen the regs on *Listeria* alone? It's three inches thick!" said one). Managing a packinghouse according to stringent bureaucratic regulation is a crushing burden for anyone, particularly if you are not terribly well connected or financially backed. Government's genuine concern over safe food has created a megalithic bureaucracy that aims to eliminate all food-borne risk at "any cost," including the elimination of local, small-scale food production.

When it comes to government fixes, we need to be careful what we ask for. Inviting authoritarian oversight into your competitor's business always seems like a good idea at the time. But when the same authorities start pounding on *your* door, the notion starts to lose some of its charm. . . .

BUILDING MARKETS

Directly marketing our product has given us tremendous leeway in how we approach our cattle operation. As Benjamin Franklin observed, however, it's impossible to have both complete liberty and complete security. Our method of selling products locally is certainly free from the vagaries of larger market forces that traditionally plague producers, but a steady paycheck it isn't.

And as for clientele, the genuine appreciation we get for our product is a large part of our compensation package. Our customers are *interested* in what they eat, justifying their purchase on far more than price-point. They love the proximity of their food production, they love the connection to it, and they are willing to pay for our lack of economies of scale. I suppose it's somewhat akin to the weekend hunter who, if he actually breaks it down, finds he's "paid" $35 a pound for elk meat (beer, gasoline, camouflage, beer, Cheetos, new scope, ammo and extra beer); what you eat is about more than just shelf price.

ETHICS AND ENVIRONMENT:

PROPERTY

Our stewardship is, importantly, tied to our sense of *ownership* of the resource. A wise man once said, "nobody owns this ground, God owns it, but *I* pay the taxes." Indeed, it is this sense of ownership that guides us toward activity that burgeons our local environment. At a deep level we understand that variety is our best insurance, diversity is our greatest asset and that if we are to prosper we must ensure that our land is prospering first. We take a holistic approach to our management and do everything we can to avoid the trap of silver-bullet solutions (and anyway, we've seen as many werewolves here as wombats). Very little of this could be accomplished if we did not have a vested interest in the land we manage. It is gratifying to note, for instance, that despite a significantly smaller budget and bearing the financial necessity of producing a saleable product, the biological diversity found on our ranch is arguably greater than that found on a Nature Conservancy preserve immediately adjoining us. The combination of maintained pastures, riparian bottomland, and native desert vegetation creates boundary zones that teem with wildlife, while the enforced "hands-off" approach used by conservationists yields ambivalent results at best.[13]

PURSUING HAPPINESS

Foregoing a comfy, predictable, well-paid lifestyle for one that depends wholly upon one's own resources is a truly frightening thing. But freedom is a strong incentive, and we now allocate our time and energy to whatever *we* deem best. We eat our meals as a family, we play and work outside, we read, ride horses, play the piano, watch chickens, and go for walks when we want to. Weekends don't mean what they used to. Every day, our time is our own, but we aren't exactly on vacation. We work longer days doing harder work than the majority. Being free from the direct caprices of bosses and bureaucracies does not mean you are free from want, from the necessity to feed and clothe one's family. Inevitably we find ourselves stressed

and unhappy at times. But there seems to be a big difference when pressure comes from within rather than without.

All in all, I suspect that we've found our own particular version of Aristotle's "middling way," while attempting to negotiate the balance between excess and deficiency. I wouldn't congratulate ourselves for doing this intentionally; we bounce through the ruts like anyone else. But I must confess a certain contentment of spirit, an appreciation for what we craft that I suspect is lacking in many lives. The model of sustainable ranching that we promote is by no means perfect. It's expensive for consumers, it's physically and financially demanding for producers. But if nothing else it is *honest*, the costs are a direct reflection of the necessary inputs. We live in intimate proximity to the processes that give (and take) life. We, in turn, give back to the land, leaving it richer and more fecund than we found it.

We have a deep-seated land ethic generated through proximity and mutual dependence. We are not hobbled by notions that Nature needs us to "leave her alone," for we see and feel the consequences of our actions at every turn. We take great and genuine pride in the health and vibrancy or our surroundings, taking pleasure in seeing a natural setting producing wealth on well-managed productive ground. I might go so far as to say that we gain the same level of satisfaction as one who appreciates an untrammeled wilderness (for I am one of those as well), for both visions are healthy, productive and stable.

CONCLUSION:

It may not be politically correct to observe, but our property interest and profit motive has probably done more for local biodiversity and ecological health than all the goodwill gestures and government mandated environmental programs combined. We genuinely strive to foster abundance, stability, and variety.

In line with this approach is a view that diversity is fostered from the bottom up, beginning with the microbes found within our soils. We harbor a general distrust toward centralized, top-down decision making and we would rather see the spontaneous arrival of a new species of nematode than an artificially reintroduced wolf or beaver. The technocratic approach to ecology management based on emotional favoritism for charismatic megafauna is a disturbing one, for it utterly fails to recognize the power and resilience of natural systems.

We think that strength comes from below rather than on high. Dispersing decision making power, whether in politics or in ecology, is always a more effective and equitable approach for it releases the hidden drive and aspiration of the individual. Information and feedback can only be adequately transmitted in an organic, reactive process. Ecologies do this all the time, reacting to changing conditions while continually seeking new niches in which to proliferate. And we, as participants in our own ecology, are no different.

NOTES

1. Center for Biological Diversity, http://www. biologicaldiversity.org/programs/public_lands/ rivers/san_pedro_river/index.html.

2. University of California Museum of Paleontology, Berkeley. http://www.ucmp.berkeley.edu/bacteria/ cyanointro.html

3. Dan Dagget, *Gardeners of Eden: Rediscovering Our Importance to Nature*, Thatcher Charitable Trust, 2005.

4. They were clearly articulated in the resource management literature by Allan Savory, "Holistic resource management: a conceptual framework for ecologically sound economic modeling" *Ecological Economics* (September 1991): Vol 3, Issue 3. 181–191.

5. See the essay in this volume by Michael Pollan.

6. National Wildlife Federation, http://www.nwf.org/ News-and-Magazines/National-Wildlife/Animals/ Archives/1999/How-Many-Species-Exist.aspx

7. University of Idaho, Rangeland Ecology & Management, "A Short Course on Rangelands": www.cnr. uidaho.edu/what-is-range/files/short_course.pdf

8. Again, see the essay by Pollan in this collection.

9. Cato Institute: "Agricultural Subsidies," http:// www.downsizinggovernment.org/agriculture/ subsidies

10. Ibid

11. http://ageconsearch.umn.edu/bitstream/35944/1/ waeasp79.pdf
http://www.ers.usda.gov/AmberWaves/March09/ Features/GrainPrices.htm

12. Laura Sayre, http://newfarm.rodaleinstitute.org/ features/0303/newzealand_subsidies.shtml

13. See the essay by Rose in this volume.

BEING A CITIZEN OF THE WORLD
A. Working Together

ELLIOTT SOBER

PHILOSOPHICAL PROBLEMS FOR ENVIRONMENTALISM

INTRODUCTION

A number of philosophers have recognized that the environmental movement, whatever its practical political effectiveness, faces considerable theoretical difficulties in justification.[1] It has been recognized that traditional moral theories do not provide natural underpinnings for policy objectives and this has led some to skepticism about the claims of environmentalists, and others to the view that a revolutionary reassessment of ethical norms is needed. In this chapter, I will try to summarize the difficulties that confront a philosophical defense of environmentalism. I also will suggest a way of making sense of some environmental concerns that does not require the wholesale jettisoning of certain familiar moral judgments.

Preserving an endangered species or ecosystem poses no special conceptual problem when the instrumental value of that species or ecosystem is known. When we have reason to think that some natural object represents a resource to us, we obviously ought to take that fact into account in deciding what to do. A variety of potential uses may be under discussion, including food supply, medical applications, recreational use, and so on. As with any complex decision, it may be difficult even to agree on how to compare the competing values that may be involved. Willingness to pay in dollars is a familiar least common denominator, although it poses a number of problems. But here we have nothing that is specifically a problem for environmentalism.

The problem for environmentalism stems from the idea that species and ecosystems ought to be preserved for reasons additional to their known value as resources for human use. The feeling is that even when

Sober, Elliott. 1986. Philosophical Problems for Environmentalism. The Preservation of Species. Edited by B. Norton. Copyright © 1986 by Princeton University Press, Princeton. Pages 173–194. Reprinted by permission of the publisher.

we cannot say what nutritional, medicinal, or recreational benefit the preservation provides, there still is a value in preservation. It is the search for a rationale for this feeling that constitutes the main conceptual problem for environmentalism.

The problem is especially difficult in view of the holistic (as opposed to individualistic) character of the things being assigned value. Put simply, what is special about environmentalism is that it values the preservation of species, communities, or ecosystems, rather than the individual organisms of which they are composed. "Animal liberationists" have urged that we should take the suffering of sentient animals into account in ethical deliberation.[2] Such beasts are not mere things to be used as cruelly as we like no matter how trivial the benefit we derive. But in "widening the ethical circle," we are simply including in the community more individual organisms whose costs and benefits we compare. Animal liberationists are extending an old and familiar ethical doctrine—namely, utilitarianism—to take account of the welfare of other individuals. Although the practical consequences of this point of view may be revolutionary, the theoretical perspective is not at all novel. If suffering is bad, then it is bad for any individual who suffers.[3] Animal liberationists merely remind us of the consequences of familiar principles.

But trees, mountains, and salt marshes do not suffer. They do not experience pleasure and pain, because, evidently, they do not have experiences at all. The same is true of species. Granted, individual organisms may have mental states; but the species—taken to be a population of organisms connected by certain sorts of interactions (preeminently, that of exchanging genetic material in reproduction)—does not. Or put more carefully, we might say that the only sense in which species have experiences is that their member organisms do: the attribution at the population level, if true, is true simply in virtue of its being true at the individual level. Here is a case where reductionism is correct.

So perhaps it is true in this reductive sense that some species experience pain. But the values that environmentalists attach to preserving species do not reduce to any value of preserving organisms. It is in this sense that environmentalists espouse a holistic value system. Environmentalists care about entities that by no stretch of the imagination have experiences (e.g., mountains). What is more, their position does not force them to care if individual organisms suffer pain, so long as the species is preserved. Steel traps may outrage an animal liberationist because of the suffering they inflict, but an environmentalist aiming just at the preservation of a balanced ecosystem might see here no cause for complaint. Similarly, environmentalists think that the distinction between wild and domesticated organisms is important, in that it is the preservation of "natural" (i.e., not created by the "artificial interference" of human beings) objects that matters, whereas animal liberationists see the main problem in terms of the suffering of any organism—domesticated or not. And finally, environmentalists and animal liberationists diverge on what might be called the $n + m$ question. If two species—say blue and sperm whales—have roughly comparable capacities for experiencing pain, an animal liberationist might tend to think of the preservation of a sperm whale as wholly on an ethical par with the preservation of a blue whale. The fact that one organism is part of an endangered species while the other is not does not make the rare individual more intrinsically important. But for an environmentalist, this holistic property—membership in an endangered species—makes all the difference in the world: a world with n sperm and m blue whales is far better than a world with $n + m$ sperm and 0 blue whales. Here we have a stark contrast between an ethic in which it is the life situation of individuals that matters, and an ethic in which the stability and diversity of populations of individuals are what matter.[4]

Both animal liberationists and environmentalists wish to broaden our ethical horizons—to make us realize that it is not just human welfare that counts. But they do this in very different, often conflicting, ways. It is no accident that at the level of practical politics the two points of view increasingly find themselves at loggerheads. This practical conflict is the expression of a deep theoretical divide.

THE IGNORANCE ARGUMENT

Although we might not now know what use a particular endangered species might be to us, allowing it to go extinct forever closes off the possibility of discovering and exploiting a future use." According to this point of view, our ignorance of value is turned into a reason for action. The scenario envisaged in this environmentalist argument is not without precedent; who could have guessed that penicillin would be good for something other than turning out cheese? But there is a fatal defect in such arguments, which we might summarize with the phrase *out of nothing, nothing comes*: rational decisions require assumptions about what is true and what is valuable (in decision-theoretic jargon, the inputs must be probabilities and utilities). If you are completely ignorant of values, then you are incapable of making a rational decision, either for or against preserving some species. The fact that you do not know the value of a species, by itself, cannot count as a reason for wanting one thing rather than another to happen to it.

And there are so many species. How many geese that lay golden eggs are there apt to be in that number? It is hard to assign probabilities and utilities precisely here, but an analogy will perhaps reveal the problem confronting this environmentalist argument. Most of us willingly fly on airplanes, when safer (but less convenient) alternative forms of transportation are available. Is this rational? Suppose it were argued that there is a small probability that the next flight you take will crash. This would be very bad for you. Is it not crazy for you to risk this, given that the only gain to you is that you can reduce your travel time by a few hours (by not going by train, say)? Those of us who not only fly, but congratulate ourselves for being rational in doing so, reject this argument. We are prepared to accept a small chance of a great disaster in return for the high probability of a rather modest benefit. If this is rational, no wonder that we might consistently be willing to allow a species to go extinct in order to build a hydroelectric plant.

That the argument from ignorance is no argument at all can be seen from another angle. If we literally do not know what consequences the extinction of this or that species may bring, then we should take seriously the possibility that the extinction may be beneficial as well as the possibility that it may be deleterious. It may sound deep to insist that we preserve endangered species precisely because we do not know why they are valuable. But ignorance on a scale like this cannot provide the basis for any rational action.

Rather than invoke some unspecified future benefit, an environmentalist may argue that the species in question plays a crucial role in stabilizing the ecosystem of which it is a part. This will undoubtedly be true for carefully chosen species and ecosystems, but one should not generalize this argument into a global claim to the effect that *every* species is crucial to a balanced ecosystem. Although ecologists used to agree that the complexity of an ecosystem stabilizes it, this hypothesis has been subject to a number of criticisms and qualifications, both from a theoretical and an empirical perspective.[5] And for certain kinds of species (those which occupy a rather small area and whose normal population is small) we can argue that extinction would probably not disrupt the community. However fragile the biosphere may be, the extreme view that everything is crucial is almost certainly not true.

But, of course, environmentalists are often concerned by the fact that extinctions are occurring now at a rate much higher than in earlier times. It is mass extinction that threatens the biosphere, they say, and this claim avoids the spurious assertion that communities are so fragile that even one extinction will cause a crash. However, if the point is to avoid a mass extinction of species, how does this provide a rationale for preserving a species of the kind just described, of which we rationally believe that its passing will not destabilize the ecosystem? And, more generally, if mass extinction is known to be a danger to us, how does this translate into a value for preserving any particular species? Notice that we have now passed beyond the confines of the argument from ignorance; we are taking as a premise the idea that mass extinction would be a catastrophe (since it would destroy the ecosystem on which we depend). But how should that premise affect our valuing the California condor, the blue whale, or the snail darter?

THE SLIPPERY SLOPE ARGUMENT

Environmentalists sometimes find themselves asked to explain why each species matters so much to them, when there are, after all, so many. We may know of special reasons for valuing particular species, but how can we justify thinking that each and every species is important? "Each extinction impoverishes the biosphere" is often the answer given, but it really fails to resolve the issue. Granted, each extinction impoverishes, but it only impoverishes a little bit. So if it is the *wholesale* impoverishment of the biosphere that matters, one would apparently have to concede that each extinction matters a little, but only a little. But environmentalists may be loathe to concede this, for if they concede that each species matters only a little, they seem to be inviting the wholesale impoverishment that would be an unambiguous disaster. So they dig in their heels and insist that each species matters a lot. But to take this line, one must find some other rationale than the idea that mass extinction would be a great harm. Some of these alternative rationales we will examine later. For now, let us take a closer look at the train of thought involved here.

Slippery slopes are curious things: if you take even one step onto them, you inevitably slide all the way to the bottom. So if you want to avoid finding yourself at the bottom, you must avoid stepping onto them at all. To mix metaphors, stepping onto a slippery slope is to invite being nickeled and dimed to death.

Slippery slope arguments have played a powerful role in a number of recent ethical debates. One often hears people defend the legitimacy of abortions by arguing that since it is permissible to abort a single-celled fertilized egg, it must be permissible to abort a foetus of any age, since there is no place to draw the line from 0 to 9 months. Antiabortionists, on the other hand, sometimes argue in the other direction: since infanticide of newborns is not permissible, abortion at any earlier time is also not allowed, since there is no place to draw the line. Although these two arguments reach opposite conclusions about the permissibility of abortions, they agree on the following idea: since there is no principled place to draw the line on the continuum from newly fertilized egg to foetus gone to term, one must treat all these cases in the same way. Either abortion is always permitted or it never is, since there is no place to draw the line. Both sides run their favorite slippery slope arguments, but try to precipitate slides in opposite directions.

Starting with 10 million extant species, and valuing overall diversity, the environmentalist does not want to grant that each species matters only a little. For having granted this, commercial expansion and other causes will reduce the tally to 9,999,999. And then the argument is repeated, with each species valued only a

little, and diversity declines another notch. And so we are well on our way to a considerably impoverished biosphere, a little at a time. Better to reject the starting premise—namely, that each species matters only a little—so that the slippery slope can be avoided.

Slippery slopes should hold no terror for environmentalists, because it is often a mistake to demand that a line be drawn. Let me illustrate by an example. What is the difference between being bald and not? Presumably, the difference concerns the number of hairs you have on your head. But what is the precise number of hairs marking the boundary between baldness and not being bald? There is no such number. Yet, it would be a fallacy to conclude that there is no difference between baldness and hairiness. The fact that you cannot draw a line does not force you to say that the two alleged categories collapse into one. In the abortion case, this means that even if there is no precise point in foetal development that involves some discontinuous, qualitative change, one is still not obliged to think of newly fertilized eggs and foetuses gone to term as morally on a par. Since the biological differences are ones of degree, not kind, one may want to adopt the position that the moral differences are likewise matters of degree. This may lead to the view that a woman should have a better reason for having an abortion, the more developed her foetus is. Of course, this position does not logically follow from the idea that there is no place to draw the line; my point is just that differences in degree do not demolish the possibility of there being real moral differences.

In the environmental case, if one places a value on diversity, then each species becomes more valuable as the overall diversity declines. If we begin with 10 million species, each may matter little, but as extinctions continue, the remaining ones matter more and more. According to this outlook, a better and better reason would be demanded for allowing yet another species to go extinct. Perhaps certain sorts of economic development would justify the extinction of a species at one time. But granting this does not oblige one to conclude that the same sort of decision would have to be made further down the road. This means that one can value diversity without being obliged to take the somewhat exaggerated position that each species, no matter how many there are, is terribly precious in virtue of its contribution to that diversity.

Yet, one can understand that environmentalists might be reluctant to concede this point. They may fear that if one now allows that most species contribute only a little to overall diversity, one will set in motion a political process that cannot correct itself later. The worry is that even when the overall diversity has been drastically reduced, our ecological sensitivities will have been so coarsened that we will no longer be in a position to realize (or to implement policies fostering) the preciousness of what is left. This fear may be quite justified, but it is important to realize that it does not conflict with what was argued above. The political utility of making an argument should not be confused with the argument's soundness.

The fact that you are on a slippery slope, by itself, does not tell you whether you are near the beginning, in the middle, or at the end. If species diversity is a matter of degree, where do we currently find ourselves—on the verge of catastrophe, well on our way in that direction, or at some distance from a global crash? Environmentalists often urge that we are fast approaching a precipice; if we are, then the reduction in diversity that every succeeding extinction engenders should be all we need to justify species preservation.

Sometimes, however, environmentalists advance a kind of argument not predicated on the idea of fast approaching doom. The goal is to show that there is something wrong with allowing a species to go extinct (or with causing it to go extinct), even if overall diversity is not affected much. I now turn to one argument of this kind.

APPEALS TO WHAT IS NATURAL

I noted earlier that environmentalists and animal liberationists disagree over the significance of the distinction between wild and domesticated animals. Since both types of organisms can experience pain, animal liberationists will think of each as meriting ethical consideration. But environmentalists will typically not put wild and domesticated organisms on a par. Environmentalists typically are interested in preserving what is natural, be it a species living in the wild or a wilderness ecosystem. If a kind of domesticated chicken were threatened with extinction, I doubt that environmental groups would be up in arms. And if certain unique types of human environments—say urban slums in the United States—were "endangered," it is similarly unlikely that environmentalists would view this process as a deplorable impoverishment of the biosphere.

The environmentalist's lack of concern for humanly created organisms and environments may be practical rather than principled. It may be that at the level of values, no such bifurcation is legitimate, but that from the point of view of practical political action, it makes sense to put one's energies into saving items that exist in the wild. This subject has not been discussed much in the literature, so it is hard to tell. But I sense that the distinction between wild and domesticated has a certain theoretical importance to many environmentalists. They perhaps think that the difference is that we created domesticated organisms which would otherwise not exist, and so are entitled to use them solely for our own interests. But we did not create wild organisms and environments, so it is the height of presumption to expropriate them for our benefit. A more fitting posture would be one of "stewardship": we have come on the scene and found a treasure not of our making. Given this, we ought to preserve this treasure in its natural state.

I do not wish to contest the appropriateness of "stewardship." It is the dichotomy between artificial (domesticated) and natural (wild) that strikes me as wrong-headed. I want to suggest that to the degree that "natural" means anything biologically, it means very little ethically. And, conversely, to the degree that "natural" is understood as a normative concept, it has very little to do with biology.

Environmentalists often express regret that we human beings find it so hard to remember that we are part of nature—one species among many others—rather than something standing outside of nature. I will not consider here whether this attitude is cause for complaint; the important point is that seeing us as part of nature rules out the environmentalist's use of the distinction between artificial–domesticated and natural–wild described above. *If we are part of nature, then everything we do is part of nature, and is natural in that primary sense.* When we domesticate organisms and bring them into a state of dependence on us, this is simply an example of one species exerting a selection pressure on another. If one calls this "unnatural," one might just as well say the same of parasitism or symbiosis (compare human domestication of animals and plants and "slave-making" in the social insects).

The concept of naturalness is subject to the same abuses as the concept of normalcy. *Normal* can mean *usual* or it can mean *desirable*. Although only the total pessimist will think that the two concepts are mutually exclusive, it is generally recognized that the mere fact that something is common does not by itself count as a reason for thinking that it is desirable. This distinction is quite familiar now in popular discussions of mental health, for example. Yet, when it comes to environmental issues, the concept of naturalness continues to live a double life. The destruction of wilderness areas by increased industrialization is bad because it is unnatural. And it is unnatural because it involves transforming a natural into an artificial habitat. Or one might hear that although extinction is a natural process, the kind of mass extinction currently being precipitated by our species is unprecedented, and so is unnatural. Environmentalists should look elsewhere for a defense of their policies, lest conservation simply become a variant of uncritical conservatism in which the axiom "Whatever is, is right" is modified to read "Whatever is (before human beings come on the scene), is right."

This conflation of the biological with the normative sense of "natural" sometimes comes to the fore when environmentalists attack animal liberationists for naive do-goodism. Callicott writes:

> . . . the value commitments of the humane movement seem at bottom to betray a world-denying or rather a life-loathing philosophy. The natural world as actually constituted is one in which one being lives at the expense of others. Each organism, in Darwin's metaphor, struggles to maintain its own organic integrity. . . . To live is to be anxious about life, to feel pain and pleasure in a fitting mixture, and sooner or later to die. That is the way the system works. *If nature as a whole is good, then pain and death are also good.* Environmental ethics in general require people to play fair in the natural system. The neo-Benthamites have in a sense taken the uncourageous approach. People have attempted to exempt themselves from the life death reciprocities of natural processes and from ecological limitations in the name of a prophylactic ethic of maximizing rewards (pleasure) and

minimizing unwelcome information (pain). To be fair, the humane moralists seem to suggest that we should attempt to project the same values into the nonhuman animal world and to widen the charmed circle—no matter that it would be biologically unrealistic to do so or biologically ruinous if, per impossible, such an environmental ethic were implemented.

There is another approach. Rather than imposing our alienation from nature and natural processes and cycles of life on other animals, we human beings could reaffirm our participation in nature by accepting life as it is given without a sugar coating. . . .[6]

On the same page, Callicott quotes with approval Shepard's remark that "the humanitarian's projection onto nature of illegal murder and the rights of civilized people to safety not only misses the point but is exactly contrary to fundamental ecological reality: the structure of nature is a sequence of killings."[7]

Thinking that what is found in nature is beyond ethical defect has not always been popular. Darwin wrote:

> . . . That there is much suffering in the world no one disputes. Some have attempted to explain this in reference to man by imagining that it serves for his moral improvement. But the number of men in the world is as nothing compared with that of all other sentient beings, and these often suffer greatly without any moral improvement. A being so powerful and so full of knowledge as a God who could create the universe, is to our finite minds omnipotent and omniscient, and it revolts our understanding to suppose that his benevolence is not unbounded, for what advantage can there be in the sufferings of millions of the lower animals throughout almost endless time? This very old argument from the existence of suffering against the existence of an intelligent first cause seems to me a strong one; whereas, as just remarked, the presence of much suffering agrees well with the view that all organic beings have been developed through variation and natural selection.[8]

Darwin apparently viewed the quantity of pain found in nature as a melancholy and sobering consequence of the struggle for existence. But once we adopt the Panglossian attitude that this is the best of all possible worlds ("there is just the right amount of pain," etc.), a failure to identify what is natural with what is good can only seem "world-denying," "life-loathing," "in a sense uncourageous," and "contrary to fundamental ecological reality."

Earlier in his essay, Callicott expresses distress that animal liberationists fail to draw a sharp distinction "between the very different plights (and rights) of wild and domestic animals."[9] Domestic animals are creations of man, he says. "They are living artifacts, but artifacts nevertheless. . . . There is thus something profoundly incoherent (and insensitive as well) in the complaint of some animal liberationists that the 'natural behavior' of chickens and bobby calves is cruelly frustrated on factory farms. It would make almost as much sense to speak of the natural behavior of tables and chairs."[10] Here again we see teleology playing a decisive role: wild organisms do not have the natural function of serving human ends, but domesticated animals do. Cheetahs in zoos are crimes against what is natural; veal calves in boxes are not.

The idea of "natural tendency" played a decisive role in pre-Darwinian biological thinking. Aristotle's entire science—both his physics and his biology—is articulated in terms of specifying the natural tendencies of kinds of objects and the interfering forces that can prevent an object from achieving its intended state. Heavy objects in the sublunar sphere have location at the center of the earth as their natural state; each tends to go there, but is prevented from doing so. Organisms likewise are conceptualized in terms of this natural state model:

> . . . [for] any living thing that has reached its normal development and which is unmutilated, and whose mode of generation is not spontaneous, the most natural act is the production of another like itself, an animal producing an animal, a plant a plant. . . .[11]

But many interfering forces are possible, and in fact the occurrence of "monsters" is anything but uncommon. According to Aristotle, mules (sterile hybrids) count as deviations from the natural state. In fact, females are monsters as well, since the natural tendency of sexual reproduction is for the offspring to perfectly resemble the father, who, according to Aristotle, provides the "genetic instructions" (to put the idea anachronistically) while the female provides only the matter.

What has happened to the natural state model in modern science? In physics, the idea of describing what a class of objects will do in the absence of "interference" lives on: Newton specified this "zero-force state" as rest or uniform motion, and in general relativity, this state is understood in terms of motion along geodesics. But one of the most profound achievements of Darwinian biology has been the jettisoning of this kind of model. It isn't just that Aristotle was wrong in his detailed claims about mules and women; the whole structure of the natural state model has been discarded. Population biology is not conceptualized in terms of positing some characteristic that all members of a species would have in common, were interfering forces absent. Variation is not thought of as a deflection from the natural state of uniformity. Rather, variation is taken to be a fundamental property in its own right. Nor, at the level of individual biology, does the natural state model find an application. Developmental theory is not articulated by specifying a natural tendency and a set of interfering forces. The main conceptual tool for describing the various developmental pathways open to a genotype is the norm of reaction. The norm of reaction of a genotype within a range of environments will describe what phenotype the genotype will produce in a given environment. Thus, the norm of reaction for a corn plant genotype might describe how its height is influenced by the amount of moisture in the soil. The norm of reaction is entirely silent on which phenotype is the "natural" one. The idea that a corn plant might have some "natural height," which can be augmented or diminished by "interfering forces" is entirely alien to post-Darwinian biology.

The fact that the concepts of natural state and interfering force have lapsed from biological thought does not prevent environmentalists from inventing them anew. Perhaps these concepts can be provided with some sort of normative content; after all, the normative idea of "human rights" may make sense even if it is not a theoretical underpinning of any empirical science. But environmentalists should not assume that they can rely on some previously articulated scientific conception of "natural."

APPEALS TO NEEDS AND INTERESTS

The version of utilitarianism considered earlier (according to which something merits ethical consideration if it can experience pleasure and/or pain) leaves the environmentalist in the lurch. But there is an alternative to Bentham's hedonistic utilitarianism that has been thought by some to be a foundation for environmentalism. Preference utilitarianism says that an object's having interests, needs, or preferences gives it ethical status. This doctrine is at the core of Stone's affirmative answer to the title question of his book *Should Trees Have Standing?*[12] "Natural objects can communicate their wants (needs) to us, and in ways that are not terribly ambiguous. . . . The lawn tells me that it wants water by a certain dryness of the blades and soil—immediately obvious to the touch—the appearance of bald spots, yellowing, and a lack of springiness after being walked on." And if plants can do this, presumably so can mountain ranges, and endangered species. Preference utilitarianism may thereby seem to grant intrinsic ethical importance to precisely the sorts of objects about which environmentalists have expressed concern.

The problems with this perspective have been detailed by Sagoff.[13] If one does not require of an object that it have a mind for it to have wants or needs, what is required for the possession of these ethically relevant properties? Suppose one says that an object needs something if it will cease to exist if it does not get it. Then species, plants, and mountain ranges have needs, but only in the sense that automobiles, garbage dumps, and buildings do too. If everything has needs, the advice to take needs into account in ethical deliberation is empty, unless it is supplemented by some technique for weighting and comparing the needs of different objects. A corporation will go bankrupt unless a highway is built. But the swamp will cease to exist if the highway is built. Perhaps one should take into account all relevant needs, but the question is how to do this in the event that needs conflict.

Although the concept of need can be provided with a permissive, all-inclusive definition, it is less easy to see how to do this with the concept of want. Why think that a mountain range "wants" to retain its unspoiled appearance, rather than house a new amusement park?[14] Needs are not at issue here, since in either case, the mountain continues to exist. One might be tempted to think that natural objects like mountains and species have "natural tendencies," and that the concept of want should be liberalized so as to mean that natural objects "want" to persist in their

natural states. This Aristotelian view, as I argued in the previous section, simply makes no sense. Granted, a commercially undeveloped mountain will persist in this state, unless it is commercially developed. But it is equally true that a commercially untouched hill will become commercially developed, unless something causes this not to happen. I see no hope for extending the concept of wants to the full range of objects valued by environmentalists.

The same problems emerge when we try to apply the concepts of needs and wants to species. A species may need various resources, in the sense that these are necessary for its continued existence. But what do species want? Do they want to remain stable in numbers, neither growing nor shrinking? Or since most species have gone extinct, perhaps what species really want is to go extinct, and it is human meddlesomeness that frustrates this natural tendency? Preference utilitarianism is no more likely than hedonistic utilitarianism to secure autonomous ethical status for endangered species.

Ehrenfeld describes a related distortion that has been inflicted on the diversity/stability hypothesis in theoretical ecology.[15] If it were true that increasing the diversity of an ecosystem causes it to be more stable, this might encourage the Aristotelian idea that ecosystems have a natural tendency to increase their diversity. The full realization of this tendency—the natural state that is the goal of ecosystems—is the "climax" or "mature" community. Extinction diminishes diversity, so it frustrates ecosystems from attaining their goal. Since the hypothesis that diversity causes stability is now considered controversial (to say the least), this line of thinking will not be very tempting. But even if the diversity/stability hypothesis were true, it would not permit the environmentalist to conclude that ecosystems have an interest in retaining their diversity.

Darwinism has not banished the idea that parts of the natural world are goal-directed systems, but has furnished this idea with a natural mechanism. We properly conceive of organisms (or genes, sometimes) as being in the business of maximizing their chances of survival and reproduction. We describe characteristics as adaptations—as devices that exist for the furtherance of these ends. Natural selection makes this perspective intelligible. But Darwinism is a profoundly individualistic doctrine. Darwinism rejects the idea that species, communities, and ecosystems have adaptations that exist for their own benefit. These higher-level entities are not conceptualized as goal-directed systems; what properties of organization they possess are viewed as artifacts of processes operating at lower levels of organization. An environmentalism based on the idea that the ecosystem is directed toward stability and diversity must find its foundation elsewhere.

GRANTING WHOLES AUTONOMOUS VALUE

A number of environmentalists have asserted that environmental values cannot be grounded in values based on regard for individual welfare. Aldo Leopold wrote in *A Sand County Almanac* that "a thing is right when it tends to preserve the integrity, stability, and beauty of the biotic community. It is wrong when it tends otherwise."[16] Callicott develops this idea at some length, and ascribes to ethical environmentalism the view that "the preciousness of individual deer, *as of any other specimen*, is inversely proportional to the population of the species."[17] In his *Desert Solitaire*, Edward Abbey notes that he would sooner shoot a man than a snake.[18] And Garrett Hardin asserts that human beings injured in wilderness areas ought not to be rescued: making great and spectacular efforts to save the life of an individual "makes sense only when there is a shortage of people. I have not lately heard that there is a shortage of people."[19] The point of view suggested by these quotations is quite clear. It isn't that preserving the integrity of ecosystems has autonomous value, to be taken into account just as the quite distinct value of individual human welfare is. Rather, the idea is that the only value is the holistic one of maintaining ecological balance and diversity. Here we have a view that is just as monolithic as the most single-minded individualism; the difference is that the unit of value is thought to exist at a higher level of organization.

It is hard to know what to say to someone who would save a mosquito, just because it is rare, rather than a human being, if there were a choice. In ethics, as in any other subject, rationally persuading another person requires the existence of shared assumptions. If this monolithic environmentalist view is based on the notion that ecosystems have needs and interests, and that these take total precedence over the rights and

interests of individual human beings, then the discussion of the previous sections is relevant. And even supposing that these higher-level entities have needs and wants, what reason is there to suppose that these matter and that the wants and needs of individuals matter not at all? But if this source of defense is jettisoned, and it is merely asserted that only ecosystems have value, with no substantive defense being offered, one must begin by requesting an argument: *why* is ecosystem stability and diversity the only value?

Some environmentalists have seen the individualist bias of utilitarianism as being harmful in ways additional to its impact on our perception of ecological values. Thus, Callicott writes:

> On the level of social organization, the interests of society may not always coincide with the sum of the interests of its parts. Discipline, sacrifice, and individual restraint are often necessary in the social sphere to maintain social integrity as within the bodily organism. A society, indeed, is particularly vulnerable to disintegration when its members become preoccupied totally with their own particular interest, and ignore those distinct and independent interests of the community as a whole. One example, unfortunately, our own society, is altogether too close at hand to be examined with strict academic detachment. The United States seems to pursue uncritically a social policy of reductive utilitarianism, aimed at promoting the happiness of all its members severally. Each special interest accordingly clamors more loudly to be satisfied while the community as a whole becomes noticeably more and more infirm economically, environmentally, and politically.[20]

Callicott apparently sees the emergence of individualism and alienation from nature as two aspects of the same process. He values "the symbiotic relationship of Stone Age man to the natural environment" and regrets that "civilization has insulated and alienated us from the rigors and challenges of the natural environment. The hidden agenda of the humane ethic," he says, "is the imposition of the anti-natural prophylactic ethos of comfort and soft pleasure on an even wider scale. The land ethic, on the other hand, requires a shrinkage, if at all possible, of the domestic sphere; it rejoices in a recrudescence of the wilderness and a renaissance of tribal cultural experience."[21]

Callicott is right that "strict academic detachment" is difficult here. The reader will have to decide whether the United States currently suffers from too much or too little regard "for the happiness of all its members severally" and whether we should feel nostalgia or pity in contemplating what the Stone Age experience of nature was like.

THE DEMARCATION PROBLEM

Perhaps the most fundamental theoretical problem confronting an environmentalist who wishes to claim that species and ecosystems have autonomous value is what I will call the *problem of demarcation*. Every ethical theory must provide principles that describe which objects matter for their own sakes and which do not. Besides marking the boundary between these two classes by enumerating a set of ethically relevant properties, an ethical theory must say why the properties named, rather than others, are the ones that count. Thus, for example, hedonistic utilitarianism cites the capacity to experience pleasure and/or pain as the decisive criterion; preference utilitarianism cites the having of preferences (or wants, or interests) as the decisive property. And a Kantian ethical theory will include an individual in the ethical community only if it is capable of rational reflection and autonomy. Not that justifying these various proposed solutions to the demarcation problem is easy; indeed, since this issue is so fundamental, it will be very difficult to justify one proposal as opposed to another. Still, a substantive ethical theory is obliged to try.

Environmentalists, wishing to avoid the allegedly distorting perspective of individualism, frequently want to claim autonomous value for wholes. This may take the form of a monolithic doctrine according to which the only thing that matters is the stability of the ecosystem. Or it may embody a pluralistic outlook according to which ecosystem stability and species preservation have an importance additional to the welfare of individual organisms. But an environmentalist theory shares with all ethical theories an interest in not saying that everything has autonomous value. The reason this position is proscribed is that it makes the adjudication of ethical conflict very difficult indeed. (In addition, it is radically implausible, but we can set that objection to one side.)

Environmentalists, as we have seen, may think of natural objects, like mountains, species, and ecosystems, as mattering for their own sake, but of artificial objects, like highway systems and domesticated animals, as having only instrumental value. If a mountain and a highway are both made of rock, it seems unlikely that the difference between them arises from the fact that mountains have wants, interests, and preferences, but highway systems do not. But perhaps the place to look for the relevant difference is not in their present physical composition, but in the historical fact of how each came into existence. Mountains were created by natural processes, whereas highways are humanly constructed. But once we realize that organisms construct their environments in nature, this contrast begins to cloud. Organisms do not passively reside in an environment whose properties are independently determined. Organisms transform their environments by physically interacting with them. An anthill is an artifact just as a highway is. Granted, a difference obtains at the level of whether conscious deliberation played a role, but can one take seriously the view that artifacts produced by conscious planning are thereby *less* valuable than ones that arise without the intervention of mentality.[22] As we have noted before, although environmentalists often accuse their critics of failing to think in a biologically realistic way, their use of the distinction between "natural" and "artificial" is just the sort of idea that stands in need of a more realistic biological perspective.

My suspicion is that the distinction between natural and artificial is not the crucial one. On the contrary, certain features of environmental concerns imply that natural objects are exactly on a par with certain artificial ones. Here the intended comparison is not between mountains and highways, but between mountains and works of art. My goal in what follows is not to sketch a substantive conception of what determines the value of objects in these two domains, but to motivate an analogy.

For both natural objects and works of art, our values extend beyond the concerns we have for experiencing pleasure. Most of us value seeing an original painting more than we value seeing a copy, even when we could not tell the difference. When we experience works of art, often what we value is not just the kinds of experiences we have, but, in addition, the connections we usually have with certain real objects. Routley and Routley have made an analogous point about valuing the wilderness experience: a "wilderness experience machine" that caused certain sorts of hallucinations would be no substitute for actually going into the wild.[23] Nor is this fact about our valuation limited to such aesthetic and environmentalist contexts. We love various people in our lives. If a molecule-for-molecule replica of a beloved person were created, you would not love that individual, but would continue to love the individual to whom you actually were historically related. Here again, our attachments are to objects and people as they really are, and not just to the experiences that they facilitate.

Another parallel between environmentalist concerns and aesthetic values concerns the issue of context. Although environmentalists often stress the importance of preserving endangered species, they would not be completely satisfied if an endangered species were preserved by putting a number of specimens in a zoo or in a humanly constructed preserve. What is taken to be important is preserving the species in its natural habitat. This leads to the more holistic position that preserving ecosystems, and not simply preserving certain member species, is of primary importance. Aesthetic concerns often lead in the same direction. It was not merely saving a fresco or an altar piece that motivated art historians after the most recent flood in Florence. Rather, they wanted to save these works of art in their original ("natural") settings. Not just the painting, but the church that housed it; not just the church, but the city itself. The idea of objects residing in a "fitting" environment plays a powerful role in both domains.

Environmentalism and aesthetics both see value in rarity. Of two whales, why should one be more worthy of aid than another, just because one belongs to an endangered species? Here we have the $n + m$ question mentioned in [the Introduction to this paper]. As an ethical concern, rarity is difficult to understand. Perhaps this is because our ethical ideas concerning justice and equity (note the word) are saturated with individualism. But in the context of aesthetics, the concept of rarity is far from alien. A work of art may have enhanced value simply because there are very few other works by the same artist, or from the same historical period, or in the same style. It isn't that the price of the item may go up with rarity; I am talking

about aesthetic value, not monetary worth. Viewed as valuable aesthetic objects, rare organisms may be valuable because they are rare.

A disanalogy may suggest itself. It may be objected that works of art are of instrumental value only, but that species and ecosystems have intrinsic value. Perhaps it is true, as claimed before, that our attachment to works of art, to nature, and to our loved ones extends beyond the experiences they allow us to have. But it may be argued that what is valuable in the aesthetic case is always the relation of a valuer to a valued object. When we experience a work of art, the value is not simply in the experience, but in the composite fact that we and the work of art are related in certain ways. This immediately suggests that if there were no valuers in the world, nothing would have value, since such relational facts could no longer obtain. So, to adapt Routley and Routley's "last man argument," it would seem that if an ecological crisis precipitated a collapse of the world system, the last human being (whom we may assume for the purposes of this example to be the last valuer) could set about destroying all works of art, and there would be nothing wrong in this.[24] That is, if aesthetic objects are valuable only in so far as valuers can stand in certain relations to them, then when valuers disappear, so does the possibility of aesthetic value. This would deny, in one sense, that aesthetic objects are intrinsically valuable: it isn't they, in themselves, but rather the relational facts that they are part of, that are valuable.

In contrast, it has been claimed that the "last man" would be wrong to destroy natural objects such as mountains, salt marshes, and species. (So as to avoid confusing the issue by bringing in the welfare of individual organisms, Routley and Routley imagine that destruction and mass extinctions can be caused painlessly, so that there would be nothing wrong about this undertaking from the point of view of the nonhuman organisms involved.) If the last man ought to preserve these natural objects, then these objects appear to have a kind of autonomous value; their value would extend beyond their possible relations to valuers. If all this were true, we would have here a contrast between aesthetic and natural objects, one that implies that natural objects are more valuable than works of art.

Routley and Routley advance the last man argument as if it were decisive in showing that environmental objects such as mountains and salt marshes have autonomous value. I find the example more puzzling than decisive. But, in the present context, we do not have to decide whether Routley and Routley are right. We only have to decide whether this imagined situation brings out any relevant difference between aesthetic and environmental values. Were the last man to look up on a certain hillside, he would see a striking rock formation next to the ruins of a Greek temple. Long ago the temple was built from some of the very rocks that still stud the slope. Both promontory and temple have a history, and both have been transformed by the biotic and the abiotic environments. I myself find it impossible to advise the last man that the peak matters more than the temple. I do not see a relevant difference. Environmentalists, if they hold that the solution to the problem of demarcation is to be found in the distinction between natural and artificial, will have to find such a distinction. But if environmental values are aesthetic, no difference need be discovered.

Environmentalists may be reluctant to classify their concern as aesthetic. Perhaps they will feel that aesthetic concerns are frivolous. Perhaps they will feel that the aesthetic regard for artifacts that has been made possible by culture is antithetical to a proper regard for wilderness. But such contrasts are illusory. Concern for environmental values does not require a stripping away of the perspective afforded by civilization; to value the wild, one does not have to "become wild" oneself (whatever that may mean). Rather, it is the material comforts of civilization that make possible a serious concern for both aesthetic and environmental values. These are concerns that can become pressing in developed nations in part because the populations of those countries now enjoy a certain substantial level of prosperity. It would be the height of condescension to expect a nation experiencing hunger and chronic disease to be inordinately concerned with the autonomous value of ecosystems or with creating and preserving works of art. Such values are not frivolous, but they can become important to us only after certain fundamental human needs are satisfied. Instead of radically jettisoning individualist ethics, environmentalists may find a more hospitable home for their values in a category of value that has existed all along.

NOTES

1. Mark Sagoff, "On Preserving the Natural Environment," *Yale Law Review* 84 (1974): 205–38; J. Baird Callicott, "Animal Liberation: A Triangular Affair," *Environmental Ethics* 2 (1980): 311–38; and Bryan Norton, "Environmental Ethics and Nonhuman Rights," *Environmental Ethics* 4 (1982): 17–36.

2. Peter Singer, *Animal Liberation* (New York: Random House, 1975), has elaborated a position of this sort.

3. Occasionally, it has been argued that utilitarianism is not just *insufficient* to justify the principles of environmentalism, but is actually mistaken in holding that pain is intrinsically bad. Callicott writes: "I herewith declare in all soberness that I see nothing wrong with pain. It is a marvelous method, honed by the evolutionary process, of conveying important organic information. I think it was the late Alan Watts who somewhere remarks that upon being asked if he did not think there was too much pain in the world replied, 'No, I think there's just enough'" ("A Triangular Affair," p. 333). Setting to one side the remark attributed to Watts, I should point out that pain can be intrinsically bad and still have some good consequences. The point of calling pain intrinsically bad is to say that one essential aspect of experiencing it is negative.

4. A parallel with a quite different moral problem will perhaps make it clearer how the environmentalist's holism conflicts with some fundamental ethical ideas. When we consider the rights of individuals to receive compensation for harm, we generally expect that the individuals compensated must be one and the same as the individuals harmed. This expectation runs counter to the way an affirmative action program might be set up, if individuals were to receive compensation simply for being members of groups that have suffered certain kinds of discrimination, whether or not they themselves were victims of discrimination. I do not raise this example to suggest that a holistic conception according to which groups have entitlements is beyond consideration. Rather, my point is to exhibit a case in which a rather common ethical idea is individualistic rather than holistic.

5. David Ehrenfeld, "The Conservation of Non-Resources," *American Scientist* 64 (1976): 648–56. For a theoretical discussion see Robert M. May, *Stability and Complexity in Model Ecosystems* (Princeton: Princeton University Press, 1973).

6. Callicott, "A Triangular Affair," pp. 333–34 (my emphasis).

7. Paul Shepard, "Animal Rights and Human Rites," *North American Review* (1974): 35–41.

8. Charles Darwin, *Autobiography of Charles Darwin* (London: Collins, 1876, 1958): 90.

9. Callicott, "A Triangular Affair," p. 330.

10. Callicott, "A Triangular Affair," p. 330.

11. Aristotle, *De Anima*, 415a26.

12. Christopher Stone, *Should Trees Have Standing?* (Los Altos: Kaufmann, 1972): 24.

13. Sagoff, "Natural Environment," pp. 220–24.

14. The example is Sagoff's, "Natural Environment," pp. 220–24.

15. Ehrenfeld, "The Conservation of Non-Resources," pp. 651–52.

16. Aldo Leopold, *Sand County Almanac* (New York: Oxford Press, 1949): 224–25.

17. Callicott, "A Triangular Affair," p. 326 (emphasis mine).

18. Edward Abbey, *Desert Solitaire* (New York: Ballantine Books, 1968), p. 20.

19. Garrett Hardin, "The Economics of Wilderness," *Natural History* 78 (1969): 176.

20. Callicott, "A Triangular Affair," p. 323.

21. Callicott, "A Triangular Affair," p. 335.

22. Here we would have an inversion, not just a rejection, of a familiar Marxian doctrine—the labor theory of value.

23. Richard Routley and Val Routley, "Human Chauvinism and Environmental Ethics," *Environmental Philosophy, Monograph Series 2*, edited by D. S. Mannison, M. A. McRobbie, and R. Routley (Australian National University, 1980): 154.

24. Routley and Routley, "Human Chauvinism," pp. 121–22.

BRYAN G. NORTON

TOWARD UNITY AMONG ENVIRONMENTALISTS

DOLLARS AND SAND DOLLARS

The poignancy of the dilemma facing advocates of environmental protection was dramatized for me in an encounter with a little girl. It was a sleepy, summer-beach Saturday and I was walking on a sandbar just off my favorite remnant of unspoiled beach on the north tip of Longboat Key, Florida. The little girl clambered up the ledge onto the sandbar, trying not to lose a dozen fresh sand dollars she cradled against her pushed-out and Dan-skinned stomach. I guessed she was about eight.

Thirty yards away, her mother and older sister were strip mining sand dollars—they walked back and forth through the colony, systematically scuffing their feet just under the soft sand on the bottom of the lagoon

TOWARD UNITY AMONG ENVIRONMENTALISTS by Norton (1991) 8,063w from pp. 3–11, 187–191, 238–243. © 1994 by Oxford University Press, Inc. By permission of Oxford University Press, USA.

and bending over to retrieve each disk as it was dis-lodged. Their treasure was held until collected by the eight-year-old transporter, whose feet were too small to serve as plowshares. Gathering the sand dollars at the point of excavation, she related them to the sand bar where a considerable pile was accumulating near the family's beached powerboat.

Many months earlier, I had noted how the fickle current through Longboat Inlet had begun to dump sand in a large crescent spit out into the Gulf of Mexico, forming a waist-deep lagoon. Next came a profusion of shore birds and the colony of sand dollars that mul-tiplied in the protected water, and then came the little girl and her family in their powerboat.

I was startled by the level of industrial organiza-tion; even the little girl executed her task with square-jawed efficiency. I engaged her as she emerged onto the sand bar. "You know, they're alive," I said.

"We can put 'em in Clorox at home and they'll turn white."

I asked whether they needed so many. She said, "My Momma makes 'em outta things."

I persisted: "How many does she need to make things?"

"We can get a nickel apiece for the extras at the craft store." I sighed and walked away. Our brief con-versation had ended in ideological impasse.

But I was troubled. How could my indignation be stilled so simply? Must the environmental con-science always give way to economic arguments? As I wandered off, I analyzed the short and unsatisfactory debate. I had begun by expressing my concern for life, for the several hundred green discs drying in the af-ternoon sun. Yet I'd have felt silly saying, "Put them back, they have a right to live." I'd have felt silly be-cause I don't think it's immoral for little girls to take a few sand dollars from the beach, any more than I had been immoral when I had red snapper for lunch that same day. I felt ill-equipped to make my point, about which I had little doubt, that the little girl should put most of the sand dollars back. If I admitted that sand dollars are just resources, like chunks of coal, salable in an available market, I could not at the same time argue that the little girl should put most of them back. Once sand dollars are economic resources, their value is counted in nickels. Therefore, I could not express my indignation in the language of economic aggregation.

Nor could I precisely express it in the language of rights of sand dollars, especially not if that language is given its accepted meaning in the tradition of John Locke and Thomas Jefferson. I did not find it self-evident that all sand dollars are created equal with little girls. Imagine instead that I had encountered the little girl with a half-dozen sand dollars sub-merged in seawater in her bucket and she had said, "We're going to cut up a couple and put the rest in our saltwater aquarium and watch 'em." If I appeal to the rights of sand dollars as individuals (or, even somewhat more weakly, to the intrinsic value of in-dividual sand dollars), I would have to object to this purely instrumental use of sand dollars in a rudimen-tary science lesson.

I faced the environmentalists' dilemma;[1] it was a dilemma, not because I did not know what I wanted the little girl to do, but because I could not coherently explain *why* she should put most of them back. If I chose the language of economic aggregation, I would have to say that she could take as many as she could use, up to the sustainable yield of the population. On this approach, more is better—the value of sand dollars is their market value, and I could not use this language to express the moral indignation I felt at the family's strip mining sand dollars and hauling them away in their powerboat. To apply, on the other hand, the language of moralism, I would have to decry the treatment of sand dollars as mere resources; I would have to insist that the little girl put *all* of them back. Neither language could express my indignation *and* my commonsense feeling that, while it was not wrong for the little girl to take a few sand dollars, she should put most of them back—the aggregationist approach to valuing sand dollars would prove too little, and the moral approach would prove too much.

Consider again the altered scenario in which the little girl takes a half-dozen home in her bucket to be cut up or imprisoned in an aquarium. Suppose the little girl takes them home, and they are, predictably, dead in a week, but that the little girl attains an inter-est in biology, eventually becoming a marine biologist who works to protect echinoids. If sand dollars had myths and legends, the sacrificed sand dollars might be worshiped as saviors of their king. And to the little girl, also, they would have been far more valuable than nickels. It is this sense of respect for sand dollars as living creatures, worth more than mere nickels but less than little, round people, that I could not express in either the strict language of moralism or in the language of simple economic aggregationism. I knew I wanted to get the little girl to put most of them back, and to respect the remaining ones as living creatures from whom we might learn something worthwhile; I was torn between two inadequate languages for expressing the value of sand dollars. In this sense, the environmentalists' dilemma is primarily a dilemma in values, conceptualizations, and worldviews more than a dilemma regarding actions and policies. It affects mainly how environmentalists explain and justify their policies, and only occasionally and tangentially does it affect those policies themselves.

My conversation on the beach represents, in microcosm, a larger dilemma facing environmentalists. I know that this practical and industrious family would not be moved by speeches for sand dollar liberation, however eloquent. That argument had been cut short, rendered irrelevant by the little girl's utilitarian reply. Sand dollars are by no means an endangered species, so that line of argument wasn't applicable.

Once I'd given up my moral high ground and asked only whether they needed so many, I'd conceded the utilitarian value of sand dollars. If a few are useful as commodities, surely more are correspondingly so. Of course I could have given her the conservationist line, that she should take only the sustainable yield of the colony. But I didn't have the faintest idea how to do a population model to show the little girl that she'd exceeded permissible levels of exploitation and, even if I could have, it wouldn't have satisfied me. I wanted to say more. So I fell silent stymied.

As in my conversation with the little girl, environmentalists often begin by implying that there is something morally wrong in the systematic exploitation of nature, something that cannot be fully expressed in the language of scientific resource management and maximum sustainable yields. When the heat is on, however, they retreat to the solid grounds of economic arguments, as I did when I tried the "How-many-do-you-need?" routine.

Environmentalists face two crises, one external and one internal. Against outsiders, they must continually defend their hard-won successes and urge new reforms against advocates of commercial interests who insist that environmental legislation ought never to disrupt "economic efficiency."

. . .

While these external challenges command the attention of environmentalists, a theoretical crisis, in language and worldviews, causes paralysis and miscommunication within the movement: There has emerged within the movement no single, coherent consensus regarding positive values, no widely shared vision of a future and better world in which human populations live in harmony with the natural world they inhabit.

The environmentalists' dilemma, which is primarily a dilemma in ultimate values, results in inarticulation when environmentalists discuss, explain, and justify their policies. To the extent that utilitarian and more preservationist approaches are seen as exclusive choices—as *opposed* rather than complementary values—it follows that I must choose between two inadequate languages to express my indignation. Neither the language of biocentric moralism nor the language of utilitarianism was adequate to explain and justify my view that the little girl should put most of the sand dollars back.

Historically, it has been useful to speak of two divisions of the environmental movement, "conservationists" and "preservationists," because some environmentalists have faced this dilemma squarely and have opted for one horn of it or the other. Most conservationists see natural ecosystems and other species as resources and are concerned mainly with the wise use of them. Finding its philosophical roots in the ideas of Gifford Pinchot, first official forester of the United States, this group judges all questions according to the criterion of the greatest good for the greatest number in the long run. The members of this faction, who are often trained as professional resource managers, have usually exerted their influence through control of governmental agencies such as the Forest Service and the Bureau of Reclamation. These environmentalists apparently diverge from the value system of their more commercially concerned opponents in industry only in insisting that costs and benefits of development and exploitative projects be computed over longer frames of time. Conservationism, or wise-use environmentalism, emphasizes avoidance of waste in the present pursuit of economic well-being. Thus, while natural ecosystems and other species are resources to be used wisely, they are very definitely to be *used* for human purposes. Pinchot once said, "The first great fact about conservation is that it stands for development. . . . [Its] first principle is the use of the natural resources now existing on this continent for the benefit of the people who live here now."[2]

Conservationists, especially those who are trained in resource management and those who work in government resource agencies, have generally applied concepts and a value system that tend toward economic reductionism, which interprets values as individual preferences expressed in free markets. The value of a sand dollar, on this view, is what someone is willing to pay for it. This reductionist approach has led to a long-standing collaboration of conservationists with economists and to a tendency to pose questions in quantified terms in which information on resource use and its consequences can be aggregated and presented in dollar terms.

Opposed to this group is another, often called "preservationists," which is committed to protecting large areas of the landscape from alteration. This faction derives its spirit and mandate from John Muir, who was the first president of the Sierra Club (in 1892). Muir saw his quest to preserve nature as a moral one. He rejected or reinterpreted the Christian views of monotheism and the Judaeo-Christian idea that nature exists for the sake of humans, arguing that the dogma "that the world was made especially for the uses of men" was the fundamental error of the age, and that "Every animal, plant, and crystal controverts it in the plainest terms." Muir railed against human arrogance that judges nature only according to human values:

> How narrow we selfish, conceited creatures are in our sympathies! how blind to the rights of our fellow mortals! Though alligators, snakes, etc., naturally repel us, they are not mysterious evils. They . . . are part of God's family, unfallen, undepraved, and cared for with the same species of tenderness and love as is bestowed on angels in heaven or saints on the earth.[3]

Initially, Pinchot, Muir, and their disparate group of followers worked together in opposition to the timber barons and other wasteful exploiters of natural resources. Both of these leaders, especially Pinchot, can today be thanked for creating the immense National Forest system. But Muir and Pinchot quarreled over grazing in the national forest preserves, and opposed each other bitterly over the plan to dam Hetch Hetchy, a beautiful canyon in Yosemite National Park. Pinchot allied himself with the developers: "As to my attitude regarding the proposed use of Hetch Hetchy by the city of San Francisco . . . I am fully persuaded that . . . the injury . . . [caused] by substituting a lake for the present swampy floor of the valley . . . is altogether unimportant compared with the benefits to be derived from its use as a reservoir."[4]

Muir stated the case for preservation: "These temple destroyers, devotees of ravaging commercialism, seem to have a perfect contempt for Nature, and instead of lifting their eyes to the God of the mountains, lift them to the Almighty Dollar."[5] "Dam Hetch Hetchy! As well dam for water-tanks the people's cathedrals and churches, for no holier temple has ever been consecrated by the heart of man."[6] Muir's pantheism implied that humans exist as part of a great spiritual whole. We worship that whole, the creator and sustainer of us all (which Muir identified with nature itself), he thought, by preserving and studying the most spectacular and beautiful areas as shrines. But Muir's heretical theological reasoning was never made explicit in his public writings. Indeed, he was referred to as a "man of God" by his contemporaries, and he appealed effectively to the powerful tradition in American protestantism, traceable to John Edwards, that saw nature as God's messenger to humans.

With scientifically trained professional conservationists lined up against Muir over Hetch Hetchy, he appealed to the public. In reviewing the revised edition of Muir's *Our National Parks* in 1909, the *New York Times* declared: "It is the sentimentalist like Mr. Muir who will rouse the people rather than the materialist."[7] And rouse them he did. Against all odds, Muir and his band of amateur preservationists held up the Hetch Hetchy Project for more than a decade. But when Woodrow Wilson took office and swung his weight in favor of the dam, the bill was forced through Congress by a narrow margin. The despondent Muir died shortly thereafter.[8] But his flaming rhetoric has created a powerful force of *moralism* in American environmentalism. That force has, from time to time, come to the fore as a political power, as when the Sierra Club, under the radicalized leadership of David Brower in the 1950s, succeeded in quashing a proposed dam in Dinosaur National Monument.

. . .

Muir's and Pinchot's respective successors in the modern environmental movement have more recently cooperated by maintaining an uneasy coalition. In general the environmental movement achieves its greatest unity when confronted with sustained attack on environmental policies, such as the one mounted by the President and his Secretary of the Interior James Watt in the early years of the Reagan presidency. The divergent elements also unify to defend specific resources and natural areas against threats of environmental degradation. In spite of these broad agreements on policy, however, the environmental movement still faces a dilemma: There has emerged within the movement no shared, positive understanding of the human relationship to the natural world; consequently, environmentalists lack a consensually accepted set of ideals and values. They therefore ricochet back and forth between two apparently exclusive worldviews and sets of value assumptions.

The choice between the legacies of Muir and Pinchot also presents itself to the environmentalist as a political dilemma: To follow Muir and grant rights to rattlesnakes is to embrace a radical ideal, one that appeals deeply to a small but committed minority that rejects the thoroughgoing anthropocentrism of our Judaeo-Christian tradition. This ideal, which elevates all nature to moral standing, calls into question the very idea motivating the American faith in Adam Smith's invisible hand, the idea that the path of economic development should be guided by a free market. Since nature has no dollars to spend, its voice cannot be heard in a marketplace; on any easily intelligible theory of the rights of rattlesnakes, these rights will limit the free choices of industrialists and consumers to buy and sell, to exploit and make profits. Embracing rights for rattlesnakes therefore damns the environmentalists, at least until there are fundamental changes in the value system of mainstream American

society, to appealing to a very small audience of quacks and cranks, who are out of step with the economic values of our period of history.

But to follow Pinchot, to forget Muir's impassioned moral rhetoric, reduces environmentalists to a role as one more interest group, fighting for clean air, for clean water, for protection of the National Parks. These activities appear, politically, as no more than spirited support for strongly felt preferences. Clean air must be "balanced" against jobs and economic growth, and if customers want clean air, they must be willing to pay for it in forgone jobs and dividends. On this side of the dilemma, environmentalists have lots of company. Everywhere there are interest groups shouting to protect their piece of a limited economic pie, and environmentalists are in danger of being entirely drowned out in the frantic melee, as everyone from profiteers to moral zealots attempts to focus governmental resources on social problems both real and imagined.

The environmentalists' dilemma, then, manifests itself in a number of ways. Among those who have opted for one or the other horn of the dilemma, it manifests itself in factionalism and distrust of those perceived to have joined the other camp. Other environmentalists remain uncommitted and uneasily embody both factions as internal personae. The resulting schizophrenia can paralyze us with inarticulation and humble us in a debate with an eight-year-old in the sand dollar business.

The dilemma is especially evident in accounts of, and commentaries on, the progress of environmentalism. Historians, social scientists, and philosophers who have discussed the movement have been quick to see dichotomies and polarities. For example, the historian Stephen Fox emphasizes that Pinchot derived his strength from professionals, scientific forest managers and bureaucrats who made their living in exploiting or regulating resource use, while Muir drew upon the enthusiasm of amateurs motivated by an almost-religious zeal for the preservation of nature. Political scientist Lester Milbrath notes that environmentalism is a value-oriented reform movement but insists that "we must make a distinction between environmentalists who wish retain the present socio-economic-political system and those who wish to drastically change it."[9] Philosophers who have discussed environmental values have concentrated almost exclusively on the dichotomy between anthropocentric (human-related) values and biocentric (nature-oriented) values.[10]

While these dichotomies do not all draw precisely the same distinction, they emphasize the polarization of environmentalists and suggest that the polarization derives from essential differences regarding values. For better or worse, these diverse but related dichotomies were given a generic characterization by Arne Naess when he distinguished a "shallow" from a "deep" ecology movement.[11] Naess' categories generally serve to characterize clusters of individuals who largely fit the Pinchot/conservationist mold and the Muir/preservationist mold, respectively. . . . When pressed for an essential difference marking this generic distinction, Naess and his followers emphasize that shallow ecologists retain the anthropocentric view that the natural world exists as resources for the use of humans, while deep ecologists adopt the biocentric view that nature, as well as man, has intrinsic value and that it should be preserved for its own sake.

While Naess's provocative and tendentious characterization of conservationists as "shallow" environmentalists represents an extreme example, it is generally true that academic and social commentary on the environmental movement has accepted and even reinforced the dilemma and the deep polarities it evokes. Historical and sociological accounts that emphasize the different training and backgrounds of conservationists and preservationists, as well as philosophical analyses that concentrate on the dichotomy between anthropocentric and biocentric value systems, conspire to reinforce these polarities. This emphasis on deep underlying differences in values forces us to wonder whether the environmental movement is a "movement" after all. If the individuals and groups often referred to as "environmentalists" embrace no common values, then why assume that the environmental movement has a true and lasting identity? If left unchallenged, these suspicions undermine the task at hand—to understand a movement. Presumably, it is a movement *toward something*. To emphasize only the disparity of visions pursued by the various contributing factions is, in effect, to deny that environmentalism is a movement at all.

. . .

THE EMERGING CONSENSUS

Environmentalists of different stripes, as far back as the days of Pinchot and Muir, have often set aside their differences to work for common goals. But those traditional cooperations were, it seemed, almost accidental collaborations originating in temporary political expediency. My hypothesis about the current environmental scene asserts a more than accidental growth in cooperation: In spite of occasional rancorous disputes, the original factions of environmentalism are being forced together, regardless of their value commitments.

For example, a growing sense of urgency led soil conservationists and preservationist groups to work together to pass the 1985 Farm Bill, even though they suffered some ill feelings along the way. Similarly, the National Wildlife Federation, a collection of sportsmen's organizations, and the Defenders of Wildlife advocate similar wetlands protection policies. While the value they place on wildlife is very different, the policy of protecting wildlife habitat represents a common-denominator objective, and the National Wildlife Federation is an effective lobbyer for legislation to protect nongame endangered species as well as game species and their habitats. Given our present scientific knowledge about wildlife populations, hunters and animal protectionists alike conclude that we must aggressively protect the remaining habitats for migrating waterfowl. Both groups would also agree on the importance of careful management to protect the reserves from the effects of human activity. This consensus signals the end of both the atomistic style of single-species game management characteristic of early conservationists and of isolationist preservationism, which in its extreme form repudiated management altogether.

Several gradual changes undermined the two extremes of management style. Not the least of these causes was the progressive development of the nation, which increased the likelihood of spillover effects of one activity on another. Another cause was the rapidly increasing demand for outdoor recreation that began in the forties and fifties and has developed steadily since. In general, as population expanded and diversified, more demands were put on more lands, and decisions to use land for productive purposes led to more and more direct conflicts. Leopold's land ethic, which recognizes that the land community is a larger system in which human activities must be integrated, has led environmentalists beyond both atomism and isolationism.

What this means, in more concrete terms, is that all environmentalists, regardless of their allegiance to diverging traditions, must seek to manage the entire mosaic that is the American landscape. If we are to maintain the productivity of American agriculture *and* protect biological diversity, if we are to maintain adequate water supplies for homes and industry *and* preserve some wild and scenic rivers, if we are to provide sufficient opportunities for outdoor activities *and* preserve the pristine nature of wilderness areas, we must make large-scale land use decisions with an eye to their larger context. A landscape that can accommodate all of the varied aspirations of Americans will have to be a patchy landscape, in which urban elements, productive elements, and pristine elements are arranged intelligently. Each of the patches must be managed according to the methods appropriate to goals that define its use, but those methods must also be designed to enhance, or at least not destroy, the values sought elsewhere in the mosaic. Further, the principles of this holistic management must be aesthetic as well as economic, and historically informed as well as forward-looking. But they must be applied to the entire context of human activities, not to specific activities viewed either atomistically or in isolation from other activities.

The forced abandonment of the two extreme styles of management associated with the old split between conservationists and preservationists provides a useful first stab at characterizing the emerging consensus. . . . [There is] a pattern of emerging policies that unite environmentalists in opposition to the policies usually favored by production-oriented developers. In each area—resource use, pollution control, protection of biological diversity, and land use policy—environmentalists advocate limits that guide the search for acceptable policy options, insisting against the simple economic Aggregators that there are constraints governing human exploitative activities. These constraints are usually stated in terms of "sustainability," but Leopold and modern environmentalists have gone beyond demand-oriented conceptions of sustainability to recognize limits inherent in the complexity and organizational integrity of larger ecological systems. Similarly, in pollution policy, environmentalists

have recognized constraints on activities that pollute the environment based on rights of other individuals to a healthy environment.

The common denominator of these obligations of resource users to limit their activities in these diverse cases cannot be understood as a commitment to any particular moral principle such as the moral equality of species or of interpersonal equity. The common element is structural: in each case, individually motivated behaviors, which can be understood as activities of economic man, are constrained because of the impacts those behaviors impose on their larger context. Environmentalists emphasize total diversity and biological complexity because the complex processes that constitute biological systems *are* the larger context of all life, human and nonhuman. Rapid alteration of those larger systems will cause serious disruption of both human and nonhuman activities. Land must therefore be used according to patterns that protect the complex processes of nature, so as to avoid destabilizing changes, changes in environing systems that are too rapid to allow human activities and nonhuman processes to respond and adapt.

This consensus represents, in one sense, a victory of Moralists over Aggregators. The essence of the simple aggregationist approach was to reduce all questions in environmental policy to calculations regarding economic efficiency, to judge all questions on a single scale. Environmentalists have rejected simple aggregationism and insist on moral constraints ranging from individual rights to clean air to imperatives to protect the integrity of ecological systems. Pinchot, however, has left his mark as well. In the spirit of the great compromiser, environmentalists play pragmatic politics—they seek their policies from among the politically viable options. In political practice, both moral and economic imperatives exercise a veto power.

. . .

In the context of political debate, individual rights, moral obligations to protect species, and scientifically articulated thresholds or constraints inherent in fragile ecological systems must all be factored into a process that sets goals, objectives, and standards for environmental programs. Economics are, of course, not irrelevant. Once goals and standards are set politically, it makes sense to use economic analysis to rank those alternative actions and policies regarding their efficiency in achieving the politically determined goal. Environmentalists know that economic interests will block environmental legislation if it is too costly. It behooves environmentalists, therefore, to propose the least costly option that will fulfill their goals.

Once the crucial distinction between setting goals and choosing means to achieve those goals is recognized, contextualism need not emphasize prohibitions and regulations in order to encourage actions that respect constraints. With an adequate conception of health for the overall ecological context in place, efforts can be shifted from prohibition and regulation to the creation of incentives that encourage individual actors to choose less polluting activities or to choose land uses that will help, rather than harm, efforts to protect biological diversity.

So, for all its emphasis on constraints, the emerging consensus among environmentalists need not operate, on a day-to-day basis, by constraining individual activities. . . . [Considering an] example of [a] farmer who clears his woodlot to plant wheat, the emerging consensus need not, when trends in farmers' behavior begin to press against thresholds inherent in the land community, regulate the farmer. It may, instead, choose to institute incentives that will encourage some farmers, either the one in question or others, to let a wheat field go fallow. The beauty of contextualism is that, once ecologically informed constraints are formulated, the society can undertake positive steps to encourage individuals to act in ways that counter dangerous trends. By combining a positive, biological conception of a healthy ecosystem with a program of incentives, the emerging consensus offers an alternative to simple reductionistic economics on the one side and onerous restrictions on the other. Following David Brower, this alternative can be called "restorationism." A positive definition of ecosystem health, one that incorporates human activities as long as they do not threaten thresholds inherent in ecological systems, opens the possibility of a truly positive ideal of humans living, creatively and freely, but harmoniously, within a larger, ecological context.

. . .

THE CONVERGENCE HYPOTHESIS

Contextual thinking encourages us to focus on environmental problems as involving impacts on multiple levels, in different scales, and it may occur that the same action can have different moral value, depending on the context in which it occurs. . . . Farmer Jones, who is deciding whether to clear his woodlot and plant wheat there, is acting within several nested systems simultaneously. On one level, he is acting within a free enterprise social and economic system, within which he will decide mainly in terms of his individual interests. Within a larger, synchronous system, Jones' action may be catastrophic to individual members of wild species, and widespread habitat destruction may raise serious moral concerns.

But the decision can also be evaluated for its impacts on the environment, or context. If Jones's woodlot is on a steep slope, or in a watershed that is prone to serious erosion of topsoil, the decision may have impacts on future uses of the land. On this level, Jones's decision can be seen as an event on the interface of a cultural and a natural system. If Farmer Jones's decision is part of a major trend, woodlot-clearing may trigger both accelerating changes in context and preemptive constraints. Since the future possibilities of individuals in the social system may depend on Jones's decision, it should be examined for impacts on this larger system, which can be expected to unfold in a longer scale of time.

A hierarchical system of value therefore opens the door to new possibilities for understanding environmental ethics. Environmentalists need not choose between the worldview of anthropocentric economic reductionism and biocentrism. Another possibility is an [sic] hierarchically organized and *integrated* system of values. Such a system aspires not to reduction to a single scale of value, but to second-level principles that explain and justify the proper realm, or system of application, of a variety of constraints associated with cultural and biological limits inherent in larger, regional systems.

Environmentalists need a unifying vision for the future. Contextualism can provide an integrative map for the consideration of environmental problems as they unfold outward into larger and larger systems, provided this structure is sufficient to support the common-denominator objectives shared by environmentalists of all stripes. I believe that an integrated system, a worldview that is unified by a commitment to a variety of values on various levels, holds more promise for unifying environmentalism than either of the monistic and exclusivist value approaches of economic or biocentric reductionists.

The key to the integrative approach . . . is a recognition that the vision of environmentalism is unified, not by a shared commitment to a single value, but by a shared belief in scientific naturalism and its associated belief that all things in nature are related in complex, hierarchically organized systems—the commitment to scientific naturalism, its associated natural aesthetic, and to a belief that humans evolve their personalities and cultures within environing systems that are, ultimately, shaped and limited by hierarchical constraints. Conservation is not a value-free science—its basic concept is ecosystem "health." But ecosystem health can be understood only in a cultural context—the land ethic is a locally determined sense of the good life, constructed with a careful and loving eye on the natural constraints imposed by the ecological and climatological context of that life.

Because of a shared commitment to scientific naturalism, environmentalists of differing value commitments gravitate toward similar policies, because they believe that a scientific understanding of ecological systems determines the available means to pursue their diverse goals. No long-term human values can be protected without protecting the context in which they evolved. Scientific naturalism thereby enforces upon all environmentalists a basically holistic, nonatomistic approach to environmental problems.

Although they are fascinated with the disagreement raging over the center, or centers, of environmental values, active environmentalists have made their peace over this issue by accepting an empirical hypothesis—the convergence hypothesis. Environmentalists believe that policies serving the interests of the human species as a whole, and in the long run, will serve also the "interests" of nature, and vice versa. When David Brower says, "Everything I have done as an environmentalist can be justified in human terms,"[12] a philosopher who assumes anthropocentrism and biocentrism are in conflict will conclude that Brower has no concern

for other species. But this is manifestly untrue. Like so many great environmentalists before him, he is relying on the convergence hypothesis.

While empirical in nature, the convergence hypothesis is not a precisely formulated hypothesis open to direct test in a series of dramatic experiments. Although cases where human interests and nonhuman interests seem to conflict are clearly relevant to the case, environmentalists will not surrender it easily. The convergence hypothesis therefore has a dual status as (1) a very general empirical hypothesis and (2) an article of environmentalists' faith. In this respect it plays a role similar to the medieval belief in the geocentric universe. It is an empirical hypothesis, but it is not to be given up at the drop of an epicycle.[13] Similarly, advocates of the convergence hypothesis, when faced with an example in which the interests of another species seem in conflict with long-term human interests, will dismiss it, claiming the example has not yet been viewed in sufficiently long temporal terms.

The convergence hypothesis functions, then, as an item of faith, guiding environmentalists' ongoing search for a rational solution to environmental problems. Since environmentalists believe that the hypothesis follows as a corollary of the systemic emphasis on contextualism, it is supported more by scientific theory than by particular observations. The convergence hypothesis rests firmly on the central insight of ecology—that all things in nature are interrelated. If humans damage the larger context shared by both humans and other species there will, eventually, be negative impacts on all species, humans included. But the hypothesis is also informed by another law of ecology, the law of complexity, which tells us that things are not equally related.

This approach is neither monistic—it posits no single moral principle determining morality in all subsystems—nor aggregative—it does not sum results across systems. It is hierarchical—it applies to each moral problem those locally determined principles determined by a careful look at the local and regional context shaping that problem. This approach integrates man into the ecological system—it avoids isolationism by recognizing that human cultures have, since time immemorial, shaped their context. Also, it avoids atomism, and tries for a broader integration of social values, including wilderness values and a hope for a future that respects and shares our values.

Ecological science, hierarchical thinking, and the convergence hypothesis work together to define the limits of individual behavior. But they do so not by meddling in every individual decision, but by encouraging local freedom and determination. Environmental constraints apply only when limits are approached. And a society with wisdom and foresight may be able to encourage enough diversity in voluntary land use decisions and careful management of publicly owned lands to require little interference with individual freedoms.

. . .

The convergence hypothesis is the hopeful hypothesis. If, in fact, there is no obligation to protect the context of human activities, or if the human species exists in fundamental opposition to the healthiness of ecological systems, there is no escape from the environmentalists' dilemma. Either we will be economic Aggregators and incrementally sell our cultural and natural heritage down the proverbial river, or we will embrace biospecies egalitarianism and be cursed with a choice between self-starvation and constant sin against that moral law. Contextualism and pluralism, however, hold out a reasonable hope for constructing a culturally *and* biologically determined conception of the good life—one recognizing that every species modifies its context, but also recognizing that the scales on which those modifications take place will determine the quality of all future life.

. . .

FRAGILE FREEDOMS

Back to the beach, one more time: When I saw the little girl with so many sand dollars, I was struck speechless because the languages readily available to an environmentalist were inadequate. Once it is admitted that sand dollars can be exchanged for nickels, the language of economic aggregation encourages the application of a maximization criterion. On that language, the little girl's utilitarian logic was unassailable: More is better. But the traditional language of morality, developed and honed over centuries and millennia to articulate rules for interpersonal behavior among human individuals, was equally inadequate: An extension of the language of individual rights and interests to apply to this interspecific situation would encourage a total prohibition on exploitation—and thus would deny the obvious fact that humans must sometimes exploit elements of nature in order to live and enjoy.

Our search for a way between the horns of the environmentalists' dilemma has led to an emphasis on the *context* of human actions. The family's strip-mining operation, on this view, is wrong primarily because it was inappropriate to its context. The exploitative activity turned the beach into the first stage of a trinket factory; building sandcastles and learning about nature had lost out to an economic perspective. That little remnant of beach was saved for little girls, but for little girls to learn to love and respect their natural context, not for them to learn to exploit its products.

I wish now that I had used the incident as an opportunity (with her parents' consent, of course) to teach the little girl some ecology and natural history. I'll bet I could have interested her in the way that sand dollars make a living. I could turn over a sand dollar so that the little girl could see and feel the kneading of the hundreds of little sucker-feet by which the sand dollars pull themselves through the sand while passing some of the particles through their bodies, digesting diatoms from the particles as they pass through and are then flushed out.

I'll bet the little girl would have been fascinated to see that the sand dollar has a pentagonal structure analogous to our head, arms, and legs, but that the sand dollar's nervous system is undifferentiated. Therefore the behavioral repertoire of sand dollars is far more limited than our own. Sand dollars' life in predator-rich lagoons encouraged them to invest in external armour rather than mobility.

This approach, turning the beach into a natural laboratory rather than a trinket factory, is in keeping with the environmentalists' long-standing commitment to the educability of the American public. They believe that if enough people adopt the ecological viewpoint, their approach to environmental policy will win out and their common-denominator goals will be achieved. The natural history approach to the situation on the beach is, in other words, to follow Thoreau, Muir, and Leopold in putting faith in the power of observation and experience to transform worldviews. Here, it is possible to say, is the single greatest failure of the environmental movement. While groups have been quite successful in educating their members through slick membership magazines, they have made less headway in educating the general population. For example, few schools teach conservation in any systematic way, and most science texts do no more than mention conservation in passing.

But I should not, as part of my lesson, insist that the little girl value the sand dollars *in their own right*. That would be like taking the little girl to a symphony concert and trying to teach her to value one note or to an art museum and trying to teach her to value one brush stroke. We must value nature from our point of view *in a total context*, which includes our cultural history and our natural history. Nature must be valued, from the ecological–evolutionary viewpoint of environmentalists, in its full contemporary complexity and in its largest temporal dynamic.

And this crucial lesson of our dependence on the larger systems of nature can be learned from sand dollars—for sand dollars, just like humans, act within an ecological context. The success of their activities depends on a relatively stable context to which they have adapted. The freedom and creativity of sand dollars is a *constrained* freedom, freedom to adapt to a limiting context. We differ from sand dollars in having a repertoire of behaviors almost infinitely more complex than theirs. But our freedom and creativity is no less than theirs a constrained freedom.

The freedom to collect sand dollars, to catch rockfish and bluefish, and to propel ourselves about the countryside by burning petroleum are all fragile freedoms. They are freedoms that depend on the relatively stable environmental context in which they have evolved. If I could, then, have used the incident on the beach to teach the little girl that sand dollars embody an ancient wisdom from which we can learn, and also to illustrate for her the way in which our activities— just like the activities of sand dollars—are possible, and gain meaning and value, only in a larger context, I would have progressed a good way toward the goal of getting the little girl to put most of the sand dollars back. The strip-mining activities of the family were not wrong in the absolute terms of interpersonal morality;

they were inappropriate on a beach set aside for relaxation and enjoyment of nature.

The family's reaction, upon finding sand dollars in the lagoon, was to treat them as an economic resource. But the power boat gave me a clue that they did not really need the nickels, and the little girl's dogged efforts convinced me that she was the loser on the beach. Trips to the beach should be explorations of a larger world than the limited sphere of economic activity in which the little girl will no doubt spend most of the rest of her life. Like Muir and Leopold I should have emphasized the ecstatic aspect of observation and natural history studies. I could have avoided the environmentalists' dilemma by encouraging the little girl to see the world through a lens larger than a cash register. Then, she might have killed some sand dollars to study them, but she would still have *respected* sand dollars as living things with a story to tell. I hope she would also have realized, then, that sand dollars are more valuable alive than dead.

Moralists among environmental ethicists have erred in looking for a value in living things that is *independent* of human valuing. They have therefore forgotten a most elementary point about valuing anything. Valuing always occurs from the viewpoint of a conscious valuer. Since I doubt that sand dollars are conscious, I doubt they are loci of value-expression. To recognize that only the humans are valuing agents at the beach, however, need not enforce the conclusion that sand dollars will be valued only from the narrow perspective of human economics. If the little girl can learn to value sand dollars in a larger perspective, an ecological context in which sand dollars are fellow travelers in a huge, creative adventure, she will have undertaken the first tentative steps toward thinking like a lagoon.

Charter captains see restrictions on the taking of bluefish as unjustified infringements of their freedoms. That, as Leopold recognized, represents a failure of *perception*, not value. The captains, used to apparently unlimited bounty from nature, are unable to think like the bay. Environmentalism will succeed if it educates the public so that all citizens are capable of seeing environmental problems at the interface of two systems—the slow-changing systems of nature that change in ecological and evolutionary time and the relatively fast-changing systems of human economics. To the extent that individual freedoms to take bluefish or rockfish depend on the complex, usually slow-changing, systems of nature, they are fragile freedoms. They depend upon, and gain meaning and value within, the larger natural context in which they are pursued.

. . .

We are left with the disturbing question: How onerous must the restrictions be on future human activities? The answer to this question, I think, must be "It depends." It depends on how we conceive those restrictions. If we, as at present, conceive nature as a machine capable of producing unlimited amounts of a small number of economically useful items, we will view nature and our opportunities statically. If charter captains, who once could offer their clients unlimited catches of bluefish, insist on that freedom indefinitely, they will destroy that freedom. Bluefish catches will eventually be limited by rules and regulations or by natural declines in bluefish stocks. The outlook for human freedom from this static viewpoint looks bleak.

But consider an analogy. Whaling is in the process of fading away as an economically feasible activity. Whale stocks are so depleted that the search becomes ever more expensive. Technology has found substitutes for all but the most esoteric uses of whale oil. Environmentalists therefore insist that whaling is no longer an appropriate activity, even if there are governments that will prop up the dying industry with economic subsidies. If environmentalists and others succeed in the desperate effort to save populations of the great whales, however, there will be a whole new, nonconsumptive, and dynamic industry, whale watching, that will take its place. Children of future generations will pay, it can be assumed, to watch a great whale swim playfully under their boat and breach a few yards away. The fragile freedom to kill whales will be replaced with a more secure freedom, a freedom constant with the life history of these great, but not reproductively prolific, creatures.

And this suggests the proper answer to charter boat captains who are justifiably wary of catch restrictions given the present attitudes of charter renters. The charter captains have an obligation to educate as well as profit from their customers. The whale-watching case suggests how salable a natural spectacle is. Participation in a bluefish run should be reward enough—and it would be if fishermen carried away information and understanding as well as a couple of bluefish. Charter captains should teach themselves some marine ecology and pass it on as a part of their explanations of why, next year, we're going to release all bluefish but three per fisherman. This is the proper response to a demand for bluefish that cannot be met indefinitely: educate the public and have them pay for it as part of the skills of a competent charter captain. If charter captains will not educate their fishermen, who will?

. . .

Our freedom and creativity may appear limited when looked at from a conservative viewpoint that insists on pressing fragile freedoms, such as the freedom to take bluefish, rockfish, or whales to their limit. But . . . we have the ability to learn, through science, the limitations of rockfish and whales to reproduce, and to encourage alternative, more adaptive behaviors before an element of nature's productive fabric is destroyed.

And here we see the potentially true nobility of the human species. Unlike the other forces of nature, which react unconsciously to their surroundings, mainly through the weeding out of unfit individuals, we are conscious beings who can adapt consciously to our changing environment. If we can progress beyond the environmentalists' dilemma, which encourages us to understand and value nature in the limited context of human economics or in the limited context of human ethics, and value nature from our point of view, but in its full and glorious context, there is yet hope for the human species.

NOTES

1. Cf. David Ehrenfeld, "The Conservationist's Dilemma," in *The Arrogance of Humanism* (New York: Oxford University Press, 1978). I have modified Ehrenfeld's terminology because . . . it has been helpful to use the term "conservationist" more narrowly, to represent only one faction of the early environmental movement.

2. Gifford Pinchot, *Breaking New Ground* (Washington, D.C.: Island Press, 1987; originally published 1947), p. 261.

3. John Muir, *A Thousand-Mile Walk to the Gulf* (Boston: Houghton Mifflin, 1981; first published 1916), pp. 98–99.

4. Roderick Nash, *Wilderness and the American Mind*, 3rd ed. (New Haven: Yale University Press, 1982), p. 161.

5. Ibid., p. 161.

6. Ibid., p. 168.

7. Stephen Fox, *John Muir and His Legacy* (Boston: Little, Brown, 1981), p. 121.

8. Ibid., pp. 145–46.

9. Lester W. Milbrath, *Environmentalists: Vanguard for a New Society* (Albany: State University of New York Press, 1984), p. 72.

10. Bryan G. Norton, "Conservation and Preservation: A Conceptual Rehabilitation," *Environmental Ethics* 8 (1986): 195–220.

11. Arne Naess, "The Shallow and the Deep, Long-Range Ecology Movement: A Summary," *Inquiry* 16 (1973): 95–100.

12. Interview with author, July 28, 1987.

13. For a more recent analogue, consider the economists' belief in the Axiom of Abundance. That axiom, which asserts that there exist suitable substitutes for every natural resource, cannot be disproven; it can always be said that we just have not found the best substitute as yet. This feature of certain beliefs—that they are empirical in form, but seem *impervious* to refutation—is common among the most basic axioms of a worldview.

KATIE MCSHANE

ANTHROPOCENTRISM VS. NONANTHROPOCENTRISM
Why Should We Care?

For at least the last 30 years now, there has been a running debate among environmental ethicists about whether anthropocentrism can serve as an adequate foundation for environmental ethics. The most recent discussions of this issue have concerned Bryan Norton's "convergence hypothesis"—the view that if we have a suitably sophisticated anthropocentrism, then in practice, anthropocentrism and nonanthropocentrism will converge.[1] That is to say, they will both recommend the same environmentally responsible behaviours and polities. If this is so, then one might think the dispute between them is merely academic—a matter for "intramural philosophical debate," but nothing more.[2]

In this paper, I grant for the sake of argument that anthropocentric and nonanthropocentric ethics will converge when it comes to the policies and behaviours they recommend. I also grant that as practical ethicists, we should demand that there be an issue of practical importance at stake before we commit our time and energy (not to mention journal space, etc.) to addressing a theoretical dispute. If two theories have exactly the same practical implications, we shouldn't spend our time worrying about what other differences there

Katie McShane, "Anthropocentrism vs. Nonanthropocentrism: Why Should We Care?" Environmental Values 16, no. 2 (2007): 169–185.

might be between them. What I want to explore here is the question of what counts as a "practical implication" of an ethical theory. In practical ethics, we often talk as though ethical questions are just questions about which actions to take or which policies to adopt. There is, however, a long history in ethics of being concerned with questions of how to feel, what attitudes to take toward different things in the world, which things to care about and how to care about them.[3] The aim of this paper is to consider what significance the differences between anthropocentrism and nonanthropocentrism might have from the point of view of these questions.

1. BACKGROUND

. . .

Proponents of nonanthropocentrism often claim that it is precisely the view that "it's really all about *us*" that got us into all of these environmental messes in the first place. In order to solve our environmental problems and avoid running into them again in the future, they claim, ethics needs to recognise the folly of such self-centeredness and develop an ethic of, as Tom Regan puts it, respect for nature rather than mere use of nature.[4] Other nonanthropocentrists claim that the wrong-headedness of anthropocentrism is evident once we take seriously what ecology has taught us about our relationship to the rest of the natural world. The more we understand about how the world works, they argue, the more evident it is that we are but one species among many, that we live interdependently with other parts of the natural world, and that we aren't as different from the rest of nature as we once might have thought. Getting clear about our ecological place in the world is humbling, and the claim is that this humility ought to carry over to claims about our moral place in the world.[5]

On the other side, anthropocentrists claim that insofar as environmental problems are due to ethical wrong-headedness, the mistake we've made isn't in thinking that only human interests matter directly, but rather in being ill-informed and short-sighted about what our interests really are. If we take seriously the interest of future generations of humans and get clear about all of the ways in which the health of the natural environment improves the quality of human lives, we will have all the arguments we'd ever need to justify

caring about the health of the environment, behaving in ways that are environmentally responsible, and adopting policies that are environmentally sustainable.[6]

Furthermore, anthropocentrists claim, anthropocentric approaches have a number of advantages over nonanthropocentric approaches. First, there are worries about whether nonanthropocentric ethics can be made philosophically viable. Though I won't rehearse these debates here, the most well-known versions of nonanthropocentrism have been charged with metaphysical, epistemological, and/or normative inadequacy.[7] Anthropocentric ethics seems to have a better track record in this regard. Second, most traditional ethical theories are roughly anthropocentric in nature, so adopting anthropocentrism makes available a wide variety of theoretical resources that have been developed to explain, defend, and apply these theories. This is not true for nonanthropocentrism. Third, as Bryan Norton has pointed out, most policy-makers and social scientists are anthropocentrists, and anthropocentric assumptions underlie most of the work that they do. By granting their assumption of anthropocentrism, environmental ethicists open the door for more productive collaborative relationships with people who have a significant impact on shaping environmental policies.[8] And finally, anthropocentrism might offer hope as a strategy for rejecting the "people vs. nature" formulation that so many environmentalists find frustrating. If what's good in nature is ultimately a matter of what's good for people, then (we might think) there can't really be any deep conflict here.

From the point of view of the anthropocentrist, then, our theory choice looks like this: We have on the one hand nonanthropocentrism, which recommends environmentally responsible behaviours, but is fairly radical, unpopular, and theoretically problematic. On the other hand we have anthropocentrism, which recommends the same environmentally responsible behaviours, but requires only minor changes in ethical beliefs that are already widely accepted, and is theoretically well worked out. If this is what we're deciding between, the choice looks obvious—only a fool would choose the nonanthropocentric route.

Before jettisoning nonanthropocentrism, however, I think it would be useful to think carefully about what exactly we would be giving up. My suspicion is that we would be giving up more than this story suggests.

In order to determine whether this is so, we should first get clear about how claims like those that constitute anthropocentrism and nonanthropocentrism fit into the structure of ethical theories in general.

2. THE CLAIMS OF ANTHROPOCENTRISM AND THE STRUCTURE OF ETHICAL THEORIES

Anthropocentrism claims that the nonhuman world and/or its parts have value only because, and insofar as, they directly or indirectly serve human interests. It is worth noticing that in the first instance, this is not a claim about how we ought to behave. It is a claim about which features of nonhuman things can make them matter in which ways. Anthropocentrism says that only one feature—serving human interests, directly or indirectly—can make a nonhuman thing valuable. Claims about why something has value are claims about why we, as moral agents, have reason to care about the thing.[9] More precisely, they are claims about why the thing is worth caring about.[10] Anthropocentrism says that when it comes to the nonhuman world, the only acceptable reasons of this kind are those that show a connection to the satisfaction of human interests. These claims about why we moral agents should care about a thing serve as the grounds for ethical norms concerning the thing. These ethical norms come in at least two flavours: norms for action (what we ought to do), and norms for feeling (how we ought to feel).[11] The picture we have so far, then, is this: anthropocentrism limits the kinds of claims we can (justifiably) make about why certain things are worth caring about. The worry about anthropocentrism can be understood as the worry that since these claims serve to ground our ethical prescriptions, limiting the claims we can make might limit the kinds of ethical prescriptions we can offer. The worry about Norton's convergence hypothesis, then, is a worry about what sorts of limits will be placed on our norms for action: if we accept anthropocentrism, will we still have a theory that can tell us to do the right things? The convergence hypothesis answers this question "yes," and I will not challenge that claim here.[12]

But if anthropocentrism and nonanthropocentrism both tell us to do the same thing, and the right thing, how much is left for us to worry about? How different *are* anthropocentrism and nonanthropocentrism at this point? To see what differences remain, let's consider how the anthropocentrist can make her case for convergence when it comes to norms for action. Anthropocentrism tells us that the nonhuman world has value only insofar as it serves human interests. On this view, if I were to claim that some part of nonhuman nature has value in its own right, independently of human interests, I would be incorrect. Likewise, if I were to claim that some part of nonhuman nature has value because it serves the interests of another part of nonhuman nature, though these two parts don't serve human interests in any way, I would also be mistaken. But to say this isn't to say that anthropocentrism can't tell me to *act as if* parts of the nonhuman world had value in their own right. It might serve human interests, for example, to treat some part of the natural world as though it had a kind of value—sacredness, say—that doesn't depend at all on nature's furthering our interests. Perhaps if we treated some parts of our world as though they were sacred, we would all be better off for it. Anthropocentrism can wholeheartedly endorse such treatment.

To grant the truth of the convergence hypothesis is to grant that, when it comes to claims about what we should do, both anthropocentric and nonanthropocentric reasons will support taking the same actions—i.e., both types of theory will produce the same action-norms. The justifications that they offer for these action-norms—i.e., the reasons they give for why we should take these actions—will be different, of course. But do we have any independent interest in differences among reasons if they lead to the same recommendations for action? Perhaps we would if we thought that some of the reasons offered were morally unacceptable. So, for example, a theory that says "be environmentally good citizens because Hitler would want you to" would be objectionable because the reason it offers is itself objectionable. But nonanthropocentrists do not find appeals to human interests troubling in their own right: they just object to the claim that these are the *only* reasons to which one can appeal.[13] So nonanthropocentrists would happily grant that reasons of human interest *are* reasons that justify environmentally responsible policies and behaviours; they just don't think these are the only reasons that do so. Nevertheless, anthropocentrists have given them good ethical recommendations on the basis of reasons they accept—what more could an ethicist want?

3. ANTHROPOCENTRISM AND QUESTIONS OF HOW TO FEEL

The answer, I think, is to be found when we consider what effect anthropocentrism might have on our norms for feeling. Questions of how to feel aren't as widely discussed in ethics as questions of what to do are, but they are clearly an important part of the ethical picture.[14] While there isn't room here to rehearse all of the arguments for the moral importance of norms for feeling, I will briefly sketch a few of the most important considerations.[15] First, and perhaps most obviously, how we feel significantly affects how we act—if I like you, I'm more likely to be nice to you, etc. If ethics cares about how we act, then it ought to care about how we feel.

Second, matters of feeling are an important part of what we care about in our social relationships, and not just because we think that how a person feels affects how she acts. For this reason, our interest in questions of how to feel isn't merely derivative of our interest in questions of what to do. I want my friends to like me, not just to act as though they do. And I don't just want them to like me because I think that their taking this attitude will make them behave more nicely toward me. My desire isn't that my friends adopt whatever attitude will produce the nicest behaviour; rather, my desire is that their behaviour express genuinely friendly feelings. As contemporary virtue ethicists have pointed out, our everyday moral judgments of people already take into account assessments of their feelings, not just their actions.[16] So, imagine someone who felt she was better than everyone else though she didn't let this smug sense of superiority affect her actions, or imagine someone who hated people of other races but never acted on these feelings. While I'm sure we would be glad that these people's feelings didn't influence their actions, we'd probably still be concerned about the fact that they had these feelings at all. People can take attitudes toward the world that we find morally troubling even when these attitudes don't lead them to perform bad actions.

Third, questions of how to feel are also central in thinking about how to direct our own lives. When I think about what I'm aiming for in trying to be morally good, I don't just think about which actions to perform. I also think about how to feel about the world. I want to be emotionally oriented toward things in the right way. I don't just want to know whether I should act in a more sympathetic manner toward my friends; I want [to] know whether I should be more sympathetic to them—and being sympathetic necessarily involves feeling sympathy. I don't just want to know whether I should act more proudly; I want to know whether I should be more proud—and being proud necessarily involves feeling pride. Our moral lives are lived from the inside, in the first person, and from this point of view we have an interest in more than just satisfying the claims that others legitimately make on us. We care not only about generating properly the "outputs" (actions, behaviours, choices, etc.), but also about the inner life of the being who produces those outputs. We evaluate the moral goodness of our lives as lived from within. In the cases of both ourselves and others, then, norms for feeling are expressions of the independent moral interest that we take in the inner lives of human beings.[17]

Finally, questions about how we should feel about the world can't be reduced to questions about which ways of feeling best serve our interests, for questions about how to feel are also in part questions about which feelings are called for by their objects—which feelings are deserved, apt, or fitting. Discovering that it would be in my interest to feel admiration for my boss doesn't fully answer the question of whether I should admire her.[18] There is also the question of whether she deserves admiration—of whether she really is admirable.

So we do have an ethical interest in answering questions about how to feel, and this doesn't just amount to wanting to know which actions to perform or which feelings it would be in our interest to have. But what effect would anthropocentrism have on the way that we answer such questions? To answer this, let's consider how the central claim of anthropocentrism might conflict with certain kinds of feelings.

4. FEELINGS AND THE SOURCES OF VALUE

Some attitudes that we can take toward a thing are incompatible with thinking that its value is entirely dependent on its satisfaction of our interests. Take the case of love, for example. Suppose that I claim to love my friend, but I also claim that she only has value to the extent that she serves my interests. If she didn't serve my interests, I claim, she would have absolutely no value whatsoever. If I said this, you might well wonder whether I was being serious when I claimed to love her. Would it help my case if I told you a long and complex story about all the ways in which she serves my interests? I could explain that she brings joy to my life, that she inspires me to be a better person, that she allows me to see the world in new ways, and that her friendship is essential to having my life go the way I had always hoped it would go. Still, the story I am telling is an entirely self-centred one, and that is precisely the problem. The love involved in friendship is an *other*-centred emotion.[19] To love something in this way is in part to see it as having value that goes beyond what it can do for you. Certainly it does serve our interests to participate in loving relationships. But to love a friend is in part to deny that her value is just a matter of her serving your interests.[20]

I think that there are other attitudes besides love of which this is also true. Respect certainly seems to work this way; awe (at least in some manifestations) might do so as well. To respect something is in part to see it as making a claim on your moral attention in its own right. It is to attribute to the thing a kind of independent standing in your scheme of "things that matter." To be in awe of something is in part to see it as having a kind of greatness that goes beyond you—beyond your needs, interests, or attitudes. In fact, the awe that we feel toward some things (the might of the ocean, the power of a volcanic eruption, the size of the universe) seems to be enhanced by the fact of their utter indifference to our interests. Thus while it might be in our interest to live lives that involve feeling love, respect and awe for certain parts of the world, to take up these valuing attitudes is precisely to see the world as valuable in ways other than serving our interests.[21] If this is right, then at least some of the attitudes that we take toward things would be undermined by the belief that they only have value insofar as they serve our interests. Holmes Rolston makes a similar point about certain religious attitudes that one might take toward nonhuman nature. He says,

> If nature is used as a hospital or school for character, that is clearly an instrumental use, but what shall we say when nature is used as a church? Is this too an instrumental use—to generate human religious experiences, nothing more? Perhaps. But some of these experiences will involve a recognition of God's creation, or the Ultimate Reality, or a Nature sacred in itself. In fact, one profanes such experiences and nature alike to see nature as merely instrumental and otherwise devoid of value.[22]

It is worth noticing that this incompatibility is much more of a problem in the case of feelings than it is in the case of actions. While anthropocentrism can tell me to act as though something has value in its own right even when I know it doesn't, it's much less clear that anthropocentrism can tell me to feel as though something has value in its own right even when I know it doesn't.[23] If I think that your only value is what you can do for me, I might be able to *act* as though I love you if I judge it in my self-interest to do so. But it's not at all clear that I can actually *love* you, for loving you requires me to see you as having a value that is independent of me. The problem here is that because many emotions have a cognitive element, norms for feeling are more tightly connected to beliefs about value than norms for action are. I can act as if A matters even while believing that A doesn't matter. But because part of what it is to feel that A matters is to think of A as mattering,[24] it's not clear that I can feel that A matters while believing that A doesn't matter. Perhaps I can; the human mind is complex enough that it may be psychologically possible to think of the world as being one way while believing that it is another. But one thing is certain: the world can't *be* both ways. While philosophers of the emotions disagree on the precise nature of the cognitive aspects of the emotions, they agree on its direction of fit. Knowledge, belief, perception, discernment: all of these cognitive states aim to fit the world—that is, they aim to accurately describe the way the world is. The problem for the person who both thinks of A as mattering and believes that A doesn't matter is that she has two cognitive states, both of which aim to be correct descriptions of the world, and they can't both be right. What kind of problem this is—whether it is a form of irrationality, logical impossibility, cognitive dissonance—will depend on one's overall theory of rationality. My only claim here is that most of us take these states to be a problem, and that if we do so, we will have reason to worry about anthropocentrism.[25]

The upshot of this is that the central claim of anthropocentrism is incompatible with certain kinds of attitudes we might want to take toward the natural world—love, respect and awe; perhaps others as well. Thus according to anthropocentrism, the way that these attitudes involve seeing the value of the natural world must be fundamentally incorrect. If to love something is to think of it as having a kind of value that doesn't depend on us and our interests, then according to anthropocentrism, to love the natural world is to make a mistake about its value.

So even if anthropocentrism doesn't change what we think it makes sense to do in the world, it might well change how we think it makes sense to feel about the world. In particular, if I am right that the central claim of anthropocentrism is incompatible with the attitudes of love, respect and awe, then insofar as anthropocentrism is true, we are making a kind of mistake when we love the land, respect nature, are in awe of the vastness of the universe, or take other attitudes that are incompatible with thinking that their object's only value is in serving our interests. On the other hand, if these attitudes are appropriate, then we have good reason to worry about the adequacy of anthropocentrism.

5. [CONCLUSION]

. . .

. . . From the point of view of norms for feeling, anthropocentrism does have very different practical implications from nonanthropocentrism, and this is a difference about which we have reason to care. Even if anthropocentrism leaves us with good policy recommendations, it will constrain the ways in which we think it makes sense to care about the natural world. . . .

Now, given the enormity of the environmental problems we currently face, I am not arguing that we should all just turn our attention inward and work on getting our feelings straight. Adopting good environmental policies and getting people to act in environmentally responsible ways should be a priority, especially given the urgency of many environmental problems. But there is room within (or perhaps alongside) that project for asking how we ought to feel about the world we live in. In that context, the differences between anthropocentrism and nonanthropocentrism are considerable and, I think, still well worth our attention.

REFERENCES

Anderson, Elizabeth. 1993. *Value in Ethics and Economics*. Cambridge, MA: Harvard University Press.

Baier, Annette. 1995. *Moral Prejudices: Essays in Ethics*. Cambridge, MA: Harvard University Press.

Bell, Michael. 2000. *Sentimentalism, Ethics and the Culture of Feeling*. Houndmills, Basingstoke, Hampshire: Palgrave.

Brentano, Franz. 1969. *The Origin of Our Knowledge of Right and Wrong*. London: Routledge & Kegan Paul.

Callicott, J. Baird. 1985. "Intrinsic value, quantum theory, and environmental ethics," *Environmental Ethics* 7: 257–275.

Callicott, J. Baird. 1989. "The conceptual foundations of the land ethic," in J. Baird Callicott (ed.), *In Defense of the Land Ethic* (Albany: State University of New York Press), pp. 75–99.

Callicott, J. Baird. 1992. "Rolston on intrinsic value: a deconstruction," *Environmental Ethics* 14: 129–143.

D'Arms, Justin, and Daniel Jacobson. 2000. "Sentiment and value," *Ethics* 110: 722–748.

Darwall, Stephen. 1995. *The British Moralists and the Internal "Ought": 1640–1740*. Cambridge: Cambridge University Press.

Donner, Wendy. 2002. "Callicott on intrinsic value and moral standing in environmental ethics," in Wayne Ouderkirk and Jim Hill (eds.), *Land, Value, Community: Callicott and Environmental Philosophy* (Albany: SUNY Press), pp. 99–105.

Gaus, Gerald F. 1990. *Value and Justification: The Foundations of Liberal Theory*. Cambridge: Cambridge University Press.

Gibbard, Allan. 1990. *Wise Choices, Apt Feelings*. Cambridge, MA: Harvard University Press.

Goodpaster, K.E. 1979. "From egoism to environmentalism," in K.E. Goodpaster and K.M. Sayre (eds.), *Ethics and Problems of the 21st Century* (Notre Dame, IN: Notre Dame University Press), pp. 21–35.

Holland, Alan. 1996. "The use and abuse of ecological concepts in environmental ethics," in N.S. Cooper and R.C.J. Carling (eds.), *Ecologists and Ecological Judgments* (New York: Chapman and Hall), pp. 27–41.

Hursthouse, Rosalind. 1999. *On Virtue Ethics*. Oxford: Oxford University Press.

Light, Andrew. 2002. "Contemporary environmental ethics: from metaethics to public philosophy," *Metaphilosophy* 33(4): 426–449.

McDowell, John. 1997. "Values and secondary qualities," in Stephen Darwall et al. (eds.), *Moral Discourse and Practice: Some Philosophical Approaches* (Oxford: Oxford University Press), pp. 201–213.

McShane, Katie. 2007. "Why environmental ethics shouldn't give up on intrinsic value," *Environmental Ethics* 29: 43–61.

Murdoch, Iris. 2001. *The Sovereignty of Good*. London: Routledge Classics.

Nichols, Shaun. 2004. *Sentimental Rules: On the Natural Foundations of Moral Judgment*. Oxford: Oxford University Press.

Norton, Bryan G. 1984. "Environmental ethics and weak anthropocentrism," *Environmental Ethics* 6: 131–148.

Norton, Bryan G. 1991. *Toward Unity Among Environmentalists*. New York: Oxford University Press.

Norton, Bryan G. 1995. "Why I am not a nonanthropocentrist: Callicott and the failure of monastic inherentism," *Environmental Ethics* 17: 341–358.

Norton, Bryan G. 1999. "Pragmatism, adaptive management, and sustainability," *Environmental Values* 8: 451–466.

Oakley, Justin. 1992. *Morality and the Emotions*. London: Routledge.

Partridge, Ernest. 1986. "Values in nature: is anybody there?" *Philosophical Inquiry* 8: 96–110.

Preston, Christopher J. 1998. "Epistemology and intrinsic values: Norton and Callicott's critiques of Rolston," *Environmental Ethics* 20: 409–428.

Rabinowicz, Wlodek, and Toni Rønnow-Rasmussen. 2004. "The strike of the demon: on fitting pro-attitudes and value," *Ethics* 114: 391–423.

Regan, Tom. 1981. "The nature and possibility of an environmental ethic," *Environmental Ethics* 3: 19–34.

Regan, Tom. 1992. "Does environmental ethics rest on a mistake?" *Monist* 75: 161–182.

Rolston, Holmes, III. 1982. "Are values in nature subjective or objective?" *Environmental Ethics* 4: 125–151.

Rolston, Holmes, III. 1983. "Values gone wild," *Inquiry* 26: 181–207.

Rolston, Holmes, III. 1988. *Environmental Ethics*. Philadelphia: Temple University Press.

Saner, Marc A. 2000. "Biotechnology, the limits of Norton's convergence hypothesis, and implications for an inclusive concept of health," *Ethics and the Environment* 5: 229–242.

Slote, Michael. 1992. *From Morality to Virtue*. Oxford: Oxford University Press.

Stenmark, Mikael. 2002. "The relevance of environmental ethical theories for policy making," *Environmental Ethics* 24: 135–148.

Steverson, Brian K. 1995. "Contextualism and Norton's convergence hypothesis," *Environmental Ethics* 17: 135–150.

Sylvan, Richard. 1973. "Is there a need for a new, an environmental ethic?" *Proceedings of the XII World Conference of Philosophy* (1): 205–210.

Taylor, Paul. 1986. *Respect for Nature: A Theory of Environmental Ethics*. Princeton: Princeton University Press.

Velleman, J. David. 1999. "Love as a moral emotion," *Ethics* 109: 338–374.

Warren, Karen. 1990. "The power and promise of ecological feminism," *Environmental Ethics* 12(2): 125–146.

Weston, Anthony. 1996. "Beyond intrinsic value: pragmatism in environmental ethics," in Andrew Light and Eric Katz (eds.), *Environmental Pragmatism* (London: Routledge), pp. 285–306.

NOTES

1. Norton's discussion of the convergence hypothesis can be found at Norton 1991: 237–43.

2. This phrase is from Light 2002: 436.

3. It is feelings rather than actions, for example, that distinguish Aristotle's virtuous person from the merely continent person. See *EN* 1147b20 *ff*. For historical treatments of the role of feeling and sentiment in ethics, see Darwall 1995 and Bell 2000. For contemporary accounts, see Oakley 1992 and Nichols 2004.

4. Regan 1981; Regan 1992. See also Sylvan 1973 and Goodpaster 1979.

5. See, e.g., Callicott 1989 and Taylor 1986, part 3. For criticisms of this type of argument, see Holland 1996.

6. See, e.g., Norton 1984.

7. See, e.g., Rolston 1988, which is criticised in Callicott 1992, as well as Rolston 1982 and Rolston 1983, which are criticised in Partridge 1986 (but see Preston 1998 for a defence of Rolston's view). See also Callicott 1985, which is criticised in Norton 1995 and Donner 2002. Of such criticisms, I think the following can fairly be said: (1) many nonanthropocentric ethical theories have run into significant theoretical problems; however, (2) nonanthropocentric theories, or at least the environmentalist versions of them, haven't been around for that long; and (3) many of these

problems seem to stem from features of the theories other than their nonanthropocentrism.

8. See Norton 1991 and 1999.

9. See Brentano 1969, Anderson 1993, D'Arms and Jacobson 2000; Gaus 1990 and McDowell 1997. Having reason to do or care, in this context, should be understood as having a *pro tanto* reason, not having an all-things-considered reason. That is to say, it counts as a reason, though one that could be outweighed, overridden, or undermined by other reasons. The "shoulds" and "oughts" that are generated by such reasons should also be understood as *pro tanto*.

10. This distinguishes them from other reasons for caring—prudential reasons, for example. It can, in some circumstances, be in my interest to care about things that aren't worth caring about. For a further discussion of this issue, see D'Arms and Jacobson 2000 and Rabinowicz and Rønnow-Rasmussen 2004.

11. Anderson 1993; Gibbard 1990; Hursthouse 1999: 108; Oakley 1992, Ch. 6. (While there is fairly widespread agreement about this claim, there is less agreement about how we should understand relationships between these two kinds of norms and the role they play in ethics.) Above, and in what follows, I do not use the term "feeling" in the sense it has taken on in the literature on philosophy of the emotions, where it has come to mean something like "sensation." I use it in the more ordinary, colloquial sense to designate emotions in general. Of course, the distinction between doing and feeling I am employing here is a fairly crude one, and there isn't room to work out an adequately detailed account of it here. I trust that there is enough content in our ordinary understanding of these concepts to make sense of the claims I wish to make involving them.

12. But see Steverson 1995, Stenmark 2002, and Saner 2000 for challenges to Norton's claim.

13. Thus I disagree with Andrew Light's claim that nonanthropocentrists are committed to the view that "even a limited endorsement of anthropocentric forms of valuation of nature would necessarily give credence to those anthropocentric values that prefer development over preservation" (Light 2002: 429).

14. Both feminists and ecofeminists have been arguing the importance of questions of how to feel for quite some time. See, e.g., Karen Warren's discussion of Marilyn Frye's distinction between "arrogant perception" and "loving perception" in Warren 1990.

15. For a more extended discussion of some of these issues, see Murdoch 2001.

16. See, e.g., Baier 1995: 30–1; Slote 1992: 89.

17. Many of those who think of people's inner lives (including their feelings) as outside the scope of moral evaluation, I think, confuse the question of what we're entitled to expect from others—i.e., what claims or obligations we can legitimately place on them—with the question of what it makes sense to evaluate in ourselves or others. (Thanks to Jeff Kasser for this way of putting the point.) As Iris Murdoch (citing Hume) points out, "good political philosophy is not necessarily good moral philosophy" (Murdoch 2001: 79).

18. Whether it answers this question at all is a matter of some debate. Some claim that it answers the question of whether I should try to get myself to admire her, though not the question of whether I should admire her. For a discussion of this issue, see Rabinowicz and Rønnow-Rasmussen 2004.

19. Notice that this claim is limited to a particular form of love, namely the love involved in friendship. The English word "love" can be used to refer to a number of very different valuing attitudes, and I do not want to claim that all of them have the structure I describe here. My love of sweet potato pie or rock climbing, for example, may well be compatible with thinking that their value is entirely instrumental. Thanks to Simon Keller for urging the importance of this point.

20. For a discussion of the structure of attitudes such as this, see Anderson 1993: 8–11, 205–7; for a discussion of the kind of valuing involved in love, see Velleman 1999.

21. Notice that here I do not make the further claim that attitudes of love, respect and awe involve seeing their objects as having value in their own right. For a discussion of this issue, see McShane 2007.

22. Rolston 1988: 25–6.

23. This might depend on how [we] distinguish actions from feelings. If we count "adopting an attitude toward something" as an action, then the

problems I raise here for feeling-norms will make trouble for some action-norms as well.

24. Or to see A as mattering, or to believe that A matters, or to judge that A matters—how one construes this will depend on one's theory of the emotions in general, and the relevant emotions in particular.

25. An anonymous reviewer raises the following objection: "I think I am able to feel awe for some impressive piece of human engineering, say the Boulder Dam or the pyramids, while believing simultaneously that the Dam itself serves only an instrumental purpose and has no value other than that of providing energy for humans." In this case, however, the reviewer believes that while the Dam is awesome, its awesomeness makes no contribution at all to its value—it would be just as good if it was small, ordinary, not very well put together, designed by a few mediocre engineers, etc., just as long as it did its job of providing energy for humans. In this case, I am inclined to doubt that what the reviewer is feeling is really awe. Insofar as awe is a valuing attitude, it isn't just the thought "My, what a large object!" It's *valuing* something in virtue of its greatness. But by hypothesis, this person thinks that its greatness isn't a reason to value it—the only aspect of it that merits valuation is its energy-producing abilities.

LYNN SCARLETT

CHOICES, CONSEQUENCES, AND COOPERATIVE CONSERVATION: A NEW ENVIRONMENTALISM?

Land management and conservation present a delicate interface of people and places, public and private actions, and persistent tensions between ecology and economy. On the landscapes where these tensions unfold, fifth-generation ranchers who know and love their land, their lifestyles, their legacy, and their communities eke out a living on semi-desert lands along the Southwest border. Thousands of miles north, Athabaskan Native populations replay centuries of subsistence fishing practices in remote camps in the wilds of Alaska on the Yukon River. Across a continent, Maine loggers intent on lightening their environmental footprint for a sustainable future re-examine their land management to strike a balance between environment and economy.

SETTING THE STAGE—CONFLICT AND COMMUNITIES

Conflict often accompanies the choices of these people and others as they draw their livelihood from public and private lands. Conflict accompanies their choices, yet, generally, these are hard-working people caring for their families, their communities, and, in their own ways, this magnificent world.

Original essay for this volume. Lynn Scarlett is a Senior Environmental Policy Analyst at Resources for the Future. She formerly has served as Deputy Secretary and Chief Operating Officer at the Department of the Interior.

Conflict is not new at the intersection of mankind and nature. The legendary words, attributed to Mark Twain, "whiskey's for drinking; water's for fightin,'" are testament to over a century of resource conflicts. Land-use conflicts are the rule, not the exception, exemplified in the thousands of lawsuits with which the U.S. Department of the Interior, manager of over 500 million acres of public lands, regularly grappled as the twentieth century drew to a close.[1]

Conflict, in part, springs from differing perceptions of what uses of lands and waters are appropriate, what impacts of those uses are acceptable, and how best to balance environmental protections with uses of lands, waters, and resources in the pursuit of economic opportunity. Conflict springs from varying views on how best to reduce the impacts of human action on lands, waters, and wildlife. Conflict also arises from ill-defined ownership of some wildlife, such as fish, and ill-defined responsibilities for land impacts.

Many of these challenges test our governing institutions. They present environmental and community conundrums. They complicate the quest for liberty, justice, contentment *and* conservation.

The first Earth Day heightened national attention to environmental matters in 1970, prompting philosophers, economists, environmental activists, political scientists, and others to probe these conundrums and debate how best to address them. The dividing lines of debate have juxtaposed federal prescriptions against performance incentives and market forces; or national mandates against local choices; or regulations against property rights regimes intended to overcome "commons" problems that accompany "unowned" resources.[2]

Each of these debate clusters zeroes in on both institutional challenges and certain features of environmental problems, offering up options for addressing them. While these long-standing debates about institutions and the environmental toolkit persist, environmental policy discussions are also moving in new directions that center on conflict resolution. These discussions have both philosophical underpinnings and practical implications. They present an emergent chapter of environmentalism.

A KALEIDOSCOPE OF CHALLENGES

Environmental challenges are diverse and extensive. On public lands, managers grapple with how to remove or contain unexploded ordinance on vacated military sites. Public-sector managers and private landowners strive to protect species amid land fragmentation, poor water quality, and the march of non-native, invasive species that upset long-standing rhythms of Nature. They struggle to enhance forest health where tree stands sometimes reach densities 20 times what they were at the time when Europeans first arrived to this continent. These densities, to the unschooled eye, give forests a rich and mysterious appeal, but they create risks of catastrophic fires and threaten human communities. Air emissions, including greenhouse gases, affect the health of lands, waters, and wildlife, and, now, even influence global climate.

Across the Nation along rivers and coasts, landowners face the consequences of years of altered water flows—in the Everglades, the Bay Delta of California, the Louisiana Gulf Coast, and elsewhere. Often, these altered flows are the product of past dreams as human communities years ago tried to minimize floods and extend agricultural opportunities. These altered water systems have to some degree performed as intended, containing floodwaters within levee banks or drying lands to give way to farming or redirecting waters to turn deserts into gardens. However, with extensive alteration have come unintended consequences. No longer are sediments from the Mississippi River deposited along the Gulf of Mexico coast to create the delta that supported marshlands that served as natural buffers against storm surges during inevitable hurricanes.[3] In the Bay Delta, dikes and levees, which opened up land for farming, have resulted in land subsidence. In the Klamath Basin, water diverted for irrigation has left traditional habitat inadequate to support some fish populations.

These unintended consequences heighten the press for environmental protection and for course corrections to restore natural landscapes and water flows. Yet therein lay many challenges. How, for example, can public and private land managers restore water flows across the Everglades while maintaining century-old communities, their homes, and their livelihoods?

How can Louisiana restore coastal sea marshes and delta water flows amid human communities that have their homes on the lands now surrounded by dikes and levees?

I came to Washington with decades of theory about how the world works and a Pollyannaish optimism about the good will of mankind and the power of private stewardship. On the one hand, I maintain that optimism. But nearly eight years of experience at the Interior Department also deepened my appreciation for how very, very hard it is to conserve lands, waters and wildlife *and* maintain places and spaces for people, their work, and their communities.

Those difficulties arise from the tensions among battling interests and competing priorities. They result from the sheer complexities of place and the complexities that reside in the dynamic interface of people with the lands. Should snowmobiles continue to traverse Yellowstone? What about mountain biking? Where? When? How? Where might ranchers graze their cattle? Or where might loggers cut timber for homes, or energy producers find energy to warm houses, or miners extract the minerals that become toothpaste, pacemakers, wedding rings, or computers? How can the nation protect silvery minnows, provide irrigation water to farmers in the West who grow two-thirds of the Nation's produce, and service 31 million residential water users, all in a context of water scarcity in the West?

Can the people of the United States access these resources and protect the environment simultaneously? Who should decide the mix of land uses and protections? Through what decision processes, institutions, ownership structures, and rules might these matters achieve resolution?

Consider one tableau in the Bay Delta of California. State and Federal water projects deliver millions of acre-feet of water to people for household drinking, to farmers who produce most of this Nation's produce, and to natural places that sustain wildlife. The Bay Delta is a re-plumbed system with vast numbers of levees and dikes and monumental canals and pumps. It is a system with a century of drained wetlands resulting in land subsidence of 20 or even 30 feet in places. Amid all this, there is the tiny delta smelt and the mighty salmon.

In headlines and the courts, it is easy to line up on the side of the smelt, or the salmon, or the farmers, or California's thirsty residents. But it is not so easy to figure out how to really manage these waters for people, places, and wildlife. In this altered system, managing the waters to protect the smelt in some circumstances could actually harm the salmon. Moreover, withdrawing water from rivers for agriculture is not about big business. It is about food for a nation. Any changes in water flows will affect people, wildlife, and the lands and habitats on which they depend. The status quo seems unsustainable—for fish populations and human communities. But whatever changes are proposed will likely result in both gains and losses.

In addressing all these issues and similar situations across the United States, the nation faces a tapestry of rights, ownerships, and responsibilities. There are places with private ownership of lands but public ownership of mineral rights. There are places with vast stretches of public ownership interrupted by centuries-old in-holdings of private property. There are places set aside by law for resource use and others, like national parks, destined for the preservation and enjoyment of the public. There are places with ill-defined ownership and responsibilities, such as the oceans. There are circumstances in which producers and consumers pay for use of some resources, like fuel and minerals, but not for other resources, like the air into which pollutants disperse.

DEFINING THE ENVIRONMENTAL PROBLEM SET—FOUR QUESTIONS

The environmental problems faced by the nation vary widely in their details, but they hold common characteristics, too. One way or another, environmental policy challenges and the policy battles surrounding them center on four implicit questions.

INFORMATION CHALLENGES

First is the information challenge—the matter of how best to generate and use information relevant to understanding and addressing environmental problems.

That quest is rendered difficult within contexts that are inevitably complex and dynamic. Think of the Everglades. To the casual visitor, the Everglades ecosystem is a flat plain of grasses with scattered trees. To the scientist, however, the Everglades is a mosaic of tree islands, ridges and sloughs, areas of subsided peat lands and invasive plants, estuaries, and mangrove swamps.

So altered is the Everglades landscape after years of canal building and installation of dikes that it is not possible, in restoring an Everglades ecosystem, to simply return water flows across south Florida to conditions of one hundred years ago. The lands are too altered, with great depressions resulting from peat subsidence and the entire eastern coast of Florida now an uninterrupted, densely populated series of cities and towns.

As public, private, and tribal land managers seek to restore some semblance of the historic "river of grass," they face questions of how much water should flow, when, and where? If land managers re-wet the land, what happens to the endangered Cape Sable Seaside Sparrow that needs high, dry nests? Reintroducing water flows across subsided lands will create deep pools, not the historic low-depth sheets of water that once traversed this Everglades landscape. Yet restoring significant water flows, for most of the Everglades landscape, is the single most important requirement for restoration.

The quest to generate relevant information is especially difficult where environmental harms are cumulative, where responsibility for harms is diffuse, and where the time lag between cause and effects observed is long. Think of nutrients seeping into the Mississippi River—the result of over a century of runoff from thousands of places. A small amount of runoff a century ago into the river produced negligible effects, but, over the decades, at some point, the cumulative effects of runoff from thousands of locations have produced severe hypoxia—oxygen-deprived waters—in the Gulf of Mexico, rendering some places akin to a "dead zone" that will not support marine life.

Generating and assembling relevant information for diverse and dispersed environmental challenges is costly, and evaluating that information often results in competing analyses and conclusions. Yet scientific information is just one informational component. Also important is information about resource management practices, techniques, and economics. A central challenge, in environmental decision making, is how to stimulate the generation and incorporation of both scientific and practical information into decision processes.

INCENTIVE CHALLENGES

A second question, often cast as a debate over "sticks" or "carrots," recurs in environmental policy debates: what institutional arrangements and policy tools best motivate conservation and better environmental performance? The flip side of this question is: why do people pollute, degrade landscapes, and "waste" resources?

Noted 20th century conservationist Aldo Leopold attributed poor environmental performance to an absence of a land "ethic."[4] Students of Garrett Hardin's treatise on the "tragedy of the commons" attribute "waste" and "pollution" to an absence of property rights such that everyone has access to the use of resources, such as ocean fish, but no one has guardianship over those resources with the ability to exclude others and the long-term management horizons to sustain and replenish the resource for continued use.[5] A variation on this theme is the economic concept of negative externalities, in which certain costs associated with an action—release of air emissions from an electric utility—are not incorporated into production costs. Emissions are, in effect, released into freely available air. There are, thus, no incentives to reduce emissions.

ACCOUNTABILITY CHALLENGES

A third dimension of environmental debate centers on how to address risks or harms imposed by some on others—what might be called an "accountability" problem. Those who drive gasoline-powered automobiles, for example, generate tailpipe emissions—carbon monoxide, volatile organic compounds, and nitrogen oxide. Collectively, the emissions of multiple vehicles create health and other environmental hazards for which no driver is held accountable. Similarly, a farmer that applies chemical pesticides, herbicides and fertilizers that migrate into streams and rivers contributes to pollution loadings, yet, often, holds little legal responsibility for resultant harms.

COORDINATION PROBLEM

Finally, much environmental policy discourse centers on how to coordinate human action across ownership and jurisdictional boundaries and among multiple often competing value sets. Invasive species, for example, respect no property boundaries. Cheat grass, inadvertently introduced onto western lands, has spread over millions of acres. These grasses increase risks of extreme fire hazards; they reduce land health. Yet actions of individual landowners to remove cheat grass are futile unless, collectively, land managers on adjacent lands also tackle the cheat grass problem. Or consider forest management. Reducing excess underbrush and thinning tree stands to reduce risks of catastrophic fire cannot be effective if undertaken randomly and occasionally by some landowners but not others.

These four questions *are not* those generally summarized by competing policy camps in environmental debates. Traditional debates are often couched as a contest of command-and-control regulations versus incentives; or they are cast as a contest between central versus local decision making; or they unfold as debates about the merits of mandates versus markets.

Instead, these four issues are the "questions behind the questions." They lurk as an often unstated set of organizational and decision making challenges. But attempts to answer these questions lie at the core of much environmental debate. Answering these questions also helps point the way to reformulating the environmental decision making framework in ways that strengthen *both* conservation commitments and private initiative and responsibility by: 1) fostering decision settings that tap local ideas and on-the-ground information; 2) inspiring a nation of stewards by ensuring that good actions are not punished and stewardship is encouraged; 3) affirming accountability; and 4) achieving integrated decisions that transcend jurisdictional and property boundaries.

PHILOSOPHY MEETS POLICY—CONTENDING FRAMEWORKS

Before exploring this framework in more detail, let us look at the theoretical landscape—the different ways different people address the four challenges I have presented. Various contenders offer varying answers to these policy questions. Consider three contending answers, here described in a highly stylized summary. In practice, of course, these contending perspectives are not mutually exclusive.

REGULATIONS AND ENFORCEMENT

First is the regulatory perspective. In a nutshell, this perspective would reduce risks and coordinate human action through use of collectively set standards. This perspective would motivate human action through the threat of enforcement measures and punishment. The institutional emphasis is on uniformity of standards and certainty in decision process (if not in actual environmental outcomes). The policy tools include requirements that landowners, firms, and other organizations adhere to certain planning and permitting processes. The emphasis, too, is on prescriptions such as smokestack scrubbers on power plants, or four-inch grass height requirements on ranch lands, or particular land-management practices. Problems are tackled one standard at a time, each with its own rule. Each land manager or other regulated entity undergoes permitting requirements separately.

This policy framework has generated some notable environmental successes. This framework largely shaped modern environmental laws such as the Clean Air Act, Safe Drinking Water Act, Clean Water Act, Endangered Species Act, and other laws. Through these laws, the nation's air is cleaner, eagles again soar in abundance, and many hazardous waste sites are now cleaner.[6]

But this framework, with its prescriptions, procedural decision making layers, and reliance on enforcement actions as a central motivator of environmental progress, also often has resulted in high conflict, high costs to achieve environmental goals, and high unintended consequences. Prescriptions can mesh poorly with the varying details of particular circumstances. This framework is, thus, not well suited to the generation and use of relevant, often location-specific knowledge. Yet that knowledge is acutely relevant to help define the doable and pinpoint the possible.

Consider albatross and the threat from certain fishing practices. In the last decade, the U.S. Fish and Wildlife Service identified certain fishing practices as harming albatross. Under a traditional regulatory framework, the Service could have invoked regulatory requirements for the fishers to cease their activities. Or they could have prescribed certain practices. But their prohibitions and prescriptions might not have taken advantage of what Nobel laureate economist F.A. Hayek referred to as the knowledge of time, place, and situation—the knowledge of on-the-ground experience.[7] In this instance, the Fish and Wildlife Service chose a non-regulatory approach. Instead, the Service approached the local fishing community and explained the albatross problem. Informed of the problem, the fishing community responded by saying they could do things differently. The outcome of this interaction was continued fishing to sustain local livelihoods and protection of albatross.

The regulatory framework is not well suited to tapping local knowledge. Nor is it well suited to enhancing self-motivated environmental stewardship or to giving expression to multiple, competing priorities. It is not merely the figment of imagination among conservative critics that the Endangered Species Act, for example, can discourage private stewardship. A growing bipartisan recognition of these stewardship disincentives gave rise in the 1990s to an innovation called Safe Harbor Agreements under the Endangered Species Act to encourage landowners to improve habitat to attract endangered species to their lands. Its first use was in the southeast, among private forest owners, to protect the red-cockaded woodpecker. These agreements, in effect, gave landowners protections against future regulatory restrictions if they undertook conservation actions to attract endangered species to their lands.

REGULATIONS PLUS MARKETS

A second environmental policy perspective is the economic efficiency model. Like the more traditional regulatory school of thought, this perspective embraces a framework that relies on collectively set standards, universally applied, to reduce risks and coordinate human action. But this school of thought introduces market trading tools within the context of those standards to create incentives for more cost-effective, pollution-reducing innovations and conservation actions.

Consider the Tualatin Basin in Oregon and Clean Water Act requirements for cool temperatures where stormwater infrastructure and wastewater treatment plants discharge effluent and water runoff. Using tradable credits under Clean Water Act regulations, a cluster of wastewater treatment plants and a stormwater utility paid farmers $6 million to plant trees along the stream rather than $60 million to add refrigeration systems. The result was the same—cooler water—but the cost difference was significant.[8]

This economic efficiency framework partly addresses the "high cost" problem resulting from the more prescriptive, traditional regulatory framework by creating incentives for innovation and the generation and use of site-specific knowledge in problem solving. This framework provides some means of addressing the four challenges outlined above—the challenges of information, motivation, accountability, and coordination. Yet both of the first two schools of thought essentially sidestep questions of liberty—and its relationship to human progress, peace, and prosperity.

FREE MARKET ENVIRONMENTALISM

A third perspective offers a free-market framework—with voluntary action as its centerpiece. Its focus is on property rights and the common law of tort as antidotes to commons problems that give rise to environmental risks and harms. A central thesis is that many environmental problems spring from what Garrett Hardin called "the tragedy of the commons." Where ownership of resources is ill-defined or nonexistent, wrote Hardin, people have no incentive to sustain the resource into the future. Instead, they have an incentive to "grab all."[9]

Under the free market framework, an oft-invoked remedy to resolve environmental problems is to establish property rights and minimize the "tragedy of the commons" problem. Think of individual tradable quotas for certain fisheries whereby fishermen and women receive a specific (and tradable) allocation for a particular amount of fish.

Within this framework, the trading of goods and services in a market context is also presented as a way to advance conservation through the discipline of competition—what might be called the "green thumb" of Adam Smith. Think of something as simple as a coke can—and its history. Four decades ago, in the popular culture of teenagers, it was a sign of virility to crush a coke can; now nearly anyone can crush a can with a single hand. Why? Competitive markets resulted in can manufacturers doing more with less. Forty years ago, manufacturers used approximately 168 pounds of metal to make 1,000 cans; today they use 28 pounds of metal for those 1,000 cans.

A decentralized, voluntary, competitive trading context creates incentives that motivate, under some circumstances, conservation, thus achieving environmental progress while minimizing conflict and keeping liberty in play. But there are gaps in the scholarship attending to this model. Though there are exceptions, the free market framework has inadequately focused on "coordination" challenges so relevant where problems span multiple property ownerships and governing jurisdictions. It has also inadequately addressed accountability challenges in which the causes of environmental harm are dispersed, time lags between causes and apparent effects are long, or effects are cumulative. These circumstances render common law legal tools of tort ill-suited as a mechanism to assure accountability.

In dwelling on the "tragedy of the commons" and the remedy that delineation of property rights sometimes provides for those problems, the free market school has pioneered understanding of conservation incentives. But this market school has overlooked persistent environmental problems in cases where clearly defined property rights exist yet transcend ownership boundaries. With the spotlight on markets and market transactions, the free market school of thought has also underplayed the role of voluntary associations in environmental problem solving.

COOPERATIVE CONSERVATION

A fourth environmental framework—cooperative (or collaborative) conservation—is gaining momentum in practice and sparking theoretical and analytic inquiry.[10] Cooperative conservation is more than a bumper sticker phrase. Many environmental practitioners now give an appreciative nod toward collaboration. But let me plumb, for a moment, why the evolution toward cooperative conservation is important.

Professionally, I came out of a "think tank" world that celebrated individual entrepreneurship and importance of liberty and responsibility as underpinnings of moral action. It might, thus, seem odd that I see collaboration, cooperation, and collective action as central to 21st century conservation. Yet this orientation is not really puzzling at all.

The free market environmental toolkit has centered on legal regimes to better define property rights and apply common law and torts to incidents of harm. But this toolkit is often a poor fit in landscape-scale, cross-boundary contexts. In these contexts, more relevant and interesting is the work of scholars like Nobel laureate economist Elinor Ostrom, who examine formal and informal collaborative governance.[11]

Formal and informal collaborative efforts tied to place-based issues are precisely important because they acknowledge that different participants in land management and environmental policy decisions have different value sets, priorities, and interests. Sustained outcomes that transcend litigation and pitched policy battles require mechanisms to give stronger expression to these differences and decision processes that enable those participants affected by or deeply interested in the outcomes of the decision process to bargain and negotiate.

But these collaborative efforts meet another test, as well. Beyond a fundamental recognition of values tensions, these collaborative efforts better conform to the current nature of land and resource management challenges. They provide a decision process that transcends property ownership and jurisdictional boundaries, better aligning with the nature of land and resource problems that confront us. They transcend boundaries—and Nature knows no boundaries.

They also facilitate introduction of "experiential knowledge"—the knowledge of situation, time, place, and practice" described by Nobel laureate F.A. Hayek. As in the earlier description of the albatross and the fishing community in Alaska, this sort of on-the-ground knowledge helps generate feasible remedies to environmental problems. It is this experiential knowledge that is so often lacking in top-down, prescriptive policies.

Earth Day 1970 unleashed modern environmental laws predicated on regulations and uniform prescriptions designed by federal agencies. Forty years later, though these laws remain the bedrock of environmental protection in the United States, a growing momentum is propelling investment in place-based collaboration to achieve environmental results.

COLLABORATIVE GOVERNANCE—A VIRTUAL TOUR OF AMERICA

To bring this institutional and governance discovery process alive, join me on a brief virtual tour of places where new forms of governance, new property institutions, and new social arrangements are emerging. These arrangements help generate holistic or integrated decisions that coordinate human action across property and jurisdictional boundaries and incorporate multiple, intersecting values and issues. They strengthen incentives for private stewardship. They create contexts that generate and foster use of relevant information. They help reduce environmental risks and harms through innovation and clearly delineated responsibilities. They also sustain liberty—a context in which individuals with competing value priorities bargain and negotiate to achieve acceptable outcomes that meet environmental goals while affirming economic, recreation, and other opportunities.

All four decision frameworks outlined earlier pertain to how decision makers—public and private—make choices, communicate information and ideas, and organize and coordinate action. Collectively, these might be called "governance" challenges. To understand their intrinsic importance to conservation, communities, and individuals, I offer a virtual tour of unfolding examples.

First on the virtual tour, let us head south to the Malpai Borderlands in Arizona and New Mexico. In Arizona, along the Mexican border, a number of ranchers participate in the Malpai Borderland Group, which has created a grassbank—an easement across hundreds of thousands of acres—through which grasslands are conserved and restored while enhancing ranching opportunities. Within the grassbank, grasslands flourish to provide prairie habitat for dozens of wildlife species and plants. Yet the grassbank is also akin to an insurance policy: during times of drought or fire, participants can move their cows, temporarily, onto the grassbank to assure their survival. This linkage of conservation with economic benefits is a natural lure for

ranchers to participate, and the grassbank offers opportunities for landscape-scale, cross-boundary land and water management.[12]

Traveling across a continent, to the northeast and the Duck Trap River in Maine, over two dozen partners, including landowners, snowmobile enthusiasts, local, state, and federal agencies, farmers, conservation organizations, and others joined in a management coalition to restore miles of the river and adjacent lands to improve salmon habitat while maintaining recreation, farming, and other land uses. The Duck Trap River Coalition unpacked problems into bite-sized chunks.[13] The Coalition applied new techniques to mitigate erosion along stream banks. Members rehabilitated gravel pits, transforming them into vernal pools. They created an education partnership with the snowmobile association to maintain recreation opportunities on trails least subject to environmental impacts and monitored by the association. They used conservation easements to achieve enduring protections. This partnership is bringing miles of restoration to the river. It has generated permanent protections of lands and waters, blended with continued landowner and community use. It has generated data and monitoring by volunteers, recognizing that the true test of conservation resides in the results achieved and sustained.

In western Pennsylvania, at Buffalo Creek, dozens of farmers, their efforts coordinated by the U.S. Fish and Wildlife Service (FWS) and a local university, are fencing off miles of streams and riparian areas. They are planting native warm spring grasses. They are installing owl boxes, wood duck boxes, and bat boxes. Stream monitoring shows dramatic reductions of bacteria in water—a 1,000-fold reduction in the bacteria count. Stream banks now display dense shrubs and brush, bringing habitat for birds and shade cover for fish. Buffalo Creek manifests another outcome: the conservation partnership is inspiring many to become citizen stewards. Farmers engage actively in conservation as partners.

Contrast this engagement to the response, if, instead, the FWS or other agencies had extended a regulatory "stick" to require the stream fencing or grass planting. The "stick" often triggers a hunkering down and door closing—a "no, thank you," while the appeal for partnerships inspires, instead, citizens to engage in stewardship. The "stick" can stop "bad stuff" from happening, but is limited in inspiring "good stuff."

At Buffalo Creek, we see accountability and co-ordinated action. We see citizen stewards applying caring hands to the landscape—across boundaries, transcending yet respecting property lines. As envisioned by 20th century conservationist Aldo Leopold, we see a blend of public and private, formal and informal governance, shared goals and partnered problem solving.

Let us continue our journey, heading to Oregon in the northwest. Citizen stewards here formed the Applegate Partnership. The Applegate River watershed is a forested area of about 500,000 acres, of which 70 percent is publicly owned. Tree stand densities are far beyond that of the pre-settlement time period.

Buildup of underbrush and dense tree stands is partly the result of the "Smokey the Bear" perspective of the 1940s and 1950s that shaped federal efforts to put out all forest fires. With decades of fuel buildup, fires don't behave as in the past. In the past, a lightening strike might have caused the fire to run down a tree and spread along the forest floor. Fires now can travel up the stands of densely configured, sometimes diseased trees, reaching the crowns of the trees. Crown fires can burn at 2,000 degrees F and release the energy equivalent of an atomic bomb. These fires burn so intensely that they can incinerate forests and burn so hot that the land becomes baked and hardened, resistant to new growth. Water cannot move through the soil to nourish the roots of sprouting vegetation.

What does the Applegate Partnership have to do with this problem? Citizens living in a wild land–urban interface joined with the Interior Department, the Forest Service, local governments, state foresters and local environmental groups to thin some of the undergrowth material to reduce the danger of catastrophic wildfire. Collaboration among partners is facilitating "landscape level" timber sales that do not involve clear cutting, reducing community risks, and restoring forest health.[14]

Let us proceed to one more stop—this time in Arizona, home of the Sonoita Valley Planning Partnership. The partnership includes a medley of public and private land managers and partners. The partners,

through many years, had conflicting visions that highlighted, respectively, recreation, ranching, preservation, and other values. After years of conflict, citizens shifted gears and collaborated with public land managers. Collectively, they defined land health outcomes and set forth a management regime to achieve those outcomes that blend recreation, economic activity, and conservation goals. They created a novel governance structure—a board of directors comprising public agencies and private citizens—to oversee implementation of a shared management plan.[15]

SHARED GOVERNANCE

All these emerging partnerships present new governance structures that shape incentives, influence accountability, and enhance coordination. These structures display some common features. They incorporate local ideas and insights and location-specific information into decisions while drawing upon science to understand conditions of land health and the relationship between management actions and possible outcomes. These efforts reflect the importance of experiential knowledge—the idea that, as poet Wallace Stevens once wrote: "Perhaps real truth resides in a walk around the lake."

These efforts also re-align incentives and inspire conservation by linking conservation to economic action, community well being, and citizen engagement. Incentives must be broadly understood, not as monetary payoffs but as arrangements that recognize that human excellence can flourish with encouragement, from a pat on the back, from someone saying, "Good job!"

Incentives spring from decision making arrangements that engage rather than confront citizens. After he put stream bank fencing up, one farmer at Buffalo Creek called the Fish and Wildlife Service, saying: "I saw a yellow warbler today." The FWS agent asked: "how do you know—I thought you had no interest in wild birds?" The farmer replied: "Since re-establishing my stream bank, I now have a bird book."[16]

Partnerships along the virtual tour outlined here are also characterized by decision making contexts that promote innovation and iterative adjustments.

All of these collaborative efforts enhance coordination while preserving the expression of individual priorities and values.

All center attention on results—not on paperwork, process, or prescription. They focus on holistic results that take into account environmental goals, thriving communities and dynamic economies. They bring together a mosaic of objectives, understanding that human aspirations and well being encompass a variety of values. Those values include a desire for healthy lands and waters. They include human aspirations for energy to warm homes and goods that make lives comfortable and convenient. They include the desire that many people have for outdoor recreation in a variety of forms.

This vision of cooperative conservation is a hopeful one. Yet cooperative conservation is neither easy nor one-dimensional. In her novel, *Ahab's Wife*, Sena Jeter Naslund has the heroine saying she wished that words were like music so we could play many strands at once. Many environmental policy advocates have reservations about cooperative conservation. Contemplating cooperation, some think: "but, but, but . . . what if everyone doesn't want to co-operate?" "What about those individuals who are ornery—who work against the common good?"

These observations have merit. Cooperation won't replace prescription everywhere and always. But the governance challenge before us is not an "either–or" one of choosing between an environmentalism of regulatory compliance and an environmentalism of cooperation. Rather, the challenge is one of emphasis, situation, and orientation.

As the discovery process of network governance unfolds, the need for new skills and different information emerges. Environmental action centered on outcomes invokes the need for better metrics. To focus on results requires the ability to define and measure them. Over the past half century, the nation's land managers have become good at tracking permits and monitoring regulatory compliance. The nation's land managers—public and private—are less adept at monitoring on-the-ground results. We are often hard-pressed to tell people exactly how to measure healthy forests or healthy grasslands. We lack widespread, consistent data on water quality.

Collaborative governance also requires that participants strengthen their skills at mediation, negotiation, and conversation. These collaborative settings require what author William Isaacs calls dialogue—conversation with a center, not sides. Dialogue requires that we listen—that, as Isaacs describes, we develop an inner silence as others speak.[17]

Finally, we need additional and sometimes different governing rules. We need tools like "safe harbor" agreements under the Endangered Species Act—agreements that provide landowners the ability to protect endangered species without invoking restrictions on their use of the land provided that protection goals are met.

Key to fulfillment of the Endangered Species Act and its purposes is both public and private land stewardship. Over 80 percent of species listed as endangered or threatened are found, at least in part, on private lands. One third may be found only on private lands. Species conservation, as conservationist Aldo Leopold anticipated a half century ago, must, therefore, be a matter for public and private action.[18]

Many ESA observers have lamented the limited successes in species conservation under the Act.[19] If removal of species from threatened and endangered lists is the metric of success, the record is not inspiring. But the simple listing and delisting metric probably conveys an incomplete picture. Steven Yaffee at University of Michigan has pointed out that under the Act, land management decisions now take into much greater account effects of actions on species.[20] The Act has motivated many large, landscape-scale conservation initiatives. Many of these partnerships link public and private actions. The Platte River conservation plan, the Upper Colorado River restoration, the Missouri River restoration, or the High Plains Partnership all involve large, regional restoration efforts that cut across governing boundaries.

That most listed species remain designated as threatened or endangered is a consequence of many, many factors. The Act's early failure to set forth a context that motivates private stewardship is an important factor. But getting those incentives right will not likely get vast numbers of species off ESA lists. The effects of a changing climate, land fragmentation, persistent environmental contaminants, and scarce water will all continue to threaten species. These challenges transcend decision making incentives within the context of implementing the ESA.

Still, clearly the Nation can do better, and private lands are keys to future success. Over the past 15 years, many innovations in implementing the Act have softened ESA disincentives for private stewardship. The Fish and Wildlife Service now uses Safe Harbor Agreements, a "No Surprises" rule, Candidate Conservation Agreements (CCAs) with Assurances (CCAAs), and Habitat Conservation Plans (HCPs) with incidental take permits to provide greater certainty to landowners and reduce their disincentives to protect at-risk species.

By 2006, Safe Harbor Agreements covered nearly 4 million acres. The Agreements covered at least 36 species, including the much celebrated case of the red-cockaded woodpecker. Candidate Conservation Agreements of various types covered nearly 200 species. Through recent guidance, FWS has outlined a way to combine CCAs and CCAAs where applicants have activities on both federal and non-federal lands. The guidance also sets forth a process to link CCA conference opinions to Section 7 consultations and biological opinions if a candidate species becomes listed.

These efforts are important steps in further reducing landowner disincentives to conserve species. Turning to HCPs, by 2005, nearly 500 Habitat Conservation Plans covering 39 million acres addressed some 590 species. All of these tools partly remedy the "uncertainty" problem. They remedy the uncertainty context in which landowners have been reluctant to undertake conservation measures out of fear that the presence of endangered species on their lands would invoke land use restrictions.

Two additional tools—conservation banking and recovery credits—now establish some value in species conservation. They not merely reduce disincentives; they motivate conservation.

These tools, though constructive, are imperfect. The imperfections cluster into several categories, including:

- Burdensome, time-consuming procedures;
- Performance requirements built upon sometimes inadequate information;
- Management prescriptions rather than performance based on species outcomes; and

- Inadequate distinctions between practices intended solely for beneficial environmental restoration and conservation and those directed toward land development and land-transforming uses.

As we think about conservation tools, we need to remind ourselves of two goals in the context of private lands. The first is the matter of performance. The fundamental goal or test of success should be species protection and recovery. The second is the matter of incentives—how to engage private landowners in conservation.

In considering incentives, let us return to the bigger picture of cooperative conservation and collaborative problem solving. We need conservation on working landscapes and across boundaries. University of Michigan scholar Steven Yaffee examines the Upper Colorado River management initiative that involves many agencies and many participants, both public and private. The management regime unfolds on an ecosystem scale, with a multi-species focus. In this setting, conservation actions occur on working landscapes in a context of both technical and financial incentives to enhance participation. These features set the foundations for 21st century environmental performance, the actual recovery of species, and enhancement of habitat health.

Some of the best prospects for stimulating private stewardship lie alongside rather than within the ESA context. Programs such as the Partners for Fish and Wildlife Program, Coastal Program, State Wildlife Action Plans, Farm Bill conservation grants and other similar programs inspire landowner stewardship through technical and financial assistance and rewards. These programs increasingly operate on a landscape scale. Many of these programs function through competitive awards. Some of the best opportunities to enhance species protection lie in strengthening the performance provisions of these programs to include goals for species protections.

The diagnosis in the 1990s of a key impediment to ESA success was the landowner incentive issue. Many new tools and resources have begun to address the disincentives issue. Further streamlining of their implementation would strengthen incentives of landowners to participate. But today's central challenge is not per se the incentive issue.

A central challenge today is, rather, how to pivot from a species by species to a multi-species focus. Another challenge is how to strengthen landscape-scale efforts. These challenges put a premium on developing tools for cross-jurisdictional, public–private, and private–private coordination and cooperation. Initiatives like the Blackfoot Challenge in Montana, the Duck Trap River collaboration in Maine, the Puget Sound Partnership, and others are the building blocks for this coordination and cooperation.

A few years back, I met a Montana farmer who told me his wife calls him a "next year country man" because he's always saying: "Next year there will be no hail; next year it will rain in July; next year there will be no snow in August." I am a "next year country person," too. I am a perennial optimist that an era of cooperative conservation is facilitating environmental problem solving while sustaining the voices and views of people in their communities and workplaces.

NOTES

1. This 3,000 lawsuit tally is an estimate generated by the Solicitor's Office of the U.S. Department of the Interior in 2008.
2. See, for example, DeWitt John, *Civic Environmentalism: Alternatives to Regulation in States and Communities*, Washington, DC: CQ Press, 1994; Michael McCloskey, The Skeptic: Collaboration Has Its Limits, *High Country News*, 28 (9), 1996; Don Snow, Coming Home: An Introduction to Collaborative Governance, in *Across the Divide: Explorations in Collaborative Conservation and the American West*, eds. Philip Brock, Donald Snow, and Sarah Van de Wetering, Washington, DC: Island Press.
3. See "Rebuilding Wisely for a Disaster-Resilient Gulf Coast: Conceptual Framework and Steps to Address Gulf Area Reconstruction and Reduce Future Risks," U.S. Department of the Interior, November 21, 2005.
4. Aldo Leopold, *A Sand Country Almanac*, Oxford University Press, 1949.
5. Garrett Hardin, "The Tragedy of the Commons," *Science* 162 (December), 1968.
6. See, for example, Gregg Easterbrook, *A Moment on Earth*, Viking, 1995.
7. F. A. Hayek, "The Use of Knowledge in Society," in *Individualism and Economic Order*, Chicago University Press, 1945.
8. Communication with Dean Marriott, Portland, Oregon, June 2009.
9. Hardin, op cit.
10. See, for example, Tomas Koontz, et al., *Collaborative Environmental Management: What Roles for Government?* Washington, DC, Resources for the Future, 2004; Philip Brick, Donald Snow, and Sarah Van de Wetering, *Across the Great Divide: Explorations in Collaborative Conservation and the American West*, Washington, DC: Island Press, 2001.
11. Elinor Ostrom, Roy Gardner, and James Walker, *Rules, Games, and Common-Pool Resources*, Ann Arbor: University of Michigan Press, 1994.
12. See www.malpaiborderlandsgroup.org
13. *Atlantic Salmon in Maine*, National Research Council, National Academies Press, Washington, D.C., 2004.
14. See www.rlch.org discussion of the Applegate Partnership.
15. For information on the Partnership, contact the Bureau of Land Management Tucson Field Office.
16. This incident was reported to the author during a visit with Buffalo Creek farmers in 2002.
17. William Isaacs, Dialogue
18. Aldo Leopold, *Sand County Almanac*.
19. *The Endangered Species Act at Thirty*, Vol. 1 & 2 (eds. Dale Goble, Michael Scott, and Frank Davis), Island Press, 2006.
20. Steven Yaffee, ADD.

B. Taking Responsibility

BAYLOR L. JOHNSON *Holding People to Collective Agreements.*

ETHICAL OBLIGATIONS IN A TRAGEDY OF THE COMMONS

Individual's action has no effect

A commons is a resource whose use is shared by several parties. Heavy use of a commons can degrade, deplete, or even destroy it. The concept is usefully elastic. Thus it can apply to a place—a pasture or forest, the Antarctic, or even the Earth; a natural resource like a fishery or the Southern Ocean whale stock; or an abstraction like the world's biodiversity. Though the concept is applicable to manmade things, for example a commons room, I shall focus in this paper on natural commons.

Many modern environmental problems are commons problems in the sense that they are caused by overuse (or overexploitation) of some shared, subtractable resource. All humans, for example, use air and water, in multiple ways. They are, inter alia, used as sinks for waste products, and this use both degrades their quality for other uses (breathing and drinking, for example) and also has side effects on resources both private and common. (So acid precipitation damages structures, both public and private, and also damages biological resources like lakes and forests.)

What ought commons users to do when their aggregate use threatens a commons? More specifically, what is the right thing for them to do ethically?

Suppose, for instance, that someone understands the problem of global warming and the contribution that autos make to it. Can she in good conscience drive an SUV (i.e., any especially large gas guzzler)? Can she in good conscience drive at all? More specifically, is it morally wrong to drive, or to drive an SUV?

Are companies that make SUVs morally obligated to stop manufacturing them? Are they immoral for making cars of any type? Are they at least obligated to make cars whose environmental effects are tolerable in some long-term picture?

The answer widely believed is a Kantian one, that every commons user ought, morally, to restrict his or her use to a level that would be sustainable if all other users reduced their use in a similar way, and to do this regardless of what others do. So, unless the earth can tolerate everyone driving SUVs, no one should. If a commons is being degraded by aggregate use, then

Adapted from Baylor L. Johnson, "Ethical Obligations in a Tragedy of the Commons," *Environmental Values* 12, no. 3 (2003): 271–287.

every firm and every factory ought voluntarily and unilaterally to reduce its emissions to the sustainable level (and to zero, if that is all that is sustainable).

While there is a kernel of truth in this answer, I think it is largely mistaken. It is mistaken because it fails to distinguish acting unilaterally from acting as one of many in a cooperative scheme to address a problem. At least in addressing commons problems, unilateral, voluntary actions typically have no reasonable chance of achieving their object. Collective efforts, by contrast, do not face the same systematic barriers. There is, of course, no guarantee that a cooperative solution to a particular commons problem can be crafted, but there is no systematic reason, of the kind faced by individual, voluntary efforts, to doubt that some collective scheme might succeed. If and when a cooperative scheme to avoid commons problems is in place, failure to adhere to it would normally be a form of free riding—an attempt to enjoy the benefits of others' sacrifices while avoiding one's own fair share of them. Free riding is immoral in the most standard and obvious ways. It is an attempt to gain an undeserved advantage by deception or force. If I am correct that unilateral action predictably has no reasonable expectation of success, then even though no one can rationally universalise use of the commons at unsustainable levels, no one has a direct moral obligation to restrict use of the commons to sustainable levels by unilateral action. Since collective, coordinated action faces no similar, systematic obstacle, and so has a greater chance of protecting the commons, one's moral obligation is to work for and adhere to a collective scheme to protect the commons.

1. THE TRAGEDY OF THE COMMONS

The term "Tragedy of the Commons" (Henceforth "T of C") comes from a classic article of that same name by Garrett Hardin.[1] A T of C occurs when many *independent* agents derive benefits from a *subtractable* resource that is threatened by their *aggregate* use.

To say that a resource is *subtractable* means that its supply of benefits can be depleted by overuse, and in the worst case, that the source of the benefits can be destroyed, as when an ecosystem or species is extinguished.

To say that the agents are *independent* means that they have no collective agreement governing use of the commons.[2] While each agent may take into account the likely actions of other agents, they have no agreed scheme for sharing use of the commons beyond mutual tolerance of mutual use.

To say that the commons is threatened by their *aggregate* use is to say that it is not threatened by each individual act of appropriation from the commons because no individual is using the commons at a rate that is unsustainable.[3] This is not a problem in which every individual act is harmful and the total of all these harmful acts is dreadful. Rather, individual acts are harmless in themselves, but harmful in aggregate.

For illustration I shall use Hardin's own parable, supposing that the agents are herders using a common pasture. Since each herder keeps all the benefit—meat, milk, wool, sale price, etc.—from each animal she pastures, each has a significant incentive to maintain or increase the size of her herd. And this incentive survives the realisation (if it occurs) that the pasture is suffering from overuse. For while each individual herder gets all the benefit from putting more animals on the commons, any improvement in the pasture that results from reducing her herd size will be shared with all other users. As a result, her individual share of these improvements will be quite small. Worse yet, even if many other herders show similar restraint, a small group (and at the limit, a single individual) can continue to increase herd size, thus appropriating the resources saved by conscientious users and undoing the good achieved by their restraint. This small group might include those who are less insightful about the damage being done to the commons, those who are too self-centred or short-sighted to care, and those who simply worry that at least some others will not restrain themselves and will thereby appropriate the resources saved by the sacrifices of others.

. . .

A rational herder therefore understands that her restraint will have a definite cost but produce a much smaller and less certain benefit. So in every decision about decreasing her herd size she sees that she will be worse off from decreasing her herd than from holding constant or increasing. The situation is nicely summed up by the phrase "use it or lose it." Resources foregone by the individual today are almost certain to be lost to some less enlightened herder tomorrow. Thus, at least where one's life or livelihood is derived from use of the commons, personal sacrifice to preserve the commons tends to be self-eliminating, as the scrupulous users lose their livelihood to the ignorant, the unscrupulous, or those who reasonably doubt that all will voluntarily reduce their use. Thus the rational herder sees that what is true in the short run is also true in the long run: merely reducing her own use of the commons to sustainable levels will have a definite cost to her, but will produce a smaller and much less certain benefit, all other herders see the same, and therefore there can be no reasonable expectation that unilateral reductions in use of the commons will be mirrored by enough other users to protect the commons.

2. THE REAL WORLD

Despite the analytical power of Hardin's parable, in the real world sharing resources does not always end in tragedy. People manage to escape from a potential T of C by a variety of stratagems, all of which can be grouped under what I call collective agreements and Hardin calls "mutual coercion mutually agreed upon."

In this paper I use terms like "collective agreement" and "cooperative scheme" interchangeably. In addressing modern environmental problems these will seldom if ever take the form of private person-to-person agreements. They will, rather, generally be legislation, or treaties between nations. Familiar examples might be green taxes, laws that regulate emissions, or treaties like Montreal Protocol pledging nations to limit emissions of ozone-depleting chemicals. They are "collective" or "cooperative" at least in the minimal sense that they coordinate the behaviour of individuals to protect the commons. This is achieved by altering the incentives that commons users face, imposing sanctions on excessive use or providing incentives for decreased use. Both of these, in turn, increase the confidence of users that their own reductions in use will not be wasted, but will be mirrored by similar reductions on the part of others.[4] When these measures are adopted within democratic regimes, they are likely

also to be "collective" or "cooperative" in the strong sense that they have the support of a majority of those affected by them.

. . .

3. MORAL OBLIGATIONS IN A TRAGEDY OF THE COMMONS—THE STANDARD ANSWER

What should a person do in a T of C? More specifically, what ought such a person to do from a moral point of view? The standard answer, the one that most people seem to accept, is that what each person ought to do is to reduce his or her use of the commons to sustainable levels and that this is true whether or not others can be expected to do so. We should (morally) do what we believe that everyone should do, and do so whether or not we believe others will actually do the same. It isn't right, after all, to follow a mob to do evil, and deeply engrained social practices can be morally wrong—slavery, for example—and it is the responsibility of individuals to resist the common wisdom and the material temptations, and to take the right stand however lonely and however costly it may be. So, too, in a T of C, most people reason, one should do "the right thing," which is to reduce one's use to the level that all could adopt while preserving the commons, and one should do this without regard to the behavior of others or the costs to oneself.

If this answer is correct, and if the situations I described in my opening are indeed T of Cs, then the answer to each of my opening questions is clear. No, we should not drive SUVs, or cars at all, unless the commons—in this case the biosphere—can sustain them for everyone, which is very doubtful. Yes, companies that pollute the commons beyond sustainable levels are acting immorally, just as manufacturers who enable us to consume beyond sustainable levels are.

By now it should be clear why I think voluntary, unilateral reductions of use have no reasonable expectation of success when the situation faced strongly resembles a T of C. . . . It is very unlikely that most commons users will adopt such widespread restraint without organised assurances that others will mirror one's own restraint. The reasons are those given above: the incentives users have in such cases; each user's knowledge that her restraint is likely only to reward less scrupulous users; each user's awareness that every other user sees the same discouraging prospect; the need for nearly universal restraint in order to effectively protect the commons or reassure users that their sacrifice is not in vain.

The only reason to adopt unilateral restraint, however, is to avert a T of C. So if unilateral restraint cannot reasonably be expected to achieve its purpose, there is no reason, and hence no moral reason, to adopt it. (I shall qualify this claim later.) I claim that averting a T of C is the only reason for adopting unilateral restraint because in a T of C there is nothing wrong with any one person's use of the commons. No one person's use is large enough to harm the commons. Harm results only from the aggregate level of use. (My argument is not meant to apply to atypical cases in which one individual's use of the commons is great enough to damage the commons independent of others' use.)

I will now consider [an objection] to this thesis.

4. [AN OBJECTION] ANSWERED

Suppose people can throw a pebble onto a pile building up on an innocent person. No individual's pebble harms the person, but if enough people cast a stone, in aggregate they will crush him to death. If each person acts independently, then just as in the commons case, no person's restraint controls the aggregate amount and no one's unilateral restraint can reasonably be supposed to prevent (or contribute to prevention of) the harm. If my reasoning about the commons is correct would it not follow, contrary to our ordinary moral intuitions, that no one has an obligation to refrain from stoning the victim?

. . .

Three parallels with the commons case clearly hold. These are as follows:

(1) No individual contribution produces harm.
(2) The harm is a consequence of the aggregation of many separate actions.
(3) No individual can prevent the harm by unilateral action.

There are three other features, however, that might differ from the typical commons case from which my

argument is derived. In a tragedy of the commons, the following three features are also found:

(1*) Each individual stands to benefit considerably (in the short run) from continuing to use the commons above sustainable levels, and will, conversely, lose appreciably from refraining.
(2*) One person's reduced use of the commons is likely to encourage others to increase use, so that her restraint becomes in effect a reward to those who are less scrupulous.
(3*) There is no collective agreement to prevent the aggregate harm by individual acts of restraint.

If all of these features were present in the pebble case, then I believe the two cases would be parallel, and my position would commit me to saying that no one else has a moral obligation to refrain from throwing his pebble. So my response to this challenge depends on claiming that these features are unlikely to hold in the pebble case, or that if they do, this excuses the individual action that would normally be morally wrong. I shall discuss each of the three in turn.

FEATURE 1*

We can imagine that 1* holds in the pebble case or that it does not. If it costs an individual little or nothing to withhold her pebble, and if she understands that throwing it on the pile will contribute to killing someone, then, ceteris paribus, it seems clear that it would be wrong to cast it onto the pile. Similarly, if users of the commons have little to gain or lose from reducing their use, then the case that each of them should do so unilaterally is strengthened. This is so for two reasons. First, if there is little at stake, the odds that enough people might unilaterally reduce use in hopes of preventing damage to the commons are increased, since people will do what is easy more often than what is costly to them. This obviously means that there is a greater chance that one's unilateral action will actually be part of a group effort that protects the commons, and so there is some good reason to take the action. Second, if the cost of restraint is small, then there is less reason for the individual to continue to use the commons, so even an improbable gamble on unilateral action is more easily justified. This follows from standard reasoning about wagers. Though numbers cannot be assigned in this case, a wager whose payoff is fixed becomes more rational as either the odds of the payoff increase or the cost of the wager decreases. So if either others are more likely to do what is necessary to protect the commons (odds of the payoff increase) or the cost to the individual of restraining use of the commons unilaterally in hopes of contributing to its protection decreases (costs of the wager decrease), then this action becomes more rational.

Suppose, however, that individuals stand to gain significantly from tossing pebbles, or to lose significantly by abstaining. Suppose, for example, that the local dictator threatens to imprison or kill those who refuse to participate, or to harm their families. In such a case it is obviously less likely that many individuals will abstain unilaterally thereby saving the victim. As a consequence, the practical point of any one individual's abstention is less, since the victim is likely to be killed no matter what the individual chooses. In this event, whereas I would admire the moral courage of a person who nevertheless refused to participate in the stoning (especially if the consequences were visited upon her alone, and not upon her innocent family), I would also tend to excuse those who participated. That is, my judgment would be harsher toward someone who threw on a stone when she could have refrained at little or no cost, than it would be for someone who threw a stone knowing that her restraint could not reasonably be expected to save the victim, while it would result in grave harm to her or to other innocents.

The latter case (where restraint is costly) is the one that parallels the typical commons situation. In judging it, I feel moral tension. On the one hand, it is difficult to say that a person who knowingly participates in the killing of an innocent person is blameless, even in the difficult conditions described. On the other, I am inclined to make allowances for the difficulty of the conditions and to see the responsibility of the participants as diminished because of those conditions. In this I draw on a long tradition that goes back in the literature at least as far as Aristotle's discussion of whether a ship's captain who jettisons cargo to save his ship in a fierce storm has acted voluntarily and so responsibly.[5] The tradition generally allows for a defense that while what one has done would otherwise be blameworthy, one has acted reasonably and with diminished fault

in the circumstances. With regard to the commons, I conclude that the moral judgment must be similar. Considered in isolation this condition (unilateral reduction in use is costly to the individual but has little chance of contributing to protection of the commons) diminishes but does not by itself remove one's moral obligation to make such a reduction.

FEATURE 2*

It is easy to imagine circumstances in which a parallel to 2* holds in the pebble case. Suppose the dictator offers a reward for each pebble tossed, so that those pebbles dropped by non-participants are likely to be picked up and thrown by less scrupulous persons. If even one person is unscrupulous enough, he can kill the victim by throwing enough stones alone. If the village idiot does not realise that all these stones will kill the victim, he might keep throwing them to collect the rewards, even if no one else did. If we imagine that no participant knows what decision the others are making, then we can even suppose that there is someone who would refrain if he thought others would also do so, but who is unwilling to pass up the reward when he thinks that his restraint will only reward the less scrupulous or less enlightened, and thus he alone throws enough stones to kill the victim in the mistaken belief that others are also throwing many stones. In such circumstances every rational person will see that her own refusal can contribute to saving the victim only if such refusal is universal, and that, given the ordinary mix of human nature, this cannot reasonably be expected. Thus she will see that her own unilateral actions will entail a cost to herself (either loss of the reward if 2* holds alone, or both punishment and loss of reward if both 1* and 2* hold), with no reasonable expectation of a good result, and hence she will be less likely to refuse to participate.

What is the moral significance of these considerations? Greed does not excuse one from moral obligations, and since I think we have a moral obligation not to contribute knowingly to the death of innocent persons, I would not argue that the promise of a reward excuses throwing of pebbles. But the line between reward and punishment is often uncertain. Suppose, for instance, that potential stone throwers cannot afford the basics of existence for themselves or for others who depend on them unless they claim the reward offered for tossing a pebble. In that case one need not be greedy to be tempted, and those who choose the reward, knowing as they do that their own restraint will not only entail serious losses, but that it cannot be expected to produce any good consequences, would have my sympathy.

I conclude that the mere fact that one must forgo a reward if one reduces one's use of the commons unilaterally plays little role in explaining why one has no moral obligation to do so. By contrast, if users must make a significant sacrifice, that would play a larger role in diminishing their moral responsibility. Taking an extreme, if other things are equal and one must choose between one's own death and that of another, or the death of some stranger and the death of someone close to us, it seems plausible to say that one has a right to choose to preserve oneself or the person close to one. I interpret this as an application of the principle that our moral responsibility to preserve the stranger is overridden by our moral right to preserve ourselves and those close to us, or more generally that a prima facie moral obligation can be overridden by the sacrifice it would entail.

FEATURE 3*

I come now to 3*, which I think is the most significant of these three features. It seems clear to me that in the pebble case we have already a collective agreement that one should, other things being equal, refrain from actions that will contribute to the harm or death of other innocent parties. Thus we have a collective agreement that one should, other things being equal, refrain from casting pebbles into the pile. In fact, as a description (I am not offering a meta-ethical theory here) of how they function, widely accepted moral beliefs are collective agreements about one's obligations in a particular kind of situation. It is because we have such agreement that I could appeal to our intuitive moral sense that one should, other things being equal, refrain from actions that cause harm to an innocent person, and a fortiori that one should refrain from actions that cause his death.

By contrast, in the typical commons case, no such collective agreement exists.

The commons problems with which I am concerned (as opposed to problems of free riding on an established agreement in a commons), occur when conditions change so that [a previously sustainable use of a commons] is seen to endanger it. Increased exploitation might endanger it, or other changes might decrease its ability to recover from use rates that were previously sustainable. Because of this, there is no pre-existing agreement about what is permissible. Heretofore individuals have been free to do what they wanted in the commons. Now that same behaviour threatens the commons. Even if awareness of the threat is widespread, agreement that one now has an obligation to refrain from previously permissible actions may be slow to emerge.

As an empirical example, think about public attitudes toward the activities producing greenhouse gases and other environmentally destructive emissions. Though many engage in self-serving denials, most people in the developed world have at least a dim awareness that their emissions are problematic. Most in the environmental community recognise that present practices are unsustainable in the long run. And some in that community believe that present practices are immoral. But it would obviously not be true that there is a public consensus that present practices must change, and still less that they are immoral.

Feature 3* seems to me to be the one of the three considered that does the heavy lifting in distinguishing a typical commons case from the pebble example, and in explaining why no one has a moral obligation to reduce use of the commons unilaterally. There is a vast difference between (a) free riding or otherwise failing to live up to an existing (and functioning) collective agreement that produces benefits, and (b) refusing to act unilaterally in the way one would like to see universalised when that is costly to oneself and cannot reasonably be expected to produce the outcome whose pursuit justifies one's action. The former is a paradigm of unethical behaviour. It may sometimes be forgiven. One's obligations may be diminished by special circumstances (such as the weight of the sacrifice demanded). But the prima facie obligation remains, forgiven, diminished, ignored, or fulfilled. By contrast, in the absence of the collective agreement that would give one's restraint a chance of securing its object, there is no point and no obligation to make the sacrifice that restraint entails.

In the pebble case we have a pre-existing agreement that one should, ceteris paribus, refrain from harming (or contributing to the harm of) innocent persons. This explains, I think, why we feel clearly that throwing pebbles is wrong, and that at best it can be understood or forgiven.

In the typical commons case, while there may be good reasons justifying an agreement about how individuals should act, and while such an agreement would give rise to a moral obligation to abide by it, in the absence of the agreement, no one has an obligation to beggar herself without purpose. One is obligated to make sacrifices for the common good, but no one has an obligation to make sacrifices without purpose, and in the circumstances of a T of C, including the absence of an [sic] collective agreement about how individuals should act to protect the commons, reducing one's own use to the sustainable level is a fruitless sacrifice.[6]

. . .

[5.] SOME QUALIFICATIONS

I promised earlier to qualify my thesis. I have argued that unilateral reduction in one's use of the commons is ineffective in averting a T of C, and therefore that it is not ethically obligatory. I have not argued that such reductions in use are, typically, immoral or unethical. They may be so if they severely deprive oneself, or other innocent persons who depend upon one, and they may be so if they become a substitute for organising efforts. Provided, however, that they do not have these consequences, individual reductions are surely morally permissible, and perhaps even praiseworthy as supererogatory actions.

Indeed, there are at least three good reasons to undertake such unilateral reductions in one's use of an overburdened commons. The first is that it may make one feel good, while doing no harm. While organizing efforts can seem impersonal, slow moving, and uncertain, when one reduces one's own burden on the natural environment, one knows that one has done something concrete and immediate. I have argued in this paper that there is little reason to think that our environmental problems will be solved by these kinds of individual, voluntary efforts, but this does not mean that they do no good at all. They

contribute, typically, a drop in the bucket, and we deceive ourselves when we think of them as analogous to the small contributions we make when we vote, or do a kind deed. Voting has a point because it is part of a collective effort, and kind deeds have immediate beneficiaries, and so both stand in contrast to ill-aimed efforts to prevent aggregate harm by unilateral efforts. But if individuals feel better because of making these individual sacrifices and are encouraged to persevere with the more important efforts to contribute to collective agreements, there is typically no reason to object to them.

This claim is strengthened by a second reason for undertaking such individual reductions, which I shall call "pioneering."[7] We need to work out new ways of living within the biosphere, and individual reductions in one's burden on an ecosystem can constitute exploration of alternative ways of life. Although full solutions to our environmental problems will almost certainly require restructuring of whole ecosystems, those who have pioneered may show where changes are most needed. Those who have lived without autos, for instance, may know best where public transit is most needed, as those who have tried solar design houses can best tell us whether, and with what adaptations, they are actually viable in a given area. Further, there may be rare cases in which technological innovations available to individuals can actually solve environmental problems, and in these cases individual purchase may strengthen the chances that a purely voluntary solution will be adopted.

A third reason for individual reductions is that it may be necessary as part of organising efforts. Those who are persuaded by the argument I have given will reject the following view, but it is still true that many people think it is hypocritical to argue that everyone should collectively undertake changes that the individual has not willingly undertaken already. Making individual reductions, therefore, may be necessary to convince others of one's sincerity and of the viability of what one proposes. Beyond this it may set an example for others and impress them with one's commitment and understanding. So as an aid to one's organising efforts, there may be a place for exemplifying the kinds of changes that one urges on others as part of a collective agreement.

[6.] CONCLUSION

There are many reasons why people believe that individual sacrifices are the proper response to a T of C. They confuse such actions with individual contributions to collective efforts like voting or pulling one's own oar in a boat. They confuse unilateral reductions in use with abstention from actions that cause immediate, individual harm, like killing and stealing. The view may be reinforced by consumer society, which encourages us to focus on sources of satisfaction that can be purchased by individuals rather than those achieved by coordinated effort with others. Not least, the belief that our obligation is primarily a personal one to reduce our own use of the commons can be comfortable. If we become involved in organising activities, we lose a certain amount of control. Others may urge us to give more—of our time, of our money—than we had planned. We may have to deal with other people in ways we find unfamiliar or unpleasant. And the process can seem interminable and therefore frustrating. It may seem, it may even be, that we are making no real progress toward our goal. By contrast, unilateral reductions in our burden on the commons are wholly within our control and hence we decide exactly how much we are obligated to do. No one badgers us to turn the heat down further or buy a still more efficient auto. And in contrast to the often frustrating uncertainty of collective efforts, individual reductions are satisfyingly certain and concrete.

For all these reasons, individual reductions are seductively inviting as a focus for our concern about threats to the natural world. If my argument in this paper is correct, however, it is a seduction we should resist. I have argued that it is a mistake to see our primary obligation as unilaterally reducing our individual burden on the environment. I have couched this in terms of a commons in order to make use of the well known and powerful reasoning that Hardin developed in discussing the Tragedy of the Commons, but it should be clear that my main concern is not with pastures but with consumer decisions, one's attitude toward polluting industries, and the like. Hardin's reasoning makes it clear why it is unreasonable to expect such uncoordinated acts of supposed virtue to achieve their object. We need to focus our efforts in the political sphere, working for changes in the

socio-economic structure that will change aggregate behaviour, and thus have effects of the magnitude needed to match the magnitude of the assaults on the integrity of ecological processes. Similarly, I believe, we must accept that we cannot expect companies to undertake costly environmental protection plans voluntarily, for they thereby put themselves at a competitive disadvantage that may only undermine their viability.[8] On the other hand, those individuals and firms that actively oppose collective agreements that could "level the playing field" and effectively address the commons problems that we face do fully deserve our condemnation. The dangers are real, and those who seek to benefit in the short run at the expense of the larger public, including future generations, are at best misguided, and at worst immoral.

REFERENCES

Aristotle. 1966. *Nicomachean Ethics*, in R. McKeon (ed.) *The Basic Works of Aristotle*. New York: Random House.

Hardin, G. 1968. "The Tragedy of the Commons," *Science* 162: 1243–48.

Ostrom, E. 1990. *Governing the Commons*. New York: Cambridge University Press.

Parfit, D. 1984. *Reasons and Persons*. Oxford & New York: Oxford University Press.

NOTES

1. G. Hardin 1968.
2. An effective collective agreement would establish rules for use of the commons, a method for monitoring compliance with the rules and sanctions for non-compliance, and a mechanism for amending all of these as required. Such an agreement can be quite formal, or merely customary. See E. Ostrom (1990).
3. This is typical in potential T of Cs. This paper is not concerned with atypical cases in which individual agents exceed sustainable rates of use of a commons.
4. Privatising a commons, either by giving property rights to the whole to one individual, or by carving it up into parcels whose property rights are assigned to multiple individuals, is a special type of

collective agreement. It is a collective agreement in that property rights are recognised and enforced by the collectivity. It alters the incentives of commons users because they acquire exclusive use of some portion of the commons and so can reasonably expect that their reductions in use will result in offsetting benefits for themselves. It is special since the scheme does not require cooperative reductions in use by others.

5. Aristotle, 1966: 1110a.

6. In *Reasons and Persons* Derek Parfit has addressed a number of the same issues that I take up in this paper. So far as I can see we have no important disagreements. Importantly his Fisherman's Dilemma (esp. pp. 101–103) is a typical T of C, and in discussing it he too endorses the claim that no one has a moral obligation to reduce use of the commons without a reasonable expectation that enough others will do likewise to gain the benefits

that only shared restraint can obtain. I am indebted to an anonymous reviewer for *Environmental Values* for bringing Parfit's work on similar issues to my attention.

7. I owe the term "pioneering" to Faye Duchin.

8. Firms can, of course, judge that environmentally desirable actions are in their competitive interest, perhaps because they will appeal to some consumers or perhaps because the firm anticipates that such actions will be necessitated by legislation or supply shortages in the future and that the firm will be better able to compete by advance preparation for these developments. Support for collective action to protect the environment encourages the latter kind of action. Conversely, such moves are discouraged when anticipated agreements are undermined, since those who took early steps have incurred costs that will not normally be compensated by the market.

TY RATERMAN — *WE SHOULD BE CONSISTENTLY TRYING TO DO BEST OR. GET OUT OF OUR COMFORT ZONE.*

BEARING THE WEIGHT OF THE WORLD
On the Extent of an Individual's Environmental Responsibility

1. INTRODUCTION

I think of myself as an environmentally-conscientious person: I walk or bicycle to work, eat a vegetarian diet,[1] recycle zealously, practically never heat or air-condition my home, and more. It is, however, not my intention to boast. In fact, I want plainly to admit that it is certainly *not* the case that I perform every

environmentally-friendly action I could. Thus, I often find myself wondering: Am I doing all that I ought to be? Is my environmental impact small enough as to satisfy the demands of morality? Now, I also wonder about how much businesses and governments should do to help promote a healthy environment. Questions about business and government, though, are not ones I will explicitly consider here—though some of what

Adapted from Ty Raterman, "Bearing the Weight of the World: On the Extent of an Individual's Environmental Responsibility," *Environmental Values* 21, no. 4 (2012): 417–436.

I argue may be relevant to them. Instead, this paper's central focus is on the actions of individual people. The primary question is: To what extent is an individual morally obligated to perform environmentally-friendly actions? In other words: At what point has an individual done what she/he ought, morally, in respect to the environment?

After motivating the question more fully, I will reject two ways of answering—views that I see as constituting two extremes. On one of these views, while we are morally obligated to act in accordance with established, sensible collective schemes that in practice require *many* people jointly to act in the environmentally-friendly way, we are not morally obligated to act in this way *unilaterally*—which is to say outside of a collective scheme, where one person's potentially-lone action has no meaningful impact. On the other view, even in the absence of a collective scheme, and so even without assurance that many other people would join in, each person is nonetheless morally obligated to act in a way that would be sustainable if everyone were to act in this way. The truth, I believe, is somewhere in the messy middle. I will argue that each individual's moral obligation, roughly, is constantly to strive to do more than she/he does currently and to push her/himself to new, uncomfortable territory, but that no one is obligated to martyr her/himself for an environmental cause.

2. SETTING UP THE QUESTION

I would never claim that one's judgments regarding the extent of one's moral responsibility is the only, or even always the primary, motivation for acting. Some people seem not to care one whit about morality. And even those of us who do so care are complicated creatures who are typically motivated by a variety of factors: social pressure, desire for pleasure, affection from others, etc. For most of us, though, how we act does often turn somewhat, and does sometimes turn largely, on our judgments about how we ought, morally, to act. In deciding what environmentally-friendly actions to perform, many of us are thus interested to know what morality requires. However, that issue is complex, particularly in light of four points.

First, the list of environmentally-friendly actions one could perform is incredibly long. One could: have a small family (even altogether abstaining from having children); drive less, and walk, bicycle or take public transit more; live close to where one works; carpool; drive the most fuel-efficient vehicle possible, and keep it tuned up and leak free, and its tyres properly inflated; minimise the number of miles one flies; eat a vegetarian diet; eat food that is local and organic; invest in the stock of only environmentally-responsible companies; buy products that are produced in an environmentally-responsible manner; buy products that are extensively reusable; buy second-hand items; recycle; properly dispose of automotive oil, batteries and tyres, and of household hazardous waste; avoid toxic or non-biodegradable products; live in a small-sized dwelling; live in a region with a moderate climate; heat and cool one's home minimally; work to ensure that one's house is as energy efficient as possible (e.g., that it is well insulated, its doors shut tightly, its windows are double-paned, . . . its appliances are efficient, that it uses compact fluorescent light bulbs, that its lights and electronics get turned off—that electronics even get unplugged—when not being used, and that it is powered by solar panels and/or renewable energy from one's power company); renovate (flooring, cabinetry, countertops, etc.) using sustainable materials; take short showers; do not flush every time one goes to the bathroom; do not wash clothes, towels, sheets, etc., unless they are genuinely sufficiently dirty; use a manual lawn mower; avoid synthetic fertilisers, herbicides and pesticides. The list could go on.[2]

Second, many of these behaviours involve some cost to the individual engaging in them. Consider, first, monetary costs. As an example, buying "green" products—organic food or clothes, say—often requires paying more than one would for the "conventional" alternative. Fixing an oil leak in one's car can also be expensive. Now, some environmentally-friendly purchases will save the consumer money in the long run. Energy-efficient products are the obvious example: a more efficient refrigerator, dual-pane windows, home insulation, etc. Often, though, these will cost more *up front*—a nontrivial fact for people whose bank account is thin enough to make it difficult to do what will pay for itself (say) a decade later. Other costs are non-monetary. Some environmentally-friendly actions involve making extra effort (e.g., bringing hazardous household waste to the appropriate municipal facility), enduring some inconvenience (e.g., walking rather than driving), or sacrificing some comfort (e.g., not air conditioning one's home on a hot day) or some enjoyment (e.g., not making a lovely sight-seeing drive). Sometimes these actions can actually save one money, but they count as costs overall when, in the individual's eyes, the value of what is lost (comfort, convenience, etc.) outweighs the value of the money saved.

Third, the fact that the environmentally-friendly action is costly (in one or more of the aforementioned senses) means that many people—not all people, certainly, but many—will not actually perform the action unless required, or at least strongly pressured, to do so. This is not to say that cost is always the factor preventing every individual from behaving in the environmentally-friendly way. Undoubtedly, people sometimes act simply out of custom.[3] Rather, the point—which I take to be uncontroversial—is just that the costliness of the aforementioned kinds of actions can in many cases be counted as a barrier against their performance.

Fourth, environmental problems are collective-action problems, and the aforementioned kinds of actions generally have no appreciable impact unless they are consistently performed by many people. I might refrain from taking a jet ski[4] onto a local lake so that I do not contribute to the pollution of the lake; but if everyone else who would normally go jet skiing there does so just the same, the effect of my refraining fails to register. Any test of the lake's water quality will produce the same results as if I had joined in the fun. Relatedly, if no one else is performing some particular environmentally-unfriendly action, the environment is not made worse off in any significant or discernible way by one single person doing so. So, if I alone jet ski, a test of the lake's water quality will come back the same as if no one *at all* jet skied. These two related points generally hold in respect to all the possible environmentally-friendly actions I listed earlier—and especially when impacts are assessed on a large scale. Consider, even, the decision regarding how many children to have. Now, it is true that over the course of a lifetime the amount of raw materials consumed, solid waste produced, and carbon gases emitted by one single person—particularly in developed countries,

and above all in the profligate United States—will measure in the thousands of metric tons. Nonetheless, an exhaustive account of environmental problems—whether global or local—is not going to differ at all according to how many children any one particular couple decided to have. No environmental scientist assessing air quality, no ecologist evaluating the health of a forest or stream, no epidemiologist gauging rates of cancer, no population biologist examining an endangered species, and no climatologist studying ambient temperatures, is going to take a measurement that would at all differ depending on one couple's reproductive choices.

The difficulty is now apparent. Given how many environmentally-friendly actions one could conceivably perform, that so many of these involve a cost to the individual performing them, and that whether or not one individual performs an action generally has no appreciable effect on the environment, it is far from clear how many such actions one is actually morally obligated to perform.

. . .

[3.] ONE WRONG ANSWER

One of the most provocative answers to the question of the extent of an individual's moral obligation in respect to the environment comes from Baylor Johnson.[5] Johnson rejects what he calls the "Kantian" principle that "every commons user ought, morally, to reduce her or his use to a level that would be sustainable if all other users reduced their use in a similar way, and to do this regardless of what others do."[6] He argues instead that "one's moral obligation is [only] to work for [the establishment of] a collective scheme to protect the commons" and to "adhere to" this once it is in place.[7] As I will explain in the next section of the paper, I agree that the Kantian principle—which constitutes what I call one of two extremes—should be rejected. This does not, however, lead me to endorse Johnson's alternative—which I count, frankly, as the extreme other end of the spectrum.

. . .

Johnson maintains that unilateral actions are never obligatory. He does acknowledge that "It isn't

right . . . to follow a mob to do evil, and deeply engrained social practices can be morally wrong—slavery,
for example—and it is the responsibility of individuals
to resist the common wisdom and the material temptation, and to take the right stand however lonely and
however costly it may be."[8] He does not, however, believe this carries over to individual actions in the context of the environment. He says that "The only reason
to adopt unilateral restraint . . . is to avert a [tragedy
of the commons]. So if unilateral restraint cannot reasonably be expected to achieve its purpose, there is no
reason, and hence no moral reason, to adopt it."[9] On
one occasion he says that in respect to big environmental problems, "no individual's use of the commons is harmful."[10] This, he notes, is what makes, e.g.,
driving a gas-guzzling car different from, say, murder
and lying: an act of murder harms and lying (at least)
often does so, whereas no matter how big a guzzler the
vehicle is, no meaningful harm is done through the
driving of it.[11]

. . .

There are, of course, numerous possible objections to
this. Johnson himself actually considers one, which
goes as follows:

> Suppose people can throw a pebble onto a pile
> building up on an innocent person. No individual's
> pebble harms the person, but if enough people cast
> a stone, in aggregate they will crush him to death. If
> each person acts independently, then just as in the
> commons case, no person's restraint controls the ag-
> gregate amount and no one's unilateral restraint can
> reasonably be supposed to prevent (or contribute to
> the prevention of) the harm. If my reasoning about
> the commons is correct would it not follow, contrary
> to our ordinary moral intuitions, that no one has an
> obligation to refrain from stoning the victim?[12]

Naturally, Johnson believes he has a satisfactory
reply: he says that in respect to the average environmental problem: (1) a person who draws on the
commons at an unsustainable level stands to benefit
considerably from doing so and would lose appreciably from refraining; (2) when a person refrains
from unsustainable use of the commons, she/he in
effect makes it easier for others to increase their use;

and (3) "there is no collective agreement to prevent
the aggregate harm by individual acts of restraint."[13]
Johnson argues that while the pebble-casting case may
or may not match the first two characteristics, it does
not match the third. "It seems clear to me," he says,
"that in the pebble case we have already a collective
agreement that one should, other things being equal,
refrain from actions that will contribute to the harm
or death of other innocent parties. Thus we have a collective agreement that one should, other things being
equal, refrain from casting pebbles into the pile."[14]

I find the objection itself quite powerful, and see
multiple problems in Johnson's reply. First, if—as
Johnson seems to believe—the agreement not to cast
pebbles onto the pile is not sui generis, and instead
falls out of a broader agreement to refrain from actions that contribute to the harm or death of innocent persons, then an agreement not to perform
environmentally-unfriendly actions plainly also falls
out. To be clear, this is not necessarily because one
person's environmentally-unfriendly actions do . . . by
themselves harm innocent persons. . . . Setting a
forest fire is an example of a single environmentally-
unfriendly action performed by a lone individual that
can cause such harm; but examples of this sort are
rare. . . . But even if we ignore these possibilities and,
with Johnson . . . , focus on harm to humans and say
that individual environmentally-unfriendly actions do
not cause such harm, we can still say that such an action
contributes to such harm. Plainly, a sufficient amount of
pollution can harm us, and so, too, can severe deprivation of access to important resources; and so even if I
am not harming an innocent person when I consume
energy (even of a non-renewable sort) by air conditioning my home, or drive my car (without crashing it into
anyone), or send a recyclable bottle to a landfill, I am
certainly contributing to such a harm when I do these
things. Not everything that contributes to a harm actually harms, just as not everything that contributes to a
tasty dish is tasty (think: pepper, all by itself). But an
action can contribute to a harm even if the action is
neither necessary nor sufficient for the harm. Consider
this example from Walter Sinnott-Armstrong: "Imagine
that it takes three people to push a car off a cliff with
a passenger locked inside, and five people are already
pushing. If I join and help them push, then my act of

pushing is neither necessary nor sufficient to make the car go off the cliff. Nonetheless, my act of pushing is a cause (or part of the cause) of the harm to the passenger."[15] When the car goes over the cliff, the passenger is surely harmed, and if one joins in as a sixth pusher, one has certainly contributed to that harm. So, in short, if the agreement not to be one of many who piles a pebble on the helpless person is part of or entailed by a general agreement not to harm *or* to *contribute* to a harm of innocent persons, then Johnson should say that behaving in environmentally-unfriendly ways is prohibited by the same general agreement.[16]

Second, it is surely not simply on account of a pre-existing agreement that it is morally wrong to toss your pebble onto the pile. The point is perhaps easiest to see in the context, again, of Sinnott-Armstrong's car-pushing example. Johnson would no doubt say that we should not join in to push the occupied car over the cliff, and he would presumably say this because we have made some prior "collective agreement that one should, other things being equal, refrain from actions that will contribute to the harm or death of other innocent parties"—as joining in pushing them over the cliff would. However, suppose we had not made such an agreement. Would it then really be permissible to join in the pushing? At least in ordinary circumstances, it plainly would not.[17] The same is true in the pebble-tossing case. The agreement—even if it exists—is clearly not as important as Johnson suggests. Even if there is no collective agreement not to contribute to the harm of innocent persons by performing environmentally-unfriendly actions, it is at least an open question whether doing so is wrong. The mere fact that there is no agreement in the environmental case—supposing this to be a fact—would not entail that there is nothing morally wrong with contributing to a harm by performing environmentally-unfriendly actions.

Johnson says that "If and when a cooperative scheme to avoid a commons problem is in place, failure to adhere to it would normally be a form of free riding—an attempt to enjoy the benefits of others' sacrifices while avoiding one's own fair share of them."[18] But—as an extension of my second point, above—surely free-riding can occur, and count as wrong, even outside of a formal cooperative scheme. Consider an apartment complex where every two weeks a paid employee scoops leaves out of the swimming pool. However, leaves accumulate in the pool quickly. There is no collective agreement that residents will scoop out leaves; in fact, the formal pre-existing agreement stipulates that the complex employees will do so. Nonetheless, imagine that as a resident I recognise the need, and so take the net and do some cleaning. Another tenant—one with whom I have never spoken—sees me doing so and the next day takes a turn of her own. The next day, another tenant—again, without any communication—takes a turn; and so on. A dozen tenants join in, but there is still nothing official about this scheme. There is, however, one person who swims every day, but who would not do so if there were leaves in the pool, and who knows both that other residents have informally started taking turns doing some cleaning and that without this there would be many leaves in the pool, but who never takes a turn cleaning. This person is free-riding, and is morally derelict. Again, this shows that Johnson is trying to get too much leverage out of what he terms a collective agreement or cooperative scheme.

At this point, Johnson might claim that the kind of scheme he has in mind as being morally relevant need not be particularly formal, and thus that what exists in my pool-cleaning case actually counts as such. There would be two problems with such a claim. First, this kind of case is very unlike the "legislation [and] treaties between nations" that Johnson himself mentioned in characterising typical collective schemes.[19] Second, were he to make such a claim, Johnson would be wielding a double-edged sword, since the more the bar is lowered on what level of formality is required for the existence of a collective agreement or scheme, the more Johnson will have needed, on pain of consistency, to say something he plainly does not believe, namely that so many (and perhaps all) of our environmental behaviours are governed by a collective agreement.

Further evidence of the unsuccessfulness of Johnson's appeal to the significance of collective schemes comes from his (quick) discussion of voting. Voting parallels the pebble-tossing and environmental cases in important ways. That citizens living in democracies ought to vote is uncontroversial.[20] This is true despite the fact that no major election is going to be decided by a single vote. (This is increasingly certain as one moves from an election within a small organisation to the level of the city, county, state and nation.) So, there is no individual whose vote is going to make a difference to the outcome of the election. On what grounds, then, can Johnson maintain that citizens in a democracy ought to vote? He says: "Individual, voluntary efforts [in respect to the environment] . . . contribute merely a drop in the bucket, and we deceive ourselves when we think of them as analogous to the small contributions we make when we vote . . . Voting has a point because it is part of a collective effort."[21] This is essentially all he says; but it is surely inadequate to establish that the analogy to voting is problematic. Again one wishes that Johnson had been clearer about what is required for a collective scheme (i.e., agreement, i.e., effort) to exist. Voting is, we can concede, part of a collective effort, if that means just that many people make the needed effort to cast a vote, and believe that it is important to do so. But a considerable number of people also make an effort to reduce their environmental impacts. If voting is "part of a collective effort," why would recycling, buying organic food and biking to work not also be? It is true that these things are not formally required; but then neither is voting. I thus cannot see grounds for saying, as Johnson does, that one has a moral responsibility to vote but not to perform even a single environmentally-friendly action outside of a collective scheme.

In addition to failing to explain what is wrong with being one of many individuals who sets a pebble onto the helpless person or with failing to vote in a large-scale election, Johnson's argument is actually self-defeating. Again, while maintaining that we are not morally obligated to make unilateral reductions in our environmental impact, Johnson argues that we *are* morally obligated to work to establish collective schemes. However, the reasons that tell against the former tell equally against the latter. Johnson considers and rejects this charge. He says: "organising efforts do not face the most intractable features of a [tragedy of the commons]. In particular no one can misappropriate the benefits of one's organising efforts in the way that one party can appropriate the resources saved by another's forbearance in a commons."[22] He adds that "Even more importantly, in a [tragedy of the commons] game the possibilities of communication between

users are, by definition, limited to decisions to increase or reduce use of the commons" whereas "organising efforts face no such artificial limits on communication."[23] In my judgment, however, these differences are not that significant. The features of a tragedy of the commons scenario that Johnson's case really rests on are present in the context of working to establish a collective scheme: there are many possible collective agreements, and fixing our environmental problems will require many actual collective agreements, not just one; doing so is costly (requiring both time and, in almost every case, money); most people will not perform this work; and it takes the work of many people to get even a single . . . collective scheme in place (so that one's individual's efforts will be fruitless if no one else is working on this and needless if many others are working on it). And here, Johnson's aforementioned tack of locating moral reasons in the terms of a pre-existing agreement will unquestionably not work. There is not a pre-existing collective agreement to work to establish collective agreements; and even if there were, the problem could then just be pushed up a level. (To avoid an infinite regress, at *some point* reasons to work to establish a collective agreement must be located outside of a pre-existing agreement.)

Now, as I will explain in the next section, I cannot get on board with what we have dubbed the Kantian principle in the context of environmentally-friendly actions. That said, to me it is now plain that the absence of a collective agreement does not entirely excuse one from the moral obligation to perform environmentally-friendly actions. Any sensible account of our moral obligations will need to make room for non-consequentialist reasons for acting. Johnson's does not do so. As noted above, he says that "The only reason to adopt unilateral restraint . . . is to avert a [tragedy of the commons]. So if unilateral restraint cannot reasonably be expected to achieve its purpose, there is no reason, and hence no moral reason to adopt it."[24] This omits so much.

. . .

Performing environmentally-friendly actions unilaterally plainly has an extremely important symbolic, expressive function. When one makes the decision to live close to where one works, one proclaims that one is not complicit in the harm (in the form of polluted air, a changing climate, etc.) that results when many people engage in long commutes. By, say, biking to work, one declares one's repudiation of lifestyles built around the rapacious, unsustainable consumption of fossil fuels. By eschewing meat, one engages in a form of protest—important more for what it symbolises than for what it accomplishes—against the wastefulness and pollution of factory farms, and indeed against a view of animals as resources existing simply for humans' benefit. By setting one's recycling bin out for pickup each week, one expresses one's disapproval of wastefulness, and symbolically announces that one cares about the future of the planet (including all those people who dwell on it). By doing nothing in respect to recycling one communicates the opposite message. And if one works for the establishment of a recycling-related collective scheme but prior to its establishment one does not actually recycle, one at best communicates a mixed message.

Now, all the examples just mentioned are ones where the performance or non-performance of the act is not private. Others see my recycling bin on the curb or see that it is not there. They see me biking to work, or driving there. And they at least sometimes see me eating meat or refraining from doing so. What work can the notion of actions' expressive or symbolic function do when the actions are more private—as, for example, adding insulation to your attic is? Here, one may be affirming something to members of one's family—perhaps children in the family, most importantly; but even if one is not doing that, it is important that by performing the action one is affirming something to oneself.

All of this, but especially the idea of affirming something to oneself, relates closely to integrity. Everyone takes integrity to be a virtue. As Marion Hourdequin has noted, integrity and integration are related notions: to be a person of integrity is, roughly, to be a person whose values and behaviours are integrated, or in other words, harmonise.[25] There are many ways one might lack integrity. As Hourdequin correctly observes, one of these is to value a healthy environment—e.g., clean air, large thriving forests, unpolluted oceans, etc.—but not to act in ways that reflect this value. If I value a healthy environment but do not recycle,

bicycle, turn down the heat in my house, reduce/eliminate meat in my diet, etc. unless there is a collective agreement requiring this of everyone, my integrity is compromised. This is true, in fact, even if I am working to establish collective agreements (as opposed to doing *nothing* that is environmentally friendly), since in this case, quite plainly—as Hourdequin notes—my actions at the personal and political levels are not integrated.

. . .

[4.] ANOTHER WRONG ANSWER

According to the argument in the previous section, Johnson's position—which constitutes one of two extremes—is wrong. Each individual has moral reasons to make unilateral reductions in his/her consumption and pollution. These reasons are strong enough that, at least sometimes, it is wrong not to make the unilateral reduction. This does not mean, however, that the view constituting the other extreme is the correct one. According to this view, which might reasonably be called Kantian, the fact that environmental problems are collective-action problems, and that many people will not join you in performing the environmentally-friendly action, in no ways excuses you from doing so unilaterally. On this view, you are morally obligated to act in a sustainable manner regardless of what others are doing. Or, to put it slightly differently, even where no collective scheme is in place, you are morally obligated to act as you would be required if the collective agreement existed.[26]

What is the problem with this view? Recall from earlier that Johnson claimed that environmental problems share the following three characteristics: (1) a person who draws on the commons at an unsustainable level stands to benefit considerably from doing so and would lose appreciably from refraining; (2) when a person refrains from unsustainable use of the commons, she/he in effect makes it easier for others to increase their use; and (3) "there is no collective agreement to prevent the aggregate harm by individual acts of restraint." Again, Johnson has maintained that his argument does not entail that putting one's pebble on the pile is permissible because that kind of case does not fit the third of those characteristics. I have argued that this is unconvincing. The first of those features, though, can do more work. In the pebble case, individuals probably do not stand to benefit considerably from putting their pebble on the pile and would not lose significantly by refraining. The same is true in respect to helping to push the car off the cliff and . . . voting. Were this different, though—that is, were there a very high cost associated with holding back one's pebble, or abstaining from helping to push the car, or voting—then it would not be nearly so obvious that one is morally obligated to do these things.

Usefully, Johnson asks us to consider the following:

> Suppose . . . individuals stand to gain significantly from tossing pebbles, or to lose significantly by abstaining. Suppose . . . the local dictator threatens to imprison or kill those who refuse to participate. . . . In this event, whereas I would admire the moral courage of a person who nevertheless refused to participate in the stoning. . . . I would also tend to excuse those who participated. That is, my judgment would be harsher toward someone who threw on a stone when she could have refrained at little or no cost, than it would be for someone who threw a stone knowing that her restraint could not reasonably be expected to save the victim, while it would result in grave harm to her.[27]

This is a reasonable point; and it has significant consequences for our discussion. I recently completed an 'ecological footprint' inventory.[28] The results indicated that if everyone on the planet lived like I do, we would need just over three Earths to sustain us! In order to satisfy the Kantian requirement, I would need to reduce my impact very significantly. As I said in my introduction, though, I think of myself as *already* behaving in many significant environmentally-friendly ways. Plainly, then, getting my footprint down to what the Kantian approach requires would take a rather monumental effort. Running my air conditioner and heater as little as I do already impinges considerably on my quality of life. Doing all that I would need to do to reduce my footprint from "three Earths" to "one Earth" would almost certainly diminish my quality of life in a very serious way. It would seemingly be inconvenient and expensive—involving actions ranging from ensuring that much more of my food is local and organic, to installing solar panels on my house, perhaps all the way to eliminating trips to visit my parents

and siblings (who live about 2000 miles from me). Now, if everyone else were similarly committed to reducing their impacts, I would be more willing to do so; and perhaps it would then even be immoral for me not to. But I am not obligated to martyr myself alone, when my serious sacrifice would be for naught—as it would be given how few other people[29] are, or would be, willing to live in a way that approaches a footprint as small as "one Earth."

. . . That one will make a difference is not the only reason one could have for acting; there are plainly meaningful non-consequentialist reasons for refraining from putting one's pebble on the prostrate innocent person, even if one's pebble would be far from necessary or sufficient for bringing about harm to this person. That is not enough to say, though, that these reasons are indefeasible. So, if enough other people are certainly going to cast their pebble onto the pile that this individual is going to die regardless of what I do with my pebble, and there are *very* serious negative consequences for me if I hold back my pebble, then it is implausible to say that I should not—i.e., that it would be seriously wrong of me to—put my pebble on the pile. Similarly, I have meaningful non-consequentialist reasons for refraining from, as it were, putting my consumption and pollution "on the pile," even if my consumption and pollution would be far from necessary or sufficient for causing environmental harm. But these reasons are not indefeasible; and they are annulled or overridden specifically in cases where the environmentally-friendly actions become—as they certainly can—sufficiently burdensome.

[5.] THE MIDDLE WAY

The critical question at this stage is: How substantial does the sacrifice to one's own welfare need to be before the non-consequentialist reasons for performing the environmentally-friendly unilateral actions are defeated? Alas, it is very difficult to specify, in general, with any high degree of exactness. There are too many variables to be able to say, e.g., that one ought to perform 117 environmentally-friendly unilateral actions, or that one ought unilaterally to devote 23 per cent of one's income to environmentally-friendly purchases/investments, or anything of this sort. Instead,

I believe it is most illuminating to proceed via a handful of analogies. In athletic training, one can generally be sure one is not exercising in a sufficiently vigorous way if there is no strain or pain involved; and, by the same token, one is doing too much if one exercises so hard as to cripple oneself. In education, if one does not push oneself to the point of discomfort—of being tired, and of confronting claims that are hard to understand and/or challenge one's longstanding commitments—one is not doing enough; but one is doing too much if one studies to the point where one emotionally collapses or forsakes all one's other projects and relationships. In employment, if one never works hard enough to be tired or stressed, and never thinks about one's job-related responsibilities when one is home in the evening, one is not doing enough; but if one works so hard that one never sees one's children or gives oneself terrible ulcers, one is doing too much. In parenting, if one is never willing to be inconvenienced by driving one's child somewhere or getting out of bed at night when one's child has a nightmare, one is not doing enough; but if one instantly drops what one is doing, no matter how personally important, every time one's child faintly requests it, then one is going further than one is obligated.

The analogies are imperfect, but are important nonetheless. They demonstrate several things. First, there are many kinds of cases in which we lack a very precise formula for determining whether we are doing as much as we ought to be—and, in fact, we are not especially surprised or disturbed by the lack of such a formula in those cases. In light of this, our inability to fix an exact extent to which we ought to perform environmentally-friendly actions should not be viewed as especially disappointing, and indeed the initial suspicion that we might be able to specify precisely how much we are morally obligated to do in the environmental context looks somewhat naïve. Second, what we can reasonably say, in so many kinds of cases in life, is that one is not expected to be as fully devoted to an end as one could possibly be, but one is plainly not doing enough if one stays entirely within the realm of comfort and convenience. So, *prima facie*, it is sensible to think that the same is true of our duties in respect to the environment.

There arises at this point a question about the degree of subjectivity in my account. Plainly, the same

action will not necessarily always strike two people as equally taxing. However, this does not mean that the account is therefore thoroughly subjective. Let us return to the exercise example. A five-mile run is a breeze for some people, and for others [it] would be brutal. But if someone says that taking one 15-minute walk a day is too arduous, we are generally incredulous. If this is indeed too arduous, it means that that individual is very unhealthy. Similarly, for some people there is little discomfort or inconvenience in biking to work or installing solar panels on their home. For others, though, this will be much more taxing. This degree of subjectivity does not particularly concern me. Indeed, it leaves room for us to say, as, for example, Lucie Middlemiss has,[30] that what exactly one's environmental obligations are turns to some degree on one's financial means and life circumstances. However, if someone says that the effort associated with recycling is enough to make her/him uncomfortable and thus is all she/he is obligated to do, she/he is either exaggerating or lazy. For the majority of us, whose recyclables are picked up at the curb outside our house, recycling is simply not cumbersome (physically or financially). As for those things which do involve discomfort, it is also relevant to note that, as with so many other things in life, the more you perform various environmentally-friendly actions, the more accustomed to these you become, and the less uncomfortable doing them seems. Carpooling to work and eating less meat are examples. Finally, we must recognise that not everything that seems like a burden truly is. As Chrisoula Andreou has explained,[31] ample psychological research has shown that so much of our environmentally-taxing material consumption fails to contribute significantly to our happiness.

So, I finally return to my initial question: Is my environmental impact small enough as to satisfy the demands of morality? I do not do all that I could—but it is not my obligation to do so. On the other hand, there are many environmentally-friendly actions I perform unilaterally, and I have strong non-consequentialist reasons for doing so. So, I am in that messy middle, which, in general, is where I should be. Indeed, I do enough as to involve some discomfort and inconvenience. However, much of what once seemed to me quite taxing is now practically second nature. I have settled into a routine, and my obligation is to strive further and challenge myself anew. I am not failing egregiously, but there is more I can do without seriously sacrificing my well-being. The crawlspace of my house is ready for insulation, and local organic farmers are ready for more of my business! It is time to stop talking and take action.

REFERENCES

Andreaou, C. 2010. "A shallow route to environmentally-friendly happiness: Why evidence that we are shallow materialists need not be bad news for the environment(alist)." *Ethics, Place and Environment* 13(1): 1–10.

Dobson, A. 2004. *Citizenship and the Environment*. New York: Oxford University Press.

Dobson, A. 2007. *Green Political Thought*. New York: Routledge.

Gabbert, L. and J. Schein (directors). 2009. *No Impact Man* [motion picture]. Oscilloscope Pictures.

Green, P. 2007. "The year without toilet paper." *New York Times*, 22 March 2007: Home & Garden section.

Hourdequin, M. 2010. "Climate, collective action and individual ethical obligations." *Environmental Values* 19: 443–64.

Ilea, R.C. 2009. "Intensive livestock farming: Global trends, increased environmental concerns, and ethical solutions." *Journal of Agricultural and Environmental Ethics* 12(3): 271–287.

Johnson, B. 2003. "Ethical obligations in a Tragedy of the Commons." *Environmental Values* 12(3): 271–287.

Middlemiss, L. 2010. "Reframing individual responsibility for sustainable consumption: Lessons from environmental justice and ecological citizenship." *Environmental Values* 19(2): 147–167.

Sinnott-Armstrong, W. 2005. "It's not my fault: Global warming and individual moral obligation," in W. Sinnott-Armstrong and R.B. Howarth (eds.), *Perspectives on Climate Change: Science, Economics, Politics, Ethics* (Amsterdam: Elsevier), pp. 285–307.

Shove, E. 2004. *Comfort, Cleanliness, and Convenience: The Social Organization of Normality*. Oxford: Berg Publishers.

NOTES

1. That a vegetarian diet is environmentally friendly will not be obvious to every reader. For an excellent account of the adverse environmental impacts of the livestock/meat industry, see Ilea, 2009.
2. Several years ago, the *New York Times* ran a story about a family—the Conlin-Beavans—in New York City who undertook a year-long "no-impact" experiment. During this time the family went so far as to avoid using toilet paper! (See Green 2007.) The undertaking was captured on film and later released as a documentary. (See Gabbert and Schein, 2009.)
3. For more on this, see, e.g., Shove, 2004.
4. Technically, Jet Ski is a brand name, but I am following the custom of using it as a general term for what are more properly called "personal watercraft."
5. Johnson, 2003.
6. Ibid.: 272.
7. Ibid.
8. Ibid.: 276.
9. Ibid: 277.
10. Ibid.: 278.
11. Assuming, of course, that it is not crashed into someone.
12. Johnson, 2003: 278.
13. Ibid. 279.
14. Ibid. 281.
15. Sinnott-Armstrong, 2005: 289.
16. It is hardly worth mentioning, I think, that if the claim were instead to be that there is a sui generis agreement not to be one of many people who put a pebble on a pile on top of an innocent person, this would be implausible on its face.
17. A case where someone is holding a gun to your head demanding that you help push is not an ordinary case; and this connects up to what I will discuss in the next section of the paper.
18. Johnson, 2003: 272.
19. Ibid: 274.
20. In any case, it is [. . .a claim] whose truth I am simply going to take for granted for the sake of this paper.
21. Johnson, 2003: 285.
22. Ibid. 284.

23. Ibid. 284.
24. Ibid. 277.
25. Hourdequin, 2010.
26. If forced, we might label Dobson (2004, 2007) as a contemporary proponent of this view. Space limitations prevent me from discussing his specific arguments in detail.

27. Johnson, 2003: 280.
28. A number of these are available online, but the one I used is at http://www.myfootprint.org, and is hosted by the Center for Sustainable Economy.
29. Or at least so few people in the "developed" world.
30. Middlemiss 2010.
31. Andreou 2010.

DAN SHAHAR

TREADING LIGHTLY ON THE CLIMATE IN A PROBLEM-RIDDEN WORLD

In the public discourses of most developed nations, trepidation about global climate change is often bound up with concerns over "personal carbon footprints." According to the conventional wisdom on responsible climate citizenship, personal choices that expand one's carbon footprint ought to be made with hesitation, since these activities are "part of the problem."[1] Likewise, opportunities to reduce one's carbon footprint ought to be pursued, since these activities are "part of the solution."

Within the last dozen years, however, doubts have been raised about the moral significance of our carbon footprints. The main source of these reservations is the idea that single individuals' impacts on the global climate system are vanishingly small in comparison with the worldwide patterns of climate forcing activities that collectively alter the global climate system. Indeed (the argument goes), our impacts as individuals are so diffuse and imperceptible that it would be essentially impossible to attribute *any* differences in the climatic dangers faced by individuals, communities, future generations, and natural ecosystems to particular persons' choices about their carbon footprints. Because of this consequential insignificance, some commentators have been led to wonder whether individuals really have an obligation to constrain their carbon footprints after all.[2]

In this essay, I aim to add to these doubts, offering a new defense of the view that we are not morally obligated to restrict our carbon footprints. I start by drawing attention to the fact that climate change is only one of a wide range of problems faced by humanity. I contend that as individuals who feel bound to make a difference in the world, we are entitled to make our own choices about which causes we will promote and in what ways. I claim further that this entitlement implies that we have the right to completely ignore many important problems, and indeed we have the right to ignore the most important problems in the world.

Adapted from Dan C. Shahar, "Treading Lightly on the Climate in a Problem-Ridden World," Ethics, Policy & Environment 19, no. 2 (2016): 183–195.

I then ask whether this right extends to problems that we are implicated in causing, as is the case with global climate change. I argue that in some cases, it does. When such problems result from large-scale patterns of individually benign actions, and when real solutions would involve institutional changes rather than personal ones, I claim that it can sometimes make sense for us to think of the problems as lacking special priority over others in which we are not personally implicated. Any obligation we have with respect to such problems is simply part of a broader obligation we have to take action to make the world a better place.

Finally, I ask how far individuals who *do* choose to combat climate change should be prepared to go in reducing their personal carbon footprints. I argue that given the insignificance of individuals' carbon footprints, climate change activists should be cautious about making significant sacrifices in order to move closer to the ideal of a "carbon-neutral" or "carbon-negative" lifestyle. Contrary to at least one author's suggestion that virtuous activists will consistently push their boundaries toward more substantial footprint reductions, I claim that many climate change activists are likely doing more to restrict their carbon footprints than they can truly justify.

In what follows, I address myself to the comparatively well-to-do citizens of wealthy, developed nations. If any segment of the population has a duty to restrict personal carbon footprints, then we should expect it to be the people meeting this description. They are the ones who have the largest carbon footprints, live in the nations most historically responsible for the problem of climate change, and are typically best positioned to reduce their emissions without threatening their abilities to satisfy other crucial needs. If it turns out that people like these have no duty to restrict their personal carbon footprints—as I will be arguing—then it seems unlikely that others will have such a duty either.[3]

PICKING OUR BATTLES

I begin with the observation that the world is full of terrible problems. Poverty, disease, human rights abuses, oppression, intolerance, war, torture, animal cruelty, food and water insecurity, pollution, environmental degradation, extinction: a list like this could go on for pages. Faced with this litany of problems, some of us may feel a sort of paralysis. It can appear as though there is simply too much badness out there for us to make any real difference. Some of us may feel tempted to retreat back into our own lives, closing the curtain on the outside world.

Although this reaction might be understandable, I suspect that most of us feel it is the wrong one to have. Of course we cannot personally solve all of the world's problems, but surely we can do *something* to help. Even small efforts can make a difference and, just as importantly, they can make a difference *to us*. We can be the sorts of people who do not back away in the face of the world's most daunting challenges, and if we are honest with ourselves, we will recognize that we *want* to be these sorts of people. We want to be them even if there is a considerable chance our efforts will prove futile, and even if the best-case scenario promises only marginal progress toward fixing our problem-ridden world.

If we are realistic as well as honest, however, we will admit that we cannot take up every cause. We have to choose carefully, with the knowledge that applying ourselves to fighting female genital mutilation in Africa may take time away from advocating the closure of a dirty coal power plant in our own city, and that contributing to the efforts of Save the Children will leave less money in our accounts for Doctors without Borders. There is obviously no formula for deciding how to balance between competing causes like these. But when we are forced to make choices, I think that we learn an important lesson: we can be sensitive, globally engaged citizens without taking any action whatsoever to combat most of the problems currently facing humanity. In fact, we must be sensitive, globally engaged citizens in this way if we are to make any progress at all, especially if we want to reserve time and resources for our own personal projects. Trying to advance every important cause all the time would ultimately mean failing to advance *any* cause in a way that is worth our while.

If this is true, then it seems appropriate to think of ourselves as having a sort of internal "budget" for activism bounded both by the limits of our own effectiveness and the limits of the place we think activism ought to occupy within our lives. Suppose, for example, that I decide to make my mark on the world by volunteering at the local food bank, organizing letter-writing campaigns against police brutality, and sending money to several carefully chosen non-profit organizations. If I have arrived at this decision with due reflection, then I believe that I would be fully within the scope of my moral prerogative to tell a solicitous wind power activist I had no intention of also getting involved with her cause—even if I recognized it as a worthy one. After weighing the various pros and cons associated with engaging with different kinds of projects, and after determining how much of my time, money, and effort I should spend on each of them, it seems to me that I could be justified in considering my "activist budget" fully allocated. I might thereafter think of myself as having no remaining duty to contribute further to the promotion of noble causes, even if I would be capable of promoting them if I so chose.

I want to make clear how strong a claim I am advancing here. In telling the wind power activist that I am not interested in contributing to her cause, I need not have in mind that wind power is a relatively unimportant issue. I take it that I would be justified in saying the same thing to someone asking for my help to address problems that are far more important and far more urgent than the ones to which I am personally devoted. If my chosen cause is, say, protecting marine wildlife, then I can snub AIDS activists even if I believe that AIDS is a more serious and pressing problem than the loss of marine wildlife. Of course, I may rightly ask myself whether I should carry forward my devotion to marine wildlife given the way I feel about its importance relative to AIDS. But if I judge the answer to that question to be yes, then I will not necessarily have made a mistake. It can be perfectly acceptable just to be "the person who protects marine wildlife" and not "the person who addresses problems in order of severity and urgency as they arise."

This may sound like an argument for myopia, but it is not. The seriousness and urgency of a particular problem obviously weighs in favor of devoting efforts to address it, and this consideration should

enter into our deliberations as we decide how to conduct ourselves as activists. But it seems just as obvious that other considerations bear on the propriety of our actions as well, including the relative marginal impacts we could make by devoting ourselves to some causes instead of others, our personal connections to certain problems, and the roles that particular kinds of activism could play in developing our skills and capabilities. Again, the challenge of weighing these factors resists being captured in a neat formula, but for our purposes what matters is that the importance and urgency of a problem are far from the only considerations that should enter into the picture.[4] It would be ludicrous for a marine wildlife activist to ignore her specific combination of experience, knowledge, and passion when deciding how to spend her time in the face of an AIDS epidemic. So too would it be ludicrous for us to focus solely on the seriousness and urgency of problems when deciding how to conduct our own lives. With appropriate decisions made, then, we might find ourselves taking no action at all to address many of the world's most important problems.

Given what I have said so far, it may seem to follow straightforwardly from my view that since climate change is only one of the many important problems we face as a society, the appropriateness of personally taking action to fight it—including by restricting our carbon footprints—depends on our personal judgments and choices. If we decide to make climate change "our cause," and if we decide to contribute to it by restricting our carbon footprints,[5] then my account would obviously support us in doing that. However, if we settle on other problems as "our causes," or if we decide to fight climate change in some other way, and if we devote ourselves fully enough to the causes we have chosen in the ways we have chosen, then we can properly say that our activist duties have been fulfilled without any action being required specifically with respect to our personal carbon footprints.

THE SIGNIFICANCE OF DIRTY HANDS

Although I believe that the line of reasoning I just articulated reaches the correct conclusion, I also believe that it does so too quickly. For there is a key feature of the problem of global climate change that may be thought to differentiate it from the other important global problems with which I have been grouping it: namely, we are personally implicated in the problem of climate change in a way that we are not implicated in many other problems which may inspire us to activism. For example, indoor air pollution in less-developed nations is a serious global problem that calls for amelioration, but most of us have not clearly contributed to that problem. By contrast, our actions do contribute to the problem of global climate change on an ongoing basis, and only by reducing our personal carbon footprints can we eliminate those contributions.

To see why this might seem to make a difference, imagine that I have just helped a few friends to push a car off a cliff onto a helpless pedestrian walking below.[6] Surely it would not do for me to shrug off my responsibility for rectifying the pedestrian's grievances on the grounds that there are many problems in the world and I have made the difficult personal decision not to focus my efforts on the rehabilitation of pedestrians who have been involved in falling car accidents. This is because the pedestrian's injuries would not just be *some problem* calling for my attention among all the others: they would be a problem that I, as one of the people implicated in causing them, have a special duty to address.

Further, we might imagine that this particular incident was actually just one episode in a long string of car-pushings in which my friends and I engage on a regular basis. In this event, not only would it seem like I have an obligation to do something about the problems faced by the victims of these actions, but I would also seemingly be obliged to stop helping my friends to push cars off cliffs in the future when doing so might harm pedestrians. It would not be appropriate for me to try to justify continued contributions to the problem of crushed pedestrians in virtue of actions I am taking to fight other problems about which I personally feel more concern.

Notice, however, that we do not think this way about every problem in which we are implicated. In particular, we tend not to think this way when we are talking about problems that are caused by broad patterns of individually benign behaviors that

are offensive only when considered at an aggregate level.[7] Take, for example, the problem of traffic congestion.[8] When I was in the process of writing this paper, I gave a presentation on its subject in Baltimore, Maryland, a city that suffers from some of the worst traffic jams in the country. These traffic jams are a serious problem: they result in higher stress, more air pollution, and millions of hours of lost productivity and family time for hundreds of thousands of Baltimore citizens. Many of the victims are people who do not regularly commute, and some do not even own a car. These people are forced to put up with crowded streets and polluted air regardless of their own personal habits.[9]

Even so, imagine that I live in Baltimore and commute to work every day. Although my personal driving habits do not make much of a difference in the overall badness of Baltimore traffic, my commutes undeniably implicate me in the city's traffic problem. Even so, let us suppose that I decide to channel my desire to do good for the city of Baltimore into projects other than reducing my driving. I become actively involved in supporting the Baltimore Child Abuse Center and I volunteer extensively with Baltimore Reads, a nonprofit that promotes literacy among local children. Now suppose that an enterprising traffic activist approaches me and insists that I am part of the local traffic problem, and so morality demands that I start driving less. I say,

I'm sorry, but I'm doing a lot to make a difference in this city, and I don't have the time or inclination to add to that burden. I have a life to live, too. Fighting traffic congestion is an important battle, but it's not one that I personally feel bound to wage. My view is that if I am truly doing my part to make Baltimore a better place in the ways that I have described, then such a response may be wholly legitimate.

The legitimacy of this response can be explained by the fact that, unlike in the car-pushing case, Baltimore traffic is not caused by activities that we would independently want to suppress. While the world would be better if no one ever pushed cars onto passersby, we do not necessarily want a Baltimore in which people have to feel badly about traveling through main thoroughfares.[10] Hence the sensible way to ameliorate Baltimore's traffic problem would be to reform its institutions so that people could make mundane driving decisions without contributing to dangerous outcomes. This could be done by building extra lanes on main highways, implementing tolls, designating lanes for carpoolers only, or expanding the city's public transit system. If these measures were adopted successfully, then people would be able to use the highway whenever they wanted without worrying about their contributions to traffic. They would simply spend more time in the newly constructed lanes, avoid the highway in order to escape the new tolls, seek out carpooling partners, or take more trips with public transportation. Or they would do none of these things, continuing to use the highway just like before, and the system would be able to accommodate them due to the actions taken by others in the new highway environment. Morally motivated unilateral cutbacks in highway driving might play no important role in a good highway regime.[11]

We can say something similar about what it would be like to solve the problem of global climate change. An effective solution could work by creating cleaner technologies for engaging in everyday activities, by increasing the cost of impact-intensive consumption, or by offering positive incentives to individuals who make climate-friendly choices like planting trees or buying electric vehicles. In such an institutional environment, people would not need to make decisions with an eye to their impacts on the atmosphere: by simply participating in a system of effective climate governance, they would end up doing their part to bring about a satisfactory outcome without directly trying.

This helps to explain why it makes sense to have different judgments about the moral implications of personal complicity when problems result from large patterns of individually benign activities. When problems are caused by actions that are objectionable all on their own—like helping to crush pedestrians with cars—it makes sense to think that people who are complicit in those problems ought to take measures to reduce their complicity. But when problems are caused by actions that are only deleterious because of the consequences of their aggregation—as is the case with global climate change—it seems as though the people who contribute to these problems are complicit only in the sense that they inhabit institutional regimes that fail to coordinate everyday activities in ways that

avoid destructive results. The solution to such problems is not to get individual people to become small contributors to collective impacts rather than large contributors: rather, the solution is to transition to an institutional environment where small contributors and large contributors alike are playing their parts in the production of favorable outcomes.

This enables us to return to the line of reasoning I presented earlier in this paper and drive home the conclusion that I said I had reached too hastily: namely that individuals have no obligation to personally take action to constrain their carbon footprints. I have hopefully shown that complicity in causing climate change does not directly imply a case for restricting one's contributions to that problem, since the individual decisions that result in climate change contributions are not the main issue. Instead, the main issue is an institutional environment that fails to coordinate citizens' activities in a favorable manner. Addressing the problem of climate change, then, would require not a revolution in the way that private citizens choose to conduct their everyday lives but rather a transition to institutions that would generate better social outcomes.

The final step in my argument is to note that although such a transition would clearly be desirable, and although the status quo is clearly problematic, the necessity of reforming basic social institutions is just one of a great number of serious problems to which individuals can apply themselves. Just as Baltimore citizens can justify concerning themselves with problems other than their city's traffic, we can justify concerning ourselves with problems other than global climate change if that is what we decide to do. Of course, the fact that we play a role in contributing to climate change may provide a reason to give this problem careful consideration in allocating our budgets as activists—just as Baltimore drivers might feel impelled to give consideration to their local traffic situation on similar grounds. But in line with my arguments in the previous section, there are a wide variety of considerations that bear on how we ought to allocate our efforts,[12] and so in the absence of a special complicity-based duty there is no reason to think that the case for attending to our carbon footprints will always win out in the eyes of conscientious individuals. The upshot is that we have a right to completely ignore the problem of climate change, and hence we have no specific obligation to restrict our personal carbon footprints.

Having established this conclusion, however, an important caveat is in order. It should be noted that a critical element of the argument I just articulated was the idea that even if we are not restricting our personal carbon footprints, we can still be doing our parts to help solve the world's problems. The centrality of this idea in my argument means that for most people, it will not be appropriate to use what I have said here as a justification for inaction. This is because most people are not doing their part in helping to solve global problems of any kind. What I have defended is *selective* inaction, not self-centered indifference in the face of a problem-ridden world.

Each of us ultimately has to decide what role we think activism should play in our lives. I suspect that most of us will admit that we are not doing enough, and not only because we find it fashionable to flaunt our bleeding hearts. For us, it will rightly feel difficult to shrug off the pleas of climate activists on the grounds that we have more important things to do. The truth for so many of us is that using some of our time and energy to restrict our carbon footprints would be more worthwhile *in our own eyes* than whatever we would be doing instead.

Even if my arguments in this paper have been on-target, it does not follow that such feelings of guilt are misplaced. The point is simply that we do not have to respond to them specifically by restricting our personal carbon footprints. Instead, we can legitimately see our guilt as embodying a more general call to action, demanding that we do something to change the world but leaving open the choice of what that something will be. If we choose to, we can respond by restricting our carbon footprints. But we may also find that, upon appraising the significance of carbon footprint reductions in comparison with our other options, our time and effort would be better spent doing something else.[13] In this case, I contend that we will do better by taking up another fight instead.

FINDING THE MEAN

At the outset of this discussion, I promised to argue not only that individuals lack a specific duty to restrict their carbon footprints, but also that many climate activists who choose to devote themselves to carbon footprint reductions are likely doing more in this regard than they can justify. To this point, however, I have offered no arguments in support of this latter claim. Given that these climate activists presumably take themselves to be acting along the lines I have been advocating—devoting themselves fully enough to the causes they have chosen in the ways they have chosen—it would seem that such a claim merits justification.

To this end, we need to ask how these individuals ought to go about delimiting the role that carbon footprint restrictions will occupy in their lives: How much is enough? How small can a carbon footprint become before one should consider one's activist budget fully allocated? The answers to these questions will depend in part on how we address the broader question of how activism ought to fit into a good human life: If activism ought to play a highly encompassing role in our lives, then an individual discharging her duties as an activist might reduce her carbon footprint to zero—or perhaps even push toward significantly negative net greenhouse gas emissions. On the other hand, if activism should be confined to a small role, then individuals may be able to fully allocate their activist budgets with less intrusive measures such as driving a Prius, installing a solar water heater, and shopping with reusable bags.

Ty Raterman has offered one possible resolution to this puzzle in a recent paper entitled, appropriately enough, "Bearing the Weight of the World." According to Raterman, individuals are not obliged to "martyr" themselves for the causes they support, but they are nevertheless required to "constantly strive to do more" than they are currently doing and to consistently push themselves into "new, uncomfortable territory."[14] Raterman observes that:

> In athletic training, one can generally be sure one is not exercising in a sufficiently vigorous way if there is no strain or pain involved; and, by the same token, one is doing too much if one exercises so hard as to cripple oneself.[15]

He suggests that activist efforts ought to be judged along similar lines: there will be a limit on how much ought to be done at any particular point, but "one is plainly not doing enough if one stays entirely within the realm of comfort and convenience."[16]

Raterman's view offers us one way to judge that some climate activists may be doing too much to restrict their carbon footprints. To the extent that these individuals are causing themselves great discomfort and stress in the service of their cause, Raterman's account would suggest scaling back. However, it is also an important feature of Raterman's view that the limits on appropriate levels of devotion are transitory. As current activities become more comfortable and even pleasant, Raterman thinks people should push themselves to do even more. Reflecting on his own circumstances, he writes that

> . . . much of what once seemed to me quite taxing is now practically second nature. I have settled into a routine, and my obligation is to strive further and challenge myself anew. I am not failing egregiously, but there is more I can do without seriously sacrificing my well-being.[17]

Raterman is correct that climate change activists ought not to push themselves too far beyond their comfort zones for the sake of carbon footprint reductions. But he is mistaken in treating activists' discomfort as the central source of limits on appropriate efforts in this domain. Although climate change is a serious problem, and although climate change activists have chosen to devote themselves to combating that problem, it is my position that the duty to make the world a better place does not always demand progressively more of activists as their capacities for devotion expand. This is because as activists increase their personal outlays in the process of reducing their carbon footprints, they tend to find themselves sacrificing increasingly valuable elements of their own lives in order to achieve further progress. At a certain point, it stops being appropriate to make additional sacrifices for the sake of smaller carbon footprints even if doing so would come with little personal discomfort. Just like the fitness freak who eventually needs to curb her inclinations to push even further, activists may eventually need to learn to set boundaries in order to avoid taking their commitments too far.

Moreover, the point at which further sacrifices are inappropriate can come more quickly than many climate activists realize, limiting proper carbon footprint reductions to a much narrower domain than is often apprehended. To see why this is the case, it will be helpful to recall that carbon footprint reductions—like many forms of activism—are not especially efficacious ways of actually solving global problems. As I said at the outset of our discussion, individuals' carbon footprints are so insignificant that it would be impossible to attribute any meaningful amplification of climatic hazards to them. Of course, there are other reasons for restricting one's carbon footprint as well: signaling one's tastes to manufacturers, expressing one's concerns to political leaders, and even insulating oneself against recriminations from other climate activists. But these considerations also do not reflect ways in which ordinary individuals' choices yield significant impacts on worldly outcomes.[18]

Given the gravity of the problem of global climate change, it can often be tempting to see carbon footprint reductions as a way of sacrificing a lesser value (one's own interests) for the sake of a greater value (the mitigation of climate change). But for climate activists, meaningfully ameliorating the problem of climate change through carbon footprint reductions is not among the range of available options. Activists are really choosing between their own interests and an array of social, political, and climatic outcomes that are more or less identical to the ones that would have obtained via their inaction. In this comparison, the greater value is undoubtedly on the side of the activists themselves, no matter how much their interests may pale in comparison to the significance of the climate crisis as a whole.

As such, the possibility of sacrificing too much in the name of a smaller carbon footprint is a very real one. Those of us who have spent meaningful time interacting with activists have encountered people who have ruined relationships, missed out on family developments, and driven themselves to illness in the names of their causes. Networks of climate activists can be particularly susceptible to these problems, since opportunities abound for expressing loyalty to the cause by refusing to travel, eschewing physical comforts, and restricting one's diet. Individuals who take up these forms of activism usually do not regard themselves as martyrs, and most of them acclimate to the sacrifices they make. But as a general rule, these activists who push themselves to bear ever more of the weight of the world do so ineffectually, often harming themselves and their loved ones in the process.

Such observations demand that we recall Aristotle's characterization of virtue as a "mean" between vicious extremes.[19] As Aristotle recognized, many beneficial qualities can prove just as pathological when expressed in excess as they are in deficiency. In such cases, aiming for constantly greater expression of some quality may lead one past the point of virtue and in the direction of vice. We may readily grant that in our society apathy is a more common problem than excessive devotion, and so it should come as no surprise that qualities such as "selflessness" and "altruism" are hailed as virtues in common parlance. But I fear that among committed activists, the opposite tendencies all too often manifest themselves: in these circles, we may find ourselves rightly praising "moderation" and "perspective" instead.[20]

The truth is that our duties as activists force us to strike a balance between insufficient and excessive devotion to our chosen causes. If we respond to our problem-ridden world with apathy, then we fail to do justice to the gravity of our tragic circumstances and, in so doing, fail to do justice to ourselves. But too many climate activists fail to realize that we also fail to do justice to ourselves if we throw away what is important and meaningful in our own lives in the name of symbolic devotion. Virtue lies in the mean between these extremes, not in the constant push toward one of them.

CONCLUSION

In this paper, I have defended the claim that as long as we are doing our part to promote worthy causes, we can legitimately avoid taking measures to specifically reduce our personal carbon footprints. In the battle against dangerous global climate change, the choices and actions that make up these footprints are not the real problems. Rather, the real problem is that our institutions do not enable people to go about their daily lives without collectively causing destruction.

Better institutions are plainly needed. But the need for these institutions is just one of the many serious problems that exist in our world. As individuals, we have a duty to try to make the world a better place, but we also have the right to choose how we want to make our contributions.

It should surely be stressed that the moral seriousness and urgency of the problem of climate change provide us with powerful reasons for devoting ourselves to its amelioration. The same is true of the fact that we ourselves have contributed to that problem and continue to do so every day. But I have argued that our choices as activists ought to be sensitive to a broad range of considerations, and that this makes the task of allocating one's efforts far more complicated than the narrative of obligatory carbon footprint reductions implies.

If we do as I have suggested and identify our causes, decide how best to contribute to them, and carry out our intentions within the scopes of our budgets for activism, then we will have no moral reason to cast our eyes downwards when climate change activists implore us to reduce our carbon footprints. Nor will we have reason to do so when international aid organizations, local homeless shelters, gay rights groups, medical research funds, and innumerable others present us with opportunities to further their respective causes. Of course, it will not do for us to simply ignore such opportunities or the underlying problems they reflect. But if we devote ourselves fully enough to the causes we have chosen in the ways we have chosen, then we will be able to look others in the eye with the confidence that we are doing our parts.

On the other hand, I have suggested that most of us are not currently doing enough to fulfill our duties to help. Our budgets for activism are routinely misallocated to self-centered activities that do little to help anyone other than ourselves. Thus it should not be surprising that we feel guilty when others call on us to reduce our personal carbon footprints. Our world is full of serious problems, and we should be doing more to solve them, even if it is up to us to decide how.

For those of us who decide to make our mark through reduced carbon footprints, I have offered an additional piece of guidance as well. Given the insignificance of individual carbon emissions, it pays to be careful about going too far in one's activist efforts. Like other forms of activism, the fight against climate change can prove incredibly—and dangerously—seductive, leading people to make great sacrifices to produce little in the way of meaningful results. We must therefore keep in mind that when we lack the power to resolve major problems, our duty is not to constantly push ourselves further as activists. Rather, our duty is to find a place in our lives for activism that leaves room for our flourishing as human beings.

REFERENCES

Aristotle. (2000). *Nicomachean Ethics*, translated and edited by Robert Crisp (Cambridge: Cambridge University Press).

Broome, John. (2012). *Climate Matters: Ethics in a Warming World* (New York: Norton & Co.).

Baatz, Christian. (2014). "Climate Change and Individual Duties to Reduce GHG Emissions," *Ethics, Policy & Environment*, 17: 1–19.

Hourdequin, Marion. (2010). "Climate, Collective Action and Individual Ethical Obligations," *Environmental Values*, 19: 443–464.

Hourdequin, Marion. (2011) "Climate Change and Individual Responsibility: A Reply to Johnson," *Environmental Values*, 20: 157–62.

Jamieson, Dale. (2010). "Climate Change, Responsibility, and Justice," *Science and Engineering Ethics*, 16: 431–445.

Johnson, Baylor. (2003). "Ethical Obligations in a Tragedy of the Commons," *Environmental Values*, 12: 271–287.

Leiserowitz, Anthony, Edward Maibach, Connie Roser-Renouf, Geoff Feinberg, and Seth Rosenthal. (2014). *Politics & Global Warming, Spring 2014* (New Haven, Conn.: Yale Project on Climate Change Communication).

Maltais, Aaron. (2013). "Radically Non-Ideal Climate Politics and the Obligation to at Least Vote Green," *Environmental Values*, 22: 589–608.

Kawall, Jason. (2011). "Future Harms and Current Offspring," *Ethics, Policy & Environment*, 14: 23–26.

Nolt, John. (2011). "How Harmful Are the Average American's Greenhouse Gas Emissions?" *Ethics, Policy & Environment*, 14: 3–10.

Nolt, John. (2013). "Replies to Critics of 'How Harmful are the Average American's Greenhouse Gas Emissions?'" *Ethics, Policy & Environment*, 16: 111–119.

Raterman, Ty. (2012). "Bearing the Weight of the World: On the Extent of an Individual's Environmental Responsibility," *Environmental Values*, 21: 417–436.

Sandberg, Joakim. (2011). "My Emissions Make No Difference," *Environmental Ethics*, 33: 229–248.

Sandler, Ronald. (2010). "Ethical Theory and the Problem of Inconsequentialism: Why Environmental Ethicists Should be Virtue-Oriented Ethicists," *Journal of Agricultural and Environmental Ethics*, 23: 167–183.

Sandler, Ronald. (2011). "Beware of Averages: A Response to John Nolt's 'How Harmful are the Average American's Greenhouse Gas Emissions?'" *Ethics, Policy & Environment*, 14: 31–33.

Schinkel, Anders. (2011). "Causal and Moral Responsibility of Individuals for (the Harmful Consequences of) Climate Change," *Ethics, Policy & Environment*, 14: 35–37.

Schwenkenbecher, Anne. (2014). "Is There an Obligation to Reduce One's Individual Carbon Footprint?" *Critical Review of International Social and Political Philosophy*, 17: 168–188.

Schmidtz, David and Elizabeth Willott. (2006). "Varieties of Overconsumption," *Ethics, Place & Environment*, 9: 351–365.

Seager, Thomas P., Evan Selinger, and Susan Spierre. (2011). "Determining Moral Responsibility for CO_2 Emissions: A Reply to Nolt," *Ethics, Policy & Environment*, 14: 39–42.

Sinnott-Armstrong, Walter. (2005). "It's Not *My* Fault: Global Warming and Individual Moral Obligations," in *Perspectives on Climate Change: Science, Politics, Ethics*, edited by Walter Sinnott-Armstrong and Richard B. Howarth (Amsterdam: Elsevier), pp. 285–307.

NOTES

1. For the sake of this discussion, I remain agnostic about exactly what "the problem" with climate change amounts to. The literature of climate ethics has been rich with attempts to characterize the nature of the issue, with authors variously drawing attention to matters of interpersonal, international, and intergenerational justice; distributions of risks and good and bad outcomes; impacts on natural ecosystems and nonhuman individuals; and the collective moral virtues of our society— as well as to difficulties in applying some of these

lenses. I have tried to write this article so that one's particular conception of the climate change problem will not make an important difference to the success of the central arguments.

2. For example, Johnson (2003); Sinnott-Armstrong (2005); Sandberg (2011); and Maltais (2013). On the other hand, see expressions of support for the conventional wisdom in Hourdequin (2010); Sandler (2010); Hourdequin (2011); Broome (2012); Raterman (2012); Baatz (2014); and Schwenkenbecher (2014). It should be noted that some authors have recently challenged the claim that individuals' contributions to global climate change are insignificant when considered on their own (e.g., Nolt, 2011; Broome, 2012, chs. 4–5). I think that these authors are mistaken and individuals' contributions really are insignificant from the standpoint of causing morally significant problems, but I will not attempt to defend this empirical claim here. However, for some recent attempts to dispute Nolt's view in particular, see Kawall (2011); Sandler (2011); Schinkel (2011); and Seager et al. (2011). On the other hand, see Nolt's response in Nolt (2013).

3. This claim is not intended to stand up to philosophers' imaginations, and indeed there may even be some real world counterexamples. If, for example, there really are certain individuals who generate greenhouse gas emissions sufficient to noticeably amplify climatic hazards, then the arguments of this paper might not apply to them. I take it, however, that the overwhelming majority of people who are generally taken to have a duty to restrict their personal carbon footprints do not fall into such a category.

4. I should stress that this point is not intended to rest on the legitimacy of ethical partiality. Even if we insist on complete impartiality in all ethical matters, it will not follow that there are no (impartial) considerations weighing in favor or against some particular individual taking on particular problems as opposed to others. To the extent that such considerations exist, a proponent of ethical impartiality will have to allow that they should be taken into account. Of course, if ethical partiality is embraced then it seems even clearer that my claim is true.

5. This second condition is important because of the fact that personal carbon footprint reductions represent only one of the ways that individuals can contribute to the fight against global climate change. It is noteworthy that according to a survey conducted by the Yale Project on Climate Change Communication and the George Mason University Center for Climate Change Communication, about a third of voting Americans—and about half of liberal Democrats—reported buying products over the past twelve months with an eye to reducing global warming (Leiserowitz et al., 2014, p. 15), but only twelve percent of Americans—and only twenty-two percent of liberal Democrats—had donated money over the same time span to political candidates on account of their shared views about global warming (ibid., p. 12). Only nine percent of Americans—and only fourteen percent of liberal Democrats—had volunteered time to campaign for candidates on climate-related grounds (ibid., p. 13). And only twelve percent of Americans—and only twenty-two percent of liberal Democrats—had contacted a government official about global warming (ibid., p. 14).

6. This illustration was originally introduced in Sinnott-Armstrong (2005, pp. 289–290). Its use as an example of the immorality of complicity in collective harms comes from Raterman (2012, pp. 424–425 and 427–428).

7. These are just a few of the factors that differentiate the problem of global climate change from paradigmatic cases of interpersonal harming. For a fuller discussion of these differences, see Jamieson (2010).

8. I owe this example to Schmidtz and Willott (2006).

9. John Broome has recently attempted to dismiss the example of traffic congestion on the grounds that the harms caused by traffic are *reciprocal* harms: they fall only upon those people who help to cause them (Broome, 2012, p. 58). As my comments here indicate, this is not an accurate characterization of the case. Traffic harms people who contribute only a tiny bit to its manifestation as well as people who contribute nothing at all. I take it that this makes the problem of traffic more

serious, but I do not think that it threatens the account that I develop here as Broome seems to imply it should.

10. Adherents to certain traditions in moral theorizing might regard this claim as puzzling. For example, a Kantian moralist might think that would-be highway drivers should behave only in ways that they could rationally will to be embraced as law by the entire moral community. A rule utilitarian might likewise think that drivers should behave in ways that would produce the best outcomes if mimicked by most or all of the population. It is my view that these counterfactual-based approaches to moral theorizing are mistaken with respect to the regulation of common pool resource systems. However, airing my grievances against them would go far beyond the scope of the present paper. For the sake of offering some response to those who sympathize with such views, it may be enough to note that they have very limited grounds for condemning an individual who follows my advice *while supporting sensible attempts to regulate their shared resources.* A community of such persons would not clearly be worse than one where people engaged in morally-motivated unilateral cutbacks like those recommended by the highway activist in my story. On the contrary, by shifting pressure for alleviating collective dangers from themselves to public officials, agents of the sort I praise in this paper would liberate themselves to tackle a wide range of other important problems while still leaving room for their personal projects.

11. This point is illustrated particularly well by John Broome, who notes that in an effective climate policy regime it might even be especially difficult to improve overall climate outcomes through morally-motivated actions, since those actions might produce responses by others in the regime that would cancel out the effects of one's choices (Broome, 2012, pp. 81–82).

12. It should be added that many of the considerations bearing on such decisions will likely be tied to our particular backgrounds, circumstances,

group memberships, and so on. As a white American, I may have particularly good reason to focus on domestic race relations. As a cisgendered male, I may have particularly good reason to act on challenges faced by gender- and sex-nonconforming individuals. Indeed, even as a member of my particular family I may have particularly good reason to devote myself to providing for some of my less fortunate relatives—or for individuals and groups who supported my family in the past. As I mentioned in footnote 4 above, I hope to avoid tying my arguments to any controversial ideas about ethical partiality. However, to the extent that distinguishing facts about individuals are relevant to the question of how they should conduct their moral lives—as surely they are—these facts are likely to ground a host of distinctive reasons for people to attend to certain causes over others.

13. For discussion of this point, see Broome (2012, pp. 65–66).

14. Raterman (2012, p. 418).

15. Raterman (2012, p. 432).

16. Raterman (2012, pp. 432–433).

17. Raterman (2012, p. 433).

18. There may be exceptions to this, as in cases involving prominent world leaders or famous celebrities. These individuals' personal choices may sometimes have the potential to influence large numbers of people—and even political decisions—in ways that are not generally possible for ordinary citizens. But even in such cases, the individuals in question may discover that they still face difficult decisions about how to use their positions of influence, with particular uses drawing time, energy, and resources away from other urgent callings. When this is so, the moral case for these individuals to reduce their carbon footprints will still be inconclusive on the grounds that there are other causes they might consider more worthy of promoting instead.

19. Aristotle (2000, II.6-9).

20. On this point, see Aristotle (2000, II.8-9).

CARING FOR THE CLIMATE

DALE JAMIESON

ETHICS, PUBLIC POLICY, AND GLOBAL WARMING

There are many uncertainties concerning climate change, but an international consensus has emerged that we are likely to see a 1.1 to 6.4 C increase in the earth's mean surface temperature by the end of this century. Such a warming would have diverse impacts on human activities and would likely be catastrophic for many plants and nonhuman animals. My claim is that the problems engendered by the possibility of climate change are not purely scientific but also concern how we ought to live and how humans should relate to each other and to the rest of nature; and these are problems of ethics and politics.

INTRODUCTION

There has been speculation about the possibility of anthropogenic global warming since at least the late nineteenth century.[1] At times the prospect of such a warming has been welcomed, for it has been thought that it would increase agricultural productivity and delay the onset of the next ice age.[2] Other times, and more recently, the prospect of global warming has been the stuff of "doomsday narratives," as various writers have focused on the possibility of widespread drought, flood, famine, and the economic and political dislocations that might result from a "greenhouse warming"–induced climate change.[3]

Although high-level meetings have been convened to discuss the greenhouse effect since at least 1963,[4] the emergence of a rough, international consensus about the likelihood and extent of anthropogenic global warming began with a National Academy Report in 1983;[5] meetings in Villach, Austria, and Bellagio, Italy, in 1985;[6] and in Toronto, Canada, in 1988.[7] In 1988 the Intergovernmental Panel on

Climate Change (IPCC) was formed to provide state of the art assessments of climate science. According to the most recent IPCC report,[8] a doubling of atmospheric carbon dioxide from the preindustrial baseline is likely to lead to a 2–4.5 degree centigrade increase in the earth's mean surface temperature. (Interestingly, this estimate is close to that predicted by Arrhenius[9]). This increase is expected to have a profound impact on climate and therefore on plants, animals, and human activities of all kinds. Moreover, there is no reason to suppose that, without policy interventions, atmospheric carbon dioxide will stabilize at twice preindustrial levels. Moreover, as the human perturbation of natural systems becomes increasingly extreme, the probability of catastrophic climate change increases.[10]

There are many uncertainties concerning anthropogenic climate change, yet we cannot wait until all the facts are in before we respond. All the facts may never be in. New knowledge may resolve old uncertainties, but it may bring with it new uncertainties. It is an important dimension of this problem that our insults to the biosphere outrun our ability to understand them. We may suffer the worst effects of the greenhouse before we can prove to everyone's satisfaction that they will occur.[11]

The most important point I wish to make, however, is that the problem we face is not a purely scientific problem that can be solved by the accumulation of scientific information. Science has alerted us to a problem, but the problem also concerns our values. It is about how we ought to live, and how humans should relate to each other and to the rest of nature. These are problems of ethics and politics as well as problems of science.

In the first section I examine what I call the "management" approach to assessing the impacts of, and our responses to, climate change. I argue that this approach cannot succeed, for it does not have the resources to answer the most fundamental questions that we face. In the second section I explain why the problem of anthropogenic global change is to a great extent an ethical problem, and why our conventional value system is not adequate for addressing it. Finally I draw some conclusions.

WHY MANAGEMENT APPROACHES MUST FAIL

From the perspective of conventional policy studies, anthropogenic climate change and its attendant consequences are problems to be "managed." Management techniques mainly are drawn from neoclassical economic theory and are directed toward manipulating behavior by controlling economic incentives through taxes, regulations, and subsidies.[12]

In recent years economic vocabularies and ways of reasoning have dominated the discussion of social issues. Participants in the public dialogue have internalized the neoclassical economic perspective to such an extent that its assumptions and biases have become almost invisible. It is only a mild exaggeration to say that in recent years debates over policies have largely become debates over economics.

The Environmental Protection Agency's draft report Policy Options for Stabilizing Global Climate[13] is a good example. Despite its title, only one of nine chapters is specifically devoted to policy options, and in that chapter only "internalizing the cost of climate change risks" and "regulations and standards" are considered. For many people questions of regulation are not distinct from questions about internalizing costs. According to one influential view, the role of regulations and standards is precisely to internalize costs, thus (to echo a parody of our forefathers) "creating a more perfect market." For people with this view, political questions about regulation are really disguised economic questions.[14]

It would be both wrong and foolish to deny the importance of economic information. Such information is important when making policy decisions, for some policies or programs that would otherwise appear to be attractive may be economically prohibitive. Or in some cases there may be alternative policies that would achieve the same ends and also conserve resources.

However, these days it is common for people to make more grandiose claims on behalf of economics. Some economists or their champions believe not only that economics provides important information for making policy decisions but that it provides the most important information. Some even appear to believe that economics provides the only relevant information. According to this view, when faced with a policy decision, what we need to do is assess the benefits and costs or various alternatives. The alternative that maximizes the benefits less the costs is the one we should prefer. This alternative is "efficient" and choosing it is "rational."

Unfortunately, too often we lose sight of the fact that economic efficiency is only one value, and it may not be the most important one. Consider, for example, the idea of imposing a carbon tax or a market in emissions permissions (i.e., "cap and trade"), as a policy response to the prospect of global warming. What we think of this proposal may depend to some extent on how it affects other concerns that are important to us. Equity is sometimes mentioned as one other such concern, but most of us have very little idea about what equity means or exactly what role it should play in policy considerations.

One reason for the hegemony of economic analysis and prescriptions is that many people have come to think that neoclassical economics provides the only social theory that accurately represents human motivation. According to the neoclassical paradigm, welfare can be defined in terms of preference-satisfaction, and preferences are defined in terms of choice behavior. From this, many (illicitly) infer that the perception of self-interest is the only motivator for human beings. This view suggests the following "management technique": If you want people to do something give them a carrot; if you want them to desist, give them a stick.[15]

Many times the claim that people do what they believe is in their interests is understood in such a way as to be circular, therefore unfalsifiable and trivial. We know that something is perceived as being in a person's interests because the person pursues it; and if the person pursues it, then we know that the person must perceive it as being in his or her interests. On the other hand if we take it as an empirical claim that people always do what they believe is in their interests, it appears to be false. If we look around the world we see people risking or even sacrificing their own interests in attempts to overthrow oppressive governments or to realize ideals to which they are committed. Each year more people die in wars fighting for some perceived collective good than die in criminal attempts to further their own individual interests. It is implausible to suppose that the behavior (much less the motivations) of a revolutionary, a radical environmentalist, or a friend or lover can be revealed by a benefit–cost analysis.

It seems plain that people are motivated by a broad range of concerns, including concern for family and friends, and religious, moral, and political ideals. And it seems just as plain that people sometimes sacrifice their own interests for what they regard to be a greater, sometimes impersonal, good.

People often act in ways that are contrary to what we might predict on narrowly economic grounds, and moreover, they sometimes believe that it would be wrong or inappropriate even to take economic considerations into account. Many people would say that choosing spouses, lovers, friends, or religious or political commitments on economic grounds is simply wrong. People who behave in this way are often seen as manipulative, not to be trusted, without character or virtue. One way of understanding some environmentalists is to see them as wanting us to think about nature in the way that many of us think of friends and lovers—to see nature not as a resource to be exploited but as a partner with whom to share our lives.

Some may think that I have exaggerated the dominance of narrow, economistic approaches to policy-making. Neo-classical economics is in retreat, it might be said, in the wake of the Great Recession of 2008. Paul Krugman has recently reported that some economists are talking about a discipline in crisis.[16] Indeed, it might be thought that the hegemony of the neo-classical paradigm has been eroding since the late 1990s, as indicated by Nobel Prizes awarded to Amartya Sen (1998), Daniel Kahneman (2002), and Elinor Ostrom (2009). I am skeptical. The events of 2008 were hardly unprecedented in demonstrating the inability of conventional neo-classical models to predict dramatic changes in the economy. In 1973–4, stocks lost 48 percent of their value; in 1987 the Dow plunged nearly 23 percent in a single day for no apparent reason. A series of "bubbles" that simply could not exist according to some influential theories, have occurred throughout the world since the 1980s. Intellectually, there has always been dissatisfaction with the neo-classical paradigm, sometimes even very close to the heart of the discipline.[17] Despite this, the President's Council of Economic Advisors is still in business, unchecked by a Council of Philosophical (or Ethical) Advisors. Public decisions of great consequence continue to be made on the basis of shallow and misleading indicators such as GDP, rather than on the basis of broader considerations such as quality of life or impacts on fundamental planetary systems. The "straw man" of neo-classical economics seems to me to have quite a lot of blood left in him.

What I have been claiming in this section is that it is not always rational to make decisions solely on narrow economic grounds. Although economic efficiency may be a value, there are other values as well, and in many areas of life, values other than economic efficiency should take precedence. I have also suggested that people's motivational patterns are complex and that exploiting people's perceptions of self-interest may not be the only way to move them. This amounts to a general critique of viewing all social issues as management problems to be solved by the application of received economic techniques. There is a further reason why economic considerations should take a back seat in our thinking about global climate change: There is no way to assess accurately all the possible impacts and to assign economic values to alternative courses of action. A greenhouse warming will have impacts that are so broad, diverse, and uncertain that conventional economic analysis is practically useless.[18]

Consider first uncertainties about the potential impacts, some of which I have already noted. Even if the 2007 IPCC report is correct in supposing that global mean surface temperatures will increase between 1.1 and 6.4 °C during this century, there is still great uncertainty about the impact of this warming on regional climates. One thing is certain: The impacts will not be homogeneous. Some areas will become warmer, some will probably become colder, and overall variability is likely to increase. Precipitation patterns will also change, and there is much less confidence in the projections about precipitation than in those about temperature. These uncertainties about regional effects make estimates of the economic consequences of climate change radically uncertain.

There is also another source of uncertainty regarding these estimates. In general, predicting human behavior is difficult. The difficulties are especially acute in the case that we are considering because climate change will affect a wide range of social, economic, and political activities. Changes in these sectors will affect emissions of greenhouse gases, which will in turn affect climate, and around we go again.[19] Climate change is itself uncertain, and its human effects are even more radically so. It is for reasons such as these that in general, the area of environment and energy has been full of surprises.

A second reason why the benefits and costs of the impacts of global climate change cannot reliably be assessed concerns the breadth of the impacts. Global climate change will affect all regions of the globe. About many of these regions—those in which most of the world's population live—we know very little. Some of these regions do not even have monetarized economies. It is ludicrous to suppose that we could assess the economic impacts of global climate change when we have such little understanding of the global economy in the first place.

Finally, consider the diversity of the potential impacts. Global climate change will affect agriculture, fishing, forestry, and tourism. It will affect "unmanaged" ecosystems and patterns of urbanization. International trade and relations will be affected. Some nations and sectors may benefit at the expense of others. Moreover, there will be complex interactions between these effects. For this reason we cannot reliably aggregate the effects by evaluating each impact and combining them by simple addition. But since the interactions are so complex, we have no idea what the proper mathematical function would be for aggregating them (if the idea of aggregation even makes sense in this context). It is difficult enough to assess the economic benefits and costs of small-scale, local activities. It is almost unimaginable to suppose that we could aggregate the diverse impacts of global climate change in such a way as to dictate policy responses.

In response to skeptical arguments like the one that I have given, it is sometimes admitted that our present ability to provide reliable economic analyses is limited, but then it is asserted that any analysis is better than none. I think that this is incorrect and that one way to see this is by considering an example.

Imagine a century ago a government doing an economic analysis in order to decide whether to build its national transportation system around the private automobile. No one could have imagined the secondary effects: the attendant roads, the loss of life, the effects on wildlife, on communities; the impact on air quality, noise, travel time, and quality of life. Given our inability to reliably predict and evaluate the effects of even small-scale technology (e.g., the artificial heart,[20]) the idea that we could predict the impact of global climate change reliably enough to permit meaningful economic analysis seems fatuous indeed.

When our ignorance is so extreme, it is a leap of faith to say that some analysis is better than none. A bad analysis can be so wrong that it can lead us to do bad things, outrageous things—things that are much worse than what we would have done had we not tried to assess the costs and benefits at all (this may be the wisdom in the old adage that "a little knowledge can be a dangerous thing").

What I have been arguing is that the idea of managing global climate change is a dangerous conceit. The tools of economic evaluation are not up to the task. However, the most fundamental reason why management approaches are doomed to failure is that the questions they can answer are not the ones that are most important and profound. The problems posed by anthropogenic global climate change are ethical as well as economic and scientific. I will explain this claim in the next section.

ETHICS AND GLOBAL CHANGE

Since the end of World War II, humans have attained a kind of power that is unprecedented in history. While in the past entire peoples could be destroyed, now all people are vulnerable. While once particular human societies had the power to upset the natural processes that made their lives and cultures possible, now people have the power to alter the fundamental global conditions that permitted human life to evolve and that continue to sustain it. While our species dances with the devil, the rest of nature is held hostage. Even if we step back from the precipice, it will be too late for many or even perhaps most of the plant and animal life with which we share the planet.[21] Even if global climate can be stabilized, the future may be one without wild nature.[22] Humans will live in a humanized world with a few domestic plants and animals that can survive or thrive on their relationships with humans.

The questions that such possibilities pose are fundamental questions of morality. They concern how we ought to live, what kinds of societies we want, and how we should relate to nature and other forms of life. Seen from this perspective, it is not surprising that economics cannot tell us everything we want to know about how we should respond to global warming and global change. Economics may be able to tell us how to reach our goals efficiently, but it cannot tell us what our goals should be or even whether we should be concerned to reach them efficiently.

It is a striking fact about modern intellectual life that we often seek to evade the value dimensions of fundamental social questions. Social scientists tend to eschew explicit talk about values, and this is part of the reason why we have so little understanding of how value change occurs in individuals and societies. Policy professionals are also often reluctant to talk about values. Many think that rational reflection on values and value change is impossible, unnecessary, impractical, or dangerous. Others see it as a professional, political, or bureaucratic threat.[23] Generally, in the political process, value language tends to function as code words for policies and attitudes that cannot be discussed directly.

A system of values, in the sense in which I will use this notion, specifies permissions, norms, duties, and obligations; it assigns blame, praise, and responsibility; and it provides an account of what is valuable and what is not. A system of values provides a standard for assessing our behavior and that of others. Perhaps indirectly it also provides a measure of the acceptability of government action and regulation.

Values are more objective than mere preferences.[24] A value has force for a range of people who are similarly situated. A preference may have force only for the individual whose preference it is. Whether or not someone should have a particular value depends on reasons and arguments. We can rationally discuss values, while preferences may be rooted simply in desire, without supporting reasons.

A system of values may govern someone's behavior without these values being fully explicit. They may figure in people's motivations and in their attempts to justify or criticize their own actions or those of others. Yet it may require a theorist or a therapist to make these values explicit.

In this respect a system of values may be like an iceberg—most of what is important may be submerged and invisible even to the person whose values they are. Because values are often opaque to the person who holds them, there can be inconsistencies and incoherencies in a system of values. Indeed much debate and dialogue about values involves attempts to resolve inconsistencies and incoherencies in one direction or another.

A system of values is generally a cultural construction rather than an individual one.[25] It makes sense to speak of contemporary American values, or those of eighteenth-century England or tenth-century India. Our individual differences tend to occur around the edges of our value system. The vast areas of agreement often seem invisible because they are presupposed or assumed without argument.

I believe that our dominant value system is inadequate and inappropriate for guiding our thinking about global environmental problems, such as those entailed by climate changes caused by human activity. This value system, as it impinges on the environment, can be thought of as a relatively recent construction, coincident with the rise of capitalism and modern science, and expressed in the writings of such philosophers as Francis Bacon,[26] John Locke,[27] and Bernard Mandeville.[28] It evolved in low-population-density and low-technology societies, with seemingly unlimited access to land and other resources. This value system is reflected in attitudes toward population, consumption, technology, and social justice, as well as toward the environment.

The feature of this value system that I will discuss is its conception of responsibility.[29] Our current value system presupposes that harms and their causes are individual, that they can readily be identified, and that they are local in space and time. It is these aspects of our conception of responsibility on which I want to focus.

Consider an example of the sort of case with which our value system deals best. Jones breaks into Smith's house and steals Smith's television set. Jones's intent is clear: she wants Smith's TV set. Smith suffers a clear harm; he is made worse off by having lost the television set. Jones is responsible for Smith's loss, for she was the cause of the harm and no one else was involved.

What we have in this case is a clear, self-contained story about Smith's loss. We know how to identify the harms and how to assign responsibility. We respond to this breech of our norms by punishing Jones in order to prevent her from doing it again and to deter others from such acts, or we require compensation from Jones so that Smith may be restored to his former position.

It is my contention that this paradigm collapses when we try to apply it to global environmental problems, such as those associated with human-induced global climate change. It is for this reason that we are often left feeling confused about how to think about these problems.

There are three important dimensions along which global environmental problems such as those involved with climate change vary from the paradigm: Apparently innocent acts can have devastating consequences, causes and harms may be diffuse, and causes and harms may be remote in space and time.[30]

Consider an example. Some projections suggest that one effect of greenhouse warming may be to shift the Southern Hemisphere cyclone belt to the south. If this occurs the frequency of cyclones in Sydney, Australia, will increase enormously, resulting in great death and destruction. The causes of this death and destruction will be diffuse. There is no one whom we can identify as the cause of destruction in the way in which we can identify Jones as the cause of Smith's loss. Instead of a single cause, millions of people will have made tiny, almost imperceptible causal contributions—by driving cars, cutting trees, using electricity, and so on. They will have made these contributions in the course of their daily lives performing apparently "innocent" acts, without intending to bring about this harm. Moreover, most of these people will be geographically remote from Sydney, Australia. (Many of them will have no idea where Sydney, Australia, is.) Further, some people who are harmed will be remote in time from those who have harmed them. Sydney may suffer in the twenty-first century in part because of people's behavior in the nineteenth and twentieth centuries. Many small people doing small things over a long period of time together will cause unimaginable harms.

Despite the fact that serious, clearly identifiable harms will have occurred because of human agency, conventional morality would have trouble finding anyone to blame. For no one intended the bad outcome or brought it about or even was able to foresee it.

Today we face the possibility that the global environment may be destroyed, yet no one will be responsible. This is a new problem. It takes a great many people and a high level of consumption and production to change the earth's climate. It could not have been done in low-density, low-technology societies. Nor could it have been done in societies like ours until recently. London could be polluted by its inhabitants in the eighteenth century, but its reach was limited. Today no part of the planet is safe. Unless we develop new values and conceptions of responsibility, we will have enormous difficulty in motivating people to respond to this problem.

Some may think that discussion about new values is idealistic. Human nature cannot be changed, it is sometimes said. But as anyone who takes anthropology or history seriously knows, our current values are at least in part historically constructed, rooted in the conditions of life in which they developed. What we need are new values that reflect the interconnectedness of life on a dense, high-technology planet.

Others may think that a search for new values is excessively individualistic and that what is needed are collective and institutional solutions. This overlooks the fact that our values permeate our institutions and practices. Reforming our values is part of constructing new moral, political, and legal concepts.

One of the most important benefits of viewing global environmental problems as moral problems is that this brings them into the domain of dialogue, discussion, and participation. Rather than being management problems that governments or experts can solve for us, when seen as ethical problems, they become problems for all of us to address, both as political actors and as everyday moral agents.

In this essay I cannot hope to say what new values are needed or to provide a recipe for how to bring them about. Values are collectively created rather than individually dictated, and the dominance of economic models has meant that the study of values and value change has been neglected.[31] However, I do have one positive suggestion: We should focus more on character and less on calculating probable outcomes. Focusing on outcomes has made us cynical calculators and has institutionalized hypocrisy. We can each reason: Since my contribution is small, outcomes are likely to be determined by the behavior of others. Reasoning in this way we can each justify driving cars while advocating bicycles or using fireplaces while favoring regulations against them. Even David Brower, the "archdruid" of the environmental movement, owned two cars, four color televisions, two video cameras, three video recorders, and a dozen tape recorders, and he justified this by saying that "it will help him in his work to save the Earth."[32] More recently, the eleven day 2009 Copenhagen climate conference produced carbon emissions equal to the annual emissions of 600,000 Ethiopians.

Calculating probable outcomes leads to unraveling the patterns of collective behavior that are needed in order to respond successfully to many of the global environmental problems that we face. When we "economize" our behavior in the way that is required for calculating, we systematically neglect the subtle and indirect effects of our actions, and for this reason we see individual action as inefficacious. For social change to occur it is important that there be people of integrity and character who act on the basis of principles and ideals.

The content of our principles and ideals is, of course, important. Principles and ideals can be eccentric or even demented. In my opinion, in order to address such problems as global climate change, we need to nurture and give new content to some old virtues such as humility, courage, and moderation and perhaps develop such new virtues as those of simplicity and conservatism. But whatever the best candidates are for twenty-first century virtues, what is important to recognize is the importance and centrality of the virtues in bringing about value change.[33]

The case that I make for the virtues is modest: Focusing on character provides a resource that may be useful for solving problems that otherwise seem intractable. Others have made more ambitious claims for the virtues. They think that acting virtuously is essential to human flourishing, which in turn is understood as resting on a teleological notion of "natural goodness."

I am suspicious of such bold metaphysical claims but I cannot address them here. In any case, their truth is extraneous to the claims that I am making.

CONCLUSION

Science has alerted us to the impact of humankind on the planet, each other, and all life. This dramatically confronts us with questions about who we are, our relations to nature, and what we are willing to sacrifice for various possible futures. We should confront this as a fundamental challenge to our values and not treat it as if it were simply another technical problem to be managed.

Some who seek quick fixes may find this concern with values frustrating. A moral argument will not change the world overnight. Collective moral change is fundamentally cooperative rather than coercive. No one will fall over, mortally wounded, in the face of an argument. Yet if there is to be meaningful change that makes a difference over the long term, it must be both collective and thoroughgoing. Developing a deeper understanding of who we are, as well as how our best conceptions of ourselves can guide change, is the fundamental issue that we face.

REFERENCES

Amy, Douglas R. 1984. Why policy analysis and ethics are incompatible. *Journal of Policy Analysis and Management* 3:573–91.

Andrews, Richard, and Mary Jo Waits. 1978. Environmental values in public decisions: A research agenda. Ann Arbor: University of Michigan, School of Natural Resources.

Arrhenius, S. 1896. On the influence of carbonic acid in the air upon the temperature of the ground. *Philosophical Magazine* 41:237.

———. 1908. *Worlds in the making.* New York: Harper & Brothers.

Bacon, F. [1620] 1870. *Works*, edited by James Spedding, Robert Leslie Ellis, and Douglas Devon Heath. London: Longmans Green.

Borza, K., and D. Jamieson. 1990. *Global change and biodiversity loss: Some impediments to response.* Boulder: University of Colorado, Center for Space and Geoscience Policy.

Callendar, G. S. 1938. The artificial production of carbon dioxide and its influence on temperature. *Quarterly Journal of the Royal Meteorological Society* 64:223–40.

Conference Statement. 1988. The changing atmosphere: Implications for global security. Toronto, Canada, 27–30 June.

Conservation Foundation. 1963. Implications of rising carbon dioxide content of the atmosphere. New York.

Flavin, C. 1989. Slowing global warming: A worldwide strategy. *Worldwatch* Paper 91. Washington, DC: Worldwatch Institute.

Hirschman, Albert. 1977. *The passions and the interests.* Princeton, NJ: Princeton University Press.

Intergovernmental Panel on Climate Change. 2007. Climate Change 2007: Summary for Policymakers. Available at www.ipcc.ch/pdf/assessment-report/ar4/wg1/ar4-wg1-spm.pdf

Jamieson, Dale. 1988a. The artificial heart: Reevaluating the investment. In *Organ substitution technology*, edited by D. Mathieu, 277–96. Boulder, CO: Westview.

———. 1988b. "Grappling for a Glimpse of the Future," in Michael H. Glantz (ed.) *Societal Responses to Regional Climatic Change: Forecasting by Analogy.* Boulder CO: Westview Press. 73–93.

———. 1990. Managing the future: Public policy, scientific uncertainty, and global warming. In *Upstream/downstream: New essays in environmental ethics*, edited by D. Scherer, 67–89. Philadelphia: Temple University Press.

———. 1991. The epistemology of climate change: Some morals for managers. *Society and Natural Resources* 4:319–29.

———. 2002. *Morality's Progress.* Oxford: Oxford University Press.

———. 2007b. "When Utilitarians Should Be Virtue Theorists," *Utilitas* 19,2 (June):160–183.

———. 2007a. "The Moral and Political Challenges of Climate Change," in S. Moser and L. Dilling (eds.), *Creating a Climate for Change: Communicating Climate Change and Facilitating Social Change.* New York: Cambridge University Press. 475–482.

———. 2010. Climate Change, Responsibility, and Justice. *Science and Engineering Ethics* 16,3: 431–445.

Krugman, Paul. 2009. How Did Economists Get It So Wrong?, *New York Times*, September 2, 2009. Available at http://www.nytimes.com/2009/09/06/magazine/06Economic-t.html

Lee, Keekok. 1989. *Social philosophy and ecological scarcity*. New York: Routledge.

Locke, John. [1690] 1952. *The second treatise of government*. Indianapolis, IN: Bobbs–Merrill.

Mandeville, B. [1714] 1970. *The fable of the bees*, translated by P. Harth. Hammersmith, England: Penguin.

Mansbridge, Jane, ed. 1990. *Beyond self-interest*. Chicago: University of Chicago Press.

McKibben, W. 1989. *The end of nature*. New York: Knopf.

Myers, Milton. L. 1983. *The soul of modern economic man*. Chicago: University of Chicago Press.

National Academy of Sciences/National Research Council. 1983. *Changing climate*. Washington, DC: National Academy Press.

———. 2002. *Abrupt Climate Change, Inevitable Surprises*. Washington, DC: National Academy Press.

Opp, Karl-Dieter. 1989. *The rationality of political protest*. Boulder, CO: Westview.

Reich, Robert, ed. 1988. *The power of public ideas*. Cambridge: Harvard University Press.

Sagoff, Mark. 2004. *Price, principle, and the environment*. New York: Cambridge University Press.

Scitovsky, Tibor. 1976. *The joyless economy: An inquiry into human satisfaction and consumer dissatisfaction*. New York: Oxford University Press.

Thomas, Chris D., Alison Cameron, Rhys E. Green, Michel Bakkenes, Linda J. Beaumont, Yvonne C. Collingham, Barend F. N. Erasmus, Marinez Ferreira de Siqueira, Alan Grainger, Lee Hannah, Lesley Hughes, Brian Huntley, Albert S. van Jaarsveld, Guy F. Midgley, Lera Miles, Miguel A. Ortega-Huerta, A. Townsend Peterson, Oliver L. Phillips & Stephen E. Williams 2004. Extinction risk from climate change, *Nature*, |VOL427|8JANUARY2004, pp. 145–8.

U.S. Environmental Protection Agency. 1989. Policy options for stabilizing global climate, Draft report to Congress, edited by D. Lashof and D. A. Tirpak. Washington, DC: GPO.

Weiskel, Timothy. 1990. Cultural values and their environmental implications: An essay on knowledge, belief and global survival. Paper presented at the American Association for the Advancement of Science, New Orleans, LA.

Wolfe, Alan. 1989. *Whose keeper? Social science and moral obligation*. Berkeley: University of California Press.

World Climate Program. 1985. Report of the International Conference on the Assessment of the Role of Carbon Dioxide and of Other Greenhouse Gases in Climate Variations and Associated Impacts: Report on an international conference held at Villach, Austria, 9–15 October 1985. Geneva: World Meteorological Organization.

NOTES

1. Arrhenius 1896; 1908.
2. Callendar 1938.
3. Flavin 1989.
4. See Conservation Foundation 1963.
5. National Academy of Sciences/National Research Council 1983.
6. World Climate Program 1985.
7. Conference Statement 1988.
8. IPCC 2007.
9. Arrhenius 1896.
10. NAS 2002.
11. Jamieson 1991.
12. There are of course other conceptions of management, for example "adaptive management," which is used primarily in the domain of natural resource management.
13. U.S. Environmental Protection Agency 1989.
14. For discussion, see Sagoff 2004.
15. See Myers 1983 for the view that self-interest is the "soul of modern economic man."
16. Krugman 2009.
17. See, e.g., Mansbridge 1990, Opp 1989, and Scitovsky 1976. I'm even inclined to enlist Adam Smith as a critic of neo-classical economics.
18. Our inability to perform reliably the economic calculations also counts against the "insurance" view favored by many who favor aggressive action on climate change, but that is another story.
19. Jamieson 1988b; 1990.
20. See Jamieson 1988.

21. Borza and Jamieson 1990; Thomas et al, 2004.
22. McKibben 1989.
23. Amy 1984.
24. Andrews and Waits 1978; Jamieson 2002, ch. 15.
25. Weiskel 1990.
26. Bacon [1620] 1870.
27. Locke [1690] 1952.
28. Mandeville [1714] 1970; see also Hirschman 1977.

29. See also Jamieson 2010.
30. Other important dimensions include nonlinear causation, threshhold effects, and the relative unimportance of political boundaries, but I cannot discuss these here, but see Lee 1989 and Jamieson 1991.
31. But see Wolfe 1989; Reich 1988.
32. San Diego Union, 1 April 1990.
33. Jamieson 2007b.

PHILIP KITCHER

THE CLIMATE CHALLENGE

Climate scientists have established beyond all reasonable doubt that our planet is warming up, and that the increase in the global mean temperature is the result of human activities. Moreover, even a relatively conservative appraisal of the likely future[1] recognizes serious threats to the lives of the inhabitants of every continent, although the hardships will be disproportionately felt by the world's poor. There are three major reasons why most people underestimate the dangers. First, in thinking about future scenarios, there is a tendency to focus on constant effects—the elevated average temperature or average sea level—and to overlook the deviations around the new mean: the unprecedented heat waves, the record storms and floods.[2] Second, the effects are taken in isolation, without considering the ways in which they will combine and interact: the coming drought is not seen in the context of the shortages and disruptions that preceded it or the tensions and conflicts with neighbors who are also competing for scarce resources. Third, by concentrating on the clear and predictable dangers, some of the most devastating scenarios—like the potential for droughts to cause water wars[3] or the possibility of devastating pandemics—are downplayed, or entirely ignored. Although it's impossible to assign sizeable probabilities to any of them, there are so many of them that it would be irresponsibly optimistic to be confident that our descendants will escape all of them.

Original essay for this volume. The ideas of this essay stem from joint work with Evelyn Fox Keller. Kitcher and Keller (2017) provides a far more extensive elaboration of them, and considers many important objections to them. Here I offer only a bare, and often dogmatic, summary. Many thanks to David Schmidtz and Danny Shahar for truly excellent constructive suggestions about earlier drafts.

All these points deserve further elaboration and defense, but for present purposes, I shall simply assume them. The principal philosophical questions about climate change emerge once we ask what should be done to mitigate the threats it poses to the welfare of future generations.

Part of the answer is obvious. There must be a period—the *transition*—during which we gradually eliminate the practices that are contributing to the concentration of greenhouse gases in the atmosphere. People all over the world will have to phase out the use of fossil fuels and modify current agriculture (estimates suggest that breeding domestic animals for meat and using standard fertilizers contribute somewhere between 10% and 30% of the current annual emissions of greenhouse gases). The program will involve both *reduction* (giving up some activities, like using carbon-intensive forms of transportation or eating meat) and *replacement* (finding ways to carry on what we want to do by using renewable sources of energy). Plainly, the more we manage to reduce, the less we have to replace, and vice versa. Perhaps the transition can also be aided by developing technologies (like carbon sequestration) that allow some continued dependence on fossil fuels without emitting greenhouse gases, although the best current assessments suppose that geo-engineering of this type[4] can only solve part of the problem. Reduction and replacement both involve large social changes, including a restructuring of economies and modifying patterns of employment. They also place obstacles in the path of development for many nations yearning for economic growth and for the benefits that come (for example) from a reliable supply of electricity. Postponing the time at which the transition begins and lowering the rate at which it occurs makes it easier to address the problems encountered by those who will live through this period. By the same token it increases the chances of dangers, even catastrophes, for the generations that will come later. If the transition is achieved by 2070, many of those who are now children will suffer; if it takes until 2120, the consequences for those born in the next century are likely to be devastating.

Humanity currently faces four duties that are extremely hard to satisfy together. The *climate challenge*, as I shall call it, is to find an acceptable approximation to meeting all of the following:

1. Our duty to future generations: we owe the people who come after us a planet on which they will not be subject to catastrophic effects of climate change.

2. Our duty to the citizens of prosperous and emerging nations who do not fully participate in the wealth of those nations: we owe to the many whose prospects are already limited and to the many more whose lives will be endangered by programs of reduction and replacement the kinds of opportunities enjoyed by their more fortunate fellow-citizens.

3. Our duty to the people whose countries have been left behind by the industrial revolution: we owe the world's poor the chance to develop so that their citizens enjoy the opportunities available to those who live in affluent nations.

4. Our duty to transmit to our descendants the most valuable parts of the human heritage: we owe to those who come after us the opportunity to benefit from the discoveries, the institutions, and the cultural achievements that have improved life prospects beyond those available to our remote ancestors. We have an obligation to consolidate these achievements and to spread their benefits more widely.

It's not hard to see that the task of discharging some of these obligations is made much easier if others are sacrificed. It would, for example, be more straightforward to meet 2–4, if we forgot about 1, or to meet 1–3 if we abandoned 4.

There's no identifiable way to satisfy all these obligations completely, even if we allow ourselves a generous time period for doing so. The climate challenge requires us to act before we know many things that bear on the merits of various options. It is absurd to suppose that the wisest reflection coupled to the most benign ethical commitment could lead us to some optimal compromise. Our task is to do as well as we can in a situation pervaded by dangers and uncertainties. The temptation, of course, is either to simplify matters by pretending that one of the duties can legitimately be forgotten, or to fling up our hands in despair. But that *is* temptation, and it will bring disastrous consequences in its train.

It's important to be very clear that all the obligations are real. Some people oppose climate activism by suggesting that maintaining economic growth is the best gift we can make to the future. Extrapolating from the increases in productivity during the past 150 years, they predict a wealthier world to come in which the resources are available to address whatever damage has been wrought by continuing business as usual. Their foolhardy assurances are flawed in two important ways. First, if the transition were seriously postponed or abandoned, some of the predicted climatic effects could not be mitigated given any foreseeable increase in global wealth. Climate refugees will hardly be recompensed by the fact that they live in a materially more affluent world. Second, not only is the extrapolation questioned by economists who see the recent upsurge in productivity as exceptional,[5] but, more importantly, it fails to take into account the shocks administered to the global economy from the expected changes in the earth's climate.[6] Betting the human future on fantasies about the prosperity and adaptive abilities of our descendants is the height of irresponsibility. What's needed is a thoroughly pragmatic attitude that starts by acknowledging the dangers, tries out potential ways of avoiding them, and evolves by absorbing the approaches that work best.

Another common reaction (at least in the affluent world) questions whether 3 is a duty. Some of those most sensitive to duty 2 argue that the governments of the more prosperous nations have the responsibility to alleviate the predicaments of their own citizens whose opportunities are severely restricted. Especially at a time when unemployment is high, when many children live in poverty, when the national infra-structure is crumbling and social mobility decreasing, there is pressure to take steps to ensure that a society's wealth is distributed more fairly. Giving aid to distant people can easily be seen as a diversion from the primary obligation to solve domestic problems. Foreign aid is a matter of benevolence not something morally required.[7]

This reaction is mistaken. To be sure, the transition will demand even more strenuous efforts to attend to the pockets of poverty within the world's prosperous nations, and to guard against the new forms of poverty that climate action can be expected to bring. There will have to be serious programs to retrain workers whose lives are disrupted by efforts at reduction and replacement. We must have a "war on coal," but we must avoid warfare against the miners: they must be offered opportunities to pursue productive and valuable lives. Duty 1 raises the bar for discharging duty 2. Nevertheless, duty 3 cannot be dismissed. Two elementary ideas about justice require the affluent world to provide funds so that the rest of the world, the world that has been left behind, may develop using green technology (as the United Nations Framework Convention on Climate Change has recommended). First, those who have created a mess are expected to clear it up, particularly when they have benefited enormously from the mess-making. Second, when a group of people faces a common threat, it is rightly expected that those with the ability to address it should do so.

Pleas for large amounts of aid for green development are often characterized as idealistic by those who see themselves as hard-headed practitioners of *realpolitik*. The charge is unfounded. It is unrealistic to suppose that those who suffer from a glaring injustice can be enlisted in any cooperative venture that fails to address that injustice. Our atmosphere is profoundly indifferent to where the increasing concentrations of greenhouse gases come from. Hence, to achieve the transition, all nations of the world need to participate. If impoverished nations are denied sufficient aid to develop as they would have been able to do, had the continued use of fossil fuels been unproblematic, they will inevitably see the situation correctly. The affluent nations that led the way in industrializing have become rich by using far more than their fair share of what should have been a common resource. For the atmosphere can be thought of as containing a sink of finite size, into which just so much carbon can safely be dumped, and calculations show that the USA, the UK, and Germany have poured into it many times the amount that would have been allotted to them on the basis of relative population size. Moreover, since 1980,[8] when the danger of climate change became evident, the emissions of the United States exceed the total it would have been assigned for its entire industrial career—and, of course, the transition isn't over yet. Under these circumstances, the argument that poorer nations must forego using fossil fuels and thus postpone the development they have hoped for is not exactly persuasive.[9]

Our planet needs a panhuman alliance in a war against a new enemy: atmospheric carbon. If the alliance is to be built and sustained, those who have played principal roles in creating the enemy will be expected to help those who are vulnerable and who have done far less harm. Because the course of the campaign cannot be predicted in advance, the strategy has to be pragmatic and experimental. Our ignorance of the economic and social consequences of potential programs of reduction and replacement requires different nations to try out different possibilities, and to discover which ones offer the best approximations to joint satisfaction of the four duties. As with experiments generally, steps must be taken to protect the lives of human subjects. We shall need safety nets within nations to help those who suffer from the reductions and the replacements. We shall need full transparency across nations, so that all may benefit from the most promising experiments. And we shall need safety nets for all nations, so that countries who try out unsuccessful programs are given new opportunities. In short, unprecedented levels of international cooperation will be required. Recognition of a common enemy has sometimes enabled people to transcend their everyday disagreements and work together. With luck, awareness that greenhouse gases are humanity's foe will work the same magic in forging the alliance we desperately need.[10]

I have argued elsewhere for a method of ethical decision.[11] Faced with any complex dilemma, the best any group of people can do is to follow the strategy that would be chosen in an ideal discussion satisfying three conditions. First, all perspectives must be represented; second, those perspectives must be reshaped in light of the best available information; third, the discussants must be mutually engaged, seeking a solution with which all can live. The climate challenge requires us to work pragmatically together, developing ways of partially addressing the four duties that all can tolerate, adapting and adjusting them in light of new information. The most obvious way to achieve that is through the broadening of democracy to an international scale, coupled to a deepening of democracy within nations, so that the voices of different constituencies are heard. Current concerns about democracy, prominent all over the world today, seem to stem from a sense that distant elites (bureaucrats in Washington or Brussels, say) ignore the values and aspirations of large groups of citizens. Some problems—like climate change—are so large that they demand concerted action among many participants, including people who live in all parts of the globe. They cannot be addressed by allowing uncoordinated constituencies to pursue what they think best. Rather, the remedy must lie in providing, for each constituency, channels through which its distinctive ideas can be represented in decision-making.

Among those who must be represented in discussing climate change are the people of the future. Any democratic discussion must include advocates for those who will come after us. There are, of course, dangers in institutionalizing representation for those who cannot speak for themselves; the advocates may pursue their own ends, rather than the goals of those they represent. Societies have had to learn how to overcome those dangers in other instances: in protecting the interests of developmentally disabled children, of old people who suffer from dementia, and of non-human animals. Similarly, it's important to learn—quickly!—how to give our descendants an effective voice in the decisions we must make on their behalf.

At a time when nationalism is resurgent, and international institutions are often targets of criticism and even scorn, a plea for global democracy is unlikely to be welcomed. Perhaps the best hope is that, as the climate threat and its links to problems of human inequality and human insecurity become more evident, a popular movement may develop, so that politicians are, at last, compelled to take up the climate challenge in all its complexities. The alternative is truly appalling. All a philosopher can do today is warn.

REFERENCES

Gordon, Robert J. 2016. *The Rise and Fall of American Growth* (Princeton: Princeton University Press).
IPPC. 2014. *Fifth Assessment Report of the Intergovernmental Panel on Climate Change*. Available online

at https://www.ipcc.ch/pdf/assessment-report/ar5/wg3/ipcc_wg3_ar5_full.pdf.

Kitcher, Philip. 2011. *The Ethical Project* (Cambridge, MA: Harvard University Press).

Kitcher, Philip and Evelyn Fox Keller. 2017. *The Seasons Alter: How to Save Our Planet in Six Acts* (New York: W.W. Norton [Liveright]).

Stern, Nicholas. 2016. "Current Climate Models are Grossly Misleading." Available online at http://www.nature.com/news/economics-current-climate-models-are-grossly-misleading-1.19416.

Welzer, Harald. 2012. *Climate Wars* (Cambridge, UK: Polity).

NOTES

1. IPCC 2014.
2. Recently, there has also been a trend towards linking actual extreme events to climate change (often in ways that aren't rigorously justified). Nevertheless, in envisaging the future, many discussions concentrate on the averages and the constant effects.
3. Welzer 2012.
4. It's important to distinguish negative geo-engineering (aimed at preventing emissions or, more ambitiously, at withdrawing carbon from the atmosphere) from positive geo-engineering (attempts to add to the atmosphere to "balance" the warming effects—e.g. by injecting sulfur particles). The former tries to return us to a state we've encountered before and know to be benign; the latter involves us in an extremely risky experiment.
5. Gordon 2016.
6. Stern 2016.
7. Despite the fact that UNFCCC calls for aid for green development, beyond the other forms of aid provided to the developing world, the poorer nations have argued again and again in international climate discussions that the affluent world is not offering enough. They see themselves as required to suspend their hopes for development if they adhere to proposed schedules for reducing emissions, and doomed to face severe consequences if they follow the paths to industrialization that have allowed prosperous nations to amass their wealth. Rich nations have repeatedly insisted that they are not *obliged* to deliver the amounts of aid requested.
8. I have chosen a date a few years before James Hansen's famous testimony to the US Senate, because, by 1980, climate scientists had a clear appreciation of the dangers and were already reporting them to policy-makers. If anything, 1980 is a conservative (late) date for the time at which the risks were already recognizable.
9. As the sharp disagreements between affluent and poor nations about aid for green development have indicated—at meetings of the IPCC and at Paris in December 2015—the UNFCCC may be the official rubric under which global climate policy is pursued, but it hardly provides the standard for effective action.
10. I see the UNFCCC, from its inception, as an attempt to forge that alliance. If it has so far failed to do so, at least some of the problems are obvious: continued doubts about the "reality" of climate change, underestimating the devastation it will bring, optimism that continued economic growth will solve the problems, and failure to appreciate the existence of *four* duties that are very hard to satisfy together.
11. Kitcher 2011, ch. 9.

DARREL MOELLENDORF

JUSTICE IN CLIMATE CHANGE MITIGATION AND ADAPTATION POLICIES

Anthropogenic climate change affects the lives and well-being of hundreds millions of people now and for the foreseeable future. The change is driven primarily by the use of greenhouse gases, most importantly CO_2. Without substantial reductions in CO_2, the most likely rise in the mean equilibrium surface temperature of the Earth over pre-industrial times by the end of this century is in the range of 2.6 to 4.8 °C, but the possible increase could go as high as 7.8 °C. That would be a rate of warming that is unprecedented in human history. And the risks would be enormous.

How bad things would get cannot be known precisely, but there would surely be widespread loss species and eco-systemic destruction, more frequent heat waves and droughts in some locations, more and more extreme precipitation events in others, sea-level rise causing inundation in some areas, and glacial melting leading to flooding, and later to the water shortages. For humans these consequences would include significant threats to food security globally and regionally, increased risks from food- and water-borne as well as vector-borne diseases, such as malaria, increased displacement due to migration from hard hit areas, increased risks of violent conflicts, slowed economic growth and poverty eradication, and the creation of new poverty traps.

There are two main kinds of policy responses to climate change. One is mitigation, which involves reducing and ultimately halting activities that produce climate change; these are mainly the burning of fossil fuels and deforestation. The other kind of policy is adaptation, which involves altering human communities and activities so that the impact of climate change is less. A variety of things may be done to adapt. Sea walls may be built or reinforced; water can be used

more efficiently; crops can be diversified and drought resistant strains can be developed; storm drainage can be improved; public health measures can be adjusted; and communities can be relocated. Mitigation and adaptation policies raise a number of important considerations of justice. It is useful to think of principles of justice as statements of what persons are owed either by others or by institutions and policies. This article briefly discusses some of the most important of considerations of justice regarding mitigation and adaptation policies.

Humans depend on a natural environment that is conducive to health and well-being. Mitigation serves this end not mainly by addressing the present effects of climate change. Instead, it mostly serves the health and well-being of people in the future. Because a transition to renewable energy will probably require assuming short-term costs associated with generating renewable energy, mitigation raises the issue of the intergenerational distribution of the costs of climate change. But because the costs of mitigation policies must be shared around the world, the distribution of those costs raises concerns of global justice. Adaptation policies can serve both present and future generations. Such policies are also relevant to development since many of the people most vulnerable to climate change live in poor countries. The question of how the costs of adaptation should be distributed around the world is also a question of global justice.

The need to mitigate climate change is especially urgent. For any particular limit on temperature increase there is a corresponding limit to the atmospheric concentration of CO_2. But almost half the CO_2 emitted into the atmosphere remains there more than a century; and about 20% of it remains there for thousands of years. Due to the duration of the residence of CO_2 in the atmosphere, for any particular

Original essay for this volume.

temperature increase limit, whether it is 1.5°C, 2°C, or 2.5°C, there is also a corresponding limit on total historic human emissions. The lower the temperature target, the fewer the remaining emissions there are.

Multi-lateral international negotiations on climate change under the auspices of the United Nations Framework Convention on Climate Change (UNFCCC) have adopted the warming limit of 2°C. Now, in order to have a better than 66 percent chance of limiting warming to 2°C, total human emissions must not exceed one trillion tons of carbon. From the beginning of the industrial revolution to the present, humans have already emitted over 600,000,000 tons. Because currently total global emissions are increasing, the date at which the trillionth ton will be emitted is coming ever nearer. At the time of the writing of this article it is in January of 2038. Consult the webpage http://trillionthtonne.org/ to see when the trillionth ton will be emitted given emissions at the time that you are reading this article.

The 2°C warming limit is at best an estimate of what intergenerational justice might require on behalf of future generations. If justice between generations requires sharing the costs of climate change policy, a precise statement of what is owed future generations would require a reasonably accurate understanding of what the costs of climate change for any given temperature increase are and what the costs transitioning to a zero carbon economy within the timeframe to limit warming to that temperature are. Given current knowledge, no such accounting of costs could be anything other than estimates. But the cost of producing energy by means of photovoltaic cells is dropping. That makes the 2°C goal less expensive for present generations and therefore more reasonable as a demand of justice. Additionally, many of the most worrying negative effects of climate change, such as rapid sea-level rise caused by the abrupt collapse of the Greenland and Antarctic ice sheets, are uncertain. These events involve processes that are so poorly understood in their details that scientists are not able to attach a likelihood to their occurrence, even though there is mounting evidence that conditions are becoming more favorable to their happening. In light of the uncertain, but not non-negligible, probability of such catastrophes it would seem reasonable to think that the temperature limit should be as low as feasible.

But what justice in mitigation requires also depends on how effective and expensive climate change adaptation is. The less mitigation, the more important adaptation becomes. We might be tempted to think that as our technology develops we can do more to adapt at a lower cost. That could be true up to an extent, but given the threat of catastrophic change, such as rapid land-based ice sheet melting, it is also possible that our capacity to adapt could be outstripped by the extent of the negative effects. So, keeping warming at a low limit once again seems reasonable.

The arguments just surveyed suggest that intergenerational justice recommends a low warming limit. Why not lower than 2°C then? Once again, there are no definite answers here. It is noteworthy that at the meeting of the UNFCCC in Paris in 2015 representatives of states agreed to limit warming to well below 2°C and possibly even as low as 1.5°C. At the time of writing this article the Intergovernmental Panel on Climate Change (IPCC) is surveying scientific studies on what would be required to limit warming that much. One possible constraint is technological capacity. Most projections of limiting warming to 2°C assume the use of a technology that would capture and withdraw CO_2 from the atmosphere to be stored in some form on or below the surface of the Earth. The problem is that such technology is only in its infancy and is certainly not ready for large scale deployment. Failing the use of such technology, another method of reducing emissions is to reduce economic activity. We know from the experience of the Great Recession of 2009 that recessions reduce emissions. Advocates of this policy refer to it as "degrowth." A major problem with that strategy is that in the financially interconnected world in which we live recessions in the developed world get transferred to poor countries through reduced investment by corporations, reduced remittances by individuals, and decreased demand for basic commodities from poor countries. The Great Recession of 2009 also taught us that. Degrowth policies then could be very harmful to the well-being of the global poor. So, we may not have the technology to make the 1.5°C feasible without imposing harmful policies on the global poor.

The matter of how much warming should be limited on behalf of future generations does not exhaust the questions of justice in mitigation policy. Another important matter is how the costs of mitigation should be distributed globally among the present generation. Although an international mitigation regime should aim for a transition to a zero-carbon global economy, regardless of the temperature limit, it is reasonable to expect it do so in a way that is consistent with not slowing the morally mandatory project of eradicating global poverty. Experience suggests that national development strategies can be effective means for addressing poverty. The Preamble to the UNFCCC affirms the importance of the "right to sustainable development." The assertion of the right to sustainable development is a claim of justice. A plausible interpretation of that claim is that underdeveloped and developing countries are owed a treaty framework in which their macroeconomic policies that aim towards development are not hindered. And because development is a very energy intensive social process, this claim would secure their access to energy.

Currently well over 24 billion people live in energy poverty. They lack either electricity or access to modern cooking fuels. 1.4 billion of these people lack access to electricity. There is a strong correlation between diminishing energy poverty and improving human development (measured in terms of per capita income, health, and educational attainments) in a country. Achieving significant human development gains in the underdeveloped and developing countries of the world will require a massive increase in the consumption of energy. If such an increase were to involve a short-term increase in the consumption of fossil fuels, which remain less expensive in most markets than renewables, allowing that would be consistent with mitigation aims to reduce and then end all CO_2 emissions only if developed countries were to reduce their emissions enough to offset the emissions increase in poor countries. Alternatively, if an increase in energy consumption in poor countries were to involve the consumption of more renewable energy, then the protection of development aims would require that developed countries subsidize the purchase of renewables so as not to increase the cost of development.

Is respect for the right to sustainable development in climate change policy required by justice? Two arguments suggest that it is. First, when states agreed to the treaty that is the UNFCCC they agreed to treaty language that includes the right. Such an agreement amounted to a promise that any further mitigation agreements under the auspices of the UNFCCC would respect the right. States are morally bound by that promise. Additionally, respecting the right is supported by considerations of fairness. Responding adequately to climate change requires international cooperation. It seems unfair that participants in such an effort should be required to take on a burden that would harm its ability to perform the morally mandatory task of eradicating poverty, unless doing so is somehow unavoidable. Hence, respecting the right to sustainable development in assigning the burdens of climate change policy seems to be required by fairness.

Mitigation policies seem then to be appropriately directed by two considerations of justice. Even if we cannot know exactly how much we should limit warming, future generations are owed policies that constrain warming considerably; and 2°C seems plausible in that regard. Moreover, in the pursuit of mitigation, underdeveloped and developing countries are owed the liberty to pursue macro-economic policies within a treaty framework that does not hinder development by significantly raising the cost of energy.

Climate change cannot be adequately addressed by mitigation policies alone. The mean surface temperature of the planet is already nearly 0.8°C higher than before the Industrial Revolution. Such a temperature increase requires adaptation policies. One important difference between adaptation and mitigation policies is that whereas mitigation benefits everyone by stabilizing the climate, adaptation can be directed towards specific groups of people who are especially vulnerable to climate change. It is useful to think of vulnerability to climate change as the product of a person's exposure to the risks of climate change and her lack of capacity to protect herself from negative outcomes. The first of these is a matter of geography; the second is often a matter of poverty. Other than relocating communities there is nothing that policy can do to affect the geographical location that exposes people to climate change related risks. So, the object of adaptation policy is typically to protect those people who will be exposed to risks. The poor will often be in greater need of protection by policy means than the non-poor because they have less capacity for self-protection.

Indeed, adaptation can often be integrated into a comprehensive development program.

Insofar as adaptation policy seeks to reduce vulnerability, policy priorities should track vulnerability. Since, unlike mitigation, adaptation policies target specific people, the distribution of the burden to fund adaptation could be assigned to states in whose territory those who are vulnerable live. But this would place much heavier adaptation burdens on poor states with especially vulnerable populations. If, as argued above, respect for the right to sustainable development is a matter of justice in climate change policy, then it is relevant to adaptation policy as well. The development prospects of states should be safeguarded by adaptation policy. States should not be left in a worse position with respect to their development agenda because of their need to adapt to climate change. If that is correct, then developing and least developed states have a claim of justice to assistance in financing adaptation insofar as adaptation costs either raises the costs of development or compete with development objectives for funding.

How much mitigation the present generation is required to undertake is a question of intergenerational justice. The aim of limiting warming to no more than 2°C seems reasonable in that regard. How the burdens of mitigation should be assigned is a matter of global justice. Funding for adaptation also raises questions of global justice. In both cases the right to sustainable development is a plausible claim of justice that protects the development ambitions of poorer states.

JOHN BROOME

THE MOST IMPORTANT THING ABOUT CLIMATE CHANGE

. . .

Climate change raises a wide range of ethical issues. It raises issues of justice, for instance. Our emissions of greenhouse gases directly cause climate change, which is already harming other people. People are losing their homes, their livelihoods, and even their lives as a result of the climate change we are causing. This is an injustice we are doing to those people.

Climate change also raises many issues of value. We are worsening the lives of future people by damaging the environment in which they will live. To help us decide how much we should reduce our emissions, we need to set a value on the badness of the harm we are doing to future people, and compare it with the badness of the sacrifices we could make to reduce it. Among the bad things future people will suffer is that many will die before their time, in floods and heat waves, in droughts and famines, and through increased poverty among the poorest. We need to set a value on the badness of those early deaths. We also need to assess the value of nature, which we are impoverishing. Those are some assessments of value we need to make, and there are many others too.

. . .

This reading is adapted from John Broome, "The Most Important Thing about Climate Change," in Jonathan Boston, Andrew Bradstock, and David Eng (eds.), *Public Policy: Why Ethics Matters* (Canberra: Australia National University Press), pp. 101–116, pp. 102–104.

However, since the 2009 Climate Change Conference in Copenhagen, I have come to the conclusion that the very most important thing about climate change is neither what is likely nor what is unlikely to result from it. The very most important thing is this fact: that the problem of climate change can be solved without anyone making any sacrifice.[1] At Copenhagen, many nations came together and failed to reach an agreement. They were asked to make sacrifices, and they declined to do so. But no sacrifice is necessary. The nations might have been more amenable if they had understood that point.

The fact no sacrifice is necessary is a consequence of elementary economics. Climate Change is what economists call an *externality*. Many of our activities cause greenhouse gases to be emitted. In deciding how many of these activities to engage in, people weigh the benefits they gain from them against the costs of engaging in them. But most of the costs of emitting greenhouse gases are not borne by the people who emit them. Instead, they are distributed across the population of the world, through the damage the greenhouse gases do. When the costs of an activity are not fully borne by the person who decides to engage in it, that is an externality.

Elementary economics tells us that externalities cause *inefficiency*. When an economist says that a situation is inefficient, she means it would be possible to make someone better off without making anyone else worse off. More precisely, there is some alternative state such that someone prefers the alternative to the existing state and no one prefers the existing state to the alternative. To adopt economists' terminology, let us say this alternative is *Pareto superior* to the existing state. Moving to the Pareto superior state involves no sacrifice on anyone's part. Because climate change is an externality, there is a Pareto superior state we could move to. It will involve emitting less greenhouse gas. Moreover, there is a Pareto superior state that is *efficient*, which means no other state is Pareto superior to it. If we get to a state like that, the inefficiency caused by the externality will have been eliminated, and no one will have made any sacrifices.

The theory of externalities tells us that achieving a Pareto superior state will often require resources to be transferred from some people to others. In the case of climate change, it is obvious in broad terms what sorts of transfer are required. We the current generation benefit from emitting greenhouse gases as we do at present. Suppose we change our policies and emit less of them. That by itself would make us worse off. But the theory tells us that resources could be transferred to us from the beneficiaries of our reduction in emissions, in such a way that no one ends up worse off. In the case of greenhouse gases, most of the beneficiaries are people who will live in the future. Therefore, resources will need to be transferred from future people to present people.

How can that happen? We the current generation are set to bequeath a lot to future generations. We shall leave them artificial resources such as roads and museums. We shall also leave them natural resources, since this generation will not exhaust all the natural resources the earth possesses. To compensate ourselves for reducing our emissions of greenhouse gases, we can use more of other resources for ourselves. We shall leave less of them for the future. By itself, that would be bad for future generations. However, those future generations will suffer less from climate change because we reduce our emissions. We know from the elementary economic theory that, if we do the transfer correctly, future generations will end up better off on balance, and we shall be no worse off.

The outcome I have described is not a nice one. It is Pareto superior to the existing state, but the existing state contains all the bad consequences of emitting greenhouse gases. For instance, it contains the injustices I mentioned: we are already harming some existing people by our emissions. If we reduce our emissions, we shall stop harming those people in that way. But it compounds the injustice to expect them to compensate us for reducing our emissions. Another example is that our emissions are damaging the conditions of life of future people. I have said it would be better if we reduced our emissions and compensated ourselves for doing so. But it would be even better if we reduced our emissions and did not compensate ourselves for doing so.

Compare three alternatives: *A*, we do nothing about the externality and continue to emit greenhouse gases profligately; *B*, we reduce our emissions to eliminate the externality, and compensate ourselves for doing so;

C, we reduce our emissions to eliminate the externality, and do not compensate ourselves for doing so.

. . .

The difference between *B* and *C* is nothing to do with climate change. Moving from *A* to *B* eliminates the problem of climate change. To move from *B* to *C* is simply to redistribute wealth from present people towards future people. No doubt outcome *C* would be best. But to reach *C* the current generation has to make sacrifices, and the experience in Copenhagen shows it is unwilling to do so.

I think we should try first to develop the institutional arrangements that will make the move from *A* to *B* possible. That will allow us to eliminate the problem of climate change. Then we should try going further to *C*. But we should not encumber the process of controlling climate change with the quite different matter of transferring resources to future people.

REFERENCES

Foley, D. 2007. *The Economic Fundamentals of Global Warming*. Working paper 07-12-044. Santa Fe, New Mexico: Santa Fe Institute. www.santafe.edu/media/workingpapers/07-12-044.pdf.

Stern, N. 2010. *A Blueprint for a Safer Planet*. Vintage Books.

NOTE

1. I take this point from Foley (2007). It is widely recognized. For instance, it is mentioned by Stern (2010, p. 85).

BJORN LOMBORG

COOL IT

. . .

[There is a] classical divide on global warming—either you believe it is an elaborate hoax or you think it is the unmitigated apocalypse. Yet both viewpoints are unsupported by the data. Indeed, we need to get our heads around the double facts that 1) global warming is both true and man-made, but 2) dramatic and fast CO_2 cuts are a poor way to deal with global warming and an extremely poor way to help the world and its inhabitants.

In *Cool It*, I try to stake out the sensible middle ground between global warming rejection and alarmism. Finding this middle ground is absolutely essential if we are to make a better future, both for people and the planet. This is why *The New York Times* described my book as part of the emerging "pragmatic center" on the global warming debate.

Most of the public debate seems to lack this center, and often it means that we end up with surprisingly inadequate positions, some of which I've been actively involved in exposing since the publication of *Cool It*.

One example has been the worldwide "lights-out" campaign from Sydney to Toronto, where environmental groups encourage entire cities to turn out their lights for an hour to emphasize the need for global warming action. Yet it seems nobody wanted to spoil the party by pointing out that the event is immensely future, underlines a horrible metaphor, and engenders extremely high pollution levels. Let's look at Denmark (the native country of the story of the "Emperor's New Clothes") for instance. The papers happily quoted WWF on how the event was an overwhelming success, yet the entire energy savings from the event (assuming people didn't use more energy later in the night to make up for lost time) was a full 10 tons of CO_2. This is equivalent of just a single Dane's annual emissions. Economically speaking, the effect of the entire collected good efforts of the Queen, the many participating companies, and Copenhagen city hall, as well as many other cities, managed to do only $20 worth of good. I'm sure this will make the future remember us fondly.

Moreover, what sort of message does turning out the lights send? As some conservative commentators like to point out, the environmental movement has indeed become the dark force, not metaphorically, but literally. Urging us to sit in darkness will indeed make us realize how utterly unlikely it is that we will be convinced to give up the advantages of fossil fuels. Indeed, it might make us realize how utterly dependent we are on fossil fuels. Curiously, nobody suggested that the lights-out campaign should also mean no air conditioning or heating, no telephones, Internet or movies, no hot food, warm coffee, or cold drinks—not to mention the loss of security when public street lights go out.

Ironically, the lights out also implies much greater energy inefficiency and dramatically higher levels of air pollution. Most of the people around the world when asked to extinguish the electrical lights, might turn to candlelights instead. It is cozy and seems oh-so-ecological. Yet, when measured on their light, candles are between ten and a thousand times less efficient than electrical lights—and this is compared to the maligned incandescent light bulb, with energy-saving lights besting candles between a hundred and a hundred thousand times.

At the same time, candles create massive amounts of some of the most societally damaging pollution, namely particulate air pollution, which in the United States is estimated by the U.S. EPA to kill more than 100,000 people each year. Yet, candles can easily create indoor air pollution levels ten to one hundred times the outdoor air pollution caused by cars, industry, and electricity production. Moreover, the whole family along with kids will conveniently be gathered around the coziness to fully inhale the extra fumes. Measured against the relative reduction in air pollution from the reduced fossil fuel energy production, candles increase the health damaging air pollution a thousand to ten thousandfold.

This seems more generally to be the state of much of our environmental debate. Because we're lacking the middle ground, we only hear the stories that fit the preconceived frameworks. You have undoubtedly read the story about a breakup of a massive glacier in the Antarctic, supposedly showing the ever-increasing effects of global warming. Yet we don't hear that the area was ice-free, possibly just some 400 years ago, without the help of global warming. We don't hear that the Wilkins glacier makes up less than 0.01% of Antarctica. And we don't hear the inconvenient fact that the Antarctic is experiencing record sea ice coverage since satellite measurements began.

While we all heard Al Gore talking about the dramatic hurricane years of 2004 and 2005, we've heard almost nothing about the complete absence of hurricane damage in 2006 and 2007. The insurance company Lloyds of London has now begun to fret that the absence of natural disasters is putting a squeeze on their premiums.

We are constantly presented with the stories underlining how temperatures are soaring, but over the past year, when temperatures worldwide have plummeted, we've seen the single fastest temperature change [ever] recorded, either up or down. Yet this rarely gets mentioned, although the stories abound. In January, Hong Kong was gripped with the second longest cold spell since 1885. Winter storms in central and southern China produced the worst winter weather in half a century. Snow fell on Baghdad for the first time in living memory.

Indeed, most of the public debate seems to lack a sensible . . . center. Instead almost all politicians in most nations are scuffling to promise ever stricter CO_2

cuts. This is evident also in the United States, where, as of this writing, all three major presidential candidates have set forward elaborate promises to deliver significant carbon reductions by 2050. However, there is very little information on both the efficiency of such policies (how much less warming will we see?) and their costs (how many billions of dollars will it cost?). And for good reason. . . . Al Gore's proposal for a $140 carbon tax would hike gas prices by $1.25 per gallon, cut the U.S. emissions by half in 2015, yet have an almost immeasurable impact on temperatures—decreasing the average temperature in 2100 by 0.2°F. And the cost would be a dramatic $160 billion annually for the rest of the century.[1]

While most U.S. politicians have only made promises but done little toward implementing them, it is perhaps worthwhile to look at politics in Europe where the extravagant promises are now beginning to be felt. A good example is the EU's newly instituted policy of cutting CO_2 emissions by 20% by 2020.

A 20% reduction in the EU, vigorously enforced throughout this century, would merely postpone global warming by two years at the end of the century. The temperature increase the world would expect to see by 2100 because of global warming would first take place in 2102. An immeasurable change. Yet the cost would be anything but immeasurable. The EU's own estimate for the cost is about €60 ($90) billion annually, which conveniently is down from its own previous estimate of almost twice that much. It is almost certainly a vast underestimate, since it requires the EU to make the reductions as smart as possible. . . . The real price will likely become much higher. An economic cost–benefit analysis indicates that for every dollar we spend on such policies like the EU's, we only help the world about 30 cents. However, the EU politicians are not content just talking about cutting emissions—they also want to decide *how*. They have decided that the renewable energy share in the union should be increased by 20% by 2020. This increase has no separate climatic effect, since they have already promised to cut emissions by 20%, and because the extra spending will go to buying current technology not to produce much better future technologies. However, it does manage to make a poor policy decision dramatically worse.

Here, the debate in my native Denmark is instructive as the relevant government ministries have outlined what this decision will end up costing Denmark, and it gives a feel for the total cost for the EU. The costs for an increase in renewable of less than 20% (18 percentage points) and with less ambition (five years later by 2025) shows the total cost will be about $4 billion annually. And the benefit? If Denmark sticks to this decision throughout the rest of this century, the end result will be to postpone global warming by the end of the century by five days. The average temperature that the globe would react by Friday, January 1, we would postpone till the following Wednesday, after having spent more than $300 billion.

Is that a sensible decision? The total advantage into the indefinite future from this Danish reduction to the world (measured on all relevant parameters such as lives saved, agricultural production increased, wetlands preserved, etc.) is about $15 million. Or for every dollar spent, we would do a bit less than half a cent worth of good for the world.

To put this into perspective, the $4 billion spending could double the number of hospitals in Denmark. And if we really wanted to do good, $3 billion could halve the number of malaria cases in the world. It would save 850 million lives over the century, avoid 250 million people getting infected every year. It would mean that the people of malaria-infected countries would live much better lives, become more productive and leave a world for the kids and grandkids in 2100 that would be much, much better. The last billion could fund an eightfold increase in R&D of CO_2-reducing energy technologies, which in the long run would make it possible for everyone to reduce CO_2 much more dramatically, at a much lower cost.

So, what should it be? Achieve one of the most remarkable improvements in history—reducing the frequency of malaria in this world by half—while dramatically increasing the possibility of solving global warming in the medium run? Or make a renewable pledge that looks good but does two thousand times less good and will change the global climate insignificantly?

And it gets worse. The price of $4 billion requires politicians to pick the cheapest way possible. Yet the politicians seem intent on often picking much more expensive solutions essentially doubling the cost or more. And the opposition—in trying to trump the government—insists that we should increase our ambitions to almost 40%. The cost would escalate to nearly $15 billion annually, with every dollar doing just a quarter of a cent worth of good for the world.

All of these considerations seem to be playing themselves out internationally. Using the Danish figures to extrapolate EU costs, the total cost is likely to be more than $225 billion annually, with every dollar doing just half a cent worth of good. And this is assuming that politicians pick the lowest cost best options and that the opposition let's-do-more attitude doesn't win. I'm not sure this is clear. How do you measure what the best options are?

The same money could triple the global development aid budget. It could easily give clean drinking water, sanitation, education, and health care to every single human being on the planet, while tenfold increasing CO_2-reducing R&D.

And there is one final risk in dealing with global warming, we need to remember. If we persistently overworry and exaggerate the problems people will eventually tire of the entire discussion. There are already ominous signs that this is happening. A recent poll from [the] National Center for Public Policy Research shows that while 18% of all Americans are willing to pay 50¢ on the prevention of global [warming], almost half are unwilling to spend even a penny more. A recent UK survey from the Environmental Transport Association showed that three in 10 people reckon there is too much publicity about global warming and more than half of these are "bored hearing about it."

Remember the bird flu? A couple of years ago, we worried extensively about a global influenza pandemic, which could kill hundreds of millions [of] people. We worried mostly about birds in Europe and the United States infected with H5N1, while the risk lay mainly with the billions of birds living in close proximity to hundreds of millions in Southeast Asia. And eventually we got fed up with the scary news stories and moved on. This doesn't mean the risk wasn't there—if anything the risk of a global pandemic is probably increasing. But the fact that we overworried, focused wrongly, and then gave up shows a disconcerting analogy with global warming. We should have focused on smart policies to gain information, sequence diseases, and ramp up investments in research for vaccines, while avoiding the hyperbole that eventually drained interest.

Not worrying about global warming is as wrong as worrying too much. But if we keep sounding the alarmist doomsday drums on global warming, we are likely to enact ineffective and enormously costly policies, that will do little to help the world but much to drain us of our long-term stamina necessary for seeing us through. Instead of focusing on how intensely we should be worrying, we need to worry correctly. We need to find the pragmatic middle ground and get smart, cost-effective policies to deal with global warming. But we will only get there, if we keep our cool.

NOTES

1. [See Lomborg, *Cool It*, p. 132.]

1 5

URBAN ECOLOGY
AND MODERN LIFE

ADRIANA ZUNIGA-TERAN

URBAN ECOLOGY

Urban ecology—or the study of the interactions between living organisms and their urban environment—is a multidimensional and interdisciplinary field of study with growing importance. Since 2008, and for the first time in history, more than half of the people of the world live in cities; and this trend is projected to continue (Grimm et al., 2008). In order for urban societies to exist and expand, energy, food, water, and other natural resources are needed. But as cities grow, fertile land is converted into urban development limiting agricultural productivity, fragmenting the natural landscape, and altering the functioning of the ecosystems that provide valuable ecosystem services to humans. In addition, global environmental change is already pressuring social and ecological systems to adapt and become resilient. Therefore, as the world urbanizes, it becomes critical to understand the ecological dynamics of human occupation.

Cities are never isolated entities. Cities engage with surrounding natural landscapes that provide food, water, energy, materials, and other necessary resources. Water, energy, and food are part of a "nexus" because these resources cannot be managed separately. For example, energy is needed to pump and transport water. Water is needed to produce electricity. Energy and water are needed to produce food, and animal waste and some types of crops can produce energy. Further, the water–energy–food nexus and infrastructure requires governance, which raises questions about political power, resource access, and social equity (Scott, Crootof, & Kelly-Richards, 2016).

In addition to the links between cities and their surrounding landscapes, cities are also connected to one another, which enable them to trade goods and services usually not found within their own landscapes and boundaries. For millennia, this connection between

Original essay for this volume.

cities was at a local or regional scale, but during the past decades, the connection between cities has widened even more to produce "global cities" (Sassen, 2005). This new concept of global cities emerges in this era of globalization, when transnational companies outsource some of their services and new technological capacities allow the dissipation of distance and a reconfiguration of workplace.

Global cities are connected to each other quite deeply, although not always evidently. A person can now live in a city, while working in a company whose headquarters are located in a different city, consuming goods produced and manufactured somewhere else, and at the same time be supporting a family in a faraway country.

Global cities may have economic advantages, yet global cities are also vulnerable to threats that affect not only their own regions, but the entire planet. Population growth is one of the main stressors of cities. As the population of the world exceeds seven billion people, there is a growing concern for the availability of natural resources. This societal concern dates back to the early 1970s when a group of scientists from the Massachusetts Institute of Technology, published their book "The Limits to Growth" in 1972. For the first time in history, urban ecology was studied using computer models in what they called "system dynamics." Their three main conclusions were: (1) if present trends continue, the limits to population growth and industrial capacity will be reached within the next century, with a sudden uncontrollable decline (2) it is possible, however, to modify these trends through what they called "sustainable development," and (3) if we choose to work towards sustainability, time is of essence and the sooner we start working towards this outcome, the better chances we get in avoiding the uncontrollable decline of our species. Their findings are very relevant today. Current concerns about a growing population involve differences in lifestyles, where people in developed countries consume more and generate more carbon emissions and waste. In turn, developing countries strive to provide this comfortable lifestyle to their own people, stressing the balance between resources and population.

One strategy to reverse growing population trends has focused on educating girls in developing countries, because the number of children that females have in poor countries is inversely related to their level of education. As young women get educated, they find more livelihood opportunities and choose to have fewer children. Other population growth concerns include the relationship between aging population with young working population groups, where developed countries face a serious challenge. In rich countries, families are smaller and consequently there is a larger aging population and fewer young people working to support them.

The scientific work by the MIT researchers evidenced the generalized awareness of rising resource scarcity. This same year (1972), the United Nations Conference on the Human Environment took place in Stockholm, prompting national governments to safeguard natural resources. There have been other influential works on urban ecology and the predicament that we live in with a growing population in a world that has a finite amount of natural resources. Some examples include "The Closing Circle" by Barry Commoner (1971), where he outlined the four laws of ecology that basically stress the connection of everything to everything else. This is particularly applicable to cities whose demands on the surrounding landscape (and the world in general) is more pronounced. Other influential works include "The Population Bomb" by the biologist Paul Ehrlich (1968); and "The Ultimate Resource" by the economist Julian Simon (1981), who eventually got into a famous bet.[1] Another influential work that paved the way for the green movement was the utopian novel "Ecotopia" by Ernest Callenbach (1975). This work is considered a protest against consumerism and materialism, two human tendencies that occur in cities. Also, Garrett Hardin's "Tragedy of the Commons" (1968) paints a future for a humanity doomed to overexploit common resources. However, three decades later, Elinor Ostrom challenged Hardin's gloomy vision introducing a framework to analyze social and ecological systems that can result in a sustainable collaborative ecosystem management (E. Ostrom, 2009; Elinor Ostrom, 1999; Elinor Ostrom, Burger, Field, Norgaard, & Policansky, 1999). Finally, "The Ecological Footprint" by Mathis Wackernagel and William Rees (1996) describes a practical tool to analyze the land area beyond the city boundary needed to sustain a certain type of lifestyle considering the carrying capacity of the earth. This approach to the analysis of resource consumption in cities has given rise to the new concept of "urban metabolism," in which cities are examined as living organisms in terms of their inputs and outputs, transformations, and waste-recycling (Scott et al., 2016).

In addition to the limits of resources accessible to rapidly growing local populations, climate change is adding global pressure. Recent climate-related disasters have dramatically affected major cities throughout the world. In many cases, urban infrastructure exacerbates the negative effects of disasters in general (climate-related or not). For example, in 2005, hurricane Katrina hit the U.S. Gulf Coast negatively affecting the City of New Orleans. The levees and flood walls that had protected the city for decades failed, causing flooding in most of the city. The 2011 tsunami that hit the coasts of Japan also illustrates the potential negative effects of infrastructure during catastrophes that extend beyond city boundaries. The Fukushima nuclear disaster affected fisheries serving the other side of the world. Further, "resource traps" can occur when cities rebuild their infrastructure after a catastrophe, but fail to build the kind of infrastructure that will be able to handle extreme events in the future. Rebuilding infrastructure that exacerbated the effects of an extreme weather event in the first place is a vicious cycle that many cities maintain. Examples of resource traps include developing along a flood plain or a wetland, paving ephemeral river beds in cities, and increasing paving that prevent the land from being able to absorb floodwaters (Scott et al., 2016).

To understand urban ecology today, it is critical to consider not only all of the challenges and threats that we are facing, but also the important opportunities that we still have to reverse these trends and adapt to the inevitable climate change. The critical components of urban ecology in the 21st century that offer opportunities for sustainability and increased resilience to climate change include water, food, energy, transportation, greenspace, and waste.

WATER

The sustainable management of water resources is critical (Scott et al., 2013). Many scientists agree that the problem with water resources is not so much the availability of water but the sustainable management of the resource and the establishment of good governance systems (Varady et al., 2013). It is tempting to think that because the solution to water security depends on policy, it should be easy, but nothing is further from the truth. We have learned that conventional water governance systems that are centralized top-down approaches result in inequity outcomes that, in turn, produce ecological degradation that damage water resources (Scott et al., 2013; Varady, Zuniga-Teran, Garfin, Martin, & Vicuña, 2016).

An alternative approach to water governance that strives for sustainability is the Integrated Water Resources Management, or IWRM. This governance model is decentralized, meaning that water management decisions are made by impacted stakeholders. More recently, the concept of *adaptive management* emerged, which allows the incorporation of uncertainty into water management and relies on long-term monitoring. Finally, IWRM was criticized for not providing a clear goal to water management. As a response to this shortcoming, the new concept of *water security* emerged that includes equity goals and environmental considerations in a quantifiable way (Varady et al., 2016). Water security is defined by Scott and colleagues (2013) as "the sustainable availability of adequate quantities and qualities of water for resilient societies and ecosystems in the face of uncertain global change" (p.281). Water security goals are included in the Sustainable Development Goals, or SDGs, developed by the United Nations and adopted by many countries in 2015 with targets for the next 15 years ("Sustainable Development Goals | UNDP," n.d.).

FOOD

As with water security, the real food security problem is not a simple matter of there not being enough food. As documented by Amartya Sen's Nobel Prize winning work, what causes famine is not a breakdown of food availability per se so much as a breakdown in food distribution networks. Sen won a Nobel Prize for documenting that 20th century famines never were caused by a lack of food, but always by imploding distribution mechanisms. Famine is caused not by eroding soil but by eroding rights. In particular, farmers have to be able to count on their crop not being confiscated. Where farmers cannot count on that, they don't plant crops, and famine results (Sen 2009, Schmidtz 2011).

Again, there are enough resources to prevent people from dying of hunger (Ingram, Ericksen, & Liverman, 2010); but, in a troubling paradox, as part of the world struggles to feed its people, another part is dying from diseases linked to overconsumption (Shaw, 2007). Current contributing factors to food insecurity include population growth, higher per capita consumption, changes in diet that include more meat (more resources are needed to feed carnivores than vegetarians), higher food prices, less available land for cultivation combined with a decline in productivity, and an increase in food waste (Godfray & Robinson, 2015; Kuyper & Struik, 2014; Westengen & Banik, 2016). In cities, food security is further challenged by an unequal distribution of food sources that creates "food deserts"—or neighborhoods where there is no healthy food available within a certain radius. This situation disproportionately stresses low-income families that do not own a car and therefore are forced to eat whatever is available, that is mostly junk food.

Urban environments provide important opportunities to increase food security through *urban agriculture*. This concept refers to the local production and consumption of food in cities, including fruits and vegetables, livestock, and even aquaculture (Mathews & Dodson, 2016; Mosquera-Losada et al., 2017). Some examples of urban agriculture include community gardens, aquaponics, horticultural precincts, household farming, and vertical farms (Mathews & Dodson, 2016). Urban agriculture allows the production of food almost anywhere in cities, helping overcome the impacts of food deserts. Producing food in cities also decreases pressure on transportation systems (and related carbon emissions), and reduces vulnerability to climate change. For example, if a city is affected by an extreme weather event that damages bridges on key access roads, food supply may be interrupted until the bridge is repaired. However, producing food locally may offset the need to bring resources by other means of transportation that can be very costly. Furthermore, using urban waste as a fertilizer reduces methane emissions (a potent greenhouse gas) and the economic and environmental cost of transport. The local production of food in cities has been promoted by the UN Food and Agriculture Organization (FAO) (Mosquera-Losada et al., 2017) and is also part of the SDGs. Producing food locally through urban agriculture shows a promising approach to enhance resilience and increase food security in cities.

ENERGY

Energy is a key resource for cities worldwide and *the* key for reversing negative trends. Cities are critical contributors to climate change because they depend on fossil fuels not only to provide electricity, but also for transportation, heating and cooling of buildings, construction materials, food supply, and maintenance of urban infrastructure. As the world strives to transition toward renewable energy sources (e.g., solar, wind, geothermal) to mitigate climate change, we also face serious challenges. For example, cities that want to move away from fossil fuels will still need a diversity of energy sources and new infrastructure that supports new technologies. Therefore, urban planning will require regulatory frameworks for decentralized energy systems (e.g., solar panels on building roofs and over parking lots, wind turbines in backyards or walls, geothermal systems) (Mathews & Dodson, 2016). They will also require the mass adoption of electric cars. Moreover, energy prices are likely to increase because renewable energy is more expensive, which may result in equity and gender issues. Therefore, cities will have to look for market incentives to lower energy prices and more equitable ways to supply this resource (Cherp & Jewell, 2011). Equity issues and the need for renewable energy are integrated in the SGDs with clear goals for affordable and clean energy.

Urban design strategies can be implemented to reduce energy consumption at the city scale. Compact development (or urban consolidation) that increases density in cities reduces distances and fuel demand for transportation. In addition, compact neighborhoods require a less extensive network of infrastructure and utility supply, which reduces vulnerability to climate-related events (Mathews & Dodson, 2016).

TRANSPORTATION

Transportation is another critical factor in urban ecology, because the functioning of the city relies on effective transportation systems and networks. Transportation connects people physically to each other and allows the flow of materials, resources, and services within and beyond city boundaries. And yet most urban travel in the world use petroleum fuels (Dodson, 2016). Since the 1950s, urban development in the U.S., Australia, and other countries has transitioned from pedestrian-centered to car-oriented communities, and from inclusive societies to exclusive or segregating communities (e.g., suburban development, gated communities). The mass adoption of the automobile that happened after World War II, allowed cities to expand rapidly in what is known as *urban sprawl* (Barnett, J., 2003). This rapid expansion combined with zoning regulations resulted in a separation of land uses that caused increased traffic, and the fierce consumption of fertile land (Randolph, J., 2004). Because in suburban neighborhoods, most services (e.g., restaurants, offices, supermarkets) are located far away from homes, people rely on the use of the automobile for their daily activities resulting in sedentary and isolated societies, and with related health impacts (Whitelegg, 2016). These negative effects of suburban development combined with the proliferation of the highway system that tear cities in the U.S. apart was captured by Jane Jacobs in her iconic book "The Death and Life of Great American Cities" published in 1961. Low density residential development, Jacobs wrote, also results in less people watching the streets, which is related to a decrease in sense of community, and an increase in crime (Jacobs, 1961).

Urban planners and designers have tried to reverse these negative trends by promoting transit-oriented development, that is, development that combines different modes of transportation, has high density, and combines different land-uses (Mathews & Dodson, 2016). Complete streets—designed to accommodate pedestrians, bicycle riders, transit users, and motorists of all abilities and ages—may reduce the use of the automobile and promote walking and biking as part of daily transport. Changes in the built environment that increase lifestyle physical activity offer a promising approach to sustainable urban development (Zuniga-Teran et al., 2017).

GREENSPACE

Greenspace plays a critical role in cities because it allows the functioning of the ecosystems, upon which human societies depend. Greenspace is sometimes referred to as "green infrastructure" especially when these vegetated areas (or green spaces) are used as stormwater infrastructure that allows water infiltration through its permeable surfaces. Examples of greenspace include parks, golf courses, sport fields, greenways, green roofs, urban forests, green streets and biophylic buildings (Mathews & Dodson, 2016). Greenspace provides a wide range of benefits for both social and ecological systems, particularly if these spaces are part of a network (Mathews & Dodson, 2016). Greenspace purifies the air (Ernstson et al., 2010), reduces noise and stress (Chu, Thorne, & Guite, 2004), and provides recreational opportunities (Herrick, 2009). In addition, greenspace provides ecosystem services including reduced flooding risk and runoff, recharged aquifers, and reduction of the urban heat island effect enhancing thermal comfort in cities (Ernstson et al., 2010; Moore, Gulliver, Stack, & Simpson, 2016). Finally, greenspace provides habitat for species and allows landscape connectivity so species can move through the urban matrix, decreasing the negative impact of habitat fragmentation (Andersson & Bodin, 2008). However, the distribution of greenspace in cities is not homogeneous, and poor neighborhoods often lack vegetation (Wolch, Byrne, & Newell, 2014). The absence of greenspace in low-income neighborhoods is a stress, raising questions of environmental and social justice.

WASTE MANAGEMENT

How we manage our waste is a critical factor in urban ecology because it offers important opportunities to reduce our ecological footprint while mitigating climate change. Organic waste produces methane—a potent greenhouse gas. Separating organic waste and converting it into compost not only reduces methane emissions, but also increases the amount of fertile soil needed for agriculture, and reduces landfill area. Another sustainable approach to waste is to convert landfill gas into biogas—a renewable energy source. Biogas production is also feasible in farms where livestock produce a considerable amount of waste. Furthermore, there are many opportunities to improve waste management at the household level by what is known as the three "Rs," that is, reducing our waste, reusing our stuff, and recycling paper, aluminum, glass, and other materials. However, recycling requires large amounts of energy, particularly if waste is shipped to other countries for recycling. Finally, as we deplete the earth's mineral resources, current mining technologies are considering *urban mining* as a way to acquire important mineral resources. For example, by retrieving electronics from landfills (also known as "e-waste") companies can get essential minerals while saving money. In addition, important elements can be extracted from human waste, including nitrogen and phosphorus, that can be used as fertilizers in urban agriculture (Mosquera-Losada et al., 2017). The urban metabolism framework considers waste a potential resource.

Urban design may provide a key to *future cities*—or cities approaching zero pollution and zero greenhouse gas emissions—in which all the waste produced is recycled, and resources are conserved and recovered (Scott et al., 2016). Such urban design would integrate strategies at the building, neighborhood, and city scales with decentralized infrastructure (or recovery facilities) that could treat waste and wastewater, while producing energy from organic solids, and at the same time sequestering carbon dioxide (Scott et al., 2016). For future cities to succeed, the cost of technologies would have to be reduced.

CONCLUSION

Urban societies currently face complex challenges and imminent threats including local population growth, limited resources, and climate change. Equity issues lie at the center of this conundrum. The actions that we take today and in the near future may determine critical outcomes for the survival of our species. Water, food, energy, transportation, greenspace, and waste offer important opportunities for sustainability in cities, as well as ways to increase climate change resilience.

In terms of water security, a promising approach includes decentralized governance systems that involve stakeholders, incorporate uncertainty and equity into decision-making, and integrate the energy and food sectors in a nexus approach. With regard to opportunities for food security in cities, urban agriculture that produces food at the local level may increase not only food security but also resilience to climate change. For energy security, urban planning systems that allow decentralized renewable systems at the household/building level, and promote compact development has the potential to mitigate climate change. In terms of transportation, promoting transit-oriented development where people can choose different modes of transportation, where land uses are combined in a high-density compact

design can reduce energy consumption in cities, promote lifestyle physical activity, and increase sense of community. Furthermore, increasing greenspace in a connected network can help maintain the functioning of the ecosystems and help us adapt to climate change. Finally, urban mining has the potential to transform waste into usable resources including valuable minerals and energy. All of these changes have the potential to direct urban societies toward sustainable development, which seems to be the most promising path for a bright future. But it is only possible if we work together, and sooner rather than later.

NOTE

1. www.nytimes.com/2013/09/08/opinion/sunday/betting-on-the-apocalypse.html

Acknowledgements: Support came from the International Water Security Network, funded by Lloyd's Register Foundation (LRF), a charitable foundation in the U.K. helping to protect life and property by supporting engineering-related education, public engagement, and the application of research. Support also came from the Inter-American Institute for Global Change Research (IAI), for project SGP-CRA005, supported by the National Science Foundation (NSF) Grant No. GEO-1138881; and for Research Project CNR3056, supported by NSF Grant No. GEO-1128040.

REFERENCES

Andersson, E., & Bodin, Ö. (2008). Practical tool for landscape planning? An empirical investigation of network based models of habitat fragmentation. *Ecography*, 32(1), 123–32.

Barnett, J. (2003). *Redesigning Cities; Principles, Practice, Implementation*. Chicago, Illinois United States: Planners Press American Planning Association.

Cherp, A., & Jewell, J. (2011). The three perspectives on energy security: intellectual history, disciplinary roots and the potential for integration. *Current Opinion in Environmental Sustainability*, 3(4), 202–212. https://doi.org/10.1016/j.cosust.2011.07.001

Chu, A., Thorne, A., & Guite, H. (2004). The impact on mental well-being of the urban and physical environment; an assessment of the evidence. *Journal of Public Mental Health*, 3(2), 17–32.

Dodson, J. (2016). A Stormy Petroleum Horizon: Cities and planning beyond oil. In N. Sipe, J. Dodson, & A. Nelson (Eds.), *Planning After Petroleum—Preparing Cities for the Age Beyond Oil*. Taylor and Francis.

Ernstson, H., van der Leeuw, S. E., Redman, C. L., Meffert, D. J., Davis, G., Alfsen, C., & Elmqvist, T. (2010). Urban transitions: on urban resilience and human-dominated ecosystems. *Ambio, 39*(8), 531–545.

Godfray, H. C. J., & Robinson, S. (2015). Contrasting approaches to projecting long-run global food security. *Oxford Review of Economic Policy, 31*(1), 26–44. https://doi.org/10.1093/oxrep/grv006

Grimm, N. B., Faeth, S. H., Golubiewski, N. E., Redman, C. L., Wu, J., Bai, X., & Briggs, J. M. (2008). Global change and the ecology of cities. *Science, 319*(5864), 756–760.

Herrick, C. (2009). Designing the fit city: public health, active lives, and the (re)instrumentalization of urban space. *Environment and Planning A, 41*(10), 2437–2454. https://doi.org/10.1068/a41309

Ingram, J., Ericksen, P., & Liverman, D. (Eds.). (2010). *Food security and global environmental change.* London and Washington DC: Earthscan.

Jacobs, J. (1961). *The Death and Life of Great American Cities* (50th Anniversary Edition). New York, NY: Modern Library.

Kuyper, T. W., & Struik, P. C. (2014). Epilogue: global food security, rhetoric, and the sustainable intensification debate. *Current Opinion in Environmental Sustainability, 8,* 71–79. https://doi.org/10.1016/j.cosust.2014.09.004

Mathews, T., & Dodson, J. (2016). Institutional planning responses to a confluence of oil vulnerability and climate change. In N. Sipe, J. Dodson, & A. Nelson (Eds.), *Planning After Petroleum—Preparing Cities for the Age Beyond Oil*. Taylor and Francis.

Moore, T., Gulliver, J., Stack, L., & Simpson, M.. (2016). Stormwater management and climate change: vulnerability and capacity for adaptation in urban and suburban contexts. *Climatic Change, 138*(3–4), 491–504. https://doi.org/10.1007/s10584-016-1766-2

Mosquera-Losada, R., Amador-García, A., Muñóz-Ferreiro, N., Santiago-Freijanes, J. J., Ferreiro-Domínguez, N., Romero-Franco, R., & Rigueiro-Rodríguez, A. (2017). Sustainable use of sewage sludge in acid soils within a circular economy perspective. *CATENA,* 149, 341–348. https://doi.org/10.1016/j.catena.2016.10.007

Ostrom, E. (1999). Coping with tragedies of the commons. *Annual Review of Political Science, 2*(1), 493–535.

Ostrom, E. (2009). A General Framework for Analyzing Sustainability of Social–Ecological Systems. *Science, 325*(5939), 419–422. https://doi.org/10.1126/science.1172133

Ostrom, E., Burger, J., Field, C. B., Norgaard, R. B., & Policansky, D. (1999). Revisiting the commons: local lessons, global challenges. *Science, 284*(5412), 278–282.

Randolph, J. (2004). *Environmental land use planning and management.* Washington: Island Press.

Sassen, S. (2005). The global city: Introducing a concept. *Brown Journal of World Affairs, 11*(2), 27–43.

Schmidtz, David (2011). Nonideal Theory: What It Is and What It Needs To Be. *Ethics* 121, 772–796.

Scott, C. A., Crootof, A., & Kelly-Richards, S. (2016). The Urban Water–Energy Nexus: Building Resilience for Global Change in the "Urban Century." In H. Hettiarachchi & R. Ardakanian (Eds.), *Environmental Resource Management and the Nexus Approach* (pp. 113–140). Cham: Springer International Publishing. https://doi.org/10.1007/978-3-319-28593-1_5

Scott, C. A., Meza, F. J., Varady, R. G., Tiessen, H., McEvoy, J., Garfin, G. M., . . . Montaña, E. (2013). Water Security and Adaptive Management in the Arid Americas. *Annals of the Association of American Geographers, 103*(2), 280–289. https://doi.org/10.1080/00045608.2013.754660

Sen, Amartya (2009). *The Idea of Justice* Cambridge: Harvard University Press.

Shaw, J. (2007). *World food security: A history since 1945.* Basingstoke: Palgrave.

Sustainable Development Goals | UNDP. (n.d.). Retrieved 2016, from http://www.undp.org/content/undp/en/home/sustainable-development-goals.html

Varady, R. G., van Weert, F., Megdal, S. B., Gerlak, A., Iskandar, C. A., & House-Peters, L. (2013). Groundwater Governance: A Global Framework for Country Action. Retrieved from http://www.yemenwater.org/wp-content/uploads/2015/04/GWG_Thematic5_8June2012.pdf

Varady, R. G., Zuniga-Teran, A. A., Garfin, G. M., Martin, F., & Vicuña, S. (2016). Adaptive management and water security in a global context: definitions, concepts, and examples. *Current Opinion in Environmental Sustainability, 21*, 70–77. https://doi.org/10.1016/j.cosust.2016.11.001

Westengen, O. T., & Banik, D. (2016). The State of Food Security: From Availability, Access and Rights to Food Systems Approaches. *Forum for Development Studies, 43*(1), 113–134. https://doi.org/10.1080/08039410.2015.1134644

Whitelegg, J. (2016). Walking the City. In N. Sipe, J. Dodson, & A. Nelson (Eds.), *Planning After Petroleum—Preparing Cities for the Age Beyond Oil.* Taylor and Francis.

Wolch, J. R., Byrne, J., & Newell, J. P. (2014). Urban green space, public health, and environmental justice: The challenge of making cities "just green enough." *Landscape and Urban Planning, 125*, 234–244. https://doi.org/10.1016/j.landurbplan.2014.01.017

Zuniga-Teran, A. A., Orr, B., Gimblett, R., Chalfoun, N., Guertin, D., & Marsh, S. (2017). Neighborhood design, physical activity, and wellbeing: Applying the Walkability Model. *International Journal of Environmental Research and Public Health, 14*(76). https://doi.org/10.3390/ijerph14010076

LYNN SCARLETT

MAKING WASTE MANAGEMENT PAY

Over the past decade, academics and industry alike have scrutinized the "greening of the economy" and its potential to advance environmental progress. Two questions loom before us: "Where is environmental entrepreneurship going?" and "What barriers stand in its way?" But before we can address those questions, we need first to establish a context. What, in fact, do we mean by environmental entrepreneurship? Many environmental champions pluck out of the general economy a subset that they have labeled "environmental entrepreneurship" activities. This subset includes recycling, hazardous waste remediation, energy efficiency, renewable energy, and other economic activities often associated with environmental investment.

I want to offer a different perspective—one that advances two key points. First, borrowing a phrase from noted management scholar Peter Drucker, environmental entrepreneurship resides "anywhere" and "everywhere," rather than amid a predefined set of activities dubbed "green businesses." Second, we should think of environmental entrepreneurship as a discovery process—a process that starts with an idea, followed by investment in that idea, implementation of the innovation, and, finally, ongoing adaptation to improve the innovation. As a discovery process, all entrepreneurship involves a constant search for ways to add value by reducing costs, improving the bundle of attributes of good and services, or assembling and conveying attributes of goods and services in new ways. In the case of environmental entrepreneurship, this discovery process centers on adding value by improving the environmental performance of a good or service.

Original essay for this volume. Lynn Scarlett is a Senior Environmental Policy Analyst at Resources for the Future. She formerly has served as Deputy Secretary and Chief Operating Officer at the Department of the Interior.

The discovery process of environmental entrepreneurship unfolds along two dimensions—technological innovations and institutional innovations. The role technological innovation plays in adding value in the marketplace is both recognized and well understood. Indeed, economic history often describes a sequence of innovations that propel economic growth.

GREENING TECHNOLOGIES—BOUNDLESS OPPORTUNITIES

"The ideal," wrote one commentator, "is to have nothing to salvage." Who penned these words: champion of the environment Al Gore; techno-environmentalist Amory Lovins; or perhaps "green designer" William McDonough?

The answer is "none of the above" nor any of their contemporaries. The author is Henry Ford, early 20th century industrialist and pioneer of assembly-line production. He wrote this praise of waste reduction in *Today and Tomorrow*, a treatise that set forth his social and economic vision. Ford went on to describe his assault on waste: "There was waste all around the factory," he lamented.

By deliberately looking for this waste, in a single year his plant managers eliminated 80 million pounds of steel scrap and millions of pounds of brass and bronze—metals of choice a century ago. They achieve this feat by trimming and slimming materials and by changing metal-cutting patterns. In short, Henry Ford was a master at what we now dub "dematerialization"—using less stuff per unit of output.

Henry Ford was, of course, not alone in this waste-reducing endeavor. From the dawn of the industrial era to the present, manufacturers have continuously sought ways to "do more with less." As early as 1835, writer Charles Babbage opined that, "amongst the causes which tend to the cheap production of any article . . . may be mentioned, the care which is taken to prevent the absolute waste of any part of the raw material." In 1862, reference books on reducing or recycling waste had begun to appear. Popular culture celebrated industrial efficiency. One 19th century ditty, commenting on the Chicago slaughterhouses of the urban jungle, proclaimed, "A cow goes lowin' softly in Armour's an' comes out glue, gelatine, fertilizer, celooloid, joolry, sofy cusions, hair restorer,

washin'sody, littrachoor an bed springs so quick that while aft she's still a cow, for'ward she may be anything fr'm buttons to pannyma hats."

Other trends in materials and energy use yielded dramatic environmental benefits. The search for more efficient fuels, for example, propelled a climb up what might be called a "clean fuel ladder." The switch from wood burning to coal burning to natural gas for heating residences in the 20th century eliminated piles of household waste ash and ushered in dramatic reductions in residential sulfur dioxide emissions.

Fast forward to the 21st century and one finds other technological wonders that have allowed people to communicate more quickly and reliably—with far fewer resources for each "consumption" unit. A single CD, for example, can carry 90 million phone numbers, replacing five tons of phone books. A mere 65 pounds of silica can create a fiber optic cable that carries 40 times the messages of a cable made from one ton of copper.

Even the humble aluminum can underwent dramatic transformations in the search by soda companies to do more with less. In the 1960s, crushing a soda can was a macho act, a sign of strength. Try crushing a can today. Just about anyone can crush a soda can single-handedly—and then rip it in half.

Why is this possible? Propelled by competitive market forces to drive down costs, new manufacturing techniques and new can designs have enabled manufacturers to reduce the thickness of the can. In the 1960s, it took 164 pounds of metal to make 1,000 cans. Today, it takes less than 30 pounds. Competition resulted in conservation.

But, even with technologies, opportunities for better environmental performance lie anywhere and everywhere rather than in a few "green" categories such as recycling or waste reduction or biodegradable products. Consider a few examples that fall outside of the traditional recycling, remediation, and renewable energy boxes.

A few years ago, at one refinery, an energy producer embraced "Nature's Capital" by creating wetlands to treat its wastewater rather than continuing to rely on the prescribed mechanical treatment system. The wetlands purification system required one-third the installation costs of traditional mechanical treatment systems. It cost $30,000 to $50,000 per year for maintenance in contrast to ten times that amount for maintenance of traditional mechanical treatment systems. The wetland purification system produced better water quality—and created habitat that became home to some 200 species.

Or consider a Dutch flower grower who shifted from traditional soil medium to grow flowers and, instead, began growing flowers in a rock wool medium with water circulating through the medium. Through this system, the nursery could substantially reduce water use through recirculation; chemical use decreased dramatically through the highly refined and controlled application in the circulating water; plant quality improved because variability in growing conditions was reduced; and labor costs declined because harvesting flowers from rock wool containers on platforms was easier than harvesting from ground-level flower beds.

Take another example: Hitachi six-screw washing machines. The machine enhances ease of disassembly and remanufacturing. It takes 33 percent less time to produce because it has fewer parts; it requires less servicing for the customer because of the reduced number of moving parts.

These industries—oil refining, flower growing, and washing machine manufacturing—fall outside traditional "green" categories. Yet these are all examples of environmental entrepreneurship. Similar opportunities lie among the many goods and services in the marketplace and among all activities and processes undertaken by governments.

GREENING AS INSTITUTIONAL DISCOVERY

Let us move from technological innovation to institutional discovery—an oft-neglected dimension of entrepreneurship. For environmental entrepreneurship, new institutional arrangements that improve environmental performance fall into several categories.

First are new relationships between manufacturers and suppliers through "green performance contracts." For example, Saturn used to buy paint by volume. Under this arrangement, paint suppliers had little incentive to make more efficient paint—paint that would adequately color cars but use less "stuff." Saturn introduced a green performance contract through which

its paint suppliers get paid on the basis of number of cars painted rather than volume of paint purchased. Paint suppliers now have an incentive to develop more efficient paint. They also have an incentive to work with Saturn to reduce overspray, which wastes paint.

Next are new relationships between producers and customers. For example, moving from purchase agreements to lease agreements can reduce waste. One firm, Interface Flooring, introduced "carpet tiles" and carpet tile leasing, whereby companies lease floor covering rather than buy it. When individual carpet tiles wear out, they can be replaced without taking up the entire carpet and discarding it.

A third institutional innovation centers on new relationships between a company and a host community. Many companies have developed "Good Neighbor Compacts" through which they work with their communities to develop agreed upon performance goals—goals that often go beyond basic compliance with state and federal regulations. These compacts help enable companies to continue or expand production and to overcome NIMBY—not-in-my-backyard—predispositions.

Finally, we are seeing the emergence of new relationships among producers through waste exchanges or development of byproduct synergy contracts. Through these relationships, one company's waste becomes another's feedstock.

What, then, are the challenges to this environmental entrepreneurship? First is the marketplace itself. While opportunities for greening are infinite, attempts that assume buyers are willing to pay a premium for environmental improvements in their goods and services will find expectations unfulfilled. Just a small percentage of the buying public is willing to pay a premium for environmental attributes. Goods or services with environmental attributes, to be widely embraced, must be cost competitive with alternatives to flourish.

Yet there is another challenge in this green marketplace: there is a "greyness" to being green. What sometimes seems green can turn out to generate more, not less, resource use. In the 1990s, the kindergartner's simple "juice box" came under scrutiny by "green" watchdogs. Maine even passed a law banning the little juice boxes, using the argument that the boxes were not recyclable. It turns out that the little juice boxes can be recycled. But there was a larger, unexamined consideration.

Filling the little juice boxes required about half the energy needed to fill glass containers. Transporting the lightweight juice boxes—aseptic packages, in the jargon of packaging manufacturers—to bottling sites dramatically reduced fuel use. For a given volume of beverage, it took 15 times as many trucks to transport empty glass bottles than the aseptic packages, which could be transported in a flat form, then assembled at the bottling site.

A second challenge to marketplace greening can be rules constraints. For example, the Resource Conservation and Recovery Act hazardous waste definitions sometimes stand in the way of creating waste exchanges among firms.

Information constraints present a third challenge. Performance contracts, for example, require good baseline information and good metrics that specify what constitutes good practices and good results. Ironically, the "old environmentalism" of the past four decades produced a lot of rules and procedures, but relatively little effort was expended on developing good environmental performance measures.

Tax law, too, can be a constraint. The current tax code treatment of leasing versus capital asset purchases can make "green performance leasing" appear more expensive than direct asset purchasing.

But let me end on a note of optimism. Opportunities for environmental entrepreneurship abound. The limits lie only in our imaginations. Five areas hold especially strong near-term possibilities.

First is in the realm of performance contracts. Such performance contracts include energy efficiency building management contracts. Such contracts also lie, for example, in land management performance contracts in which, for example, environmental experts provide performance measures for farmers with confined animal feeding operations, audit the farmers' performance against those measures, and propose improvements. Already, such contracts have been used with potential cost savings for farmers when the Environmental Protection Agency and other agencies substitute performance contracts for prescriptive rules.

A second area of opportunity is in conservation land transactions. Demand is growing for the services of those skilled in arranging conservation easements, purchase-of-development rights transactions, mitigation banks, grass banks, and so on.

A third area of opportunity lies in development and application of metrics and monitoring. The growing emphasis on environmental indicators requires more monitoring and more measurement information and technologies.

Fourth, there is a growing demand for alternative dispute resolution, mediation, and arbitration of environmental conflicts. The evolving shift to cooperative conservation in which landowners and agencies partner to achieve shared environmental outcomes is generating demand for mediation skills.

Finally, though remediation of hazardous wastes is likely a non-growth field, we can expect to see demand for remediation and restoration in new arenas—especially in riparian restoration. We will also see a growing demand for biotechnology applied to remediation challenges. And we will see a growing demand for "natural engineering," such as wildlife friendly culverts, or permeable infrastructure in building complexes to permit natural drainage and percolation of water into the ground. The 20th century was a time of paving over our cities. The 21st century will be a time of re-creating natural landscapes, natural urban streams, and other permeable landscapes.

Yogi Berra once quipped that "the future ain't what it used to be." Environmental entrepreneurship, including waste reduction, is a search for new ways to add value through environmental improvements. These improvements take the form of cost reductions through waste exchanges or energy and water efficiencies. They take the form of providing new bundles of customer value, such as through hazards reductions or conservation enhancements. The opportunities lie anywhere and everywhere as we enter an era of the viridian verge—the coming together of environmental and economic values.

BILL MCKIBBEN

DEEP ECONOMY

AFTER GROWTH

For almost all of human history, said the great economist John Maynard Keynes, from "say, two thousand years before Christ down to the beginning of the
eighteenth century, there was really no great change in
the standard of living of the average man in the civilized centers of the earth. Ups and downs, certainly visitations of plague, famine and war, golden intervals, but
no progressive violent change." At the utmost, Keynes
calculated, the standard of living had increased 100
percent over those four thousand years. The reason was,
basically, that we didn't learn how to do anything new.
Before history began we'd learned about fire, language,
cattle, the wheel, the plow, the sail, the pot. We had
banks and governments and mathematics and religion.

And then, in 1712, something new finally happened. A British inventor named Thomas Newcomen
developed the first practical steam engine. He burned
coal, and used the steam pressure built up in his boiler
to drive a pump that, in turn, drained water from coal
mines, allowing them to operate far more cheaply and
efficiently. How much more efficiently? His engine replaced a team of five hundred horses walking in a circle.
And from there—well, things accelerated. In the words
of the economist Jeffrey Sachs, "The steam engine
marked the decisive turning point of human history."
Suddenly, instead of turning handles and cranks with
their own muscles or with the muscles of their animals
(which had in turn to be fed by grain that required
hard labor in the fields), men and women could exploit the earth's storehouse of fossilized energy to do
the turning for them. First coal, then oil, then natural
gas allowed for everything we consider normal and
obvious about the modern world, from making fertilizer to making steel to making electricity. These in turn

fed all the subsidiary revolutions in transportation and
chemistry and communications, right down to the
electron-based information age we now inhabit. Suddenly, one-hundred-percent growth in the standard of
living could be accomplished in a few decades, not a
few millennia.

In some ways, the invention of the idea of economic growth was almost as significant as the invention of fossil fuel power. It also took a little longer.
It's true that by 1776 Adam Smith was noting in *The
Wealth of Nations* that "it is not the actual greatness
of national wealth, but its continued increase" which
raises wages. But, as the economist Benjamin Friedman points out in *The Moral Consequences of Economic
Growth*, his recent and compelling argument for economic expansion, it's "unclear whether the thinkers of
the mid-18th century even understood the concept of
economic growth in the modern sense of sustained increase over time," or whether they thought the transition to modern commerce was a onetime event—that
they'd soon hit a new plateau. The theorists didn't
control affairs, though; and the dynamic entrepreneur-
ial actors unleashed by the new economic revolution
soon showed that businesses could keep improving
their operations, apparently indefinitely. By the early
twentieth century, increasing efficiency had become
very nearly a religion, especially in the United States,
where stopwatch-wielding experts like Frederick Taylor
broke every task into its smallest parts, wiping out in-
efficiencies with all the zeal of a pastor hunting sins,
and with far more success. (Indeed, as many historians
have noted, religious belief and economic expansion
were soon firmly intertwined: "economic effort, and
the material progress that it brought, were central to
the vision of moral progress," notes Friedman.) Soon,

as Jeremy Rifkin observes, the efficiency revolution encompassed everything, not just factory work but homemaking, school teaching, and all the other tasks of modern life: "efficiency became the ultimate tool for exploiting both the earth's resources in order to advance material wealth and human progress." As the nation's school superintendents were warned at a meeting in 1912, "the call for efficiency is felt everywhere throughout the length and breadth of the land, and the demand is becoming more insistent every day." As a result, "the schools as well as other business institutions, must submit to the test of efficiency." It was a god from whom there was no appeal.

Even so, policy makers and economists didn't really become fixated on growing the total size of the economy until after World War II. An economic historian named Robert Collins recently described the rise of what he called "growthmanship" in the United States. During the Great Depression, he pointed out, mainstream economists thought the American economy was "mature." In the words of President Franklin D. Roosevelt, "our industrial plant is built. . . . Our last frontier has long since been reached. . . . Our task now is not discovery or exploitation of natural resources, or necessarily producing more goods. It is the soberer, less dramatic business of administering resources and plants already in hand . . . of adapting economic organizations to the service of the people." It was left to former president Herbert Hoover to protest that "we are yet but on the frontiers of development," that there were "a thousand inventions in the lockers of science . . . which have not yet come to light." And Hoover, of course, did not carry the day. Even a decade later, as the country began to emerge from hardship with the boom that followed Pearl Harbor, many businessmen—the steelmakers, the utility executives, the oilmen—were reluctant to build new plants, fearing that overproduction might bring on another depression.

But they were wrong. Mobilization for war proved just how fast the economy could grow; by 1943, even in the midst of battle, the National Resources Planning Board sent this report to Roosevelt: "Our expanding economy is likely to surpass the wildest estimates of a few years back and is capable of bringing to all of our people freedom, security and adventure in richer measure than ever before in history." From

that point on, growth became America's mantra, and then the world's. Hoover had been right—there were all kinds of technological advances to come. Plastics. Cars that kept dropping in price. Television. Cheap air-conditioning that opened whole regions of the country to masses of people.

Per capita gross national product grew 24 percent between 1947 and 1960, and during that year's presidential election John F. Kennedy insisted he could speed it up if the voters would only reject "those who have held back the growth of the U.S." Indeed, he proved correct: between 1961 and 1965, GNP grew more than 5 percent a year while the percentage of Americans living in poverty dropped by nearly half. Economists scrambled to catch up, and in doing so they built the base for modern growth theory. The general mood was captured by Lyndon Johnson, who, not long after moving into the White House, told an aide: "I'm sick of all the people who talk about the things we can't do. Hell, we're the richest country in the world, the most powerful. We can do it all. . . . We can do it if we believe it." And he wasn't the only one. From Moscow Nikita Khrushchev thundered, "Growth of industrial and agricultural production is the battering ram with which we shall smash the capitalist system."

There were hiccups along the way, as Robert Collins points out in his account. LBJ's belief that we could do anything led us deep into Vietnam, which in turn led us into inflation and recession. The oil shocks of the 1970s and the spectacles of burning rivers and smoggy cities led some, even outside what was then called the counterculture, to question the idea of endless expansion. In 1972, a trio of MIT researchers published a series of computer forecasts they called Limits to Growth, and a year later the German-British economist E. F. Schumacher wrote the best-selling *Small Is Beautiful*, with its commitment to what he called "Buddhist economics" and its exhortation to people to "work to put our own inner house in order." (Four years later, when Schumacher came to the United States on a speaking tour, Jimmy Carter even received him at the White House.) By the end of the 1970s, their message resonated: the sociologist Amitai Etzioni reported to President Carter that 30 percent of Americans were "pro-growth," 31 percent were "anti-growth," and 39 percent were "highly uncertain."

That kind of ambivalence, Etzioni predicted, "is too stressful for societies to endure," and in 1980 Ronald Reagan's election proved his point. Reagan convinced us it was "Morning in America" again, and under various banners—supply-side economics, globalization—it has stayed morning ever since. Out with limits, in with Trump. The collapse of communism drove the point home, and now mainstream liberals and conservatives compete mainly on the question of what can flog the economy faster. The British prime minister Margaret Thatcher used to use the acronym TINA to underscore her contention that There Is No Alternative to a world fixated on growth. But conservatives weren't the only ones enamored of growth. Lawrence Summers, who served as Bill Clinton's secretary of the Treasury, put it like this: the Democratic administration "cannot and will not accept any 'speed limit' on American economic growth. *It is the task of economic policy to grow the economy as rapidly, sustainably, and inclusively as possible.*" (Emphasis added.) Even that was not enough—in the vice presidential debates during the 1996 campaign, Republican Jack Kemp shouted, "We should double the rate of growth."

People kept seeing new opportunities for faster growth: microtechnology, nanotechnology. (Sometimes the speeding up is literal: "microediting," for instance, now allows call centers and radio stations to edit out pauses and speed up speech with no discernible changes. "We call it the 66-second minute," the president of one firm said recently. "In normal conversation only a small part of the brain is taxed.") The evangelism for efficiency and growth grew louder, too. It was not just, as Benjamin Friedman insists, that a growing economy gets us more stuff—"better food, bigger houses, more travel"—but that it makes us better people: more open, more tolerant, more confident. The "quality of our democracy—more fundamentally, the moral character of American society—is at risk," he said, unless we grow the economy more vigorously. As the new millennium began, growth had become the organizing ideology for corporations and individuals, for American capitalists and Chinese communists, for Democrats and Republicans. For everyone. "Harnessing the 'base' motive of material self-interest to promote the common good is perhaps the most important social invention mankind has achieved,"

said Charles Schultze, a former chair of the president's Council of Economic Advisers. George Gilder, the fervent apostle of tech-driven high-growth economics, went further: entrepreneurs, he said, "embody and fulfill the sweet and mysterious consolations of the Sermon on the Mount." The so-called Washington consensus dominated far more of the world than the Union Jack ever had; it was an empire of the mind.

And it is easy to understand why. For one thing, under present arrangements any faltering of growth leads quickly to misery: to recession and all its hardships. For another, endless growth allows us to avoid hard choices, to reconcile, in Collins's words, the American "love of liberty with its egalitarian pretensions." The administration of George W. Bush assures us that we can have tax cuts and still protect Social Security because the tax cuts will stimulate economic growth so much that we'll have more than enough cash on hand to take care of our old. No need to choose. Having found what has been truly a magic wand, the strong temptation is to keep waving it.

But, as readers of fairy tales know, magic can run out. Three fundamental challenges to the fixation on growth have emerged. One is political: growth, at least as we now create it, is producing more inequality than prosperity, more insecurity than progress. This is both the most common and least fundamental objection to our present economy, and I will spend relatively little time on it. By contrast, the second argument draws on physics and chemistry as much as on economics; it is the basic objection that we do not have the energy needed to keep the magic going, and can we deal with the pollution it creates? The third argument is both less obvious and even more basic: growth is no longer making us happy. These three objections mesh with each other in important ways; taken together, they suggest that we'll no longer be able to act wisely, either in our individual lives or in public life, simply by asking which choice will produce more.

. . .

It's useful to remember what Thomas Newcomen was up to when he launched the Industrial Revolution. He was using coal to pump water out of a coal mine. The birth of the Industrial Revolution was all about fossil fuel, and so, in many ways, was everything that followed. We've learned an enormous amount in the last two centuries—our body of scientific knowledge has doubled so many times no one can count—but coal and oil and natural gas are still at the bottom of it all.

And no wonder. They are miracles. A solid and a liquid and a gas that emerge from the ground pretty much ready to use, with their energy highly concentrated. Of the three, oil may be the most miraculous. In many spots on the face of the earth, all you have to do is stick a pipe in the ground and oil comes spurting to the surface. It's compact, it's easily transportable, and it packs an immense amount of energy into a small volume. Fill the tank of my hybrid Honda Civic with ten gallons—sixty pounds—of gasoline and you can move four people and their possessions from New York to Washington, D.C., and back. Coal and gas are almost as easy to use, and coal in particular is often even cheaper to recover—in many places it's buried just a few feet beneath the surface of the earth, just waiting to be taken.

That simple, cheap, concentrated power lies at the heart of our modern economies. Every action of a modern life burns fossil fuel; viewed in one way, modern Western human beings are flesh-colored devices for combusting coal and gas and oil. "Before coal," writes Jeffrey Sachs, "economic production was limited by energy inputs, almost all of which depended on the production of biomass: food for humans and farm animals, and fuel wood for heating and certain industrial processes." That is, energy depended on how much you could grow. But fossil energy depended on how much had grown eons before, on all those millions of years of ancient biology squashed by the weight of time till they'd turned into strata and pools and seams of hydrocarbons, waiting for us to discover them.

To understand how valuable, and how irreplaceable, that lake of fuel was, consider a few figures. Ethanol is one modern scientific version of using old-fashioned "biomass" (that is, stuff that grows anew each year) for creating energy. It's quite high-tech, backed with billions of dollars of government subsidy. But if you're using corn, as most American ethanol production does, then by the time you've driven your tractor to plant and till and harvest the corn, and your truck to carry it to the refinery, and then powered your refinery to turn the corn into ethanol, the best-case "energy output-to-input ratio" is something like 1.34 to 1. That is, you've spent 100 BTU of fossil energy to get 134 BTU of ethanol. Perhaps that's worth doing, but as Kamyar Enshayan of the University of Northern Iowa points out, "It's not impressive. The ratio for oil (from well to the gas station) is anywhere between 30 and 200," depending on where you drill. To go from our fossil fuel world to that biomass world would be a little like going from the Garden of Eden to the land outside its walls, where bread must be earned by "the sweat of your brow."

And east of Eden is precisely where we may be headed. As everyone knows, the last three years have seen a spate of reports and books and documentaries insisting that humanity may have neared or passed the oil peak—that is, the point where those pools of primeval plankton are half used up, where each new year brings us closer to the bottom of the bucket. The major oil companies report that they can't find enough new wells most years to offset the depletion of their old ones; worrisome rumors circulate that the giant Saudi fields are dwindling faster than expected; and, of course, all this is reflected in the rising cost of oil. The most credible predict not a sharp peak but a bumpy ride for the next decade along an unstable plateau, followed by an inexorable decline in supply. So far that seems to be spot-on—highly variable prices, trading higher over time.

One effect of those changes, of course, can be predicted by everyone who's ever sat through Introductory Economics. We should, theory insists, use less oil, both by changing our habits and by changing to new energy sources. To some extent that's what has happened: SUV sales slowed once it appeared high gas prices were here to stay, and the waiting lists for Toyota Priuses were suddenly six months long. Buses and subways drew more riders. People turned down their thermostats a touch, and sales of solar panels started to boom. This is a classic economic response. But it's hard for us to simply park our cars, precisely because cheap oil coaxed us to build sprawling suburbs. And Americans can switch to hybrids, but if the Chinese and the Indians continue to build auto fleets themselves, even if they drive extremely small cars, then the pressure on oil supplies will keep building. Meanwhile, solar power and the other renewables, wondrous as they are, don't exactly replace coal and oil and gas. The roof of my home is covered with photovoltaic panels, and on a sunny day it's a great pleasure to watch the electric meter spin backward, but the very point of solar power is that it's widely diffused, not compacted and concentrated by millennia like coal and gas and oil.

It's different: if fossil fuel is a slave at our beck and call, renewable power is more like a partner. As we shall eventually see, that partnership could be immensely rewarding for people and communities, but can it power economic growth of the kind we're used to? The doctrinaire economist's answer, of course, is that no particular commodity matters all that much, because if we run short someone will have the incentive to develop a substitute. In general, this has proved true in the past—run short of nice big sawlogs and someone invents plywood—but it's far from clear that it applies to fossil fuel, which in its ubiquity and its cheapness is almost certainly a special case. Wars are fought over oil, not over milk, not over semiconductors, not over timber. It's plausible—indeed, it's likely—that if we begin to run short, the nature of our lives may fundamentally change as the scarcity wreaks havoc on our economies. "The essence of the first Industrial Revolution was not the coal; it was how to use the coal," insists Jeffrey Sachs. Maybe he's right, but it seems more likely that fossil fuel was an exception to the rule, a onetime gift that underwrote a onetime binge of growth. In any event, we seem to be on track to find out.

JOSHUA COLT GAMBREL AND PHILIP CAFARO

THE VIRTUE OF SIMPLICITY

In what follows, we argue that simplicity is a virtue, because its cultivation is necessary if we hope to achieve human flourishing, both individually and collectively, in the broad sense outlined above; and to sustain nature's ecological flourishing, also understood broadly. This seems to us the proper framework in which to consider the status and specify the details of any virtue. However, we recognize that conceptions of flourishing and appreciation of nature vary widely, and we believe a strong case can be made for simplicity as a virtue even for those holding quite different conceptions of human flourishing or nature's value.

For example, those who would deny that appreciating and promoting nature's flourishing is a necessary criterion of human virtue must still acknowledge material simplicity's role in furthering the development of a full range of human capabilities. You may be uninterested in species loss and protected by your society's wealth from the most serious dangers of ecosystem collapse (at least temporarily); still, if you are an American, you must navigate the pitfalls of a high consumption society. Personal bankruptcy, unhealthy obesity and a focus on possessions rather than relationships and achievements, all remain dangerous pitfalls to your flourishing. Again: those who define human flourishing fairly narrowly may perhaps ignore questions of autonomy or meaning, as they focus on the bare essentials of human flourishing. Still, material overconsumption can undermine our hedonistic well-being and the good functioning of

Adapted from Joshua Colt Gambrel and Philip Cafaro, "The Virtue of Simplicity," Journal of Agricultural and Environmental Ethics 23, nos. 1–2 (2010): 85–108. Copyright © Springer Science+Business Media B.V. 2009. Reprinted with permission from Springer.

society (Hursthouse's criteria 3 and 4) in fairly obvious ways. Health can be undermined by overeating; savings accounts can be emptied out by overspending; banking systems, apparently, can be overwhelmed by greed and its attendant overreaching.

Material simplicity points us toward a nobler conception of human flourishing and facilitates its accomplishment. But it also improves our chances of achieving more modest or conventional forms of well-being. It is a virtue for eco-saints and moral strivers, but also for just plain folks.[1] This strengthens its claim to virtue-hood. In what follows, we ask our readers to consider material simplicity's potential contributions to happiness, flourishing, or human well-being however *you* understand them, and over the full range of what *you* consider to be morally acceptable kinds of good human lives; also (if this matters to you), simplicity's potential contribution to the continued survival and flourishing of the five to ten million other species with whom we share the earth. Your assessment of these contributions should control your answers as to whether or not simplicity is a virtue, its relative importance in our lives, and its further detailed specification.

SIMPLICITY

In her seminal article "Non-Relative Virtues: An Aristotelian Approach," Martha Nussbaum provides a useful way to define and distinguish the virtues. "Isolate a sphere of human experience that figures in more or less any human life, and in which more or less any human being will have to make *some* choices rather than others, and act in *some* way rather than some other," she suggests. Crucially, to require the specification of a virtue or a range of virtuous behavior in this area, these choices must be important to people's happiness or well-being. "The 'thin account' of each virtue is that it is whatever being stably disposed to act appropriately in that sphere consists in" (Nussbaum 1993, p. 245). The "full or 'thick' description" of the virtue examines the opportunities and pitfalls that await in the realm of experience under analysis. It specifies the characteristic thought processes, habituation and emotional development, ways of looking at the world, and other aspects of human character and training that help us choose well in that particular sphere.

Following Nussbaum's schema, we define simplicity as the virtue disposing us to act appropriately within the sphere of our consumer decisions, from food and drink to stereo and housing purchases to cars and airplane travel. As we understand it, simplicity is a conscientious and restrained attitude toward material goods. It typically includes (1) decreased consumption and (2) a more conscious consumption; hence (3) greater deliberation regarding our consumer decisions; (4) a more focused life in general; and (5) a greater and more nuanced appreciation for other things besides material goods, and also for (6) material goods themselves.

As Aristotle noted long ago, people may be much more likely to err in one direction rather than another in particular spheres of human choice, either due to human nature or to the pathologies of their particular societies (*Nicomachean Ethics*, book II, chapter 8). In Athens in Aristotle's day, men were apparently more likely to err on the side of irascibility than "inirascibility"; hence Aristotle named the virtue with regard to anger "mildness" (book IV, chapter 5). In wealthy western democracies today, people are more likely to err on the side of overconsumption than underconsumption. Hence the term "simplicity" is arguably a good one for this virtue (as long as we remember that underconsumption can also be a problem).

Simplicity overlaps with such traditional virtues as temperance (moderation in food and drink), frugality (the responsible and restrained use of wealth), prudence and self-control. In what follows, we make no attempt to systematically relate our treatment of simplicity, focused on overall material consumption, to traditional discussions of these virtues, which often ranged more narrowly or broadly than ours; and which took place in comparatively poor societies whose economies of scarcity have been replaced by economies of abundance throughout the modern industrialized world. We note, however, that within the tradition, philosophers once routinely claimed that temperance, frugality and simplicity were keys to living justly and wisely. They were right. We see it as a glaring weakness of contemporary discussions of justice and wisdom that they rarely make this connection.

It is often helpful to consider simplicity as a virtuous mean between vicious extremes. However, like other complex virtues, simplicity appears to be a mean along

Vice	Virtue	Vice
	Simplicity	
Underconsumption (poverty?)		overconsumption (gluttony)
unthinking consumption (carelessness)		overthinking consumption (obsession)
none; or crude consumption (asceticism, "monkish virtue")		luxurious consumption
inefficient or pointless consumption (wastefulness)		hyper-efficient consumption (penny-pinching)
immoral consumption (callous, disproportional)		none; or, moral finickiness ("moral foppery")

several axes. Some of its associated vices have obvious names, others do not, perhaps owing to their rarity:

Obviously, there is more than one way to go wrong in our stance toward consumption!

AN EXAMPLE

Treating simplicity as a virtue presupposes that through reflection, we can discover our deeper, more significant needs and goals; recognize some goals as ignoble, foolish, or trivial, and replace them with better ones; and pursue our goals more efficiently, with less waste and harm to others. By way of illustration, consider some steps a person might take to practice voluntary simplicity in relation to food consumption, as these relate to the six aspects of simplicity noted above.

Americans consume on average 25% more calories than necessary, on a conservative estimate (Putnam et al. 2002). Today, three out of five Americans are overweight and one out of five is obese. This excessive consumption of food harms our health and quality of life (US Department of Health and Human Services 2001). Food overconsumption also causes direct and indirect environmental degradation, through habitat loss and increased pollution from agricultural fertilizers and pesticides (Cafaro et al. 2006). Twenty percent of American greenhouse gas emissions come from growing and transporting our food (Pollan 2007). So here simplicity clearly demands decreased consumption (aspect 1).

However, whether we are talking about personal health, healthy communities, or healthy land, consuming less is not enough. We also need to consume *differently*. We may buy and prepare more healthy foods for ourselves; buy organic foods and local foods and eat less meat, all of which decrease environmental harms; purchase more food directly from farmers at farmers' markets or as part of community-supported agriculture co-ops, to support small farmers and keep local agriculture vibrant. Such changes demand attention: a more conscious consumption, involving greater deliberation about our consumer decisions (aspects 2 and 3)

Many food simplifiers combine more conscious consumption with greater participation in food *production*: gardening, raising chickens or keeping bees, joining CSA cooperatives. Research shows that food produced in these ways is more environmentally sustainable and often more nutritious than conventionally-grown food (Felice 2007). These activities are also often enjoyable and interesting, and connect people to their neighbors and to the earth. Similarly, taking time to prepare our own food and eating meals together offer important opportunities to connect to loved ones. Consciously taking such steps leads to a more focused life (aspect 4). It can further gratitude toward the many other species that sustain us; tune us in to nature's rhythms and details; and enrich our relationships with other people. In these ways, food simplifiers explore and sustain a wide range of nonmaterial goods (aspect 5) and come to better understand and appreciate the material realities of food production and consumption (aspect 6).

The example should begin to suggest how simplicity can contribute to human and nonhuman flourishing in important ways. It also illustrates several important points about simplicity as a virtue.

First, living simply is not necessarily simple. It requires deliberation: thinking through our choices and acting on our best judgment, rather than following the herd, or the blandishments of advertisers, or doing what we have always done, or what comes easiest. Thinking about our food consumption and improving it typically involve research and planning, and some of what we learn about how our food is grown will probably be discouraging or disgusting. Still, it is better to know the ugly facts and act in full consciousness of what we are a part of, rather than in ignorance. Simplicity is better than simple-mindedness, the default setting of the American food consumer (an ignorance that the food industry spends many millions of dollars a year cultivating).

Second, though, simplicity *is* often simple; or rather, it often involves working our way back to simpler, less convoluted ways of doing things. When I plant and tend a garden, ride a bicycle and fix it myself, or sing songs with my children on family outings, these are relatively simple ways of satisfying some of my food, transportation and entertainment needs. The simplicity of such activities makes them less likely to stray from their goals and more likely to involve thoughtful activity rather than passive consumption. Their simplicity may make them particularly appropriate vessels for finding meaning, or expressing happiness and gratitude.

Third, simplicity is not a call to "return to nature" in any romantic or primitivist sense. Old ways can be wasteful, or harmful; new ways can be an improvement. Similarly, simplicity is not opposed to technology, or to new technologies. It just asks that we consciously develop and appropriately incorporate technologies into our lives with reference to our real purposes and to their full effects on the world around us. Hydroponics has a role to play, along with sharing heirloom tomato seeds with the neighbors.

Fourth, simplicity is not poverty. Poverty is a state defined by lack, where people find it difficult to obtain the means to satisfy even the essential human needs—food, water, shelter, basic physical safety—let alone higher needs for self-actualization or creative personal development. Poverty means living in deprivation, against one's will. Simplicity is consciously and freely chosen.[2] It provides greater opportunities than conventional materialism to achieve human flourishing, while poverty limits those opportunities.

Fifth, simplicity is a process, not an endpoint. Although we are *arguing* here for simplicity, we have not forgotten Aristotle's reminders that habituation is more important than arguments in developing virtue; and that virtue demands *phronesis*, practical wisdom, applied to the details of life. Anyone who has tried to cultivate simplicity in their own life knows that Aristotle was right. Creating a character, a personal infrastructure, and daily habits that regularly result in less consumption and less dumb consumption are difficult and ongoing affairs. Hence it is a mistake to look for particular markers that indicate the presence of this virtue (although a Hummer in the driveway pretty clearly indicates its absence. And it is not a mistake, but good practice, to set down markers for ourselves and strive to achieve them.)

Sixth, simplicity is not uniformity. There are as many ways to cultivate simplicity in our food or other consumption decisions as there are ways to complicate them. Different people will focus on different aspects of these problems, and our solutions should play to our individual interests and strengths (maybe you'd rather brew beer than raise tomatoes; perhaps you're the cook, not the gardener, in the family). Hence lives and lifestyles will legitimately differ. Simplicity need not limit diversity.

Seventh, simplicity, like all the virtues, needs to be cultivated by individuals and families, but also encouraged and sometimes mandated by society, if we hope to secure human and nonhuman flourishing. The very term *voluntary* simplicity emphasizes voluntarism, while most of the literature on material simplicity focuses on individual and small-group action. But this is arguably a failure of this literature (Claxton 1994). Jerome Segal (1999) argues convincingly that creating less materialistic societies will demand fundamental political changes. Discussing the United States, Segal emphasizes changes in economic policy that would help safeguard basic physical and economic security, and thus make it easier for individuals to freely choose less materialistic paths. Because we often "consume because others consume" (Lichtenberg 1998) and because "what counts as necessary [consumption] in a given society" depends in part on "what the poorest members of society require for credible social standing" (Schudson 1998), enacting simplicity has an important political component.

Eighth, we're not arguing that we should eliminate or minimize material goals within our lives. Human beings have essential needs that must be met, so we must devote a certain amount of our time and attention to meeting them. Simplicity actually represents a better way of meeting these needs. In the case of food, "better" means in ways that are healthier, more morally justifiable, and more interesting than business as usual. Simplicity can help us really understand our material needs and meet them efficiently, morally, and even joyfully.

Ninth (and at the risk of sounding grandiose), our short discussion of food simplicity suggests that material simplicity does indeed further justice and wisdom, as philosophers have long maintained. Modern industrial agriculture is callous toward farmers and farm communities, and grossly unjust toward its animal "production units." These injustices are sustained in large part by the ignorance of consumers. Voluntary food simplicity can help reverse this process, as we learn about food and act on what we have learned, try to appreciate the processes involved in feeding us, and honor the various participants in those processes (Berry 1990). To the extent we use resources, take life, or cause pain when we raise or eat food, simplicity enables us to do so consciously and honestly. This opens up a space within which we *may* act justly and wisely. Note that simplicity does not *guarantee* justice and wisdom in this important area of our lives; it makes them possible. Casual participants in the industrial food status quo, however, cannot act justly or wisely in their food consumption decisions. Those options aren't on the menu.

True, few people in our society would look to a person's eating habits to discern whether they are just or wise. But we believe this is a measure of how distracted we have become and how confused about what is really important in life.

Again, others might say that what are really needed are better rules for how farmers should be compensated, food animals treated, and so forth. Then we could follow the rules and eat whatever we wanted, with a clean conscience. We certainly agree on the need

for better rules: they are essential to furthering material simplicity politically, and thus helping create more virtuous and just societies. But rules will only get us so far. The world is an unjust place and seems likely to remain so for the foreseeable future; hence we cannot completely rely on "the rules" to tell us how to behave. Further, the idea of purely economic spheres of life, where we can choose freely—that is, without the need to consult anything but our own desires and whims, perhaps restrained by a few basic moral rules—is deeply flawed; part of the economistic view of life that has given us modern industrial agriculture in the first place. Setting up such "duty free zones" blinds us to both responsibilities and opportunities. We think we are increasing our options and our freedom of action; instead, we find we have lost the ability to distinguish right from wrong, or quantity from quality. But acting on such distinctions, in all areas of our lives, is the very definition of wisdom.

. . .

(1) Freedom and Autonomy—Freedom is a basic human good and a fundamental human desire. Material possessions sometimes increase and sometimes decrease our freedom; it requires wisdom to decide which, in particular instances. Henry Thoreau claimed that "a man is rich in proportion to the number of things he can afford to leave alone"; he is free, that is, both from the craving for those things and from having to earn the money to buy them. But even Thoreau appreciated being able to take the train from Concord to Boston when he had an errand there. He appreciated the freedom a well-built canoe provided in the Maine backcountry.

Full human freedom includes the ability to see and set limits to our pursuit of material goods. We do not deny the value of some stuff for increasing freedom. But we insist that consciously deciding the role of possessions in our lives is one important key to freedom.

. . .

Take the important example of the automobile, a powerful symbol of freedom for many people, particularly Americans.[3] Today most Americans simply expect that every adult should own their own car and drive it whenever and wherever they want; anything less is seen as seriously cramping our freedom. In reality, given common financial constraints, not owning a car can free up vital resources for students and poorer workers—provided they can get where they need to get without one. Commuting by bicycle or train can be more relaxing and enjoyable, even for wealthier commuters. Millions of people have these options but are unaware of them, so *auto*matic have their transportation decisions become. This cluelessness limits their freedom. Similarly, the development of auto-centric urban areas and our society's failure to provide adequate mass transportation may force many people to buy, drive and maintain cars who would have preferred not to. It may take away their freedom *not* to drive, *not* to make car payments, *not* to subsidize environmental destruction by the oil companies.

All this is not to say that every American should junk his or her car. We only suggest that in some cases, limiting our automobile use, either individually or collectively, may make Americans more free—but that for the most part, we are unable to think clearly about this, because our society tends to confuse us concerning the connections between freedom and consumption. At a minimum, we should try to recognize all the consequences of our transportation and other consumption choices. Acting on the basis of such recognition, personally and politically, is an important part of freedom.

(2) Knowledge—Simplicity also can aid in the acquisition of two important kinds of knowledge. First, simplicity assists us in becoming more self-aware. Simplifying our lives requires us to look within ourselves to distinguish our true needs and most important goals from what is inessential or positively harmful in our lives. It may force us to confront some of our less charming weaknesses and obsessions and some of our more important moral failings. Attempting to practice simplicity can force us to find the proper balance between demanding more from ourselves and showing charity toward our own failings.

Know thyself! It is an essential human task and will help you live a better life, however you define that. People with greater self-knowledge are better positioned to achieve happier and more meaningful lives and develop the full spectrum of human potentials: physical, emotional, mental and spiritual.

Self-knowledge facilitates the self-control necessary to combat materialism and live more focused lives. All this increases our ability to flourish.

Second, simplicity facilitates local, place-based, ecological knowledge. Make this simple experiment. Select a stretch of road that you have often traveled by car, and bicycle along it instead. Next, take even more time and walk it. One of this article's authors once did this along a 10-mile stretch of rural highway in coastal Oregon. Having roared down it every day for a whole summer to and from work, the next summer he traded in his motorcycle for a bicycle, commuting along the same route. There were a thousand and one things that he only noticed once he began to bicycle. People, houses, trees; smells, sounds; the pitch of the terrain, the different water levels in the river at high and low tides. Not all that he noticed was pretty. There were trash dumps and junked cars. But traveling slower, he noticed new construction and shoddy logging practices along the way that made possible informed participation in local zoning hearings and town debates.

This is just an example, but we find it suggestive. Because he no longer owned a motorcycle, your author didn't have the choice of driving to work, and was forced to bicycle on days when he often would not have. Here less choice equaled more experience, and less convenience equaled greater knowledge of the local landscape. Modern microeconomics unequivocally says that more choice is better: give an individual a greater number of choices and more money to spend on them, and he can more fully satisfy his preferences (Heyne 1994, p. 178). Modern advertising sends the same message: look at the many new, improved cars, computers, or shaving creams to choose from! But this is unconvincing. For we can choose wrongly, and in ways that lead to less pleasure, less health and less knowledge of the world around us. One of the ways we can choose wisely is in deciding to limit our options and leaving them limited. Choosing correctly also involves limiting the amount of time we spend choosing, thus leaving our minds free to deal with more important things (Schmidtz 2008). We believe it involves simplifying our lives so that we maximize knowledge and appreciation of the world, rather than consumption and wealth.

(3) Meaning—Cultivating simplicity can also enhance meaning in our lives by connecting us in rich ways to our inner hopes, visions and potential. Living meaningfully involves acting in service to goals and ideals that we are convinced are important. Living a life devoted to things and the status they provide is deeply unsatisfying to many people. What people tend to find most meaningful is having good relationships with other people and achieving personal and career goals that make them proud. Materialistic pursuits tend to trivialize our lives, instead of enriching them with meaning. We've already seen that materialism increases the likelihood that we will grow up to be non-nurturing parents, that we will live in fear, and that we will doubt our own self-worth. In order to connect to people and activities that we find meaningful, it helps to get off the materialistic treadmill.

In this regard, we should remember our natural tendency to use material acquisitions to make up for perceived deficiencies. One-third of all shoppers are "shopping therapeutically"; that is, they are shopping to feel better about themselves (De Graaf 2002). Unfortunately, this often leads to further dissatisfaction and discontent (Kasser et al. 2004; Lane 1998). If we keep in mind what human flourishing really requires, we'll remember that money and possessions are merely means, of limited usefulness, and not ends in themselves. Money cannot buy self-esteem, wisdom, or love. It cannot buy the friendship or respect of people whose friendship and respect matters. Before we purchase anything, we should ask ourselves what contribution, if any, the purchase might make toward meeting our highest goals or important projects. We should ask whether our material purchases bring meaning into our lives.

(4) Promoting the Flourishing of Nonhuman Beings—Simplicity promotes human flourishing. Just as clearly, it is necessary to create and preserve space and resources for nonhuman species and ecosystems to flourish (Wensveen 2001). Due primarily to overpopulation and overconsumption, humans are extinguishing animal and plant species a thousand times faster than natural background extinction rates (Millennium Ecosystem Assessment 2005). Along with many scientists and environmentalists, we believe that this loss of biodiversity is the most significant environmental problem facing humanity today. The ability of our global biosphere to sustainably provide for human and non-human flourishing is stressed by continued population growth and by growing global overconsumption. These two trends are negatively synergistic; if we don't reverse them, we may lose up to one-third of the world's species of plants and animals within 50 years (ibid.).

In the face of this overwhelming extinction threat, most people recognize the need to "do something." Buy and set aside more public lands as wildlife habitat; find alternative technologies to limit air and water pollution. These steps are necessary, but not sufficient. We cannot set aside land if we need it to feed our appetites for food, fuel, or other material goods (Cafaro et al. 2006). Technological improvements can alleviate pollution, but without some limits to human demands, the improvements are swamped and pollution increases (as happened in the U.S. over the past thirty years with carbon emissions, as increased energy efficiency was swamped by greater per capita energy demands and by ever more "capitas"; Camarota and Kolankiewicz 2008).

Limiting consumption must be part of the solution to the extinction crisis, reining in global climate change, and meeting the other environmental challenges we face in the 21st century (Cafaro 2010). Better planning, technological improvements, and other efficiency gains have important roles to play in creating sustainable societies, but they will not succeed alone. We must find ways to embrace less consumption—or accept responsibility for creating a more ecologically degraded world. Environmental protection is an important example of the more general rule that individuals and societies which can intelligently moderate their consumption open up a space to preserve and enhance their preeminent values. Preserving the flourishing of nonhuman species should be one of those values. However, even people who do not care about protecting wild nature tend to care about the safety and security of their children and grandchildren. So we conclude this section with the reminder that evidence is rapidly accumulating that our posterity's wellbeing will depend on keeping human demands on the biosphere within ecological limits (IPCC 2007). That means learning to live more simply.

REFERENCES

Bennett, W. J. (1993). "Quantifying America's Decline." *Wall Street Journal,* March 15.

Berry, W. (1990). *What Are People For?* New York: North Point Press.

Cafaro. P. J. (1998). "Less Is More: Economic Consumption and the Good Life." *Philosophy Today* 42, pp. 26–39.

Cafaro, P. J. (2001). "The Naturalist's Virtues." *Philosophy in the Contemporary World* 8 (2), pp. 85–99.

Cafaro, P. J. (2005). "Gluttony, Arrogance, Greed, and Apathy: An Exploration of Environmental Vice." In R. Sandler & P. Cafaro (eds.), *Environmental Virtue Ethics.* Lanham, MD: Rowman & Littlefield.

Cafaro, P. J., R. B. Primack & R. L. Zimdahl (2006). "The Fat of the Land: Linking American Food Overconsumption, Obesity, and Biodiversity Loss." *Journal of Agricultural and Environmental Ethics* 19, pp. 541–561.

Cafaro, P. J. (2010). "Beyond Business as Usual: Alternative Wedges to Avoid Catastrophic Climate Change and Create Sustainable Societies." In D. Arnold (ed.), *The Ethics of Global Climate Change* (Cambridge University Press).

Camarota, S. A. & L. Kolankiewicz. "Immigration to the United States and World-Wide Greenhouse Gas Emissions." *Center for Immigration Studies,* 2008, http://www.cis.org/GreenhouseGasEmissions, accessed 9/28/08.

Claxton, G., (1994). "Involuntary Simplicity: Changing Dysfunctional Habits of Consumption." *Environmental Values* 3, pp. 71–78.

Cross-National Collaborative Group (1992). "The Changing Role of Depression: Cross-National Comparisons." *Journal of the American Medical Assoc.* 268, pp. 3098–3105.

De Graaf, J., D. Wann, & T. H. Naylor (2002). *Affluenza.* San Francisco: Berrett–Koehler.

Felice, J. (2007). "Food for Thought." *Acta Neuropsychiatrica* 19 (5).

Goleman, D. (1995). *Emotional Intelligence: Why It Can Matter More than I.Q.* New York: Bantam Books.

Heyne, Paul (1994). *The Economic Way of Thinking,* 7th ed. New York: MacMillan Press.

Honore, C. (2004). *In Praise of Slowness.* San Francisco: HarperCollins.

Hursthouse, R. (1999). *On Virtue Ethics.* New York: Oxford University Press.

Intergovernmental Panel on Climate Change (IPCC) (2007). *Fourth Assessment Report: Climate Change 2007: Synthesis Report: Summary for Policymakers.* Access at www.ipcc.org.

Jacka, F. (2007). "Food for Thought." *Acta Neuropsychiatrica* 19 (5).

Kasser, T (2002). *The High Price of Materialism.* Cambridge: MIT Press.

Kasser, T., R. M. Ryan, C. E. Couchman & K. M. Sheldon (2004). "Materialistic Values: Their Causes and Consequences." In T. Kasser and A. D. Kanner (eds.), *Psychology and Consumer Culture: The Struggle for a Good Life in a Materialistic World* (Washington, D.C.: American Psychological Association).

Lane, R. E. (1998). "The Road Not Taken: Friendship, Consumerism, and Happiness." In D. Crocker and T. Linden (eds.), *Ethics of Consumption: The Good Life, Justice, and Global Stewardship.* Lanham, MD: Rowman & Littlefield.

Lichtenberg, J. (1998). "Consuming Because Others Consume." In D. Crocker and T. Linden (eds.), *Ethics of Consumption: The Good Life, Justice, and Global Stewardship.* Lanham, MD: Rowman & Littlefield.

Murray, B. (2004). "Pill-Popping Pre-Schoolers." *Psychiatric Services* http://www.upliftprogram.com/h_depression.html#h77, accessed 2/01/08.

Nash, J. A. (1998). "On the Subversive Virtue of Frugality." In D. Crocker and T. Linden (eds.), *Ethics of Consumption: The Good Life, Justice, and Global Stewardship.* Lanham, MD: Rowman & Littlefield.

Nussbaum, M. (1993). "Non-Relative Virtue: An Aristotelian Approach." In M. Nussbaum and A. Sen (eds.), *The Quality of Life.* Oxford: Oxford University Press.

Peterson, C. & M. E.P. Seligman (2004). *Character Strengths and Virtues.* New York: Oxford University Press.

Pollan, M. (2007). *The Omnivore's Dilemma: A Natural History of Four Meals.* New York: Penguin Books.

Putnam, J., Allshouse, J., and L. S. Kantor (2002). "U.S. per Capita Food Supply Trends: More Calories, Refined Carbohydrates, and Fats." *Food Review* 25 (3), pp. 2–15.

Rolston III, H. (1988). *Environmental Ethics: Duties to and Values in the Natural World*. Philadelphia: Temple University Press.

Sandler, R. L. (2007). *Character and Environment: A Virtue-Oriented Approach to Environmental Ethics*. New York: Columbia University Press.

Schmidtz, D. (2008). "Choosing Strategies." In D. Schmidtz, *Person, Polis, Planet: Essays in Applied Philosophy*. New York: Oxford University Press.

Schor, J. (1992). *The Overworked American*. New York: Basic Books.

Schudson, M. (1998). "Delectable Materialism: Second Thoughts on Consumer Culture." In D. Crocker and T. Linden (eds.), *Ethics of Consumption: The Good Life, Justice, and Global Stewardship*. Lanham, MD: Rowman & Littlefield.

Seager, J. (1995). *The State of the Environment Atlas*. London: Penguin Books.

Segal, J. (1998). "Consumer Expenditures and the Growth of Need-Required Income." In D. Crocker and T. Linden (eds.), *Ethics of Consumption: The Good Life, Justice, and Global Stewardship*. Lanham, MD: Rowman & Littlefield.

Segal, J. (1999). *Graceful Simplicity: Toward a Philosophy and Politics of Simple Living*. New York: Henry Holt)

Seligman, M. E.P. (2000). "Positive Psychology: An Introduction." *American Psychologist* 55 (1).

Thoreau, H. D. (1971) [1854]. *Walden*. Princeton: Princeton University Press.

U.S. Department of Health and Human Services (2001). *The Surgeon General's Call to Action to Prevent and Decrease Overweight and Obesity*. Rockville, MD: Office of the Surgeon General.

U.S. Fish and Wildlife Service (2007). *USFWS Threatened and Endangered Species System*. http://ecos.fws.gov/tess_public/summarystatistics.do, accessed 03/13/08.

Wensveen, L. V. (2001). "Attunement: An Ecological Spin on the Virtue of Temperance." *Philosophy in the Contemporary World* 8 (2), pp. 67–78.

Wheeler, S. M. & T. Beatley (2004). *The Sustainable Urban Development Reader*. New York: Routledge).

World Advertising Research Center (2007). "World Advertising Trends: Ad Spending by Country." Accessed 9/08 at www.warc.com.

World Resources Institute (2005). *World Resources 2005— the Wealth of the Poor: Managing Ecosystems to Fight Poverty*. World Resources Institute, Washington, D.C.

NOTES

1. Compare courage, a virtue for the soldier facing death on the battlefield and for the nervous applicant looking to make a good impression in a job interview.

2. However, we want to leave room for *communities* to choose simplicity, not just individuals. We do not agree with a purely voluntaristic view of the cultivation of virtue. The primary purpose of law is to force citizens to act more virtuously than they otherwise would.

3. For a more detailed discussion of consumption and cars, see Cafaro (1998).

MARK SAGOFF

DO WE CONSUME TOO MUCH?

OVERCONSUMPTION—ETHICS OR ECONOMICS?

Do we consume too much? To some, the answer is self-evident. If there is only so much food, timber, petroleum, and other material to go around, the more we consume, the less must be available for others. The global economy cannot grow indefinitely on a finite planet. As populations increase and economies expand, natural resources must be depleted; prices will rise, and humanity—especially the poor and future generations at all income levels—as a result will suffer.[1]

Other reasons to suppose we consume too much are less often stated though also widely believed. Of these reasons the simplest—a lesson we learn from our parents and from literature since the Old Testament—may be the best: although we must satisfy basic needs, a good life is not one devoted to amassing material possessions; what we own comes to own us, keeping us from fulfilling commitments that give meaning to life, such as those to family, friends, and faith. The appreciation of nature also deepens our lives. As we consume more, however, we are more likely to transform the natural world, so that less of it will remain for us to learn from, communicate with, and appreciate.

During the nineteenth century preservationists forthrightly gave ethical and spiritual reasons for protecting the natural world. John Muir condemned the "temple destroyers, devotees of ravaging commercialism" who "instead of lifting their eyes to the God of the mountains, lift them to the Almighty dollar."[2] This was not a call for better cost–benefit analysis: Muir described nature not as a commodity but as a companion. Nature is sacred, Muir held, whether or not resources are scarce.

Philosophers such as Emerson and Thoreau thought of nature as full of divinity. Walt Whitman celebrated a leaf of grass as no less than the journeywork of the stars: "After you have exhausted what there is in business, politics, conviviality, love, and so on," he wrote in *Specimen Days*, and "found that none of these finally satisfy, or permanently wear—what remains? Nature remains."[3] These writers thought of nature as a refuge from economic activity, not as a resource for it.

Today many biologists say we are running out of resources or threatening the services ecosystems provide. Predictions of resource scarcity and ecological collapse appear objective and scientific, whereas pronouncements that nature is sacred or has intrinsic value can appear embarrassing in a secular society. One might suppose, moreover, that prudential and economic arguments may succeed better than moral or spiritual ones in swaying public policy. This is especially true if the warnings of resource-depletion, global famine, and plummeting standards of living are dire enough—and if a consensus of scientists vouch for them.

In the 1970s, prominent scientists saw mankind's relationship to the environment as a zero-sum game; they wrote that anything people did—to build houses, schools, or hospitals, to farm, to cultivate or create new plants and animals, indeed, even to cure disease—was bad for nature, bad for the environment, and thus bad for humanity. If humanity is defined as distinct from and apart from the natural world, logically every human action disrupts and degrades it. The Back Bay in Boston, the Foggy Bottom in Washington, DC, and hundreds of other masterpieces of architectural design and urban living—virtually anywhere humanity can live decently—has required such actions as the filling of malarial swamps, the clearing of woods, or the damming of rivers—all examples of the degradation

Mark Sagoff, "Do We Consume Too Much?" Atlantic Monthly 279, no. 6 (1997): 80-96. Reprinted with permission of the author.

of nature. In 1993, a group of fifty-eight of the world's scientific academies issued a statement making this point. "Environmental degradation has primarily been a product of our efforts to secure improved standards of food, clothing, shelter, comfort, and recreation for growing numbers of people,"[4] these scientists said.

Many environmental scientists have argued that technology has no longer the potential to improve the quality of life—because it can no longer push back limits that nature sets. "In an agricultural or techno-logical society," two scientists said in a much-cited article in 1971, "each human has a negative impact on his environment."[5] The more we consume, the less we have left, scientists said. Progress in knowledge or technology, these authors wrote, had already exhausted the possibility of economies of scale with respect to most resources. Because of the growth of population and affluence, "we are on the diminishing returns part of the most important curves."[6]

Predictions of resource depletion, food scarcity, and falling standards of living, however, may work against our moral intuitions. Consider the responsibility many of us feel to improve the lot of those less fortunate than we. By declaring consumption a zero-sum game, by insisting that what feeds one mouth is taken from another, environmentalists offer a counsel of despair. Must we abandon the hope that the poor can enjoy better standards of living? The Malthusian proposition that the earth's population already overwhelms the carrying capacity of the Earth—an idea associated for fifty years with mainstream environmentalist thought—may make us feel guilty but strangely relieves us of responsibility. If there are *too many people* some must go. Why not them?[7]

A different approach, which is consistent with our spiritual commitment to preserve nature and with our moral responsibility to help each other, rejects the apocalyptic narrative of environmentalism. The alternative approach suggests not so much that we consume less but that we invest more. Environmentalists could push for investment in technologies which increase productivity per unit energy, get more economic output from less material input, provide new sources of power, increase crop yields by engineering better seeds, and move from an industrial to a service economy. Technological advances of these kinds account

for the remarkable improvements in living conditions most people in the world have experienced in the last decades—and this was the period over which environmentalists had predicted the steepest declines. They also account for the preservation of nature—for example, the remarkable reforestation of the eastern United States.

What should environmentalists do? Should we insist with many conservation biologists and other scientists that the earth has reached its limits and "the end is in sight although we can quibble about the details and the schedule?" Should we instead leave the End Days to the saints and work with the kinds of knowledge-based high-tech industries that seek to engineer solutions for—or if necessary ways to adapt to—the local and global challenge of preserving nature while promoting prosperity?

BUST OR BOOM?

In the 1970s, a group of intellectuals, primarily biologists, supported the Malthusian view that humanity had already exceeded the carrying capacity of the earth. In 1970, Paul Ehrlich predicted that global food shortages would cause four billion people to starve to death between 1980 and 1989, 65 million of them in the United States. In *The End of Affluence* (1974), Paul and Anne Ehrlich wrote that "before 1985 mankind will enter a genuine age of scarcity in which many things besides energy will be in short supply." Crucial materials would near depletion during the 1980s, the Ehrlichs predicted, pushing prices out of reach. "Starvation among people will be accompanied by starvation of industries for the materials they require."[8]

These ideas created great excitement—a bandwagon effect—at the time. Ehrlich himself appeared about 20 times on the Johnny Carson show, then the most popular TV program. In a best-selling 1972 study, *The Limits to Growth*, the Club of Rome predicted that the world would effectively run out of gold by 1981, mercury by 1985, tin by 1987, zinc by 1990, petroleum by 1992, and copper, lead, and natural gas by 1993, occasioning drastic price increases.[9] Similar warnings, representing what seems to have been the scientific consensus of the time, poured forth in widely-read studies, including *Small Is Beautiful* (1973), the *Global 2000 Report* (1980), and the annual *State of the World* reports by Lester Brown and the Worldwatch Institute. Apocalyptic pronouncements brought celebrity, prizes, grants, and honors. The direr the prophecy the higher the lecture fee. Skeptics or "contrarians" were shunned.

The authors of some of these studies have released more recent books with the same message. Paul Ehrlich's *One with Nineveh* (2004) repeats the warning, according to *Booklist*, that "an escalating human population places ultimately unsustainable demands on the natural resources necessary for survival."[10] Gus Speth, chief author of *Global 2000*, issues the jeremiad in a new version, *Red Sky in the Morning* (2004). In *Limits to Growth: the 30-Year Update* (2004), the Club of Rome team renews its warning "that if a profound correction is not made soon, a crash of some sort is certain. And it will occur within the lifetimes of many who are alive today."[11] In *Plan B: Rescuing a Planet under Stress* (2003), Lester Brown reiterates that "our claims on the earth have become excessive." Unlike the first editions, these "updates" are not best-sellers. The best-seller at the time was Michael Crichton's *State of Fear*, a diatribe *against* environmentalism.

Why have the "updates" of the warnings of the 1970s not sold so well? The predictions proved far off-base. Indeed, some researchers had all along questioned the apocalyptic narrative. The World Resources Institute, in a 1994–1995 report, referred to "the frequently expressed concern that high levels of consumption will lead to resource depletion and to physical shortages that might limit growth or development opportunity." Examining the evidence, however, the Institute said that "the world is not yet running out of most nonrenewable resources and is not likely to, at least in the next few decades."[12] A 1988 report from the Office of Technology Assessment concluded, "The nation's future has probably never been less constrained by the cost of natural resources."[13] Advancing technology and increasing wealth, far from destroying the planet, helped to clean up the air and water—in the United States to the lowest levels of "criteria" pollutants ever recorded.[14]

Far from vindicating the environmental narrative of inevitable decline and collapse, the last fifty or sixty years have seen a remarkable improvement in standards of living except in those specific countries in which oppression, corruption, and civil war deprive people of the blessings of technological advance and global prosperity.[15] According to an authoritative report, "Global economic activity increased nearly sevenfold between 1950 and 2000. Despite the population growth . . . , average income per person almost doubled during this period."[16] According to a World Bank report, "Global economic output grew 4 percent a year from 2000 to 2007, led by record growth in low-and middle-income economies. Developing economies averaged 6.5 percent annual growth of GDP from 2000 to 2007, and growth in every region was the highest in three decades."[17]

War, oppression, ethnic violence will cause famines, but it is wrong to conclude, as some environmentalists have done, that there is not enough food to go around. As a major report states, "our ability to provide sufficient food and to do so in increasingly cost-effective ways has been a major human and humanitarian achievement. . . . And according to most projections, it appears likely that growing food needs can be met in the foreseeable future.[18]

The reasons for poor standards of living can be traced to the absence of economic development—not to a lack of resources. As the world has grown wealthier, it has become healthier. At the world level, life expectancy at birth has risen from about 30 years a century ago to 47 in 1950, 58 in 1975, and stands at 67 (for men) and 71 (for women) today.[19] In high-income nations, a child born today can expect (on average) to live at least 80 years.[20] This could greatly increase with advances in medical knowledge and technology. Access to clean potable water has also improved globally over the past 50 years although—as with food and longevity—many people lack adequate access to water in nations locked in civil war and trapped in poverty, corruption, and oppression.[21]

The apocalyptic narrative is logically irrefutable—as is any prophecy that is easily postponed. The better things get, the worse they shall become. The concept of "overshoot" explains away or accommodates any amount of progress—making the apocalyptic prophecy immune to empirical evidence. Paul Ehrlich, when he lost his famous bet with Julian Simon about the price a basket of minerals (which declined over a decade), dismissed the results. "The bet doesn't mean anything. Julian Simon is like the guy who jumps off the Empire State Building and says how great things are going so far as he passes the 10th floor," Ehrlich said.[22]

The idea that increased consumption will inevitably lead to depletion and scarcity, as often as it is repeated, is mistaken both in principle and in fact. It is based on five misconceptions. The first is that we are running out of non-renewable resources, such as minerals. The second is that the world will run out of renewable resources, such as food. The third contends that energy resources will soon run out. The fourth misconception argues from the "doubling time" of world population to the conclusion that human bodies will bury the Earth. The fifth misconception supposes the wealthy North exploits the impoverished South. These misconceptions could turn into self-fulfilling prophecies if we believed them—and if we therefore failed to make the kinds of investments and reforms that have improved standards of living in most of the world.

ARE WE RUNNING OUT OF NON-RENEWABLE RESOURCES?

While commodity markets are volatile—with petroleum especially sensitive to political conditions—the prices of minerals generally declined between 1980 and the terrorist attack on September 11, 2001. From 1980 to 1990, for example, the prices of resource-based commodities declined (the price of rubber by 40 percent, cement by 40 percent, and coal by almost 50 percent), while reserves of most raw materials increased.[23] They increased because technologies greatly improved exploration and extraction, for example, the use of bacteria to leach metals from low-grade ores. Reserves of resources "are actually functions of technology," one analyst has written. "The more advanced the technology, the more reserves become known and recoverable."[24]

For this reason among others, as the World Bank reiterated in 2009, while commodity prices are volatile, "Over the long run, demand for commodities is not expected to outstrip supply."[25] While commodity prices rose in 2007 and 2008 they began to fall back to normal levels—comparable in real terms to those of the 1990s—in 2009. In its 2009 report on commodity prices, the World Bank opined "Real food prices are projected to decline by 26 percent between 2008 and 2010, energy prices to fall by 27 percent, and metals prices to decline by 32 percent."[26]

. . .

If price is the measure of scarcity, then metals and minerals have become more plentiful over the past decades. According to a 2004 World Bank report, the price of its index of minerals and metals (in 1990 dollars) fell from a high close to $160 in 1965 to a low of about $80—a decline of 50 percent—in 2001.[27] One reason for this persistent decline is that plentiful resources are quickly substituted for those that become scarce and the price of which therefore rises. Analysts speak of an Age of Substitutability and point, for example, to nanotubes, tiny cylinders of carbon whose molecular structure forms fibers a hundred times as strong as steel, at one sixth the weight.[28] As technologies that use more-abundant resources do the work of those dependent on less-abundant ones—for example, ceramics in place of tungsten, fiber optics in place of copper wire, aluminum cans in place of tin ones—the demand for and the price of scarce resources decline.

One can easily find earlier instances of substitution. During the early nineteenth century whale oil was the preferred fuel for household illumination.[29] A dwindling supply prompted innovations in the lighting industry, including the invention of gas and kerosene lamps and Edison's carbon-filament electric bulb.[30] Whale oil has substitutes, such as electricity and petroleum-based lubricants. From an economic point of view, technology can easily find substitutes for whale products. From an aesthetic, ethical, and spiritual point of view, in contrast, whales are irreplaceable.

The more we learn about materials, the more efficiently we use them. The progress from whale oil to candles to carbon-filament to tungsten incandescent lamps, for example, decreased the energy required for and the cost of a unit of household lighting by many times. On perfecting the electric bulb which made lighting inexpensive, Thomas Edison is widely quoted as saying that "only the rich will burn candles." Compact fluorescent lights are four times as efficient as today's incandescent bulbs and last ten to twenty times as long.[31] Comparable energy savings are available in other appliances: refrigerators sold in 1993 were 23 percent more efficient than those sold in 1990 and 65 percent more efficient than those sold in 1980, saving consumers billions in electric bills.[32] Robert Solow, a Nobel laureate, says that if the future is like the past, "there will be prolonged and substantial reductions in natural-resource requirements per unit of real output." He asks, "Why shouldn't the productivity of most natural resources rise more or less steadily through time, like the productivity of labor?"[33]

WILL THERE BE ENOUGH FOOD?

A prominent agricultural economist, Gale Johnson, wrote in 2000, "People today have more adequate nutrition than ever before and acquire that nutrition at the lowest cost in all human history, while the world has more people than ever before—not by a little but by a lot."[34] This happened, he argued, because "we have found low-cost and abundant substitutes for natural resources important in the production process."[35] By around 2000, the price of food and feed grains, in real dollars (adjusted for inflation) has declined by half from what it was fifty years ago in international markets.[36] Contrary to the apocalyptic narrative,[37] at the global level "soil loss and degradation are not likely to represent a serious constraint on agricultural production." Agronomist Vernon Ruttan notes, "Water and wind erosion estimates are measures of the amount of soil moved from one place to another rather than the soil actually lost."[38]

From 1961 to 1994 global production of food doubled.[39] "The generation of farmers on the land in 1950 was the first in history to double the production of food," the Worldwatch Institute reported. "By 1984, they had outstripped population growth enough to raise per capita grain output an unprecedented 40 percent."[40] From a two-year period ending in 1981 to a two-year period ending in 1990 the real prices of basic foods fell 38 percent on world markets, according to a 1992 United Nations report.[41] In the developing world, the production of food outpaced population growth, almost tripling between the periods 1948–1952 and 1994–1996.[42] The production of staple crops worldwide continues to increase as more people emerge from poverty and can pay even minimal prices. On June 4, 2009, the U.N. Food and Agriculture Organization reported, "With the new 2009–2010 marketing season commencing, prospects continue to be positive as world cereal production is expected to be the second largest, after last year's record."[43]

. . .

Before one heads to Morton's to tuck into a Double Filet Mignon, Sauce Béarnaise—followed quickly by postprandial stupor and a triple-bypass—one should acknowledge three problems for this optimistic account. First, the essential input onto agriculture is money. Money is not spread evenly over the earth; it is concentrated in the wealthier nations. According to the *Millennium Ecosystem Assessment*, "Despite rising food production and falling food prices, more than 850 million people still suffer today from chronic undernourishment."[44] Many of the poorest countries, such as Chad and Congo, possess more than enough excellent agricultural land but lack social organization and investment. Institutional reform—responsible government, peace, the functioning of markets, the provision of educational and health services—in other words, development, is the appropriate response to poverty and therefore malnutrition.[45]

Second, the *Assessment* observes, "Among industrial countries, and increasingly among developing ones, diet-related risks, mainly associated with over-nutrition, in combination with physical inactivity now account for one third of the burden of disease."[46] (By comparison, "worldwide, under-nutrition accounted for nearly 10% of the global burden of disease."[47]) Third, to make 9 billion people obese, biotech-based agriculture would have to convert the earth to a feedlot for human beings. Farmers can now provide a healthful diet for that many people on less acreage than they use today—thus sparing land for nature.[48] In other words, we can spare nature by sparing ourselves.[49]

By locking themselves into the Malthusian rhetoric—by predicting impending world-wide starvation and using the plight of the very poor as evidence of it—environmentalists ignore and even alienate groups who emphasize the quality and safety rather than the abundance of food and who understand that under-nutrition represents a local not a global problem. The discussion has moved from the question whether the earth sets "limits" to the question of how to get wealthy people to eat less and poor people to eat more.[50] Animal rights advocates deplore horrific confined animal feedlot operations and related factory-farm methods required to overfeed people. Environmentalists have obvious allies in advocates of human development, public health, and animal rights. To have any credibility, however, environmentalists must lose the apocalyptic narrative.

ARE WE RUNNING OUT OF ENERGY?

. . .

The most persistent worries about resource scarcity concern energy. "The supply of fuels and other natural resources is becoming the limiting factor constraining the rate of economic growth," a group of experts proclaimed in 1986. They predicted the exhaustion of domestic oil and gas supplies by 2020 and, within a few decades, "major energy shortages as well as food shortages in the world."[51]

In stark contrast with the dire projections of the 1980s, the U.S. Department of Energy projected in 2009 that U.S. domestic production of petroleum would continue to increase slowly to a plateau over the following decades. "U.S. crude oil production increases from 5 million barrels per day in 2008 to over 6 million barrels per day in 2027 and remains at just over 6 million barrels per day through 2035."[52] The same report projects domestic natural gas production to "grow from 20.6 trillion cubic feet in 2008 to 23.3 trillion cubic feet in 2035," owing largely to new methods of mining.[53]

The most abundant fossil or carbon-based fuel is coal, and some of the largest reserves of it are found in the United States. These will last for more than a century. In this respect, no global shortages of hydrocarbon fuels are in. "One sees no immediate danger of 'running out' of energy in a global sense," writes John P. Holdren, a professor at Harvard University who became the principal science advisor in the Obama administration. He concludes that "running out of energy resources in any global sense is not what the energy problem is all about."[54]

For decades, environmental "Cassandras" have reiterated that we are running out of energy—thus directing attention to sources rather than sinks. By this time, however, everyone knows Holdren is correct. The real energy problem is two-fold: global climatic instability and global political instability. Reasonable minds can disagree about which problem is worse—but both require that the world move away from its dependence on fossil fuels and toward reliance on cleaner and smarter kinds of energy, as well greater efficiencies in its use.

First, the burning of hydrocarbon fuels contributes to global warming and climate change. In 1958, the concentration of carbon dioxide (CO_2) stood at 315 parts per million (ppm). Today, it has reached 380ppm, which is about one-third higher than the historical norm over 400,000 years. Levels of CO_2 are increasing so fast that in four or five decades concentrations may be twice as great as historic levels.[55] Since the planetary climate may already be changing in response to current CO_2 loadings, scientists consider the situation urgent. The global energy problem has less to do with depleting resources than with controlling pollutants.

The second problem has to do with geopolitical stability, in other words, world peace. Thomas Friedman observes that oil-rich states tend to be the least democratic—and the wealthier the ruling class gets, the more tyrannical, truculent, obstructive, and dangerous it becomes.[56] The petrocracies destabilize global balances of power while holding oil-dependent states hostage. While the food problem is best understood as local—giving the very poor access to nutrition—the energy problem is global. The principal concern is not the supply of energy but the effects of its use on geopolitics and climate.

Although leading environmentalists have focused on scarcity issues, they also join nearly everyone else in deploring the effects of the consumption of carbon-based fuels on the political as well as atmospheric climate. In a much-discussed essay, "The Death of Environmentalism," consultants Michael Shellenberger and Ted Nordhaus have argued that the environmental community while bewailing these problems has offered virtually no solutions for them except such gestures as tighter fuel economy (CAFE) standards for cars and trucks and calls for greater energy efficiency.[57]

If gasoline was taxed more (in February 2009 the global price of petroleum actually sank to $30 a barrel) higher prices would drive people into lighter and to hybrid vehicles and force industry to be more fuel efficient. When oil prices spiked in the early 1970s as a result of the embargo, the economy adjusted. From 1973 to 1986, for example, energy consumption in the United States remained virtually flat while economic production grew by almost 40 percent. Compared with

Germany or Japan, this was a poor showing.[58] The Japanese, who tax fuel more heavily than do Americans, use only half as much energy as the United States per unit of economic output. (Japanese environmental regulations are also generally stricter; if anything, this improves the competitiveness of Japanese industry.) The United States wastes hundreds of billions of dollars annually in energy inefficiency. By becoming as energy-efficient as Japan, the United States could expand its economy and become more competitive internationally.[59]

To provide leadership and direction—rather than simply reiterate their apocalyptic projections—environmentalists should advocate investment in some mix of power-producing climate-sparing technologies. There is a smorgasbord of suggestions. These include hybrid, plug-in hybrid, and electric vehicles; greater energy efficiency in housing, appliances; and the production of liquid fuels from renewable sources, some produced by genetically engineered or synthesized microorganisms capable of creating biomass cheaply or even directly splitting the carbon dioxide molecule. Other approaches include the expansion of nuclear power generation, including smaller "distributed" and sealed units, the development of geothermal and wind energy, and basic and applied research in battery technology, fuel cell technology, tidal, and other forms of power. Efforts are underway to construct a "smarter" and more efficient electric energy transmission grid.

In the American Reinvestment and Recovery Act of 2009, the Obama administration threw a staggering amount of money at clean energy technologies. It is impossible at this time to pick "winners" among the scores of innovations. Some of this money will stick. Amory Lovins, among others, has described commercially available technologies that can "support present or greatly expanded worldwide economic activity while stabilizing global climate—and saving money." He observes that "even very large expansions in population and industrial activity need not be energy-constrained."[60]

. . .

ARE THERE TOO MANY PEOPLE?

In the 1970s, the population crisis was easy to define and dramatize. The Malthusian logic of exponential

growth or "doubling times," so forcefully presented in books such as *The Population Bomb* (1968) and *The Population Explosion* (1990), proved that the "battle to feed all of humanity is over," and analogized the spread of population with cancer. "A cancer is an uncontrolled multiplication of cells; the population explosion is an uncontrolled multiplication of people. . . . The [surgical] operation will demand many apparently brutal and heartless decisions. The pain may be intense. But the disease is so far advanced that only with radical surgery does the patient have a chance of survival."[61]

By emphasizing the exponential mathematics of population growth—as if people were cancerous cells whose reproductive freedom had to be controlled by radical surgery—environmentalists made four mistakes. First, they missed the opportunity to endorse the belief that people should have all—but only—the children they want. The goal of assisting parents world-wide to plan for their children might appeal to "family values" and thus to social conservatives in a way that concerns about "too many people" did not. Efforts to improve the status of women—a key factor in fertility—may enjoy more political support and may be more effective than conventional fertility-control policies.

Second, by inveighing against economic growth—by demanding a small economy for a small earth—environmentalists alienated potential allies in the development community. Leading environmentalists explicitly rejected "the hope that development can greatly increase the size of the economic pie and pull many more people out of poverty." This hope expresses a "basically a humane idea," Paul Ehrlich wrote, "made insane by the constraints nature places on human activity."[62]

. . .

Third, by invoking "doubling times" as if that concept could be as meaningfully applied to people as to tumors, environmentalists ignored science and reason, that is, everything demographers knew about the transition then underway to a stable global population. As people move to cities—where children are not needed to do agricultural labor—and as they are assured their children will survive (so they can have fewer), and as the status of women improves, families become smaller. World population growth, which resulted from lower mortality not higher fertility, had been decelerating since the 1950s and dramatically after the 1970s. The United Nations now projects the global population "to reach 7 billion in late 2011, up from the current 6.8 billion, and surpass 9 billion people by 2050," at which it will stabilize and probably decline.[63] Most demographers believe that population will stop increasing during this century and then decline slowly to perhaps 8.4 billion in 2100.[64]

In almost all developed countries today fertility has fallen below 2.1 births and is expected to decline. European women have on average 1.4 births. According to the Population Reference Bureau, as of 2002, fertility fell "below replacement level in 33 less developed countries—mostly in Latin America and the Caribbean and parts of Asia—and is declining steeply in many others."[65] Most people live "in countries or regions in which fertility is below the level of long-run replacement."[66]

Fourth, the environmental community has yet to respond to the principal moral problem that confronts population policy—one that involves longevity not fertility.[67] The oldest segments of the population increase the fastest as science and technology extend the length of life. A U.N. report observes that in developed regions of the world, "the population aged 60 or over is increasing at the fastest pace ever (growing at 2.0 per cent annually) and is expected to increase by more than 50 per cent over the next four decades, rising from 264 million in 2009 to 416 million in 2050." The developing world is aging even more rapidly. "Over the next two decades, the population aged 60 or over in the developing world is projected to increase at rates far surpassing 3 per cent per year and its numbers are expected to rise from 473 million in 2009 to 1.6 billion in 2050."[68]

According to a U.N. report, over 2 billion of us will be over 60 years old at the middle of this century—which equals the entire population increase between 2011 and 2050. "In developed countries as a whole, the number of older persons has already surpassed the number of children (persons under age 15), and by 2050 the number of older persons in developed countries will be more than twice the number of children."[69]

In several countries, such as Japan, people 65 and older already are more numerous than those under 15; by 2030, residents 65 years and over will outnumber those under 15 in nearly every developed country—and by a 2:1 ratio in Japan and several European nations. In those countries by 2030 the median age will be 52 and grandparents will outnumber of grandchildren under 18 years of age. And these estimates do not account for possible cures for dread diseases like cancer—which could push longevity further.

Anyone interested in "doubling times" or "exponential growth" may consider the following statistic. In industrialized countries the number of centenarians has doubled every decade since 1950. According to the Population Reference Bureau, "The number of Chinese ages 65 and older is projected to swell from 88 million in 2000 to 199 million in 2025—and to 349 million in 2050." In many countries, those ages 80 or over (the "elderly") constitute the fastest-growing segment of the population. In 1900, 374,000 people in the U.S. had attained age 80; today, 10 million Americans are elderly; by 2030, that number is expected nearly to double, making huge demands on younger workers, whose labor may be needed and incomes taxed to pay for their care.

Environmentalists confront population growth with an entrance strategy, that is, birth control. Bill McKibben's *Maybe One: A Case for Smaller Families* (1999) now sets the pace. Even with one-child-per-couple, however, world population will continue to increase if families reach four, five, or more generations. Environmentalists need to develop an exit strategy. A book with the title *Maybe Eighty: A Case for Shorter Life-Spans* could provide one approach to the question environmentalists must confront. The problem is no longer Malthus—it's Methuselah. What do environmentalists say about this? Oddly the writers of the 1960s and 70s in the updated versions of their original studies—published 30 to 40 years later—have little to say about this. As long as environmental leaders argue there are "too many people" without suggesting how long a life should last, they seem self-serving. They appear to comprise a vast and growing gerontocracy outraged that younger people whom they may need to take care of them presume to raise their own children.

. . .

DOES THE NORTH EXPLOIT THE SOUTH?

William Reilly, when he served as administrator of the Environmental Protection Agency in the Bush the Elder Administration, encountered a persistent criticism at international meetings on the environment. "The problem for the world's environment is your consumption, not our population," delegates from the developing world told him. Some of these delegates later took Reilly aside. "The North buys too little from the South," they confided. "The real problem is too little demand for our exports."[70]

The delegates who told Reilly that the North consumes too little of what the South produces have a point. "With a few exceptions (notably petroleum)," a report from the World Resources Institute observes, "most of the natural resources consumed in the United States are from domestic sources."[71] Throughout the later decades of the 20th century, the United States and Canada were the world's leading exporters of raw materials.[72] The United States consistently leads the world in farm exports, running huge agricultural trade surpluses. The share of raw materials used in the North that it buys from the South recently stood at a thirty-year low; industrialized nations trade largely among themselves.[73] The World Resources Institute reported that "the United States is largely self-sufficient in natural resources." Again, excepting petroleum, bauxite, "and a few other industrial minerals, its material flows are almost entirely internal."[74]

Sugar provides an instructive example of how the North excludes—rather than exploits—the resources of the South. Since 1796 the United States has protected domestic sugar against imports.[75] American sugar growers, in part as a reward for large contributions to political campaigns, have long enjoyed a system of quotas and prohibitive tariffs against foreign competition.[76] American consumers paid about three times world prices for sugar in the 1980s, enriching a small cartel of U.S. growers. Forbes magazine has estimated that a single family, the Fanjuls, of Palm Beach, reaps more than $65 million a year as a result of quotas for sugar.[77]

The sugar industry in Florida, which is larger than that in any other state, makes even less sense environmentally than economically.[78] It depends on a publicly built system of canals, levees, and pumping stations. Fertilizer from the sugarcane fields chokes the Everglades. Sugar growers, under a special exemption from labor laws, import Caribbean laborers to do the grueling and poorly paid work of cutting cane.[79]

As the United States tightened sugar quotas (imports fell from 6.2 to 1.5 million tons annually from 1977 to 1987), the Dominican Republic and other nations with ideal environments for growing cane experienced political turmoil and economic collapse. Many farmers in Latin America, however, did well by switching from sugar to coca, which is processed into cocaine—perhaps the only high-value imported crop for which the United States is not developing a domestic substitute.[80]

Before the Second World War the United States bought 40 percent of its vegetable oils from developing countries. After the war the United States protected its oilseed markets—for example, by establishing price supports for soybeans.[81] Today the United States is a leading exporter of oilseeds, although until recently it imported palm and coconut oils to obtain laurate, an ingredient in soap, shampoo, and detergents. Even this form of "exploitation" ceased. In 1994 farmers in Georgia planted the first commercial crop of a high-laurate canola, genetically engineered by Calgene, a biotechnology firm.[82]

About 100,000 Kenyans make a living on small plots of land growing pyrethrum flowers, the source of a comparatively environmentally safe insecticide of which the United States has been the largest importer. The U.S. Department of Commerce, however, awarded $1.2 million to a biotechnology firm to engineer pyrethrum genetically. Industrial countries will synthesize pyrethrum and undersell Kenyan farmers.[83]

An article in the *New Yorker* magazine describes the efforts of thousands of Asian and African farmers to raise *Artemisia annua*, or sweet wormwood, the herb that contains artemisinin, "the world's most important malaria medicine."[84] Biologists have recently created novel genetic sequences synthetically which, combined with wormwood genes in a bacterium fabricated for the purpose, produce through fermentation large and inexpensive amounts of amorphadiene, a chemical precursor to artemisinin. Laboratories are expected soon to produce artemisinin at about 20 cents a course, a fraction of the price of the "natural" product.

. . .

MAKING A PLACE FOR NATURE

According to Thoreau, "a man's relation to Nature must come very near to a personal one."[85] For environmentalists in the tradition of Thoreau and John Muir, stewardship is a form of fellowship; although we must use nature, we do not value it primarily for the economic purposes it serves. We take our bearings from the natural world—our sense of time from its days and seasons, our sense of place from the character of a landscape and the particular plants and animals native to it. An intimacy with nature ends our isolation in the world. We know where we belong, and we can find the way home.

In defending old-growth forests, wetlands, or species we environmentalists make our best arguments when we think of nature chiefly in aesthetic and moral terms.[86] Rather than having the courage of our moral and cultural convictions, however, we too often rely on economic arguments for protecting nature, in the process attributing to natural objects more instrumental value than they have. By imputing to an endangered species an economic value or a price much greater than it fetches in a market, we "save the phenomena" for economic theory but do little for the environment. When environmentalists make the prices come out "right" by imputing market demand to aspects of nature which in fact have moral, spiritual, or aesthetic value, we confuse ourselves and fail to convince others.

There is no credible argument that all or even most of the species we are concerned to protect have any economic significance or that they are essential to the functioning of the ecological systems on which we depend. (If whales went extinct, for example, the seas would not fill up with krill.) David Ehrenfeld, a biologist at Rutgers University, points out that the species most likely to be endangered are those the biosphere is least likely to miss. "Many of these species were never common or ecologically influential; by no stretch of the imagination can we make them out to be vital cogs in the ecological machine."[87]

Species may be profoundly important for cultural and spiritual reasons, however. Consider the example of the wild salmon, whose habitat is being destroyed by hydroelectric dams along the Columbia River. Although this loss is unimportant to the economy overall (there is no shortage of farmed salmon), it is of the greatest cultural significance to the Amerindian tribes that have traditionally subsisted on wild salmon, and to the region as a whole. By viewing local flora and fauna as a sacred heritage—by recognizing their intrinsic value—we discover who we are rather than what we want. On moral and cultural grounds society might be justified in making economic sacrifices—removing dams, for example—to protect remnant populations of the Snake River sockeye, even if, as critics complain, hundreds or thousands of dollars are spent for every fish.

Even those plants and animals that do not define places possess enormous intrinsic value and are worth preserving for their own sake. What gives these creatures value lies in their histories, wonderful in themselves, rather than in any use to which they can be put. Biologist E. O. Wilson elegantly takes up this theme: "Every kind of organism has reached this moment in time by threading one needle after another, throwing up brilliant artifices to survive and reproduce against nearly impossible odds."[88] Every plant or animal evokes not just sympathy but also reverence and wonder in those who know its place, properties, and history.

. . .

The world has the wealth and the resources to provide everyone the opportunity for a decent life. We consume too much when market relationships displace the bonds of community, compassion, culture, and place. We consume too much when consumption becomes an end in itself and makes us lose affection and reverence for the natural world.

NOTES

1. See, for example, Herman E. Daly, "From Empty-world Economics to Full-world Economics: Recognizing an Historical Turning Point in Economic Development," in Robert Goodland, Herman E. Daly, and Salah El Serafy, eds., *Population, Ecology, and Lifestyle* (Washington, DC: Island Press, 1992), pp. 23–37.

2. John Muir, *The Yosemite* (New York: Century Co., 1912), p. 256.

3. Walt Whitman, *Specimen Days* (Boston: David R. Godine, Publisher, 1971), p. 61.

4. National Academy of Sciences, Population Summit of the World's Scientific Academies: *A Joint*

Statement by Fifty-eight of the World's Scientific Academies (Washington, DC: NAS Press, 1993), p. 5. . . .

5. P. R. Ehrlich and J. Holdren, "Impact of Population Growth," *Science* 171(1971): 1212–1217; quotation at p. 1212.

6. Ibid. p. 1213.

7. See Paul R. Ehrlich, *The Population Bomb* (New York: Ballantine Books, 1971), pp. 146–8, endorsing an end to food aid to impoverished areas.

8. Paul R. Ehrlich and Anne H. Ehrlich, *The End of Affluence* (New York: Ballantine, 1974), p. 33.

9. Donella Meadows, et al., *The Limits to Growth: A Report for the Club of Rome's Project on the Predicament of Mankind*, Universe Books, 1972.

10. See publisher's blurb at http://www.amazon.com/ exec/obidos/ASIN/1559638796/ref=pd_sxp_elt_l1/ 002-8426557-5628017

11. Donella H. Meadows, Jorgen Randers, Dennis L. Meadows, *Limits to Growth: The Thirty-Year Update* (White River Jct., VT: Chelsea Green Publishing, 2004), p. 1.

12. The World Resources Institute, *World Resources 1994–95*, p. 5.

13. Quoted and cited in Stephen Moore, "The Coming Age of Abundance," in Ronald Bailey, ed., *The True State of the Planet*, p. 137.

14. Steven Hayward et al., *Index of Leading Environmental Indicators* April 2005 Pacific Research Institute for Public Policy San Francisco, California and American Enterprise Institute for Public Policy Research Washington, DC, 2005, p. 5. Criteria pollutants are those at the time controlled under the Clean Air Act. http://www.pacificresearch.org/pub/ sab/enviro/05_enviroindex/2005_Enviro_Index.pdf

15. The World bank, *World Development Indicators 2005* (Washington, DC, 2005) reports: "Since 1990 extreme poverty in developing countries has fallen from 28 percent to 21 percent. Over the same time population grew 15 percent to 5 billion people, leaving 1.1 billion people in extreme poverty. If economic growth rates in developing countries are sustained, global poverty will fall to 10 percent—a striking success. But hundreds of millions of people will still be trapped in poverty, especially in Sub-Saharan Africa and South Asia and wherever poor health and lack of education deprive

people of productive employment; environmental resources have been depleted or spoiled; and corruption, conflict, and misgovernance waste public resources and discourage private investment."

16. Millennial Ecosystem Assessment, *Ecosystems and Human Well-being: Current State and Trends*, p. 74.

17. World Bank, *2009 World Development Indicators* (Washington, DC, 2009). "World View," p. 2.

18. Millennial Assessment Chapter 8, "Food", p. 212.

19. Millennial Ecosystem Assessment, Ecosystems & Human Well-Being: Volume 1: Current State and Trends: Chapter 28, "Synthesis," p. 829. United Nations Population Division, World Population Prospects: The 2002 Revision (February 2003). On line at: http://www.un.org/esa/ population/publications/wpp2002/WPP2002-HIGHLIGHTSrev1.PDF (Also noting that because of HAV/AIDS and other scourges, "But whereas more developed regions, whose life expectancy today is estimated at 76 years, will see it rise to 82 years, that of less developed regions will remain considerably below, reaching 73 years by mid-century (up from 63 years today)."

20. For these statistics, see World Bank, *World Development Report 2010: Development and Climate Change* (Washington, DC, 2009), pp. 378–379.

21. Millennial Ecosystem Assessment, *Ecosystems and Human Well-being: Current State and Trends*.

22. John Tierney, "Betting the Planet," *New York Times*, December 02, 1990, Section 6; Page 52; Column 3; Magazine. This irrefutable argument is commonplace. See, for example, C. Folke, M. Hammer, R. Costanza, and A. Jansson, "Investing in Natural Capital—Why, What, and How?" Pages 1–20 in A. Jansson, M. Hammer, C. Folke, and R. Costanza, eds. *Investing in Natural Capital: The Ecological Economics Approach to Sustainability.* Island Press, Washington, DC (analogizing optimists to "the man who fell from a ten story building, and when passing the second story on the way down, concluded 'so far so good, so why not continue?'") quotation at p. 3.

23. See Stephen Moore, "The Coming Age of Abundance," in Ronald Bailey, ed., *The True State of the Planet*, pp. 126–27.

24. Thomas H. Lee, "Advanced Fossil Fuel Systems and Beyond," in Jesse H. Ausubel and Hedy E.

Sladovich, eds., *Technology and Environment* (Washington, DC: National Academy Press, 1989), pp. 114–136; quotation at p. 116.

25. World Bank, Global Economic Prospects 2009 (Washington, DC, 2009), p. xi.

26. Ibid., p. 5.

27. World Bank, *Global Economic Prospects 2004* (Washington, DC): Appendix 2. http://siteresources.worldbank.org/INTRGEP2004/Resources/appendix2.pdf

28. H. E. Goeller and Alvin M. Weinberg, "The Age of Substitutability," *Science* 191 (February 20, 1976): 683–689. Curt Suplee, "Infinitesimal Carbon Structures May Hold Gigantic Potential," *Washington Post*, Dec. 2, 1996, p. A3.

29. See Daniel Yergin, *The Prize: The Epic Quest for Oil, Money, and Power* (New York: Simon and Schuster, 1992), p. 122.

30. See Jesse Ausubel, "The Liberation of the Environment," in Jesse Ausubel, ed., The Liberation of the Environment, *Daedalus* 125(3)(Summer 1996), pp. 1–19.

31. See Jesse Ausubel, "Can Technology Spare the Earth?" *American Scientist* 84 (March–April 1996): 166–78; esp. pp. 164–170. For further information see, Solstice: Internet Information Service of the Center for Renewable Energy and Sustainable Technology, http://www.crest.org/.

32. See "Appliance Standards are Getting Results," *Energy Conservation News*, Vol. 18, No. 2, Sept. 1, 1995.

33. Robert M. Solow, "Is the End of the World at Hand?" in Andrew Weintraub, Eli Schwartz, and J. Richard Aronson, eds., *The Economic Growth Controversy* (White Plains, N.Y.: Institute of Arts and Sciences Press, 1973), p. 49.

34. D. Gale Johnson, "Population, Food, and Knowledge," *American Economic Review* 90:1(March 2000): 1–14; quotation at p. 1.

35. Ibid p. 2.

36. Robert E. Evenson, "Besting Malthus: The Green Revolution," *Proceedings of the American Philosophical Society* 149(4) (December 2005): 469–486; see p. 471.

37. See, for example, D. Pimentel et al., "Environmental and Economic Costs of Soil Erosion and Conservation Benefits," Science, 267 (24 February 1995).

38. Vernon W. Ruttan, "Scientific and Technical Constraints on Agricultural Production: Prospects for the Future." *Proceedings of the American Philosophical Society* 149(4) (December 2005): 453–468. Quotations at pp. 457–458.

39. See Lester R. Brown, Christopher Flavin, and Hal Kane, Vital Signs 1996 (New York: W.W. Norton, 1996), p. 25; see also Ronald Bailey, ed., *The True State of the Planet*, p. 409.

40. Lester Brown et al., State of the World 1995 (New York: W.W. Norton), p. 7; Amartya Sen, "Population: Delusion and Reality," *New York Review of Books*, Sept. 22, 1994, pp. 62–67. . . .

41. UNCTAD VIII, Analytical Report by the UNCTAD Secretariat the Conference (United Nations, 1992), Table V-S, p. 235.

42. Johnson, "Population, Food, and Knowledge," p. 12.

43. U.N. Food and Agriculture Organization (FAO) press release, June 4, 2009, "Global food supply gradually steadying," at http://www.fao.org/news/story/en/item/20351/icode/

44. Millenium Ecosystem Assessment, Ecosystems and Human Well-being: Current State and Trends, p. 212.

45. See for example Jeffrey Sachs, *The End of Poverty: Economic Possibilities for Our Time* (Penguin Press: New York, 2005).

46. Millennial Ecosystem Assessment Report, Ecosystems & Human Well-Being: Volume 1: Chapter 8, "Food and Ecosystem Services," pp. 233–34. (reporting an epidemic of obesity. "At present, over 1 billion adults are overweight, with at least 300 million considered clinically obese, up from 200 million in 1995").

47. Ecosystems and Human Well-Being Synthesis, p. 51.

48. Waggoner, *How Much land Can 10 Billion People Spare for Nature?* Task Force Report 121 (Ames, IA: Council for Agricultural Science and Technology, February, 1994). . . .

49. Paul Waggoner, *How Much Land Can Ten Billion People Spare for Nature?* Task Force Report 121 (Ames, IA: Council for Agricultural Science and Technology), pp. 26–27. . . .

50. See Nikos Alexandros, Countries with rapid population growth and resource constraints: issues of food, agriculture, and development.ee T. Lang, "Food Policy and Markets: Structural Challenges

and Options," paper presented at the OECD Conference on Changing Dimensions of the Food Economy: Exploring the Policy Issues, The Hague, Netherlands, 6–7 February.

51. John Gever, Robert Kaufmann, David Skole, Charles Vorosmarty, *Beyond Oil: The Threat to Food and Fuel in the Coming Decades* (a Project of Carrying Capacity, Inc.) (Cambridge, MA: Ballinger, 1986) pp. 9, xxix, and xxx. . . .

52. U.S. Energy Information Administration (EIA), "EIA Energy Outlook Projects Moderate Growth in U.S. Energy Consumption, Greater Use of Renewables, and Reduced Oil and Natural Gas Imports." Press Release December 14, 2009. . . .

53. Ibid.

54. John Holdren, "The Energy Predicament in Perspective" in Irving M. Mintzer, ed., *Confronting Climate Change: Risks, Implications and Responses* (New York: Cambridge University Press 1992), pp. 163–169; quotation at p. 165.

55. These data are widely available. See, for example, Jonathan Shaw, Fueling Our Future, Harvard Magazine 108(3)(May–June 2006), p. 43.

56. Thomas L. Friedman, "As Energy Prices Rise, It's All Downhill for Democracy," *New York Times*, p. 23, Section A, col. 1.

57. Shellenberger and Nordhaus, "The Death of Environmentalism," p. 3; http://www.thebreakthrough.org/images/Death_of_Environmentalism.pdf

58. See Michael Brower, *Cool Energy*, esp. pp. 13–15.

59. For data comparing energy efficiency in the U.S. with that of its trading partners and relevant analysis and recommendations, see Joseph J. Romm and Amory B. Lovins, "Fueling a Competitive Economy: Profiting from Energy," *Foreign Affairs*, Winter 1992, pp. 46–60. For further evidence and argument, see Michael E. Porter and Claas van der Linder, "Green and Competitive: Ending the Stalemate," *Harvard Business Review*, September–October 1995, pp. 120–130.

60. Amory B. Lovins, "Energy, People, and Industrialization," in Kingsley Davis and Nikhail S. Bernstam, eds., *Resources, Environment, and Population: Present Knowledge, Future Options* (New York: Oxford University Press, 1991): 95–124; quotation at p. 95. For further evidence and testimony to this effect, see Thomas B. Johnsson et al. eds.,

Renewable Energy: Sources for Fuels and Electricity (Washington, DC: Island Press, 1993).

61. Paul Ehrlich, *The Population Bomb* (New York: Ballantine Books, 1971), p. 152.

62. Paul R. Ehrlich and Anne H. Ehrlich, *The Population Explosion* (New York: Simon and Schuster 1990), p. 269, n. 29.

63. Social Affairs, Population Division (2009). World Population Prospects: The 2008 Revision, Highlights, Working Paper No. ESA/P/WP.210. Page vii. On line at: http://www.un.org/esa/population/publications/wpp2008/wpp2008_highlights.pdf

64. See W. Lutz, W. Sanderson, and S. Scherbov, "The End of World Population Growth," *Nature* 412(2001): 543–546.

65. Population Reference Bureau, Population Bulletin 60(1) (2005) "Global Ageing: The Challenge of Success," p. 15.

66. Chris Wilson, "Fertility Below Replacement Level" *Science* 304, no. 5668, (9 April 2004), pp. 207–209.

67. http://www.silvereconomy-europe.org/daten/demographie_en.htm

68. United Nations, Department of Economic and Social Affairs, Population Division (2009). World Population Prospects: The 2008 Revision, Highlights, Working Paper No. ESA/P/WP.210. Page viii. On line at: http://www.un.org/esa/population/publications/wpp2008/wpp2008_highlights.pdf

69. Ibid. p. x.

70. In a phone interview, December 21, 1994, Mr. Reilly vouched for these remarks, noting that this incident happened more than once.

71. World Resources Institute, *World Resources 1994–95*, p. 16.

72. World Resources Institute, *World Resources 1994–95*, p. 291.

73. World Resources Institute, *World Resources 1994–95*, pp. 13–16.

74. Albert Adriannse et al., *Resource Flows*, p. 13.

75. See "America's Farm Subsidies," *The Economist*, June 27, 1992.

76. Sean Holton, "Sugar Growers Reap Bonanza in Glades," *Orlando Sentinel Tribune*, September 18, 1990, p. A1.

77. Phyllis Berman & Alexandra Alger, "The Set-aside Charade," *Forbes*, March 13, 1995: 78.

78. Keith Maskus, "Large Costs and Small Benefits of the American Sugar Programme," *World Economy* 12(1989): 85–104.

79. Holton, "Sugar Growers Reap Bonanza in Glades."

80. For an excellent account of the political costs of the sugar program internationally, see Anne O. Krueger, "The Political Economy of Controls: American Sugar," in Maurice Scott and Deepak Lal, eds., *Public Policy and Economic Development: Essays in Honor of Ian Little* (New York: Oxford University Press, 1990).

81. See Luis Llambi, "Opening Economies and Closing Markets: Latin American Agriculture's Difficult Search for Place in the Emerging Global Order," in Alessandro Bonanno et al., *From Columbus to ConAgra* (Lawrence, KA: University of Kansas Press, 1994), esp. pp. 184–194.

82. See "Calgene Get Canola OK," *Sacramento Bee*, November 2, 1994, p. D5; "Calgene Begins World's First Commercial Planting of Genetically Engineered Plant Oil," BIOTECH Patent News, November 1994. See also, "Calgene Completes Talks with FDA on Laurate Canola," *Genetic Engineering News*, April 15, 1995, p. 9.

83. For this and other examples, see Kate de Selincourt, "Future Shock: Effects of Biotechnology on Developing Countries," *New Statesman & Society* 6(281)(December 3, 1993). De Selincourt's larger study, "Genetic Engineering Targets Third World Crops," is available from the Panos Institute, 9 White Lion Street, London N1 ORP. . . .

84. Michael Specter, "A Life of Its Own: Where Will Synthetic Biology Take Us," *The New Yorker*, September 2009.

85 H. D. Thoreau, *The Journal of Henry David Thoreau*, vol. 10, ed. by Bradford Torrey and Francis H. Allen (Boston: Houghton Mifflin Company, 1949); quotation at page 252.

86. Aesthetic, cultural, and moral terms, of course, may also have economic and prudential significance. For an insightful discussion of normative terms such as "health" and "integrity" as applied to ecological communities and systems, see Laura Westra, *An Environmental proposal for Ethics: The Principle of Integrity* (Lanham, MD: Rowman and Littlefield, 1994).

87. David Ehrenfeld, "Why Put a Value on Biodiversity?" in E. O. Wilson, ed., *Biodiversity* (Washington, DC: National Academy Press, 1988), pp. 212–216; quotation at p. 215.

88. Edward O. Wilson, *The Diversity of Life* (Cambridge, MA: Harvard University Press, 1992), p. 345.

FREYA MATHEWS

LETTING THE WORLD GROW OLD

"Nature" is here understood, for environmental purposes, in terms of process rather than in terms of things: *nature* is whatever happens when we, or other agents with the capacity for abstract thought, let things be, let them unfold in their own way, run their own course. *Artifice*, in contrast, is understood as that which happens when such agents intentionally intervene to change the course of events for the sake of abstractly conceived ends of their own. . . . Modern civilization, on the other hand, rests on a deeply entrenched preference for artifice, for the abstractly imagined over the given, and the substitution of

Freya Mathews. 1999. Letting the World Grow Old: An Ethos of Countermodernity. Worldviews 3 (1999): no. 2. Reprinted by permission of White Horse Press, Cambridge, U.K. Revised for this volume.

the possible—the planned, the "improved," the redesigned—for the actual.

LIVING WITH NATURE

The trap for environmentalists, in thinking about nature, has generally been to reify it, to conceive of it in terms of things rather than processes. When we think of it in this way, we understand it as consisting of all those things which are not the product of abstract human design: forests, swamps, mountains, oceans, etc. We then contrast nature with the human-made environment, consisting of cities, artifacts, technologies, etc. We make the same mistake in thinking about nature at the level of the self: the *natural* self is equated with the body, the instincts, intuitions, emotions, etc, and this is contrasted with the civilized self, consisting of the controlled rational ego. The environmentalist's defence of nature is accordingly read as a project not only to save existing swamps, forests, etc, but to restore lost ones. Introspectively it is taken to imply a counter-cultural ethos of spontaneity, eros, intuitiveness and instinctuality. From the present point of view, this is a mistaken reading. To "return to nature" is not to restore a set of lost things or attributes, but rather to allow a certain process to begin anew. This is the process that takes over when we step back, when we cease intervening and making things over in accordance with our own abstract designs. Such a process can recommence anywhere, any time. It . . . can start to unfold again in the midst of the most intensively urbanized and industrialized environments on earth and in the most controlled and civilized of persons.

In a world already urbanized, "returning to nature" means not tearing down the cities and factories, and planting woods and gardens in their stead. Such action would merely perpetuate the cycle of making the world over in accordance with abstract designs—albeit in this case ecological designs—and would reinforce the mind-set involved in living against nature. Rather, "returning to nature" in an urbanized world means allowing this world to go its own way. It means letting the apartment blocks and warehouses and roads grow old. Yes, we shall have to maintain them, since we shall need to continue to use and inhabit them. Inhabitation will also call for adaptation and aesthetic enhancement. But this is compatible with a fundamental attitude of letting be, of acquiescence in the given, and of working within its terms of reference, rather than insisting upon further cycles of demolition and "redevelopment." Gradually such a world, left to grow old, rather than erased for the sake of something entirely new, will be absorbed into the larger process of life on earth. Concrete and bricks will become weathered and worn. Moss and ivy may take over the walls. Birds and insects may colonize overhangs and cavities within buildings. Green fingers will open up cracks in pavements. Bright surfaces will fade, acquiring natural patinas. Under the influence of gravity, the hard edges of modern architecture will soften, and imitate the moulded contours of landforms. Given time, everything is touched by the processes of life, and eventually taken over by them, to be fed into the cycle of decay and rebirth.[1]

. . .

When the world is allowed to grow old, when things are retained, or left to unfold in their own way, then it is possible truly to *inhabit* places, to come to belong to them, in ways that are undreamt of in change-based societies. As years pass, and places retain their identities, they can, if we let them, come to be inscribed with our histories and the histories of our families and communities. They acquire meaning for us as our life experiences are woven into them. Here, on this road going down to the creek, where I walk my dog every week, is the house my great grandfather built. I have a faded photograph of it on lock-up day, sometime late in the 19th century. Around the corner is the store my grandfather ran, and over there is the park in which my parents walked, each evening, holding hands, for sixteen years. Here, alongside it, is the cemetery where I roamed in my gothic youth, looking for the grave of that same great grandfather, keeping trysts in the peppercorn groves, composing poems about roses. And it was along the tree-lined avenue at the edge of this cemetery that I pushed my baby son to creche. Layers and layers of significance accrete as our lives unfold amidst familiar spaces, significance that can for us never be reproduced in any other setting. The setting itself infiltrates our identity. This irreplaceable significance of our own place or places for us binds us to them. We become their natives.

This belonging is reinforced in another way when we let our world—whether urban or rural—grow old. For when the lay-out and structures and constellation of physical features that define a particular place are allowed to endure for a long time, then not only can it become interwoven with our individual and collective identity in a way that binds us to it, but, from a panpsychist point of view, *it* can come to know *us*. In time, and only in time, a place can, if we commit to it, come to accept us, open its arms to us, receive us—it agrees to be our place, attentive to us, attuned to us. We become its people. The land, or place, claims its own. It can never receive the casual or expedient sojourner or stranger in such familiar fashion. In this way too then, through time, and the reinhabitation of places that are allowed to be, we become native to our world.[2]

The self-realization of the biosphere—which is to say, the unfolding of nature on earth—involves a pattern of gradual but continuous change—a pattern of aging and decomposition followed by spontaneous reconstitution into new forms. This is what happens to things when we let them be. Artifice, as here understood, correspondingly consists in any regime of abrupt, wholesale change, change that involves the erasure of one environment, or order of things, and its replacement with an entirely new one.

. . .

I should note here that by making the point that "nature" in its deeper sense connotes not trees and grass and wildlife, but the processes which occur to any and all things when they are no longer subject to intentional control, I am by no means wanting to say that the conservation of trees and grass and wildlife—which is to say, environmentalism in its traditional form—becomes superfluous. Existing ecosystems should, like cities and selves, be allowed to unfold in their own way, free from undue human disturbance. Where such ecosystems have already been modified by the introduction of exotic species however, the present view entails that the new and old species should in principle—though there may be many countervailing considerations in practice—be left to sort it out. To respect nature in this connection does not imply that we should eradicate the exotics and restore the

indigenous. It means that we should forego interventionist "management" and allow natural processes to reassert themselves. It may be deeply distressing to watch native plants and animals disappearing under the onslaught of aggressive invaders, and there may be many compassionate and practical reasons for attempting to temper this onslaught, but, to the extent that we opted out of the whole affair, we would at any rate have the satisfaction of knowing that what we were witnessing was in fact a return to nature.

. . .

A certain stepping back, then, is what is involved in "returning to nature" in the outer world. At the level of self, making the transition from civilization to a more natural state is no more a matter of trying to reinstate an instinctual, free-and-easy, impulsive regime than returning the world to nature is a matter of restoring lost forests and swamps. . . . The way for a self-censoring self to "return to nature" is simply for it to stop altogether the business of attempting to make itself over in accordance with abstract ideals, and surrender instead to what it already is. When we give up being dissatisfied with ourselves, and reconcile ourselves to our "unnaturalness," our tedious uptightness, for instance, then, ironically, we start to relax anyway; as we stop forcing ourselves to follow the latest social prescriptions, our own instinctual conatus has a chance to make itself felt again. Gradually we become re-animated with our native will to self-realization.

The point I am making here, at the level of both self and world, is that it is never too late to return to nature. No matter how artificial our self or world has become, they can always, at any given moment, become subject again to natural processes, simply by our decision to call a halt to "development" and "progress" and "self improvement," and to allow things to remain as they are, to be retained rather than replaced. In saying this I am not of course intending to ban change altogether, but to insist that change should not disrupt the general unfolding of things. It should not raze the old and superimpose on the space that is left something unrelated to what preceded it. Change should carry us gently and smoothly into the future, respecting the cycles of creation, decay and regeneration. It should grow from within the shell of the given.

It might be objected at this point that the attitude of letting things be that I am recommending here is too passive to be of use to the environment movement, that in the end it amounts to little more than a laissez-faire acquiescence in the political status quo. To dispel this fear, let me explain in a little more detail how such an attitude would, if adopted by a significant proportion of the populace, in its quiet way thoroughly disable the present world-destroying order of capitalism, by systematically negating the following values on which that order rests.

Consumerism. When we embrace those things that are already at hand, we do not seek to replace them with new ones. Such embracing of the given is thus an antidote to the culture of disposability and conspicuous consumption fostered by capitalism. From the viewpoint of letting things be, we would be most pleased, not with our brightest and newest things, but with those that were our oldest and most well-worn, things which had long figured in our lives, and mingled their identity and destiny with ours. "Keeping up with the Joneses," if it applied at all in the letting-be scenario, would entail having fewer and older things than the Joneses. . . . Acquisitiveness, and hence consumerism, melt away in the face of an attitude of letting be.

Commodification. When we value things and places for the meaning that our own lives have invested in them, via our relationship with them, this removes them from the market place. They cannot be replaced by other things and places, even things and places of the same type, since the substitutes will not share our history nor hence be imbued with the same meaning for us. From this point of view, I could no more buy or sell things or places which had become part of the landscape of my life, part of my very identity, than I could buy or sell members of my family. Thus the pool of commodities is continually diminished.

Productivity. When we embrace the world as it is, and are no longer forever seeking to make it better, according to abstract (generally egocentric or anthropocentric) conceptions of the good, then greed is effectively abolished. We no longer crave bigger and better houses, cars, roads, cities, whatever. We are instead attached to what is already given. There is thus no call for ever-increasing productivity.

Progress. When people no longer believe that the world can always be improved, the slate wiped clean and a better world, a better society, inscribed on it, then the ideological rationalization for capitalism viz that it can continue to improve peoples' "standard of living" indefinitely, collapses.

Efficiency. In late capitalism, efficiency—patently a notion pertaining to means—has acquired an almost fetishistic status. Tools (where this includes all kinds of techniques and procedures as well as implements and technologies) are valued not so much for what they do as for their efficiency, and they are retained only so long as their efficiency is perceived as maximal. When the attitude of letting be is assumed however, tools are valued not merely for their efficiency, but for their meaning. I may continue to use an old plough, or a leaky fountain pen, or a certain laborious method for making dough, simply because this is the plough, or pen, or method, that my mother or grandfather used. Efficiency may still be a consideration, but it will be only one factor determining the means I choose to achieve my ends.

Industry/business. These are the two definitive modalities of capitalism—industriousness and busyness—both connoting a certain kind of externally driven, externally focussed, hectic state of doing or acting. Those who are busy and industrious act on the world, they take initiatives and make things happen. When we assume the attitude of letting be however, we let the world do the doing, and we fit in with it. We favour "inaction,"[3] which is not passivity, but action which is effortless. . . .

Development. When we understand "development" in terms of the transformation and regeneration that eventually transpires when things are left to grow old, to unfold in their own way, then we will not tolerate the erasure of the given which is the precondition and prelude to "development" in the capitalist sense, i.e., the replacement of the given by the decontextualized abstractly imagined new.

Profit. If we do elect to let things be, it is on the assumption, as I explained earlier, that nature knows best—that nature, left to itself, conserves itself, does not exhaust itself, but rather replenishes itself, in accordance with the law of birth, decay and rebirth. To sustain itself in this way, nature returns *everything* to the life cycle, it recycles everything. There is no "surplus" in this system, and hence no accumulation. The law of return makes nonsense of the notion of "profit." "Profit" in one part of the system merely signals loss and depletion in another part.

Automation. For the capitalist, labour is merely a means to production; if automation provides a cheaper, more efficient means, it will be preferred. From the viewpoint of letting things be, human labour is, or can be, a vehicle for meaning. Things become significant to us partly as a result of our building, making, repairing or decorating them ourselves.... To "mix our labour" with things is, as Locke said, though with entirely different intent, to make them ours, in a sense analogous to that in which our family is ours. To make things ourselves, or to have them made by the hands of others, then, is in certain respects preferable, from the present point of view, to mechanization of the processes of production.

Property. When people honour the world as it is— honour its immanent telos, its capacity to unfold in its own way—they no longer seek to *own* the world, but rather to *belong* to it. They belong to their world by being faithful to the things it contains, keeping and tending them and letting the world manifest through them as they endure. The world expresses itself, reveals itself, through the changes it induces in these things, through the lichen on the walls, the cracks in the glaze, the slow, stooping, inevitable return to earth. By continually replacing things we never witness the way the world reclaims its own, so we miss out on knowing it, encountering it. Strangers to the world, we do not belong, we are anything but natives. We comport ourselves as invaders, conquerors, buying up the matter which means nothing to us, and trashing it when we are tired of it. We treat ourselves, our own bodies, in the same way, truculently professing to own them and reluctant to allow them to be reclaimed by the world, reluctant to see the world tenderly revealing itself to us through them, through the fading and crazywork and mute surrender of flesh to gravity. But of course, at the final call, the world claims us anyway, and we go, back into the earth, but no wiser, and a lot lonelier, strangers to the end.

...

An economics in accordance with the principle of letting be is an economics of the given, an economics which respects the world as it is, and finds metaphysical sufficiency in it.

THE POLITICS OF REINHABITATION

I have argued that when we assume the attitude of letting things be, we cease to be interested in consumerism and the pursuit of wealth and become defectors from capitalism. We become children of nature again, true natives, of our cities, of our world. When a significant proportion of the population adopts this attitude, the capitalist system, robbed of its consumers, would presumably wither away. But is such "inaction" enough? In a society in which this is not the majority position, a society dedicated to relentless progress and development, with the insatiable bulldozers and chainsaws and toxic spills that this entails, can we stand by and "do nothing"? Wouldn't our attitude of letting things be merely abet the destruction in this scenario? Isn't *resistance* rather than acceptance the appropriate political response to a system which will not let things be?

I think there is indeed a place for resistance in the politics of letting be. The impulse to let things be, after all, springs from cherishing the given, embracing the world as it is. This commitment to the given is primarily a commitment to *things*, to concrete particulars and places. It implies a commitment to protect those things and places against arbitrary erasure undertaken for the sake of abstract ideals. We will thus defend the things and places to which we have pledged our loyalty, and we will do so, not in the name of an abstract ideology, but simply because a world which is allowed to grow old claims us as its own, and we shall spring to its defence as surely as natives have perennially sprung to the defence of their lands.

But how can we neo-natives, a tiny minority, conduct such defence against the forces of capitalism? Our defensive resources are no greater than those of a small country facing a large-scale foreign invasion. But just as civilian defence seems to be the principal strategy for small populations in this situation, so such a form of defence might provide a key to imagining resistance from the perspective of letting things be. Civilian defence, of course, involves bands of individuals from the occupied territories withdrawing to secret, often inaccessible, locations in the countryside or city, and, through sniping and ambush, making it impossible for the invaders to move freely through the occupied regions. By analogy, followers of the politics of letting be could block the expansionism of capitalist interests by *reinhabiting* places earmarked for the inevitable "development."

What does reinhabitation mean in this context? It signifies people acknowledging particular places as the inalienable landscape of their lives. Just as civilian defence requires of citizens that they get to know the lie of their own land intimately, so that they can live off it, and disappear into it when the heat is on, so the politics of reinhabitation requires of its followers that they explore and research their own homeplace or region thoroughly, discovering its secrets and substrata, checking titles offices and municipal and historical records, for instance, so that the offensives of planners and developers can be anticipated. It involves finding means of sustenance, on every level, within their own neighbourhood.

. . .

So a politics of reinhabitation calls for us to find creative and forceful ways of both re-establishing and proclaiming ourselves as natives in the midst of the industrial and urban devastation of the world today. It also calls on us to recognize that global capitalism represents nothing short of an *invasion* of our world, and requires that we organize and comport ourselves with corresponding tenacity in our world's defence.

FROM MODERNITY TO COUNTERMODERNITY

From a panpsychist perspective, respect for nature, as we have seen, is not a matter of protecting only ecosystems, but *all* material things, from undue human disturbance, including things that do not usually arouse the concern of environmentalists, even non-anthropocentric environmentalists, such as deep ecologists. This view of nature, and what it is to live with rather than against it, implies an ethos that is far more encompassing than that of the traditional environment movement. It is an ethos as encompassing in fact as the ethos of modernity that it seeks to reverse. For the hallmark of modernity is radical change—in the form of development,

control, management, design, intervention, progress, improvement, even salvation. (This is reflected in the very etymology of the word, "modern," which is derived from "mode," meaning "of the present," as in "a la mode," keeping up with the latest. Modernity is that period which can be characterized in terms of its commitment to the ever-emerging new, its dissatisfaction with the given, its radical discontinuity with the past and its dissociation from tradition.) The ethos of letting be challenges modernity head on, trusting as it does the innate wisdom of things, and eschewing as it does the definitive ambition of modernity, to remake the world in accordance with abstract ideas. From the present point of view, not only is environmentalism, even in its deep-ecological forms, missing the larger metaphysical picture in its approach to modernity; it is also itself deeply entangled or imbued with the modernist ethos in its understanding of its own mission; it needs to extricate its legitimate concern for nature from heroic modernist assumptions about its own world-changing, world-saving role.

I am suggesting that instead of perpetuating this profoundly modernist ethos of changing or saving the world, the environment movement could assume what I would venture to describe as a *counter*modern attitude of letting things be. We could step right outside the presuppositions of modernity, and dare *not* to try to make things better, at any rate if "making things better" is a rationalization for continually replacing one regime with another. When we say, "let's fix the world up—let's pull down these slummy old tenement blocks and build a brand new eco-permacultural-urban-village in their stead"—we are just as much in the grip of the old ethos of domination and control as the city fathers were. We are rejecting the given in favour of an abstract or imagined alternative of our own—we are refusing to "let things be"—and it is this hubristic mentality which is the motor of modern civilization and the source of the environmental crisis. In remaining in the grip of the old ethos, in nursing the desire to make things better, we are simply continuing to water the deeper modernist roots of the present predatory economic system.

An ethos which tries to avoid the pitfalls of this mentality will, of course, be an ethos of conservatism rather than radicalism. This conservatism has always been implicit in the environment movement, as plainly betokened by the fact that the term "conservation" is often regarded as synonymous with "environmentalism." However, such conservatism does not imply that the attitude of letting be is aligned with the political right. The political right has historically, of course, been conservative, that is, committed to the given, while the left has been opposed to the given, and committed to the abstract possible or ideal. The historical right however, though conservative, differed from the present position inasmuch as it was socially rather than ontologically motivated—it was at heart a defence of social, political and economic privilege, rather than a defence of the world for its own sake. In other words, the right insisted on the preservation of traditions and institutions because it was through these traditions and institutions that the upper classes retained their privileges. A degree of ontological conservatism—the conservation of architecture and landscapes, for instance—was implicit in this position, but this ontological conservatism was in reality a mere spin-off from a self-interested politics of oppression. The historical left rejected this politics of oppression, and demanded the overthrow—and ongoing readjustment—of the existing social order, in order to end the systematic privileging of the powerful few at the expense of the many. This revolutionary or radical politics however sustained an unremitting antagonism not only to traditions and institutions, but to the world that these traditions and institutions had built, and this legacy has served, in the long run, to legitimate a rapacious contempt for the given in all its social and ontological forms, where this contempt is the hallmark of late capitalist modernity.

The attitude of letting things be, in contrast, is conservative out of genuine respect for the world, for the capacity of things to unfold in their own way. Its conservatism is ontologically rather than socially motivated, and it extends primarily to material things rather than to cultures, traditions and social institutions.[4] This attitude certainly does not spring from a desire to preserve the privileges of the few, as that of the historical right has done. . . . The attitude of letting things be effectively inverts this nightmare and, by stepping outside the game of left and right altogether, inadvertently combines the essence of the upside of each of the old right and left.

The aim of such a conservative ethos then is not a brave new world, but an old world, a world unfolding naturally, redolent with meaning, beauty, and its own life and terms. The only way of achieving such a world, without engaging in further interventions, is, as I have explained, to let the present world grow old—to let the cities weather and fade, and the ivy creep up the walls.

. . .

DISCOVERING THE TAO IN AUSTRALIA

The position that I have outlined in this paper is basically a Taoist one. Nature, according to my definition, is more or less equivalent to the Tao: it is the wise way the world unfolds when left to its own devices (Mathews 1996). The Taoism of Lao Tzu does not announce itself as panpsychist, but clearly a world animated by the Tao is one which is possessed of some intelligent inner principle, a principle that can be trusted to guide us into the deepest channels of life.

It is not my place to comment in detail here on the affinities between the broadly Taoist attitude of letting be and certain fundamental characteristics of Aboriginal thought. Suffice it to say that Aboriginal cultures evince a powerful engagement with the given that ensures their continuity with their own past but also their flexibility in the face of an almost unimaginable scale of externally imposed change. For while not *craving* the possible and the ideal, they exhibit a genius for accommodating the new once it has become actual. One of the flashpoints in the evolution of my own thinking occurred when a non-indigenous friend who had married into an Aboriginal family in the far north-west of Australia told me about an elder there who included *motorboats* in his Dreaming stories. Years later I happened to find myself living for a while in the very community to which the old man—by now deceased—had belonged, and I was enchanted by the way in which the people in this community refused nothing. They accepted—though they never craved—anything and everything that drifted their way, all the trappings and junk of modern civilization. But in the process of accepting this tawdry stuff, they also uncannily Aboriginalized it, so that it assumed an entirely different significance in the context of their community from its intended significance within the framework of a capitalist culture. Somehow, through this affectionate trust in the given, the everyday was rendered numinously spiritual, and the spiritual unpretentiously everyday.

Mary Graham has declared that one of the most taken-for-granted assumptions of Aboriginal thought is that spirit is real; another is that land is all there is (Graham 1992). That is to say, spirit has a status, in Aboriginal thought: . . . spirit animates the given rather than existing in the realm of the abstract, so we connect with spirit by engaging—and not unnecessarily interfering—with the given. By embracing the given even in its most adulterated forms, we reinhabit our own contemporary, mundane reality in the same kind of profound way that traditional Aboriginal peoples inhabited their reality. . . . by remaining attuned to the wisdom that this peaceful old land imparts to those who pay attention to it.

NOTES

1. I have observed a similar attitude to junk and rubbish in Aboriginal communities in Australia. Lots of litter and old machinery and cars and fridges and so on are left lying around in some of the remoter communities, apparently on the assumption that these things, like all others, have their place in the world, so there is no point in pretending that they do not exist by putting them out of sight. They will in time, again like everything else, be received back into the land, back into the cycles of life.

2. For a comparable account of the way the land claims its native sons and daughters in the Aboriginal world, see Deborah Bird Rose 1992.

3. I intend "inaction" here in the Taoist sense of the term.

4. There is a great deal more to be said than I can say here concerning the ultimate scope of the principle of letting be. See *Reinhabiting Reality.*

REFERENCES

Mary Graham, 1992, interviewed on *Aboriginal Perspectives*, Caroline Jones and Stephen Godley, ABC Religious Program.

Freya Mathews, "The Soul of Things," *Terra Nova* 1 (1996): 55–64.

Freya Mathews, "Letting the World Grow Old: an Ethos of Countermodernity," *Worldviews* 3 (1999): 2.

Freya Mathews, *Reinhabiting Reality*, Albany: SUNY Press (2005).

Deborah Bird Rose, *Dingo Makes Us Human*, (Cambridge: Cambridge University Press, 1992).

ADRIANA ZUNIGA-TERAN

WALKABLE NEIGHBORHOODS

Neighborhood design affects lifestyle physical activity. The design of a neighborhood determines whether a person has to use the automobile for daily trips and errands or whether he/she can walk, bike, and/or use public transportation. This relationship between the built environment and physical activity is usually known as "walkability" and higher levels of walkability are thought to increase lifestyle physical activity and improve human health. Therefore, neighborhood design affects public health and health care costs.

Walkable neighborhoods also have the potential to reduce some of the negative effects of urbanization and mitigate climate change. Walkable neighborhoods not only reduce sedentary societies that depend on the

This reading is adapted from Adriana Zuniga-Teran, Barron J. Orr, Randy H. Gimblett, Nader V. Chalfoun, Stuart E. Marsh, David P. Guertin, and Scott B. Going, "Designing Healthy Communities: Testing the Walkability Model," Frontiers of Architectural Research 6, no. 1 (2017): 63–73.

use of the automobile, but also traffic, noise, and pollution generated by cars, which are also detrimental to human wellbeing. If more people choose to walk or bike as their method of transportation, it will also result in less CO_2 emissions from vehicles, which mitigates climate change. Finally, walkable neighborhoods are compact and reduce urban sprawl that consumes the natural landscape.

What is a walkable neighborhood? Can we measure walkability? In Zuniga-Teran, Orr, Gimblett, Chalfoun, Marsh, et al. (2017), we examine interactions between the built environment and physical activity and find significant correlations between different aspects of the built environment and people reporting an increased level of physical activity. The neighborhood design elements that we thought would be related to people walking, were in fact significantly related. We called this the Walkability Model. Walkability in a neighborhood can be assessed through a conceptual framework that contains nine categories: (1) connectivity, (2) land-use, (3) density, (4) traffic-safety, (5) surveillance, (6) parking, (7) experience, (8) greenspace, and (9) community. Most of these categories and the design elements contained in them are based on previous studies (Saelens, Saliis, and Frank 2003; Cerin et al. 2013; Frank et al. 2009; USGBC 2014; Handy et al. 2002; Barton, Grant, and Guise 2003; Sandifer, Sutton-Grier, and Ward 2015).

1. *Connectivity* refers to the directness and shortness of routes. This category includes all the neighborhood design elements that allow people to reach a destination directly and where there are alternative routes to do so. Some examples include the use of a grid street network over the cul-de-sac street

network (Figure 1). Other connectivity elements include small blocks or short distances between street intersections, and lack of fences and gates.

2. *Land-use* refers to the proximity of different land uses that provide multiple destinations for walking (shops and restaurants close to dwelling units). The distance between dwelling units and destinations should be less than 400 meters or ¼ mile, because ½ mile is the distance that most people would walk (to and from destination adds ½ mile). It is recommended that walking destinations are diverse (some restaurants, some shops, some offices), and that they have different working hours (bakeries that open early and bars or theaters that close late) so there are people on the streets at all times. Other design elements of land use are related to size, where small-size services are recommended. It encourages people to be out shopping in the community on a daily rather than a weekly basis.

3. *Density* refers to the number of dwelling units per unit of area, where higher density is related to higher walkability. Density also refers to commercial uses; a commercial street is more walkable if there is more store floor area in relation to parking. This category also includes infill development (building on vacant lots) and brownfield development (rehabilitating contaminated lots that were previously used for industrial uses, for example). It is important that new neighborhood projects are located within the urban boundary, reducing urban sprawl and increasing density.

4. *Traffic-safety* refers to the infrastructure that minimizes the risk of pedestrians, cyclists, and patrons of the transit system from being involved in traffic

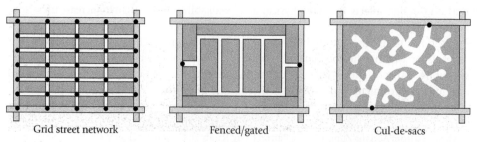

Grid street network   Fenced/gated   Cul-de-sacs

FIGURE 1 A grid street network with multiple access points (red dots) provide more direct and alternative routes to different destinations.

FIGURE 2 Separating pedestrians and bikers from the road increases safety from traffic injuries. Design elements include speed limits, speed bumps, and strips of vegetation or on-street parking between sidewalks, bike lanes, and vehicle traffic.

accidents. Some neighborhood design elements in this category include sidewalks and bike lanes buffered from the road by a strip of vegetation or on-street parking, safe and comfortable bus stops close to homes, and traffic calming treatments (crosswalks, roundabouts, speed limits, speed bumps, pedestrian-only streets, etc.) (Figure 2).

5. *Surveillance* refers to the sensation of people watching the street from inside the buildings. This feeling is thought to increase the perception of safety from crime. Examples include shops with clear glass windows, where entrances occur close to one another and with façades close to the street (or short building setbacks). It is recommended to have outdoor cafes, front porches, balconies, lighting, and on-street parking, in order to increase surveillance. (Figure 3).

6. *Parking* refers to the availability of parking, where less parking is more walkable. Other than on-street parking—that buffers vehicle traffic from pedestrians—locating parking along street fronts is not recommended. Walking through a parking lot or by a parking garage is not interesting to pedestrians. Also, if there is low availability of parking, people may choose a different mode of transportation (e.g., walk, bike, transit) to reach different destinations. If parking is essential, it is recommended to locate parking lots and garages on the rear of buildings with access from secondary streets because car access interrupts sidewalks and reduces walkability (Figure 4a, 4b). Also, shared parking (e.g., parking that is used during the day by offices and during the night by theaters) decreases the area required for parking.

7. *Experience* refers to the sensorial experience while walking (e.g., thermal comfort, aesthetics, fumes, noise, way-finding). Examples of this category include the streetscape that consists of a building-height-to-street-width ratio of 1:3 (Figure 5). This ratio means that for every unit of building height there are three units of street width or less (Figure 5). This ratio feels snug. It provides a feeling of enclosure to the public space and is usually achieved by reducing building setbacks to a minimum and avoiding parking (again, other than on-street parking) in the front of the buildings (e.g., avoid strip malls that locate parking in the front of the buildings).

FIGURE 3 Surveillance can be enhanced with lighting, short building setbacks, front porches, balconies, outdoor cafes, and on-street parking.

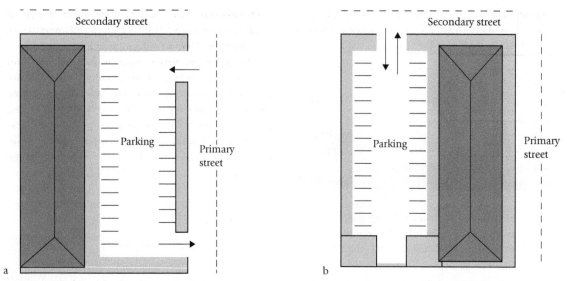

FIGURE 4 Locating parking at the rear of buildings increases walkability. Figure 4a shows a low walkability example where parking is located at the front of the buildings with access to parking lot interrupting the sidewalk of the primary street. Figure 4b shows a more walkable example where parking is located at the rear of the buildings with access through a secondary street, leaving a continuous sidewalk with storefront along the primary street.

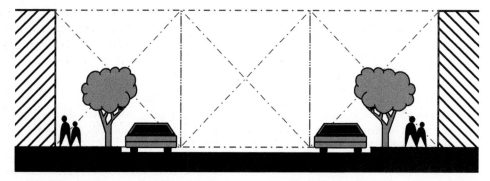

FIGURE 5 A building-height-to-street-width ratio of 1:3 (one unit of building height for three units of street width) is thought to increase the feeling of enclosure and walkability.

This category also includes vegetation and trees, beautiful buildings and sights, landmarks, signage, water bodies, art, and street furniture.

8. *Greenspace* refers to the proximity and access to greenspace. This is a destination that is closely related to physical activity because it provides opportunities for recreational activities, but the design of the neighborhood directly affects its access. For example, a park may be located across

the street of a neighborhood, but if there is a busy intersection to cross and the neighborhood entrance is located on the other side, residents will not visit this park as often.

9. Finally, *community* refers to spaces that allow community interaction that include plazas, community centers, churches, etc. Neighborhoods that provide spaces for community interaction are not only related to walkability but also to an increased

sense of community. For a list of neighborhood design elements for the nine categories see Appendix A in Zuniga-Teran (2015).

The graphic representation of the Walkability Model (Figure 6) connects all the categories with a circle to represent that the categories are all equally important and that they are interconnected and interdependent. By interconnected we mean that one design element may be listed in several categories. Examples include *on-street parking*, which is listed as a neighborhood design element for traffic safety (buffering pedestrians from vehicle traffic), parking (recommended type of parking), and surveillance (more people accessing cars provides eyes on the street). Another example is a *strip of vegetation* along the sidewalk. This neighborhood design element is listed under traffic safety (buffers pedestrians), and experience (provides thermal comfort and beautiful sights). The interdependence of categories means that one category cannot exist without others. For example, mixing land-uses is possible if there is high density (shops and restaurants need many people for their business to succeed) and that the neighborhood is connected (people can access shops and restaurants directly from homes).

Urban design solutions that enhance walkability can be found by just looking at the past. Before World War II and the mass adoption of the automobile, people planned their days around walking, and neighborhood form followed that function. Traditional

neighborhoods score highly along most if not all dimensions of the Walkability Model (Zuniga-Teran, Orr, Gimblett, Chalfoun, Guertin, et al. 2017).

Designing walkable neighborhoods may not only increase lifestyle physical activity, but also increase safety from traffic-related injuries, and provide a feeling of surveillance and security. It may result in more people visiting greenspace more frequently, and may increase a sense of community. In other words, walkable communities are vibrant and healthy communities.

REFERENCES

Barton, Hugh, Marcus Grant, and Richard Guise. 2003. *Shaping Neighborhoods. A Guide for Health, Sustainability and Vitality*. London and New York: Spon Press.

Cerin, Ester, Terry Conway, Kelli Cain, Jacqueline Kerr, Ilse De Bourdeaudhuij, Neville Owen, Rodrigo Reis, Olga Sarmiento, Erica Hinckson, and Deborah Salvo. 2013. "Sharing Good NEWS across the World: Developing Comparable Scores across 12 Countries for the Neighborhood Environment Walkability Scale" *BMC Public Health* 13 (1): 309.

Frank, L. D., J. F. Sallis, B. E. Saelens, L. Leary, K. Cain, T. L. Conway, and P. M. Hess. 2009. "The Development of a Walkability Index: Application to the Neighborhood Quality of Life Study." *British Journal of Sports Medicine* 44 (13): 924–33. doi:10.1136/bjsm.2009.058701.

Handy, Susan L., Marlon G. Boarnet, Reid Ewing, and Richard E. Killingsworth. 2002. "How the Built Environment Affects Physical Activity: Views from Urban Planning." *American Journal of Preventive Medicine* 23 (2): 64–73.

Saelens, B. E., Saliis, J. F., and Frank, L. D. 2003. "Environmental Correlates of Walking and Cycling: Findings from the Transportation, Urban Design and Planning Literatures." *The Society of Behavioral Medicine* 25 (2): 80–91.

Sandifer, Paul A., Ariana E. Sutton-Grier, and Bethney P. Ward. 2015. "Exploring Connections among Nature, Biodiversity, Ecosystem Services, and Human Health and Well-Being: Opportunities to Enhance Health and Biodiversity Conservation."

FIGURE 6 A walkable neighborhood includes neighborhood design elements from nine categories.

Ecosystem Services 12 (April): 1–15. doi:10.1016/j.ecoser.2014.12.007.

USGBC. 2014. "LEEDv4forNeighborhoodDevelopment." http://www.usgbc.org/sites/default/files/LEED%20v4%20ND_10.01.14_current_0.pdf.

Zuniga-Teran, Adriana A. 2015. "From Neighborhoods to Wellbeing and Conservation: Enhancing the Use of Greenspace through Walkability." Tucson, AZ: U of Arizona.

Zuniga-Teran, Adriana A., Barron Orr, Randy Gimblett, Nader Chalfoun, David Guertin, and Stuart Marsh. 2017. "Neighborhood Design, Physical Activity, and Wellbeing: Applying the Walkability Model." *International Journal of Environmental Research and Public Health* 14 (76). doi:10.3390/ijerph14010076.

Zuniga-Teran, Adriana A., Barron J. Orr, Randy H. Gimblett, Nader V. Chalfoun, Stuart E. Marsh, David P. Guertin, and Scott B. Going. 2017. "Designing Healthy Communities: Testing the Walkability Model." *Frontiers of Architectural Research*, January. doi:10.1016/j.foar.2016.11.005.

TAKING ACTION

PAUL WATSON

TORA! TORA! TORA!

On December 7, 1941, the Imperial Japanese First Naval Air fleet launched a surprise attack against the US Naval base at Pearl Harbor on the Hawaiian island of Oahu.

As the Japanese planes swooped in low, their wing commander gave his orders. The Japanese words "Tora, Tora, Tora" crackled through the cockpits of the torpedo bombers.

"Attack, attack, attack." Such was the battle cry of a people who had mastered the martial strategies of Asia. The attack was swift, surprising, ruthless, and effective.

As an ecological strategist, I have faced the Japanese as adversaries on numerous occasions. For this reason, I have studied Japanese martial strategy, especially the classic work entitled *A Book of Five Rings* written by Miyamoto Musashi in 1648. Musashi advocated the "twofold way of pen and sword," which I interpret to mean that one's actions must be both effective and educational.

In March 1982, the Sea Shepherd Conservation Society successfully negotiated a halt to the slaughter of dolphins at Iki Island in Japan. Contributing to this success was our ability to quote Musashi and talk to the Japanese fishermen in a language they could understand—the language of no compromise confrontation.

During our discussion, a fisherman asked me, "What is of more value, the life of a dolphin or the life of a human?"

I answered that, in my opinion, the life of a dolphin was equal in value to the life of a human.

The fisherman then asked, "If a Japanese fisherman and a dolphin were both caught in a net and you could save the life of one, which would you save?"

All the fishermen in the room smirked. They had me pegged a liberal and felt confident that I would say that I would save the fisherman, thus making a mockery of my declaration that humans and dolphins are equal.

Paul Watson. 1995. Tora! Tora! Tora! Earth Ethics. Edited by. J. Sterba. Englewood Cliffs, NJ: Prentice Hall. 341–346. Reprinted with permission of the author.

I looked about the room and smiled. "I did not come to Japan to save fishermen; I came here to save dolphins."

They were surprised but not shocked by my answer. All the fishermen treated me with respect thereafter.

Why? Because the Japanese understand duty and responsibility. Saving dolphins was both my chosen duty and my responsibility.

Sea Shepherd had already established a reputation in Japan as the "Samurai protector of whales." This came in an editorial that appeared in the Tokyo daily *Asahi Shimbun* in July 1979, a few days after we rammed and disabled the Japanese owned pirate whaler, the *Sierra*, off the coast of Portugal.

That incident ended the career of the most notorious outlaw whaler. In February of 1980, we had the *Sierra* sunk in Lisbon harbor. A few months later, in April, our agents sank two outlaw Spanish registered whalers, the *Isba I* and the *Isba II*, in Vigo Harbor in northern Spain.

We then gave attention to two other Japanese pirate whalers, the *Susan* and the *Theresa*. Given the controversy of the *Sierra*, and the fact that the *Susan* and the *Theresa* were owned by the same Japanese interests, the South Africans, who had just publicly denounced whaling did not want the stigma of harboring illegal whaling ships. The South African Navy confiscated and sank the *Susan* and *Theresa* for target practice after we publicly appealed to them to do so, in 1980.

The last of the Atlantic pirate whalers, the *Astrid* was shut down after I sent an agent to the Spanish Canary Islands with a reward offer of $25,000 US to any person who would sink her. The owners saw the writing on the wall and voluntarily retired the whaler.

Because of these actions many have labeled us pirates ourselves. Yet we have never been convicted of a criminal charge nor have we ever caused injury or death to a human. Nor have we attempted to avoid charges. On the contrary, we have always invited our enemies to continue the fight, in the courts. Most times they have refused and the few times that they complied, they lost.

Vigilante buccaneers we may well be but we are policing the seas where no policing authority exists. We are protecting whales, dolphins, seals, birds, and fish by enforcing existing regulations, treaties and laws that heretofore have had no enforcement.

In November 1986, when two Sea Shepherd agents, Rod Coronado and David Howitt, attacked the Icelandic whaling industry, they were enforcing the law. The International Whaling Commission (IWC) had banned commercial whaling, yet Iceland continued to whale without a permit. We did not wish to debate the issue of legality with the Icelanders. We acted instead. Coronado and Howitt destroyed the whaling station and scuttled half the Icelandic whaling fleet.

Iceland refused to press charges. I traveled to Reykjavik to insist that they press charges. They refused and deported me without a hearing. The only legal case to result from the incident is my suit against Iceland for illegal deportation.

In March of 1983, the crew of the *Sea Shepherd II* were arrested under the Canadian Seal Protection Regulations, an Orwellian set of rules which actually protected the sealing industry. The only way to challenge these unjust rules was to break them. We did and at the same time we chased the sealing fleet out of the nursery grounds of the Harp Seals. We beat the charges and in the process helped the Supreme Court of Canada in its decision to dismiss the Seal Protection Act as unconstitutional.

In the years since, we have intervened against the Danish Faeroese fishermen in the North Atlantic to save the Pilot Whales they kill for sport. We have shut down seal hunts in Scotland, England and Ireland. We have confronted Central American tuna seiners off the coast of Costa Rica in an effort to rescue dolphins.

In 1987, we launched our first campaign to expose drift net operations in the North Pacific. Our ship the *Divine Wind* voyaged along the Aleutian chain documenting the damage of the drift nets and ghost nets (abandoned nets). We helped convince Canada to abandon plans to build a drift net industry.

For new supporters who do not know what drift nets are, I will briefly explain. Drift nets are to the Pacific Ocean what clear-cuts are to the Amazon Rainforest or the Pacific Northwest Temperate Rainforest. Drift netting is strip-mine fishing.

From May until late October, some 1800 ships each set a net measuring from 10 to 40 miles in length! These monofilament nylon gill nets drift freely upon the surface of the sea, hanging like curtains of death to a depth of 26 or 34 feet. Each night, the combined fleet sets between 28,000 and 35,000 miles of nets. The nets radiate across the breadth of the North Pacific like fences marking off property. The nets are efficient. Few squid and fish escape the perilous clutches of the nylon. Whales and dolphins, seals and sea lions, sea turtles, and sea birds are routinely entangled. The death is an agonizing ordeal of strangulation and suffocation.

Drift nets take an annual incidental kill of more than one million sea birds and a quarter of a million marine mammals each year, plus hundreds of millions of tons of fish and squid. A few short years ago, the North Pacific fairly teemed with dolphins, turtles, fur seals, sea lions, dozens of species of birds and uncountable schools of fish. Today it is a biological wasteland.

The Japanese say their nets are taking fewer incidental kills now than a few years ago. This is true, but the reason the kills are down is simply that there are now fewer animals to kill.

For many years, governments and environmental groups have talked about the problem. Nobody actually did anything about it. Sick of talk, the Sea Shepherd Conservation Society decided to take action.

The *Sea Shepherd II* moved to Seattle, Washington, in September 1989 to prepare for an expedition to intercept the Japanese North Pacific drift net fleet. We set our departure date for June 1990. Overhauls and refitting were completed by May to meet the targeted date.

We were unable to leave Seattle. One of our crew was a paid infiltrator working, we believe, for the Japanese fishing industry. He successfully sabotaged our engine by pouring crushed glass into our oil, destroying our turbo-charger, and destroying electrical motors. Although we discovered the damage and identified the saboteur, we faced extensive repairs.

The saboteur fled to Britain. We asked Scotland Yard to track him down and investigate the incident. However, the damage was done and we were hardly in a position to cry foul. After all, we had already been responsible for destroying six whaling ships ourselves. The enemy had succeeded in striking a blow—it was as simple as that. We were down, but not for long.

We immediately set to work to repair the damage. Thanks to an appeal to Sea Shepherd Society members, funds were raised to purchase a replacement turbocharger.

The *Sea Shepherd II* was prepared for departure again on August 5. We left Seattle and stopped briefly in Port Angeles on the Olympic Peninsula. Port Angeles resident and Sea Shepherd veteran David Howitt stopped by to visit us. He could not bring himself to leave. The ship departed with David on board. He had left his job and an understanding wife on the spur of the moment. We needed him and he knew it and that was reason enough to return to the eco-battles. He took the position of 1st Engineer.

It was with confidence that I took the helm of our ship and headed out the Strait of Juan de Fuca for the open Pacific beyond. I had a good crew, including many veterans.

Myra Finkelstein was 2nd Engineer. A graduate zoologist, Myra had worked for weeks in the bowels of the engine room to repair the damage to the engine. She was a veteran of the 1987 drift net campaign and the 1989 tuna dolphin campaign. In addition she had been a leader of the Friends of the Wolf campaign in northern British Columbia where she had parachuted into the frigid and remote wilderness to interfere with a government sponsored wolf kill.

Sea Shepherd Director Peter Brown was on board with the camera gear to document the voyage. Peter was also helmsman and my deputy coordinator for the expedition.

Marc Gaede, who had sailed with us a year ago on the campaign off the coast of Costa Rica, returned as our photographer. Trevor Van Der Gulik, my nephew, a lad of only 15 from Toronto, Canada, became—by virtue of his skills—our 3rd Engineer. Trevor had helped to deliver the *Sea Shepherd* from Holland to Florida in 1989.

Also sailing with us this summer was Robert Hunter. Bob and I had both been founders of Greenpeace and he had been the first President of the Greenpeace Foundation. Bob had been the dynamic force behind the organization and ultimate success of Greenpeace. Like myself, he had been forced out of Greenpeace by the marauding bureaucrats who in the late 1970s ousted the original activists and replaced us with fundraisers and public relations people.

With Bob on board, I felt a little of the old spirit which got us moving in the early 70s. We had no doubts: we would find the drift net fleets.

Five days out to sea, we saw a military ship on the horizon, moving rapidly toward us. We identified her as a large Soviet frigate. The frigate hailed us and asked us what we were about. I replied that we were searching for the Japanese drift net fleet and asked if they had seen any Japanese fishing vessels.

The Russians said they thought the Japanese were a few days to the west. Then, surprisingly, the Soviet officer, who spoke impeccable English, said, "Good luck, it is a noble cause that you follow. We are with you in spirit."

ECO-GLASNOST?

Only a few years ago we battled the Russian whalers. In 1975 Bob Hunter and I had survived a Russian harpoon fired over our heads by a Soviet whaler we had confronted. In 1981, we had invaded Siberia to capture evidence on illegal whaling by the Russians. We had narrowly escaped capture. Now, here we were being hailed by the Soviets with a statement of support. We have indeed made progress.

In fact, the Soviets were allies in more than just words. On 29 May 1990, the Russians had seized a fleet of North Korean fishing boats with drift nets in Soviet waters. Japan was diplomatically embarrassed when it was discovered that the 140 supposedly North Korean fishermen in Soviet custody were in fact Japanese.

On the eighth day out from Seattle, I put the *Sea Shepherd II* on a course of due west and decided not to correct the drift. I felt that the drift would take us to the outlaws. Slowly we began to drift north on the course line. Forty-eight hours later, my intuition proved itself right. The sea herself had taken us directly to a drift net fleet.

At 2030 Hours on August 12, we sailed into the midst of six Japanese drift netters. The fleet had just completed laying their nets—more than 200 miles of net in the water. The Japanese ships were each about 200 feet long, equal in size to our own.

As we approached, the Japanese fishermen warned us off, angrily telling us to avoid their nets. Our ship is a large 657 ton North Atlantic trawler with an ice strengthened bow and a fully enclosed protected prop. We were able to cruise harmlessly over the lines of floating nets. We made close runs on the vessels to inspect them closely.

With darkness rapidly closing in, we decided to wait until morning before taking action against the ships. The Japanese vessels had shut down for the night. They drifted quietly. We waited out the night with them.

An hour before dawn they began to move. We moved with them. For three hours, we filmed the hauling in of mile after mile of net from the vessel *Shunyo Maru #8*. We watched the catch of two-foot-long squids being hauled into the boat along with incidental kills of sharks, sea birds and dolphins. The catching of the sea birds violated the Convention for the Protection of Migratory Birds, a treaty signed between the US and Japan in March 1972. The nets impact more than 22 species of birds, 13 of which are protected by the treaty. It was to enforce this treaty that our ship and crew had made this voyage.

The fishing boats were brilliantly illuminated and the work on the deck could be adequately filmed. As the power blocks pulled in the nets, the bodies of squid, fish and birds fell from the nets to the deck or back into the sea.

We had the evidence we needed. We had seen the bodies of protected species in the net. For the next step we needed more light. It was painful to continue watching but it was imperative that we wait for dawn and the light we needed to properly film events.

At 0540 Hours, there was enough light. We prepared the deck and the engine room for confrontation. We positioned our cameramen and photographers. I took the wheel. We brought the engine up to full power and charged across the swells toward the *Shunyo Maru #8* whose crew were still hauling in nets. Our objective was to destroy the net retrieval gear. To do so, we had to hit her on an angle on her port mid-side.

We sounded a blast on our horn to warn the Japanese crew that we were coming in. I piloted the *Sea Shepherd II* into position. We struck where intended. The ships ground their hulls together in a fountain of sparks amidst a screeching cacophony of tearing and crushing steel. The net was severed, the power blocks smashed. We broke away as the Japanese stood dumbfounded on their decks.

One fisherman, however, hurtled his knife at photographer Marc Gaede. The knife missed Marc and hit the sea. The same fisherman grabbed a second knife and sent it flying at cameraman Peter Brown. Peter's camera followed it as it came toward the lens. It fell at Peter's feet.

As we pulled away, I looked with satisfaction on the damage we had inflicted. One ship down for the season. On board our own ship, a damage control party reported back that we had suffered minimal injury. The Japanese ships were no match for our ice-strengthened steel reinforced hull.

We immediately targeted a second ship, the *Ryoun Maru #6*. The Japanese were attempting to cut a large shark out of the net. Looking up, they saw us bearing down at full speed upon them. Eyes wide, they ran toward the far deck.

We struck where intended. Again to the roaring crescendo of tortured metal, the power blocks and gear were crushed; the deck and gunnels buckled. The net was severed.

We broke off and immediately set out for the third ship. By now, the Japanese realized what was happening. The first and second ships had been successfully Pearl Harbored. The third was not to be surprised. As we approached, she dropped her net and fled. We pursued.

We then turned and targeted a fourth ship. She also fled, dropping her net in panic. We stopped and pulled up alongside the radio beacon marking the abandoned net. We confiscated the beacon. We then grappled the net, secured a ton of weight to one end and dropped it, sending the killer net to the bottom, two miles beneath us. We watched the cork line drop beneath the surface, the floats disappearing in lines radiating out from our ship toward the horizon.

On the bottom the net would be rendered harmless. Small benthic creatures would literally cement it to the ocean floor over a short period of time.

We cleaned up the remaining nets and then returned to the chase. For the next twenty hours, we chased the six ships completely out of the fishing area.

The next morning, we could look at what we had achieved with pleasure. Two ships completely disabled from further fishing, a million dollars' worth of net sunk and destroyed and all six ships prevented from continued fishing and running scared.

We had delivered our message to the Japanese fishing industry. Our tactics had been both effective and educational. Effective in that we directly saved lives by shutting down a fleet, and educational in that we informed the Japanese fishing industry that their greed will no longer be tolerated.

Our ship was only slightly damaged. Most importantly, there were no injuries on any of the ships involved.

I turned the bow of our ship southward to Honolulu to deliver the documentation to the media and to begin again the tedious task of fundraising which will allow us to mount further attacks against these mindless thugs slaughtering our oceans.

As we headed south, we stopped repeatedly to retrieve drifting remnants of nets. In one we found 54 rotting fish. In another a large dead mahi-mahi. In another a dead albatross. These "ghost nets" present an additional problem for life in the sea. Each day the large fleets lose an average of six miles of net. At present an estimated 10,000 plus miles of ghost nets are floating the seas. These non-biodegradable nets kill millions of fish and sea creatures each year. Decaying fish attract more fish and birds . . . a vicious cycle of death and waste.

Arriving in Honolulu, we berthed at pier eleven ironically just in front of two fishery patrol vessels, one from Japan, the other from Taiwan. The crew of each scowled at us.

We were prepared for the Japanese to attempt to lay charges against us or failing that to publicly denounce us. Instead, they refused to even recognize that an incident took place.

We contacted the Japanese Consulate and declared that we had attacked their ships and had destroyed Japanese property. We informed the Consulate that we were ready to contest charges, be they in the International Court at the Hague or in Tokyo itself. The Consulate told us he had no idea of what we were talking about.

The Japanese realize they have nothing to gain by taking us to court and much to lose. Which means that we must return to the oceans and must escalate the battle.

The Taiwanese drift netters are beginning to move into the Caribbean Sea. We must head them off. We must continue to confront the Japanese fleets, and we must take on the Koreans. Each net we sink will cost the industry a million dollars. Each vessel we damage will buy time for the sea animals. Each confrontation we mount will embarrass the drift net industry. This summer, we won a battle. However, the war to end high seas drift netting continues.

The Japanese, Taiwanese, and Korean drift net fleets can be driven from the oceans. We need only the will, the courage, and the financial support to do so.

J. BAIRD CALLICOTT

ENVIRONMENTAL PHILOSOPHY IS ENVIRONMENTAL ACTIVISM
The Most Radical and Effective Kind

Here is one picture of philosophy. It goes on in an ivory tower pursued by cloistered academics who endlessly dispute the contemporary equivalents of questions like "how many angels can dance on the head of a pin?" It is far removed from the "real world," even when philosophers spin theories about what is "real." (In the real world, everyone knows what's real, without needing philosophers to inform or misinform them.) Here is another picture of philosophy. Socrates is hauled into court and sentenced to death—not for anything he might have done, such as sell state secrets to the Lacedaimonians or assassinate Kleon—but for questioning religious ideas and moral ideals, thus bringing about the precipitous transformation of Athenian society. In the first picture, philosophy seems socially irrelevant. In the second, it seems to be the most potent force of social change imaginable.

There does seem to be a lot of ivory tower philosophy—a kind of new scholasticism—going on today in academe. But only future historians will be in a position to judge whether it will prove to have actually been socially transformative. But let's grant, for the sake of argument, that the test of time will prove that what seems to be irrelevant ivory tower philosophy is indeed just that. The post-sixties "applied" movement in late twentieth-century philosophy has been an attempt, on the part of many academic philosophers, to descend from the ivory tower and directly engage real-world issues. The advent of business ethics, biomedical ethics, animal welfare ethics, engineering ethics, and environmental ethics illustrates two points. First, that many young academic philosophers then believed that business-as-usual analytic philosophy, phenomenology, philosophy of science, and the like are, as many nonphilosophers suspect, socially irrelevant; and second, that an attempt was deliberately made to reorient philosophy so as to apply its rich heritage of theory and powerful methods of argument to illuminate and help solve real-world problems.

The "pure" philosophers, as if to confirm the suspicion that their preoccupations are ivory tower

J. Baird Callicott. 1995. Environmental Philosophy Is Environmental Activism: The Most Radical and Effective Kind. Environmental Philosophy and Environmental Activism. Edited by D. Marieta and L. Embree. Lanham, MD: Rowman & Littlefield. Pages 19–35. Reprinted with permission of the publisher.

irrelevancies, have responded with contempt. Applied philosophy is scorned as not "real"' (that is, genuine) philosophy and as merely yeoman's (and yeowoman's) work, appropriating the creative ideas of the true, the pure, the real philosophers and mechanically applying them to current social "issues." Applied work is perhaps suitable for academic philosophers toiling in bush-league undergraduate departments, but not for those holding prestigious chairs in major-league research departments.

Since environmental philosophy came into being in such circumstance—in deliberate reaction to what was perceived as the reigning neoscholasticism and in a deliberate attempt to help society deal with real-world problems—it is surprising to find some people now suggesting that environmental philosophy is itself an ivory tower preoccupation of little practical moment. Though the people I have in mind occupy positions in philosophy departments and publish papers in philosophy journals, I hesitate to call them philosophers, since they seem to think that philosophy, even environmental philosophy, is worse than an irrelevancy, it's a subterfuge.

One such environmental antiphilosopher is Kenneth Sayre. He writes,

> In no case does the reasoning of an ethical theorist actually cause a norm to be socially instituted or cause a norm once in force to lose that status. Whether a moral norm is actually in effect within a given community depends not at all on ethical theorizing. . . . If norms encouraging conservation and proscribing pollution were actually in force in industrial society, it would not be the result of ethical theory; and the fact that currently they are not in force is not alleviated by any amount of adroit ethical reasoning.[1]

Sayre's understanding of ethical theory is very narrow and formal. No doubt there is a kernel of truth in his claim, if by "ethical theory" we refer to some arid inferential exercise in which a philosopher deduces that (4) action X should be proscribed, since (3) X is wrong, because (2) X has the property A and (1) all actions that have A are wrong. The alternatives to ethical theorizing, so conceived, that Sayre suggests would seem to dissolve environmental ethics into various social sciences, much as sociobiology would

absorb the social sciences into biology. "Environmental ethics," he writes, "should join forces with anthropology, economics, and other areas of social science in hopes of generating a basis for empirical information about how moral norms actually operate."[2]

For Sayre "moral norms" seem just to exist in splendid isolation from the larger cognitive culture. Sayre's example of a norm that is socially "in place" is honesty. An example of an environmental ethical norm that is not in place is recycling. Sayre seems to think that eventually people may just up and adopt the recycling norm, and a new breed of environmental ethicists transformed into sociologists, social psychologists, and economists can empirically describe the mysterious process by which such a norm shift will have occurred, if it does. Or empirically examining how new norms, such as antislavery, came to be adopted in the recent past, environmental ethicists can help socially engineer new environmental norms, such as recycling, in the near future. One thing Sayre is sure of is that no amount of theorizing is going to induce most people to believe that recycling is simply the right thing to do in the same way that most people believe that honesty is simply the best policy.

Doubtless he is right if environmental ethical theory conforms to Sayre's caricature. But such formal reasoning is not what actually goes on in theoretical environmental philosophy. Environmental philosophers, rather, are attempting to articulate a new worldview and a new conception of what it means to be a human being, distilled from the theory of evolution, the new physics, ecology, and other natural sciences. On this basis, we might suggest how people ought to relate to the natural environment, but there is rather little deducing of specific rules of conduct. People come to believe that old norms (such as stone adulterers and burn witches) should be abandoned, and new ones adopted (such as abolish slavery and feed the hungry) only when their most fundamental ideas about themselves and their world undergo radical change. Much of the theoretical work in environmental ethics is devoted to articulating and thus helping to effect such a radical change in outlook. The specific ethical norms of environmental conduct remain for the most part only implicit—a project postponed to the future or something left for ecologically informed people to work out for themselves.

Bryan Norton, another environmental antiphilosopher, thinks that theoretical environmental ethics is not only an irrelevant subterfuge, but that it is also downright pernicious. Environmental ethicists arguing with one another about whether nature has intrinsic as well as instrumental value and about whether intrinsic value is objective or subjective divide environmentalists into deep and shallow camps. While these two camps spend precious time and energy criticizing one another, their common enemy, the hydra-headed forces of environmental destruction, remains unopposed by a united and resolute counterforce. But according to Norton a long and wide anthropocentrism "converges" on the same environmental policies—the preservation of biological diversity, for example—as nonanthropocentrism. Hence the intellectual differences between anthropocentrists and nonanthropocentrists, deep ecologists and reform environmentalists are, practically speaking, otiose. Environmental philosophers, in Norton's view, should therefore cease spinning nonanthropocentric theories of the intrinsic value of nature and, as Norton himself does, concentrate instead on refining environmental policy. Norton opts for anthropocentrism because it is the more conservative alternative. Most people are anthropocentrists to begin with, and when the instrumental value of a whole and healthy environment to both present and future generations of humans is fully accounted, anthropocentrism, he believes, is sufficient to support the environmental policy agenda.[3]

Norton's "convergence hypothesis," however, is dead wrong. If all environmental values are anthropocentric and instrumental, then they have to compete head-to-head with the economic values derived from converting rain forests to lumber and pulp, savannahs to cattle pasture, and so on. Environmentalists, in other words, must show that preserving biological diversity is of greater instrumental value to present and future generations than lucrative timber extraction, agricultural conversion, hydroelectric empoundment, mining, and so on. For this simple reason, a persuasive philosophical case for the intrinsic value of nonhuman natural entities and nature as a whole would make a huge practical difference. Warwick Fox

explains why. Granting an entity intrinsic value would not imply "that it cannot be interfered with *under any circumstances*."[4] Believing, as we do, that human beings are intrinsically valuable does not imply that human beings ought never be uprooted, imprisoned, put at grave risk, or even deliberately killed. Intrinsically valuable human beings may—ethically may—be made to suffer these and other insults with sufficient justification. Therefore, Fox points out,

> the mere fact that moral agents must be able to justify their actions in regard to their treatment of entities that are intrinsically valuable means that recognizing the intrinsic value of the nonhuman world has a dramatic effect upon the framework of environmental debate and decision-making. If the nonhuman world is only considered to be instrumentally valuable then people are permitted to use and otherwise interfere with any aspect of it for whatever reasons they wish (i.e., no justification is required). If anyone objects to such interference then, within this framework of reference, the onus is clearly on the person who objects to justify why it is more useful to humans to leave that aspect of the nonhuman world alone. If, however, the nonhuman world is considered to be intrinsically valuable then the onus shifts to the person who wants to interfere with it to justify why they should be allowed to do so: anyone who wants to interfere with any entity that is intrinsically valuable is morally obliged to be able to offer a sufficient justification for their actions. Thus recognizing the intrinsic value of the nonhuman world shifts the onus of justification from the person who wants to protect the nonhuman world to the person who wants to interfere with it—and that, in itself, represents a fundamental shift in the terms of environmental debate and decision-making.[5]

Just as Sayre seems to think of moral norms as hanging alone in an intellectual void, so Norton seems to think of environmental policies in the same way. We environmentalists just happen to have a policy agenda—saving endangered species, preserving biodiversity in all its forms, lowering CO_2 emissions, etc. To rationalize these policies—to sell them to the electorate and their representatives—is the intellectual task, if there is any. (Much of Norton's research for his book, *Unity Among Environmentalists*, consisted of interviewing the Washington based lobbyists for "big ten" environmental groups. Such cynicism may be characteristic of lobbyists who are hired to pitch a policy, but starting with a policy and looking for persuasive reasons to support it is not how sincere environmentalists outside the Beltway actually think.) People just don't adopt a policy like they decide which color is their favorite. They adopt it for what seems to them to be good reasons. Reasons come first, policies second, not the other way around.

Most people, of course, do not turn to philosophers for something to believe—as if they didn't at all know what to think and philosophers can and should tell them. Rather, philosophers such as Thoreau, Muir, Leopold, and Rolston give voice to the otherwise inchoate and articulate thoughts and feelings in our changing cultural Zeitgeist. A maximally stretched anthropocentrism may, as Norton argues, rationalize the environmental policy agenda, but anthropocentrism may no longer ring true. That is, the claim that all and only human beings have intrinsic value may not be consistent with a more general evolutionary and ecological worldview. I should think that contemporary environmental philosophers would want to give voice and form to the still small but growing movement that supports environmental policies for the right reasons—which, as Fox points out, also happen to be the strongest reasons.

Granted, we may not have the leisure to wait for a majority to come over to a new worldview and a new nonanthropocentric, holistic environmental ethic. We environmentalists have to reach people where they are, intellectually speaking, right now. So we might persuade Jews, Christians, and Muslims to support the environmental policy agenda by appeal to such concepts as God, creation, and stewardship; we might persuade humanists by appeal to collective enlightened human self-interest; and so on. But that is no argument for insisting, as Norton seems to do, that environmental philosophers should stop exploring the real reasons why we ought to value other forms of life, ecosystems, and the biosphere as a whole.

The eventual institutionalization of a new holistic, nonanthropocentric environmental ethic will make as much practical difference in the environmental arena as the institutionalization of the intrinsic value of all human beings has made in the social arena. As recently as a century and a half ago, it was permissible to own human beings. With the eventual institutionalization of Enlightenment ethics—persuasively articulated by Hobbes, Locke, Bentham, and Kant, among others—slavery was abolished in Western civilization. Of course, a case could have been made to slaveowners and an indifferent public that slavery was economically backward and more trouble than it was worth. But that would not have gotten at the powerful moral truth that for one human being to own another is wrong. With the eventual institutionalization of a holistic, nonanthropocentric environmental ethic—today persuasively articulated by Aldo Leopold, Arne Naess, Holmes Rolston, and Val Plumwood, among others—the wanton destruction of the nonhuman world will, hopefully, come to be regarded as equally unconscionable.

. . .

In my opinion, the seminal paper in environmental ethics is "The Historical Roots of Our Ecologic Crisis" by Lynn White Jr. His brassy and cavalier critique of Christianity as the ultimate cause of our contemporary environmental malaise overshadows a more general (and more credible) subtext in that essay. Four or five times he reiterates the claim that what we do depends upon what we think and thus that if we are to effect any lasting changes in behavior, we must first effect fundamental changes in our worldview: "What shall we do?" he asks, about our environmental crisis. "No one yet knows. Unless we think about fundamentals, our specific measures may produce new backlashes more serious than those they are designed to remedy."[6] Is he right about this? Sure. For example, the Green Revolution and Eucalyptus afforestation programs, couched in the modern industrial paradigm, have proved to be socially and environmentally disastrous in recipient countries.[7] Certainly they created "new backlashes more serious than those they were designed to remedy." In the next paragraph, White adds, "The issue is whether a democratized world can survive its own implications. Presumably we cannot unless we rethink our axioms."[8]

Toward the middle of his infamous essay, White returns to this subtext:

What people do about their ecology [that is, how people treat their natural environments] depends on what they think about themselves in relation to things around them. Human ecology is deeply conditioned by beliefs about our nature and destiny—that is, by religion. To Western eyes this is very evident in, say, India or Ceylon [that is, Sri Lanka]. It is equally true of ourselves and of our medieval ancestors.[9]

And in his peroration White writes, "What we do about ecology [that is, what we do about environmental problems] depends on our ideas of the man–nature relationship. More science and more technology are not going to get us out of the present ecologic crisis until we find a new religion or rethink our old one."[10]

White, of course, rejects the first alternative, finding a new religion, and opts for the second, rethinking our old ones, Judaism, Christianity, and Islam. Finally, in his penultimate sentence, he writes, "We must rethink and refeel our nature and destiny."[11]

The agenda for a future environmental philosophy thus was set. First, we identify and criticize our inherited beliefs about the nature of nature, human nature, and the relationship between the two. White himself initiated this stage with a critique of those most evident biblical ideas of nature, "man," and the man–nature relationship. Other environmental philosophers, I among them, went on to identify and criticize the more insidious intellectual legacy of Western natural and moral philosophy going back to the Greeks. Second, we try to articulate a new natural philosophy and moral philosophy distilled from contemporary science. We try, in other words, to articulate an evolutionary–ecological worldview and an associated environmental ethic.

This two-phase program of environmental philosophy has been gaining momentum for the past two decades. In that amount of time—which is really not very much time to bring off a cultural revolution comparable to the shift from the medieval to the modern world—how effective has environmental philosophy been? In so short a time, the rethinking of our old religion that White called for is virtually a fait accompli. The stewardship interpretation of the God–"man"–nature relationship set out in Genesis is now semiofficial religious doctrine among "people of the Book"—Jews, Catholics, Protestants, even Muslims. Such an interpretation and its dissemination would

not have come about, or at least it would not have come about so soon, had White's despotic interpretation not provoked it. The currently institutionalized Judeo-Christian–Islamic stewardship environmental ethic was a dialectical reaction to White's critique. It has now trickled down into the synagogues and churches, and may be on its way into the mosques. Children learning about God's creation and our responsibility to care for it and pass it on intact to future generations may never hear White's name, or the names of John Black, James Barr, Robert Gordis, Jonathan Helfand, Francis Schaeffer, Albert Fritsch, Thomas Berry, Wendell Berry, Matthew Fox, Iqtidar Zaidi, and the other Jewish, Christian, and Islamic theologians whom White provoked, but what they are being taught—and as a result of that teaching how in the future they may try to be good stewards of God's creation—owes a lot to Lynn White and those whom he challenged to reconceive Judeo-Christian–Islamic attitudes and values toward nature.

But if you think I'm impossibly biased—a philosopher affirming the power of ideas and defending the practical efficacy of philosophy—then perhaps you can trust Dave Foreman, environmental activist extraordinaire, to provide a candid assessment of the role that environmental philosophy has played in shaping the contemporary environmental movement. Remember that it was Foreman who wrote, "Let our actions set the finer points of our philosophy."[12] And in a 1983 debate with Eugene C. Hargrove about the wisdom of monkey-wrenching, it was Foreman who dismissed environmental philosophers in the following terms: "Too often, philosophers are rendered impotent by their inability to act without analyzing everything to absurd detail. To act, to trust your instincts, to go with the flow of natural forces, is an underlying philosophy. Talk is cheap. Action is dear."[13]

Eight years later, Foreman changed his tune. In "The New Conservation Movement," Foreman identified four forces that are shaping the conservation movement of the 1990s. They are, and I quote, first "academic philosophy," second, "conservation biology," third, "independent local groups," and fourth, "Earth First! " That's right, "academic philosophy" heads the list. This is some of what Foreman has to say about it:

During the 1970s, philosophy professors in Europe, North America, and Australia started looking at environmental ethics as a worthy focus for discussion and exploration.... By 1980, enough interest had coalesced for an academic journal called *Environmental Ethics* to appear.... An international network of specialists in environmental ethics developed, leading to one of the more vigorous debates in modern philosophy. At first, little of this big blow in the ivory towers drew the notice of working conservationists, but by the end of the '80s, few conservation group staff members or volunteer activists were unaware of the Deep Ecology–Shallow Environmentalism distinction or of the general discussion about ethics and ecology. At the heart of the discussion was the question of whether other species possessed intrinsic value or had value solely because of their use to humans. Ginger Rogers to this Fred Astaire was the question what, if any, ethical obligations humans had to nature or other species.[14]

And part of the way that Earth First!—last but not least on Foreman's list—helped to shape the new conservation movement was by bringing "the discussion of biocentric philosophy—Deep Ecology—out of dusty academic journals."[15]

Clearly Foreman understands the power of ideas. Of course, we philosophers do not simply create new environmental ideas and ideals ex nihilo. Rather, we try to articulate and refine those that the intellectual dialectic of the culture has ripened. To employ a Socratic metaphor, we philosophers are the midwives assisting the birth of new cultural notions and associated norms. In so doing we help to change our culture's worldview and ethos. Therefore, since all human actions are carried out and find their meaning and significance in a cultural ambience of ideas, we speculative environmental philosophers are inescapably environmental activists.

All environmentalists should be activists, but activism can take a variety of forms. The way that environmental philosophers can be the most effective environmental activists is by doing environmental philosophy. Of course, not everyone can be or wants or needs to be an environmental philosopher. Those who are not can undertake direct environmental action in other ways. My point is that environmental philosophers should not feel compelled to stop thinking, talking, and writing about environmental ethics, and go do something about it instead—because talk is cheap and action is dear. In thinking, talking, and writing about environmental ethics, environmental philosophers already have their shoulders to the wheel, helping to reconfigure the prevailing cultural worldview and thus helping to push general practice in the direction of environmental responsibility.

NOTES

1. Kenneth M. Sayre, "An Alternative View of Environmental Ethics," *Environmental Ethics* 13 (1991): 200.
2. Sayre, "An Alternative View of Environmental Ethics," 195.
3. Bryan Norton, *Toward Unity Among Environmentalists* (New York: Oxford University Press, 1991).
4. Warwick Fox, "New Philosophical Directions in Environmental Decision-Making," unpublished manuscript, 18, emphasis added.
5. Fox, "New Philosophical Directions in Environmental Decision-Making," 18–19, emphasis in original.
6. Lynn White Jr., "The Historical Roots of Our Ecologic Crisis," in *Ecology and Religion in History*, ed. David Spring and Eileen Spring (New York: Harper Torchbooks, 1974), 18, emphasis added. See White's essay in this volume.
7. See Ramachandra Guha, *The Unquiet Woods: Ecological Change and Peasant Resistance in the Himalaya* (Berkeley: University of California Press, 1990) and Vandana Shiva, *The Violence of the Green Revolution: Third World Agriculture, Ecology, and Politics* (London: Zed Books, 1991).
8. White, "The Historical Roots," 19.
9. White, "The Historical Roots," 23.
10. White, "The Historical Roots," 28.
11. White, "The Historical Roots," 31.
12. Dave Foreman, "More on Earth First! and the Monkey Wrench Gang," *Environmental Ethics* 5 (1993): 95.
13. Foreman, "More on Earth First!", 95.
14. Dave Foreman, "The New Conservation Movement," *Wild Earth* 1 (Summer 1991): 8.
15. Foreman, "The New Conservation Movement," p. 10.

KATE RAWLES

THE MISSING SHADE OF GREEN

According to *The Collins Paperback English Dictionary*, an activist is someone who takes direct action to achieve a political or social goal. Philosophy, on the other hand, "is the academic discipline concerned with making explicit the nature and significance of beliefs, and investigating the intelligibility of concepts by means of rational arguments." These definitions coincide rather neatly with those offered by many from outside academia (and some from inside)—the consensus here being that while activists get on and do something, philosophers just think. In this paper, I am particularly concerned with activists who get on and do something about animals or the environment and philosophers who take these as the focus of their thoughts. I suppose paradigmatic, if slightly caricatured, cases might be Paul Watson and the crew of *Sea Shepherd* releasing dolphins from drift nets and a philosopher in an office thinking about the concept of nature.

There is, of course, something not quite right about a straight contrast between thinking and doing. Thinking is doing; it is, in some sense, an activity. Here, the kind of activity to be contrasted with thinking is the kind that has, and intends to have, a direct effect on the world. But deciding what will qualify as a desirable effect clearly requires some thought. "She acted blindly" presumably means she acted without thinking, and blind or mindless action isn't what we are after when we talk of activism. So thinkers and activists will not be cleanly separated.

Nevertheless, a person could be described as an environmental philosopher without having any intentions to "save the world." And Paul Watson does not have a philosophy degree—and seems to get along pretty well without it. So one question concerns the extent to which philosophical thought does, or can,

bear constructively upon activism. In the early part of this paper I want to explore the suggestion that philosophy can contribute to activism (1) by motivating it, in the sense of encouraging people to take action on various issues; (2) by guiding it, in the sense of helping to ensure that the actions taken are thoughtful or skillful ones; (3) by offering reasoned and systematic justification for action and hence helping to legitimize it.

Presumably we are interested in activism because we want to see changes made or prevented from occurring in the world. So a broader question might be that of the extent to which philosophy does or can contribute to such change, whether directly through activism or indirectly, by other means. I will consider two suggestions: first, that philosophy can contribute to constructive change by facilitating dialogue between opposing sides; second that philosophy may help by changing people's perceptions of the world.

I start, then, by singing philosophy's praises, albeit tentatively. In the second part of the paper I will exercise various reservations about the usefulness of philosophy in this context. For example, I suggest that it may paralyze action rather than galvanize it, and that its potential efficacy is limited when set in an academic context.

PHILOSOPHY AND ACTIVISM

In this paper, I take various things for granted. First, that species extinction, climate change, pollution, widespread hunger, persecution of humans and nonhumans, and many other things are really happening. Second, that it would be better if they were not. Third, that activism which contributes to constructive change (which may of course sometimes mean conservation) is important and valuable. Any of these claims taken singularly might be disputed. For example, there is

Kate Rawles. 1995. The Missing Shade of Green. In Environmental Philosophy and Environmental Activism. Edited by D. Marieta and L. Embree. Lanham, MD: Rowman & Littlefield. Pages 149–167. Reprinted with permission of the publisher.

much well-known contention about whether global warming is a genuine threat, and not everyone will agree with my position vis-à-vis the treatment of animals. But what concerns me here is the general claim that, on the environmental front, things could be better. This does not seem particularly contentious.

Perhaps I should also say that I am a philosopher, in the sense that I teach and study philosophy, and also in the sense that it is a subject I am attached to for reasons other than its potential effect upon the world's environmental problems. But if I had to prioritize my concerns, then trying to contribute something to the resolution of these problems would come first. A question which runs throughout this paper, then, is whether working as a philosopher in an academic department is really a viable way of helping to change things out there in the world. This question is for me a vivid and often troublesome one.

DOES PHILOSOPHY MOTIVATE ACTIVISM?

Can philosophy prompt people to take action on particular issues? (I'm not talking about the whole of philosophy. It would be a strange thesis that mathematical logic led to environmental activism.) My own interest in environmental issues developed out of an involvement with animal rights issues and this was initially sparked off by a philosophy book, Peter Singer's *Animal Liberation*.[1] Here, then, is an initial suggestion; philosophers write books and articles and (sometimes!) people read them. Philosophers also take courses. If Singer's lectures are as powerful as his book I would guess that many of his students have changed their eating habits.

An objection to this might be that it is not the philosophy in Singer's book that motivates action as much as the facts. In addition to the famous argument condemning speciesism, *Animal Liberation* contains several chapters that give vivid information about intensive agriculture, slaughterhouses, and the less salubrious aspects of medical research. The facts are in many cases so horrific that they seem to make any argument redundant. Surely in this kind of context, just knowing what goes on is sufficient to lead to the judgment that it is wrong, and that it should stop. To claim that it is philosophy which is motivating activism here is to give philosophy credit where it is not due.

In my own case I do not think I can say to what extent I was swayed specifically by the argument against speciesism and to what extent by the information. I certainly found the information very distressing, and I also felt very angry that until then I had no idea that the animals I ate lived such unnecessarily miserable lives. This lack of knowledge resulted in my being a party to something I deeply objected to. Moreover, it turned out that this was just the beginning of the trail. I did not know about all sorts of practices that I certainly did not wish to condone once I did know about them. I now think that this was not (just) ignorance on my part; rather that what might be called the Western lifestyle has implications for other animals, other people, and the environment that are often both very negative and well concealed. If this is correct, then the sort of information deficit I uncovered will be pretty common, and giving people access to this information will be an important task.

An objection here might be that I am not on the payroll as a philosopher in order to act as a consciousness raiser! Well, yes and no. It is hard to discuss ethical issues in our treatment of animals without knowing what this treatment is. Similar points can obviously be made in the context of environmental or developmental issues. Raising awareness of environmental problems may not be the primary goal of, say, an applied ethics course, but it may well be a welcome and inevitable side effect. To return to the argument, we might agree that the facts are powerful but add that the arguments are embedded in the facts. It seems rather unjust to say that it was not really the philosophy in the philosophy book that influenced me.

The suggestion that facts alone will motivate action, that we only need the information about intensive farming or environmental degradation to be convinced that it ought to be stopped, can in any case be challenged. The facts "by themselves" will sometimes motivate, but often they will not. A suggested explanation of this might amount to a stronger claim, namely, that we don't really have "facts by themselves" nor are we motivated by such things. Rather, it might be said that we receive—and select—information through a filter of beliefs, values, and assumptions that we may or may not be aware of, and that will affect how we respond to the information in question. A simplified example: learning about environmental degradation will not trouble me if I believe that the environment is only important insofar as humans need it, and I am reassured that this degradation does not constitute a threat to something which humans need.

What philosophy can do in this context is, of course, to draw attention to these values and assumptions and subject them to a critical scrutiny. This might lead to activism first by viewing the facts in a new way and, second, by leading to a change in values.

Identifying beliefs and assumptions, and starting to look at them critically, can create a space between those beliefs and the person who holds them; it can lift the assumptions off the person so that the facts can sneak in underneath. Whatever, in the end, is made of the argument against speciesism, just thinking about it can startle someone away from the "oh, it's just a chicken" response for long enough to let information about intensive farming appear in a new light. I witnessed a particularly striking example of this taking place in a student of Professor Bernie Rollins at Colorado State who, after debating the moral status of animals in Bernie's philosophy class, went, on his own initiative, to all the local slaughterhouses. As a result of this, he became a vegetarian and campaigned for better conditions for the animals still being eaten by others. What makes this a particularly striking case is that Geoff was a cowboy from a ranching community. The attitude toward animals he had been brought up with was extremely different from the one he eventually endorsed. It might be added that very many people in Europe and North America are brought up with the belief that nonhuman animals are vastly inferior to human ones and that the environment is essentially a resource for people. So this may be a particularly vivid example but it will not necessarily be a particularly unusual one.

It might be said, then, that philosophy can open the way for the facts to get in, and that this may prompt action. But I also suggested that it may be misleading to talk about facts motivating single-handedly. It was a suspension of his society—inherited beliefs and attitudes about animals that prompted Geoff to discover for himself what happens at slaughterhouses and this suspension also allowed the information to really hit home. But presumably this would not have developed

into a systematic and long-term campaign unless his original beliefs about the moral status of animals had also changed.

But to what extent can philosophical thought lead to a change in values and moral beliefs? As a philosopher, am I entitled to throw my weight behind one set of moral beliefs rather than another? Clearly, there is a great deal that could be said on this topic alone. Here I will do no more than sketch the beginnings of a response.

I take it that we are thoroughly imbued with values and attitudes and that many of these come from our background in various ways. We are influenced in this respect by our parents, school, religion, and society in a broader sense. I take it that the sort of independence of thought or integrity that results from identifying and examining these values and assumptions is something of value in its own right, and that philosophy, insofar as it leaves people better able to decide for themselves what to think, is a liberating discipline, which enhances people's autonomy. But what is the relationship between this and environmental activism? Is there any guarantee or even likelihood that critical reflection will lead to the endorsement of "green" values, say, rather than some other set? No doubt if we are brainwashed it is not in a green direction. So removing the brainwashing is a start. But does philosophy have the means to take us further than this?

The suggestion is that it is the role of philosophy to present the correct facts—"thick" facts—and that this will lead to specific values and appropriate action is one I will take up in the next section. First, I want to consider the objection that as a philosopher one's function is not to take sides, but simply to encourage critical debate by laying out the arguments. In *Moral Literacy* Colin McGinn writes, "If you finish this book with a totally opposite set of beliefs to mine, but with an enhanced capacity to articulate and justify your moral position, I will be happy."[2] So do I have to be happy when a slave-owning, mahogany-exporting chicken farmer emerges from my course on environmental ethics better able to justify her position?

I do not think so. The claim that I do rests on the supposition that all moral positions can be equally well justified. But my position on intensive chicken farming includes the conviction that the arguments against it are stronger than the arguments for it. So the student who concludes that it is acceptable either has a different idea about the relative strength of the arguments and ought to be able to persuade me of it—or she has missed something. What arguments deserve from philosophers is impartial rather than equal treatment. The conclusion of the argument should not automatically influence my assessment of it but I am not expected to consider all arguments to be equally valid. Hence, I am not expected to consider all conclusions to be equally correct. Indeed, McGinn himself hints at this in his book's subtitle—*How to Do the Right Thing*—that rather suggests the view that there is a right thing and that thinking clearly can put you in touch with it.

As a philosopher, then, it seems that I am at least entitled to indicate where I think the stronger arguments lead. Of course, this leaves open the question of whether careful and critical reflection has any tendency to lead to environmentally friendly conclusions. It may turn out that the stronger arguments lead to Thatcherite materialism. I believe that this is unlikely, but have to admit that I would be hard pressed to offer good grounds for this conviction.

PHILOSOPHY AS LEGITIMIZING ACTIVISM

I have suggested that philosophy may prompt people to take action on various issues by raising awareness of these issues, by encouraging people to take a critical look at their beliefs and values, and by offering support for sets of values which will have implications for action and ways of living. The next question I want to raise is that of whether and how philosophical skills are of value to those who are already activists.

One suggestion is that the ability to offer reasoned and systematic justification for any particular action can help to legitimize it in the eyes of other people. For example, to return to Paul Watson, a recent documentary showed pictures of whales being harpooned and gutted on boat decks awash with blood. It then showed Watson and the *Sea Shepherd* sabotaging whaling ships. The viewers' inevitable sympathies for the saboteurs were abruptly suspended by the suggestion that for Watson to tell the Norwegian people they ought not to kill whales, because of their intelligence and rarity, is comparable to an Asian Indian enjoining

North Americans not to kill cows in virtue of their status as sacred animals.[3] The program did not offer Watson's response. But a convincing response was clearly called for, and this would have involved a careful analysis of the claims showing, perhaps, why the analogy is not a good one. The point is obvious: activists are often called upon to justify their actions, and to do this convincingly presumably requires a certain amount of philosophical skill.

This particular issue has recently acquired an even more complex twist to it. "Sustainable development," this year's apple-pie and motherhood buzzword for all things undeniably good, has been invoked on the side of the whalers, against environmentalists, by none other than Gro Harlem Brundtland.[4] To unravel this issue, Paul Watson may need a philosophy degree after all.

PHILOSOPHY AS GUIDING ACTIVISM

Clearly, activists need to think about what they are doing, and why. This is not just so that they can offer reasoned and convincing defenses of their actions if challenged—but also because mindless or confused activism can be useless or even harmful. In this context, philosophy may be able to guide activism by helping to ensure that actions taken are thoughtful or skillful ones, and by helping to define the problem and what might count as a solution to it. Indeed, it is hard to see how constructive activism is possible without some thought about what counts as change for the better—and this sort of thought is philosophical. The point might be illustrated by a cartoon I once saw on a notice-board at the Glasgow vet school—which showed a member of the Animal Liberation Front exclaiming "don't worry, mate, we'll soon get you out of there," as he took a crowbar to a tortoise.

A more complex version of the tortoise case would be the development of Third World countries. The assumption that development can be equated with an increase in GNP and that the questions to be asked about development are purely technical ones, i.e., how to achieve such increase, has caused and continues to cause much social and environmental mayhem. The normative questions inherent in development— what are and ought to be its goals, aims, and acceptable means—are still urgently in need of debate.

Development activists, for example, are busy building the Narmada Dam, in western India, as a monument to progress, while local people who have not been consulted and who certainly will not benefit from it have said they will drown when the monsoon arrives rather than leave their villages.[5] "Don't worry, mate, we will help you develop" may be a most threatening cry.

PHILOSOPHY AS INDIRECT ACTIVISM

Philosophy, then, can help in the skillful direction of activism. Indeed, it can be argued that constructive activism is not possible without a certain amount of reflection on what constitutes valuable change or conservation.

A rather different suggestion is that philosophy may sometimes be indirect activism. For example, philosophy may be able to provide the means by which dialogue can be generated between opposing sides, or within an institution that normally manifests a particular attitude. A case of the latter with which I am familiar is veterinary colleges. My experience of "teaching ethics" at a Scottish vet school is really a case of promoting discussion about the moral status of animals within an institution that typically—and perhaps surprisingly—endorses the view that animals are essentially resources, albeit ones which should, within certain limits, be treated humanely. Where these limits are to be drawn is a contentious subject badly in need of discussion given that many vets will be effectively employed by the agricultural industry.

The use of animals in medical research is a case that has led to deep polarization. Often, those who oppose such research are written off as lunatics while those who condone it are condemned as sadists. Verbal warfare and physical intimidation has led to much defensiveness and retraction on the part of the medical establishment. But this does not lead to change. Here, dialogue is activism and a philosopher is well placed to promote this by identifying the assumptions that each party is making, the common ground they may share, and so on.

PHILOSOPHY AND WORLDVIEWS

The suggestion that I want to look at in slightly more detail, however, is that philosophy constitutes activism insofar as it changes worldviews.

To return to the ALF activist taking a crowbar to the tortoise, it might be objected, again, that what he lacks is not philosophical aptitude but certain facts about the nature of tortoises. Now suppose the picture were of an antitortoise activist, deliberately crushing the tortoise with the crowbar. What is interesting is that one might be tempted to say much the same thing; that this person cannot really know what it is like to be a tortoise. If she did know, for example, how much pain and fear tortoises experience when their shells are battered then, other things being equal, she would not be doing it.

This takes us back to the idea that facts influence action. The notion this time is that if one really knows about the way animals and the environment are, a certain sort of response to them will naturally follow. I want to briefly explore this idea with reference to Hume and Callicott.

Hume says "we cannot form to ourselves a just idea of the taste of a pineapple, without having actually tasted it."[6] Certainly, one problem in discussing issues having to do with our treatment of animals is, to bend Hume more than a little, that people form ideas of animals without ever having had impressions of them. People who have had little contact with animals can say the oddest things about them, for example, that "they are not really conscious of what they are doing"; "their behavior is all instinctive, they don't learn anything"; "animals don't have feelings." Moral beliefs about animals may thus be based on a false picture of what animals are actually like, for these beliefs are built on ideas and ideas depend on impressions. For Hume the only exception to this might arise were someone to be presented with a color chart in which tones of blue are graded from light to dark; with one tone missing. In this case, Hume thought, it might be possible to have an idea of that particular color of blue without ever having had the impression of it. "The missing shade of blue" is, however, a case which Hume thought to be "so particular and singular that it is scarce worth our observing, and so does not merit that for it alone we should alter our general maxim."[7]

I take it, then, that we can't get a good idea of the natural world by extrapolating from a series of impressions of streets with fewer and fewer houses on. Rather, we need, let's say, to experience it and to have some ecological understanding of it. Without this, we may reach ethical conclusions about the natural world which are based on a false picture of what it is. This seems uncontroversial.

I am less sure about variations on the claim that experience and/or understanding of animals or the environment is a sufficient condition for believing that, and acting as if, animals and the environment have a high moral status. Deep Ecologists, for example, may suggest that recognition of the intrinsic value and moral standing of the natural world will follow from certain sorts of experience of it. The position of J. Baird Callicott, as I understand it, is that a good ecological and evolutionary understanding of animals and the environment will engender a positive moral attitude toward them or, to put it another way, that the claim that animals and the environment are morally irrelevant is underpinned by "facts" which are "false." Replace the false facts with true ones and anthropocentrism will be replaced by an attitude of benevolence and respect toward the nonhuman world.

I would not want to dispute that changing the general way in which we perceive animals and the environment is important. In *Man and the Natural World* Keith Thomas writes, "as for cattle and sheep, Henry More in 1653 was convinced that they had only been given life in the first place so as to keep their meat fresh 'till we shall have need to eat them.'"[8] In *Last Chance to See* Douglas Adams writes, "The giant tortoises were eaten to extinction because the early sailors regarded them much as we regard canned food. They just picked them off the beach and put them in their ship's hold as ballast, and then, if they felt hungry they'd go down to the hold, pull one up, kill it and eat it."[9] If Paul Watson is to become redundant, our attitude to marine and other creatures must become such that drift-netting is no longer considered to be an acceptable practice. This will involve seeing such creatures as something other than substitutes for canned food.

What troubles me is that on Callicott's view all normative disputes are in the end reducible to disputes about facts, albeit what he refers to as "thick facts." His position implies that, as long as someone is not a psychopath, if she genuinely understands and accepts that from an evolutionary perspective animals are kin and from an ecological perspective the land is

a community, she will agree that she has strong moral obligations toward land and animals and will treat them accordingly. What the tortoise aggressor and the general anthropocentrist need is fact-therapy.

But what if the fact-therapy fails? Is it true that, other things being equal, a person would not attack a tortoise, if she really knew what tortoises are like? I think it is quite possible to imagine various nonpsychopathic anthropocentrists stubbornly maintaining their anthropocentrism in the face of such fact-therapy, assenting to the evolutionary and ecological perspectives on animals and the environment, but insisting nevertheless that they have moral obligations only toward humans. In this case an argument is needed, to show why anthropocentrists ought to feel morally inclined to treat the environment better than they in fact do. And such an argument will not be forthcoming from a Humean theory. To put it another way, the sort of changed worldview required will include irreducibly normative components.

Another reservation concerns the possibility of the fact-therapy operating in the wrong direction. I spent some months working on a farm and left disliking chickens intensely. This was because I came to see that these creatures, which I had until then rather liked, are typically mean, stupid, aggressive, and greedy. In this case, my positive sentiments toward chickens were based on a false picture of them, which, when corrected, drained my compassion and respect entirely. However, I would argue, presumably against the Humean, that such a response to chickens is no basis for treating them badly.

These problems, then, are to do with the kind of view which says, first, that a human being's informed and uncorrupted response to animals and the environment is a positive one; and second, that this positive response forms the basis of our ethical obligations. The first is a claim that I would like to believe, but about which I am skeptical. The second is worrying because it may leave one defenseless against those who fail to respond positively despite being well-informed, as well as vulnerable to the claim that well-informed negative responses sanction bad treatment. All these issues have clear practical implications, relating, for example, to the viability of Callicott's and the Deep Ecologists' program for change, and to any suggestion that exposing people to animals or the environment will necessarily help to produce a positive orientation toward them.

A third problem relates to the claim that changed worldviews will necessarily be accompanied by changed action. Again, I think that there are many reservations to be expressed about such a claim, some of which have been famously explored by Byron Earhart in "The Ideal of Nature in Japanese Religion and Its Possible Significance for Environmental Concerns."[10] Here, however, I will only say that I think that alleged links between worldviews and action merit cautious treatment and that the issue would be worth returning to.

To conclude this section, if it is true that changing people's world views results in better treatment of animals and the environment, the philosophers who change people's worldviews will surely qualify as activists. While I would agree that an alternative to the canned food view of animals—and the resource view of the environment in general—is a necessary component of change, I am not convinced that this will be achieved by fact-therapy alone. Moreover, even if one's conception of the world, or worldview, is changed, I am not sure that this will guarantee changed action. In this context, then, we might conclude that philosophers are necessary but not sufficient.

RESERVATIONS

I have suggested that philosophy may motivate, legitimize, and guide activism; that it may help to create dialogue effective in bringing about desirable change; and that it may help to alter our perceptions of animals and the environment—in some cases at least, a necessary if not sufficient condition of treating them better. If this is correct, the claim that while activists do something, philosophers just think, needs to be revised.

What follows, however, are various reservations about the extent to which philosophy either does or can contribute to desirable change. Some of these reservations are to do with philosophy as a skill or subject and some are to do with philosophy as it is practiced in contemporary academic institutions—though these are of course connected.

An obvious preliminary is that there is no necessary connection between particular environmental philosophers and environmental activism. An environmental philosopher may have little to do with the great outdoors but commute to work and spend all day in her study; she may discuss the concept of the environment at a very abstract level so that students who are already actively inclined find the course interesting from a philosophical point of view but irrelevant to their activism. Moreover, just as, according to the introduction of a popular dictionary of philosophy, there is no logical contradiction involved in being an immoral moral philosopher, an environmental philosopher could without contradiction live an extremely ungreen lifestyle, refusing to recycle, driving a sports car, deliberately eating chemically saturated vegetables, taking airplanes to conferences, and so on. However, even if we are concerned exclusively with environmental philosophers who are concerned about environmental issues, there may be ways in which the philosophy proves to be more of a hindrance than a help.

PHILOSOPHY AS A SKILL OR SUBJECT

Philosophy has a way of retreating away from the question it is trying to answer. Take the issue of the relationship between environmental philosophy and environmental activism. If one tackles this as a philosopher, it is very difficult not to ask: what, exactly, is activism? What is action? How do thinking and acting relate? What did Aristotle have to say about this? It is also difficult not to feel that these questions all have to be resolved before one can attempt to answer the initial question. A. A. Milne perhaps captures the essence of this in the poem "The Old Sailor," which begins,

> There once was a sailor my grandfather knew
> Who had so many things which he wanted to do
> That, whenever he thought it was time to begin,
> He couldn't because of the state he was in.[11]

A related problem is that it seems part of the internal logic of the subject to become increasingly focused on fine-grained questions. It is very difficult to stay with a big, broad problem like the one under discussion. To get on with it requires giving rather cavalier treatment to concepts like "nature" and "environment," batting them about as if there were no conceptual questions to be asked. But a more conventionally philosophical approach might never get beyond the question, what do we mean by "the environment"?

Such an approach will not necessarily lead to action, for action is often motivated by simplifying the issues, rather than by revealing their complexities. Consider what Allison Pearson of *The Independent* has to say about John Pilger's documentary *Return to Year Zero*: "Shawcross' film [also about Cambodia] was fine journalism but it was Pilger's that made you angry. After his last one, 18,000 viewers wrote to Margaret Thatcher about Cambodia. That's what he does best, *choosing to find truths where there is uncertainty*" (my emphasis).[12] It is this, she suggests, that motivates. On the other hand, one might say that philosophers choose to find uncertainty. This is a feature of philosophy that is actually extremely attractive. A philosophical gaze turned upon concepts so familiar they are hardly noticed not only brings them vividly back into focus but may reveal them as troublesome or illusory. What is nature? What is wilderness? What is it that nature conservationists are supposed to be conserving? And of course a philosopher's film about Cambodia might be in some sense more honest than Pilger's, and this might be a reason for thinking it preferable. But whatever merits this aspect of philosophy has, they probably do not include inspiring action. Telling the truth, the whole truth and nothing but the very, very complicated truth is likely to paralyze action rather than galvanize it.

PHILOSOPHY IN CONTEXT

These problems may all be exacerbated by the academic context within which much philosophical thinking takes place. Here, one's remit is not to think about this problem until it is no longer useful to do so. Rather one often ends up following the problem wherever it goes and for the sake of the problem rather than for the light it may be able to shed on external issues. Consider the question of the metaphysical status of value in nature. The question is of interest in its own right. But from the perspective of improving states of affairs in the world, the complex and convoluted trail one embarks upon in order to try to answer it seems, after a certain point, to become quite unrelated to the starting point. If philosophy is to contribute to change, it needs a constant pulling back to the question, how

does this help?—so that philosophy runs in its own direction and is then returned, runs on again, and so on.

In an academic context, however, it is relatively easy just to run with the problem. The question how does this help may be lost, or may not even be asked. Moreover, it might be suggested that many academic journals actually require complexity beyond what is useful as a condition of publication and that, in general, to ask how helpful a given project is may be considered a sort of betrayal of the academic endeavor. Clearly there is more to be said on what counts as "helpful," and I am not suggesting that philosophy should be exclusively concerned with being "helpful," whatever this turns out to mean. But neither, surely, should philosophy amount to no more than a clever and beautiful game or, to use Kingsley Amis's wonderful phrase, a discipline concerned merely with "shining a pseudo-light on a nonproblem."[13]

The feeling that philosophers must continuously struggle to resist strong undercurrents which pull toward increasingly abstract and remote shores might be less frustrating if contemporary environmental problems were less serious or less immediate. But this is not the case. The monsoon that may end the lives of many Indian villagers if the construction of the Narmada Dam continues will arrive in June, and ours is the last decade which will have the chance to prevent complete destruction of the world's rain forests. In these and many other cases we do not have time to solve all the philosophical problems before we act—nor would this be necessary. We do not need to know the precise status of value in nature, nor exactly what is meant by nature, before we can conclude that rain forests should not be destroyed at the rate of a football field per minute. Philosophy and activism, then, can seem to operate within quite different time frames and this can lead one to become impatient with philosophy, or even to feel dragged under by it. On the other hand, activists can also become trapped, both in their own institutions and in the present moment, a problem which philosophical thought may help to redress. Some sort of dynamic equilibrium between philosophical thought and practical issues seems to be called for. At the moment, however, at least within British philosophy departments, the process is often lopsidedly biased toward the theoretical and the abstract.

Moreover, even if attention were focused on keeping philosophy useful, philosophers may be handicapped by the fact that, in the main, they have little to do with activists. Nor will they necessarily have a great knowledge of biology, ecology, or animals. Philosophers may be weak on both facts and experience, and this may be an obstacle to successfully relating their work to particular problems in the field. The response that this is up to individuals to remedy is too glib. The amount of published material is doubling exponentially every seven years, but no one supposes that the amount of time available for reading is increasing at the same rate.[14] Staying on top of the literature in any particular area is a genuine problem, and current academic arrangements regarding teaching and administrative loads hardly lend themselves to taking on an additional clutch of new subjects.

Finally, an obvious point is that philosophers' audiences are actually rather small. Few philosophical books, even in the environmental sphere, are best-sellers while the audience for academic journals is even more restricted. On the other hand, writing for "popular" journals that do have a wider readership is not encouraged by current research rating systems.

PROBLEMS WITH ACADEMIA?

Mary Midgley in *Wisdom, Information and Wonder* offers a critique of academic pursuits in general.[15] This critique, I think, is a revealing one, and it may be helpful to consider environmental philosophy in this broader context.

Midgley argues that one result of the massive increase in information I have already referred to is increasing specialization. We have more knowledge, so each individual has a smaller percentage of it. But, she says, if a thousand individuals each know a thousandth of something and nobody knows it in its entirety, we do not really have knowledge at all. Knowledge involves understanding and this involves knowledge of the whole, not just of specialized bits.

Clearly, each individual cannot master details of all subjects. Rather, "what is needed," according to Midgley, "is that all should have in their minds a general background map of the whole range of knowledge as a context for their own specialty, and should integrate this wider vision with their practical and emotional attitude to life. They should be able to place

their own small area on the map of the world and to move outside it freely when they need to." If this is not the case, when we talk about accumulating knowledge, we are simply talking about storing information, holding onto it like inert property or "handing it on like a dead fish to students."[16] This cannot be our ideal of knowledge, nor what we really think knowledge is for.

The question of the purpose of knowledge is one Midgley thinks we urgently need to ask. She writes, "the question is not a demand for a simple, hedonistic pay-off at a given moment. The gratification it looks for may be something much wider, slower, vaster, and more pervasive. But it still does have to touch down somewhere in the sentient lives of those who seek it."[17] The way in which it should touch down is in relation to the question of how we are to live. Thus, while bits of knowledge only make sense in relation to all knowledge, knowledge as a whole gains its meaning and value from the role it plays in helping us live well. Knowledge correctly understood, then, is an aspect of wisdom: "an understanding of life as a whole, and a sense of what really matters in it."[18]

What Midgley fears is that academia tends to pursue knowledge in the sense of a passive store of specialized bits of information. For this reason, academic knowledge can become irrelevant (and of course the word "academic" is sometimes used in a derogatory manner to mean precisely this). Moreover, given this notion of knowledge, it makes perfect sense to contrast knowledge with action, thinking with doing. But if knowledge is taken to be an active process aiming at wisdom, both the contrast and the criticism are undermined.

Thus Midgley rebukes Marx for implying, in his famous "The philosophers have only interpreted the world in various ways; the point is to change it,"[19] that we need to change the world *rather* than understand it. Proper understanding, she says, is a necessary condition of proper change. But understanding is different from information storing, and understanding is not always going on in academic institutions for the reasons sketched above.

If Midgley's analysis is correct, one problem with environmental philosophy is that the academic endeavor in general has become increasingly specialized and dislocated, in such a way that its pursuits have become increasingly pointless and unhelpful. This is a radical claim and seems to suggest the need for a radical restructuring of universities in response to it. If this were undertaken, part of the very purpose of environmental philosophy would presumably be to explicitly address the question "how ought we to live" in relation to the environment. This would certainly help to counteract some of the problems of relevance discussed earlier—though it would not amount to an alternative to activism. Understanding may be active, but it is not necessarily the same sort of thing as that prescribed by activists. We might conclude that the best philosophy and the best activism complement each other, and that neither is capable of achieving desirable change single-handedly. However, in the context of academic institutions, we are not always witnessing the best philosophy, and the helpfulness of philosophy may thus be compromised.

This last suggestion can be put in another way. Suppose you wanted to encourage the development of wise and effective activists. Would you do it by sending them to study environmental philosophy in a university philosophy department? Probably not. A better choice might be a multidisciplinary course involving not just separate modules of ecology, biology, politics, and policy in addition to philosophy but these and other subjects taught so that the connections between the subjects are also revealed. In addition, the course might include active contact with animals and the environment, and it would combine activism with philosophy not just in the sense of bringing activists and philosophers together in the same room—but also by encouraging these skills in the same person. This course—let us call it 301, Applied World Saving— would certainly raise awareness and understanding of environmental problems. But it would also seek to facilitate a translation of this into effective action in both immediate and long-term ways.

Would this be the kind of course that could be legitimately held within an academic institution? I suppose that how this is answered will depend partly on whether you agree with Midgley and on how far you think the "Midgley reforms" would take you. I don't think anyone would suppose that academic life should be entirely taken over with this kind of course. But I would argue that there has to be a legitimate space for such a course within it. On our planet currently we have extremely complex and pressing environmental problems and also institutions containing collections of highly intelligent people. It seems simply perverse for the one not to address the other.

CONCLUSION

I want to conclude by returning to the activists releasing dolphins from drift nets. I have said that philosophy, however well conceived and practiced, will never amount to a replacement for this kind of immediate action. But not everyone agrees that such direct action should take place and drift-netting as a practice still continues. There is a need for activism to be legitimized and for the practice of drift-netting to cease. For this to happen, critical reflection and debate about our ethical relationship to the rest of the natural world is called for, and this surely indicates a key role for philosophy. Working to change the canned food attitude to animals will not free those dolphins stuck in drift nets right now. But endlessly cutting drift nets is not a long-term solution either. Moreover, we do not want mindless activism nor do we want our horizons in terms of time and imagination to be limited to the horizons of those working in the present on compelling issues. Activists may be trapped and limited by their institutions as much as philosophers.

I would argue, then, that philosophy is both crucial to and a component of activism and that thinking and acting are both essential components of long- and short-term constructive change. However, philosophy also has the potential to be quite unhelpful or even obstructive, and these tendencies in the subject may be exacerbated by the academic institutions within which much philosophizing takes place. Keeping philosophy useful requires, I think, deliberate effort, and this in a direction that may be counter to the general academic flow. Moreover, specialization within universities can result in philosophy and philosophers becoming increasingly abstract and out of touch. The missing shade of green in academic institutions may be the one that deliberately sets itself to address contemporary environmental problems, in an interdisciplinary way.

I want to end, however, with something of a qualification to the above. The most effective green activists might be produced by some form of relentless media campaign and I left quite open the question of whether there are any necessary links between independence of thought and greenness of values. I am just not sure what I think about this. But a large part of my commitment to philosophy in any case derives from the belief that the sort of greenness that may be evoked by assaulting people with new age music, the smell of pine cones, and stirring rhetoric, so that everyone emerges with firm resolve and inanely beatific smiles is just as offensive as the advertisement-induced conviction that success in life is defined by the make of your running shoes. Philosophy, I maintain, is an antidote effective against both complaints. But it may leave us with an ongoing tension between the desire to encourage the resolution of environmental problems as rapidly and effectively as possible and the desire to foster and promote integrity, autonomy, and independence of thought.

NOTES

1. Peter Singer, *Animal Liberation* (London: Thorsons, 1976).
2. Colin McGinn, *Moral Literacy or How to Do the Right Thing* (London: Duckworth, 1992), p. 16.
3. "Defenders of the Wild," Channel 4 Television (April, 1993).
4. John Vidal, "Weeping and Whaling," *The Guardian*, May 7, 1993.
5. Reported, for example, in *The Guardian*, April 1993.
6. David Hume, *A Treatise of Human Nature* (London: Collins Fontana, 1962), p. 48.
7. Hume, *A Treatise*, p. 50.
8. Keith Thomas, *Man and the Natural World* (London: Penguin, 1983), p. 20.
9. Douglas Adams, *Last Chance to See* (Pan, 1991), p. 193.
10. Byron Earhart, "The Idea of Nature in Japanese Religion and Its Possible Significance for Environmental Concerns," *Contemporary Religions in Japan*, 11.1:26.
11. A. A. Milne, *Now We Are Six* (London: Methuen, 1927), p. 36.
12. Allison Pearson, "Not on a Level Filming Field," *The Guardian*, April 25, 1993.
13. Kingsley Amis, *Lucky Jim* (New York: Penguin, 1993).
14. Mary Midgley, *Wisdom, Information and Wonder* (London: Routledge, 1989), p. 6.
15. Midgley, *Wisdom*.
16. Midgley, *Wisdom*, p. 8.
17. Midgley, *Wisdom*, p. 17.
18. Midgley, *Wisdom*, p. 13.
19. Karl Marx, "Theses on Feuerbach," in *Karl Marx: Selected Writings*, ed. David McLellan (Oxford: Oxford University Press, 1977), p. 158.

ANDREW LIGHT

TAKING ENVIRONMENTAL ETHICS PUBLIC

At present, environmental ethics, especially in North America, is dominated by a concern with abstract questions of value theory, primarily, though not exclusively, focused on the issue of whether nature has "intrinsic value," or more generally noninstrumental value, understood in a nonanthropocentric scheme of valuing. Such work, as the introduction to this volume suggests, not only makes environmental ethics a form of normative ethics, but also creates a body of metaethical work which challenges the traditional assumptions of normative ethics. If nature has such noninstrumental value, then a wide range of duties, obligations, and rights may obtain in our treatment of it.

While this goal in the field is philosophically sound it has tended to engender two unfortunate results: (1) the focus on the value of nature itself has largely excluded discussion of the beneficial ways in which arguments for environmental protection can be based on human interests, and relatedly (2) the focus on somewhat abstract concepts of value theory has pushed environmental ethics away from discussion of which arguments morally motivate people to embrace more supportive environmental views. As such, those agents of change who will effect efforts at environmental protection, namely humans, have been oddly left out of discussions about the moral value of nature. As a result, environmental ethics has become more abstract, less concrete, and less able to contribute to cross-disciplinary discussions with other environmental professionals on the resolution of environmental problems, especially those professionals who also have an interest in human welfare.

In recent years a critique of this predominant trend in environmental ethics has emerged from within the pragmatist tradition in American philosophy.[1] The force of this critique is driven by the intuition that environmental philosophy cannot afford to be quiescent about the public reception of ethical arguments over the value of nature. The original motivations of environmental philosophers for turning their philosophical insights to the environment support such a position. Environmental philosophy evolved out of a concern about the state of the growing environmental crisis, and a conviction that a philosophical contribution could be made to the resolution of this crisis. But if environmental philosophers spend all of their time debating non-human centered forms of value theory they will arguably never get very far in making such a contribution. For example, to continue to ignore human motivations for the act of valuing nature causes many in the field to overlook the fact that most people find it very difficult to extend moral consideration to plants and animals on the grounds that these entities possess some form of intrinsic, inherent, or otherwise conceived nonanthropocentric value. It is even more difficult for people to recognize that non-humans could have rights. Claims about the value of nature as such do not appear to resonate with the ordinary moral intuitions of most people who, after all, spend most of their lives thinking of value, moral obligations, and rights in exclusively human terms. Indeed, while most environmental philosophers begin their work with the assumption that most people think of value in human centered terms (a problem that has been decried since the very early days of the field), few have considered the problem of how a non-human centered approach to valuing nature can ever appeal to such human intuitions. The particular version of the pragmatist critique of environmental ethics that I have endorsed recognizes that we need to rethink the utility of anthropocentric arguments in environmental moral and political theory, not necessarily because the traditional nonanthropocentric arguments in the field are false, but because they hamper attempts to contribute to the public discussion of environmental problems, in terms familiar to the public.

If the pragmatist critique is taken seriously then environmental ethics (and perhaps environmental philosophy more broadly) necessarily encompasses both a traditional philosophical task involving an investigation into the value of nature, and a second public task involving the articulation of arguments which will be morally motivating concerning environmental protection. This chapter will briefly overview the case for a demarcation of these tasks and make a claim about their relative importance in relation to each other in the context of my methodological form of environmental pragmatism. The set of arguments I will suggest here answer the call of "The Last Man and the Search For Objective Value" (the editors' introduction to Part I of this volume) to consider not only which values in the environment matter, but also to "figure out what really works." I take this to mean that we should not only worry about how to apply a new scheme of valuing nature, but also consider testing our schemes of valuing nature on the grounds of whether they could ever be convincing to a critical mass of other humans.

1. WHO IS ENVIRONMENTAL PHILOSOPHY FOR?

An open question that I believe still plagues most environmental philosophers is what our discipline is actually for, and consequently, who our audience is. In their "General Introduction to Ethics" with which this volume begins, the editors suggest that environmental ethics is not like other fields of applied ethics—such as medical or business ethics—because it is not tied to a particular profession. Not coincidentally, I believe, environmental ethics has evolved largely as a conversation that occurs mostly among philosophers, directed primarily toward other environmental philosophers and our students (as most traditional philosophical sub-fields are usually directed), often untethered by the burdens of everyday environmental disputes. But given the history of the field, one would think that the ambitions would be greater.

As has been demonstrated in this collection, environmental ethics got off the ground in the early 1970s through the work of thinkers as diverse as Arne Naess, Val Plumwood, Holmes Rolston III, Peter Singer, and Richard Sylvan, who all seemed concerned with how philosophers could make some sort of contribution to the actual resolution of environmental problems, not simply contribute new ideas on nature to theories of value. While it is certainly true that a contribution to value theory could help to resolve environmental problems, the worry is that such discussions usually have little impact beyond those who actually participate in the development of such theories.

But if environmental philosophy is for an audience other than philosophers, who is it for? There are a number of candidates. Realizing this other potential however requires reevaluating the thought with which this volume began, regarding the relative difference of environmental ethics from other applied fields. While surely the editors are correct that environmental ethics is not tied to a profession, there certainly are professions, and other kinds of human activity, concerned with the environment that the field could be in a position to assist. Environmental philosophy might also serve as (i) a guide for environmental activists searching for ethical justifications for activities in defense of other animals and ecosystems, (ii) an applied ethic for

natural resource managers, (iii) a general tool for policy makers, helping them to shape more responsible environmental policies, or, beyond this still further, (iv) be directed at the public at large, attempting to expand their notions of moral obligations beyond the traditional confines of anthropocentric moral concerns.

For reasons that I will save until later, my usual answer to the question of who environmental philosophy is for is "all of the above," though I think that most importantly environmental philosophers should focus their energies more on category (iii) policy makers and (iv) the general public. While it is undeniable that the work of environmental philosophers on topics like value theory could be helpful for all of these audiences, these contributions have, by and large, not been delivered in a manner that is very useful for them to use since the theories are often unconnected to how humans actually think about environmental questions. But I think environmental ethicists, perhaps more so than other applied ethicists, should pay closer attention to the issue of whether their work is useful to the public and policy makers.

My rationale goes something like this: if the original reasons for philosophers starting this field in the first place was principally to make a philosophical contribution to the resolution of environmental problems (consistent with the flurry of activity in the early 1970s around environmental concerns), then the continuation (indeed, the urgency) of those problems demands that philosophers do all that they can to actually help change present policies and attitudes now involving environmental problems rather than restrict their work to the traditional task of theory building. If we philosophers only end up talking to each other then we have failed as environmental professionals. But if we can somehow help to convince policy makers to form better policies—or, more accurately, come up with reasons to morally ground better environmental policies—and aid in making the case to the public at large to support these policies for ethical reasons, then we will have made a contribution to the resolution of environmental problems similar to the sorts of contributions made by other environmental professionals though constituted through our particular talents as philosophers. This goal of moving closer to other environmental professionals is also very important.

At present, the focus in environmental philosophy on the search for a description of the nonanthropocentric value of nature also separates it from other forms of environmental inquiry. Most other environmental professionals look at environmental problems in a human context rather than trying to define an abstract sense of natural value outside of the human appreciation or interaction with nature. Fields such as environmental sociology and environmental health, for example, are concerned not with the environment per se but the environment as the location of human community. This is not to say that these fields reduce the value of nature to a crude resource instrumentalism. It is to say instead that they realize that a discussion of nature outside of the human context impedes our ability to discuss ways in which anthropogenic impacts on nature can be understood and ameliorated. If environmental philosophers continue to only pursue their work as a contribution to value theory only then they cut themselves off from the rest of the environmental community which seeks to provide practical solutions to environmental problems, solutions that it is almost trite these days to suggest must be interdisciplinary. Further, if environmental philosophers define the terms of their work in language radically different from that of other environmental professionals, then they will quickly find themselves operating in isolation, unable to make a contribution to the interdisciplinary discussion of environmental issues.

Now, one may fairly wonder how environmental philosophers can make a contribution to something other than value theory. After all, what else are they trained to do as philosophers? My claim is that if philosophers could help to articulate moral foundations for environmental policies in a way that is translatable to the general public then they will have made a contribution to the resolution of environmental problems commensurate with their talents and in a fashion compatible with the work of other environmental professionals. But making such a contribution may require doing environmental philosophy in some different ways. At a minimum it requires a more public philosophy, as the American pragmatist philosopher John Dewey envisioned, though one specifically more focused on making the kind of arguments that resonate with the moral intuitions which most people carry around with them on an everyday basis. A public environmental philosophy would not rest with a mere description of the value of nature (even a description that justified a secure foundation for something as strong as a claim for the rights of nature). A public environmental philosophy would further question whether the description of the value of nature it provided could possibly cause human agents to change their moral attitudes about nature taking into account the overwhelming ethical anthropocentrism of most humans.[2] As such, a public environmental philosophy would have to either embrace an enlightened anthropocentrism about natural value or endorse a pluralism which admitted the possibility, indeed the necessity, of sometimes describing natural value in human centered terms rather than always through nonanthropocentric conceptions of natural value.

In a strong sense, this suggestion is consistent with this volume's opening essay on "A General Introduction to Ethics" that "doing environmental ethics without pertinent facts is . . . unethical." The editors no doubt have in mind the idea of doing environmental ethics without recourse to facts about nature. Here I am suggesting that another pertinent set of facts to take into account is how humans think about nature.[3] And whether we like it or not, most humans think about nature in human centered terms.

In a survey by Ben Minteer and Robert Manning about the sources of positive attitudes toward environmental protection in Vermont, respondents overwhelmingly indicated that the reason why they most thought the environment should be protected is because they think that we have positive obligations to protect nature for *human* future generations.[4] More exhaustive surveys of American attitudes toward environmental protection have also found such results. In the preparatory work for their landmark study of American environmental attitudes in the U.S., Willett Kempton and his colleagues found that obligations to future generations was so powerfully intuitive a reason for most people to favor environmental protection that they would volunteer this view before they were asked. In a series of interviews which helped determine the focus of their questions for the survey, the authors remarked:

> We found that our informants' descendants loom large in their thinking about environmental issues.

Although our initial set of questions never asked about children, seventeen of the twenty lay informants themselves brought up children or future generations as a justification for environmental protection. Such a high proportion of respondents mentioning the same topic is unusual in answering an open-ended question. In fact, concern for the future of children and descendants emerged as one of the strongest values in the interviews.[5]

The larger survey conducted by Kempton which included questions about obligations to the future confirmed these findings. Any philosophical views which would extend such intuitions would of necessity have to start with anthropocentric premises.

But does my suggestion that we begin to make arguments closer to anthropocentric, everyday, moral intuitions mean that environmental philosophers must give up their pursuit of a theory of nonanthropocentric natural value in order to make their philosophy more publicly useful? I don't think so. It only requires that philosophers be willing to rearticulate their philosophical views about the value of nature in terms which will morally motivate policy makers and the general public even when they have come to their views about the value of nature through a nonanthropocentric approach. A public environmental philosophy requires a certain skill at translation, and a tolerance for pluralism in moral theory—that is to say, it requires philosophers to accept that there will be more than one way to express the value of a given natural object or environmental practice and some of those ways may be anthropocentric, such as the value of preserving nature out of obligations to human future generations.[6]

I call the view that makes it plausible for me to make such an argument, "methodological environmental pragmatism." As I will explain in more detail below, by this term I do not mean an application of the traditional writings of the American pragmatists—Dewey, William James, Charles Sanders Pierce, etc.—to environmental problems. Instead, I mean that environmental philosophy of any variety ought to be pursued within the context of a recognition that a responsible and complete environmental philosophy includes a public component with a clear policy emphasis. It is perfectly fine for philosophers

to continue their search for a true and foundational nonanthropocentric description of the value of nature. But we are remiss if we do not set aside that search at times and try to make other, perhaps more pedestrian ethical arguments in a public context which may have an audience with an anthropocentric public. Environmental pragmatism, as I see it, is, properly speaking, a methodology permitting environmental philosophers to consistently endorse a pluralism allowing for one kind of philosophical task inside the philosophy community—searching for the "real" value of nature (though this is not a task that all environmental philosophers will have to take up)—and another task outside of that community—articulating a value to nature that resonates with the public. Environmental pragmatism in my sense is agnostic concerning the existence of nonanthropocentric natural value or the relative superiority of one form of natural value verses another. Those embracing this view can either continue to pursue nonanthropocentric theories or they can take a more traditional pragmatist stance denying the existence of such value.[7]

A more traditional pragmatist would be more inclined to engage in the debates over intrinsic value mentioned in the introduction to this volume. Such theorists would argue, for instance, that the question of whether a Redwood has intrinsic value is answered by the pragmatist claim that nothing has value apart from the act of human valuing of a thing. But if environmental pragmatism in my sense is truly concerned with making environmental philosophy relevant to the actual public discussion and resolution of environmental problems, then it cannot afford to serve as a launching pad for yet another round of metaethical debates in environmental ethics. To insist that all environmental philosophers give up their nonanthropocentric commitments in favor of a Deweyian naturalism, for example, would be an invitation to plunge further into debates that can only be resolved (if ever) through a long and protracted discussion of the metaphysical relationship between humans, nature, and the act of valuing. As such, I believe that the principle task for an environmental pragmatism is not to philosophically obviate the metaethical and metaphysical foundations of current trends in environmental ethics, but rather to impress upon environmental philosophers the need to take up the largely empirical question of what morally motivates humans to change their attitude, behaviors, and policy preferences toward those more supportive of long-term environmental sustainability.

But my discussion so far has been exceedingly general. If we are to justify a shift in focus in environmental philosophy at least partly toward a public task, then how will this shift be justified in philosophical terms? What are its parameters, and what are the acceptable limits of this philosophical project so that it will remain a philosophical project and not just a project in rhetoric or communication studies? What is the relationship between the traditional task in environmental ethics of finding a moral foundation for valuing nature, often in nonanthropocentric terms, and the public task of appealing to anthropocentric intuitions? I cannot fully justify my methodological pragmatism in the space provided here, so for now will simply sketch out how such a form of public philosophy might work.

2. TWO TASKS, TWO COMMUNITIES

It should be clear by now that endorsing a methodological environmental pragmatism requires an acceptance of some form of anthropocentrism in environmental ethics, if only because we have sound empirical evidence that humans think about the value of nature in human terms and pragmatists insist that we must pay attention to how humans think about the value of nature. Indeed, as I said above, it is a common presupposition among committed nonanthropocentrists that the proposition that humans are anthropocentrists is true, though regrettable. There are many problems involved in the wholesale rejection of anthropocentrism by most environmental philosophers. While I cannot adequately explain my reservations to this rejection, for now I hope the reader will accept the premise that not expressing reasons for environmental priorities in terms more familiar with human schemes of value seriously hinders our ability to communicate a moral basis for better environmental policies in a language familiar to the public. Both anthropocentric and non-anthropocentric claims should be open to us.

But of course we cannot simply pick and choose our application of philosophical conceptions of value willy-nilly, without some reason for our choices. We

must have reasons which back up and make coherent a public environmental philosophy which is able to support anthropocentric reasons and appeals to human centered moral motivations without a wholesale and necessary endorsement of crass versions of anthropocentrism (and a concomitant rejection of nonanthropocentrism). How then can a methodologically pragmatic endorsement of anthropocentrism be endorsed so as to make it systematically palatable even to those who hold out a general skepticism of anthropocentrism as an adequate basis for an environmental ethic?

As suggested before, for a variety of reasons, environmental ethics has evolved over the course of the last thirty years as a fairly abstract philosophical activity. Certainly the reasons for why the field has evolved primarily as a branch of value theory are understandable. Like other areas of applied ethics, environmental ethicists have long sought intellectual credibility as a branch of philosophy, or, in other words, as part of the larger philosophical community. While some may disagree, environmental ethics has done a good job of situating itself as part of that community (and I will use "community" in what follows in a very ill defined and general sense) while remaining quite distinctive, especially given its emphasis on nonanthropocentric theories of value.

But we are also part of another community as well, namely, the environmental community. And while the connection has never been clear, the field continues to be part of at least an on-going conversation about environmental issues, if not an outright intentional community of environmentalists. The necessity of engaging in a policy, or at least problem-oriented environmental ethics, is driven by the particular exigencies of the environmental community and the problems that it orients itself around. The drive to create a public environmental philosophy is thus not only motivated by a desire to actively participate in the resolution of environmental problems, but to hold up our philosophical end, as it were, among the community of environmentalists.

But how should environmental ethicists serve the environmental community? The answer for the pragmatist begins in a recognition that if philosophy is to serve a larger community then it must allow the interests of the community to help to determine the philosophical problems which the theorist addresses.[8] This does not mean that the pragmatic philosopher necessarily finds all the problems that a given community is concerned with as the problems for her own work. Nor does it mean that she assumes her conclusions before analyzing a problem like a hired legal counsel who doesn't inquire as to the guilt or innocence of her client. It only means that a fair description of the work of the pragmatic philosopher is to investigate the problems of interest to their community and then articulate the policy recommendations of the community on these problems to those outside of their community, that is, to the public at large.

Knowing how to forge this connection with a larger community and understanding its relationship to more traditional philosophical projects is a tricky, but not insurmountable problem. To begin with, we can take Bryan Norton's convergence hypothesis as a plausible point of departure. First expressed in Norton's *Toward Unity Among Environmentalists* (excerpted earlier in this section of this book), and then later explicated in a series of papers and defenses of the view, the convergence hypothesis is an empirical claim about the likely overlap between environmentalists of different orientations. After spending some time studying the various demands of different environmental organizations, from radicals to liberals, Norton came to the conclusion that there was more that was agreed upon between anthropocentrists and nonanthropocentrists than many people had assumed. The convergence hypothesis encapsulates this overlap inside a practical framework:

> Provided anthropocentrists consider the full breadth of human values as they unfold into the indefinite future, and provided nonanthropocentrists endorse a consistent and coherent version of the view that nature has intrinsic value, all sides may be able to endorse a common policy direction.[9]

Norton's convergence hypothesis has been often misunderstood as an overly optimistic claim. Commentators have lined up to provide Norton with examples of where anthropocentrists and nonanthropocentrists disagree. But this is to miss the point of the suggestion: empirically, there is much agreement among a wide variety of environmentalists of what

they want to achieve. Assuming that this claim holds up under empirical scrutiny—and so far it has—then we can begin to build an agenda for a public environmental philosophy on top of this claim and orient it around two clear tasks for environmental philosophers: (1) to help express the environmental community's position on some environmental problem to those outside the community who may not even see some problem as a problem and (2) to attempt to influence the views within the environmental community of a problem of interest to that community. But more detail is needed.

Task 1. The first task of a methodologically pragmatist environmental philosophy is its public task. Here, following the convergence hypothesis, the role of environmental philosophers is to take those issues that the environmental community agrees upon, for whatever reasons, and communicate these issues to the larger public. These issues will be the relatively easy ones which most environmental philosophers, if not all, also already endorse. But our role here is not just rhetorical, it is necessarily philosophical. The goal is to come up with ethical grounds upon which environmental policies can be justified. Not just any grounds, however, but those grounds which will motivate the broader public to act on or assent to the passage of environmental policies even if they do not count themselves as environmentalists. The successful pursuit of this task requires environmental philosophers to endorse, at least publicly, a robust and consistent pluralism which allows for both anthropocentric and nonanthropocentric arguments, and attention to research in moral psychology on what reasons morally motivate people to actually change their lifestyle or behavior. Since many people are motivated by anthropocentric reasons, environmental pragmatists engaged in task 1 will of necessity have to endorse anthropocentrism in a public policy oriented context. I call this form of anthropocentrism a "strategic anthropocentrism" which operates according to the following rule of thumb: (i) Always first pursue the anthropocentric justification for the environmental policy in order to persuade a broader array of people to embrace the view, because (ii) anthropocentric justifications can most plausibly speak to people's ordinary moral intuitions more persuasively than nonanthropocentric justifications. But just as the convergence hypothesis is empirical, so is the endorsement of strategic anthropocentrism. If it turns out to be the case that the best social science research on why people act on environmental policies in general, or even on a particular issue, tells us that a nonanthropocentric justification will better provide a warrant for action, then a strategic anthropocentrism must give way to a strategic nonanthropocentrism.

No doubt many will object to describing task 1 as philosophical at all. Is this not simply rhetoric driven by an unreasoned and careless endorsement of substantial policy goals? But I believe this objection fails. What is being asked of philosophers here is not an endorsement of ends that they do not agree with, but rather the pursuit of a reasonable project of engaging the public on the moral grounds of better environmental policies, which surely any environmental philosopher would see as a worthy goal. An environmental philosopher at work at task 1 cannot offer just any reason for endorsing a given environmental policy, but must stick to the traditional criteria of what counts as a good philosophical argument, such as coherence, consistency and adequacy.

A philosopher engaging in this task must also not stray from other expected ethical norms. If a methodological pragmatist were an atheist, and was called by a Christian church group to speak at a Sunday service on the importance of voting on a referendum expanding a local forest preserve, the pragmatist could not say, "Jesus sent me here today to tell you to vote for this bill," because she thought it would be more convincing to the congregation. What she could do is come to the congregation with an awareness of how seriously they took the Christian Bible and try to make an argument for why there is a directive for an ethic of stewardship in the old testament that would encourage a favorable view on the forest preserve bill. Sincerity is also clearly an issue. No one endorsing this methodology would be required to say things that they felt very strongly were false, simply to convey a reason to support a policy agreed on by the larger environmental community. But a philosopher endorsing this view would still have a warrant to articulate a multiplicity of arguments for a converged upon policy which presumably would go beyond those reasons that she firmly stood against.

Task 2. Because the environmental community does not always agree on its priorities, our second task is the traditional one of searching for better philosophical foundations for environmental values. As Norton says, "The convergence hypothesis does not, of course, claim that the interests of humans and interests of other species *never* diverge, only that they *usually* converge."[10] When environmentalists are at an impasse about how to proceed then environmental ethicists must go back into the more private philosophical task of discerning the best assessment of the truth about whatever aspect of environmental value is at issue. The pluralism in public argumentation warranted in task 1 is then not granted when convergence does not exist. We could call task 2 "environmental first philosophy." Such a project is more in line with traditional philosophical practices in the field as they have been engaged in for the last thirty years. And while there is no guarantee that such a project will ever achieve a resolution between anthropocentrists and nonanthropocentrists on any given issue, it is, at first gloss, the only recourse of philosophers who are committed to trying to respond to the problems of the environmental community. Here, the environmental ethicist is acting more as a member of the philosophical community, though importantly they are still driven by the needs of the environmental community.

It is important to note however that the relation of task 1 to task 2 is not necessarily linear: it isn't as if pragmatist philosophers can only turn to task 2 after task 1 is not warranted by a lack of convergence in the environmental community. We must always instead engage in both tasks simultaneously. Even when the environmental community agrees on its ends it is appropriate for philosophers to continually think about the foundations of environmental value and push on the converged ends to make sure that they can stand up to critical scrutiny. As we learn more about how the environment works, and consequently how we have effects on it, we will need to continually revise our understanding of what counts as right action in relation to the environment. Pointing out the separable importance of task 1 from task 2 is simply a way of reminding us that if we only engage in task 2 then we are not fulfilling our full potential as philosophers taking part in the environmental community. It is also a reminder that those more interested in the value theory debates of task 2 ought not to continually put up roadblocks for those doing the more public work of environmental philosophy.

This last comment further opens the discussion of the relationship between task 1 and task 2 which surely deserves more treatment than I can provide here. For example, what if someone comes to the conclusion that they have discerned the exclusive truth of the matter about how we are to value nature and that truth can only be expressed in terms of a nonanthropocentric as-cription of the value of nature? If ever such a view was discerned, and if it had the force of argument to be per-suasive over all competitors, then I would assume that it could serve as the basis for a strong set of obligations, policies, even laws which could stand above and beyond the predilections of human preferences (and I am cer-tainly open to the claim that a body of law acknowledg-ing something like the rights of nature would be the most stable foundation for environmental protection). But assuming the view did not have such force—and I am skeptical that a nonanthropocentric view could ever get such agreement on a description of the value of nature—then our best recourse will be some kind of pluralism (task 1) aimed at making arguments which morally motivate people embedded within the regulat-ing context of a methodological pragmatism. This view can justify articulating reasons for an end, even when we think that the end will most properly be justified for other reasons, while still working within the context of a consistent and coherent philosophical practice.

One thing more for now. Are the tasks of the envi-ronmental philosopher exhausted by these two tasks as they have been described so far? I don't think so. For one thing, a fair question could be who counts as the envi-ronmental community to which the pragmatist envi-ronmental philosopher should respond in gauging the relative propriety of task 1 or task 2 at any given time? This is a serious problem for this view. There seems to be no fair way of discerning who counts as an environ-mentalist. At best, it seems that all we can fairly say at present is that someone counts as an environmentalist if they claim to be an environmentalist. (Other options for segregating "real" environmentalists seem implau-sible. What policy, for example, must someone endorse in order to claim that they are an environmentalist?)

But this will be an unsatisfactory answer. Is there no way to exclude the "wise use" movement which cloaks anti-environmental policies in the language of envi-ronmentalism? This is a particularly important ques-tion for my view where the environmental ethicist's first task is driven by those policies which the envi-ronmental community comes to converge upon. How can there be convergence in a community when anti-environmentalists count as environmentalists?

This worry has led me to further develop the terrain covered by task 2. Even though the convergence hypoth-esis is a nice starting point for describing the appropri-ate work of environmental philosophers, it need not drive the end of all philosophical inquiry or set up rigid marching orders for philosophical work. As philoso-phers, we ought not only to wait on convergence and then go about our public work, we should also help to fashion the converged ends of the environmental com-munity. Specifically, environmental ethicists can help to fashion ends by working on the problem of what we might call "environmental intuitions." Before the dis-putes which may divide the environmental community begin, or maybe because of the ones which already have divided the community, we need an account of what counts as an environmental intuition, or a fair starting place for an environmental claim, as a way of getting to a narrower description of who counts as an environmen-talist. "Environmentalists" could be defined as those who begin their arguments with such intuitions even though the specific arguments made by any given en-vironmentalist could differ from those made by others.

The details of such an account will need to be more clearly laid out, but at minimum we can imagine that this account of intuitions would have to be one that assumes the inherent revisability of intuitions as well as articulates a relationship between environmen-tal intuitions and environmental science as mediated through experience and experimentation. The more we know about nature, the better off we are to assess what-ever nonanthropocentrists would imagine are nature's "interests," and whatever anthropocentrists would imagine are our interests in relationship to nature. For example, the horrific Yellowstone fires of several years ago settled the debate among environmentalists over the merits of fire suppression in wilderness areas. We now understand much more about fire and its role in ecosystems and know that excessive suppression actually hinders rather than helps preservation efforts by creating surplus brush matter which can fuel a fire. Any environmentalist today who maintains support for a policy of fire suppression—perhaps because they think the purpose of national parks is to preserve some bit of wilderness as an unchangeable aesthetic ideal—does so only through a willful ignorance of the best that experience and science have to offer on this issue. Legitimate environmental intuitions then must at minimum be sensitive to the received views of environmental science, as those views change over time. The challenge will be figuring out what other criteria we ought to use to describe such intuitions.

Let me close with a slogan. As a philosopher interested in the revival of a public philosophy, I'm rather fond of slogans. To date, if environmental philosophers thought that they were serving any interests, they would best be described as the interests of nature. Some, such as the deep ecologists, have been explicit about this, others have been less so. If we can conceive of environmentalism in general as being interested in two broad concerns, namely the preservation of the nature still around and the restoration of that which has been degraded by anthropogenic causes, then environmental philosophers, even when they are engaged in pedestrian and traditional debates in value theory, have been concerned primarily with the preservation and restoration of nature for nature's sake.

But the pragmatist environmental ethicist asks that we complicate this neat picture a bit and broaden the overall scope of environmental philosophy to include other interests as well. These are not the interests of those who want to destroy the environment through crude discussions of the utility of natural resources (criticized through task 2), but those who, as humans, want to work for long term environmental sustainability for a variety of reasons (promoted through task 1). So rather than thinking about environmental philosophy as being in the service of the preservation and restoration of nature itself, we should think about environmental ethics as working toward (and here's the slogan) the preservation and restoration of a human "culture of nature." Surely no progress on environmental issues, from any quarter, can succeed without the flourishing of that culture.

NOTES

1. The term "environmental pragmatism" was first used in *Environmental Pragmatism*, eds. Andrew Light and Eric Katz (London: Routledge Press, 1996) to refer to a broad range of approaches to environmental ethics, capturing under one label the similarities between the work of figures like Norton, Anthony Weston, and more historically oriented theorists like Kelly Parker, Sandra Rosenthal, and Larry Hickman. See "Environmental Ethics and Environmental Pragmatism as Contested Terrain," in *Environmental Pragmatism*, op. cit., pp. 1–18. For a more recent summary of the development of this loosely amalgamated "school" in environmental philosophy, see Ben A. Minteer, "No Experience Necessary: Foundationalism and the Retreat from Culture in Environmental Ethics," *Environmental Values* 7 no.3 (August 1998): 333–348. As we will see below, I think there are at least two identifiable strains of environmental pragmatism whose compatibility is yet to be proven. This is why I hesitate to call the collection of this work a "school" of thought in the proper sense.

2. In addition to the claims that most environmental ethicists have made decrying the anthropocentrism prevalent in contemporary human societies and forms of thought which point to this palpable hurdle, Anthony Weston has argued that committed nonanthropocentrists have failed to adequately describe what a nonanthropocentric culture would possibly look like. Weston takes this failure to be indicative of the need to relax the severe denigration of anthropocentrism in the field. See Weston, "Before Environmental Ethics," in *Environmental Pragmatism*, op. cit., pp. 139–160.

3. Several essays in the second half of this volume do attempt to discuss what it would mean to treat humans as more integral parts of the nature rather than leaving them out of these discussions entirely. Also, on the importance of taking human interests seriously, see David Schmidtz's paper, "Natural Enemies: An Anatomy of Environmental Conflict," *Environmental Ethics* 22 no.4 (2000): 397–408. Reprinted with nine commentaries in *Ethics, Policy, and Environment* 14 (2011) 127–38.

4. Ben Minteer and Robert Manning, "Pragmatism in Environmental Ethics: Democracy, Pluralism, and the Management of Nature," *Environmental Ethics* 21 no.2 (1999): 191–207.

5. Willett Kempton, et. al. *Environmental Values in American Culture* (Cambridge, MA: Massachusetts Institute of Technology, 1997), p. 95.

6. For a longer justification of my approach to pluralism in environmental ethics, as connected to policy concerns, see my "Callicott and Naess on Pluralism," *Inquiry* 39 no.2 (June 1996): 273–94.

7. See for example Kelly Parker, "Pragmatism and Environmental Thought," in *Environmental Pragmatism*, op. cit., pp. 21–37, and Anthony Weston, "Before Environmental Ethics," op. cit.

8. While developed independently of each other, some readers will no doubt see a similarity between my focus on taking seriously the interests of the environmental community and Avner de-Shalit's similar endorsement of what he calls "public reflective equilibrium" for environmental ethics. See de-Shalit's *The Environment Between Theory and Practice* (Oxford: Oxford University Press, 2000).

9. Bryan Norton, "Convergence and Contextualism," *Environmental Ethics* 19 (1997): 87.

10. Bryan Norton, "Convergence and Contextualism," *Environmental Ethics* 19 (1997): 100.